Society in Focus

An Introduction to Sociology

Sixth Edition

William E. Thompson
Texas A & M University–Commerce

Joseph V. Hickey
Emporia State University

PEARSON

Boston   New York   San Francisco
Mexico City   Montreal   Toronto   London   Madrid   Munich   Paris
Hong Kong   Singapore   Tokyo   Cape Town   Sydney

To our children, with love and affection:
Mica and Brandon Thompson
Christopher Parrish Hickey

Executive Editor: Jeff Lasser
Editorial Assistant: Lauren Houlihan
Senior Marketing Manager: Kelly May
Senior Development Editor: Leah Strauss
Supplements Editor: Deb Hanlon
Composition Buyer: Linda Cox
Manufacturing Buyer: Megan Cochran
Production Supervisor: Karen Mason
Full-Service Production: WestWords/PMG
Photo Researcher: Katharine S. Cebik
Cover Administrator: Linda Knowles

Between the time website information is gathered and published, some sites may have closed. Also, the transcription of URLs can result in typographical errors. The publisher would appreciate notification where these occur so that they may be corrected in subsequent editions.

Library of Congress Cataloging-in-Publication Data
Thompson, William E. (William Edwin), 1950-
    Society in focus : an introduction to sociology / William E. Thompson, Joseph V. Hickey. — 6th ed.
      p. cm.
   ISBN13: 978-0-205-51689-6
   ISBN10:   0-205-51689-0
  1.   Sociology.   I. Hickey, Joseph V.   II. Title.
  HM586.T47 2008
  301—dc22

                                           2007014452

Printed in the United States of America

10 9 8 7 6 5 4 3 2 1   RRD-OH   11 10 09 08 07

Photo credits appear on page 649, which constitute an extension of the copyright page.

Brief Contents

Contents

PART 3 Social Differentiation and Inequality

Preface

These are exciting and challenging times for sociologists and sociology students alike. In the twenty-first century, there is a growing consensus on campus and in society that many traditional approaches to understanding our social world are no longer very useful. Changing times require new emphases in textbooks. In this Sixth Edition of *Society in Focus*, we emphasize how society and social forces affect everything from international policies to our everyday lives. This makes the subject matter of this book seemingly familiar and ordinary.

Sociologist Peter Berger's admonition, "The first wisdom of sociology is this—things are not what they seem"—serves as a challenge to our teaching and provided special inspiration in writing this book. To help meet this challenge, our chapter-opening vignettes focus students on the concept that "things are not what they seem." The questioning of "commonsense notions" and the "official interpretation" of issues and events are at the heart of the sociological enterprise, and we emphasize this in the vignettes and throughout the text. *Society in Focus* shows students that sociological thinking is much more than an ivory-tower enterprise. Because sociology is about all of us and our daily lives, it is an eminently practical discipline.

Our diverse research interests and experiences illustrate the fact that, for sociologists, all the world is a laboratory. Individually and collaboratively, our research projects include field studies of the Fulani in West Africa, American cowboys, African American settlements, ethnic communities, and the Old Order Amish in Oklahoma and Kansas. We have also worked in a beef slaughtering plant, interviewed topless dancers and morticians, and even played Santa Claus and the Easter Bunny at suburban shopping malls. Over 50 years of combined experience in teaching Introduction to Sociology has taught us what "works" and what does not work in class.

In this edition, we go beyond the mere questioning of issues to take a closer look at the social world in which we live. We provide an integrated approach that uses sociological thinking to help students analyze and understand every chapter component from the opening vignette, which is the chapter focus, to theoretical perspectives, boxed material (Sociological Focus), and even the photographs, maps, and cartoons. To focus increased attention on sociological thinking and research methods, we have chosen four key areas that reviewers have told us are of greatest interest to students and instructors alike: Mass Media, Globalization, Cultural Diversity, and the Future.

THEMES

THE MASS MEDIA AND TECHNOMEDIA

In earlier editions we pioneered a critical analysis of the mass media—especially television—to help students grapple with sociological concepts and methods. In this edition we continue our critical analysis of mass media in every chapter, by exploring issues such as the possible link between television violence and aggression in children (see Chapter 7) and over half a century of patriarchal portrayals of women in television (see Chapter 11). Virtually all sociologists today recognize student interest in this area as well as the potency of the media that broadcast a standard message to widespread audiences in shaping, defining, and influencing our social world. Most introductory textbooks have followed our lead, including a chapter or at least some examples that acknowledge the media's importance.

In *Society in Focus,* we coined the term *technomedia* to better describe emerging media technologies and their special role in contemporary society. Technomedia include a host of newer, more personalized forms of information and entertainment technologies, such as personal computers, fax machines, video games, cellular phones, the Internet, and interactive television.

In Chapter 1 we introduce all forms of media and then include a section on their powerful social influence in every chapter of the book. Whether these various forms of media use technology to collect, interpret, and disseminate information, or for entertainment, they shape and give meaning to the world in which we live. Moreover, for many people the problem with media is no longer in finding information but in dealing with "information overload" and in developing the necessary critical thinking skills to make sense of diverse perspectives. For example, we look at differential access to and use of the Internet by various social classes (Chapter 8) and racial and ethnic groups (Chapter 10). We ask whether new technologies may be the solution or merely part of the problem in our educational system today and in the future (Chapter 14). We look at the blending of what some call the "old media" (radio, television, magazines, newspapers, and books) with the "new media" (cellular phones, computers, the Internet, and others). For example, today, the major television networks and major newspapers and magazines can be accessed 24 hours a day around the world through the World Wide Web. We believe that any introductory sociology book that fails to acknowledge and critically examine all forms of the media is ignoring one of the most powerful and influential institutions in contemporary life.

Globalization

In the past few decades modern technology and economic development have facilitated the flow of people, goods, ideas, and money across old national boundaries and from one end of the earth to the other. This process of globalization has altered social relations and societies everywhere. Today, people reside and work in geographic locations far removed from where they were born. The annual migration of more than one million immigrants into the United States—and a population shift from the rust belt to the sunbelt—has altered America's social landscape. Moreover, today's complex global economy has blurred not only the lines that once distinguished one major corporation from another, but also the political and economic boundaries that once separated nations. We explore these important developments in Chapter 9, "Global Stratification," and in Chapter 17, "The Economy and Work." In addition, we weave comparative material from the diverse cultures of the world into every chapter to demonstrate how globalization has made all of our lives increasingly complex and interdependent.

Cultural Diversity

In an effort to acknowledge and affirm the rich tapestry of human culture and achievement, in this edition of *Society in Focus* we expand the emphasis on social and cultural diversity. Reflecting fundamental changes in the social composition of American cities and most other major cities of the world, we have expanded our coverage of race, ethnicity, gender, sexual orientation, and many other forms of cultural diversity. At the same time, we illuminate social inequality and what it means to be at the margins or even outside of the cultural mainstream in various parts of the world. We have expanded coverage of the important issues of sexual orientation, disability, and problems with identity in postmodern society as well.

Here are just a few of the diversity issues that we ask you to examine in various chapters: Chapter 7 differentiates between diversity and deviance and illustrates how entire categories of people are sometimes labeled and treated as deviants and thus become victims of prejudice, discrimination, and even hate crimes simply because of their differences. Chapter 10 raises the question: given increasing rates of interracial marriages, should the current U.S. racial classification system be changed to include new biracial and multiracial categories? In Chapter 13, you are asked to take positions for and against the long high-standing tradition of spanking children.

THE FUTURE

Our final theme is called Looking to the Future. While predicting the future is a risky venture, we are convinced that critical thinking and sociological perspectives can improve the accuracy of anyone's forecasts. We pioneered this popular feature in our first edition, and we continue to provide cutting-edge and comprehensive sociological projections of the future in each chapter. This section also has another goal: it is designed to increase student awareness of the importance of collective action, as well as the ability of ordinary people to alter public policy and improve society. In Chapter 1, for example, we look at the future of sociology and what important issues are likely to dominate the discipline. We show how the future of sociology, and the future of society itself, are tied to a better understanding of the impact of the technomedia, globalization, and cultural diversity.

PLAN OF THE BOOK

Society in Focus is designed to help students think clearly and critically about sociological issues, concepts, and methods. Questioning is at the heart of this approach and as students read this book they are encouraged to become part of the sociological enterprise—rather than remain passive observers. Every element of the text is designed to challenge students to evaluate social issues and, guided by the sociological imagination, to clearly formulate their own positions. By asking questions that demand sociological and creative thought, we want to remind students that their conclusions and decisions, as well as their nondecisions and inaction, may have important social consequences. The following features have been chosen to help students achieve these goals.

Organization

Society in Focus is divided into five parts. In Part I, "The Sociological Perspective," Chapter 1, "Discovering Sociology," introduces sociology and the history of the discipline. Chapter 2, "Doing Sociology," describes the methods and theories of sociological research.

Part II, "The Social Framework," discusses the influence of "Culture and Society" (Chapter 3), "Socialization" (Chapter 4), "Social Interaction in Everyday Life" (Chapter 5), and "Social Groups and Organizations" (Chapter 6) on individual and social behavior.

Part III, "Social Differentiation and Inequality," details how people are rewarded differentially in society. This section includes "Deviance and Conformity" (Chapter 7) and the extent to which behavior is sanctioned according to whether people conform to or deviate from established norms. Chapter 8, "Social Stratification and the U.S. Class System," discusses class inequality in the United States; and Chapter 9, "Global Stratification," examines stratification on a global scale. Chapter 10, "Race and Ethnicity," Chapter 11, "Sex and Gender," and Chapter 12, "Age and the Elderly," explore how people are treated (and rewarded) differently because of their socially defined physical attributes.

In Part IV, "Social Institutions," we discuss major social institutions and their vital roles in the social order. The traditional institutions discussed are "Families" (Chapter 13), "Education" (Chapter 14), "Religion" (Chapter 15), "Politics and War" (Chapter 16), and "The Economy and Work" (Chapter 17). Chapter 18, "Health and Medicine," looks at medicine and health care in contemporary society.

Part V, "Social Change," contains two chapters. Chapter 19 explores issues related to "Population, Urbanization, and Ecology," and Chapter 20, "Social Change, Collective Behavior, and the Future," looks at collective behavior, social movements, social change, and the future.

Special Features

Opening Vignettes   Each chapter opens with an interesting case study, anecdote, or other example to capture the reader's interest and introduce the chapter topic. The material is also meant to stimulate sociological thinking by raising a variety of important social issues and questions. Opening vignettes illustrate our theme that things are not necessarily what they seem, and introduce students to important concepts that follow, as well as set the tone for the entire chapter. For example, Chapter 5, "Social Interaction in Everyday Life," begins with a vignette about surfing the Net and interaction in cyberspace between millions of people worldwide. This vignette explores the power of new media in society and introduces the concept of technomedia. More important, it shows how easily people can be deceived while interacting through cyberspace, and it raises questions that are at the very heart of the sociological enterprise. For example, is a person alone at a computer who anonymously chats online with others participating in "social interaction," as sociologists have traditionally defined the term? Who has and who should have access to these media—which raises fundamental questions of power, freedom, and equality?

Theoretical Perspectives   To enhance sociological thinking, we include a comprehensive examination of what are considered the three major perspectives in sociology: *interactionism, functionalism,* and *conflict theory.* In addition, throughout the book, we present new paradigms, conflicting research findings, and controversial approaches. This encourages students to look beneath the surface of complex issues and recognize how the various perspectives alter both sociological questions and answers. For example, feminist theory is introduced in Chapter 1, "Discovering Sociology," and then is applied to special topics, such as "Doing Sociology" (Chapter 2), "Sex and Gender" (Chapter 11), "Families" (Chapter 13), and "The Economy and Work" (Chapter 17). In this edition, we list our theoretical coverage in the Detailed Contents, as well as in each chapter outline. More important, with many more examples from contemporary social theorists, we provide new, cutting-edge models and approaches that are both interesting and accessible to students.

Sociological Focus: Controversial and Thought-Provoking Boxes   We have added new boxes to this edition that encourage students to take a closer look at society and selected social issues. In each chapter there are three or more Sociological Focus boxes that challenge students to focus on major sociological concepts or examine contemporary social issues, such as euthanasia, abortion, genital mutilation, and capital punishment. These boxes ask students to peer beneath the surface of common sense and official views and use their sociological skills to decipher and analyze the issue in question. For example, Chapter 3, "Culture and Society," examines female genital mutilation and asks students to decide if the custom is a universal human rights violation.

Photographs, Maps, Tables, Figures, and Cartoons   Full-color illustrations, tables, figures, photographs, maps, and cartoons have been selected to capture interest while visually underscoring major sociological concepts and ideas. Also, we do more than simply present these visual materials as if they offered obvious conclusions. Instead, we provide questions for students to analyze and critique. For example, in Chapter 7, a map of the United States illustrates rates of violent and property crimes in various sections of the country, and students are encouraged to think about what social and cultural variables might help explain the geographic variations in crime rates. In the same chapter, the FBI's official crime data are graphically displayed, and students are asked to analyze why these data do not necessarily give an accurate picture of crime in the United States. Similar thought-provoking questions accompany many visuals in each chapter.

Pedagogical Features There are additional aids to reinforce and expand student learning.

- A **summary** that highlights the most important material for reflection and review is provided at the end of each chapter. Further, it helps boost sociological thinking skills by providing a thumbnail sketch of the most important components with their logical connections within each chapter.

- **Key terms and concepts** are boldfaced and defined within the text at first mention and are listed at the end of each chapter with cross-reference page numbers. Key terms and their definition are also positioned in the margin, generally at the bottom of the page or page spread at their point of usage.

- A comprehensive **glossary** and complete **bibliography** are included at the end of the book.

- Separate **subject** and **name indexes** are included at the end of the book.

SUPPLEMENTS

Instructor Supplements

- **Instructor's Manual.** The print Instructor's Manual includes chapter at-a-glance grids, learning objectives, lecture outlines, key terms and people, suggested discussion questions, weblinks, additional references, and recommended videos.

- **Test Bank.** The print Test Bank includes multiple choice, true-false, fill-in-the-blank, matching, and essay questions for making up quizzes and exams.

- **Computerized Testing.** The test bank is also available through Allyn and Bacon's computerized testing system, TestGen EQ. This fully networkable test generating software works with both Windows™ and Macintosh™ computers. The user-friendly interface allows you to view, edit, and add questions, transfer questions to tests, and print tests in a variety of fonts. Search-and-sort features allow you to locate questions quickly and to arrange them in whatever order you prefer.

- **PowerPoint® Presentation.** These PowerPoint presentations on CD-ROM, created for the Fifth Edition, feature lecture outlines for every chapter and artwork from the text. The PowerPoint presentation is also available at the instructor's resource center: *www.ablongman.com/irc*

- **Allyn and Bacon/ABC News Sociology Videos.** If you like to use news footage and documentary-style programs to illustrate sociological themes, this series of videos contain programs from *Nightline, World News Tonight,* and *20/20.* Each video has an accompanying User's Guide (available electronically). Available titles are *Poverty and Stratification, Race and Ethnicity, Gender, Deviance,* and *Aging.* Videocassettes are available on request to adopters.

- **Allyn and Bacon Video Library.** Qualified adopters may select from a wide variety of high-quality videos from such sources as Films for the Humanities and Sciences and Annenberg/CPB.

- **Allyn and Bacon Transparencies for Introductory Sociology.** This package includes over 125 color acetates featuring illustrations from the text or from other sources.

- **The Video Professor: Applying Lessons in Sociology to Classic and Modern Films** (Anthony W. Zumpetta, West Chester University). This manual describes hundreds of commercially available videos that represent nineteen of the most important topics in introductory sociology textbooks. Each topic lists a number of movies, along with specific assignments and suggestions for class use. Adopters can request a print copy or download the electronic file by logging in to the instructor's resource center: *www.ablongman.com/irc*

● **InterWrite PRS (Personal Response System).** *http://www.ablongman.com/catalog/ academic/product/0,1144,0205436951,00.html* Assess your students' progress with the Personal Response System—an easy-to-use wireless polling system that enables you to pose questions, record results, and display those results instantly in your classroom. Designed by teachers, for teachers, PRS is easy to integrate into your lectures:

- Each student uses a cell-phone-sized transmitter, which they bring to class.

- You ask multiple-choice, numerical-answer, or matching questions during class; students simply click their answer into their transmitter.

- A classroom receiver (portable or mounted) connected to your computer tabulates all answers and displays them graphically in class.

- Results can be recorded for grading, attendance, or simply used as a discussion point.

Our partnership with PRS allows us to offer student rebate cards bundled with any Allyn & Bacon/Longman text. The rebate card is a direct value of $20.00 and can be redeemed with the purchase of a new PRS student transmitter. In addition, institutions that order 40 or more new textbook plus rebate card bundles will receive the classroom receiver—a $250 value—including software and support at no additional cost. Contact your Allyn & Bacon/Longman representative or visit *http://www.ablongman.com/prs* for more information.

Student Supplements

● **Study Guide.** This print manual provides learning objectives, chapter outlines, key terms and people, self-tests, and glossaries.

● **Themes of the Times: Technomedia and Society.** This brief anthology, created specifically for this text, consists of current articles from the *New York Times* that pick upon and expand one of the major themes in the text: the impact of mass media and information technology on society. This reader is packaged free with the text on request.

● **Study Card for Introduction to Sociology.** Compact, efficient, and laminated for durability, the Allyn & Bacon Study Card for Introductory Sociology condenses course information down to the basics, helping students quickly master fundamental facts and concepts or prepare for an exam.

Online Course Management

● **—CourseCompass Version.** MySocLab is a state-of-the-art interactive and instructive solution for introductory sociology, delivered within CourseCompass, Allyn & Bacon's course management system (powered by Blackboard and hosted nationally on our server). MySocLab is designed to be used as a supplement to a traditional lecture course, or to completely administer an online course. Customize your course or use the materials as presented. Built around a complete e-book version of the text, MySocLab enables students to explore important sociological concepts, by watching television news stories, listening to interviews with prominent researchers and social scientists, reading current newspaper articles, analyzing data from graphs and maps in the text, and performing other hands-on activities. Available at no additional cost to students when the text is packaged with a MySocLab CourseCompass Student Access Code Card.

● **mysoclab—Website Version.** Provides virtually the same online content and interactivity as the CourseCompass MySocLab, without any of the course management features or requirements. Available at no additional cost to students when the text is packaged with a MySocLab CourseCompass Student Access Code.

● **WebCT™ and Blackboard™ Test Banks.** For colleges and universities with **WebCT™** and **Blackboard™** licenses, we have converted the complete Test Bank into these popular course management platforms. Adopters can request a copy on CD or download the electronic file by logging in to the instructor's resource center: *www.ablongman.com/irc*

Additional Supplements

● **Research Navigator™** (Access Code Required). This online research database is available free to students when the text is packaged with a MySocLab Access Code Card, or the *ResearchNavigator.com Guide: Sociology* (see below). Searchable by keyword, it gives your students access to thousands of full-text articles from scholarly social science journals and popular magazines and newspapers included in the *ContentSelect Research Database*, as well as a one-year archive of *New York Times* articles.

● **ResearchNavigator.com Guide: Sociology** (Joe Jacoby, Bowling Green University). This manual, which is packaged on request at no additional cost with this text, includes tips, resources, and URLs to aid students conducting research on Pearson Education's research website, *www.researchnavigator.com*. Each copy contains a student access code for the Research Navigator database, offering students free, unlimited access to a collection of more than 25,000 discipline-specific articles from top-tier academic publications and peer-reviewed journals, as well as the *New York Times* and popular news publications. The Guide introduces students to the basics of the Internet and the World Wide Web, and includes tip for searching for articles on the site, and a list of journals useful for research in their discipline. Also included are hundreds of web resources for the discipline, as well as information on how to correctly cite research.

● **Building Bridges: The Allyn and Bacon Guide to Service Learning** (Doris Hamner). This manual, packaged on request at no additional cost with this text, offers practical advice for students who must complete a service-learning project as part of their required course work.

● **Careers in Sociology, Third Edition** (W. Richard Stephens, Eastern Nazarene College). This supplement, packaged on request at no additional cost with this text, explains how sociology can help students prepare for careers in such fields as law, gerontology, social work, business, and computers. It also examines how sociologists enter the field.

● **College and Society: An Introduction to the Sociological Imagination** (Stephen Sweet, Ithaca College). This supplemental text uses examples from familiar surrounding—the patterns of interaction, social structures, and expectations of conduct on a typical college campus—to help students see the ways in which large society also operates. Available for purchase separately or packaged with this text at a special discount.

ACKNOWLEDGMENTS

Society in Focus: An Introduction to Sociology, Sixth Edition has benefited from the wisdom and friendship of many people. We are grateful to Harriet Prentiss for signing the original book, and to Alan McClare for his help on the first three editions. Additionally, we want to thank the many Allyn and Bacon staff members whose efforts enhanced the quality, timeliness, and look of the text. Special thanks go to Jeff Lasser, who served as editor for this edition. We also want to thank Leah Strauss, development editor, Karen Mason, production supervisor, and Melena Fenn and the team at WestWords/PMG, for guiding the production of this edition. For the photo research, we'd like to thank Katherine Cebik for her work on this edition and Sarah Evertson, PoYee Oster, and Julie Tesser for their work on previous editions. We also thank Eric Madfis who provided valuable research assistance.

Without the love and encouragement of our wives, Marilyn Thompson and Mary R. Hickey, and our children, Brandon and Mica Thompson and Christopher Hickey, this book would not have been possible. We are indebted to our many friends and colleagues for their unstinting support.

Finally, we want to thank our colleagues from across the country who reviewed the manuscript and who generously shared their time and wisdom gained through many years of teaching sociology. For their help on this edition, we are deeply grateful to: Adriana Leela Bohm, Delaware Country Community College; Betty J. Daughenbaugh, Wor-Wic Community College; Susan Dobyns, Pima Community College; Risa Lynn Garelick, Coconino

Community College; Edmond C. Johnson, Barton County Community College; Michael V. Miller, University of Texas–San Antonio; and Terrence Stewart, Mott Community College.

For their help on previous editions, we would like to thank: Bonnie Ach, Chapman University (CA); William Arnold, University of Kansas, Lawrence; George E. Arquitt, Oklahoma State University; Roger Barnes, University of the Incarnate Word (TX); Diane Barthel, State University of New York, Stony Brook; William Beaver, Robert Morris College; Marshall Botkin, Frederick Community College; Janet Boyce, Idaho State University; Suzanne Brandon, College of St. Catherine (MN); Cliff Brown, University of New Hampshire, Durham; Alyce Bunting, Texarkana College; William D. Camp, Luzerne County Community College (PA); Karen Conner, Drake University (IA); Dr. Denise Dalaimo, Mt. San Jacinto College; Raymond DeVries, St. Olaf College (MN); Lois Easterday, Onondaga Community College (NY); Susan Farrell, City University of New York Kingsborough Community College; Charles Faupel, Auburn University; Barbara Feldman, Seton Hall University (NJ); Jan Fiola, Moorhead State University (MN); Robin Franck, Southwestern College (CA); Pamela Gaiter, Collin County Community College (TX); Carol Gardner, Indiana University-Purdue University, Indianapolis; Michael Goslin, Tallahassee Community College (FL); Debbie Hanna, Lander University; Roxanna Harlow, Indiana University, Bloomington; Emily Ignacio, University of Illinois, Urbana; Miho Kawai, SUNY Ulster County Community College; Joseph A. Kortaba, University of Houston (TX); Larry Lance, University of North Carolina, Charlotte; Diana Larkin, South Puget Sound Community College (WA); Richard Leveroni, Schenectady Community College (NY); Diane E. Levy, University of North Carolina, Wilmington; Sandra Lopez, Trident Technical College; Kim MacInnis, Bridgewater State College (MA); Rick Malloy, St. Joseph University (PA); Marcella Mazzarelli, Massachusetts Bay Community College; Kristy McNamara, Furman University (SC); Michael Miller, University of Texas, San Antonio; Richard Miller, Missouri Southern State College; Edward V. Morse, Tulane University (LA); Craig J. Nauman, Madison Area Technical College (WI); Ronald Penton, Sr., Gulf Coast Community College (FL); Anne Peterson, Columbus State College (OH); Howard Robboy, The College of New Jersey; Helen Rosenberg, University of Wisconsin, Parkside; Rudy Sanfilippo, Canada College (CA); Tahmoores Sarraf, Idaho State University; Caroline Schacht, East Carolina University; Jennifer Crew Solomon, Winthrop University (SC); Brenda Still, College of Charleston; Marcella Thompson, University of Arkansas; Charles Tolbert, Louisiana State University, Baton Rouge; Robert Tournier, College of Charleston (SC); Lisa Troyer, University of Iowa; Steven L. Vassar, Mankato State University (MN); Mel Wallace, McHenry County College (IL); Dwight Wood, Marshall University; Robert Wood, Rutgers University, Camden (NJ); Diane Zablotsky, University of North Carolina, Charlotte, and Anthony W. Zumpetta, West Chester University.

William E. Thompson
Joseph V. Hickey

About the Authors

The cooperative writing efforts of Thompson and Hickey began more than a decade ago, when they decided to explore the mall Easter Bunny and Santa Claus as well as other "taken-for-granted" roles, social settings, and everyday social interactions.

William E. Thompson was born and raised in Tulsa, Oklahoma, and was the first member of his family to receive a high school diploma. He received his bachelor's degree from Northeastern State University, a master's degree from Missouri State University, and a Ph.D. from Oklahoma State University. Professor Thompson has authored and coauthored more than 30 articles in professional journals, including several reprinted in sociology textbooks and readers. He has coauthored a textbook on juvenile delinquency that is in its seventh edition, and has coedited an anthology on juvenile delinquency. Thompson also is the author of *The Glass House*, a nonfiction account of his mother's two year battle with cancer and the lessons about life and living learned from her death and dying.

Professor Thompson began his college teaching career at the University of Tulsa. He spent the next ten years at Emporia State University in Emporia, Kansas. He is currently a professor of sociology and criminal justice and Director of Mayo College, a residential learning community for first-year students, at Texas A & M University–Commerce. He has also taught in the British Studies Program at Kings College, University of London. In 1993 Thompson received an Outstanding Teaching Award from the Texas Association of College Teachers, and in 1994 he won the Distinguished Faculty Award for Research and Teaching at Texas A & M University–Commerce. For fun and relaxation Thompson plays the drums.

Joseph V. Hickey received his bachelor's and master's degrees from George Washington University and his Ph.D. from the University of New Mexico. A native New Yorker and Midwest transplant, Professor Hickey has won both writing and film awards. He has authored and coauthored two dozen articles and has written and produced numerous videotapes on such diverse subjects as popular culture, racial and ethnic communities, and cross-cultural studies.

Joseph Hickey is currently professor Emeritus in the Department of Sociology–Anthropology at Emporia State University in Emporia, Kansas, where for more than two decades he taught introductory courses in sociology and cultural anthropology to undergraduates.

Chapter 1

Discovering Sociology

"The first wisdom of sociology is this— things are not what they seem."
—Peter Berger, *Invitation to Sociology*

The premise is simple. Sixteen total strangers are dropped off in the middle of nowhere with only the most rudimentary supplies—usually a knife, a pot or pan for boiling water, enough rice for one or two meals, and a flint for starting a fire. They must start from scratch and build shelter, find a fresh water supply, or at least build a fire to boil water and protect themselves from wildlife. More important, they must build some type of society and establish some rules for living, because for the next 39 days their survival depends on one another. Cooperation is paramount. Teamwork is essential. And, by the way, they are competing *against* each other for a grand prize of one million dollars that will be awarded to the "sole survivor."

The so-called "reality" television show, *Survivor,* has enjoyed several successful seasons as one of the most popular and highest rated programs shown around the world. Viewers are vicariously transported to exotic locations such as Palau Tiga island, the outback of Australia, and the tropical rain forest of the Amazon. Contestants range from 20-something bikini-clad swimsuit models and bare-chested personal fitness trainers to 50-something grandmothers, ex-professional football players, and goat farmers. Survival skills are tested as participants build shelter, forage for food, and compete in "reward challenges" involving athletic and mental contests and "immunity challenges" to avoid getting voted out of the "tribe." Each season has pitted young against old, blacks against whites and other racial and ethnic groups, men against women, blue-collar workers against professionals, devout Christians against atheists, and one season even featured a hearing-impaired contestant. First they compete in teams; later it becomes an individual competition.

At first, it seems that the "fittest" will survive, so young, athletic, muscular ex-military types seem to have a clear advantage over

This is a scene from an episode of the popular television show *Survivor, Cook Islands.*

How do so-called "reality shows" such as *Survivor* reflect some of the basic principles of sociology?

weaker, less physically gifted opponents. Yet, both contestants and viewers soon realize that survival skills involve far more than youth, vigor, and physical fitness. In each episode alliances are made and broken; rumors run rampant; hunting, fishing, and cooking skills become less important than diplomacy and the ability to "fly under the radar" to avoid making enemies. In the end, various *Survivor* millionaires have included the most obnoxious and hated tribal member (Richard from season 1), one of the most popular and friendly tribal members (Tina from season 2), and a self-confessed "spoiled brat" in a 22-year-old swimsuit model (Jenna from season 6). In fact, most viewers, contestants, and winners agree that each season's "sole survivor" has been totally unpredictable.

You may ask, "What does the television program *Survivor* have to do with sociology?" At first, the answer seems to be, "nothing," yet, if one looks beneath the surface of the mere voyeuristic and entertainment aspects of the program, the answer is, more accurately, "everything." While "reality television" may be far removed from most people's *reality,* the program underscores what sociologists have always known: age, race, ethnicity, sex, gender, social class, religion, groups, and social networks are but a few of the important variables that affect how people interact and literally *survive* in the real world. More important, each season and every episode of *Survivor* has illustrated the first wisdom of sociology and the guiding theme of this book: *things are not necessarily what they seem* (Berger, 1963).

WHAT IS SOCIOLOGY?

Sociology is *the systematic and scientific study of human behavior, social groups, and society.* Sociologists examine the structural and institutional forces that shape our everyday lives, behaviors, and social values and look at how we help create those social structures and institutions. Table 1.1 compares and contrasts sociology to other social and behavioral sciences and related disciplines. Sociology is an academic discipline, but this does not mean that it is simply "a thing to be studied . . . sociology is, first of all, a thing lived" (Lemert, 2005:xv). Perhaps sociologist Peter Berger (1963:4) said it best when he wrote, "Sociology is not a practice but *an attempt to understand.*" This requires that sociologists look at everyday events a little differently from the way most people do. Our goal in this book is to help you better understand the world in which you live and your place in it by helping you to develop your *sociological imagination* and to learn to *think sociologically.*

Do you sometimes enjoy the peace and solitude of being alone? At other times do you like being with other people, celebrating your achievements or sharing your concerns? If you are like most people, the answer to both questions is probably "Yes." While all of us enjoy some time alone, we also need and actively seek the company and security of other people. We congregate to establish families, groups, tribes, communities, nations, and many other organizations, some of which transcend national boundaries. This *social imperative* sets us apart from other animals, and, though it is survival-related, it greatly transcends mere biological or instinctive drives to cluster for survival. As we form collectivities we make both conscious and unconscious choices to sacrifice some of our individual freedoms, but at the same time we derive many social benefits from the process. This interdependence between society and the individual is the primary focus of sociology, and understanding it requires the development of a **sociological imagination**—a *quality of mind that provides an understanding of our-*

TABLE 1.1
SOCIOLOGY AND OTHER SOCIAL AND BEHAVIORAL SCIENCES AND RELATED DISCIPLINES

All social and behavioral sciences focus on the behavior of people and attempt to explain, at least to some extent, *what* they do, *how* they do it, and *why* they do it. Yet each discipline has a different exphasis and primary focus that sets it apart from the others.

SOCIOLOGY	PSYCHOLOGY	ANTHROPOLOGY (CULTURAL)	HISTORY	ECONOMICS	POLITICAL SCIENCE	CRIMINAL JUSTICE	SOCIAL WORK
Studies human behavior with emphasis on social structure, social groups, interaction, and society.	Studies human behavior with emphasis on individuals, personality, and biology.	Studies past human behavior with emphasis on past cultures and preindustrial societies.	Studies human behavior with emphasis on people and events of the past.	Studies human behavior with emphasis on the economy and the exchange of goods and services.	Studies human behavior with emphasis on political institutions, government, power, and authority.	An applied field that uses sociological and criminological theories to explain the creation, causation, and control of crime. Focuses on criminal procedures, law enforcement, and corrections.	An applied field that uses sociological and psychological theories to explain social problems and to operate agencies designed to alleviate some of the consequences of these problems.

selves within the context of the larger society (Mills, 1959). Focus box 1.1 describes how one of the authors had his sociological imagination sparked and became a sociologist.

The Sociological Imagination

By using our sociological imaginations we can better see the relationship between ourselves and the society in which we live. Sociologist C. Wright Mills (1959) contended that this requires that we grasp the connection between *history* (events that have shaped an entire society's values and beliefs) and *biography* (an individual's life experiences within a particular society). This important link is often overlooked, but it is essential for sociological understanding, because it places individual behavior in a larger social context. It reminds us that we, as individuals, are to some extent *products* of the particular society and historical period in which we live, but also acknowledges that we are *history makers,* who help produce and change society by our actions. We can only guess what would have happened to the Civil Rights movement of the 1960s if the late Rosa Parks had given up her seat to the white man and moved to the back of the bus in Montgomery, Alabama, in 1955. Or what might have transpired if she had refused to do so 30 years earlier, in the 1920s. Sociology teaches us that everything, from the most heroic and spectacular actions to the most mundane and taken-for-granted features of our existence, reflects the dynamic interplay between the individual and society.

Rosa Parks made history in 1955 when she violated an Alabama law by refusing to give up her seat to a white person and move to the back of the bus.

How does this solitary act illustrate C. Wright Mills's contention that a sociological imagination requires the understanding of the link between history and biography?

Personal Troubles versus Social Issues   A sociological imagination allows us to see the important relationship between *personal troubles*, which affect an individual (e.g., being an alcoholic), and *social issues*, which reflect a problem for the entire society (e.g., alcoholism) (Mills, 1959). This distinction is a critical component of sociology, because it enables us to see the *general* in the *particular* (Berger, 1963). Sociologists study patterns of behavior in order to draw general conclusions about a social issue that transcend the effect of the problem or issue on any particular individual. For example,

Where did I go wrong? I could have been almost anything—a jet pilot, sky diver, firefighter, surgeon—you name it, I could have done it. So how did I end up a sociologist? Bad genes? Bad instincts? Bad choices? Or just bad timing? Oh, yes; now I remember. It was the fall of my freshman year, and I took that general education class, Sociology 101, Principles of Sociology.

I tried not to like the class. After all, my choice of major had changed from history to physical education to premed and back to history. I knew where I was headed and resented a college curriculum that forced me to waste my time on "useless" subjects such as the humanities, fine arts, and social and behavioral sciences. I would complete my history major and physical education minor, complete teacher certification requirements, and teach high school history and coach baseball like my high school idol had done.

Then came Sociology 101. The teacher obviously knew her subject—and loved it. Here was a class that acknowledged the social world in which I lived. The country was torn by racial tension, and we were reading and discussing Eldridge Cleaver's *Soul on Ice;* students were seizing administration buildings on college campuses, and we were reading and discussing Jerry Farber's *Student as Nigger;* the Vietnam War orchestrated by the American military-industrial complex was tearing the nation apart, and we were reading and discussing C. Wright Mills's *The Power Elite;* and finally, I was searching for my academic niche, and we were reading and discussing Peter Berger's *Invitation to Sociology.* That was it; I was hooked. In sociology there was something I could embrace—something I could live.

In his *Invitation to Sociology,* Berger describes a sociologist as a person

intensively, endlessly, shamelessly interested in the doings of [people] . . . naturally . . . interested in the events that engage people's ultimate beliefs, their moments of tragedy and grandeur and ecstasy. But he [or she] will also be fascinated by the commonplace, the everyday. . . . [The sociologist] is the [person] who must listen to gossip . . . who is tempted to look through keyholes, to read other people's mail (1963: 18–19). And he warns that people who like to avoid shocking discoveries, who prefer to believe that society is just what they were taught in Sunday School, who like . . . the world-taken-for-granted, should stay away from sociology" (1963:24).

In some ways I had always been a sociologist at heart; I simply lacked the academic training. I had never been able to walk past a closed door without wondering what was behind it. People fascinated me, and I delighted in watching them interact. The rest of my undergraduate years sped by. I took more than the required number of sociology courses for my major—in fact, I took all that my small school offered.

Even though I took a few detours along the way, which included teaching high school social studies (and even coaching a little baseball), my goal was a Ph.D. in sociology. During my doctoral studies and after receiving the degree, I actively pursued the role of sociologist—teaching, researching, writing, and publishing.

My passion for sociology sometimes annoys those around me as they realize that I am always plying the crafts of my trade. Whether at a wedding, funeral, party, or faculty meeting, I am always observing, analyzing, and interpreting human social interaction. My research has covered everything from playing the Easter Bunny and Santa Claus in shopping malls to hanging cows' tongues on the "kill floor" of a beef processing plant. My enthusiasm is infectious, and I delight in seeing friends, colleagues, and students become interested and sometimes excited when I share my research findings with them.

One Christmas my wife gave me a coffee mug. On one side of the mug is the phrase "Success is doing what you love"; on the other side is "Success is loving what you do." I am a success.

Sociology is not for everyone. If you have no curiosity about the social world in which you live, you will find little satisfaction in sociology. However, if the investigation of the subjects of sociology—family, school, religion, politics, economics, crime, delinquency, prostitution, urbanization, gender roles, health care, aging, terrorism, war, and peace—intrigues you, you too might want to reflect on becoming a sociologist.

TAKING A CLOSER LOOK

What aspects of sociology appeal to you the most? Are you interested in accepting Berger's invitation to sociology? If not, how might this sociological curiosity benefit you in other aspects of your life?

---

while alcoholism may have devastating consequences for the alcoholic and his or her immediate family, sociology focuses on the larger problem of alcoholism and its impact on society. This broader sociological focus may include cross-cultural values and attitudes toward alcohol consumption, alcohol use and abuse on college campuses, drinking and driving, the differences and similarities between alcoholism and other forms of drug abuse, and other sociological issues. This is not to say that sociologists are unconcerned about individuals and their lives, but sociology's emphasis is on the way individuals relate to others, peoples' positions in society, and the interdependence between society and individuals.

Making Generalizations while Avoiding Stereotypes As noted in the example of alcoholism, one goal of sociologists is to identify and understand general patterns of social behavior by studying the actions of specific individuals and groups. As a result of sociological studies, we know that nationality, race, age, gender, sexual orientation, political preference, religion, and a host of other social factors greatly affect our viewpoints and actions. For example, as we discuss in Chapter 16, African Americans, women, the elderly, and labor union members are more likely to vote for Democrats than Republicans in national elections. In making generalizations, however, we must be careful not to fall prey to overgeneralizations and inaccurate stereotypes (oversimplified ideas about a group) that can seriously distort our thinking and cloud our understanding. Consider some of the ways we think about and act toward people based on their race, age, sex, social class, and other characteristics, and how these thoughts and actions can be potentially damaging and even dangerous. Many of our stereotypes come from the mass media, especially television. Throughout this book we illustrate how to examine the media more critically from a sociological perspective. Stereotypes also come from our myopic view of the world. The sociological imagination and locating individuals in a larger social context require that we understand that we live in a global society.

Recognizing diversity and understanding its impact on society is a critical component of sociological thinking.

How does this photo of the United Nations building in New York City serve as a daily reminder of life in a global society?

Understanding Life in a Global Society

One of the most significant social consequences of the twentieth century was the transformation of a world of separate nation-states with unique histories, cultures, and social experiences into a massive global village. In the sixteenth century the Portuguese navigator Ferdinand Magellan led a Spanish expedition that was the first to circumnavigate the globe. The treacherous journey took approximately 3 years. Today, ships can make the same journey in less than a week and airplanes in less than 24 hours; communication satellites orbit the earth in less than 2 hours and send electronic signals around the world in seconds.

The world has changed, and understanding the nature of these changes is essential for developing a sociological understanding of our lives and the world around us. Nowhere is that change more apparent and powerful than in our ability to communicate information, transport people, and move huge sums of capital around the globe quickly. Technological advances in communication, transportation, importation, and exportation have rendered the ideology and policies of *social isolationism* not only ridiculous, but also impossible. As one sociologist noted, globalization changes everything: "some social things may be reshaped or threatened . . . they can't any longer be taken for granted" (Lemert, 2005:181).

Look around you. Two of the most popular brands of Japanese automobiles, Toyota and Honda, are manufactured in Ohio and Kentucky, while many General Motors cars are made from parts manufactured in Mexico and Canada. The best-selling American athletic shoes, Nike, are headquartered in Oregon but made in China and Indonesia. Reebok shoes bear the symbol of the British flag but are manufactured in China and Indonesia. Designer clothes with European labels are made in Central and South America, as are some of the least expensive brands sold under American labels in huge discount stores in the United States.

The recognition that we live in a global society is an integral part of thinking sociologically and developing our sociological imaginations—that is, understanding ourselves in a larger social context. Throughout this book we focus on the global aspects of the issue under study and draw on a wealth of studies and examples from around the world. Global awareness also helps us to question cultural misconceptions and media stereotypes about people who live in countries with cultures very different from our own. It accentuates diversity and helps us challenge views that our particular way of doing things is the only way, or even the best way, of doing them.

Recognizing Diversity

Imagine a world where everybody is exactly the same: everyone looks alike, acts alike, talks alike, and thinks alike. What a simple and uninteresting world it would be. While it may sometimes be comforting to be around people with similar backgrounds and interests, the world is far more complex than that. We live in a world where variety is indeed the "spice of life." Globalization has increased mobility, providing in many places a social mosaic of people from different racial and ethnic backgrounds, nationalities, religions, and cultures.

How does this diversity affect you and me? It requires that we look at ourselves and the world in which we live a bit differently. We must realize that complex social issues cannot be viewed in simple terms of *right* or *wrong, black* or *white,* and *good* or *evil,* but require that we understand and consider other points of view that may be dramatically different from our own. Just as sociology makes generalizations about how common powerful social forces act on all of us, it also recognizes the importance of diversity for understanding social interaction and human society. Throughout this book we underscore the diversity of society by focusing on research and examples that include people from both sexes, the entire range of gender roles, a wide variety of racial and ethnic groups, diverse sexual orientations, different levels of physical and mental abilities, and representatives from diverse national, cultural, religious, and political affiliations, as well as all social classes.

As noted, sociologists are interested in how variables such as age, race, sex, and social class, as well as a host of other social characteristics, influence social interaction and shape the society in which we live. These and other aspects of social diversity are at the heart of the sociological enterprise. As with an understanding of globalization, this appreciation for diversity quashes numerous misconceptions and stereotypes about various categories and groups of people and leads us to question many aspects of social life often taken for granted. Questioning "commonsense" understandings is at the heart of sociology and sociological thinking.

SOCIOLOGY AND CRITICAL THINKING

Thinking sociologically is a form of **critical thinking** that *involves objectively assessing ideas, statements, and information.* It entails defining problems, looking beneath the surface of commonly held ideas, questioning assumptions, logically and systematically analyzing evidence, recognizing biases, avoiding emotional knee-jerk reactions to issues and arguments, forming reasonable solutions to problems, and developing tolerance for a certain amount of uncertainty and ambiguity (Ruggiero, 2000). Simply put, **sociological thinking** involves *asking questions and questioning answers.* It requires *taking a closer look* at our social world.

Taking a Closer Look: Things Are Not Necessarily What They Seem

The subject of sociology is people and what they do in groups, organizations, and societies—subject matter familiar to all of us. Unfortunately, much of our understanding of the social world is very individualized and limited to personal experience, hearsay, and our preconceived notions about the way we think things are and the way we might want them to be. Sociology looks beyond the commonly accepted understandings of human social action to discover different levels of meaning that may be hidden from the consciousness of everyday life. It may even require a bit of suspicion and skepticism about the way human events are interpreted both personally and officially.

CRITICAL THINKING
Objectively assessing ideas, statements, and information.

SOCIOLOGICAL THINKING
Asking questions and questioning answers.

This sometimes creates a problem for sociologists. If they study a commonly experienced social institution such as the family, for example, and find that children tend to adopt the religious and political views of their parents, many people respond with a resounding "So what? Everybody knows that." On the other hand, if sociological findings contradict a commonly held assumption—for example, that child molestation is more likely to be perpetrated by a family member or a close friend of the family than by a stranger—they are likely to be met with skepticism, disbelief, or even anger. As one sociologist noted, applying the sociological imagination may make you "a rude, improper guest who crashes someone else's well-planned party" (Lemert, 2005:215).

This "damned if you do, damned if you don't" dilemma is faced by virtually all who undertake the sociological enterprise. The study of sociology does not require that we abandon our values, thoughts, ideas, and accumulated knowledge, but it does necessitate being open-minded and tolerant of values, thoughts, ideas, knowledge, and experiences that may be dramatically different from our own. This allows us to see the *strange* in the *familiar*—an important aspect of thinking sociologically. This is not to say sociologists are interested only in the bizarre or sensational aspects of human life. Quite the contrary. The sociologist is as interested in the priest as in the thief, in the hero as in the mass murderer, in the executioner as in the death row inmate (Berger, 1963). But when we study these people and their roles sociologically—that is, systematically and scientifically, we find that many of our preconceived notions are totally inaccurate and that much of what passes for *common sense* is nothing more than *common nonsense* (see Focus box 1.2 for examples). Sociology differs from everyday observation because it uses systematic, scientific methods to obtain information for research and study. Sociological thinking requires looking beneath the surface to question what we think we already know about people and their roles in society. When we do this, more often than not we find that *things are not necessarily what they seem.*

Analyzing assumptions and challenging personal experiences can be quite unsettling; sociology often raises more questions than it answers. Those who demand concrete answers and absolute certainties may become frustrated with sociology. Those who enjoy the search for elusive answers to the riddles of social life, however, will find sociology very appealing.

Sociological thinking also demands that we look beyond commonsense assumptions, media portrayals, and official data, to assess critically how such information is reported, collected, and interpreted. Any attempt to think sociologically about contemporary society must include a focus on mass media and the new information technologies (or "technomedia"). These media not only reflect our society but also play an important role in shaping and defining it. Now, more than ever, we need the critical thinking skills of sociology to analyze the "lies, distortions, and calculated fantasies" that have become part of "the normal content of mass communication" (Connell, 2000: 214). One sociological study of television talk shows concluded:

It's surprising how many ideas that seem to make sense are actually wrong. Sociologists have found that many widely held beliefs about the world, other people, and even ourselves are based on preconception, not fact.

When sociologists take a look beneath the surface of our taken-for-granted world, we find that much of what passes for "commonsense" understandings in our society is nothing more than common nonsense. This box provides a few examples and points to chapters in the book where more information on these topics can be found.

Common (Non)Sense: The larger a researcher's sample, the more accurately findings can be generalized to the population.

Fact: Representativeness is far more important than size for accurate sampling. Samples of 100–200 carefully selected subjects are better than 1,000–2,000 selected haphazardly (see Chapter 2).

Common (Non)Sense: An individual's personality is fully determined by age 6 and remains relatively unchanged as he or she becomes an adult.

Fact: Even as adults, individuals have multiple selves that change through the process of socialization according to social situations and cultural expectations (see Chapter 4).

Common (Non)Sense: Following the adage that "Two heads are better than one," the more people in a group, the better decisions that group is likely to make, because more alternatives will be considered.

Fact: Groups often become subject to *groupthink,* where the strong desire for consensus and group harmony causes members to ignore alternative solutions and go along with the group (see Chapter 6).

Common (Non)Sense: The majority of people on welfare are members of minorities who have been on welfare for generations and are too lazy to get a job.

Fact: The largest category of welfare recipients are female heads of households with young children, and most of them have been on welfare for less than 2 years (see Chapter 8).

Common (Non)Sense: Prejudiced people discriminate against members of minority groups; nonprejudiced people do not.

Fact: In some circumstances, because of peer pressure, expediency, and other social factors, nonprejudiced people may practice discrimination and prejudiced people may refrain from it (see Chapter 10).

Common (Non)Sense: The majority of people in the United States over age 65 live in nursing homes.

Fact: Less than 5 percent of the elderly in the United States live in nursing homes today, and less than 10 percent will ever live in a nursing home (see Chapter 12).

Common (Non)Sense: The United States provides equal educational opportunities for everyone regardless of race, ethnicity, or socioeconomic status.

Fact: Members of racial and ethnic minorities and the poor still suffer from unequal and inadequate educational opportunities in many parts of the United States (see Chapter 14).

Common (Non)Sense: In national elections in the United States, most voters vote, and winning candidates are elected by a majority of voters.

Fact: Often fewer than half of registered voters vote in national elections; although winners receive a majority of votes cast, they are usually elected by a minority of eligible voters and sometimes even by a minority of those who cast votes as was the case in the 2000 Presidential election (see Chapter 16).

Common (Non)Sense: In the United States, adequate health care is available to any person who needs it.

Fact: The United States is the only industrialized nation in the world that does not provide a national health insurance system for all of its citizens. Millions of Americans have no health insurance and cannot afford even the most basic medical care (see Chapter 18).

Common (Non)Sense: Social movements and revolutions are most likely to occur in poverty-stricken nations where people have little or no hope for peaceful social change.

Fact: Social movements and revolutions are far more common in relatively affluent societies where social situations seem to be improving and people see prospects for a better life (see Chapter 20).

TAKING A CLOSER LOOK

Why are so many "commonsense" notions perpetuated despite social scientific evidence to the contrary? How can critical thinking and a sociological imagination help us analyze commonsense assumptions and distinguish them from common nonsense?

A decade of the "confrontational" contemporary television talk show has provided, however unintentionally, an ideal laboratory for the study of "the social construction of reality." . . . Since it is already well documented that Americans get most of their "information" from television . . . it seems that sociology could well use its unique conceptual framework to help the public "see through" the talk shows and similar media messages. (Abt and Seesholtz, 1997:4)

Taking a Closer Look at the Mass Media

The critical thinking characteristic of sociology is especially useful in evaluating the mass media, because of their profound impact on virtually every aspect of social life. By **mass media,** we mean *forms of communication that transmit standardized messages to widespread audiences,* including newspapers, magazines, books, radio, television, and motion pictures. Communications expert Wilson Dizard (1997) refers to these as the "old media"; combined with the new technomedia they constitute one of the most powerful social influences in the world.

Perhaps the first major technological development in creating a powerful mass media occurred in the mid-nineteenth century, when the invention of steam-powered printing presses led to widespread distribution of affordable newspapers, magazines, and books. Literacy rates increased dramatically, news and information traveled much more rapidly and reached much greater audiences, and for the first time ordinary people turned to reading as a source of information and entertainment.

The second significant technological advancement occurred with the introduction of radio broadcasting in 1920 and television in 1939. From 1920 to the early 1950s the radio was a centerpiece in almost every American home and served as a primary source of news and entertainment. When the Pioneer Corporation introduced television sets to America with the words "We bring the revolution home," many doubted that television could ever replace the popular medium of radio. In 1946, motion picture mogul Darryl F. Zanuck of Twentieth Century Fox declared that television would never be successful because people would tire of staring at a plywood box every night.

Today, almost every American home has at least one television set; the average home has between two and three sets (see Table 1.2). Studies reveal that children spend as many as 40 hours per week viewing television. Adults are also ardent television viewers; it has been estimated that they spend between one-fourth and one-third of their lives in front of a television set (see Figure 1.1). Through the use of satellites and other communication technology, television literally links every portion of the globe into one mass-mediated society.

Sociological analysis can help us understand that while society has a tremendous impact on the mass media, the media—especially television—not only reflect the society but also exert tremendous influence in shaping society. The media influence social and political agendas by deciding what tiny bit of a tremendous amount of information is important. Moreover, when people have not experienced an event firsthand, media reports often constitute their "first draft of reality" (Graber, 1993:21). For some, it may also constitute their *final* draft. It can be argued that mass

MASS MEDIA
Forms of communication that transmit standardized messages to widespread audiences (e.g., newspapers, magazines, books, radio, television, and movies).

TABLE 1.2
TELEVISION SETS IN AMERICAN HOUSEHOLDS

YEAR	TELEVISION SETS IN HOMES (IN MILLIONS)	PERCENTAGE OF HOUSEHOLDS WITH TELEVISION SETS	NUMBER OF TELEVISION SETS PER HOUSEHOLD
1950	3.9	9.0	1.01
1960	45.8	87.1	1.13
1970	81.0	94.9	1.39
1980	128.0	97.9	1.68
1990	193.0	98.2	2.00
2000	245.0	98.2	2.40
2003	260.0	98.2	2.40

Source: Adapted from TABLE 1117, U.S. Bureau of Census, *Statistical Abstract of the United States: 2006* (122nd ed.), Washington, D.C. 2002.

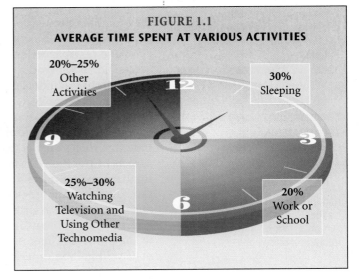

FIGURE 1.1
AVERAGE TIME SPENT AT VARIOUS ACTIVITIES

20%–25% Other Activities

30% Sleeping

25%–30% Watching Television and Using Other Technomedia

20% Work or School

media, especially television, may in fact be the most powerful social force in American society today—and perhaps in the world, since it now reaches even the most remote areas of the globe.

Several key media formats serve to filter what we see, read, and hear. First and foremost, media presentations, including those of "serious information" like the evening news, must be entertaining to attract viewers. For example, there appears to be little difference between stories aired by the major networks on the nightly news and those shown on popular television programs such as *Inside Edition* and *Extra*. Second, information must be packaged and presented within severe time constraints. After the time devoted to commercials, for example, the evening news has 23 minutes to convey the day's most important events. Usually each major story gets two minutes or less; stories that might take more than three minutes are considered too long for network news and are more appropriate for documentaries. Thus, if the media act as a mirror, they are a clouded and distorted mirror at best.

As a consequence of these and other agendas and formats, media presentations almost always emphasize (1) *personal* over *social* issues; (2) *emotional* over *intellectual* issues; (3) *concrete* over *abstract* events; and (4) *dynamic* and *fast-paced* stories over "talking heads" and *thought-provoking* pieces. The media rarely display a *sociological imagination;* instead, they personalize issues by using the most sensational, emotional, and extreme examples possible.

TECHNOMEDIA IN FOCUS

Although the traditional mass media, especially television, are still among the most powerful and pervasive forms of media today, we are bombarded with new forms of information technology that greatly influence our individual lives and change the world around us. Whereas communication and the exchange of information were once limited to face-to-face interaction, or standardized and more structured channels, now we can access a wealth of information and data almost instantaneously and can communicate with people around the globe. We define **technomedia** as *the newer and more personalized information technologies,* including personal computers, CD-ROMs, fax machines, video games, handheld databanks, cellular phones, the Internet, fiber optic communications, and interactive television—what Dizard (1997) calls the "new media."

The technomedia are of particular interest to sociologists because they combine elements of both the "old" and "new" media. *Time, Newsweek, U.S. News & World Report,* the *New York Times, Washington Post,* and a host of other major magazines and newspapers, as well as the networks ABC, CBS, NBC, Fox, and CNN, are fully accessible on the World Wide Web; the so-called new media now include all the major players from traditional mass media.

Sociologists are interested in technomedia for other reasons as well. Although computers and other electronic media appear to have a unifying effect on society by making communication and social interaction faster and easier than ever before, they also illustrate that *things are not necessarily what they seem.* The technomedia combine all the aspects of traditional mass media—print, sound, and video—but rather than sending standardized messages to massive audiences, technomedia are interactive and aimed at providing much more personalized services to smaller groups and individuals. Or, as one media expert asserted: television is the primary medium for *broadcasting,* but the Internet is the ultimate in *narrowcasting,* offering websites and chat groups that appeal to the particular interests of individual users (Sandberg, 1996). Thus while approximately 50 million Americans may use the Internet annually, the largest percentage are

Mass media, especially television, have helped bring about the globalization of society.

What impact do you think television may have on the lives of people in developing nations?

TECHNOMEDIA
Newer and more personalized information technologies (e.g., personal computers, CD-ROMs, fax machines, video games, handheld databanks, cellular phones, the Internet, fiber optic communications, and interactive television).

white men over age 40. Racial and ethnic minorities, women, the elderly, and the poor are the least likely to have access to or to use the new technomedia (Reuters, 1997). In 1998, almost half of all white homes had computers (44.9%), but less than one-third (29.0%) of African American households were equipped with computers—a phenomenon dubbed "the racial divide on the information highway" (Harmon, 1998:A1) or what sociologists refer to as the *digital divide*. That gap narrowed somewhat a year later, as 36 percent of African Americans gained access to the Internet (Goldstein, 2000). The fastest growing category of computer and Internet users, however, is youth ages 10 through 18; because of their ease with technology, experts predict that age group may soon become the major users of all technomedia.

In 1949, the magazine *Popular Mechanics* predicted that sometime in the future computers might weigh as little as 1.5 tons, making them more practical for use in business and industry. Today, most laptop computers are no larger than a purse or small briefcase, and handheld calculators and palm pilots are as small and lightweight as a credit card. It took radio 15 years to penetrate 25 percent of American households; television did it in only 7 years; the Internet took less than 3 years (CBS News, 1999). It is estimated that nearly 70 million households around the world are wired for Internet access (two-thirds of that number in the United States and Canada alone) (see Figure 1.2). Of greater sociological interest than these figures is the fact that different racial, age, gender, ethnic, and socioeconomic groups have differential access to and use patterns of technomedia (Reuters, 1997; Goldstein, 2000).

Online chat rooms are so commonplace that they are being replaced with "virtual communities." In 1996, for example, Howard Rheingold, a San Francisco–based writer, created a "town" in cyberspace called *Electric Minds*. According to its creator, a virtual community goes a step beyond chat rooms by providing more structure, long-term bulletin boards and message centers where messages remain for months at a time, and a place where "communities are built on sustained conversations, as opposed to more ephemeral chat" (Hafner, 1997:72). These

Why do you think Asia, Europe, and North America lead the world in Internet use?

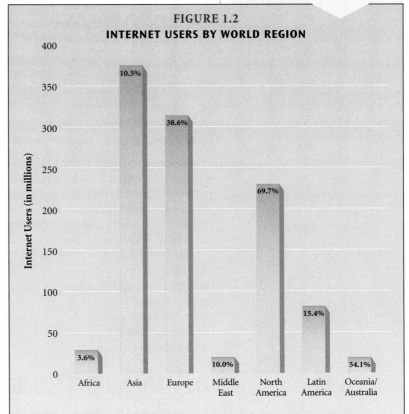

**FIGURE 1.2
INTERNET USERS BY WORLD REGION**

Internet Users (in millions)

- Africa: 3.6%
- Asia: 10.3%
- Europe: 38.6%
- Middle East: 10.0%
- North America: 69.7%
- Latin America: 15.4%
- Oceania/Australia: 54.1%

Note: Displayed in each bar is the number of internet users as a percentage of the total population for that world region.
Source: © Copyright www.internetworldstats.com, Nov. 15, 2006. Reprinted by permission of Miniwatts Marketing Group.

cyberspace "communities" are emerging at an amazing rate and attract "residents" from all over the United States, Tokyo, Berlin, and other major cities around the world (Hafner, 1997). Social norms arise in chat rooms and in virtual communities, creating what some have dubbed as "cyber civility" (Minerd, 2000).

Not only computers have made their way into the hands of individuals, but also a wide variety of other information technologies, including personal fax machines, cellular telephones, fiber optic communications, and interactive television, which combines aspects of the old media with the new. Unlike the traditional mass media, which were phased into society slowly, new forms of technomedia burst onto the scene almost daily. They have certainly changed people's lives in terms of activities if not also in substance and content (May, 2002). New media technologies permeate every aspect of society and have become imbedded in our very social fabric (Howard and Jones, 2004). Moreover, unlike many of the older forms of mass media, much of the new technomedia is relatively unregulated. Today, anybody who secures a website can disseminate research findings and data, or express opinions as facts, with virtually no checks or restraints.

These rapid technological developments pose some interesting sociological questions. For example:

- How has society changed now that daily newspapers and weekly magazines can be instantly accessed along with other online news and information services?
- What will be the social impact if traditional publishing companies, books, and libraries disappear in the wake of desktop publishing, CD-ROM, and online information services?
- How will television viewing change if networks and cable systems cannot compete with interactive television, computervision, personalized video, and online entertainment options?
- What are the First Amendment issues related to regulation of the Internet and other forms of technomedia? How will we resolve these issues?
- What are the social implications of online chat rooms and virtual communities? How will they alter our understandings of communication and social interaction?
- Do the mass media and technomedia provide us with access to too much information? If so, what are the sociological implications of this information overload? On the other hand, do the mass media and technomedia provide too little information as they edit and package news and information into brief capsules?
- How will interaction over the Internet alter the importance of race, age, sex, and social class?
- Is interaction in cyberspace *social* interaction?

These questions call attention to the need for sociological analysis of the mass media and technomedia. This is true today and will be even more important in the future as we attempt to select, interpret, and understand the media and their impact on society.

In each chapter of this book, we take a sociological look at the influence of the traditional mass media and technomedia as they relate to the topic covered in that chapter. This is neither an exercise in the popular sport of "media bashing" nor an attempt to promote mass media or technomedia. Rather, it is designed to help you sharpen your sociological imagination and critical thinking skills in order to better decipher, analyze, and understand the countless messages you receive every day as well as to realize how modern information technologies affect individuals and society. This involves thinking sociologically, looking beneath the surface, questioning the official view, and critically analyzing what is commonly taken for granted—activities that have been at the heart of sociology since its inception.

THE DEVELOPMENT OF SOCIOLOGY

Writings of philosophers, poets, and religious leaders of the ancient civilizations of Babylon, Egypt, India, and other parts of the world reflect substantial interest in interpreting social life. Most of the early writers, however, were less concerned with discovering what society *was* than with describing what it *should be*. Although social thinkers had long pondered the influence of society on human behavior, and the tenets of sociology probably have been practiced informally since humans first appeared, the term *sociology* was not coined, and the formal discipline of sociology did not emerge, until the early nineteenth century. Sociology was born in France, gained impetus in Great Britain and Germany, and eventually made its way to the United States as each of these countries experienced radical changes in social conditions and the intellectual explanations for them.

The Changing Social Climate: The Industrial Revolution

Prior to the Industrial Revolution, European society was characterized by a feudal system consisting of wealthy landowners (lords), who owned huge manors, and large numbers of peasants (serfs), who tilled the land and were thus economically tied to the lords and their manors for subsistence. As the lords died, were displaced, or drove one another off their lands, the manors were divided into small farms tilled by their new owners and their families, and small villages with an emerging merchant class developed as important economic centers and social communities.

One of the driving forces that led to the development of sociology in Europe was the dramatic social upheaval linked to the processes of *industrialization, urbanization,* and *immigration.* With the advent of new technology, especially steam-driven machines, factories developed, luring people from small villages and the less productive farms to more centralized locations to work for the new factory owners. Thus *industrialization,* the transformation from a predominantly agriculture-based economy to a manufacturing one, was accompanied by rapid *urbanization,* the growth of large cities. These two factors were accompanied by massive waves of *immigration,* as increased mobility encouraged people to cross political borders to escape oppressive conditions or pursue perceived opportunities elsewhere.

New problems emerged, such as inadequate housing; inordinate wealth beside abject poverty; crime; air, water, and noise pollution; and disease. Moreover, wherever industrialization, urbanization, and immigration have occurred, they have been linked to enhanced political awareness and demands for greater political, economic, and social participation. Consequently, nineteenth-century Europeans experiencing dramatic social upheaval sought explanations for, and workable solutions to, the day-to-day problems they were experiencing.

The Changing Intellectual Climate: The Rise of Science

Scholars often describe the eighteenth century as the *Age of Reason,* or *Enlightenment,* because during this time Western culture emerged into a new era of social thought. Over several centuries, and as a result of much struggle, the dominant way of explaining social events shifted from *theological* to *scientific.* Rather than attribute human behavior and social conditions to supernatural forces, people searched for logical, rational, and cause-and-effect explanations. As a result, universities replaced the church as the primary source of knowledge.

Early European Sociology

The works of several nineteenth-century scholars provided the foundation for contemporary sociology. One of the first was Auguste Comte, often credited with being the founder of sociology.

Auguste Comte (1798–1857)   Auguste Comte grew up in the aftermath of the French Revolution. Observing the social turmoil of his native country, he believed the new scientific approach to problem solving that was sweeping Europe might also be applied to the study of society. He coined the term *sociology* and wrote *Positive Philosophy,* the first systematic sociological approach to the study of society. Comte's new science emphasized **positivism,** *the use of observation, comparison, experimentation, and the historical method to analyze society.* Comte also identified two major areas of study for sociologists: *social statics,* which focuses on social structure, or the relatively stable elements found in every society, and *social dynamics,* which focuses on social change. These two areas remain part of the primary focus of contemporary sociology, and they contributed to the development of the structural functionalist perspective introduced later in this chapter and applied throughout the book.

Comte envisioned sociology as being much more than an intellectual enterprise. He dreamed of a utopian society fine-tuned by social engineers (sociologists) who would apply sociological knowledge to cure society's ills. In his later years, his devotion to sociology became so intense that he envisioned it almost as a religion, with sociologists the "high priests of positivism." While later sociologists tempered Comte's idealistic and zealous vision, most continue to believe in sociology's promise as a vehicle for positive social change.

Harriet Martineau (1802–1876)   Harriet Martineau grew up in England. In 1853, she translated Comte's six-volume *Positive Philosophy* into English and condensed it into two volumes, thus introducing sociology to England (Webb, 1960). Martineau made her own contribution to sociology with *Society in America,* one of the first and most thorough sociological treatises on American social life and one of the first to compare the system of social stratification in Europe to that in America. She took sociology from the realm of ideas to the arena of practice in *How to Observe Manners and Morals,* published in 1838 and one of the first books to focus on sociological research methods.

Auguste Comte (1798–1857) coined the term *sociology* and launched the positivistic approach to the study of sociology.

Harriet Martineau (1802–1876), one of the founders of sociology, translated Comte's work and helped establish a strong theoretical foundation for sociological research.

POSITIVISM
The use of observation, comparison, experimentation, and the historical method to analyze society.

Karl Marx's tomb in Highgate Cemetery in London, England. Sociologists embrace Karl Marx (1818–1883) as the founder of the conflict perspective in sociology although his academic training was in history, economics, and philosophy.

How did Marx's understanding of these disciplines contribute to his influence on sociology?

Émile Durkheim (1858–1917) with his emphasis on social structure and social solidarity provided a strong theoretical basis for the functionalist perspective in sociology.

Although Martineau introduced sociology to England, it was Herbert Spencer's controversial application of sociology that gained attention and support from wealthy industrialists and government officials in England and throughout Europe.

Herbert Spencer (1820–1903)

Observing the negative aspects of the Industrial Revolution in England—the struggle, competition, and violence—Herbert Spencer developed a theoretical approach to understanding society that relied on evolutionary doctrine. To explain both social structure and social changes, he used an *organic analogy* that compared society to a living organism made up of interdependent parts—ideas that ultimately contributed to the structural functionalist perspective in sociology. Using the phrase "survival of the fittest" even before Charles Darwin's landmark *On the Origin of Species* ([1859] 1964) was published, Spencer's *social Darwinism* concluded that the evolution of society and the survival of those within it were directly linked to their ability to adapt to changing conditions. According to Spencer, a free and competitive marketplace without governmental interference was essential so that the best and the brightest would succeed and, in turn, help build a stronger economy and society. Spencer opposed welfare or any other means of helping the weak or the poor, believing such efforts would weaken society in the long term by helping the "unfit" to survive. These ideas appealed to wealthy industrialists and government officials, who used Spencer's theory to scientifically support policies and practices that helped them maintain their wealth, power, and prestige at the expense of those less fortunate.

Karl Marx (1818–1883)

Marx was trained in history, economics, and philosophy, but his ideas reflect sociological thinking. Observing the same social conditions as Spencer, he drew very different conclusions about their origins. Marx declared that the unequal distribution of wealth, power, and other limited resources in society was not the result of "natural laws" but was caused by social forces—specifically, the exploitation of one social class by another. He insisted that social structure and the political and economic institutions that people took for granted were not the result of natural evolution or social consensus but reflected the opposed interests of different social classes.

Marx believed society consisted of two basic social classes: the "haves" and the "have-nots." According to Marx's viewpoint, the *bourgeoisie* (haves), the powerful ruling class, had assumed power not because they were the "fittest" but because they owned and controlled the means of production. He believed the bourgeoisie used deception, fraud, and violence to usurp the production of the *proletariat* (have-nots), or working class, whose labor created most of society's goods—and hence, its profits.

Marx was not a detached social observer but an outspoken social critic. He concluded that a slow, natural evolutionary process would not bring about necessary social changes. Rather, his analysis called for a major social revolution in which the proletariat would rise up, forcibly overthrow the bourgeoisie, and form a new, classless society. In such a society, Marx wrote, everyone would contribute according to his or her abilities and receive from society based on need. Marx's contributions to sociological understanding provided the foundation for the conflict perspective in sociology, discussed later in this chapter and throughout the book. Marx's focus on social conflict was unsettling to many—especially those whom he described as the bourgeoisie. They were relieved when Émile Durkheim's more palatable social analysis emerged and shifted the focus of sociology back to a more conservative approach called *functionalism*.

Émile Durkheim (1858–1917)

Unlike Marx, who focused on social conflict, French sociologist Émile Durkheim was primarily concerned with social order. He believed that *social solidarity,* or the social bonds developed by individuals to their society, create social order. Durkheim believed that social solidarity could be categorized into two types: *mechanical solidarity,* the type found in simple rural societies based on tradition and unity, and *organic solidarity,* which was found in urban societies and was based more on a complex division of labor and formal organizations.

One of Durkheim's most important contributions to sociology was his study *Suicide* ([1897] 1951), which demonstrated that abstract sociological theories can be applied to a very real social problem. More important, it showed that suicide, believed to be a private, individualized, and personal act, can best be explained from a sociological viewpoint. By looking at suicide rates instead of individual suicides, Durkheim linked suicide to *social integration*—the extent to which individuals feel they are a meaningful part of society. Those with the strongest social bonds are less likely to commit suicide than those who are less meaningfully integrated and have weaker social bonds. For example, his data demonstrated that married people had lower suicide rates than those who were single or divorced; people in the workforce had lower rates than those who were unemployed; and church members had lower rates than nonmembers. Moreover, those religions that promote the strongest social bonds among their members (e.g., Catholicism and Judaism) had much lower suicide rates than less structured religions (e.g., Protestantism). Today, over a century later, these patterns in suicide, and others discerned by Durkheim's early study, still persist.

Max Weber (1864–1920) Max Weber, a contemporary of Durkheim, was concerned that many sociologists, especially his fellow German, Karl Marx, allowed their personal values to influence their theories and research. Weber insisted that sociologists should be *value-free*—analyzing what society is, rather than what they think it should be. Weber did not advocate a cold, impersonal approach to sociology, however; he argued that understanding the meaning of social interaction requires *Verstehen,* an empathetic and introspective analysis of the interaction. In other words, Weber believed that researchers should avoid their personal biases and put themselves in the place of those they study, to understand better how they experience the world and society's impact on them.

One of Weber's most important contributions to sociology was his concept of the **ideal type,** *a conceptual model or typology constructed from the direct observation of a number of specific cases and representing the essential qualities found in those cases.* By ideal type, Weber was referring to a generalization based on many specific examples, not implying that something was necessarily desirable. For example, Weber used bureaucracy as an ideal type to analyze and explain the increasing rationalization and depersonalization that is part of formal organizations. Weber contended that to maximize efficiency, formal organizations such as private businesses, educational institutions, and governmental agencies had become and would continue to be increasingly bureaucratic. Although Weber contended that bureaucracy as an ideal type represented the most rational and efficient organizational strategy, he also warned of its depersonalizing and dehumanizing aspects.

Sociology Crosses the Atlantic

As in Europe, the onset of rapid industrialization and urbanization, and accompanying social problems, gave impetus to the development of sociology in the United States. American sociologists built on and expanded the theories and ideas of the European founders of sociology.

Lester F. Ward (1841–1913) Lester Ward is often considered the first systematic American sociologist. He attempted to synthesize the major theoretical ideas of Comte and Spencer, and differentiated between what he called **pure sociology**—*the study of society in an effort to understand and explain the natural laws that govern its evolution*—and **applied sociology,** which *uses sociological principles, social ideals, and ethical considerations to improve society.* The distinctions between these two areas of sociology are still made today.

Jane Addams (1860–1935) Although not a sociologist, Jane Addams practiced applied sociology and put sociological theory to work when she established the famous Hull House in Chicago in 1889 to aid the poor and homeless. One of the founders of American social work, in 1931 Addams's devotion to applied sociology and social activism earned her a Nobel Prize.

Perhaps no early sociologist had a more powerful influence on the study of social interaction than Max Weber (1864–1920).

Do you think Weber's insistence on "empathetic understanding" is important for sociology today?

IDEAL TYPE
A conceptual model or typology constructed from the direct observation of a number of specific cases and representing the essential qualities found in those cases.

PURE SOCIOLOGY
The study of society in an effort to understand and explain the natural laws that govern its evolution.

APPLIED SOCIOLOGY
Using sociological principles, social ideals, and ethical considerations to improve society.

William E. B. DuBois studied under Max Weber and helped establish African American sociology and the National Association for the Advancement of Colored People (NAACP).

Margaret Sanger (1883–1966) Another notable social reformer, Margaret Sanger applied sociological theories to problems of population, health, and women's rights. After watching a poor working woman die from a self-induced abortion, she began publishing *Woman Rebel,* a journal aimed at raising the consciousness of working-class women. Her articles covered topics ranging from personal hygiene, venereal disease, and birth control to social revolution.

William E. B. Dubois (1868–1963) William E. B. Dubois earned his doctorate from Harvard and pursued postgraduate study in sociology, history, and economics at the University of Berlin, where he studied under Max Weber. After returning to the United States, Dubois applied Weber's methodological technique of *Verstehen* to sociological studies of blacks in the United States. He is considered the founder of "Afro-American sociology" (Collins and Makowsky, 1993). Dubois was also one of the founders of the National Association for the Advancement of Colored People (NAACP), where he applied his theories, empirical research, and sociological imagination to empower African Americans to achieve social justice and equality in the United States.

CONTEMPORARY SOCIOLOGY

Sociology came of age in America during the 1920s, 1930s, and 1940s—a period of radical social change that included the Roaring Twenties, the Great Depression, and World War II. During that period, some of the most prominent sociologists and social psychologists of the twentieth century were either faculty members or students in the first sociology department in the United States, at the University of Chicago. They used Chicago as a dynamic sociological laboratory to observe and analyze the social impact of urbanization and industrialization.

The theoretical and methodological contributions of these scholars became known as the *Chicago School,* and provided sociology with symbolic interactionism, one of the three major **theoretical perspectives**—a *viewpoint or particular way of looking at things*—that dominate sociology today. The other two are: structural functionalism, and conflict. These three overriding perspectives serve as **paradigms,** *sets of assumptions and ideas that guide research questions, methods of analysis and interpretation, and the development of theory.* Let's take a brief look at each and compare their relative strengths and weaknesses. Table 1.3 gives a brief comparison of these three perspectives.

THEORETICAL PERSPECTIVE
A viewpoint or particular way of looking at things.

PARADIGM
A set of assumptions and ideas that guide research questions, methods of analysis and interpretation, and the development of theory.

TABLE 1.3
MAJOR THEORETICAL PERSPECTIVES IN SOCIOLOGY

PERSPECTIVE	VIEW OF SOCIETY	MAJOR CONCEPTS AND IDEAS	STRENGTHS	WEAKNESSES
Symbolic Interactionism	Society is like a stage where people define and redefine meaning as they interact with one another.	Meaningful symbols; definition of the situation; looking-glass self; symbolic interaction; dramaturgical analysis; labeling	Microlevel analyses; face-to-face interaction; day-to-day activities	Macrolevel analyses; ignores structure and larger social forces
Structural Functionalism	Society is a social system made up of interdependent parts, all of which must fulfill certain functions to operate properly.	Organic analogy; manifest and latent functions; equilibrium; dysfunctions	Macrolevel analyses; structure; institutions	Microlevel analyses; ignores conflict and diversity
Conflict	Society is a social arena in which diverse groups with conflicting values and interests compete for scarce resources, especially wealth, power, and prestige.	Social class; class consciousness; vested interests; alienation; power; coercion; domination; negotiation	Macrolevel analyses; social stratification; inequality	Microlevel analyses; ignores cooperation

The Symbolic Interactionist Perspective

The **symbolic interactionist perspective** *views social meaning as arising through the process of social interaction.* Contemporary symbolic interactionism rests on three basic premises:

1. Human beings act toward things on the basis of the meanings that they attach to them.

2. These meanings are derived from, or arise out of, social interaction with others.

3. These meanings may be changed or modified through the processes of interaction and interpretation. (Blumer, 1969b:2)

Proponents of this perspective, often referred to as the *interactionist perspective,* engage in **microlevel analysis,** *which focuses on the day-to-day interactions of individuals and groups in specific social situations.* Three major concepts important for understanding this theoretical approach include meaningful symbols, the definition of the situation, and the looking-glass self. In addition, two important types of theoretical analysis fit within the interactionist perspective: dramaturgical analysis and the labeling approach.

Meaningful Symbols   George H. Mead (1863–1931) insisted that the ongoing process of social interaction and the creating, defining, and redefining of meaningful symbols make society possible. *Meaningful symbols* are sounds, objects, colors, and events that represent something other than themselves, and are critical for understanding social interaction. Language is one of the most important and powerful meaningful symbols humans have created, because it allows us to communicate through the shared meaning of words.

Definition of the Situation   *Definition of the situation* refers to the idea that "if [people] define situations as real, they are real in their consequences" (Thomas and Thomas, 1928:572). Simply put, people define social reality through a process of give-and-take interaction. Once a definition is established, it shapes all further interactions. For example, have you ever decided that you were "in love" with someone? If so, how did that change the way you interacted with that person? Conversely, what happens when a married couple decides they are no longer in love? If they define their marriage as meaningless or decide they have irreconcilable differences, how does that affect their relationship? Is a marriage likely to survive if both partners have defined it as "over"?

The Looking-Glass Self   The *looking-glass self* refers to the idea that an individual's self-concept is largely a reflection of how he or she is perceived by other members of society (Cooley, [1902] 1922). Society is used as a mirror to reflect a feeling of self-pride, self-doubt, self-worth, or self-loathing. These important elements of symbolic interactionism contribute to socialization and the process of becoming human as we establish our personal and social identities.

Dramaturgical Analysis   A useful theoretical framework within symbolic interactionism, **dramaturgical analysis,** *uses the analogy of the theater to analyze social behavior.* In this approach, people are viewed as actors occupying roles as they play out life's drama. In real life, people do not passively accept others' definitions of the situation nor the social identities assigned to them. Rather, they take an active part in the drama, manipulating the interaction to present themselves in the most positive light. Thus, people often use *impression management* to communicate favorable impressions of themselves (Goffman, 1959).

The Labeling Approach   Another theoretical viewpoint within symbolic interactionism is the **labeling approach,** which *contends that people attach various labels to*

People rarely interact and communicate only with their voices.

What meaningful symbols might sociologists identify as important in helping to give meaning to the conversation between these two people?

SYMBOLIC INTERACTIONIST PERSPECTIVE
Views social meaning as arising through the process of social interaction (often referred to as *interactionism*).

MICROLEVEL ANALYSIS
Focuses on the day-to-day interactions of individuals and groups in specific social situations.

DRAMATURGICAL ANALYSIS
Uses the analogy of the theater to analyze social behavior.

LABELING APPROACH
Contends that people attach various labels to certain behaviors, individuals, and groups that become part of their social identity and shape others' attitudes about and responses to them.

certain behaviors, individuals, and groups that become part of their social identity and shape others' attitudes about and responses to them. For example, in *Outsiders* (1963), Howard Becker explored the fascinating world of jazz musicians and how their non-traditional music, penchant for marijuana, and open racial integration during the 1950s led mainstream Americans to label them "deviant."

The influence of the Chicago School and symbolic interactionism waned in the late 1950s, when a faction of sociologists argued that its approach was too dependent on ethnographic studies, personal observations, interviews, and subjective interpretations. Insisting that sociology must be more scientific, or at least, as Comte had envisioned, more positivistic, this group believed that sociology should rely more heavily on quantifiable data, facts, figures, and statistics. This led to the development of the Iowa School of symbolic interaction and also fueled a revival of structural functionalism.

The Iowa School of Symbolic Interaction Manford H. Kuhn argued that the theoretical assumptions of symbolic interactionism can be operationalized and applied in more positivistic scientific ways. While sharing the theoretical assumptions of the Chicago School, the Iowa School sought to lend more scientific credibility to symbolic interaction and its research methods. Meanwhile, the desire to make sociology return to its positivistic roots provided the impetus for Talcott Parsons and others at Harvard University to revive the structural functionalist perspective of early European sociologists.

The Structural Functionalist Perspective

Heavily influenced by the ideas of Comte, Spencer, and Durkheim, the structural functionalist perspective shifted the focus of sociology from the study of day-to-day social interaction to a **macrolevel analysis,** which *examines broader social structures and society as a whole.* This perspective emphasizes social structure and order. Often referred to as the functionalist perspective, or functionalism, the **structural functionalist perspective** *views society as a system of interdependent and interrelated parts.* Within the overall *structure* of the system, each part fulfills a specific *function,* which thereby contributes to the overall functioning of the entire system.

The example of a stereo system helps illustrate this view. A stereo system consists of various components: an amplifier, tuner, compact disk player, and speakers. Each component has a specific function to perform so that the overall stereo system can perform its function: the playing of music. If any component fails to function properly—for example, if one of the speakers rattles—the entire system fails to function properly. It is then necessary to isolate and identify the problem (in this case, a bad speaker) and repair or replace it. Once the problem with the speaker is fixed, the stereo system resumes its normal functioning. An emergency room in a contemporary hospital serves as a more human example where doctors, nurses, technicians, and other specialists work together as a team, each performing specific tasks, in an effort to save a patient's life.

Social Structure The structural functionalist perspective contends that society has a *structure* consisting of a variety of important components—for example, basic social institutions such as the family, religion, education, politics, and the economy. These institutions are interrelated and interdependent. Each performs an important *function* contributing to the overall structure of society. A problem in one area creates a problem for the entire system, and for society to function properly all social institutions must fulfill their basic functions. When all aspects of society are functioning properly, they are in a state of *social equilibrium,* or balance. In addition to the emphasis on structure, three basic concepts of the structural functionalist perspective are manifest functions, latent functions, and dysfunctions.

Manifest and Latent Functions Contemporary sociologists who use the structural functionalist perspective differentiate between **manifest functions,** *the anticipated or intended consequences of social institutions,* and **latent functions,** *the unintended or unrecognized consequences of social institutions.* As an example of the two,

MACROLEVEL ANALYSIS
Examines broader social structures and society as a whole.

STRUCTURAL FUNCTIONALIST PERSPECTIVE
Views society as a system of interdependent and interrelated parts (often referred to simply as the functionalist perspective or functionalism).

MANIFEST FUNCTIONS
Anticipated or intended consequences of social institutions.

LATENT FUNCTIONS
Unintended or unrecognized consequences of social institutions.

let's consider higher education. Its obvious manifest function is to transmit knowledge and prepare students for life in a complex industrial society. Higher education also serves a variety of latent functions. For instance, though usually unacknowledged by administrators, faculty, and students, a college campus provides a setting for meeting a marriage partner.

Dysfunctions   From the functionalist perspective, some aspects of society are viewed as *dysfunctional* because they threaten to disrupt social stability and order. It is important to note that "functional" and "dysfunctional" do not represent value judgments and are not synonymous with "good" and "bad." Crime can be viewed as dysfunctional in that it threatens social order, hurts people, and costs society a lot of money. But functionalists point out that crime is also functional. For example, laws are reinforced when criminals are caught and punished, and crime creates many jobs in law enforcement and related careers.

An alternative macrolevel analysis of society and human behavior is the conflict perspective. Whereas the structural functionalist perspective focuses on balance, harmony, and cooperation, the conflict perspective sees societal structure as much more diverse and characterized by competition and conflict. The turbulent times of the 1960s and early 1970s revived an interest in the ideas of Karl Marx and gave impetus to the conflict perspective in sociology.

The Conflict Perspective

The assassinations of President John F. Kennedy, Robert Kennedy, and Dr. Martin Luther King Jr., along with the Civil Rights movement, the Vietnam War, and rising crime and poverty rates in major cities, focused renewed attention on the problems of urban industrial America. The United States was in a state of social upheaval, as were many other countries, and people were seeking answers to sociological questions. Interactionism's emphasis on microlevel issues and functionalism's focus on stability and order seemed inadequate. Problems of racism, poverty, crime, and delinquency threatened the very fabric of the society, and their negative consequences were felt around the world.

The **conflict perspective** *views society as composed of diverse groups with conflicting values and interests.* In any society, these groups have differential access to wealth, power, and prestige. The most important aspects of the conflict perspective are the Marxian approach, which focuses on economic determinism and the importance of social class, and the neoconflict approach, which focuses on differential power and authority.

The Marxian Approach to Conflict   The theoretical roots of the conflict perspective can be traced to Karl Marx. Often, the values and interests of different groups conflict with one another. According to Marx, these conflicts are determined by economics and are based on social class, and the struggle between the different values and interests of the bourgeoisie and the proletariat is inevitable. When these battles occur, the dominant group attempts to force its values and ideology on less powerful groups. The result is the domination and exploitation of the masses (the proletariat) by the rich and powerful members of society (the bourgeoisie). The conflict perspective is not solely Marxist sociology, however; today conflict theorists often take a neoconflict approach.

The Neoconflict Approach   Social conflict can be viewed as a necessary and even functional social process. From this perspective, conflict necessitates negotiation and compromise, hence it can produce order and a reaffirmation of the social structure. In a diverse nation like the United States, conflict between racial, ethnic, religious, age, gender, and political groups is inevitable but not necessarily destructive. For example, attempts to balance the national budget have typically been thwarted by bickering over what areas of the budget should be increased and which should be cut. Those dependent on Medicare and Social Security resist cuts to those programs and would rather see cuts in, for example, the defense budget or federal aid to tobacco growers. Meanwhile,

CONFLICT PERSPECTIVE
Views society as composed of diverse groups with conflicting values and interests.

Pentagon officials and cigarette manufacturers are not about to sit back and allow legislators to balance the budget at their expense. Both sides employ powerful lobbyists to persuade legislators to vote for their relative interests. These political and ideological quarrels are marked by compromises or trade-offs that may not satisfy either group but also do not allow one interest to totally dominate the other. When society is confronted by an external threat, these internal conflicts may decrease, for, as is often said, nothing unites a group like a common enemy. From this perspective, conflict is dysfunctional only if it threatens one or more of society's core values (Coser, 1956).

Neoconflict theorists also contend that class conflict in industrialized countries is not so much a struggle over the means of production (as Marx argued) but rather a result of the unequal distribution of authority (Dahrendorf, 1959). For example, the differing power and prestige of college professors and students sometimes lead to tension and conflict between the two groups that has nothing to do with the ownership of property or the means of production. This version of the conflict perspective focuses on differences in power and authority and the exploitation of some groups by other, more powerful groups. A good example of this approach can be seen in the work of C. Wright Mills.

C. Wright Mills and the "Power Elite"   C. Wright Mills promoted the conflict perspective for analyzing the distribution of power and authority in the United States. In *The Power Elite* (1956), he contended that its post–World War II society was dominated by a powerful military, industrial, and political elite that shaped foreign and domestic policy for the benefit of the wealthy and powerful class. His approach focused on historical and structural analyses of class conflict and the uses of ideology for domination.

C. Wright Mills (1916–1962) wrote *The Sociological Imagination, The Power Elite,* and several other important works that have contributed to the contemporary conflict perspective in sociology.

How does the image of Mills on his motorcycle reflect his iconoclastic social theories?

Which Perspective Is Best?

Symbolic interactionism, structural functionalism, and the conflict perspective offer very different explanations for society and human behavior. This often prompts students to ask which one is best. However, since each contributes a distinctive interpretation, a more appropriate question might be, how does each theory help us better analyze and understand particular aspects of society or social behavior? By asking this question, we are thinking sociologically and developing our sociological imaginations. To illustrate, let's look at how each of the three major perspectives might analyze the role of the media in society.

The Functionalist View of the Media   From the functionalist perspective, the media perform a host of social functions, first and foremost the dissemination of information and ideas and the provision of almost instantaneous communication around the globe. This function is heightened during times of crisis, such as war, natural disasters, and social instability. Of course, the media also have dysfunctional consequences, as they may encourage passivity, promote stereotypes, discourage physical activity and critical thinking, and misinform people. Thinking sociologically, how do the media fit into the overall structure of American society? How do the media function to help create a global society? In what ways do the media contribute to social order and stability? In what ways are they dysfunctional?

The Media and Social Conflict   From the conflict perspective, the media, especially traditional mass media, are tools of power that help maintain the status quo, cultivate consumers, and disseminate information that serves the vested interests of the wealthy and powerful people and corporations that own or control the media. Sociologists using the conflict perspective point out that despite their egalitarian rhetoric and appeal, the technomedia are disproportionately available to the elite class. What other insights does the conflict perspective offer in regard to the media? Do the media help dissolve and blur class distinctions in the United States and around the world? Or do they accentuate these differences? How do the new technomedia reinforce or alter these class differences?

The Media from an Interactionist Perspective Symbolic interactionists point out that the media provide the quickest and most effective methods of "defining the situation" to promote commercial products through mass advertising in newspapers, magazines, radio and television commercials, and over the Internet. Likewise, politicians stage "media events" to popularize their agendas and promote their careers, and every major social movement or activist organization has a website. How do the media help shape the definition of a particular social situation? Do the media unduly influence and shape thinking and social behavior? Or do the media merely reflect one version of social reality?

None of these analyses is entirely correct, nor entirely wrong. They are merely three different theoretical approaches to the same topic.

Feminist Theory: An Example of Combining the Three Perspectives

Quarrels over which theoretical paradigm is best have been nonproductive. Increasingly, the three dominant paradigms are being linked, integrated, and synthesized to take sociological theory in new directions.

An example of an approach that combines elements of all three of the major perspectives can be found in **feminist theory,** which *studies, analyzes, and explains social phenomena from a gender-focused perspective.* This approach, used by both women and men, emphasizes the fundamental importance of gender for understanding society and social relationships. Feminist theories reflect and synthesize much of the rich diversity among other theoretical perspectives in sociology (Chafetz, 1997; Beasley, 1999; Delamont, 2003). Feminist theory, for example, uses elements of the interactionist perspective to study the ongoing social meanings of gender and to question commonly accepted definitions and symbols of femininity and masculinity. Like functionalists, however, sociologists who use feminist theory also argue that gender is incorporated into the basic social structure of every society. They also study how traditional gender roles and sexism function to maintain the status quo in most societies, yet may be dysfunctional in the way they inhibit some people from achieving their full potential. One of the "hottest" topics among feminist scholars today focuses on "the intersection of race, class, and gender" (Chafetz, 1997:115). Feminist theory is most closely aligned with the conflict perspective, however, especially in the way it draws on the historical and contemporary subordination of women and analyzes differential power and authority and the exploitation of one group by another based on gender. Shifting the focus of sociology away from a male-dominated view of the world, feminist theory has emerged as an important theoretical tool for analyzing all aspects of society, but especially in understanding problems of gender inequality, poverty, domestic abuse, pornography, sexual harassment, and violence.

Thinking Sociologically: Taking an Integrated Approach

Throughout this chapter we have used the phrase *thinking sociologically* to describe the type of critical thinking we encourage to understand society and the social world. In our view, this type of thinking can be achieved only by taking an integrated approach to sociology that encompasses all three of the major theoretical perspectives, as well as drawing on theories and ideas from numerous other academic disciplines. All three of the major sociological paradigms are valid ways of analyzing society, and alone or in combination they enhance our sociological imaginations and understanding of human social behavior. And, as feminist theory illustrates, elements of the three approaches can be combined to provide a more eclectic understanding of our social world.

Because of different assumptions and approaches, the weaknesses of one perspective are often the strengths of the other two. Also, because of their different approaches to

FEMINIST THEORY
Studies, analyzes, and explains social phenomena from a gender-focused perspective.

society and human behavior, one perspective may be more helpful than another, depending on what you wish to study.

While the interactionist perspective provides tremendous insight into the day-to-day, face-to-face interactions of individuals and groups, it has been criticized for somewhat ignoring the constraints of the larger social structure in which this interaction occurs. Meanwhile, whereas the structural functionalist approach corrects that deficiency, its focus on structure, stability, harmony, and equilibrium, along with its emphasis on pre-dictability and "natural laws" that govern society, tends to ignore the importance of diversity and how social variables such as race, ethnicity, and gender may lead to poten-tial tension and conflict among groups. Functionalism also downplays the ability of indi-vidual actors to create spontaneously their social realities as they interact with one another. Finally, the conflict perspective emphasizes the struggles for power among vari-ous classes and groups of people and helps explain social inequality. Yet it, too, tends to ignore the importance of day-to-day and face-to-face interaction—especially the tremendous amount of daily cooperation and harmony among diverse groups and indi-viduals as they interact. Given these relative strengths and weaknesses, which theoretical perspective might be most helpful in studying small group dynamics, say the workings of a criminal jury or the president's cabinet? Would that same perspective be as helpful in understanding the breakup of the former Soviet Union, or the ethnic cleansing in Bosnia? How might a more integrated approach that draws from all three perspectives help us better understand all of these?

For the most balanced approach to sociological understanding, and to encourage you to think sociologically, we use all three major theoretical approaches throughout this book. Our goal is to help you develop a strong *sociological imagination* and encour-age *sociological thinking,* rather than to promote any particular paradigm.

the FUTURE
LOOKING to

SOCIOLOGY IN THE TWENTY-FIRST CENTURY

The new millennium sparked widespread public speculation and some concern as to what the future may hold. Sociology was born during a period of rapid social change associated with industrialization, and historically sociologists have taken the lead in analyzing and interpreting social change and its impact on society. The challenge for sociology in the twenty-first century is to avoid complacency and to face the challenge of public conservatism on the one hand and the pressures of "political correctness" on the other. In the twenty-first century, sociology has been plagued by attacks both from the "new know-nothings," who resist or outright attack science and scientific findings about human behavior because those findings threaten their religious beliefs or their social status and power, and from the "know-it-alls," who claim far more for their scientific findings than are warranted by their data (Curra and Paolucci, 2004). Both of these social trends have hampered meaningful research and open discussion of sensitive issues such as racial, ethnic, and gender tensions, as well as serious efforts to study and analyze the powerful influence of mass media and technomedia on society. Avoiding discussion about these sensitive issues supports the status quo, whereas openly talking about them is viewed by some as tantamount to an act of war. Sociolo-gists must use and encourage the critical thinking approach we have described in this chapter to resolve this dilemma if they are to shed light on these issues in the twenty-first century (Williams, 1996; Portes, 2000).

There is much disagreement on the shape of societies of the future, but some com-mon elements run through most futurist literature. Although some futurists are highly pessimistic and others very optimistic, virtually all agree that in the future, sociologists will be studying a vastly different society. That society, characterized by enhanced geographic mobility, increased globalization and diversity, more sophisticated tech-nology, and powerful forms of technomedia that link people and places everywhere on earth, will provide new and interesting challenges to sociologists. This will require

Students often ask, "What can I do with a degree in sociology?" The question annoys academic sociologists to the point that it sometimes elicits a flippant answer such as "You can frame it" or "Anything that you are imaginative enough to do with it." Actually, those two answers, especially the latter, are not all that bad. For a degree in sociology, like almost any college degree, does not represent vocational training for a particular job, as does a certificate from a beauty college or welding school. Sociology is a broad-based liberal arts discipline. Its concepts, theories, and methods can be used in virtually any aspect of one's life. Whether a person is a shoe shiner, a shoe salesperson, or a shoe company magnate, an individual who has an understanding of society, social groups, and human behavior is likely to be more successful than one who lacks such insights. Course work and the degree in sociology do have some career-oriented applications, however.

About 70 percent of those who have obtained a doctoral degree in sociology choose careers in academic settings, some teaching in high school but most teaching at community colleges, four-year colleges, or universities. Others with advanced degrees in sociology are employed by governmental and private corporations in a variety of specialties ranging from conducting and analyzing research to directing human resources, consulting, and serving in a wide array of supervisory and management positions. Students don't have to achieve an advanced degree to put their sociology to work, however.

People with bachelor's degrees in sociology are finding increased employment opportunities in state, county, and local social service agencies, court services, probation and parole, law enforcement, corrections, human resources, health care, business consulting, state and local government, city management, gerontology and eldercare, and the military. In 1988, the U.S. Office of Personnel Management established a "Sociology-GS-184" classification that outlines the standards for sociologists seeking employment in federal agencies, and officially recognizes the specific contributions of sociology to the federal workforce.

Additionally, the bachelor's degree in sociology provides an excellent academic background for pursuing advanced degrees in areas such as law, social work, demography, gerontology, human resources, and business administration. Business and industry leaders increasingly recognize the value of a strong liberal arts education, as opposed to the narrower, more highly focused curricula of vocationally oriented programs. Students with degrees in sociology are increasingly being sought and recruited for their critical thinking skills, their ability to read and synthesize vast amounts of diverse and contradictory information, their understanding of human social behavior, and especially their knowledge of how people interact in groups, institutions, and bureaucracies. Consequently, sociology majors are increasingly being employed as bankers, human resource directors, consultants, and for other important jobs in business and industry. Moreover, research on finding, getting, and keeping jobs increasingly indicates that the abilities to use social networks and to "get along with others on the job" are among the most valued assets for employees today. Who better than sociologists should understand the importance of social networks and social interaction?

In short, people can use their academic backgrounds in sociology and their sociological imaginations in countless ways to meet career goals. More important, sociological knowledge, understanding, and skills can prove personally rewarding in helping people better understand the social world in which they live.

TAKING A CLOSER LOOK
What other occupations and careers might sociologists pursue? Even if you do not major in sociology or pursue a career in a sociology-related field, how might a basic understanding of sociology benefit you in your choice of career or occupation?

Source: Stephens, W. Richard Jr. *Careers in Sociology* (3rd ed.), Boston: Allyn & Bacon, 2002.

---

increased internationalism of sociology and a return to its critical analysis of social institutions and social life (Abbott, 2000; Wallerstein, 2000). We believe the sociological approach introduced here will be essential for understanding social life in the twenty-first century.

Sociologists are not fortune-tellers, but we can construct theoretical models that can be used to plan and shape the societies of tomorrow. For sociology to remain viable, it must demonstrate its utility to society not only in interpreting but also in changing the world. This also addresses a pragmatic question often posed by students of sociology: "Wow, sociology is really interesting. But can I make a living at it?" Focus box 1.3 focuses on some of the careers pursued by sociologists that involve the practical application of important sociological concepts, theories, and research skills.

Sociological models, as opposed to those of futurists, will be guided by a legacy that includes careful observation, critical thinking, and other scientific principles developed over many centuries. Sociologists' goals, however, will continue to be those of sociology's founders: to understand society and to formulate social policies that enhance the quality of human life. While sociology is not about creating utopia, it is interested in what people think that might be (Shostak, 2000b). If sociology is to remain on the cutting edge of scientific inquiry, we must continue to challenge the commonsense assumptions and taken-for-granted explanations of the world in which we live. We encourage you to apply critical thinking skills and to use your sociological imagination as you embark on your study of sociology.

Summary

1 Sociology is the systematic and scientific study of human behavior, social groups, and society. It is based on the *sociological imagination,* which allows us to locate ourselves within a larger social context. It helps us to recognize the *general* in the *particular* and the *strange* in the *familiar* as well as to distinguish between *personal troubles* and *social issues.* An important aspect of sociological thinking is the ability to understand the significance of globalization while also recognizing the importance of diversity in human society.

2 Sociology differs from popular notions of human behavior in that it uses systematic, scientific methods of investigation and encourages sociological thinking that questions many of the commonsense and taken-for-granted views of our social world. Sociological thinking involves taking a closer look at our social world and recognizing that most often things are not necessarily what they seem. This approach is especially beneficial for analyzing the powerful influence of the mass media and their impact on society. *Mass media* refers to the traditional forms of media—newspapers, magazines, books, radio, television, and motion pictures. *Technomedia* refers to the newer, more individualized forms of information technology such as personal fax machines, cellular phones, fiber optics, and, most important, personal computers. Combined, the media do not merely reflect society but also shape it, by filtering information and framing events in ways that lead individuals to develop a sense of reality created by "media logic." The mass media and technomedia have also made it possible to disseminate information almost instantaneously around the world, helping to link unique and diverse nations and cultures into a global society.

3 The discipline of sociology arose out of a changing social climate that reflected problems associated with widespread industrialization, urbanization, and immigration and a changing intellectual climate that turned to science for explanations for the accompanying economic, political, and social upheaval experienced in both Europe and the United States.

4 Three overriding theoretical perspectives, or paradigms, have dominated contemporary sociology: symbolic interactionism, structural functionalism, and conflict. While debates continue over which theoretical perspective is best, all three have made important contributions to sociological understanding. Functionalism and conflict focus on social structure and society as a whole, thus providing better analyses of macrolevel events, whereas interactionism focuses on interpersonal communication and provides keen insights into microlevel, small group, and day-to-day activities. Other important theoretical approaches and offshoots of the major paradigms, including dramaturgical analysis, labeling theory, and feminist theory, which combine elements of all three of the major paradigms, are making valuable contributions to the sociological enterprise. We believe that thinking sociologically is enhanced through an integrated approach that uses all three major perspectives as well as theories from other disciplines when appropriate.

5 Future sociologists must use the sociological imagination to fulfill the promise of sociology: to make the world a better place. Sociology's success in that effort is influenced by the extent to which sociologists recognize how sociology has become institutionalized and tied to important elements of the social structure. Not only must sociologists develop a better understanding of history, but they are also beginning to construct theoretical models that can be used to plan and shape the societies of tomorrow. These models will build on a rich scientific foundation and a desire to enhance the quality of human life.

Key Terms

applied sociology (p. 15)
conflict perspective (p. 19)
critical thinking (p. 6)
dramaturgical analysis (p. 17)
feminist theory (p. 21)
ideal type (p. 15)
labeling approach (p. 17)
latent functions (p. 18)

macrolevel analysis (p. 18)
manifest functions (p. 18)
mass media (p. 9)
microlevel analysis (p. 17)
paradigm (p. 16)
positivism (p. 13)
pure sociology (p. 15)
sociological imagination (p. 2)

sociological thinking (p. 6)
sociology (p. 2)
structural functionalist perspective
    (p. 18)
symbolic interactionist perspective
    (p. 17)
technomedia (p. 10)
theoretical perspective (p. 16)

Chapter 2

Doing Sociology

"There are three kinds of lies—lies, damned lies, and statisitics."

—*Benjamin Disraeli*

*O*n a Friday night, most high school students and the majority of the townspeople go to the local stadium to watch the varsity football team. The stadium lights blare and the din of the crowd can be heard throughout the small community, and the game seems to be the *only* event of consequence that evening—evidence of the sociological premise that *things are not necessarily what they seem*. On the outskirts of town beneath a small abandoned bridge, a group of students who call themselves *The Coven* congregate for their weekly satanic ritual, meeting by the light of "sacred" candles and a campfire to call forth demons to do their bidding.

Sociologist Kathleen Lowney spent five years conducting ethnographic field research on a satanic adolescent subculture in a Southern community. Lowney began her research by interviewing members of the press, local law enforcement officials, and school administrators. She read both academic and popular books as well as articles on Satanism and developed a list of teenagers suspected of being members of a satanic cult. She observed these youths from a distance and then, over time, chatted with some of them as they "hung out" or played video games at the mall. Lowney arranged interviews with members of the group; these interviews ranged from one to several hours. She ascertained that the Coven had approximately 35 members; all were white; all were from middle- or upper-middle-class families; about one-third of the members were female; and one of the females had emerged as the group's charismatic leader.

Lowney's analysis indicated that contrary to popular belief, members of the Coven showed no evidence of being "mentally disturbed," nor did they engage in any serious criminal activities—although they did participate in underage drinking, minor vandalism, and other law-violating activities frequently committed by nonsatanic youths. While specific reasons for joining the Coven varied, Lowney concluded that membership in the group served several important functions for its members. Most important, in a community steeped in conventional Christian values and symbols and in which athletes and cheerleaders held the highest status among high schoolers, it provided a visible challenge to the community's dominant value system. Moreover, it provided a social clique in which its members could achieve social status and recognition as well as a sense of social identity.

Lowney's research on teenage Satanism is interesting to sociologists for several reasons. First and foremost, it provides insight into a phenomenon surrounded with sensationalism, fear, misunderstanding, and even hysteria (Lewis, 2001). It also demonstrates some important features of sociological research: it illustrates the processes involved in selecting a research topic, reviewing literature, developing a workable research strategy by combining several data-gathering techniques, and analyzing and interpreting research findings—topics we discuss in this chapter.

Lowney also faced several ethical dilemmas during her study: interviewing minors without their parents' consent; risking harm to her subjects if their activities became known to the parents, school officials, or police; maintaining her subjects' privacy; and what to do if she witnessed members engaged in any illegal activities. In each case, Lowney made important decisions that allowed her to continue her research without violating the law, her personal ethics, or the ethical code of the American Sociological Association.

Finally, Lowney's study of the Coven reveals that, contrary to popular belief, research is not something conducted only in sterile laboratories by scientists in white lab coats; sociological research may be conducted anywhere that social interaction takes place. The entire world serves as a laboratory for sociologists.

The goal of sociology is to reach a better understanding of the social world in which we live and, ultimately, to make it a better place. Sociologists conduct research in an effort to gain the knowledge that will contribute to achieving that goal. Our focus in this chapter is on **methodology,** *the rules and guidelines followed in sociological research,* and the way sociologists develop theories and gain knowledge about human behavior, groups, social interaction, and society.

Lowney's research on teenage Satanists found that many of them were seeking conformity to a group, much like the cheerleaders and athletes.

What do the "uniforms" of these students indicate about their need to belong to a social group?

METHODOLOGY
The rules and guidelines followed in sociological research.

GLOBALIZATION, DIVERSITY, AND TYPES OF KNOWLEDGE

Most of us tend to be curious about ourselves and others. We want to know how and why things happen. As we become more aware that we live in a global society comprised of people from diverse racial, ethnic, religious, political, and social backgrounds, this curiosity is increased because we discover that although other peoples' daily lives are dramatically different from our own, there still are many social trends and patterns that occur with remarkable regularity. Around the globe and within any particular culture, people use a variety of types of knowledge, including experience, cultural tradition, faith, authority, and science. While sociologists use all of these forms of knowledge, science is the primary tool of the discipline.

Experience

A common way of gaining knowledge is through *experience,* which relies on trial-and-error learning. One of the authors is reminded of a time when he was interviewing an Old Order Amish farmer while their two 5-year-old sons played with a small snapping turtle. As the Amish boy held the turtle in one hand he would reach out with the other and tap the turtle's beak with his index finger, jerking it away as the animal snapped harmlessly in the air. Several times, the farmer interrupted his conversation to warn his son that if he continued teasing the turtle, he would be sorry. Suddenly, the boy squealed out in pain and dropped the turtle to the ground. As the father retrieved a handkerchief from his pocket and attended to the young boy's bleeding finger, the man looked into his son's eyes and said in German what roughly translates into "Maybe the turtle has taught you what your father could not." The author could not help but feel that his son, who stood in horror looking at his Amish friend's bleeding finger, had also learned something from the experience.

Groups like the Old Order Amish place much more emphasis on experience, tradition, and faith than on modern science.

An old adage claims, "Experience is the best teacher." If our knowledge is limited to personal experiences, however, then it is limited indeed, for experience is the best teacher only if we cannot also find other paths to knowledge. Since experience is a very personal and individualistic way of gaining knowledge, it is influenced by our social and cultural backgrounds. Experiential knowledge is punctuated by diversity as people of different racial, ethnic, gender, and socioeconomic backgrounds not only experience vastly different things in life, but, more important, often interpret similar experiences quite differently.

Cultural Tradition

A second way of gaining knowledge is through *cultural tradition,* whereby an accepted body of "facts" is passed from generation to generation. Farmers and ranchers in the American Midwest, for example, "know" that burning their pasturelands early each spring helps remove dead underbrush so that nutritious pasture grasses can get a better start for summer grazing. Farmers in Iran, however, move their herds into the mountains during the spring and summer months and then back onto the plains in the fall and winter, allowing nature to kill off undesirable weeds and underbrush and replenish the desirable grasses.

Many cultural traditions have far less practical applications. For example, in the United States cultural tradition dictates that a groom should not see the bride before the ceremony on the day of their wedding. Many people believe that violation of this tradition will lead to bad luck and "doom" the marriage, while others see it as a silly superstition. Nevertheless, even those who fall into the latter category often honor the tradition—just in case.

While cultural traditions and folklore may be modified, or even discarded as personal experiences require, in most cultures tradition plays an important role in everyday social life. Going against accepted ways of doing things may be tolerated, but questioning or violating important cultural traditions may result in ostracism, punishment, or even death. This is most likely to occur when the cultural tradition is linked to religious beliefs.

Faith

Faith—a strong belief in "truths" that cannot be verified by personal experience—serves as an important source of knowledge in almost every culture. The smaller and more homogeneous a society, the more agreement as to what constitutes truth; the larger and more heterogeneous the population, the more diversity of faiths and, hence, many more different *truths, untruths,* and even *heresies.*

Faith goes beyond tradition, however, because it is often supported by intense emotional commitment. The belief in a supernatural being, or in life after death, for example, requires faith beyond personal experience. Yet surveys show that the vast majority of Americans (80 to 90 percent) believe in God, the power of prayer, and an afterlife (Woodward, 1997; Adler, 2005). Because of its emotional and moral connotations, faith is a powerful source of knowledge, and those who question it may suffer some of the most serious social consequences a society has to offer. History is replete with religious wars, inquisitions, hangings, and burnings at the stake motivated by religious convictions and conflicts. In order for people to enforce their beliefs formally, they must have the support of those in positions of power and authority.

Authority

Authoritative knowledge is gained by listening to people who are recognized as authorities or experts. Authority is often linked to power; those in leadership positions may be viewed as more knowledgeable than others and can use their power to influence others. Parents usually serve as our first source of authoritative knowledge, and children often are dismayed to discover that their parents do not know everything. Elementary school-aged children often view their teachers as the ultimate source of knowledge, while teenagers rely more on their peers for information and advice. Adults have a much wider range of authorities to whom they can turn for answers to their questions.

In contemporary society, a wide variety of "experts" are considered sources of authority, and many people turn to them as the ultimate source of knowledge and truth. For medical questions we turn to doctors, nurses, and pharmacists; we get our weather information from certified meteorologists; we consult licensed counselors for emotional problems and attorneys for legal advice. These experts share a common trait: their training, expertise, and credentials are linked to the rational problem-solving techniques of science and the scientific method.

Science

Science *bases knowledge on empirical evidence gained through direct, systematic observation.* Unlike tradition, faith, and authority, scientific knowledge requires tangible evidence and *empirical verification* before it is affirmed. Experience, tradition, and faith may also require some type of verification to be widely accepted, but unlike science they involve personal and subjective interpretations of events. While science may also have subjective elements, the goal of scientists is to observe, measure, and interpret data as systematically and objectively as possible. Science is built on the logic of *cause-and-effect* explanations for understanding events and an insistence that, for every event that occurs (an effect) there is at least one knowable cause that precedes it.

Experience, tradition, faith, authority, and science are not mutually exclusive ways of knowing, and all of us use them at various times. For example, despite the fact that scientific thinking dominates most of the Western world, it can be argued that scientists rely heavily on *tradition* and *experience,* and that they put a great deal of *faith* in *authority* (especially other reputable scientists). Still, the focus of science is on systematic observation, objectivity, and empirical verification. Sociology, as a science, attempts to adhere to those criteria.

SOCIOLOGY AND SCIENTIFIC KNOWLEDGE

In an effort to demonstrate their scientific credibility, social and behavioral scientists emphasize sophisticated research procedures and statistical techniques for collecting, analyzing, and interpreting data. The goal of science is to gain knowledge about a particular phenomenon in order to more accurately predict and control outcomes in certain situations. Some have argued, however, that, because the subjects of sociology are free-willed, thinking human beings, their behavior cannot be predicted, much less controlled. This has led to the claim that sociology and other social and behavioral sciences are somehow inferior to the natural sciences.

SCIENCE
Knowledge based on empirical evidence gained through direct, systematic observation.

Sociology as a Science

Fritz Machlup (1988), former professor of economics at Princeton and New York Universities, addressed this issue by comparing the social sciences to the natural sciences on seven criteria: (1) invariability of observations, (2) objectivity of observations and explanations, (3) verifiability of hypotheses, (4) exactness of findings, (5) measurability of phenomena, (6) constancy of numerical relationships, and (7) predictability of future events. Machlup pointed out that in each of these areas it is erroneous to conclude that the social sciences are inferior to the natural sciences. Rather, it can be concluded only that the social sciences are *different* from the natural sciences. And in four of the areas the two are not even very different. With regard to invariability, verifiability, and numerical constancy, Machlup conceded that the natural sciences may be superior to the social sciences. However, he asserted that saying sociology is inferior to physics in its numerical constancy is like saying "champagne is inferior to rubbing alcohol in alcoholic content" (Machlup, 1988:64). This "inferiority" refers to a particular quality, not to overall quality or other specific qualities. Machlup also pointed out that social science disciplines such as sociology may be superior to the natural sciences in predicting the future. He noted that social sciences sometimes predict human behavior accurately over long periods of time (such as Durkheim's findings that suicide rates vary by race, marital status, gender, age, and social class, as discussed in Chapter 1). In contrast, the natural science of meteorology, despite its state-of-the-art scientific technology, rarely predicts the weather accurately even within a period of 24 hours.

Sociology, which once insisted that *all* human behavior is learned, is today more cognizant of the important relationships among biology, chemistry, physiology, and social behavior. This acknowledgment, along with a vast amount of research linking genetics, diet, chemical imbalances, and other variables to human social behavior, has given rise to the creation of *sociobiology,* a subfield of sociology that explores relationships between biological and environmental influences on humans. Today, most sociologists concede that the only way to understand the limitations of existing knowledge is through more interdisciplinary training and research. As a science, sociology follows many of the same systematic procedures as the natural sciences to guide its research efforts to develop scientific theories that explain society and human behavior.

Today's technomedia allow sociological researchers to access a remarkable amount of information and data in a matter of seconds.

How have computers changed sociological research?

The Theory-Building Process

Sociological knowledge is amassed through the process of building, developing, and testing theories that attempt to explain human social behavior. A theory is much more than speculation or a hunch about how or why certain events occur. A **theory** is *a set of interrelated propositions, or statements, that attempt to explain some phenomenon.* It has been argued that the "acid test of the scientific status of a discipline is the quality of its theory" (Lenski, 1988:163). Thus a major goal of sociological research is to generate theories that explain human social behavior. These theories, then, "give order and insight to research activities" (Denzin, 1970:5).

Building theory is a basic part of any scientific process. In sociological analysis, theory-building requires critical thinking that involves both inductive and deductive reasoning.

Inductive and Deductive Reasoning Robert Pirsig described the difference between inductive and deductive reasoning in *Zen and The Art of Motorcycle Maintenance:*

> [inductive reasoning] start[s] with observations of the machine and arrive[s] at general conclusions. For example, if the cycle goes over a bump and the engine misfires, and then goes over another bump and the engine misfires . . . and then goes over a long smooth stretch of road and there is no misfiring, and then goes over [another] bump and the engine misfires again, one can logically conclude that the

THEORY
A set of interrelated propositions, or statements, that attempt to explain some phenomenon.

misfiring is caused by the bumps. That is induction: reasoning from particular experiences to general truths. (Pirsig, 1974:99)

Sir Arthur Conan Doyle's fictional detective, Sherlock Holmes, praised the merits of inductive reasoning when he noted, "It's a capital mistake to theorize before one has data" (Doyle, [1892] 1987:13). Much of the theory-building process uses **inductive reasoning,** which *puts the sociologist in the role of a detective who pieces together "clues" from specific observations in order to develop a general understanding* of the overall puzzle of human behavior, or, as we discussed in Chapter 1, to see the *general* in the *particular.*

Some sociologists believe that sociology relies too heavily on inductive studies; they assert that general theoretical models based on deductive reasoning are also very important (Kiser and Hechter, 1991). **Deductive reasoning** *begins with a general understanding or theory that is then tested through the observation or study of specific situations.* Pirsig noted that deductive inferences

> start with general knowledge and predict a specific observation. For example, if, from reading the hierarchy of facts about the machine, the mechanic knows the horn of the cycle is powered exclusively by electricity from the battery, then he can logically infer that if the battery is dead the horn will not work. That is deduction. (Pirsig, 1974:99)

Deduction is an important way in theory-building to test and evaluate existing sociological understandings and theories. Sociological research usually involves a process of interweaving both inductive and deductive reasoning in an effort to increase our knowledge, develop our understanding, and gain insight into the problem and concepts under study.

Identifying and Defining Concepts Theory-building begins with the identification of important concepts about what is being studied (see Figure 2.1). A **concept** is *an abstract idea or general thought.* To conduct meaningful research, sociologists must identify and define concepts, which may be rather vague. For example, sociologists interested in studying juvenile delinquency must first define two important concepts: "juvenile" and "delinquency." The initial process in clarifying concepts is developing a **conceptual definition**—that is, *defining a concept through the use of other concepts.* A conceptual definition of "juvenile" might be "a person who is not yet legally considered an adult." A conceptual definition of "delinquency" could be "any illegal acts committed by youths." While these definitions help clarify the concepts of "juvenile" and "delinquency," they do not provide a precise enough definition for scientific inquiry.

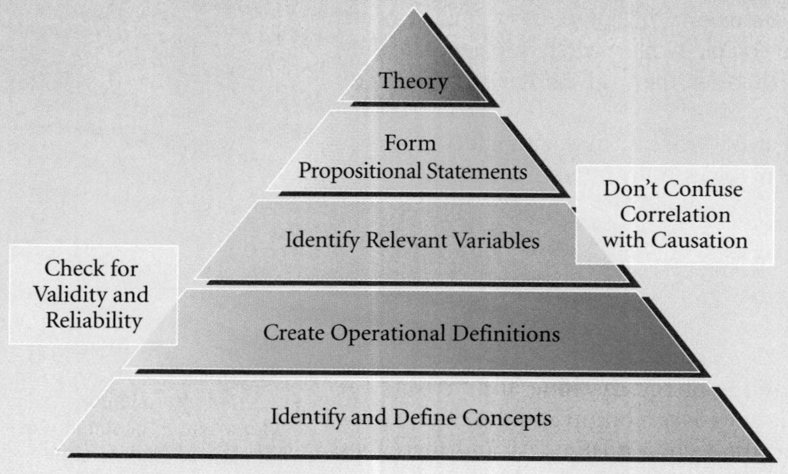

Creating Operational Definitions The sociologist's next task involves developing **operational definitions** *that specify how a concept is measured.* For example, a sociologist studying delinquency might operationalize the term "juvenile" on the basis of legal statutes. In many states, juveniles are defined as youths age 7–18. This age range could serve as an operational definition of juvenile because the concept can now be measured. The concept of "delinquency" also needs to be operationally defined. One possible operational definition of a juvenile delinquent is any juvenile who has been adjudicated delinquent by a juvenile court. These

INDUCTIVE REASONING
The use of specific observations to develop a general understanding.

DEDUCTIVE REASONING
Reasoning that begins with a general understanding or theory that is then tested through the observation or study of specific situations.

CONCEPT
An abstract idea or general thought.

CONCEPTUAL DEFINITION
Defining a concept through the use of other concepts.

OPERATIONAL DEFINITION
A definition that specifies how a concept is measured.

FIGURE 2.1
THE THEORY-BUILDING PROCESS

Theory

Form Propositional Statements

Identify Relevant Variables

Create Operational Definitions

Identify and Define Concepts

Check for Validity and Reliability

Don't Confuse Correlation with Causation

definitions allow the concepts to be measured, but can you think of some problems and limitations with them?

Checking for Validity and Reliability   Operational definitions provide specific techniques to measure what is being studied. Two important criteria for sociological measurements are that they must be both valid and reliable. **Validity** refers to *the extent to which a technique accurately measures what it purports to measure;* **reliability** refers to *the consistency of measurement.* A measure that is reliable should produce the same results each time it is used. A measure can be reliable without being valid. For example, although measuring delinquency as the number of youths officially adjudicated delinquent should give consistent results, it is not a valid measurement, since we know that a large number of youths who commit delinquent acts each year do not come to the attention of the police or the juvenile courts.

Identifying Variables   The next step in the theory-building process is to identify variables. A **variable** *represents ways in which concepts vary or differ.* For example, while juveniles might be defined as all youths age 7–18, some important variables that a sociologist might consider include the juveniles' sex, race, age (within that range), and socioeconomic status. All of these variables have been shown to be related to juvenile delinquency. Can you think of other important variables that might be important?

Forming Propositional Statements: Correlation Versus Causation
When concepts have been defined and operationalized, and variables identified, propositions can be formulated. A **proposition** is *a statement that interrelates two or more variables.* The statement "Delinquency rates are higher among males than among females" states a relationship between two variables: sex and delinquency rates. Since a goal of science is to identify cause-and-effect relationships, the linking of variables is an important step in theory building. In linking variables, however, sociologists must be careful not to confuse **correlation** *(two variables that are related in such a way that a change in one is accompanied by a change in the other)* with **causation,** *when a change in one variable creates a change in another variable.* To establish causation: (1) the two variables must be related; (2) the *cause* must precede the *effect;* and (3) the relationship between the two variables must persist when all other relevant variables are controlled.

Sometimes an apparent relationship between two variables is meaningless. We call this type of relationship *spurious.* For example, it could be demonstrated that as the deadline for filing income taxes approaches, the sale of swimsuits increases. Despite the strong statistical correlation between the two, it would be ludicrous to assume that filing income taxes causes people to want to wear swimsuits. A much more likely explanation is that because the tax filing deadline falls on April 15, about the same time summer clothing debuts in department stores, people begin to anticipate the oncoming swimming season. Can you think of examples of spurious relationships that are commonly accepted and may go unchallenged? For example, does watching violence on television lead to aggressive and violent behavior? Does capital punishment deter crime? We take a closer look at these sociological questions in Chapter 7.

The Scientific Method

Most sociological studies follow the general guidelines outlined in the eight steps of the scientific method, which provides a systematic framework to guide research.

1. *Statement of the Problem.* The first step in sociological research is to formulate a research question.

2. *Review of the Literature.* After stating a research problem or developing a research question, the sociologist seeks out previous studies to determine what is already known about the problem.

3. *Development of Hypotheses or a Statement of Research Objectives.* Based on what is already known about a topic, the researcher develops **hypotheses,** which are *propositional statements about the relationships between the concepts or variables under*

VALIDITY
The extent to which a technique accurately measures what it purports to measure.

RELIABILITY
The consistency of measurement.

VARIABLE
A construct that represents ways in which concepts vary or differ.

PROPOSITION
A statement that interrelates two or more variables.

CORRELATION
A measure indicating that two variables are related in such a way that a change in one is accompanied by a change in the other.

CAUSATION
A relationship in which a change in one variable creates a concomitant change in another variable.

HYPOTHESES
Propositional statements about the relationships between the concepts or variables under study.

Every 10 years the U.S. Bureau of the Census conducts one of the most extensive survey research projects in the world.

What are some of the benefits of using survey research for this type of data collection? What are some of the drawbacks?

study. These hypotheses are written in such a way that they can be tested and either supported or rejected, according to the research findings. Sometimes instead of theoretical hypotheses researchers develop **research objectives,** which *outline specific goals or purposes for the research project.*

4. *Choice of Research Design.* To test theories and hypotheses or to achieve research objectives, sociologists gather data: facts and information. A variety of research methods can be used, including a secondary analysis of the available data; experiments; surveys; and field research, such as ethnographic interviews, participant observation, and case studies. These research designs are discussed in more detail later in this chapter.

Researchers often must grapple with the problem of time in gathering research data. In devising a *cross-sectional study,* the researcher studies a phenomenon by "freezing the action" and collecting data at a particular point in time. The major population study conducted every 10 years by the U.S. Bureau of the Census is a good example of a cross-sectional study. The other option is to conduct research over an extended period of time; this is called a *longitudinal study.* The ongoing data collection of the Census Bureau that is summarized annually is an example of a longitudinal study. Longitudinal studies allow researchers to identify social processes, trends, and patterns, but they are costly and time-consuming and, in some cases, may not yield better data than carefully designed cross-sectional studies.

5. *Data Collection.* In this step, the researcher collects the observations, facts, and information to use in testing the hypotheses or fulfilling the research objectives.

6. *Data Analysis and Interpretation.* At this stage, the researcher considers the study's findings and determines what they mean. Data analysis can be divided into two general categories: quantitative and qualitative. *Quantitative analysis* converts data to numerical form so they can be subjected to a variety of statistical techniques and measurements (see Focus box 2.1). Field methods may produce data that cannot be easily translated into numerical form; in that case, the researcher uses *qualitative analysis* to observe and interpret data. In qualitative analysis, the researcher analyzes observations, interviews, and/or behaviors to discover trends, patterns, and other generalizations.

7. *Development of Conclusions.* On the basis of research findings and data analysis, the researcher makes generalizations and draws conclusions regarding the research hypotheses or objectives.

8. *Posing New Research Questions.* Science is a never-ending venture, and a good sociologist realizes that the conclusion of a specific research project does not end the research enterprise. Thus part of the research process is identifying new problems for future research. In this sense, each of the eight steps of the research process is a building block for the next, and when step 8 is completed it becomes the foundation for beginning step 1 all over again. Figure 2.2 portrays the steps of the scientific method.

Sociological research is a dynamic process of discovery. It is important to understand that the scientific method is

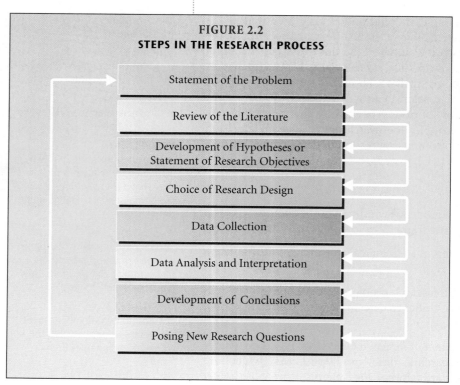

FIGURE 2.2
STEPS IN THE RESEARCH PROCESS

Statement of the Problem

Review of the Literature

Development of Hypotheses or Statement of Research Objectives

Choice of Research Design

Data Collection

Data Analysis and Interpretation

Development of Conclusions

Posing New Research Questions

Quantitative sociological studies convert data into numerical form and subject them to numerous mathematical and statistical operations to analyze research findings. Statistical techniques can be quite sophisticated, and sociologists are usually required to complete several courses in research methods and statistics during their professional training. There are a few very basic statistics that are relatively simple to calculate and understand, however, they can help you read and better understand sociological studies.

Among the most fundamental statistics used in sociological research are **measures of central tendency,** which *describe statistical averages of numerical data.* Sociologists frequently use three different measures of central tendency: the mean, the median, and the mode. The following example illustrates how sociologists might use these statistical measures.

Sociology majors frequently ask, "What kind of starting salary can I expect to make after I complete my degree?" Although the question is impossible to answer definitively, one approach to it might be to look at the starting salaries of nine students who graduated with a bachelor's degree in sociology last year:

Professional basketball player	$1 Million
Research staff worker	30,000
Court services officer	29,000
Juvenile probation officer	28,000
Coordinator of family services	27,000
College admissions counselor	26,000
Management trainee	24,000
Graduate teaching assistant	10,000
Graduate research assistant	10,000

What is the average starting salary of these students? The **mean** is *an arithmetic average* calculated by adding up all the figures and dividing by the number of cases. The starting salaries total $1,184,000. Dividing by 9, we find that the mean salary is approximately $131,556. It should be readily apparent that the mean is a misleading figure in this case,

because eight of the nine graduates earn much less than that amount. The unusually high starting salary of the sociology major who went on to play professional basketball grossly distorted the mean. A weakness of using the mean is that it is dramatically affected by extreme scores.

The median income might provide a more realistic "average" starting salary. The **median** represents *the midpoint; half the scores fall above and half the scores fall below it.* In this case the median salary is $27,000. Four salaries are above that figure and four are below it. (If there were an even number of salaries, the median would be the midpoint between the two middle figures.) The median is not affected by extreme scores, and in this case it gives a much more representative picture of the starting salaries.

The third measure of central tendency is the **mode,** which is *the figure that occurs most often.* In this case the mode is $10,000. Although this figure occurs most often, you can see that it is not representative of the starting salaries (unless a student is planning on going to graduate school), because it does not take into account the range of the data. There can be more than one mode in a data set.

All three measures of central tendency are used in sociology. Some data more readily lend themselves to one type of measure than the other two; sometimes it is useful to look at all three measures. In the case of incomes or similar data, the median is usually the preferred measure. If you were looking at standardized test scores or similar data, the mean might be a better statistic. The mode is less often used in sociology, but it is the easiest of the three measures to identify; it is useful if a sociologist simply wants to know which figure occurs most frequently.

TAKING A CLOSER LOOK
It has been said that "statistics don't lie, but liars use statistics." What are some of the pitfalls that must be avoided when reading and interpreting statistics?

---

an *ideal type,* designed to serve as a general guideline for scientific research rather than a recipe to be rigidly followed. We would be wise to remember the comments of Polykarp Kusch and Percy Bridgman when they accepted their Nobel Prize in physics; they declared that there is no such thing as "*the* scientific method" and that scientists must do the utmost with their minds, "*no holds barred*" (Mills, 1959:58).

Some of the most significant findings in both the natural and social sciences have developed out of serendipitous observations during research. The discovery of penicillin, for example, occurred quite by accident when scientists became curious about the mold growing in samples they were using in other medical research. Similarly, sociologist Howard Becker (1963) was attempting to explain the use of marijuana among jazz musicians when he realized that virtually all the actions of this group were viewed as deviant by the larger society. Concluding that jazz musicians were considered "outside" the mainstream of conventional society, he wrote *Outsiders,* a significant contribution to the development of the labeling perspective on deviant behavior.

A wide range of research procedures falls somewhere between rigid adherence to the scientific method and serendipity. Joel Smith (1991) echoed a recurring theme in contemporary sociology that urges a combination of scientific rigor and methodological flexibility in the quest for knowledge. He asserted that there are five important questions for sociological researchers: (1) What does one want to know and why? (2) What is to be observed? (3) Which and how many objects are to be examined? (4) How are the phenomena to be observed? (5) How are answers to be decided? These questions not only pose methodological issues, but also raise ethical issues related to sociological research.

Ethical Issues in Sociological Research

Because sociologists study people and what they do in the course of their everyday lives, certain ethical considerations apply to every sociological study. Laud Humphreys's study of covert homosexuality in *Tearoom Trade* (1970) sparked heated debate over the rights and responsibilities of sociological researchers (see Focus box 2.2). For example:

1. Do sociologists have the right to study people who do not know they are being studied?

2. Do sociologists have the right intentionally to deceive the people they are studying?

3. Do sociologists have the right to break the law while conducting sociological research?

4. Do sociologists have the right to collect data under the guise of one type of study when they are actually collecting it for another, clandestine research purpose?

How would you respond to these questions? In an attempt to clarify ethical issues and provide ethical guidelines for sociological research, the American Sociological Association (ASA) adopted a comprehensive Code of Ethics for its members. It was last revised in 2001, and its essential elements include the following research guidelines:

1. Maintain objectivity, integrity, confidentiality, and social responsibility in research.

2. Respect and protect the privacy, dignity, and safety of research subjects.

3. Do not discriminate or misuse or abuse the research role.

4. Disclose all assistance and support.

5. Disassociate from any research that violates the ASA Code of Ethics. (ASA, 2001)

This ethical code is supposed to be applied to all types of sociological research and research designs.

TYPES OF RESEARCH AND RESEARCH DESIGNS

Because sociologists conduct research for different purposes, there are different types of research designs; the four most common types in sociology are exploratory, descriptive, explanatory, and evaluative.

Types of Research

Exploratory research *attempts to answer the question "What?"* The first sociological study of any phenomenon—hula hoops, test-tube babies, or children with AIDS—is likely to be exploratory, focusing on what takes place. Exploratory research provides a foundation on which future research is built, and while it may not answer all our questions about a topic, it is in some ways the most important type of research in that it involves breaking new ground and asking previously unasked questions.

Descriptive research *answers the questions "What?" and "How?"* It describes what takes place and how it happens, as accurately and objectively as possible. Many of the most fascinating studies of religious cults, motorcycle gangs, or teenage Satanists are descriptive in nature.

EXPLORATORY RESEARCH
Research that attempts to answer the question "What?"

DESCRIPTIVE RESEARCH
Research that answers the questions "What?" and "How?"

When Laud Humphreys decided to study homosexual behavior in public men's rooms, he had to find a way to get unbiased information while protecting his subjects' privacy and his own safety. The choices he made raised important ethical questions.

Sociologists studied gay bars and male prostitution before 1970, but until Humphreys conducted the research reported in *Tearoom Trade,* no systematic study of the covert homosexuality in public restrooms (called "tearooms" by participants) had ever been undertaken. Sociologists might have avoided this area of behavior because of the many emotional and methodological problems it presents.

Humphreys noted that his was not a study of homosexuals but of participants in homosexual acts. The subjects had only one thing in common: Each was observed by Humphreys in the course of a homosexual act in a public park restroom.

Humphreys studied park facilities because earlier research on the homosexual subculture indicated that they were all known for being the scene of quick, impersonal homosexual acts. His research had two distinct stages: an ethnographic and participant observation stage, which lasted a little over two years on a part-time basis, and the administration of interview schedules to more than 100 respondents, which took six months of full-time work.

In the first phase of research, Humphreys

> assumed the role of the voyeur—a role superbly suited for sociologists and the only lookout role that is not overtly sexual. Although it avoids sexual pressure, this role is problematic for the researcher; it is short-lived and invariably disrupts the action he has set out to observe. (1970:27–28)

Humphreys gathered a sample of 100 "tearoom" participants by tracing their automobile license plates. Once his face had become familiar, he entered into verbal relationships with 12 of the participants, whom he referred to as the "intensive dozen." After initial conversations with the intensive dozen, he informed them of his research objectives, and all agreed to subsequent interviews.

Realizing that the majority of his participant sample were married—and nearly all of them quite secret about their homosexual activity—he was faced with the dilemma

of how to interview more than the 12 respondents. Humphreys noted, "Clearly, I could not knock on the door of a suburban residence and say, 'Excuse me, I saw you engaging in a homosexual act in a tearoom . . . and I wonder if I might ask you a few questions?'" Having already been jailed, locked in a restroom, and attacked by a group of teenage "gay bashers," Humphreys did not wish to risk physical harm at the hands of his subjects.

It was then that Humphreys made one of his most controversial research decisions. He had been asked to develop a questionnaire for a social health survey of men in the community, including questions about family background and socioeconomic factors, personal health and social histories, religious and employment data, social and political attitudes, friendship networks, and marital relationships and sex.

After obtaining permission from the director of the research project, Humphreys added his sample of 100 men to the overall sample of the health survey. His findings showed that the participants in the covert homosexual encounters of the tearooms were very ordinary people from virtually all walks of life—teachers, doctors, mechanics, and truck drivers, to name but a few. They came from all religious backgrounds and socioeconomic classes, and they were as likely to vote conservatively as not.

While Humphreys's research added valuable information about a heretofore unstudied phenomenon and demonstrated how a variety of research methods could be combined advantageously, it also raised a host of ethical questions pertaining to sociological research that are still debated in sociological circles today.

TAKING A CLOSER LOOK

What are some of the ethical issues raised by Humphreys's research on covert homosexuality in public restrooms? How should sociologists reconcile the dilemma between scientific investigation and a researcher's "need to know" and a subject's right to privacy? Did Humphreys cross that line? Are there certain areas of human social behavior that should be off limits to sociological investigation? If so, who decides?

Source: Laud Humphreys. *Tearoom Trade: Impersonal Sex in Public Places.* New York: Aldine, 1970, Chap. 2, pp. 16–44.

Explanatory research *attempts to explain social phenomena by answering the questions "What?" "How?" and "Why?"* Explanatory studies not only analyze and explain what takes place and how it occurs but examine why people behave the way they do in given social circumstances. This is the ultimate goal of any science: to understand not only what is happening and how, but also why. This is often difficult in social and behavioral sciences due to the wide variety of possible explanations for human behavior.

Evaluation research *measures the effectiveness of a program;* it doesn't ask "What?" or "How?" or "Why?" Rather, it asks "Does it work? Is it accomplishing the specific goals and objectives set out for the program?" Evaluation research is used widely in sociology

EXPLANATORY RESEARCH
Research that attempts to explain social phenomena by answering the questions "What?" "How?" and "Why?"

EVALUATION RESEARCH
Research that measures the effectiveness of a program.

today, and in this era of limited resources and accountability is often more likely to be funded by governmental or private agencies than the more traditional types of sociological research already discussed. For example, Head Start is a national preschool program designed to prepare underprivileged inner-city children for a successful school experience. Evaluation research can be used to study Head Start's accomplishment of that goal to determine the effectiveness of spending money on it and similar programs.

Quantitative Research Designs

An important step in the sociological research process is choosing a research design that meets the goals and objectives of the study. **Quantitative research designs** *emphasize the use of numbers and statistics to analyze and explain social events and human behavior.* Sociologists who use quantitative designs believe that the most objective and systematic way to study and analyze a phenomenon is through quantification of observations and use of statistical techniques. Computer technology and sophisticated mathematical models lead some researchers to argue that the vast possibilities for quantitative research in sociology remain unrealized (Blalock, 1989; Black, 1999). Some of the more commonly used quantitative methods in sociology are secondary analysis, experiments, and surveys.

Secondary Analysis

Secondary analysis *makes use of existing data and is often used in comparative/historical studies.* The population data collected by the U.S. Bureau of the Census every 10 years are some of the most commonly used data for secondary analysis. Because these data have been systematically collected for over 200 years, sociologists can use them to analyze population characteristics and trends. Focus box 2.3 gives an example from the *Uniform Crime Reports,* another commonly used source of secondary data, to explain how to read tables.

An advantage of secondary analysis is that it saves the time and expenses associated with data collection. With today's computerized technology, millions of pieces of research data are literally at the sociologist's fingertips. Such convenience has its drawbacks, however. Because the data were collected by somebody else, and for some other purpose, any weaknesses in the data collection process place limitations on its use by the secondary researcher.

Experiments and Quasi-Experimental Designs

When we think of scientific research, we often think of the experimental method. In practice, ethical considerations and the problem of control severely limit the use of experiments in sociological research. **Experimental designs** *attempt to discover a cause-and-effect relationship between two variables.* The standard format for an experiment is to manipulate an **independent variable**—*a variable that brings about change in another variable*—to measure its effect on a **dependent variable,** which is *changed by the independent variable.* This format requires controlling for **intervening variables,** *variables that might come between the independent and dependent variables.* Because it is difficult to control extraneous variables outside the laboratory, sociologists sometimes use a *quasi-experimental design,* which approximates an experimental design but lacks the rigid control required by laboratory experiments.

Suppose your sociology instructor believes that showing videos will enhance the learning process and increase your understanding of sociology. How might he or she test this hypothesis? Your teacher could develop an experiment to test the effects of viewing videos on classroom learning. In this case, showing videos would be the independent variable and classroom learning the dependent variable. For the purposes of this experiment, your instructor might use exam scores as a way of operationalizing the extent of classroom learning. He or she could use your class as a **control group,** which is *not exposed to the experimental variable,* and another section of introductory sociology students as the **experimental group,** which is *exposed to the independent variable.* That class would receive the same lectures and reading assignments as you, but, in addition, would be shown supplementary videos on relevant topics. At the end of the study unit,

QUANTITATIVE RESEARCH DESIGN
A research design that emphasizes the use of numbers and statistics to analyze and explain social events and human behavior.

SECONDARY ANALYSIS
The analysis of existing data.

EXPERIMENTAL DESIGN
A research design that attempts to discover a cause-and-effect relationship between two variables.

INDEPENDENT VARIABLE
A variable that brings about change in another variable (i.e., the cause).

DEPENDENT VARIABLE
A variable that is changed by the independent variable (i.e., the effect).

INTERVENING VARIABLES
Variables that may come between the independent and dependent variables in an experiment.

CONTROL GROUP
Subjects not exposed to the experimental variable in an experiment.

EXPERIMENTAL GROUP
Subjects exposed to the independent variable in an experiment.

Sociologists often present their research findings in the form of tables that are intended to summarize data for quick and easy analysis. Consequently, it is important for sociology students to develop basic skills in reading tables. Tables appear in a variety of formats. We have borrowed part of a table from the *Uniform Crime Reports* that includes data a sociologist might use in studying crime.

PARTS OF A TABLE

Title Every table should have a title that indicates what is included in the table. In this case the title indicates that the table includes data on the distribution of total arrests by age for the year 2005.

Headnotes/Footnotes Headnotes and footnotes tell how the data were collected or give additional information about the data included in the table. In this case, the footnote indicates that 8,009 agencies reported the data in the table, and that the estimated population served by those agencies in 2005 was 178,017,991.

Column Headings Column headings identify the type of information included in each column. This table has four columns. Listed in the first column is the offense with which arrestees were charged. The second column gives the total number of people arrested for each offense. The third column indicates the number of arrestees under age 18 for each offense; and the fourth column indicates the number of arrestees age 18 or older.

Row Headings Row headings are located on the left-hand side of a table and indicate that data are included in each row under each column heading. Our table contains nine rows. The first row shows the total number of people arrested. Below are eight rows of specific criminal offenses and the number of people arrested for each. For example, the table indicates that 739 people under age 18 were arrested for murder and nonnegligent manslaughter in 2005.

Source The source of the data is usually listed directly below the table. In this case the table came from FBI's *Uniform Crime Reports: Crime in the United States, 2005,* published by the U.S. Government Printing Office in 2006.

Interpreting Tables Once all parts of a table have been identified, you can look at the data in specific columns and rows and draw some preliminary conclusions. In looking at this table, you can discern several patterns. For example, in 2005 more people age 18 or older were arrested than people under age 18; more people were arrested for larceny-theft than for any other crimes listed; and of the eight crimes listed, arson is the only offense for which more offenders were under 18 than were age 18 and older.

TAKING A CLOSER LOOK

Beyond simply reading the information presented in a table, critical thinking requires that we analyze and interpret the data. Does a table on total arrests for particular crimes provide an accurate picture of the total number of those crimes committed? For example, according to the table, 15,129 arrests for forcible rapes were made in 2005. Do you believe that accurately reflects the number of rapes committed in that year? Why is arson the only major crime for which more people under the age of 18 than age 18 and over are arrested? Does this table indicate that violent crimes (especially homicides) are committed primarily by teenage gang members, as the media sometimes lead people to believe? What other sociological questions about crime are raised by the data presented in this table?

Total Arrests, Distribution by Age, 2005

Offense Charged	Total All Ages	Ages Under 18	Ages 18 and Over
Total	8,244,321	1,278,948	6,965,373
Murder and nonnegligent manslaughter	7,989	739	7,250
Aggravated assault	282,003	36,967	245,036
Forcible rape	15,129	2,392	12,737
Robbery	67,841	16,791	51,050
Burglary	180,973	47,416	133,557
Larceny-theft	692,593	182,813	509,780
Motor vehicle theft	82,160	19,755	62,405
Arson	9,716	4,915	4,801

Note: 8,009 agencies; 2005 population 178,017,991.

Source: FBI *Uniform Crime Reports: Crime in the United States, 2005,* Table 32. Washington, DC: U.S. Government Printing Office, 2006.

your instructor would administer identical examinations to both classes. If the overall grades for the other class were higher than the grades for your class, your instructor would probably conclude that the use of videos indeed enhanced learning. But would that necessarily be an accurate conclusion?

The problems with this analysis reflect some of the weaknesses of the quasi-experimental design in sociological research. How does the instructor know the use of videos explains the difference in exam scores between the two classes? The apparent relationship may be spurious. It may be that the students in the other class are more

intelligent than the members of your class and would have scored higher on the same exam even if they had not seen videos. In fact, it is possible they would have scored even higher if they had not seen the videos. Test scores may also have been affected by the times the classes met, the rooms in which the exams were administered, different study habits, and a multitude of other unidentified and uncontrolled variables.

Another problem that arises in sociological experiments is that *the mere fact that subjects know they are being studied may influence their behavior.* The **Hawthorne effect,** as it is called, was discovered when Western Electric conducted a series of experiments at its Hawthorne factory (Roethlisberger and Dickson, 1939). Researchers hypothesized that worker productivity (the dependent variable) would increase if the lighting in the work area (the independent variable) was improved. Sure enough, when the lighting was increased, so was productivity. Then the lighting was decreased. To the researchers' surprise, and contrary to their hypothesis, worker productivity continued to increase. The researchers discovered that the amount of lighting was not causally related to worker productivity. Rather, the fact that they were being studied was an intervening variable that caused the workers to increase their productivity—a phenomenon that continues to appear in more contemporary research (Jones, 1990). Nevertheless, experimental and quasi-experimental designs remain viable quantitative methods in sociology if conducted carefully (Killias, Abei, and Reiband, 2000; Thye, 2000; Neuman, 2007).

HAWTHORNE EFFECT
The phenomenon where subjects' behavior is influenced by the fact that they are being studied.

SURVEY RESEARCH
Research using a questionnaire or interview to obtain data.

Survey research can be conducted by using questionnaires or by interviews.

Why is survey research the most popular research method in sociology? What are some of its strengths? What are some of its weaknesses?

Surveys At one time or another, you probably have participated in **survey research** that uses *questionnaires or interviews to obtain data.* As a college student, you may have completed a questionnaire for a student or faculty member, or one of the administrative units on campus may have surveyed you on a particular aspect of college life. Many colleges and universities use a standardized form for students to evaluate courses and instructors. These are examples of survey research.

The two most common survey instruments are questionnaires and interviews. A *questionnaire* is a series of statements or questions to which an individual is asked to respond. Questions may be *closed-ended,* asking the respondent to choose from several standardized responses, or *open-ended,* requiring the respondent to create an answer. Closed-ended questions are much easier to tabulate and analyze because the responses are standardized and need only be counted. Open-ended questions have the advantage of allowing respondents to answer more freely and to explain their answers.

The phrasing of questions is important in survey research. Researchers may influence responses by the way they word questions. For example, a *New York Times* poll showed that only 29 percent of respondents were "for" and 67 percent were "against" a constitutional amendment "prohibiting abortions," but when the question was reworded, 50 percent were "for" and 39 percent were "against" a constitutional amendment "protecting the life of the unborn" (Budiansky et al., 1988:44).

An interview is a questionnaire administered to respondents by the researcher. Interviews are more expensive and time-consuming than self-administered questionnaires, but they offer the advantage of having face-to-face contact with respondents.

Researchers must be careful, however, not to coach or influence responses by interpreting questions.

Sampling An important aspect of sociological research is sampling. In order to make generalizations about a **population**—*the entire body of people to which the sociologist would like to generalize research findings*—it is important to select a large enough and representative **sample,** or *segment of the population.*

Suppose you want to survey students at your college or university to determine their attitudes toward capital punishment. It would not be feasible, nor would it be necessary, to survey every student on campus. While it would be possible to obtain a sample by standing in the student union and asking students to participate in your survey, such a sample would probably not be representative of your school's student population. This is called *availability sampling;* it involves using whoever is readily available as research subjects. Although it is sometimes used for pretesting a questionnaire, it is rarely considered an adequate sampling technique for serious sociological research.

More likely to provide a representative sample is *random sampling,* in which each member of the population has an equal opportunity of being selected. If you obtain a list of all the students enrolled in your school, place their names in a large container, mix them thoroughly, and then draw 100 names, based on the laws of mathematical probability you are likely to get a representative sample of the student body. Today's computers provide less cumbersome ways of generating a random sample that work on the same principle.

In an attempt to ensure the representativeness of your sample, you might find it necessary to select a *stratified random sample,* which includes proportionate representation of the different categories of people from which a random sample is drawn. For example, you could stratify your sample by race, sex, or classification (seniors, juniors, sophomores, and first-year students) and randomly select from each category so that the right proportions are represented in your sample. There are other methods of sampling, but whatever the strategy the goal is the same: to choose a sample that accurately represents the population to be studied. This is one of the major challenges faced by the U.S. government as it plans future census surveys as arguments over the viability of sampling techniques became a $100 billion issue (M. Miller, 1998). Despite sampling procedure arguments, the 2000 Census was conducted almost identically to the 1990 Census, and the government has no plans to change procedures for the 2010 Census.

Qualitative Research Designs

Qualitative sociologists use an *interpretive paradigm,* and use the scientific method only as a general guideline for observation and analysis. Rather than state and test specific research hypotheses, they usually develop research objectives to guide their studies. **Qualitative research designs** *use systematic observation and focus on the meanings people give to their social actions.* Despite the subjective interpretation demanded in qualitative research, sociologists remain vigilant in their attempt to analyze and assess their findings objectively, and to generate meaningful sociological theories (Denzin and Lincoln, 2000).

Ethnographic Interviews Earlier we discussed interviews as a type of survey research where the researcher reads a questionnaire to respondents. In field research the ethnographic interview follows quite a different procedure. Rather than *"studying people,"* ethnography means *learning from people"* (Spradley, 1979:3). An **ethnographic interview** is *a technique where the researcher talks with people in an effort to learn as much as possible about them and their behavior.* Ethnographic researchers focus on a particular culture or subculture and attempt to understand what

POPULATION
An entire body of people to which the sociologist would like to generalize research findings.

SAMPLE
A segment of the population.

QUALITATIVE RESEARCH DESIGN
A research design that uses systematic observation and focuses on the meanings people give to their social actions.

ETHNOGRAPHIC INTERVIEW
A qualitative technique where the researcher talks with people in an effort to learn as much as possible about them and their behavior.

Field research is much more difficult and time consuming than survey research.

What are some of the strengths and weaknesses of field research?

its members do, how they do it, and the meanings they attach to their behaviors. The study of the coven by Kathleen Lowney, described in the opening to this chapter, is a good example of qualitative research using ethnographic interviews.

Ethnographic interviewers rely on locating and interviewing knowledgeable informants. An *informant* is a member of a particular culture or subculture who is willing to share his or her experiences, knowledge, and understanding with a researcher. Ethnographic interviewers are careful to maintain objectivity in their research and analysis. Since their method requires that they become familiar with people in order to learn more about them, researchers must build trust and empathy with the people they study. But they must not allow this to distort their analyses or allow subjective observations and interpretations to distort their findings.

Participant Observation In **participant observation,** the *researcher systematically observes the people being studied while participating with them in their activities. Nonparticipation* occurs when the researcher observes social action but does not participate in it or interact with participants (Spradley, 1980). For example, a sociologist might set up a hidden camera to record the behaviors of people at a vending machine, or, acting as an observant bystander, might watch children interacting in a classroom or on a school playground.

In *limited participation,* the researcher's participation in the interaction is restricted. *Full participation,* in which the researcher becomes actively and completely involved in the behavior being studied, is the highest level of involvement for the sociologist (Spradley, 1980). In *Tearoom Trade* (1970), Laud Humphreys assumed the role of voyeur who observed covert homosexual behavior between two men in a public restroom while simultaneously being a "lookout," warning the participants when someone approached.

Case Studies Qualitative field researchers also use **case studies,** which involve *the intensive observation of a particular person, group, or event.* The researcher gathers as much detailed information as possible. Case studies often use other research methods, including ethnographic interviewing or participant observation. William Foote Whyte took a case study approach when he investigated a Boston slum neighborhood in his classic work *Street Corner Society* (1943). By studying and interacting with a particular group on a personal level, Whyte discovered that, contrary to public assumptions that immigrant slum dwellers had no norms or values, the group of first- and second-generation Italian immigrants who inhabited "Cornerville" had a highly structured set of values, attitudes, beliefs, and norms that governed their daily lives. Lowney's study of the Coven could also be considered a case study of a particular adolescent satanic subculture.

Qualitative sociologists contend that numbers and statistics are dehumanizing and that when observations are reduced to numbers the essence of human social behavior is lost. They embrace the sentiment that "if you can measure it, that ain't it" (Kaplan, 1964:206). Quantitative sociologists argue that qualitative methods lack scientific rigor and that instead of providing explanations of behavior these methods reveal the subjective interpretations and biases of the researcher.

Combining Research Methods

To overcome methodological weaknesses, whether quantitative or qualitative, sociologists sometimes combine techniques from several different methodologies. **Triangulation** is *the use of multiple (usually three) techniques to gather or analyze research data.* For example, a common procedure among qualitative researchers is to combine ethnographic interviews with participant observation. Lowney's research on teenage satanism combined these methods. Another method is *team field research,* which involves more than one researcher in order to combine "the cool detachment of the outsider and the committed view of the insider" (Douglas, 1976:218).

THE FAR SIDE® By GARY LARSON

© 1986 FarWorks, Inc. All Rights Reserved/Dist. by Creators Syndicate

The Far Side® by Gary Larson © 1986 FarWorks, Inc. All Rights Reserved. The Far Side® and the Larson® signature are registered trademarks of FarWorks, Inc. Used with permission.

"So, you're a *real* gorilla, are you? Well, guess you wouldn't mind munchin' down a few beetle grubs, would you? ... In fact, we wanna see you chug 'em!"

PARTICIPANT OBSERVATION
A qualitative method in which the researcher systematically observes the people being studied while participating with them in their activities.

CASE STUDIES
Qualitative techniques that involve intensive observation of a particular person, group, or event.

TRIANGULATION
The use of multiple (usually three) techniques to gather or analyze research data.

It is also possible to combine quantitative and qualitative research methods to provide both statistical and interpretive insights. Researchers who focus on how social structure shapes peoples' behavior should also seek to understand how people interpret their worlds, and the field researcher who attempts to capture the social lives of people through their eyes should also make every effort to see how those lives are embedded in the social structure (Pearlin, 1992).

The study of covert homosexuality discussed in Focus box 2.2, although qualitative field research, also used quantitative data collected from survey research. By tracing license plate numbers, Humphreys learned the identities of the men he observed. He then included these individuals in a health-care survey, in which he visited their homes and interviewed their wives while they were away. This approach allowed him to collect demographic data that he could not obtain during participant observation. Humphreys's research demonstrates at least one way to combine qualitative and quantitative research designs.

Researchers employing **content analysis,** which *examines and analyzes communication,* may use either qualitative or quantitative methods or a combination. Content analysis can be used to study the content of poetry, literature, newspaper and magazine articles, television programs, commercials, and movies. The analysis may focus on words, themes, or patterns of communication. For example, qualitative content analyses of television programs may study the portrayal of gender roles and the different themes reflected between 1950 and 2000 (see Chapter 11).

A quantitative approach to content analysis often involves counting and carefully coding elements of communication. Studies that have explored the relationship between television violence and aggressive behavior in children, for example, have typically used content analysis of television programming. One method is to count and categorize the number of violent scenes per minute or the average number of minutes of television violence aired per day. In studying the effects of television violence, researchers have found that it is important not only to count the number of violent scenes but also to look for more subtle and symbolic aspects of violence on television. This requires the careful qualitative analysis of themes, stereotypes, jokes, and situations that might promote violence, without being explicitly violent themselves. Research on this topic is covered in Chapter 7.

THE RELATIONSHIP BETWEEN THEORY AND METHODS

Sociologist Norman Denzin (1970:56) stated, "Theory guides research while research guides theory." Sociologists' theoretical perspectives influence the topics they study, how they frame their research questions, the methods they use to collect and analyze their data, and how they interpret their findings. Because of the interdependence of theory and method, let's briefly examine how the major theoretical perspectives introduced in Chapter 1 relate to doing sociology.

The Interactionist Perspective

The interactionist perspective focuses on analysis at the microlevel. Sociologists who use it are most interested in the meanings people attach to human behavior; consequently they are most likely to use qualitative research methods. Ethnographic interviews, participant observation, and case studies are trademarks of interactionist research.

The interactionist perspective's focus on symbols puts certain demands on its methodologies. The interactionist perspective suggests that:

1. Symbols and interactions must be combined before an investigation is complete.

2. The researcher must take the "role of the other" and view the world from the subjects' point of view, but must maintain the distinction between everyday and scientific conceptions of reality.

3. The researcher must link subjects' symbols and definitions with the social relationships and groups that provide those conceptions.

CONTENT ANALYSIS
Research that examines and analyzes communications.

4. The behavior settings of interaction and scientific observation must be recorded.

5. Research methods must be capable of reflecting process or change as well as more stable behavioral forms.

6. Conducting research and being a sociologist are best viewed as an act of symbolic interaction. The personal preferences of sociologists shape their activities as investigators (Denzin, 1970:19).

Although the interactionist approach is most often linked to qualitative research methods, it does not use them exclusively. The Chicago School, which gave birth to symbolic interactionism, insisted that researchers use introspection and subjective interpretation. In sharp contrast, the Iowa School, a branch of symbolic interactionism founded by Manfred H. Kuhn, argues that the theoretical assumptions of symbolic interactionism can be operationalized and used in quantitative, empirical scientific research. While sharing the basic theoretical assumptions of the Chicago School, the Iowa School favors different research strategies, insisting that even the meanings and understandings of human behavior can be quantified and statistically analyzed.

Dr. Phil, who gained notoriety through appearances on the *Oprah Winfrey Show*, has developed into a media personality who dispenses advice to millions on his syndicated radio and television programs.

How might a sociologist analyze America's seeming obsession with media personalities who offer advice on personal issues ranging from dating and marriage to obesity, childrearing, and a wide range of other personal and relationship matters?

The Functionalist Perspective

Functionalists take a macrolevel approach to the study of society and human behavior. Their emphasis on structure, social institutions, manifest and latent functions, and entire societies influences their selection of research problems, choice of research designs, and analysis and interpretation of results. Sociologists who adopt the functionalist perspective often use quantitative research designs and statistical techniques for data analysis. The most popular method among functionalists is the use of questionnaires in large-scale surveys. Survey data collected from representative samples of large populations (e.g., census data) are especially appealing because they provide a picture of a society as a whole.

Evaluation research is often guided by the functionalist perspective, as there is a natural theoretical and methodological link between the two. The role of evaluation research is to determine whether a particular agency, service, or program is functioning properly. Evaluation research identifies strengths and weaknesses, the functional and dysfunctional aspects of programs.

Functionalists' preference for quantitative research methods can be traced to Émile Durkheim ([1893] 1964), who emphasized that sociological theory must be derived from the study of *social facts*. Distinguishing sociology from the "armchair theorizing" of philosophy and the emphasis on "psychological facts" of psychology, Durkheim insisted that social facts are the products of social institutions. His emphasis on rates as opposed to individual behaviors laid the groundwork for functionalists' general disdain for qualitative methods that focus on microlevel analysis. While qualitative research designs also may be used by functionalists, the theoretical assumptions behind those techniques are less compatible with the major premises of structural functionalism. However, the functionalist approach and qualitative methods are not totally antithetical. Cultural anthropologists, for example, with their holistic studies of communities, long have demonstrated that qualitative methods such as ethnographic interviews, participant observations, and case studies can be conducted and interpreted from a structural functionalist perspective.

The Conflict Perspective

The conflict perspective also uses macrolevel analysis, and traditionally its followers have preferred quantitative research methods designed to gather and analyze data on social institutions over qualitative designs geared more toward studying smaller groups and small-scale interactions. Secondary analyses, surveys, and other methods used by conflict theorists do not usually focus on the functioning of different parts of society, however. Research from the conflict perspective focuses on social diversity, conflict, alienation, exploitation, and social change. Conflict theorists attempt to assess the impact of social variables such as age, race, sex, and socioeconomic status on people as they participate in groups and institutions; these theorists want to know how these variables relate to the exploitation of less powerful groups by more powerful ones. Thus the major differences between research conducted by conflict theorists and that by functionalists are related more to their theoretical analyses than to their particular methodologies.

Conflict theorists often use census data, crime rates, and data from other large-scale surveys to document the extent of social inequality and class conflict in American society. From a conflict perspective, these data indicate that age, race, sex, and socioeconomic status determine one's life chances and ability to compete for desired resources and goals. Conflict theorists show how ageism, racism, and sexism in society account for differences in the education, occupational level, income, and arrest rates of different groups.

Like functionalists, conflict theorists do not limit themselves to the use of quantitative methods, but many of the theoretical assumptions of the traditional conflict perspective are less compatible with qualitative designs. Steeped in the tradition of Karl Marx, research from the conflict perspective is most interested in understanding and explaining large-scale social change. This emphasis encourages a preference for the secondary analysis of data and a strong emphasis on historical studies.

Contemporary conflict theorists, however, are less tied to macrolevel analysis and the use of quantitative methods than their predecessors were. They believe that strict adherence to traditional scientific methodology is much less important than an unwavering commitment to the discovery of knowledge. Consequently, they use historical, quantitative, qualitative, and even experimental models where appropriate. An example of the neoconflict approach can be seen in contemporary feminist sociology.

Feminist Theory and Research

In Chapter 1, we discussed feminist theory as an example of contemporary sociological theory that combines elements of all three major theoretical perspectives in sociology. Similarly, when it comes to research there is no single feminist method. The most prominent feature of feminist research is the importance it places on gender in all phases of the research process—from selection of a topic through choice of design, data collection and analysis, and interpretation of findings. Feminist research reconceptualizes knowledge to encompass the female experience. It points out that the world of scientific enterprise historically and cross-culturally has been viewed as the domain of men. Sexism in scientific research tends to be subtle, and feminists note that the questions scientists choose to ask and the way they ask them often determine the types of answers the investigation will yield (Spanier, 1997; Fisher, 2005). Consequently, sociological research dominated by men and conducted primarily on men may produce male-biased theories of society and human behavior (Scheider, 2000). And, as feminists have noted, women have been ambivalent toward science—at times trying to embrace it and other times outright rejecting it (Sayers, 1987; Tetrault, 1993). Perhaps Marjorie DeVault (1996:30) put it most succinctly when she pointed out, "Feminist sociologists are committed to both feminism and social science, and they use the tools of the discipline to 'talk back' to sociology in a spirited critique aimed at improving the ways we know society." Sociology, in fact, may be one of the few scientific disciplines in which a critical mass of women have earned Ph.D.'s and have conducted sufficient research that structural barriers based on gender have been reduced, especially in regard to publishing and other academic endeavors (Stack, 1994; Singley, Firebaugh, and Chase, 1998; Stack, 2002; Hesse-Biber and Yaiser, 2004).

Perhaps one of the most distinguishing features of feminist theory is its unwavering commitment to gender research. While there is no single paradigm in feminist theory most agree that research guided by the feminist approach can be summarized as attempting to remedy three major problems that have consistently plagued sociology throughout all but its most recent existence:

1. Most sociological studies were conducted by men who studied men but then generalized their findings to everybody. Feminists remind us that our experiences, even

Traditional sociological research has come under criticism from the feminist perspective for primarily involving men conducting research on other men. Contemporary sociological research includes numerous studies conducted by women with both male and female subjects.

In what other ways has the feminist perspective affected sociological research?

those guided by the objectivity of science, are shaped in important ways by our gender; consequently they urge scientific research to "bring women in" (DeVault, 1996:32). While there may be good reason to target one sex or the other in a particular study, it is important in such cases not to generalize the findings to both sexes.

2. For many years, gender was considered neither an important topic for research nor a serious subfield of sociology, and women were ignored. Women's activities and contributions are often less visible, especially in the formal social structure, than are men's. Therefore, it often takes in-depth ethnographic inquiry to bring women's experiences and social activities to light. Moreover, in many cultures only female researchers are allowed to enter the private, domestic, behind-the-scenes world of women.

3. Often when women have been studied their attitudes and behaviors have been analyzed by men and compared to male standards of "normality" and correctness. While feminists do not argue that only women can study women, they emphasize the importance of gender in choosing a research topic, developing a research design, and shaping our perceptions, analyses, and interpretations (Renzetti and Curran, 1995; Fisher, 2005). This may make a good case for men and women collaborating, especially in participant observation and ethnographic studies. For example, John Hostetler and Gertrude Huntington (1971) teamed up to study childhood socialization in Old Order Amish communities, assuming women would be more likely to confide in Huntington and men would more likely share certain information with Hostetler.

Two good examples of sociological research from the feminist theoretical perspective are found in Arlie Hochschild and Anne Machung's *The Second Shift: Inside the Two-Job Marriage* (1990) and Hochschild's later work, *The Time Bind: When Work Becomes Home and Home Becomes Work* (1997). These insightful studies of families where both adults work outside the home show the dramatic differences in the way men and women perceive careers, responsibility for household chores, and the level to which each spouse contributes to maintenance of the home and child care.

Sociologists working from all theoretical perspectives and using a variety of research methods are concerned about how their research findings are used. Over 40 years ago, Mills (1959) warned that sociologists and their research would be used increasingly for bureaucratic and ideological purposes. One of the greatest concerns facing sociologists today is how the mass media, especially television, present, use, interpret, and often distort sociological findings.

SOCIAL RESEARCH AND THE MEDIA

Just as sociology discovered the mass media in the 1960s and 1970s, the mass media, especially television, discovered sociology. While sociologists were attempting to assess television's impact on society, television was attempting to "study," "analyze," and "explain" major social issues. When the major networks broadcast special reports on crime in American cities, sociologists specializing in criminology were often called in as expert analysts. Similarly, prominent sociologists were interviewed in special reports on social issues ranging from poverty and teenage runaways to drugs, violence, terrorism, and war. Research findings previously buried in academic journals were published in prominent newspapers, popular magazines, and supermarket tabloids as well as aired on nightly news reports and prime-time specials.

Infotainment: Information and Entertainment

Sociologists disagree about the effects of media attention on sociology and sociological research, but most agree that the media's penchant for brief, sensationalistic, and entertaining reports have combined to create a new phenomenon: *infotainment.* Serious sociological studies of crime, prostitution, drug cults, youth gangs, and other important social issues are not as interesting or entertaining to television viewers as the sensationalistic and superficial reports by television "journalists," whose personal and editorial opinions are often given at least as much emphasis as the findings of scientific investigators (Cundy, 1989). As two researchers noted, the media make little effort "to distinguish 'good' research from 'bad'; they are concerned less with the scientific value of the information communicated than with its entertainment value" (Weiss and Singer, 1988:253). "Newsworthiness" is determined by editorial "gate keepers" based on a variety of personal and social factors (Clayman and Reisner, 1998).

For example, there have been several magazine and television reports on the problem of newborn babies who, because of their mother's drug addiction during pregnancy, are born addicted to crack cocaine. The media report that these so-called "crack babies" suffer from lifelong inability to function normally, yet there is no scientific evidence that they fare any worse than other children born in poverty or whose mothers lacked adequate prenatal care. In fact, there is medical evidence that these babies actually do better than babies afflicted with fetal alcohol syndrome (ABC News, 1997a).

Besides a penchant for sensationalism and entertainment over information, the media tend to mix findings from scientific research with those from pseudoscientific polls and even mere speculation. It is important for us to understand the difference between pseudoscientific polling and systematic survey research.

Pseudoscientific Polling versus Survey Research

The media are intrigued by public opinion polls and often report them as if they represent serious scientific research; in fact, however, they are "part science and part art" (Singer and Endreny, 1986; M. Moore, 1992:ix). There are well over one thousand polling organizations in the United States, with estimated earnings of several billion dollars annually. It is virtually impossible to read a major newspaper or magazine or to listen to a newscast without discovering the results of some poll. These polls measure everything from the popularity of presidential candidates to attitudes toward a host of social issues, including abortion, capital punishment, gun control, foreign aid, same-sex marriage, and nuclear energy. Given the competition among the media, there is tremendous pressure to be the first to report the results of a new poll. Many of these topics are also researched by sociologists and other social and behavioral scientists. Unfortunately, the media (especially television) indiscriminately mix the findings from polls with those from scientific research, giving equal credibility to both.

The results of media polls are usually presented in the form of percentages of people "for" or "against" a particular issue, and they are reported with great fanfare and the appearance of statistical precision. At least two major problems arise from these polls: (1) They oversimplify and misrepresent the research process; and (2) their findings are often distorted and misinterpreted. Polling, especially as it is used by politicians, advertisers, and the mass media, represents at best a *tainted truth* (Crossen, 1996).

The first problem can be attributed to format, which places greater emphasis on entertainment than on accurate information. Information is condensed, simplified, and packaged with pizzazz, glitz, and entertainment value in order to appeal to a mass audience. Methodological issues related to sampling technique, sampling size, representativeness of the sample, problems in data collection, and so on are typically ignored or glossed over in media accounts. Instead, research findings are presented in an attractive, pseudoscientific way that appeals to the masses but requires little or no thought.

Politicians, newspeople, and others often cite "official" statistics to make a point, support a cause, mobilize people, or otherwise sway public opinion.

What are some of the problems that can occur with this type of use and misuse of statistical data and research?

This problem is not limited to media polls. A sociological research study that may have taken months to design and years to complete may be given less than 30 seconds on a newscast. The media tend to gloss over qualifying statements and to make dramatic assertions that may be unwarranted. If a study captures wide media attention, the researcher may be interviewed on television talk shows. Some sociologists may jump at the chance to discuss their research, especially if they believe their findings have been distorted or misinterpreted. The perception of an opportunity to "set the record straight" is usually short-lived, however, as researchers discover that the host and the audience do not want to be "bored" with scientific jargon and technical discussions about data collection and analysis. Rather, researchers are expected to be entertaining, and they are encouraged to respond spontaneously to questions from the audience and the host; in the long run, such exposure may distort the researchers' findings even further.

Another problem stems from the public's lack of understanding of statistics. It is not fair to blame statistics for the distortions they suffer at the hands of the mass media, but statistics can contribute to falsehoods. Americans are fascinated by numbers, and once a statistic is cited it often takes on a life of its own. Focus box 2.4, "Lies, Damned Lies, and Statistics," provides some examples of how distorted statistics can create "virtual truth."

Sociologists must be vigilant in correcting inaccurate reporting and discouraging the reporting of pseudoresearch, and greater efforts must be made to publicize important sociological studies in addition to those that lend themselves to journalistic adaptation (Singer and Endreny, 1986). Technological advances make that job simultaneously easier and more difficult. Let's look at the impact on research of the new technomedia discussed in Chapter 1.

THE TECHNOMEDIA AND RESEARCH

Technological advances, especially in computers and interactive media, may have the greatest impact of all on research methodology. Computers provide a wealth of information about people's financial resources, preferences, and opinions, and much of this information is accessible to government planners, merchants, sociologists, and even ordinary citizens. Just three decades ago computers were so large and expensive that only the largest universities and corporations had the space needed to house them and the funds necessary to purchase and maintain them. Today, microcomputers are in most offices and homes, and people around the world can collaborate on research projects simply by using the telephone or the Internet. Access to data analysis has become much less expensive and cumbersome. On the other hand, one downside of technology is that because so many people use answering machines to screen their calls, poll results are skewed and extended telephone interviews are far more difficult to conduct (Barta, 1998).

The impact of the media, especially the technomedia, on sociological research will probably be greater in the future. They may have a tremendous impact on the types of research funded by government and private agencies, by helping define what is in the "public interest." How has this new technology affected you? Who has access to information about you? How is that information used? How difficult is it for you to gain access to information about your family, friends, or classmates?

Technological advances also raise new ethical issues for sociological researchers. The widespread use of computers makes it much easier to collect information about people, and technology makes it possible to study people without their knowledge or consent. The widespread use of video cameras and other forms of covert surveillance and the popularity of multimedia voyeuristic home pages on the Internet led one sociologist to declare that contemporary society is dominated by the *culture of surveillance* (Staples, 1997). Nevertheless, if a picture is worth a thousand words, the use of digital cameras,

In *Dragnet,* a popular television series of the 1950s and 1960s, one of the lead characters, Sergeant Joe Friday, implored people to give him the facts, "just the facts." He preferred his witnesses not to embellish or in any way interpret the events of the crime that had occurred. Sergeant Friday believed that the only way to discover the truth was to deal with the cold hard facts, free of any interpretation. Many sociologists and other social scientists striving to better understand the complex social world in which we live may also seek the truth by attempting to discover and study social facts. And, albeit a difficult task, some believe that this requires a value-free approach in which scientists allow the facts to speak for themselves.

Sociologist William Gamson (1999:23), however, points out that "facts are institutionally validated claims about the world . . . [and they] lead one to interpret evidence in particular ways." These facts, then, as they are revealed become subject to validation. In this case, sociologists or other social scientists become the primary validators. Gamson goes on to indicate, however, that scientists are not the only validators. In today's mass-mediated world, those who disseminate the so-called facts become important secondary validators, a role that is played primarily by the mass media, especially newspaper and television reporters. And, as sociologist Judith Stacey (1999:18) laments, once the media become involved, "the search for truth is a creative process." In fact, Stacey asserts that today, with the help of mass media, many sociologists have taken on the role of social advocates as opposed to merely researchers and reporters of facts. She calls this new phenomenon *virtual social science,* which involves "the application of sophisticated technologies of public relations and mass media to culturally construct social scientific 'truth'" (Stacey, 1999:18).

Stacey relates this new virtual social science to a political cartoon that illustrated the creative process of searching for truth:

First, you create a premise. Next, you create a statistic to back it up. Then, you create an audience by repeating it over and over again . . . until the media pick it up. That's when you know you've done it—created a fact! (1999:19–21)

Stacey uses the sociological topic of fatherlessness to illustrate her point of how research and interpretation in many cases has given way to blatant advocacy—in this case, of traditional marriage patterns. Other sociologists indicate similar occurrences of social science research being used for social policy advocacy in reporting on divorce (Furstenberg, 1999), homelessness (Rossi, 1999), and countless other sociological topics of public interest (Gamson, 1999).

Budiansky and his co-authors pointed to the often-cited figure of $140 billion in illegal drug trafficking as an example. The figure is impressive and precise—not "over $100 billion," or "approximately $150 billion," but "$140 billion." Yet as Budiansky pointed out, this figure was derived from a guess dating back to 1978, when it was estimated that the illegal drug trade was about $50 billion. Two years later it was estimated the figure had jumped to $80 billion, and in 1982 it was estimated at $90 billion. John Cusack, former director of the National Narcotics Intelligence Consumers Committee, the government commission charged with tracking illegal drug trafficking, indicated that "adding $10 billion a year seemed to make sense," so the committee has done so ever since (Budiansky et al., 1988:45). The figure of $140 billion was cited by virtually every government agency and publication as if it were empirically derived and statistically accurate.

Joel Best (2001) provides yet another example citing the example of a report that approximately 150,000 American women were anorexic. Concerned activists and media reports distorted that statistic by claiming that approximately 150,000 American women die from anorexia annually, when, in fact, approximately 70 women die from anorexia each year.

Can sociological research be truly objective? Most sociologists today agree that it probably cannot. In fact, Frank Furstenberg asserts that because sociologists are human beings, "a fundamental sociological axiom reminds us that social position influences personal perspective" (1999:10). He notes:

Men and women, old and young, rich and poor will see the world differently from one another. Thus, our professional role of fact finder, neutral data analyst, and fair-minded interpreter—the basis of our claims to be expert witnesses—collides, at least to some degree, with sociological theory. (Furstenberg, 1999:10)

Source: From Frank F. Furstenberg, Jr. "Children and Family Change: Discourse between Social Scientists and the Media," *Contemporary Sociology* 28 (January), 1999:10–17. William A. Gamson. "Beyond the Science-versus-Advocacy Distinction," *Contemporary Sociology* 28 (January), 1999:23–26. Peter H. Rossi. "Half Truths with Real Consequences: Journalism, Research, and Public Policy," *Contemporary Sociology* 28 (January), 1999:1–5. Judith Stacey. "Virtual Truth with a Vengeance," *Contemporary Sociology* 28 (January), 1999:18–23.

video cameras, and other visual media has a valid place in contemporary sociological research (Becker, 2000; Holliday, 2000). Increasingly, sociologists must weigh the ethical issue of the scientist's "right to know" against the individual's right to privacy. This is likely to become an even more controversial issue in the future.

SOCIAL RESEARCH IN THE TWENTY-FIRST CENTURY

Regardless of the methodological strategies used, all sociological research has one paramount goal: to understand society better. Hence it is appropriate to look to the research methods that will shape how we may think about society in the future.

Technological developments have given rise to an increased emphasis on quantitative research designs, because of the speed and ease with which they can be conducted. With such widespread use, however, the prestige once accorded quantitative and sophisticated statistical analyses has diminished somewhat, and interest in qualitative studies is increasing. Some of sociology's most distinguished scholars have urged their colleagues to devote more time and energy to qualitative research (Gans, 1989; Portes, 2000), and researchers have acknowledged that subjective information is often used even in some of the most sophisticated statistical models (Angel and Gronfein, 1988). A concerted movement is being mounted to combine quantitative and qualitative methods to create innovative designs that incorporate the strengths of both approaches and to provide as much useful information as we can discover. There is some evidence that the distinction between quantitative and qualitative research methods are now less important in structuring the discipline than they were in the past (Cappell and Guterbock, 1992; Neuman, 2007). Many contemporary researchers believe sociology has suffered from the quarrels over methodological approaches—especially the debate over quantitative versus qualitative methods—and argue that the most meaningful research in the future will combine various research strategies (Smith, 1991; Zhao, 1991; Portes, 2000).

Today many sociologists use the so-called information highway and various techno-media both as a research tool and as a way of disseminating research findings. To that end, sociologist Karl Schonborn broke from the long-standing tradition of reporting research findings in professional journals and books and developed "socumentaries" to convey the results of his research in a sophisticated video format. These videos combine quick video cuts from in-depth interviews on subjects ranging from prostitution to the plight of California migrant workers. Unlike documentaries, they make no effort to draw final conclusions or make value judgments about the subjects. Rather, they are presented in a systematic format derived from the scientific method, beginning with a statement of the problem and a brief review of the literature, and they conclude by posing further possible research questions on the topic (Alesci, 1994). Also, today all major sociological journals can be accessed online. Creative uses of media technology are likely to increase and to have tremendous impact on the nature of sociological research.

Another factor that will affect the future direction of sociology is the role government and industry will play in funding sociological research. There is a distinguishable difference between the sociological specialties supported by research agencies and those that draw their support from intellectual, ideological, and political opposition (Cappell and Guterbock, 1992). What types of studies do you think are most likely to be funded by government and industry in the future? What types are least likely to receive funding? How is this likely to affect sociological research in the twenty-first century?

If sociology is to realize its promise, rigid adherence to any one methodology or type of analysis must give way to eclectic methods that reflect a scientific commitment to knowledge and understanding. The reality is that no single research method or theoretical interpretation can ever capture the true complexity of human social interaction. Throughout this book, we draw on findings from the widest possible variety of sociological research methods.

Summary

1 People are curious about human behavior and have long attempted to explain how and why people behave the way they do. This is especially true in the diverse, global society in which we live today. In their quest for understanding, people have turned to traditional knowledge, faith, authoritative knowledge, and science.

2 Science uses both inductive and deductive reasoning in the theory-building process. Building theory involves defining and operationalizing concepts and identifying relevant variables. Relationships between variables are then stated in propositional form, and these propositions are used to develop, test, and verify theories. Sociologists use the scientific method as a general guideline for their research procedures. The eight steps in this process are: stating the problem, reviewing the relevant literature, developing hypotheses or research objectives, choosing a research design, collecting data, analyzing and interpreting the data, developing conclusions, and posing new research questions. Studying people raises a number of ethical issues. Sociologists must strive to maintain objectivity and integrity in their research, protect their subjects, use the research role properly, disclose assistance and support, and disassociate themselves from unethical research.

3 Sociological research generally falls into one of four types—exploratory, descriptive, explanatory, and evaluative—which can be conducted through either quantitative or qualitative research designs. Quantitative designs emphasize the use of numbers and statistics, and they include secondary analysis, experiments (and quasi-experiments), and surveys. Qualitative designs focus on social interaction and the meanings people impute to their behavior, and they include ethnographic interviews, participant observations, and case studies. Triangulation involves combining multiple research strategies (usually at least three) to gather research data and may combine both quantitative and qualitative methods. Content analysis is a research technique that often combines the quantitative and qualitative approaches.

4 There is a strong relationship between sociological theory and research methods. A researcher's theoretical perspective shapes what is studied, the choice of research design, and interpretations and conclusions drawn from the data. Sociologists who conduct research guided by the functionalist and conflict perspectives tend to focus on macrolevel analysis and often use quantitative research methods to collect and analyze data. Research conducted from the interactionist perspective is more likely to use qualitative methods more conducive to microlevel analysis. Researchers who use feminist theory to guide their research remind us of the importance of gender in all phases of research and may use any of the methods discussed in this chapter.

5 The media, especially television, have become increasingly interested in sociological research. A positive result is that sociologists have found a public forum for communicating the sociological perspective and its insights. A negative result is that the mass media focus on brief and sensationalistic reports, often distorting research findings or drawing erroneous and unfounded conclusions. The use of computers and technomedia such as interactive media and surveillance pose additional ethical issues for sociological researchers and will probably have even more profound influence on social research in the future.

6 In the ongoing quest for knowledge, sociologists must renew their scientific commitment to developing new and creative research designs and methods aimed at an increased understanding of our social world in the twenty-first century.

Key Terms

case studies (p. 42)
causation (p. 33)
concept (p. 32)
conceptual definition (p. 32)
content analysis (p. 43)
control group (p. 38)
correlation (p. 33)
deductive reasoning (p. 32)
dependent variable (p. 38)
descriptive research (p. 36)
ethnographic interview (p. 41)
evaluation research (p. 37)
experimental design (p. 38)
experimental group (p. 38)

explanatory research (p. 37)
exploratory research (p. 36)
Hawthorne effect (p. 40)
hypotheses (p. 33)
independent variable (p. 38)
inductive reasoning (p. 32)
intervening variables (p. 38)
mean (p. 35)
measures of central tendency (p. 35)
median (p. 35)
methodology (p. 28)
mode (p. 35)
operational definition (p. 32)
participant observation (p. 42)

population (p. 41)
proposition (p. 33)
qualitative research design (p. 41)
quantitative research design (p. 38)
reliability (p. 33)
research objectives (p. 34)
sample (p. 41)
science (p. 30)
secondary analysis (p. 38)
survey research (p. 40)
theory (p. 31)
triangulation (p. 42)
validity (p. 33)
variable (p. 33)

Chapter 3

Society and Culture

"America is the only culture that went from barbarism to decadence without civilization in between."

—Oscar Wilde

*C*ongratulations! You have decided to take an overseas teaching job at Lingnan University in Hong Kong. Your assignment is to teach undergraduate students about other cultures. You might be thinking, How hard can this be? Hong Kong is a major global banking center that literally depends for its existence on international commerce and a keen understanding of diverse cultures and societies. But as we have stressed: *Things may not be what they seem*. When Rozanna Lilley, an anthropologist with many years of research and teaching experience, began a "Comparative Cultures" course she almost immediately experienced difficulties. She decided to discuss Australian Aborigines, who placed little value on material goods—almost the polar opposite of the intense consumerism in Hong Kong society. She noted that her effort did not seem to have the desired effect. One student wrote on an exam, "they [Australian Aborigines] just live like an animal because they don't worry about the future . . ." (2001:136). Then students began to complain that the study of other cultures was "boring." Many pleaded with her, "Can't we just do something about Hong Kong?" (Lilley, 2001:136). The exception was Japanese culture, which at the time had become part of a Hong Kong commercial craze—Hello Kitty products and Japanese horror movies were all the vogue.

Lilley also found that although there is a sizeable minority population in Hong Kong, few students saw any need to discuss them because, despite a great deal of evidence to the contrary, relations between the majority Hong Kong Chinese and other ethnic groups were almost universally believed to be harmonious and free of racial tensions. At the conclusion of the first lecture, two students complained that they found the Comparative Cultures course very hard: when Lilley asked why they found it challenging, "one despairingly replied 'You were talking about East Africa; I've never even thought of East Africa'" (Lilley, 2001:146). Even the popular classroom exercise on social change fell flat. In the exercise called "Chinese Whispers," a single sentence is repeated, in whispers, from student to student, with the last person stating out loud what she heard. Lilley remarked that in her teaching experiences in Australia, there was always great amusement when students compared the original sentence to the final one. But Hong Kong students refused to whisper to one another; and "If someone didn't hear the sentence 'properly', they asked their neighbor to repeat it more loudly . . . people continued to repetitively shout the sentence, with crystal clear enunciation, . . . Until . . . The final person repeated the original sentence verbatim" (Lilley, 2001:147). While Lilley (2001:147) may have been disappointed that the exercise produced no social change, her students finally had found something in her cultures course they could relate to: "everyone felt pleased that the whole class was correct."

Today, the foods and cultures of the world are so common in cities that few people notice the extraordinary cultural diversity all around them.

Are these Hong Kong students unique in their views of culture and appreciation of global social diversity? Because of the media and globalization, few people are unaware of the extraordinary diversity of societies and cultures in the world today. They can be seen in television shows, movies, and on the Internet on any given day. Or they can be experienced during a walk through almost any large city and many small towns throughout the world. Far-reaching global changes have tremendous local impact (Savage et al., 2005), and today, few people have much difficulty comprehending how different cultures and societies affect others. However, most of us find it much harder to understand how culture and society affect our thoughts and behaviors. Even seasoned teachers of culture, like Rozanna Lilley, acknowledge that they have learned a great deal about their own values and cultural assumptions by teaching in undergraduate classrooms in diverse societies like Hong Kong. This is because culture is so pervasive and taken for granted that it rarely enters into our consciousness. But more is involved: if asked, most people around the world would probably agree that their societies and cultural beliefs and values are either "natural" or the "best."

WHAT IS SOCIETY?

For much of history, people lived in small, relatively autonomous societies and made their living by hunting and farming. Traditional definitions of **society,** as *people who live in a specific geographic territory, interact with one another, and share many elements of a common culture,* were well suited to these lifestyles. Today, any definition of society must be broader and more flexible.

Until about 10,000 years ago, all societies were hunting-gathering societies, and they were pretty much alike with respect to size, structural complexity, technology, and other aspects of social and cultural life. In the first great technological revolution that sociolo-

SOCIETY
People who live in a specific geographic territory, interact with one another, and share many elements of a common culture.

gists call the agricultural revolution, however, farming societies emerged and began to supplant them. Farming societies were more complex, technologically sophisticated, and more densely populated than hunting-gathering societies and far more competitive.

These trends, in turn, accelerated in the late eighteenth century as part of a second great revolution, the Industrial Revolution, which produced much larger populations, many more goods and services, urbanization, militarization, and the erosion and disappearance of thousands of rural communities. Today, many sociologists believe computers and other advanced technologies have produced a third major revolution—the information revolution—that is generating two very different social trends. On the one hand, new information technologies encourage greater social consolidation, perhaps the beginning stages of life in a truly "global village," where patterns of social interaction instantaneously crisscross the globe. On the other hand, new technologies encourage a more privatized and individualistic society, where more people may work, socialize, and spend much of their lives at home. They are also creating many more flexible and tentative statuses and identities than in any previous period (Caplow, 1991; Kumar, 1995; Turkle, 1995).

These great transformations are all part of what sociologists call **sociocultural evolution,** *a process in which societies grow more complex in terms of technology, social structure, and cultural knowledge over time.* Although there is nothing inevitable about this process, and at any given time a society may decline or collapse, in the course of human history there has been a progressive trend toward more complex and more geographically far-reaching sociocultural arrangements.

TYPES OF SOCIETIES

The type of society in which we live helps determine who we are, what we become, what is expected of us, and what we expect from others. In fact, it has profound impact on every aspect of our lives. Nevertheless, society is taken-for-granted, and we seldom contemplate it unless forced to do so. Sociologist Charles Lemert (2005:xii) asserts:

Most of the time [people] have no good and practical reason to think about so abstract a consideration as "society." Then, unexpectedly, something happens. One day, we are caught unawares by the unusual arising out of the ordinary and we are brought home to the reality of social things. when people are thus surprised, they become sociologists as best they can.

Because of globalization, social boundaries among groups and societies are much harder to define and cultural complexity rather than homogeneity is the rule everywhere. All contemporary societies, however, share one thing in common: they all are characterized by large-scale social structures that span the globe and link billions of people. Let's take a closer look at some major kinds of societies, from the simplest societies of the past to today's complex postindustrial societies. Table 3.1, on the next page, lists six major types of societies and some of their defining characteristics:

1. A **hunting-gathering society** is *a society in which people make their living by hunting, collecting wild foods, and fishing with simple technologies.*

2. A **pastoral society** is *a society that depends for its livelihood on domestic animals.*

3. A **horticultural society** is *a society in which hand tools are used to grow domesticated crops.*

4. An **agrarian society** is *a society that depends on crops raised with plows, draft animals, and intensive agricultural methods.*

5. An **industrial society** is *a society that relies on machines and advanced technology to produce and distribute food, information, goods, and services.*

6. A **postindustrial society** is *one in which service industries and the manufacture of information and knowledge dominate the economy.*

SOCIOCULTURAL EVOLUTION A process in which societies grow more complex in terms of technology, social structure, and cultural knowledge over time.

HUNTING-GATHERING SOCIETY A society in which people make their living by hunting, collecting wild foods, and fishing with simple technologies.

PASTORAL SOCIETY A society that depends for its livelihood on domestic animals.

HORTICULTURAL SOCIETY A society in which hand tools are used to grow domesticated crops.

AGRARIAN SOCIETY A society that depends on crops raised with plows, draft animals, and intensive agricultural methods.

INDUSTRIAL SOCIETY A society that relies on machines and advanced technology to produce and distribute food, information, goods, and services.

POSTINDUSTRIAL SOCIETY A society where service industries and the manufacture of information and knowledge dominate the economy.

	HUNTING-GATHERING	HORTICULTURAL	PASTORAL	AGRARIAN	INDUSTRIAL	POSTINDUSTRIAL
Period of historical dominance	10,000–50,000 years ago	5,000–10,000 years ago	5,000–10,000 years ago	5,000 years ago to A.D. 1750	18th–20th century	Late 20th and early 21st centuries
Population size	50–150	150–3,000	150–10,000	Millions	Millions to over a billion	Millions to over a billion
Technology	Stone, wood	Sickle, hoe	Domesticated animals	Animal-drawn plow agriculture; irrigation agriculture; animals	Machine power; electric, petroleum, nuclear power	Computer information technologies; photonics; robotics; biogenetics
Economy	Subsistence; several-week surplus	Horticulture; several-month surplus	Surplus on the hoof	Agriculture; market exchange surplus	Industrial; mass production and market economy	Global information—service economy
Settlement pattern	Nomadic	Semipermanent villages	Nomadic; seminomadic camps	Cities and empires; large rural populations	Majority of the population in cities	Megalopolises
Social organization	Family or kin bands	Chiefdoms; specialized religious-military roles	Chiefdoms and marked inequality	Complex division of labor; complex economic, military, and religious institutions; marked social inequality	Distinct institu-tions; growth of state power	Growth of scientific and technical institutions; emerging global classes; social networks and power structures
Contemporary examples	Mbuti of Central African Republic; Ju/'hoansi of South Africa prior to 1970	Yanomamo of Brazil; Dani of New Guinea highlands	Masai of Kenya and Fulani of Nigeria; Navajo of American Southwest	Ancient Egypt; feudal Europe; most Third World nations; rural China	Brazil; Eastern Europe; urban Russia	United States; Canada; Japan; and much of Western Europe

Source: "A Nip Here and Tuck There." From the March 2003 issue of *American Demographics.* Copyright, Crain Communications Inc. 2003. Used by permission.

How is the evolution of societies from simple to complex (as shown in this table) reflected in the numbers and varieties of social statuses in each type of society?

TECHNOMEDIA AND POSTINDUSTRIAL SOCIETIES

Many sociologists believe that the postmodern condition has generated new social structures, with most people having multiple, often temporary connections to groups and organizations (Bell, 1973; Pescosolido and Rubin, 2000). Postindustrial societies require the most advanced technologies in order to function. High-tech computers, robotics, biogenetic engineering, laser technology, and other high-cost, high-return industries are now basic to life in postindustrial societies. Transnational corporations, which link the world in a global market economy, become dominant, and corporate giants like General Motors and Toyota relinquish their national identities and assume global ones in pursuit of profit.

The influence of several institutions expands dramatically in postindustrial societies. Science is the cornerstone of the new order, for it produces both the technology and technical skills necessary for the efficient functioning of postindustrial societies. The educational institution is no less important; in postindustrial society education becomes a lifelong process as ideas rapidly become obsolete and new forms of knowledge must be learned. The media, however, becomes the central institution, affecting all other institutions—everywhere on earth.

In postindustrial society, the mass media and technomedia move from the background to center stage and becomes vitally linked to all social institutions. The media are key parts of life in the United States, and it is impossible to think of sports, medicine,

CULTURE
The learned set of beliefs, values, norms, and material goods shared by group members.

MATERIAL CULTURE
Artifacts, art, architecture, and other tangible goods that people create and assign meanings.

NONMATERIAL CULTURE
Mental blueprints that serve as guidelines for group behavior.

politics, the economy, and even religion without computers and the ubiquitous television monitor. Today, e-mail, teleconferencing, and new interactive media also expand individual and group contacts and make it possible for a growing segment of the population to hear the perspectives of many groups—from people with diverse sexual orientations to people with disabilities— whose voices formerly have been ignored by the mainstream media.

Some scholars contend that instead of creating a global village, new technomedia promote trends already evident in most postindustrial societies: (1) a polarization of society into "haves" and "have-nots" in terms of both wealth *and* information, and (2) a growing individualism and widespread disengagement from face-to-face social interactions and collective action.

For many people—from children and teenagers to urban professionals and retirees—*virtual communities* have supplanted local community life. For reasons of convenience and safety, many people shop at home and spend a great deal of leisure time in front of a computer or television monitor (Kumar, 1995).

Some sociologists go further, and argue that proliferating virtual communities are in reality "lifestyle enclaves" that provide isolated individuals with a sense of community and unique subcultures that may begin even in early childhood. This leads us to a discussion of culture.

"If you are calling from a touch tone telephone, press 1. If you are calling from a rotary phone, you probably don't even own a computer or a fax machine, and we strongly recommend that you get with it."

WHAT IS CULTURE?

Culture is *the learned set of beliefs, values, norms, and material goods shared by group members.* On the surface, the concept of culture is not difficult to understand. Culture consists of everything we learn in groups during the life course—from infancy to old age. Culture therefore includes ideas about what is real and what is not, what we may and may not eat, the clothing we wear, the music we listen to, and the games we play. Culture shapes our understandings of good and evil, health and sickness, and life and death. It lays down rules for serious social concerns as well as guidelines for everyday life. Culture is much more than ideas and rules of behavior, however. It gives our lives meaning, telling us why we should get out of bed each morning, obey the rules, and live from infancy to old age. Culture provides rewards for proper behavior and may promise that these rewards will continue beyond this physical world.

Material and Nonmaterial Culture

Culture has two major components: material and nonmaterial culture. **Material culture** includes *artifacts, art, architecture, and other tangible goods that people create and assign meanings.* Technology, art, architecture, clothing, television sets, and consumer goods at malls and supermarkets are all part of material culture in advanced industrial societies. **Nonmaterial culture** refers to *mental blueprints that serve as guidelines for group behavior.* They include the collective assumptions, languages, beliefs, values, norms, and attitudes of groups (see Figure 3.1, on the next page).

Symbols are humans' greatest achievement. The application of symbols to the physical world—specifically, the invention of material culture and technology—follows closely. Material and nonmaterial culture are interrelated in that all societies express their beliefs, values, and understandings in artifacts, architecture, and art. In simple societies material culture usually supports a consistent view of reality.

For example, the Lakota (Sioux) and other traditional Plains Indians believed that everything that was vitally important in nature—the sun, moon, earth, and stars—was round, and the "sacred circle" represented completeness, wholeness, health, and harmony with nature. Much of their material culture reflected this ideology: their houses (tepees)

How have new forms of technomedia affected interpersonal and group relationships in the United States and around the globe?

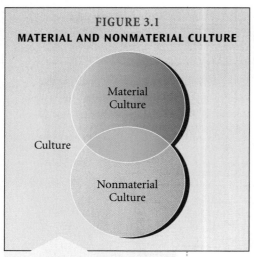

FIGURE 3.1
MATERIAL AND NONMATERIAL CULTURE

Material Culture

Culture

Nonmaterial Culture

Do material and nonmaterial culture typically change at the same rate?

were circular and were always placed in a circle; battle shields and drums were circular; circular objects were used to process the bison; circular amulets warded off evil spirits; and hoops, rings, and spinning tops were favored for recreation and sport (Lowie, 1963; Geertz, 1968b; Neihardt, 1984).

In modern industrial societies, values and norms are expressed in technology, architecture, and art, although the relationship is more complex than in simple societies. A century ago, Max Weber ([1904–1905] 1958a) demonstrated how values such as thrift, hard work, individuality, and savings, part of what he called the "Protestant ethic," played a central role in the birth and expansion of industrial capitalism. Mass production and the proliferation of objects, gadgets, implements, and devices of every type is a reflection of American values, norms, and "mass society." For example, can you describe the nonmaterial and material culture of a McDonald's or other fast-food restaurant and show how they are interrelated?

If values and beliefs influence material culture, the reverse is equally true. Material culture, especially technological innovations, can have dramatic and often unintended effects on values, beliefs, and social relationships. The invention of the automobile provides a classic example. Originally seen as little more than a convenience, cars revolutionized almost every aspect of American life. The auto provided people with more personal freedom, economic opportunities, and easy access to the bright lights of the city. Even those who thought it might be dangerous, however, could never have envisioned the 40,000 or more traffic fatalities in America each year, the smog and pollution, and the auto's role in the destruction of thousands of rural villages and later in the devastation of the central city. Automobiles also expanded people's social worlds by providing increased mobility, became new status symbols, and even altered the dating patterns and sex lives of teenagers. In recent years, new technologies and globalization have brought even greater cultural changes, and challenges. Let's look at how culture evolved and proliferated over millions of years, eventually enabling people to survive virtually everywhere on earth.

The Origin of Culture

A little more than a century ago, biologist Charles Darwin's essay titled *On the Origin of Species* ([1859] 1964) brought about a revolution in scientific thinking about all living things. Borrowing ideas from biology, paleontology, and natural history, Darwin proposed a radical new view of our relationship to animals and the rest of the natural world.

The Evolution of Culture   First, Darwin observed that species produce far more offspring than can be supported by the environment. Second, he found that while offspring closely resemble their parents and each other, they differ in some traits. He proposed that it is from this pool of sibling differences that new life is formed; according to the *theory of evolution,* the environment, or "nature," selects those traits that are advantageous and rejects those that are not. This endless process of adaptation and competition and the "survival of the fittest" have generated the great diversity of life on earth, from the simplest bacteria to more complex creatures, including humans.

From the beginning of life on earth, the success of animal species has depended on instincts or genetic programming. Humans are believed to be the only species that combine genes and culture to solve the problems of living. For example, higher primates, such as chimpanzees, our closest relatives in the animal world, sometimes use stones to process food or defend themselves, but these rudimentary forms of culture are not essential for species survival. For humans, both material and nonmaterial culture clearly are.

The first clear evidence of culture is from about 2 million years ago on the plains of Africa. Crude stone tools found at several sites show that our prehuman ancestors gradually adapted to the environment with tools and traditions that were passed on from generation to generation. In this sense, technology helped transform human biology, with each small technological advance altering both the structure and size of the brain, until learning and cultural solutions became the primary way that all humans adapt to the world.

Nature and Nurture Today, most human behaviors are learned and culturally patterned within groups. Only a handful of behaviors are genetically determined, and in the course of our everyday lives we hardly consider them important. For example, humans are born with the ability to grasp, suck, and cry, but "even these elementary responses in newborns fade after a few weeks and must . . . [be] replaced by learned responses if infants are to survive" (Schultz and Lavenda, 2005:31). Likewise, we inherit simple reflexes, such as blinking, and drives, which include self-preservation, sex, and the need for nourishment. But even powerful drives can be delayed or overridden by rules for proper behavior; people may willingly sacrifice their lives for others, abstain from sex for religious and other reasons, and diet for days, weeks, or a lifetime. The influence of nature and nurture on human behavior is explored further in Chapter 4, Socialization.

Fashion models and the "multicultural look."

Cultural Worlds Everywhere on earth, groups transform nature into "cultural worlds" that guide their members' understandings of reality. In this sense, when one of the authors was in Nigeria standing side by side with a cattle-herding friend, each person could be said to inhabit different "sensory worlds." Each had been taught to look for, hear, and experience different things, and this affected how they perceived the environment. The same is true of their ideas of space and time. The Western visitor operated "by the clock" and perceived time as linear, which meant it could be divided up, "lost," or squandered. His cattle-herding friend, by contrast, saw time as more circular, consisting of natural rhythms and seasons that repeated themselves.

Is a smile universally recognized as a sign of friendly intentions? Sociologists caution that, like most human behaviors, smiles are complex and groups may interpret them in various ways. For example, think of the possibilities of a smile in interactions with your friends. When you smile it may reflect friendliness, but it may also express uncertainty, derision, or even contempt. And, of course, your friends may or may not agree with your interpretation. Add to that the ways various groups from around the world may interpret a smile and you have some idea of the complexity of what is popularly assumed to be a "universal behavior."

When you look at this photo do you see the various standards of beauty of many ethnic groups from around the world?

Beauty is often described as universal as well—especially by the media. For example, *Newsweek* reported that research had shown that "body symmetry and a .7 waist-hip ratio" were universally recognized as "beautiful" (Cowley and Hager, 1996). Are they indeed essential to *every group's* standard of beauty? Knowing the extraordinary variation in people's ideas of beauty around the world and even in the United States, where ethnicity, sex, and other factors influence people's ideas of beauty, beauty treatments, and cosmetic surgery (see Table 3.2, on the next page), most sociologists doubt it. In some cultures women are seen as beautiful; in others it is men. Some associate ideal beauty with facial and body scarification. Others—including Americans 100 years ago—consider plumpness and obesity marks of beauty. Today, models are mostly tall, thin, and athletic-looking, and in the United States the "multiracial look" has become increasingly popular; it, too, is becoming a popular standard of beauty in the United States and worldwide (Cowley, 1996; Halter, 2000).

COMPONENTS OF CULTURE

Although different groups and societies around the world may have very different cultural understandings, all create worlds of meaning with the same basic components: symbols, language, beliefs, values, norms, and material culture. Let's take a closer look at each of these elements and how they affect people's thoughts and actions.

TABLE 3.2
COSMETIC SURGERY IN THE UNITED STATES

HAVE DONE OR WOULD LIKE TO DO:	MEN	WOMEN	WHITE*	HISPANIC	BLACK*
Laser eye surgery	34%	42%	39%	41%	34%
Tummy tuck	11%	35%	23%	34%	19%
Liposuction	12%	28%	20%	34%	12%
Chemical peel/skin resurfacing	8%	25%	15%	26%	21%
Breast augmentation	3%	24%	13%	23%	13%
Face-lift	7%	18%	15%	—	—
Hair implants	11%	5%	7%	—	—
Nose job	5%	9%	7%	—	—
Botox injections	3%	9%	7%	—	—
Collagen injections	2%	8%	6%	—	—

*White and blacks are non-Hispanic.

—Sample size too small

Source: From *American Demographics*, March 2003, Copyright 2003 PRIMEDIA Business Magazines & Media Inc. All rights reserved. Reprinted by permission.

Symbols

For animals, information is conveyed almost exclusively through *signs,* which are biological forms of communication. Animals use signs to express fear, hostility, and other emotional states. For example, when a dog bares its teeth and raises the hair on its back, every dog from California to China knows it is a threat. But animal communication has a very narrow range of expression: animals cannot combine signs, nor can they use signs to refer to the past or future (Swartz and Jordan, 1976).

Humans, of course, also use signs to express emotions, but somewhere in antiquity we began to convert them to symbols to communicate messages about emotional states and everything else. A **symbol** is *anything to which group members assign meaning.* It may be an object, color, sound, gesture, person, or anything else. The important difference between signals and symbols is that the latter are purely arbitrary. For example, water has real physical properties, but as a symbol the same water may be defined as pure water, dirty water, holy water, or spring water with curative powers. With only a slight chemical change, the same water may also be transformed into an expensive beverage that may be used to express one's social standing.

Colors also may be interpreted in diverse and even opposite ways because of symbolic behavior. In the United States and other Western cultures, white is a symbol of life, purity, and goodness. "Good guys" wear white hats. Black can symbolize something serious and solemn. For example, black is worn at graduation ceremonies and in courts of law by judges. But black in Western culture more generally symbolizes evil and death: people wear black at funerals, "bad guys" wear black hats, and football teams with black uniforms have menacing reputations. In China and many other parts of Asia, many of these meanings are reversed. White is a symbol of mourning and death, and people wear white, not black, to funerals (Rosman and Rubel, 2001). Wearing a green baseball cap, a symbol of a sports team in the West, might cause embarrassment in China, because there it mocks a man's masculinity and is a symbol for a cuckold (Smith, 2002).

Clothing is symbolic as well, although most of the time we hardly notice what classmates, professors, and our friends wear. But look more carefully at the symbolic mes-

Color symbolism varies from culture to culture.

Do you think that black uniforms have helped the Oakland Raiders sustain their menacing reputation?

SYMBOL
Anything to which group members assign meaning.

sages people convey through clothing. Some t-shirts carry obvious messages, but every item of apparel makes some kind of statement. Of course, symbols may change over time. Today blue jeans are so common on campus that few people notice them. Had you worn jeans to class a century ago, however, you would have shocked and angered almost everyone because they were "working-class" apparel. And only a few decades ago, jeans were considered appropriate for males but not females.

Harley-Davidson motorcycles were once significant symbols as well—of deviance and "outlaw bikers." Today, most Americans consider them socially acceptable, because in the past few decades stockbrokers, attorneys, dentists, and other Harley enthusiasts have redefined the term "Harley-Davidson" to mean "mainstream." And because they are as expensive as some luxury automobiles, they now are status symbols to the rich and successful. Of all symbols that people use, language is by far the most important in preserving and transmitting the cultural heritage of groups.

Language

A **language** is *a complex system of symbols with conventional meanings that people use for communication.* Language is often thought to include only the spoken word, but in its broadest sense language contains verbal, nonverbal, and written symbols.

Spoken Language   There are an estimated 3,000–5,000 languages worldwide today, and within these languages there is often linguistic variation based on regional, class, ethnic, and other subcultural differences. Most spoken languages make use of 15–60 distinct sounds to communicate messages. English, for example, uses 44 distinct sounds. These few sounds and the rules for combining them into words, sentences, and more complex structures are the primary basis of all social traditions (Howard and Dunaif-Hattis, 1992).

Humans are biologically predisposed to learning language. Infants are born with the ability to produce many sounds, hear subtle differences among these sounds, and process this information in the brain. As with all symbols, the sounds chosen by a culture and how they are arranged to produce meaning is decided by social convention. Every healthy 4-year-old child who is a member of the Hausa ethnic group in West Africa knows the meaning of the phrase *na sayi abinci* ("I bought food"). To a visiting American who does not know Hausa, of course, the phrase means absolutely nothing.

Nonverbal Communication   Not all language is spoken. To be an effective speaker in any society or group, it is not enough to know the sounds and arrangement of its words and sentences. We also must learn the nonverbal symbols—the proper uses and the meanings of gestures, eyes, posture, and space. *Body language* is often used to reinforce spoken messages, but at times it may be used independently. For example, many Americans shake their head from side to side when they mean "no," whereas Greeks express "no" with a sudden upward jerk of the head. Likewise, while raised eyebrows is an appropriate way to greet another in American culture, it is considered "indecent" in Japan and is rarely used, except as an insult (Haviland, 2005). Moreover, every culture has clear rules about touching—some are deemed high-touch cultures, others low-touch (Ferraro, 2001).

Some argue that nonverbal communication is such an art form in Italy that entire conversations can be conducted without the use of spoken words. For example, when Italians want to express anger, they need only curl an index finger and appear to bite down to make the point. Likewise, the appropriate way to signify that something is weird is to tap the forehead lightly a few times with one's fingers. To ask, "What do you want?" in nonverbal Italian you merely pinch your fingertips together. And at the conclusion of bargaining, when you want to say that an agreement has been reached, all you have to do is grip the skin under your right eye with the index finger and pull down slightly; the deal is done (*Wichita Eagle,* 1994b).

The Power of Language   Language, thought, and culture are interrelated (Kottak, 1987). Without language there would be no culture, for language enables groups to store meanings, communicate with one another, and transmit knowledge between generations.

LANGUAGE
A complex system of symbols with conventional meanings that people use for communication.

Moreover, language plays an important role in how various cultures think about their "worlds." According to the *Sapir-Whorf hypothesis,* the language of each culture does not merely influence how people understand the world; it shapes perceptions and leads people to think in particular ways (Sapir, 1929, 1949; Whorf, 1956). From this perspective, people who speak different languages live in different sensory worlds, for the structure of their languages and the words highlight some things and ignore others. This theory has generated much controversy among scholars, but research suggests that languages do facilitate particular ways of thinking because they make it easier to code or symbolize some events and objects, which as a result are easier to remember (Michener et al., 1986).

While each language shapes reality, it does not, however, imprison its speakers in a narrow and changeless world. This is because all languages are flexible and acutely sensitive to change. New words and ideas are regularly adopted by speakers of any language to fill various cultural needs. For example, computers have influenced our speech and thoughts noticeably. We speak of sound bites, networking, and interfacing, and computer terminology is commonly used on the nightly news to describe everything from business transactions to politics. Similarly, non-computer-users would find it mystifying—if not almost impossible—to read the abbreviations and symbols that appear regularly in e-mails and chat room conversations.

At the same time, most people speak "many languages" each day, altering forms of communication to suit business, family, and other group needs. For example, even well-advertised soft drinks are referred to differently in various regions in the United States (see Map 3.1). And in the past few decades, not only in Texas and California but also throughout the United States, Spanish and Latino cultural themes have proliferated as well. Between 1980 and 1990 the number of Spanish-speakers increased 50 percent, and this dramatic expansion will continue throughout the twenty-first century (Wallraff, 2000:54). Today, Spanish-speaking America is already the world's fifth-largest Hispanic nation. With these trends in mind, what do you think is the likelihood that the growing use of Spanish will profoundly influence U.S. culture—not only the media and popular culture—but also the nation's most deeply felt beliefs and values?

MAP 3.1
A NATION DIVIDED

The map illustrates, by color, the term used to refer to carbonated beverages by the majority or plurality of each state's residents. The numbers on the map represent the percentage of respondents from each state that refer to carbonated beverages as "coke" (even when it's a Pepsi), "pop," or "soda," respectively.

Source: "A Nation Divided." Reprinted with permission from the February 2003 issue of *American Demographics.* Copyright, Crain Communications Inc. 2003.

Beliefs

Beliefs are *assertions about the nature of reality.* They provide groups with a fundamental orientation to the world and answer questions about proper relations among people, good and evil, and the destiny of humans and the universe.

Unlike scientific knowledge, which is based on empirical understandings, many beliefs may be seen as "truths" by group members; they are based not on objective reality but on social agreement. Moreover, yesterday's beliefs and the common sense of the moment are the falsehoods and "myths" of tomorrow. For example, the word *lunatic* is derived from the popular nineteenth-century belief that a full moon caused madness, a belief that had folk origins in European farming and hunting societies. Today, such thinking is derisively labeled "superstition"—although police officers, mental health professionals, and emergency room personnel tell of bizarre happenings during full moons.

Belief systems in complex societies—particularly advanced industrial and post-industrial societies—include multiple and competing belief systems that often contain many contradictions. Think about your membership in family, school, and peer groups alone. Do they all share a common vision of reality and have similar goals? For example, scientific knowledge and religious beliefs present very different approaches to reality. One demands that we consider only what is empirical and observable in the "natural world." The other stresses a world beyond nature, and how the "supernatural" affects our lives. Cultural contradictions often require that people rationalize one set of beliefs in order to accommodate others. Likewise, beliefs typically change at a much faster rate. So do values.

Values

Values are *shared ideas about what is socially desirable.* For all groups, values define what is desirable by ranking behaviors, people, events, objects, and social arrangements. These rankings define what is good or bad, beautiful or ugly, moral or immoral, just or unjust, and desirable or undesirable. In modern pluralistic societies, such as the United States, with its many ethnic, religious, and other groups, value orientations are complex. Some values may be widely shared, but others may be hotly disputed by various groups. Over the years, sociologist Robin Williams (1970) has charted several core values that he maintains exert a particularly strong influence on the national culture and are especially prominent in the popular media.

BELIEFS
Assertions about the nature of reality.

VALUES
Shared ideas about what is socially desirable.

U.S. Core Values

According to Williams, the following values are widely shared in the United States:

1. *Individualism and Freedom.* Self-reliance, individualism, and the freedom to achieve whatever goals we may set for ourselves are particularly important. Americans value their independence and the ability to make personal choices that are free of social constraints. Hollywood has made a fortune portraying "rugged individualists" who pay a heavy price for resisting conformity to the group but in the end prove to be "right" and prevail over "society."

2. *Equality.* According to the American definition of equality, people should be able to compete openly and have a fair chance to achieve society's rewards. This definition stresses "equality of opportunity" and does not require "equality of outcome"—for example, that people have similar amounts of wealth, power, and prestige.

3. *Achievement.* Most people desire to get ahead and to better the circumstances of their birth. This requires that each person compete with others for society's limited prizes. Consequently, we expect that there will be "winners" and "losers"; most attribute success or failure to personal talent, intelligence, and "character."

4. *Efficiency and Practicality.* People value a simple and direct approach to life and what are understood as "commonsense,"

Numerous American celebrities have brought attention to developing countries and their cultures by making high-profile visits accompanied by the media.

"down-to-earth" approaches to problem solving. In organizations of every type—especially those of business and government—these values are evoked with terms like "streamlining," "downsizing," and the "elimination of fat and waste."

5. *Progress and Technology.* Americans value what is new and progressive and place a high value on technology as a solution to the problems of modern life. They demand "state-of-the-art" products and believe that, as a general rule, future products will be superior to those manufactured today and the future will be brighter than the past.

6. *Material Comfort and Consumerism.* In the United States, success and personal worth are measured in large part by the quality and quantity of material possessions. For many, material possessions such as autos, homes, and clothes are important measures of personal identity and self-worth.

7. *Work and Leisure.* Americans value hard work and labor and laud the efforts of those who put in long hours to accomplish goals and "make something of themselves." However, Americans also value leisure and periods of "free time" in which to relax with family and friends and get away from work and its stresses. For many, work and leisure are related, as is suggested by the phrase "work hard and play hard." Another novel blend is leisure, consumerism, and work, the essence of which is captured in another popular phrase, "shop till you drop."

Do you agree that these values are shared by most people in the United States? If you answered yes, did you consider the values of minority groups? For example, what about many Latino and Japanese American groups—do they subscribe to American "core values" as we have defined them? Let's take a closer look.

Latino and Japanese Cultural Orientations

The values of particular ethnic groups in the United States may be in accord with some "core values" but not others. For example, many Latino groups have a strong work ethic and value technology and progress, but do not value the extreme materialism that is so highly valued in the mainstream media. Moreover, many Latino groups emphasize that in numerous social contexts the individual should defer to the group. This is especially true of family and kin obligations but also extends to the workplace, church, school, and other social arenas.

In the workplace, for example, Latinos place great emphasis on consensus and harmony and are often willing to sacrifice task achievement and formal goals for the sake of interpersonal relationships. Latinos also place a high value on trust and open communication. And most Latino groups follow a *simpatia script,* in which people place a special emphasis on dignity, honor, respect, and positive attitudes and behaviors in social relations (Ferdman and Cortes, 1992).

Some Japanese Americans go a step further and maintain that the individual must be submerged in a group. In traditional Japanese culture, individuals should not stand out, and they should neither expect nor demand recognition for their special talents and skills. In Japanese-owned auto plants—including those in the United States—Japanese management measures a person's worth not by what the individual accomplishes, but by what the team produces. In Japan this collectivist orientation goes beyond the workplace and is a pervasive feature of social life.

Value Tensions and Conflicts

In all complex societies, there are many inconsistencies and conflicts in cultural values. In addition to conflicting ideas based on ethnicity, religion, and other social divisions, there are conflicts in core values themselves. Some U.S. values—for example, freedom, achievement, progress, and individuality—may be logically consistent. Many others, however, are inconsistent and may even be contradictory. For example, while most Americans value work they also value leisure; consequently, people may simultaneously resent *and* admire lottery winners and people with inherited wealth.

"Pro-life" advocates may see no contradiction in their positions on abortion and capital punishment: that it is always wrong to kill (the unborn) yet appropriate and just to kill people for certain offenses. An environmentalist may protest the destruction of the tropical rain forest on Monday and on Tuesday purchase mahogany and rattan furniture without the slightest pang of guilt.

Conflicts in core values are but one aspect of value conflict in complex modern societies. According to the conflict perspective, social class, age, occupation, gender, race, and ethnicity all influence a person's value orientation. Because each of us is a member of many social categories, at any given moment our values may or may not all be in agreement. For example, the same elderly farmer who is opposed to "welfare handouts" may expect and demand federal farm subsidies and protest even the slightest changes in Social Security policy. We also regularly choose among alternative values in the course of our daily lives. In some social situations, total honesty may be required. In others—for example, when acquaintances casually ask how you are doing and you are in a terrible mood—they neither expect nor desire the "truth."

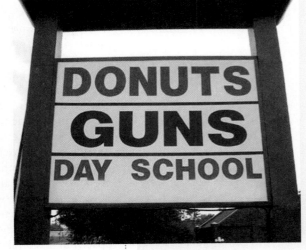

What cultural values and potential value conflicts are represented on this sign at a strip mall in a small community outside of Dallas, Texas?

Often, social situations demand that we choose a particular value over others, and there are many ways to justify our decisions. At times we may rank certain values, believing that in a particular context one value is more appropriate than another. We may rationalize why we have chosen one value or another or even deny that our values conflict. Sometimes powerful groups decide issues for us, or in some cases public opinion may resolve difficult issues. If the issue is sufficiently important, the vague abstractions and guidelines that are the basis of all values may be converted into specific rules, or norms.

Norms

Norms are *expectations and rules for proper conduct that guide the behavior of group members.* Among all groups, norms provide guidelines that tell members how they should think and act in any given social situation. There are four major kinds of norms: folkways, mores, laws, and taboos.

Folkways   The most common norms are **folkways,** *informal rules and expectations that guide people's everyday behavior.* They include such things as etiquette, table manners, proper appearance, and many other simple, everyday behaviors that in American culture are indicators of "self-control." While people find violations of folkways annoying, they typically tolerate them. Moreover, when sanctions are applied they are usually *informal sanctions* that are loosely defined and applied by individuals rather than by an authorized social body. When a child holds a fork in the proper hand, a parent may sanction the behavior with praise. Conversely, if the child spreads butter on bread using fingers instead of a knife, negative sanctions may be applied; the child may be ridiculed, threatened, or sent away from the table.

A breach of folkways is not ordinarily considered a threat to society, nor is the individual who occasionally violates them subjected to serious penalties. Nevertheless, the persistent violation of folkways may be interpreted by others as evidence of social deviance, and this could have serious consequences. The cumulative effect of many violations may be recognized as sufficient grounds for divorce, termination of employment, incarceration, or even confinement to a mental institution.

How would you and your classmates respond if tomorrow, at the end of your Introduction to Sociology lecture, a student in the front row began to applaud? It is likely that you and your classmates would become mildly annoyed, but the first time it happened you would be surprised by the student's behavior and you might not respond. If the same student were to repeat the applause after the following class, the second episode would almost certainly be met with "dirty looks." A third incident probably would elicit even stronger sanctions, possibly including sarcastic applause.

This example illustrates the importance of norms in our everyday lives. Norms are basic to every social situation, yet because they are so tightly woven into the fabric of

NORMS
Expectations and rules for proper conduct that guide behavior of group members.

FOLKWAYS
Informal rules and expectations that guide peoples' everyday behavior.

social life we often take them for granted. Typically we conform to norms, and in most social situations we expect others to do the same. Some norms tell us what we should *not* do, for example, that students should not cheat on exams; these are called *proscriptive norms.* Others spell out what we *should do,* for example, take and pass exams; these are *prescriptive norms.*

Mores   Mores (pronounced more-ays) are *salient norms that people consider essential to the proper working of society.* Mores have considerable moral (and sometimes religious) significance and are closely tied to values. People believe that mores protect what is right and good. *Formal sanctions,* which are clearly defined rewards or punishments administered by specialized agents of society, are often employed to ensure conformity to mores. Medals and awards may be given in recognition of heroic acts and special contributions to society. Conversely, people who commit serious violations of mores may be imprisoned, tortured, and executed.

A large number of mores have their roots in ancient religious traditions, and these include many proscriptive norms that have near-universal application. The "Thou shalt not's"—steal, commit adultery, or commit murder—and other "sacred commandments" are serious mores, and their violation brings strong and immediate public response. The desecration of important public symbols, such as burning the American flag, elicits similar responses. Unethical conduct may sometimes be recognized as a breach of mores as well. If an auto body shop does a sloppy paint job the owner of the vehicle may become upset, but it is unlikely others would feel offended. If a mechanic is careless while adjusting an automobile's brakes, however, and a family is seriously injured, most people would consider the lapse morally reprehensible and demand punishment.

Conformity is ensured partly by public understandings that mores are important to everyone and that detection and punishment for wrongdoers is almost a certainty. No society relies on coercion alone, however, to get people to conform to and uphold its most serious norms. During childhood, individuals are taught the rules of proper conduct. People internalize the rules and in effect become society's police—society's standards become "our" standards, and adherence to norms strongly influences how we view ourselves. When we conform to societal norms, we feel good knowing that we have done the "right thing"; when we violate norms, we feel bad, even if we are certain our offenses will never be known.

Laws   Important mores typically become encoded into **laws.** Laws are *formal rules enacted and enforced by the power of the state, which apply to members of society.* Laws that codify mores are usually recognized as vital to society, and most people believe that without them public order would be impossible. The relationship between laws and mores is complex, however. Sometimes laws and mores correspond closely; for example, it is both immoral and illegal to steal another's property. In other cases, laws may reflect the power of one group or segment of society relative to another, and their legitimacy may be challenged by opposition interests or groups. For example, prior to 1972 and *Roe v. Wade,* abortion was illegal in the United States. After the landmark Supreme Court decision that year, women gained the legal right to have an abortion. While this law is supported by a large segment of American society, another portion has challenged it because according to their views of morality it violates the societal norm that we not take another's life.

Sometimes laws may not correspond to a society's mores, and these laws are the most difficult to enforce and most subject to change. For example, in the United States there is little public consensus regarding the morality of gambling. In some states gambling is illegal, but in others state-sponsored lotteries and horse racing not only are legal but also contribute important revenues to the state. Thus, a police officer may make a gambling arrest in Utah on Friday, then cross the border into Nevada, go to Las Vegas, and gamble all weekend without seeing the slightest inconsistency in the two behaviors.

Taboos   Taboos are *prohibitions against behaviors that most members of a group consider to be so repugnant they are unthinkable.* Eating human flesh, for example, is considered to be such a heinous act that in most societies neither sanctions nor laws are

MORES
Salient norms that people consider essential to the proper working of society.

LAWS
Formal rules enacted and enforced by the power of the state, which apply to members of society.

TABOOS
Prohibitions against behaviors that most members of a group consider to be so repugnant they are unthinkable.

needed for compliance with the taboo against this behavior. Another taboo is the incest taboo, especially parent-child and sibling sex, that is widely shared around the world; incest is also a serious breach of the law in most nations.

Sanctions   Norms are enforced by the use of **sanctions,** which are *penalties or rewards society uses to encourage conformity and punish deviance.* For example, parents are expected to feed, clothe, and care for their children. If they do not, they may not only be punished for their neglect, they may lose custody of the children. Some norms apply in certain situations but not in others. In the United States, for example, people should not spit on the floor of a home, nor should they spit on a crowded street. During baseball games, however, spitting is so common among the players that people who do not know the sport might think it is an essential part of the game.

We have divided beliefs, values, and norms in this discussion, but we want to emphasize that the three are vitally linked, and it is impossible to separate what people value from their interpretations of reality. This is evident in the abortion debate: those who support the "pro-life" position believe that the fetus is a person, whereas many "pro-choice" advocates believe it is not. The values of both groups play a major role in how they interpret "reality." We focus more specifically on the importance of norms and social control in Chapter 7.

ETHNOCENTRISM AND CULTURAL RELATIVISM

Small children are acute observers of human behavior, and for a few years they are receptive to every cultural tradition on earth. Children learn languages—even 10 or 15 languages in some parts of the world—and are able to imitate hundreds of gestures with ease. Young children willingly sample foods, wear different clothing styles, and accept as fact an extraordinary variety of beliefs. As we discuss in greater detail in Chapter 4, during socialization, families and other groups narrow these possibilities. For example, children learn that only some plants and animals can be eaten, and that some are better than others. Children also learn to distinguish and rank houses, clothing apparel, automobiles, people, and virtually everything else.

Culture Shock

Once created, these cultural categories serve as lenses or filters of reality throughout our lives. From this point on, we rarely recognize culture's powerful impact on our thoughts and behavior. The exception, of course, is when we encounter a culture that takes a radically different approach to reality. For some Americans, a visit to a developing country with teeming markets and strange sights and smells may encourage cultural comparisons and questions about our own customs. Of course, with globalization, people no longer have to travel abroad to discover surprising diversity in the food, dress, and other customs of one's neighbors. In *Crossing the Blvd,* the authors mention that in Queens, New York, an estimated 138 languages are spoken and that the Queens area has become so ethnically diverse that whatever your ethnic background, you are a minority (Lehrer and Sloan, 2003; Kilgannon, 2003). New arrivals in the United States are often confused and dismayed by many aspects of American life—especially family life and parent-child relations. In extreme cases, such encounters may produce what sociologists call **culture shock,** or *feelings of confusion and disorientation that occur when a person encounters a very different culture.*

If we carefully observe another culture, however, we realize that the same things that cause us shock and confusion provide order, security, identity, and meaning to the people of that culture. Do visitors to the United States experience cultural shock? One of the authors discovered the answer when he served as a tour guide for a visitor from rural China, who was shocked by the many goods and affluent lifestyles that she witnessed in malls and suburban communities, which most Americans consider "ordinary."

Although people today have a much greater understanding of cultural diversity than they did just 100 years ago, many continue to believe that the customs and beliefs of others are backward, inferior, or even degenerate when compared to their own. Likewise,

SANCTIONS
Penalties or rewards society uses to encourage conformity and punish deviance.

CULTURE SHOCK
Feelings of confusion and disorientation that occur when a person encounters a very different culture.

although Americans may be more tolerant of other cultures than they were in the past, no individual or group is value-free and open to *all* customs. For example, what do you think about the custom in some countries of eating dogs and cats, or the practice of eating dirt (actually clay) that is enjoyed by some people in the southern United States? If you are like most Americans, you probably find these practices either repulsive or ridiculous.

Ethnocentrism

Sociologists call this kind of thinking **ethnocentrism**—*the tendency to evaluate the customs of other groups according to one's own cultural standards.* As Focus box 3.1 illustrates, ethnocentrism is such a strong tendency that when social scientists encounter particularly exotic cultures, even they are not always able to restrain their cultural biases.

Ethnocentrism has a positive side. It can enhance group stability by providing members with roots and a strong sense of meaning and purpose. The tendency to view one's culture as "the best" also has provided humans with many different solutions to the problems of living. If groups had taken their cultures lightly or even pragmatically, cultural homogeneity rather than cultural diversity would now be the norm. But most people are attached to their religious beliefs, foods, clothing, and other customs and are unwilling to give them up, except under extreme conditions. Even social researchers may experience difficulty identifying their own cultural assumptions and biases—especially when there are strong emotional responses to people, groups, and places (Cylwik, 2001).

Throughout history, ethnocentrism's negative side has been equally pronounced. Viewing one's values and customs as natural and right, and those of others as inferior and wrong, often contributes to prejudice and discrimination, interethnic conflict, exploitation, and even ethnic cleansing and genocide.

Cultural Relativism

One important way that we can guard against ethnocentric biases is by adopting a perspective called **cultural relativism**, which *asks that we evaluate other cultures according to their standards, not ours.* For example, a highly unusual custom to most Americans is the extension of lips that once marked ideal beauty in Central Africa. Circular plugs were inserted into the lips and then gradually enlarged until the lips were stretched 4 inches or more. On the surface, this custom seems to make little sense, but let's examine it more carefully.

First, sociologists have found that most cultures modify the face and lips in some way to achieve beauty. For example, many American women use lipstick; some enhanced their lips surgically. But why did so many villages in Central Africa take what may seem to Americans a more extreme approach to beauty? Some functionalist scholars attribute the custom of placing large circular objects in the lips to intense slave raiding a century ago. They contend that villages that practiced lip extension were often avoided by slave raiders, and this may have encouraged villagers to exaggerate lip extension as a symbol of beauty.

The Relativist Fallacy

Conflict theorists caution that we should be careful about associations between customs and the proper functioning or good of "society." In some cases, perhaps including lip extension, customs may be far more beneficial to one group than to another, or continue because they give advantages to men or the rich and powerful. We should also guard against viewing all cultural practices as being equally valid and worthy of respect. This is called the *relativist fallacy,* and in its most extreme form it would treat even the most severe social pathologies, such as Nazi gas chambers and apartheid in South Africa, as legitimate cultural practices. Focus box 3.2 takes a close look at female genital mutilation that many sociologists believe is another example of the relativist fallacy.

GLOBALIZATION AND CULTURAL DIVERSITY

During the past half century, expanded global trade, advances in telecommunications, tourism, and large-scale emigration from one end of the earth to the other have introduced virtually everyone to the extraordinary array of customs, values, beliefs, and

ETHNOCENTRISM
The tendency to evaluate the customs of other groups according to one's own cultural standards.

CULTURAL RELATIVISM
A perspective which asks that we evaluate other cultures according to their standards, not ours.

In the following article, anthropologist Horace Miner reviews the ritual life of the Nacirema, a society he describes as so magic-ridden that it is a wonder they still survive.

They are a North American group living in the territory between the Canadian Cree, the Yaqui and Tarahumare of Mexico, and the Carib and Arawak of the Antilles. . . . Nacirema culture is characterized by a highly developed market economy which has evolved in a rich natural habitat. While much of the people's time is devoted to economic pursuits, a large part of the fruits of these labors and a considerable portion of the day are spent in ritual activity. The focus of this activity is the human body, the appearance and health of which loom as a dominant concern in the ethos of the people. . . . The fundamental belief underlying the whole system appears to be that the human body is ugly and that its natural tendency is to debility and disease. Incarcerated in such a body, man's [people's] only hope is to avert these characteristics through the use of powerful influences of ritual and ceremony. Every household has one or more shrines in their houses. . . . Most houses are of wattle and daub construction, but the shrine rooms of the more wealthy are walled in stone. Poorer families imitate the rich by applying pottery plaques to their shrine walls. . . .

While each family has at least one such shrine, the rituals associated with it are not family ceremonies but are private and secret. . . . The focal point of the shrine is a box or chest which is built into the wall. In the chest are kept many charms and magical potions without which no native believes he [or she] could live. . . . Beneath the charm-box is a small font. Each day every member of the family, in succession, enters the shrine room, bows his [or her] head before the shrine-box, mingles different sorts of holy water in the font, and proceeds with a brief rite of ablution.

. . . The Nacirema have an almost pathological horror and fascination with the mouth, the condition of which is believed to have supernatural influence on all social relationships. Were it not for the rituals of the mouth, they believe that their teeth would fall out, their gums bleed, their jaws shrink, their friends desert them, and their lovers reject them. . . . The daily body ritual performed by everyone includes a mouth-rite. . . . It is reported to me that the ritual consists of inserting a small bundle of hog hairs into the mouth, along with certain magical powders, and then moving the bundle in a highly formalized series of gestures.

In addition to the private mouth-rite, the people seek out a holy-mouth-man once or twice a year. These practitioners have an impressive set of paraphernalia, consisting of a variety of augers, awls, probes, and prods. The use of these objects in the exorcism of the evils of the mouth involves almost unbelievable ritual torture of the client. . . . In the client's view, the purpose of these ministrations is to arrest decay and to draw friends. The extremely sacred and traditional character of the rite is evident in the fact that the natives return to the holy-mouth-men year after year, despite the fact that their teeth continue to decay.

It is to be hoped that, when a thorough study of the Nacirema is made, there will be a careful inquiry into the personality structure of these people. One has but to watch the gleam in the eye of a holy-mouth-man, as he jabs an awl into an exposed nerve, to suspect that a certain amount of sadism is involved. If this can be established a very interesting pattern emerges, for most of the population shows definite masochistic tendencies. It was to these that Professor Linton referred in discussing a distinctive part of the daily body ritual which is performed only by men. This part of the rite involves scraping and lacerating the surface of the face with a sharp instrument. . . . The theoretically interesting point is that what seems to be a predominantly masochistic people have developed sadistic specialists.

The medicine men have an imposing temple, or *latipsoh,* in every community of any size. The more elaborate ceremonies required to treat very sick patients can only be performed at this temple. . . . Few supplicants in the temple are well enough to do anything but lie on their hard beds. The daily ceremonies, like the rites of the holy-mouth-men, involve discomfort and torture. With ritual precision, the vestals awaken their miserable charges each dawn and roll them about on their beds of pain while performing ablutions, in the formal movements of which the maidens are highly trained. At other times they insert magic wands in the supplicant's mouth or force him [or her] to eat substances which are supposed to be healing. From time to time the medicine men come to their clients and jab magically treated needles into their flesh. The fact that these temple ceremonies may not cure, and may even kill, the neophyte, in no way decreases the people's faith in the medicine men.

. . . In conclusion, mention must be made of certain practices which have made their base in native esthetics but which depend upon the pervasive aversion to the natural body and its functions. There are ritual fasts to make fat people thin and ceremonial feasts to make thin people fat. Still other rites are used to make women's breasts large if they are small, and smaller if they are large. General dissatisfaction with breast shape is symbolized in the fact that the ideal form is virtually outside the range of human variation. A few women afflicted with almost inhuman hyper-mammary development are so idolized that they make a handsome living by simply going from village to village and permitting the natives to stare at them for a fee.

. . . Our review of the ritual life of the Nacirema has certainly shown them to be a magic-ridden people. It is hard to understand how they have managed to exist so long under the burdens which they have imposed on themselves. . . .

TAKING A CLOSER LOOK

Who are these strange people? Has ethnocentrism influenced Miner's description of the Nacirema? Had Miner avoided such a strong focus on the Nacirema's magical practice, would this group have appeared more human by your cultural standards? Might your own daily life and the lives of your friends be described in similar terms—as magic-ridden and filled with superstitions and rituals? Take a position and support it with empirical evidence.

Source: Horace Miner. "Body Ritual Among the Nacirema." *American Anthropologist* 58 (June) 1956:503–507.

In today's global society, cultural relativism is a vital necessity. It promotes understanding and opens our vision to the extraordinary range of human imagination, creativity, and achievement. It also helps us guard against negative stereotypes and intolerance when we encounter group practices that are very different from our own. But adopting cultural relativism does not mean that sociologists like or endorse every custom and practice. Cultural relativism is about understanding, not approval.

The issue of violence against women—especially the practice of female genital mutilation—highlights the "perils of cultural relativism," wrote Carolyn Fluehr-Lobban (1997:33). Currently, female genital mutilation is performed on perhaps as many as 130 million women and girls in more than two dozen nations in Africa and other parts of the world. Although the custom takes many forms, it typically involves folk doctors removing a portion of or the entire clitoris of young girls (without anesthesia), usually when they are 6 to 8 years old. Female genital mutilation often results in severe health problems. The operation itself can cause acute pain, hemorrhaging, urinary infections, and blood poisoning that may cause severe illness or death. But for most women health problems last a lifetime and may include cysts, chronic pelvic infections, urinary tract infections, abscesses, and many other medical problems. Painful intercourse, difficult deliveries, frustration, anxiety, and depression are equally common among women who have been subjected to this centuries-old tradition (Mackie, 1996; Fluehr-Lobban, 1997).

Rather than diminishing with globalization, the practice is spreading—even to the United States and Europe, where hospitals are sometimes contacted by African women, not knowing that the practice is illegal, and asked to perform the operation. Cultural persistence suggests how deeply embedded the practice is in many cultures. Genital mutilation is said to enhance nature and make women more beautiful, hard-working, modest, and chaste. Ironically, the practice is also believed to promote health and fertility.

Many believe that it also protects society from the voracious sexual appetite of women, safeguards virginity, promotes fidelity (of women), and enhances a woman's marriage prospects. The custom is also powerfully tied to family, kinship, and ideas of honor—especially male honor and the prestige and "honor" of patriarchal kin groups (Mackie, 1996; Fluehr-Lobban, 1997).

Fluehr-Lobban makes the important point that it is not always easy to achieve a consensus on whether a particular cultural practice has crossed the line and is a violation of "human rights." Genocide clearly fits this description. Many sociologists would agree that female genital mutilation does also despite the fact that some African scholars have criticized the term *female genital mutilation* as being ethnocentric, while others around the world claim the term is yet another example of "post-colonial imperialism" (Boyle, 2002:154). This raises questions about many other cultural practices that alter the body and may harm individuals and groups. For example, is male circumcision a legitimate cultural practice or a human rights violation? How about the widespread custom of spanking—does it violate children's human rights? And, as non-Western critics suggest, are the many forms of cosmetic surgery that are currently popular in the United States, such as breast enhancement, liposuction, and lip enhancement, human rights violations or legitimate cultural practices?

TAKING A CLOSER LOOK
Examine one of the American customs mentioned and argue whether it should or should not be considered a human rights violation.

Source: Carolyn Fluehr-Lobban. "Cultural Relativism and Human Rights." *Annual Editions: Anthropology,* 20th ed. Guildford, CT:Dushkin Publishing, 1997:33–35. Gerry Mackie. "Ending Footbinding and Infibulation: A Convention Account." *American Sociological Review* 61 (6) (December) 1996:999–1017. Elizabeth H. Boyle. *Female Genital Cutting: Cultural Conflict in the Global Community.* Baltimore, MD: Johns Hopkins University Press, 2002.

lifestyles worldwide. This process has greatly accelerated *cultural borrowing*. Across the globe billions of people now share many elements of culture in common—especially elements of popular and consumer culture that are promoted by the mass media (see Table 3.3). But cultural diversity has dramatically increased as well.

Today, because of global emigration, in most large cities and even many small towns, peoples' values, beliefs, food, and clothing may have much more in common with people who live thousands of miles away than with their neighbors who live only a few blocks away. In this sense, contemporary culture is a complex mosaic, with members of different cultures and subcultures living side-by-side, sometimes in harmony, relishing each other's special contributions, but at other times in opposition and conflict with these value orientations. Sociologists have discovered numerous factors that make special contributions to the rich tapestry of culture today. In this section, we examine how subcultures, the multicultural movement, postmodern culture, countercultures, the media, and strains between ideal and real culture affect culture in the United States and globally.

SUBCULTURES
Groups that share many elements of mainstream culture but maintain their own distinctive customs, values, norms, and lifestyles.

Subcultures

Subcultures are *groups that share many elements of main-stream culture but maintain their own distinctive customs, values, norms, and lifestyles.* There are subcultures based on age, gender, wealth, sexual orientation, education, and occupation, to name only a few. Within organizations, management and workers maintain their own symbols, specialized languages, and material culture, as do subcultures in rural and urban areas. Even within a 10-block area in most cities there may be hundreds or thousands of subcultures, including jazz musicians, street people, inner-city gangs, investment bankers, garment workers, and topless dancers.

Every region of the United States is a mosaic of ethnic and religious subcultures as well. For example, although Lowell, Massachusetts, is famous as the birthplace of the Industrial Revolution, from its beginnings it has also been the crucible for an important and continuing multicultural experiment. The town, founded in 1826, was initially the home of Boston-based English gentry who financed and built the textile mills that attracted immigrants from all over the world. Jewish, Greek, Polish, and Portuguese people arrived first, along with over 30,000 Irish Catholic immigrants who moved to Lowell during the Irish potato famine of the 1840s (Kiang, 1994). French Canadians arrived next and created the Little Canada community. In the 1950s, large numbers of Puerto Ricans and Dominicans relocated to Lowell to work in the garment industry. The most dramatic and rapid growth in Lowell, however, occurred in the 1980s. At that time, more than 25,000 Cambodians and several thousand Vietnamese and Laotians moved from other states to work as entry-level assemblers in new high-tech industries, bringing with them Buddhism, Confucianism, and many other forms of ethnic and religious diversity (Kiang, 1994).

You might attempt to chart the diversity in your town or city. You may be surprised at the degree of cultural diversity, expressed in such things as architectural designs, clothing, foods, family patterns, and religious beliefs.

Countercultures

Countercultures *reject the conventional wisdom and standards of behavior of the majority and provide alternatives to mainstream culture* (Berger, 1981; Yinger, 1982). For these reasons, they are considered threats to society, their members are labeled "deviant," and they are subjected to a variety of negative sanctions. Inequalities of class, race, age, gender, and other forms of social differentiation in contemporary postindustrial societies provide fertile ground for the development of countercultures. For example, political and social protests in the 1960s spawned dozens of countercultures, including the Black Panthers and the hippie movement. More recently, skinheads, the Aryan Brotherhood, and the Christian Identity Movement have emerged to challenge multiculturalism, nonwhite immigration, and racial harmony with calls for a return to white domination and "racial purity."

A number of sociologists suggest that the marginal status of adolescence has contributed to the proliferation of youth subcultures and even countercultures. This theory of *marginality* was first used to explain the predicament of second-generation immigrants (Park, 1928; Stonequist, 1937) "who seek to emulate dominant patterns but retain some visibility as minorities" and consequently are not fully acculturated. Nor are they fully accepted members of either cultural system (Marden et al., 1992:17). This has encouraged the formation of adolescent subcultures and sometimes countercultures in the United States and worldwide (Bynum and Thompson, 2007). Throughout

TABLE 3.3 GLOBAL VALUES: A ROPER POLL COMPARES AMERICANS' VALUES WITH GLOBAL VALUES	
Top 10 Values for Americans	**Top 10 Values Globally**
1. Honesty	1. Protecting the Family
2. Protecting the Family/ Freedom	2. Health and Fitness
3. Health and Fitness	3. Honesty
4. Friendship	4. Self-Esteem
5. Justice	5. Justice
6. Stable Peer Relationships	6. Friendship
7. Knowledge	7. Freedom
8. Enjoying Life	8. Knowledge
9. Self-Esteem	9. Self-Reliance
10. Learning	10. Wisdom

Source: "Global Values," 2005 *Roper Reports® Worldwide*, GfK Custom Research North America. Reprinted by permission.

This music festival in New York City's Central Park celebrates cultural diversity, including musical traditions from Africa, Latin America, the Caribbean, and other parts of the world.

Could contemporary rap, rock and roll, and jazz music exist without the benefits of cultural diversity?

COUNTERCULTURES
Groups that reject the conventional wisdom and standards of behavior of the majority and provide alternatives to mainstream culture.

the twentieth century, numerous youth countercultural movements, from heavy metal in the 1970s and 1980s to gangster rap and grunge in the 1990s, to rave subcultures with their drug use, all-night "rave" dance parties, and computer-generated music (Wilson, 2003) have attacked traditional adult norms and values. Some sociologists believe that traditional ways of distinguishing between subculture and countercultures may be confusing and even ethnocentric where some "countercultures" are involved. According to James and Laura Dowd (2003:34), "rather than continuing to think of countercultures as constituting an altogether different entity from the more common and less deviant subcultures, . . . [we] would emphasize the key distinction of a group's likelihood of assimilating into the surrounding culture. That is, countercultures publically and actively resist assimilation, whereas other types of subcultures are far less likely to do so" (Dowd and Dowd, 2003:34).

Multiculturalism

Multiculturalism recognizes cultural diversity as a national asset rather than a liability. Further, it recognizes that in different regions of the country much of the population is considered "multicultural" (see Map 3.2). The movement emerged in the 1980s, on campuses and in other social arenas, during the second largest wave of immigration in American history. **Multiculturalism** *encourages respect and appreciation for cultural difference.* In many ways, the multicultural movement seeks to reverse centuries of cultural intolerance and oppression of minority groups in the United States, Canada, and Europe. The majority historically has taken an *assimilationist approach* to immigrant groups, demanding that they abandon their cultural heritages and adopt the traditions of the host group. In the United States, this meant adopting the English language and the foods, dress, religion, and other cultural practices of the dominant European (Anglo-Saxon) groups, which established the early colonies and dominated American institutions (Gitlin, 1995).

MULTICULTURALISM
A movement that encourages respect and appreciation for cultural differences.

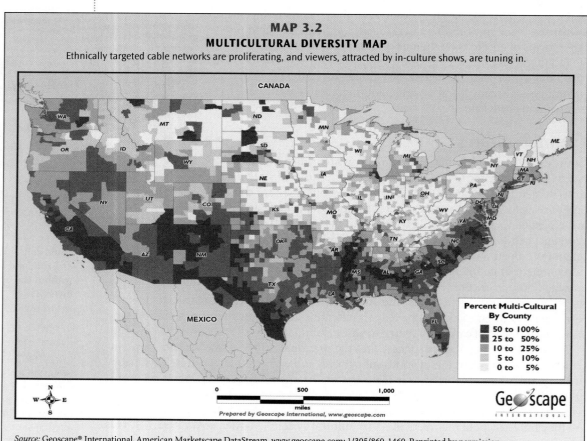

MAP 3.2
MULTICULTURAL DIVERSITY MAP
Ethnically targeted cable networks are proliferating, and viewers, attracted by in-culture shows, are tuning in.

Source: Geoscape® International, American Marketscape DataStream, www.geoscape.com; 1/305/860-1460. Reprinted by permission.

Some call this one-sided approach to minority groups and their cultures **Eurocentrism**—*the belief that European cultures have contributed the most to human knowledge and are superior to all others.* This perspective is especially pronounced in the U.S. educational system, where European accomplishments, interests, and perspectives have dominated history, literature, and all other subjects from grade school through college. In recent years, some minority groups have sought to balance these views with educational programs that emphasize their unique perspectives and accomplishments. **Afrocentrism**, for example, *emphasizes the preeminence of African and African American culture in human development.* Like Eurocentrism, however, it suffers from a unidimensional view of history, literature, and art by placing African culture above all others (Schlesinger, 1992).

Multiculturalism has brought fundamental changes to American education and "developing the ability to adapt to different cultural contexts may be one of the key learning areas of the curriculum of the future" (Campbell, 2000:31). The shift toward the appreciation of cultural diversity is reflected in a new emphasis on global languages in most school curricula and in efforts to bring the literatures and perspectives of many ethnic groups to human understanding—especially those that have been ignored in history and education, such as Native American cultures. Multiculturalism also has raised peoples' consciousness about the importance of gender, disability, sexual orientation, and other cultural differences that were previously neglected. The movement has also led to ethnic revival in many cities and in the nation as a whole, as evidenced by the celebrations of ethnic foods and folk customs, and by the holiday parades that celebrate ethnicity. Nowhere is this celebration more apparent than in popular culture and media celebrations of global diversity, from Disneyland to the Olympics, that are now beamed to billions of people worldwide.

The introduction of multiculturalism has not been without controversy, and there has been a strong backlash to the movement in politics and education. For some, *affirmative action, welfare,* and *multicultural* have become "code words" that license more subtle forms of racial and ethnic exclusion (Macedo and Bartolomé, 1999). Some conservative politicians have called multiculturalism misguided and even dangerous to the nation's future. Robert Bork (1996), for example, called challenges to Eurocentrism "ignorant and perverse," noting that "European American culture is the best the world has to offer." More tangible effects of the conservative backlash have been anti-immigrant legislation and efforts in many states to legislate "English only" in schools and government offices. At the national level, several bills have been introduced in Congress to make English the "official language" of the United States and in 2006, Congress passed a law stating that English was the "common language" that unites the United States.

From Modern to Postmodern Culture

For much of the twentieth century *modern values* were associated with industrial societies. Industrial societies essentially follow an assembly-line model. They are hierarchical, carefully ordered, with clear rules and a common vision that pervades major social institutions from politics to education and religion. Beginning in the 1970s in the most advanced postindustrial nations, new information technologies ushered in very different cultural trends that sociologists have labeled *postmodern values.*

Postmodern values are associated with prosperous high-tech societies that have a high degree of security. They emphasize quality of life and greater openness to change and diversity. They also place more stress on equality and creativity and promote more individualist orientations than any previous society. In postmodern culture, there is a shift from rugged individualism to *expressive individualism,* which emphasizes "style" rather than "taste." Likewise, social life becomes highly fragmented and the pace of social life accelerates (Bertman, 1998).

As journalist James Gleick remarked, technology has conditioned us to perform multiple tasks at the same time. Today people drive cars, eat, talk on cellular phones, and read newspapers and business reports at the same time—sometimes with disastrous results. According to Gleick (2000:18), "Technology has conditioned people to expect

EUROCENTRISM
The belief that European cultures have contributed the most to human knowledge and are superior to all others.

AFROCENTRISM
The perspective that emphasizes the preeminence of African and African American culture in human development.

instant results. Internet purchases arrive by next-day delivery . . . the microwave delivers a hot meal in minutes, [and] faxes, e-mails and cell phones make it possible—and increasingly obligatory—for people to work faster." In an era of high-speed change, many seek greater control of their lives (Bertman, 1998). For others, the desire for control and order is less important than personal improvement. As Bartos (1996:32) remarked, in the new postmodern culture we are aware that everything that we do or possess sends a message—our clothes, homes, cars—and, like media messages, we change and reinvent ourselves continually.

In a *World Values Survey* of 43 societies, Ronald Inglehart (1997) found a worldwide shift toward postmodern values. A shift in this direction is neither uniform nor assured, however. As in previous periods, globalization and immigration have generated opposite tendencies, including cultural segmentation, a resurgence of local cultures, ethnic and religious revival, and, in some cases, militant nationalism. For example, in many parts of the former Soviet Union, and especially in the former Yugoslavia, radical political and economic restructuring have sparked the revival of nationalist, ethnic, and religious groups and values.

In advanced postindustrial societies many groups at the edge of the mainstream—in economically depressed cities and many rural areas—have also responded to global change with calls for a return to traditional values and "universal morality" as the best approach to the present (and future). Another important challenge to postmodern culture has been the emergence of countercultures that reject the mainstream and offer their own visions of a better future.

Culture, Class, and the Media

During much of the twentieth century, and typical of *modern culture* described earlier, cultural variation was reflected in the different aesthetic standards and tastes of social classes. According to Herbert Gans (1975), during this period there were three major kinds of "taste cultures" in all advanced industrial societies: high culture, folk culture, and popular culture.

High Culture   *High culture* includes tastes and creations supported and used by the upper classes and intelligentsia to make fine distinctions within their ranks and to distinguish themselves from those beneath them in the social hierarchy. High culture demands elaborate training, technical proficiency, and considerable resources. Consequently, it has long been used by elites as social indicators of refinement, education, and style. Examples in Western cultures include classical music, opera, ballet, novels by the "great authors," and works by artists defined as possessing extraordinary skills and creative talents.

Conflict theorists argue that the belief that high culture is far superior to folk and popular culture reflects elite definitions of the situation. One English scholar, for example, wrote that "the differences between trash culture and high culture show only that storytelling adapts to changing economic, social, and political conditions" (Simon, 1999:2). Those who play a key role in constraining artistic diversity and keeping highbrow genres distinct from folk and popular tastes are *aesthetic gatekeepers,* including critics, reviewers, taste makers, and opinion makers, whose reviews, disseminated through the mass media, "may be more widely experienced than the artwork itself" (Shrum, 1991:373).

Folk Culture   *Folk culture* is in most ways the opposite of high culture; it includes the art, dance, music, and other creations of working-class and minority group members in their home environments. Folk culture includes such things as doll and quilt making, subway art, customized low-rider automobiles, and dancing. Folk culture is spontaneous, familiar, and practical, and is produced for and by ordinary people (Real, 1977). It also includes various forms of graffiti that Susan Phillips (1999) in her book *Wallbangin'* has classified into: gang graffiti, political graffiti, and hip-hop graffiti, the latter what she calls "subway art."

Popular Culture *Popular culture* comprises tastes and creations that appeal to the masses. Because popular culture consists of products and creations designed for leisure, entertainment, and mass consumption, it includes a bewildering assortment of things that critics say favor "vulgarity," "the commonplace," and the "lowest common denominator" (Bogart, 1991:63). Examples of popular culture include prime-time television, Elvis statues, live concerts by popular artists, tractor pulling contests, mud wrestling, baseball cards, NASCAR, and the mall Easter Bunny and Santa Claus.

Some sociologists contend that globalization and new information technologies have blurred "taste cultures." Anthropologist Terry Eagleton (2000:125) believes that traditional high culture has been supplanted by new media combinations and that there is "almost no popular culture outside commercial forms." At least one scholar argues that the Disney model has had such profound effect on social structure and culture that it has created a *Disneyization* of global society (Bryman, 2004). Technomedia, from fax machines to interactive videos and the World Wide Web, have given anyone with a personal computer access to virtually all of the arts, from the great books to comic books and graffiti. A recent study suggests that members of the upper class (highbrows) no longer limit themselves to the fine arts to distinguish themselves from other classes (lowbrows), as they did in previous periods. Instead, upper- and upper-middle-class professionals have become "cultural omnivores," who appreciate a great variety of art, music, and dance from around the world. Cultural eclecticism, of course, is highly functional in a global economy and can be used to express such things as a broad-based education, international experience, and cultural tolerance and understanding (Peterson and Kern, 1996).

This is not to say that every kind of cultural production has become equal, however. One researcher found that art, music, dance, and other leisure activities that are considered highbrow culture in nations such as the United States, Israel, and Sweden may be considered "popular culture" in nations like Germany and Italy, where they receive considerable funding by the state, cities, and even towns. Further, in pluralistic societies today, class divisions and cultural consumption are differentiated by national context but "there are significant linkages between race, religion, and gender" (Katz-Gerro, 2002:224). Moreover, "taste," now in the guise of a broad knowledge of global music and fine arts, continues to be useful in class ranking. For example, corporate employers may use evidence of "cultural eclecticism" as one important measure of managerial competence. Cultural tolerance, however, has its limits, and this too may reinforce class and other social boundaries.

BREVITY: © Guy & Rodd/Distributed by United Feature Syndicate, Inc. Used by permission.

Ideal and Real Culture

Another important source of cultural variation in every contemporary society are contradictions and disagreements between **ideal culture**—*what people should do, according to group norms and values*—and **real culture**—*what people do in everyday social interaction.* Value conflicts create strains and tensions in society, social problems, and sometimes even wars. Ideally, the United States is a land of opportunity where everyone is given an equal chance to succeed. In fact, social barriers such as age, gender, class, and race inhibit the chances of some and enhance the chances of others. Parents are expected to love and care for their children, yet it is estimated that 1.5 million children each year are victims of abuse (Straus et al., 2006; Gelles and Cornell, 1990).

Contradictions between ideal and real culture can be an important source of social change. For example, for many years police tolerated drunk-driving violations. Conforming to the public view that occasional excessive drinking was not socially harmful, police may have ignored violations or subverted the law by taking drunk drivers to their

IDEAL CULTURE
What people should do, according to group norms and values.

REAL CULTURE
What people do in everyday social interaction.

homes. The efforts of some individuals and the social movement Mothers Against Drunk Driving (MADD) led to changes in public opinion on this issue, resulting in much stricter enforcement of the law.

Almost 100 years ago, well before television, computers, and cellular phones, William Ogburn (1922, 1964) noted that material culture tends to change more rapidly than nonmaterial culture and that this can cause cultural strains and even contradictions. This may result in **cultural lag**—*inconsistencies in a cultural system, especially in the relationship between technology and nonmaterial culture.* Recent advances in medical technology have had precisely the effects Ogburn proposed. We now have the ability to keep terminally ill patients alive indefinitely, using heart pumps, human and animal organ transplants, and artificial respirators. Cultural lag is obvious in such cases, for neither doctors nor family members are entirely sure of their responsibilities to the patient. Laws vary widely as well, for medical innovations have so redefined the fundamental nature of human existence that judges and juries regularly decide these issues. Recent experiments with genetic engineering and cloning have raised even more complicated questions that will provide new challenges in the future.

SOCIOLOGICAL APPROACHES TO SOCIETY AND CULTURE

Sociologists view culture from several different perspectives. Functionalism and conflict approaches tend to be particularly useful in examining large-scale cultural patterns as well as cultural diversity in complex societies. Symbolic interactionism is better suited to understanding the powerful role of symbols and cultural interpretation in face-to-face interaction.

Society, Culture, and Functionalism

To understand why customs and traditions vary so widely around the world, it is important to know that all cultures are, in part, practical responses to environmental conditions. The **cultural ecological approach,** which *examines the relationship between a culture and its total environment,* best exemplifies this perspective. At first glance, the Hindu custom that prohibits the slaughter of India's estimated 120 million cows because they are "sacred" may seem maladaptive and irrational. Functionalists contend, however, that we must examine the full context of the practice to understand it.

Although this practice may not seem rational in the context of advanced industrial and postindustrial societies, in India's preindustrial society the benefits outweigh the liabilities. For one thing, in a country with few tractors, draft animals pull plows and transport people and goods to market. Cattle also provide manure, which is dried and used for fertilizer, fuel, and housing; and after they die their hides are processed into sandals and leather goods. Most important, according to one anthropologist, "cow veneration" contributes to the adaptive resilience of Indian society by protecting a vital commodity that otherwise would have been consumed in any number of famines and droughts (Harris, 1974:30).

Such an approach to culture and society is clearly useful in tracing the origin of customs and provides important checks against ethnocentrism. Functionalism also shows how the cultural practices of groups tend to "fit together," something sociologists call *cultural integration.* Changes in one element may have broad repercussions for the culture of any group. For example, the automobile, television, and computers clearly had a broad impact on almost every aspect of American culture and society, from family and work patterns to preferences for fast food and countless other elements of material and nonmaterial culture.

Society and Culture from the Conflict Perspective

According to the conflict perspective, the values, beliefs, and traditions of a nation or society are not necessarily a product of consensus and "social need," as some functionalists claim. Instead, in all stratified societies, culture is highly complex, with many strains

CULTURAL LAG
Inconsistencies in a cultural system, especially in the relationship between technology and nonmaterial culture.

CULTURAL ECOLOGICAL APPROACH
An approach that examines the relationship between a culture and its total environment.

and contradictions that reflect conflicting group interests and needs. Because of their abundant resources, however, groups at the top of society commonly have a disproportionate influence over national culture. As Marx and Engels ([1846] 1947:39) noted, "The ideas of the ruling class are in every epoch the ruling ideas." In the slave era, for example, the dominant *ideology* promoted slavery and praised its virtues for both slaveholder and slave alike. Today, corporate capitalism extols the merits of individuality, consumerism, and free enterprise, which provide great benefits to corporate and governing elites.

Sociologists refer to more subtle, contemporary forms of elite cultural control—**cultural hegemony,** or *the domination of cultural industries by elite groups. Cultural industries* include the educational system, religion, the family, and, most important in contemporary society, the media. Today, the mainstream media, which reach most people, are disproportionately influenced by large corporations and government officials. Through *media framing* of the "news" and popular entertainment, elite groups around the world daily "help" the public recognize and interpret important issues and events.

American corporate symbols permeate the globe.

For example, after the Tiananmen Square massacre in 1989, one might think the last image the Chinese leadership would have shown on television would be the lone man confronting a line of tanks near the Beijing Hotel. Yet with proper framing it became one of their favorite images, and they showed this dramatic incident repeatedly on television—not to show the man's bravery, courage, and support for freedom and democracy as portrayed in the Western media, but to show the "extreme restraint" exercised by Chinese soldiers in restoring order (Snow and Benford, 1988; Lull, 1991). One scholar believes that corporations, advertisers, and mainstream media have even found a way to turn countercultures and social protest into commercial products and fantasies. "Hip consumerism" and anything with an edge that hints at rebellion have become highly marketable. For example, Ozzy Osbourne, the seventies "shock rocker" and former symbol of anarchy, has, along with his family, become repackaged as "hip in an odd way" and perfectly suitable for mainstream television and even a White House visit (Hadnot, 2003:J1; Frank, 1998).

What influences do American products have on other cultures besides those obvious to the product?

Even in the most rigidly controlled media systems, however, audiences have considerable room for interpretation as well as many opportunities to challenge and protest establishment views. For example, the music industry pours forth a steady stream of records and music videos that promote system-supporting images and themes, but on any given day, a cacophony of dissent can also be heard or seen in heavy metal, grunge, rap, country, and many other forms of music and music videos.

Symbolic Interactionism, Society, and Culture

The *interactionist approach* focuses on how individuals and groups use symbols to define and interpret reality. This approach emphasizes that people everywhere live in "symbolic worlds" that are created and reproduced by diverse social groups, from Wall Street bankers to gangs and cab drivers. James Henslin (1993) provides an excellent example of the "cultural world" of cab drivers, where cabbies use time of day, dress, age, race, and "body language" to determine whether someone will be a trustworthy ride or a potential threat.

According to interactionists, our daily lives are structured by the symbols and meanings of many groups. These symbolic worlds shape reality and truths, whether or not they are real or scientifically valid. According to interactionism, if groups define something as real, whether or not they truly exist, "they are real in their consequences." For example, in 1997, 39 members of a UFO religious group in San Diego committed mass suicide, believing that visitors from outer space had summoned them to a spaceship that was trailing the Hale-Bopp comet.

CULTURAL HEGEMONY
The domination of cultural industries by elite groups.

SOCIETY AND CULTURE IN THE TWENTY-FIRST CENTURY

Today, there is no society on earth so remote that its inhabitants have not heard of radios, televisions, blue jeans, automobiles, and soft drinks; in fact, most people already possess them. Pygmies in the heart of the African rain forest wear Pepsi and Coca-Cola t-shirts; Inuit Eskimos drive snowmobiles, drink beer, and watch *Survivor*. By no means are cultural contacts one-way. From the beginning, American and other Western cultures have borrowed from traditional cultures and non-Western foods, clothing styles, architecture, art, and many other elements of material and non-material culture have greatly enriched our lives. Some argue that with globalization and the spread of English as the language of business, science, and computers, English *and* American customs and ideas will become dominant as well. Such thinking may be misguided. For one thing, computer programs like *Microsoft Millennium* feature more than two dozen languages and their spell checker offers not one but "four varieties of English" (Wallraff, 2000:66). Moreover, writer Barbara Wallraff (2000) contends that as English spreads around the world, English itself will be transformed, because ordinary people will coin new words and usages in their local languages and adapt English to suit their cultural and social environments.

Likewise, in the popular view, the media now bind together the diverse elements of American and global society into a seamless whole. People from different occupations, races, social classes, and even nations may have little else in common, but because of the media they share many values, beliefs, and norms. Few people in the world do not know about Coca-Cola Classic and the "golden arches," and almost anyone can express an opinion on a story about child abuse or capital punishment that was broadcast last night or last week on CNN or network television. Is this "Americanization" of the world a dangerous trend, as some European scholars have suggested, one that may lead to "cultural extinctions" all over the globe (Goldsmith, 1998:104)?

Many scholars take the opposite view, arguing that while media and popular culture provide entertainment and pleasure for audiences, they create neither identification with social authority nor shared values. Instead of uniting audiences by exposing them to common values, mass media and postmodern culture fragment audiences with a smorgasbord of contradictory images and meanings that reinforce social divisions and make it difficult for ordinary people to see their common interests. "American popular culture is capitalist culture," where commodities are produced to spur desire and profit. This, of course, makes it a highly disruptive standard-bearer of modernity and change (Rothstein, 2002:1).

Global popular culture is no less fragmented. Even if elites wished to use the media to promote a homogeneous "global culture," media texts can be read in a variety of ways. And while global audiences may sometimes interpret messages to agree with the interpretations of media producers, at other times they may disagree or even transform the intended messages to conform to traditional values and beliefs (Tetzlaff, 1992; Barker, 1999). This prompted sociologist George Ritzer (2004) to assert that the *globalization of everything* leads to the *globalization of nothing*. Aviad Raz, in his study of Tokyo Disneyland, contends that this process is a form of "glocalization." According to Raz (1999:199), with global commodities—video, television, Hollywood, Coke, MTV, McDonald's—these symbols spin webs of interaction that become "imbued with local meanings." Focus box 3.3 takes a closer look at the presence of McDonald's in Asia and how both adaptation and conflict are the norm.

What effect will transnational corporations and the mass media have on developing countries, and how will people in these countries respond to the flood of ideas and goods from the West? Of special interest to sociologists is the expansion of "consumer culture" and related ideas of freedom, individuality, and progress—especially among young people, who comprise the fastest growing segment of the population in most developing countries. Will the young in developing countries emulate the West and

Many people believe that McDonald's is such a potent source of American fast-food culture and American culture in general that when it transplants itself overseas, "American values" are widely adopted. In effect, this thesis holds that no matter the cultural setting, the arrival of the Golden Arches inevitably leads to cultural homogenization in the American model, a trend that is supposedly sweeping the globe. Several researchers have put this hypothesis to the test by conducting personal interviews and informal conversations with consumers in Beijing, China, Hong Kong, Taiwan, and other East Asian countries. Not surprisingly, they found that some elements of culture were transferred from West to East relatively intact while others did indeed supplant traditional cultural practices. However, they also discovered that McDonald's adapted to local cultural biases, preferences, and customs, modifying many company practices—even some of its most basic understandings of how a fast-food restaurant should operate (Watson, 1997).

Today, virtually all East Asian McDonald's restaurants have added features to accommodate local cultures. Teriyaki burgers are popular from Japan to China, and local owner-operators are the norm. Likewise, Ronald McDonald is known throughout much of the region as "Uncle McDonald," a wise and understanding figure—not unlike similar figures in traditional Chinese folklore. Another novel twist that reflects a long-standing East Asian value is the nature of staff-customer interactions. In Beijing, for example, each restaurant has between five and ten female "receptionists" who talk to parents and care for their children during their visits. One receptionist in Beijing had over 100 young friends. Moreover, borrowing from traditions that value close and long-term personal interactions in business and elsewhere, the receptionists' care goes well beyond company time. Many visit children's homes and classes after work, send cards on their birthdays and holidays, and otherwise become part of their families. Because of this, they are called "Aunt McDonald" in many parts of East Asia (Watson, 1997).

Joe Kincheloe, in his book *The Sign of the Burger,* contends that such adaptations are a well-calculated part of a "global reeducation campaign." He writes, "contemporary advertising intends for consumers to make their own meanings of products" but also to convince people everywhere that burgers and fries are good food and that McDonald's restaurants are fun, "cool," and ultramodern (Kincheloe, 2002). In China, for example, parents are obsessed with their children's education, believing that schools and the family must prepare them for life in a global society. So

McDonald's encourages parents to bring their children by the restaurant for a lesson in "modernization," even supplying paper and pens for the children, sponsoring essay contests, and presenting educational children's programs (Kincheloe, 2002:112).

Advertisers have a second objective as well—to "counter and dismiss criticism from detractors"—a sizeable task in the global community where it is never totally successful. First, virtually everywhere, McDonald's is powerfully associated with America, transnational corporations, capitalism, and the "Americanization of the planet" (Kincheloe, 2002:3). So powerful are these associations that immediately "after the terrorist-controlled airplanes crashed into the World Trade Center Towers and the Pentagon, all McDonald's regional offices were closed and evacuated" (Kincheloe, 2002:4).

And activists at home and abroad regularly challenge its wholesome images, spotlighting not "consumption" but "production," and focusing on health and environmental concerns, low wages for workers, and a host of other problems. Kincheloe (2002:10) mentions that one social activist website, "McSpotlight," was visited 65 million times over a three-year period—"making it one of the most important monitors of corporate behavior on the planet." In France protestors have attacked and dismantled fast-food restaurants, and in Italy a food critic and leader of a "slow-food" antiglobalization movement said McDonald's "symbolized oppression of the palate" [and] "the potatoes were obscene" (Truelsen, 2003:5). The regional headquarters in Italy subsequently filed a $25 million lawsuit against the food critic and decided to revamp its global advertising messages. According to Kincheloe (2002:17) "confused by the mixed reception of its signifiers, the corporation is struggling to formulate new ways of representing itself in a rapidly changing world."

TAKING A CLOSER LOOK

In contemporary society, can any advertising images and messages of McDonald's satisfy both local and global audiences?

Source: James L. Watson. "Introduction: Transnationalism, Localization, and Fast Foods in East Asia," in *Golden Arches East: McDonald's in East Asia,* James L. Watson (ed.) Standard, CA: Stanford University Press, 1997:1–38. Joe L. Kincheloe. *The Sign of the Burger: McDonald's and the Culture of Power.* Philadelphia: Temple University Press, 2002.

demand a greater share of material benefits? If their desires are not met, will this lead to a worldwide crisis of rising expectations or, conversely, a rejection of Western culture and a reemphasis on traditional values and beliefs? Further, there are a growing number of new immigrants who wish to maintain dual identities and cultural practices that may clash with majority cultures in both Europe and America. For example, in Miami, some recent arrivals from Cuba and Haiti practice Santeria, which involves animal sacrifice; it not only is prohibited by law but is deemed "cruel to animals" by many in the population. Likewise, in Berlin, some Turkish parents have questioned "why Islamic classes cannot be made available as an elective in Germany," with its tradition of religious instruction in public schools (Coles, 2003:14).

Some sociologists see considerable potential in grassroots movements that advocate a new global consciousness and "world culture." Many seek to promote social structures and cultural values that stress "universalism, individualism, voluntaristic authority, and rational progress" (Boli and Thomas, 1997:171). To some, these cultural values are the essential ingredients of world citizenship, and they will become much more pronounced in this twenty-first century.

What about cultural change in advanced postindustrial societies where populations are growing older? At the turn of the last century, people age 65 or older accounted for only 4 percent of the U.S. population. It is estimated that by 2030 this age cohort will increase to 20 percent and in Japan and Germany one in three persons will be older than 64 (Bosworth and Burtless, 1998). The mainstream media have already shifted their emphasis from youth culture toward middle-aged and elderly consumers. One journalist contends that "as the entire population of the developed world grows older, the attributes of personal aging may come to define the tone and pace of the culture at large" (Peterson, 2000b:21). Or perhaps the elderly will splinter into a variety of subcultures or counter-cultures that challenge dominant cultural values—perhaps including the ideas of progress and consumerism—much as youth countercultures did in the 1960s?

Finally, the impact of technological changes on culture and society will be closely monitored. How will improvements in computers, robotics, lasers, and countless other high-tech industries influence postindustrial societies of the future? Will genetic and biomedical research bring fundamental changes to our ideas of life and death and what it means to be human? What new technological developments will radically alter our visions of the natural and supernatural worlds and our relations with one another? Will the rapid pace of technological change in this twenty-first century reinforce traditional values and beliefs, or will cultural lag eventually lead to social and political chaos and perhaps even fundamental changes in American ideology? Do technology and technicians, in fact, hold the key to the future? Some in the popular media lend strong support to the idea that technological advances eventually will solve all social problems and ultimately produce utopian societies. Others believe dystopian societies are more likely and that unbridled technological change will eventually lead to environmental destruction and global terrorism and war. What do you think?

Summary

1 All human societies can be grouped into six types based on their technologies and social lives: hunting-gathering, pastoral, horticultural, agrarian, industrial, and postindustrial.

2 Technomedia are fundamental to postindustrial society. They create the possibility of both a global village and a home-centered society with much greater individualism and social fragmentation than is characteristic of industrial society.

3 Culture consists of the learned set of practices, beliefs, values, rules for proper conduct, and material objects that are shared by group members. Sociologists divide culture into material and nonmaterial culture.

4 All contemporary people live in culturally constructed worlds that are largely their own creation. This includes group understandings of time, space, beauty, and virtually everything else.

5 All groups create worlds of meaning with the same basic elements: symbols, language, beliefs, values, norms, and material culture.

6 In today's global society, cultural diversity both shapes and is shaped by subcultures, the multicultural movement, postmodernism, countercultures, the media, and conflicts between ideal and real culture.

7 Sociologists take three major approaches in studying cultural diversity. Functionalists tend to emphasize the origin of customs and how culture contributes to social order. Conflict theorists emphasize cultural conflict and change, while interactionists stress how groups create and give meaning to symbols and how they affect face-to-face interaction.

8 The globalization of the economy and demographic change will have an important impact on virtually all cultures in the future. Likewise, technological changes will continue to alter traditional beliefs, values, and norms around the world—perhaps at an unprecedented rate.

Key Terms

Afrocentrism (p. 73)
agrarian society (p. 55)
beliefs (p. 63)
countercultures (p. 71)
cultural ecological approach (p. 76)
cultural hegemony (p. 77)
cultural lag (p. 76)
cultural relativism (p. 68)
culture (p. 56)
culture shock (p. 67)
ethnocentrism (p. 68)
Eurocentrism (p. 73)

folkways (p. 65)
horticultural society (p. 55)
hunting-gathering society (p. 55)
ideal culture (p. 75)
industrial society (p. 55)
language (p. 61)
laws (p. 66)
material culture (p. 56)
mores (p. 66)
multiculturalism (p. 72)
nonmaterial culture (p. 56)
norms (p. 65)

pastoral society (p. 55)
postindustrial society (p. 55)
real culture (p. 75)
sanctions (p. 67)
society (p. 54)
sociocultural evolution (p. 55)
subcultures (p. 70)
symbol (p. 60)
taboos (p. 66)
values (p. 63)

Chapter 4

Socialization

"Learning is not compulsory—
neither is survival."
—W. Edwards Deming

As a brand-new student at Hofstra University, Tamara was surprised that so many people waved, smiled, and spoke to her as if they knew her. At first she just assumed people at Hofstra were very friendly; later it began to bother her when people would approach her, act as if they knew her, and then walk off seemingly perturbed when she failed to call them by name or know what they were talking about. Obviously, they had her confused with somebody else.

Then, at her twentieth birthday party, at the insistence of a friend of one of her guests who claimed Tamara looked and acted identically to his friend Adriana, Tamara agreed to contact Adriana through e-mail. After a few electronic exchanges, they learned that both were adopted, both were slightly over 5 feet 3 inches tall, both had adopted fathers who had died of cancer, both loved Mexican food (especially chicken fajitas), both liked to dance, and both wore silver hoop earrings. The girls exchanged photos, which both described as like looking in a mirror, and eventually the two met. There was no doubt about it, they were identical twins who had been separated at birth (Gootman, 2003).

At first, even sociologists who read an account such as the story of Tamara and Adriana may be tempted to assume their similarities are more than mere coincidence or the result of social experiences. But the critical thinking of sociology demands further investigation and questioning of such taken-for-granted assumptions. For example, how many students in your sociology class had fathers who died of cancer? Do you or any of your classmates love chicken fajitas? How many like to dance and own silver hoop earrings? Surely nobody would suggest that all those who fit these categories are long-lost brothers or sisters of Tamara and Adriana. While genetics and heredity play an important part in our lives, the powerful influence of our social experiences cannot be underestimated.

We know that babies are born with very few instinctive behaviors and cannot survive without the care, nurturance, and guidance of other humans. It is through the process of socialization, in interacting with others, that we become human beings. **Socialization** is *a process in which we learn and internalize the*

Identical twins separated at birth, Tamara and Adriana accidentally discovered one another on the Hofstra campus and were amazed at many of their similarities that extended beyond mere physical appearance.

How might sociologists explain many of the similarities between Tamara and Adriana as opposed to how they might be viewed by biologists or geneticists?

attitudes, values, beliefs, and norms of our culture and develop a sense of self. This lifelong procedure begins at birth and continues until death. Socialization provides a vital link between an individual and society. Societies provide "rough scripts and casts of characters whose interactions tend to shape individual lives" through the socialization experience (Clausen, 1991:805).

THE SOCIALIZATION PROCESS

Have you ever been told that you walk just like your father? Does your laugh sound just like your mother's? Do you like the same foods as your older brother or sister? Is your sense of humor just like your father's and your Uncle Fred's? Or do you take after your mother, who represents the more serious side of the family? Are any of these characteristics inherited, or are they all learned? Sociologists attribute most, if not all, of these personal and social attributes to the socialization process, but questions such as these have fueled a long-standing debate over the importance of nature versus nurture.

Nature and Nurture

Scientists have debated the influence of **nature** (*heredity*) versus **nurture** (*environment*) in personality development for many years. During the late nineteenth and early twentieth centuries, the argument was dominated by those on the side of heredity. In *On the Origin of Species,* Charles Darwin ([1859] 1964) contended that all organisms are in a constant struggle and that to survive species must make continuous biological and physiological adaptations to their environments. Some social scientists used Darwin's ideas to argue that human organisms are driven by biology and physiology. By the 1920s, several thousand so-called human instincts that determine human behavior had been identified (Bernard, 1924).

During the twentieth century the pendulum swung in the opposite direction; the influence of environment and learning was viewed as paramount in human development. Many behaviorists went so far as to declare that humans are totally devoid of instincts and *all* behavior is learned (Watson, 1924).

Research on identical twins who have been reared apart indicates that rather than thinking of nature versus nurture, it is more productive to acknowledge the dynamic interplay between the two (Farber, 1981; Donahue, 1985; Gallagher, 1994). As organisms, we have certain genetic, biological, and physiological attributes that establish behavioral constraints and boundaries. At the same time, as social beings with the ability to think, learn, rationalize, and interpret our behavior, we have the ability to develop countless unique characteristics within our biological and physiological makeup.

The studies on identical twins as well as research in health, medicine, language development, sexual orientation, and other areas indicate that the old debate over nature versus nurture is no longer relevant. As one writer put it, "Asking whether nature or nurture is more important is like a political debate where neither candidate is credible and both are simultaneously right and wrong" (Siegfried, 2003:1E). Or, as another writer observed,

Is it nature? Is it nurture? Are we controlled by our genes? And, do parents even matter? Scientists have a long way to go, but the answers are starting to roll in, and so far it looks like they are yes, yes, yes and yes. (Hayden, 2000:57)

Today, there is much more agreement that both nature and nurture are important and that as humans, we are products of both our heredity and environment, or as Matt Ridley (2003) so succinctly put it, it is no longer nature versus nurture, but nature *via* nurture.

SOCIALIZATION
A process in which we learn and internalize the attitudes, values, beliefs, and norms of our culture and develop a sense of self.

NATURE
Heredity.

NURTURE
Environment.

Sociobiology and the Importance of Heredity and Environment

Since the mid-1970s, a more balanced approach to personality and social development has emerged, with social scientists acknowledging that the nature versus nurture debate has been futile and unproductive. A controversial approach that has gained popularity is **sociobiology,** which *integrates theories and research from biology and sociology in an effort to better understand human behavior.* Much of the sociobiological literature concludes that genetics, biology, and physiology set parameters on a wide range of human characteristics, traits, and even temperament; environment, socialization, and experience then shape the final product (Wilson, 1978; Fisher, 1991; Gallagher, 1994). Clearly all of us are affected by our biology and physiology, but our personalities and behavior are largely shaped by social and cultural variables. Consequently, it can be stated with confidence that who we are and what we do represent a dynamic interplay among (1) genetic traits and characteristics, (2) the environment, and (3) what we learn in interaction with others (Cherry, 1994; Ridley, 2003).

The interplay between heredity and environment is important, and nowhere is this better demonstrated than in the process of early childhood socialization. At conception and during prenatal development, we are genetically programmed for characteristics such as sex, race, skin color, hair and eye color, and even height and weight. In addition, neurobiological research indicates that, contrary to previous beliefs that infant's brains are fully developed at birth, during the first two to three years of life a baby's brain is literally being "wired" for skills and activities such as thinking, mathematics, music, and, most important, language. These studies show that the brains of institutionalized children and infants who are ignored or not spoken to often are less active and hence do not physically develop in the same ways as the brains of children whose parents talk to them a great deal, play music for them, and otherwise stimulate brain activity (Begley, 1997; Kantrowitz, 1997; Cowley, 2000; Siegfried, 2003).

From birth, people are bombarded with cultural and social experiences that shape their development. Since newborn infants are totally dependent on others and seemingly totally malleable, the earliest stages of socialization are critical in the development of personality and the process of becoming human. Because we must learn the distinctive behaviors associated with being human (especially the use of language), early childhood socialization takes on compelling significance. Have you ever wondered what would happen to children if they were deprived of all contact with other people? Since the beginning of civilization people have been curious about the effects of social isolation. A number of cases support the view that when children are raised in isolation they either die or fail to develop acceptable human behavioral characteristics.

The Effects of Social Isolation

In cultures all over the world, people are fascinated by the idea of children being reared by animals in the wild. Stories abound of so-called feral children, who were briefly raised in the presence of people and then abandoned to be cared for by animals.

Feral Children   *The Legend of Greystoke,* the story of a young boy lost in the jungle and reared by apes, has given us the popular book, television, and movie characterizations of Tarzan. On a similar theme, moviegoers in late 1994 were mesmerized by Jodie Foster's performance in the motion picture *Nell,* in which she portrayed a young girl abandoned in the wilds of North Carolina who developed her own language.

In France, the "wild boy of Aveyron" was intensively studied, and in Burundi, Africa, a boy believed to have been raised by chimpanzees aroused much scientific curiosity (Shattuck, 1980). Cases of feral children have been difficult to substantiate, however, and scientific research on them has suffered from numerous theoretical and methodological flaws.

Sociological Case Studies: Anna and Isabelle   While stories of feral children are questionable, there are some documented cases of children raised in social isolation.

SOCIOBIOLOGY
A field that integrates theories and research from biology and sociology in an effort to better understand human behavior.

The first sociologist to study systematically the effects of social isolation on children was Kingsley Davis (1940, 1947). One of the cases he studied was that of a young girl named Anna, the illegitimate daughter of a farm woman who lived alone with her father. After Anna's mother unsuccessfully attempted to have her adopted, the child was, at her grandfather's insistence, banished to a small room in the attic. Her mother gave Anna just enough physical care to keep her alive and apparently ignored all but her most basic social and psychological needs.

When Anna was discovered by social workers at age 6, she was in poor physical health; she was covered with filth and excrement and was unable to walk, talk, or perform any other routine behaviors considered normal for 6-year-olds. Anna was placed in a county home, and after about a year and a half of intensive socialization learned to walk, understand simple commands, and interact with a few people whom she recognized, although she did not learn to speak. It is impossible to guess whether Anna could have "caught up," for she suffered from numerous health problems and died at about age 10 (Davis, 1947).

Isabelle was discovered about the same time as Anna. She, too, was an illegitimate child who was isolated until approximately age 6 under remarkably similar circumstances. Isabelle spent her first 6 years in a dark attic room inhabited only by her and her deaf-mute mother. When discovered, she could not speak, could barely walk, and appeared to be severely mentally retarded, acting more animal-like than human. After she was removed from the attic, Isabelle was given a battery of psychological and IQ tests, which indicated that she was virtually uneducable and probably would never learn to speak.

Nevertheless, Isabelle responded to an intensive socialization program. She began to vocalize after only a week and, within 2 months, was forming sentences. Within a year, she had learned to read, write, and do simple mathematics. By age 8, Isabelle had gone through almost all of the normal developmental sequences, and according to Davis gave all appearances of being a bright, energetic, and cheerful little girl. Davis used the functionalist perspective to emphasize how dysfunctional social isolation was for cultural transmission and human development (Davis, 1947).

The cases of Anna and Isabelle underscore the importance of social interaction in human development. While healthy individuals are born with all the genetic, biological, and physiological potential to become full human beings, it is the socialization process that completes their transformation. As one author summarized the research on early childhood development: "genetics provides the raw material; life molds the spirit and the soul" (Kantrowitz, 1997:8). These cases also underscore the fact that socialization is indeed a *process,* not an *act.*

Developing a Social Self

The process of becoming human involves the development of a **personality**—*a dominant pattern of attitudes, feelings, and behaviors*—and what sociologists call a *concept of self.* Sigmund Freud ([1923] 1947), noted physician and psychologist, writing at a time when most people viewed personality as being unidimensional, contended that there are three important components of personality: the *id,* the *superego,* and the *ego.* George Herbert Mead, a contemporary of Freud, also saw personality as being multidimensional, but he viewed its development as a social process. Mead (1934) contended that an individual's mind and conception of self are inseparable from society and social interaction. Research indicates that almost half of all parents (43 percent) think that children's personalities are genetically determined, but that same research demonstrates that how parents and others treat children has dramatic impact on personality development and shaping a sense of self (Hayden, 2000). These studies emphasize the importance of the socialization process on personality development and the powerful influence of society on the individual. According to Mead, the **self,** *a person's conscious recognition that he or she is a distinct individual who is part of a larger society,* emerges through social experience. Using the symbolic interactionist perspective, Mead divorced the self from any biological components and viewed people's ability to think of themselves as social objects in relation to others as the characteristic that distinguishes

PERSONALITY
A dominant pattern of attitudes, feelings, and behaviors.

SELF
A person's conscious recognition that he or she is a distinct individual who is part of a larger society.

human beings from animals. Behaviorists such as John B. Watson (1924) and Ivan Pavlov (in Wade and Tavris, 1998) had demonstrated that animals could be trained to react to certain stimuli; Mead insisted that humans not only react to stimuli in their environment but, more important, *interpret* them. Human actions are then based on the meanings that humans impute to stimuli.

The "I" and the "Me"   Mead contended that the self is composed of two related and interdependent components: the *I* and the *me*. The **I** is *the unsocialized self as subject.* More spontaneous, creative, and uninhibited than the me, the I is the initiator of social action. Young children tend to be "I-dominated," in that they usually see themselves as the center of the social universe. Correspondingly, much of their conversation is punctuated with the word *I:* "I'm hungry," "I want a drink," "I want a toy," and so forth.

Through socialization, however, as the sense of self develops more fully, the **me** component, or *the socialized self as object,* develops. The sense of me represents people's ability to realize that they are members of a social world and that, while they have the ability to act in a way that has an impact on others, others can also act in ways that have an impact on them. Although the I is spontaneous and creative, the me is reactive; it is based on our perception of how others will respond to our actions. The I and the me are the basis of thought and allow the individual to experience social interaction even in the absence of others. Through effective socialization, the I and the me work in harmony to allow us to act, react, and interact while taking others into account.

The "Looking-Glass Self"   Mead's conception of the self was influenced by his colleague Charles Horton Cooley, who coined the term **looking-glass self** to describe *the process in which individuals use others like mirrors and base their conceptions of themselves on what is reflected back to them during social interaction.* Also working from the interactionist perspective, Cooley ([1902] 1922) described three successive steps in the process:

1. The imagination of our appearance to others.

2. The imagination of their judgment of that appearance.

3. The development of feelings about and responses to these judgments (see Figure 4.1).

For example, if you approach a group of college classmates, you are immediately aware that you are giving off an impression. Generally you want that impression to be as favorable as possible, and you may view yourself as being friendly, witty, and charming. As you interact with members of the group, you "read" both their verbal and nonverbal reactions to assess whether they view you in the way you imagine you appear to them. If their feedback is positive and they include you in the group, you will have your positive concept of self reaffirmed. On the other hand, if they suddenly stop talking, seem to feel ill at ease, look away, or make a hasty retreat, you might reassess your feelings about yourself and wonder if maybe you are less friendly, witty, and charming than you thought.

Many of our feelings about ourselves are attributable to our interpretations of others' impressions of us. Do you think you are ugly or overweight or have a big nose? Where did these ideas come from? Or do you think you are attractive, physically fit, and charming? What led you to this view? Most likely, these perceptions have been conveyed to you during interactions with others. Of course, some people's opinions mean more to

I
In Mead's schema, the unsocialized self as subject.

ME
In Mead's schema, the socialized self as object.

LOOKING-GLASS SELF
Cooley's concept that individuals use others like mirrors and base their conceptions of themselves on what is reflected back to them during social interaction.

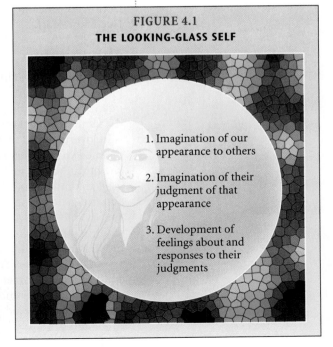

FIGURE 4.1
THE LOOKING-GLASS SELF

1. Imagination of our appearance to others

2. Imagination of their judgment of that appearance

3. Development of feelings about and responses to their judgments

People use mirrors to evaluate their physical appearance to others.

How did sociologist Charles Horton Cooley use this analogy in his concept of "looking-glass self"?

us than others'. The opinions of family and friends usually have a greater impact on our concept of self than the opinions of strangers.

It is possible to misinterpret the feedback we receive from others. We have all experienced the uneasy feeling of not being quite sure how people were responding to us as we interacted with them. Did their laughter mean they enjoyed my joke? Or were they laughing at me in ridicule? How a person answers those questions relates to his or her conception of self based on past social experiences and particular social situations.

The Situated Self Because our most important identities lend continuity and unity to our behavior, we tend to think of our "selves" as fixed and changeless. In fact, social interaction requires that the selves we present to others vary from situation to situation; that is, we all have multiple selves. **Situated self** describes *the self that emerges in a particular situation.* For example, being African American and being a woman are both important identities. Nevertheless, when an African American woman interacts with African American men, she is most likely to think of herself as a woman; when she interacts with white women, she is more likely to activate her African American identity (Michener et al., 1986).

How does this social self develop? It is taught and learned through the process of socialization by the major agents of socialization: family, school, church, peers, and in many cases, the mass media.

MAJOR AGENTS OF SOCIALIZATION: A GLOBAL VIEW

Socialization is considered too important to leave to chance, so every society has institutionalized ways of carrying out the process. **Agents of socialization** are *those groups and institutions that both informally and formally take on the task of socialization.* We will discuss six major agents of socialization. Three of them—the family, the school, and religion—are widely accepted as legitimate socializing agents. The other three—peers, the workplace, and the mass media—are not specifically charged with the task of socialization but in contemporary society play an important role in the socialization process (see Figure 4.2).

The Family

In all societies, the first major agent of socialization for most individuals is the family. From birth, parents and siblings influence the social development of the newborn infant, helping him or her to internalize culture and develop a social identity. Much of the family's impact on socialization is intentional and carefully designed, but some of it is inadvertent and unrealized. For example, studies show that children of women who married young, were pregnant when married, or cohabited before marriage learn values and attitudes that make them more likely to do the same (Thornton, 1991).

The family also provides an ascribed social status for its young members. In some societies, such as in India, where social mobility has historically been limited, people continue to be educated, marry, and live out their entire lives within the same social stratum into which they are born. Even in countries like the United States, where social mobility and opportunity are highly valued, a child's initial social class is an important aspect of his or her identity and is one of the most important variables in determining educational attainment, the selection of marital partner, place of residence, religious and political preferences, occupation, and even life expectancy. As the saying goes, "It's easier to climb the ladder of success if your parents own the ladder."

Parents and older siblings also play a key part in early sex-role socialization. In the United States, often the infant's bedroom is decorated according to whether the baby is a

SITUATED SELF
The self that emerges in a particular situation.

AGENTS OF SOCIALIZATION
Those groups and institutions that both informally and formally take on the task of socialization.

boy or a girl, and clothing and toys deemed appropriate to the child's gender are chosen. As the child develops a sense of self, same-sex parents and siblings serve as important role models for gender identity (Berryman-Fink et al., 1993; Bryant and Check, 2000; Marshall, 2003).

In less complex societies, parents play an even more important role in sex-role development. For example, whereas the average American infant under the age of 6 months spends approximately 20 percent of his or her time in close contact with his or her mother, among the Ju/'hoansi (formerly referred to as the !Kung) of South Africa's Kalahari Desert, infants spend about 70 percent of their time in close contact with their mothers. From birth, Ju/'hoansi girls spend almost all of their waking hours with their mothers, initially mimicking their actions and behaviors and later assuming many of the tasks they will be expected to perform as wives and mothers. Ju/'hoansi boys spend their infancy (at least while nursing) with their mothers, but as soon as they are old enough they begin to imitate their fathers and to learn the skills they will need as Ju/'hoansi men (Haviland, 2005).

FIGURE 4.2
MAJOR AGENTS OF SOCIALIZATION

School · Family · Religion · The Self · Peers · Media · Workplace

Socialization within the family is not a one-way street. As parents and older siblings are socializing younger family members, they are simultaneously being socialized themselves. Harriet Rheingold (1969) contended that human infants are social by nature and that socialization is always a mutual process. She believes that during the first months of life babies socialize others more than they are socialized. She pointed out that the birth of a baby affects all other family members, who must learn to modify their routines and needs to fit those of the baby. Rheingold suggested that an infant's cry is an important social signal. It is the first way the child learns to communicate with others and to exert some control over the environment. Parents learn to distinguish cries of hunger from cries of pain and discomfort. The child also learns that crying is a way to manipulate others. Similarly, a baby uses a smile as a social signal to indicate recognition, comfort, or pleasure. Babies soon discover that through crying and smiling they can significantly control the behavior of others. Anyone who doubts Rheingold's thesis need spend only a few minutes in a household with a baby to test its validity.

As children develop and progress through adolescence, their contributions to the socialization of other family members, especially their parents, become even more obvious. One of the authors was reminded of this when his teenage son, who had just received permission to spend a week with a friend, said to his 10-year-old sister, "Don't worry, Sis, by the time you become a teenager, I'll have Mom and Dad completely trained."

The School

The second major agent of socialization encountered by most children is the school. All societies have an institutionalized process for teaching important knowledge to new generations. It may involve youngsters sitting at the feet of the eldest and wisest tribal member while he or she provides them with an oral history of their cultural traditions, or it may involve a complex bureaucracy that includes preschools, kindergartens, elementary and secondary schools, community colleges, universities, and graduate and professional schools.

The school's primary charge in the socialization process is the transmission of the cognitive aspects of culture (i.e., knowledge and ideas) from one generation to another and preparation for assuming future roles. In a preindustrial society such as the Mbuti of the Democratic Republic of the Congo, education is informal and often takes the form of games. Men and women are equally involved in teaching children the hunting and gathering skills necessary for individual and group survival. The *bopi,* a large playground in the village, is set aside for play but also becomes a training ground where adults pretend to be wild animals that the children must learn to drive into nets, capture, and pretend to kill and prepare for consumption. Adults also encourage the children to play house, mimicking adult domestic roles they will be expected to fulfill after reaching puberty (Turnbull, 1983).

In an industrial society like the United States, education is formalized and highly structured. Language and mathematical skills as well as scientific and technological knowledge are taught. The culture's art, music, literature, and history are also usually considered essential.

The school's role in socialization is not limited to the "three R's"—readin', 'ritin', and 'rithmetic. Usually the school attempts to teach at least two other R's: right and 'rong. It is this second area, the teaching of the normative aspects of culture, that is most controversial. Some resent the "hidden curriculum" of the school and believe that the school should limit its socialization efforts to teaching academic skills and knowledge, leaving the teaching of values and beliefs to the family and church. Others argue that the school has an obligation to socialize young people into the roles of "good and productive citizens," believing that intellectual knowledge should be supplemented with the teaching of values, ethics, and morality. Moreover, some research indicates that moral intervention with effective communication enhances social cognitive growth as well as moral development (Santilli and Hudson, 1992). This is not much of an issue in small, homogeneous societies such as the Mbuti, where there is widespread consensus on norms, values, attitudes, and beliefs. In large, complex, heterogeneous societies such as the United States, however, the question of whose norms, values, and beliefs will be taught becomes important.

Beyond teaching culture, the school also plays an important role in the development of social identity. Whether a student is viewed as "gifted" or "dumb," "good" or "bad," "cooperative" or "a troublemaker" influences his or her sense of self. Jonathan Kozol (1967) described what he called "the destruction of the hearts and minds" of black children who were subjected to the racial prejudice and discrimination of teachers and administrators in the Boston public schools during the 1960s. The children were labeled "dumb," "dirty," and "failures"; their self-esteem was crushed; and they followed a self-fulfilling prophecy of illiteracy, truancy, and vandalism, eventually dropping out of school in large numbers.

In a country like the United States, socialization experienced within the family tends to result in a more diverse population; the public school experience contributes to uniformity. Because of the school's bureaucratic structure, much individuality must be sacrificed. Students learn that to be successful they must conform to a fairly rigid set of rules, guidelines, and expectations. Harry Gracey (1977) said kindergartens are "academic boot camps," where the primary goal is to teach young children the student role. Today, many children learn that role in preschool. The educational experience is supposed to develop intellectual skills, creativity, and the ability to think critically. Unfortunately, as most college students know, much of the socialization experienced in school emphasizes conformity, unquestioned obedience, and successfully "playing the game." A sign on a college professor's door that reads, "Question

This mother reads to her preschool-age daughter every evening.

How can socialization at home complement socialization at school? Can socialization at home also conflict with socialization at school?

Authority—But Raise Your Hand First," summarizes the paradox in American higher education.

Religion

Not all societies have organized churches, but all have institutionalized religious practices. Functionalists point out that an important role of religion is to contribute to the socialization of societal members by instilling in them a sense of purpose in life and providing them with moral instruction. This function is so important that according to anthropologists, over the past 100,000 years no group of people anywhere on earth have been found that did not practice some form of religion (Haviland, 2005).

One outcome of religious socialization is the development of a *lifetheme,* an overriding way of viewing and interpreting the world (McNeil, 1969). The teachings of the church may influence eating habits, dating practices, mate selection, birth control practices, funeral customs, and many other elements of lifestyle. For example, the powerful influence of religious socialization on developing a lifetheme can be found among the Old Order Amish (see Focus box 4.1). While the family serves as the primary socialization agent in Amish communities, their religious beliefs permeate every aspect of everyday life.

Consider the pronounced differences in values, beliefs, attitudes, behaviors, and lifestyles of "born-again" Christians, the Old Order Amish, Orthodox Jews, Roman Catholics, Muslims, Buddhists, and members of other religious groups. Clearly many of these differences are directly attributable to the socialization provided by religious institutions. Most families hope the church will help reinforce the socialization children receive at home, and religious leaders generally assume the family will provide socialization in harmony with the teachings of the church. Both institutions hope to shape children's values, attitudes, and beliefs before they form peer groups, which exert tremendous influence over the socialization process.

Peers

A child's first peer group is made up of children of roughly the same age who live in the same village or neighborhood or attend the same day-care center. In small hunting and gathering societies, a child's peer group remains fairly stable throughout life and often consists of people related to him or her by blood or by marriage. In industrialized nations, however, when a child enters school, the peer group expands markedly, as does the influence of those peers on the child's personality and behavior. Peer influence is most pronounced during adolescence. No longer children but not yet adults, youths at this stage band together to achieve a meaningful sense of social identity.

The peer group is unique as a socializing agent. Parents and older siblings, teachers and school administrators, and church officials and religious leaders all have more power than those they are attempting to socialize. Peers, however, are relatively equal in social status and have no recognized authority to sanction behavior. Also, the peer group is a voluntary association, usually the first one experienced by children. Thus youths have the option of leaving their peer group, unlike their family or their school, at any time. Nevertheless in the United States, peers, especially during adolescence, often emerge as the most powerful among the major agents of socialization. Fear of losing friends is a strong element of social control because people tend to evaluate themselves on the basis of the number of friends they have (Feld, 1991).

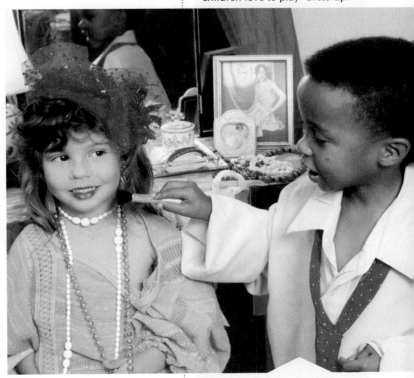

Children love to play "dress-up."

How does the game of dress-up contribute to anticipatory socialization?

Religious socialization has been an important and powerful influence on human behavior throughout history. The Old Order Amish are a conservative religious sect that live in small rural communities primarily along the Ohio River Valley in Pennsylvania but also in 23 other states. At the core of Amish socialization are strong religious beliefs that focus on living a plain, simple life. Religion is such a central theme of Amish socialization that they hold worship services in their homes rather than separate church buildings. This practice symbolically emphasizes the important connection between church and family and reinforces the idea that religion is lived every day, not practiced once a week in a special setting. Amish dress, language, modes of transportation, farming practices, and everyday activities reflect this powerful religious socialization.

One of the authors once asked several Amish men whether many of their children were tempted to leave the Amish community when they reached young adulthood. The men were unfamiliar with the sociological term *socialization,* but to a man their answers indicated that it was the intensive socialization experienced by Amish youths at the hands of the family, church, and community that prevented many from leaving the Amish faith. They indicated that although some Amish teenagers succumbed to the temptation to go to town, drive cars, drink alcohol, and date non-Amish peers, they soon discovered they did not "fit" with the outside world. More important, most experienced strong feelings of guilt and were anxious to return to a lifestyle that was consistent with their moral upbringing.

As with all people, Amish socialization begins at birth and continues throughout the life course. Amish babies are nurtured by all family members and the entire community. As they grow, Amish children are taught to respect authority, share with others, and enjoy work and that although they live *in* the world they are not *of* the world. This separation from larger society and the importance of family and community are emphasized throughout the socialization process, instilling a feeling of "differentness" that is internalized by virtually all who experience it. Consequently, even during adolescence, when peers are of paramount importance, most Amish children's peer groups are comprised of other Amish youths who have experienced the same powerful socialization and have "accepted being Amish as part of [their] identity" (Hostetler and Huntington, 1971:30).

TAKING A CLOSER LOOK

How does Amish socialization differ from the socialization that you experienced as a child? Would the influence of the Amish family and community change if the Amish used electricity and allowed televisions, radios, and other forms of mass media in their homes? Will the Old Order Amish be able to maintain their boundaries with larger society and survive as separate communities in the twenty-first century? If so, what role will socialization play in their survival?

Source: From John Hostetler. *Amish Society,* 3rd ed. Baltimore: John Hopkins University Press, 1980. John Hostetler and Gertrude Enders Huntington. *Children in Amish Society: Socialization and Community Education.* New York: Holt, Rinehart & Winston, 1971. William E. Thompson. "The Oklahoma Amish: Survival of an Ethnic Subculture." *Ethnicity* 8 (December) 1981:476–487. William E. Thompson. "Old Order Amish in Oklahoma and Kansas: Rural Tradition in Urban Society." *Free Inquiry in Creative Sociology* 12 (May) 1984:39–43.

Peers teach some important attributes that are not taught by the family, school, or church. For example, peers emphasize independence from authority (especially parents and teachers) while simultaneously demanding conformity to peer group standards, and they demand a sense of social cooperation and loyalty. One step in establishing freedom from adult authority is the formation of a youth subculture, which because of mass media extends around the globe, complete with distinctive language, music, dress, grooming, fads, values, and behaviors (Sebald, 1968, 1986; Richards, 1988; Bynum and Thompson, 2007). This subculture does not have to lead to a direct conflict between youths and their parents, teachers, and other adults, although it often strains those relationships. Sebald (1986) found that peers exerted the most powerful influence over social activities such as dating and joining clubs, but youths usually consulted their parents for advice on financial matters and choosing colleges and occupations. Peers have been documented as powerful influences in juvenile delinquency for several decades (Sutherland and Cressey, 1978; Kim and Goto, 2000; Bynum and Thompson, 2007).

There are times when parents, teachers, and the church come into direct conflict with peers in the socialization process. For example, these different agents of socialization often disagree on values and attitudes toward truancy, drinking, taking drugs, listening to rap and heavy metal music, and sexual activity. Adults generally view these activities as serious norm violations, but peers often see them as harmless and may encourage participation in them. Research indicates that much of what constitutes delinquency among middle-class adolescents may be largely attributable to the importance of belonging to and identifying with the youth subculture (Bynum and Thompson, 2008).

The Workplace

The workplace provides an important arena for the socialization of adults. This is usually the case in industrialized nations and is especially true in the United States, where a person's occupation becomes an integral part of his or her personal and social identity. One of the authors was struck by how differently occupations are viewed in Great Britain, when riding on a train through Wales engaged in idle conversation with a distinguished-looking Englishman who appeared to be in his late forties or early fifties. When the author asked the gentleman, "What do you do?" he was surprised at the answer: "I like to read, collect stamps, and ride my bicycle." Noting the perplexed look on the author's face, the gentleman then responded, "Oh, I'm sorry, you mean my occupation . . . I work for a publishing company." Unlike in the United States, the British do not equate their occupation with "what they do." More important, they do not equate their occupation with "who they are." We discuss work and its impact on identity more thoroughly in Chapter 17.

In the United States, much of our anticipatory socialization as children and young adults is oriented toward preparing us to assume work and occupational roles. Once we enter the workplace, a more specific socialization into occupational roles occurs. The socialization process usually follows two lines. First, formal socialization by supervisors teaches us the policies, rules and regulations, and perhaps the technical skills needed to complete the assigned work successfully; second, informal socialization by co-workers teaches us the "unofficial rules" we must abide by to be accepted by our peers on the job (Hughes, 1958; Ritzer, 1977). Have you ever experienced these contradictory socialization experiences when the boss informed you of the proper way to perform your job, only to have a co-worker come by later and show you a totally different way of doing it? How did you respond? In the long run, do you think most employees follow the formal or the informal socialization most faithfully?

While socialization into a work role may take place at a college or training program, when individuals enter the workplace they experience additional socialization by those with whom they work. Research shows that effective socialization into a group has an important impact on the level of commitment to that group (Hellman and McMillin, 1994). Most employers realize that the socialization of employees as they enter the workplace is important, and research indicates that employees may view training and socialization as even more important than do their employers (Jacobs et al., 1996). Sometimes this necessitates the shedding of former attitudes, values, beliefs, and behaviors, and socialization into almost an entirely new identity. We address this topic later in this chapter when we discuss desocialization and resocialization.

Assuming a work role is an important part of one's social identity and hence is a continuation of the process of developing a self. Work experiences during adolescence have been linked to self-esteem (Steitz and Owen, 1992). There is mounting evidence that socialization experienced in the workplace is important and "has diverse psychological consequences, including effects on intellectual flexibility, self-concept, worldview, and affective states" (Miller, 1988:350). As we have alluded, when adults meet for the first time—especially in the United States—one of the first questions they ask one another is "What do you do?" A person's occupation—doctor, lawyer, garbage collector, police officer, or mortician—affects how he or she is perceived by others and the nature of the interaction that will follow. Similarly, when college students meet, they often ask, "What's your major?" This is essentially the same question, in that it implies, "What occupation do you plan to enter after you graduate?"

THE MASS MEDIA AND TECHNOMEDIA

One of the important goals of socialization is the transmission of culture from one generation to the next. This involves communication, and communication is what the mass media and the technomedia are all about.

Mass Media Newspapers, magazines, radio, television, and movies are important creators, transmitters, and interpreters of culture. They are among the most powerful agents of socialization. You may remember from Table 1.2 that over 98 percent of American households are equipped with televisions and that the average household has between two and three television sets.

The media help tell us who we are and help shape our identities; they give us aspirations and provide us with a means of escape. They also promote traditional cultural values and serve to maintain the status quo. Research shows that in the United States, for example, the major television networks and newsmagazines such as *Time* and *Newsweek* portray the news so as to promote ethnocentrism, social order, rugged individualism, responsible capitalism, and altruistic democracy (Gans, 1979a; Real, 1989).

We are only beginning to understand the influence of the mass media on the socialization process. In a report issued in the 1960s, the National Commission on the Causes and Prevention of Violence concluded that the mass media are powerful agencies of socialization (Stephens, 1994). **Social learning theory** suggests that *much human behavior is learned from modeling others* (Bandura, 1977), and studies show that when children identify strongly with media characters they are influenced by them (Williams et al., 1981; Stephens, 1994; Patterson, 2004). Moreover, research indicates that the mass media, especially television, should not be underestimated as a source of racial, ethnic, and sex-role stereotypes (Williams et al., 1981; Evra, 1990; Stephens, 1994). In short, the media penetrate our daily lives and shape our consciousness. This fact was taken to the point of absurdity in the 1998 movie *The Truman Show,* which starred Jim Carrey as a young man whose entire life took place in a huge artificial studio environment and was broadcast live to a worldwide television audience. Later, the popularity of television shows such as *Survivor* and *Real World* illustrated that Americans could indeed succumb to the voyeurism of watching ordinary people carry out both ordinary and extraordinary routines in front of cameras.

Television has become the single most powerful medium in the world for communicating a standardized message to millions of people in a matter of moments. Its possibilities for socialization are mind-boggling. A 2003 study showed that 73 percent of all American children under the age of 6 watch television and 83 percent used some form of screen media (see Figure 4.3). The Kaiser Foundation found in 2006 that 40 percent of children under the age of 2 watch television daily, and that one-third of all children between the ages of 6 months and 6 years have a television in their bedroom (Churnin, 2006). At the age of 3 or 4, American children often spend 4 to 6 hours a day watching television, and by mid-adolescence they average approximately 25 hours per week, some watching as many as 40 hours in a single week (Hodge and Tripp, 1986; Stephens, 1994; McGinn, 2002; AP Washington, 2003d). This is more time than is spent with any other agent of socialization.

What are the positive and negative aspects of children viewing so much television? Nobody knows for sure because studies show mixed results. It is clear, however, that television has an impact on the socialization process. And research shows that while viewing television in small blocks of time may have little direct impact on behavior, over a long period of time it seems to have a cumulative effect that does influence thinking and

How do you explain the popularity of so-called "reality shows" such as *Dancing with the Stars?* How do shows featuring competitions among celebrities differ from shows like the *Real World, Big Brother*, and others that depict ordinary people participating in day-to-day activities?

SOCIAL LEARNING THEORY
The idea that much human behavior is learned from modeling others.

behavior (Graber, 1993). Educational programs for children, such as *Sesame Street, Blue's Clues,* and *Barney,* help teach children the alphabet, counting, and other skills they will need later in school. These programs have been shown to help teach children to internalize prosocial values and behaviors such as sharing, helping others, cooperation, honesty, and sincerity (Johnston and Ettema, 1986; McGinn, 2002). Children also witness and vicariously experience events on television that may help them cope with similar events in their lives and those of their friends. For example, a number of made-for-television movies and documentaries focus on problems such as teenage suicide, alcoholism, drug abuse, and coping with the death of a loved one.

Television also socializes its viewers to become mass consumers, linking an individual's social identity with the number and type of "things" he or she owns. Children's programming is accompanied by a huge array of commercials aimed at them as young consumers, and the content of many children's programs is so closely linked to consumer products that one researcher called them "program-length commercials" (Englehardt, 1986:75). Of course, not only children are targeted for such socialization by advertisers; specific adult audiences are also targeted. Sports programs are usually sponsored by the makers of athletic equipment and beer, whereas daytime television programs run commercials aimed at women and the unemployed. During the course of any given day, television viewers are bombarded with the necessity to brush after every meal, use deodorant, color their hair, eat high-fiber cereals, and, if unemployed or stuck in a dead-end job, pursue vocational or occupational training.

A Federal Trade Commission investigation found that movie studios, record companies, and video game producers aggressively market their products to children even though they may label them as inappropriate for young audiences (*Washington Post,* 2000). Many adults are concerned about the large amount of violence in the media and its potentially

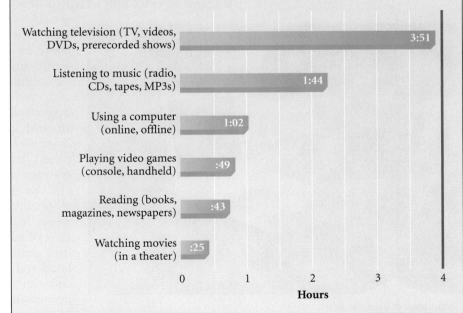

FIGURE 4.3 (A)
CHILDREN'S USE OF TELEVISION, COMPUTERS, AND VIDEO GAMES

Percentage of children 6 and younger who ...

Use any screen media — 83%
Play outside — 83%
Read/are read to — 79%
Listen to music — 79%
Watch TV — 73%
Watch videos/DVDs — 73%
Use a computer — 18%
Play video games — 9%

Percentage (0–100)

FIGURE 4.3 (B)
MEDIA EXPOSURE

A Henry J. Kaiser Family Foundation survey of 2,032 Americans ages 8–18 showed that the average young person spends 6 hours, 21 minutes every day exposed to various forms of media. Amounts of time devoted to the following activities:

Watching television (TV, videos, DVDs, prerecorded shows) — 3:51
Listening to music (radio, CDs, tapes, MP3s) — 1:44
Using a computer (online, offline) — 1:02
Playing video games (console, handheld) — :49
Reading (books, magazines, newspapers) — :43
Watching movies (in a theater) — :25

Hours (0–4)

Note: Due to overlapping media use, these figures cannot be summed. Average times are among all young people, not just those who used a particular media that day.

What impact does such heavy exposure to television, computers, and video games have on early childhood socialization?

THE BABYSITTER...

impact on children. In particular, they fear that watching television violence may encourage violent and aggressive behavior in children (Chapter 7 explores violence in the media and its potential impact on deviant behavior). Studies in the United States, England, and Belgium indeed suggest that viewing television violence may be linked to aggressive behavior in children and adolescents (Bandura and Walters, 1963; Leyens et al., 1975; Belson, 1978; Eron and Huesmann, 1980, 1985; Patterson, 2004). Young males, in particular, may identify with actors playing violent parts, especially if they have no other influential male role models (Stephens, 1994). Advertisers appear to be aware of the potentially negative aspects of violence. Despite sponsoring programs that contain violence, they rarely use violence in their commercials as they do not want their products associated with it (Maguire et al., 2000). Others, however, suggest that viewing television violence may in fact have positive effects, providing a catharsis that allows viewers to vent their aggressions and hostilities by viewing violence on television rather than participating in it themselves (Myers, 1993).

Marie Winn (1977) argued that the content of television programming should not be of as much concern as the amount of television viewed. She said that watching television is a passive activity and a one-way transaction. Thus children are socialized to be passive recipients of information, lulled into an almost hypnotic state, acting much as if they were under the influence of a drug. A study by the American Medical Association found that children who viewed television more than 10 hours per week were more likely to be overweight and slower to learn in school (Springen, 2002). Hodge and Tripp (1986) countered this argument by insisting that children interact with television in much the same way they interact with their toys. These authors contended that children

What impact have the new technomedia had on the socialization of children?

are able to separate fact from fiction and interpret what they see on the screen. They concluded that television socializes children to the dominant norms and values of society and that rather than diminishing their ability to think it provides them with much to think about. Similarly, other research suggests that "television has not seriously constrained children's intellectual achievement and interests [and that] in homes where literacy is prized, television becomes another resource to enhance children's knowledge and critical thinking" (Neuman, 1991:159). A major study conducted at Stanford University concluded that although television may provide children with an erroneous view of adult life and, in some ways, even hasten their entrance into adulthood, children who are loved and respected at home and active in school and with their peers are unlikely to suffer any harm by watching television (Stephens, 1994).

Other forms of mass media also serve as socializing agents. Popular movie stars and entertainers often serve as role models for children and adults, especially in the areas of grooming and dress. Parents are often concerned about their children emulating rock stars such as Pink, 50 Cent, and Eminem, forgetting that their generation did the same thing with Elvis Presley and the Beatles, just as their parents imitated Frank Sinatra and others.

For teenagers, radio and magazines play an important part in the socialization process (see Figure 4.4). Most rock-and-roll stations have disk jockeys who become heroes to their young listeners, even though some of them are fat, bald, and over 40 years old. The banter of these radio celebrities often shapes the specialized language of youths. Similarly, many magazines are aimed at the teenage market. *Seventeen, Teen, Teen Beat, Spin, Glamour,* and others set the trends for dress, grooming, and fads while also offering advice to their young readers about sex, drugs, and getting along with their parents. Research indicates that these publications encourage teens to become consumers by acting as "social mirrors": teens measure their looks and body shapes against ideal cultural standards, and they are encouraged to purchase products to help them reach those standards. At least half the content of magazines is advertising. Some sociologists question whether the print media aimed at adolescents should be so commercially driven, asking whether magazines should acknowledge their role in socialization by helping youths examine values and explore alternatives to materialism and self-indulgence (Evans et al., 1991). And Deborah Tannen (1998) suggests that all forms of media are contributing to an "argument culture" in which getting information becomes more about attacking and winning than about communicating.

Mass media not only have a powerful socializing influence on children and adolescents but also are an important socialization agent for adults. During political elections, voters are influenced by television advertising, especially the visual images portrayed on the screen (Noggle and Kaid, 2000). Advertisers are aware of the powerful influence of television commercials on adults, as billions of dollars are spent each year in an attempt to not only influence purchasing practices but also influence values, attitudes, and beliefs related to consumerism.

Whether the mass media establish cultural norms and values or merely reflect them can be debated ad infinitum. Probably elements of the mass media do both. We are socialized by television, radio, movies, and magazines, and at the same time, through our power as consumers, we influence what appears in and on them. Today, the traditional mass media are being overshadowed by the powerful new forms of technomedia, which not only have changed our ability to communicate but also have transformed the way we think and re-create who we are.

The Technomedia Computers and electronic telecommunications have created what one social observer calls an *electronic republic* (Grossman, 1995). A significant aspect of the electronic republic is a change in how people view society, government, and themselves, and the relationship among the three. The media have undergone a massive transformation that involves computer links, the Internet, MP3 players, and interactive media in the form of cellular phones, personal fax machines, and interactive television, which allow people to interact with one another,

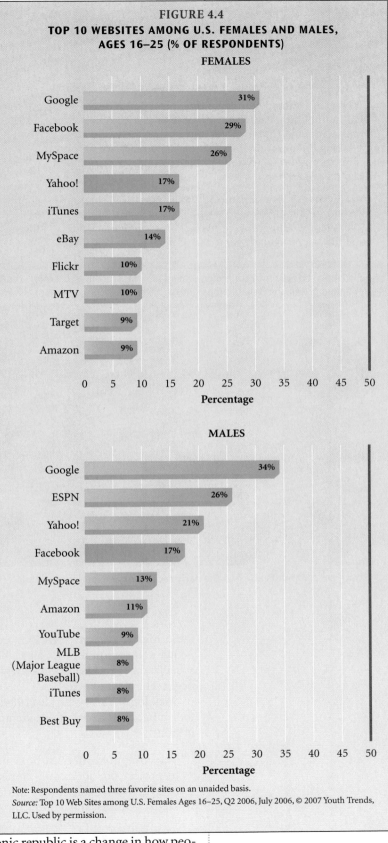

FIGURE 4.4

TOP 10 WEBSITES AMONG U.S. FEMALES AND MALES, AGES 16–25 (% OF RESPONDENTS)

FEMALES

Website	Percentage
Google	31%
Facebook	29%
MySpace	26%
Yahoo!	17%
iTunes	17%
eBay	14%
Flickr	10%
MTV	10%
Target	9%
Amazon	9%

MALES

Website	Percentage
Google	34%
ESPN	26%
Yahoo!	21%
Facebook	17%
MySpace	13%
Amazon	11%
YouTube	9%
MLB (Major League Baseball)	8%
iTunes	8%
Best Buy	8%

Note: Respondents named three favorite sites on an unaided basis.

Source: Top 10 Web Sites among U.S. Females Ages 16–25, Q2 2006, July 2006, © 2007 Youth Trends, LLC. Used by permission.

At what age should babies get their first stuffed toy? How about their first ball? What about their first computer? Parents across the United States and around the world are now asking the question "When is my child ready for his or her first computer?" And some of the answers are startling. A PC data research firm notes,

Already, there's an estimated $30 million software market for children 3 and younger. It's only a small slice of the $500 million youth-software market. But the demand for baby titles—particularly for kids 1½ to 3—is growing faster than any other software segment. (Sandberg, 2000:78)

A study conducted by the Kaiser Family Foundation and Children's Digital Media Centers found that children between the ages of 6 months and 6 years spend approximately 2 hours per day watching television, playing video games, or using a computer (AP, Washington, 2003). That is more time than they spend playing outside and more than three times as long as they spend reading.

These facts pose some interesting sociological questions regarding the usage of computers by young children and what, if any, its impact on the socialization process is. As with most issues related to the technomedia, there are conflicting views. So far, there have been no comprehensive studies on the impact of computing on small children, especially those of preschool age. So much of the information is anecdotal.

Advocates of early computer usage and proponents of baby software contend that in today's technological world, the earlier children get started on computers, the better. They argue that early exposure to computers and the use of the software programs for children help to promote technical literacy and instill confidence and self-

This 2-year-old is using a computer game that helps teach him his colors through a simulated drawing and painting program.

How have computers affected the early socialization experience of toddlers?

radio and television celebrities, government officials, and even computer-simulated people and communities around the globe. The potential impact of technomedia on the socialization process is mind-boggling. Toddlers start using computers before they even begin school (see Focus box 4.2).

Sociologist Sherry Turkle (1984; 1995) notes that the computer is much more than a tool. It becomes a part of our identity, what she calls the *second self*. According to Turkle (1995:9):

The computer offers us both new models of mind and a new medium on which to project our ideas and fantasies. . . . [It] has become even more than tool and mirror: We are able to step through the looking glass. . . . In cyberspace we can talk, exchange ideas, and assume personae of our own creation.

In the world of cyberspace, people create new identities that may be part reality, part fiction, or total fantasy. They operate in MUDs (multiuser domains) with others who are simultaneously creating, re-creating, and revealing their thoughts, ideas, values, and selves—both real and imaginary. During the course of this interaction participants are continually reshaping their concepts of self and, in fact, changing who they are and who they hope to become. What is emerging, Turkle believes, is a new sense of identity—one

assurance. Others say that computers can be every bit as stimulating for children as toys or even books and, because they are interactive, are probably far more stimulating than television. As the mother of a 22-month-old who bought her daughter a computer and the *Sesame Street* CD-ROM, hoping to encourage and develop intellectual skills long before kindergarten, asserted, "[It's] not that I expect her to turn around and start speaking Spanish to me, but it seems a little more educational than cartoons" (Sandberg, 2000:78). Others agree that the computer, computer games, and the Internet are far more intellectually challenging than television and that, whereas television is controlled by adults and children are typically passive observers, in contrast, children, particularly as they get a little bit older, are in control of much of their world on computers and the Internet:

> It is something they do themselves; they are users, and they are active. They do not just observe, they participate. They inquire, discuss, argue, play, shop, critique, investigate, ridicule, fantasize, seek, and inform. (Tapscott, 1998:25)

Observing the trend toward earlier computer use by children, even some babies, some child psychiatrists and early childhood educators are much less supportive. Samuel Meisels, president of Zero to Three, a Washington, D.C., nonprofit group for parents asserts:

> Babies have none of the motor skills. It's unlikely they're even absorbing, because they can't assimilate. The big step for children under 3 is language. To learn it, kids have to interact. Sitting your very young child in front of a computer won't be very helpful, even if you put in a so-called learning program. (Sandberg, 2000:79)

Others emphasize the need for human interaction in early childhood development and see the use of computers and their programs as possibly detrimental, especially to the development of language and other important social skills. Some educators fear that the computer and its software, like television, may help to shorten attention spans and hinder imagination. Many of the computer programs for toddlers are extensions of their television viewing, featuring *Barney, Blue's Clues, Teletubbies,* and other children's television characters. Many experts view these computer programs as no more challenging than simply watching television.

Although there is much debate and disagreement over the pros and cons of computer usage by preschool-age children, especially those under the age of 3, there is one thing upon which almost all child-development experts agree: Early childhood socialization is critical, and the most productive and important socialization occurs when parents and children interact together.

TAKING A CLOSER LOOK

What are some of the potentially positive aspects related to toddlers using computers? What are some of the potentially negative outcomes? Sociologically, how is the increased use of computers, interactive television, and other forms of technomedia likely to affect early childhood socialization?

Source: AP, Washington. "Study: Media Glut Starts Early," *Dallas Morning News,* October 29, 2003. Sandberg, Jared. "Multimedia Childhood," *Newsweek, Special Edition,* Fall/Winter, 2000:78–79. Tapscott, Don. *Growing up Digital: The Rise of the Net Generation,* New York: McGraw-Hill, 1998.

that is decentralized and multiple in nature. As they interact in cyberspace, people create multiple selves, one of which they usually refer to as RL (real life). As one daily computer user noted:

> I split my mind. . . . I just turn on one part of my mind and then another when I go from window to window. . . . RL is just one more window . . . and, it's not usually my best one. (Turkle, 1995:13)

Reality has a whole new meaning as a result of the technomedia. As Turkle (1995:23) notes, "We now not only have to deal with things at *face value, but have learned to take things at interface value.*" This learning is a result of socialization. As one concerned parent notes, "Children's technological abilities far exceed their judgment" (Stone, 1998:74). Consequently, parents, who often are less computer literate than their children are faced with problems of regulation, supervision, and control of Internet use. Social psychologists note that evolving technologies may discourage social interaction and encourage isolation by reducing peoples' interdependence. Children often play games with computers instead of siblings or friends, and many adults have found it more productive to work at home than in an office with all of its distractions. What impact do you think the technomedia are having on socialization? How have they affected your social identity? If the media have indeed become "the central nervous system of modern society" (Real, 1989:13), then their impact, especially the effect of the new technomedia on socialization throughout the entire life course, certainly warrants more sociological investigation.

SOCIALIZATION AND THE LIFE COURSE

Socialization is a lifelong process. Sociologist Arnold Van Gennep ([1908] 1960) was one of the first to explain the **life course** as *a process in which individuals move from one biological and social stage to another as they grow and develop.* He pointed out that life can be seen as a kind of journey in which people pass through a series of stages that involve social and psychological transitions as well as biological and physiological changes. The interaction of these social, cultural, physical, and psychological aspects shapes the life course of individuals (Clausen, 1991). Most societies celebrate **rites of passage,** which are *ceremonies that symbolically acknowledge transitions from one life stage to another.* For example, baptismal ceremonies, bar mitzvahs, weddings, and funerals are rites of passage that denote important transitions in people's lives. Socialization teaches us the normative expectations associated with each life stage and prepares us for entry into the next stage.

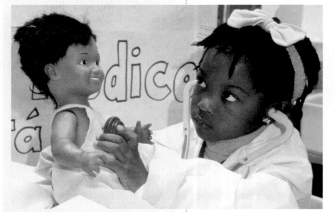

This 4-year-old girl takes on the role of doctor with her doll.

Where did this child learn to play the role of doctor? What American values and norms are reflected by this young girl's play?

Socialization in Childhood and Adolescence

Early childhood socialization involves a complex process through which children form important attachments, or bonds, with their parents, while simultaneously developing a concept of self that is separate and apart from them. As discussed earlier, the first 2 to 3 years of a child's life are critical for both physical and social development. Despite over 100 years of so-called expert advice on raising children, little of the anxiety and unpredictability of childhood socialization has been relieved (Hulbert, 2003).

Our preliminary discussion of socialization and the works of Mead and Cooley focused on **primary socialization,** *the learning of human characteristics and behaviors and the development of a concept of self.* Beginning at birth and extending through childhood, primary socialization is important because it provides the foundation for our personality and the development of our social selves, which influence our behavior throughout our lives. It also teaches us some of the basic norms, values, and behavioral expectations of our culture.

Role Taking: Significant and Generalized Others Mead believed that the most important outcome of socialization was **role taking,** *the ability to anticipate what others expect of us, and to act accordingly.* According to Mead, role taking develops in stages over a period of time. These stages are not based on biology or physical maturity as much as they are related to the extent of one's social experience. During childhood, because our social interaction is limited, we first learn to respond to **significant others,** *specific people with whom we interact and whose response has meaning for us,* such as parents, siblings, and perhaps a few close playmates. As our social world expands, we learn to anticipate and internalize the expectations of **generalized others,** *the dominant attitudes and expectations of most members of society.* It does not matter that we have not interacted with all of these people, for that is no longer necessary. Rather, we have conceptualized our place in the social world and base our actions on how we think they will be received by others.

Stages of Social Development Mead outlined three developmental stages involved in the process of learning roles (see Figure 4.5). Stage 1, the *imitative stage,* is a period when children mimic the behaviors of others. During this stage, little children

LIFE COURSE
A process in which individuals move from one biological and social stage to another as they grow and develop.

RITES OF PASSAGE
Ceremonies that symbolically acknowledge transitions from one life stage to another.

PRIMARY SOCIALIZATION
The learning of human characteristics and behaviors and the development of a concept of self.

ROLE TAKING
The ability to anticipate what others expect of us, and to act accordingly.

SIGNIFICANT OTHERS
Specific people with whom we interact and whose response has meaning for us.

GENERALIZED OTHERS
The dominant attitudes and expectations of most members of society.

often imitate their parents or older brothers or sisters. Stage 2 is the *play stage,* in which children begin to play at the roles of specific other people. Elementary school-age children often come home and line up their dolls and stuffed animals, assume the role of teacher, and "teach" the toys how to say the alphabet or how to count to ten. The play stage is the beginning of **anticipatory socialization,** which involves *learning designed to prepare an individual for the fulfillment of future statuses and roles.* Stage 3, which Mead called the *game stage,* involves the assumption of different roles (often as part of an organized game). For example, a child who plays on a soccer team not only must understand his or her position as forward but also must understand the role expectations of halfbacks, fullbacks, the goalie, and other players. The game also demands an understanding of the rules and the roles played by coaches, officials, and others connected with it.

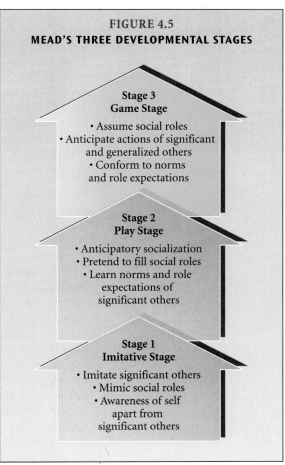

FIGURE 4.5
MEAD'S THREE DEVELOPMENTAL STAGES

Stage 3
Game Stage
• Assume social roles
• Anticipate actions of significant and generalized others
• Conform to norms and role expectations

Stage 2
Play Stage
• Anticipatory socialization
• Pretend to fill social roles
• Learn norms and role expectations of significant others

Stage 1
Imitative Stage
• Imitate significant others
• Mimic social roles
• Awareness of self apart from significant others

Stages of Cognitive and Moral Development Both primary and anticipatory socialization involve the development of the cognitive skills and intellectual abilities necessary to fulfill certain social roles. Jean Piaget (1954) contended that individuals pass through successive stages of cognitive development characterized by different levels of intellectual processes and abilities. In the first stage, the *sensorimotor stage,* the child can experience the world only through the senses. For the first year or two of life, the child's experience of the world is limited to things he or she can see, touch, taste, smell, and feel. Lawrence Kohlberg (1981) believed this stage also represented a "preconventional level" of moral reasoning at which judgments about "right" and "wrong" are pretty much a matter of expediency, based on whatever the child desires at a particular time.

By age 2, most children have moved into the *preoperational stage,* which lasts until about age 7. In this stage, children are inquisitive and begin developing the necessary cognitive and language skills for reading, mathematics, and other intellectual activities. In the *concrete operational stage,* roughly ages 7 to 12, children can understand their surroundings in about the same way adults do. They lack the ability to understand abstract and hypothetical situations, however, and have not developed critical thinking skills.

The final stage in Piaget's framework, the *formal operational stage,* begins in adolescence and is characterized by the ability to achieve abstract thought. During this stage, important anticipatory socialization occurs that prepares youths for their future roles as spouses, parents, voters, workers, professionals, and community members. Kohlberg (1981) contended that young people in this stage reach a conventional level of moral development, using a much broader set of criteria than just their personal wants or needs to determine what is right or wrong. Kohlberg contended that as adults people enter a *postconventional level* of moral reasoning, where they ponder abstract ethical ideals that allow them to question the status quo, rules and laws, and the existing social structure.

A Comparative Evaluation of the Theories of Stages of Development

Mead's, Piaget's, and Kohlberg's theories of developmental stages share some theoretical assumptions, but there are some important differences among them. All three theorists saw the development of the mind as social in origin. Piaget linked cognitive development to physical development and used fairly discrete age categories to delimit his developmental stages. Kohlberg used similar age-graded criteria as the basis for different stages of moral development.

Mead, on the other hand, divorced his stages from physiology and biology. He did not suggest at what age an individual might move from the imitative stage to the play stage, or from the play stage to the game (role-taking) stage, because he believed age was irrelevant to the process. Rather, Mead viewed the developmental process as purely social. By interacting with others, an individual develops a self; then, as a result

ANTICIPATORY SOCIALIZATION Learning designed to prepare an individual for the fulfillment of future statuses and roles.

of further social experience, he or she learns to see the world through the eyes of others.

As noted earlier, socialization in childhood and adolescence varies from one culture to another. For example, while parents in the United States tend to encourage children to become independent and "stand on their own two feet," Japanese parents emphasize dependence on parents and the family throughout childhood and adolescence (Lebra, 1994). How do these two contrasting views reflect and reinforce the different cultural values of the two countries? In every culture, the socialization process is not confined to childhood and adolescence, but continues throughout the life course.

Adult Socialization

We have discussed developmental stages important to the socialization of infants, children, and adolescents. What about adults? If socialization is indeed a lifelong process, do adults also pass through a series of developmental stages? For the most part, sociologists and psychologists agree that they do.

Erik Erikson: Resolving Crises in Adulthood

As we noted, Kohlberg believed that stages of moral development extended into adulthood, and Mead viewed socialization as a lifelong process. Erik Erikson (1963, 1975) identified three developmental stages in adult life that focus on a series of crises that must be resolved. According to Erikson, during early adulthood—roughly age 20–40—people must contend with conflicts between family life and work. We are socialized to pursue the roles of spouse and parent, yet during the same period we are expected to earn a living and pursue a career. Consequently we are faced with reconciling the conflict between spending time with our spouses and children and establishing a career. In American society, traditional sex-role expectations have made this dilemma particularly pronounced for women (see Chapter 11).

Middle adulthood (about age 40–60) is characterized by conflict between "generativity" and "stagnation." Erikson contended that, on the one hand, adults in this age range are aware that they are getting older and that death is in their future. On the other hand, they may want to feel a sense of rejuvenation. They may change jobs or otherwise pursue some of their youthful ambitions. If unable to do so, they run the risk of becoming depressed and stagnant and of acting much older than their chronological age. Late adulthood, from age 60 on, provides the final challenge of attempting to achieve a sense of integrity and satisfaction with one's life while not sinking into despair over impending death. Erikson contended that during this stage adults tend to wrestle with the conflict between being satisfied with their accomplishments in life and despairing over missed opportunities and "could-have-beens."

Levinson's Developmental Approach to Adult Socialization

Daniel Levinson (1978) and his research associates also applied a developmental approach to the study of adulthood, identifying three distinct stages in the life cycle of an adult: early adulthood, about age 17–45; middle adulthood, roughly age 45–65; and late adulthood, from age 65 on. Focusing most of their interest on men age 35–45—calling this the "midlife decade"—Levinson contended that this period marks one of the most crucial stages of adult development. During this period, a midlife transition occurs that involves important changes in biological and psychological functioning as well as in social status. It marks an important turning point in which individuals reappraise their life goals, assess their accomplishments or failures, and consider the possibilities of a better or worse future. Levinson concluded that it is virtually impossible for a person to go through the midlife transition without experiencing at least a moderate crisis.

Young Adults: Betwixt and Between

Until the beginning of the twenty-first century, 18- to 30-year-olds were ignored by social and behavioral scientists studying socialization. If addressed at all, they were simply considered young adults, and were lumped in with other adult populations. As the new millennium dawned, however, a social phenomenon, too pronounced to be ignored, arose in American society and in other parts of the postindustrial world. More and more young people were graduating high school and refusing to leave home. Enjoying the lack of responsibility and stress associated with parents in a lifestyle they could never afford out on their own. Many went off to college and graduated, only to return home to live with their parents. Sociologists coined terms such as "twixters," "tweens," and "kidults" to describe those who had entered a new life-stage sometimes referred to as "youthhood" or "adultescence"—a period between adolescence and adulthood (Grossman, 2005).

Differing explanations have arisen for this ever-increasing phenomenon. Many concerned, stunned, and even embarrassed parents attribute it to laziness. Why should my grown kids go out and work and pay their own bills when we're willing to do it for them? Researchers suggest the trend may be far more complex than that. Sociologists, psychologists, and economists who study this age group contend that twixters are not growing up because the social and cultural mechanisms that used to turn children into adults have broken down or no longer exist. They argue that growing up is much harder than it used to be and that society no longer provides the social and moral background or the financial wherewithal for young adults to take a meaningful place in the adult world. In short, the socialization process, for whatever reasons, has failed (Grossman, 2005).

Understanding the Gender Dimension

An important criticism of theories of socialization that outline stages of development through childhood, adolescence, and adulthood is that they are based on research conducted almost exclusively on males. As noted in Chapter 2, much of the research conducted in sociology, and science in general, has been conducted *by* males *on* males. Yet the findings and conclusions from these studies often are generalized to all people. This is not always the case, however; Charles Horton Cooley derived much of his concept of looking-glass self by observing his daughters at play.

Nevertheless, sociologists whose research is guided by feminist theory argue that gender is an important but often overlooked variable in the socialization process, because it affects not only personality traits but also how people think (Gilligan, 1982; Gilligan et al., 1989; Thorne, 1993; Marshall, 2003). They contend that the stages of social and psychological development—especially moral development—differ in important ways for males and females. Carol Gilligan's research, for example, shows that males tend to rely on rules and abstract ideals when determining right from wrong—what she called a "justice perspective on morality." Females, on the other hand, develop more of a care and responsibility perspective, preferring to use personal experience and social relationships as important criteria in developing moral judgments about social situations. Unfortunately, and inexcusably, Kohlberg and others have tended to evaluate this type of moral reasoning as inferior to that of males. Conversely, according to some early childhood researchers, "even normal boy behavior has come to be considered pathological in the wake of the feminist movement" (Kantrowitz and Kalb, 1998:56). In either case, the gender dimension of socialization cannot be ignored. While Gilligan's and her students' research focuses on childhood and adolescent socialization, their findings suggest that important gender differences in socialization persist throughout the entire life course.

Gail Sheehy (1976) outlined a set of adult developmental stages for both men and women in *Passages.* Sheehy

Women have a long and proud history in the U.S. military. In Afghanistan, and in the Iraqi wars, women have fulfilled combat roles and have been taken as prisoners of war. All branches of the military struggle today with issues related to basic training and resocialization of women and men for combat.

described the "trying twenties" as a time of making a break from parents, selecting mates, and starting careers—a time of high expectations, hopes, and dreams. The "catch thirties" are the years when bubbles often burst and people realize their mates and jobs are not exactly perfect. This difficult period is characterized by high divorce rates and sudden career changes. The "forlorn forties" follow, when adults enter their midlife crises. Sheehy described these as dangerous years during which the dreams of youth must be reassessed. It is common for men to become dissatisfied with their jobs and to want to stay home; it is a time when women who have not worked outside the home become dissatisfied and want to take jobs. Sheehy focused more on this development stage—especially the social and psychological effects of menopause—in *The Silent Passage* (1993). Next come the "refreshed" (or "resigned") "fifties." Sheehy contended that for those who free themselves from their old roles and embrace life with a renewed sense of purpose, this can be the best stage of life. It may also be a time when people face the fact that they have not accomplished their youthful ambitions and simply resign themselves to the status quo.

Works on adult socialization point out that we spend a great deal of our research and socialization efforts studying children and preparing them for their developmental stages so that they can make successful transitions to adulthood. We do not, however, spend an equivalent amount of time in socializing adults for the developmental stages they will experience. The works described above emphasize the need for **developmental socialization,** *learning better to fulfill the roles we already occupy,* and possibly even **desocialization,** *the "unlearning" of previous normative expectations and roles,* and **resocialization,** *learning a radically different set of norms, attitudes, values, beliefs, and behaviors.*

DESOCIALIZATION AND RESOCIALIZATION

Desocialization requires that an individual discard his or her former self and undergo resocialization in order to acquire a new and different self. The most dramatic examples of desocialization and resocialization take place in the context of **total institutions,** *places where people carry out virtually all of their activities.* Total institutions are cut off from the wider society and hence become a society unto themselves (Goffman, 1961a). Prisons, hospitals, mental hospitals, monasteries, military bases (especially during boot camp), and, to some extent, hospitals and private boarding schools are all examples of total institutions. Focus box 4.3 describes some of the desocialization and resocialization experienced in U.S. Marine Corps boot camp and looks at the important role gender plays in that process.

Total institutions are unique social settings; it is unusual for us to work, play, eat, sleep, and carry out all routine daily behaviors within the context of one social institution. For example, most college students leave their homes to live in residence halls or apartments and then leave these to attend classes in different social environments and may even take part-time jobs. If students go out in the evening, they go to places other than the classrooms or workplaces they inhabit during the day. In other words, their different life activities take place in a variety of social spheres. An inmate in a maximum security prison, however, does not

DEVELOPMENTAL SOCIALIZATION
Learning better to fulfill the roles we already occupy.

DESOCIALIZATION
The "unlearning" of previous normative expectations and roles.

RESOCIALIZATION
Learning a radically different set of norms, attitudes, values, beliefs, and behaviors.

TOTAL INSTITUTIONS
Places where people carry out virtually all of their activities.

DEGRADATION CEREMONY
A process in which an individual is stripped of his or her former self, publicly stigmatized, and assigned a new identity.

Juvenile boot camps have become popular methods of dealing with young criminal offenders in many states as correctional officials hope that the dramatic resocialization will alter values, attitudes, beliefs, and behaviors of the young people who go through the experience.

Not everybody experiences the dramatic impact of reso-cialization, but people who enter total institutions are often "stripped" of their former selves and resocialized in order to ensure conformity to a new and dramatically different role. Sociologists Peter I. Rose, Myron Glazer, and Penina Migdal Glazer described the resocialization experienced by young Marines in boot camp.

The armed forces prepare men and women to develop the physical and emotional attributes necessary to endure hardship, obey orders, promote group solidarity, and acquire the attitudes and skills necessary for war. This preparation requires both the desocialization of recruits, to eradicate their civilian selves, and intensive resocialization into the role of combat-ready military personnel. Thus new recruits are required to leave behind their families, as well as most of their personal possessions and other remnants of their civilian selves.

Rose and his colleagues described a young U.S. Marine Corps recruit's experiences in boot camp:

An initial part of the resocialization began with *depersonalization.* The young men were no longer called by their names. Their possessions were taken away, and a hundred rules or new norms were thrown at them. Merging with the group was stressed, rather than individual identity. Recruits were no longer treated as individuals, but had to speak, look, and act like every other recruit—or else. Uniforms and haircuts were important components of the transformation. To accomplish depersonalization, the men had to do some *unlearning.* It no longer mattered whether a recruit had been a high school baseball star, a talented carpenter, a big man on campus, or his parents' pride and joy. Former roles and

identities simply did not count. The sooner they were forgotten, the better the recruit would get along.

It is not enough, of course, for new recruits simply to abandon their former identities. At the same time, they must forge new identities as U.S. Marines. This involves learning an entirely new set of role definitions and behavioral expectations. After being broken down and physically exhausted, the recruits begin to reconceptualize themselves as stronger than ever, relatively impervious to pain, and able to face virtually any physical challenge with the certainty of success. In addition, a sense of camaraderie with other Marines is forged—an esprit de corps that encourages the willingness to sacrifice for the good of the group and success of the mission.

TAKING A CLOSER LOOK

Why is it so critical for the Marine Corps to desocialize and resocialize its recruits? Notice that the study by Rose and colleagues was conducted at a time when only men experienced the traditional Marine Corps boot camp. How has the increased number of female recruits changed the boot camp experience? Should men and women be trained together? In the twenty-first century, do you think the Marine Corps may need to alter its philosophy and approach to boot camp? What changes might you anticipate or suggest?

Source: Peter I. Rose, Myron Glazer, and Penina Migdal Glazer. "In Controlled Environments: Four Cases of Intensive Resocialization," in Peter I. Rose (ed.), *Socialization and the Life Cycle.* New York: St. Martin's Press, 1979, pp. 323–325. Vicki Allen. "Armed Forces Chiefs Defend Same-Sex Training," Washington (Reuter), online, June 6, 1997.

have this flexibility. He or she lives within the confines of the institution and works, eats, sleeps, and plays there—in short, carries out all day-to-day activities there.

Recognizing the unusual nature of total institutions and the perceived need for total conformity, administrators and staff emphasize the necessity to desocialize individuals from the identities they have developed outside the institution and to resocialize them to the appropriate role identity within the institution. Often, the first step in this process is what sociologists call a **degradation ceremony,** in which *an individual is stripped of his or her former self, publicly stigmatized, and assigned a new identity* (Garfinkel, 1956). An example of the degradation ceremony is the criminal trial, in which accused criminals are publicly charged and convicted and their identities changed from "law-abiding citizens" to "criminals." This is an important step preceding their induction into a correctional facility, which then further strips them of their previous social identities in order to prepare them for socialization into the inmate role. Military boot camps, mental hospitals, some isolated private schools, and other total institutions use similar techniques in their resocialization efforts.

Total resocialization seldom occurs. Despite the adverse circumstances of total institutions, people still play an active role in shaping their identities through interaction with others (Paterniti, 2000). Even prisoners of war who are subjected to systematic brainwashing often resist its effects and maintain a sense of their former identities. Research indicates that people confined in total institutions form an assortment of subcultures that provide alternative social roles. For example, John Irwin (1970) described the social world of convicts in maximum security prisons, indicating that they undergo two resocialization processes simultaneously. They are formally socialized into the inmate role as it is defined by the warden, staff, and guards; at the same time, they are informally socialized into the inmate subculture as it is defined by the other inmates. Not surprisingly, many of the expectations are at odds with one another. For example, in the inmate world some may become "merchants" of contraband on the black market while others become "enforcers" of the inmate codes, both roles that violate official rules and expectations of the prison. Goffman (1961a) described a remarkably similar "inmate subculture" among patients in a mental hospital.

Although they provide the most dramatic examples, total institutions are not the only places where desocialization and resocialization occur. As people change their social statuses, switch roles, or otherwise assume new or different identities, there is almost always some need for "unlearning" old ideas and behaviors and learning the new. For example, when young children leave the family to attend school for the first time, a certain amount of desocialization and resocialization must occur for them to make the transition successfully from the role of son or daughter to that of student.

Likewise, as noted earlier, when students leave school and enter the world of work they must make another important social transition, discarding the role of student to assume the role of employee. Almost all professions contain elements of a subculture and require a certain amount of desocialization and resocialization at the entry level. For example, research shows that medical students must overcome much of their previous socialization about the human body if they are successfully to assume the role of physician (Smith and Kleinman, 1989). A particular problem for medical students is removing any sexual connotation from physical contact with intimate body parts. This is done by desocializing students from thinking of breasts and genitals as sex organs and resocializing them to think of these body parts as distinct parts of an organism, totally devoid of any sexual implication. One male third-year medical student described how he overcame his uneasiness in giving a young female patient a pelvic exam: "You can't tell what's wrong without looking under the hood. It's different when I'm talking with a patient. But when I'm examining them it's like an automobile engine" (Smith and Kleinman, 1989:61). It also can be seen that this resocialization experience may have unintended consequences, such as promoting the sexism of a male-dominated profession, as is reflected in the medical student's use of an "automobile" metaphor to describe a woman's body.

Finally, it might be argued that in the United States and many other modern nations the changing attitudes toward gender roles over the past several decades may require a certain amount of desocialization and resocialization for those who grew up during the immediate post–World War II era, the 1950s, and 1960s. Traditional notions about what is appropriate for little girls and boys as well as for grown women and men have changed dramatically and require different attitudes, values, beliefs, and behaviors from those which millions of people may have been taught as they were growing up.

These examples illustrate how life experiences within any particular culture may necessitate desocialization and resocialization. But what are the chances that people are going to live their entire lives within the culture in which they were born and socialized? In today's global society people are far more likely than not to travel, work, and live in countries with cultures different from those in which they were socialized. Those who make the most successful adjustment to their new social environments are those who most readily learn and adopt the new customs and norms. This may require discarding some of the attitudes, beliefs, and norms they were originally taught.

Even if people live their entire lives in the same country, state, and city, they are very likely to interact with people from parts of the world whose socialization experiences are as diverse as the people themselves. This, too, requires a certain amount of desocialization and resocialization to attitudes, values, beliefs, and norms if people hope to interact with one another successfully.

Globalization and cultural diversity require a certain amount of desocialization and resocialization as "we" become more like "them" and "they" become more like "us" through the process of social interaction—no matter who "we" and "they" are. The acquisition of additional languages is an example of desocialization and resocialization, as it involves far more than simply learning new words and vocabularies. Understanding a language, especially thinking in another language, requires an understanding and appreciation of the culture that produced it. This is one reason it is generally easier for young children to learn and speak languages than it is for adults, who are often more culture-bound and hence reluctant to change long held attitudes, beliefs, customs, and ways of thinking.

UNDERSTANDING SOCIALIZATION: A COMPARATIVE ANALYSIS

As with most aspects of human behavior, there are a variety of theoretical frameworks for analyzing and understanding socialization. We began this chapter by looking at the nature versus nurture argument and the combined influences of the natural and social sciences on the sociobiological approach to human development. We also looked at how psychologists emphasize personality development whereas sociologists view early childhood socialization and the development of a social self as the key to understanding our personal and social identities. While all sociologists emphasize that socialization is a social process, let's take a brief look at how the three major theoretical perspectives in sociology differ in how they view socialization.

Becoming Human: A Symbolic Interactionist Approach

Perhaps symbolic interaction's major contribution to sociology has been in the area of socialization. Emphasis on microlevel analysis of social interaction, the importance of primary groups, interpretation of meaningful symbols, the development of a social identity, and viewing the self as an object is ideal for analysis of the socialization process. Consequently, much of this chapter has focused on the symbolic interactionist perspective.

As noted earlier, Cooley's looking-glass self, with its insistence that our self-image develops as a result of how we interpret other peoples' impressions of us, provides an important theoretical framework for the interactionist perspective on socialization. Mead built on this framework with his work on the I and the me, significant and generalized others, developmental stages leading to role taking, and the indistinguishable link among mind, self, and society.

While symbolic interactionism dominates the sociological approach to socialization and human development, it is not the only theoretical perspective interested in the process. Structural functionalists view socialization, especially the transmission of culture and internalization of norms, as critical for the overall functioning of a social system.

Perpetuating Society and Culture: A Structural Functionalist Viewpoint

From a functionalist's perspective, socialization serves the important function of reinforcing the social structure, perpetuating society, and transmitting culture from one generation to the next. The socialization process is viewed much like inoculation: members of society are injected with the attitudes, values, beliefs, and norms that will allow them to assume and successfully fulfill the roles of full and productive citizens. Functionalists identify motivation and ability to perform role expectations as one of the basic prerequisites for survival of the social system, and these motivations and abilities are acquired through socialization (Parsons, 1951).

Resocialization is also important from the functionalist perspective, because it serves the critical function of helping an individual abandon a previous role in order to fulfill a

What impact do media celebrities such as Paris Hilton have on the socialization of young girls?

new one. This process is viewed as essential in order to make successful transitions from home to school, school to work, civilian to military life, the "free world" to prison, and so on.

From the functionalist's perspective, a breakdown in socialization leads to a breakdown in the social system. Hence, as we discuss in Chapter 7, functionalists attribute various forms of deviant behavior to inadequate socialization and failure to internalize society's norms. Thus, resocialization is viewed from this perspective as one way to rehabilitate deviants and help ensure society's survival. This differs dramatically from the view of the conflict perspective.

Maintaining Existing Inequalities: The Conflict Perspective

From a conflict perspective, socialization is one of the most powerful and effective tools used by those in power to maintain the status quo and legitimize existing social inequalities. At a very fundamental level, socialization prepares people for class-related roles they will fill throughout their lives. For example, even as children, members of the upper class are socialized for positions of authority and leadership roles. They are trained how to interact among members of the same class as well as how to deal with servants, staff, and members of the lower classes. Similarly, members of the lower class may be socialized from childhood to show deference to those above them in the social hierarchy and may be trained in skills that will increase their opportunities for serving those who are higher on the social ladder.

We noted earlier that stereotypes are often learned through socialization, and the mass media play a powerful role in this capacity. The media promote age, race, and gender stereotypes and socialize people in how to see and act toward the elderly, racial and ethnic minorities, and women. Moreover, they tend to provide a dichotomous view of society that simplifies complex issues into conflicts between right and wrong, good and bad, moral and immoral. In most media scenarios, the side of right, good, and moral eventually prevails. Not coincidentally, the conflict theorists point out, these are almost always represented by those viewed as having legitimate power and authority over others: the government, the police, the rich, and the powerful. Criminals, drug addicts, lunatics, and others who pose a threat to the existing order are often portrayed in the media as coming from the lower social strata, foreign evil empires, or other planets (Parenti, 1992).

The conflict perspective also points out that socialization is not a unidimensional process. Throughout the life course, especially during adolescence, people are bombarded with contradictory and conflicting attitudes, values, beliefs, and behaviors. Most of us remember at some time being told "Do as I say, and not as I do" by someone in authority whom we may have caught violating one of the rules he or she had taught us. We probably all remember being told by our parents, teachers, and religious leaders that certain behaviors were wrong, and perhaps forbidden, only to find that our peer group insisted they were not only okay but also mandatory. Most adolescent boys, for example, are taught that fighting is improper, but they are considered cowards by their peers if they walk away from a fight. Similarly, while teenage girls may be taught that premarital sex is immoral and will ruin their reputation, they realize boys are not held to the same standard and may feel tremendous pressure from both male and female peers to be sexually active in order to be "normal" or enter "adulthood."

Sociologists who use the conflict perspective view resocialization as an example of how those in power attempt to coerce and exploit others and attempt to perpetuate their own authority. Resocialization in total institutions such as the military, prisons, and mental hospitals reaffirms the importance of status hierarchies and obedience to the rules established by those in power. Moreover, they legitimate the status quo by rewarding unquestioned conformity and punishing those who challenge existing authority structures, question social inequalities, or even dare to be different. As we look to the future and anticipate an even more diverse and complex society, these various sociological perspectives become even more important for looking beneath the surface assumptions in the socialization process.

SOCIALIZATION IN THE TWENTY-FIRST CENTURY

The importance of the mass media and technomedia as socializing agents will continue to increase in the twenty-first century as technological advances ease communication with mass audiences around the world. For members of most industrialized and postindustrial nations, television is the primary source of information about the world around them, and the influence of television is increasing in developing countries as well. How interactive television, in which the viewer can participate in television broadcasts, will influence socialization remains to be seen.

Schools have become increasingly dependent on mass media and technomedia for educational purposes. Videotapes, newspapers, magazines, and big-screen televisions hooked to satellite dishes are standard features in many schools today and will become even more commonplace in the future. Schools also have become dependent on computers, which supplement instruction by teachers in many school systems. In the future, computers may become the primary means of instruction and hence major agents of socialization. This aspect of socialization is discussed further in Chapter 14.

The media's impact on the way people think may be one of the most important, relatively untapped areas for future research. For example, the format of television news, which demands short, sensational stories, more suited to sound bites than to complex, thoroughly developed explanations, may socialize viewers to think in disconnected segments, as opposed to grasping the big picture. Moreover, television and other media presentations discourage critical thinking and looking beneath the surface. This area is ripe for more thorough sociological research.

The technomedia may have even more influence on socialization than the traditional mass media throughout the twenty-first century. Children are exposed to computers and other technologies at earlier ages. What changes in socialization do you anticipate as people increasingly interact through cyberspace as opposed to face-to-face? How will the technomedia change our conceptions of self? Will RL (real life) be just one of the many social selves we develop? How do the technomedia affect the way we think? It has been suggested that the widespread use of technomedia may require even more critical thinking for meaningful understanding than do traditional mass media. We are bombarded with thousands of uncontrolled and unstandardized data from almost unlimited sources; to make sense of any of it requires looking beneath the surface and realizing that in the technomedia, more than perhaps anywhere else, things are not necessarily what they seem.

As the demands of work and careers increase, as family structure changes and more women enter the workforce, families are increasingly abdicating their role in their children's socialization to other social groups, agencies, and institutions. Robin Leavitt and Martha Power (1989) opened an important avenue for future research with their study of the impact of day-care centers on children's emotional development. Subsequent studies suggest that day-care centers are just as important as the family and, more important, just as capable of providing primary socialization, teaching verbal skills, and teaching young children to think (*Washington Post,* 1997). Past sociological research on early childhood socialization concentrated on the family; future research must include day-care centers, preschools, and other surrogate family settings.

Another area that demands more attention is sociobiology. The debate over nature versus nurture is being revived by new discoveries about the influence on human behavior of hormones, chromosomes, and genes. New research suggesting that there are physiological differences between the brains of males and females and between heterosexual and homosexual males that may account for differences in behavior has stirred a great deal of controversy and given impetus to additional research in the arena of sociobiology. Discovery of the human genome has provided even more stimulus for sociobiological research.

Sociologists also need to renew their interest in the role of government and nation-states in the socialization of individuals. In the early part of the twentieth century,

Aldous Huxley's novel *Brave New World* and George Orwell's *1984* drew frightening scenarios in which governments of the future intervened at birth and became the only officially recognized agents of socialization. Through technology and the use of sophisticated methods of thought control, the governments indoctrinated citizens with a standardized set of beliefs, ideas, customs, and rules of behavior. The year 1984 passed, and Orwell's literary nightmare was not realized. But technological developments and the potential for government or media intervention in the lives of private citizens now surpass even Huxley's and Orwell's wildest dreams. As governments become increasingly involved in socialization, it will be interesting to see how nations with various political and economic ideologies differ in their approaches to molding individuals in relation to state goals. What do you envision as some of the possibilities for socialization in this area in the future?

Two related questions that sociologists are now exploring promise to provide stimulating debates in the future: To what extent are individuals products of their society? And to what extent should individuals be held responsible for their actions? How would you respond to these two questions? Dennis Wrong (1961) critiqued what he called the "oversocialized" conception of people held by contemporary sociological theory, which implies that humans are the passive recipients of socialization. He argued that basic drives are never fully suppressed by socialization and that the major agents of socialization are far from unanimous and harmonious in their approach to the socialization process. The view of socialization as an inoculation process oversimplifies the diversity of experiences that human beings encounter during their lifetime. This view fails to acknowledge the reciprocal nature of the socialization process and ignores the widespread cultural diversity in our global society. As we have discussed throughout this chapter, human beings are thinking creatures actively involved in their own socialization and that of others. The mass media and technomedia, along with globalization, have transformed our world into a rich mosaic of cultural diversity. Consequently, in the future, socialization becomes an even more important and complex process than ever before.

Summary

1 Socialization is the lifelong process through which individuals internalize culture and develop a personality and sense of social identity. The nature versus nurture debate over explanations of human behavior has proved futile, as sociobiological research indicates that humans are affected by both their genetic potential and the environmental influences that shape their personalities and behaviors. The process of becoming human involves developing a concept of self, which is largely based on our interactions with others.

2 The major socializing agents are the family, schools, religion, peer groups, the workplace, and the mass media and technomedia. All play prominent roles in transmitting culture and influencing personality development and a person's social self.

3 Socialization occurs throughout the life course. Primary socialization occurs in early childhood and teaches us human characteristics as we develop a concept of self. Anticipatory socialization usually occurs during adolescence and young adulthood and prepares us to assume future roles. Developmental socialization helps us better to fulfill the roles we occupy and to make transitions through the various life stages. It is important to understand the role of gender in the socialization process throughout all stages of the life course.

4 Some individuals experience desocialization and resocialization, in which they must shed previously learned attitudes, values, beliefs, and norms to assume a new social identity. This often occurs within the context of a total institution, but in today's global society it may also occur as a result of cultural diversity.

5 The symbolic interactionist perspective emphasizes that socialization is the process by which we become human. This approach focuses on the development of a social self through the course of social interaction. Structural functionalists view socialization as a fundamental way of perpetuating society and transmitting culture from one generation to the next. Sociologists who use the conflict approach agree that socialization perpetuates society, but also point out that it perpetuates and reinforces existing social inequalities and encourages maintenance of the status quo.

6 Sociological research on socialization is shifting its focus from the traditional family to surrogate family settings such as day-care facilities. The role of the mass media and technomedia in socialization is becoming even more prominent, and future research must explore the impact of new technological developments in interactive television and computers on the socialization process. Sociologists in the future should also focus on the government's role in socialization. People are far more than mere products of their society; as thinking beings, people have the ability to make decisions and judgments and consequently are accountable for their behavior.

Key Terms

agents of socialization (p. 88)
anticipatory socialization (p. 101)
degradation ceremony (p. 104)
desocialization (p. 104)
developmental socialization (p. 104)
generalized others (p. 100)
I (p. 87)
life course (p. 100)

looking-glass self (p. 87)
me (p. 87)
nature (p. 84)
nurture (p. 84)
personality (p. 86)
primary socialization (p. 100)
resocialization (p. 104)
rites of passage (p. 100)

role taking (p. 100)
self (p. 86)
significant others (p. 100)
situated self (p. 88)
socialization (p. 84)
social learning theory (p. 94)
sociobiology (p. 85)
total institutions (p. 104)

Chapter 5

Social Interaction in Everyday Life

"You can observe a lot just by watching."
—*Yogi Berra*

Fred's hands perspire as he sits at the keyboard and prepares to type a response to Nina's last correspondence. They have "known" each other for almost 3 months, and what started as a casual acquaintance has blossomed into an important and caring relationship based on common interests, shared humor, mutual understanding, and, most important, love. Fred is ready to pop the big question, but he is nervous—in fact, he's downright afraid. What if she says no? Or, more frightening, what if she says yes?

As a confidence builder, Fred rereads the ad that brought the two of them together: *Attractive, single African American female in early twenties, likes bicycling, body surfing, long walks along the beach on warm moonlit nights seeking young attractive like-minded male for conversation, friendship, and whatever else may develop. I'm a 5-foot 8-inch, 115-pound aerobics instructor who has an open mind and will try almost anything once. If you're interested, meet me poolside at the Cybercity Hotel (nonsmokers only, please). Ask for Naughty Nina.*

How can Fred pose this important question? After all, he hasn't been totally honest with her. He told her that he is vice president of accounting at a major firm but he is only 1 of 40 assistant accountants who work there. They celebrated when he passed the CPA exam a month ago. What will she do when she discovers he was actually so frightened that he didn't even take the exam? Fred hates to admit it, but much of his relationship with Nina is based on deception.

Fred takes a deep breath, summons all his courage, and types: *Nina, I think it is time we meet in person. What do you think? Love, Fred.*

Fred's consternation is nothing compared to the humor produced at the other end when his e-mail is received by Nina. Nina is neither African American nor an aerobics instructor. And although

Nina is indeed 5 feet 8 inches tall, *he* weighs a little over 175 pounds. While Fred may not have taken the CPA exam, "Nina," whose real name is Frank, earned his CPA on his thirty-fifth birthday. He and his wife and two daughters celebrated by going out to dinner that night. That was 32 years ago. Frank, now retired, gets bored, so while his wife watches television, he plays on the computer. For the last three months, he has "surfed the Net" dropping in and out of chat rooms under various pseudonyms, including *Wicked Walt, The Iceman, Lovely Lucy*, and one of his favorites, *Naughty Nina*. To date, "Nina" has received over 300 marriage proposals and more than 1,000 requests for personal meetings, and has provided dozens of hours of "harmless" entertainment for Frank.

There is no race . . . there is no age . . . there is no gender . . . On the World Wide Web, there are only minds . . . (popular television ad for the Internet)

Computers and the Internet have dramatically affected social interaction. Today, people can communicate instantaneously with others in the next room, across the street, across the nation, and across the globe.

What impact has the Internet had on some of the most important sociological variables in interaction such as age, race, sex, and social class?

It's impossible to determine precisely how many people in the United States and around the world have access to personal computers and at some time or another go online to use the Internet; the number changes daily—or, more accurately, by the minute. (See Map 5.1 for per capita Internet connections around the world.) We do know, however, that computers and the World Wide Web have dramatically altered our understanding of the world and how we interact with one another in our everyday lives. Think about the fictitious vignette involving Fred and "Nina." Would such deception have been possible before the use of personal computers? Is the hoax perpetuated by "Nina" harmless fun? What are the possible consequences of such a hoax? Would you even categorize the correspondence between Fred and "Nina" as social interaction?

Sociologists know that age, race, ethnicity, sex, gender, and social class are but a few of the important variables that significantly affect how people interact in our everyday lives. Do these variables come into play when people interact over the Internet? If so, in what ways? Or, as one television advertisement for the Internet declares, is cyberspace a place for interaction where these social characteristics do not matter? These and other questions spring to mind when the vignette is viewed from a sociological perspective. The vignette also illustrates the guiding theme of this book: *things are not necessarily what they seem.* This may be especially true when it comes to social interaction in everyday life.

SOCIAL STRUCTURE

Despite the extraordinary complexity of social life in all contemporary societies, social relations are not random. If you look carefully, you will see that your life and everyone's life has certain patterns of social interaction that are repeated over and over again. Sociologists calls this **social structure**—*the ordered relationships and patterned expectations that guide social interaction*—and it is fundamental to life in all societies.

What would happen if these nearly invisible patterns of interaction were suddenly suspended? The authors discovered the answer when, during a visit to a large publishing company, a tornado alarm sounded. Until the alarm, our interactions with editors, salespersons, and business managers were routine. Bureaucracies, of which the publishing

SOCIAL STRUCTURE
The ordered relationships and patterned expectations that guide social interaction.

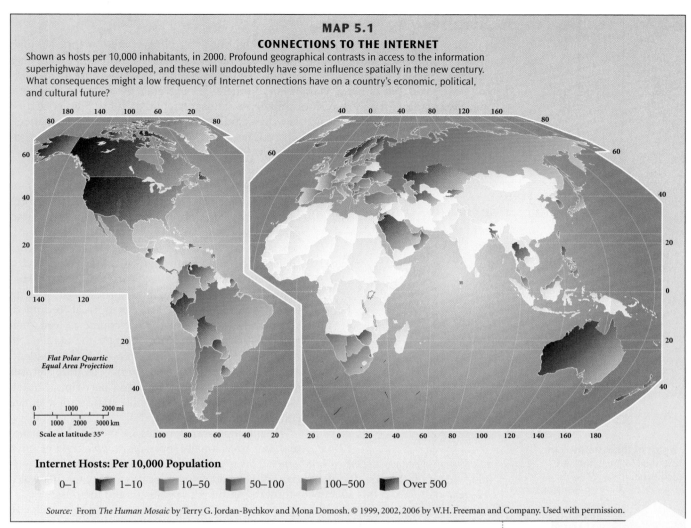

MAP 5.1
CONNECTIONS TO THE INTERNET

Shown as hosts per 10,000 inhabitants, in 2000. Profound geographical contrasts in access to the information superhighway have developed, and these will undoubtedly have some influence spatially in the new century. What consequences might a low frequency of Internet connections have on a country's economic, political, and cultural future?

Flat Polar Quartic Equal Area Projection

Scale at latitude 35°

Internet Hosts: Per 10,000 Population

0–1   1–10   10–50   50–100   100–500   Over 500

Source: From *The Human Mosaic* by Terry G. Jordan-Bychkov and Mona Domosh. © 1999, 2002, 2006 by W.H. Freeman and Company. Used with permission.

Thinking sociologically, how would you explain the dramatically unequal distribution of Internet connections around the globe?

company is one, give the appearance of rigid order, and this allows people to respond to others in predictable ways. We had clear ideas of how we ought to behave in the presence of vice-presidents of the company and how to act in the presence of janitors and cafeteria workers, and they knew how to behave toward visiting professors. That is, until the siren began to roar.

In an instant, the tornado alert shattered the illusion of order. The alarm transformed us from visiting professors, editors, and salespersons to a seamless, faceless crowd. In the tornado drill, we found there were no vice-presidents, professors, cafeteria workers, or janitors. From our vantage point, in fact, there were neither clear-cut roles nor expectations. Someone directed us to the basement, but no one had any idea who this person was. People who a moment earlier were in total command now were confused, and no matter how exalted their rank in the company, all blindly followed orders to proceed to the basement. A senior vice-president asked, "Where are we going? Is this a drill, or the real thing?" No one answered, because no one knew.

When we arrived in the basement, people stood in silence looking at co-workers as if they had never seen them before, each of us looking to others for cues as to which behaviors might be appropriate in the situation. It was apparent that although we were visitors, at that moment we could have taken charge of the situation and a hundred or more employees, including the company president, would have followed our orders. When the alarm ended, though, people returned to their offices and became editors and salespersons, and we again became prospective authors; we resumed our familiar routines as if nothing had happened. As sociologists, it was apparent that once social structure was restored, people assumed their social statuses and roles and went about the routine social interactions of their everyday lives.

115

Statuses

People often use the word *status* to refer to high social standing or prestige (one has high status or possesses status symbols, such as a Mercedes Benz or a Rolex). Sociologists define **status** as *a socially defined position in a social structure.* A status is not an individual possession, but rather a *relationship* to others. For example, the status of mother is socially meaningful only in relationship to the statuses of child or father. Statuses define a multitude of other relationships as well, including those of father-son, doctor-patient, teacher-student, and shopper-merchant. These and other statuses affect the expectations and behaviors of others, a person's social identities, and even one's sense of self.

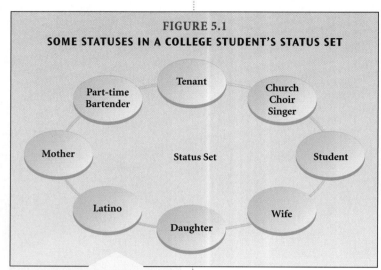

FIGURE 5.1

SOME STATUSES IN A COLLEGE STUDENT'S STATUS SET

Part-time Bartender — Tenant — Church Choir Singer — Mother — Status Set — Student — Latino — Daughter — Wife

Which of these statuses are ascribed? Which ones are achieved?

Status Set Statuses, which may be ranked high or low, determine where a person fits in society. Moreover, every person occupies a variety of statuses and each status has an appropriate social context. Sociologists call *all of the statuses a person has at a given time* that person's **status set.** In the course of a day, a woman may occupy the statuses of mother, Hispanic, friend, shopper, and attorney. The statuses that people occupy change not only according to social context, but over the life course as well. As a young person, a child may occupy the statuses of daughter, girl scout, soccer player, ballet student, and 4-H leader. In college, she may assume statuses such as college student, wife, and part-time worker. Figure 5.1 depicts some possible statuses of a female college student.

Usually a person's statuses are more or less consistent, but occasionally *a person occupies two or more statuses that society deems contradictory.* This is called **status inconsistency.** For example, what if on the first day of class you discovered your college sociology teacher was a 12-year-old? Would this affect your thinking about your professor and the class?

Ascribed and Achieved Statuses Every society limits access to statuses. **Ascribed statuses** are *statuses assigned to individuals without reference to their abilities or efforts,* such as age, gender, race, ethnicity, and family background. Although these statuses influence how a person is defined, they allow the individual few options or choices. Being born a member of the British Royal Family entitles one to a number of highly ranked social positions should he or she desire to claim them. On the other hand, being born poor, black, and a Haitian refugee places severe limits on one's chances of securing valued statuses.

Some societies allocate a great many statuses on the basis of ascription. For example, in the traditional Indian caste system, family background determined one's occupation, marriage choice, neighborhood, political affiliation, and most statuses a person could claim during life. By contrast, modern industrial societies favor more competitive access to social positions.

Achieved statuses are *statuses secured through effort and ability.* College coach, church member, spouse, janitor, priest, juvenile delinquent, and fashion model are all examples of achieved statuses—statuses usually gained by education and training.

In all societies, a person's ascribed statuses influence those statuses he or she might achieve. For example, gender, age, and race have either restricted or boosted a person's opportunities of gaining entry to a college, country club, job, or the position of President of the United States.

Master Statuses

Often, a particular status in an individual's status set dominates the thinking of others. This status is called a **master status,** *a status that dominates all other statuses.* It defines who that person is and his or her limitations and opportunities. Sometimes a person's master status is revealed by self-definition. For example, if

STATUS
A socially defined position in a social structure.

STATUS SET
All of the statuses a person has at a given time.

STATUS INCONSISTENCY
Two or more statuses that a society deems contradictory.

ASCRIBED STATUSES
Statuses assigned to individuals without reference to their abilities or efforts.

ACHIEVED STATUSES
Statuses secured through effort and ability.

MASTER STATUS
A status that dominates all other statuses.

you ask a boy who he is, he will usually respond by noting his age and sex ("I am a 6-year-old boy"). Most people in college describe themselves as students, and the master status of most adult Americans is their occupation. Occupation is so important that many years after retirement, people continue to define themselves and others in terms of their former occupations—ex-professor, ex-nurse, or ex-auto worker. Likewise, students often identify themselves by their academic major—which identifies their future occupation.

Because rather strong expectations are attached to a person's master status, they may have either positive or negative consequences. For example, those with a master status of surgeon or bank president, gain access to many other social positions. That is, by virtue of their master statuses, surgeons and bank presidents may be asked to become church elders, members of the Rotary Club, girl scout troop leaders, and so on. By contrast, those with master statuses that are negatively labeled may be denied access to many social situations.

For example, the master status of judge is highly regarded. A judge convicted of or even accused of child molestation, however, is a child molester, a master status with severe social limitations. Likewise, no matter what other statuses they may occupy, people with the status of ex-convict are usually labeled ex-convicts—ex-convict painters, ex-convict fathers, and ex-convict neighbors—and this master status denies them many opportunities. This is not always the case, however. Increasingly, in contemporary industrial societies deviant identities, such as "former substance abuser," are being transformed into what J. David Brown (1991:219) called "professional ex-s," who capitalize on a deviant past by transforming it from a liability to an occupational asset—in this case, for example, substance abuse counselors. The concept of master status is further developed in Chapter 7.

O.J. Simpson's master status has changed over the years from Heisman Trophy winner, to Pro Bowl running back, to football Hall of Famer, and to movie and television celebrity.

What would you say is O.J.'s master status today?

Roles

A status is a social category and as such is somewhat fixed. Roles, which are dynamic, bring statuses to life. As Ralph Linton (1936) put it, we *occupy* statuses, but we *play* roles. A **role** is *a set of expectations, rights, and duties that are attached to a particular status.* Some sociologists use the metaphor of the theater to describe how roles influence social life (this is discussed later in this chapter in more detail). Like actors on a stage, all of us play roles in our daily lives—sons, friends, pizza deliverers, students, sorority sisters, and a multitude of other roles. Attached to each role is a script that tells us how we should behave toward others and how they should act toward us. But, as noted earlier, social life is far more complex than any stage, and in most roles people are allowed considerable latitude in how they interpret their "scripts."

Without roles, human social life would be almost impossible, for roles guide our interactions in virtually every social situation. Roles simplify the process of interaction because we do not have to base our actions on the unique personality of each individual with whom we interact. Rather, we respond to their roles, and they respond to ours. For example, in the role of traveler, when we arrive at a toll booth we have a duty to give the attendant the proper toll, and he or she is obligated to receive it and allow us to proceed. Think of what it would be like to travel if there were no clear guidelines in this one social arena, and we could never be sure how a particular toll booth operator might behave. With such uncertainty, we would make every effort to avoid toll roads altogether. Today, most toll roads are even more predictable, using automated toll booths, eliminating the need for social interaction altogether.

ROLE
A set of expectations, rights, and duties that are attached to a particular status.

Actors and Their Roles Although expectations are attached to roles, the *role performance,* or how each occupant of a status fulfills his or her role, may vary widely. One reason is that people's emotional commitment to and identification with roles may vary. A college athlete, for example, may never miss tennis or basketball practice but cut classes because he or she considers the student role to be of minor importance. Another reason role performance varies is that role expectations are usually flexible enough for individual interpretation. Some roles, for example the role of Buckingham Palace guard, allow a narrow range of individual expression. By contrast, artists are expected to be creative and as a result are given great latitude in how they behave. This too is restrictive, however, in that artists must be creative to be judged competent in the role. Focus box 5.1 examines a classic experiment in role playing that involved students "playing" the roles of prisoners and guards.

Most roles constrain certain behaviors but allow freedom of expression in others. For example, all toll booth operators must collect money, but expectations concerning their other behaviors are less clearly defined. Some are polite and cheerful; others are curt and abrasive. Although fast-food chains make an effort to standardize employee roles and minimize elements of personality as well as regional, class, and ethnic influences on role performances, they have not been entirely successful. This is because during interaction people evaluate their performances by imagining how others view them, and adjust their behavior accordingly. This process, called *role taking,* gives the individual some influence in how a role is defined.

Role performance also may be affected by our knowledge of a role. The expectations for some roles, for example the roles of daughter and student, are widely understood. The expectations for many other roles, however, are ambiguous or unclear. Do you sometimes occupy roles that you play so rarely that you are uncertain how they should be played? How does this make you feel?

Some roles are entered into or discarded with little effort or commitment. At other times, in cases of **role distance,** *people play a role but remain detached from it to avoid any negative aspects of the role.* Erving Goffman used the example of adults riding a merry-go-round with their children to describe role distance. According to Goffman (1961b), because their adult role might be threatened if they appeared to enjoy the ride, adults express their detachment by exaggerating the performance of merry-go-round rider, or by acting bored and disinterested. How might students use role distance in the classroom? Might professors, too, sometimes use role distance during class? Can you think of other social situations that might require role distance? How about at a fast-food restaurant?

Role embracement occurs *when a person's sense of identity is partially influenced by a role.* Sometimes **role merger** occurs when *a role becomes central to a person's identity and the person literally becomes the role he or she is playing.* For example, one of the authors had a friend who fully embraced the role of business owner, so much so that the role influenced his relations with friends, his children, and even his wife. One day after work he returned home and found his house untidy, so he demanded that his wife treat the home like a warehouse. His wife's reply was, "I'm a wife, not one of your employees, and this is our home and not a warehouse!"

Role Sets People try to fulfill their roles as they understand them, but role performances also are influenced by the fact that *multiple roles are attached to almost every status,* which sociologists call a **role set.** Figure 5.2 shows linkages among a person's status set and role set.

The student role, for example, includes all of the patterned expectations of all people with whom the student interacts. The role set of a student includes rights and duties toward professors, classmates, roommates, friends, parents, employers, and many others in reciprocal roles. In everyday interaction, we play many roles simultaneously. Sometimes we move from role to role with relative ease. For example, during a conversation with a fellow student, do you sometimes shift from the role of classmate, to friend, to roommate in a matter of seconds based on the context of the conversation? Not all roles, however, are logically consistent.

Role Strain and Role Conflict In cases of **role strain,** there are *contradictory expectations and demands attached to a single role,* which is quite common in everyday

---

ROLE DISTANCE
When people play a role but remain detached from it to avoid any negative aspects of the role.

ROLE EMBRACEMENT
When a person's sense of identity is partially influenced by a role.

ROLE MERGER
When a role becomes central to a person's identity and the person literally becomes the role he or she is playing.

ROLE SET
Multiple roles that are attached to almost every status.

ROLE STRAIN
Contradictory expectations and demands attached to a single role.

ROLE CONFLICT
When a person cannot fulfill the roles of one status without violating those of another.

Experiments in role playing rarely generate much controversy, but there is one major exception in the annals of social psychology: Philip Zimbardo's notorious experiment on how roles affect prison behavior. During the early 1970s, in an attempt to understand what it means to be a prisoner or a prison guard, Zimbardo and his Stanford University colleagues screened over 70 volunteers who had answered an ad in a Palo Alto newspaper. They ended up with about two dozen young men whom they described as mature, emotionally stable, normal, intelligent, middle-class students from the United States and Canada—"the cream of the crop of this generation."

Half were arbitrarily designated as prisoners by a flip of the coin; the others became guards in the experiment's simulated prison. Researchers told the "guards" about the seriousness and danger of the situation and recommended that they create their own formal rules to maintain law, order, and respect during their 8-hour, 3-man shifts. The "prisoners" were picked up at their homes by a city police officer in a squad car; they were searched, handcuffed, fingerprinted, booked at the Palo Alto station house, and taken blindfolded to the simulated jail. There they were stripped, deloused, put into a uniform, given a number, and placed, along with two other prisoners, into a cell that was to be their home for the next two weeks.

How did the experiment fare? Zimbardo had to discontinue the experiment after only 6 days because of the frightening behavior of the mock prisoners and guards. The students could no longer clearly distinguish where reality ended and their experimental roles began. Dramatic changes occurred in the thinking and behavior of virtually every subject. In less than a week, "self concepts were challenged and the ugliest, most base, pathological side of human nature surfaced," wrote Zimbardo. The entire research team was horrified because the "guards" treated the "inmates" as if they were less than human; correspondingly, the "prisoners" acted like "servile, dehumanized robots who thought only of escape, of their own individual survival, and of their mounting hatred for the guards."

TAKING A CLOSER LOOK

Zimbardo's study seems to suggest that there is a fundamental "pathology of imprisonment" that impacts on roles. In everyday life, are prisoners and guards antagonistic—as mainstream media cop shows would have us believe? Or are they generally cooperative, with the members of each group performing their roles with a great deal of "face work," each cooperating to make the system work? If Zimbardo's experiment was a true reflection of how guards and prisoners actually interact in prisons around the country, do you think prisons could work?

Is it possible the experiment might have had different results had guards and prisoners been not white men, but women, Latinos, or members of another minority group? Substitute one of these groups and describe how you think gender, ethnicity, or some other social factor could have produced different results.

Source: From Philip Zimbardo. "Pathology of Imprisonment," *Society 9* (April) 1972:4–8.

life. The student role offers a good example, for it includes numerous expectations that pull students in opposite directions. Professors expect students to study, but when friends visit they expect students to put away their books and talk or go out for fun. Your roommate may expect you to remain on campus during the weekend while your parents demand that you return home. In the course of our everyday interactions, all of us must make such difficult choices.

Role conflict occurs *when a person cannot fulfill the roles of one status without violating those of another.* Television dramas probably could not exist without role conflicts—such as the cop show favorite where a police officer responds to a burglary only to discover that the thief is a child, sibling, or close friend.

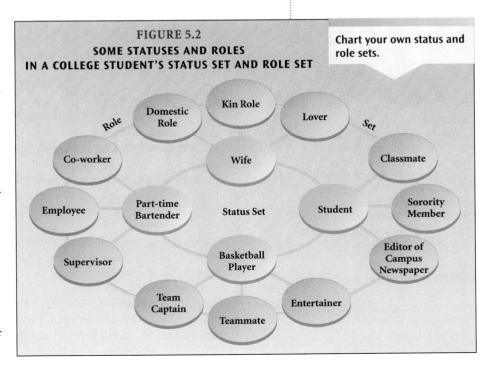

FIGURE 5.2

SOME STATUSES AND ROLES IN A COLLEGE STUDENT'S STATUS SET AND ROLE SET

Chart your own status and role sets.

Role Set

Domestic Role · Kin Role · Lover · Co-worker · Wife · Classmate · Employee · Part-time Bartender · Status Set · Student · Sorority Member · Supervisor · Basketball Player · Editor of Campus Newspaper · Team Captain · Teammate · Entertainer

One of the authors witnessed a dramatic example of role conflict during the 1968 urban riots following the death of Dr. Martin Luther King Jr. He, another white soldier, and two African American National Guardsmen were assigned to an army patrol, and one of the first disturbances they were sent to investigate was in a neighborhood of one of the black soldiers. When they arrived on the scene, the protesters spotted their neighbors and friends in uniform and shouted, "Hey, brother, what are you doing with the enemy? Take off those uniforms and join your brothers!" At that moment their roles of neighbor, friend, and fellow African American were in direct conflict with the military role.

Role strain, conflict, and the choices they demand are important forces in social change. In everyday interaction people must tiptoe through a minefield of role conflicts and strains and make choices they may or may not wish to make. That people play their roles so well, and adhere so strongly to them despite the costs, tells us much about the power and necessity of roles. They provide the vital framework of social interaction that links individuals to others in reciprocal roles, patterned relationships, and social networks.

Social Networks

All of us fulfill many social roles, and a large part of our lives is spent developing a **social network,** which includes *the total web of an individual's relationships and group memberships.* Social networks include our families, friends, and neighbors, as well as all other people and groups with whom we have ongoing relationships. People often create and maintain social networks for functional reasons, such as advancing their careers, for social support, and to promote a host of other interests and needs.

Social networks do not have clear boundaries, and their members may or may not interact on a regular basis. Moreover, people in social networks do not always have a sense that they belong together, nor do they necessarily have common aims and goals, as do members of a group. Nevertheless, social networks are a vital part of social structure and are extremely important in our everyday lives. Social networks radiate out from individuals and groups, and through them groups, organizations, and nations are bound together. Social networks also provide linkages between one individual and another, and then through other people's social networks to still others, until, in theory, people everywhere are linked together.

Every person's social network is unique. The social networks of husbands and wives differ, as do those of brothers and sisters. For example, a husband's social network might include family members, neighbors, people in his car pool, co-workers, and members of his bowling league. A wife's network overlaps with her husband's to some extent; she and her husband share ties with some family members, neighbors, and friends. But her network may also include members of her car pool, her co-workers, and friends and acquaintances with whom she alone maintains a relationship.

Each person's social network also includes two kinds of relationships. One kind, which is characterized by *strong ties,* is a relationship that is intimate, enduring, and defined by people of special importance. A person typically has strong ties to family members, some neighbors, and a small circle of intimate friends. People in this kind of network usually exert considerable influence on each other; they share information and resources and usually can be counted on if needed. In effect, they are a person's primary social support system and provide "our security and sense of well-being, and even our health" (Fischer, 1982:3; Seeman et al., 1985).

The classroom is a place where students fulfill one set of role expectations while professors fill another.

What status and role expectations conform to popular stereotypes about a university classroom in this photo? How do the roles and statuses depicted in this photo differ from the university classroom of the 1950s?

SOCIAL NETWORK
The total web of an individual's relationships and group memberships.

When you complete your degree, what is the best approach to finding a good job? Sociologists have conducted research on this subject for almost half a century, and survey results have been remarkably consistent. In *Getting a Job,* Mark Granovetter notes that there are three main ways to find professional jobs with high salaries and many benefits: direct application to businesses, using formal means (newspaper ads, the Internet, and employment agencies), and through personal contacts (social networks). Of the three, which do you think offers the best formula for success?

If you answered social networks, you are correct. Granovetter's surveys revealed that people find almost 56 percent of all professional jobs through social networks compared to about 18 percent found by direct application. The classified ads, Internet, and employment agencies were a distant third: they were the source of only about 16 percent of peoples' jobs. Social networking plays such an important role in successful job hunting and throughout one's career, that most career counselors agree that it is the most effective job-search method (Tullier, 2004). You need to know something more about social networks, however, if you want to conduct a successful job search.

Social networks can be characterized as consisting of either strong or weak ties. Those marked by strong ties are made up of close kin and friends, whereas weak ties usually involve acquaintances of various kinds, such as a friend of a friend and other distant acquaintances, whom we may see infrequently and barely know. Each kind of network provides its own advantages in the job search. For example, surveys have found that strong ties and close friends "are most likely to be used by job seekers who are unemployed or in a great need of a job" (Granovetter, 1995:149). When searching for professional jobs, weak ties that expand one's circle of acquaintances as widely as possible usually offer a better chance of success.

Another way to find a job is to participate in as many organizations as possible—both business and voluntary, mindful that they, too, expand one's social networks. One researcher contends that membership in neighborhood groups, hobby clubs, and other professional and social networks outside the firm may hold the key to finding and keeping a job in the highly competitive job markets of the future. As Charles Sabel (1991:43) wrote,

> Only those who participate in such multiple, loosely connected networks are likely to know when their current jobs are in danger, where new opportunities lie, and what skills are required in order to seize these opportunities. The more open corporate labor markets become, the greater the burden these networks will have to bear and the greater will be the economic compulsion to participate in the social activities they organize.

When it comes to getting a job, there is some truth to the old adage "It's not *what* you know, but *who* you know."

TAKING A CLOSER LOOK

Upper-middle-class professionals are encouraged to join numerous organizations to boost their job prospects and career mobility. If this becomes every volunteer's primary motivation for joining social clubs and organizations, how might this affect voluntary organizations like the League of Women Voters, the Girl Scouts, and the Rotary Club?

Source: Mark Granovetter. *Getting a Job: A Study of Contacts and Careers,* 2nd ed. Chicago: University of Chicago Press, 1995. Charles Sabel. "Moebius-Strip Organizations and Open Labor Markets: Some Consequences of the Reintegration of Conception and Execution in a Volatile Economy," in Pierre Bourdieu and James Coleman (eds.), *Social Theory for a Changing Society.* Boulder, CO: Westview Press, 1991, pp. 23–54. Michelle Tullier. *Networking for Job Search and Career Success* (2nd ed.) NY: Jist, 2004.

A person's network also includes *weak ties* to distant kin, co-workers, acquaintances, and even people who have only interacted through cyberspace on the Internet (Warschauer, 2003). Internet sites such as *Facebook, MySpace,* and others may increase a person's social network exponentially. While they are more tenuous and impersonal, they provide the individual with many contacts beyond family and friends that offer a wide range of information and services which would not be available otherwise. In Focus box 5.2 we examine the special importance of "weak ties" in finding a good job.

Social networks are useful to individuals and of critical importance in most societies. Contrary to popular thought, social networks are just as important to city dwellers as they are to rural folks. While urbanites are likely to have fewer family members in their social networks, they are nevertheless just as likely to use networks for procuring goods and services and finding jobs (Greeley, 2002). It is through social networks that information, knowledge, and resources are shared among individuals and groups. For example, many companies prefer these networks in hiring, and pay bonuses to employees for recruiting friends and acquaintances, believing social networks produce savings in screening costs (Fernandez et al., 2000). In both small-scale and complex societies, social networks can be very useful for such things as getting a promotion, mobilizing political support, gaining entry to a club, getting a date, or finding a marriage partner. For example, if you notice an attractive person in your sociology class you might announce in the personal ads of the school newspaper that you are interested in meeting the student. You usually will be far more successful, however, if you use social networks. While you may not know the other person, a friend or an acquaintance may know him or her, and through that contact (your friend's network), the two of you may be introduced.

In addition to serving the needs of ordinary people, conflict theorists see social networks as being particularly useful to those at the top of the social hierarchy. Personal networks are influenced by gender, race, social class, and a variety of other social factors that can serve to expand or limit one's access to information, resources, and power.

In many societies networks composed exclusively of men who are members of dominant class, racial, and ethnic backgrounds routinely exclude women and minorities from becoming members of their clubs and associations, thereby denying them access to information and other resources. And, as John Scott (1991) noted for the larger political economy, "informal social networks of social connection" are becoming an increasingly important means through which corporate decision makers (and the capitalist class as a whole) maintain and reproduce their power and influence not only nationally but globally.

Social Institutions

A popular American television advertisement proclaims that "Americans want to succeed, not just survive." To most viewers the message is obvious: Americans have progressed beyond mere survival and are now concerned with the more lofty goals of prosperity and personal success. Nothing could be further from the truth. No society, that of the United States included, can ever take its survival for granted. To this end, all societies create **social institutions**—*relatively enduring clusters of values, norms, social statuses, roles, and groups that address fundamental social needs.*

Sociologists generally identify five major social institutions that exist in every society: family, education, religion, government, and the economy (Chapters 13, 14, 15, 16, and 17 provide in-depth looks at each of these institutions). These institutions along with the mass media and technomedia serve as powerful social forces that shape and alter our social structure and impact social interaction in our everyday lives.

SOCIAL INTERACTION

It may be tempting to argue that social roles, groups, institutions, and other social forces have such powerful influence on human behavior that we as individuals have no choice but to do what society demands. Yet it is clear that while people often conform to social expectations, in everyday social interaction we also interpret the rules to suit ourselves, create and manipulate meaningful symbols, present ourselves to others in a variety of ways, and are constantly interpreting and redefining the meaning of our actions. These processes are what guide and provide meaning to the social interaction in our everyday lives.

Imagine that you are strolling across campus absorbed in thought. What happens when out of the corner of your eye you notice that someone lounging on a bench is looking at you? Does your behavior change in any way? Unless you are totally engrossed in thought, the answer is probably yes. There is a basic change as you and the other person acknowledge and respond to each other's presence. This is but one of countless forms of **social interaction**—*the mutual influence of two or more people on each other's behavior*—that profoundly affect our lives. Social interaction is the building block of the entire social order.

Patterns of Social Interaction

Sociologists recognize that among individuals, groups, organizations, and societies there are five fundamental patterns of social interaction: exchange, cooperation, competition, conflict, and coercion. Robert Nisbet (1970:50) described these elements as the "molecular cement" that binds people, groups, and societies together.

SOCIAL INSTITUTIONS
Relatively enduring clusters of values, norms, social statuses, roles, and groups that address fundamental social needs.

SOCIAL INTERACTION
The mutual influence of two or more people on each other's behavior.

1. *Exchange.* *Exchange* is perhaps the most basic form of social interaction (Blau, 1963, 1964). Social exchange theorists maintain that our interactions with others are guided by the "profit motive"—that is, we seek to maximize rewards and minimize costs (Homans, 1961). Social exchange is based on the *norm of reciprocity*—that we help and not harm those who have helped us (Gouldner, 1960). This norm establishes the expectation that gifts, recognition, love, and other favors will be returned. In the course of a day, people exchange smiles, waves, and other simple courtesies. Exchanges of this kind are most often taken for granted—at least until people fail to meet our expectations. The norm of reciprocity, of course, has a negative side, which includes the expectation that hostilities, threats, social slights, and other acts meant to harm will be reciprocated.

A college student checks out messages on her *MySpace* web page.

Exchange theorists believe that people, groups, organizations, and nations keep a running account of what they are owed and what they owe others. Top priority is given to exchange relationships with business partners, political allies, friends, kin, or lovers who provide the greatest benefits at the lowest costs. Because people have an interest in searching for the most favorable cost-benefit ratios in their dealings with others, relationships are forever shifting. Nevertheless, exchanges and ties of mutual obligation are a vital social glue.

How have popular websites such as *MySpace, Facebook, Friendster, Livejournal,* and others expanded and altered the social networks of youths?

2. *Cooperation.* *Cooperation* is a pattern of interaction in which individuals, groups, and societies work together to achieve shared goals. Cooperation is fundamental to human survival; without it social life would be impossible. Cooperation sustains routine, face-to-face encounters. It is also necessary if people are to make love, raise children, protect themselves, and make a living. Some societies place greater emphasis on cooperation than others. For example, the Japanese, whose norms and values promote sharing and "selflessness," have altered the American version of baseball, which stresses individualism and encourages "stars" to stand out from the group. In Japan, people expect all players to exhibit *wa,* a sense of team spirit that obligates the individual to subordinate everything to the group. Team members *always* eat together and sleep together; one ex-player claimed that even the players' sex lives might be sacrificed during the season to conserve energy for the team (Hillenbrand, 1989; Whiting, 1989).

3. *Competition.* *Competition* is much like cooperation, in that both individuals and groups strive to achieve a shared goal. It differs from cooperation, however, in that in competition, instead of joining with others to achieve valued goals, people or groups contest for them, recognizing that society's prizes are in limited supply and only one person or group can attain them.

Competitive relationships are especially common to capitalist economies and pervade almost all aspects of people's lives. For example, corporations compete for customers, professional athletes vie for prizes, students compete for grades, political rivals contest for votes, and even pastors must win converts from competitors.

4. *Conflict.* *Conflict* is a pattern of interaction in which people or groups struggle to achieve a "commonly prized object or goal" (Nisbet, 1970:75). Conflict is especially common when competitors violate rules and seek to gain their objective by any means available. Robert Nisbet (1970:76) wrote, "There is no group or relationship, however small and intimate, in which conflict does not occasionally occur." We most often consider conflict to be opposed to human interests, harmful to the social order, and something to be avoided or resolved as quickly as possible. Yet, as conflict theorists emphasize, conflict has a positive side. It may enhance social solidarity, for nothing reduces conflicts and strains within a relationship (whether marital or between nations) better than an external threat (Simmel [1908] 1955; Coser, 1956; Nisbet, 1970). As Robert Nisbet (1970:76) observed, it also may serve as a vehicle for social change in which stagnant beliefs and values are dissolved, old tyrannies loosened, and individuals released to achieve new and higher goals.

5. *Coercion.* When people or groups are compelled to interact with each other, *coercion* is the glue that binds them together. Coercion is the actualization of the threat of force that those with power sometimes use to achieve their objectives. For example, in the United States, education is compulsory; children must attend school whether they want to or not. The relative strength of coercion as a cohesive force lies not so much in blatant expressions of power and authority as in the myriad expressions it may assume in everyday life. Ridicule, gossip, the silent treatment, and withdrawal of affection are but a handful of coercive devices people use in their daily interactions with others. Coercion involves an individual or group that dominates another, the *superordinate,* and a person or group that is dominated, the *subordinate.* There cannot be one without the other for, as Georg Simmel ([1908] 1955) noted, the behavior of one is conditioned by the other.

People often form social perceptions and develop stereotypes based on first impressions.

What do you think is the first impression made on the young woman in the center of the photo by the young man in the tie-dyed T-shirt with the long dreadlocks?

SOCIAL PERCEPTION
The process by which we form impressions of others and of ourselves.

The five patterns of social interaction discussed here are neither distinctive nor mutually exclusive. In everyday life, there is a fine line between competition and conflict, coercion and exchange, and the same is true concerning other patterns of social interaction. For example, if a classmate asks you to help him or her move into an apartment, this is potentially an exchange relationship. But what if your professor asks you to help him or her move? Is this exchange or coercion? Certainly, power influences whether it is one or the other, but this may not be the only factor involved; people's definitions, too, may influence the nature of the interaction— what is exchange to one may be coercion to another. Consequently, much of our social interaction is guided by social perception and stereotypes.

Social Perception and Stereotypes

In addition to defining a situation, we must decide who we have encountered before we activate what we believe to be the appropriate self. We attempt to answer this question through **social perception,** which is *a process by which we form impressions of others and ourselves.* In everyday life, we both give off and receive cues about the kinds of persons we are. We do this in almost every situation: when we enter a class, during a stroll across campus, while shopping at the mall, or when trying to flag down a taxi. How we perceive others and how we are perceived by them depend on such symbolic elements as physical appearance, clothing, gestures, tone of voice, facial expressions, posture, and other elements that reveal our various statuses, attitudes, and expectations.

Social perception depends in part on our impressions of other people's personal characteristics, such as whether they are attractive or ugly, good or bad, strong or weak. At the beginning of an encounter, people appear to devote considerable energy to discovering with whom they are dealing. Once people feel they have enough information, their attention to this assessment wanes, and early impressions continue to dominate their thinking and behavior (Dreben et al., 1979).

Our initial impressions of others also depend on our perceptions of people's social identities. When we encounter others, we mentally make a checklist of their various statuses, such as gender, age, and race, as well as search for clues to their less obvious identities. We scan clothing, hair style, body posture, and hand and eye behaviors for clues to occupational identity, social class, group membership, and other social statuses. Since we cannot know everything about everyone we meet, we cut corners by fitting people into ready-made categories.

In everyday life, we use a variety of **stereotypes,** which are *static and oversimplified ideas about a group or social category,* that influence our expectations and behaviors. In American society, there are stereotypes of women, men, jocks, the elderly, racial and ethnic minorities, college students, and countless other groups and social categories. When people are identified as belonging to a particular category, we assume they possess particular traits, and we act accordingly. Thus many people believe that redheads should be approached with caution, for they have hot tempers and can "explode at any time." By the same measure, negative stereotypes influence our interactions with racial and ethnic groups. As we discuss more fully in Chapter 10, if Scots are believed to be cheap, Italians passionate, and African Americans violent, in the early stages of interaction people will respond to them as if they possess these and other traits associated with their group, whether or not they have them.

Where do these generalized perceptions and stereotypes of other groups and individuals come from? Many are formed spontaneously as we interact in specific social situations. Yet that experience alone cannot account for some of the powerful perceptions and stereotypes that many people hold toward certain groups and categories of people—some of whom they have never encountered personally. Many of these assumptions have been taught and learned through the process of socialization, discussed in Chapter 4, and help shape and influence our social acts.

Social Acts

When you wake up in the morning and prepare for school you perform many acts—solitary behaviors that seemingly affect no one but yourself. You might stretch and yawn, scratch yourself in a place that you would never touch in front of another person, look out the window, and eat a bowl of cereal. In everyday life such behaviors are common. But if we could examine everything we do in the course of a day, we would discover that **social acts,** which are *behaviors influenced or shaped by the presence of others,* are far more numerous and important. When people enter our presence, we alter our behavior based on their expectations and demands, or at least on what we think they will consider appropriate. Social acts include countless daily behaviors that are usually taken for granted—such behaviors as walking across campus, shopping at a mall (see Focus box 5.3 on interacting with Santa Claus at the mall), or merely standing in a crowded elevator. Whether we feel that an elevator is crowded or not is also socially and culturally determined, based on our attitudes and values regarding personal space.

Personal Space and Nonverbal Communication

Have you ever had anybody approach you to talk and you felt the uncontrollable urge to take a step backward to put more distance between you and him or her? Or, have you ever reached out to touch someone during conversation and they seemed very uncomfortable and withdrew? These are common occurrences, especially when people from different cultures interact with one another, or when people of different ages, sexes, races, or social classes interact. Each of us surrounds ourselves with an invisible "bubble" that constitutes what we consider our **personal space,** *an area around our body that we reserve for ourselves, intimate acquaintances, and close friends.* On occasion we must allow others to "invade" this personal space, for example, when a doctor examines us, or perhaps when we are standing on line or in a crowded elevator. These situations often make us uncomfortable, however, and may call for "defensive strategies" such as folding our arms across our chest, placing an obstacle (an umbrella, a briefcase, or a backpack) between us and the other person, or at the very least, avoiding eye contact and verbal communication.

STEREOTYPES
Static and oversimplified ideas about a group or a social category.

SOCIAL ACTS
Behaviors influenced or shaped by the presence of others.

PERSONAL SPACE
An area around our body that we reserve for ourselves, intimate acquaintances, and close friends.

Each year between Thanksgiving and Christmas, countless Santas magically appear at shopping malls across the country. Most observers see Santa's visit as serving three obvious purposes: to help put people in the Christmas spirit, to amuse and entertain the public, and to make holiday shopping more fun. Sociologists, however, see much more, knowing that things are not necessarily what they seem. With this in mind, we decided to conduct team research and take a closer look at how people interact with Santa Claus at shopping malls.

Using the method of triangulation, we combined the qualitative techniques of ethnographic interviewing, nonparticipant observation, limited participant observation, and full participant observation at several shopping centers in small towns, medium-sized cities, and a large metropolitan area in the Midwest. Santa actors were observed and interviewed by both authors, who discussed with them their interactions with the public. At other times, both individually and as a team, the authors observed Santa's interactions with the public and then interviewed mall visitors about their perceptions of the encounters. At one point, Thompson went "undercover," donned the Santa Claus outfit, and played the role of Santa for an entire evening shift at one of the malls. Only Hickey, who observed the interactions, and the professional photographer working the Santa booth were aware that Santa was conducting sociological research.

What did we find? As you might guess, we learned several things that go well beyond the aforementioned three simple assumptions. Santa actors tended to be white, middle-aged or older men, although we observed a few college students, one or two African American men, and one woman who played Santa. Once inside the suit, however, virtually all Santas looked alike.

The public's reactions to Santa were revealing, with the variables of age and sex the most influential in shaping the interaction. Young children and senior citizens became excited when they saw Santa, the younger children clearly believing in the fantasy character and the elderly seemingly enjoying playing along with the Santa fantasy. Among other age cohorts, noticeable differences emerged between males and females. Adult men, unless accompanied by young children, almost uniformly ignored Santa, refusing to wave, respond to his greetings of "Merry Christmas," or otherwise acknowledge his presence. Adult women, by contrast, seemed quite comfortable waving to Santa and often stopped to speak or sometimes even shouted a greeting across the mall. Teenagers were the most interesting group. It seemed important to them to use Santa to demonstrate publicly that they were no longer children. Boys either tried to ignore Santa (like adult men) or (especially if in groups) felt compelled to ridicule Santa, pull on his beard, or otherwise publicly challenge the Santa fantasy. Teenage girls openly flirted with Santa; many sat on his lap and posed for pictures; many seemed to use Santa to confirm that they were budding young women who were more interested in the man in the Santa suit than in his fantasy role.

TAKING A CLOSER LOOK

Given the discussion of social interaction in this chapter, why did teenage boys feel compelled to publically challenge the Santa Claus fantasy?

Source: "Encountering Santa Claus at the Mall," by William E. Thompson and Joseph V. Hickey, from *Qualitative Sociology* 12(4), 1989: 371–389. With kind permission of Springer Science and Business Media.

How does Santa Claus at the mall illustrate sociology's theme that things are not necessarily what they seem?

Anthropologist Edward Hall (1959) discovered that Americans surround themselves not with one, but with four "invisible bubbles" and identified four different zones of comfort regarding social interaction (see Figure 5.3):

1. *Intimate Distance.* For most Americans this distance extends from the body outward approximately 18 inches. Generally we protect this space fiercely and allow it to be penetrated only by loved ones, very close friends, and our family pets. In the course of our daily interactions, this intimate zone is reserved for hugging, kissing, lovemaking, or comforting. Occasionally, medical professionals such as doctors, nurses, and dentists must invade this intimate space, sometimes making us feel rather uncomfortable. When strangers invade this space, we defend the space and our bodies by either retreating to a safer and more comfortable distance or by striking out in defense.

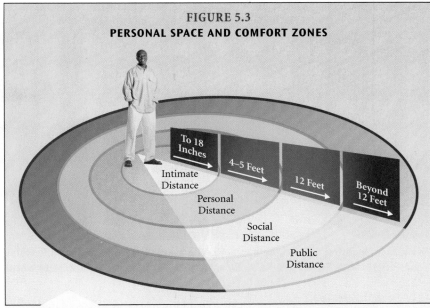

FIGURE 5.3
PERSONAL SPACE AND COMFORT ZONES

To 18 Inches — Intimate Distance
4–5 Feet — Personal Distance
12 Feet — Social Distance
Beyond 12 Feet — Public Distance

What happens when people "invade" your intimate distance? How do these "invisible bubbles" around us shape our interactions with others?

Criminologists and law enforcement officials, for example, know that deaths by stabbing and strangulation are more often committed by intimates, family members, or friends than total strangers, because of the nature of intimacy involved in the crime.

2. *Personal Distance.* This zone extends from approximately 18 inches from the body out to about 4 or 5 feet. While not reserved for intimates, we tend to feel most comfortable allowing friends and acquaintances within this space for any length of time. Generally when we are being introduced to people for the first time, we like to maintain somewhere between 2 to 4 feet between our bodies and theirs, not coincidentally the most comfortable distance for two people to shake hands. Again, criminologists and police figure that if a person is shot from this distance that the perpetrator was probably a friend or family member.

3. *Social Distance.* A distance of 4 or 5 feet out to approximately 12 feet is commonly used for impersonal and formal interactions. This is a common distance used in job interviews (sitting across a 36-inch desk with each person approximately a foot from it), for example. It also is the distance that podiums are usually set from the front row to separate speakers and audience, and if you observe the professor in your classroom, probably about the distance from which he or she lectures or leads class discussions. Shootings from this distance are as likely to have been committed by casual acquaintances or total strangers as friends or family members.

4. *Public Distance.* This distance, beyond 12 feet, is open to just about anybody and rarely do we feel threatened when somebody is 12 or more feet away from us. We can walk past total strangers, acknowledging them only with a glance or a nod, or ignoring them altogether if we choose to do so. Secret Service agents and bodyguards like to keep this much distance between dignitaries and the general public. Killings that take place from this distance often involve total strangers, as in the case of drive-by shootings, or random sniper shootings.

As we mentioned earlier, these "comfort zones" identified by Hall vary from one culture to another and within cultures when people of different age, race, sex, and social class categories interact. Middle Easterners, for example, have much smaller distance requirements for casual interaction and men often embrace or kiss on the cheek when introduced for the first time—something that makes American men very uncomfortable.

Americans generally greet one another with a handshake whereas Asians usually bow.

How do these differences in greetings both reflect and dictate the comfortable social distances of the two cultures?

Despite living in a densely populated country, the Japanese often maintain a larger social space when interacting with strangers. When two Japanese men are introduced, they bow toward one another, an act that requires a distance of about 6 feet to prevent bumping heads.

In the United States, women are generally far more comfortable touching, hugging, or kissing one another than are men, and women will allow other women within their intimate distance, something a man rarely allows from another man, even if they are blood related. Also, not all men are comfortable with the same amount of personal and social distance. We found, for example, in our research on the demeanor of contemporary cowboys, that cowboys out on the Great Plains have a much larger "invisible bubble" surrounding them, and although they will allow others closer to them on their side, they generally keep 5 to 6 feet (coincidentally, about the length of a horse) between them and others during face-to-face interaction (Hickey and Thompson, 1988).

The difference in attitudes toward personal space between the sexes can cause some awkward situations. For example, if a woman touches a man, he often misreads this gesture as a sexual overture because she has invaded his intimate space; hence, he considers it an intimate gesture—something she may not have intended at all. Similarly, older people often feel comfortable touching younger people, but children often feel uncomfortable approaching adults they do not know. While members of the lower socioeconomic classes often hug one another, embrace upon meeting, and feel comfortable in close proximity, members of the upper class usually maintain a "proper" distance between themselves and others, especially when interacting with members of lower social classes. All of these examples involve **nonverbal communication**—*the body movements, gestures, and facial expressions that we use to communicate with others.* Smiles, nods, winks, eye contact, hand gestures, and other forms of nonverbal communication can be just as important, if not more so, than words in shaping our interactions with others. They are especially important in helping social actors to define social situations and give meaning to everyday interactions.

Defining Social Situations

When we interact with others, we constantly define and redefine the social situation in order to provide meaning to our actions and theirs. As we noted in Chapter 1, William I. Thomas (1928) contended that a critical element of everyday social interaction involves creating a **definition of the situation,** *the idea that when people define situations as real they become real in their consequences.* For example, do you consider your sociology class to be interesting, informing, and exciting? If so, you probably read all the assignments, come to class regularly, and participate in class discussions. And, guess what? Your sociology class is interesting, informing, and exciting. On the other hand, if you

NONVERBAL COMMUNICATION
The body movements, gestures, and facial expressions that we use to communicate with others.

DEFINITION OF THE SITUATION
The idea that when people define situations as *real* they become real in their consequences.

think a class is dull, boring, and a waste of time, you probably do not read the assignments, go to class, or participate in class. Consequently, that class is indeed dull, boring, and a waste of your time. Of course, not everybody defines situations in the same way. So, a class that is fun and exciting to some is dull and boring to others, and vice versa.

Also, because we constantly define and redefine social situations in ways that are meaningful to us, we always run the risk of misinterpreting other people's actions, especially their nonverbal forms of communications. Did that girl just wink at me, or does she have something in her eye? Did that person just hold up an index finger toward me, or was it the middle finger? Does holding up two fingers signify victory, peace, or simply the number two? The meanings imputed to these actions and gestures become critical in shaping the meaning of our present and future interactions with others. How we define social situations becomes an important part of our presentation of ourselves to others and how we attempt to manage their impressions of us. In that sense, to paraphrase Shakespeare, life becomes much like a drama, with each of us performing various roles on the stage of life.

Dramaturgy: Presentation of Self and Impression Management

We all have been encouraged to "put our best foot forward" when meeting somebody for the first time. Similarly, we have all heard that "you only get one chance to make a first impression." These admonitions acknowledge that much of our day-to-day interaction constitutes a performance—one that is judged by others and, as a result, has tremendous impact on how we are viewed by others and how we view ourselves. As we noted in Chapter 1, Erving Goffman (1922–1982) introduced the theoretical framework of *dramaturgical analysis,* which uses the analogy of the theater to analyze social behavior as a way of understanding these social performances. Dramaturgical analysis focuses on the ways we present ourselves to others and our attempts to manage their impressions of us in a favorable light.

Contemporary Iraqi war protesters rejuvenate the antiwar symbols of the Vietnam war era.

President Nixon often triumphantly displayed what his generation viewed as the "victory sign" by making a "V" with the first two fingers. During the Vietnam War, millions of baby boomers and so-called "hippies" used the same symbol to mean "peace." Nixon would flash the "victory sign" to crowds implying that if the U.S. continued and stepped up the military action in Vietnam, victory would eventually be achieved. Meanwhile, youths in the crowd would flash the "peace sign" back shouting, "Hell no, we won't go!"

In everyday life, some interactions are simple and direct and people's behaviors are fairly predictable. Casual greetings are a good example. Most other face-to-face interactions, however, require more of participants, and people's responses may be highly variable. According to symbolic interactionists, who study how symbols, language, and gestures shape social behavior, we do not respond directly to individuals, events, acts, and objects, but to our images of them (McCall and Simmons, 1979:66). As Herbert Blumer (1969a) wrote, in social interaction the key to a person's response is how he or she organizes, defines, and interprets another's behaviors. William Swann (1998:399) noted that people's identities and self-views are not like bowling balls that are unaffected by either people or objects they encounter in their travels. For people, the exact opposite is true; we are acutely sensitive to those with whom we share ongoing relationships. This may explain the remarkable consistency of "self" over time—even over a lifetime. People usually cling to their self-views because dramatic changes would disrupt relationships with those we deem important—in some cases, even relationships with others that may sustain negative self-views and behaviors (Swann, 1998).

Many everyday interactions appear as if they were scripted minidramas, in which people encounter one another, assess each other's personal and social characteristics, assume identities, and behave in appropriate ways. Given the complexity of most social situations and the fact that spontaneity and surprise are integral features of virtually all social interactions, however, improvisation is usually required (Flaherty, 1990).

Using the analogy of the theater, **dramaturgy** *analyzes social interaction as though participants were actors in an ongoing drama.* Dramaturgy, however, emphasizes that in real life "actors" passively accept neither the definition of the situation nor the identities granted by others. Instead, people take an active part in social interaction, manipulating it to their perceived advantage. Erving Goffman (1959) called this **impression management,** *ways that people use revelation and concealment to make a favorable impression on others.*

Dramaturgists note that people not only have an interest in presenting their best "selves" to others but also tacitly agree to support each other's performances and help each other maintain face. Teamwork requires that people overlook or ignore poor performances (a professor who stutters), embarrassing acts (a growling stomach), and deceits (excuses for being late). Also, we may sometimes be called on to do remedial work or help out by agreeing with others, even though we may totally disagree with their definition of the situation. Why we do these things should be obvious. When a "bad actor's" performance is called into question, the entire social interaction may be threatened. Few cultures are more aware of this fact than the group-oriented Japanese, who recognize that when emotional outbursts occur, those present must realign their behaviors to suit the individual's goals, rather than those of the group.

Daniel and Cheryl Albas (1988) provide an example of impression management that is very familiar to college students everywhere—when graded exams are returned in class. They called their research report "Aces and Bombers," noting that students who receive A's want to tell others about their success—and they usually do—whereas those who receive D's and F's take great pains to cover up their failure. Can you think of some of the ways that aces and bombers might accomplish these goals, using your sociology class as an example?

Ethnomethodology: The "Taken-for Granted" Aspects of Interaction

The self that we present in one social situation may be inappropriate in another. This discrepancy is illustrated in a series of experiments conducted by Harold Garfinkel (1967) who introduced **ethnomethodology,** which literally means *people's methods,* or is more generally described as *a way of analyzing the "taken-for-granted" aspects that give meaning to social interaction.* Ethnomethodologists contend that much of what transpires when we interact with others relies on unspoken and commonly understood assumptions about the meanings of our words and actions. For example, when walking across campus, you often pass somebody who may nod and say, "What's up?" You probably nod in response and say, "not much," and go on about your business. What really transpired in that brief conversation? Basically, two people just acknowledged one another in an informal greeting and response. What would have happened, however, if you had no understanding of the taken-for-granted aspects of the other person's question? When he or she asked, "What's up?" what if you had stopped and replied "the sky is up and so is the North Pole, at least on a map." No doubt your fellow actor would either think you were incredibly stupid, or a smart aleck, and probably the next time you passed him or her on campus you would be ignored to avoid such an awkward situation again. Occasionally these types of interactional miscues occur when people from other cultures or with language barriers interact with one another. One of the authors remembers, for instance, a situation when he asked a Chinese student entering class, "What's happenin'?" and the student paused, got a very concerned look on his face, and then somberly responded, "Students are being massacred in Tiananmen Square by soldiers because they are demonstrating for human rights." Not exactly how the author meant to greet the student—a situation that required what Goffman called *remedial work,* an explanation that clarified the situation and put both the author and the student more at ease before class began.

To illustrate the taken-for-granted aspects of everyday interaction, Garfinkel had his students act as though they were boarders when they returned home from college dur-

DRAMATURGY
Analyzes social interaction as though participants were actors in an ongoing drama.

IMPRESSION MANAGEMENT
Ways that people use revelation and concealment to make a favorable impression on others.

ETHNOMETHODOLOGY
A way of analyzing the "taken-for-granted" aspects that give meaning to social interaction.

ing a visit, instead of behaving as sons or daughters. Pretending to be strangers in their own homes, the experiments tended to last only a few minutes because parents could not comprehend why their children were behaving so courteously and formally, and so "out of character." In some cases, tempers flared, and parental responses included, "What's the matter? Are you sick? Are you out of your mind or are you just stupid?" (Garfinkel, 1967:47).

In today's world the presentation of self, impression management, and the taken-for-granted aspects of interaction now involve interacting through cyberspace. As our opening vignette involving Fred and "Nina" illustrated, the advent of the technomedia has dramatically affected social interaction in our everyday lives.

SOCIAL INTERACTION, MASS MEDIA, AND THE TECHNOMEDIA

Mass media and the technomedia have had tremendous influence in shaping social interaction in our everyday lives. Our social perceptions and stereotypes have been influenced by portrayals of institutions (i.e., family, education, religion, the economy, and government) and various categories of people on television. In later chapters we explore these media portrayals, especially television dramas and situation comedies, and how they have shaped our perceptions of the various institutions in some detail.

Today, perhaps no genre of television programming is more popular than the so-called "reality" shows. Every night of the week at least one, if not all, of the major networks, and several cable stations offer some type of "reality" programming. *Survivor, Big Brother, The Real World, The Bachelor, The Bachelorette, The Apprentice, The Amazing Race,* and a host of other programs put noncelebrities in both conventional and unconventional social situations while viewers watch their every move and sometimes become involved in these programs by calling in or logging on to specialized websites. Program participants live together, date, have sex, argue, fight, and in some cases compete for prizes of over a million dollars. Viewers "interact" with the people on these programs by helping to select their mates or determining whether they remain in the competition or are "voted off" the show. For many Americans and other people around the world, participants in these programs vicariously become friends, enemies, partners, and adversaries. Social attitudes, values, beliefs, norms, and stereotypes are simultaneously reinforced, challenged, questioned, redefined, and shattered. From a sociological perspective, however, the question looms as to whose reality is this? What lasting impact do these programs have on our values, attitudes, beliefs, and norms? To what extent is the so-called reality displayed in these programs shaped and altered by television producers, directors, film editors, and corporate sponsors? More important, how do these programs affect our social interactions with others in our everyday lives? And remember, television is but one form of the ever increasing technomedia that influence our day-to-day interactions with others.

The technomedia, especially the Internet, have expanded our daily social interactions from personal face-to-face encounters to the realm of cyberspace and interaction in virtual communities. College students expand their social network on *MySpace* and *Facebook* and evaluate their teachers on *Rate My Professor.* On-line shopping allows people to browse and shop from the comfort of their own homes without the need to interact with salespeople or other customers. E-mail, chat rooms, and other forms of communication through cyberspace have made letter writing almost a lost art, and

Shows like *American Idol* transform ordinary people into instant celebrities replete with fan clubs, critics, and stalkers.

"Sorry, honey, but I won't be home for dinner tonight. Instead, however, I'm sending over a virtual version of myself on CD-ROM."

despite the widespread use of cellular phones, with widespread computer access, even the telephone is losing its importance as a means of communication. Moreover, as our opening vignette with Fred and "Nina" illustrated, on the World Wide Web people can be anybody they want. Thus, influential variables and potential barriers to social inter-action, such as age, race, ethnicity, sex, gender, social class, and others are at least temporarily suspended as people interact with one another through cyberspace.

In an experiment in an upper-middle-class suburb of Toronto, Canadian residents were provided with high-speed Internet services to create a virtual community that became known as "Netville" to see if widespread access to the Internet promoted or reduced community social interaction. The study found that those who used the Internet most extensively developed broader social networks, but these networks and most of the interaction over the Net did not contribute to creating a so-called global community, because most of the online communications were within the boundaries of the original community or with residents who lived within a 50- to 100-mile radius (Hampton and Wellman, 2002; Warschauer, 2003).

The influence of mass media and especially technomedia on social interaction will increase in the future and we discuss this in the Looking to the Future section of this chapter. How sociologists view this influence, and analyze social interaction in general, however, varies greatly depending upon which often major sociological perspectives they use.

SOCIOLOGICAL APPROACHES TO INTERACTION IN EVERYDAY LIFE

We have discussed social interaction in our everyday lives. Sociologists view interaction differently, depending on which theoretical perspective they adopt.

The Structural Functionalist Approach

According to functionalists, for society to exist, whether it is a colony of ants, a pack of dogs, a swarm of bees, or a human society, it must have a *structure*—patterned and recurrent relationships among group members. Much of social life is repetitive and enduring. A university, for example, is stable because it is structured. It has a president, vice-presidents, department heads, and specialists in many areas, and all have fairly clear ideas about their rights and duties relative to other members of the campus community. People are hired and fired, some retire and others die, yet the university endures. To some, this suggests that social structures, whether families, schools, or sororities, are relatively rigid and changeless structures.

Functionalists take a similar approach to social institutions: institutions are basic to the proper functioning of contemporary societies. Therefore, institutions provide the framework for social interaction in our everyday lives. Of all social institutions, the family is perhaps the most important. It regulates sexual activity and it produces new members and socializes and cares for them. In some societies families also transmit cultural knowledge, but in modern societies the educational institution fulfills the basic need of training each new generation. The economic institution produces and distributes goods and services, the political institution provides order and defense, and the religious institution fulfills the social need for meaning, social solidarity, and control. Religion (and the family) provided for the health of people in small-scale societies, but in modern industrial societies the medical institution, which includes a relatively stable cluster of norms and values, medical specialists, administrators, insurance companies, and other groups and organizations, maintains people's health.

To functionalists, institutions are a society's blueprint for solving basic needs, and any particular institutional structure channels experience along certain lines; it prohibits certain possibilities, tolerates or ignores others, and encourages still others (Williams, 1970). To say that a social arrangement is "institutionalized" means it is deeply embedded in the fabric of a group or society and is surrounded by customary beliefs, values, and norms. Institutions provide solutions to what are defined as long-term problems, and as such they are comfortable and familiar. Institutions provide the illusion of order and stability that is necessary if people are to have and rear children, plan, build, and invest in the future.

Analyzing interaction at the macro level, functionalists focus on the first two patterns of social interaction we introduced earlier in this chapter: exchange and cooperation. In this view of "you scratch my back and I'll scratch yours," if a friend or roommate helps you study for an algebra exam, you may reciprocate later by typing his or her sociology research paper, or by letting him or her borrow your favorite sweater. From the functionalist perspective, interaction is governed by the norm of reciprocity and people tend to cooperate as much as possible to ensure smooth day-to-day interaction as well as the perpetuation of their society and the survival of the species.

The Conflict Perspective

Conflict theorists disagree with this line of reasoning, noting that it is a fiction that institutional arrangements benefit all individuals and society as a whole. Instead, institutional arrangements grant a disproportionate share of wealth, power, and privilege to certain individuals and classes, and it is they who seek to maintain the status quo by defining particular institutional arrangements—whether slavery, feudalism, or the capitalist system—as vitally important to "society."

Conflict theorists agree that society is structured but emphasize that roles, statuses, and institutions do not exist for the good of "society." Instead, they are used by superordinates to exploit and dominate subordinates as well as to maintain and perpetuate elite wealth, power, and privilege. Conflict theorists agree with functionalists on one point, however; once institutional patterns develop into a coherent system, their "commonsense" logic may come to pervade all social institutions and make them highly resistant to change. Moreover, linkages among institutional complexes reinforce conservative tendencies. For example, the dominance of the economic complex in American society reflects its multiple ties to all other institutional complexes (Form, 1990). Hence, changing the American economic institution would require more than economic change, because capitalism pervades every American institution: the economy emphasizes free enterprise, and religion free will; the family system promotes high mobility and individual choice; the educational system stresses competition and being first; the mass media glorify stars and heroes, and the political system, with its democratic ideology, emphasizes the personal "character" of political candidates, as well as "one person one vote." Conflict theorists argue that it is impossible to understand human behavior without reference to social stratification, for people's positions in the social hierarchy influence virtually everything they think and do. From the conflict perspective, roles such as teacher and business owner have advantages and in various ways are used to exploit those in linked roles—student and worker. Social networks and institutions operate in much the same way. In each case, those at higher levels in the social hierarchy use their wealth, power, and influence to dominate and exploit those at lower levels—whether locally, nationally, or globally.

How might the conflict perspective be used to explain the nature of the interaction displayed in this photo?

Conflict theorists also tend to view social interaction from a macro level, but they focus on the last three patterns discussed earlier: competition, conflict, and coercion. From the conflict perspective, the unequal distribution of power and economic resources shape not only institutional configurations, but influence our day-to-day, face-to-face interactions with one another. From this viewpoint, social classes as well as individuals enter interactions with different vested interests and different goals. In this "dog-eat-dog" view of the world, the strong and powerful use daily interaction to dominate those who are weaker and less powerful. In contrast to the functionalist view, from this perspective, survival of the individual, society, and the species resides not in cooperation but in intense competition, with the "fittest" becoming the ultimate winner.

The Symbolic Interactionist Approach

Symbolic interactionists contend that all of social life—including social institutions—are in a constant state of flux. This is because people continually define and redefine relationships, and even those social arrangements that appear to be deeply embedded in social structure change. For example, American religious institutions are undergoing radical changes as more women enter divinity schools, especially elite schools that play a major role in shaping public opinion.

By the 1990s, more than half of the student seminarians at Yale and Harvard were women, and they and other female seminarians across the country have begun to reshape traditional notions of gender and liturgical practices, in some cases those that are centuries old (Woodward, 1989). For example, in 1989, the Reverend Barbara Harris was consecrated the first female bishop in the Anglican church. Female seminarians, priests, and ministers also have made substantive changes in the language of the church. At many seminaries generic nouns such as "mankind" have been replaced with "humankind" and "God 'the Father' is acceptable only if twinned with God 'the Mother', [or] God 'the parent'" (Woodward, 1989:59).

Interactionists contend that there is more flexibility in roles and relationships and much greater possibility for change than either functionalists or conflict theorists would allow. Interactionists stress that human social structure is built of collections of people who interact with one another according to expectations rather than certainties. This results in a constant reordering of society as people in interaction define and redefine social relationships and expectations change.

Because symbolic interactionists focus on the micro-level day-to-day, face-to-face interactions of individuals, much of this chapter has emphasized the interactionist approach. Personal space, nonverbal communication, definition of the situation, dramaturgical analysis, presentation of self, impression management, and ethnomethodology are all important elements of the symbolic interactionist perspective. Interactionists primarily view social structure and social institutions as mutually agreed-upon fabrications of social interaction. The seeming permanence of these institutions and their impact on our daily lives relies on us, as social actors, continuing to define them as stable and important. The stock market, for example, seemingly a stable aspect of the American economic institutions, fluctuates daily, based far less on economic earnings and corporate profits than on investors' faith in the market and their belief that it is a wise and sage investment. The stock market crash of 1929 and the more recent "crashes" in the 1980s and the early 2000s reflect waning consumer confidence in the market. When people define the market as "unsafe" and an unwise investment, they take their money out of the market, sending the Dow Jones Index and NASDAQ plunging to all-time lows. On the other hand, when consumer confidence is high and investors view the market as a wise and safe place to put their money, prices soar, and the stock indexes reach record highs. Even the most highly educated economic analysts now admit that it is the public's definition of the situation that governs the economy more than the so-called law of supply and demand or other standard economic principles.

the FUTURE
LOOKING to

SOCIAL INTERACTION IN THE TWENTY-FIRST CENTURY

If recent decades are any indication, the future of social interaction in our everyday lives promises some fascinating possibilities. As society changes so rapidly, new statuses and roles emerge on a daily basis and our constantly increasing status and role sets provide more potential for role strain and role conflicts than ever before. Social institutions, once thought of as stable and enduring aspects of society, now undergo rapid change and are continually being defined and redefined on an ongoing basis. Governments and regimes are toppled, maps become obsolete, the meaning of family is redefined, and social stereotypes are simultaneously reinforced and shattered on a daily basis. The future promises more instability in social institutions as we know them and the impact on our daily lives will be substantial.

As our opening vignette illustrated, perhaps no single aspect of society has more dramatically influenced and changed social interaction in our daily lives than the new technomedia. Manuel Castells (2002:xx) noted that the new "Internet Society" is:

. . . a social structure built on networks. But not any kinds of networks, since social networks have been an important dimension of social life since the origins of humankind. The networks that characterize contemporary social organization are information networks powered by microelectronics-based information technology. . . . The emerging pattern is one of self-directed networking . . . it does not substitute for face-to-face sociability or for social participation. It adds to it.

The impact of technomedia on social interaction will increase in the future as more technological developments alter our ability to communicate with one another locally, nationally, and around the globe. Parents can monitor their baby's every activity whether in the next room or at work across town by the use of two-way radios, video cameras, and computer programs. Elementary school children as well as university students wear pagers and carry digital phones, blackberries, and other electronic devices that keep them in contact with babysitters, parents, friends, drug dealers, parole officers, and anybody else with whom they feel the need to communicate. Computers and the Internet have revolutionized comtemporary education and the use of e-mail, on-line

chat rooms, and the creation of virtual communities have permanently altered our abilities to communicate and interact with others in our everyday lives. In the future, these and other technological advancements will create more and not fewer changes in our interaction capabilities.

We posed the question at the beginning of this chapter as to whether the communications between Fred and "Nina" should even be categorized as social interaction. Is a person sitting all alone in front of a computer engaged in social interaction? If so, how does this type of interaction differ from face-to-face interaction? What happens to those ever important variables such as age, race, ethnicity, sex, gender, and social class that traditionally have had such powerful influence on social interaction in our daily lives? Howard Rheingold (2002:xxviii) poses some additional questions that will be of increasing interest to sociologists in the future:

- Does using the Internet make people happier or unhappier?
- Is the Internet empowering, or is it a tool of social control?
- Is the Internet addicting?
- Does virtual community erode face-to-face community?

Based on the reading of this chapter and your personal experiences, how would you answer these questions? Do technology and technicians hold the key to the future? Some in the popular media lend strong support to the idea that technological advances eventually will solve all social problems and ultimately produce utopian societies. Others believe dystopian societies are more likely and that unbridled technological change will eventually lead to environmental destruction and global terrorism and war. Visions of the future, however, are never passive reflections of historical reality, but are often self-fulfilling prophecies that influence and shape the future.

Summary

1. The basic elements of social structure that provide the framework for interaction are statuses, role networks, and institutions.

2. Social interactions tend to fall into patterns of exchange, cooperation, competition, conflict, or coercion.

3. Much of the social interaction in our everyday lives is guided by social perception and stereotypes.

4. Personal space and nonverbal communication play important roles in shaping and influencing our interactions with others.

5. During social interaction, we continually define and redefine situations in such a way as to give meaning to the interaction.

6. Dramaturgy uses the analogy of the theater to analyze interaction as social performances involving the presentation of self and impression management.

7. Ethnomethodolgy examines the taken-for-granted aspects of social interaction showing how we "fill in the gaps" and use common understandings to interact with others.

8. The mass media and technomedia have had tremendous influence on social interaction and will continue to alter social institutions and the ways we interact with one another in the future.

9. Structural functionalists tend to focus on exchange and cooperation as the most important aspects of interaction, while conflict theorists emphasize competition, conflict, and coercion. Meanwhile symbolic interactionists focus on the micro-level aspects of day-to-day, face-to-face interaction and how actors manipulate symbols to give meaning to their actions and the actions of others.

10. In the future, increased technology and the ability to "interact" through cyberspace will redefine the meaning of social interaction in our everyday lives.

Key Terms

Chapter 6

Social Groups and Organizations

"A committee can make a decision that is dumber than any of its members."
—David Coblitz

*T*he request, "May I take your order, please?" is familiar to everyone in the world today. Obviously you are in a McDonald's, Burger King, Starbucks, or some other fast-food restaurant, where global corporations have programmed worker greetings, worker routines, and even worker attitudes to a standardized formula. Jennifer Talwar's study of immigrant fast-food restaurants in New York City, however, suggests, once again, that *things may not be what they seem*. Talwar found that in places like Chinatown and Little Dominican Republic in New York City, fast-food organizations have somehow managed to combine rigid standardization with remarkable flexibility to market their products in some of the largest and most ethnically diverse cities in the world (Talwar, 2002).

In Chinatown, for example, new consumer marketing strategies present McDonald's as an "authentic Chinese" fast-food restaurant. The sign outside is in Chinese, a two-story Chinese arch inside is painted red for good luck, and the "front wall displays four Chinese characters that symbolize long life, happy marriage, lots of children, and lucky money" (Talwar, 2002:22–23). Mandarin Chinese is spoken in addition to English, and, just as in Beijing, China, the outlet hires "hostesses" to greet families and entertain children. "Cultural managers" represent the neighborhood and most workers are from China, although a "United Nations staff" (from more than a dozen countries including Malaysia, Dominican Republic, Honduras, and Togo, Africa) now pool their talents to portray McDonald's as an "American and Chinese eatery"—all in one (Talwar, 2002:18). Likewise, select "Chinese values" including teamwork and loyalty are emphasized at some restaurants, "United Nations" potluck dinners are held to promote "organizational unity," and employees—regardless of ethnicity—"are more apt to be dismissed or suspended . . . for having poor school grades than for refusing to work when not scheduled" (Talwar, 2002:140).

Restaurants in Little Dominican Republic demonstrate similar sensitivity to ethnic heritage and community life and the McDonald's in the very heart of the neighborhood has almost completely reinvented itself as a "Latino-American" experience. Spanish is spoken almost exclusively by workers and customers alike, and ironically, McDonald's has redefined itself as a place of "leisure," where Dominicans and other Latinos can munch on a chicken fajita and chat with friends for long periods. Talwar (2002:34) remarks that she "stood on line at one McDonald's in Little Dominican Republican for twenty minutes . . . and then waited another ten minutes for a table." Employees have been instructed to say "permisso," not "excuse me," and "honor and respect" have infiltrated worker-customer relations, with some managers instructing employees on how to tactfully "defend themselves" against rude customers behavior and insults.

McDonald's is as standard a feature in Chinatown as anywhere else today. Customers recognize the famous golden arches and can find standard fare such as Big Macs and fries, but they also will find localized and regionalized cultural symbols reflecting different group and organizational values and goals.

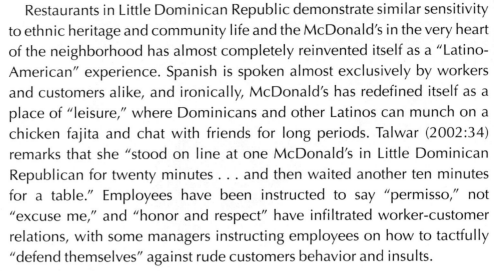

From the very beginning of the discipline, sociologists have highlighted the powerful influence of groups and organizations on people's thoughts and behaviors. Virtually all important human activities are embedded in groups and organizations; we could not function, let alone prosper, without them. As we discuss in this chapter, diverse groups and organizations establish a range of possibilities for what all of us can think and feel, as well as become and achieve—and that includes the proliferating fast-food organizations that are currently sweeping the globe.

SOCIAL GROUPS

When standing in line waiting to purchase a ticket to a movie, are you part of a group? What if you notice that the person in front of you is left-handed, and that she is wearing a wrist watch just like yours? Would these shared traits make the two of you members of a group? The first example, people waiting to buy a ticket, is not a group but an **aggregate,** which is *a collection of people who happen to be in the same place at the same time.* In an aggregate, as opposed to a group, the interaction is brief, expectations are limited, and people have no sense of belonging together. Left-handed people who own identical watches also are not a group but a **category**—*people with similar social characteristics or a common status.* A category includes people who have common characteristics but do not necessarily have patterned relationships, such as students, farmers, ministers, and Asian Americans.

Although left-handed people, farmers, and students may sometimes recognize others with these characteristics and may occasionally be mobilized into groups, for the most part they rarely interact and remain strangers. If you own a Mustang convertible and you pass someone on the highway driving an identical car, you may wave at him or her. That wave, however, represents the entire interaction, for you may never see each other again.

In the course of our daily lives, there are many chance encounters with strangers who make brief appearances and then disappear, never to reenter our lives. But patterned interactions are more common and more socially significant. Most human activity occurs in a **social group,** which consists of *two or more people who interact in patterned ways, have a feeling of unity, and share interests and expectations.*

Group interactions are fundamental to human existence. We spend most of our lives in groups. We are born in the presence of a group, we work and play in groups, and in large and complex societies like the United States, a multitude of groups, including hospital employees, funeral directors and their staffs, church congregations, and insurance workers, ensure that we make a proper exit. Groups are literally everywhere. Two lovers are a group, and so are three or four friends who spend an afternoon hanging out on a street corner or at a shopping mall. Your family is a group, and cafeteria workers who serve food at the cafeteria are one of many groups that enable your college to function.

AGGREGATE
A collection of people who happen to be in the same place at the same time.

CATEGORY
People with similar social characteristics or a common status.

SOCIAL GROUP
Two or more people who interact in patterned ways, have a feeling of unity, and share interests and expectations.

Because human activities of every kind are embedded in social groups, they are highly variable. Social groups may be large or small, temporary or long-lasting, intimate or impersonal, loosely organized or tightly knit. Some groups have a strong influence on peoples' behaviors and their members are deeply committed to the group. Others have little influence, and people do not much care whether they continue or disband. If we combine group dimensions of every kind, all groups can be classified into two major categories: primary and secondary groups.

Primary and Secondary Groups

A **primary group** consists of *people who regularly interact and have close and enduring relationships.* When he coined the term, Charles Horton Cooley (1909:23) used the word *primary* because he believed small, intimate groups were "fundamental in forming the social nature and ideas of the individual."

In primary groups people interact with one another on an informal basis, and relationships are flexible and enduring. Moreover, people are treated as total social persons, not just in terms of particular social identities, such as student or customer. In primary groups, relationships are valued not for what they can do for members, but for the relationships themselves. These *expressive* relationships usually have deep emotional significance and meaning for people. People develop strong attachments to primary groups and often use the word *we* when referring to them (Cooley, 1909). Two lovers, a family, close friends, and neighbors who see each other regularly and who care about each other's welfare are good examples of primary groups.

In simple, preindustrial societies, most interactions occur in primary groups of kin, friends, and neighbors. By contrast, in modern industrial and postindustrial societies, secondary group interactions are very important. A **secondary group** consists of *two or more people who interact on a formal and impersonal basis to accomplish a specific objective.* Sociologists call these activities *instrumental behavior,* because people interact with others not as an end in itself, but to achieve specific goals. In most secondary relationships, interactions are limited and often brief, rules are important, and people relate to one another in terms of specific roles. For example, professors and students may get to know each other pretty well during a semester, but primarily in terms of their reciprocal roles. It is rare for either to know where the other lives, the names of spouses and children, or how the other person spends his or her leisure time. Secondary groups may be small or large, but all large groups in which regular face-to-face interaction is impossible are secondary groups.

If you examine your daily routines, you will discover that whereas a few hours each day may be devoted to your family and friends, much of the day's activities are embedded in secondary groups. When you visit a restaurant, attend class, shop at the mall, go to church, participate in a club meeting, or have a brief chat with the mail carrier, you are engaging in secondary group activities. The distinction between primary and secondary groups, however, is not always clearcut, and in everyday life groups may include elements of each *ideal type.*

For example, when co-workers begin to see each other after work and engage in multifaceted relationships, office relationships often come to include both primary and secondary traits, and primary groups may emerge. When this occurs, co-workers often bend the rules and sometimes even subvert the group's formal objectives in order to accommodate each other's personal talents, interests, and needs. Table 6.1 lists important primary and secondary group characteristics.

PRIMARY GROUP
People who regularly interact and have close and enduring relationships.

SECONDARY GROUP
Two or more people who interact on a formal and impersonal basis to accomplish a specific objective.

Is your Introductory Sociology class a primary or secondary group?

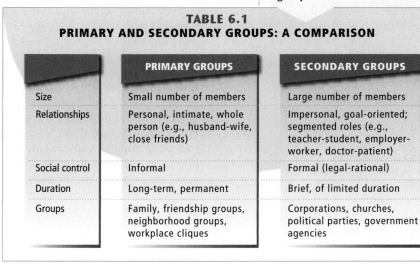

TABLE 6.1
PRIMARY AND SECONDARY GROUPS: A COMPARISON

	PRIMARY GROUPS	SECONDARY GROUPS
Size	Small number of members	Large number of members
Relationships	Personal, intimate, whole person (e.g., husband-wife, close friends)	Impersonal, goal-oriented; segmented roles (e.g., teacher-student, employer-worker, doctor-patient)
Social control	Informal	Formal (legal-rational)
Duration	Long-term, permanent	Brief, of limited duration
Groups	Family, friendship groups, neighborhood groups, workplace cliques	Corporations, churches, political parties, government agencies

In-Groups and Out-Groups

Even groups that we are not members of may have a strong influence on our behavior. This is because all groups distinguish and maintain their boundaries with the help of outside groups. An **in-group** is *a group with which people identify and have a sense of belonging.* In contrast, an **out-group** is *a group that people do not identify with and consider less worthy and less desirable than their own.* In-group boundaries are commonly maintained by challenges and threats—either real or imagined—from out-groups. Likewise, the "we-ness" or cohesiveness of a group is often proportional to the nature and intensity of these threats (Sumner, 1906; Lamont and Fournier, 1992).

At the heart of the in-group–out-group distinction is the concept of **social boundaries,** *material or symbolic devices that identify who is inside or outside a group.* In some cases groups are distinguished and interactions regulated by means of actual physical barriers, such as the Great Wall of China. In others, territories such as neighborhoods, regions, and nation-states may contain fences, gates, and other physical barriers to keep some people in and others out (see Map 6.1).

Social distinctions and symbolic barriers are equally effective in boundary maintenance. In Northern Ireland, for example, religion distinguishes one group from another; Roman Catholics paint their front doors green, and Protestants paint their doors blue (Gelman, 1989). Athletic teams, fraternities and sororities, and youth gangs use colors, language, emblems, mascots, insignias, and other symbols to set themselves apart from others as well.

Reference Groups

Are you attractive? Are you a good person? Are you rich or poor? There is no objective answer to any of these questions. Rather, the answer depends on the *groups that people refer to when evaluating their personal qualities, circumstances, attitudes, values, and behaviors.* Sociologists call these **reference groups,** and they may serve both positive and negative functions. For example, when Little League players choose Major League baseball players as their reference group they may copy their best behaviors and become cooperative, honest, and fair. Of course, the Little Leaguers may also learn to curse, chew tobacco, throw temper tantrums, and exhibit other socially disapproved behaviors.

Some reference groups give us a sense of *relative gratification* (Singer, 1981). For example, people of average income may judge themselves rich if they use people on welfare or the homeless as reference groups. On the other hand, most people would experience a sense of *relative deprivation*—feelings of dissatisfaction based on the gap between what they have and what they would like to have—if they used billionaires Bill Gates or Warren Buffet as their reference group. In much the same way, if we judge our looks by how well we compare to top fashion models on the covers of *Vogue* and *GQ,* we are unlikely to feel very good about our appearance.

Many people boost their self-esteem and social standing by associating with successful groups (Felson and Reed, 1986). A good example is some peoples' strong identification with winning athletic teams. Many fans proudly display the banners, flags, coffee mugs, and license plates of these teams—not only to declare their allegiance but to make a public statement about themselves: that they, too, are winners. Of course, reference groups can be used in the opposite way. Parents are notorious for comparing their children's unacceptable behaviors to those of reference groups that are paragons of virtue and high achievement.

Sports fans provide excellent examples of in-group and out-group behavior.

IN-GROUP
A group with which people identify and have a sense of belonging.

OUT-GROUP
A group that people do not identify with and consider less worthy and less desirable than their own.

SOCIAL BOUNDARIES
Material or symbolic devices that identify who is inside or outside a group.

REFERENCE GROUPS
Groups that people refer to when evaluating their personal qualities, circumstances, attitudes, values, and behaviors.

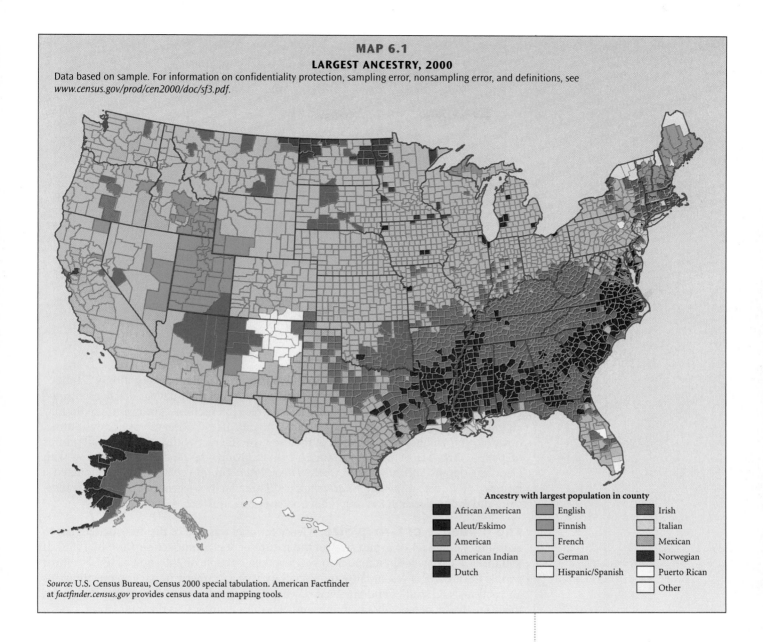

MAP 6.1

LARGEST ANCESTRY, 2000

Data based on sample. For information on confidentiality protection, sampling error, nonsampling error, and definitions, see www.census.gov/prod/cen2000/doc/sf3.pdf.

Ancestry with largest population in county

African American	English	Irish
Aleut/Eskimo	Finnish	Italian
American	French	Mexican
American Indian	German	Norwegian
Dutch	Hispanic/Spanish	Puerto Rican
		Other

Source: U.S. Census Bureau, Census 2000 special tabulation. American Factfinder at *factfinder.census.gov* provides census data and mapping tools.

In modern, complex societies people may choose from among a multitude of reference groups, and these groups may conflict with or reinforce one another. For example, early in their college careers, when parents are an important reference group, college students tend to have conservative attitudes about sex. By contrast, sexual attitudes and behaviors become much more permissive as peers become a more important reference group (Walsh et al., 1976, cited in Worchel et al., 1991). Likewise, corporate marketers depend on trendsetters as well as peer group influence "to encourage" teenagers and preteens to purchase and display luxury brands like Christian Dior, Polo, and Gucci—brands that they aim "to register so strongly in kids' minds that the appeal will remain for life" (Holstein, 2003:1). Figure 6.1 demonstrates the influence of peer groups on consumer behavior. Because there are so many choices, people also can be creative when it comes to selecting a reference group. For example, a student who received a C on an exam may choose as his or her reference group students who got an F—at least for parental consumption. Parents, on the other hand, rarely accept the worst students as their children's reference group; instead, they almost always choose A students.

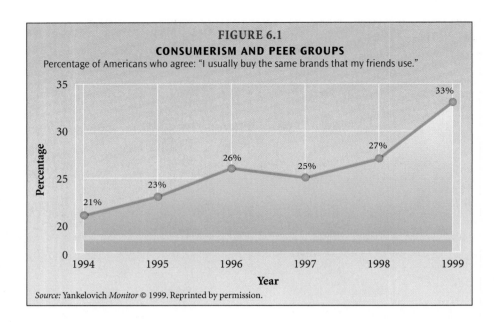

FIGURE 6.1
CONSUMERISM AND PEER GROUPS
Percentage of Americans who agree: "I usually buy the same brands that my friends use."

Source: Yankelovich *Monitor* © 1999. Reprinted by permission.

Small Group Dynamics

Although groups may range in size from two friends to a giant corporation with thousands of workers all over the globe, most people conduct their day-to-day lives in *small groups* in which members have regular face-to-face interactions. For example, you may attend a university that has 20,000–30,000 students. If you observe your daily routine, however, you will notice that much of the time you interact with the same small groups of people. Because of the importance of small groups, researchers—beginning with George Homans and his classic work, *The Human Group* (1950)—have conducted a number of studies of *small group dynamics.* Three factors—group size, group leadership, and group decision making—have received the most scholarly attention.

The Influence of Group Size Georg Simmel was one of the first sociologists to examine the impact of group size on the nature of social interaction ([1908] 1955). If you threw a party, would it matter to you whether 2 people or 200 showed up? For most people the answer is yes, because numbers can have a dramatic impact on our thoughts and actions. Lab studies and our everyday experiences tell us that the smaller the group, the more direct, personally satisfying, and emotionally intense is the interaction.

The smallest possible group is a **dyad**—*a two-person group.* In the dyad, the individual must take account of no one but the other person, thus "individuals can give themselves to each other totally" (Palazzolo, 1981:69). However, because the relationship is totally dependent on the continued participation of both parties, it is also the most fragile, demanding, tension-filled, and precarious of all relationships. Should either party even temporarily ignore the other, the relationship may be threatened; if one withdraws, the dyad ceases to exist.

When another person is added and a **triad,** or *a three-member group,* emerges, the nature of the interaction becomes less intimate but more flexible. In a triad one member may temporarily withdraw, daydream, or become silent without harming the group. Moreover, within the triad various coalitions are possible that cannot be found in a dyad. A third person may mediate conflicts, join with one member to gang up on the third, or take power by manipulating the other two. Even small increases in group size can have a dramatic impact on social interaction.

In a dyad there is only one relationship, but with each added member the number of relationships increases dramatically. For example, if a group expands to four there are six possible relationships; with the addition of only one more member—a group of five—there are ten possible relationships (see Figure 6.2) (Palazzolo, 1981).

DYAD
A two-person group.

TRIAD
A three-member group.

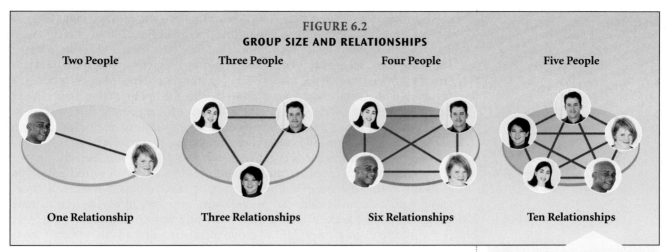

FIGURE 6.2
GROUP SIZE AND RELATIONSHIPS

Two People — One Relationship

Three People — Three Relationships

Four People — Six Relationships

Five People — Ten Relationships

Which size group do you believe is ideal for working together on a class project?

A number of studies suggest that 5 members make the ideal discussion or work group. When a group exceeds 7, direct interaction among members becomes difficult, and, as any observant person knows who has attended a party, the group begins to fragment into smaller groups. If the group exceeds 12, it becomes impossible for people to interact with all members of the group, and usually someone is chosen to direct group activities. At the same time, members' participation decreases, and people begin to treat others in a more formal and rigid way, addressing the group as a whole rather than as individual members (Levine and Moreland, 1998). With these problems in mind, why do you think the American criminal justice system chose 12 as the typical jury size?

As group size increases, there is also an increased chance for a specialized division of labor. With more individuals and more talent and specialized skills available, proportionately greater results can be achieved in many social spheres. Studies have shown that this is not always the case, however. As groups grow, people often reduce their efforts, a phenomenon sociologists call *social loafing*. People seem to do this because they think their efforts cannot be monitored or appreciated or because they expect that others will loaf and they do not want to carry more than their share of the load or be exploited. Experiments also have shown that in the presence of large public groups, people are less willing to assist someone in need than they would be if they were the only one available to help. In large groups, witnesses often assume that someone else will help out, so they shift responsibility to others (Latané and Nida, 1981; Jackson and Harkins, 1985; Levine and Moreland, 1998).

Group Leadership Most groups have leaders. Even many small informal groups include a leader, although we do not always recognize them as such. For example, have you noticed that when you and two other students decide to meet for a coffee break, one person usually suggests where and when to meet and the others tacitly follow the suggestion? Charles Palazzolo (1981:213) wrote that *leadership* is a group process in which an individual, in a given situation, "is able to direct and control group interaction more influentially than any other group member." It is often assumed that leaders possess special traits that distinguish them from followers, but this may not be the case. This is because leadership is situational and task-specific, and leadership qualities and skills that are appropriate in one situation may be inappropriate in another. Moreover, leadership is a two-way street. Any understanding of leadership must include knowledge of how followers perceive their leaders, as well as how this affects group processes and the behavior of leaders.

Leaders often vary according to their leadership style, which may assume any one of three basic forms: authoritarian, democratic, and laissez-faire (Lippitt and White, 1958).

Authoritarian leaders give orders and direct activities with minimal input from followers. In extreme cases, they may be said to rule with an iron fist that crushes all dissent. In cultures where it is customary for authoritarian leaders to make decisions in both political and domestic spheres, this leadership style may be preferred. In egalitarian societies authoritarian leaders may be tolerated, but members of small groups typically prefer individuals with a *democratic* leadership style, who attempt to involve others in decision making. Laissez-faire style leaders take a "hands-off" approach; they neither set the agenda nor try to direct followers in any obvious way. Instead, they allow group members the freedom to choose whatever direction the group thinks is best.

No single leadership style is effective in every social situation. Because they require neither agreement nor support, authoritarian leaders often fail to recognize conflicts and strains within the group that may reduce its effectiveness. But when a situation is unclear, authoritarian leaders can provide structure and, in emergencies, immediate action. Democratic leaders operate well under ordinary circumstances, where there is time for leaders to gain input from all group members and then take action (Chemers et al., 1975). Laissez-faire leadership seems to be the least effective of the three styles, at least in lab experiments with American youngsters. Laissez-faire leadership can be productive if group members are highly motivated, but without direction group members eventually work at cross-purposes and interpersonal tensions and conflicts may threaten the group.

Conformity and Group Decision Making To function properly, group members must cooperate to accomplish a task. Leaders can help define and coordinate group activities, but something more is required if groups are to achieve their goals—individuals must conform to the group's opinions and expectations. One of the most important discoveries in the area of small group dynamics is that there are intense pressures on individuals to conform.

In an early study of conformity, Muzafer Sherif (1936) asked subjects to stare at a stationary point of light that, because of the autokinetic effect, appeared to be moving. First, individuals were asked how far they thought the light had moved, and their estimates were plotted. Next, groups of two or three people were asked to do the same thing. Sherif found that when subjects were uncertain about their own judgments, they relied on the opinions of others and that estimates in groups converged on a common judgment (Sherif, cited in Michener et al., 1986).

The classic experiment on group conformity is the Asch experiment. Asch (1952) created an experiment in which groups of various size were selected and coached to give the wrong answer about the length of lines on various cards. He found that these groups of perfect strangers were able to pressure individuals into agreeing with their distorted view of reality. The pressure to conform was so intense that more than one-third of the subjects, though convinced their judgments were correct, changed them to accommodate to the majority opinion.

To what extent might some of the policies and decisions regarding the Iraqi war have been a result of what sociologists call *groupthink*?

If individuals can be persuaded by strangers, there should be much more intense pressure to conform to primary groups, in which individuals are committed to others. Irving Janis (1972) found that in tightly knit groups the pressures to conform are indeed strong, because they are reinforced by intense feelings of loyalty. According to Janis (1972), this can result in **groupthink,** *decision making that ignores alternative solutions in order to maintain group harmony.* Janis wrote that groupthink can have disastrous results. His favorite example is the decision of President John F. Kennedy and a small group of advisers to attempt an overthrow of the Castro regime in the Bay of Pigs invasion of Cuba in 1961. Janis discovered that although several members had serious reservations about many aspects of the plan, once a consensus was reached they neither voiced their concerns nor sought outside opinions. The result was a swift and embarrassing defeat for 1,400 CIA-trained Cuban refugees. Some journalists argue that groupthink may have been an important factor in several NASA space shuttle disasters—including the loss of the Challenger in 1986 and the Columbia disaster in 2003. For example, the journalists claim that once engineers and important decision makers in the Columbia case reached a consensus that the falling foam insulation did not endanger the shuttle, the missions were allowed to proceed, although "other engineers who had been consulted became increasingly concerned and frustrated" (Schwartz and Wald, 2003:1). One nuclear engineer contends that similar problems may characterize nuclear power plants as well: "As you go up the chain, you're asked harder and harder questions by people who have more and more control. The group answering the questions then tend to agree on a single answer, and to be reluctant to admit it when they don't have an answer (Schwartz and Wald, 2003:2).

The Bay of Pigs fiasco and perhaps even NASA's shuttle disasters seem to support the popular notion that groups are inherently conservative, but researchers have found that this is true only in certain situations. Experiments have shown that during the decision-making process, group members often shift toward extreme positions—either conservative or high-risk—a tendency that is called the *group polarization phenomenon* (Myers and Lamm, 1978). But, as in social life in general, the opinions of group members are not all equal. Any model of social influence must allow for inequalities of interpersonal influence, for situations where there is no initial consensus and where no group members' opinions are fixed (Friedkin, 1999).

When the choice is culturally favored, a *risky shift* often occurs; that is, people take greater risks in groups than they might have had they acted independently. For example, James Stoner (1961) presented subjects with a hypothetical case in which an engineer could continue in a secure but low-paying job or take a high-risk job in a newly formed company. He found that after group discussions, individuals typically took the high-risk course of action. However, when a group had to decide on a socially disapproved or unpopular course of action, group members became more cautious, often because group discussion and debate alerted them to problems they might not have anticipated as individuals. In general, "subjects who are exposed to mostly risky arguments become more risk-taking, whereas those who hear mostly conservative arguments become more cautious" (Michener et al., 1986). The study of group dynamics is beginning to shift to an important new area, "cybergroups" on the Net, which we discuss in Focus box 6.1. Of course, job and career shifts involve more than personal factors. Most depend on the larger economy and the relative fortunes of large formal organizations.

FORMAL ORGANIZATIONS

In some parts of the world small primary groups of kin, neighbors, and friends continue to play a central role in people's lives, not only providing emotional support but fulfilling most of their members' basic needs. In modern societies, though, primary groups often form the backdrop rather than center stage in people's day-to-day lives.

GROUPTHINK
Decision making that ignores alternative solutions in order to maintain group harmony.

A colleague returned home recently to find his 14-year-old son alone at the computer, playing a game. When he asked his son how his day had been, the boy responded, "Just a minute, Dad, I'm with two other guys." The father was confused. As it turned out, the son was playing a computer game with two other people, but this play group was a cybergroup that consisted of a 14-year-old boy in the United States and two adult men—a U.S. serviceman in England and a 60-year-old mechanic in Poland.

In 2001, the Kyodo News Service in Japan reported, "Police arrested five teenage members of 'Mad Wing Angels,' a virtual motorcycle gang that met via media texting, including members who didn't own motorcycles, and had never gath- ered in one place at the same time. The leader had never met the four Tokyo girls she ordered to beat and torture a fifth gang member who asked permission to leave the group to study abroad" (Rheingold, 2002:4).

Sociologists are beginning to conduct research in this important new area. Several exploratory studies have examined how a limited social presence (compared to face-to-face interaction) affects group dynamics and decision making. In cybergroups, most of the social cues that help to guide everyday interactions are either absent or unclear. For example, in cybergroups there are neither verbal cues nor body language to help with the interaction. Likewise, observable information about social contexts and social characteristics (e.g., race, class, gender, age) of group members may also be lacking, ambiguous, or potentially false.

This is not to say that there are no detectable status differences in cyberspace. People can provide status cues like titles (senior vice-president) and can demonstrate status and competence through computer language, prestigious e-mail addresses, and names that protect anonymity but are well-known on-line. A new computer lexicon that is developing includes icons for all sorts of emotions, from smiling faces to express happiness or agreement to flames to express anger or contempt. But most of the trappings and seeming certainties of real-life power and authority become less certain in computer-mediated

Japanese teens "texting."

Are they participating in small group behavior—although their close friends are not actually present? And are these cybergroups altering the very nature of face-to-face interaction—as this photo suggests?

In modern societies, people's lives are largely shaped by **formal organizations,** which are *secondary groups that are formally organized to achieve specific goals.* Such organizations are the fundamental building blocks of the contemporary social order— they produce and distribute goods and services, maintain order, and fulfill our spiritual and physical needs (Aldrich and Marsden, 1988). If you are injured on the way to school you would appreciate the help of a group of bystanders. However, your survival depends on formal organizations—the telephone company that enables people to notify an emergency crew, hospital workers to assist in your recovery, and insurance companies to help you pay hospital and emergency care bills.

Moreover, as Charles Perrow (2000:474) observed, since the beginning of the nineteenth century, large organizations have played the key role in shaping stratification systems across the globe. Today, more than "half of the working population works for

FORMAL ORGANIZATIONS
Secondary groups that are formally organized to achieve specific goals.

interactions, where people are both socially and physically distant. Perhaps the most noteworthy difference between cybergroups and face-to-face groups is "the emphasis on shared interests rather than social characteristics" (Wellman, 1996:225).

Another major difference between cybergroups and face-to-face interaction relates to group size. In real life, most people regularly interact with fewer than 25 kin, friends, and coworkers, whereas they are acquainted with perhaps as many as 1,000 people. Computers have expanded these numbers dramatically, making it possible to interact with an unlimited number of people and groups, all across the globe, and to create new groups and terminate others instantaneously. Research in the 1990s suggested that participation in on-line groups might reduce off-line social interaction—especially interaction with kin, friends, neighbors. Research in the twenty-first century, however, suggests the opposite is the case. Studies have found that numerous "virtual" social connections actually "reinforce pre-existing social, political, and cultural patterns." That is, for people who are already active members of numerous "off-line groups" the Internet adds a new layer of communication opportunities (Matei and Ball-Rokeach, 2002:405). "Interestingly, one study of ethnically diverse neighborhoods in Los Angeles found that most new on-line social connections tended to be made within one's ethnic group. Asian Americans in particular seemed more cautious in venturing outside their groups and social networks, with some believing that on-line relationships outside one's in-groups were shallow, unsavory, or even dangerous. As one Korean woman put it, "On-line friends are just for fun, not for serious relationships" (Matei and Ball-Rokeach, 2002:420).

Studies have found cybergroups to resemble both primary and secondary groups—but not to fit either ideal type very well. One sociologist defined cybergroup ties as "moderately strong intimate secondary relationships" (Wireman, cited in Wellman et al., 1996:222). They can be simultaneously detached and intensively emotional, enduring or brief. Most cybergroup interactions are relatively superficial, yet they can also produce powerful emotional bonds and lasting ties—even marriages, as in the case of an American woman who quit her job and flew to England to marry a fellow Net user whom she had never met (Wellman et al., 1996).

This strange comingling of primary and secondary group traits is explained in part by the special nature of computer-mediated interactions. They tend to be more open, egalitarian, and creative than groups in everyday life. People communicate more freely and easily in cybergroups, and relative anonymity makes it easier to express inner thoughts and feelings. This gives cybergroups the potential of becoming very effective support groups. Likewise, because individuals are less constrained by group pressures and opinions on-line, cybergroups tend to be very creative. People seem to be more willing to take risks on-line than they would in real life.

Such freedoms, of course, have a downside. Without clear patterns of authority and leadership, group consensus is often difficult to reach on-line. And cybergroups seem to have difficulty reaching decisions that would be considered simple and routine in face-to-face interactions. Moreover, the social solidarity that is associated with traditional work groups is often lacking in cybergroups, where "each person is at the center of a unique personal community and work group" (Wellman et al., 1996:232). Sociologists also want to know what new dilemmas will emerge as more people shift back and forth between cybergroups and groups in real life.

TAKING A CLOSER LOOK
How might the proliferation of cybergroups affect people's understandings of groups in the future? Use your own experiences on-line and off-line to chart future directions.

Source: Barry Wellman, Janet Salaff, Dimitrina Dimitrova, Laura Garton, Milena Gulia, and Caroline Haythornthwaite. "Computer Networks as Social Networks: Collaborative Work, Telework, and Virtual Community." *Annual Review of Sociology* 22, 1996:213–238. Nancy K. Baym. "The Emergence of Online Community." *Cyber-Society 2.0: Revisiting Computer-Mediated Communication and Community.* Thousand Oaks, CA: Sage, 1998:35–68.

highly stratified organizations . . . and the organizations themselves exist in a highly stratified population of organizations."

Sociological Approaches to Organizations

Are organizations important and necessary to modern society? Or do they cause more harm than good, primarily benefiting bureaucrats and the wealthy and powerful and only sometimes serving people's needs? In sociology, the answer depends on which approach you take to organizations.

The Structural Functionalist Approach
From the functionalist perspective, formal organizations are necessary to the proper functioning of large and complex societies, which currently include millions or even billions of people. We typically associate

formal organizations with large-scale endeavors, such as NASA space projects, but organizations play a vital role in every social sphere. Without formal organizations there would be no radio to wake us in the morning, and we could not drive to work because there would be neither cars nor highways. We would have to depend on our gardens for food because there would be no supermarkets, and children would discover they had huge amounts of time to fill, for there would be no schools, churches, recreation leagues and clubs, or, most of all, no televisions and computers.

Of course, not all formal organizations serve such positive and socially beneficial purposes. Some formal organizations, such as gangs, may represent an alternative social order that mainstream society defines as deviant and threatening. Functionalists stress that they are dysfunctional and a threat to the larger society as a whole.

The Conflict Perspective From the conflict perspective, organizations emerged not because they benefited "society," but because they offered elites greater ability to meet the challenges of competitors, and more effective ways to control subordinates (Perrow, 1986). From the conflict approach, organizations reflect and reinforce social inequality, because most are hierarchically ranked in terms of their access to scarce but valued resources. Conflict theorists see organizations primarily as defenders of the status quo—not "society"—from giant government and corporate bureaucracies down to the smallest community clubs, which carefully screen membership lists to keep out minorities and other "have-nots."

To conflict theorists, organizational goals, rules, and regulations function to perpetuate the wealth, prestige, and power of those at the top of the hierarchy and to exploit those at lower levels—a process that is characteristic of capitalistic societies as a whole. Such inequalities reverberate throughout society and produce tensions, conflicts, and social problems at every level of society: worker alienation, feelings of isolation, and powerlessness are just a few of the costs people have paid for efficiency, consumer products, and other benefits that large organizations contribute to contemporary life (Bensman and Rosenberg, 1976; Hummel, 1977).

Symbolic Interactionism From the symbolic interactionist perspective, it is people—not organizations—that have goals. Further, these goals are often more complex and dynamic than the formal objectives of any organization. In addition, while organizations have rules and constraints that limit individual choices and behaviors, it is people and the meanings they bring to their everyday interactions with co-workers, bosses, and others that produce and reproduce organizational structures. Interactionists contend that organizations are often so large and complex that few workers understand the many rules and regulations. They manage to function, they say, not because of rules, but with the help of people and small groups who in everyday interaction negotiate, compromise, reach agreements, and even redefine rules to suit their purposes and needs (Maines, 1977; Fine, 1984).

Types of Organizations

Formal organizations may be classified into three major types: voluntary, coercive, and utilitarian (Etzioni, 1975). Organizations that people join freely to accomplish goals are called *voluntary organizations*. They typically contain like-minded people who pursue shared goals because they find them personally and socially rewarding. According to sociologist John Wilson (2000:223), "extensive social networks, multiple organizational memberships, and prior volunteer experience all increase the chances of volunteering" in organizations such as soccer clubs, the PTA, a church choir, Mothers Against Drunk Drivers, and countless others.

Coercive organizations are those that people are forced to join. Prisons, mental institutions, elementary schools, and, where military service is compulsory, the armed forces are examples of coercive organizations. People join *utilitarian organizations* for practical reasons. For example, we may join a company to earn income or attend college to increase our knowledge and skills. Utilitarian organizations are in some ways intermediate between voluntary and coercive organizations, but such a scheme may be too simplistic. For example, most students think of universities as utilitarian organizations. But are they purely utilitarian in today's workplace, which demands many skills and advanced degrees to get and keep a job? Or are the penalties for not having a college degree so severe that universities have become coercive organizations? Gangs can be seen in much the same way. While some may be voluntary, others use physical intimidation and violence against those who resist becoming members.

Contemporary Organizations

Formal organizations are complex and difficult to classify. Richard Hall (2002) believes that any classification system must acknowledge a number of key ways that organizations differ in contemporary society. Size is one way to distinguish organizations: some organizations are small with relatively few members, resources, and clients; others may include tens of thousands of people with vast resources, like global corporations and military organizations. Some organizations are public and constrained by political authority, like schools and government agencies; others are private and constrained by economic authority—such as business. Likewise, some dominate their market or environment, while others have little influence or power. Hall remarks that organizations may be rigidly structured with a centralized power structure, or loosely structured and highly democratic, like some employee-owned business firms. Most of all, contemporary organizations are dynamic. As Hall (2002:105) wrote, organizations have the ability to "change in size, adopt new technologies, face changing environments and internal and national cultures, adopt new strategies or find old ones, and adjust to other organizations in their field." Our opening vignette concerning global fast-food restaurants attests to the remarkable ability of modern organizations to adapt to changing circumstances.

In this photo, members of the Vice Lords, Latin Kings, Bloods, and Crips gangs put their hands together in solidarity at the conclusion of a "peace summit" in Kansas City.

How might organizational structures influence the success or failure of this summit?

BUREAUCRACIES

Large-scale formal organizations came into being at least 6,000 years ago in Egypt and Mesopotamia, when cities and trade networks became so complex that regional centers developed. Religious elites began to coordinate the activities of many villages, and more complex organizations appeared to regulate water and maintain irrigation canals. Still others emerged to defend city-states against a growing list of enemies. Over the millennia, as organizations increased in size and complexity, a special kind of organization developed, which sociologists call a **bureaucracy,** *a large-scale organization that uses rules, hierarchical ranking, and a rational worldview to achieve maximum efficiency.* Throughout the preindustrial era there was a progressive trend toward a bureaucratic form of organization. However, it was not until the Industrial Revolution that almost all large-scale organizations became structured in a bureaucratic way and rationality and efficiency became guiding principles for society.

Bureaucracies: The Ideal Type

What do you think of when you hear the word *bureaucracy*? For many of us, it evokes images of long lines and delays and petty officials adhering to rules at the expense of reason. In the late nineteenth century, when Max Weber began his sociological investigation of bureaucratic organizations, he recognized that they had limitations. He warned that bureaucracy could become an *iron cage* "that shrinks a person's moral capacity into a mere duty to obey" (Otten, 1981:30). At the same time, however, Weber and his contemporaries were most impressed with bureaucracy's ability to

BUREAUCRACY
A large-scale organization that uses rules, hierarchical ranking, and a rational worldview to achieve maximum efficiency.

coordinate the activities of large groups of people—especially in business, medicine, and the military—and to outperform and outproduce all other forms of organization. This may include contemporary state structures. Evans and Rauch (1999:760) found: "state bureaucracies characterized by meritocratic recruitment and predictable rewarding career ladders are associated with higher growth rates." Weber was certain of bureaucracy's future, for he lived at a time when old-fashioned, personal organizations of every description, from mom-and-pop grocery stores to old-fashioned cavalry units, were being swept aside by a bureaucratic revolution.

Weber analyzed bureaucracy as an ideal type, which isolated for study only the essential characteristics of this form of organization. That is, instead of describing the various kinds of bureaucracies in government, education, business, and religion, Weber abstracted from them certain features that were common to all. To Weber (1978), bureaucracies owed their technical superiority to other forms of organization because of five basic characteristics:

1. *Specialization and Division of Labor.* Tasks are accomplished by people trained to perform specific duties. There is a clearcut division of labor among workers, with each person held responsible for a small portion of the total operation.

2. *Hierarchical Structure.* Positions are arranged in a hierarchical fashion. Rank and authority increase as one moves from the bottom to the top of the bureaucracy, and authority is clearly defined at every level. That is, people take orders from supervisors immediately above them until the head of the organization is reached. Conversely, directives and orders flow downward.

3. *Formal Rules, Regulations, and Procedures.* Written rules and regulations specify the goals of the organization, the work to be performed, and what workers can and cannot do. In principle, formal, written rules ensure uniformity of operations and provide continuity regardless of changes in personnel or organizational goals.

4. *Impersonality.* Interactions with clients and co-workers are guided by rules, not personal feelings. Ideally, emotional detachment ensures that everyone will be treated equally and that personal considerations will not cloud official judgments or subvert organizational goals.

5. *Merit and Careers.* Positions in the bureaucracy are based on qualifications and performance, which benefit the organization and gives people a sense of continuity and security; a "meritocracy" enables people to plan for careers, which ideally ensures a stronger worker identification and a greater commitment to the organization and its goals.

Contemporary Bureaucracies: The Reality

To be perfectly efficient and rational, Weber's ideal bureaucracy would have required that almost all traces of humanity be eliminated and that people consistently act in a cold and calculating manner—a scenario that seems better suited to robots than to humans. Sociologists have found that even in the largest bureaucracies, regular face-to-face contact often transforms impersonal secondary relationships into primary ties, and these in turn lead to the development of *informal structures,* with their own statuses, beliefs, norms, practices, and goals (Lehman and Etzioni, 1980; Perrow, 1986).

This process occurs in environments as diverse as the university classroom, the kill floor at a beef packing plant, and the army barracks, where soon after people have joined to accomplish an organization's formal goals, they develop their own ways of doing things. Informal structures sometimes promote greater bureaucratic efficiency. At other times they may have the opposite effect.

Numerous other forces may hinder bureaucracies from approaching Weber's ideal type. Organizational charters and rules may initially produce results, but if conditions change and workers remain attached to them, they may be transformed from assets into liabilities. In some cases **bureaucratic ritualism** may occur, where *workers conform to rules and procedures to such a degree that they become more important than goals* (Mert-

BUREAUCRATIC RITUALISM
Workers conform to rules and procedures to such a degree that they become more important than goals.

on, 1938). Bureaucracies are also geared to typical, routine cases, and when confronted with exceptions or extraordinary circumstances they may grind to a halt.

C. Northcote Parkinson found that bureaucracies not only waste time and money, they also are just as efficient at wasting human talent and energy. Calling it *Parkinson's Law,* he wrote that work expands to fill the time available for its completion (1957:15). Parkinson discovered that often in bureaucracies workers give the appearance of being busy, because if they appear otherwise they may be given additional work or even lose their jobs. This begins a vicious bureaucratic cycle. Because everyone scurries around frantically performing their duties, management assumes they are working to capacity and that more workers may be needed. According to Parkinson's Law, however, although the workforce steadily grows, very little additional work is ever produced. Of course, the Internet, too, may contribute to organizational efficiency and worker productivity or it may provide employees endless hours of distracting entertainment—during work. Likewise, it may facilitate worker sabotage. For example, all one disgruntled worker needed was access to e-mail to summon fellow employees and managers to "endless phantom meetings," which seriously disrupted company routines and morale until he was caught (Civin, 2000:162).

What do you think these people would think of Weber's description of bureaucracy as an ideal type for organizational efficiency?

Large and impersonal bureaucracies also can hide incompetents of every description, sometimes because they are hard to detect in large groups and sometimes because workers often cover up one another's failings. In what is now known as the *Peter Principle,* Laurence Peter and Raymond Hull (1969) asserted that in bureaucracies individuals are promoted until they reach their level of incompetence. In other words, bureaucracies reward people for doing a good job at a particular level by moving them up in the hierarchy, but there is never a guarantee that at the next level they will be able to perform satisfactorily. Many people eventually assume a position that demands more than they can handle; when this point is reached their progress stops. There, ineligible for further promotions, they perform jobs that are beyond their skills. Taking this to its logical conclusion, Peter and Hull asserted that most bureaucracies are filled with incompetent people at every bureaucratic level. How, then, do bureaucracies continue to function? According to Peter and Hull, at any given time there are usually plenty of workers who have *not* reached their level of incompetence—and they are responsible for keeping bureaucracies running.

Another problem that may have grave social consequences is that within large bureaucracies individuals often believe they can avoid responsibility for their actions. Activities that people would not do in small groups, because others would hold them accountable, are routinely performed in bureaucratic organizations, often to the detriment of others. For example, an individual who would not throw a candy wrapper in a neighbor's yard because his behavior would be sanctioned may, without the slightest fear or moral pangs, work for a chemical company that dumps tons of toxic chemicals into a river that supplies that same neighbor's drinking water. Today, in the name of national defense and shielded from responsibility by legions of officials and files marked top secret, defense contractors may threaten the public's well-being. At Rocky Flats, Colorado, for example, defense contractors were found not only to have contaminated local environments with hazardous materials, but to have routinely emitted high levels of radiation into the air for decades. Focus box 6.2 examines media images of government bureaucracies.

MEDIA ORGANIZATIONS AND CHANGE

In contemporary society, people continue to interact face-to-face. Moreover, in interaction we still give and receive messages, interpret them, and try to act in socially appropriate ways. However, as Bensman and Rosenberg (1976) noted, small, intimate groups no longer play the same role in shaping attitudes, values, and beliefs that they did before the advent of mass communication. Today, our attitudes, beliefs, and the very content of our daily conversations reflect the influence of the media—both the mass media and the technomedia (Bensman and Rosenberg, 1976; Dizard, 1997).

As an experiment, in conversations with family and friends one day, try to avoid any mention of something you learned on radio or television, on the Internet, or in a newspaper or magazine. You will be surprised at how difficult it is to carry on a conversation without media help.

Mass-Media Organizations

Mass communication contrasts markedly with face-to-face interaction in many ways. First, neither the communicator (medium) nor the receiver (audience) is a single person. The sender is usually a formal organization and its spokesperson a professional communicator, whereas the receiver is a large, heterogeneous, mass audience whose members are anonymous to one another (Dominick, 1987). Second, the communication does not involve give and take, with spontaneous and unpredictable elements, but instead is unidirectional, with the sender transmitting a standardized message and thousands or even millions of individuals receiving it. Mass communication thus allows extensive influence and, as Denis McQuail (1983:35) wrote, "much less variability of response than occurs with slow and sequential person-to-person diffusion of information."

Sociologists have focused much attention on the mass media as organizational systems. Following Etzioni's (1961) typology of organizations, sociologists classify most media organizations as *utilitarian,* for the majority operate for profit and people who receive their messages do so voluntarily. Many media organizations, however, are oper-

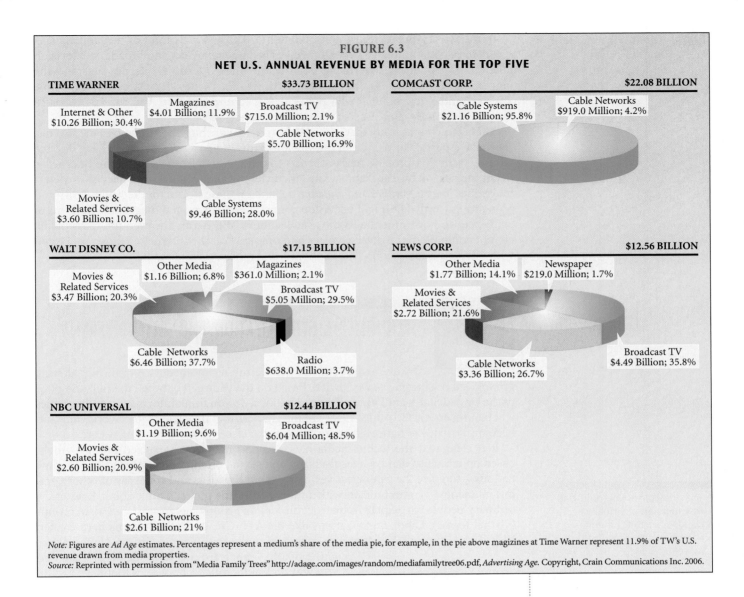

FIGURE 6.3

NET U.S. ANNUAL REVENUE BY MEDIA FOR THE TOP FIVE

TIME WARNER $33.73 BILLION

Internet & Other $10.26 Billion; 30.4%
Magazines $4.01 Billion; 11.9%
Broadcast TV $715.0 Million; 2.1%
Cable Networks $5.70 Billion; 16.9%
Movies & Related Services $3.60 Billion; 10.7%
Cable Systems $9.46 Billion; 28.0%

COMCAST CORP. $22.08 BILLION

Cable Systems $21.16 Billion; 95.8%
Cable Networks $919.0 Million; 4.2%

WALT DISNEY CO. $17.15 BILLION

Movies & Related Services $3.47 Billion; 20.3%
Other Media $1.16 Billion; 6.8%
Magazines $361.0 Million; 2.1%
Broadcast TV $5.05 Million; 29.5%
Cable Networks $6.46 Billion; 37.7%
Radio $638.0 Million; 3.7%

NEWS CORP. $12.56 BILLION

Other Media $1.77 Billion; 14.1%
Newspaper $219.0 Million; 1.7%
Movies & Related Services $2.72 Billion; 21.6%
Broadcast TV $4.49 Billion; 35.8%
Cable Networks $3.36 Billion; 26.7%

NBC UNIVERSAL $12.44 BILLION

Other Media $1.19 Billion; 9.6%
Broadcast TV $6.04 Million; 48.5%
Movies & Related Services $2.60 Billion; 20.9%
Cable Networks $2.61 Billion; 21%

Note: Figures are *Ad Age* estimates. Percentages represent a medium's share of the media pie, for example, in the pie above magizines at Time Warner represent 11.9% of TW's U.S. revenue drawn from media properties.

Source: Reprinted with permission from "Media Family Trees" http://adage.com/images/random/mediafamilytree06.pdf, *Advertising Age.* Copyright, Crain Communications Inc. 2006.

ated for both utilitarian and ideological ends, because they wish not only to make a profit but also to promote certain values and beliefs. In cases where media organizations are owned and operated by governments and messages must conform to an official view, the media appear to be more like *coercive* organizations. However, while governments can package information to suit their ends, it is much more difficult to force people to receive their propaganda and interpret it as officials wish. Consequently, media organizations are never completely coercive (McQuail, 1983). Ironically, although bureaucracies perform important functions, the media often present them either as faceless, cold, or in the case of government bureaucracies, as irrational, incompetent, and wasteful (see Focus box 6.2).

Sociologists are particularly interested in how media organizations and bureaucratic structures shape and define information. Contemporary mass communication is studied as a big business that requires large sums of operating capital and includes formal organizations that closely approach Weber's bureaucratic ideal type. Media organizations include a specialized division of labor, a hierarchy of authority, and formal objectives, among which profit is central. This means their messages are bureaucratic products that have been filtered through various committees at ascending levels of bureaucracy, screened and modified by each, with end results "that seldom resemble the original idea of the creator" (Dominick, 1987). Some media experts claim that megamergers among already giant media enterprises may make media messages even more uniform than in the past. Today, there are five megamedia corporations (see Figure 6.3) and even they are adding to their holdings and merging with each other.

In the twenty-first century, consolidating media and a handful of megamedia survivors have great influence over all media. The large networks and broadcast television take in most political advertising dollars and "the 20 leading Internet sites and the biggest cable channels are already owned by G.E., Disney, Fox, Gannett, and Time Warner" and a few other media powerhouses (Safire, 2003:1). And the 16,000 or so radio stations have consolidated with similar owners as well.

There is a certain irony that while all mass media are huge bureaucracies themselves, they take a particular delight in finding and exposing bureaucratic flaws. Each day, the wire services that provide news capsules for all media—from radio to the Internet— detail stories of bureaucratic waste, inefficiency, and corruption. Television newsmagazines like *60 Minutes* and *Dateline* depend on these stories for their popularity and high ratings, as do late-night television comics, newspapers, and magazines. In terms of challenges to government and the establishment in general, however, the mass media cannot compare to the diverse voices and opinions on the Internet or those associated with interactive television, cellular phones, and other evolving media.

TECHNOMEDIA, GLOBALIZATION, AND SOCIAL DIVERSITY

Many media scholars believe the technomedia are radically altering groups and organizations worldwide. Based on the wide gap between the rich and poor in the United States and other advanced nations, do you think information technologies will be universally available? What are the chances that they will spread worldwide and become available to nations that are still without electricity and running water?

It is clear that the technomedia have enabled many marginalized groups—those based on ethnicity, gender, age, disability, and sexual orientation, as well as low-income nations—to voice their perspectives, learn about the ideas and concerns of others, and instantaneously communicate with others across the globe. Think about how many ordinary people participate in Internet discussion groups (netgroups) and work groups (virtual teams). Labor organizations like the AFL-CIO and other unions have created Web-based communities that join members and social activists in the United States and globally. Glance around your sociology class and you will find numerous technologies that have had an impact on your classmates: cellular phones, pagers, Black Berries and laptop computers abound, and they have altered the nature of groups and organizations in the United States and worldwide.

Some scholars contend that the technomedia have brought even greater changes to bureaucracies. For example, economist Lester Thurow (1997) contended that with the new media's help, *debureaucratization* will proceed at an accelerated rate in the twenty-first century, that bureaucracies will become smaller and more manageable, and that some will become obsolete. He maintains that few organizations—in business, education, government, and other social institutions—will escape these trends.

Electronic communication has already produced dramatic changes in many bureaucracies. In many large corporations it has facilitated the removal of middle management and eliminated millions of jobs. For example, bank tellers are being replaced by automated teller machines (ATMs), automated checkouts are replacing grocery clerks, and on-line classes are replacing classrooms with teachers and students inter-

Technomedia are becoming an essential part of virtually every classroom setting, altering education and other institutions as well.

acting face-to-face. As more people shop by computer, the number of department stores and supermarkets may decline.

Thurow also believed that inexpensive, high-quality videos and teleconferencing may eliminate educational bureaucracies at all levels. For example, he predicted that the thousands of degree-granting universities will soon be replaced by a small number of education centers with high-tech media capabilities and media-savvy instructors, who will teach and offer degrees to students all over the globe. One scholar predicted that one-third of independent universities will close in the next 10 years and 50 percent will cease to exist by midcentury (Dunn, 2000). This same logic can be applied to virtually every other organization in the twenty-first century: most will operate out of a few regional and international centers in a handful of "megacities" to reach vast markets and audiences all over the globe. Is this a realistic portrait of organizational life in the future? Some scholars claim that new media—especially mobile wireless technologies that allow instant and ubiqituous communication—will encourage the dispersal and fragmentation of groups, organizations, and community (Rheingold, 2002). Today, technomedia drives "network individualism"—where each person becomes a kind of switchboard using networks "to obtain information, collaboration, orders, support, sociability, and a sense of belonging" (Haythornthwaite and Wellman, 2002:34).

the FUTURE

LOOKING to

GROUPS AND ORGANIZATIONS IN THE TWENTY-FIRST CENTURY

Many writers and scholars believe that despite their record of achievement and success during the twentieth century, the days of giant bureaucratic organizations are almost over. In the 1960s, for example, Warren Bennis and Philip Slater (1968) predicted that future technological changes would become so rapid and unpredictable that bureaucracies, which are geared to relatively stable and routine conditions, would be replaced by smaller, more egalitarian groups and organizations. Highly skilled workers would periodically join forces, solve a problem, and then disband until their skills were needed elsewhere. For a small segment of highly educated and highly skilled workers, these predictions have become a reality.

The expansion and merger of transnational corporations, which now routinely cross political and cultural boundaries to make a profit, have altered bureaucratic organizations as well. During the 1990s, mergers produced giant corporations with complex bureaucracies that spanned the globe. At the same time, an organizational pattern of decentralization and flexibility has become more common among small and large businesses alike. Many corporate CEOs believe flexibility will be essential to adapt to rapidly changing and diversified global markets— especially international labor and money markets. One sociologist claims that the new economy has created a "network society," where work, employment, and much of social life are marked by relentless change. One key component of the network society is the: "[f]eminization of paid labor . . . and the rise of the 'flexible woman,' gradually replacing the 'organization man'" (Castells, 2000:11).

On-line classes are proliferating—not just for the busy professional—but for ordinary college students across the nation and globally.

In *Bowling Alone*, Robert Putnam and colleagues (2000) contended that in the past few decades there has been a dramatic decline in social and civic participation in the United States. All groups and organizations have been affected by the globalization of the economy and technological change, but these changes "have rendered obsolete a significant stock of America's social capital" (Putnam, 2000:367). According to Putnam, these agents of change, especially the electronic media and changes in the workplace that require that both spouses be employed outside the home to maintain a decent standard of living, have encouraged a greater emphasis on individualistic values and goals and declining participation in community affairs and collective life. According to Putnam (2000:195):

Comparing two women of the same age, education, financial security, and marital and parental status, full-time employment appears to cut home entertaining by roughly 10 percent, club and church attendance by roughly 15 percent, informal visiting with friends by 25 percent, and volunteering by more than 50 percent.

Putnam remarks that debates about the disintegration of American society and social life have been raging for centuries, and large-scale change often activates this discussion. He asks, "Is social life in the 1990s really so different than it was in the past?" Putnam's research seems to answer this question in the affirmative, confirming a widespread popular belief that Americans are becoming less engaged in virtually every sphere of community life. This includes declining attendance at Parent-Teacher Association (PTA) meetings that once had more members than any other voluntary organization. Putnam (2000:56) notes that between 1990 and 1997, "the PTA lost half a million members . . . even though the number of families with children under eighteen grew by over two million." Civic organizations such as the Elks and the Knights of Columbus experienced a similar decline: Their membership has decreased by about half since World War II. Religious and political participation has dwindled as well, and so has

people's participation in a host of social clubs and community activities like neighborhood parties, card games, and picnics. According to Putnam (2000:56) even "bowling leagues that flourished a few decades ago have now become passé."

Putnam notes that not all associations are in decline, but those gaining new members tend to have personal rather than collective goals. For example, professional organizations such as the American Medical Association (AMA) and the American Bar Association (ABA) have doubled or tripled their membership in the past few decades. However, even though membership in these organizations grew in the 1990s, many became "mailing list organizations."

Putnam found that one type of group has bucked the trend in declining membership: the small group movement. Half of these groups were religion-based, such as prayer fellowship and Bible study groups. Many others were self-help groups such as Gamblers Anonymous and Alcoholics Anonymous, and crime-fighting neighborhood watch groups also flourished. So did emotional support groups and encounter groups, which proliferated in the 1990s. (See Table 6.2.) In the same period, there was an explosion of cybergroups and virtual neighborhoods that offered millions of Americans an "antidote to social disconnectedness" (Putnam, 2000:148). But, as Putnam remarked, few of these groups focused on collective needs, and even fewer offered face-to-face interactions of any kind.

Soon after the terrorist attacks on the World Trade Center in 2001, Putnam and his colleagues (2001:20–21) reinterviewed people they had talked to in 2000 to see if that event had revived patriotic sentiment and civic engagement—as the media seemed to show. Putnam found that following the attack there was indeed greater trust in government and interest in politics, people volunteered more in their communities, and even church attendance increased—but apparently not for long, as most people soon returned to their normal

Another major trend that has changed patterns of work and industrial organization is the success of Japanese and other Pacific Rim corporations. Their bureaucratic structures and decision-making processes have already brought significant social and cultural changes to bureaucratic organizations worldwide (Hickson, 1987). More than 1 million Americans work for Japanese corporations, and they and American business leaders have witnessed many of the competitive advantages of teams, consensus, collective decision making, and worker loyalty and commitment.

The team (and virtual team) have become important in automobile, electronics, and other high-tech industries. These industries have attempted to make decision making much quicker and more participatory and consensual, with more initiatives coming from the "bottom up" rather than the "top down." Given globalization and demographic trends, effective organizations have become more open to social diversity and the special contribution of people with disabilities and ethnic minorities to organizational efficiency (Prasas and Mills, 1997). And, high-speed technologies have filtered into every group and organization—accelerating every aspect of people's lives. Even fast-food

TABLE 6.2

ASSOCIATIONS AND AGE

Older Americans are more likely than younger Americans to be members of a club or an association.

PERCENT OF ADULTS WHO BELONG TO SELECT ORGANIZATIONS, BY AGE:

ASSOCIATION	ALL	18–34	35–49	50+
Church, temple, or synagogue	41%	32%	40%	49%
Union	9%	6%	10%	10%
PTA	8%	5%	14%	5%
Fraternal order	5%	2%	3%	9%
Art association	5%	3%	4%	6%
Veterans' club	5%	1%	2%	11%
Civic club	3%	2%	2%	4%
Business club	3%	2%	4%	4%
Country club	3%	2%	2%	3%
Environmental organization	3%	3%	3%	4%
Religious club	2%	1%	2%	4%
Human rights organization	1%	2%	1%	1%
Regional development committee	1%	—	1%	1%
Any organization	56%	44%	57%	66%

Note—Sample size too small

Source: "Elder Members." Reprinted with permission from the March 2003 issue of *American Demographics.* Copyright, Crain Communications Inc. 2003.

ment, given the many obstacles involved. As Scott McLean (2002:285) wrote, "community sentiments or allegiance to the values of American institutions are necessary for democratic revival, but they are not sufficient. . . . Consumerism, television, declining cities, economic inequalities, globalization, and the role of corporate America in politics are persistent realities that cannot be wished away by good community feelings. Ironically, after September 11, 2001, the gap between community sentiments and civic engagement seems wider than ever."

TAKING A CLOSER LOOK

Have community organizations and civic participation declined in the United States? Or, as Putnam acknowledges, have people merely shifted to new forms of social engagement and community participation? Support your case by examining your own neighborhood or community and the nature of that social life today.

Source: Robert D. Putnam and Lewis M. Feldstein. *Bowling Alone: The Collapse and Revival of American Community.* New York: Simon & Schuster, 2000.

routines. In the same period, President George W. Bush called on every American to volunteer a minimum of 4,000 hours of community service in "faith-based" and government-sponsored organizations to help the needy and boost civic involvement across the country (McLean, 2002). Most sociologists laud these efforts but doubt that they will shift the pendulum toward greater civic involve-

organizations are trying to get faster, with many adding "express lanes." Likewise, "uptempo living" has become a characteristic of every facet of daily life. As *The Futurist* magazine observed, people everywhere are becoming "multitaskers"—"eating while driving, writing an e-mail while talking on the phone, or skimming dozens of television programs on split screens" (*The Futurist,* 2000:18).

Several British sociologists argue that new technologies are creating new "hybrid organizational forms." They are even more flexible than matrix organizations based on project teams and "more responsive to a constantly shifting and unpredictable market" (Heath et al., 2000:303).

Another trend that sociologists will follow is the growing interdependence of bureaucratic organizations. For example, scientific research is no longer conducted by single organizations but by a set of interdependent agencies that includes universities, corporations, and the federal government. Sociologist Stanley Aronowitz (2000) observed that for decades these organizations cooperated as part of a vast military-industrial complex. Today, however, they must justify their existence on commercial, profit-making grounds.

Sociologists want to know not only how organizations establish such linkages, but the potential consequences of these partnerships. For example, will they make American businesses more competitive, as some have suggested, or merely increase the power and influence of transnational corporations and national governments and result in even larger, more complex, and perhaps more oppressive bureaucracies?

Some new bureaucratic models reflect the shift from an industrial to a postindustrial information and service economy, and thus far they have had significant consequences for only a few dozen advanced nations such as the United States. One major trend that has been exported to many parts of the world, however, is the "McDonaldization of Society" (Ritzer, 2000): expansion of the fast-food model of bureaucratic organization, with its heavy emphasis on efficiency, predictability, quantification, and control of employee and customer behavior, is now common to many organizations. What this may mean for bureaucracies, American society, and societies across the globe, will be decided by all of us in the coming century.

Bureaucratic decentralization may also boost small, grassroots social movement organizations in the twenty-first century. At the grassroots level, people and communities have already begun to experiment with new organizational forms to find more humane and efficient means of accomplishing collective goals. For example, many collectives and employee-owned companies have appeared in the past decade to make bureaucracies more responsive to worker and community needs. And information technologies should continue to affect organizations in ways we can only imagine. One trend is clear, however: the convergence of domestic and work environments. The alternative workplace of "nontraditional" work practices and settings affects "30 to 40 million people in the U.S., . . . who are either telecommuters or home-based workers" (Apgar, 1998:121). (There is of course a dark side to organizational change, which we examine in Focus box 6.3 on pages 158–159.)

Can bureaucratic corporations make money, be efficient, and provide people with humane and personally satisfying environments? At least one kind of corporation, the network organization, which sells products directly to consumers, seems to have found a way. Sociologist Nicole Biggart (1989), who studied Mary Kay Cosmetics, Amway, Avon, and other *network organizations,* discovered that they were successful not because they adhered to traditional bureaucratic principles, but because they violated them. For example, Mary Kay workers could not make a profit without developing close personal ties to clients and co-workers, and being emotionally committed to Mary Kay products and even the "Mary Kay lifestyle."

This perversion of Weberian bureaucratic logic seems due to the fact that unlike mainstream companies, which can give employees such incentives as raises and promotions, network organizations must rely on belief and loyalty to maintain worker commitment. Mary Kay workers do not just sell soap and hairspray, they sell "a superior way of life, a life of independence, and loyalty to family, God, and country" (Coughlin, 1989).

Network organizations combine belief, emotion, and the personal touch to sell products. Can this model be transferred to other profit-making companies? Lester Thurow contended that computers may soon make mall shopping obsolete. Does the Mary Kay approach suggest that this technological vision of the future may be wrong? Network companies seem to show that both buyers and sellers want something more than products and conveniences—especially the interpersonal contact that network companies provide.

Perhaps continued corporate downsizing and emphasis on part-time work, teams, and virtual teams will lead to a proliferation of network organizations in the immediate future. Likewise, they may expand into many new social arenas—just as the fast-food model infiltrated people's lives in the past few decades. In the postindustrial societies of the future, we should expect rapid change in all organizational models and much greater organizational diversity as corporations, groups, and grassroots organizations search for new ways to meet people's collective needs.

Summary

1 Most human activity occurs in groups, which consist of two or more people who interact with each other in patterned ways, have a feeling of unity, and share certain expectations and interests. Primary groups include a small number of people who interact regularly and are emotionally committed to the relationship, whereas secondary groups operate on a formal and impersonal basis to achieve a specific objective.

2 Formal organizations are large secondary groups organized to achieve specific goals. Formal organizations are highly diverse and include everything from gangs to civic and other voluntary organizations.

3 A bureaucracy is a special kind of organization that employs formal rules, hierarchical ranking, and a rational worldview to achieve maximum efficiency.

4 Today, the mass media provide a first draft of reality for most people on earth. In recent years there has been a steady consolidation of the global media into a few giant corporations. At the same time the technomedia have given people, particularly formerly marginalized groups, access to a wealth of information and contacts with others that were undreamed of just a few decades ago.

5 Several trends are reshaping the fundamental nature of bureaucracies. Particularly important are the fast-food model, the Japanese team concept, global social diversity, and perhaps egalitarian and network organizations whose members join forces to sell products or accomplish other goals.

Key Terms

aggregate (p. 140)
bureaucracy (p. 151)
bureaucratic ritualism (p. 152)
category (p. 140)
dyad (p. 144)

formal organizations (p. 148)
groupthink (p. 147)
in-group (p. 142)
out-group (p. 142)
primary group (p. 141)

reference groups (p. 142)
secondary group (p. 141)
social boundaries (p. 142)
social group (p. 140)
triad (p. 144)

Deviance and Conformity

"Humanity can be quite cold to those who see the world differently."

—*Eric A. Burns*

*M*ore than 250 total strangers assembled in the lobby of the Hyatt Hotel in Manhattan and, at a precise moment, burst into 15 seconds of loud applause, and then dispersed, never talking or otherwise interacting with one another. By the time hotel security arrived the "mob" had come and gone. Some guests were offended, but most were amused, although hotel staff and management were perturbed and viewed the behavior as deviant and disruptive (Bedell, 2003).

Approximately 200 tourists from all over the world crowded into a McDonald's restaurant in downtown Tokyo. Befuddled workers and patrons looked on in disbelief when, with no visible or verbal cue, the tourists performed what seemed to be an unrehearsed and poorly executed form of ballet. Just as quickly as they had appeared, the dancers stopped dancing and dispersed. Police were called, but all the dancers had disappeared, and as one of the officers explained to the restaurant's manager, he wasn't sure that anything could have been done anyway because the spontaneous dancers had not broken any laws. The manager later told a news reporter, "It may not have been illegal, but people just don't do that sort of thing in this city." A Japanese patron indicated that the perpetrators should be "caught and punished," while an amused American tourist said he "enjoyed the floor show" (CNN *Headline News,* August 25, 2003).

At an upscale shoe store in the Soho district of New York City, approximately 75 people entered and pretended to be tourists. As quickly as they had gathered, the group dispersed. Later the same day, over 100 people flooded the ninth floor of Macy's Department Store and sat on a huge Oriental rug for approximately 10 minutes, and then arose and left the store. Customers did not know what to think and store employees worried that perhaps the action was designed to distract them so that somebody could shoplift or perhaps even rob the store (Bedell, 2003).

"Flashmobbing," impromptu meetings of people coordinated over the Internet, often disrupts businesses and shocks unsuspecting observers. Here, a "flashmob" gathered at a Philadelphia bookstore supposedly looking for "Aaron,"and then quickly dispersed after the store manager called the police.

These sudden and seemingly spontaneous events are known as "flashmobbing," and according to Howard Rheingold (2002b), these "flash mobs" or "smart mobs" as he calls them, may represent a new form of social protest. Business owners, police, and others who have experienced the disruption associated with this new phenomenon are both perplexed and frustrated. They view the actions of those involved as deviant, but since the activities take place in public places, and no laws are broken, nobody seems to know what to do about them. Others see flashmobbing as harmless fun, and can't imagine what the fuss is about. Moreover, the flash mob "events" seem to be spontaneous, and consequently, impossible to predict or prevent—another example of the first wisdom of sociology, that *things are not necessarily what they seem.*

As it turns out "flashmob" activities are neither unplanned nor spontaneous. Instead, they are well-orchestrated events planned over the Internet and through the use of cellular phones. In fact, entire websites are devoted to flashmobbing, and Rheingold (2002b) points out that the phenomenon is a natural outgrowth of a highly technological society where groups, social reformers, protesters, newshounds, and others can organize, demonstrate, make political statements, or just have fun without ever having met or interacted on a face-to-face basis.

Is "flashmobbing" deviant behavior? Does it cause any harm? Is it illegal? Should it be?

Is flashmobbing deviant? Do these types of events pose a threat to social order? Should participants be punished? Is it harmless fun? As this vignette illustrates, deviance and conformity are powerful yet elusive concepts on which there is not unanimous agreement. Nevertheless, the extent to which people conform to or deviate from the rules of society is one of the criteria by which we set them apart for differential and unequal treatment. In this chapter we look at popular explanations for deviance, and then analyze deviance and conformity from the three major theoretical perspectives. We also look at the powerful mechanisms of social control people use to discourage deviance and encourage conformity.

DEFINING DEVIANCE AND CONFORMITY: A GLOBAL VIEW

What comes to mind when you hear the word *deviance?* What mental image do you picture when you think of a deviant? If you are like most people you probably consider yourself to be a conformist and may equate deviance with bizarre behaviors such as heinous murders, mass suicides, and incest. Your image of deviants may include members of strange religious cults, organized crime bosses, and mass murderers. Certainly, all of these qualify. But in reality everybody is both a deviant and a conformist, as on almost a daily basis we violate some of society's rules and guidelines and adhere to others. And sometimes it is not even clear whether a particular act is deviant. What about Annette Sorensen? (See Focus box 7.1) Did she commit a deviant act when she left her baby unattended outside a New York restaurant? What does it say about the levels of deviance in New York City when people assume an unattended baby will be kidnapped, harmed, or murdered? What do we mean when we use the terms *deviance* and *conformity?*

Onlookers were horrified as the couple parked the stroller outside a New York City restaurant, pulled the blanket up under the chin of the sleeping baby, then nonchalantly entered and gave their drink orders to the waiter as they were seated at a table near a window. Less than an hour later, Annette Sorensen and her husband, Exavier Wardlaw, were equally horrified when they emerged from the restaurant to find the stroller and their 14-month-old daughter missing. The couple were relieved to find police officers nearby, and tried to squelch their worst fears as they reported that their baby had been kidnapped. Imagine their surprise when the officers interrupted them midstory to inform them the child had been turned over to Child Protective Services, and that they were being placed under arrest for child abandonment and endangerment. Public outrage exploded across the country that night as every major television network reported the story of the Danish couple who recklessly abandoned their baby on the streets of New York City. Meanwhile, when the news spread across the Atlantic, residents of Denmark were at first thoroughly confused, and later outraged over the fact that the baby had been placed in foster care and the couple jailed for such a common and innocent act.

In a nation where thousands of infants are abandoned each year and thousands more are kidnapped, the response to the story of 14-month-old Liv Sorensen being left unattended outside a restaurant in the heart of New York City is understandable. After all, this appears to be a blatant example of a deviant, if not criminal, act. Yet this story underscores the first wisdom of sociology—that things are not necessarily what they seem. From the outset, Annette Sorensen, a Danish actress who was visiting her husband in Brooklyn, was astonished at the reaction of the police and public, and insisted she had done absolutely nothing wrong. Sorensen explained that in her home country of Denmark it was common practice for parents to leave infants unattended in their strollers outside restaurants and shops; indeed her attorney produced a videotape to support her claim. Eventually a New York judge dismissed all charges against Annette Sorensen and reunited her with her baby, declaring the whole thing a serious cultural misunderstanding (Marcano, 1997; Ojita, 1997; Sullivan, 1997).

TAKING A CLOSER LOOK

What does it say about American cultural values and norms when it is assumed that if a baby is left unattended it will be abducted and harmed? Can you think of other behaviors that might be considered deviant by American cultural standards, but perfectly acceptable in another country?

Source: Tony Marcano. "Judge Drops Charges Against Danish Mother." *New York Times*, May 14, 1997:B3; Ojita, Mirta. "They're Not in Denmark Anymore." *New York Times*, May 18, 1997:D2; Sullivan, John. "Charges Against Danish Mother Dropped." *New York Times*, May 17, 1997:A23.

In their simplest terms, **deviance** refers to *violation of a social norm* and **conformity** to *adherence to social norms.* Every society uses these or similar definitions to differentiate people on the basis of their levels of deviance and conformity. But, as we have noted throughout this book, life is rarely as simplistic as it seems, and the social processes involved in defining deviance and conformity are far more complex than these definitions imply.

DEVIANCE
Violation of a social norm.

CONFORMITY
Adherence to social norms.

CATFISH

THERE'S ALWAYS ONE!

What norms are being violated at this wedding? How does this photo also reflect conformity?

Norms and a Range of Tolerance

In Chapter 3, we defined *norms* as the guidelines that govern our thoughts, beliefs, and behaviors. It may be helpful to review the importance of norms, especially in regard to defining deviance and conformity. Then we will look at how members of society use norms to establish a range of tolerance to determine what is and what is not socially acceptable.

Norms Some norms are *prescriptive*—they tell us what we should do. For example, informal norms that encourage Americans to say "excuse me" after bumping into another person, as well as formal laws that require us to pay a portion of our income each year in taxes, both fall into this category. Not doing these things would be considered deviant.

Other norms are *proscriptive*—they tell us what we should not do. They also range from informal rules, such as "Don't put your feet up on the dinner table," to potent religious commandments such as "Thou shalt not kill," to even more powerful *taboos,* which are prohibitions against behaviors that most members of a society consider so repugnant they are unthinkable. Doing any of these things is generally considered deviant.

There are three major types of norms. *Folkways* are informal norms that reflect cultural traditions and guide our everyday interactions. *Mores* (pronounced *morays*) are informal but salient norms that are linked to value judgments about the rightness and wrongness of particular acts. Mores almost always have moral connotations and include norms prohibiting acts such as incest, adultery, murder, and stealing. Because mores are so important, they often are codified into the third type of norm: *laws,* which are formal rules enacted and enforced by the state.

Although folkways and mores are informal norms and laws are formally codified, laws are not necessarily more important. The norm violations that are most likely to disrupt routine social interaction, cause problems between friends, break up marriages, or lead to placement in a mental institution are far more likely to involve violations of informal folkways and mores than of formal laws.

An emphasis on norms in defining deviance and conformity (sometimes called the *normative approach*) illustrates how members of society evaluate behavior in reference to some pre-established standard of behavior. It also implies that there is some set of absolute norms, the violation of which automatically constitutes deviance. In this regard, we should be mindful of the three baseball umpires who were asked to describe the job of calling balls and strikes during a game. The first umpire responded, "Some's balls and some's strikes and I calls 'em as they is." The second umpire said, "Some's balls and some's strikes and I calls 'em as I sees 'em." The third declared, "Some's balls and some's strikes but they ain't nothin' till I calls 'em" (cited in Nimmo, 1978:77). Many people, like the first umpire, believe that deviance and conformity are objective conditions that need only to be identified. Others, in harmony with the second umpire, insist that defining deviance and conformity is a subjective process that relies on interpretation. Like the third umpire, many view deviance and conformity as labels placed on some actions and people by others with the power to do so. These three viewpoints illustrate some of the complexities of defining deviance and conformity.

While we tend to think in simple dichotomies, social life is rarely divided into neat, discrete categories of good and bad, right and wrong, or deviance and conformity. It may be comforting to think the "good guys" wear white hats and "criminals" are locked away in prison so "decent, law-abiding citizens" can go about their daily lives, but the issue of defining deviance and conformity is not that simple. From a sociological viewpoint, deviance and conformity are socially defined; rather than viewing them as two opposing categories, it is more insightful to think of them as representing the two ends of a continuum. As sociologist Émile Durkheim ([1893] 1964) concluded, even in a nation of "saints," some saints would be considered "less holy" than others.

Range of Tolerance We expect people to conform to social norms because this allows us to anticipate what others will do in certain situations and provides guidelines for what we are expected to do. In most societies, however, people are not expected to adhere to every single norm in every situation; in some cases adhering to one norm may even require violation of another. For example, when a friend asks your opinion of a bad haircut, you might find that the norm of politeness conflicts with the norm of honesty, thus complicating your response. Consequently, members of society establish a **range of tolerance,** or *a scope of behaviors considered acceptable and defined as conformity,* although they may involve violation of a norm. For example, despite posted maximum speed limit signs, police departments and even individual officers establish acceptable ranges beyond the maximum speed that they are willing to tolerate. If the posted speed on an interstate is 70 miles per hour, do you think most officers would issue you a ticket if you were traveling 71? Almost assuredly not. While you may have violated a norm, an officer who gives you a ticket for driving 1 mile over the speed limit is just as likely to be considered deviant by fellow officers as by you. What if you are driving 75? Maybe you will get a ticket. What about 80? There's a good chance. What about 100? You can count on it.

Sociologist Ruth Cavan (1961) created a behavioral continuum model that illustrates how societal members create an acceptable range of tolerance around a social norm (see Figure 7.1). Society's range of tolerance varies from one culture to another. Whereas the previous example is familiar and clear in illustrating the flexibility of speed limits to most American drivers, it would be confusing and serve as an example of the rigidity of American traffic laws to most European drivers, especially those from Germany, where speed limits are rarely posted and almost never enforced. Sociologists also point out that deviant and criminal activities such as recreational marijuana use and ticket scalping often are tolerated by both the public and law enforcement (Hathaway and Atkinson, 2001).

Cavan's model shows how *overconformity* as well as *underconformity* can be viewed as deviance. For example, have you ever had a class with a student who never missed a single class period, completed all assignments before they were due, knew the answer to every question, and scored 100 percent on every examination and paper? While this

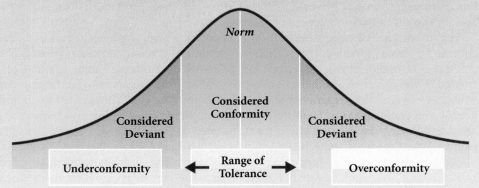

FIGURE 7.1

RANGE OF TOLERANCE

If you hypothetically plotted all human behavior on a continuum, most would be very close to what the norm governing that behavior described. Society members create a range of tolerance around a norm, and as long as behavior falls within that range of tolerance it is considered conformity. When behavior falls outside the range of acceptable limits, it is no longer tolerated and is considered deviant.

Norm

Considered
Conformity

Considered
Deviant

Considered
Deviant

Underconformity

**Range of
Tolerance**

Overconformity

Source: From "The Concepts of Tolerance and Contraculture as Applied to Delinquency," by Ruth Shonle Cavan. © 1961 by Midwest Sociological Society. Reprinted from *The Sociological Quarterly,* Spring, 1961, pp. 243–258 by permission of Blackwell Publishing Ltd.

Can you think of scenarios other than the speed limit example that fit this model? When does overconformity become regarded as deviant? How does a society's range of tolerance change for young children? teenagers? adults? the elderly? Can you think of variables other than age that affect society's range of tolerance?

RANGE OF TOLERANCE
A scope of behaviors considered acceptable and defined as conformity.

student would appear to be the model conformist, most of the other students would probably think he or she is a bit weird, and they may gossip about or ridicule the student. Just as maximum speeds are enforced if exceeded beyond reasonable limits, so too are minimum speeds, and a driver is more likely to be pulled over and issued a citation for driving 30 miles per hour on an interstate highway than for driving 75.

Deviance and *conformity* are not absolute terms. Rather, they are terms that we apply to people and behaviors based on a wide variety of circumstances. In defining deviance and deciding the range of tolerance for acceptable and unacceptable behaviors we must take into account time, place, situation, and most important, the culture in question.

Importance of Time, Place, Situation, and Culture

What is considered conformity at one point in time may be viewed as deviance at another. Hence, today's conformist may be tomorrow's deviant, and vice versa. This illustrates the importance of time in defining deviance and conformity.

Time Folkways governing fashion and grooming are excellent examples of how norms change over time. For example, America's founding fathers wore long hair, ruffled shirts, and silk stockings—appropriate attire for men of that period; a similarly dressed man today would attract much attention and would more likely be a famous athlete, rock musician, or female impersonator than a politician.

Place The place where behavior occurs is also an important determinant of whether an act is viewed as appropriate or deviant. Whistling, shouting, cheering, and booing are acceptable at Yankee Stadium but would evoke strong disapproval in the Mormon Tabernacle, at the Wailing Wall in Jerusalem, or at the end of a college lecture.

Situation Situation often takes precedence over place in determining the appropriateness of actions. For example, although whistling, shouting, and booing may be deemed appropriate at Yankee Stadium during a baseball game, they would not be okay when it is the site of a religious crusade. Likewise, reading a newspaper is acceptable at home, but not in class, in church, or while watching a child's soccer match.

Culture Perhaps no other variable is more influential in defining deviance and conformity than the cultural context in which behavior occurs. Take, for example, appropriate greetings between two men in various parts of the world. In the United States we expect that two men will shake hands when they are introduced. In Japan, they are expected to bow in greeting; in many Middle Eastern countries they embrace; in many European countries they might kiss each other on the cheek; and in Russia it is acceptable for two men to kiss on the lips in greeting.

The importance of culture becomes very apparent when people socialized in different cultures come into direct contact. One of the authors is reminded of a story told by a cultural anthropologist who described her fieldwork on a remote Pacific island. Confronted by the choice of whether to "go native" and bare her breasts or to conform to her American socialization experience and keep her breasts covered, she decided to discard her top and conform to local cultural norms. Much to her chagrin, her visit to the market the following day elicited stares from the men in the village and glares from the women. When she went home, two women from the village followed her inside and cautioned her about sexually stimulating their husbands. The anthropologist apologized and said that she would cover her breasts. Imagine her surprise when the women explained to her that it was not her bare breasts that aroused the men of the village, but her bare calves. On the island, women were expected to cover their legs at all times; only husbands were allowed to see one of their wives' most erotic body parts: the calves. Focus box 7.1 provides another example of the importance of culture in defining deviance and conformity.

It should be clear that norms vary greatly from one culture to another, and definitions of deviance and conformity vary among different groups and subcultures within a culture. In all cultures, however, at least three important elements are important in defining deviance and conformity: the actors, their audience, and the mass media.

This Samburu tribesman of Kenya has painted and adorned his body in order to conform to the norms of his culture.

Hromi Nakano, however, is regarded as deviant for having her entire body covered with decorative tattoos.

How do these two people from different cultures illustrate the relativity of deviance and conformity?

Significance of Actors, Audience, and the Media

It is important to understand that deviance does not refer simply to the extraordinary. For example, it is unusual for scientists to win the Nobel Prize or for pilots to become astronauts, but these people are not considered deviant. In fact, their behaviors may be statistically rare but they are regarded favorably by most members of society. Thus, who commits the act is often as important as the act itself in defining deviance and conformity. The tremendous emphasis placed on social actors in defining deviance led one sociologist to proclaim that the analysis of deviance has largely focused on the study of "nuts, sluts, and preverts [sic]" (Liazos, 1972).

Actors and Deviance   Most people consider murder to be one of the most heinous acts, and they cannot imagine the intentional killing of another person not being considered deviant. Yet there are many times when taking another person's life is not viewed negatively and in fact may be rewarded by society. Soldiers who kill during war and law enforcement officers who kill in the line of duty are not considered deviant by most members of society, and often they are regarded as heroes.

An individual's age, sex, race, ethnicity, social class, physical appearance, demeanor, and other variables all may enter into the deviance–conformity equation. In everyday life, we can see that certain behaviors considered deviant in children (e.g., smoking, drinking, and gambling) may be tolerated in adults. Likewise, a double standard may tolerate premarital sexual activity for boys but not for girls. Members of racial and ethnic minorities often find that their behaviors are scrutinized more closely than those of the dominant group, and they are more likely to be labeled deviant for participating in activities tolerated in others. A person's social class also may affect deviant labels and may provide the resources that in court could mean the difference between acquittal and life imprisonment or execution. Consider some high-profile criminal cases—the Menendez brothers, O. J. Simpson, Jon Benet Ramsey, Scott Peterson, Kobe Bryant, and Robert Blake. How were public perceptions and official views of

The relativity of deviance is illustrated in ceremonies where soldiers receive medals for bravery for acts committed during combat that might be deemed as deviant if committed by civilians in non-combat situations.

deviance affected by the age, sex, race, and social class of the principal actors? These cases illustrate the critical role of the actor as well as the audience in defining deviance and conformity.

The Role of the Audience What is deviant to one audience may be regarded as conformity by another. This reflects the diversity of values and interests of different groups. For example, while the jury in the O. J. Simpson criminal trial found him not guilty in the murder of Nicole Brown Simpson and Ronald Goldman, the jury in the later civil case found him liable for their deaths. Using the critical thinking approach of sociology, what role do you think race, sex, and social class played in these two trials? Even though the jury acquitted Simpson in the criminal case, millions of people around the world concluded that he was "deviant" and guilty of a crime. The Simpson case also illustrates the extraordinary influence of the mass media in defining deviance in contemporary society.

The Power of the Media The mass media play a powerful role in defining social reality. In today's global society virtually all parts of the world are linked by mass media. Consequently, the audience involved in defining an act as deviance or conformity is potentially comprised of millions of people from hundreds of cultures. The Sorensen case in Focus box 7.1 serves as a good example. With the help of the media, what began with a handful of people and a couple of New York City police officers defining an act as deviant became an international debate. Every major television network carried the story, relaying it around the globe via satellite, and every major newspaper in the world reported the incident. Within a few days, a website was established on the Internet and people from all parts of the globe either supported or condemned the handling of the incident on-line.

Today media and technomedia images are fundamental to public perceptions of deviance and conformity. Folk wisdom tells us, "A dog biting a person is not news, but a person biting a dog is." Because we are inundated with stories about the most bizarre forms of deviance, we tend to forget that the vast majority of norm-violating behavior is fairly mundane and often of little consequence. Media sensationalism—especially in the tabloids, on the Internet, and on popular TV shows—contributes to the popular belief that people can be divided into two neat and distinct categories: deviants and conformists. Numerous sociological studies indicate that public perceptions of morality and immorality, conformity and deviance, as well as what constitutes crime and who is likely to be a criminal, are shaped by media portrayals and social constructions of reality presented by the media (Dotter, 2002; Cavender, 2003; Lowney, 2003). The media also tend to equate deviance and crime and to reinforce stereotypes about deviants and criminals—that they are almost exclusively from lower socioeconomic classes and most are minorities, that they are all violent, and that controlling them costs taxpayers huge amounts of money. These stereotypes do not hold up under scrutiny. In fact, each year white-collar and occupational crimes account for more lost revenue than all the burglaries, larceny-thefts, auto thefts, and arsons combined (FBI, *Uniform Crime Reports,* 2006).

The Difference between Deviance and Crime

Popular wisdom often equates deviance and crime—two related but distinct concepts in sociology. *Deviance* refers to *all* norm violations. *Crime,* on the other hand, refers only to violations of one type of norm: laws. Even the majority of violation of laws involve civil laws covering contracts, real estate, and other noncriminal activities. Consequently, **crime,** which is *any act that violates a criminal law,* is divided into violent offenses (against persons) and nonviolent offenses (against property). Therefore, we can see that while all crime is deviance, not all deviance is crime.

Although crime is a major social problem, most of the deviance that occurs in society does not involve any type of criminal activity. We consider crime in more detail later in this chapter when we discuss formal social control and the criminal justice system. First, let's explore another concept that is sometimes confused with deviance—diversity.

CRIME
Any act that violates a criminal law.

Distinguishing between Diversity and Deviance

Up to this point, our discussion of deviance and conformity has focused on *behaviors* that are judged to either violate or conform to the norms that govern a particular situation. But deviance and conformity represent broader categories, and some people are considered to be deviant simply for being who they are. For example, individuality is considered to be a highly valued and positive trait in American society, especially if it involves unique talents or skills. On the other hand, Americans encourage conformity to dominant values and beliefs, and those who challenge the status quo, question mainstream beliefs, or violate norms of the dominant group often are viewed as deviant.

Sometimes entire categories of people are viewed as deviant by those who are intolerant of social and cultural diversity. While most of us are aware of the prejudice, discrimination, and inequality faced by the poor, racial and ethnic minorities, women, and the elderly, we may be less cognizant of the fact that the same is true for millions of people who may be labeled deviant because of their sexual orientation, physical or mental infirmities, religious beliefs, or other characteristics considered outside the mainstream. This devaluation results in *stigma*—a powerful social label that negatively affects every aspect of a person's life. It also sometimes leads to **hate crimes**—*criminal acts against people and their property that are motivated by racial and ethnic prejudices and other social biases.*

Deviance and Stigma

Stigma is *any characteristic that sets people apart and discredits or disqualifies them from full social acceptance and participation.* Sociologist Erving Goffman (1963) identified three principal types of stigma experienced by those considered beyond society's range of acceptability:

1. *Abominations of the Body.* This category includes any physical limitation, deformity, or other visible and identifiable physical characteristic deemed beyond "normal." For example, people may be stigmatized because they are too fat or too thin; too short or too tall; because they are bald, have a noticeable scar or birthmark, or use a wheelchair. Goffman notes that even though others may be sympathetic toward those in this category, they still may regard them as deviant and sanction them. Subsequent research indicates that possessing a physical stigma may amplify other deviance and evoke even stronger negative sanctions (e.g., if a person in a wheelchair smokes cigarettes) (Stiles and Kaplan, 1996).

2. *Blemishes of Individual Character.* This category includes those who are stigmatized on moral grounds, such as those who are thought to be dishonest, liars, cheaters, or thieves, as well as people who suffer from mental disorders, alcoholism, drug addiction, or even a terminal illness such as AIDS. The latter is particularly stigmatized if it is believed to be linked to some other type of deviant behavior associated with the disease (e.g., smoking and lung cancer, or illegal drug abuse or homosexuality and AIDS) (Nack, 2000).

3. *Tribal Stigma.* This category includes all those who are discredited because they are members of a socially disapproved category or group. For example, many people are stigmatized because of their race, ethnicity, religion, sexual orientation, or affiliation with a group or organization deemed outside the mainstream. Sometimes family members of deviants are stigmatized simply because of their relationship to the norm violator (May, 2000). Furthermore, an entire category of people can be stigmatized by the actions of a very few, as is the case of postal workers who often hear the expression "going postal" used to describe the actions of someone who goes on a murderous rampage (Mittelstadt and Enders, 2000).

Goffman (1963:5) asserted that not only are stigmatized individuals considered deviant, but they are regarded as "not quite human." The social ramifications of stigma are devastating, and in many cases people go to extreme lengths to hide

HATE CRIMES
Criminal acts against people and their property that are motivated by racial and ethnic prejudices and other social biases.

STIGMA
Any characteristic that sets people apart and discredits or disqualifies them from full social acceptance and participation.

Although physical deformities often elicit sympathy, they also stigmatize people and cause them to be viewed as deviant. The so-called "Elephant Man" serves as a classic example.

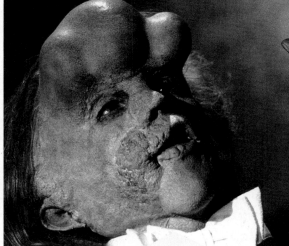

Can you think of others?

stigmatizing attributes and avoid negative social consequences. In today's global society many people confuse diversity with deviance and seek to punish those who pose no real threat to society simply because they are "different." Critical thinking and sociological understanding can expand the range of tolerance, but they must compete with a variety of popular theories that often take narrower and more punitive approaches to deviance.

POPULAR EXPLANATIONS FOR DEVIANCE

Before the rise of science, the understanding of deviance tended to be linked to so-called "human nature" and whether people are basically "good" or "evil." If people are naturally evil, then deviant behavior can be readily explained: give people rules, and they will violate them. On the other hand, if people are basically good, they will abide by society's norms. These popular notions persist, and many people believe it is just that simple: there are two kinds of people in the world—good and bad; good people are conformists and bad ones are deviant.

Deviants Are Different: From Demonology to Biology

For much of history, deviance and conformity were explained in theological terms. Deviant behavior was attributed to demonic possession, and it was believed that the devil or evil spirits took possession of people's bodies and souls. There is evidence that Stone Age humans drilled holes in the skulls of wrongdoers so that evil spirits could escape and that the ancient Hebrews, Egyptians, Greeks, and Romans all practiced rites of exorcism. Today, many people still equate deviance with sin and the devil. Others allude to demonology in a more figurative way, linking deviance and crime with declining moral values, and many blame the mass media—especially television, which has emerged as a contemporary demon.

During the eighteenth and nineteenth centuries, theological explanations for deviance and conformity gave way to scientific and pseudoscientific ones. Particularly influential were some of the early biological and genetic theories offered by physicians and surgeons. For example, toward the end of the nineteenth century, an Italian surgeon, Cesare Lombroso, posited that much criminality was the result of *atavism*—a package of genetic traits that distinguished violent and habitual criminals from the "normal," noncriminal population. These physical attributes included a low and protruding forehead, prominent cheekbones, a large protruding lower jaw, small ears set low on the side of the head, long arms and large hands, excessive hairiness, and relative insensitivity to pain. Another popular biological theory of the time was *phrenology*—the scientific study of the bumps and protrusions of the skull believed to be linked to violence, mental illness, and criminality. We may laugh at these ideas today, but they were accepted as "scientific facts" by much of society for many years. Then, in the early twentieth century, the "family pedigree" became the focus of attention as it was decided that genes and family background were the keys to understanding deviance and conformity.

While most of these early biological theories of deviance and criminality are dismissed by serious social scientists today, remnants can be found in some of the popular notions, stereotypes, and misconceptions held by those who believe deviants are markedly different from conformists. Today many people still may contend that an individual has the "beady eyes" of a criminal, or that a notorious serial killer doesn't look like the kind of person who could do such a horrible thing. Moreover, aspects of these early biological theories can be found in some of today's controversial genetic theories that attempt to link deviance and crime with biological, genetic, and medical causes. Today, the medical model has emerged as one of the most powerful popular explanations for deviance and conformity.

The Medical Model: Equating Deviance with Illness

The **medical model** *views deviance as analogous to illness* and uses terminology associated with disease. From this view, if society is to understand and control deviance and deviants, *symptoms* associated with the problem must be identified, *diagnoses* must be

MEDICAL MODEL
Views deviance as analogous to illness.

made, and appropriate *treatments* must be *prescribed.* In keeping with the medical model, each treatment elicits a *prognosis,* and eventually, the deviant (*patient*) is either *cured, made better,* or declared *incurable.*

Many adherents of the medical model take the analogy literally. To them, deviance has made the transition from being *like* an illness to *being* an illness. Today, it is common to hear the terms *sick* and *deviant* used interchangeably. Think of some of the most bizarre and heinous crimes you have heard or read about—mass murders, serial killings, acts of cannibalism, and others. What was your first reaction when you learned what the offenders had done? Many people's immediate response is, "They are sick!"

This medical model approach to deviance is part of a sweeping *medicalization* of society (see Chapter 18), where problems once thought of as social or behavioral in nature are now attributed to disease. Unruly children in school may be diagnosed as having ADHD (attention deficit hyperactivity disorder), and drinking problems, drug addiction, attempted suicide, and many types of crimes may lead to hospitalization and medical treatment.

The widespread use of the term *mental illness* and the view that deviants are "sick" demonstrate the power and pervasiveness of the medical model. Part of its popularity is due to the fact that the public tends to hold biology, chemistry, and other sciences linked to medical research in high esteem. Moreover, powerful organizations and money are involved, and the medical establishment has claimed "ownership" of most contemporary forms of deviance. The media has assisted this process by embracing and disseminating research findings and promoting its explanations, no matter how tenuous, controversial, and questionable they may be. Because they too are a powerful institution, the media themselves are now seen as both a cause of and possible solution to deviance.

Many people blame the media for teaching children and adolescents to be violent.

Do you think programs such as *Jackass* encourage violence and other forms of deviant behavior?

Blame It on the Media

In addition to the media's role in defining deviance, sociologists are interested in the popular view that the media help create, promote, and perhaps even cause deviance. The mass media—television, movies, magazines, radio, comic books, advertising, video games, and rock music—have been linked to such problems as robbery, burglary, poor grades at school, antisocial fantasies, drug abuse, rebellion, declining test scores, lack of moral standards, poor diet, passivity, hyperactivity, wasting time, desensitization to violence, amorality, war, rape, and murder. Since it is impossible to look at all of these issues here, let's focus on three: the possible link between pornography and sex crimes; the purported connection between media violence and aggressive behaviors; and the alleged negative effects of heavy metal and some forms of rap music.

Pornography and Sex Crimes   Many people believe that the use of **pornography**—*sexually explicit materials intended solely for sexual arousal*—not only is morally deviant but also leads to crimes of violence against women and children. They cite studies which contend that pornography dehumanizes sexuality, degrades those who make and use it, and desensitizes consumers to sexual violence (e.g., Attorney General's Commission on Pornography, 1986; Hughes and McMickle, 1997; Nichols, 1997; Jensen, 2004; Taverner, 2006). Yet numerous other studies dispute these claims, indicating that sex offenders are no more likely to be users of pornography than anybody else and claiming that pornography may have beneficial effects in helping some people explore and understand their sexuality (Best and Luckenbill, 1994; Strossen, 1995; McElroy, 1997; Jensen, 2004).

Assertions made by those on both sides are very difficult to prove or disprove, for several reasons. First and foremost is the problem of defining pornography. The U.S. Supreme Court wrestled with this problem for years, deciding that only members of a local community can define obscenity by determining what types of materials violate their moral standards. Thus, while popular magazines such as *Playboy, Playgirl,* and *Penthouse* may be found in university and public libraries in some communities, they

Different cultures have very disparate attitudes and laws regarding pornography and sex-related businesses. In many large cities adult bookstores, video stores, topless bars, and other adult entertainment industries congregate in one particular area where activities and businesses are tolerated that would not be allowed to operate in other parts of the same community.

may be banned as pornography in others. In 2003, however, the U.S. Supreme Court ruled that libraries receiving federal funding must filter Internet pornography or risk losing their funds (McCaffrey, 2003).

Assessing the effects of pornography, however it is defined, is also problematic. While numerous laboratory experiments attempting to relate pornography to aggression and violence have been conducted, their results have been mixed. As one sociologist surmises, even if laboratory results were consistent, "their significance for pornography's effects outside the experimental lab seems trivial" (Felson, 1996).

If we look at the issue of pornography cross-culturally, defining it and assessing its social impact become even more difficult. For example, in Islamic countries such as Iran, censorship is very stringent and the government bans any material that shows partial nudity or is sexually suggestive. In countries such as Japan, Amsterdam, and Denmark, where censorship is almost unheard of, explicit sexual magazines, videos, and other materials are unregulated and extremely popular. Interestingly, rates of abuse and violence against women are much higher in the Islamic countries where pornography is suppressed or banned than in Japan, Amsterdam, and Denmark, where almost "anything goes" (Wekesser, 1997).

Another problem in attempting to relate pornography to violence or other forms of deviance is the vast "underground" network involved in its manufacture, sale, and distribution. While *Playboy* magazine has a circulation of approximately 3.5 million and can be purchased in most bookstores and delivered to a subscriber's home by mail, this is not true of much of the estimated $7 billion per year industry that includes everything from 900 phone sex numbers and explicit materials available over the Internet, to triple-X videos that contain everything from bestiality and pedophilia to rape and murder. Today, thousands of computer bulletin boards, chat rooms, and other sexually explicit and "deviant" materials are also available in cyberspace (Durkin and Bryant, 1995; Wekesser, 1997; Taverner, 2006). Quinn and Forsyth (2005) suggest that due to the Internet and other technologies, we may have to rethink and redefine what constitutes conforming and deviant sexual behaviors.

The debate over pornography has created some unusual coalitions between religious conservatives who oppose it on moral grounds and feminists who oppose it because it exploits women and treats them as sexual objects. They are pitted against an equally diverse alliance between civil libertarians who oppose censorship and other feminists who believe pornography liberates both women and men (Best and Luckenbill, 1994; Palac, 1997).

Media Violence and Aggressive Behaviors A hotly debated issue today centers on the possible link between violence on television and aggressive behavior in children (see Focus box 7.2). The proposed link between media violence and social aggression is not limited to children, however. There is some evidence that portrayals of violence in the mass media provoke aggression in the real world as well as in the laboratory. David Phillips (1983) produced data showing that homicide rates exhibited a brief but sharp increase immediately after televised heavyweight fights. Other studies have linked increased imitative suicides to televised and newspaper accounts of suicides, particularly those involving celebrities, and still others have shown that media violence may be linked to everything from aggression in children to violent crime (Phillips, 1974; Stack, 1987b, 2000; Wekesser, 1995; Patterson, 2004; Boyle, 2005).

Research findings on the possible link between viewing television violence and aggressive or violent behavior are mixed, and the methodological limitations of these studies make it difficult to draw any clearcut conclusions (Felson, 1996; Boyle, 2005). Nevertheless, television violence has become popularly defined as a social problem, prompting the U.S. Congress to create the Television Violence Report Card Act in 1993. In 1997, the four largest American television networks agreed to rate programming based on violence and sexual content, similar to the motion picture rating system. Also, a federal law was passed requiring that all television sets manufactured in the United States must contain a "V-chip" that enables parents to block out violent programming from their children.

The Effects of Heavy Metal and Rap Music   Debates also have been waged over the impact of heavy metal and certain forms of rap music—especially so-called *gangsta rap*. With lyrics promoting suicide, racism, rape, murder, and other forms of violence, these forms of music have opened the floodgates of negative responses from adults across the country, many of whom indicate they view heavy metal and rap music as audio pornography (Lynxwiler and Gay, 2000). Several states have introduced legislation to label offensive recordings and ban their sale to minors, with legislators asserting that music glorifying deviant behavior such as murder and suicide must be strictly controlled (Hinton, 1990; Binder, 1993; Leland, 1993; Epstein, 1994; Wekesser, 1995; Newton, 1997). Some sociologists argue that condemnation of this music as deviant makes it even more appealing to the youth subculture (Moore, 2005).

Other countries are also concerned about the possible link between heavy metal music and deviance. Egyptian officials are concerned that young fans of heavy metal music are imitating the deviance of their American and European counterparts, tattooing their bodies, wearing deviant hair and dress styles, being sexually promiscuous, possibly engaging in satanic rituals, and otherwise rejecting Egyptian and Islamic culture (Jehl, 1997).

A 1989 American Medical Association report concluded that music had more influence over teenagers than television and other forms of mass media. That report and similar studies prompted Barbara Hattemer, president of the National Family Foundation, to launch a movement against heavy metal rock music and gangsta rap, contending that they promoted sexism, racism, hatred, suicide, drug abuse, and violence (Hattemer and Showers, 1993). At least one social psychological study concluded that violent lyrics are indeed linked to feelings of hostility and aggression (Anderson et al., 2003).

Sociological research, however, suggests that attempts to censor heavy metal and rap music may be motivated more by race and social class than by genuine concern for their potential effects. The racial and class composition of the artists and audiences of the two types of music tend to be quite different and shape their portrayal by the media and how they are perceived. Heavy metal is often associated with stereotypical images of troubled lower- and middle-class white youths, whereas the dangers associated with rap music are exaggerated by whites' fears of stereotypical media portrayals of poor, angry, and violent black youths (Binder, 1993). Historian Tricia Rose (1995) contends that gangsta rap has become a convenient scapegoat for society's violence and that efforts to censor it reflect a demonization of young black males.

Researchers are divided on the question of a link between the mass media and violence, but none deny that media portrayals influence public perceptions of what constitutes deviance. Media attention to crime, drugs, pornography, eating disorders, suicide, and AIDS affects public attitudes toward these issues and contributes to both public understanding and misunderstanding.

All of these popular explanations for deviance operate on the oversimplistic idea that we can dichotomize the world into two types of people: deviants and conformists. They fail to acknowledge the complex sociological processes involved in defining deviance and conformity. For that, we turn to sociology.

SOCIOLOGICAL ANALYSIS OF DEVIANCE AND CONFORMITY

Since the discipline's earliest inception sociologists have asked: Why do some people violate norms while others do not? Why do people conform to some norms while violating others? Let's look at how the three major theoretical perspectives in sociology might provide answers to these questions.

The Structural Functionalist Perspective

Sociologists who use the structural functionalist perspective view both deviance and conformity as integral components of the basic structure of society. Because norms provide guidelines for human behavior, their violation almost always has important consequences for the deviant and the rest of society. From a structural functionalist perspective, some of these social consequences are dysfunctional (having a potentially

Violence, in a variety of forms, has become a part of social reality across the United States and throughout the world. Nowhere, however, is violence more prevalent than in the world of mass media. On Saturday mornings, children ranging in age from toddlers to teenagers watch cartoon mice explode pesky cats with dynamite; watch the Road Runner pulverize Wile E. Coyote; and watch multitudes of superheroes pummel, shoot, laser-beam, and disintegrate their enemies. These programs are often followed by a barrage of football, basketball, or hockey games, professional boxing and wrestling matches, and a variety of other sporting events highlighted by violence and aggression. The nightly news follows, with videotape of brutal beatings, murders, and perhaps a massive terrorist attack, and then viewers can watch a variety of "reality" shows depicting police chases and violent automobile crashes captured on videotape. During prime time, cable viewers can watch a popular Emmy-winning series such as *The*

Sopranos where they are treated to mob-hits as a standard program feature.

The television set is on an average of 8 hours a day in the typical American home but may double that on the weekends. One-third of all children live in a home where the television is on all the time during waking hours (Churnin, 2006). When the television set is off, youngsters may spend their time playing a host of computerized video games featuring hand-to-hand mortal combat or the simulated use of high-powered explosives and laser-guided weapons. What effect do such heavy doses of indiscriminate and senseless violence have on viewers? Nobody knows for sure. Many people believe that explicit violence in the mass media, especially on television, contributes to violence and aggression in society, and parents and teachers are particularly concerned that media violence may negatively affect children.

Albert Bandura's studies using the "Bobo doll" were among the first attempts to link television violence to aggressive behavior in children. There is much disagreement over the interpretation of Bandura's findings as well as that of subsequent research on the effects of media violence on children.

What do you think? Do the media help create, or merely reflect, violence in society?

The National Institute of Mental Health (1982) and other research (e.g., Gerbner, 1995; American Academy of Pediatrics, 2001; HND, 2003; Boyle, 2005) indicate that these fears are not totally unfounded, and that viewing violence in the media may contribute to aggressive behavior, especially among young viewers. There is general consensus that "exposure to television violence can cause short-term arousal and modeling effects" (Tan, 1986:41). Experiments with the "Bobo doll" indicate that children learn and imitate aggressive and violent modes of play from watching television programs as children repeatedly beat and kicked the Bobo doll after viewing similar behavior on television (Bandura et al., 1963; Bandura, 1965). Other studies have also shown that there is a relationship between media violence and aggressive behavior, especially when viewers understand and remember the violence, and believe that the perpetrator was in some way rewarded for the violence and aggression (Bandura, 1973; Gerbner and Gross, 1976; Fenigstein, 1979; Geen, 1983; Medved, 1992; American Academy of Pediatrics, 2001; HND, 2003; Boyle, 2005).

Robert Hodge and David Tripp (1986) argued, however, that the fear of media violence is exaggerated. They contend that children are very much aware that television violence is not real and consequently view it only as entertainment. Others even suggest that media violence may have a cathartic effect, believing that watching violence on television and in motion pictures or playing violent video games may provide a vicarious outlet for aggression and in fact reduce the amount of actual violence engaged in by the viewer (DeFleur, 1983; Brown, 1990). In fact, one psychiatrist used "slasher movies," such as the *Friday the 13th* and *Nightmare on Elm Street* series, as therapy for disturbed youths, contending that the films helped youths deal with their anger (Brown, 1990).

Most studies seem to refute the catharsis theory, however. When a link between viewing violence in the media and aggressive behavior can be determined, it is almost always in a positive direction (the more violence viewed, the more aggressive behavior) rather than a negative direction (the more violence viewed, the less aggressive behavior) (Liebert and Sprafkin, 1988). Although there is no clear evidence that media violence causes aggressive behavior, there is mounting evidence that the persistent and relentless depiction of violence in the media and the unrealistic and stereotypical portrayal of victims and victimizers desensitize viewers and cultivate values that contribute to aggression, fear, and gloom (Evra, 1990; Gerbner, 1995; Patterson, 2004; Boyle, 2005). Research indicates that long-term heavy viewing of violence-laden media contributes to increased apprehension, mistrust, alienation, and the "mean-world syndrome," which may lead to the purchase of new locks, guard dogs, and guns for self-protection (Gerbner, 1995:553).

From a sociological viewpoint, it seems clear that mass media are but one component of a society that is permeated by violence. Moreover, any relationship that may exist between watching violence in the media and actually perpetuating violence is likely to be a very complex one involving a wide variety of social factors (Erwin, 1997). Violence in the media has become an integral part of our global society, and with the advent of increasingly sophisticated computer technology and ever widening media markets around the globe, media violence is likely to continue to be a hot commodity.

TAKING A CLOSER LOOK

Why does violence play such a prominent, pervasive, and persistent role in the media? How does participating in violence in video games and other electronic media differ from watching violence on television or in motion pictures? Why is American culture so fascinated by violence? Should media violence be censored? If so, who decides? What roles does the government play? What other issues (e.g., First Amendment) are raised by media censorship?

*For an excellent collection of essays debating the issue of violence in the media, see Carol Wekesser (ed.). *Violence in the Media*. San Diego: Greenhaven Press, 1995.

Source: Albert Bandura, J. D. Ross, and S. Ross. "Imitation of Film-Mediated Aggressive Models." *Journal of Abnormal and Social Psychology* 66, 1963:3–11. Albert J. Bandura. "Influence of Models' Reinforcement Contingencies on the Acquisition of Imitative Responses." *Journal of Personality and Social Psychology* 1, 1965:589–595. Albert J. Bandura. *Aggression: A Social Learning Analysis*. Englewood Cliffs, NJ: Prentice-Hall, 1973. George Gerbner and L. Gross. "Living with Television: A Violence Profile." *Journal of Communications* 26 (2), 1976:173–200. A. Fenigstein. "Does Aggression Cause a Preference for Viewing Media Violence?" *Journal of Personality and Social Psychology* 37, 1979:2307–2317. National Institute of Mental Health, *Television and Behavior: Ten Years of Scientific Progress and Implications for the Eighties*, Vols. 1 and 2. Washington, DC: U.S. Government Printing Office, 1982. Melvin DeFleur. *Social Problems*. Boston: Houghton Mifflin, 1983. R. G. Geen. "Aggression and Television Violence" in R. G. Geen and E. I. Donnerstein (eds.). *Aggression: Theoretical and Empirical Reviews*, Vol. 2. New York: Academic Press, 1983:103–125. Robert Hodge and David Tripp. *Children and Television: A Semiotic Approach*. Cambridge, UK: Polity Press, 1986. Alexis S. Tan. "Social Learning of Aggression from Television" in Jennings Bryant and Dolf Zillmann (eds.). *Perspectives on Media Effects*. Hillsdale, NJ: Erlbaum, 1986:41–55. Robert M. Liebert and Joyce Sprafkin. *The Early Window: Effects of Television on Children and Youth*, 3rd ed. New York: Pergamon, 1988. Heidi Nolte Brown. "Can Violent Films Help Troubled Teens?" *Dallas Morning News*, March 11, 1990:4C. Judith Van Evra. *Television and Child Development*. Hillsdale, NJ: Erlbaum, 1990. Michael Medved. *Hollywood vs. America: Popular Culture and the War on Traditional Values*. New York: Harper-Collins/Zondervan, 1992. George Gerbner. "Television Violence: The Power and the Peril," in Gail Dines and Jean M. Humez (eds.). *Gender, Race and Class in Media: A Text-Reader*. Thousand Oaks, CA: Sage, 1995:547–557. American Academy of Pediatrics. "Media Violence." *Pediatrics* 108 (November), 2001:1222–1226. HND. "Media Violence Predicts Aggressive Behavior." *Health News Digest*, <http://www.healthnewsdigest.com/, 2003>. Kirstin J. Erwin. "Children's Attitudes Toward Violence on Television." *Journal of Psychology* 131 (4), 1997:411. Karen Patterson. "Piling on the Violence." *Dallas Morning News*, April 12, 2004: IE. Nancy Churnin. "Tot TV comes with Parental Guidance." *Dallas Morning News*, May 25, 2006: IA. Karen Boyle. *Media and Violence: Gendering the Debates*. Thousand Oaks, CA: Sage, 2005.

disruptive impact) and others are functional (contributing to the overall functioning of society). For example, functionalists contend that when norms are violated:

1. People may be harmed or injured.
2. Norms may be threatened.
3. There can be enormous financial, social, and emotional costs.
4. Social order often is disrupted.
5. There is concern that violation of one norm may lead to the violation of others. (Liska and Warner, 1991; Bynum and Thompson, 2007)

Because of their negative consequences, most of us are well aware of these dysfunctional aspects of deviance, but we may be unaware that social deviance can also be functional and have positive consequences for society and individuals. Émile Durkheim ([1893] 1982) viewed deviance as an integral part of social structure and believed that even severe forms of deviance, such as crime, could be functional because they enhanced social cohesion and solidarity. Moreover, functionalists note that in some cases deviance may:

1. Reaffirm and reinforce norms because the deviants are punished.
2. Promote social solidarity as people unite either against or on behalf of the deviants.
3. Provide a contrast effect because conformity assumes meaning only when it is contrasted with deviance.
4. Act as a "safety valve," relieving pressure and preventing more serious deviance.
5. Lead to innovation and social change. (Dentler and Erikson, 1959; Bynum and Thompson, 2007)

The 1995 bombing of the federal building in Oklahoma City, with its devastating loss of lives, massive destruction, terror, fear, and hatred, serves as a stark and chilling example of all five of the dysfunctions of deviance. Yet the incident and subsequent arrest, trial, conviction, and sentencing of Timothy McVeigh illustrate how deviance can unite survivors, a community, and almost an entire nation in the effort to reinforce norms and punish the deviant. The 9/11 attacks on the World Trade Center and the Pentagon reinforce this concept. They also illustrate how some factions in society unite on behalf of norm violators.

Deviance as Social Pathology An early version of the structural functionalist approach to deviance is found in Herbert Spencer's assertion that deviance is a form of social pathology. Like most functionalists, Spencer viewed society as consisting of a basic structure that included a variety of interconnected and interdependent parts. To Spencer, a problem in one part of the organism affected the entire organism. Building on Spencer's *organic analogy* (see Chapter 1), many early sociologists viewed deviant behavior as a form of **social pathology,** *a problem that potentially threatens the survival of society.* Crime, mental illness, drug abuse, suicide, and other forms of deviance were viewed as social pathologies in need of study and remedy. Spencer's approach to deviance provided a theoretical basis for the structural functionalist approach to deviance that later became known as *structural* or *strain theories.*

Strain theories *view deviance as a result of the tensions or strain experienced by people because of their position in the social structure.* Émile Durkheim's sociological analysis of suicide serves as a good example of this structural functionalist approach to deviance and conformity.

Durkheim's Theory of Suicide Émile Durkheim's ([1897] 1951) classic study of suicide showed that what seems to be an individualistic and personal act is in fact influenced by a person's place in the social structure and can be viewed as both socially dysfunctional and functional. Insisting that suicide could be understood only through a

SOCIAL PATHOLOGY
A problem that potentially threatens the survival of society.

STRAIN THEORIES
The view that deviance is a result of the tensions or strain experienced by people because of their position in the social structure.

study of overall rates, not individual suicides, Durkheim defined four categories of suicide: egoistic, altruistic, anomic, and fatalistic. He wrote that *egoistic suicide* occurs in large, complex, and loosely integrated urban societies in which individuals feel they are not meaningfully integrated into a social group or into society as a whole. Despite some contradictory findings regarding the role of religion (e.g., Van Poppel and Day, 1996), numerous other studies of suicide have confirmed the influence of social integration, especially marriage, on differing suicide rates (e.g., Gibbs, 1982; Stack, 1990b; Stockard and O'Brien, 2002).

Conversely, *altruistic suicide,* which is more characteristic of smaller "folk societies" or closely bonded small groups, occurs as a result of extreme social integration, when suicide may be viewed as necessary and even functional for the survival of the overall group. Every major religion has its martyrs. Military folklore, too, is replete with stories of soldiers jumping on live grenades to save their comrades in the heat of battle. The famous Japanese kamikaze pilots in World War II went through a ritual, then strapped themselves into planes loaded with explosives and flew into U.S. warships, sacrificing their lives for their country. Modern suicide bombers are motivated by similar ideological commitments.

In *anomic suicide* people take their lives as a result of a lack of social regulation and control. Durkheim insisted that people want norms to govern and regulate their behavior so that they know what is expected of them and others. He coined the term **anomie,** which refers to *a state of social strain, normative confusion, or rapid change in norms, when people's behavior is no longer restrained by conventional norms.* In times of natural disasters, war, stock market crashes, and other major social upheavals, suicide rates tend to increase.

Fatalistic suicide was mentioned only briefly by Durkheim and is overlooked by many sociologists today. Durkheim insisted that people need social constraints, but he also acknowledged that they need a certain amount of autonomy and freedom from social control. Prisoner suicides, suicidal "love pacts," and similar circumstances where people believe they have no freedom or choice and that their futures are doomed are examples of fatalistic suicide.

Merton's Anomie Theory   Sociologist Robert Merton borrowed from Durkheim to develop a general structural functionalist theory to explain conformity and deviance. To Merton (1938), the primary causes of deviance were social situations in which people, because of their place in the social structure, were unable to pursue socially accepted goals through culturally approved means.

According to Merton, Americans are socialized from birth to strive for material possessions (e.g., nice homes, new cars, fashionable clothes, expensive jewelry) and high social status (usually based on the prestige of one's occupation). Although Americans are encouraged to internalize these measures of success, some find it impossible to attain them by culturally approved means (staying in school, hard work, thriftiness, and deferred gratification). When individuals experience the strain associated with the discrepancy between socially approved goals and the approved means of pursuing them, anomie results. Merton's typology describes five possible ways in which people respond to their anomic situation (see Table 7.1).

One adaptation is *conformity,* in which people accept socially approved goals and pursue them by culturally acceptable means— even if they find that the means

ANOMIE
A state of social strain, normative confusion, or rapid change in norms, when people's behavior is no longer restrained by conventional norms.

TABLE 7.1
MERTON'S TYPOLOGY OF MODES OF ADAPTIVE BEHAVIOR

ADAPTATION	SOCIALLY ACCEPTED GOALS	CULTURALLY APPROVED MEANS
Conformity	Accepts and pursues	Accepts and uses
Innovation	Accepts and pursues	Rejects, or finds them unavailable; substitutes deviant means to achieve goals
Ritualism	Rejects and does not pursue	Appears to accept; confuses the means with the goals
Retreatism	Rejects and does not pursue	Rejects and does not use
Rebellion	Rejects and replaces with deviant goals	Rejects and replaces with deviant means

Source: Adapted from Robert K. Merton. "Social Structure and Anomie." *American Sociological Review* 3, 1938:676.

are not readily available to them. In contrast, the other four adaptations in Merton's typology result in the violation of social norms, and their perpetrators are usually defined as deviants.

Merton's second adaptive strategy is *innovation,* which can be defined as finding a new way to do an old thing. Innovators internalize the goals of society, but they either reject the culturally approved means of achieving them or, because they find the approved means unavailable, develop alternative means of pursuing the goals. For example, most Americans have internalized the goal of accumulating lots of money. The culturally prescribed way of realizing that goal is to stay in school, work hard, save, and defer gratification. Other ways to amass a fortune include robbing banks, dealing in illegal drugs, embezzling, participating in insider trading, and committing a host of other white-collar crimes with big financial payoffs.

Merton's third adaptive strategy is *ritualism,* in which a person either rejects society's goals or realizes that he or she cannot achieve them but still "goes through the motions" so as not to get into trouble or be disappointed. In this adaptation, the individual's allegiance shifts from the goals to the means; for example, a petty bureaucrat may become more concerned about following rules and completing the appropriate forms than about accomplishing the broader goals associated with his or her work.

Merton's fourth adaptation is *retreatism,* which involves the rejection of both socially approved goals and culturally approved means of achieving them. Like ritualists, retreatists have not internalized the success goal; unlike ritualists, retreatists are unwilling to "play the game." Instead, some retreatists drop out of mainstream society by becoming vagrants, hermits, or members of deviant subcultures or they retreat from society through the use of drugs and alcohol.

Merton's fifth adaptive strategy is *rebellion,* which rejects society's goals and replaces them with antithetical goals. Rebels also reject society's culturally approved means and replace them with deviant means. Of all of Merton's categories, rebels are usually viewed as the most threatening because they represent an overt threat to social order. Terrorists, for example, often evoke the most powerful emotions and most severe sanctions of all deviants.

It is important to understand that Merton was not describing personality types in his modes of adaptive behavior. Rather, he described patterns of behavior and pointed out that individuals and groups readily shift from one adaptive scheme to another. Merton's anomie theory, especially his categories of retreatists and rebels, provided the basis for another set of functionalist explanations for deviance: *deviant subcultures.*

Deviant Subcultures

Albert Cohen (1955) and Richard Cloward and Lloyd Ohlin (1960) expanded on Merton's anomie theory of deviance. Focusing on juvenile delinquency, they theorized that the reason lower-class boys may become involved in property offenses and even violent crimes is because they find few legitimate opportunities to achieve some of the middle-class goals (especially material possessions) to which they aspire. These blocked opportunities lead to the formation of deviant subcultures that provide increased social status through illegitimate means and support deviance such as dropping out of school, joining gangs, stealing, dealing drugs, or otherwise pursuing status and material possessions through illegitimate means.

Deviant subcultures are not unique to juveniles. Practitioners of many forms of deviance (e.g., religious cults, drug users, nudists) may feel "cut off" from larger society and consequently find it functional to band together for social purposes, mutual support, and protection (McCaghy and Capron, 1994; Clinard and Meier, 2003).

Taking a Closer Look at the Structural Functionalist Perspective

What do you perceive as the major strengths of the structural functionalist perspective on deviance? Can you identify some weaknesses? Spencer's organic analogy and comparison of deviance to pathology emphasizes the interdependence of society and the importance of "healthy" social institutions for the overall functioning of society. Durkheim's study of suicide is considered a classic, and while it has both supporters and detractors, no one can deny its importance in defining suicide as a social rather than a personal act. Merton's anomie theory and the deviant subculture theories it spawned have been very productive in shedding light on various forms of deviance, especially juvenile delinquency committed by lower-class boys.

Nevertheless, while structural functionalist theories provide important sociological insight into deviance and conformity a common weakness of this perspective is that it infers that there is widespread consensus about what constitutes deviance and conformity and assumes that everyone is socialized to have common values, aspirations, and goals. These assumptions downplay the impact of social inequality and ignore the diversity of a complex global society—two things addressed by the conflict theories of deviance.

Conflict Theories of Deviance

Karl Marx ([1867] 1975) argued that society is comprised of two distinctive social classes and that a person's social class largely determines every aspect of life. From this view, norms do not arise out of general consensus but represent the values and interests of the ruling class and are designed to exploit and control members of the working class. According to Marx, the ruling class treats as deviant any activities that threaten their privileged position. Consequently any norms at odds with those of the ruling class are viewed as deviant (and usually illegal) and will be punished. **Conflict theories of deviance** *view deviance as arising when groups with power attempt to impose their norms and values on less powerful groups.* Contemporary conflict theories focus on power, thus concentrating more on the origin of norms and their enforcement than on the behavior of individuals; hence they are theories of *deviance* more than theories of *deviant behavior* (Clinard and Meier, 2003).

Power and Deviance   Although it may be more pronounced and obvious in some countries than in others, inequality exists in every society throughout the world. Great Britain maintains the Royal Family and titles of nobility; many Middle Eastern countries have their kings or sheiks; and despite its legal dissolution, Indian society retains many remnants of its rigid caste system. Whereas Marx focused on economic inequality and the differential power between the social classes, inequality of power goes well beyond social class. In most cultures power is differentially distributed on the basis of age, race, sex, religion, and politics as well as social class. In work environments, supervisors and bosses enjoy more power than employees, and in academic environments, at least in terms of academic decisions, administrators have more power than the faculty and teachers have more power than students. Contemporary conflict theorists focus much of their attention on the role that power plays in creating and enforcing the rules of society and consequently defining deviance and conformity.

Power theories explain deviance in two very important ways. First, those in power have more opportunity to make and enforce the norms that govern their and others' behavior. Hence they often have the power to say what and who are and are not deviant. Second, because of their loftier social positions, only certain people have the power to commit certain types of deviance.

Turning to the first point, conflict theorists insist that criminal justice systems reinforce inequality and define as deviant any behavior that threatens those in power. For example, capitalistic countries place tremendous emphasis on laws that protect property (e.g., theft, vandalism) and may even make it illegal to be poor (e.g., vagrancy, panhandling, hitchhiking). Criminologist Jeffrey Reiman asserts that the American criminal justice system creates an image of crime that portrays the poor as dangerous to individual safety and a threat to the security and stability of society. According to Reiman, this ideological approach to crime diverts attention from those in power, allowing them to continue their participation in white-collar crimes and other forms of elite deviance. Asserting that "nothing succeeds like failure," Reiman (2007:5) developed the *Pyrrhic defeat theory,* which contends that those in power have designed the criminal justice system to fail because "the failure of the criminal justice system yields such benefits to those in positions of power that it amounts to success." In other words, as long as crime rates are high, prisoners are not rehabilitated, and fear for personal property and safety remain high, very little attention is focused on who makes the laws, how

CONFLICT THEORIES OF DEVIANCE
View deviance as arising when groups with power attempt to impose their norms and values on less powerful groups.

they are enforced, and why crimes committed by the poor and powerless are punished severely while those committed by the wealthy and powerful are largely ignored.

The point that only the powerful are in a position to commit certain types of deviance is also of sociological interest. Have you ever thought of embezzling millions of dollars from a bank or multinational corporation? Are you tempted to violate antitrust acts in order to monopolize an entire market and strip your competitors of the opportunity to perform the same services or sell in the same markets you do? Have you ever rigged a bid, taken a bribe, or accepted a kickback on a multimillion dollar construction project? Have you ever abused the power of your position, job, or office to benefit yourself or harm others? If you are like most college students, the answer to all of these questions is "No," but this may not be solely because of your high moral standards or commitment to conformity. The answer may, at least in part, be attributed to the fact that you have never had the power to commit any of those crimes, because they constitute what sociologists call elite deviance.

Elite Deviance   Only certain people in society can commit **elite deviance,** which *includes all aspects of white-collar crime as well as other deviant acts perpetrated by those in power.* This includes environmental pollution, deceptive advertising, fraud, insider trading, manufacture of harmful products, political corruption, and a host of other deviant activities. Elite deviance is not new, and the general public has long been aware of political scandals, corporate crimes, and other forms of crime and deviance committed by those in power. What does the conflict perspective contribute to the understanding of elite deviance? The answer lies in what has always been sociology's major strength: rather than focusing on the individuals who commit elite deviance and explaining their actions as being a result of individual immorality, greed, or pathology, the conflict perspective focuses on the basic social structure and identifies social inequality as the major explanation for this type of deviance (e.g., Turk, 1969; Quinney, 1975, 1980; Chambliss and Mankoff, 1976; Vold and Bernard, 1986; Reiman, 2006; Simon, 2006).

Drawing on the work of C. Wright Mills (1956; 1959), conflict theorists attribute elite deviance to a social structure where those who control the dominant social institutions—governments, militaries, major national and multinational corporations—have amassed inordinate amounts of wealth, power, and prestige that allow them to protect their vested interests, control the mass media, and promote their values over those of less powerful social institutions such as the family, education, and religion. The conflict perspective also contends that the power elite who control those dominant institutions use their wealth, power, and prestige to control and manipulate the mass media to reinforce their definitions of deviance and conformity (Ermann and Lundman, 1996; Simon, 2006; Dotter, 2002).

ELITE DEVIANCE
Includes all aspects of white-collar crime as well as other deviant acts perpetrated by those in power.

Elite deviance usually attracts far less public attention and often elicits lesser legal penalties than do street crimes and other forms of highly visible deviance. Here, the late Kenneth L. Lay, former Chairman and CEO of Enron, exercises his fifth amendment right to avoid self-incrimination while testifying before the U.S. Senate Committee on Commerce, Science, and Transportation about the collapse of Enron.

Taking a Closer Look at the Conflict Theories of Deviance

What do the conflict theories contribute to our understanding of deviance and conformity? Certainly one of their strengths is the recognition that we live in a diverse society where various groups have different opinions about what is right and what is wrong, what is acceptable and what is not, and what constitutes deviance and what is conformity. They also provide a framework for analyzing the roles of social inequality and differences in power in creating and enforcing norms as well as defining deviance and conformity. And the conflict perspective's emphasis on elite deviance and white-collar crime challenge many of the functionalist theories' assumptions about deviance being a lower-class phenomenon.

Nevertheless, the conflict theories, with their reliance on Marxian philosophy and emphasis on economic determinism, ignore many of the day-to-day microlevel aspects of creating and re-creating norms, defining and redefining deviance and conformity. Moreover, while their emphasis on power is enlightening, it fails to explain how those who have very little power can be involved in labeling acts and people as deviant or conformist. These microlevel issues are addressed by the symbolic interactionist perspective.

Interactionist Explanations

The interactionist perspective views deviance and conformity as flexible and symbolic terms that must be defined and redefined through the process of interaction. From the interactionist perspective, three of the most important explanations of deviance and conformity involve labeling, social learning, and social control.

Labeling Theories As their name implies, **labeling theories** *view deviance and conformity as labels assigned to certain people and certain acts.* From this perspective, attention is shifted from the actor and the act to the audience. Labeling theories are less concerned with explaining what causes deviant behavior than with understanding how labels are applied and why some norm-violating people and behaviors are labeled as deviant while others are not. For example, labeling theorists contend that Durkheim's study of suicide ignored how deaths become labeled as suicides in the first place. Durkheim emphasized religion as a measure of social integration because Protestant suicide rates were much higher than those of Catholics and Jews. Subsequent research, however, points out that at least part of the discrepancy in suicide rates among Protestants and Catholics may be attributed to the reluctance on the part of Catholics to label a death as a suicide. Consequently, in the absence of a note or other solid evidence of suicide, many unattended deaths among Catholics were labeled as "accidental deaths" than as suicides (Van Poppel and Day, 1996).

Primary and Secondary Deviance Edwin Lemert (1951) emerged as one of the leading proponents of the labeling approach with his analysis of how being labeled deviant may shape subsequent behavior. According to Lemert, **primary deviance** occurs *when an individual violates a norm and is viewed as deviant but rejects the deviant label and maintains a conformist conception of herself or himself.* If the person's self-concept is unaltered by the deviant label, he or she is no more likely to engage in future deviance than before the label was attached. Lemert acknowledged that others' perceptions are important, and it is difficult to maintain a conformist self-image after being labeled deviant. As a result, many people become involved in **secondary deviance,** which is *the internalization of a deviant label and the assumption of a deviant role.* Lemert (1972) argued that social control, which invariably involves the application of the deviant label, may be more likely to lead to future deviance than to prevent it.

Deviance as a Master Status Howard Becker developed a *career model of deviance* that demonstrates how the application and subsequent internalization of the deviant label leads to continued and increased deviance. Becker's emphasis on the developmental process underscored the idea that deviance often becomes a *master status,* a status that overpowers and in many cases supersedes any other statuses an individual holds that might run counter to it.

Edwin Schur (1971) pointed out that individuals often internalize the deviant identity to the extent that they, too, view themselves as generally deviant, rather than deviant in relation to a specific act or attribute. Describing this process as *role engulfment,* Schur explained that people often become so absorbed in their deviant identity that this shapes their subsequent behavior, and they fulfill expectations associated with the deviant role. Likewise, Becker concluded that treating a person as generally rather than specifically deviant produces a self-fulfilling prophecy.

Labeling "Mental Illness" as a Master Status D. L. Rosenhan, professor of law and psychology at Stanford University, designed and participated in a study on mental illness that resembled a Hollywood film plot. What if a perfectly "normal" person were diagnosed as "crazy" and locked in a mental institution against his or her will? Would doctors and nurses recognize the mistake and release the misdiagnosed person immediately? Or, as some movies suggest, could a "sane" person languish for years in a mental institution, unable to prove his or her sanity? Rosenhan and his research team of four men and three women, including two psychologists, a graduate student, a psychiatrist, a pediatrician, a homemaker, and a painter, visited 12 mental institutions in five states on the East and West Coasts, reporting to hospital admissions staff that they heard voices.

LABELING THEORIES
View deviance and conformity primarily as labels assigned to certain people and certain acts.

PRIMARY DEVIANCE
When an individual violates a norm and is viewed as deviant but rejects the deviant label and maintains a conformist conception of himself or herself.

SECONDARY DEVIANCE
The internalization of a deviant label and the assumption of a deviant role.

All eight "pseudopatients" were admitted to the hospitals. Except for giving a false name and faking the initial symptom, each pseudopatient gave an accurate history and made no additional attempts to fool hospital staff. In fact, all acted as normal as possible. Despite their "normal" actions once admitted to the hospital, none of the pseudopatients was detected by hospital staff. The length of hospitalization ranged from 7 to 52 days. On release, all but one "manic-depressive" were discharged as schizophrenics "in remission"—a label that stays with an ex-mental patient for the rest of his or her life. Rosenhan concluded that once someone is diagnosed as "mentally ill," the structure and environment of the hospital serve to maintain and confirm the original diagnosis.

Social Learning Theories

Social learning theories *contend that all behavior (including deviance) is learned through social interaction.* They assume that some people learn to become deviant through the complex process of socialization. One of the most prominent social learning theories is *differential association theory* (Sutherland and Cressey, 1978).

Differential Association   Many sociologists consider Edwin Sutherland the first criminologist to provide a sociological explanation of individual-level and macrolevel differences in crime and delinquency (Laub and Sampson, 1991). Sutherland argued that deviant behavior is learned through interaction with other deviants in a social context where deviance is viewed as acceptable. Differential association theory elaborates on the old adage "Birds of a feather flock together" by showing that our behavior is influenced by the people with whom we associate. The theory stresses that primary relationships, such as those with our parents, siblings, and close friends, have the greatest impact on our behavior. At least moderate support for differential association theory has been found in studies of delinquency (e.g., Orcutt, 1987; Kim and Goto, 2000).

Differential Reinforcement   Ronald Akers (1985) pointed out that depending on whom an individual associates with, norm-violating behavior may be either positively rewarded or negatively sanctioned. For example, suppose a teenage girl shoplifts a compact disk. If she is not caught, she may experience a sense of gratification by getting something she wanted for nothing. If her friends praise her deviant behavior, she is likely to shoplift again. On the other hand, if her friends are outraged by her behavior and threaten to withdraw their friendship, she is much less likely to repeat the deviant behavior. To Akers, then, *differential reinforcement* is the key to deviant or conformist behavior and acts as a method of social control.

Social Control Theories

Whereas most theories of deviant behavior ask what causes deviance, control theorists argue that a more important question is: What causes conformity? From this viewpoint, people have a natural propensity toward deviant behavior. Further, control theorists assert that much of what constitutes deviance (especially minor rule violations) is exciting and fun. The question, then, is not "Why does anybody do it?" but "What keeps everybody from breaking the rules?" The answer is social control. **Social control theories** *contend that deviance is normal and conformity must be explained.*

Hirschi's Social Bond Theory   Travis Hirschi (1969) concluded that the main reason some people do not commit deviance is that they have developed a strong *social bond,* consisting of an attachment to parents, school, church, and other institutions aligned with conformity; a commitment to conventional norms; an involvement in conventional activities; and a belief in the validity of social norms. Hirschi asserted that the stronger a person's social bond, the less likely his or her involvement in deviant activities. Conversely, the weaker the social bond to conformist groups and institutions, the easier it is for the individual to violate society's norms. Research on delinquency, crime, and deviance over the life course finds modest to impressive support for social bond theory among both adolescents and adults (Sampson and Laub, 1990; Free, 1994; Osgood et al., 1996; Sharp, 1998).

Containment Theory   Walter Reckless (1961) contended that during the socialization process individuals develop the first barrier against deviance, which he called *inner con-*

SOCIAL LEARNING THEORIES
Contend that all behavior (including deviance) is learned through social interaction.

SOCIAL CONTROL THEORIES
Contend that deviance is normal and conformity must be explained.

tainment. Inner containment is the extent to which an individual internalizes the norms, attitudes, values, and beliefs of his or her culture. Most people can control their impulses to deviate. For some, however, inner containment is not strong enough, so society provides a second layer of control in the form of *outer containment,* which consists of parents, teachers, police officers, and others who serve as agents of social control. Reckless's containment theory also recognizes the importance of the social environment. In some social situations people with weak inner containment are subject to a vast array of external agents of social control. In many others outer containment is minimal, and if an individual's inner containment is not sufficiently strong deviance is likely to occur.

Techniques of Neutralization   Gresham Sykes and David Matza (1957) theorized that much deviant behavior can be explained by people's ability to rationalize it and hence neutralize their inhibitions. From this perspective, individuals sometimes ignore conventional norms because they view them as flexible guidelines for behavior rather than as rigid rules. Depending on the situation, the greater the ability of an individual to rationalize (and therefore neutralize) norm violation, the more likely he or she is to engage in deviant behavior. Sykes and Matza identified five *techniques of neutralization:*

1. *Denial of Responsibility.* People may rationalize deviant acts by claiming they were caused by forces beyond their control. For example, have you ever explained to your professor that you were late for class or missed an exam because of a flat tire, a faulty alarm clock, or heavy traffic?

2. *Denial of Injury.* If a person cannot deny responsibility for a deviant act, he or she may argue that no harm was done. Usually, the less serious the infraction, the greater the chance it will be neutralized, but this technique is also used to rationalize crimes such as vandalism and shoplifting.

3. *Denial of the Victim.* When somebody is hurt and harm cannot be denied, the deviant may rationalize that the victim deserved to be hurt. Rapists, for example, often contend that their victims were "asking for it," and social attitudes and legal processes may reinforce that idea (Davis and Stasz, 1990).

4. *Condemnation of the Condemners.* A common assertion by many deviants is that those who condemn them are even more worthy of condemnation. This argument often is used by prison inmates, who assert that police and judges are corrupt and that white-collar and corporate criminals commit more serious offenses but almost never serve hard time.

5. *Appeal to Higher Loyalties.* Many forms of deviance can be rationalized as altruistic acts for the good of a particular group or for some higher cause. Terrorists, for example, rationalize their deviance as serving some higher cause and greater good.

Focus box 7.3 illustrates how topless dancers use techniques of neutralization to manage the stigma associated with their deviant occupation.

We find that all of us, as a society, are to blame, but only the defendant is guilty."

In contemporary industrial societies, occupation is one of the most important elements of an individual's personal and social identity. When encountering strangers, one of the first questions most of us ask is "What do you do for a living?" For some people, jobs are badges of honor. Physicians, architects, and engineers, for example, readily admit their occupations and through language, dress, and demeanor define themselves as members of these socially acceptable, highly skilled, and well-paid professions. For others, occupation is a badge of shame. As William Thompson and Jackie Harred (1992) demonstrated in their study of seven topless bars in a major metropolitan city in the Southwest, many of the distinctive features of topless dancer subculture directly reflect the fact that although the profession can be highly lucrative, it also is a "stigmatized occupation"—one that "discredits or disqualifies its members from full social acceptance" (Goffman, 1963).

All dancers in the study were female. They ranged in age from 19 to 41, with a median age of 22. The vast majority were white and married, and about half of the women had at least one child. All the dancers indicated that they were aware that most people considered the occupation of topless dancer "improper" or "immoral," and they recognized it as a stigmatized occupation. Consequently, in addition to employing a specialized language, dress, demeanor, and symbols, as is characteristic of all subcultures, they also adopted a variety of strategies to manage and overcome the stigma associated with their work. Many of these techniques served to highlight and further differentiate this occupational subculture from those deemed acceptable by the dominant culture.

Thompson and Harred discovered that topless dancers coped with the stigma associated with their profession in two major ways. First, they divided their social world into two groups: a small group with whom they were able to reveal their "real" occupation and "true identities" and "be themselves" and the vast majority from whom this information had to be concealed at all times, lest their "spoiled identities" be exposed (Goffman, 1963). Information control and "passing" were common strategies, with most dancers describing themselves to acquaintances, casual friends, and sometimes even parents and spouses as "entertainers" and "waitresses."

Second, most employed a variety of techniques that attempted to rationalize and neutralize the stigma associated with their occupation. One common technique used was the *denial of harm,* or, for some, the assertion that topless dancing actually benefits society by providing therapy, educational services by displaying the female anatomy, and, as one dancer put it, "keeping . . . perverts off the streets" (Thompson and Harred, 1992).

Another neutralization technique was the *condemnation of the condemners.* Virtually all dancers indicated that they resented that their occupation was negatively viewed and considered both their customers and the general public "hypocrites." As one dancer put it, "They come in here on Saturday nights, get drunk, and play grab-ass, . . . and then go to church on Sunday and condemn what we do" (Thompson and Harred, 1992). Many also *appealed to higher loyalties,* contending that while they worked in an occupation that violated middle-class norms, they did so only for the benefit of others—children, husbands, or, for some, to relieve parents of having to pay for their college expenses.

A Decade Later. . . A decade later, Thompson, Harred, and another researcher, Barbara Burks, replicated the study in five "gentlemen's clubs" in the same metropolitan area. Interviews with 28 topless dancers produced findings that were quite consistent with those of the earlier study with a couple of interesting additions. By the time of the second study, topless dancing had become a $15-billion-dollar-per-year industry in the United States (Fairbank, 2003). The city in which the clubs were located had launched a major "cleanup" campaign against the adult entertainment industry, specifically targeting topless clubs, citing them for numerous health code violations and writing tickets to dancers and patrons for participating in "lewd behavior." This citywide campaign led by the mayor and city council resulted in even more stigma for topless dancers. In addition to dividing the social world and using the neutralization techniques discovered in the first study, it was discovered that dancers a decade later also relied heavily on *cognitive* and *emotive dissonance* to reduce the emotional strain of the work and to alternately embrace their role as dancer and distance themselves from it as the situation seemed to dictate. Almost unanimously, the dancers reported that they disliked their jobs, would not want their daughters to do it, and that they tried to hide their occupation from as many people as possible. Nevertheless through cognitive and emotive dissonance the dancers were able to separate true feelings from feigning emotions and go about their jobs flirting with customers who they routinely referred to as "perverts," "horny bastards," "arrested adolescents," or as one dancer so eloquently put it, "a bunch of frustrated married guys who just come in here to get a hard-on" (Thompson et al., 2003:16).

TAKING A CLOSER LOOK

Do male dancers such as the Chippendales and Chunkendales experience the same social stigma as female dancers? If not, why not? If so, would they employ the same techniques of rationalization and neutralization that are used by female dancers? What social factors might reduce the stigma associated with male seminude dancing?

Source: Erving Goffman. *Stigma: Notes on the Management of Spoiled Identity.* Englewood Cliffs, NJ: Prentice-Hall, 1963. William E. Thompson and Jackie L. Harred. "Topless Dancers: Managing Stigma in a Deviant Occupation." *Deviant Behavior* 13 (Summer) 1992:291–311. William E. Thompson, Jack L. Harred, and Barbara E. Burks. "Managing the Stigma of Topless Dancing: A Decade Later." *Deviant Behavior* 24(6), 2003:1–20. Katie Fairbank. "Dancing for Dollars." *Dallas Morning News,* February 22, 2003:2F, 3F.

Taking a Closer Look at the Interactionist Perspective The interactionist approach focuses on how deviance and conformity are defined and emphasizes social reactions to people and their behaviors. Labeling theories acknowledge the relativity of norms and emphasize the social processes involved in defining deviance and conformity. Social learning theories have made important contributions to understanding deviance and conformity and show how both are learned through socialization and social interaction with others. Their emphasis on the influence of peers has been insightful for explaining various types of deviance, especially juvenile delinquency. Control theories also provide insight into delinquency because they explain how some juveniles can overcome their socialization to rationalize and neutralize their deviance.

A shortcoming of the interactionist approach is its inability to explain the initial motivations for deviance, and how members of a society decide which norms to enforce and what activities to label as deviant or not. For example, while labeling deviance as a master status and role engulfment help explain secondary deviance and career deviance, they shed little light on why the first act of deviance occurred and how society decides which norms to enforce and which activities can or cannot be tolerated. The impact of negative labels also may vary according to the age, race, and sex of those who are labeled (Adams et al., 1998).

As interactionist theories suggest, conformity is no more "natural" than deviance. When people come together to form societies anywhere in the world, they form rules and guidelines to provide a sense of order and social control.

DEVIANCE, CONFORMITY, AND SOCIAL CONTROL

Every society creates ways to encourage conformity and deter deviance. **Social control** refers to the *mechanisms people use to enforce prevailing social norms.* This process involves the imposition of *positive sanctions* to reward conformity (e.g., encouragement, awards, medals, certificates, diplomas) and *negative sanctions* to punish deviance (e.g., discouragement, ridicule, fines, imprisonment). In most societies far more effort goes into negatively sanctioning deviance than in positively rewarding conformity.

Social Control and Deterrence

Some sociologists contend that deterrence is the most important element of social control and that social control is the most important aspect of sociological inquiry. **Deterrence theory** *states that deviance will be deterred if negative social sanctions (especially punishment) are perceived to be certain, swift, and severe* (Gibbs, 1975). Deterrence theorists differentiate between *specific deterrence,* which are punishments that discourage the individual from committing similar acts in the future, and *general deterrence,* which discourages others from committing similar acts. For example, as a specific deterrent, capital punishment is 100 percent effective. There has never been a case where someone who was executed committed another offense after the execution. On the other hand, there is very little evidence that capital punishment serves as an effective general deterrent: states with capital punishment have higher violent crime rates than those without it. Moreover, a state may execute an individual at 12:01 for committing capital murder, and at 12:02 someone else may commit the same offense. Ideally, social control mechanisms should accomplish both specific and general deterrence.

Voluntary (or Internalized) Social Control

One of the most effective methods of regulating human behavior is for people to internalize society's values and norms and voluntarily restrain themselves. For example, most of us have never committed murder, but that is due more to the fact that we believe it is morally wrong to take another person's life than because it is illegal and we fear being caught and punished. Most people voluntarily conform most of the time. What psychologists refer to as "conscience" represents the sense of guilt we feel when we violate or even consider breaking social norms. Sociologists take this reasoning a step further, explaining that we not only take into account the norms, values, and beliefs of others, but that we also anticipate social reactions to our acts before we commit them.

SOCIAL CONTROL
Mechanisms people use to enforce prevailing social norms.

DETERRENCE THEORY
States that deviance will be deterred if negative social sanctions (especially punishment) are perceived to be certain, swift, and severe.

Informal Social Control

When voluntary social control is insufficient and folkways or mores are violated, informal social control measures may be implemented. *Gossip,* for instance, is a very effective means of penalizing behavior. In small towns or groups where everybody knows everybody else, gossip may be a powerful deterrent to straying from the straight and narrow.

Ridicule, or *shame,* is another common and effective method of informal social control. Few people enjoy being the butt of others' jokes. American teenagers seem particularly adept at this form of informal control over their peers. Research indicates that shame, especially in the form of informal but pervasive social control by others, is linked to conformity (Scheff, 1988).

Perhaps one of the most effective methods of informal social control is *ostracism—* excluding someone from social acceptance or group membership. For the Old Order Amish ostracism (shunning) is the most powerful negative sanction against church members who seriously deviate from the moral and social codes of their faith. The shunned individual is not allowed to take meals with others, is neither spoken to nor acknowledged, and cannot participate in any community activities. In small, interdependent communities such as those created by the Old Order Amish, primary interaction is essential to daily living, and shunning amounts to "social death" (Hostetler, 1980; Thompson, 1986).

Informal social control can be very powerful and is often all that is necessary to dissuade deviance and encourage conformity. When formal norms are violated, however, informal social control may be supplemented and reinforced by formal controls.

Formal Social Control: Crime and the Criminal Justice System

We discussed earlier how crime differs from other forms of deviance. The violation of formally codified laws elicits a different response than the violation of informal folkways and mores. Before we look at the formal mechanisms of social control we have incorporated into a highly complex criminal justice system, we need to look briefly at the types of deviance it was designed to control. In the United States we classify crime into three major categories: violent crimes, property offenses, and public order (so-called victimless) crimes.

Violent Crimes *Violent crimes* are considered the most threatening because they involve offenses against persons. They include homicide (the willful taking of a person's life), aggravated assault (an attack with the intent to inflict severe bodily harm), forcible rape (sexual intercourse against the victim's will), and robbery (stealing from a person by the use or threat of force).

The media portray the United States as a violent, crime-ridden society, and most people shudder at daily reports of rape, murder, and mayhem on American streets. The United States is, in fact, the most violent industrial/postindustrial nation in the world and one of the easiest nations in which to acquire a gun. It is nonetheless interesting that while media coverage and public awareness of violent crime are increasing, official data indicate that overall crime rates, including violent crimes, have actually decreased

" ...AND THIS IS WHERE MY DAD KEEPS THE GUN THAT WE DON'T KNOW ABOUT. "

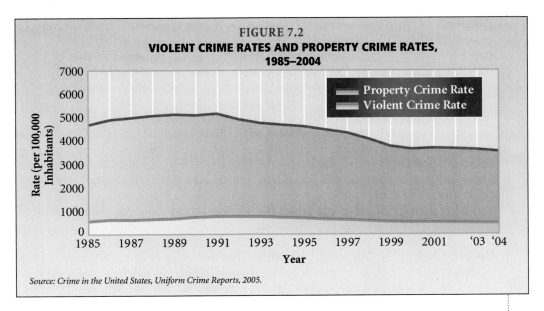

FIGURE 7.2
VIOLENT CRIME RATES AND PROPERTY CRIME RATES, 1985–2004

Source: Crime in the United States, Uniform Crime Reports, 2005.

rather dramatically since 1995 and murder reached a 40-year low in 2004 (see Figure 7.2) (FBI, *Uniform Crime Reports,* 2005; *Associated Press* Washington, 2005). Of course, it also is important to realize that official crime statistics represent only those crimes reported to the police, and sometimes only those that resulted in arrests, so they, too, do not provide an accurate picture of crime. Map 7.1 shows how violent and property crime rates vary by region.

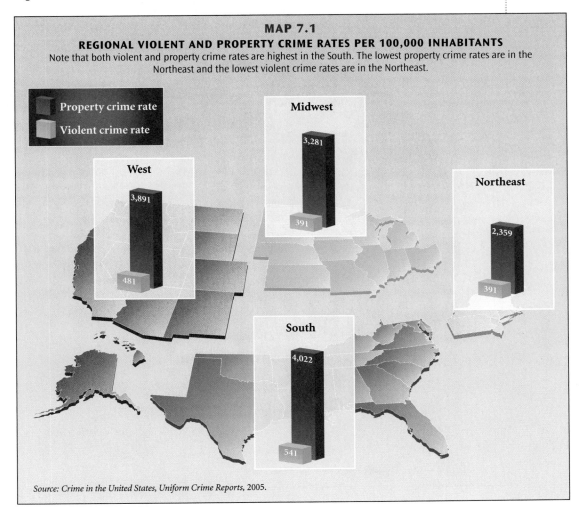

MAP 7.1
REGIONAL VIOLENT AND PROPERTY CRIME RATES PER 100,000 INHABITANTS
Note that both violent and property crime rates are highest in the South. The lowest property crime rates are in the Northeast and the lowest violent crime rates are in the Northeast.

Source: Crime in the United States, Uniform Crime Reports, 2005.

Property Offenses Although people fear violent crimes the most, they are far more likely to become victims of property offenses, which occur much more frequently (see Figure 7.3). *Property offenses* are nonviolent crimes, the most serious of which include burglary (unlawful entry with the intent to steal), larceny-theft (the theft of anything valued in excess of $100), auto theft, and arson (intentionally setting a fire).

While the media and public attention focus on the "street-level" property offenses mentioned here, it is important to realize that white-collar crime victimizes far more people and costs billions of dollars each year. White-collar crimes include embezzlement, fraud, insider trading, copyright and patent violations, and the violation of antitrust laws. These crimes are committed by people of higher socioeconomic status, but at least one criminologist insists it may be a mistake to differentiate between white-collar crime and conventional street crime because both are violations of criminal law, and other than social status and power the offenders share more common characteristics than they do differences (Poveda, 1994).

Public Order/"Victimless" Crimes The third type of crime is *public order,* or *victimless, crime,* such as prostitution, illegal gambling, and illegal drug use. Since these crimes do not involve a clear-cut victim, the average citizen feels much less threatened

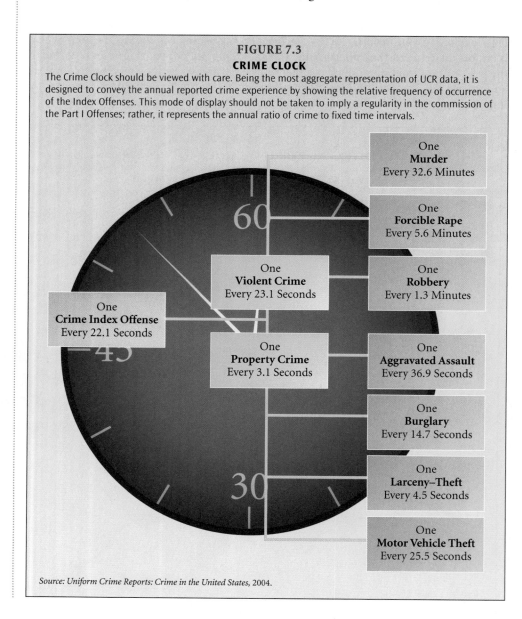

FIGURE 7.3
CRIME CLOCK

The Crime Clock should be viewed with care. Being the most aggregate representation of UCR data, it is designed to convey the annual reported crime experience by showing the relative frequency of occurrence of the Index Offenses. This mode of display should not be taken to imply a regularity in the commission of the Part I Offenses; rather, it represents the annual ratio of crime to fixed time intervals.

One **Murder** Every 32.6 Minutes

One **Forcible Rape** Every 5.6 Minutes

One **Robbery** Every 1.3 Minutes

One **Violent Crime** Every 23.1 Seconds

One **Crime Index Offense** Every 22.1 Seconds

One **Aggravated Assault** Every 36.9 Seconds

One **Property Crime** Every 3.1 Seconds

One **Burglary** Every 14.7 Seconds

One **Larceny–Theft** Every 4.5 Seconds

One **Motor Vehicle Theft** Every 25.5 Seconds

Source: Uniform Crime Reports: Crime in the United States, 2004.

by them. Nevertheless, many people argue that these crimes are not victimless because they disrupt social order and threaten society's moral fiber, thus victimizing all members of society.

Émile Durkheim ([1893] 1964) observed that crime is a normal part of all societies, and all societies institutionalize measures to control criminals. In the United States, social concern about crime and efforts to sanction criminals have led to the creation of one of the most complex and elaborate criminal justice systems in the world. Criminal justice procedures can be divided into law enforcement, the courts, and corrections.

Although British Bobbies are most often seen in informal roles giving directions to tourists, they represent the most highly visible element of social control in Great Britain just as American police officers do in the United States.

Law Enforcement Police officers are the most visible and most direct link between the criminal justice system and the public. They take primary responsibility for the enforcement of laws. The police have two important roles: to catch criminals and to maintain order with the hope of preventing crime. Although the media emphasize the "crime-fighter" image of police work, police officers spend far more time in the second role.

During the 1960s, police went from walking "beats" to riding in squad cars. While cars provided a faster response to emergency calls, they also changed the nature of social interaction between police officers and the public. Police work had been highly personal, as officers strolled the sidewalks talking to storekeepers and homeowners, but it became much more impersonal, with less contact between officers and citizens. In contrast, the British police, after which the American police were modeled, continue to walk beats (usually in pairs), allowing them to interact with residents and businesspeople on a personal basis. This tends to create greater understanding and cooperation between the officers and the people they are policing.

Since the 1960s, technological advances have provided more elaborate means of communication and surveillance, better-equipped squad cars, and more sophisticated weaponry. Of course, criminals have benefited from increased technology as well. This and other developments have led many city leaders to question contemporary policing practices and some to accentuate the need to reemphasize police-community relations. Thus, in the early 1990s, many cities adopted *community policing* strategies and reassigned police officers to walk beats in an effort to regain community trust and cooperation. Today, community policing is a major part of law enforcement in almost every American city.

When someone is arrested, police officers begin pretrial investigations, and staff in the district attorney's office decide whether to file charges and which charges to file. Criminal charges lead to the next component of the criminal justice system—the courts.

The Courts Although every criminal is entitled to his or her day in court, almost 90 percent of criminal cases never go to trial. Instead, prosecuting attorneys representing the state and defense attorneys representing the accused usually negotiate a plea bargain, whereby the defendant agrees to plead guilty to a specific charge (usually less serious than the one originally filed).

Even with only about 10 percent of cases going to trial the criminal court dockets are crowded, and it may take a year or more for a case to go to trial. Judges play a key role in the court phase of criminal justice. They have a great deal of discretion in accepting pleas, admitting evidence, instructing jurors, and setting sentences for those who are convicted of crimes. Private citizens also play an important role in this aspect of the criminal justice system, as they make up the juries when cases go to trial.

When criminal cases are resolved through plea bargaining or convictions, a judge or jury must decide what type of sentence the criminal will receive. This begins the third and final stage of the criminal justice process: corrections.

Corrections   As the name implies, a correctional system represents society's attempt to "correct" those who have violated its laws. Corrections may be linked to *rehabilitation* and an effort to *reform* criminals, but most often they take the form of *retribution,* or *punishment.*

The most common sentence for nonserious offenses and petty property crimes is *probation,* in which people pay fines or make restitution to the victim and are allowed to return to public life with restrictions on their freedom. For more serious property offenses and violent crimes, offenders are more likely to have their freedom restricted by incarceration in a local, state, or federal institution. Despite consistent research findings that imprisonment has little effect on crime (DeFina and Arvanites, 2002; Travis, 2005), the United States has one of the highest imprisonment rates of any country in the world, with over 2 million inmates, more than 125,000 of which are over the age of 55 (Gilliard and Beck, 1998; AP, Washington, 2003a, 2005b). What problems do you foresee as the criminal justice system must continue to provide prison space for teenage offenders while also being faced with housing an increasingly aged population of inmates?

Most prisoners are released on *parole* before they serve their entire sentences. Like people on probation, parolees must periodically report to an officer of the court and must live within a set of rules that restricts their personal freedom. Altogether, 3.1 percent of the American population—1 of every 32 adults—were on some form of supervised release by federal, state, or local authorities as we entered the twenty-first century (Levinthal, 2000a). The large numbers of people on probation and parole, along with the high rates of *recidivism*—repeated offenses by those who have already been convicted of crimes—have led to a "get tough" movement that has had a controversial impact on American corrections.

The most extreme form of social control is capital punishment, that is, execution of the criminal offender. Until the 1960s, capital punishment was an integral part of the British criminal justice system, and during the eighteenth century there were over 200 crimes, ranging from high treason to petty pickpocketing, for which people could be executed. These executions were held in full public view in the belief that the witnesses would be deterred from committing similar acts.

The American criminal justice system, which borrowed heavily from Great Britain, also incorporated capital punishment and used it widely until 1972. That year, the U.S. Supreme Court ruled in the case of *Furman v. Georgia* that execution practices were discriminatory and had been applied arbitrarily and capriciously. Executions were halted in the United States and did not resume until 1977, the year after *Gregg v. Georgia,* in which the court ruled that executions could be carried out as long as they did not inflict unnecessary pain and suffering or constitute cruel and unusual punishment as outlined in the Eighth Amendment to the U.S. Constitution. Over 1,000 inmates have been executed in the United States since the reinstatement of the death penalty in 1977. Map 7.2 shows the states that had the death penalty in 2005 and the number of executions in each state since 1977.

Debate continues over the appropriateness of capital punishment: Does it deter crime, or does it have the opposite effect of "brutalizing" the members of society? While the debate may never be resolved, most contemporary research on capital punishment finds little evidence of general deterrent effects, confirms the accusations of its opponents that the poor and members of racial and ethnic minority groups are disproportionately put to death, and concludes that it has failed as a social policy (Costanzo, 1997). In 1997, the American Bar Association voted that its members should stop seeking the death penalty until these issues could be resolved. The ABA has no means to enforce such a resolution, however, and on the day they took their vote in San Antonio, Texas, a young woman received the death sentence in a courtroom only 30 miles away. Later that year Timothy McVeigh received the death penalty in a federal court after being convicted of the bombing of the federal building in Oklahoma City. McVeigh was executed on June 11, 2001, the first execution carried out by the federal government in almost 40 years. In 1998 the debate over capital punishment intensified and focused on gender, when Texas executed Karla Faye Tucker—the first woman put to death since the

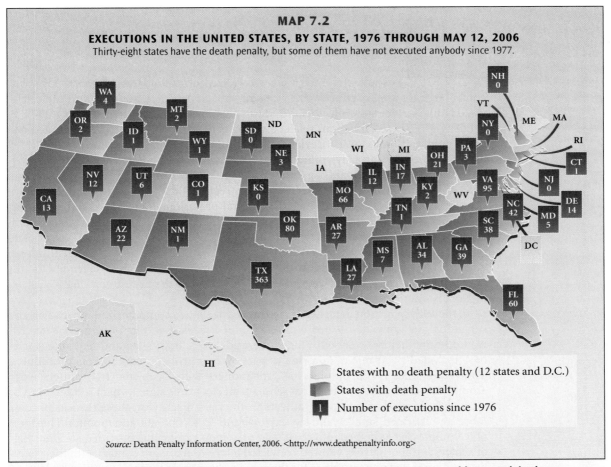

MAP 7.2

EXECUTIONS IN THE UNITED STATES, BY STATE, 1976 THROUGH MAY 12, 2006

Thirty-eight states have the death penalty, but some of them have not executed anybody since 1977.

States with no death penalty (12 states and D.C.)

States with death penalty

1 Number of executions since 1976

Source: Death Penalty Information Center, 2006. <http://www.deathpenaltyinfo.org>

As you look at this map, what regional patterns emerge in regard to executions? How would you explain these patterns?

Civil War (Hancock, 1998). Although executions continue, there was a slight decline in executions from 1999 to 2000, leading some experts to believe that attitudes toward capital punishment might be changing in the United States (New York Times News Service, 2000). In 2002, the U.S. Supreme Court ruled that executing mentally retarded persons violated the constitutional ban on cruel and unusual punishment, and in 2003, the American Bar Association reiterated its stance that death penalty laws should be revised or prosecutors should stop seeking capital punishment altogether (AP, Seattle, 2003). In 2005, the U.S. Supreme Court ruled that it was unconstitutional to execute persons who were under the age of 18 when they committed the offense. Sociological research indicates that support for the death penalty is linked to conservative values and perceived threats from racial and ethnic minorities (Jacobs and Carmichael, 2002), and that the media, especially television, bolster an illusion that Americans support the death penalty far more than is the case, especially if alternative sentences are available (Niven, 2002).

Most sociologists agree that it is difficult to determine whether formal social control and punishment act as effective deterrents to crime and other forms of deviant behavior. Although many of us come into contact with either the police, the courts, or corrections at some time in our lives, most citizens' ideas about deviance, crime, and the criminal justice system come from images presented by the mass media: newspapers, magazines, movies, and, especially, television. As we discussed earlier, it is popular to blame much of the deviance in society on the media. Just as the media are often viewed as part of the problem, however, they also are viewed as being part of the solution. Today more than ever media—especially computers and other sophisticated technomedia—are being developed and used in efforts to control, deter, and prevent deviance and crime.

SOCIAL CONTROL THROUGH THE TECHNOMEDIA

The technomedia are recognized as potential mechanisms of social control and are used in efforts to reduce and prevent deviance. Today, for example, televised public service announcements discourage drinking and driving, smoking, and illegal drug use. These campaigns reflect a strong belief in the power of the mass media to shape public attitudes toward deviance and to influence peoples' behavior.

Technomedia, especially computerized information technology, have become common weapons in the "wars" against drugs, crime, and other forms of deviance. In 1968, the Omnibus Crime Control and Safe Streets Act that was part of President Lyndon Johnson's "war on crime" included several provisions for telephone wiretapping, "bugging," and other forms of electronic surveillance. Closed circuit television cameras are used extensively throughout Great Britain and other European countries to help patrol streets, subways, and other public areas. Despite potential constitutional questions, they also are gaining popularity with law enforcement agencies in the United States—especially private security firms, one of the fastest growing industries in North America.

In the 1950s, cartoon detective Dick Tracy spoke into a computerized wristwatch and suggested that convicted felons wear electronic bracelets so that government officials would know their whereabouts. Since the mid-1980s, both state and federal agencies have included electronic monitoring as part of their probation and parole procedures. They sometimes equip parolees or probationers with electronic transmitters worn around the wrist, ankle, or neck that send out an electronic signal which is monitored by a centrally located computer or officers in the field. Each year, these devices become more sophisticated, smaller, and less expensive to build, operate, and monitor. This form of technomedia has helped reduce jail and prison overcrowding; provided a wider range of sentencing alternatives; allowed convicted felons to maintain contact with their families; and provided opportunities for them to work, provide for their families, and otherwise be productive citizens without the stigma of incarceration. On the downside, electronic monitoring raises several constitutional issues related to privacy and in the minds of many people reduces the deterrent effect by removing the stigma of incarceration and providing too much freedom and too few restrictions for those who have violated the law and are supposedly being punished.

Computers are at the forefront of the technomedia's contributions to law enforcement and the deterrence of crime and deviance. Every police department is now equipped with computerized information systems, and most national governments cooperate with Interpol's vast computer crime network. PAVNET (Partners Against Violence NETwork) is an on-line service created by several federal agencies and the U.S. Department of Justice to combine information and techniques for combating violence (National Institute of Justice, 1995). Other on-line services provide a wealth of information

Technology allows probationers to wear electronic tracking bracelets or anklets so that they can live at home and go to work, and still have their whereabouts constantly monitored.

about crime, drug abuse, mental disorders, suicide, child abuse, and virtually any other form of deviance imaginable. As we continue in the twenty-first century reliance on computerized information technology and other forms of the technomedia for social control will continue to increase.

DEVIANCE AND CONFORMITY IN THE TWENTY-FIRST CENTURY

Sociologist Desmond Ellis (1987:4–5) wrote in *The Wrong Stuff* that once moral evaluations are formed, a "moral hierarchy" is created, against which people's behaviors—and, indeed, people themselves—are judged. These social judgments lead to different and unequal treatment. The more effective one group of people is in defining another group's values, norms, and behavior as deviant (and therefore wrong), the more successful they are in defining their own behavior as conformist (and consequently right and good).

Once moral judgments are made and the mechanisms of social control are activated, those whose behavior falls outside society's range of tolerance find themselves in a precarious social situation. Today, many turn to each other for help; this action may diffuse public hostility, but it can do the opposite by bringing a group of deviants together in one place. Those labeled deviant often form support groups to help shield them from public wrath and protect them from social discrimination. In addition to the more traditional Alcoholics Anonymous and Narcotics Anonymous, a person can join Overeaters Anonymous, Depressives Anonymous, the National Association to Aid Fat Americans, the National Organization of Rare Disorders, Compulsive Shoppers, Trichotillomania Support Network (for people who pull out their hair), Hot Flashes (for menopausal women), Parents of Sex Offenders, Cross Dressers, Gamblers Anonymous, Schizophrenics Anonymous, and a host of other self-help and social and psychological support groups. Millions of Americans (perhaps as much as 40 percent of the U.S. population) belong to various support groups that hold regular meetings and feature websites on the Internet. This "quiet revolution" is dramatically changing human relationships; support groups have become "part of the glue that now holds society together" (Wuthnow, 1994b).

If current trends persist, we can expect crime rates to stabilize, but because of the "get-tough" attitude toward criminal offenders and changes in the types of crimes committed, the number of people incarcerated and on probation and parole is projected to increase. The Bureau of Justice statistics indicate that the number of persons under correctional supervision has steadily increased since the 1980s, and this increase is projected to continue during the first decade of the twenty-first century. Polls show that Americans are fed up with crime, support the death penalty in record numbers (over 70 percent, although, as we indicated earlier, that figure may be misleading), and are infuriated by a criminal justice system they view as inept against violent crime. Meanwhile, media portrayals of sensational violent crimes reaffirm the message that Americans must get even "tougher" on criminals and other deviants. When probation, parole, and incarceration are combined, the United States has more than 7 million people under supervision by the criminal justice system. While violent offenses are expected to stabilize, drug offenses, white-collar crime (especially computer-related), and crimes committed by the elderly are expected to add significantly to the work load of police and prosecutors in the future (Conly and McEwen, 1990; *New York Times*, 2004).

Predicting future attitudes toward deviance, crime, and social control is risky. However, it is almost certain that the mass media and technomedia will play an even greater role in shaping public perceptions of deviance and conformity as well as providing new methods both for committing deviance and controlling it. As one expert said, "With regard to crime and justice, as well as other social concerns, the critical issue is ultimately the media's role in the social construction of reality" (Surette, 1992:251). Sociological research indicates that in the future the media, especially television, are likely to continue to construct a social image of rampant crime and random violence because of their rhetorical appeal to the public and their political value to politicians (Best 2003; Sasson, 2003). From a sociological view, specific behaviors—either conforming or deviant—are much less important than the social processes involved in defining them as one or the other. Perhaps the only certainty for the future is that in all societies people will continue to be set apart for different treatment because of their perceived levels of deviance and conformity.

Summary

1 Every society creates norms and a range of tolerance of acceptable behaviors to help regulate human behavior and make social life more predictable. Time, place, situation, and culture are all important in defining deviance and conformity, as are the actor, the social audience, and the mass media. The mass media play an important role in defining deviance in the United States and other industrialized and technological societies. Sometimes people equate deviance, which refers to all norm violation, with crime, which refers only to the violation of criminal laws. Similarly, sometimes diversity is confused with deviance and people are stigmatized simply because they are different.

2 Some of the most popular explanations for deviance range from demonology and biology to the medical model, which equates deviance with illness, and the ever popular sport of media bashing, which blames deviant behavior on the negative influence of the media.

3 A sociological analysis of deviance and conformity from the structural functionalist perspective shows that deviance can be both functional and dysfunctional. Structural functionalist theories point to the social strain experienced by some people because of their place in the social structure, calling this the primary cause of deviant behavior. Conflict theories of deviance focus less on deviant acts and more on inequality and power in the process of creating and enforcing norms. The interactionist perspective includes social learning theories, which contend that conformity and deviance are learned through socialization, as well as social control theories, which contend that to understand deviance we must ask what causes conformity. The answer,

according to this perspective, is social control in the form of a social bond and the development of both internal and external methods of containment. Some people overcome those constraints, however, by rationalizing deviant behavior and neutralizing its potentially negative impact on them. Finally, labeling theorists contend that deviance and conformity do not reside in acts or people but are simply labels placed on acts and people as a result of the social reaction to them.

4 People are expected to internalize society's norms and exercise voluntary control to conform to societal expectations. When people's behavior violates society's norms beyond acceptable limits, external mechanisms of social control are implemented. These methods may be informal (gossip, ridicule, ostracism, and stigma) or formal (fines, probation, detention, imprisonment, corporal punishment, or execution). The most complex formal social control in response to crime in the United States is the criminal justice system. A major emphasis of the criminal justice system is deterrence, and sociologists have developed deterrence theory as an explanation of conformity. The technomedia are sometimes viewed as part of the problem of creating deviance but are also seen as part of the solution, especially in the areas of computerization, electronic surveillance, and other forms of social control.

5 Future trends are difficult to predict, but social norms and social control are inherent in every society, and people have always been and will continue to be treated differently and unequally on the basis of their levels of conformity to and deviation from social expectations.

Key Terms

anomie (p. 179)
conflict theories of deviance (p. 181)
conformity (p. 165)
crime (p. 170)
deterrence theory (p. 187)
deviance (p. 163)
elite deviance (p. 182)

hate crimes (p. 171)
labeling theories (p. 183)
medical model (p. 172)
pornography (p. 173)
primary deviance (p. 183)
range of tolerance (p. 167)
secondary deviance (p. 183)

social control (p. 187)
social control theories (p. 184)
social learning theories (p. 184)
social pathology (p. 178)
stigma (p. 171)
strain theories (p. 178)

Chapter 8

Social Stratification and the U.S. Class System

"People who work sitting down get paid more than people who work standing up."

—Ogden Nash

Katrina was the eleventh named tropical storm and the first Category 5 hurricane to hit the United States in 2005. Katrina's 175-plus-mile-per-hour winds caused over $300 billion in damages, killed over 1,300 people, and displaced over 1 million Americans, ranking it as one of the most deadly and most expensive natural disasters in American history.

One thing we know about natural disasters is that they are equal opportunity. They do not discriminate on the basis of age, race, sex, social class, or any of the other variables of interest to sociologists. Therefore, analyses and explanations of the massive devastation of a natural disaster such as Hurricane Katrina seem to be the domain of the natural sciences, and little light could be shed on the subject by sociology. On the other hand, a closer look at the destruction of hurricane Katrina is another good example of the first wisdom of sociology: *things are not necessarily what they seem.*

Hurricane Katrina and its aftermath were as much a *social* disaster as a *natural* one. Although age, race, sex, and social class may not matter to a hurricane, they do to city planners, government officials, contractors, levee builders, and, in some cases, even emergency relief agencies and workers. Make no doubt about it: everyone in the path of hurricane Katrina suffered—old, young, black, white, male, female, rich, and poor. Analyses of the most hard-hit victims, however, indicate that they were disproportionately the elderly and the very young, racial and ethnic minorities, females, and the poor. Although New Orleans' plush upper-middle- and upper-class Garden District suffered tremendous wind and flash flooding damage, most of its occupants had the wherewithal to flee the city before the hurricane hit. Moreover, when the levees of New Orleans were breached, it was the city's infamous Ninth Ward, the most poverty-ridden area of the city, that was almost

Hurricane Katrina, one of the
most devastating natural
disasters in recent history, not
only demonstrated the powerful
forces of nature, but also the
powerful influence of social
class as the poor suffered
disproportionately in terms of
loss of life and livelihood.

totally vanquished. Similarly, New Orleans' historical and financially
profitable French Quarter emerged almost unscathed, while over 80 percent of the city was submerged under water. Live televised rescue operations, subsequent media accounts, and the official death and damage
statistics reflected what all Americans already suspected or knew, but
most Americans did not want to admit: even when it comes to natural
disasters, a person's social class may be the most important thing in their
life, or for that matter, their death.

I t is impossible to understand people's behavior in any society
without the concept of social stratification, because class position has a pervasive influence on almost everything that we
think and do. Our religious beliefs are affected by class. So is political affiliation and whether we vote or ignore politics altogether.
Class position affects the foods we eat, the clothes we wear, and the
television shows we watch. Social class affects whether we own a
computer, and if we do, what we do with it. Even the most trivial
matters are influenced by class, such as the colors we paint our
homes and the names we give our pets. Much more is involved,
however. Our position in the social hierarchy affects our health,
happiness, personal safety, and even how long we will live.

UNDERSTANDING SOCIAL STRATIFICATION

All societies, past and present, are characterized by **social differentiation,** *a process in which people are set apart for differential treatment by virtue of their statuses, roles, and other social characteristics.*
The process of social differentiation does not require that people
evaluate certain roles and activities as being more important than
others. Nevertheless, social differentiation sets the stage for **social
inequality,** *a condition in which people have unequal access to
wealth, power, and prestige.* As Daniel Rossides (1998:12) noted,
even in the simplest societies "the old are usually given authority
over the young, parents over children, and males over females."

As societies became more complex and surpluses grew, there was
a fundamental change in the nature of inequality—stratification
appeared. **Social stratification** is *a form of inequality in which categories of people are systematically ranked in a hierarchy on the basis of their access to scarce
but valued resources.* In stratification, as opposed to other forms of inequality, social
positions are ranked in terms of their importance, rewarded differentially, and transmitted from generation to generation through inheritance.

Social strata give the appearance of rigidity and permanence, but, unlike geological
layers that are hardened in place, they are composed of human beings who continuously
define and redefine social reality during interaction. Therefore, boundaries between
social strata are "semipermeable" (Beeghley, 2005:59)—they can be crossed, but with
difficulty. The relative permeability of boundaries and the opportunities available for
people to move up or down in the social hierarchy depend much more on the nature of
the stratification system than on the amount of individual effort.

SYSTEMS OF STRATIFICATION

All contemporary societies distinguish between categories of people who are entitled to
a greater share of wealth, power, and prestige and categories of people who are less
deserving. In the principal types of stratification systems, however, one of three factors
of inequality (wealth, power, or prestige) tends to receive special emphasis. Stratification

SOCIAL DIFFERENTIATION
A process in which people are
set apart for differential
treatment by virtue of their
statuses, roles, and other social
characteristics.

SOCIAL INEQUALITY
A condition in which people
have unequal access to wealth,
power, and prestige.

SOCIAL STRATIFICATION
A form of inequality in which
categories of people are
systematically ranked in a
hierarchy on the basis of their
access to scarce but valued
resources.

systems also differ in the relative permeability of boundaries between social strata. In *closed systems,* boundaries are relatively impermeable—statuses are ascribed, and custom, law, and public attitudes tend to place severe limitations on *social mobility.* In *open systems,* boundaries are less firm, social statuses are largely determined by achievement, and legal and ideological supports give people opportunities to change their social ranking. There are four major types of stratification systems: slavery, castes, estates, and social classes.

Slavery

Slavery is one of the oldest and most resilient systems of stratification. It existed in many early agrarian civilizations, including Greece and Rome, and for centuries it flourished in such disparate political economies as the United States, Korea, Russia, and Saudi Arabia. Slavery persists in parts of Asia, Africa, and Latin America; even today, there are perhaps as many as 3 million slaves in the world.

A **slave system** *includes two distinct strata—a category of people who are free and a category of people who are legally the property of others.* The low rank of slaves is based on economic considerations and the fact that they are productive resources used as their masters see fit. But most important, it is a function of slaves' complete lack of power (Patterson, 1982).

Throughout history, the treatment slaves received and the amount of social mobility afforded them varied, depending on economic and political circumstances. In some societies slaves had legal rights, were well treated, assumed important political positions, and could gain freedom and become respected members of society. Slavery in the United States was very different because of racism and a supposed link between biology and class position. Some sociologists maintain that when slavery was abolished in the United States, Southern blacks entered the second major system of stratification—the caste system (Heller, 1987).

Castes

When Portuguese explorers arrived in India in the fifteenth century they were struck by the fact that categories of people could not intermarry. They called the separate groups *casta,* or members of distinct families and lineages. In time, these endogamous (inmarrying) groups became known as castes. Compliance with India's restrictive sexual code was ensured by a belief in ritual pollution, which held that even casual contact among people from different social strata caused those of higher ranks to be contaminated. If an upper-caste woman had sex with a lower-caste man, her defilement could not be removed. This belief was very important in protecting the integrity of caste boundaries (Kottak, 1998).

In a **caste system,** *rank is hereditary and permanent, and marriage between members of different categories is prohibited.* As an ideal type, the caste system is totally closed: status is ascribed, and no matter what they might do to change it, people inherit the social position of their parents. In traditional India there were four major castes, or *varna:* Brahmins (priests and scholars), Kshatriyas (warriors and royalty), Vaisyas (merchants), and Sudras (peasants, craftworkers). Although Harijans, or Untouchables, were very much a part of the caste system, their ancestry and occupations, which included cleaning latrines and being responsible for the dead, were seen as so defiling that they were symbolically placed outside the caste system.

Within each *varna* there were many subcastes associated with occupational specializations. Social mobility was possible within subcastes, but one's caste position could not be improved—at least during one's lifetime. The caste system was formally abolished in 1950, but it remains influential and continues to serve as a guide to behavior in many social arenas.

Estates

In Europe, feudalism, or the estate system, was born of the violent dissolution of the Roman empire. Initially, the **estate system** *was a social hierarchy centered on the monopoly of power and ownership of land by a group of religious and political elites.*

SLAVE SYSTEM
A society with two distinct strata—a category of people who are free and a category of people who are legally the property of others.

CASTE SYSTEM
Ranking is hereditary and permanent, and marriage between members of different categories is prohibited.

ESTATE SYSTEM
A social hierarchy centered on the monopoly of power and ownership of land by a group of religious and political elites.

Those at the top of the early estate system were victorious warriors (lords) who were entitled to labor, goods, and military service from peasants—the vast majority of the agrarian population. Feudalism became fully developed in the twelfth century in response to the growing wealth and power of urban merchants who aspired to noble status. To defend their privileges, the nobility defined three estates by law: priesthood, nobility, and commoners, which included peasants, artisans, merchants, traders, and townspeople (Bloch, 1961).

Because of technological advances, the estate system was marked by extreme inequality, well beyond that of most caste and slave systems. At the same time, though, the estate system afforded somewhat greater opportunities for social mobility. There were no formal barriers to peasants entering the priesthood, but "rank gave the nobleman exclusive access to high religious position" (Rossides, 1998:30). Upward mobility into the noble estate was much more difficult, because at the top, status was largely defined by heredity. Historically, a number of wealthy commoner families were able to purchase titles, and others gained them through marriage and military valor. Conversely, impoverishment sometimes resulted in noble families descending into commoner ranks.

Social Classes

The shift from an agrarian to an industrial economy led to the development and spread of a new form of worldwide stratification called the class system. In a **class system,** *the economic factor and achieved statuses (gained by ability and merit) are the principal means of ranking.* Class systems are more open to social mobility than caste or estate systems, and boundaries between social strata are less clear. They may take several forms, depending on political and economic conditions, history, and culture. Most contain a small upper class, which owns the bulk of a nation's assets and has a great deal of influence and power. Beneath this level there may be major differences in the size, wealth, and power of the middle class as well as the conditions of those at the bottom of class hierarchies.

DETERMINING SOCIAL CLASS RANKING

Where do you fit in the U.S. class system? If your answer is consistent with sociological surveys, you probably answered "in the middle class." What criteria did you use to decide your class standing? Money? In the United States, many believe that people can be sorted into three major categories—a tiny segment of the population that is super-rich, an equally small number of very poor people, and the vast majority of the population that is financially "comfortable"—especially when compared to people in most other nations.

Is the United States a "middle-class nation"? And is money the sole criterion used to determine class ranking? Let's take a closer look at the "money is everything" approach

CLASS SYSTEM
The economic factor and achieved statuses (gained by ability and merit) are the principal means of ranking.

Would you rank this lottery winner, who had such phenomenal luck that she won the New Jersey lottery twice, on the same rung of the social ladder with Caroline Kennedy Schlossburg, whose father was John F. Kennedy, a former president of the United States?

to social class. If you believe money and wealth determine class ranking, would you agree that millionaires such as a cocaine dealer, a lottery winner, a rock star, and a member of the Rockefeller family are all on the same rung of the social ladder? If you are like most Americans, you would be unwilling to accord equal rank to a lottery winner or rock star and a member of one of America's most distinguished families.

Moreover, most people would place cocaine dealers, no matter how much money they had, near the bottom—not at the top—of the social hierarchy. Why is this so? Sociologist Max Weber (1946) was among the first to argue that economic status, or wealth, is not the only factor that determines a person's rank. Power and prestige are also basic ingredients in the ranking process, and each dimension can operate independently of the others in determining social rank.

Wealth and Income

Weber believed that differences in wealth lead to the formation of classes, which have similar lifestyles, or ways their members consume goods and express their social worth. Differential wealth also gives social classes different life chances, or opportunities for securing such things as health, education, and long lives. We often use the word *wealth* to mean "money," but Weber defined it more broadly. To Weber, **wealth** includes *a person's or family's total economic assets.* In advanced industrial societies wealth in the form of stocks, real estate, trusts, yachts, and other goods and services is vitally important to class standing. For most people, however, income, which includes money earned in the form of wages and salaries, is the primary economic asset.

Power

Power is the second dimension of class ranking. **Power** is *the ability to realize one's will, even against resistance and the opposition of others.* Sociologists differentiate between *personal power*—the ability to make decisions that affect one's life—and *social power*—the ability to make decisions that affect the lives of others. Of course, power can refer to physical force, or the threat of violence by a person or group against others. But Weber believed *authority,* or legitimate power, carried far more weight in the conduct of human affairs.

Sociologists agree that, like wealth, power is unequally shared. Those who take a *pluralist perspective* maintain that classes and interest groups vote their interests and sometimes vote against others to keep them from dominating the political process. Conflict theorists disagree, maintaining that power is concentrated at the top. Some sociologists go even further, maintaining that there is a "governing class" in the United States whose members are drawn from the upper class. But political power only hints at the extent of the upper class's influence and power. Their members also dominate America's giant industries, banks, foundations, and virtually all other important policymaking institutions. These and other "duties" help boost the prestige of the upper class as well.

Prestige

Prestige, which is *the respect and admiration people attach to various social positions,* is the third dimension of stratification. In every society some categories of people are regarded as deserving more respect and honor than others, because of ascribed statuses (e.g., race, sex, ethnicity), achieved statuses (e.g., occupation, marital status), possessions, or personal qualities (e.g., holiness, intelligence). In the United States, such things as material possessions, education, family background, and occupation have a major impact on everyone's class ranking.

When we meet strangers, we usually ask them what kind of work they do. For almost a century, the relative prestige of occupations has been stable not only in the United States but in most nations. As Table 8.1 demonstrates, jobs that require extensive formal education and provide much authority and autonomy rank highest, but surveys conducted over the past two decades show surprising changes in the prestige of different occupations. Unskilled manual labor jobs, which are usually poorly paid and heavily supervised, rank lowest (Treiman, 1977).

WEALTH
A person's or family's total economic assets.

POWER
The ability to realize one's will, even against resistance and the opposition of others.

PRESTIGE
The respect and admiration people attach to various social positions.

TABLE 8.1

27–YEAR TREND FOR "VERY GREAT" PRESTIGE
"I AM GOING TO READ OFF A NUMBER OF DIFFERENT
OCCUPATIONS, FOR EACH, WOULD YOU TELL ME IF IT IS AN OCCUPATION OF VERY GREAT PRESTIGE,
CONSIDERABLE PRESTIGE, SOME PRESTIGE OR HARDLY ANY PRESTIGE AT ALL?"

BASE: ALL ADULTS	1977	1982	1992	1997	1998	2000	2001	2002	2003	2004	2005	2006	Changes since 1997
	%	%	%	%	%	%	%	%	%	%	%	%	%
Fire fighter	NA	NA	NA	NA	NA	NA	NA	NA	55	48	56	63	NA
Doctor	61	55	50	52	61	61	61	50	52	52	54	58	−3
Nurse	NA	NA	NA	NA	NA	NA	NA	NA	47	44	50	55	NA
Scientist	66	59	57	51	55	56	53	51	57	52	56	54	−12
Teacher	29	28	41	49	53	53	54	47	49	48	47	52	+23
Military Officer	NA	22	32	29	34	42	40	47	46	47	49	51	NA
Police Officer	NA	NA	34	36	41	38	37	40	42	40	40	43	NA
Priest/Minister/Clergyman	41	42	38	45	46	45	43	36	38	32	36	40	−1
Farmer	NA	NA	NA	NA	NA	NA	NA	NA	NA	NA	NA	36	NA
Engineer	34	30	37	32	34	32	36	34	28	29	34	34	0
Member of Congress	NA	NA	24	23	25	33	24	27	30	31	26	28	NA
Architect	NA	NA	NA	NA	26	26	28	27	24	20	27	27	NA
Athlete	26	20	18	21	20	21	22	21	17	21	23	23	−3
Lawyer	36	30	25	19	23	21	18	15	17	17	18	21	−15
Entertainer	18	16	17	18	19	21	20	19	17	16	18	18	0
Accountant	NA	13	14	18	17	14	15	13	15	10	13	17	NA
Banker	17	17	17	15	18	15	16	15	14	15	15	17	0
Journalist	17	16	15	15	15	16	16	19	15	14	14	16	−1
Union leader	NA	NA	12	14	16	16	17	14	15	16	15	12	NA
Actor	NA	NA	NA	NA	NA	NA	NA	NA	13	16	16	12	NA
Bussiness executive	18	16	19	16	18	15	12	18	18	19	15	11	−7
Stockbroker	NA	NA	NA	NA	NA	NA	NA	NA	8	10	8	11	NA
Real estate broker/agent	NA	NA	NA	NA	NA	NA	NA	NA	6	5	9	6	NA

Source: By permission of Harris Poll and Creators Syndicate, Inc.

What can we learn by taking a closer look at occupational prestige rankings? First, with the exception of a handful of highly skilled blue-collar jobs, such as computer or aircraft technician, white-collar jobs confer much greater prestige. Second, "education is by far the most important determinant of prestige" (MacKinnon and Langford, 1994:231). However, in the new economy, while "education remains important in adult occupational rank, its importance is in decline" (Rytina, 2000:1270). Third, occupational prestige is affected by gender. Christine Bose (1985), for example, found that survey respondents ranked occupations much lower if they perceived them to be "female jobs" rather than "male jobs"—a topic we examine in greater detail in Chapter 11.

Finally, although the most prestigious jobs typically are associated with high incomes and a great deal of authority, this is not always the case. For example, college professors are often ranked near the top of the prestige hierarchy—well above accountants and engineers—but accountants' and engineers' annual incomes are typically much greater. Moreover, social and political change can have an effect. For example, look at changing public views over the past two decades regarding the occupation of military officer. Why do you think survey respondents became more positive about this occupation over the past two decades? This supports Weber's multifaceted view of stratification and challenges the popular notion that in America "money is everything."

Occupational prestige rankings in the United States have been remarkably consistent over the past century. This includes the occupations of police officer and social worker, which have maintained midlevel rankings. Police officers rank just below electricians and above bookkeepers, whereas social workers are sandwiched between funeral directors and computer programmers. Both occupations reflect a multifaceted approach to ranking. For example, their incomes are less than those of many occupations that rank lower on the prestige scale, but their emphasis on community service somewhat elevates their social standing.

Traditionally, law enforcement has drawn its members from the working class, attracting high numbers of ethnic minorities (especially the Irish). Social work has historically attracted a more diverse population, though it has relied primarily on women to fill its ranks. Initially, these occupations required little formal education and appealed most to those who were faced with limited job opportunities. In addition, they attracted people who not only wanted to help their own lot in life but were also committed to making society a better place.

Over the past four decades, police officers and social workers have worked diligently to increase their occupational prestige. Perhaps their greatest efforts have been directed at transforming their work from an occupation to a profession. Although there are numerous definitions of what constitutes a profession, sociologists generally agree that professions share some common characteristics: mastery of a body of theoretical knowledge, a self-regulating organization, and an emphasis on people and community.

Although some police departments require only a high school diploma, many require at least some college, and most prefer to hire college graduates. Criminal justice is one of the fastest growing college majors, and many law enforcement agencies provide incentives to their members to complete their college degrees. Most agencies require that officers attend a police academy and complete a minimum number of in-service training hours periodically to maintain licensure and certification. This is especially true for those who wish to move into administrative positions or any of the growing list of law enforcement specialties (e.g., criminal investigations, surveillance, forensics). Whereas police officers of the past were most likely to be union members, today membership in a host of other professional law enforcement organizations is common.

Similarly, social work now requires a minimum of a bachelor's degree for entry-level positions and a Master's in Social Work (MSW) or even a doctorate for administrative and senior-level positions. Most states require licensure and certification to become a recognized member of this profession, especially to specialize in geriatrics, psychiatric social work, or child welfare, and social workers generally belong to more than one professional organization.

Despite these efforts at professionalization, law enforcement officers and social workers continue to struggle to enhance their occupational prestige ranking. Both occupations deal with a clientele comprised mainly of the poor, the powerless, and others at the margins of society. These occupations increasingly draw their members from these same categories, a factor that makes it unlikely they will increase their salaries, power, or prestige in the near future.

TAKING A CLOSER LOOK

Can you think of other occupations that have sought to enhance their ranking by redefining their work as "professions"? Consider occupations near the bottom of the ranking system, such as garbage collector and maid. What might members of these occupations do to become professional and boost their prestige rankings? Do you think the terrorist attacks on 9/11 affected the prestige of police officers?

Source: F. Ellen Netting, Peter M. Kettner, and Steven L. McMurtry. *Social Work Macro Practices,* 2nd ed. New York: Longman, 1998. Frank Smallenger. *Criminal Justice Today,* 4th ed. Upper Saddle River, NJ: Prentice-Hall, 1997.

Socioeconomic Status

There are often inconsistencies in the three dimensions of stratification. A person may rank high in one dimension but low in another. For example, in terms of occupational prestige, police officers and social workers have maintained midlevel rankings. They are both low-paying jobs but deemed socially important, and people in these positions often have power over people in more prestigious occupations. Focus box 8.1 takes a closer look at how police officers and social workers attempt to elevate their occupational rank. Trust, an increasingly scarce and shifting commodity in contemporary life, may also complicate occupational prestige, as we show in Figure 8.1.

Over the years, sociologists have used three major methods to identify social classes. One of the earliest used was the *reputational method,* which asked selected members of

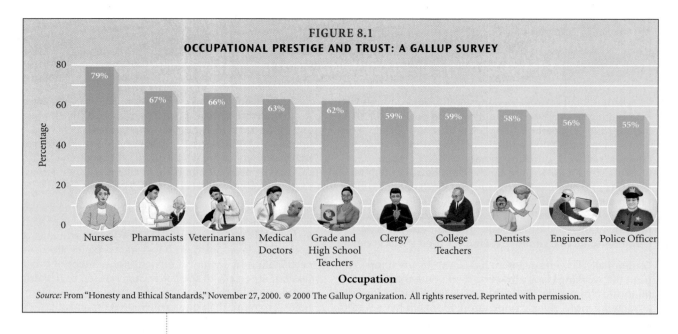

FIGURE 8.1
OCCUPATIONAL PRESTIGE AND TRUST: A GALLUP SURVEY

a group to socially rank people in their community. The *subjective method* asks people to locate themselves in the class system. The *objective method* assigns individuals to social classes on the basis of more objective measures. One objective approach is **socioeconomic status,** *a ranking that combines income, occupational prestige, level of education, and neighborhood* to assess class ranking.

By measuring socioeconomic status, we not only can make distinctions among people—for example, people in different occupations—but also can demonstrate how people in the same line of work may rank differently. For example, if only occupational prestige is used, two professors may be judged as occupying the same social rank. If socioeconomic status is used, however, their ranking may be very different, for one may live in a rental apartment while the other, who ranks higher, may have inherited a fortune and live in a prestigious neighborhood. This method produces a hierarchy that can be used to distinguish the major social classes in the United States.

SOCIAL CLASSES IN THE UNITED STATES

American social classes are distinguished in part by wealth and income. This distinction is particularly important in differentiating those at the top of the class hierarchy from those at lower levels. Whereas the majority of Americans depend on wages and salaries, the wealthiest Americans derive most of their revenues from income-producing assets.

Wealth and Income: The Twenty-First Century

According to economic data, a tiny segment of the American population owns most of the nation's wealth. The wealthiest 1 percent (900,000 households with about $6 trillion net worth) own more than the least affluent 90 percent of Americans (84 million households with about $5 trillion net worth). Or, from another angle, the top 1 percent of the population owns about 38 percent of all wealth in the United States while the bottom 80 percent of the population accounts for about 17 percent of the national wealth (Mishel et al., 2001). To give you a more personalized view of the gap between rich and poor consider this: Bill Gates owns "more wealth than America's 100 million poorest people" (Greider et al., 1998:39). Annual household income is unequally distributed as well (see Figure 8.2): the 400 wealthiest taxpayers accounted for more than 1 percent of all the income in the United States—double their share just eight years earlier" (Johnston, 2003:1).

SOCIOECONOMIC STATUS
A ranking that combines income, occupational prestige, level of education, and neighborhood to assess people's positions in the stratification system.

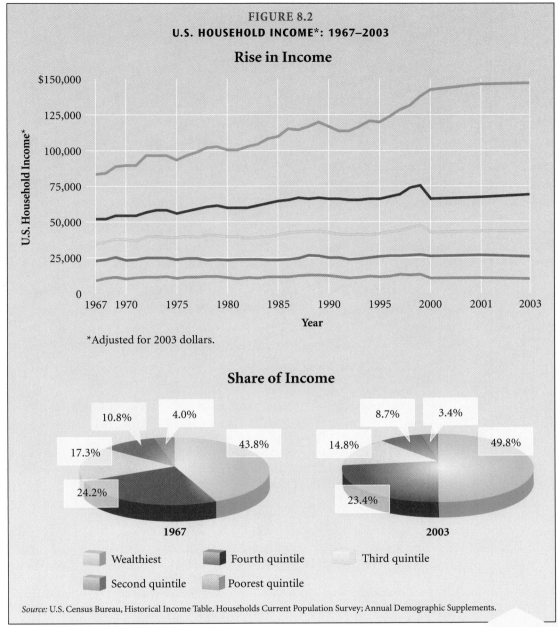

FIGURE 8.2

U.S. HOUSEHOLD INCOME*: 1967–2003

Rise in Income

U.S. Household Income*

$150,000

125,000

100,000

75,000

50,000

25,000

0

1967 1970 1975 1980 1985 1990 1995 2000 2001 2003

Year

*Adjusted for 2003 dollars.

Share of Income

10.8%   4.0%
17.3%
24.2%
43.8%

1967

8.7%   3.4%
14.8%
23.4%
49.8%

2003

Wealthiest   Fourth quintile   Third quintile

Second quintile   Poorest quintile

Source: U.S. Census Bureau, Historical Income Table. Households Current Population Survey; Annual Demographic Supplements.

> **Do the household income figures support the belief that the rich are growing richer and the poor are becoming poorer?**

Even media hype about widespread stock ownership among ordinary Americans is deceptive. Whereas nearly half of all American households own some stocks (most of it in small retirement accounts), the wealthiest 10 percent of households own 80 percent of the nation's stocks. And the top 10 percent of households "appropriated 86 percent of the stock market gains since 1989" (Hahnel, 1999:8). A relatively few wealthy individuals, families, and corporate heads have so much stock that they exert great influence over the world's major corporations (Leland, 1998).

In 2005, the median net worth of all Americans was about $100,000. This is the total worth of most American households, if they had to pay off all consumer debts, including home mortgages. As you might expect, there are significant differences in net worth based on age. As Figure 8.3 shows, those under 35 years of age have few assets, and those 65 and older have the most assets. Married couple households have many times the assets of all other household types, especially female-headed households, which have the lowest net worth of all groups. There were significant differences by race and ethnicity with the median net worth of white households at $45,470, the figure for black households was $4,418, and Latino households had about $4,656.

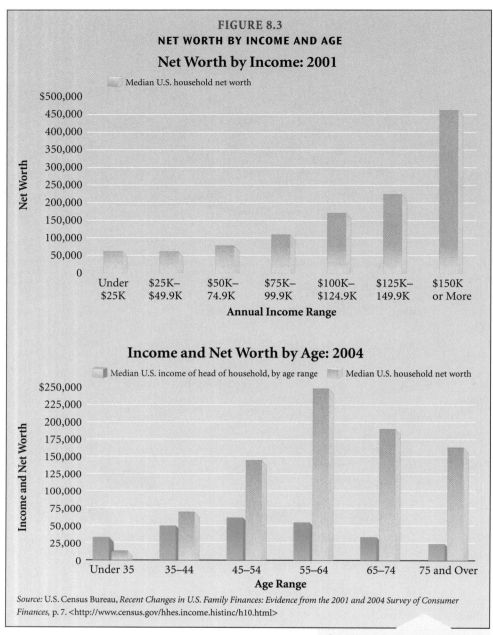

FIGURE 8.3

NET WORTH BY INCOME AND AGE

Net Worth by Income: 2001

Source: U.S. Census Bureau, *Recent Changes in U.S. Family Finances: Evidence from the 2001 and 2004 Survey of Consumer Finances*, p. 7. <http://www.census.gov/hhes.income.histinc/h10.html>

If at the end of your career you possessed about $100,000 in net worth—would you consider yourself well-off and secure?

American Social Classes

Today, sociologists identify five major class groupings in the United States, each with very different life chances and lifestyles. Focus box 8.2 (on page 210–211) illustrates how these five groupings would affect the popular board game of Monopoly.

The Upper Class The upper class constitutes around 5 percent of the population and its members have incomes of $150,000 or more. See Figures 8.2 and 8.3 for changes in net worth and income and share of wealth in 2001 and over the past three decades. Note the top 5 percent of wealthy households (those with earnings of more than $150,000) account for more than 20 percent of total income (Brimelow, 2000). Figure 8.4 shows the "Top 400": their average incomes and tax bills. The upper upper class, with incomes of $250,000 or more, comprises less than 1 percent of the population.

More important, members of the upper upper class have net worths in the millions or even billions of dollars. Household wealth, however, is not their only resource. Upper-class families also dominate corporate America and have a disproportionate influence over the nation's political, educational, religious, and other institutions. Of all social classes, members of the upper class also have a strong sense of solidarity and "consciousness of kind" that stretches across the nation and even the globe. In the life course, many enroll in the same private prep schools and attend a handful of prestigious Ivy League colleges. They also are active in the same social clubs and vacation at the "right" retreats and resorts around the world (Domhoff, 1974; Baltzell, 1990).

There are several subgroups within the upper class. At the top are Old Money families whose wealth goes back a century or more, such as the Duponts and Rockefellers. Some members of this exclusive group still manage giant corporations. Many elite families, however, take a less active role in business, using trusts, real estate income, and other inherited investments to fund lavish lifestyles, philanthropic activities, and, in some cases, public service.

Old Money families can trace their elite heritage for many generations and have a family background that may include marriages to European aristocrats, and a history of distinguished national service. During the past century, most members of this group were listed in various blue books or in the *Social Register,* which validated Old Money status. Most also went to the same schools, clubs, and resorts. They tended to marry each other as well.

Just below them are families of great wealth who have made their fortunes in the past generation or so. They are often called New Money, and some of their more prominent members would include the Walton family (Wal-Mart) and Microsoft billionaire Bill Gates. Much of their wealth is in stock and stock options in their own corporations.

Prominent government officials, CEOs of major American corporations, media and sports celebrities, and others who make many millions form the next tier of the upper class. They may or may not have elite backgrounds. The bottom rung of the upper class includes millionaires who exist in virtually every community: bank and factory owners, large-scale farmers, even lottery winners who have amassed instant fortunes. This group also includes professionals whose incomes exceed a quarter of a million dollars per year.

Upper Middle Class

The upper middle class, which constitutes about 15 percent of the population, includes corporate executives, physicians, attorneys, white-collar management, and professional employees. Many in this class have household incomes of $100,000 or more as well as advanced college degrees. There are some exceptions, however. For example, many college professors have relatively low incomes but are in the upper middle class by virtue of occupational prestige. Likewise, a successful small business owner may not have a college degree but may gain entry to the upper middle class by virtue of high income.

In many American communities this group represents the elite, for small-town America may have relatively little contact with the upper class. Within rank, age is an important variable. Young professionals often have heavily mortgaged homes, luxury autos, and some income-producing investments. Even the types of restaurants they frequent and the types of food they eat reflect conspicuous consumption (Wright and Ransom, 2005). Those late in their careers may also have substantial investments and assets. Members of the upper middle class often belong to country clubs, live in expensive homes in elegant neighborhoods, and are active in politics and community affairs.

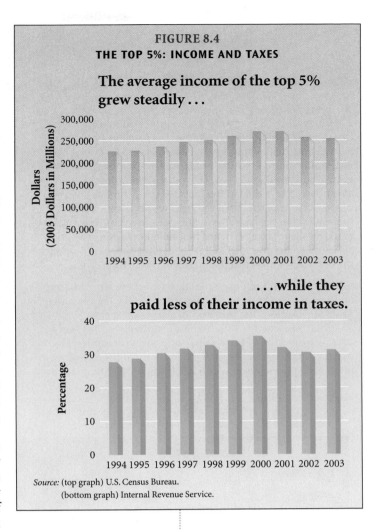

FIGURE 8.4
THE TOP 5%: INCOME AND TAXES

The average income of the top 5% grew steadily . . .

. . . while they paid less of their income in taxes.

Source: (top graph) U.S. Census Bureau.
(bottom graph) Internal Revenue Service.

Billionaire Bill Gates is one of the world's richest and most philanthropic people. Nevertheless, like Gates, CEOs of major corporations use both their personal fortunes and the resources of their companies to influence public policy and ensure that their class interests are served.

Monopoly is one of the most successful board games ever invented. The reason for the game's popularity is obvious to most Americans. Like games in virtually every society, it is fun and challenging, and it can be played by young and old, family members and friends. But much more is involved than leisure and family fun. The game's phenomenal success also owes a great deal to the fact that many Americans also see it as a primer for life in the "real world." Americans believe that in the game, as in life, people compete for valued resources, and that by means of intelligence, determination, skill, and luck, some rise to the top while others, deficient in these qualities, move in the opposite direction.

Is Monopoly an accurate reflection of American economic and social life? While most Americans would say yes, once again we caution that things may not be what they seem and that "obvious truths" can be deceptively wrong. Let's take a closer look at how well Monopoly corresponds to real life. In the game everyone has an equal chance of winning, each player starts with $1,500, and everyone plays by the same rules. Is this true in real life? Does everyone begin with the same amount of money, follow the same rules, and have the same chances of winning?

To reflect real world conditions more accurately, sociologist Leonard Beeghley (2005) reinvented the game. In Beeghley's version, which we have altered slightly, five groups compete. See Table 8.2. Group 1 has few players, but even before rolling the dice group 1 owns Park Place and Boardwalk, and each of its members starts the game with $5,000. Group 1 also takes care of the bank, and this added responsibility entitles its members to an extra roll of the dice each turn. Group 2 is larger than group 1; each member starts the game with a small amount of property and $2,000. Group 3 is larger still; its members start with no property and only $1,000, but they believe that with hard work and a little luck they can purchase property and move into group 2. Group 4 also is quite large, but its members begin the game with no property and only $500, and their behavior is carefully monitored by members of groups 1–3.

Group 5 is smaller than groups 2, 3, and 4, but it still contains many people. Its members begin the game with $100, and because they are unsure of the rules they sometimes pay too much for properties and fines. Members of group 5 occasionally lose a turn, and some spend most of the game in jail.

Although it might not be as much fun to play, if Beeghley's game were commercially available, it would be far more instructive than the Parker Brothers version of Monopoly. The original game, with its focus on the individual, competition, equal opportunity, and fair play, provides an inaccurate picture of social reality. To succeed in Beeghley's game, hard work, intelligence, and other personal skills are desirable, but one also must be aware of cultural and institutional arrangements that promote inequality in wealth, power, and prestige. In games we can ignore what is confusing, unpleasant, or even threatening; sociology teaches that in real life we cannot.

The Monopoly board game has made a fortune because many Americans see it as a primer for real life.

Lower Middle Class   A large and diverse lower middle class (33 percent of the population) occupies the next rung on the social ladder. Its members emulate the upper middle class and share many of its values, but they lack the resources to copy their more affluent lifestyles. Many in the lower middle class worked their way through college and have degrees from community and state colleges and universities.

Teachers, bank employees, midlevel supervisors, and salespeople—who generally have household incomes of $30,000–75,000—make up a large part of this class. Although most are white-collar, nonmanual workers, they have considerably less autonomy and on-the-job decision-making power than upper-middle-class professionals. In terms of America's core values, members of the lower middle class play it by the book. People in this class tend to live in modest but well-groomed homes and neighborhoods and they try to keep up with the Joneses. They watch the right TV shows, drive sports utility vehicles, take the kids to scouts and soccer matches, and are members of the PTA.

In recent years, many in this class have become "overworked" and "overspent." According to economist Julia Schor, members of this class—and many in the working class as well—who once desired to "live comfortably" now have adopted the consump-

TABLE 8.1
THE REPRODUCTION OF CLASS STRUCTURE: RULES FOR A REAL-LIFE GAME OF MONOPOLY

GROUP	NUMBER OF PLAYERS	$$ AT BEGINNING OF THE GAME	MOVEMENT AROUND THE BOARD	MISCELLANEOUS	LIKELIEST RESULT
Group 1 (Uncle Sam's Top Hat)	Smallest group, statistically insignificant.	$5000 each. Already own property.	Two rolls of dice per turn.	-Control the bank. -Occasionally "borrow" money when other players aren't looking. -Have extra "Get Out of Jail Free" cards.	-Stay within group 1, unless very unlucky or foolish.
Group 2 (Car)	Very large.	$2000 each. No property.	One roll of dice per turn.		-Stay within group 2. -Attribute their position to hard work and ability.
Group 3 (Apple pie)	Very large.	$1000 each. No property.	One roll of dice per turn.		-Limited movement up to group 2. -Most members work hard and accept their position. -Some become alienated and lose enthusiasm for the game, or allow others to move their tokens. -A few use violence to alter their economic situation; most of their victims are other members of groups 3 and 4. -If caught, spend long periods in jail.
Group 4 (Taxi)	Smaller than groups 2 and 3, but significant.	$500 each. No property.	-One roll of dice per turn. -Don't know all rules of the game. -Often miss turns.	-Often pay more than other players for properties and fines.	Same as group 3.

Source: Adapted from Leonard Beeghley. *The Structure of Social Stratification in the United States.* Boston: Allyn & Bacon, 2005. The name of the game, Monopoly, is the trademark of Parker Brothers for its Real Estate Trading Game (Beverly, MA: Parker Brothers Division of General Mills Fun Group, Inc., 1935, 1946, 1961).

TAKING A CLOSER LOOK

Does the Parker Brothers game provide insights about social stratification that are very much a part of "real life"?

Source: Adapted from Leonard Beeghley. *The Structure of Social Stratification in the United States.* Boston: Allyn & Bacon, 2005.

tion patterns of those who earn three or four times more and who have benefited from rising stock and real estate markets. For example, in one survey "one in three adults believes a family of four with an income under $50,000 is poor . . . and one in five considered an annual income of $200,000 as the bare minimum required for wealth" (Austin, 2000:32).

By choosing to emulate consumer behaviors of the rich (especially the rich on prime-time TV), many members of the lower middle class have had to make liberal use of their credit cards and borrow heavily. As one study found, while middle-class families captured almost 3 percent of stock market growth in the 1990s, they also accounted for almost 40 percent in the rise of household debt (Mishel et al., 2001).

Working Class The working class (30 percent of the population) includes both blue-collar and clerical workers who work for low wages in unpleasant and sometimes dangerous environments, usually under close supervision. Truck drivers, machine operators, laborers, and service and factory workers, whose household incomes range from $16,000 to $30,000 per year, are all members of the working class.

For most, job security is tenuous, and many of the benefits routinely enjoyed by the middle classes are rare or nonexistent. Although few have more than a high school education and their jobs are often demeaned by others, many blue-collar workers take pride in doing "real work." Their self-respect hinges on hard work, but members of the working class are most vulnerable to layoffs and long periods of unemployment. In recent years, with the globalization of the economy, many have also lost a large share of the benefits that were once associated with manufacturing and union jobs, such as health care and pensions. For many, there is the ever present threat of impoverishment and a free fall to the very bottom of the class system.

Lower Class The lower class includes the "poor" ($16,000 or less), who constitute about 14 percent of the population. If all people who lose their jobs and enter the ranks of the poor in any given year are counted, however, the figure is probably closer to 20 percent. The working poor, according to the government, are those who work 27 weeks per year, but have family incomes below the poverty line. Most work at jobs— sometimes two or three—that are erratic, pay minimum wage, and have no benefits, and nearly half of the nation's poor family heads did not work at all during the early twenty-first century, because of family responsibilities, illness, or disability (Mangum et al., 2003). At the very bottom of the class system are the chronically unemployed, the homeless, and people on "welfare," who are so much in the news today. This group is estimated to number slightly less than 3 million people, or about 1 percent of the U.S. population (U.S. Bureau of Census, 2006).

POVERTY: MEDIA IMAGES AND REALITY

Suppose you were given the task of helping the poor in the United States. How would you go about identifying those who are truly needy? According to media portraits, poverty is clearly about a lack of food, housing, and other basic necessities. However, if you look more carefully you will see that in the United States poverty is also seen as "failure," degradation, insecurity, and being at the very margins or even "beneath" mainstream society, as the term *underclass* clearly implies (Katz, 1995; Turner, 1997).

In your assessment of who is and who is not poor, you can take either an absolute or a relative approach. **Absolute poverty** occurs *when people fall below a minimum subsistence level and are unable to function as members of society.* For example, adults require at least 1,500 calories each day to function, and those who fall beneath this daily minimum may be defined as poor (and at the edge of survival) in absolute terms. **Relative poverty** is *a lack of resources relative to others and the overall standards of a society.*

As you probably have noticed, absolute measures tend to put the spotlight on the poor and their condition. By contrast, relative poverty compares classes and what each has, as well as the overall economic condition of society. Which approach do you think is used by the government to decide whether a person or household is truly needy? If you answered an absolute measure, you are correct.

A half century ago, when President Lyndon Johnson declared a War on Poverty, he discovered that no one in government had a clear understanding of the nature and size of the "enemy." He therefore commissioned the Social Security Administration to devise an "objective measure" of poverty. Government officials decided the best way to do that was to multiply a person's food budget by three and make adjustments for family size and cost of living, thereby establishing what became known as the *poverty line.*

The poverty line gives some measure of poverty in America, but it can also be misleading. For one thing, the poverty count shows the number of residents in households whose incomes are below the poverty threshold— "but it does not measure how poor they are." In 2001, for example, many of the severely poor had incomes that were 41 percent or more below the poverty threshold, which suggests that government assistance had done little to alleviate their poverty (Mangum et al., 2003:7). In the 1960s, eggs, milk, bread, and similar foods were used to determine poor people's food needs. Today, while the government continues to use supermarket foods to determine whether a family is living beneath the poverty line, the public

ABSOLUTE POVERTY
When people fall below a minimum subsistence level and are unable to function as members of society.

RELATIVE POVERTY
A lack of resources relative to others and the overall standards of a society.

This photo of a runaway teenager in Times Square belies the image of the poor often portrayed in the media as living fun-loving, happy-go-lucky lives—despite a condition of impoverishment surrounded by opulent wealth.

does not: most Americans recognize breakfast cereals, soft drinks, and fast foods as basic staples. If a poor family of four spent one-third of its $18,267 income on fast food at McDonald's, do you think they would live high off the hog at taxpayer expense, as many Americans believe? By Leonard Beeghley's (2005:99) calculations, assistance money would entitle each family member "to purchase a Big Mac and a medium coke (but no french fries) each day."

Moreover, in the past two decades, housing costs have risen in virtually every American community. By the 1990s, families spent much more than they did in the 1960s on transportation, clothing, health care, child care, and most other living expenses. If there was indeed a war against poverty, do you think we won the struggle?

Who Are the Poor? Media Images

Polls conducted during the past decade have consistently shown that most Americans believe inner-city minorities constitute the vast majority of the poor and people on welfare. Since the majority of Americans have little contact with the poor, where do they get their opinions and "facts"? For many, the answer is that they watch television cop shows, Hollywood movies, and the evening news, or they listen to talk radio, which daily informs millions of people about poverty and other social problems.

Overwhelmingly, these mainstream media focus on inner-city minorities as the "prototypical poor." According to the media spotlight, the vast majority of the poor are either young African American men or ghetto single moms (with many young children) who are portrayed as preferring welfare to work. Examine the evening news or a Hollywood movie and its portrayal of poverty. Who are the poor and why are they poor? Are these portraits consistent with the government's profile of the poor, which we now examine?

Poverty: The Reality

By 2005, over 33 million Americans—or about 12 percent of the population—had incomes below the poverty line. Because of the high turnover in the indigent population, however, the percentage of people who experience poverty each year is closer to 20 percent of all Americans. Moreover, in the past four decades the poverty rates have edged higher—except in a handful of economic boom periods (see Figure 8.5). Contrary to

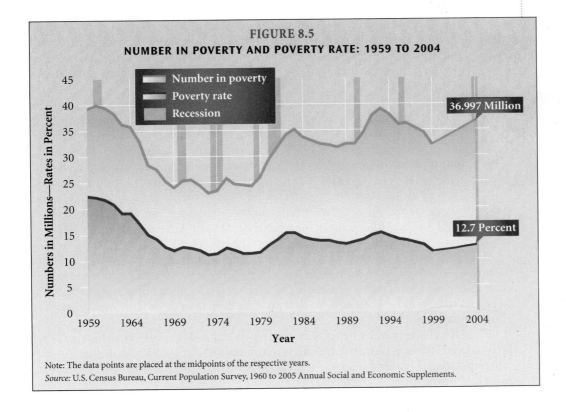

FIGURE 8.5
NUMBER IN POVERTY AND POVERTY RATE: 1959 TO 2004

Note: The data points are placed at the midpoints of the respective years.
Source: U.S. Census Bureau, Current Population Survey, 1960 to 2005 Annual Social and Economic Supplements.

TABLE 8.3
MEDIAN HOUSEHOLD INCOME AND POVERTY RATES FOR WHITES, AFRICAN AMERICANS, LATINOS, AND ASIAN AMERICANS, 2001

	WHITES	AFRICAN AMERICANS	LATINOS	ASIAN AMERICANS
Income	$44,517	$29,470	$33,565	$53,635
Percent in poverty	9.9	22.7	21.4	10.2

Source: U.S. Census Bureau, Current Population Survey, 2001 and 2002 Annual Demographic Supplements.

Which category has the most poor people? If you answered white (who comprise about 80 percent of the overall population) you are correct.

With factory and other jobs moving overseas as a result of increased globalization, young families with little education constitute a disproportionate share of the poor. Despite public perception that the poor do not work, the majority are employed—but in jobs that do not provide basic subsistence needs for their families.

FEMINIZATION OF POVERTY
Women and girls constitute a disproportionate share of the poor.

media accounts that highlight poverty and race, about 46 percent of all poor persons in the United States are white. However, poverty rates for African Americans, Latinos, and other ethnic minorities are disproportionately high. Whereas about 10 percent of all white Americans live in poverty, approximately 23 percent of African Americans and 22 percent of Latinos have incomes below the poverty line. Native Americans also have poverty rates of around 25 percent, though they soar to 60 percent on some reservations. With only about 10 percent of their members below the poverty line, only Asian and Pacific Islanders of all minorities have a poverty rate that is comparable to that of whites (see Table 8.3). However, there are sizable gaps in income between Asian American families that have been here for many generations and those who recently emigrated to the United States. Moreover, for many Asian Americans, household incomes include the earnings of numerous kin.

During the past two decades poverty rates have risen faster for children than for any other group. Children 18 years of age or younger, about one-fourth of the total U.S. population, now account for 36 percent of all poor in the United States—and nearly half of them reside in female-headed families (Lichter et al., 2005). According to James Patterson (1994:226), by the early 1990s the U.S. poverty rate for all children under 18 was "twice as high as Canada's and ten times higher than Sweden's." Moreover, the United States also has the highest rate of young children (under 6 years of age) living in poverty than all other industrial nations do. In the late 1990s, about 22 percent of young children were poor, whereas "in Finland and Denmark, the rates were so low (2 and 4 percent, respectively) that it is rare to encounter a poor child" (Shirk et al., 1999:243).

During the past two decades poverty rates have risen faster for children than for any other group. Children 18 years of age or younger, about one-fourth of the total U.S. population, now account for 36 percent of all poor in the United States—and nearly half of them reside in female-headed families (Lichter et al., 2005). According to James Patterson (1994:226), by the early 1990s the U.S. poverty rate for all children under 18 was "twice as high as Canada's and ten times higher than Sweden's." Moreover, the United States also has the highest rate of young children (under 6 years of age) living in poverty than all other industrial nations do. In the late 1990s, about 22 percent of young children were poor, whereas "in Finland and Denmark, the rates were so low (2 and 4 percent, respectively) that it is rare to encounter a poor child" (Shirk et al., 1999:243).

The poverty of children, of course, is linked to the economic circumstances of their families, and changes in the structure of American families over the past three decades have influenced the increasing proportion of children among the poor. Since the 1960s, there has been a progressive trend toward the **feminization of poverty,** whereby *women and girls constitute a disproportionate share of the poor.* The most dramatic statistics combine race, ethnicity, sex, and age and include teenage mothers, elderly widows, divorced women, and female heads of single-parent households. If only children under the age of 6 are considered, 72 percent of Latino children and 73 percent of African American children living in single-parent families are poor (Thomas, 1994; DiNitto, 1995).

As media images suggest, poverty is primarily an urban problem—but it is not exclusively confined to metropolitan areas. Approximately 60 percent of the nation's poor live in central cities, 15 percent in the suburbs, and 25 percent outside metropolitan areas, mainly in rural areas. The rural poor are almost equally distributed across the United States (see Map 8.1).

What about the public's belief that single-parent families exist on welfare rolls for generations? It, too, is inconsistent with government statistics, which show that the welfare population is highly dynamic. People who are disabled and cannot work account for most long-term poverty (18 percent of the poor). Much of the rest of the welfare popula-

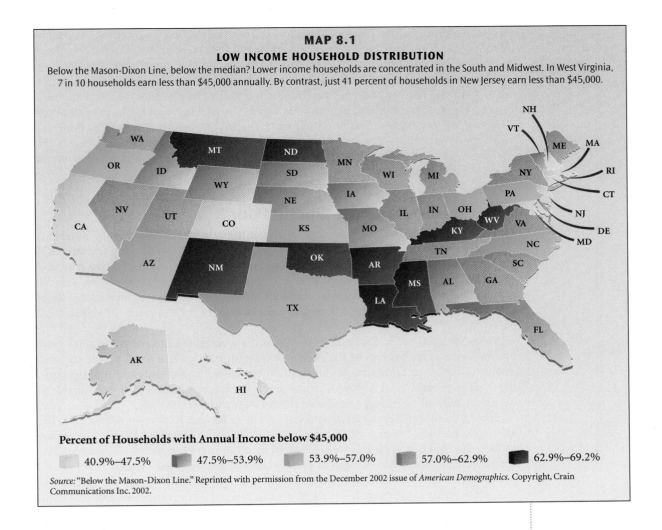

MAP 8.1

LOW INCOME HOUSEHOLD DISTRIBUTION

Below the Mason-Dixon Line, below the median? Lower income households are concentrated in the South and Midwest. In West Virginia, 7 in 10 households earn less than $45,000 annually. By contrast, just 41 percent of households in New Jersey earn less than $45,000.

Percent of Households with Annual Income below $45,000

40.9%–47.5%	47.5%–53.9%	53.9%–57.0%	57.0%–62.9%	62.9%–69.2%

Source: "Below the Mason-Dixon Line." Reprinted with permission from the December 2002 issue of *American Demographics.* Copyright, Crain Communications Inc. 2002.

tion receives government support for only brief periods (see Figure 8.6). For example, the average length of time families receiving Temporary Assistance for Needy Families (TANF) is 18.3 months. Moreover, there is a 4-year lifetime limit on cash assistance under TANF and adult recipients with a child over 1 year of age must participate in a work activity that will lead to self-sufficiency in order to receive benefits (Department of Health and Human Services, 2006).

Many other media-generated stereotypes are also false. Despite media horror stories about public housing, three-quarters of all poor families receive no housing assistance of any kind. Further, less than half the poor receive public assistance, and about the same number receive food stamps. Moreover, very few TANF recipients have children to expand their welfare benefits. Instead, 82 percent of all TANF single parents have one or two children, and less than 7 percent have more than four children.

How about public perceptions that welfare is overly generous? Government data show that the average woman on TANF with two children received around $223 per month in benefits, or about $2676 a year. And 27 percent of the poor received no assistance of any kind, either cash or other benefits (U.S. Bureau of the Census, 2002; Department of Health and Human Services, 2006).

Moreover, around 38 percent of poor householders worked, nearly 12 percent of them full time. This is even more true of African American males, so often the target of negative media stereotypes. By 2001, most African American men were in the working class, many with two or more jobs, but that did not move many of them above the poverty line. Katherine Newman's (2002a) book, *No Shame in My Game,* documented the willingness of Harlem residents to take whatever jobs

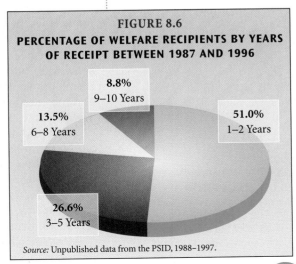

FIGURE 8.6

PERCENTAGE OF WELFARE RECIPIENTS BY YEARS OF RECEIPT BETWEEN 1987 AND 1996

8.8%
9–10 Years

13.5%
6–8 Years

51.0%
1–2 Years

26.6%
3–5 Years

Source: Unpublished data from the PSID, 1988–1997.

were available in the low-pay service sector, and how, despite their best efforts, few managed to make ends meet. And African Americans and others were not on welfare because of laziness, but because of labor market problems (unemployment, underemployment, and low earnings). In fact, "workers at the bottom decile of the employment distribution earn a paltry 38 percent of the national median, as against 68 percent for European workers and 61 percent for their Japanese counterparts"—and most are without health care, pensions, or any other benefits (Wacquant, 2002:1519). Even many homeless people work full or part time—and many more would work if jobs were available (Ropers, 1991; Patterson, 1994; Shea, 1995; Feldman, 2006). Let's take a closer look at another media favorite during the past decade—homelessness in America.

Homelessness and the Ghetto Poor

During the 1980s a disturbing and highly visible ingredient was added to the inner-city landscape: individual and entire families of homeless people wandering the streets in search of food and sleeping in subways, autos, and in the open. Conservative estimates of the homeless are in the 250,000 range. However, if all people who experience periods of homelessness in a given year were included, even by the strictest definitions, perhaps as many as 2 million people are homeless each year (Blau, 1992; Jencks, 1994; Feldman, 2006).

Powerful stereotypes dominate people's thinking about the homeless. Network news and newsmagazine profiles of the homeless often imply that "personal problems" such as alcoholism, drug addiction, and mental illness "cause" homelessness. Similarly, terms like "bag lady" and "skid row bum" continue to reinforce popular views that homelessness primarily affects middle-aged and elderly men and women.

Few of these stereotypes are true today. Between 60 and 70 percent of the homeless are single, and adult men comprise the largest share of the homeless. Most, however, are in their 20s and 30s, with the average age of all adult homeless people about 35. Some are adolescent "throwaways" who have been abused and rejected by their families and forced to live on the streets. Others live on the streets with family members. Families, in fact, account for somewhere between 30 and 40 percent of the homeless, many of them single mothers and their children. And close to 50 percent of the homeless are minorities (Blau, 1992; Sweeney, 1993; Dreier and Appelbaum, 1994; Feldman, 2006).

Likewise, economic and political factors—not personal flaws—are largely responsible for homelessness. Deinstitutionalization of mentally ill people, released from hospitals without adequate care and community support, account for some recent gains in homelessness. The exodus of manufacturing firms, chronic unemployment, and declines in real wages in many American cities have pushed many others onto the streets. At the same time, real estate speculation and high rents have made it impossible for large segments of the poor to find housing. Today the majority of the poor pay more than half of their incomes for housing, and many single moms pay almost three-fourths of their meager earnings just to keep a roof over their family's heads.

Government officials have also made many decisions that concentrated poverty in many cities. In the past decade, the federal government has terminated billions of dollars of support to inner-city communities. Likewise, many welfare programs for the poor have been abolished and converted to workfare programs. These have benefited some, but ironically, many welfare recipients have not taken jobs specifically created for them. Instead, they have been given the jobs of the working poor, whose working hours and incomes have been severely reduced to make room for those on "workfare" (*New York Times,* 1997).

After studying the urban poor in the Bronx, New York, and other cities around the world, anthropologist Oscar Lewis (1959, 1966) concluded that many poor people were held back by a **culture of poverty,** *a set of norms, beliefs, values, and attitudes that trap a small number of the urban poor in a permanent cycle of poverty.* Lewis believed that some of the distinctive attitudes and values of the "hard-core poor" include immediate gratification, apathy, and distrust, which encourages people to "blow" their earnings and live for the moment, making it hard to respond to opportunity.

Most sociologists disagree with Lewis's argument that the poorest of the poor have distinctive values, and most are opposed to the idea that the "culture of poverty" is

CULTURE OF POVERTY
A set of norms, beliefs, values, and attitudes that trap a small number of the urban poor in a permanent cycle of poverty.

structural and therefore highly resistant to change. In fact, sociologists have found that on those rare occasions when economic opportunities arise in the inner city, the poor respond to them without hesitation. Some also point to drug dealers and others in "deviant occupations" who respond to limited opportunity structures in the informal economy and sometimes illegal trade with remarkable entrepreneurial skills that, if they were not illegal, would be the envy of corporate America.

In his research on urban poverty, William Julius Wilson (1996, 1999) found that it is not long-term cultural patterns that fuel ghetto poverty, where poverty rates are at least 40 percent, but a relatively new phenomenon: a severe shortage of jobs and social isolation and dislocation that now affect the majority of adults in many inner-city neighborhoods, especially in the Northeast and Midwest. During the past few decades, well-paying factory jobs and much of the African American middle class have drifted to the suburbs, withdrawing both money and community leaders from the inner city. In the same period, those left behind have had to face severe reductions in government assistance programs, as well as continuing patterns of housing segregation and other forms of discrimination. Perhaps the only enduring legacy of the past are public attitudes that the poor are responsible for their own circumstances.

SOCIAL CLASS IN THE UNITED STATES: MYTH AND REALITY

As noted in Chapter 3, individualism is a dominant cultural orientation in the United States. Many Americans value their independence and the chance to compete as individuals and make personal choices that are free of social constraints. Related to this is an *ideology of personal responsibility,* which maintains that each person is responsible for his or her own actions, successes or failures, and social standing.

American ideology also takes a distinctive approach to equality. It does not require that people have equivalent resources, only *equal opportunities.* According to the *ideology of equal opportunity,* everyone should have the chance to compete on an equal basis and to win any of society's rewards. Because most Americans stress opportunity and a "level playing field," they tend to see the unequal distribution of wealth, power, and prestige as inevitable and even socially beneficial, with the gifted and hard-working rising to the top and those lacking in these qualities falling to the bottom.

Life Chances and Social Class

What evidence is there that people compete as individuals and that each must bear full responsibility for his or her own success or failure? Most sociologists would say, not much. **Life chances** are *opportunities for securing such things as health, education, autonomy, leisure, and a long life,* and they are directly related to social class. People at the top of the social hierarchy have resources that enable them to respond to opportunities when they arise. Their superior resources are equally important in helping them resolve personal problems, such as illnesses, lawsuits, or periods of unemployment.

Advantages begin early and persist throughout life. Childhood mortality rates are higher at the bottom of the social hierarchy. For example, "Black infants were 2.4 times as likely to die as white infants . . . and in 2000 it [was] estimated [they died] at three times the white rate" (Scanlon, 2000:29). Impoverished children more often suffer chronic illnesses and receive inferior health care than those at higher socioeconomic levels. Life expectancy, too, is affected by class: the higher the ranking in the class system, the longer the life. Those at the top of the hierarchy also attend better schools. Teachers and administrators expect more of upper-class and upper-middle-class students and encourage them to pursue the most rigorous academic programs and to attend college. By contrast, working-class and lower-class students get less encouragement, and most find themselves placed in vocational tracks. In addition, divorce and illegitimacy occur at higher rates among the lower classes. Police scrutiny is far more common among the poor than the rich. Moreover, people have a greater chance of being labeled a criminal, being a victim of a crime, and spending time in prison if they are members of the lower classes (Hannon, 2005). Add racial and ethnic stratification to the equation, and much stiffer penalties are involved, including the death penalty (Rainwater, 1974; Reiman, 2007). (In Focus box 8.3, two Yale professors offer a plan to boost every American's life chances.)

LIFE CHANCES
Opportunities for securing such things as health, education, autonomy, leisure, and a long life.

Two Yale law professors have a plan to reduce inequality in America and strengthen democracy that might appeal to you. In their book *The Stakeholder Society*, Bruce Ackerman and Anne Alstott trace the growing gap between rich and poor in America and how globalization and the new economy may be increasing this ominous trend. The question they ask is how growth can be sustained in the new economy while reversing what amounts to the creation of two societies in America: a small group of fabulously wealthy, highly educated and high-skilled haves and 80 percent or more of American households that are struggling to maintain what they have or are losing ground.

Their plan is quite simple. It would boost "equal opportunity" by granting everyone a stake in America at that moment in life when it may have the most impact. The authors would guarantee as a fundamental right to every American citizen—both rich and poor—at his or her twenty-first birthday a grant from the government of $80,000. For college-bound students, the grant would start at age 18 and be paid over four years—"provided the person . . . stays out of trouble" (Ackerman and Alstott, 1999:62–63). They note that such a sum is unlikely to have a major impact on the fortunes of the already rich. But it would give poor and minority households enough wealth to compete—if the money were used as intended. There would be no strings attached to how this money could be spent: a person could invest in mutual funds, start a business, or buy a home. For most people, however, the money would clearly be meant to be used to gain the necessary skills through education and job training that will be needed in the new economy. In fact, that is where they came up with the $80,000 figure—that is, "enough to pay for four years of tuition at the average private college in the United States" (Ackerman and Alstott, 1999:58). There

would be one price to be paid to society and future generations: If it was financially possible, the money would have to be paid back with interest at death, in effect recycling wealth to the needy indefinitely.

And where would the money come from to fund a program that would be almost the size of the current defense budget? Ackerman and Alstott would levy an annual wealth tax of 2 percent on the top 40 percent of American households. However, because most wealth is concentrated at the top, more than 90 percent of the money would be contributed by the wealthiest 20 percent of American households— those prospering in the new economy and most able to bear the tax burden.

Ackerman and Alstott note that granting young Americans money to finance their futures is not new. After World War II, the GI Bill of Rights provided many Americans with sufficient money to get an education, purchase homes, and start businesses, and millions moved up the social ladder. Although the authors do not believe that everyone will use the money wisely, they are convinced that the vast majority of high school graduates—minority group members in particular— would benefit by being given "a cushion in hard times and a source of entrepreneurial energy in better ones" (Ackerman and Alstott, 1999:10).

TAKING A CLOSER LOOK

On the basis of your experiences, will this plan produce the desired results: increase economic freedom, equal opportunity, and boost social participation and democracy in the United States?

Source: Bruce Ackerman and Anne Alstott. *The Stakeholder Society.* New Haven, CT: Yale University Press, 1999.

Social Mobility in the United States

In the United States there is a long tradition that celebrates upward mobility—from Horatio Alger stories to accounts of poor boys moving from log cabins to the White House. These myths suggest that any poor but hard-working person can easily move up the social ladder, even from the very bottom to the top. Today these myths are reinforced by media stories of ghetto children becoming star athletes, Hollywood celebrities, and generals. Yet, cross-national studies show that the United States has the highest overall social inequality of any postindustrial nation in the twenty-first century (Smeeding, 2005).

Can anyone who works hard and has talent become wealthy and move from the bottom to the top of the social hierarchy? Studies have shown that over the last century, the United States class system has been dynamic and fluid, with relatively high rates of **social mobility,** *the movement of people from one social position to another in the stratification system.* There are two major kinds of social mobility: horizontal and vertical. *Horizontal mobility* is movement from one social status to another of equivalent rank. For example, when the daughter of a biologist becomes a civil engineer, this is horizontal mobility. *Vertical mobility* involves movement, either up or down, from one social status to another. When a lawyer is disbarred and becomes a janitor, or a peanut farmer's son becomes president, this is vertical mobility.

SOCIAL MOBILITY
The movement of people from one social position to another in the stratification system.

As these examples demonstrate, vertical mobility can be either intragenerational or intergenerational. *Intragenerational mobility* refers to changes in an individual's social ranking over the course of his or her lifetime, whereas *intergenerational mobility* involves differences in the social status of parents and their offspring. Intergenerational mobility is of particular interest to sociological researchers because it provides a measure of the relative dynamism and openness of the class system.

Most studies of intergenerational mobility compared fathers' and sons' occupations. The influx of women into the workplace in the last few decades, however, has led to studies that incorporate women in class analysis and social mobility studies. Data suggest that the conventional analysis of male-only tables to represent the whole population underestimates the degree of openness in family mobility, though the bias is not large. Likewise, while women's employment has been shown to influence mobility, in a four-nation study, the husband's class location remained the primary determination of the family's class ranking (Baxter, 1994). During the past three decades in the United States, both husbands' *and* wives' incomes have begun to influence family class position. But other socioeconomic measures seem to be weighted differently. For example, "husband's occupational prestige—but not [a] wife's—affects class identification." By contrast, "men and women do not agree about the contributions of the husband's and wife's education." Likewise, self-employed women have a more independent basis of class identification" (Yamaguchi and Wang, 2003:440).

Virtually all mobility studies in the twentieth century found that while class position is largely inherited, the rate of upward mobility also has been relatively high. For example, of those billionaires who made the *Forbes 400* in 1997, 112 inherited their fabulous wealth directly—like the members of the Walton family. Many others also inherited at least a portion of their wealth, even some of those 219 individuals on the list that *Forbes* labeled "self-made" billionaires or millionaires (*Forbes*, 1997). (See Table 8.4).

Most people think that the superrich and rich alike inherit their fortunes at the death of parents or other benefactors, but in fact, nearly 90 percent of wealth transfers occur while wealthholders are alive. Moreover, sociologists argue that "inheritance" involves more than intergenerational wealth transfers. For example, cultural capital is transferred through formal and informal education, and social capital is transferred in the form of social networks and access to the rich and powerful as well (Keister and Moller, 2000:75–76).

Peter Blau and Otis Dudley Duncan (1967) found that 68 percent of the sons of salaried professionals became white-collar workers and 72 percent of laborers' sons had blue-collar jobs. Roughly the same figures were obtained in a later study by Featherman and Hauser (1978). Despite these findings, upward mobility rates were fairly high—especially when compared to those of many other industrial nations. For example, Blau and Duncan (1967) found that roughly 40 percent of the sons of blue-collar workers had white-collar jobs, a figure that increased to 45 percent in Featherman and Hauser's (1978) study. While this upward mobility is impressive, both studies found that short-range, one-step moves were more common than long-range moves and that most mobility was in the middle levels of the social class system (Kurz and Muller, 1987).

President Bush 41 and President Bush 43 enjoy a relaxing day on the golf course. Although people of the United States take great pride in not having royal families or aristocracies, some political and social analysts contend that families such as the Kennedys, Rockefellers, Bushes, and Clintons represent America's version of "ruling elites".

What do you think?

TABLE 8.4

WHY THE RICH GET RICHER: PERCENT OF POPULATION RECEIVING INHERITANCES

INHERITANCE AMOUNT

INCOME	$0	$1–$25,000	$25,000–$50,000	$50,000–$100,000	MORE THAN $100,000
Less than $10,000	54.9%	2.0%	0.4%	0.5%	0.7%
$10,000–$25,000	6.4%	0.5%	0.1%	0.0%	0.2%
$25,000–$50,000	14.1%	0.7%	0.2%	0.2%	0.2%
$50,000–$75,000	9.0%	0.5%	0.1%	0.2%	0.2%
$75,000–$100,000	3.9%	0.3%	0.2%	0.1%	0.1%
More than $100,000	3.6%	0.3%	0.1%	0.1%	0.2%
Total	91.9%	4.3%	1.1%	1.1%	1.6%

Source: "Why the Rich Get Richer." Reprinted with permission from the May 2003 issue of *American Demographics*. Copyright, Crain Communications Inc. 2003.

Moreover, while it is not discussed as often as upward mobility, the incidence of downward mobility also was moderately high. Katherine Newman (1993) found that more than half of the population has suffered falling incomes and almost one-third plunged far down the income ladder.

Despite our fondness for rags-to-riches tales, Blau and Duncan (1967) also found that fewer than 1 percent of those sampled moved from the bottom to the top of the status hierarchy. Several other findings deserve mention. First, mobility rates of black men were considerably lower than those of white men, although black mobility increased somewhat between 1960 and the early 1970s. For example, in 1990, the percentage of white men in the middle class was 29 percent; in the same year only 13 percent of black men had attained this level of class ranking (Horton et al., 2000:132). This is true even for blacks who have climbed the highest mobility ladder (from unskilled parents to professional status) and is evidenced by substantial differences in wealth; black net worth was only one-quarter that of whites who were of similar social backgrounds (Oliver et al., 1995).

There were regional differences as well. Both black and white Southerners were found to have lower mobility rates than the same groups in other sections of the country (Blau and Duncan, 1967; Featherman and Hauser, 1978).

Popular opinion maintains that high mobility rates reflect individual efforts to get ahead, but this is not the case. As Beeghley noted (2005:75), without industrialization "most people would still be farmers today and the rate of social mobility would be very low." Most gains, then, are the result of **structural mobility,** or *large-scale changes in occupational, educational, and corporate social structures that enable people to move up or down in the stratification system* (Lipset, 1982). In the twentieth century, three factors were particularly important to occupational advancement and the vast expansion of the middle class: improved technology and the creation of many more higher-status, white-collar jobs than blue-collar jobs; low birthrates among those at the top of the social hierarchy, which allowed those at lower levels to move up in the occupation hierarchy; and large-scale immigration, which pushed the native-born at the bottom of the job market to slightly higher positions than they might otherwise have attained (Gilbert and Kahl, 1987).

Blau and Duncan (1967:163) asked, "How does status attained (whether by ascription or achievement) at one stage of the life cycle affect the prospects for a subsequent stage?" They concluded that parental status indirectly affects people's occupational attainment, primarily by influencing the level of education they achieve, and that education level strongly determines people's first and subsequent occupations and how far they advance. In the new economy, a father's occupation and the occupational advantages it confers on children seems to be increasing (Rytina, 2000). Later studies found that other factors influence *status attainment,* including ability (as measured on achievement tests); parental, teacher, and peer expectations; size and structure of families; birth order; and age of parents (Hout and Morgan, 1975; Hauser et al., 1989; Mare and Tzeng, 1989).

Some sociologists question whether we should call it upward mobility when the sons and daughters of blue-collar workers find employment in low-level service positions such as salesclerk and bank teller. Others argue that when we focus on short-distance occupational gains, we forget the more important distinction between property owners and the working class. They argue that the focus on occupational gains may be yet

"*Actually, Lou, I think it was more than just my being in the right place at the right time. I think it was my being the right race, the right religion, the right sex, the right socioeconomic group, having the right accent, the right clothes, going to the right schools . . .*"

Source: © The New Yorker Collection 1992 Warren Miller from cartoonbank.com. All Rights Reserved. Used by permission.

STRUCTURAL MOBILITY
Large-scale changes in occupational, educational, and corporate social structures that enable people to move up or down in the stratification system.

another example of false consciousness, as we ignore the inequities of the class system and fail to acknowledge that although industrial and postindustrial economies have created a multitude of occupational statuses, the class system itself has been reproduced with relatively minor changes.

PERSPECTIVES ON SOCIAL STRATIFICATION

Why does inequality exist? Popular wisdom maintains that inequality is the result of personal motivation and "natural" differences among people. According to this view, those who are gifted and motivated inevitably claim a disproportionate share of a society's valued resources, while those with less talent and desire assume lower levels and get less. Many Americans favor this belief as it relates to the poor, who they believe end up with little because of mental, moral, or physical deficiencies.

The Functionalist Perspective

Sociologists recognize that there are differences between individuals, but most agree that social forces, rather than personal factors, are responsible for the fate of the rich and the poor. Kingsley Davis and Wilbert Moore (1945) argued that inequality is not created by natural differences but by the needs of society. Adopting the functionalist perspective, they argued that some positions are more important to social well-being and require longer training and greater skills. To their thinking, it is through a differential reward structure that all societies motivate people to defer gratification and spend many years in training or at work.

The Davis-Moore hypothesis has generated much controversy among sociologists. While many agree that incentives are important in complex societies, not all agree that they have to take the form of unequal access to scarce goods. Most sociologists are especially opposed to the idea that those at the top of the social hierarchy gained their wealth and privilege because of talent and efforts—with the implication that the poor are failures and their contributions to society are "unimportant."

Herbert Gans (1971, 1994) offers an alternative approach to functionalism. He asks whether it is possible that poverty is in some way socially beneficial. While most Americans would answer this question with a resounding "no," Gans argues that poverty may be functional and beneficial—not for society but for certain segments of society. He contends that poverty is very functional for those who make their living assisting the poor, such as public health workers, social workers, and many people in government. It is no less important to those who control the poor, including police officers, probation and parole workers, and prison officials. Landlords who provide minimal housing services for the poor at high rents also benefit, as do many inner-city grocers, who do not have to compete with giant supermarket chains and can charge the poor much more than middle-class suburbanites.

The Interactionist Perspective

Interactionists agree that members of all classes use symbols, language, clothing, and other things to differentiate themselves from those at other social levels. Fundamental to class are **lifestyles,** which are *the distinctive ways in which group members consume goods and services and display rank.* Thorsten Veblen (1899) noted that those at the top of the hierarchy typically convert wealth into prestige through *conspicuous consumption* and *conspicuous leisure.*

Drive through different parts of any American town and you will observe social class enclaves as well as obvious lifestyle differences. If you can see through the gates or over the walls of upper-class neighborhoods, you will observe massive homes of brick or stone, well-manicured lawns, and perhaps pools and tennis courts. Upper-middle-class neighborhoods are similar, though neither as grand nor as ostentatious, with much less property, more wooden frame homes, and strong preferences for earth tone colors. Working-class homes are also frame homes, though they are highly uniform, closely spaced, and often painted in bright colors such as canary yellow and hot pink. (Focus box 8.4 (on page 222) takes a closer look at the rise of gated communities in recent years.)

LIFESTYLES
The distinctive ways in which group members consume goods and services and display rank.

Can you imagine a future in which a growing segment of the population lives apart from the majority of Americans in oases of prosperity that are walled off and heavily policed to prevent intrusion into their private domains? Well, that is a vision of America painted in *Fortress America* and *Behind the Gates*. Both books imply that this residential pattern—the gated community—reflects much more than housing preferences; it may mark the beginning of a social transformation that affects American society and culture in fundamental ways.

Gated communities have been springing up around the country since the 1980s and are becoming even more popular in the early twenty-first century. The economic boom of the 1990s, media horror stories about urban crime, and more recently, terrorism have all fueled middle-class desires for gated communities. In 1995 there were only about 4 million private enclaves in America. Two years later there were 8 million and a year after that 16, increasing at near exponential rates each year into the twenty-first century. Today, Los Angeles, Houston, and Dallas have over 1 million walled residential units and the Western and Southern parts of the country lead the nation in this new housing trend. In 2001, the American Housing Survey found that 7 million—or about 6 percent—of all households were now in gated communities that included one or several of these features: high walls, fences, barricades, controlled entrances, video monitors, guardhouses, and security patrols (Blakely and Snyder, 1997; Low, 2003). These gated communities represent much more than physical barriers, according to Blakely and Snyder (1997). They allow the wealthy and privileged—and, increasingly, members of the middle class and working classes—to secede from public contact and, if they wish, to interact largely with those of similar social status.

There are three kinds of gated communities: lifestyle communities, prestige communities (the original gated community), and security zone communities. The first (lifestyle communities) have a long history in the United States—especially in the Sunbelt. They emphasize leisure and golf activities, often for retirees, and may expand dramatically as baby boomers retire over the next decade or so. With the current economic boom and proliferation of new economy millionaires, high-end prestige communities have also experienced rapid growth in recent years. They include traditional enclaves for the rich and famous in Hollywood Hills and along the Northeast coast and the less exclusive but still ostentatious digs for top-fifth executives, attorneys, physicians, and other upper-middle-class professionals. The third type (security zone communities) are relatively unique, in that fences and barricades are constructed by residents, not building contractors, often in inner-city neighborhoods that residents believe are deteriorating or are being overrun by "outside forces" (traffic, criminals and drug dealers, foreign immigration, and a perceived growing underclass) (Blakely and Snyder, 1997). Some security zone communities have been accused of attempting to use barricades as a contemporary means of resegregation—by both race and class.

What kind of America can we expect in the future if these trends continue? For example, when the community of responsibility stops at the barricade or subdivision gates, what happens to the idea of the public good and the general welfare? Put another way, "Can this nation fulfill its social contract in the absence of a social contract?" (Blakely and Snyder, 1997:3). Setha Low (2003:26) contends that gated communities may be a microcosm of contemporary American society. They reflect "social concerns and conflicts as well as pleasures and desires of modern middle-class life. But it is the American dream with a twist, one that intentionally restricts access and emphasizes social control and security over other community values."

TAKING A CLOSER LOOK

Are there any of the three kinds of gated communities in your area? If so, do they exist apart from the rest of the community and reflect the authors' worst fears of social fragmentation, privatization, and exclusion? If there are no gated communities in your area, explain why this is the case.

Source: Edward J. Blakely and Mary Gail Snyder. *Fortress America: Gated Communities in the United States.* Washington, D.C.: Brookings Institute Press, 1997. Setha Low. *Behind the Gates: Life, Security, and the Pursuit of Happiness in Fortress America.* New York: Routledge, 2003.

Class boundaries are also maintained by language, speech patterns, and pronunciation. Members of the upper class speak more directly and in a more assured manner than do members of the working and lower classes. Their confident demeanor, in turn, enables upper- and upper-middle-class speakers to project images of credibility, honesty, and competence that are important in all social arenas—especially the workplace. More subtle elements of nonverbal behavior (e.g., the use of eyes, hands, and posture) distinguish classes and serve as important social barriers as well. For example, members of the upper class rarely use their hands to give orders or directions. That is more typical of the working class and many ethnic groups, who issue directives by pointing and by making arm motions.

Patterns of sociability and community participation also are class based. One consistent research finding is that working-class people tend to have strong ties with family and large numbers of kin. By contrast, middle- and upper-class members have diverse and wide-ranging associations and social networks that enhance career opportunities and social mobility (Granovetter, 1995).

Why are there different patterns of class associations? Kerbo (1991) maintains that they are the result of several factors. First, middle-class patterns of socializing often reflect high geographic and social mobility and the absence of kin. By contrast, many in the working class remain in the communities where they were born, and this allows them to maintain contacts with kin. But clearly more is involved. Middle-class people have more education and wealth and much more leisure to expand their horizons and participate in community activities. Likewise, their occupations produce far less alienation and feelings of powerlessness than do working-class jobs. Social class promotes a multitude of other lifestyle differences, including food preferences, sexual practices, musical and artistic interests, dating patterns, sleeping arrangements, and almost everything else.

The Conflict Perspective

The conflict perspective owes much to the writings of Karl Marx, who at the beginning of the Industrial Revolution witnessed extreme inequality. Marx ([1848] 1964) wrote that history is marked by class struggles. He believed only two major groups were involved in that struggle: those who owned the major productive resources, and a much larger part of the population who did not—and who were exploited. In industrial society, capitalists, or the bourgeoisie, expropriated the surplus value produced by the working class, or proletariat, who owned little and thus were forced to sell their labor power to survive.

Capitalism has proved to be far more resilient than Marx ever could have imagined. Marx's model of class conflict and his future projections were primarily based on family-owned companies and *competitive capitalism,* which prevailed in the nineteenth century. Beginning in the twentieth century, however, this system gave way to *monopoly capitalism,* in which large multinational corporations dominated various sectors of the economy. In the twenty-first century, with major advances in technology, communication, and transportation, multinationals are giving way to giant transnational corporations that search for profits all over the globe.

Globalization, Diversity, and Class Today, with globalization, deindustrialization, and factory transfers to low-income nations the gap has widened between high- and low-wage earners in the United States and other advanced industrial nations. Factories have moved overseas and skilled blue-collar jobs have been replaced by clerical and nonmanual service occupations associated with lower incomes, fewer job benefits, and much less job security.

At the same time, skilled professionals from all over the world are relocating to new global cities, such as San Francisco and New York, altering traditional class structures that were once dominated by white men. Immigrants formed the very bottom of the class hierarchy in the past and they continue to do so today. However, with the current ease of mobility across the globe, many new immigrants—especially from Asia—have emigrated to the United States with considerable fortunes, "eclipsing somewhat the image of the Chinese laundry worker and illegal alien" (Ong, 1996:747).

The top photo is an American shopper at a U.S. Nike store, and the bottom photo shows a Nike factory on the outskirts of Ho Chi Minh City in Vietnam. Global corporations like Nike have great influence in developed and developing countries. In poor countries, because often they are a major source of nonfarm jobs and capital, they are especially powerful.

Currently in the United States, immigration policy facilitates the entry of men and women who have $1 million or more and have the ability to employ many people. This policy is producing a large-scale movement of wealthy Asian families from Hong Kong and other parts of the Pacific Rim to coastal cities in the United States and Canada. They include highly educated professionals who work in Silicon Valley, as well as property developers, financiers, and industrialists. Most assume positions at the top of the class structure by purchasing multimillion-dollar homes often "with cash," as well as luxury autos and other "global symbols" of elite ranking (Ong, 1996).

Conflict theorists emphasize that elites—whether Old or New Money—derive the most benefits from the class system, because they have the greatest influence on the political economy. Some conflict theorists point to the subsidies and tax benefits that are routinely enjoyed by large corporations and the super-rich as sufficient proof of upper-class dominance.

Money and power, however, are not the only weapons in the arsenal of the upper class. Members of this class also maintain influence over all important institutions and use them to reinforce their class standing and privileges. As Michael Parenti (1978:84) wrote: "The interests of an economically dominant class never stand naked. They are enshrouded in the flag, fortified by law, . . . nurtured by the media, taught by schools, and blessed by the church." For example, John D. Rockefeller Sr. was certain that his great oil fortune was more than mere money: it was a trust from God to improve the human condition (Chernow, 1998).

The Media and Class Ideology   Today, the mass media have become vital instruments of ruling classes everywhere on earth. Ostensibly in democratic societies the media are under neither government nor corporate control, and on the surface there appears to be a relatively open expression of views. But some voices are louder than others, and while corporate and political elites cannot control every news item, they can filter out news they deem unfit to print, marginalize dissent, as well as flood the media with messages that support their interests and views (Herman and Chomsky, 1988).

It is noteworthy that in the late 1980s, 7 of the top 10 wealthiest Americans had made all or a significant portion of their fortunes in communications and entertainment, and 72 of 400 (18 percent) possessed media fortunes. A decade later, in the late 1990s, this trend continued, with 5 of 6 of the wealthiest people in the United States having made their fortunes in computers, software, and telecommunications (*Forbes,* 1989, 1997).

The 1989 film *Roger and Me* told the grim tale of Flint, Michigan, after Roger Smith, the head of General Motors, eliminated 30,000 jobs there. Movies like this that challenge the class system rarely interest Hollywood; they are produced on shoestring budgets and almost never attract large audiences.

Most mainstream media avoid important social and political issues altogether, but this does not mean their messages are value-neutral. Despite the extraordinary diversity of media offerings, almost all proffer a similar homogenized fare of free enterprise, equality of opportunity, hard work, and upward mobility. One journalist contends that popular television shows also promote consumerism and a false image of middle-class prosperity, with their fancy apartments and designer clothing. She contends that at the dawn of the middle-class expansion in the 1950s and 1960s, shows tended to reflect "real people" in more realistic settings (Austin, 2000:31).

The mass media also bombard the public with class images that show the terrible fate of the poor and homeless alongside the glorious "lifestyles of the rich and famous." Television images of the working class are somewhat kinder, but rarely are flattering and are almost never realistic. "Blue-collar" sitcom families—the Kramdens in the 1950s; the Bunkers in the 1970s; the Simpsons, Bundys, and Conners in the 1990s; and the Heffernans, Romanos, and Hughleys in the 2000s—exploit what sociologist Mik Moore described as a "working-class inferiority complex," which holds that members of this class do not have what it takes "to get it right or do it right" (H. Waters, 1990:60).

Many claim that the new media have dramatically altered this equation, since anyone with a personal computer, fax machine, or cellular phone now has access to information on any subject—including accurate information on the reality of class in the

Sociology exam 2 essays   November 17, 2009

1. Corporation workplace in U.S. vs. Japan

   J- Corporation & workers: lifetime commitment between the two, stay w/ a company until retirement employee-to-employee relationships are stronger, more supportive of eachother.

   US- Corporation & workers: jobs are temporary, although employees hope to be employed by a company for as long as possible

   J- decision making is colective between the employees & employers

   US- decisions are made for employees with little to no input from them

   Corporations in Japan have been able to adapt to their style of work & management because it's what the workers want. These ideal conditions keep them happy & therefore more productive.

2. Deviance- violation of a more that brings about widspread disaproval
   aside from criminal behavior & downright law breaking there are other forms of deviance that are frowned upon.
   Stigma- social mark that hinders a group; obesity, tattos & piercings, physically handicapped. extreme dress

WAS: homosexuality, single motherhood, interracial relations, cohabitation, divorce
NOW: overt racism, homophobia, steroid abuse, smoking indoors, physical punishment

3. <u>Ideology</u>-

United States and globally. As one social scientist noted, for the first time in history members of all social classes have a direct means of challenging elite opinion makers and the official view.

Given the long-term persistence of class divisions, we should be skeptical about claims that technology will soon eradicate class. As we noted earlier, social class is a pervasive feature of all aspects of life—including the Internet. Currently, three-quarters of all Internet users are white, more than half are male, the majority have high incomes, and most run Internet businesses.

the FUTURE

LOOKING to

THE U.S. CLASS SYSTEM IN THE TWENTY-FIRST CENTURY

As in the past, politicians and the mass media continue to frame the debate over poverty and inequality almost exclusively in economic and technological terms. Not surprisingly, many are very supportive of Daniel Bell's (1973) predictions about the future of postindustrial society—especially the belief that a technical and professional class would emerge as the largest single group in American society. And, in the new social order, politicians would finally consider the claims and needs of the truly disadvantaged.

At present, there is little evidence to support either claim. Instead, the United States has the greatest wealth and income inequality in the developed world (Schwartz, 1999:34; Smeeding, 2005). In fact, global competition, a recurring national debt, and other economic changes have challenged the dreams of boundless prosperity and unlimited social mobility that have a long history in the United States. These negative trends are reflected in public opinion polls, in which three-quarters of respondents agreed that the gap between rich and poor would widen in the twenty-first century in the United States as well as globally. Some sociologists even contend that "class polarization" in the new economy has obliterated the middle class and that, today, there is a small "privileged class" and a working and lower class (most other households) (Perrucci and Wysong, 1999; Skocopol, 2000). And the "privileged class" may have grown richer, not only with tax cut benefits in 2003 and 2005 but with the reduction and possible repeal of the inheritance tax, which will exacerbate wealth inequality. As one researcher noted, while there is a natural tendency of wealth to regress to the mean over time, generous intergenerational transfers may make "the long run long indeed" (Wahl, 2003: 294) (Table 8.4 explores inheritance in the United States).

By 2005 the stagnant economy boosted unemployment rates to levels not seen in over a decade. In their survey "The Disposable Worker: Living in a Job-Loss Economy," researchers Carl Van Horn and Kenneth Dautrich found that while some middle-class professionals received small severance packages from former employers and small $300-per-week or so unemployment checks from the government, nearly one in five received nothing at all. And, "Barely one-fourth of those surveyed said their employer extended their health benefits after they were laid off, and less than one-fifth said they received help finding a job, career counseling, or skills training" (Johnston, 2003:2). In addition during the 2003 economic slowdown, workers remained unemployed longer than in previous recessions, and most of those who lost their jobs believed that "it will happen again in the next three to five years" (Johnson, 2003:2).

Early in the twenty-first century, the mainstream media revived the debate over whether the media has become too conservative or too liberal. One journalist contends that as entertainment and corporations seep into journalism and the news, "the problem that many media organizations face is not to stay in business, but to stay in journalism" (Schell, 2003:2).

Rather than exploring how the actions of corporations and those at the top of the social hierarchy influence inequality, the mainstream media and politicians have focused on those at the bottom. Once again, the media spotlight is on "undeserving poor"—stereotypic ghetto welfare cheats, illegal immigrants who are said to be a heavy burden on social services and the "American way of life," and single mothers who some talk show radio hosts claim "prefer having children to finding work." Such rhetoric has done much to fan the flames of white middle-class anger and resentment and has created a public mood receptive to punitive welfare reform measures.

During the 1990s, new federal welfare legislation ended more than 60 years of federal guaranteed cash assistance for the poor. It also established a 5-year lifetime limit on federal welfare benefits and, just as former President Clinton promised in the early 1990s, linked welfare benefits with work. Within 2 and a half years of going on welfare, welfare recipients have to work a minimum of 30 hours per week to continue benefits.

Because of media emphasis on welfare costs and abuses, most of these experiments have widespread public approval. "Workfare" is perhaps the most popular of all reforms. However, as Christopher Jencks (1993) observed, for workfare to work over the long term there will have to be jobs—and jobs that pay considerably more than the minimum wage. An economic boom during the 1990s coincided with workfare programs and "welfare rolls have fallen to nearly half their early 1990s levels" (Edin, 2000:113). Unfortunately, by early 2003, with the economy stagnant and the unemployment rate increasing to 6 percent, politicians in Washington, D.C., attempted to increase welfare recipients' work from 30 to 40 hours per week. They also maintained the $17 billion per year provided to states under Temporary Assistance to Needy Families, despite the fact that states were facing deep cuts in services because of the economy and big budget deficits. One research group predicted, "The likely result would be reductions in job training, child care and other services in the years ahead, especially for working poor families" (Stevenson, 2003:2). As welfare rolls shrink, the number of children living in poverty increases (Acs et al., 2005).

Sociological research suggests that minimum-wage jobs may actually lead to declining living standards for many poor families. For example, studies of the poor in Chicago suggest that once women take full-time but low-paying jobs, many lose low-cost child care and other services provided by their social support networks. Equally important, many lose their supplemental, "off-the-books" income that, before workfare, enabled many women to support their families at bare subsistence levels (Edin and Lein, 1997).

Today, about two-thirds of the jobs available to those who exit welfare pay minimum wage or less, many do not provide health benefits, and about half are part-time jobs. During the economic boom in the 1990s, many coped with these conditions, but Mary Corcoran and her colleagues (2000:263) ask, How will welfare reform and workfare affect child poverty, homelessness, and child neglect in an economic downturn, "or when the 'hard core' welfare cases bump up against time limits"?

In the future, it is likely that more rather than less generous welfare assistance programs will be needed. Unfortunately, in addition to economic instability, there is a good chance that there will be much greater competition for social welfare benefits than there was in the past. As baby-boomers age, they likely will seek a greater share of public spending for elderly social welfare programs and health-care needs, with the very real possibility that other age cohorts may experience more reductions in federal assistance and increasing poverty. It is likely that state welfare policies will become even more stringent. For example, Indiana and North Carolina have 2-year limits—not 5 years in the federal welfare program—and at least 19 states "refuse to increase benefits to women who have additional children" (Seccombe, 1999:13).

Some have suggested that we borrow from European models and adopt universal rather than means-tested criteria. Such programs would provide more benefits to the needy, including child allowance, health care, and cash assistance to all the poor, "regardless of family status or income" (Hurst, 1998:385). At another level, Hurst (1998) argues that to address problems of poverty and inequality, we need to recognize that the two are vitally linked rather than being separate issues, as many people understand them. Further, instead of stressing equality of opportunity, which has benefited only a small segment of the population, we need to focus on the problem of inequality and implement public policies that address this serious national issue. Theda Skocopol (2000:163) contends that for positive changes to occur, there will have to be shifts from corporate influence, a media obsessed with entertainment and scandal, and public debates dominated by professionally run advocacy groups to a new "family-oriented populism" that will explore real problems and provide real solutions for all American families.

The gap between the rich and poor is not just a national trend, however, but one that is occurring across the globe. With globalization in the past few decades, all people and all nations are now part of a global social hierarchy. Today, if we are to understand the life chances and lifestyles of any individual, group, or nation, we must look beyond national borders and explore how global inequality—the topic of the next chapter— now affects everyone on earth.

Summary

1 Social stratification is a form of inequality in which categories of people are systematically ranked on the basis of three major dimensions: wealth, status (prestige), and power.

2 There are four principal types of stratification systems: slavery, caste, estate, and social class.

3 Sociologists measure class ranking by using a multifaceted approach. A popular approach to determine class ranking is using socioeconomic status— income, education, occupation, and neighborhood.

4 Sociologists distinguish five major classes: upper, upper middle, lower middle, working, and lower.

5 Approximately 14 percent of Americans live in poverty and, because of economic, political, and social factors, homelessness is increasing—among individuals and families. The root cause of inner-city poverty is chronic unemployment—not personal flaws or racial or ethnic deficiencies.

6 Class position influences a person's life chances, lifestyles, and opportunities of moving up or down in the social hierarchy.

7 Sociologists approach class from the functionalist, interactionist, and conflict perspectives. Functionalism sees class as fulfilling the needs of society by differentially rewarding effort. Interactionists focus more on class symbols and boundaries, and conflict theorists stress that inequality mainly benefits the rich and powerful.

8 Most sociologists anticipate a widening gap between the rich and poor in the next century and less generous welfare assistance for the poor and needy. Some suggest that we should borrow European approaches to inequality. Others see more hope in a coalition of social movements that may remedy poverty and inequality in the United States and globally.

Key Terms

absolute poverty (p. 212)
caste system (p. 201)
class system (p. 202)
culture of poverty (p. 217)
estate system (p. 201)
feminization of poverty (p. 214)
life chances (p. 217)

lifestyles (p. 221)
power (p. 203)
prestige (p. 203)
relative poverty (p. 212)
slave system (p. 201)
social differentiation (p. 200)

social inequality (p. 200)
social mobility (p. 218)
social stratification (p. 200)
socioeconomic status (p. 206)
structural mobility (p. 220)
wealth (p. 203)

Chapter 9

Global Stratification

"Poverty is the parent of revolution and crime."

—*Plato*

New meanings have been added to the holiday expression "Santa's Little Helpers." Today, with globalization and sweatshops, the term is not only associated with mythical elves who work for Santa at the North Pole, but real-life Chinese sweatshop workers, who produce 70 percent of the world's toys—including billions of dollars worth of holiday toys, Santa suits, plastic bells and angels, and other Christmas decorations. About half of these goods are exported to the United States. More than 3 million Chinese women, most between 17 and 23 years of age, work 12 or even 14-hour shifts for wages that range from 30 cents to 12 cents an hour. The wages are so low because toy factories tend to hire "temporary migrant workers" from a pool of perhaps 150–200 million migrant workers from China's impoverished countryside. They are the least-skilled workers in the Chinese factory system, and perform dull and repetitive chores like painting, spraying, or attaching toy components with glue that often results in their inhaling spray paint, glue fumes, and toxic dust during the few years that most women work (*The Irish Times,* 2002).

Some claim that conditions in the toy factories are the worst in China, but shoe and garment factories are not far behind. Despite new Chinese labor laws and global protest movements, most factories continue to provide low wages and few benefits, job security is nonexistent, and conditions in worker dormatories and on the factory floor are often overcrowded, dirty, and dangerous. Strange new symptoms have been observed at some Chinese toy and shoe factories in recent years. In 2002, The *Washington Post* reported the fate of Wang Xiao, who had worked in a factory in Southern China putting in 17-hour days gluing sneakers together. After only a few months, she noticed a tingling in her hands that later spread to her ankles and legs. Unable to work, she quit and, weeks later, she woke up paralyzed, unable even to wiggle a finger—apparently the result of toxins in the glue. Now, despite a yearlong search for treatment, Wang remains confined to a hospital bed. Her misfortune has been compounded by medical bills that have wiped out years of savings and knocked her family, once on the verge of escaping poverty, back into debt and destitution (Pan, 2002:1).

Although almost every American purchases toys and wears sneakers, jeans, and other apparel, few have much knowledge of overseas factories. The media spotlight, however, can alert the public to problems anywhere on earth in an instant. That's what it did in 1996, when a labor activist told a congressional hearing that a factory in Central America employed children and pregnant women who sewed garments for the Kathie Lee clothing line. When she heard the story, a shocked Kathie Lee Gifford announced on her morning television show that she had no idea her clothing had any connection with sweatshops and that she would sever the relationship immediately. Later, with her usual zeal and high energy, she declared war on the sweatshop industry, and with corporate help, she helped found the Fair Labor Association, which started "setting up an independent monitoring system that includes human rights groups" (Roberts and Bernstein, 2000:124).

The Kathie Lee controversy highlights the basic theme of this chapter—that we must look beyond national boundaries and examine the larger framework of global stratification to understand any contemporary issue or problem. With economic globalization, the fate and fortunes of all nations and all people are now linked. This is most obvious when we visit shopping malls and find many clothing items, toys, and other consumer goods with labels from Honduras, China, and other parts of the world. Much of the food we eat is raised abroad. There is also a good chance that you will spend part of your working life overseas, perhaps in Hong Kong, Brazil, or London. And professionals from these countries now routinely spend a part of their careers in places like Houston and Boston, or they communicate daily with co-workers in these cities via the Internet.

Today, there is considerable optimism that development and prosperity will finally reach most if not all of the nations of the world. Certainly, there have been extraordinary success stories in the past two decades. The end of the Cold War, international trade agreements, and the expansion of corporations across the globe have contributed to an economic boom in China, East Asia, and many Latin American nations as well, which has dramatically improved the living standards of millions of people.

Sweatshops are not confined to developing countries but exist in many American cities. Garment workers—most of them immigrants—work for meager wages in dark, crowded, and often dangerous environments, like those shown in this photo.

But as the opening vignette illustrates, *things are not necessarily what they seem.* Globalization has not been entirely positive. Many Americans have benefited from inexpensive goods manufactured abroad, but the shift in manufacturing jobs to poor nations where labor is cheap has led to the exploitation of many workers. It has also cost many Americans their jobs; in some parts of the United States entire communities have experienced social upheavals and severe hardships because factory jobs have been exported to low-wage nations.

In this chapter, we explore global stratification and unequal relationships between rich and poor nations: how the system began, how it is maintained, and how it affects the lives of everyone on earth. Pay particular attention to the role of governments and corporations in national development. We also peer into the future and consider some of the possible directions globalization may take in the future. Will it bring a new international consciousness and prosperity for all nations? Or will the current gap between rich and poor nations widen and poverty worsen, which may have serious consequences for the vast majority of people on earth?

GLOBALIZATION AND ECONOMIC DEVELOPMENT

In Chapter 8 we discussed social stratification in the United States. With globalization, however, we need to look beyond national boundaries and consider how the global political economy—and the worldwide distribution of jobs, capital, power, and wealth—affects our lives and the lives of people everywhere. Today, the 200-plus nations of the world are part of a **global stratification system,** where *nations are ranked in a hierarchy on the basis of their access to the world's wealth, power, and prestige.*

Just as members of the upper class in the United States possess most of the nation's income, so do a handful of the world's nations. However, the distribution of income is even more concentrated at the global level than it is nationally. As noted in Chapter 8, the top 20 percent or so of Americans own most of the nation's assets and nearly half of its income; by contrast, the poorest 20 percent earn less than 4 percent of the national income and most have few assets. At the global level, a similar percentage of wealthy nations possess most of the world's income and the poorest share a tiny fraction of global resources and income. And a tiny portion of the global population—225 people—own more than do 2½ billions of people. Moreover, extraordinary levels of population growth in Asia and Africa may make the equitable distribution of global incomes more difficult in this twenty-first century (see Figure 9.1) (Human Development Report, 2003; World Bank, 2006).

The consequences of such stratification are experienced most acutely in poor nations, where much of the world's population reside. While poverty is a significant problem in the United States, affecting nearly 40 million people, it pales in comparison to conditions in low-income countries. In these nations, more than a billion people must try to survive on annual incomes of $500 or less, and hundreds of millions of people have no regular access to basic necessities—food, clean water, clothing, housing, and safety.

The Language of Development

What images come to mind when you hear a television or radio report about a "Third World" nation? If you are like most people, the associations are probably negative. This should alert you to the power of language and labels—especially when they are used to describe or rank nations.

For more than a half century, Western government officials, international banks, and development agencies have used a popular *Three Worlds model* to classify (and rank) all

GLOBAL STRATIFICATION SYSTEM
Nations are ranked in a hierarchy on the basis of their access to the world's wealth, power, and prestige.

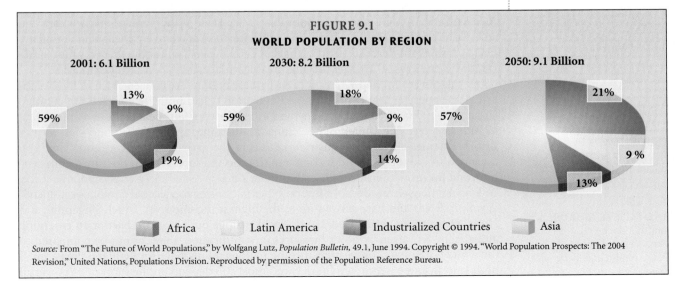

FIGURE 9.1
WORLD POPULATION BY REGION

2001: 6.1 Billion — 13%, 9%, 59%, 19%

2030: 8.2 Billion — 18%, 9%, 59%, 14%

2050: 9.1 Billion — 21%, 9%, 57%, 13%

Africa   Latin America   Industrialized Countries   Asia

Source: From "The Future of World Populations," by Wolfgang Lutz, *Population Bulletin,* 49.1, June 1994. Copyright © 1994. "World Population Prospects: The 2004 Revision," United Nations, Populations Division. Reproduced by permission of the Population Reference Bureau.

"*The poor are getting poorer, but with the rich getting richer it all averages out in the long run.*"

of the nations of the world. They labeled advanced industrial, democratic, and rich nations—such as the United States, France, and Japan—*First World* nations. In the *Second World* were socialist and communist nations, such as the former Soviet Union and China, that experienced moderate levels of industrial growth and living standards. Development analysts placed emerging nations in Asia, Africa, and Latin America in the *Third World*, a label that defined most as preindustrial and poor.

Today, sociologists see few advantages to this model. For one thing, most now recognize that the Three Worlds scheme creates powerful labels that reinforce, rather than address, global inequality. This is particularly true of the "Third World" label, which for many years meant backward, politically unstable, and high-risk in the development community. The end of the Cold War and collapse of the Soviet Union, which swept away most Second World nations, have been just as damaging to the scheme. Today, Russia and most of its former Eastern European allies, Cuba and especially China, are in a state of economic and political transition. All, however, are very much a part of the global economy.

To address the shortcomings of the Three Worlds model and highlight the dynamic nature of the global economy, we have adopted the United Nations' Development Program's classification system, which ranks nations by income and other measures. For income, this is done by dividing each nation's annual gross domestic product by its total population to give the *average income* of its citizens. By this measure, and by converting all currencies to an "international dollar" that gives real purchasing power throughout the world, all nations can be ranked as *high-income, middle-income,* or *low-income nations.* Map 9.1 shows the geographic distribution of countries in the three major income groups. The "Human Development Index" ranking also includes other variables, such as life expectancy, literacy rates, and other social measures.

High-Income Nations

High-income nations are *nations with advanced industrial economies and high living standards.* They are similar to the upper classes in that they receive a disproportionate share of global wealth and income, which is quite evident in the lives of the majority of their citizens. In high-income nations a large segment of the population own cars and well-furnished homes and apartments. Likewise, food is relatively cheap and abundant, and consumer goods are so plentiful that few people even think about them. By the world's standards, the lives of "average citizens" are not average; they are more like fantasies.

As you can see in Map 9.1, most high-income nations are concentrated in the Northern Hemisphere, where the Industrial Revolution began in the late eighteenth century. Great Britain, France, Italy, Germany, and other Western European nations were the first to industrialize. The United States, Canada, Australia, and New Zealand—all former British colonies—became industrial nations in the early nineteenth century and also ascended to the top of world income ranking. So did Japan late in the nineteenth century, and for more than a century it has been a major Asian and global economic force.

During the past few decades several other nations have succeeded in major industrialization drives and have moved up to the highest income level. Israel, Singapore, and Hong Kong were once labeled Third World nations but today are part of an emerging global elite. However, by other measures of stratification, they cannot be compared to the United States and other high-income nations. Many have limited land areas, small populations, and emerging militaries, and most still depend on the support of powerful nations, and Hong Kong has been reincorporated into the People's Republic of China.

HIGH-INCOME NATIONS
Nations with advanced industrial economies and high living standards.

MIDDLE-INCOME NATIONS
Nations that are newly industrialized and have moderate wealth and living standards.

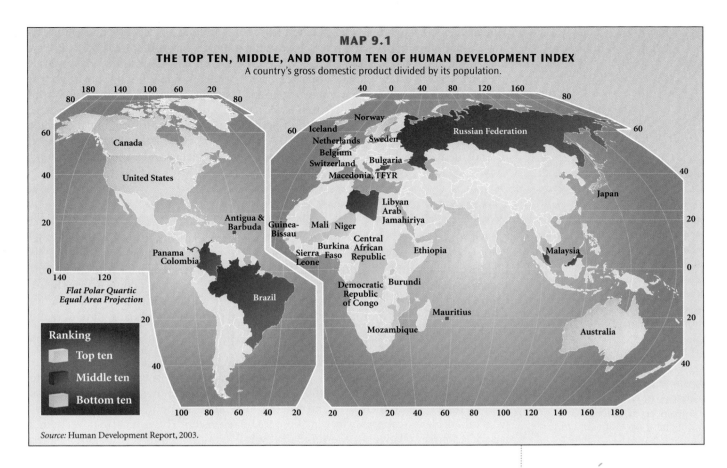

MAP 9.1

THE TOP TEN, MIDDLE, AND BOTTOM TEN OF HUMAN DEVELOPMENT INDEX

A country's gross domestic product divided by its population.

Flat Polar Quartic Equal Area Projection

Ranking
- Top ten
- Middle ten
- Bottom ten

Source: Human Development Report, 2003.

Middle-Income Nations

Middle-income nations are *nations that are newly industrialized and have moderate wealth and living standards.* In this diverse group of nations, per capita incomes vary greatly. Life in these nations can be dramatically different. In middle-income nations a tiny elite lives in great luxury that differs little from that of the wealthiest families in the United States. But beyond this world, most people have access to some credit and what people in high-income nations would consider basic necessities: small homes and apartments, local and regional foods, public transportation—though they do not necessarily own late-model cars—and most consumer goods. In countries like Saudi Arabia and Kuwait, the government subsidizes housing and provides other support to families, and most are assured of the basics. In most other middle-income nations this kind of support is unusual, and based on housing and material possessions the average person's life would be seen as "humble" indeed by most Americans.

Mexico, Brazil, Columbia, and several other Latin American nations are in this income bracket. So are several Pacific Rim nations, such as South Korea and Taiwan, and several oil-rich nations in the Middle East, including Saudi Arabia and Kuwait. Likewise, Poland and Bulgaria, which currently are shifting from state-managed to market economies, are in the middle-income group. With their strong industrial base and assistance from Western Europe and U.S. banks and corporations, both nations have the potential of moving up. Because of ethnic, religious, and nationalist conflicts, other newly independent nations may move in the opposite direction toward the bottom of the global hierarchy.

Low-Income Nations

Low-income nations are *nations that are poor, agrarian, and benefit least from their participation in the global economy.* In nations like Bangladesh and Pakistan, with large populations of peasant farmers,

This photo of rich and poor residential districts in a Latin American city should alert you to some of the problems with the label "middle-income nation." In this case, there are very wealthy and very poor people and only a small middle class.

annual surpluses are small and the majority of the population has little access to consumer goods, health care, and most other things you would consider to be bare necessities. In much of Sub-Saharan Africa, where hoe agriculture is still common, surpluses are even smaller, as are people's incomes. Much of the population may subsist almost exclusively on vegetarian diets, many experience periods of starvation, and millions of people live in temporary shelters that lack electricity, water, and sanitation. Currently, approximately 22 percent of the world's population live in South Asia, but this single region includes nearly half of the world's poor (*World Bank Atlas,* 2006). Moreover, despite media hype, the rich nations seem to be getting richer and poor nations poorer (Smeeding, 2005; World Bank 2006).

GLOBAL STRATIFICATION AND QUALITY OF LIFE

Global stratification not only affects people's household budgets, it also has broad social consequences. Because they are resource-rich, high-income nations can provide the majority of their citizens good health, relative prosperity, and long lives. Middle-income nations benefit less from international politics and trade, and low-income nations benefit the least. For nations at the bottom, this usually translates into a host of negative social consequences from high infant mortality rates, health problems, illiteracy, and chronic hunger and malnutrition for a significant portion of the population.

In Chapter 8, we noted that resources, which are distributed by class, largely determine people's life chances, or opportunities for living long and healthy lives and solving personal problems. We also discussed the important distinction between absolute and relative poverty. We noted that in the United States and most other advanced industrial nations people judge their lives and whether they are rich, poor, or "middle class" by what others have—especially by what they see on television. This is relative poverty, or a lack of resources relative to others and the overall living standards of a society. Further, most high-income nations are *welfare states,* which means they have "safety nets" and social welfare systems that attempt to provide for people's basic needs.

In most low- and middle-income nations there is no social welfare system and absolute poverty prevails. When people have problems, family and kin usually stretch their scarce resources to the limit to provide help, but there is no institutional support structure. **Absolute poverty** exists *when people lack food and other basic necessities of life.* Development officials often use a minimum of 1,500 calories per day as one measure of absolute poverty—the number of calories many Americans consume for breakfast. This near-starvation diet is not the exception but the rule in many poor nations, where at any particular time as much as 20–40 percent of the population may be malnourished.

In poor nations, absolute poverty affects every aspect of people's lives, from birth to death. Widespread malnutrition produces high miscarriage and infant mortality rates. Likewise, large segments of the population are chronically ill. Most people in low-income nations can expect to live around 50 years, compared to life expectancies of 75 years or more in high-income nations. And historically when cutbacks occur in poor nations, the largest share of the burden has been borne by those at the bottom of the global social hierarchy—poor women and children.

The Global "Haves" and "Have-Nots"

The World Bank (2006) reports that despite many global success stories, per capita gross domestic product had fallen in nearly 50 countries—most of them in the low-income bracket. If current population and economic trends continue, living standards in these poor nations—which contain one-sixth of humanity, or about 1 billion people—may seriously deteriorate in this century, even though they are already marginal at best.

One way to assess people's life chances in rich and poor nations is to compare them using a number of social and economic indicators (see Table 9.1). The top, middle, and bottom ten nations provide a global snapshot of conditions in 2003.

ABSOLUTE POVERTY
When people lack food and other basic necessities of life.

Poverty in many parts of the world is absolute and people have virtually no access to basic necessities like food and water. This evocative photo shows the poverty and suffering of a child in the Sudan, a nation in the midst of civil war and near the bottom of the global social hierarchy.

TABLE 9.1
HUMAN DEVELOPMENT INDEX : A GLOBAL SNAPSHOT, 2003

HDI RANK	HUMAN DEVELOPMENT INDEX (HDI) VALUE 2003	LIFE EXPECTANCY AT BIRTH 2003	ADULT LITERACY RATE (% AGES 15 AND ABOVE) 2003	COMBINED GROSS ENROLLMENT RATIO FOR PRIMARY, SECONDARY, AND TERTIARY SCHOOLS (%) 2002–03	GDP PER CAPITA (PPP US$) 2003	LIFE EXPECTANCY INDEX	EDUCATION INDEX	GDP INDEX	GDP PER CAPITA (PPP US$) RANK MINUS HDI RANK
High Human Development									
1. Norway	.963	79.4	*	101	37,670	.91	.99	.99	2
2. Iceland	.956	80.7	*	96	31,243	.93	.98	.96	4
3. Australia	.955	80.3	*	116	29,632	.92	.99	.95	7
4. Luxembourg	.949	78.5	*	88	62,298	.89	.95	1.00	−3
5. Canada	.949	80.0	*	94	30,677	.92	.97	.96	2
6. Sweden	.949	80.2	*	114	26,750	.92	.99	.93	14
7. Switzerland	.947	80.5	*	90	30,552	.93	.96	.96	1
8. Ireland	.946	77.7	*	93	37,738	.88	.97	.99	−6
9. Belgium	.945	78.9	*	114	28,335	.90	.99	.94	3
10. United States	.944	77.4	*	93	37,562	.87	.97	.99	−6
Medium Human Development									
58. Libyan Arab Jamahiriya	.799	73.6	81.7	96	--	.81	.86	.72	9
59. Macedonia, TFYR	.797	73.8	96.1	70	6,794	.81	.87	.70	16
60. Antigua and Barbuda	.797	73.9	85.8	69	10,294	.82	.80	.77	−7
61. Malaysia	.796	73.2	88.7	71	9,512	.80	.83	.76	−3
62. Russian Federation	.795	65.3	99.4	90	9,230	.67	.96	.76	−3
63. Brazil	.792	70.5	88.4	91	7,790	.76	.89	.73	1
64. Romania	.792	71.3	97.3	72	7,277	.77	.89	.72	4
65. Mauritius	.791	72.2	84.3	71	11,287	.79	.80	.79	−16
66. Grenada	.787	65.3	96.0	96	7,959	.67	.96	.73	−3
67. Belarus	.786	68.1	99.6	88	6,052	.72	.95	.68	17
Low Human Development									
146. Madagascar	.499	55.4	70.6	51	809	.51	.64	.35	24
147. Swaziland	.498	32.5	79.2	60	4,726	.12	.73	.64	−47
148. Cameroon	.497	45.8	67.9	55	2,118	.35	.64	.51	−19
149. Lesotho	.497	36.3	81.4	66	2,561	.19	.76	.54	−26
150. Djibouti	.495	52.8	65.5	24	2,086	.46	.52	.51	−18
151. Yemen	.489	60.6	49.0	55	889	.59	.51	.36	15
152. Mauritania	.477	52.7	51.2	45	1,766	.46	.49	.48	−13
153. Haiti	.475	51.6	51.9	--	1,742	.44	.50	.48	−9
154. Kenya	.474	47.2	73.6	52	1,037	.37	.66	.39	7
155. Gambia	.470	55.7	37.8	48	1,859	.51	.41	.49	−19

* For purposes of calculating the HDI, a value of 99.0% was applied.
-- Data unavailable

Source: Table 1 "Human Development Index" (pp.219–222): first 10 countries from High, Medium, and Low Development from *Human Development Report 2005* (2005) by the United Nations Development Programme. By permission of Oxford University Press, Inc.

The average person in high-income nations earns over 60 times the income of people in low-income nations. The *lifetime earnings* of most people in poor nations do not approach the *yearly* income of people in many industrial nations. In the United States, for example, high incomes have created "problems" that would be incomprehensible to people in poor nations. For example, a large number of Americans suffer from "overnutrition" each year, and by the early twenty-first century, about two-thirds of Americans were overweight, more than one-quarter were trying to lose weight by dieting, and many had become members of fitness and weight loss centers that were part of a diet industry that annually costs an estimated $42 billion (Kurth and Upton, 2004:2).

At the other end of the global hierarchy, people must try to subsist, educate their children, and remain healthy on annual incomes of a few hundred dollars, and do so in the face of extreme environmental and political instability. A few nations such as Vietnam and China have improved incomes per person well above $1.00 a day—"the current world standard for dire poverty." Most nations in Africa, for example, have not advanced. During the civil wars in Rwanda, Liberia, and other parts of Africa in recent years millions of people who were already severely impoverished were forced to migrate back and forth across national borders in search of food, and in some cases, to escape threats of genocide (*The Economist,* 2000:46).

National Class Systems and Poverty

The nature of each nation's class system also influences people's life chances. In some nations a large share of income and wealth is absorbed by the upper classes and, in many newly industrializing countries, by emerging middle classes as well. In others, even those that have little, national income is more equitably distributed and people live longer, more satisfying lives. It is not enough to ask the average per capita income of a nation without also asking how a nation's income is divided by class, sex, age, and other measures of stratification.

For many low-income nations this means that while average per capita incomes may be in the $1,000 range, virtually all of it goes to elites and very little trickles down to those at the bottom. The quality of people's lives in middle-income nations is affected by the nature of the class system as well.

Population Growth and Poverty

Today, more than three-fourths of the world's population inhabits low- and middle-income nations. However, people in these countries have access to only about 16 percent of the world's income. One of the greatest challenges for many of these nations is dealing with burgeoning populations. In the past two decades, political efforts and women's movements have reduced fertility rates in many low-income countries. For example, in 1970, women averaged about five children over a lifetime; today, most women in low- and middle-income nations average around three children. However, populations continue to surge because of better health care and nutrition. Moreover, so many have reached childbearing age in low-income nations that annual population increases of over 70 million people are common.

Most future population growth will occur in Asia and Africa, where the majority of poor people live. By 2025, South Asia's population is expected to double and reach nearly 4 billion. Africa also has a disproportionate share of the world's poor, and many nations in Sub-Saharan Africa currently rank among the poorest of the poor. To give you an idea of the depressed conditions in these countries consider this: Since the 1970s, food production has tripled in much of the world, but in Sub-Saharan Africa it fell during much of the past few decades. And of the fifty-four nations with declining incomes, "twenty are from Sub-Saharan Africa" (United Nations Development Report, 2003:3). And while jobs are scarce, "a phenomenal 44% of the population of Africa is under 15" (Foot, 2000:266).

During the next 25 years it is expected that world population will increase by 2 or 3 billion, for a total population of about 9 billion. By 2100, 12 billion is possible—if the environment, and poor nations in particular, can sustain such increases. See Table 9.2 for a listing of the world's ten most populous nations.

The Poorest of the Poor: Women and Children

In its 2003 Human Development Report, the United Nations announced that development in the second half of the twentieth century was unprecedented in human history. In this period, the average income increased, and in most nations many years were added to life expectancies, and child mortality rates declined dramatically in many nations (2003:3). Much of this improvement reflected technological and economic growth worldwide. But they were not the only factors involved. Some nations—including many low-income nations—made a major effort to improve the conditions of women and children. So did activists in the women's and poverty movements (United Nations Human Development Report, 2003).

Although aspects of their modernization drive have been controversial, the Chinese government's campaign to enhance the quality of women's lives has produced many positive results. In the past few decades, women's literacy rates have doubled and life expectancies have increased from 63 years in 1970 to around 70 years today. Women's employment has steadily increased, to about 45 percent of total employment, and one-fifth of China's parliamentary deputies are women, which is high by most national standards (United Nations Development Report, 2003).

During the past few decades, efforts to reduce gender inequality were not unique in low- and middle-income nations. For example, Botswana in Africa ranks very low in terms of per capita income. However, because of government and activist efforts, public health has improved and the nation's gross primary school enrollment ratio has more than doubled (United Nations Development Report, 2003:86). In parts of Brazil, social activism has helped improve the quality of life for ordinary people, as well. Entering the 1990s, in Porto Alegre, Brazil, for example, less than half of city residents had access to clean water. By late in the decade, under pressure from various social movements, almost every home had water, primary school enrollment had doubled, and public transportation had expanded to include the poor in outlying areas (United Nations Development Report, 2003:2).

Many other nations in the Southern Hemisphere also made significant strides in the past two decades. In Latin America, Asia, and Africa, women's life expectancy increased by 9 years, and female adult literacy and school enrollment increased by almost two-thirds—especially in Arab states, which made the greatest progress, nearly doubling women's literacy rates. Similar gains were made in higher education. For example, in the mid-1990s in Latin America and the Caribbean, women's college enrollments increased from 9 to 26 percent (United Nations Development Report, 2003).

TABLE 9.2
THE TEN MOST POPULOUS COUNTRIES

COUNTRY	POPULATION
China	1,313,973,713
India	1,095,351,995
European Union	456,953,258
United States	298,444,215
Indonesia	245,452,739
Brazil	188,078,227
Pakistan	165,803,560
Bangladesh	147,365,352
Russia	142,893,540
Nigeria	131,859,731

Source: The *CIA 2006 World Factbook,* "Rank Order: Population".

Many children in low-income nations subsist by foraging in garbage dumps, like this one at the edge of Cairo, Egypt. The children and their families are known as "zabbeleen," literally "trash people," and daily they are exposed to toxic wastes and deadly diseases.

Despite these remarkable achievements, a widespread pattern of gender inequality persists, and with limited resources the penalties associated with these disparities are especially severe in low- and middle-income nations. Further, as we noted in the opening vignette, many recent economic gains have come at the expense of women and children, whose labor in factories and sweatshops have helped fuel the economic miracle in many Asian nations and elsewhere in the world. In recent years there has been an increasing migration of millions of women from south to north, and from poor countries to rich ones, where they serve as nannies, maids, and sometimes sex workers. The lifestyles of industrial countries, in fact, now depend on these global service providers. While many women are attracted by the opportunities and money, others are pushed by extreme poverty into the emerging global economy (Ehrenreich and Hochschild, 2002:4).

Poverty and Malnutrition　The United Nations Development Report in 2003 observed that "More than 1.2 billion people—one in every five on earth—survive on less than $1 a day. While the number of people experiencing extreme poverty fell slightly during the global economic boom of the 1990s, if China is excluded, the number of extremely poor people actually increased by 28 million" (United Nations Development Report, 2003:5). Most poor people in the world live in South and East Asia and the majority are women and girls. During the nineties both regions made gains, especially India and China. For example, China lifted 150 million people, or 12 percent of the population, out of poverty. Nevertheless, most of these gains were negated by increased poverty in Latin America, the Arab States, Sub-Saharan Africa, and several other regions where the number of those subsisting on less than $1 a day actually increased (United Nations Development Report, 2003:5).

Because of severe malnutrition, a child from a poor nation is 50 times more likely to die before the age of 5 than a child in a rich country; and women in poor countries are 150 times more likely to die in pregnancy or childbirth than their European and North American counterparts (United Nations Development Report, 1995; Seabrook, 1996).

Economic Opportunities and Rewards　Despite major gains in education in rich and poor countries alike, women's labor force participation worldwide is only about 40 percent. Nevertheless, women and girls are responsible for two-thirds of hours worked—much of it in farm labor and unwaged, domestic work and community activities. For their efforts, women and girls receive an estimated 10 percent of the world's income and an even smaller share of the world's assets (see Figure 9.2).

Worldwide, the average wage for women is about three-quarters that of the male wage. In the nonagricultural sector women earn far less than that, in some cases, as in Bangladesh, less than half of what men earn. The reason is the same in rich and poor nations alike—occupational segregation, with women occupying mainly low-skill, low-wage, and temporary jobs. But there is more to it than that. Women are also denied access to credit, and in many developing nations women's opportunities are further constrained by unequal property rights, inheritance patterns, and marriage and divorce laws that favor men.

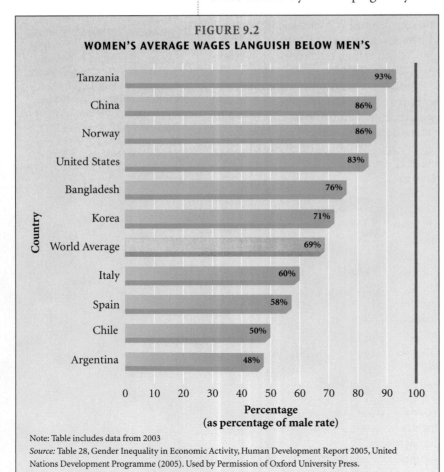

FIGURE 9.2
WOMEN'S AVERAGE WAGES LANGUISH BELOW MEN'S

Country	Percentage (as percentage of male rate)
Tanzania	93%
China	86%
Norway	86%
United States	83%
Bangladesh	76%
Korea	71%
World Average	69%
Italy	60%
Spain	58%
Chile	50%
Argentina	48%

Note: Table includes data from 2003

Source: Table 28, Gender Inequality in Economic Activity, Human Development Report 2005, United Nations Development Programme (2005). Used by Permission of Oxford University Press.

In low-income nations children are exploited as well, and current population trends suggest that the problem may soon grow much worse. According to the United Nations, in Sub-Saharan Africa, where levels of unemployment are currently among the highest in the world, there will be a need for 6 million new jobs (menial, minimal-wage jobs) in the next decade. And as young people enter the labor force India will require more than 100 million jobs. What do you think are the chances that these jobs will materialize?

Conditions are not much better in Latin America. In Mexico, for example, population growth rates have declined from well over 3 percent in the 1960s to about 2 percent today. Nevertheless, almost 40 percent of Mexico's population is under 15 years of age, and most young people are concentrated in the impoverished southern parts of the state—not in the booming industrial north. But even in the booming Maquiladoras where work is steady, young women face rigid gender roles and labor discipline that might include corporate dormitories and literally "a twenty-four hour system of complete regulation" (Cravey, 1998:109).

Literacy Rates and Street Children

On the surface, development statistics show impressive gains in education among developing countries. By the early twenty-first century, more than 80 percent of children were enrolled in primary school, and five out of six of the world's adults were literate, according to the United Nations Development Report in 2003. Yet the same report notes that only slightly over one-half of children attend school in Sub-Saharan Africa and in many developing countries few children ever graduate from primary school. And, the report noted, a gaping gender gap remained: "three-fifths of the 115 million children out of school are girls, and two-thirds of the 876 million illiterate adults are women" (United Nations Development Report, 2003:6).

Illiteracy rates in most middle-income nations are much lower, typically less than 20 percent. However, millions of rural and urban children receive no education whatsoever. In 2003, the United Nations Children's Fund (UNICEF) estimated that a little over one million children were "trafficked" each year—for $6 billion pounds. Europe was the major market, where as many as 500,000 women and young girls were traded or sold, but the trade was not limited to girls. Hundreds of thousands of boys as young as 5 were traded from West Africa, Bangladesh, India, and Pakistan to the Middle East and Europe to work as domestic slaves, herd boys, and in other occupations (Lovell, 2003). Many other poor children are abandoned or leave abusive families and flock to cities to become "street children." Most eke out a desperate living begging and stealing, while others are lured into the world of drugs and prostitution, where they are exposed to violence, disease, and death. Development groups estimate that there are 60–70 million street children globally, most of them in Latin America. Prior to the 1980s, street children were less common in Asia, where children were a productive farming asset. However, the booming cities of Asia now attract thousands of children each day who seek to escape extreme poverty. Many others are sold by poor and drug-addicted parents to proliferating sweatshops and brothels that cater to the booming tourist sex trade that flourishes in many parts of Asia (United Nations, 1993). Thailand's sex tourist industry, for example, expanded from approximately 2 million tourist arrivals in the 1980s to over 7 million in 1996 (Bales, 2002:219).

Life Expectancy and Health

Since the 1950s, life expectancy has improved in low- and middle-income nations. Nevertheless, people in rich nations such as the United States can expect to live around 77 years, compared to 50 years in much of Africa and 40 years in war-torn Afghanistan. Diseases such as smallpox, which once killed 5 million people per year, have been virtually eliminated. In low- and middle-income countries, however, stunted growth, low birth weight, and signs of low-protein diets are common. Infectious and parasitic diseases continue to be the leading causes of death, accounting for about one-half of all deaths—compared to about 1 percent of deaths in high-income industrial nations.

Every year, more than 10 million children die of preventable illnesses—30,000 a day. Likewise, more than 300,000 women die in pregnancy and childbirth, with such deaths 100 times more common in Sub-Saharan African nations than in

Brothels like this one in Vietnam, a low-income nation, are part of the booming global sex trade that attracts poor women and girls who cater to tourists from Japan, the United States, and other wealthy nations.

high-income countries. Moreover, of the 42 million people with HIV/AIDS in the world, 39 million live in developing countries, with Sub-Saharan Africa experiencing the majority of the world's cases. The United Nations points to an "underfunding" of health care in much of the developing world as the root cause of these and other health problems. According to a 2003 report, by the late 1990s, when global economic conditions were promising, "public spending on health in the poorest nations was about $6 per capita ($13 in other low-income nations) compared to $125 in upper-middle-income countries and $1356 in high-income countries (United Nations Development Report, 2003:8).

Even diarrhea, which is caused by drinking polluted water, annually kills millions of children in poor nations. Millions more die in urban areas from acute respiratory infections caused by air pollution. These numbers may dramatically increase in booming cities like Mexico City, where some schools already issue gas masks to children to protect them against carbon monoxide from trucks, autos, and over 35,000 factories (World Bank, 2006).

EXPLAINING GLOBAL STRATIFICATION

Why are some nations rich and others poor? When we ask students this question in class, we usually get two very different responses. Most students from the United States and other Western industrial nations cite abundant resources as the key to national prosperity. Rich nations such as the United States, Britain, and France, they say, have good land, hard workers, and lots of money, and that explains their success. By contrast, nations such as Somalia and Bangladesh have few resources and a great many people—so they are poor.

Students from poor countries have equally strong opinions, but they emphasize power and conflict as being far more important than natural resources. "Rich nations are wealthy because they exploit the poor—that's all there is to it," a black South African student announced in one of our classes. To emphasize his point, he repeated a popular folk expression among black South African miners that he had heard many times in his youth: "The Crown Jewels of the British monarchy were put there by the sweat and blood of the poor; without us, the tiny British Isles would be nothing!" The ideas of both groups are reflected in the functionalist and conflict perspectives in sociology and are represented by modernization, dependency, and world system approaches.

MODERNIZATION THEORY
Recognizes global development as a process in which advanced industrial nations and technology help poor nations advance.

Tibetan monks now use handheld phones. According to modernization theory, Western technology will eventually become commonplace in many low-income nations. The mass media promote the idea that new technologies, like the ones shown here, are universally desired and beneficial everywhere on earth.

Modernization Theory: A Functionalist Approach

For almost a half-century, economists and government officials have explained the conditions of rich and poor nations with modernization theory, which highlights the critical role of technology in national development. Borrowing ideas from evolutionary theory and functionalism, **modernization theory** *recognizes global development as a process in which advanced industrial nations and technology help poor nations advance.*

Most early models emphasized that each nation's rank in the global hierarchy was influenced by *internal factors.* That is, many low-income nations were poor because of some national "deficiency." In some cases, the climate was blamed for producing too much or too little rainfall for economic development. In other cases, modernization theorists pointed to poor soil or a terrain that impeded modern farming, the building of roads or deep seaports, and the economic infrastructure necessary for industrialization and trade. Political factors were cited as well. Many poor nations were said to be held back by political corruption and "warlords," who wasted money and drained wealth from the business sector.

Some modernization theorists also blamed traditional customs and institutions for the slow progress of many poor nations. In some cases, religion and otherworldly concerns were seen as special impediments to progress. For example, many blamed religious authorities in poor countries for excessive spending on "nonproductive" religious buildings and festivals that might have been used for business growth. In others, "irrational" commitments to kin and children were said to squander capital and deplete national surpluses.

Still others blamed a culture of poverty that supposedly was common among the urban poor everywhere in the world. As noted in Chapter 8, the culture of poverty was said to include an extreme orientation to the present, apathy, and waste that some development officials believed severely retarded poor people's (and poor nations') ability to build capital. Some modernization theorists argued that if people in developing countries would adopt a more individualistic approach and a strong work ethnic, it would be hard for them not to save money and advance (Lewis, 1966).

Contemporary modernization theorists have rejected many of these views. Modernization produces a shift in values from more absolute norms and values to those that are increasingly rational. However, Western and American values are not the only path to global development. Studies have shown that under some circumstances—as in the Pacific Rim—traditional values, such as paternalistic management, authoritarian rule, and an emphasis on the group, may boost rather than retard economic progress. Perhaps no nation supports this thesis better than Singapore, which until recently has had one prime minister for more than 30 years, and whose rigid authoritarian rule guided the nation from a poor agrarian nation to one of the most advanced, high-tech nations in Asia (So, 1990; McCord, 1991; Inglehart and Baker, 2000).

Subsequent studies maintain that modernization depends on a variety of factors, both internal and external. In addition to national efforts to industrialize in the Pacific Rim, the United States and Britain have exerted key roles in modernization by shifting huge amounts of capital and arms to South Korea, Taiwan, and other allies in the area. This new emphasis on geopolitics and external factors has led to a possible convergence of modernization theory and several major conflict theories that stress how global development is strongly influenced by economic competition and power (McCord, 1991; So and Chiu, 1996).

Conflict Approaches to Global Inequality

Many people in developed nations see international trade and development in positive terms. In much of the Southern Hemisphere popular opinion is more mixed, and large segments of the public in low-income nations insist that a legacy of colonialism and imperialism is largely responsible for their lack of advancement. According to this view, poor nations are not poor because of a lack of resources or internal factors, but because of unequal relations with powerful neighbors like the United States, Japan, and European nations.

Colonialism and Imperialism

The capitalist world economy and global social hierarchy originated during the sixteenth century, when Britain, Spain, and other European powers used superior militaries and "gunboat diplomacy" to subjugate and dominate smaller, weaker societies in the Southern Hemisphere. Gradually, they incorporated their economies to suit their needs. This system is called **colonialism,** *an economic and political system in which powerful nations dominate and exploit weaker ones in trade and other relations.* Early on, the basic colonial pattern was established in Africa, India, and the Americas. After conquest, government or business agents were appointed to regulate and tax indigenous farmers and shift large agricultural surpluses and raw materials from south to north. Where conditions were favorable, colonial agents also created plantations with slave labor to raise coffee, sugar, rubber, and other tropical products for export.

COLONIALISM
An economic and political system in which powerful nations dominate and exploit weaker ones in trade and other relations.

The Industrial Revolution—especially advances in transportation and military technologies—widened the gap between the global haves and have-nots even further. By the nineteenth century, the colonial system was shifting so much wealth from south to north that colonies had become fundamental to European economies and their citizens' living standards. European nations sought to expand their colonies through conquest in order to absorb ever larger territories from their rivals. By late in the century, to avert war and economic chaos, European powers carved up most of the Southern Hemisphere among themselves. For example, at the Berlin Conference of 1887, each of the major European powers literally put their flags on a giant map of Africa and claimed sole rights to the minerals, labor, and everything else in "their" territories. A decade later, in the Spanish American War, the United States too became an imperial power by defeating Spain and forcing it to surrender most of its colonies in the Pacific, Latin America, and the Caribbean (Kerbo, 1991).

By this time mineral resources had become especially important, and they too were extracted in the same profitable formula that had been used in the plantation economy. European colonial powers used cheap labor and low-cost technologies to extract tin, gold, and other raw materials, which they then shipped to industrial mills in their home countries for processing into more expensive consumer goods. The finished products were then sold back to the colonies at many times the cost of the raw materials (Berberoglu, 1992; 1994).

One of the authors lived in a tin-mining area of Nigeria, where this centuries-old pattern was very obvious. When he traveled about the area, he saw low-tech plants to dig tin out of the ground but could find no manufacturing plants to make tin pots and pans, tin roofing, or any other high-profit–high-wage enterprises. Moreover, colonial powers wasted no money on infrastructure in Nigeria or other colonies unless it was directly related to extracting and shipping raw materials. Consequently, while there were good roads and electricity in the mining districts, beyond them there were few traces of modernization.

Beginning in the 1950s, with national liberation movements throughout the world, the colonial system began to be dismantled. By the 1970s leaders in most developing nations had assumed political control of their territories. Independence movements, however, did not fundamentally alter the global political economy. According to conflict theorists, in the new system, which some have called *neocolonialism*, advanced industrial nations use economic clout in trade, finance, and business, rather than direct political and military intervention, to maintain their privileged position in the world economy. Conflict theorists argue that although they may be more subtle than in the past, dependency relations remain fundamental to contemporary forms of global stratification.

Dependency Theory   **Dependency theory** *maintains that rich industrialized nations keep poor countries from advancing through various dependency relationships.* One scholar maintains that three international organizations—the International Monetary Fund (IMF), The World Bank, and the World Trade Organization (WTO), all dominated by the most advanced industrial nations—are fundamental to "globalization" and unequal relations between rich and poor nations (Stiglitz, 2002). According to dependency theorists, wealthy nations use such things as foreign aid, weapons and military assistance, and educational grants to cultivate alliances and dependency relations. Today, three of the most important forms of dependency are trade, industrial, and investment dependency.

1. *Trade Dependency: A Continuation of Colonialism.* Industrial nations perpetuate former colonial patterns by purchasing raw materials—coffee, sugar, and minerals—at the lowest possible prices and then processing them at home and selling the finished products back to developing nations at many times the cost of the agricultural produce or raw materials. Trade dependence also is sustained by most favored nation treaties and other agreements that facilitate trade among wealthy nations—but are not extended to poor nations.

2. *Industrial Dependency: The Corporate Search for Advantage.* Corporations establish factories in the Southern Hemisphere to take advantage of cheap labor, gain access to local markets, gain tax advantages, and circumvent environmental and other govern-

DEPENDENCY THEORY
Maintains that rich industrialized nations keep poor countries from advancing through various dependency relationships.

ment regulations in their home countries. Some relationships between poor nations and corporations have been mutually beneficial. In others, capital for factories and other improvements is raised by diverting funds from agriculture and the development of domestic enterprises, while most of the profits end up in rich nations.

3. *Investment Dependency: Vicious Cycles of Credit and Debt.* International financial institutions also contribute to dependency relations, since over one-half of the World Bank's lending capital is supplied by a handful of major industrial and postindustrial nations. For nations such as Mexico and Brazil—with debts ranging from $100 to $130 billion—this means most of their export earnings are used to service debts rather than to provide for development or citizens' needs. In the past two decades, Western banks and the International Monetary Fund have alternated between policies of liberal credit followed by draconian measures to reduce debts. These austerity measures have retarded development and have been inconvenient for the rich. However, they have had a devastating impact on the lives of the poor, producing widespread poverty and periods of starvation.

World System Theory **World system theory** *maintains that all nations are part of a worldwide division of labor.* This conflict approach was developed by economist Immanuel Wallerstein (1974, 1984). He contends that since the sixteenth century all nations have been part of a capitalist world economy. According to Wallerstein, just as some people have more wealth, power, and prestige than others, so do nations in international commerce and trade. Wallerstein terms those highly industrialized nations that are headquarters for the world's major corporations and banks *core nations.* Nations like the United States and Japan are similar to the upper class in that they receive the lion's share of the world's income and most other benefits from their privileged position at the heart of the global economy. *Semiperiphery nations* occupy the next level. Nations like Saudi Arabia and Brazil that are moving toward industrialization and a diversified economy have midlevel participation in the world economy, and they benefit accordingly. *Periphery nations,* such as Ethiopia and Afghanistan, are at the very edge of the world economy; since they have very little to offer it, they get the least.

One of the major advantages of the *world system model* is its portrayal of the global economy as a dynamic system. Today, most nations have been incorporated into the world economy, but ties with nations can be loosened or even terminated. Global political stratification is especially important. Western nation-states dominate global networks and organizations and play a disproportionate role in "setting policy agendas, framing international debates, and enacting policies that benefit their interests" (Beckfield, 2003:404). While many non-Western states are excluded from full organizational participation because of major "cultural and geopolitical fault-lines," a growing list of nations are choosing to remain apart or are actively resisting incorporation—at least on terms set by core nations (Beckfield, 2003:404). Likewise, economic shifts and cycles of expansion and stagnation have created conditions for social mobility among nations. This is especially true in recent decades with the rise of giant corporations. Focus box 9.1 takes a closer look at globalization and one author's thesis of why it has produced conflict and violence among many developing countries.

TRANSNATIONAL CORPORATIONS: THE MAKING OF NEW "HAVES" AND "HAVE-NOTS"

For most of the twentieth century, development was associated with individual nations and their efforts to industrialize and advance. But giant global corporations are changing this formula. Today, these transnational corporations have expanded beyond national boundaries and their actions and decisions are becoming increasingly important in the distribution of global income and wealth.

Transnational corporations are *corporations that own companies and search for profits all over the globe.* The major companies that you see daily in television advertisements—McDonald's, Coca-Cola, Toyota, and Nike—are transnational corporations. If you doubt the influence and power of corporate giants today, consider this: if we were to rank the top organizations according to their wealth, half would be nations and the

WORLD SYSTEM THEORY
Maintains that all nations are part of a worldwide division of labor.

TRANSNATIONAL CORPORATIONS
Corporations that own companies and search for profits all over the globe.

During the 1990s, proponents of globalization, free markets, and democracy predicted that these "inevitable forces" would soon usher in an era of peace and prosperity for rich and poor nations alike. In her book, *World on Fire,* Yale law professor Amy Chua proposes some of the reasons why just the opposite occurred. She contends that the global spread of markets and democracy, which many in the West see as a "cure for poverty and ethnic violence," "is the principal aggravating cause of group hatred and ethnic violence throughout the non-Western world." Chua's special focus of the book is on ethnic violence that has impacted her own family. Her Aunt Leona, her father's twin sister, who was a member of the wealthy Chinese minority in the Philippines, was murdered by her chauffeur in 1994. While money and jewels were stolen from her aunt's hacienda-style house, the entry in the police report listed "revenge" as the motive for the murder (Chua, 2003:5). According to Chua, her aunt was a casualty of a struggle between "market-dominant ethnic minorities" whose vast fortunes dramatically expanded during the 1990s' economic boom, and poor majorities like most Filipinos, who live on less than $2 a day and who experience few of the benefits of globalization.

In the current globalization push, the United States and other advanced industrial nations favor raw "laissez-faire" capitalism, which the West abandoned years ago. While globalization and unfettered markets have indeed benefitted millions and raised living standards in some developing nations, they have also concentrated fabulous wealth in the hands of "market-dominant minorities" along with their foreign-investor partners. For example, in the Philippines an already rich Chinese minority, which comprises 1 percent of the population, controls 80 percent of the nation's wealth. Likewise, the Chinese comprise only 3 percent of the Indonesian population but control "70 percent of the private economy" (Chua, 2003:6). Ethnic minorities hold or recently held similar shares of wealth in many Latin American countries, Nigeria, South Africa, Zimbabwe, Sierra Leone, Rwanda, and other nations. And, if the designation is broadened to include small ruling elites and even the United States, which is seen by many as "the world's market-dominant minority," the list would be expanded.

Introducing democracy (immediate elections and universal suffrage) under these circumstances rarely transforms voters into "co-citizens in a national community." Instead, the competition for votes and power tends to set the stage for antimarket pressures and results in confiscation of property and wealth, social unrest, authoritarian backlash, and popular violence. It may also produce demagogues, who scapegoat resented minorities and foment active ethnonationalist movements against "outsiders," demanding that the nation's wealth and identity be reclaimed by the rightful owners of the land—the people (Chua, 2003:10). For elites, democracy has very different meanings. In the elite version of "democracy" there would be a very gradual process of majority inclusion "but always with overriding concern for the stability of property rights, foreign investment, and the status quo" (Chua, 2003:260). Global market-dominant minorities like the United States view democracy in much the same way—and believe that its reach should be limited "within individual countries." As Chua (2003:260) put it, "Does the U.S. desire 'true world democracy', in which our economic and political fate is determined by the majority of the world's countries or citizens?"

How would Chua address these problems—especially where tiny ethnic minorities dominate national economies? She proposes several immediate plans that would address the most glaring market and political imbalances. Eliminating political favoritism, monopolies, and other economically corrupt practices that favor elites and foreign investors would be a start. Likewise, government interventions in the market, like Malaysia's sweeping ethnic quota system that gave different groups a share of equity ownership, land, commercial employment, and participation in many other areas, would improve the conditions of the poor as well. So would giving people a stakehold in land and corporate ownership. In developing countries, tax and transfer programs would provide some help, but in many countries, formal, legally defensible property rights, including squatters' legal titles, would be even more useful. But, as Chua (2003:266) noted, change from the "top down" has been "notoriously unsuccessful." According to Chua (2003:278), the best hope for global free-market democracy lies with market-dominant minorities themselves. They must expand voluntary generosity and end decades or even centuries-old patterns of insularity and indifference. She concludes that by applying this formula to the United States:

> Rightly or wrongly, for millions of people around the world, the World Trade Center symbolized greed, exploitation, indifference, and cultural humiliation. Against a background of growing U.S. wealth, relative to the size of our economy, the U.S. has the smallest aid budget of any advanced country. Perhaps America should try to turn symbolism around in our favor. There is no longer promise in retreating into isolationism . . . It is difficult to see, in any event, how a little generosity and humility could possibly hurt. (Chua, 2003:288)

TAKING A CLOSER LOOK

What do you think of Chua's remedies for the future of free-market democracy? If you agree, provide some of the reasons why you think her plan might work—both at the national and global levels. If you disagree, discuss some of the reasons why her plan may not work. You might want to focus on some of the key players that may be missing in her proposal—or as conflict theorists' claim, examine "structural flaws" in the system.

Source: Amy Chua. *World on Fire: How Exporting Free Market Democracy Breeds Ethnic Hatred and Global Instability.* New York: Doubleday, 2003.

other half would be corporations. Put another way, the top 25 global corporations are richer than the majority of nations on earth. See Table 9.3 for a comparison of corporate and national wealth.

Most large corporations such as Ford, Colgate-Palmolive, and General Electric earn half or more of their revenues from sales outside the United States, and joint ventures with overseas corporations are now routine. For example, Ford Motor Company owns 33 percent of Mazda stock and General Motors Corporation owns more than 40 percent of Isuzu of Japan. Foreign corporations have an equally large stake in American businesses. For example, Smith & Wesson, whose pistols helped tame the American West, is now owned by the British, and a German firm owns Allis-Chalmers tractors. A Japanese firm owns the Las Vegas Dunes Hotel, and "foreigners" own 46 percent of downtown Los Angeles, 36 percent of Houston's urban property, and 21 percent of Manhattan (Phillips, 1990). Globalization seems to be producing scores of global transnational mergers—including Daimler-Chrysler in 1998. "The largest target of the global M & A [mergers and acquisitions] binge has been the United States. In 1999 foreigners paid $233 billion to buy American companies" (Samuelson, 2000:55).

With globalization and multinational corporations, Fords and Chevys are as common throughout Europe and Asia as they are in the United States, and even Great Britain's luxury Jaguar has made its way to Asian nations.

Corporations and the New Global Assembly Line

A brief excursion to the local supermarket or mall reveals the presence of these new directors of the "global assembly line." In the new international division of labor, corporations have broken down the process of production into various work operations, which are then located wherever goods and labor are cheapest—typically in low-income nations or depressed areas in industrial nations. As in the earlier colonial system, however, control of the process and most profits are channeled to corporate headquarters in high-income nations (Ehrenreich and Fuentes, 1997).

For example, with the help of transnationals, florists in the United States now grow flowers in Latin America, use Madison Avenue to market them, and sell them at thousands of supermarkets across the globe. Likewise, your credit card transactions may be made locally, but they may be processed as far away as India or the Caribbean. An increasing share of the fruits you eat and orange juice you drink is imported from Brazil and other countries in the Southern Hemisphere. Most of the juice is, in fact, reconstituted from concentrates—"Only the water, added to the concentrate, is local" (Bonanno et al., 1994:11).

Likewise, "made in America" labels now mean that autos, refrigerators, running shoes, and dresses are "assembled" in America. Most product components have their origins in many nations. This is because, in the past decade or so, American corporations have increased their investments abroad and have farmed out operations to countless smaller dealers across the globe. For example, while the Boeing 777 is assembled in Everett, Washington, the main body of the aircraft is manufactured by Mitsubishi in Kobe, Japan, and scores of companies in 12 different countries also contribute to the finished product (Greider, 1997). In fact, "by the early 1990s, about a fifth of the total output of American firms was being produced by non-Americans outside America" (The Economist, 1998f:4).

Emerging global banks, insurance companies, and credit agencies are fundamental to the global assembly line as well. Every day many trillions of dollars are exchanged across global computerized networks, altering personal and national fortunes. Most of this exchange is between wealthy nations, or from rich countries to a handful of emerging economies like those in East and Southeast Asia. Capital transfers to poor nations have been much rarer. Moreover, because of high rates of return in rich nations, many business owners and elites in poor nations prefer to put their capital in U.S. and European banks, rather than recycle profits and wealth into their own economies. This might have disastrous consequences for the poor, were it not for the billions of dollars in capital transfers that immigrant workers currently send every year from industrial to developing nations (Braun, 1991; Rumbault, 1995).

TABLE 9.3
CORPORATE AND NATIONAL WEALTH

WORLD'S 25 COMPANIES WITH THE LARGEST MARKET VALUE ($ IN BILLIONS)		SELECTED NATIONS AND THEIR GROSS NATIONAL INCOME ($ IN BILLIONS)	
1. ExonnMobil (U.S.)	362.53	1. United States	11,013
2. General Electric (U.S.)	348.45	2. Japan	4,361
3. Microsoft (U.S.)	279.02	3. Germany	2,086
4. Citigroup (U.S.)	230.93	4. United Kingdom	1,680
5. BP (U.K.)	225.93	5. France	1,522
6. Royal Dutch/Shell Group (Netherlands)	203.52	6. China	1,417
7. Proctor & Gamble (U.S.)	197.12	7. Italy	1,243
8. HSBC Group (U.K.)	193.32	8. Canada	774
9. Pfizer (U.S.)	192.05	9. Spain	701
10. Wal-Mart Stores (U.S.)	188.86	10. Mexico	637
11. Saudi Basic Inds. (Saudi Arabia)	184.73	11. India	571
12. Gazprom (Russia)	184.37	12. Brazil	480
13. Bank of America (U.S.)	184.17	13. Australia	437
14. Toyota Motor (Japan)	175.54	14. Netherlands	426
15. American International Group (U.S.)	172.24	15. Russia	375
16. PetroChina (China)	172.23	16. Switzerland	299
17. Johnson & Johnson (U.S.)	171.51	17. Sweden	259
18. Total (France)	154.74	18. Saudi Arabia	208
19. Altria Group (U.S.)	149.57	19. Poland	202
20. GlaxoSmithKline (U.K.)	147.42	20. Turkey	198
21. JPMorgan Chase (U.S.)	144.13	21. Hong Kong	176
22. Mitsubishi UFJ Finl (Japan)	143.01	22. Iran	133
23. Berkshire Hathaway (U.S.)	133.67	23. Egypt	94
24. Roche Group (Switzerland)	127.51	24. Pakistan	78
25. Chevron (U.S.)	126.80	25. Ethiopia	6

Source: From *Forbes Global 2000*, www.forbes.com. Reprinted by Permission of Forbes Magazine © 2007 Forbes Media LLC.

Note: Data is from 2003.

Source: Table 1327, Gross National Income by Country, 1990 and 2003; U.S. Census Bureau, *Statistical Abstract of the United States:* 2006.

Another social trend that may adversely affect low- and middle-income nations is the rapid growth of the global credit card industry. Today, emerging middle classes in Brazil, Indonesia, and many other parts of the world are purchasing so many goods on credit that they have accumulated a huge private debt. Much of this is driven by recent advances in global telecommunications that have enabled corporate advertisers to induce consumers in rich and poor nations alike to spend more money than they have, often for goods and services they may not need or even want (Ritzer, 1995). Given the nature of stratification, can you predict who will bear the major burden of this debt?

Media, Corporations, and Inequality

During the 1970s, as European nations surrendered their few remaining colonies in the Southern Hemisphere, Western corporations initiated a major drive to market films and television shows and to create new consumers for their products. One researcher claims that the giant media are "transforming the public sphere into an

Transnational
Corporations: The
Making of New
"Haves" and
"Have-Nots"

247

increasingly denationalized, visual and emotional public stage" (Urry, 2000:201). Because of a history of colonialism, it is not surprising that many leaders in newly independent nations saw the media invasion as a potential new way for rich nations to dominate the poor. So they joined forces to create the New World Information and Communication Order (NWICO), which has as its goal "the decolonization of information," as well as collective efforts to limit media offerings from advanced industrial nations and monitor negative media stereotypes (Merrill and Dennis, 1996). In 2003, prior to the World Trade Organization meeting, representatives from over 35 countries met to campaign for preservation of a "cultural exception" to free-trade agreements that would permit dozens of countries to subsidize national media to compete with American media. They also sought to "promote adoption of a global convention on a cultural diversity by UNESCO as a way to remove 'culture' from the World Trade Organization" (Riding, 2003:1).

Global Stratification and the Mass Media   So far these efforts have produced few results. In fact, the end of the Cold War, advances in telecommunication technologies, and a 1997 global telecommunications agreement that effectively ended national restrictions on "foreign ownership" of high-tech media have made Western media more accessible and influential than ever. Today, fewer than 10 telecommunications firms, including Time Warner (CNN), News Corporation, Disney, and a few other communication giants, control much of the information and entertainment that global audiences receive. In the past few decades, even countries with well-developed media such as England and France have felt the impact of media conglomerates Time Warner, Viacom, and Disney. American movies take in nearly 80 percent of the film industry's worldwide profits, and even in France, which has a well-developed media industry and a traditional "belief in native cultural superiority," Hollywood movies account for between 50 to 70 percent of annual box office receipts (Gabler, 2003:1).

This is not to say, however, that corporate messages reign supreme everywhere. As in the United States, there are alternative media, and people may change channels or turn off the TV when they encounter offensive messages. In countries such as China, regional television and radio shows from nearby Taiwan and Hong Kong are much more important than Hollywood in defining the good life and possibilities for the future (Ong and Nonini, 1997). One media scholar noted that while the United States can claim 75 percent of global TV exports, "regionalization of markets is growing" (Barker, 1999:53).

Perhaps because of anti-American sentiment, a general resentment of American cultural dominance, or even the new "niche programming" trend in television, people in countries as diverse as Malaysia, France, and Latin America are watching less American television programs than they did just a few years ago. As Neal Gabler (2003:1) wrote, American television shows like *Dallas* and *Baywatch* dominated prime-time viewing in Europe and Asia for decades. Now "top-rated shows in the U.S. like *C.S.I.* cannot attract even 3 percent of the viewers in South Korea," and other shows "have been consigned to the late-night fringes of the schedule."

In addition, people around the world may interpret the "news" and popular television shows in ways that disagree with the intended message. They may even redefine these shows to reinforce rather than challenge traditional beliefs, values, and customs. Further, new information technologies have begun to provide much greater possibilities for the free exchange of information. In China, as in the rest of the world, the Internet and other media offer people the opportunity to "shut off state messages and wander imaginatively across the globe" (Ong and Nonini, 1997:311). Focus box 9.2 discusses more practical benefits of the Internet in some of the poorest regions of India.

Technomedia and Global Stratification   Global stratification operates on the Web as well. Of the more than 60 million subscribers to the World Wide Web, most inhabit wealthy industrial nations, and most are members of the upper-middle and upper classes. A survey in the mid-1990s found that two-thirds of Internet users lived in North America, and the majority were university-educated with average incomes of about $60,000. By contrast, Algeria had 16 registered users, Bulgaria had 639, and only 11 of 54 African nations had Internet access. By the twenty-first century there was some

In 2003 the United Nations Development Report noted that slightly more than 40 percent of India's 1 billion people were illiterate. But India is also the home of some of the most advanced computer firms in the world, and the media has dubbed New Delhi "Silicon Valley East" (*PBS Frontline/World*, 2003). In 2000, *Frontline/World* on PBS and network newsmagazines touted a novel government and business experiment, called "Hole-in-the-Wall," that introduced computers and the Internet to street children from one of New Delhi's poorest slums. The project was initiated by Sugata Mitra, a researcher for an Indian software and education company, who took a PC and placed it in a concrete wall that separates the company's grounds from a garbage-strewn empty lot that had been used by street children as a public bathroom. Later, five outdoor kiosks were added, along with computer monitors protruding through holes in the wall. Each was equipped with specially designed joysticks and buttons that substituted for computer mouses. There were no teachers and no instructions on computers—the street kids had to learn basic computer skills and decide how to go on-line and use software programs (Peterson, 2000).

Experimenters and global media hailed the Hole-in-the-Wall experiment "as a groundbreaking model on how to bring India's and even the world's poor into the Internet Age" (Warschauer, 2003:1). If street kids could teach themselves the rudiments of computers within days and find out what is happening in the world on the Internet, then global illiteracy might be eradicated; or, as Mitra told *PBS Frontline World,* perhaps "it will have changed our world forever." In studying the experiment, Mark Warschauer (2003:2) is less sanguine. He contends that "Internet access was of little use because it seldom functioned." Further, while the children did learn to use the joysticks and buttons, since no instructors or educational programs were available and the content was in English, not the children's native Hindi, "almost all their time was spent drawing with paint programs or playing computer games" (Warschauer, 2003:2). In an interview with *BusinessWeek Online* editor Thane Peterson, Mitra himself noted other potential problems that poor kids might encounter. One is access to e-mail: "I'm really seriously scared about what would happen if suddenly the whole wide world had access to the kids. I don't know who would talk to them and for what purpose" (Peterson, 2000:7).

While it received little media attention, Warshauer discovered another Internet experiment in India, called the Gyan-doot Project (which in Hindi means "purveyor of knowledge") that may truly benefit the world's poor. The experiment was conducted in Dhar villages in the rural district of Madhya Pradesh—the second poorest state in India, where illiteracy is high and 60 percent of the population live below the poverty line. The project was initiated by local government officials, without the aid of corporations, foreign donors, or international agencies to enhance local development. Like the Hole-in-the-Wall project, kiosks and computers were placed throughout the district for the benefit of the rural poor. But unlike the urban experiment, these kiosks were owned by local entrepreneurs, who helped villagers by selling them Internet information and services. Warschauer (2003:179) remarks, "the principle exception to this is the large number of children, who are sent by their parents for individualized computer instruction from the kiosk managers."

Warschauer (2003) notes that in this experiment a special districtwide intranet in the Hindi language was created for the rural poor that included land deeds, government records, and tax information. There was also a section on "e-education," that included educational quizzes, math puzzles, career guidance information, and other practical information. Most important is the process of communication that allows poor farmers two-way communication with government agencies and economic and social services. Farmers can now sell cows and bicycles on-line, there is an "online matrimonial service, and an online complaint service with a pull-down menu with categories such as: non-payment of services, school district teacher absent, hand pump or transformer not working" (Warschauer, 2003:181). Warschauer offers the Gyandoot Project as a notable experiment in "e-governance"; with schools, as well as with hand pumps, villagers now feel they are in a position to defend their rights" (Warschauer, 2003:179).

TAKING A CLOSER LOOK

Warschauer clearly favors the Gyandoor Project over the Hole-in-the-Wall experiment. Critically examine what you believe are both the potential benefits and problems associated with each Internet experiment's attempt to alter the lives of India's poor.

Source: Thane Peterson. "A Lesson in Computer Literacy from India's Poorest Kids." *Business Week Online,* Daily Briefing, edited by Paul Judge, March 2, 2000:1–7. Mark Warschauer. *Technology and Social Inclusion: Rethinking the Digital Divide.* Cambridge, MA: MIT Press, 2003.

improvement. Around 5 percent of the world's population had Internet access but more than 60 percent of the on-line population was in North America alone. Or, put another way, while developing countries accounted for 85 percent of the world's population, they had "only 20 percent of Internet users" (Chen, Boase, and Wellman, 2002:78). Moreover, there were substantial differences in Internet use within developing countries. China, for example, had more than 20 million Internet users, but most of them were highly educated, young, urban, single males. And some parts of the the globe, like Africa, still had fewer Internet users than New York, Tokyo, and even "fewer e-mail addresses allocated to it than the Massachusetts Institute of Technology" (Chen, Boase, and Wellman, 2002:78). Moreover, many nations, both low- and high-income, have begun to restrict access to the Internet and monitor and censure discussions and messages (Wellman et al., 1996; Jensen, 2000). In 2003, to stem the tide of American and English media, the French government even banned the use of the term *e-mail*, substituting the French "courrier."

Nevertheless, the Internet is a growing force for free expression. For example, the Chinese government periodically closes down on-line sites and tries to filter out information it does not like, like blocking all e-mail containing the word "Falon Gong." But, as one corporate security expert noted, "like all attempts to control the Internet, newer technologies will eventually defeat it" (Crampton, 2002:3). Because electronic networks produce conditions that cannot be controlled, they may encourage democratic practices. Moreover, they may provide grassroots movements with powerful new means of contestation and resistance (Sassen 1998).

Take a moment to browse the Web for global sites and you will discover websites that deal with global inequality. An easy way to start is to use Yahoo!, Google, or another major search vehicle and enter <global inequality>. Another way to find information is to use a gopher that links related websites. A human rights or social justice gopher will give you access to up-to-date information from groups such as Amnesty International and the Children's Freedom Network. Women's Net and the Human Rights Internet provide up-to-the-minute information on the conditions of men, women, and children around the world.

Corporations, Diversity, and a World on the Move

The ascendancy of transnational corporations has also accelerated mobility patterns at every level of the global socioeconomic system. According to economist Jeremy Brecher (1999:vii):

> When corporations and private wealth can move without regulation in the global free market, work forces, communities, and countries are forced to attract footloose capital. The result has been called a "race to the bottom" in which environmental standards, social protections, and incomes are drawn down toward those of the poorest and most desperate.

The upper classes from rich and poor nations alike conduct business in New York and Switzerland one day, shop in Paris or London the next, and ski in Colorado and visit with upper-class friends from Indonesia, Mexico, and Hong Kong during the remainder of the week. In terms of life chances and lifestyles, those at the top share much more in common with each other than they do with most citizens in their home countries.

The same is true of high-level managers, highly skilled technicians, and other professionals who may live in one nation but work in many, setting up computer networks, solving organizational problems, and performing other tasks wherever their services are required. Even though unskilled labor—and the world's poor—are much less mobile than capital or the upper classes, they too have become "immensely more mobile" in the transnational phase of the world economy (Bonanno et al., 1994:16).

For the most part, migration has been in two major directions: from rural to urban areas in developing nations and—globally—from the Southern to the Northern Hemisphere. Although peasants have been moving from farms to cities for centuries, during the past two decades they have done so at unprecedented rates. In some cases, agribusinesses have replaced people with machines and impoverished peasants have been forced from their homes and villages. In others, the hope of better wages in the new factories that have cropped up all over the world have been the primary magnets (Mingione and Pugliese, 1994).

Millions of poor farmers have moved to cities in the past decade, but no part of the world can compare to China, where 100 million people have moved from the countryside to cities and coastal areas in pursuit of the new factory jobs. Many of them constitute a "floating population" of unskilled laborers, who move from job to job and from city to city. Economic and

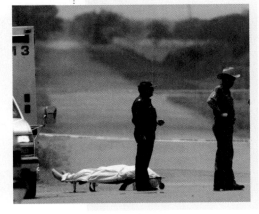

Desperate for jobs, some Mexican immigrants risk everything in the back of trucks that have neither food nor, in this case, oxygen, which can have tragic results, as this photo shows.

political instability around the world has affected the global refugee population as well. In 1970, the world's refugee population stood at about 3 million. Today, the number is closer to 30 million refugees, and millions more are classified as "displaced people": they reside in their home countries but are always on the move, driven from place to place by civil wars, ethnic animosities, and other factors.

The activities of transnational corporations also have contributed to population shifts from south to north. Historically, most population movements were cross-border movements, or from colonies to European metropolitan centers. Today, migration has become large-scale, long-distance, and increasingly illegal, as wealthy nations erect more and more barriers to emigration. Great migrant streams of tens of millions of undocumented workers annually shift back and forth from poor countries to North American and European cities in search of jobs and opportunities. See Figure 9.3 for foreign labor force as a percentage of the total population in various industrial nations.

Paul Ong and colleagues (1994) contend that *global cities* are another product of corporate activities. These cities are emerging focal points of world finance, trade, and communication, which has made them more prosperous and more socially diverse than other cities—those of both past and present. For example, Miami has expanded its financial and trade links to many Latin American nations and has attracted so many people from Cuba, South America, and the Caribbean that it is sometimes called the "capital of Latin America" (Portes and Stepick, 1993).

New York City and Los Angeles serve similar roles in the emerging global economy. Both cities attract professionals from Egypt, India, Korea, Hong Kong, and scores of other emerging nations. But their numbers do not compare to the millions of immigrants and undocumented workers who move north to serve professionals and the rich as housekeepers, nannies, dog walkers, maids, garment workers, and in many other minimum-wage jobs with no benefits (Baubock, 1994; Mahler, 1995). Focus box 9.3 takes a closer look at the growing number of immigrants working in Los Angeles's booming sweatshop industry. Many powerful cities also exist in Europe and Asia, including London, Paris, Tokyo, Zurich, and Hong Kong.

Transnational activities provide many benefits in both developed and developing countries. In emerging countries alone, more than 30 million people have found steady employment in high-tech industries in the past few decades. Yet they constitute less than

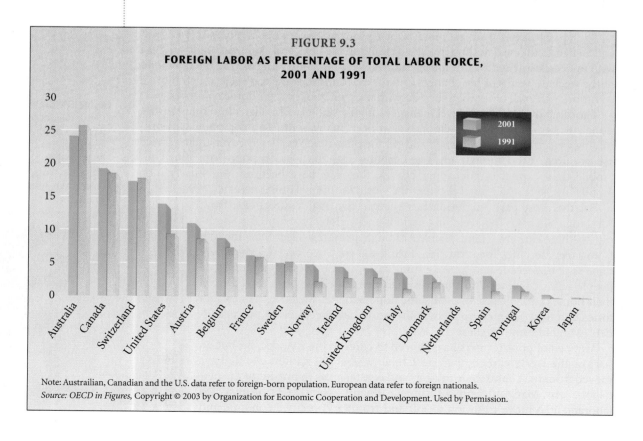

FIGURE 9.3

FOREIGN LABOR AS PERCENTAGE OF TOTAL LABOR FORCE, 2001 AND 1991

Note: Austrailian, Canadian and the U.S. data refer to foreign-born population. European data refer to foreign nationals.
Source: OECD in Figures, Copyright © 2003 by Organization for Economic Cooperation and Development. Used by Permission.

Much has been written about sweatshops overseas and the terrible conditions that workers face in China, Southeast Asia, and many other developing nations. In their book *Behind the Label,* Edna Bonacich and Richard Appelbaum (2000) describe how globalization is leading to a revival of sweatshops in many large cities in the United States as well—especially in Los Angeles.

Bonacich and Appelbaum (2000:3) define "sweatshops" as factories that engage in multiple violations of the law. Typically, these companies fail to pay the minimum wage or overtime, offer no benefits, and violate workplace health and safety regulations, often threatening workers with serious injury or even death. By this definition the majority of Los Angeles garment factories would qualify as sweatshops. According to a 1997 survey and a U.S. Department of Labor survey conducted the following year, 61 percent of garment-making firms were found to be violating wage and hour regulations, and 96 percent were found to be in violation of health and safety regulations (Bonacich and Appelbaum, 2000:3).

Few Americans are aware that Los Angeles is a manufacturing leader in the United States or that the apparel industry is the largest of all manufacturers in Los Angeles, employing one in five manufacturing employees. Most of the 122,000 workers are immigrants from virtually everywhere on the globe. The vast majority are women (72 percent of sewing machine operators), and Mexican immigrants constitute nearly half of all workers. Moreover, as researchers found, many are dark-skinned, with an Indian rather than Spanish heritage, and occupy lower-status positions both in their home countries and on the shop floor.

The authors interviewed 46 people during the early 1990s about working conditions and wages. Perhaps surprising to many Americans, they found that although wages were somewhat better than abroad, working conditions often differed little from those of developing nations. In the early 1990s, for example, Los Angeles garment workers averaged $7,200 a year, with men taking home around $8,160 and women earning $6,500.

In 1995 the media described the deplorable conditions at the El Monte factory east of downtown Los Angeles, where immigrants from Thailand worked 80 hours a week at $2.00 per hour, virtually enslaved behind barbed-wire fences. Such conditions are extreme, but harsh working conditions are the norm in the industry. Most immigrant workers toil in old high-rise office buildings that were not constructed for manufacturing. Consequently, the vast majority of factories are dirty, dangerous, and overcrowded. People rarely get breaks—even for visits to the restroom—and the noise levels are extreme, including shouts and threats by foremen, who harass and intimidate

women sewing machine operators. Bonacich and Appelbaum (2000:192) mention one interview in which a woman told the story of a Mexican girl's last day at work:

> The manager shouted at her all day long. . . . Finally, the manager shouted close to her ear and it shocked her. She screamed, and then she started crying. . . . She stood up, grabbed her purse, and she left. She never came back or said anything, just like everybody does.

Have sweatshops come full-circle with globalization, returning to the United States a century after they originated in large American cities such as New York and Los Angeles? And are they throwbacks to the earliest stages of the Industrial Revolution? The authors think not. Contemporary sweatshops are both old and new, according to Bonacich and Appelbaum (2000:3). Working conditions have improved little, but technology and the global reach of the industry have encouraged the proliferation of sweatshops in both developing and developed countries. Further, these trends have brought dramatic changes that have conspired against those at the bottom of the international labor economy. The changes include the global expansion of the wealth and power of transnational corporations, the decline of organized labor, the dismantling of the welfare state, and the vast movement of the poor in search of jobs—usually from poor to rich countries. And wherever they go in the United States, unskilled immigrant workers have to compete with low-priced imports from abroad.

Bonacich and Appelbaum contend that the way in which apparel production is organized may be a predictor of things to come in many other industries; they believe that more and more American workers may face similar wages and conditions as globalization proceeds. Perhaps NAFTA and continuing regional development will encourage decent wages and work standards for immigrants and other workers in the garment industry. There is even the possibility of regional citizenship and regional worker rights being discussed by governments and social movement activists that may bring needed reforms. As Bonacich and Appelbaum (2000:319) wrote, "a movement of workers and the community together, should it gain some political power, will be the means of doing so."

TAKING A CLOSER LOOK

Do you agree or disagree with the authors that as globalization proceeds, the way the apparel industry is organized and worker wages and conditions are predictors of things to come in many other American industries?

Source: Edna Bonacich and Richard P. Appelbaum. *Behind the Label: Inequality in the Los Angeles Apparel Industry.* Berkeley, CA: University of California Press, 2000.

1 percent of the population in low-income nations—more than 3 billion people have been untouched by industrialization. And for millions of others, corporate activities have brought instability and declining fortunes—not the dream of prosperity and advancement.

GLOBAL STRATIFICATION IN THE TWENTY-FIRST CENTURY

Current trends suggest that the power and influence of transnational corporations will grow stronger in the future. What this will mean for rich and poor nations is difficult to predict. In the past century or so, nations such as Britain, the United States, and Japan have played dominant roles in the global political economy, and China is joining their ranks. Will they retain their influence in world affairs? Or will some other organization that is larger than any nation, perhaps emerging regional trading blocks, become dominant in the twenty-first century?

The trend toward trading blocks is well underway, and they will likely have a major say in how global wealth is distributed in the future. Since the passage of the North American Free Trade Agreement (NAFTA) in 1994, few Americans are unaware of how their jobs, wages, and "futures" are influenced by economic and other relations between the United States, Canada, and Mexico. The North American trading block is the world's largest trading block, with a combined annual production of $6 trillion and a population fast approaching 400 million. But the European Union is not far behind, and a third huge trading block developing in the Pacific Rim includes several of the most rapidly growing economies in the world. Will this region become dominant in the next few decades and make the twenty-first century "The Asian Century," as some journalists predicted in the early 1990s? Or, was the 1998 "Asian monetary crisis" a harbinger of a more turbulent economic future—not only for Asia but perhaps for the world (Greider et al., 1998)?

Transnational corporations and regional trading blocks offer new possibilities and new challenges—but for the first time in history, their activities have the power to affect the lives of *everyone* on earth. The beneficiaries of this new order are highly skilled technical and managerial professionals. Members of this exclusive group have prospered in both high- and low-income nations, as have many national elites that have chosen to participate in the global economy. Even in some of the poorest nations, the living standards of millions of ordinary people have improved with the growth of global manufacturing and service industries.

For billions of others in rich and poor countries alike, globalization has not been so kind and the gap between the rich and poor is unchanged or wider. For example, while a few Latin American nations have prospered in recent years, many other nations have not advanced (and global population trends do not bode well for the future of developing countries [see Table 9.4]). Further, the economic boom of the 1990s turned to global stagnation in the early twenty-first century, and job losses and lower standards of living have become more common in rich and poor countries alike. By 2003 the flow of goods and investments across borders were declining and traditional industries in many poorer nations "were being overwhelmed by efficient multinational giants" (Leonhardt, 2003:1).

Globalization also seems to be shifting problems associated with low-income nations to advanced industrial nations. In recent years, factory transfers from rich to poor countries have resulted in lost jobs and declining revenues in many parts of the United States and Europe. In the inner city and many rural areas, officials have attempted to revive failing industries and declining tax revenues with *enterprise zones.* In others, the official response has been to institute a range of austerity measures that include severe cutbacks in social welfare benefits for the poor and immigrants (Barnet and Cavanaugh, 1994; Sassen, 1994; Leonhardt, 2003).

Former U.S. Secretary of Labor Robert Reich (1994) predicted that this process could lead to a new, three-tiered class system in the United States and globally. At the top will be a small "overclass" of wealthy, highly skilled workers who, symbolized by the gated communities in which they live, will exist apart from the majority. At the next level, but with far fewer resources and prospects than the current middle class, would be the "anxious class." People in the anxious class might have some college training or technical skills, but global competition would severely reduce their bargaining power in the job market. At the

Corporate advertisements are globally ubiquitous, even in downtown Beijing, China. In this photo several Chinese workers prepare for the day with exercise (tai chi), with the familiar Pepsi Cola advertisement in the background.

TABLE 9.4
POPULATION FOR WORLD AND MAJOR AREAS, 1750–2050

MAJOR AREA	1750	1800	1850	1900	1950	2000	2050
Population Size (millions)							
World	791	978	1,262	1,650	2,521	6,086	9,076
Africa	106	107	111	133	221	812	1,937
Asia	502	635	809	947	1,402	3,676	5,217
Europe	163	203	276	408	547	728	653
Latin America and the Caribbean	16	24	38	74	167	523	783
Nothern America	2	7	26	82	172	315	438
Oceania	2	2	2	6	13	31	48
Percentage Distribution							
World	100	100	100	100	100	100	100
Africa	13.4	10.9	8.8	8.1	8.8	13.3	21.3
Asia	63.5	64.9	64.1	57.4	55.6	60.4	57.5
Europe	20.6	20.8	21.9	24.7	21.7	12.0	7.2
Latin America and the Caribbean	2.0	2.5	3.0	4.5	6.6	8.6	8.6
Nothern America	0.3	0.7	2.1	5.0	6.8	5.2	4.8
Oceania	0.3	0.2	0.2	0.4	0.5	0.5	0.0

Source: Population Division of the Deparment of Economic and Social Affairs of the United Nations Secretariat (2004). *World Population Prospects: The 1998 Revision, vol. II, Sex and Age* (United Nations publication, Sales No. E.99.XIII.8). Also *World Population Prospects: The 1998 Revision, vol. III, Analytical Report* (United Nations pulication, Sales No.E.99.XIII.10). Reprinted with permission.

bottom, Reich sees proliferating urban and rural "underclasses," who would exist at the very edge of the global economy and whose living standards may steadily converge with those of the poor in low-income nations (Aubrey, 1994). At the dawn of the twenty-first century, two researchers adopted a similar view. They maintained that the three tiers include: 30 to 40 percent of the population in core countries who hold "tenured employment in the global economy" and reap most of its benefits; a similar number in the second tier of "casualized workers" who face chronic insecurity in the workplace; and a third tier of 30 percent or so of the population in industrial nations and more than 50 percent in developing countries, "the superfluous population of global capitalism." People in the third tier, they claimed, are structurally excluded from productive activity and completely unprotected with the dismantling of welfare and developmentalist states (Robinson and Harris, 2000:50).

If globalization is adversely affecting the middle class in rich nations, how might it affect people around the world who have nothing to offer in a high-tech global economy? In 2003, for example, President Bush's "Millenium Challenge" offered to double America's spending on development aid to nations that purchased American goods and services as well as to "well-governed" poor countries (*The Economist*, 2003b:67). What will be the fate of those poor nations that are deemed unworthy of aid? Will they become a new *global underclass*?

What about political efforts to create a New World Order that might address global inequality? There have been some important changes in the United Nations that may benefit poor nations. The U.N. Security Council is becoming more representative of global interests. Five new standing members have been added, two from high-income countries and one each from Africa, Asia, and Latin America. It has been proposed that the long-standing veto powers of permanent Security Council members like the United States and France be abolished. Might this finally give poor nations real clout in international politics and enable them to address global inequality and poverty?

What does it mean to be poor in one of the poorest nations on earth? Most Americans immediately think of the slums of Calcutta or of starving refugees in Africa or Asia waiting in long lines for food relief. These images emphasize how poverty incapacitates people and transforms them into "victims" who are incapable of coping with their circumstances. But this portrait is misleading and incomplete. Across the globe social activists have joined together to alleviate suffering and address poverty—even in the poorest nations on earth. And with the support of grassroots movements, millions of poor people have found ways to escape poverty and dependence.

Perhaps the most extraordinary success story to date is in Bangladesh. One day, during a walk in a village near his university, an economics professor, Muhammad Yunus, encountered a poor widow weaving bamboo stools. During a conversation with her, he found that she earned only two cents per day at her craft, mainly because she was unable to get the necessary credit to free her from a trader who set prices and bought her product. Yunus wanted to dig into his pocket and give her the few coins necessary to launch her business enterprise. Instead, he decided to survey the village to see whether other women craftworkers were in a similar position. He found that there were 42 women craftworkers and that $26 was all that was needed to launch their careers as small business entrepreneurs.

The Grameen ("Village") Bank began with an outrageous idea: that poor, landless women in one of the poorest nations on earth were reasonable credit risks and potential entrepreneurs.

Borrowing on his years of training at Vanderbilt University during the 1960s and his experience with student activism and the civil rights movement, Yunus tried his hand at grassroots organizing. First, he got his graduate students involved. Initially, they distributed Yunus's money to the women as well as collected the small installment loans. Two years later, when he had sufficient funds, he opened the first branch of the Grameen Bank. In 2006, Yunus and the bank received the Nobel Peace Prize.

Today, there are more than 1,050 branches serving more than 35,000 villages and 2 million customers—94 percent of them poor, rural women. In almost two decades of making loans, Grameen has distributed over $2 billion, with a 97 percent repayment rate, despite strict rules that would be the envy of most banks: Interest rates are 4 points above those of commercial rates, there are no free services to borrowers, and loans are never forgiven, although they may be restructured in cases of major disaster.

Why has the Grameen Bank been so successful, when so many other projects—both large and small—around the world have failed? One factor identified by Yunus and his students is a long tradition of self-employment, craft production, and market sales experience for men and women in Bangladesh. Entrepreneurship was deeply ingrained in rural culture; all women needed were capital and freedom from traders to launch their businesses.

But this raises another question. What political and social conditions allowed women to break free of the male trading networks that also had a long tradition? More important, in this patriarchal and Islamic society, why did husbands and religious leaders permit economic advancement among women without serious resistance? In many other parts of the world, even small gains by peasants and women involved in grassroots farm projects have been met with violence—even death squads sponsored by the authorities. Why did Bangladeshi interests not react to a massive rural experiment that threatened to alter the ownership of wealth and the balance of power?

Today, the Grameen Bank model is being used elsewhere. Will these and similar efforts affect the real source of poverty: global inequality?

TAKING A CLOSER LOOK

Might the concept of microcredit and small loans to the poor be extended to blighted inner cities in wealthy industrial nations like the United States? Would they create entrepreneurs and alleviate poverty, as they did in Bangladesh? Take a position for or against such a plan.

Source: David Bornstein. "The Barefoot Bank with Cheek." *Atlantic Monthly,* December 1995:43–47. Paul Lewis. "Small Loans May Be Key to Helping Third World." *New York Times,* Sunday, January 26, 1997: Section 1, p. 4.

Many sociologists see more hope in grassroots movements that are proliferating across the globe. Some of the largest movements, with strong links to labor, are called "citizenship movements." They seek to develop public institutions that defend and rebuild communities in an increasingly globalized economic and political order" (Johnston, 2002:241). At present, citizen movements have "no governing body, official ideology, or charismatic leader"; what they have, according to scholars and activists who participated in an "International Forum on Globalization," is a "shared belief that there is a human capacity for cooperation, compassion, creativity, and responsible choice that will make a better world possible, even though it is all too often suppressed by the culture and institutions of corporate globalization" (Cavanagh and Mander, 2002:1). A related movement called the "Jubilee Movement," which focuses on crushing debt loads

Transnational
Corporations: The
Making of New
"Haves" and
"Have-Nots"

255

in poor nations, has pushed for and won debt reduction for dozens of poor nations (Stiglitz, 2002:9). Others include global women's movements, human rights movements, social justice movements, poor people's movements, environmental movements, and others, many of them closely allied. Focus box 9.4 introduces one successful grassroots approach to remedying poverty in one of the poorest nations on earth.

An optimistic scenario sees a movement away from the insular boundaries of nation and region and an emerging respect for human dignity, justice, frugality, honesty, moderation, and equality. A darker vision sees individualistic competition, class conflict, and global consumerism leading to a less equitable distribution of resources in the United States and globally as nations compete over steadily dwindling resources—not only luxuries, but food, clean air, water, and other basic necessities.

As in the past, racial and ethnic groups—and immigrants in particular—may become convenient targets of public hostility in rich and poor nations alike. Moreover, as minorities become numerically dominant in many U.S cities and in the entire nation in the new century, we should expect race, ethnicity, and multicultural issues to become fundamental national and global concerns. In the next chapter, we explore some of these issues and how people experience unequal treatment because of socially defined physical or cultural characteristics.

Summary

1 Modern nations are part of a world economy and global stratification system. Upper-income industrial nations are at the top, newly industrializing countries occupy the second tier, and low-income agrarian nations are at the bottom of the global socioeconomic system.

2 Economic inequality and income ranking among the nations of the world have important social effects: on population patterns, levels of hunger and malnutrition, and national health, education, and literacy—especially for poor women and children.

3 Sociologists explain global inequality by using three major perspectives. Modernization theory sees global development as a process in which rich nations and technology help poor nations advance. World system and dependency theories, however, maintain that the global economy mainly benefits rich nations that exploit the poor and keep them in various dependency relations.

4 Transnational corporations are reshaping the global economy. This has created uneven development around the world, large-scale movements of people, and greater social mobility—especially within nations.

5 What direction the global socioeconomic system will take is uncertain. Global competition will likely benefit some nations and regions and impoverish others. Whether people see the world as a global village or identify with nations and attribute their problems to the poor, immigrants, and other minorities will play a major role in determining life in this twenty-first century.

Key Terms

absolute poverty (p. 234)
colonialism (p. 241)
dependency theory (p. 242)
global stratification system (p. 231)

high-income nations (p. 232)
low-income nations (p. 233)
middle-income nations (p. 233)
modernization theory (p. 240)

transnational corporations (p. 243)
world system theory (p. 243)

Chapter 10

Race and Ethnicity

"I note the obvious differences between each sort and type, but we are more alike, my friends, than we are unalike."

—*Maya Angelou*

Nina Boyd Krebs (1999) calls biracial and multiracial people "edgewalkers." Like Tiger Woods, who proudly proclaims his African American, Thai, and other racial and ethnic heritages, millions of other Americans now do the same. As one author put it, the phenomenon is "passing" for who you really are (Powell, 2005). The media—and especially advertisements—highlight multicultural themes and images for global audiences, and even Betty Crocker has become multiracial—even if she "only reflects General Mills' attempts to tap into a broader market" (Krebs, 1999:38). Likewise, in 2000, for the first time in its 200-year history, the U.S. Census Bureau permitted Americans to list multiple races when indicating their racial heritage. But for Basho Fujimoto, whose mom is Irish-Welsh and whose dad is Japanese American, and his friend Wendell Fishman, whose mom is African American and whose dad is white and Jewish, the multiracial experience has been both positive and challenging.

Basho Fujimoto's experiences are common among "edgewalkers." As he put it, "it would always arises in people's throats, . . . our ethnicity that's one of the first things put on the table: What are you? Where are you from? people are always asking" (Krebs, 1999:40). Some have mistakenly identified him as a Puerto Rican, while others have guessed that he is from Persia, Mexico, or somewhere in the Middle East. Basho spent a semester in England and then went to Denmark, where he had similar experiences: "People thought I was a Middle Eastern refugee. Oftentimes, Middle Easterners would say, 'Ah, Salaam!' (Krebs, 1999:40). He had some Iranian friends and Palestinian friends, and situations like that only reinforced his belief that 'being mixed' can be positive" (Krebs, 1999:40). As Basho Fujimoto put it: "My friends and I are mixed bloods but we're not a new race. People have been mixing for a long time" (Krebs, 1999:42).

Many Americans think that race is about biology and that prejudice and discrimination are a thing of the past. Once more, sociologists warn that *things are not necessarily what they seem*—particularly in the area of race and ethnicity, where there are deeply held myths that are false and socially harmful. In the twenty-first century, prejudice and discrimination remain one of the most serious social problems in the United States as well as globally. Although people's understanding of racial and ethnic "differences" vary around the world, they continue to provide some categories of people with advantages while penalizing and diminishing the life chances of others. Stereotypic views of racial and ethnic minorities are often translated into acts that range from avoidance and personal insults to "ethnic cleansing" and genocide.

UNDERSTANDING RACE AND ETHNICITY IN A GLOBAL SOCIETY

Over the past 50,000 years humans have colonized and adapted to most environments on earth. For a time, natural barriers such as oceans, tropical forests, and deserts limited contacts among many groups, but with improvements in transportation and communication these barriers gradually dissolved. In nature, diversity enhances survival of species. For human relationships, however, the record has been mixed. Some groups welcome those defined as racially or ethnically different; many others greet them with rejection, exploitation, and oppression. For some minorities unequal treatment has meant violent death and mass slaughter; for others it has brought a more or less permanent assignment to the bottom of the social ladder—not because of a lack of ability or effort, but because of ascribed racial or ethnic statuses.

"Black" and "white" racial distinctions that are common in the United States would make no sense to the Brazilians shown here. They and other Brazilians recognize many "races" based on skin color and wealth, and even siblings may be classified in different "races."

Race

Over the years, when discussing race in class, we often have asked students to tell us which racial classification system is "best"—the traditional American system, which recognizes a few distinct races based on skin color (black, white, yellow, red, and brown), or the Brazilian system, which recognizes many more color gradations *and* permits people to change their race as they move up or down the socioeconomic ladder. Most students respond that the American system is far superior, because they believe race to be a "biological concept." The American system uses only physical differences, whereas Brazilians mix biology and "money." Consequently, many students are certain the American system is "scientific" and better than the Brazilian one.

Is the American system "scientific," and does it accurately portray important biological differences among groups? To answer both questions, we must distinguish between race as a *biological* and a *social* concept.

Biological Races   According to biologists, a **biological race** is *a population that differs from others in the frequency of certain hereditary traits.* Because races are open and gene flow has taken place among them for millennia, no race has exclusive possession of any gene or genes and there are no "pure races." In 2003, for example, geneticists cautioned health officials that they should not base drug and health policies on American ideas of race—which have little to do with biology. Using but one example, scientists have found that "there are more genetic differences among Africans from different regions of Africa than there are between Africans and Europeans" (Fox, 2003:1). Likewise, while there may be genetic variation in populations there is no scientific evidence that the possession of a few distinctive genes by any segment of the population has any significant effect on human behavior. Of course, we can't see genetic variation within populations; the current system uses observable physical differences.

In the United States, many African Americans have European ancestors, and many of those who define themselves as "white" have African, Asian, and Native American ancestors. In terms of people's physical appearance this means individuals in one race are not

BIOLOGICAL RACE
A population that differs from others in the frequency of certain hereditary traits.

Gregory Howard Williams, dean of Ohio State University's School of Law, has experienced dramatic changes in his 50-year life, moving from the bottom to near the top of the social hierarchy. Williams's youth was spent in relative poverty as his father tried and failed at various business ventures, including running a small tavern and briefly owning a one-truck septic tank company. When he was 10, Williams learned that he had an even greater roadblock to overcome that would dramatically alter his life and very identity. While relocating from Virginia to the home of his father's aunt in Muncie, Indiana, his father suddenly announced to Greg and his brother Mike, "Boys, I've got some bad news for you. Your mother and I are getting a divorce. There's something else I want to tell you. Remember Miss Sallie who used to work in the tavern? It's hard to tell you boys this. But she's really my momma. That means she's your grandmother." "But that can't be, Dad! She's colored!" I whispered. "That's right—she's colored. That makes you part colored, too. Life is going to be different from now on. In Virginia you were white boys. In Indiana you're going to be colored boys. I want you to remember that you're the same today that you were yesterday. But people in Indiana will treat you differently" (Williams, 1995:33).

How differently, Williams could not have imagined. Once he became "black" and moved in with his black relatives, his mother (who was "white") and her family virtually ignored him and his brother. Many schoolteachers had low expectations for his academic future, and most demanded that he avoid white girls or suffer the consequences. And as he would soon discover, because he was white-skinned but defined as black, he often incurred the wrath of people of both races—especially during childhood, when many white children physically attacked him because he was "black," as did black children because he was "white."

TAKING A CLOSER LOOK

Today, do people who define themselves as biracial and multiracial experience prejudice and discrimination? How have celebrities like Tiger Woods and others changed our perceptions of race and ethnicity?

Source: Gregory H. Williams. *Life on the Color Line: The True Story of a White Boy Who Discovered He Was Black.* New York: Dutton, 1995.

easily distinguishable from others. To establish racial divisions, therefore, people must make choices. First, they must decide which physical traits are significant. Then—despite the fact that no clear boundaries exist—they must promote the understanding and gain general social agreement that they do. This process is what interests sociologists, for when people assign meanings to physical differences—whether they are real or imaginary—they become socially significant.

Social Races To sociologists, race is a social construction, and **races** are *categories of people set apart from others because of socially defined physical characteristics.* This is true in the United States and globally, where groups use physical traits such as skin color, hair texture, and other *incidental biological traits* and transform them into *significant symbols* of purported racial differences. *Social races* may seem to be about biology, but they are in fact *pseudobiological classification systems.* For example, in the United States, if one parent is "black" and the other "white," the child is genetically 50 percent white and 50 percent black. If American ideas of race are indeed based on biology and "science," why does the current racial classification system fail to recognize this child and millions of others as members of a distinctive "racial group"? Focus box 10.1 takes a closer look at racial identities and what it means to be on the "color line."

There has been very little consistency in the racial classification of groups over the years in the United States or other nations. For example, historian James Loewen (1988) found that whites in the Mississippi Delta have changed the "race" of Chinese residents not once but several times during the past century. When they first arrived in Mississippi in the late nineteenth century and worked as poor sharecroppers, whites defined the Chinese as blacks. By the early twentieth century, after they had left the fields and opened grocery stores, Chinese were redefined as neither white nor black but as *exceptions*, which resulted in them having their own separate schools, churches, and cemeteries. Then, with many successes in business and education over the last few decades, whites reclassified the Chinese again: today, both blacks and whites recognize the Chinese as white.

RACES
Categories of people set apart from others because of socially defined physical characteristics.

No one understands that race is a social construction better than Dr. Gregory Howard Williams (pictured below at left), President, The City College of New York, and author, *Life on the Color Line*. When he and his younger brother Michael (shown here with their father) grew up in Virginia, they believed that they were "white." After their parents divorced, however, they moved to their father's kin in Indiana, and discovered they were "black."

Symbolic interactionists insist that racial classification systems are much more than simple ordering devices; they also affect our perceptions of reality. For example, when one of the authors lived in Nigeria, he informally polled several local people to see if they could detect any important physical differences between him and a Japanese researcher who worked in the area. All respondents agreed that they could detect no differences. To them, Japanese and Americans looked the same. Yet local people were certain that the half dozen ethnic groups in the area were very different in appearance—though neither researcher could detect them.

Almost everywhere in the world, when people encounter others they see them as white, black, or yellow, despite the fact that most are various shades of brown. Or they stress some other "obvious traits" that set groups apart for differential and unequal treatment. Moreover, once racial traits become significant symbols, their biological functions are de-emphasized and skin color and other physical features become indicators of moral, intellectual, physical, emotional, and other capabilities.

So-called yellow skin may have some unexplored biological benefits, but as a racial marker many Americans believe it enhances math and engineering skills. In America and many other parts of the world it matters little that black skin (melanin) protects people against the harmful effects of ultraviolet radiation; what is most important are shared stereotypic beliefs by many that black skin enhances athletic performance, improves sexual performance, induces criminal behavior, and is associated with a variety of other behaviors.

Race in the 2000 U.S. Census

The U.S. Census Bureau (2001a) considers "Race" and "Hispanic Origin" to be separate and distinct categories. Consequently in the 2000 census, the question on Hispanic origin asked respondents to list separately their "race." About 48 percent of Hispanics, who comprised about 13 percent of the population, listed their race as "only white," 42 percent listed "some other race only," less than 4 percent reported black or African American alone, and approximately 6 percent of all Hispanics reported two or more races—compared to only about 2 percent of non-Hispanics. The 2000 census marked a fundamental change in how people record and perhaps perceive "race" in the United States. For the first time in over two centuries, the Census Bureau did not demand that people choose a single racial group, but permitted each person to mark one or more races to indicate what the person considered himself or herself to be (U.S. Census Bureau, 2001b). For the first time, the Census Bureau also split the Asian/Pacific Islanders into two separate categories and it combined the Indian, Eskimo, and Aleut categories into "American Indian or Alaska Native."

How did Americans respond to these new "racial" categories? Those who reported only one race (more than 97 percent of the population) included: white, 75 percent; black, 12 percent; American Indian or Alaskan Native, 1 percent; Asian, 4 percent; Native Hawaiian or Other Pacific Islander, one-tenth of 1 percent; and, "some other race," nearly 6 percent. In the new Census Bureau scheme, almost 7 million people or 2.4 percent of Americans "identified with two or more races." Those who reported more than one race were young, about one in three were of Hispanic origin, and most lived in the West. In fact, more than two-thirds of those who listed multiple races lived in just 10 states, with particularly large concentrations of multiracial people in California, New York, and Texas. Further, those who reported more than one race overwhelmingly (93 percent) reported two races: white/some other race, 32 percent; white/American Indian and Alaskan Native, 16 percent; white and Asian, 13 percent; and white and black or African American, 11 percent. And of all those marking more than one race only about 7 percent listed three or more races (U.S. Census Bureau, 2001b).

It should be clear that the new government racial classification system is anything but simple. From the beginning of the Census, government officials have made it clear that neither "science" nor "bureaucratic rationality" has offered much guidance in racial classification. As one demographer observed, "where science is weak, politics flourish" (Skerry, 2000:43). Moreover, the new system has taken on an added dilemma: in the new race and ethnic classification system, "one's racial and ethnic 'identities' have become defined as "a matter of private self-definition." How the public will respond to these new freedoms remains to be seen. At the same time, the salience of race and ethnic Census data has grown more important in politics and public policy: access to education, employment, housing, the organization of elections, and local, state, and federal funding are all "directly affected by racial classifications and the recognition of legitimate groups" (Skerry, 2000:77). Because of this importance, the government is unlikely to leave race and ethnicity up to the personal preferences of respondents and, as in the past, politicians and bureaucrats will create, stretch, and contort racial and ethnic boundaries to suit their needs. So will ordinary people and social activists, who will continue to challenge, resist, or reject these definitions for their own purposes (Skerry, 2000; Harris and Sim, 2002; Graves, 2004).

Ethnicity

Whereas race is a category of people who share socially recognized physical characteristics, **ethnicity** refers to *statuses based on cultural heritage and shared "feelings of peoplehood"* (Gordon, 1964:24). An **ethnic group** is *a category of people set apart from others because of distinctive customs and lifestyles.* Most important for all ethnic groups is that their members have a consciousness of kind and a belief in a common origin and shared fate. Members of different ethnic groups may look very much alike—as do warring Protestants and Catholics in Northern Ireland—but have very different views of where they came from, where they are going, and how they should get there (Rose, 1990).

People often believe that ethnic identities have long histories, but in fact they constantly change as they are defined and redefined in the course of social interaction. In the American Southwest, for example, some people shift their ethnic identity between Hispanic and Indian, depending on the social circumstance (Tomasson, 2000). Likewise, when they first arrived in America most Italian Americans referred to themselves as Venetians, Calabrians, or Sicilians, not as Italians. To members of the host culture, however, these distinctions had no meaning, so they lumped all Italian immigrants together into one group. In time, the dominant group's definition took hold and, responding to a common experience, the many ethnic groups coalesced to form the Italian ethnic group (Parrillo, 2006).

As a rule, it follows that when an ethnic group approximates the culture of the dominant society acceptance will loosen the bonds of ethnic identity. Conversely, ethnic groups that the dominant group perceives as being vastly different experience rejection and persecution, which in turn often strengthens ethnic consciousness and enhances ethnic solidarity.

In everyday life, people may emphasize ethnicity or downplay and ignore it. Some scholars contend that with the current celebration of diversity and multiculturalism in the United States, having an ethnic heritage is important for many people. Further, it encourages the appreciation of other ethnic heritages as well (R. Wood, 1998; Halter, 2000). In many parts of the nation, ethnic traditions are nurtured within large urban neighborhoods, such as Irish American neighborhoods in Boston and Polish American neighborhoods in Chicago (see Map 10.1). But in many other parts of the nation, increasing proportions of persons refuse to claim an ethnic identity, or when filling out

Today. many groups celebrate their ethnic heritages in parades and festivals that are attended and recognized by not only members of that ethnic group, but others as well.

What is meant by the adage, "Everybody's Irish on St. Patrick's Day"?

ETHNICITY
Statuses based on cultural heritage and shared "feelings of peoplehood."

ETHNIC GROUP
A category of people set apart from others because of distinctive customs and lifestyles.

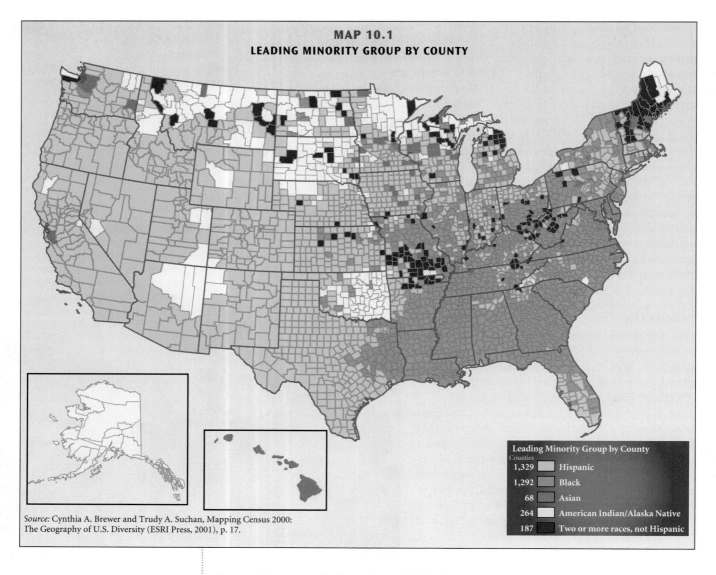

MAP 10.1
LEADING MINORITY GROUP BY COUNTY

Leading Minority Group by County	
Counties	
1,329	Hispanic
1,292	Black
68	Asian
264	American Indian/Alaska Native
187	Two or more races, not Hispanic

Source: Cynthia A. Brewer and Trudy A. Suchan, Mapping Census 2000: The Geography of U.S. Diversity (ESRI Press, 2001), p. 17.

Census forms, mark the category "other" (Tomasson, 2000:10). For example, in some parts of the American Midwest, many people define themselves as "American"—and claim no ethnic heritage whatsoever. Dominant group members may acknowledge and accept these identities, or if it suits their purposes, they may disagree and even ignore or condemn them.

At other times, dominant groups may define a group as being both racially and ethnically distinct—which often serves as a double handicap. Ethnic groups also may be redefined as "races" for political or economic purposes. For example, when the Nazis found it impossible to distinguish Jews from their German neighbors on physical grounds, they mandated that all Jews wear yellow stars. The fact that they could not identify them did not dissuade the Nazis from arguing that Jews were "biologically inferior," nor did it hinder their wartime attempts to exterminate all members of the "Jewish race."

Because ethnicity is based on cultural distinctions, members of ethnic groups often are able to join the majority by adopting the dress, manners, and customs of the dominant group. By contrast, because racial identities are based on socially defined physical characteristics, racial minorities often find it more difficult to blend with the dominant group and gain full social acceptance (Schaefer, 1993; Powell, 2005).

Minority Groups

Today, the word *minority* is a media favorite that has many meanings. Some newscasters treat minorities as groups or categories of people that comprise less than half of some population. Defined in this way, *numerical minorities* are everywhere: redheads, CPAs, teenagers, and rock musicians are all numerical minorities. Sociologists are interested in these statuses, but when they use the word **minority group,** they mean *a category of people who are set apart for unequal treatment because of physical or cultural characteristics.*

While there are many kinds of minorities, including religious groups, people with disabilities, the elderly, and others, race and ethnicity are particularly important minority statuses. Sociologists have identified five basic qualities of racial and ethnic minority groups including: (1) identifiability; (2) membership based on ascription; (3) group awareness; (4) differential power; and (5) differential and unequal treatment.

PREJUDICE

Studs Terkel (1992:3) introduced his book *Race* with a story about a white woman who became lost and drove through a black neighborhood. As she drove down the street, she noticed people on corners frantically waving their arms and gesturing wildly at her so "she became frightened, turned up the windows, and drove determinedly. She discovered, after several blocks, she was going the wrong way on a one-way street and they were trying to help her."

Prejudice refers to *preconceived judgments about a category of people.* All forms of prejudice employ stereotypes that ignore the great variation in individual behaviors and focus on a handful of traits that all group members supposedly possess. People usually have positive prejudices about their own group and the dominant group—whether or not they are members. By contrast, they tend to have negative prejudices toward minority groups, because they are "different" and are usually recognized as inferior.

In class, most students laugh at and ridicule minority group stereotypes. Nevertheless, every student can list the "essential traits" of all major ethnic groups in the United States. For example, when Native Americans are mentioned, students invariably think of the stereotypic alcoholic, much as they associate excessive drinking with the Irish. How about African Americans? Do certain group traits come to mind? Can you think of any behaviors associated with *all* Latinos? After you have listed the so-called traits of all of these groups, ask yourself whether certain traits dominate your thinking about each minority group.

When it comes to popular stereotypes, Asian Americans are somewhat unusual. First, the Asian American label includes great ethnic diversity, including scores of groups from India, China, Japan, and the Pacific Islands, among others. Yet stereotypes ignore this diversity. Second, Asian American stereotypes transform dominant group virtues, such as intelligence and family values, into vices. This is accomplished with claims that Asian Americans are "too committed" to these principles—Asian Americans are "too smart," "too family-oriented," and "too competitive." The media have made much of the latter trait, at various times transforming all Asians into a "yellow menace" intent on world domination. Can you think of any positive stereotypes for whites? How about negative stereotypes? If you are a minority group member, we predict that you will have a fairly long list. If you are a member of the dominant group your list of negatives probably will be much shorter. Why do you think that is the case?

Racism

Racism, which includes *beliefs and attitudes that one racial category is inherently superior or inferior to another,* is the most potent form of prejudice. Typically, racist beliefs include the notion that minorities are "inferior" because of physical and social traits that are intrinsic to those minority groups. For example, many in the United States continue to believe that corporate and government decisions have little to do with the extreme poverty of many minority group members in the inner city. Instead, they attribute inner-city poverty to stereotypic behaviors that supposedly are linked to the biological heritages of minority groups. Blatant racist attitudes, however, are on the decline and white support for racial equality has improved over the past few decades. Racism is more than attitudes, however; it involves differential power as well. Some scholars contend that "white" power and privilege is maintained by a majority belief that whites as a people do not have a race, and that racial identity (and associated penalties) is something others have (Fears, 2003:AO1).

MINORITY GROUP
A category of people who are set apart for unequal treatment because of physical or cultural characteristics.

PREJUDICE
Preconceived judgments about a category of people.

RACISM
Beliefs and attitudes that one racial category is inherently superior or inferior to another.

Approaches to Prejudice

Early scientists once believed that prejudice was a basic part of our biological makeup. After almost a century of research, however, most social scientists agree that prejudice is socially learned and that numerous factors, including personality factors, culture, and group competition and conflict, contribute to prejudice and discrimination.

Psychological Perspectives In 1950, T. W. Adorno and his colleagues reported strong correlations among harsh and rigid child rearing, an "authoritarian personality," and high levels of prejudice. Follow-up studies provided some support for this thesis, but, as Peter Rose (1990:101–102) noted, prejudice and discrimination are not confined to those with rigid, conservative, or "pathological" personality structures, but "characterize the attitudes and behavior of many 'normal people.'"

To social psychologists, unsatisfied expectations and desires are fertile ground for prejudice and discrimination. According to the *frustration-aggression hypothesis,* people are goal-directed, and when their desires are blocked they become angry and frustrated and seek to find an outlet for their hostilities. If people cannot pinpoint the source of their problems, or if they discover the source is too powerful to challenge, they may direct their anger at a **scapegoat,** *a weak, convenient, and socially approved target.* Historically, scapegoats (usually minorities) have shouldered the blame and have paid terrible penalties for "causing" society's ills.

Culture, Stereotypes, and Prejudice A noteworthy characteristic of all autonomous racial and ethnic groups is **ethnocentrism**—*the tendency to judge the customs of others according to one's own cultural standards.* Groups that share values, norms, and beliefs with the dominant group are highly regarded, while those judged to violate important norms are scorned and rejected.

People are not born with prejudices. They acquire them during the socialization process. The remarkable persistence of prejudicial attitudes toward minorities owes much to the fact that prejudice and interaction patterns are mutually reinforcing. When **stereotypes,** which are *static and oversimplified ideas about a group or a social category,* define a group as being "very different" from one's group, then their members tend to be avoided. Of course, if we rarely encounter members of an out-group, we will have few opportunities to modify our prejudices and negative stereotypes will persist. By contrast, there is some evidence that when different racial and ethnic groups interact on relatively equal terms, there is a tendency for members of both sides to become less prejudiced. But even in such cases, fears of the gradual homogenization of diverse cultures and threats to traditional ethnic identities may lead to the deterioration of intergroup relations, which is so evident in many parts of the world today (Amir, 1969; Clore et al., 1978; Forbes, 1997).

Conflict Approaches to Prejudice From the conflict perspective, the basic source of prejudice and discrimination is competition among racial and ethnic groups for scarce resources. As a rule, the more intense the competition, the more negative the prejudices and the greater the degree of discrimination. For example, with the collapse of the Soviet Union there has been intense competition for power in Eastern Europe, with some groups conducting "ethnic cleansing" campaigns to exterminate ethnic and religious rivals.

Marxist scholars contend that in contemporary society prejudice and discrimination persist because they serve the economic interests of the capitalist elite. For capitalist owners, they argue, prejudice and discrimination can be very profitable. First, racism and beliefs of ethnic inferiority enable capitalists to exploit minorities: minorities are assigned the lowest paying, dirtiest, and most dangerous jobs, and because of the racist ideology there is general social agreement that that is all they are capable of doing.

Second, immigrants and minorities comprise a "reserve labor force" that can be called up and put to work when the economy is expanding, or dismissed in recessions. Elites also use racial and ethnic hostilities to divert and distract white and minority

SCAPEGOAT
A weak, convenient, and socially approved target.

ETHNOCENTRISM
The tendency to judge the customs of others according to one's own cultural standards.

STEREOTYPES
Static and oversimplified ideas about a group or a social category.

SPLIT-LABOR MARKET
An economic situation in which two groups of workers are willing to do the same work for different wages.

DISCRIMINATION
Unequal treatment of people because of their group membership.

workers from recognizing their shared interests. Instead of challenging corporate owners who exploit them, poor whites direct their hostilities at minorities and attempt to take what little wealth, status, and power they may have.

Sociologist Edna Bonacich (1972; 2000) contends that although owner exploitation of workers fuels ethnic unrest, so does a **split-labor market,** which is *an economic situation in which two groups of workers are willing to do the same work for different wages.* According to Bonacich, there are two laboring groups—higher-paid labor (e.g., whites) and cheaper labor (e.g., African Americans, Puerto Ricans, Chinese). Further, contrary to Marxist claims that their economic interests are the same, they are fundamentally opposed (McLemore, 1980). According to Bonacich (1972:554), when one ethnic group is decidedly cheaper than another, the higher-paid workers face a very real economic threat—either wage reductions or job loss. From this perspective, white laborers in America often have considered themselves under attack on two fronts—"from above and below" (Limerick, 1987:262). This pattern may be extended to contemporary societies, where many members of the working and lower-middle classes attribute their declining fortunes to "big government," minorities on welfare, and immigrants.

DISCRIMINATION

Whereas prejudices are attitudes, discrimination refers to acts. **Discrimination** is *unequal treatment of people because of their group membership.* In everyday life people sometimes discriminate in favor of a group. For example, a banker may give a man or woman of Scottish ancestry a loan because he assumes all Scots are frugal and careful with money. The same banker may disqualify other people from receiving loans because they are members of a particular racial or ethnic group believed to be less reliable.

For many years, Native Americans have protested "cultural imperialism." In this photo, members of the American Indian Movement (AIM) and the National Coalition on Racism in Sports voice their concerns about the use of American Indian mascots in sports. Effective in 2006, with a few notable exceptions, such as the Florida State Seminoles who received the Seminole tribe's blessing, the NCAA required schools with potentially offensive Native American mascots to change their team's logos and mascots—or they would be banned from all postseason tournaments and championship play.

Types of Discrimination

Discrimination may be personal, legal, or institutional. **Personal discrimination** includes *attacks on minority group members, from social slights and insults to murder.* In **legal discrimination,** *minority group members are denied lawful access to public institutions, jobs, housing, and social rewards.* The third major and most subtle and pervasive kind of discrimination is **institutional discrimination,** *unequal treatment of a group that is deeply embedded in social institutions.* Typically, it includes many discriminatory practices and traditions that have such a long history they just "seem to make sense."

In *Black Power,* Carmichael and Hamilton (1967:4) provided a startling illustration of the insidious nature of institutional discrimination. They noted that when white terrorists bombed a black church and five black children were killed, the act was widely deplored by most members of American society. In that same community, however, when 500 black babies die each year because of a lack of proper food, shelter, and medical facilities, few whites see any connection between these deaths and racial discrimination. In fact, many attribute the children's deaths to their poor families, something sociologists call "blaming the victim" (cited in Steinberg, 1995:76).

For quite a long time, a similar "logic" was used by police and fire departments when they set minimum height requirements that excluded qualified Asian American men and women from these jobs (Marden et al., 1992). No less discriminatory is the commercialization of Native American cultures. For many years—and continuing in much of the nation—sports teams, corporations, and schools used Native American names, traditions, and even spiritual concepts as mascots or to sell products. Many Americans deem these practices perfectly acceptable. It was only after Native American social activists identified such practices as "cultural genocide" and condemned them that some Americans began to see that they were harmful and demanded that these practices be stopped (Churchill, 1994). In 2005, the NCAA ruled that all references to Native Americans had to be removed from team mascot names.

Prejudice and Discrimination in Everyday Life

The relationship between prejudice and discrimination often is complex. In everyday life, a prejudiced person may loathe and detest members of a certain group yet rarely discriminate against them. Conversely, a nonprejudiced person may discriminate out of economic self-interest or because of peer pressure, rules, or traditions. Robert Merton (1949, 1976) identified four major ways in which prejudice and discrimination can be combined (see Table 10.1.).

1. *Unprejudiced nondiscriminators (all-weather liberals)* adhere to the American ideal of equal opportunity for all and neither are prejudiced nor discriminate against others. Whatever the situation, they abide by their beliefs.

2. *Unprejudiced discriminators (fair-weather liberals)* are free of prejudice, but when it is expedient, profitable, or otherwise seems justifiable, they may discriminate against others. For example, a salesperson with no prejudices may tolerate ethnic jokes and racial slurs from customers out of fear that telling them to stop might lose their business.

PERSONAL DISCRIMINATION Attacks on minority group members, from social slights and insults to murder.

LEGAL DISCRIMINATION Minority group members are denied lawful access to public institutions, jobs, housing, and social rewards.

INSTITUTIONAL DISCRIMINATION Unequal treatment of a group that is deeply embedded in social institutions.

TABLE 10.1
MERTON'S TYPOLOGY OF PREJUDICE AND DISCRIMINATION

	No Discrimination	Discrimination
Not Prejudiced	1 All-weather liberal	2 Fair-weather liberal
Prejudiced	1 Fair-weather bigot	2 All-weather bigot

Source: Myers, *Dominant-Minority Relations in America* 2/e, © 2007, Pearson Education 0-205-48241-4.

3. *Prejudiced nondiscriminators (fair-weather bigots)* do not believe in equality of opportunity and hold many prejudices toward racial and ethnic groups, but they do not discriminate because they fear the consequences. Spike Lee's popular movie *Do the Right Thing* focused on this kind of individual, who had contempt for his black customers but kept his feelings to himself and did not discriminate, because it would have been "bad for business."

4. *Prejudiced discriminators (all-weather bigots)* are unashamed bigots who do not believe in equality of opportunity—at least for certain groups—and discriminate against racial and ethnic minorities freely.

Contemporary Discrimination in the United States

During the 1960s, largely due to the efforts of the Civil Rights movement and government action, many forms of racial and ethnic discrimination declined in the United States. In the twenty-first century, however, the pendulum appears to be shifting in the opposite direction. There is much support for this thesis, including the reappearance of white hate groups, the firebombing of black churches and synagogues, and continuing patterns of discrimination in the workplace, housing, education, sports, the criminal justice system, and the media.

White Hate Groups The reemergence of white hate groups and their blatant attacks on minority groups are perhaps the strongest evidence of deteriorating race relations. During the early 1990s, the number of hate groups increased from 273 to 346 in the United States, with perhaps as many as 30,000 hard-core members. They include the 6,000 or so members of the Ku Klux Klan as well as several thousand neo-Nazis. The most well-known neo-Nazi group is Aryan Nations, which has a large branch in California (White Aryan Resistance) (Chambers, 1995; Ezekiel, 1995; Nelkin and Lindee, 1995). (See Map 10.2 for active hate groups in the United States.)

Skinhead groups with names like Youth of Hitler, United White Youth, Las Vegas Skins, and Confederate Hammer Skins have also been at the forefront of racial violence. Most Americans know about skinheads from the media, especially their well-publicized racist name calling on the *Oprah Winfrey Show* and a chair throwing incident on *Geraldo.* Such violence can hardly compare to that experienced by minorities who have encountered skinheads in real life.

In 1992, for example, a homeless black man was stabbed to death when a group of skinheads with ties to the Klan and White Aryan Resistance (WAR) decided to "bash" minorities "following a celebration of Adolph Hitler's birthday" (Farley, 1995:417). More disturbing was the 1993 plot by six Fourth Reich Skinheads to kill Rodney King and members of the First African Methodist Church in Los Angeles to start a "race riot" (Chambers, 1995:213).

Shortly after the brutal murder of an African American man by alleged White Supremacists in Jasper, Texas, a member of the Texas Department of Public Safety stands guard at a demonstration that includes the Ku Klux Klan and the New Black Panthers.

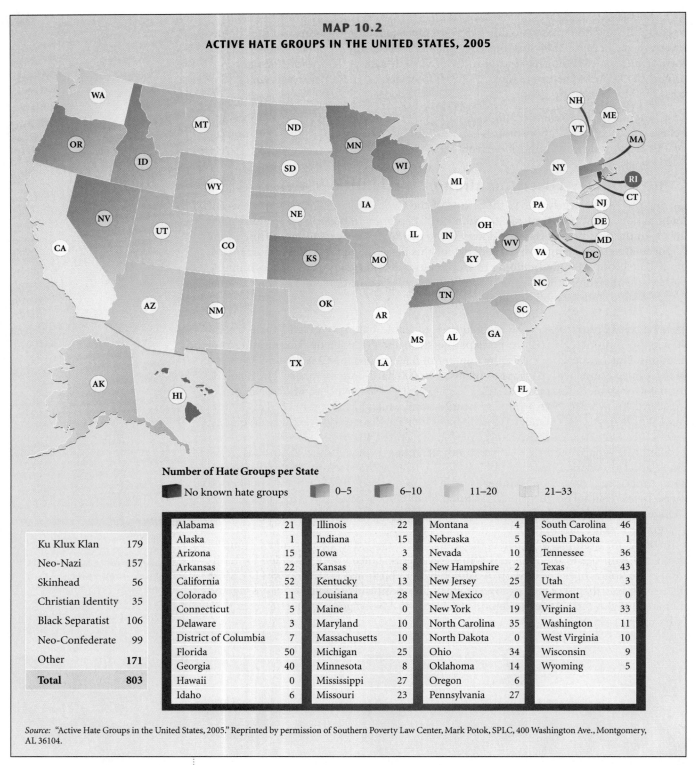

MAP 10.2

ACTIVE HATE GROUPS IN THE UNITED STATES, 2005

Number of Hate Groups per State

No known hate groups   0–5   6–10   11–20   21–33

Ku Klux Klan	179
Neo-Nazi	157
Skinhead	56
Christian Identity	35
Black Separatist	106
Neo-Confederate	99
Other	**171**
Total	**803**

State	#	State	#	State	#	State	#
Alabama	21	Illinois	22	Montana	4	South Carolina	46
Alaska	1	Indiana	15	Nebraska	5	South Dakota	1
Arizona	15	Iowa	3	Nevada	10	Tennessee	36
Arkansas	22	Kansas	8	New Hampshire	2	Texas	43
California	52	Kentucky	13	New Jersey	25	Utah	3
Colorado	11	Louisiana	28	New Mexico	0	Vermont	0
Connecticut	5	Maine	0	New York	19	Virginia	33
Delaware	3	Maryland	10	North Carolina	35	Washington	11
District of Columbia	7	Massachusetts	10	North Dakota	0	West Virginia	10
Florida	50	Michigan	25	Ohio	34	Wisconsin	9
Georgia	40	Minnesota	8	Oklahoma	14	Wyoming	5
Hawaii	0	Mississippi	27	Oregon	6		
Idaho	6	Missouri	23	Pennsylvania	27		

Source: "Active Hate Groups in the United States, 2005." Reprinted by permission of Southern Poverty Law Center, Mark Potok, SPLC, 400 Washington Ave., Montgomery, AL 36104.

Many survivalist militia groups are also blatantly racist; they fear not only "government conspiracies" but a "minority takeover" of the United States (Zellner, 1995). So do a few racist religious groups, such as the Christian Identity Sect, which contends that only whites were created by God and that people of color arose "through the mating of humans and animals" (Ezekiel, 1995:xxvi). The Christian Identity group is part of a larger white supremacy movement, which has as many as 150,000 supporters who purchase movement literature, attend rallies, and provide financial support for hate group causes. In addition, there are at least one-half million covert, low-profile supporters who read hate literature, generally agree with white superiority views, and support the activities of racist hate groups whenever they can (Flowers, 1990). White supremacist groups have even gone high-tech to reach young people and potential supporters, creating computer games like "Ethnic Cleansing"—"which encourages players to kill blacks, Jews, and Hispanics as they run through gritty ghetto and subway environments" (Godinez, 2002:13A).

In 2001, the *Chicago Tribune* reported that some militia and white supremacist group members expressed support and solidarity with terrorists in their e-mail correspondence—within hours of the 9/11 attack. For some, 9/11 may even have signaled a transformation of the radical right: instead of "looking back fondly to Southern apartheid," some appear to be looking forward to a revolutionary, anti-capitalist, anti-American struggle, "and most remarkably, to seeing itself in solidarity with the anti-imperialist struggles of the Third World people" (Brandon, 2001:2). Another white supremacist website claimed it supported both Afghanistan's former Taliban regime and Al Qaeda. As one member of the Jewish Defense League in Chicago observed, "These are strange bedfellows, to say the least, but by no means is it surprising when hate is the common denominator" (Brandon, 2001:2).

In the Workplace and Economically The Civil Rights Act of 1964 dramatically altered historic patterns of discrimination. Not only did it prohibit racial and ethnic discrimination in the workplace, it mandated that the government take *affirmative action* to ensure "equality of employment opportunity" (J. E. Jones, 1993:350). For several decades, affirmative action accomplished a great deal. For example, in 1960, only about 10 percent of African American households were in the middle class. By 1990, 30 percent of African American households had middle-class incomes and their number in high-paying professional and technical occupations had increased by over 100 percent. The strongest gains by far were in federal and state employment, where one-fourth of the entire African American labor force, or 1.6 million African American men and women, were employed (Steinberg, 1995:197).

A comparison of the net worth of whites and African Americans, however, shows that even with these gains there remains a sizeable economic gap between whites and most other minorities. For example, in the mid-1990s the median African American family's net worth was $8,300, compared to $56,000 for white families (Oliver and Shapiro, 1995). Put another way, "the typical black family had 15 cents of wealth for every dollar owned by the typical white family" (Oliver and Shapiro, 1995:7). Income statistics reveal similar racial disparities. With a median household income of $25,000, African Americans earned roughly 55 percent of white incomes (about $40,000). Moreover, the gap in income between blacks and whites at every educational level remains substantial (see Figure 10.1).

Likewise, black unemployment in the mid-1990s stood at about 12 percent—double that of white unemployment (5 percent). At various times during the early 1990s, almost 50 percent of black teenagers were unemployed. Black folk wisdom maintains that "when the United States

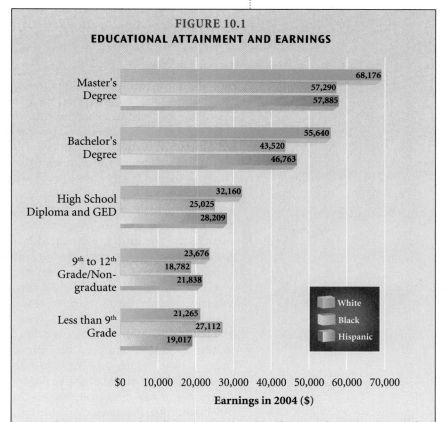

FIGURE 10.1
EDUCATIONAL ATTAINMENT AND EARNINGS

	White	Black	Hispanic
Master's Degree	68,176	57,290	57,885
Bachelor's Degree	55,640	43,520	46,763
High School Diploma and GED	32,160	25,025	28,209
9th to 12th Grade/Non-graduate	23,676	18,782	21,838
Less than 9th Grade	21,265	27,112	19,017

Earnings in 2004 ($)

Source: "Minorities Earn Less than Whites at Every Educational Level" as appeared in *American Demographics,* June 2000:23, from U.S. Bureau of Labor Statistics. Income in 2001 by Educational Attainment for People 18 Years Old and Over, by Age, Sex, Race, and Hispanic Origin. March 2002, http://www.census.gov/population/www/socdemo/education/pp1-169.html. Updated with the U.S. Census Bureau, Current Population Survey, 2005 Annual Social and Economic Supplement.

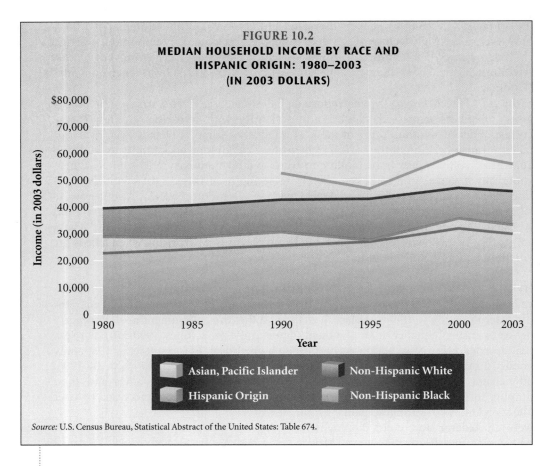

FIGURE 10.2
MEDIAN HOUSEHOLD INCOME BY RACE AND
HISPANIC ORIGIN: 1980–2003
(IN 2003 DOLLARS)

Asian, Pacific Islander   Non-Hispanic White
Hispanic Origin   Non-Hispanic Black

Source: U.S. Census Bureau, Statistical Abstract of the United States: Table 674.

experiences a recession, Black Americans have a depression," and statistics from every era—including much of the 1990s, when "blacks were the only racial group to experience a net loss of jobs"—support these claims (Chambers, 1995:83). (See Figure 10.2 for U.S. household income, race, and ethnicity over three decades.)

By most economic measures, Latinos fare only slightly better. Poverty among Mexican Americans is still more than twice the national average, and Latino incomes remain almost $10,000 below those of whites as the gap between proportions of Latinos and whites in high-paying professions is widening (Solis and Morales, 2005). Only Asian Americans seem to have experienced major gains. By 2001, about one of five whites were professionals, managers, and executives. For Asian Indians, Chinese Americans, and Japanese Americans, the percentages were 47 percent, 30 percent, and 28 percent, respectively. The median household income of Asian Americans was also higher than that of whites ($53,635 compared to around $46,305)—but this statistic is deceptive. In addition to the wages of husbands and wives, many other Asian American family members often contribute to household income. Moreover, many recent immigrants from Asia have incomes below the poverty line—even with multiple income earners.

In Housing Many Americans believe that residential segregation is a product of the economy and jobs, or a holdover from a racist past rather than current discrimination. There is little evidence to support either view. Although almost four decades have passed since the passage of the Fair Housing Act of 1968, which banned discrimination in housing, many minorities remain in segregated neighborhoods across the nation (Adelman, 2005; Freeman, 2005).

Housing studies show that discrimination persists, although in more subtle forms than the past. For example, John Yinger (1998) notes that among numerous forms of discrimination, African Americans and Hispanics may be denied information about available housing. Further, banks sometimes require higher escrow for minorities, and they reject minority loan applications at higher rates than they do for white customers. Yinger (1998:916) estimates that a black household must pay, on average, "a discrimination 'tax' of roughly $3,700." If all black households—owners and renters—were included, the "tax" would total "about $3 billion," whereas discrimination would cost Hispanics "roughly $1.7 billion." Even in Prince George's County, Maryland, the largest and richest black county in America, the effects of discrimination are evident. In predominantly black suburban neighborhoods, the homes of doctors and attorneys cost around $400,000—"but that's still about half the cost of similar developments in white suburbs" (Clemetson, 2000a:61).

In another study, Oliver and Shapiro (1995) estimated that over the next generation the price of being a black homeowner will cost $21.5 billion more in interest than being a white homeowner. Minority renters experience similar patterns of discrimination: African Americans "were refused any sort of information ('door slamming') 15 percent of the time, while Latino renters were treated this way 12 percent of the time" (Fix et al., 1993:20).

Although Latinos have become less segregated in the past three decades, Latino housing segregation still averages in the 30–40 percent range. By contrast, Asian Americans, who for almost a century were confined to Chinatowns, experience fairly low segregation rates in most cities and suburbs (Massey and Denton, 1993).

Today, black-white residential segregation averages almost 70 percent across the nation, with many metropolitan statistical areas—including both central cities and suburbs—having black-white segregation indices of 80 percent or more. The Gary-Hammond-East Chicago metropolitan area has the highest level of segregation in the nation, followed by Detroit, Cleveland, Newark, Milwaukee, and New York. In all of these cities at least 80 percent of blacks would have to move to achieve desegregated residential patterns (Massey and Denton, 1993). In these "hypersegregated cities," contact with whites are for the most part brief and superficial. "Indeed 73% of whites in the Detroit area claimed to have no black friends at all, and 57% of blacks said they had no white friends" (Welch and Sigelman, 2000:69).

This conclusion received additional support from Wisconsin researchers who used data from the 2000 Census to a make a "block-level analysis" of African American and white housing patterns in American cities. They found that most previous urban segregation indexes, which ranked entire cities, was biased and underrepresented housing segregation. By counting "how many blocks were black-white integrated" (at least 20 percent white and at least 20 percent black), they discovered that "almost a third of blacks and more than half of whites lived in blocks whose inhabitants were at least 90 percent of their own race. Moreover, block-by-block analysis reversed some earlier rankings: Norfolk, Virginia, ranked highest in residential integration, and some metropolitan areas like St. Louis and Birmingham, which were near the bottom in studies that used "metropolitan areas," moved up to the top third. And some cities "praised as less segregated, such as Albuquerque and Orange County, California, dropped "to near the bottom, partly because they have relatively few blacks" (Quinn and Pawasarat, 2003; *The Economist*, 2003a:35).

Things are not much different in many other multiethnic metropolitan areas. Camille Charles's study of Los Angeles found that in addition to social class variables, two major reasons for low levels of contact among whites, African Americans, and other minority groups, were persistent negative stereotyping and a "racial preference hierarchy."

When Charles asked respondents—both whites and minority group members—to create neighborhoods that they believed were ideal in racial composition, she found that whites were the most favored out-group and blacks were the least favored out-group. According to Charles (2000:401), on average, whites constituted between 23 and 33 percent of minority group members' ideal neighborhood. Conversely, 40 percent of Asians, nearly 33 percent of Latinos, and 20 percent of whites would create "ideal neighborhoods" that excluded blacks. It is noteworthy that in Los Angeles, where the Latino population is sizeable and growing, Latinos were excluded from a large percentage of white (17 percent) and Asian (26 percent) neighborhoods as well (Charles, 2000:401).

In Education   During the 1990s, there were many challenges to job training programs, school desegregation, and college affirmative action programs, as well as

In the United States, affirmative action has been the subject of heated debate for almost four decades. Some minority group members contend that racial preferences are the only way to reverse a long history of racial discrimination—as well as address current discrimination. According to this view, hiring preferences are necessary to reverse centuries of discrimination and are vital to creating a more level playing field that will help minorities compete and, in some cases, even enter the "contest." Conservative politicians counter that preferences based on race, ethnicity, and gender amount to "reverse discrimination," in that they often become quotas that deny white males opportunities because of what they define as past rather than present discrimination.

Some also contend that affirmative action preferences encourage the hiring of less qualified workers, which undermines the quality of the workforce and reduces American business competitiveness. A few conservative black scholars go a step further and contend that affirmative action not only harms whites, it also harms minorities and women because it reinforces negative stereotypes that minorities are less capable than whites and may create self-doubt and resentment among minority group members who must react to white skepticism about their abilities (Farley, 1995).

During the late 1970s, the Supreme Court attempted to find a middle ground, both supporting minority preferences and arguing that quotas were unconstitutional. With the appointment of more conservative justices during the 1980s, the Supreme Court applied stricter standards for federal minority preferences. In 1995, for example, in *Adarand v. Pefia,* the Court struck down an affirmative action plan in a federal highway construction program, arguing that "federal and state affirmative action programs must be narrowly tailored to redress specific cases" of discrimination. This decision brought renewed conservative calls for the complete end to affirmative action and counterclaims by minority leaders that challenges to affirmative action were "blatant acts of racism."

In the same year, President Clinton sought to restore the middle ground by asserting that affirmative action was "good for the nation" but in need of reform in three areas: "there should be no quotas, all affirmative action recipients must be qualified, and reverse discrimination must be vigorously prosecuted" (*USA Today,* 1995:1A). Then, as noted in the text, California passed what amounts to an anti-affirmative action bill (Proposition 209), and the U.S. Supreme Court let the law stand. In 1996, Cheryl Hopwood and three other students sued Texas (*Hopwood v. Texas*) over the use of "racial preferences" in admissions to enhance racial diversity; they won. The court ruling produced dramatic declines in minority group representation in Texas medical and law schools. For example, at the University of Texas School of Law, black admissions dropped from 65 in 1996 to 5 in 1997 (Feinberg, 1998:ix). Equally large declines have occurred at some schools in the University of California system, especially at the University of California, Berkeley, the state's elite institution. In the fall of 1998, African Americans, Latino, and Native Americans made up about 10 percent of those admitted, less than half the percentage of the previous fall. African Americans experienced the greatest decline: down nearly 66 percent in a single year (Ramage, 1998:A43). By 2000, with the exception of Asian Americans, who made up about 45 percent of incoming freshmen, minority enrollment had

renewed debates about race and intelligence. In this period, Richard Herrnstein and Charles Murray (1994) published a national bestseller, *The Bell Curve,* that used charts, tables, and other data to "prove" that "blacks" tested lower than "whites" on IQ tests. Most scholars who reviewed this "evidence," however, found "almost no support for genetic explanations of the IQ difference between blacks and whites" (Nisbett, 1998:89).

Most civil rights leaders were more concerned with legal challenges and Supreme Court decisions that seemed to signal a broad political retreat from affirmative action. For example, in 1995 the Supreme Court ruled that federal plans to attract white suburban students to minority inner-city schools could be used only if there was sufficient proof that both city and suburban schools still showed the

declined. Latino students accounted for 9 percent of the class, and African American students for only 4 percent (Peraino, 2000:61).

In 2003, the U.S. Supreme Court upheld the principle of affirmative action in higher education, in one of two cases involving the University of Michigan. In the law school case, the high court ruled that the university may consider race as part of its complex admissions process—"as long as they engaged in a highly individualized, holistic review" (Winter, 2003:1). However, in the undergraduate case, the court voted 6–3 that the university "must abandon its current system of undergraduate evaluations that award applicants points based on race" (Wertheimer and Hoppe, 2003:1A). Justice O'Connor noted that the court decisions reflected the fact that the "law school had considered each applicant individually, whereas the undergraduate school had reported to a mechanical selection process—the point system" (Wertheimer and Hoppe, 2003:16A).

What will be the long-term impact of these laws on affirmative action? Most agree that the high court affirmed the right of universities to create a diverse student population, using race as one factor in admissions. Justice O'Connor, for example, wrote, "cross-racial understanding . . . helps to break down racial stereotypes and better prepare graduates for the working world" (Steinberg, 2003:3). The court did not consider alternative higher education plans like those in Texas, California, and Florida, which accept the top 10 percent or some other set percentage of students from every high school. And college officials and civil rights leaders could not help but notice the justices' statement: "We expect that 25 years from now, the use of racial preferences will no longer be necessary" (Winter, 2003:3).

James Jones (1993:365) contends that the survival of affirmative action is neither about morality and justice nor about past grievances and reparations: "it is a matter of the survival of this nation." The Labor Department's demographic projections in *Workplace 2000* show that white men will constitute about 15 percent of new entrants to the workforce, the other 85 percent being women, minorities, and immigrants—the current targets of affirmative action programs.

TAKING A CLOSER LOOK

Take a position on affirmative action—for or against. As you make your case, make sure that you provide tangible evidence that there is or is not discrimination in many social arenas. Examine the implications of your position: how might your views—if they were translated into public policy—affect race and ethnic relations in the future?

Source: John E. Farley. *Majority-Minority Relations*, 3rd ed. Englewood Cliffs, NJ: Prentice-Hall, 1995. Walter Feinberg. *On Higher Ground: Education and the Case for Affirmative Action*. New York: Teachers College, Columbia University, 1998. James Ramage. "Berkeley and UCLA See Sharp Drops in Admission of Black and Hispanic Applicants." *The Chronicle of Higher Education* 64(31) April 10, 1998:A43. "Clinton Backs Bias Benefits." *USA Today*, Thursday, July 20, 1995:1A. Kevin Perainu. "Berkeley's New Colors." *Newsweek*, September 18, 2000:62. James E. Jones, Jr. "The Rise and Fall of Affirmative Action" in Herbert Hill and James E. Jones, Jr. (eds.), *Race in America: The Struggle for Equality*. Madison: University of Wisconsin Press, 1993:345–369. Greg Winter. "Ruling Provides Relief, but Less Than Hoped." *The New York Times on the Web*, Education, June 24, 2003:1–3. Linda K. Wertheimer and Christy Hoppe. "College Race Policy Withheld." *The Dallas Morning News*, Tuesday, June 24, 2003:1A, 16A. Jacques Steinberg. "After 25 Years, a Road Map for Diversity on Campus." *The New York Times on the Web*, Politics, June 24, 2003:1–4.

effects of prior segregation. This decision and the flight of many middle-class whites to private or religious schools accelerated the resegregation of many inner-city schools.

Minority gains were challenged in higher education as well. During the 1990s, the "anti-political correctness" movement of the 1980s continued. According to Noam Chomsky (1993:53), the "hysteria about political correctness" was part of the larger conservative agenda to return to the old core curricula, the classics, Western history and Western literature—and white privilege (Farley, 1995; Williams-Myers, 1995). In the same period there were calls to end "minority preferences" in hiring and admissions; a few succeeded. In 1995, for example, the University of California regents voted no longer to use race, religion, sex, color, ethnicity or national origin as criteria for hiring. A year later, California voted to end affirmative action, and in 1997 the U.S. Supreme Court let this decision stand. In 1998 another measure was introduced in Congress to end affirmative action and eliminate race and gender preferences at all public colleges and universities. That measure, however, was defeated. Focus box 10.2 takes a closer look at the affirmative action debate in the United States.

These changes have had a dramatic impact on minority enrollments. In 1990, black enrollment accounted for 4 percent at the nine University of California campuses. Today black enrollment is closer to 2 percent. Latino enrollments declined as well, by nearly 15 percent. Only Asian American enrollments increased, from 25 percent to

TABLE 10.2
RACE AND PROFESSIONAL SPORTS

RACE	PLAYERS	OWNERS	MANAGERS	COACHES
White				
MLS	64%	N/A	100%	100%
NBA	22%	95%	83%	63%
NFL	29%	100%	94%	91%
MLB	63%	96%	77%	73%
WNBA	33%	94%	77%	69%
Black				
MLS	17%	N/A	0%	0%
NBA	76%	4%	17%	37%
NFL	69%	0%	6%	9%
MLB	9%	0%	10%	12%
WNBA	66%	6%	23%	31%
Latino				
MLS	14%	N/A	0%	0%
NBA	1%	0%	0%	0%
NFL	<1%	0%	0%	0%
MLB	26%	3%	13%	13%
WNBA	1%	0%	0%	0%
Other				
MLS	5%	N/A	0%	0%
NBA	0%	0%	0%	0%
NFL	1%	0%	0%	0%
MLB	2%	0%	0%	0%
WNBA	1%	0%	0%	0%

Note: *Abbreviations*: MLS: Major League Soccer; NBA: National Basketball Association; NFL: National Football League; MLB: Major League Baseball; WNBA: Women's National Basketball Association.

Source: 2004 Racial and Gender Report Card by Richard E. Lapchisch, prepared by the Center for the Study of Sport in Society, Northeastern University, Richard E. Lapchisch, Director, Updates: The 2004 Racial and Gender Report Card, The Institute for Diversity and Ethics in Sport, DeVos Sport Business Management Program, Richard E. Lapchisch, Director.

Will demographic change and an increasingly global audience improve the Racial Report Card in the twenty-first century?

nearly 30 percent (Jaschik, 1995). In the nation as a whole, while black high school graduation rates were about the same as whites (85 percent), only about 14 percent of blacks had college degrees, compared to 29 percent of whites (U.S. Bureau of Census, 2000).

In Sports Is there any institution in American society more free from racial prejudice and discrimination than professional sports? Most Americans would say no. Sports appear to be based on talent and achievement—not ascribed statuses. In fact, many Americans believe minorities have fared better in this social arena than the white majority, and some cite statistics to prove it. For example, blacks constitute about 12 percent of the population but account for 61 percent of the players in the Women's National Basketball Association (WNBA), 65 percent of National Football League (NFL) players, and 78 percent of National Basketball Association (NBA) players. Moreover, black and other minority group superstars, such as LeBron James, Shaquille O'Neil, Barry Bonds, and Tiger Woods, are among the highest paid athletes in the world and make many millions more in product endorsements. But believing that American sports are free of racism and prejudice is further evidence of the sociological principle that *things are not necessarily what they seem.*

As Eitzen and Sage (2003:276) observed, while black athletes have made significant advances in recent years, "with the exception of professional basketball, the corporate and decision-making structure of professional sports is as white as it was before Jackie Robinson entered major league baseball in 1947."

As we show in Table 10.2, most positions of power in sports—team owners, general managers, head coaches, and directors of player-personnel—remain predominantly white. Superbowl XLI made sports history when it featured two teams with black head coaches.

In the Criminal Justice System In the past two decades, there also have been numerous examples of overt discrimination by law enforcement officials against minorities. While media coverage of the Rodney King trial gave this form of discrimination widespread national attention, it only hinted at the scope of the problem. In *Beyond the Rodney King Story,* the NAACP (1995:xvi) reported that despite the good work of most police officers, "in almost every major urban rebellion of the last three decades, it was some police action directed against African Americans that was the precipitating cause of civil disorder."

Discrimination against minorities in the criminal justice system takes many forms. In 1988, election campaign photos of Willie Horton, a black criminal who committed a brutal rape while on furlough from prison, attempted to link crime and minorities—and reinforced the prejudices of many U.S. voters (Reiman, 2007). Equally insidious is the long-standing practice of whites attributing their criminal acts to minorities. In 1994, for example, Susan Smith of Union, South Carolina, accused a fictitious black man of kidnapping her two young sons. If you are uncertain about whether this case reflects discrimination, ask yourself whether the police, community, and media would have responded in similar ways had the victims been black and the purported kidnapper been identified as white.

There also have been many cases of direct police discrimination against minorities in the past decade, with the FBI annually investigating almost 3,000 cases of civil rights

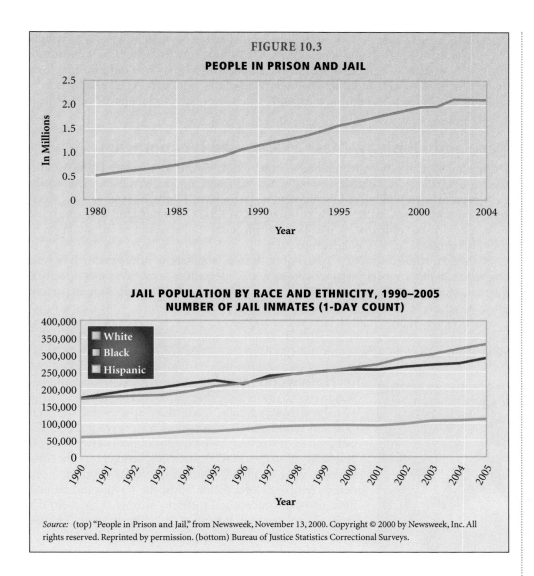

FIGURE 10.3
PEOPLE IN PRISON AND JAIL

JAIL POPULATION BY RACE AND ETHNICITY, 1990–2005
NUMBER OF JAIL INMATES (1-DAY COUNT)

- White
- Black
- Hispanic

Source: (top) "People in Prison and Jail," from Newsweek, November 13, 2000. Copyright © 2000 by Newsweek, Inc. All rights reserved. Reprinted by permission. (bottom) Bureau of Justice Statistics Correctional Surveys.

violations by police officers. The Los Angeles Police Department (LAPD) has had a disproportionate share of these complaints. For example, in the first two months of 1991 alone—the year of the Rodney King beating—the LAPD tallied 127 complaints (which cost taxpayers millions of dollars paid out to victims) (Feagin and Vera, 1995:90).

In 1995, videotape footage of a "Good Ol' Boys Roundup" reinforced minority group concerns about prejudice and discrimination among law enforcement officials. That year, an antigovernment militia member gave the media a video that showed several deputies of the Alcohol, Tobacco and Firearms (ATF) and other law enforcement officers at an annual retreat in the Tennessee mountains that had a "Nigger Check Point" sign, t-shirts with Martin Luther King Jr.'s face behind a target, O. J. Simpson in a hangman's noose, and a black man sprawled across a car with the words "Boyz on the Hood" (*USA Today,* 1995a:4A; Seper, 1995).

Racial bias operates at every level of the criminal justice system. For example, minorities are suspected and arrested for more crimes than whites. Likewise, minorities face more serious charges and are given more serious penalties and longer sentences than whites for the same crimes. In 2000, a coalition of juvenile justice researchers found that "nationally, in every category of offense, minority-youths were more likely than whites to be waived from juvenile to adult courts." Moreover, nearly two-thirds of those sent to state prison for drug offenses were black, "though white users outnumber them more than 5 to 1, according to Human Rights Watch" (Cose, 2000:46). See Figure 10.3 for incarceration rates by race.

Prison and capital punishment statistics provide other grim measures of racial discrimination. One study, "The Death Penalty in Black and White," found that black defendants were 38 percent more likely to be sentenced to die than others who committed similar crimes (Fields and Jones, 1998:3A). Although African Americans constitute slightly more than 12 percent of the American population, they account for more than 50 percent of all federal and state prisoners. And of the more than 4,000 prisoners executed in the United States during the past 70 years, over half of them have been African Americans.

Race and Ethnicity, Mass Media, and Technomedia

During most of the twentieth century white Anglo-Saxon Protestants (WASPs) and their interests and concerns have dominated the mass media. By contrast, minorities have been underrepresented, misrepresented, or presented only in terms of "the social problems they create for the majority" (Riggins, 1992:2). To understand why, one must recognize that not only do WASPs have a disproportionate share of wealth and power, they also control society's "cultural industries."

WASPs constitute less than 25 percent of the U.S. population. White males, however, constitute 90 percent of newspaper editors and 77 percent of television news directors. Further, white Anglo-Saxon men own, finance, produce, and write scripts for 80 percent of what viewers see daily on television and in feature films. Moreover, white men are disproportionately represented as lead actors and heroes, whereas minorities continue to be cast in the roles of sidekicks, villains, criminals, and losers (Barcus, 1983; Perkins, 1990; Blank and Slipp, 1994; Hunt, 2004; Wilson et al., 2004).

In early Hollywood movies, white and black romances were nonexistent and white women could not even touch black men. Today, interracial love affairs and marriages are standard fare, as is evident in *Monster's Ball,* in which Halle Berry and Billy Bob Thornton portray lovers.

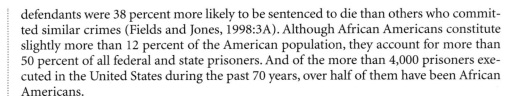

In Hollywood Movies In early Hollywood movies blacks were so unwelcome that whites had to play their parts. When real blacks finally made their appearance between 1900 and World War II, black women were relegated to the background or made occasional appearances as hypersexual "Jezebels" or submissive "mammies," content with their domestic roles and lowly stations in life. By contrast, black men were objects of ridicule, as in the Rastus and Sambo films, or were condemned in films such as D. W. Griffith's *Birth of a Nation* for lusting after white women (Hooks, 1992; Jewell, 1993).

Asians, too, were portrayed as having a special fondness for white women, but in contrast to blacks, who were portrayed as being gullible and inferior, Asians were depicted as a yellow menace intent on world domination. Mexicans represented the most direct and serious threat of all. In early "greaser" films, Mexican bandits were forever crossing the border to rob, murder, rape, pillage, and perform every other known vice (Pettit, 1980; Woll, 1980; Noriega, 1991).

During the 1960s, civil rights protests against racism initiated a shift toward ethnic tolerance and accommodation in both films and real life. Negative stereotypes of African Americans took on new guises in black action movies that typified black inner-city life as violent and drug infested. So did media portrayals of Asian American men as "gangsters, gooks, and geeks" (Zia, 2000:133).

On Television Many media critics contend that black situation comedies perpetuate old racial stereotypes of blacks as sex-crazed and irresponsible. On prime time, Latinos have not fared any better: with the exception of the *George Lopez* show, most Latino characters are either unskilled laborers or violent and menacing gang members and criminals. A 1990s study of "prime-time ethnicity" found that Latinos were four times more likely to commit a crime and twice as likely to be violent on TV than either blacks or whites (Lichter et al., 1994; Gable, 1994). Do you think such images have any influence on the real-life decisions of police officers, judges, and the general public?

Although the government and minority groups monitor programs for negative ethnic stereotypes, studies have been inconclusive regarding how the mass media affect viewer attitudes. Positive television images of racial and ethnic groups appear to alter children's attitudes. For example, in a study made during the 1970s, when positive black roles on television were expanded and blacks assumed a greater number of primary roles, children were asked to name up to three people on television they would like to be. "Forty-three percent of white children between the ages of nine and ten named a black" (Greenberg, 1972).

Research on adults is harder to interpret. Studies showed that liberal and bigoted viewers who watched *All in the Family,* a popular television show in the 1970s, watched, in effect, two different shows. Whereas liberal viewers laughed at Archie Bunker's crude racist views, bigoted viewers agreed with them, and thus their prejudices were reinforced (Vidmar and Rokeach, 1974). What do minority group members think of how they are portrayed on the evening news? A 1994 Gallup poll found that African Americans, Latinos, and Asian Americans were all dissatisfied with their images, and most blacks told pollsters that the "news" worsens rather than improves their image (McAneny, 1994). This sentiment continued into the twenty-first century (Alexassensoh and Hanks, 2001).

Even seemingly benign media messages about race and ethnic relations may have harmful effects. Robert Lichter and colleagues (1994) called most prime-time images of contemporary race relations "pluralism without pain." Their study demonstrated that most prime-time shows focused on "individual bigots"—not widespread racism. Further, while racism is certain to be condemned on prime time, shows rarely suggest ways to eliminate it; that might offend viewers and lower rating points (Lichter et al., 1994). Yanick St. Jean and Joe Feagin (1998) contend that for many media stereotypes, critiques of old shows still apply. Few shows depict everyday minority experience and even fewer depict working and family life. Further, according to James Waller (1998:75) while blatant media racism has declined, more subtle forms remain embedded in American culture. For example, while black actors appear on television in a variety of roles, their interactions with whites often are emotionally distant and detached, with fewer romantic implications—particularly in relationships outside the workplace.

What about television advertising? Mastro and Stern (2003) studied prime-time commercials on six U.S. networks (ABC, CBS, Fox, NBC, UPN, and WB) to see if racial and ethnic minorities were proportionately represented in commercials, and how they were portrayed. They found that African Americans were proportionately represented and were most often seen in commercials for financial services. Asians were under-represented and most frequently appeared in commercials featuring technology. Latinos comprise 12 percent of the population, but they appeared in only 1 percent of commercials, usually as scantily clad young women, and Native Americans were almost nonexistent in prime-time commercials.

Some argue that the twenty-first century has brought revolutionary changes that have turned old media formulas regarding race upside down. Leon Wynter (2002), for example, contends that minority purchasing power and global trade have produced a "browning" of mainstream commercial and popular culture that for centuries had been virtually white-only. In the twenty-first century, "transracial" images dominate advertising, music, and prime-time television, and superstars like Tiger Woods and global celebrities like Colombian pop singer Shakira, will market products to "global consumers" (Wynter, 2002; Day, 2002; Hunt, 2004). Do you agree or disagree that these new "transracial" media images may indeed alter race relations and may even produce racial equality in America and across the globe?

On the World Wide Web Some analysts claim that the Internet and other technomedia may level the playing field by enabling minorities to reach mass audiences and dispel old stereotypes. Technomedia have considerable potential, however, the users of technomedia do not represent a cross-section of the population (see Table 10.3). In 2000, for example, one survey found that 56 percent of whites had Internet access. By contrast, only 33 percent of blacks had access. And the racial divide increased dramatically when household income was included. For those households "with annual incomes

Media celebrities and stars such as Beyonce blur arbitrary racial categories and are popular with audiences of all races and ethnicities.

TABLE 10.3
ADULT HOME COMPUTER AND INTERNET USE BY RACE/ETHNICITY, UNITED STATES CURRENT POPULATION SURVEY, 2003

	PERCENT WITH HOME COMPUTER	PERCENT USING INTERNET AT HOME
White	71.5%	64.3%
Black	49.6%	40.0%
Latino	46.7%	37.3%
Native American	50.1%	40.5%
Asian	76.5%	69.7%

Note: All estimates are calculated using sample weights provided by the CPS.
Source: From "Explaining Differences in Access to Home Computers and the Internet; A comparison of Latino Groups to the Other Ethnic Racial Groups," Electronic Commerce Research. Reprinted by permission of Robert Fairlie.

below $40,000, whites were six times as likely as blacks to have used the World Wide Web in the week prior to the survey" (Harmon, 1998:1A). In a 2005 study, race was found to be one of the strongest factors related to access to the Internet (Wasserman and Richmond-Abbott, 2005).

Today scores of websites and chat groups examine the reality of race and ethnicity. In the United States, virtually all minority groups are on-line, including the NAACP, Southern Christian Leadership Conference, and the Anti-Defamation League, to name a few. All of these groups actively promote more positive and accurate views of minority groups and race relations. Racist hate groups and individuals, however, have proliferated on the Internet as well. On any given day, it is not difficult to find blatant racism in chat room discussions, in usenet newsgroups, and on many Internet bulletin boards.

DOMINANT-MINORITY GROUP RELATIONS

When different racial and ethnic groups come in contact they may welcome the other and emphasize shared beliefs and practices, or they may recognize differences but acknowledge the other group's special talents and abilities. A third possibility is for each group to emphasize cultural differences and define the other as an actual or potential threat. Because the dominant group has greater power than the minority, its actions are particularly important. But minority groups are not powerless, and their cultural orientations and actions also influence intergroup relations.

Cultural Pluralism

Cultural pluralism occurs *when racial and ethnic groups cooperate while still retaining their distinctive identities and lifestyles.* Cultural pluralism often reflects the desires of minority groups to cooperate with others, yet preserve their distinctive cultural heritages. They may do so in relative equality, as in Switzerland, where Germans, French, and Italians live together in harmony despite differences in language, religion, and customs. In many other cases, though, cultural pluralism reflects tolerance and accommodation on the part of dominant groups, or their attempts to promote ethnic diversity to maintain power by a system of divide and rule (Marden et al., 1992).

Assimilation

Powerful ethnic groups also may encourage or demand that a minority group modify its way of life to conform to the dominant group. **Assimilation** is *a process in which minority groups lose their distinctive identities and conform to cultural patterns of the dominant group.* Milton Gordon (1964, 1978) identified three major variants of assimilation: *cultural assimilation,* in which a minority is encouraged or required to adopt the host group's culture; *structural assimilation,* where members of the minority group are encouraged or required to participate in the dominant group's social organizations, schools, and churches; and *marital assimilation,* where the minority is encouraged or permitted to marry members of the dominant group. Given less than 3 percent of all U.S. marriages are interracial, "the conclusion is inescapable . . . a European–non-European distinction remains a central division of [American] society" (Lieberson and Waters, 1998:248) (see Table 10.4).

CULTURAL PLURALISM
When racial and ethnic groups cooperate while still retaining their distinctive identities and lifestyles.

ASSIMILATION
A process in which minority groups lose their distinctive identities and conform to cultural patterns of the dominant group.

Most social scientists believe that for much of U.S. history, the "melting pot" concept was a myth. While minorities may have altered the national culture in some areas such as religion, cuisine, recreation, and music, for the most part the melting has meant "Anglo-Conformity" (Parrillo, 2006).

Segregation

In some cases, the dominant group may decide to enforce **segregation,** which is *the physical or social exclusion of minority groups from dominant group activities.* This may be done by law (*de jure* segregation) or by customs and norms (*de facto* segregation) that are deeply embedded in social institutions.

TABLE 10.4
DEGREE OF ASSIMILATION OF AMERICAN ETHNIC GROUPS

	CULTURAL ASSIMILATION	SECONDARY STRUCTURAL ASSIMILATION	PRIMARY STRUCTURAL ASSIMILATION
Anglo-Protestants (core group)	High	High	High
Northwestern Europeans	High	High	High
Irish Catholics	High	High	Moderate
Southern and Eastern European Catholics	Moderate	Moderate	Moderate
Jews	Moderate	High	Moderate
Asians	Moderate	Moderate	Moderate
Hispanics	Moderate	Low	Moderate
American Indians	Moderate	Low	Moderate
Blacks	High	Low	Low

Source: From *Race and Ethnic Relations, American and Global Perspectives* 7th edition by Marger, 2006. Reprinted with permission of Wadsworth, a division of Thomson Learning: www.thomsonrights.com. Fax 800 730-2215.

In the future, will all forms of assimilation become moderate or high for all American ethnic groups?

Sometimes the dominant group may find "population transfer"—a euphemism for the forced expulsion of a minority group—preferable (Simpson and Yinger, 1972). On the surface, the *expulsion* of a people seems more humane than mass slaughter, but in many cases the costs are as high. For example, in 1838, white land hunger led the U.S. government to forcibly remove the Cherokee Indians from their homes in the southeastern United States, and in what is today known as the *Trail of Tears* almost one-quarter of the thousands of Cherokee marchers perished on their way to Indian territory in Oklahoma (Divine et al., 2007).

Over the past century, it has been routine policy of many governments to expel "foreigners" to gain possession of their lands and businesses, reduce economic competition, or achieve other objectives. Minority expulsion is rarely described in these terms, however. When Japanese Americans were removed forcibly from their American and Canadian homes and moved to "relocation camps" during World War II, both governments claimed they did it for "national security" reasons.

When a minority group believes it has the power to do so, it may attempt to *secede* from the dominant group. Alternatively, they may respond to oppression through *avoidance.* Chinatowns in the United States, for example, are in part an avoidance response by the Chinese to many years of white hatred and discrimination. More commonly, minority groups challenge and defy the dominant group.

Defiance may involve *organized protests.* In the 1960s, some of the most effective *nonviolent protests* that African Americans used to end racial segregation were sit-ins, marches, and freedom rides in areas that practiced discrimination. Economic boycotts against businesses that would not serve or hire minorities also helped end segregation (Parrillo, 2006). At other times, *armed confrontations* or *violent protests* may be used to oppose dominant group policies and actions. The latter include strategic bombings of public buildings and spontaneous outbreaks of violence, such as riots that occurred in many American cities following Dr. Martin Luther King Jr.'s assassination on April 4, 1968.

When all else fails, a minority group may resort to *rebellion,* as did black preacher Nat Turner and his fellow slaves, who, responding to a holy vision to destroy their white oppressors, killed nearly 60 plantation owners and members of their families before white forces counterattacked, and Turner and his followers were executed (Divine et al., 2005).

SEGREGATION
Physical or social exclusion of minority groups from dominant group activities.

Genocide

Where conflict between groups is intense and the dominant group recognizes no alternatives, a racial and ethnic minority may be completely rejected and its members targeted for *extermination*. The annihilation of a minority may be unintentional, as when Puritans brought deadly diseases to which Native Americans had no immunity. **Genocide,** by contrast, is *the deliberate and systematic elimination of minority group members.* The practice of eliminating minorities is older than civilization but is by no means a relic of the dim past. There are numerous cases of genocide in the twentieth century, including the mass murder of more than 6 million Jews during World War II by German Nazis.

At various times one or more of these patterns have prevailed in the United States. In the next section we provide a demographic snapshot of ethnicity in the twenty-first century, as well as a historical portrait of race and ethnic relations that continue to have a strong influence on American society and culture.

RACE AND ETHNIC DIVERSITY IN THE UNITED STATES

What does it mean to be an American? Your answer probably depends not only on your personal experiences but also on your racial and ethnic heritages. No other nation has permitted such high levels of immigration, nor has any nation given immigrants such a range of choices—to retain their heritages, to assimilate and become "American," or to invent their own rules for living in a pluralistic society. Over the years, however, not all groups have been welcome, nor have they been treated the same, as we discuss in this abbreviated history of racial and ethnic relations in the United States. Although it is inexact, demography provides one measure of national policy toward different racial and ethnic groups. Table 10.5 lists American racial and ethnic groups in 2000, their approximate numbers, percentage of the total population, and changes during this period. It also gives population projections for 2050.

TABLE 10.5
INTO THE FUTURE: U.S. POPULATION (IN MILLIONS)

	2000	2050	% change 2000–2050
White (Non-Hispanic)	195.7	210.3	+7%
Black (Non-Hispanic)	35.8	61.4	+71%
Hispanic (Any Race)	35.6	102.6	+188%
Asian/Pacific Islander	10.7	33.4	+213%

Source: Table 094, "United States Population Projections by Race and Hispanic Origin, 2000–2050," U.S. Census Bureau, International Database.

White Anglo-Saxon Protestants

The term *White Anglo-Saxon Protestant (WASP)* has many meanings. In sociology it reflects that segment of the U.S. population that founded the nation and traced their heritages to England, Scotland, and other parts of Western Europe. Today, the term *WASP* has negative connotations: for many, it is associated with racism and intolerance. Sociologist E. Digby Baltzell, a WASP and a member of the upper class, however, had more positive associations in mind. To Baltzell, WASP heritage was associated not only with wealth and power but also with public service and a special obligation to lead the nation and keep it running smoothly (Baltzell, 1958, 1990).

WASPs have indeed dominated the U.S. political economy for many centuries. Not only did the English create the original 13 colonies, they also filled it with Anglo-Saxon Protestant settlers. In 1790, when the first U.S. census was taken, 78 percent of the population claimed descent from England, Scotland, or Wales. During the nineteenth and twentieth centuries, waves of Irish Catholic, Italian, Polish, and other non-Anglo groups emigrated to America and WASPs became a numerical minority. Today, there are about 60 million WASPs, or less than 25 percent of the U.S. population. Nevertheless, they continue to dominate the nation's political economy and have disproportionate influence over most other American institutions. Moreover, the term *WASP* has become much more inclusive in recent years. To many people, WASPs now include most "white" people who are not acknowledged to be members of any minority group (Parrillo, 2006).

American Indians and Native Alaskans

In 2000, over 2.5 million people claimed to be all or part American Indian or Native Alaskan. In the United States, one in four lived in Oklahoma or California, with Cherokee (over 700,000) and Navajo (nearly 300,000) listed most often (U.S. Census Bureau,

GENOCIDE
Deliberate and systematic elimination of minority group members.

2001a). No minority group has suffered more at the hands of the dominant group than the original inhabitants of North America. Between 1800 and 1850, 500,000 Native Americans perished—some from European-introduced diseases but many others at the hands of settlers, the American military, and corrupt or misguided government officials.

To Europeans, the 300 or so diverse Native American cultures were obstacles to their vision of the land as profit. Moreover, Native American cultures were so diverse that the European invaders used every tactic to deal with them—from genocide to segregation, expulsion, assimilation, and cultural pluralism (Axtell, 1981).

Both on and off reservations, Native Americans continue to be penalized for being Indians. In housing, income, employment, and health, they are among the poorest of the poor. Nearly 30 percent of Native Americans live below the poverty level, and the unemployment rate on many reservations is over 50 percent. Native Americans also have the highest infant mortality rates, and the average life span for Native Americans is about 10 years below the national average. Indians are among America's least healthy, most accident-prone, and most poorly educated citizens, and Indian suicide, homicide, and alcoholism death rates are well above those of the general population (Axtell, 1981; Marden et al., 1992; Parrillo, 2006).

Against this background, Native American accomplishments and self-help efforts continue to be remarkable. In 1828 Sequoyah, the son of a Cherokee mother and British father, invented a system of writing in Cherokee and published the first Native American newspaper, *The Cherokee Phoenix,* which is still published today. Permitted to re-create self-governing political units and economic corporations in 1934, many Native American groups became competitive in agriculture, industry, education, and tourism. After World War II, with the help of political movements such as the National Congress of American Indians (NCAI) and the American Indian Movement (AIM), many Native Americans began to reclaim political power, which in 1992 included the election of the first-ever Native American U.S. Senator—Ben Nighthorse Campbell of Colorado and the Cheyenne tribe (Garbarino, 1976).

Latinos

Today, the Latino population is America's largest minority group, having overtaken the African American group. In 2002, there were approximately 39 million Latinos in the United States, or about 13 percent of the population (see Figure 10.4). In addition, various studies estimate that there are about 6 million undocumented workers in the United States, most of them Latino. The Census Bureau estimates that by 2050, the Latino population will have grown to 183 million and approximately one out of every four persons in the United States will be a Latino American. This would result in the Latino population being greater than "those of all other minority groups combined" (Gracia and DeGreiff, 2000:1).

Latinos form both one of America's oldest and one of its newest immigrant groups. Spanish speakers were in Florida in the fifteenth century and in the Southwest before the Pilgrims landed at Plymouth Rock in 1620. Most, however, arrived in the last few decades, and currently nearly 85 percent of all Latinos are first-generation Americans.

While the media prefer the term *Hispanic* and often treat Hispanics as a homogeneous group, this label includes many ethnic groups with diverse histories and cultures. Mexican Americans, Puerto Ricans, Cubans, and many other groups from South and Central America and the Caribbean rarely use the term *Hispanic:* they make finer

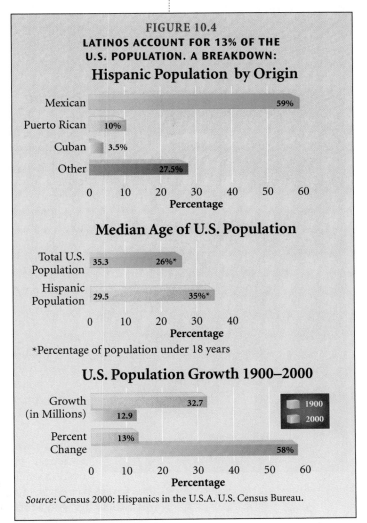

FIGURE 10.4

LATINOS ACCOUNT FOR 13% OF THE U.S. POPULATION. A BREAKDOWN:

Hispanic Population by Origin

Origin	Percentage
Mexican	59%
Puerto Rican	10%
Cuban	3.5%
Other	27.5%

Median Age of U.S. Population

Total U.S. Population: 35.3, 26%*
Hispanic Population: 29.5, 35%*

*Percentage of population under 18 years

U.S. Population Growth 1900–2000

Growth (in Millions): 32.7 / 12.9
Percent Change: 13% / 58%

1900
2000

Source: Census 2000: Hispanics in the U.S.A. U.S. Census Bureau.

distinctions based on language, race, nationality, and subgroups within nationalities. In Miami, for example, most Cubans identify themselves simply as Cubans. Some, however, refer to themselves as Afro-Cubans, Cuban-Jews (Jubans), or other labels. Many Texans with Mexican ancestry, by contrast, refer to themselves as *Tejanos*. Others with Mexican ancestry call themselves *Chicanos*, and still others in New Mexico prefer *Hispanos* to describe themselves. Many people who have recently moved to the United States from Central America use none of these labels but typically prefer national identities—such as Nicaraguan or Guatemalan (Heyck, 1994; *The Economist*, 1998c).

Mexican Americans, who are descendants of Spanish colonists and Native Americans, today number more than 13 million, or 67 percent of the Latino population. Today, 80 percent of the Mexican American population lives in cities. Until recently, most Mexican immigration centered on five states: Texas, Arizona, California, New Mexico, and Illinois. During the 1990s, however, "Mexican immigration was transformed from a regional to a national phenomenon, with nearly one-third of new arrivals going to places other than the five traditional gateway states" (Durand et al., 2000:1). Despite their long history in the United States, Mexican-origin people continue to perform as badly as, or worse than, other American minorities—in wages, poverty rates, and other measures of well-being (Livingston and Kahn, 2002:1003). In 2006, illegal immigration from Mexico into the United States became a hotly debated political issue.

Cuban Americans and Puerto Ricans, who account for about 20 percent of the Latino population, tend to have opposite effects on the overall socioeconomic status of the Latino population. While many Puerto Ricans arrived with few skills and no money, perhaps as many as 70 percent of all Cuban immigrants were skilled workers and white-collar professionals (Dinnerstein and Reimers, 1988). The more than 100,000 Cubans who arrived in the 1980 Mariel Boatlift were not as skilled as their predecessors, but because the latter had built a strong institutional support system in Miami and throughout South Florida, many were able to make a much smoother and more rapid transition to American life.

Condoleezza Rice succeeded the first U.S. African American Secretary of State, Colin Powell, and many of her supporters urged her to run for president.

African Americans

People who trace their ancestry to Africa constitute America's second largest racial minority. In 2000, the U.S. Census Bureau recorded around 36 million African Americans, or slightly more than 12 percent of the total population. By 2050, government estimates suggest that African Americans will total 61 million, or around 14 percent of the population (U.S. Census Bureau, 2001a).

Some early settlers (like many whites) arrived in the country as indentured servants; others were classified as slaves. Planter dependence on slave labor, a widespread fear of black competition by white colonists, and a massive relocation of men, women, and children from west and central Africa to the 13 colonies, however, ended America's brief experiment with "a genuinely multiracial free society" (Divine et al., 2006:79). Beginning in the 1660s, laws were passed that made blacks slaves for life, and children who were born to a slave woman became slaves regardless of their father's race.

In 1863, in the midst of the Civil War, President Lincoln issued the Emancipation Proclamation, which freed all slaves in Confederate territory; 2 years later, near the end of the war, Congress approved the Thirteenth Amendment to the Constitution, which outlawed involuntary servitude everywhere in the nation. For the 4 million or so former slaves, however, the dream of freedom in America was brief. By the turn of the century, Southern vigilante terrorism and Jim Crow laws produced two societies—a white one of privilege and power, and a black one of "utter destitution in money, knowledge and rights" (Stengel, 1985). In the South, blacks were barred from voting, using public facilities, attending schools with whites, and associating with whites for reasons other than economic necessity. Politically disenfranchised and facing grinding poverty and violence, many blacks voted with their feet.

In 1900, 90 percent of blacks lived in the South—most on farms and in rural communities. Over the next few decades, more than 4 million blacks pushed north to cities to find work in factories, educate their children, and regain their political rights (Pinkney, 1987). At the forefront of these efforts was the National Association for the Advancement of Colored People (NAACP), organized in 1905 by sociologist W. E. B. DuBois and other black leaders (Collins and Makowsky, 1993).

African Americans took a major step in securing their constitutional rights in 1954 when future Supreme Court Justice Thurgood Marshall and others challenged segregated schools in *Brown v. Board of Education of Topeka, Kansas*—and won. The Civil Rights movement in the 1960s added to these gains. On the surface, black progress has been dramatic—especially in the political arena.

In 1964, there were only about 170 black elected officials in the United States; by 1988, there were almost 7,000 (Beeghley, 1989:369). Today, there are more than 250 black mayors, and blacks head America's largest and most influential cities. Blacks also have made important gains in government, possibly the most significant being the appointment of Clarence Thomas to the U.S. Supreme Court, General Colin Powell as head of the Joint Chiefs of Staff and Secretary of State, and Condoleezza Rice as Secretary of State. For many Americans, though, black celebrities such as Bill Cosby and Tiger Woods are the strongest proof that discrimination is a thing of the past and that members of any race can make it—if they are willing to put forth the effort.

To evaluate claims that blacks have achieved equality in America, however, we must look beyond the handful of black celebrities and government officials and examine the economic and social conditions of ordinary African Americans. Some statistics are positive. Black men have moved into the middle class in increasing numbers and the mobility of black women has been even greater (Horton et al., 2000). A *Washington Post* (2006) poll showed that black men have mixed feelings about their progress, with 6 in 10 saying it is a "good time" to be a black man in the United States and a majority saying they believe in the American dream. At the same time, however, 60 percent say they have been discriminated against, and two-thirds tell their sons that they will have to be better and work harder than whites for equal rewards. Most sociologists agree that over the last three decades civil rights legislation and affirmative action programs have helped narrow—but have not closed—the gap between whites and blacks in terms of income, average years of schooling, and more equal opportunities.

Asian Americans

In 2000, the U.S. Census Bureau listed slightly more than 10 million Asian Americans and under a separate category about 400,000 Native Hawaiians and Pacific Islanders; together they constituted nearly 4 percent of the population. Asian Americans are the fastest growing minority group in the United States. Between 1980 and 1990, the Asian American population grew from 3.5 million to 7.3 million, a gain of more than 107 percent (U.S. Bureau of the Census, 2001a, 1991a; Marden et al., 1992). By 2050, the Census Bureau estimates that the Asian American population will increase to 33.4 million, more than triple the current population (Meacham, 2000:40).

The Asian American label lumps together more than a dozen ethnic groups with diverse histories, national origins, languages, religions, and customs. The Chinese, Filipinos, Koreans, and Japanese who

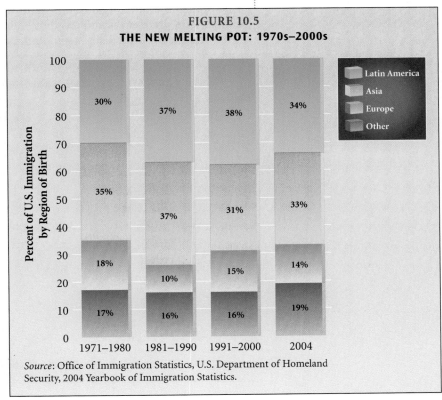

FIGURE 10.5
THE NEW MELTING POT: 1970s–2000s

Source: Office of Immigration Statistics, U.S. Department of Homeland Security, 2004 Yearbook of Immigration Statistics.

have lived in America since the nineteenth century are the largest groups. Groups of Koreans, Asian Indians, and numerous Southeast Asians who migrated to America in the second half of the twentieth century, however, are expanding. Since the passage of the Hart-Celler Act in 1965, more than 40 percent of all immigrants to America have been from Asia (Parrillo, 2006). Figure 10.5 depicts the home regions and numbers of immigrants who moved to the United States between the 1960s and 1990s.

Few Americans are unaware of Asian American successes in education and business. By 2000, 85 percent of Asian Americans had high school degrees, an astounding 50 percent had college degrees, and Asian Americans were disproportionately represented as winners of most major scholastic prizes and honors. As a group, Asian Americans have outpaced whites as professionals, managers, and executives. While one in five whites have attained these statuses, for Asian Indians, Chinese, and Japanese, the percentages are 47 percent, 30 percent, and 28 percent, respectively (U.S. Bureau of Census, 2000). Moreover, Asian Americans had advanced in politics as well. In 1998, for example, "More than 300 Asian Americans and Pacific Islanders were elected to office in the United States and its territories" (Zia, 2000:308).

These successes have led politicians, journalists, and newscasters to confer on Asian Americans the title "model minority" or sometimes, "America's trophy population" (Winnick, 1990:23). While sociologists agree that Asian Americans have made impressive gains in the last half-century, most caution against accepting a new Asian stereotype that all Asian Americans are math geniuses and prosperous white-collar professionals. In fact, vast differences separate both individuals and Asian American groups. According to Louis Winnick (1990:23–24), "Beneath a thick crust of scientists, professionals, and entrepreneurs are thicker layers of struggling families . . . who eke out a bare living by dint of double jobs and the presence of multiple wage earners."

Euro-American Ethnics

Euro-American ethnics are for the most part non-WASP groups who migrated to America from Europe during the past century. Aided by immigration quotas that favored European groups during the nineteenth and much of the twentieth centuries, Euro-American ethnics are numerically dominant in America (see Figure 10.6).

It is easy to understand why ethnicity is so important to first-generation Euro-American ethnics: the adjustment to becoming an American is made easier by personal networks and ethnic organizations and by living and working with those who share similar food preferences and customs (Alba, 1990). The persistence of ethnicity among Euro-Americans who have been in America for generations is harder to explain,

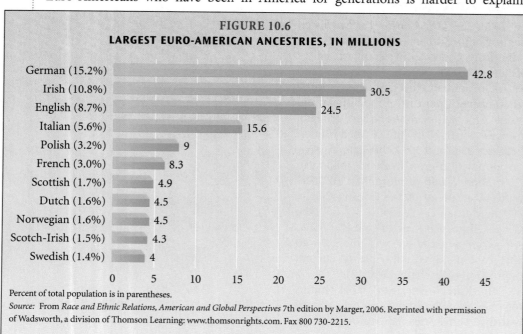

FIGURE 10.6
LARGEST EURO-AMERICAN ANCESTRIES, IN MILLIONS

German (15.2%) — 42.8
Irish (10.8%) — 30.5
English (8.7%) — 24.5
Italian (5.6%) — 15.6
Polish (3.2%) — 9
French (3.0%) — 8.3
Scottish (1.7%) — 4.9
Dutch (1.6%) — 4.5
Norwegian (1.6%) — 4.5
Scotch-Irish (1.5%) — 4.3
Swedish (1.4%) — 4

Percent of total population is in parentheses.

Source: From *Race and Ethnic Relations, American and Global Perspectives* 7th edition by Marger, 2006. Reprinted with permission of Wadsworth, a division of Thomson Learning: www.thomsonrights.com. Fax 800 730-2215.

however. Historian Marcus Hansen (1952) proposed that ethnicity passed through three historic stages: in the first generation ethnicity is dominant as immigrants adapt to a new environment; in the second generation the immigrants' children discard their ethnic heritages and assimilate into mainstream culture; by the third generation, the immigrants' grandchildren—Americanized and secure in their socioeconomic status—seek to rediscover their roots, which in turn leads to ethnic revival.

There is much evidence that ethnic revival began in the 1960s and peaked during America's bicentennial celebrations, when it seemed that white middle-class Americans were searching for their "roots." Gans (1979b) called this "symbolic ethnicity," a low-cost, minimal commitment version of ethnicity in which people occasionally marched in parades, attended group ceremonies and ate ethnic foods, and in other symbolic ways acknowledged their ethnic heritages.

Another way of explaining ethnic persistence and revival is to view ethnicity as a process rather than something fixed and unidirectional. For example, conflict theorists emphasize that for some Euro-American groups, ethnic revival was a backlash to the Civil Rights movement and affirmative action programs, which threatened to diminish the tenuous class positions of the Irish, Italian, and other Euro-Americans in many urban areas. These struggles are by no means over, and we should expect ethnic consciousness and group actions to ebb and flow as groups jockey for power and their "fair share" of jobs, benefits, and prestige.

the **FUTURE**

LOOKING to

RACE AND ETHNIC RELATIONS IN THE TWENTY-FIRST CENTURY

What will race and ethnic relations be like in this century? A poll taken in 2006 showed that 75 percent of white Americans and 60 percent of black Americans believe there is greater racial equality in the United States than ever before, and that most people were optimistic about the future, although African Americans were not nearly as sanguine about achieving racial equality anytime soon (AP, Washington, 2006). Clearly, white attitudes have changed in the last half-century. In some polls, taken during the 1990s, more than 90 percent of whites said they would vote for an African American presidential candidate—something that would have been inconceivable only a few decades ago.

There are similar trends in attitudes concerning interracial dating and marriage. In a 1980 Gallup Poll that surveyed teens about interracial dating, only 17 percent noted that they had dated someone of another race. Toward the end of the 1990s, 57 percent of teenagers surveyed reported that they had dated interracially. Moreover, only 13 percent of teenagers told pollsters they would not consider dating a member of another race (*USA Today*, 1997b:1). Likewise, in the 1950s, only 4 percent of Americans said they approved of interracial marriage. By the end of the twentieth century, more than 60 percent voiced approval of black-white marriages. These attitudes are supported by statistics that showed well over a million interracial couples in 2000—four times as many as 1970 (see Figure 10.7). Nevertheless, as noted earlier, fewer than 3 percent of all marriages in the United States were interracial (*USA Today*, 1997a, 1997b; *The Economist*, 1998e) and social barriers still exist against interracial dating (Vahquera and Kao, 2005).

As you are by now well aware, we should be cautious about polling data—especially on sensitive subjects such as race, and even public understandings of American racial groups. Few Americans want to be associated with unpopular views like being a racist, and this influences poll results. Opinion polls may be helpful to measure racial progress, but we should also examine public policies and social trends that promote or retard racial and ethnic equality. By this measure, the signals are mixed.

FIGURE 10.7

U.S. INTERRACIAL COUPLES IN MILLIONS AND AS PERCENT OF ALL MARRIED COUPLES, 1970–2000

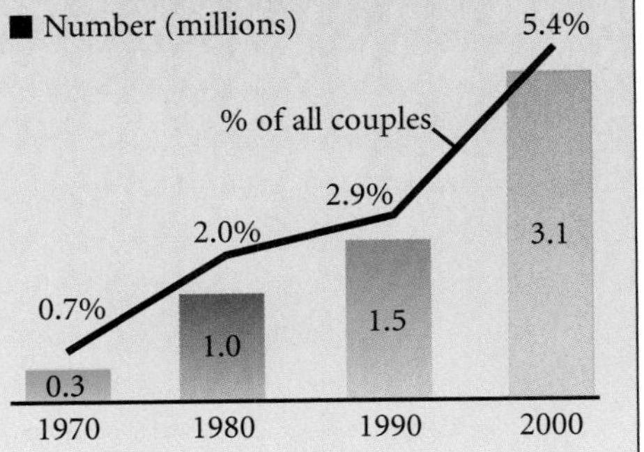

■ Number (millions)

5.4%

% of all couples

2.9%

2.0%

0.7%

0.3   1.0   1.5   3.1

1970   1980   1990   2000

Source: From *Population Bulletin*, Vol. 60, No. 2, 2005. Reproduced by permission of Population Reference Bureau.

In the past decade or so, minorities and immigrants have been the special target of white anger and resentment. White hate groups have proliferated and have become more violent, with increasing attacks on schools, churches, homes, and individuals. Deeper currents of prejudice and discrimination are reflected in numerous white challenges to minority incursions into traditional bastions of white privilege. Across the nation there have been many calls to halt immigration, as well as successful challenges to affirmative action. Likewise, there have been many attempts to make English the nation's official language.

In California, Texas, and other states there are citizen initiatives that would deny public services such as medical care and public assistance to legal and illegal immigrants. Will these trends continue in this twenty-first century, further widening the gap between whites and nonwhites?

Some writers, such as Peter Brimelow, appear to blame immigrants and the Immigration Act of 1965 in particular for much of the nation's problems. The act eliminated a long-standing pro-European immigration bias and opened the golden door to people of color from the Southern Hemisphere. Since the new policy began, "the proportion of foreign-born residents . . . has tripled, . . . today, one in ten Americans are foreign born" (Talwar, 2002:4). Brimelow claims that because new immigrants are more racially and culturally diverse than those of any previous era, they are not assimilating to "American culture." Moreover, their numbers are growing so rapidly that they and other people of color are becoming numerically dominant, something that nativists claim may threaten the nation's future. (See Figure 10.8.)

Many sociologists argue that this thesis is yet another attempt to blame the victim. Some sociologists maintain that American popular culture, which has spread across the globe, has actually made new immigrants more familiar with the many facets of American life than their predecessors (Wrong, 2000). However, many agree that demographic trends that project steady declines in both white and Anglo-Saxon segments of the population will affect future race and ethnic relations. Already, people of color are numerically dominant in California. To reflect the new ethnic reality in California, "the San Diego City Council decided to ban [the word] 'minority' from official documents and discussions, claiming the term was 'outmoded and demeaning'" (Rodriguez, 2002). Do you agree that "minority" has little meaning now that whites are a numerical minority

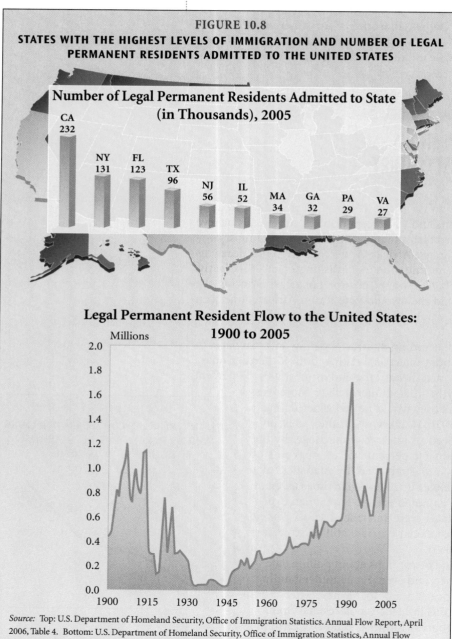

FIGURE 10.8

STATES WITH THE HIGHEST LEVELS OF IMMIGRATION AND NUMBER OF LEGAL PERMANENT RESIDENTS ADMITTED TO THE UNITED STATES

Number of Legal Permanent Residents Admitted to State (in Thousands), 2005

CA 232, NY 131, FL 123, TX 96, NJ 56, IL 52, MA 34, GA 32, PA 29, VA 27

Legal Permanent Resident Flow to the United States: 1900 to 2005

Source: Top: U.S. Department of Homeland Security, Office of Immigration Statistics. Annual Flow Report, April 2006, Table 4. Bottom: U.S. Department of Homeland Security, Office of Immigration Statistics, Annual Flow Report, April 2006, Figure 1.

in California? In addition to California, people of color have become numerically dominant in New Mexico and Hawaii, and in most major American cities (Gitlin, 2000).
Demographers predict that other states will soon follow: Texas in 2015 and, within a few
decades, Arizona, New York, Nevada, and New Jersey, among others. By 2050 whites will
no longer be a numerical majority—not only in most cities and states, but in the nation as
a whole.

One writer contends that in the twenty-first century the rising number of biracial
and multiracial Americans will hasten the demise of the legitimacy of traditional racial
systems such as the "one drop of blood system" and the contemporary scheme that is
based on "appearance." According to Korgen (1998:118):

> The United States will never again be a predominantly white monoracial society.
> This fact either can bring us closer together or tear us further apart. No matter what
> the outcome, though, one thing is certain regarding our monoracial past: it is over.
> Our multiracial future is at hand.

Will these changes lead to a more equal distribution of social rewards among ethnic
groups and more permeable group boundaries—especially those separating whites and
nonwhites? Or will whites become more protective of their wealth and privileges as
their numbers shrink, leading to more subtle or more rigid racial and ethnic distinctions and boundaries. There is support for both arguments. Of course, minority group
members will play a major role in defining racial and ethnic identities, as we discuss in
Focus box 10.3.

A Gallup poll conducted in 2000 suggested considerable pessimism about future race
relations, with many respondents answering in the affirmative that "race relations will
always be a problem" (Ludwig, 2000:56). And the most advantaged blacks (those with
the highest household income and greater amounts of formal education) hold the most
pessimistic opinions (Ludwig, 2000; Simmons and Parsons, 2005). Moreover, perceptions of white and black Americans about race relations, and how blacks are treated in
the United States, "continue to diverge." In one survey in the early twenty-first century, a
gap of 38 percentage points separated black and white respondents on the question of
whether "blacks and whites were treated the same way in local communities" (Ludwig,
2000:53) and research shows that racial empowerment does not ameliorate perceptions
of unfairness (Overby et al., 2005). Some scholars see positive trends in Supreme Court
decisions supporting affirmative action as well as a growing number of employers and
human resource personnel who recognize diversity in employment and education as
essential to America's future. These affirmative action advocates are having "a direct and
positive influence on African American employment, particularly in higher-level jobs
where blacks are relatively rare" (Button and Rienzo, 2003:13). Perhaps these same attitudes can gain traction in the larger society and "diversity management" may reach
minority populations as a whole. Indeed younger generations of whites seem to embrace
diversity, but it is important to understand, one writer noted, that listen to "hip-hop" and
wearing an Allen Iverson jersey does not mean racism is dead (Tarsant, 2006).

Some even see a pronounced shift away from old ideas of "melting" and Anglo conformity, toward more open and tolerant forms of pluralism. One popular model sees
future ethnic relations as a kind of *salad bowl*, a metaphor which stresses that in a true
multicultural society the values of the majority or dominant group would serve as a
kind of dressing that unifies and gives flavor to the whole. However, unlike previous systems these values would enhance, rather than overwhelm or destroy, the uniqueness and
special contributions of ethnic groups.

As you can see, there will be no easy answers to race and ethnic relations in this century. Neither a return to a more favorable economic climate nor more enlightened government officials will solve long-standing problems of prejudice and discrimination.
Perhaps as a first step we should follow the advice of Margaret Andersen and Patricia
Hill Collins (1992:455), who recommend that "building coalitions across differences
and empowering historically marginalized groups requires seeing the connections
among groups differentiated by inequalities of race, class, and gender. Doing so fosters
much-needed social change and eventually empowers us all."

In 2000 the U.S. Census Bureau decided that, for the first time, people would be given the option of checking multiple racial boxes instead of having to choose only one race. Today, there are 6 major racial categories and 63 possible racial and ethnic Census categories, including "11 subcategories under 'Hispanic ethnicity'" (Meachan, 2000:40). And because this system produces many new combinations (black/white, American/Indian/black/white), the Census Bureau reports racial and ethnic group numbers as "ranging from some low, say, of 32 million . . . to high, say, of 60 million (those who identify as partly black)" (Skerry, 2000:196). In fact, in the 2000 Census only about 7 million people chose the multiracial category, with about 5 percent of blacks, 6 percent of Hispanics, 14 percent of Asians, and 2.5 percent of whites identifying themselves as multiracial (Schmitt, 2001:3). This decision by the Census Bureau reflects increases in intermarriage rates among racial groups during the past few decades. It also demonstrates the growing influence of some branches of the Civil Rights movement that insist the current system is false and inaccurate and perpetuates racial stereotypes. These activists seek to end racism and racial inequality by changing the language, labels, and stereotypes that Europeans and Americans have associated with race for centuries.

There are more than 30 grassroots Civil Rights organizations that seek new language and understandings to portray race in contemporary America more accurately. Many of those who are most active in the movement are black and white interracial couples and their children, who want to redefine and broaden the language of race to acknowledge the complexity of contemporary races, as well as to celebrate racial diversity. One of them is superstar golfer Tiger Woods, who stresses his multiracial and multicultural origins—Thai, African American, Native American, and European—and claims that whatever special gifts and talents he may have are a product of all these heritages (Zack, 1995).

A top priority for many activists is to change current racial attitudes and myths that claim that black, white, Asian, and other "races" are mutually exclusive and biologically distinct. Others seek to challenge pseudobiological myths that claim that it is unnatural to mix races or that mixed marriages produce unfit offspring. Such myths have a long history in the United States. For example, proponents of the eugenics movement in the early twentieth century claimed that multiracial children were tormented by their "genetically divided selves and that their identities, social lives, and loyalties are inevitably divided and confused." (Nakashima, 1992:165)

If activists are successful, a new language of race will recognize race as more open, fluid, and holistic. Ideas of race will also be both biologically accurate and socially beneficial for the millions of people whose ancestry is derived from multiple regions of the world. As G. Reginald Daniel (1992:334) wrote:

> Whether they call themselves "mixed," "biracial," or "multiracial," these [movements] represent . . . the next logical step in the progression of civil rights, the expansion of our notion of affirmative action to include strategies not only for achieving socioeconomic equity, but also for affirming a nonhierarchical identity that embraces a "holocentric" racial self.

These activists are not without opposition, however. Not only are some groups determined to retain traditional black-white distinctions that promote white privilege, but groups within the civil rights movement also have challenged new racial labels as potentially damaging to African American political unity and minority advancement. Many opponents, for example, are concerned that new racial labels and consciousness, despite some benefits, may widen the divide between the "less privileged Black masses and the privileged few," who have tended to be disproportionately of lighter skin color and often "less Afrocentric in consciousness and cultural orientation" (Daniel, 1992:335). Others see more flexible racial labels, perhaps an emerging global system that is very much like the Brazilian model, which emphasizes "whitening and blackening"—to the continued advantage of those labeled white (Ong, 1996). Still others, such as Maria Root (1999:451), argue that biracial or multiracial people "have the right to declare how they wish to identify themselves racially—even if this identity is discrepant with how they look or how society tends to perceive them."

TAKING A CLOSER LOOK

Labels have a powerful influence on behavior, and racial labels are particularly potent. Decide which racial terms, if any, should be used by the Census Bureau and explain why your plan will enhance race relations and help reduce prejudice and discrimination.

Source: John Meacham. "The New Face of Race." *Newsweek*, September 18, 2000:38–41. Peter Skerry. *Counting the Census? Race, Group Identity, and the Evasion of Politics.* Washington, DC: Brookings Institution Press, 2000. G. Reginald Daniel. "Beyond Black and White: The New Multiracial Consciousness," in Maria P. Root (ed.), *Racially Mixed People in America.* Newbury Park, CA: Sage, 1992, pp. 333–341. Cynthia L. Nakashima. "An Invisible Monster: The Creation and Denial of Mixed-Race People in America," in Maria P. Root (ed.), *Racially Mixed People in America*, Newbury Park, CA: Sage, 1992, pp. 162–178. Aihwa Ong. "Cultural Citizenship as Subject Making." *Current Anthropology* 17(5), 1996: 737–762.

Summary

1 Minority groups are categories of people who are defined as being physically or culturally different than dominant group members, which results in their being treated unequally. Dominant groups have responded to minorities with behaviors that range from genocide to cultural pluralism. Historically, minority groups rejected by the majority have sought to secede, or rebel or, at the other extreme, accept their subordinate status.

2 Prejudice refers to preconceived judgments toward a category of people, whereas discrimination is the unequal treatment of people because of their group membership. There are three major kinds of discrimination: personal, legal, and institutional.

3 Three major perspectives are used to explain prejudice and discrimination: the psychological perspective, cultural approaches, and conflict perspectives, which emphasize intergroup competition for wealth, power, and prestige.

4 Many forms of discrimination exist in American society including the rise of racist hate groups, as well as in the workplace, education, housing, the criminal justice system, and the media.

5 For much of the twentieth century the mass media promoted and reinforced racial and ethnic prejudices. Some analysts believe the Internet and minority groups' websites will challenge traditional stereotypes and provide more accurate portrayals of minority groups. Others see a continuation of media racial and ethnic stereotypes.

6 Some popular writers anticipate severe racial and ethnic conflicts in this twenty-first century. Others predict a growing climate of racial and ethnic tolerance as people of color become statistically dominant. Sociologists maintain that coalitions based on race, class, and gender will be needed if we are to achieve a true multicultural society.

Key Terms

assimilation (p. 274)
biological race (p. 258)
cultural pluralism (p. 274)
discrimination (p. 264)
ethnic group (p. 261)
ethnicity (p. 261)
ethnocentrism (p. 264)

genocide (p. 279)
institutional discrimination (p. 266)
legal discrimination (p. 266)
minority group (p. 263)
personal discrimination (p. 266)
prejudice (p. 263)
races (p. 259)

racism (p. 263)
scapegoat (p. 264)
segregation (p. 279)
split-labor market (p. 264)
stereotypes (p. 264)

Chapter 11

Sex and Gender

"Women need a reason to have sex, men just need a place."
—Billy Crystal

Although soccer (or football, as it is called in most countries) is perhaps the single most popular spectator sport around the world, prior to 1999 few Americans had ever watched a women's soccer game, and fewer still could name any of the best female soccer players in the world. All that changed in an instant. It was the final game of the Women's World Cup Soccer Championship. The United States and China had battled for 120 minutes, including two overtime periods, only to end in a scoreless tie. In a best-of-five "shoot-out," the first four Chinese players drilled their shots past the American goalie and into the net, as did the first four American players against the Chinese goalie. The fifth Chinese player's shot was deflected by a diving American goalie's fingertips, and Brandi Chastain, a 30-year-old with a blonde ponytail, dubbed by her teammates "Hollywood," lined up for the final kick of the game, and blasted a shot past the Chinese goalie to give America its first World Cup victory. That was the moment that changed women's soccer and perhaps women's sports in America forever, or so it seemed. But, as we have repeatedly noted, *things are not necessarily what they seem.*

You see, while Americans were thrilled that the women's team had won the championship, it is not the scoring of the goal that is permanently etched into American sports history and the minds of American sports fans, but what came next. In what she calls "momentary insanity" (Starr and Brant, 1999:50), Brandi Chastain ripped off her jersey and waved it over her head in jubilance (something that male soccer players had done for years) revealing a black sports bra as she ran around the field and was stormed by her celebrating teammates. While there were approximately 90,000 fans in the stands who witnessed the event, millions watched the highlights on every major network—not the scoring of the goal, but

Brandi Chastain made sports history and media replays around the world when she ripped off her jersey after scoring the winning goal that gave the United States its first World Cup victory.

the ripping off of the jersey and the sports bra–clad celebration. That scene was shown over and over throughout the next several days and weeks as Brandi and her famous teammate, Mia Hamm, made the talk show circuits. Very few interviewers or fans seemed interested in the strategy or play of Brandi and Mia, as most of the questions focused on the famous sports bra photos and Mia's physical beauty, as both were bombarded with offers to pose nude for posters, calendars, and magazines. *The Late Show*'s David Letterman quipped, "in the future fans will come for the Hamm, but they'll stay for the Brandi."

Four years later, just prior to the 2004 World Cup Championships, the World Cup Committee announced several rule revisions. One new rule was that players would be penalized for removing any part of their uniform while on the field. When asked if this was a direct response to Brandi Chastain's famous sports bra–clad celebration, a World Cup official grinned, and responded, "No, not really [pause] we just think that removing the jersey needlessly delays the game" (NBC News, 2003). Interestingly, that was never considered a problem when thousands of male players had done it *during* the middle of matches, but suddenly became a concern when a female did it *after* a game was over.

SEX AND GENDER IN A GLOBAL SOCIETY

When Mazda opened its new production plant in Flat Rock, Michigan, its top-level managers brought more than Japanese technology, manufacturing techniques, and management style to the United States. They also brought their attitudes and values about sex and gender roles to the new plant.

American men working in the plant reported high satisfaction with working conditions, believed they benefited from the team concept of production, and indicated they enjoyed the camaraderie and friendship they had developed with their Japanese trainers, both inside and outside the plant. The 560 American women who worked there, however, told a different story.

The women believed the Japanese yelled at them more than they did at the male workers and treated them more harshly. One female worker said, "If a machine broke down and there was a woman around, the Japanese just naturally assumed it was her fault" (Fucini and Fucini, 1990:112). Initially, some of the women reported being physically and sexually harassed by the Japanese trainers and supervisors and indicated there seemed to be a pervasive attitude among the Japanese that women factory workers must be sexually "loose" and permissive. This problem was quickly addressed and eliminated by the upper levels of management at the plant.

Part of the problems at the Mazda plant stemmed from the fact that Mazda prohibited women from working as production employees in their Japanese plants. Consequently, none of the men sent to the United States to train plant workers had ever worked with women. But a sociological analysis of the situation reveals that the source of many of the problems ran much deeper. At the heart of the issue were deeply ingrained cultural differences between how the Japanese men and the American women viewed appropriate gender roles and behavior.

Notions about sex and gender vary around the world. Many of the problems encountered by American women working with Japanese men at the Mazda plant illustrate some of these differences. Almost all of the Japanese trainers and supervisors indicated that they were surprised by the "assertiveness" of the American women. They admitted that they perceived women as the weaker sex and acknowledged that they often ignored female trainees in classes while showing great interest and patience in training their male counterparts. When a group of American hirees traveled to Hofu for a month-long visit, they were offered an opportunity to attend classes in the Japanese ceremonial tea ritual, Japanese flower arranging, and samurai sword drills. The Japanese were shocked that about half of those who chose the sword drills were women. Moreover, they were astonished that several of the men in the group signed up for the flower-arranging classes. The deputy general manager of Mazda's human development division commented: "I believe women are very gentle and beautiful, and man is strong and not so beautiful. So man should go out into the mountains and battle with a bear or something, not do flower arranging" (Fucini and Fucini, 1990:113).

Over time, the Japanese at the Flat Rock plant modified their attitudes, or at least their behaviors toward the female workers, and not only were the intimidation and harassment stopped but the women also received more fair and equitable treatment. Being set apart for different and unequal treatment on the basis of sex is not unique to Japanese society. In the United States, where there is much more emphasis on equality between the sexes and numerous laws are in place to guard against gender bias, there are a wide range of attitudes about sex and gender roles. For example, in early 1995, the newly elected Speaker of the U.S. House of Representatives, Newt Gingrich, incurred the wrath of both women and men across the country when he told a college history class that women are unsuitable for military combat because they lack upper body strength and are biologically more susceptible to disease and infections. Men, on the other hand, he contended, like to wallow in the mud like piglets and are genetically programmed to go out and hunt giraffes (*Newsweek*, 1995).

These sentiments sound very similar to those expressed by Mazda's deputy general manager of human development, the main difference being only the type of animal men are supposed to hunt. Moreover, incidents at the U.S. Mitsubishi plant reveal that American women experienced similar problems of sexual harassment from their American bosses and co-workers, who, unlike the Japanese, denied and tried to cover up the allegations when confronted with them. We explore the issue of sexual harassment later in this chapter when we look at the problem of sexism in the workplace.

Women and men are different. This undeniable fact has contributed to innumerable myths, stereotypes, and arguments concerning what these differences mean. How much of the difference is based on genetics, biology, and physiology and how much is based on cultural values and social practices? Sociologists pursue answers to these questions when they attempt to differentiate between *sex* and *gender*.

Much of the debate over the differences between women and men stems from people's confusing the terms *sex* and *gender*. **Sex** is based on *biological and physical differences between females and males;* **gender** refers to a *cultural understanding of what constitutes masculinity and femininity in a society.*

Gender became a major issue when Mazda opened its production plant in the United States. Most of the Japanese men sent to train and supervise personnel were surprised to find women working in jobs that violated traditional Japanese expectations of femininity. As a result, many of the American women who worked in the plant felt that they were treated differently from their male co-workers.

Sex: Biological Differentiation

While there is no scientific evidence to support claims that women are unfit for military combat or that men are driven to hunt large animals, at least part of the difference between females and males must be attributed to genetics and biology. Humans have 23 pairs of chromosomes. Two of these are the sex chromosomes, X and Y. The normal chromosomal pattern in females is XX; in males it is XY. During prenatal development, different hormones trigger physical changes in the male and female genitalia and reproductive systems. In rare cases, a hormone imbalance during this period may produce a *hermaphrodite,* a child born with some combination of male and female genitalia. Although the practice is now controversial, for years their genitals were surgically altered to conform to the designation of female and the child was reared to accept the gender identity of female. Such cases have contributed to the nature versus nurture debate discussed in Chapter 4. Most scientists now agree that gender identity is partly innate (linked to chromosomal influence) and partly cultural—a result of socialization.

SEX
Biological and physical differences between females and males.

GENDER
Cultural understanding of what constitutes masculinity and femininity in a society.

Later in life, people develop sex-linked disparities in height, weight, body and facial hair, physical strength, and endurance. And, although research suggests that the brains of females and males may be both structurally and operationally different, most researchers acknowledge that women and men are far more alike than they are different (Phillips, 1990; Shapiro, 1990; Begley, 1995). Since we cannot see people's chromosomes, hormones, or brains, all sex-linked differences are of far less consequence than the cultural and social expectations linked to them. These social and cultural expectations include sexual orientation, sexual activities, and mate selection.

Sexual Orientation and Diversity

Every society creates and enforces norms regarding human sexual behavior, including appropriate sexual objects, desirable qualities in mates, sequences of mating patterns and gestures, and appropriate times, places, and scenarios for sexual activities. Consequently, a person's **sexual orientation,** or *preference of sex partners,* is socially significant. Preference does not necessarily mean *choice.* In Western culture sexual orientation signifies the identity an individual has based on the sexual partners he or she "tends to pair with—either at a particular time or over a lifetime" (Schwartz and Rutter, 1998:32). To ensure procreation, all societies encourage **heterosexuality,** *attraction to partners of the opposite sex,* and most believe that sexual relations should occur within the context of marriage.

Homosexuality and Bisexuality
Homosexuality involves *sexual attraction to partners of the same sex.* Attitudes and norms regarding homosexuality range from acceptance and open participation in some cultures to horror, outrage, and strict legal punishment in others. In Melanesia and New Guinea, homosexuality is practiced in male rituals and is linked to a traditional cultural antagonism between males and females, the superior status of males, and a fear by men that any contact with menstrual blood will weaken them (Herdt, 1984). Among the Etoro of New Guinea, homosexuality is not only accepted but deemed necessary for survival. Etoro men believe semen is the source of men's strength and that each man has a limited supply. Men are not born with semen, however, so as boys they must acquire it by performing oral sex on older men. Sexual intercourse with their wives is necessary for procreation, but since the resulting loss of semen is equated with weakening the male it is participated in very sparingly (Harris, 2003; Miller, 2005). Among some Plains Indians in North America, high status was granted to homosexual men known as *berdache* who dressed as women and provided sexual favors to tribal warriors (Williams, 1986). In these cases, norms for men supported **bisexuality,** *attraction to partners of both sexes.*

In Mombasa, Kenya, because the social worlds of women and men overlap so little, both male and female homosexuality are viewed as a rational decision in Swahili society, and many men and women switch from heterosexuality to bisexuality to homosexuality throughout their lives. Not only are lesbian relationships tolerated there, but after a married woman has become widowed or divorced it is very acceptable for her to choose a lesbian partner for her remaining years. In Swahili culture, social status is more important than love in choosing a marital partner. Thus it may be considered more shocking for a rich woman to marry a poor man than it would be for a poor woman to seek out a wealthy lesbian mate to enhance her social rank (Schultz and Lavenda, 2005).

Although tolerance has increased, in most Western cultures homosexuality is discouraged and often negatively sanctioned. Social changes reflected in the so-called sexual revolution of the 1960s and 1970s made homosexuality more visible as many covert gays and lesbians "came out," publicly declaring their homosexuality. As a result, the gay and lesbian community in most major cities grew from a few isolated bars and bathhouses to fairly large, well-defined *homosocial environments* consisting of shops, hotels, bars, real estate and insurance firms, legal offices, and apartment complexes owned and operated by homosexuals. In the United States lesbians, who faced both homophobia and sexism, were typically viewed as the invisible homosexuals, less likely to admit their homosexuality openly. In the 1990s, however, women came out of the closet in larger numbers and became more visible socially and politically (Salholz et al., 1993; Kushner, 1994). Perhaps one of the most celebrated cases involved comedian Ellen DeGeneres

SEXUAL ORIENTATION
Preference of sex partners.

HETEROSEXUALITY
Attraction to partners of the opposite sex.

HOMOSEXUALITY
Sexual attraction to partners of the same sex.

BISEXUALITY
Attraction to partners of both sexes.

when in 1997 she came out on a highly publicized episode of her popular TV sitcom, *Ellen.* For several weeks before the program aired, it was the topic of discussion in newspaper and magazine articles, on television talk shows, and even on the nightly news. Before the end of that television season, *Ellen* was cancelled. While network executives contended the show's cancellation was related to lowered ratings and not the star's sexual orientation, eventually they conceded that the show had been cancelled because it had become highly controversial and had moved from being entertainment to social advocacy. DeGeneres insisted the show was a victim of homophobia. Nevertheless, by the year 2000, several popular prime-time sitcoms included homosexual characters in leading roles. And, in 2003, DeGeneres launched her own daytime talk show, which has become a consistent Emmy winner. Meanwhile, movies such as *TransAmerica* and *Brokeback Mountain* became box office hits and won Golden Globe and Academy Awards.

Homophobia Because homosexuality and bisexuality challenge strong norms, many homosexuals and bisexuals find that their lifestyle carries heavy social penalties. Conservative attitudes in the 1980s—fueled in part by the discovery of the deadly acquired immune deficiency syndrome (AIDS)—spawned a sexual counterrevolution, and homosexuals encountered renewed widespread prejudice and discrimination. A growing **homophobia**—*hatred and discrimination directed against homosexuals, based on exaggerated fears of homosexuality*—gripped the nation, and homosexuals became the targets of renewed ideological, religious, and physical attacks. Some people contended that AIDS was "God's revenge" for sins against nature perpetrated by homosexuals. Others, often young men insecure about their own sexuality, participated in *gay bashing,* openly assaulting gays. Some rationalized their actions by the apparent link between AIDS and homosexual contact, saying it is "kill or be killed"; others viewed gay bashing as a sport and did it for fun (ABC News, 1995). Harassment, violence, and hate crimes against gays and lesbians increased dramatically in the 1990s, and one observer noted that the nature of the violence changed from slurs and drive-by egg tossings to attacks with switchblades and nail-studded baseball bats (Turque et al., 1992). Hate crimes against homosexuals have continued into the twenty-first century.

As a result, some gays and lesbians choose to hide their homosexuality rather than risk the social repercussions of disclosure. This tactic prompted a new movement in the gay community, known as *outing.* Gay and lesbian newspapers and magazines "out" (publicly reveal) covert homosexuals, especially public figures in politics, business, or entertainment. Another response has been the reinforcement of gay and lesbian solidarity and a push for more research on, better medical treatment of, increased social awareness of, and factual information about all sexually transmitted diseases, as well as equal treatment under the law. Some bisexuals feel that the new solidarity movement on the part of homosexuals may make them the most marginal group of all, because they may experience rejection from both homosexual society and the gay and lesbian communities.

Explaining Sexual Orientation How and why an individual develops a heterosexual, homosexual, or bisexual orientation is not clearly understood (Wilton, 2005; Omoto and Kurtzman, 2006). Alfred Kinsey's landmark studies on sexual behavior in human males (1948) and females (1953) as well as Fritz Klein's research in sexuality (1979, 1994) suggest that sexual orientation is better understood on a continuum ranging from exclusively heterosexual to exclusively homosexual at the two ends of the spectrum with a wide range of variations of bisexuality and sexual preferences in between, rather than thinking of sexual orientation as dichotomous—either heterosexual or homosexual. There is growing evidence that biological factors may play a role in sexual orientation. Neuroscientist Simon LeVay's (1992) controversial research suggests that the brains of homosexual men may be different from those of heterosexuals. Some scientists even argue that there may be a "gay gene" (Hamer and Copeland, 1994). Yet, other researchers insist that sexual orientation is not biologically determined but is a result of socialization and social experiences. As discussed in Chapter 4, like most sociological issues related to human behavior, sexual orientation reflects the dynamic interplay between nature and nurture, heredity and environment, and biology and culture.

HOMOPHOBIA
Hatred and discrimination directed against homosexuals, based on exaggerated fears of homosexuality.

Gender: Social and Cultural Differentiation

A popular nineteenth-century nursery rhyme tells us that little girls are made of "sugar and spice and everything nice," while little boys are made of "frogs and snails and puppy dogs' tails." Newborn baby boys are often described as "bouncing," while baby girls are "beautiful." Why do we make these distinctions between boys and girls? Males and females are biologically and physiologically distinct at birth; these differences become more pronounced as humans develop to maturity, but they do not explain the important social and cultural distinctions that are made on the basis of sex. As indicated in Chapter 4, the most important differences between the sexes are acquired through socialization as we all learn to fulfill our **gender roles,** *the social and cultural expectations associated with a person's sex.* These gender roles affect every aspect of our lives, from our eating behavior and the type of neighbor we are likely to be, to how long we live and our cause of death—in short, the way we think about and live life itself.

Masculinity and Femininity   **Masculinity** refers to *attributes considered appropriate for males.* In American society, these traditionally include being aggressive, athletic, physically active, logical, and dominant in social relationships with females. Conversely, **femininity** refers to *attributes traditionally associated with appropriate behavior for females,* which in America include passivity, docility, fragility, emotionality, and subordination to males. Research conducted by Carol Gilligan and her students at Harvard's Gender Studies Department indicate that children are acutely aware of and feel pressure to conform to these powerful gender stereotypes by the age of 4 (Kantrowitz and Kalb, 1998). And, Peggy Giordano's research indicates they are firmly in place by adolescence (Giordano et al., 2006). (Focus box 11.1 discusses what happens when these gender roles are violated.) Remember our opening vignette and the contro-

GENDER ROLES
The social and cultural expectations associated with a person's sex.

MASCULINITY
Attributes considered appropriate for males.

FEMININITY
Attributes traditionally associated with appropriate behavior for females.

"Sex brought us together, but gender drove us apart."

The waitress in a small restaurant confided to her manager, "There's a totally cute girl smoking a f****** cigar in my section." The look of disgust on her face could only be matched by the disdain in her voice. The manager glanced in the young girl's direction and then showed his revulsion by shrugging his shoulders and scrunching up his eyes and nose. Little did the waitress or the manager know that the "totally cute girl" was a sociology student doing a gender norm violation project for her sex and gender class.

Joyce Nielsen, Glenda Walden, and Charlotte Kunkel (2000) provide a qualitative sociological analysis of students' written narratives as part of their gender norm violation projects over a 15-year period. In addition to smoking cigars, female students chewed tobacco, sat with their legs apart, changed tires, fought physically in public, spat in public, belched and burped out loud, didn't shave their legs or underarms, went as customers to topless bars, and participated in a variety of other activities and behaviors that are traditionally considered masculine—or at least nonfeminine. Conversely, male students wore bright red nail polish, shaved their legs, wore makeup, did needlepoint in public, cried in public, wore earrings, carried a purse, wore pink shirts every day for a week, or engaged in other behaviors or activities that are generally thought inappropriate for men. Students collected, recorded, and reported their data in textual narrative form. Additionally, each student was required to have an accomplice who served as an independent observer and recorded reactions that might have been hidden from or missed by the participant. All data and narratives were then coded and analyzed by the three sociologists.

Their findings? Not surprisingly, in almost every case, people who witnessed the gender-norm-violating activities or behaviors showed open disapproval. In many cases the stigma was so acute that the student felt the need to make a disclaimer such as "I'm only doing this for a class" or "This is not what you think." What was somewhat surprising, however, was the extent to which the gender norm violation was sexualized and how consistently different the pattern was for females and males. Female gender norm violation was consistently *heterosexualized*. Their behavior was viewed either as being heterosexually promiscuous (as in the case of going to a topless bar or sitting in an "unladylike" position) or as making them somewhat less attractive to the other sex (such as being viewed as "less cute" or "unkissable" when smoking a cigar or chewing tobacco). By contrast, male gender norm violation was almost always *homosexualized*. In other words, a male who wore makeup, painted his fingernails, shaved his legs, or even wore two earrings almost always was assumed to be gay. In their final discussion, Neilson et al. (2000:292–293) concluded, "For men a gender violation threatens loss of masculine heterosexual privilege; for women, it generates evaluations of their sexual availability and desirability to men."

TAKING A CLOSER LOOK

What does this research tell us about the power of gender roles? Why do you think gender role norm violation tends to be sexualized by those who observe it? Why is gender role violation viewed in heterosexual terms for females and homosexual terms for males? How does the reaction to Brandi Chastain's ripping off her jersey in the World Cup championship support or refute these findings? What might you have done differently if you had conducted this research?

Source: Joyce McCarl Neilsen, Glenda Walden, and Charlotte A. Kunkel. "Gendered Heteronormativity: Empirical Illustrations in Everyday Life." *Sociological Quarterly* 41 (Spring), 2000:283–296.

versy that ensued when Brandi Chastain violated a gender expectation at the World Cup championship. Some people insist that gender traits such as male aggressiveness are innate characteristics linked to sex and do not depend on cultural definitions (Maccoby, 1980). However, the preponderance of research indicates that females and males can be equally aggressive under different social and cultural conditions and that levels of aggression vary as widely within the sexes as between them (e.g., Fry, 1988; Melson and Fogel, 1988; Butler, 1990; Wilton, 2005). Rachel Simmons (2003) in her book *Odd Girl Out* contends that girls are just as naturally aggressive as boys but have been taught to hold their aggression in.

Anthropologist Margaret Mead ([1935] 1963) demonstrated that gender roles in other cultures varied dramatically from those in western Europe and the United States. In researching three New Guinea tribes, Mead reported that the Arapesh were very gentle and passive, and that both sexes displayed what would be considered feminine characteristics by Western standards. The Mundugumor were fiercely aggressive and combative; by American standards, both females and males exhibited exaggerated "masculine" attributes. The Tchambuli, like Western cultures, showed clear-cut, specific gender traits based on sex. The members of one sex shaved their heads, wore no jewelry, provided most of the food, and dominated the other sex; the members of the subordinate sex wore jewelry and ornaments, were quite passive, and spent most of their time

gossiping about the opposite sex. Americans who read Mead's account were surprised to discover that among the Tchambuli it was the women who fulfilled the former gender roles, while the men adhered to the latter.

Other studies confirm that gender roles vary greatly cross-culturally. For example, among the Plains Indians of North America many women became famous hunters and warriors. The Crow tribe created a special status for brave and aggressive women they deemed to be "manly-hearted"; one such woman was even made chief because of her bravery and leadership skills. Among some hunting and gathering societies, such as the Ju/'hoansi, the men forage for wild plants and berries, help collect water, and build huts, although these have traditionally been viewed as women's roles (Haviland, 2005).

We have established that women and men are genetically and biologically distinct but concluded that they share more commonalities than differences. Similarly, we have explored gender roles and discovered that definitions of masculinity and femininity vary greatly both within and across various cultures. While many people in society may take sex and gender differences for granted, the critical thinking approach of sociology demands that we take a closer look.

EXPLAINING GENDER DIFFERENCES

In almost every culture, expectations related to work, household duties, child rearing, politics, and economics vary by sex. This prompts the question: Why do gender differences exist? The answer depends on the perspective applied to it. Symbolic interactionists, for example, tend to link gender differences to the socialization process and the development of a gender identity.

Socialization and Gender Identity: An Interactionist Approach

As children grow they are bombarded with information from parents, school, church, peers, and the mass media about appropriate gender behavior. In the United States, this means they learn at a very early age that girls don't get into fistfights and that boys don't cry; in Japan it may mean girls are expected to learn flower arranging or tea preparation while boys learn Samurai sword fighting or how to build cars. In every society, as conformity to gender expectations is rewarded and deviance from them is punished children begin assuming their gender identities.

Developing Gender Identity
A powerful dimension of fulfilling gender roles involves the development of a **gender identity,** or *acknowledging one's sex and internalizing the norms, values, and behaviors of the accompanying gender expectations.* Gender roles are the primary way people are socially differentiated on the basis of their sex; gender identity is the mechanism by which individuals differentiate themselves.

Symbolic interactionists assert that a person's sense of identity develops through social interaction and socialization. For example, in most cultures names are gender-specific, so a person's name is often the first and most important symbol of gender identity. Some American parents experiment with exotic or faddish names, but most are careful to select gender-appropriate names for their children (Lieberson et al., 2000). In other cultures, in addition to acknowledging various kinship or clan connections, names may symbolize individual character traits, such as fierceness, courage, shyness, or humility. Gender identity goes far beyond our names, however. Marked differences in language, communication, play, dress, and grooming encourage girls to develop feminine identities and boys to develop masculine characteristics.

Gender and Communication
Communication styles are distinctive. Boys tend to define goals as they talk, exert control, express independence, and assert social status. Girls tend to be more tentative in their communication, more supportive and inclusive, and more responsive to others' ideas and feelings. In her research on gender and language, Deborah Tannen (1990, 1998, 2001, 2006) asserts that women and men may be

GENDER IDENTITY
Acknowledging one's sex and internalizing the norms, values, and behaviors of the accompanying gender expectations.

two categories of people separated by a common language. According to Tannen, men operate in a hierarchical world of one-upmanship, and their conversations are punctuated by conflict, negotiation, and a struggle to maintain independence and avoid failure. Women, on the other hand, approach the world as a network of connections, and their conversations reflect intimacy, negotiations for closeness, support, confirmation, and a search for consensus.

What happens when these worlds collide? Just listen as women and men engage in conversation, and you will find out. What occurs is a "balancing act" that juggles the competing needs for independence and intimacy. Because boys and girls are socialized differently from birth, they learn to think and converse in different social worlds. It is common for men and women to share the same event or to be engaged in conversation with one another and yet come away with dramatically divergent interpretations (Tannen, 1990, 1998, 2001).

Gender and Play Girls and boys play differently as well. Girls' games generally involve pairs or small groups and encourage collaborative, cooperative interaction that focuses on communication and understanding. Boys' play tends to involve large groups and to emphasize competition, winning, territoriality, and accomplishing clear-cut goals. Male dress is less restrictive, and boys do not have to worry about exposing their underwear or violating norms of modesty while they play. Almost from infancy, boys are encouraged and expected to develop physical skills and coordination, while girls are rewarded for linguistic and social skills (Tannen, 1990, 2006; Andersen, 1993; Wood, 1998; Kelle, 2000).

Gender and Social Learning Theory How do little girls and boys learn appropriate gender roles and develop their gender identities? *Social learning theory* contends that gender identity develops through the process of imitation and is reinforced by rewards and punishments for particular behaviors (Lengermann and Wallace, 1985). Consequently boys learn to act like their fathers and brothers, not like their mothers and sisters, and girls learn the opposite. In today's mass mediated society, children learn much about gender roles and identity from television. Focus box 11.3 on page 318 discusses how gender roles have been portrayed on television for the past half-century and how this may affect socialization and gender identity.

Gender and the Looking-Glass Self Charles Horton Cooley's ([1902] 1922) concept of the *looking-glass self* recognizes the cognitive processes by which individuals use society as a mirror to reflect their self-image: individuals project a gender image to society that is then reflected back to them as being appropriately masculine or feminine. The individual then interprets these social judgments as either validating or invalidating his or her masculinity or femininity. Mass media may also operate as a looking-glass to reflect attitudes and ideas about gender.

Gender Identity and Role Taking George Herbert Mead (1934) asserted that a sense of self follows a progression through the *imitative, game,* and *role-taking* stages. Very young girls may imitate both their mothers and their fathers, but they soon identify themselves as females and pursue behavior that confirms the social identity. Hence, when they play house, they fulfill the role of mother not only by imitating behaviors and mannerisms but also by creating social situations in which they anticipate how a "mother" would act. By their early teens, most girls wear makeup, go to parties, and begin dating, thus performing roles considered appropriate for young females. Likewise, boys move from imitating their fathers to pretending to be police officers, firefighters, and soldiers.

Gender socialization begins at birth and is very prominent during childhood. Research consistently shows that young children show little or no preference for "girls' toys" or "boys' toys," but that it is parents who often insist on buying their little girls so-called feminine toys such as baby dolls and stuffed animals and their little boys the traditionally masculine trucks, trains, and guns.

Why are parents, especially fathers in regard to their sons, so concerned that their children play with gender-specific toys?

Androgyny: Redefining Gender Have you ever wondered why we place so much emphasis on distinctive gender identities and gender roles? Many people do, and in an effort to reduce social differentiation and inequality based on sex and gender some people advocate **androgyny,** *a blending of masculine and feminine attributes.* Androgyny is not role reversal, where boys are taught to act feminine and girls to behave more masculinely. It embraces the full range of human emotions and behaviors rather than only those traditionally considered appropriate to a specific sex. This involves redefining gender roles and attaching new meanings to the concepts of masculinity and femininity. Boys are taught that it is okay to cry and that it is natural to display their emotions and sensitivity when circumstances warrant. Likewise, girls are taught to be aggressive and assertive when social situations call for such behavior. It also means no longer sex categorizing and gender categorizing everybody all the time (Ridgeway and Correll, 2000).

In the world of androgyny, children's first names do not serve as clear gender markers (Lieberson et al., 2000). Moreover, children are not chastised for being tomboys or sissies, and there are no such things as "boys' toys" and "girls' toys." Similarly there is neither "women's work" nor "men's work"; whatever its nature, work is performed by whoever is capable, regardless of sex. Ideally, in a culture where androgyny is the norm, human potential would not be limited by narrow cultural stereotypes.

Despite more androgynous views of gender and the weakening of some gender stereotypes, as the vignette that opened this chapter illustrates, powerful cultural distinctions between masculinity and femininity persist. Today, women must "prove" that they are capable of performing traditional "men's work" in the military and in the fields of law, medicine, science, sports, and politics. Similarly, social and cultural attitudes often discourage or ridicule men who pursue "feminine roles" such as homemaker, secretary, nurse, flight attendant, and housekeeper. From a functionalist perspective, distinctive and complementary gender roles are important to preserving social structure and ensuring that society functions properly.

Gender Complementarity: The Functionalist View

The structural functionalist perspective argues that gender roles provide clear-cut, complementary social norms for individuals based on their sex. Because these roles are based on both real and imagined biological and physiological differences between the sexes, they provide a society with what are seen as "natural" divisions of labor.

Gender Roles as a Division of Labor Functionalists note that women face some physical limitations during pregnancy and, unlike men, are naturally equipped to nourish infants, so it is pragmatic for women to take primary responsibility for the care of young children. While at home, it is convenient for women to assume most of the duties of maintaining the domicile—doing the cooking and cleaning and performing other domestic chores. Men do not experience the same physical limitations during the gestation period, and if left alone with a newborn infant a man cannot provide for its

ANDROGYNY
A blending of masculine and feminine attributes.

B.C.   By Johnny Hart

IT'S A SOCIOLOGICAL FACT THAT MEN HUNT AND WOMEN GATHER!

YOU WERE SAYING, PERFESSOR?

© 2004 By permission of John L. Hart FLP and Creators Syndicate, Inc.

most basic survival needs. Therefore men can more easily take responsibility for duties outside the home, such as hunting, fishing, and protecting the family from enemies. Because these masculine and feminine roles are complementary, functionalists argue that they function to bind men and women together into a family unit, solidifying the structure of the family; that, in turn, contributes to the overall functioning of society.

The level of societal development is crucial to this functionalist argument of role complementarity. The functionalist perspective may explain some of the gender stratification in traditional preindustrial societies. It falls short, however, in explaining why differences persist in highly technological industrial and postindustrial societies. With readily available birth control techniques, infant formulas, and technological advances that have all but eliminated the strenuous physical aspects of work for most people, the functionalist explanations seem inadequate.

Functionalists and the Nature versus Nurture Debate Contemporary functionalists contend that biology may play a more important role than was previously acknowledged. Steven Goldberg (1986), for example, argues that the differences between the endocrine and central nervous systems of males and females determine why men seem to have a much stronger drive than women to achieve dominance and social superiority. According to Goldberg, this phenomenon transcends cultural boundaries and therefore cannot be attributed to culture and socialization alone. He does not attribute these differences solely to biology; he asserts that physiology only sets the parameters within which interaction takes place. Because of their biology and physiology, he concludes, men are more aggressive and more willing to make sacrifices and to do whatever is necessary to achieve dominance and social status. Thus, according to Goldberg, male dominance and female subordination are genetically and culturally programmed into human nature.

Goldberg's critics point out that while it is true there are biological and physiological differences between males and females no society has ever left gender stratification to nature (e.g., Epstein, 1986). Moreover, a large body of research indicates that while there may be noticeable differences in the behavior of boys and girls even at birth, they are relatively small compared to the wide variations of behavior within each gender (Bryant and Check, 2000; Bates et al., 2005).

Rather, through socialization and, in many cases, coercion, gender roles are based on cultural tradition and are taught and reinforced by those in power. The conflict perspective refutes Goldberg's position and offers an alternative explanation of gender differences that focuses on social inequality.

Gender Stratification: A Conflict Perspective

From the conflict perspective, the persistence of traditional gender roles that place women in socially inferior positions is another form of social stratification. Those who control the means of production also control and manipulate the social structure. Because of their vested interest in maintaining wealth and power, the elite reinforce the prevailing social hierarchy by limiting the opportunities of those beneath them. In the case of gender roles, men have enjoyed numerous economic, political, and social advantages, and they have a vested interest in keeping women in a subordinate role.

Gender and the Economy Friedrich Engels ([1884] 1902) contended that initially, despite their distinctive roles, men and women shared more equally in the economic survival of the family and thus experienced more egalitarianism. It was not until the emphasis shifted to owning and exchanging goods and property, Engels argued, that men began to enjoy an advantage over women. Almost immediately, men defined themselves as the primary producers of goods and women as secondary, being the consumers.

From the conflict perspective, this phenomenon increased with capitalism and the emergence of industrialized societies. Initially men, women, and children worked in factories (men were paid more than women and children). When child labor laws were passed, women were expected to give up their jobs to stay home and care for the children. Consequently, men filled the factories to be exploited for their labor, while women stayed home to be exploited for theirs (Eisenstein, 1979; Vogel, 1983). Although both

sexes were exploited, from the conflict perspective men, because they produced commodities that possessed exchange value in a market economy, enjoyed higher status, which translated into dominance in most major social arenas. Today, feminist researchers point out that work has become institutionalized in such a way as to be incompatible with child-rearing in capitalist countries. This not only helps explain the persistent wage gaps between men and women but also helps explain the general stratification between the sexes (Glass, 2000; Bates et al., 2005).

The Feminist View   The feminist approach in sociology aligns closely with the conflict perspective in explaining gender differences. Feminists contend that gender inequality is rooted in the structure of society and represents social stratification on the basis of sex and gender roles. While feminists, like most conflict theorists, acknowledge the economic links to gender stratification, their focus is more on differential power between the sexes. Men have created and perpetuated the idea that they are superior to women. This idea has created a sexist ideology that reinforces gender inequality and limits both social opportunities and outcomes for women. Feminists argue that the differences between women and men are rooted not in biology, but in this sexist ideology and how it translates into social inequality.

SEXISM: INEQUALITY BASED ON SEX AND GENDER

Sexism refers to *the ideology that one sex is inherently superior or inferior to the other.* It fosters both individual and institutionalized prejudice (attitudes) and discrimination (actions). Sexism, much like racism (see Chapter 10) and ageism (see Chapter12), is an ideology that supports the differential and unequal treatment of individuals based on ascribed characteristics—in this case, their sex.

Sexism does not apply exclusively to females; in some cases males are victimized by sexism as well, as they find their pursuits socially limited by attitudes, norms, rules, regulations, and policies based on traditional gender expectations (Goldberg, 1976; Franklin, 1988; Pollack and Shuster, 2000). As feminist scholar Carol Gilligan noted, "both sexes suffer when one is not understood—this is not a zero-sum game" (Gilligan, 2006:53). But sexism like any other "ism" is about *power,* and in the United States the sexism experienced by women is far more prominent than the sexism men may experience. In American society, sexism permeates all major social institutions, including the family, religion, education, the workplace, sports, politics, government, the military, and the mass media. Despite some costs to males and alleged discrimination against them based on affirmative action policies or even alleged "quota systems," men are the primary beneficiaries of institutional sexism.

In the Family

Much of the gender differentiation found in the American family structure can be attributed to the Western cultural tradition of **patriarchy,** *a system in which males dominate females in most spheres of life* (politics, economics, family, and so on). As Joan Huber (1990) noted, those who are perceived as producers have always enjoyed more power and prestige than those considered consumers. Men have traditionally taken an *instrumental* role in the family, assuming primary responsibility for economic support and contact with the rest of society, while women have been relegated to an *expressive* role based on providing love, nurturing, emotional support, and maintenance of the home. These traditional roles are being challenged as American families experience numerous changes. Today, the majority of American women over the age of 16 work for pay outside the home, and there are more single-parent households headed by women than at any other time in U.S. history (U.S. Bureau of the Census, 2000). Thus more American women are thrust into the instrumental role of providing economic support for the family.

Working the Second Shift   This change has not meant that men share equally in domestic responsibilities. Instead, the primary responsibility for daytime child care has been turned over to babysitters and preschools; in the evening children and housework

SEXISM
The ideology that one sex is inherently superior or inferior to the other.

PATRIARCHY
A system in which males dominate females in most spheres of life (politics, economics, family, and so on).

largely remain the mother's responsibility (Wilkins and Miller, 1985; Brines, 1994; Lennon and Rosenfield, 1994; South and Spitze, 1994). Arlie Hochschild and Anne Machung (1990) referred to women's return to the home after a full day of work as the beginning of the "second shift"—another full-time job of wife and mother. One study found that, ironically, the more a man is economically dependent on his wife, the less likely he is to help with housework (Brines, 1994). Conversely, there is no empirical evidence that marriage is any less desirable for women as they become economically independent (Oppenheimer, 1997). Although they comprise a small percentage of American households, the economic downturn of the early twenty-first century resulted in numerous situations where men lost their jobs and their wives became the sole breadwinners. Or, in some cases, both the husband and wife work, but because she holds higher educational credentials and has more professional skills, the wife makes significantly more money than her husband. This situation sometimes creates marital tension, especially in the case of African American families where more and more women are pursuing professional careers and the unemployment rates among black men are soaring (Cose, 2003; Doyle, 2003; Tyre and McGinn, 2003).

In *The Time Bind,* Hochschild (1997) contends that in the United States both men and women are experiencing the strains of trying to maintain a precarious balance between work and home. Concluding that many couples find it impossible to devote quality time to either career or family, her research shows that in some cases women go to work to flee the stress of home, whereas many men view home as the sanctuary from work. Cross-national research indicates this phenomenon may not be unique to the United States (Treas and Widmer, 2000). At least one study refutes the "time-bind" hypothesis, however, finding that contrary to Hochschild's assertions, there was little evidence that parents dissatisfied with home life worked more hours or desired to do so (Brown and Booth, 2002).

Caring for and nurturing infants has been traditionally associated with mothers, but today many men realize the joy and importance of bonding with their children.

Does this make a man any less masculine? Why is nurturing usually associated with mothers and not fathers in the United States and many other cultures?

Gender Roles and Marital Satisfaction   Women tend to be more personally, morally, and structurally committed to marriage than men (Kapinus and Johnson, 2002). A longitudinal study used a national sample of married persons to assess how changing attitudes toward gender roles affect perceptions of marital quality. As women adopt less traditional attitudes toward gender, they tend to report lower perceived quality in their marital relationship. Men, on the other hand, perceive higher quality in marriage as they adopt less traditional gender role attitudes (Amato and Booth, 1995). What are the implications of this research? One probability is that as men and women begin to share more responsibilities both inside and outside the home, they will be forced to renegotiate traditional divisions of labor. Sociologists suggest that this may lead to two potential outcomes. Many couples will experience decreased marital satisfaction and may decide to seek a divorce. Others, however, will enjoy the increased flexibility of gender equity and find marriage a much more gratifying experience (Coltrane, 1997; Zuo and Tang, 2000).

Passing Sexism on to the Next Generation   Since the family is the initial agent of socialization, gender roles and identities are first learned within the family context. Through imitation, role modeling, and intentional as well as inadvertent socialization, most families perpetuate and reinforce the traditional gender roles of their culture. Even in households where both parents work outside the home, children may see traditional roles being enacted in the home. Studies show that since the 1970s American men have roughly doubled their time spent on household chores such as cooking, cleaning, and washing, from 2–3 hours per week to about 5–8. Correspondingly, women have cut their time on these tasks from approximately 40 hours per week to about 20 (Coltrane, 1997). Nevertheless, the disparities in time spent on these tasks speak for themselves.

Despite the tendency for teenagers and young adults to swear they are going to parent their children differently than they were parented, the reality is that the most influential role models from which we learn parenting skills are our parents. And although we live in a changing society and each generation reflects those changes, the family is one of the most influential institutions in perpetuating traditional sex roles.

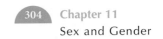

In Religion

Though scientific research disputes such beliefs, in many cultures it is believed that males are spiritually superior to females, who often are thought to be weak, untrustworthy, and dangerous. Further, the majority of religions connect male-dominated rituals and spiritual myths with the political, economic, and social supremacy of men. This trend of male dominance is reflected in church hierarchies and has been carried forward in Islam, Hinduism, Judaism, Christianity, and all other major religions (Haviland, 2005). Yet, research shows that women tend to be more religious than men (Miller and Stark, 2002).

Patriarchal Beliefs In the Judeo-Christian tradition, the ideology of male superiority begins with the story of Genesis, in which God is referred to as "He" and we are told that man was created in his image. Woman, on the other hand, was made from man and, we are told, tempted man to succumb to evil, hence bringing about the fall from grace and the expulsion from the Garden of Eden.

Moreover, the important prophets in the Bible are all men, while women are portrayed as either temptresses and harlots or helpmates and nurturers. The most important New Testament woman is Mary, who gave birth to Christ. It is important to note, however, that Mary's esteemed position is derived from her being the virgin mother of the male Christ child. Research indicates that sexism in religion transfers to other aspects of life, and both individual and group fundamentalism has been linked to sexism (Peek et al., 1991).

Toward the end of the nineteenth century, Elizabeth Cady Stanton and others wrote *The Woman's Bible,* which attempted to eliminate sexism in religion. It met with great controversy, even among other feminists who feared it would alienate people to the point they would withdraw their support for women's suffrage (Doyle, 1985). More recent attempts have been made to eliminate sexist language from the Bible, and today several gender-neutral versions are available.

Patriarchal Structures The hierarchical structure of most contemporary churches reflects the ideology of male superiority. In the Roman Catholic church, for example, the roles of pope, bishops, and priests are reserved for men; women may become nuns and serve as nurses or teachers. Other denominations, too, are dominated by males; men are found in the roles of ministers, deacons, and church elders, while women are more likely to be Sunday school teachers, organists, and choir members. The ordination of women by the United Methodist, Episcopal, and Anglican churches sparked controversies among their denominational leaders (Doyle, 1985; Woodward, 1989), but by the end of the twentieth century church seminaries nationwide were admitting large numbers of women (Niebuhr, 1999).

Centuries-old family and religious patriarchy is being challenged today in the United States and elsewhere. Even in China, where cultural differences in gender roles have been institutionalized for several centuries, women express the desire for equality (Chia et al., 1994). As women pursue nontraditional social roles, schools must adjust their educational strategies to help prepare youths for changing gender roles.

In Education

In many schools, the first day of class begins with the reminder "You are in school now, so act like ladies and gentlemen." It is clear the rules of etiquette are different for the two. Boys are admonished to let the girls go first, and while the boys can run, play, jump, and sprawl on the floor in any position, girls are reminded to sit and act "ladylike." Moreover boys are called on more and receive more encouragement from their teachers than girls (Kantrowitz et al., 1992), and the most popular boys and girls in school are those who most closely conform to the traditional gender stereotypes (Adler et al., 1992).

Sexism in the Curriculum Schoolbooks and children's literature often reinforce traditional gender stereotypes by portraying women in expressive roles as homemakers, secretaries, nurses, and elementary school teachers, while presenting men in instrumental roles as doctors, lawyers, and scientists (Richmond-Abbott, 1986; Kortenhaus and Demarest, 1993). Most authors and publishing companies are aware of the sexism in textbooks and may guard against sexist language and photos, but gender stereotypes are so ingrained in the culture of the United States that it is difficult to eliminate them entirely.

Despite a number of legal rulings and important legislation that withholds federal funds from any educational agency that discriminates on the basis of sex, school curricula still reflect sexism based on gender stereotypes. Boys continue to be discouraged from taking home economics courses and girls from taking shop or auto mechanics classes, and while these courses are open to coeducational enrollments, they remain largely segregated by sex. In addition, despite studies that provide evidence to the contrary, stereotypes persist that boys are more adept than girls at science and mathematics. Boys receive more help and encouragement in those areas, so that a self-fulfilling prophecy begins to create a real gap in those areas by secondary school age (Felson and Trudeau, 1991; Vetter, 1992; Entwisle et al., 1994; Spanier, 1997). This idea gained national attention when Harvard's president said in a speech at an educational conference that women lacked "innate ability" in math and science (Kantrowitz, 2005:36). Later, in 2006, the president resigned amid a storm of controversy and faculty votes of no-confidence. He was replaced by Drew Gilpin Faust, the first woman president of Harvard in its 371 year history.

Women have broken many gender barriers in sports.

Why do you think it is still unusual to see women competing with men in both amateur and professional sports?

Sex-Segregated Schools

Many educators believe that males and females benefit from single-sex educational environments. Private schools have a long tradition of sex segregation, and throughout the 1990s a number of states (most notably California, Illinois, Maine, New Hampshire, New York, and Virginia) experimented with sex-segregated schools or classrooms. In 2002, Houston, Texas, experimented with a boys-only public elementary school, claiming that it allowed the boys to stay focused and experience fewer distractions (Lee and Nichols, 2002). For 25 years, feminist professor and theologian Mary Daly allowed only women to take her courses at Boston College. She contended that opening her classes to men would harm the academic growth of her women students: "Even if there were only one or two men . . . the young women would be constantly, on an overt or subliminal level, giving their attention to the men because they've been socialized to nurse men" (AP, Boston, 1999:14A). In 1999 the college administration ordered Professor Daly to open her classes to men, but she refused, prompting a lawsuit in which a Massachusetts judge sided with Boston College. After a 2-year legal dispute, rather than open her classes to men, Mary Daly retired (*Boston College Chronicle,* 2001).

While there is much debate over the research findings on same-sex schools or classes, Maggie Ford, president of the American Association of University Women, concluded that "the research shows that separating by sex is not the solution to gender inequality in education . . . when elements of a good education are present, [both] girls and boys succeed" (AP, Washington, 1998a:8A). Research indicates that there is indeed a global trend toward desegregation and democratization of higher education (Charles and Bradley, 2002).

Two major universities made headlines in the late 1990s regarding their sex segregation practices. The Citadel retained its exclusively male admissions policy until 1995; Virginia Military Institute (VMI) held out until 1997. Both schools tried legal maneuvers to retain their single-sex status but eventually accepted women into their ranks. The Citadel, a state school in South Carolina with no official military affiliation, garnered widespread national attention when the first female cadet in the school's 150-plus-year history quit after a week of psychological and physical hazing and alleged death threats to her family (Faludi, 1994; Van Biema, 1994; Wingert, 1994). The Citadel was in the news again 2 years later, when four women were accepted into the freshman class. Two of the young women completed their "knob" year, so-named because of the required short-cropped haircut, but the other two quit midyear among charges of physical hazing (including having their uniforms set afire while they were wearing them), sexual harassment, and discrimination (AP, Charleston, 1996; ABC News, 1997b; Robinson, 1997). The U.S. Department of Justice decided not to prosecute anybody in the hazing cases (AP, Charleston, 1998). The Citadel graduated its first female cadet in 1999 (AP, Charleston, 1999). Virginia Military Institute ended its 158-year-old all-male admissions policy in 1997, admitting 30 women after a 1996 U.S. Supreme Court ruling that the

Women were not allowed to join the corps at the Citadel until 1995, 20 years after women were first admitted to West Point, Annapolis, and the Air Force Academy.

state-supported school must accept women (AP, Lexington, 1997). Two years later, VMI's superintendent stated that he was committed to following the Supreme Court's mandate to admit women, but believed them to be a disruptive influence on the school (Wire Reports, Washington, 1998). Two years later, however, a female cadet was chosen as one of the school's two battalion commanders—the highest rank a cadet can hold (AP, Lexington, 2000). In 2001, VMI graduated its first class of female cadets, and in 2006, Valley Forge Military College, the last all-male military college in the United States, opened its doors to women (Evelyn, 2005).

Sex-segregated universities struggling with issues of gender inequality are neither exclusively male nor exclusively military-style. There also are women's colleges that prohibit male attendance. In the spring of 1990, because of financial woes, the board of trustees at prestigious Mills College voted to end the school's 138-year women-only tradition and announced it would admit male undergraduates in 1991. This announcement brought a protest from many women students, who boycotted classes, seized buildings, and mounted demonstrations with the refrain "Better Dead than Coed!" (*Time,* 1990:27). In the end, the students won, and Mills refused to admit male students. In late 1994, the board of regents of Texas Woman's University (TWU) voted to admit men to undergraduate programs there, thus eliminating the only exclusively state-supported women's university in the United States. Although men had been admitted to certain graduate programs at TWU for quite some time, the decision to admit them to undergraduate programs was met with tremendous hostility and resentment from many female students and alumni.

The Educational Hierarchy   If verbal, written, and curricular messages in coeducational school settings are less sexist today than in the past, the status hierarchy of most schools is not. Elementary schools are primarily populated by women teachers, but the vast majority of school principals (over 75 percent) are men (National Center for Education Statistics, 2005). In high schools, men occupy most high-status positions: principals, assistant principals, coaches (often even of girls' sports), and athletic directors. They also teach the "most important" subjects, such as mathematics and science. Women occupy lower-status positions—secretaries, cafeteria workers, and school nurses—and teach subjects deemed appropriate to their gender, such as English, speech, and home economics. Despite the facts that girls out achieve boys at every level of schooling and females make up more than 56 percent of university students, men still outnumber women at the highest levels of academia (Tyre, 2006; Gilligan, 2006).

Does sexism in the curricula and status hierarchy of the schools shape the attitudes, values, and behavior of the students toward appropriate gender roles? Research indicates that the answer is a resounding yes. Schools with patriarchal curricula and structures reinforce and reproduce rather than challenge gender inequality (E. W. Kane, 1995). Conversely, children who attend schools with female principals and less sexist curricula have been found to be less likely to adhere to gender stereotypes (Koblinsky and Sugawara, 1984; Lengermann and Wallace, 1985; Paradiso and Wall, 1986). Career counseling is an area where schools are increasing their efforts to combat sexism. School counselors are taking a more egalitarian approach to career guidance, but because of the lack of adequate role models and the built-in sexism in the curriculum many young women are ill-prepared to enter some traditionally male occupations, especially those that demand a strong background in mathematics and science (Astin, 1990; Long, 1990). This problem perpetuates some of the sexism in the workplace.

In the Workplace

In most stratified societies, occupation is one of the important determinants of where people fit into the social class system. Traditional gender stereotypes promote the idea that women and men are suited to perform different kinds of work, and traditionally the view has been that women are best suited to occupy the lowest-paying and least powerful jobs (Reskin and Roos, 1990; Lips, 1991; Andersen, 1993; Heckert et al., 2002). The myths that "women who are full-time housewives are not working; that women who work for wages work for extra money, not because they must; and that women's work is not as valuable as men's" have caused the work of women to be devalued (Andersen, 1993:101). Map 11.1 compares women's wages to men's from a global perspective.

Pink-Collar Occupations   At the beginning of the twentieth century, only about 20 percent of all women were in the labor force; today there are well over 70 million women in the workforce (U.S. Bureau of the Census, 2000). Despite their large representation in the workforce, almost half of all women employed outside the home are in clerical or service work. Sociologist Jessie Bernard (1981) coined the term *pink-collar occupation* to describe clerical work; over 80 percent of all secretaries, typists, stenographers, and other clerical workers are women. The service work category includes occupations such as nursing, child care, household service, and restaurant work. Jobs in clerical and service work come with far less income, power, and prestige than most male-dominated occupations. Both verbal and nonverbal communications are shaped by gender as well as dominant-subordinate positions in the work arena (Johnson, 1994). Patterns in women's employment and incomes are changing, and occupational and other economic opportunities for women are increasing (Huber and Stephens, 2000). For the first time in human history, technology has made it possible for women's economic productivity to equal men's (Huber, 1990). Nevertheless there still exists a distinctive gender-poverty gap, and a higher proportion of women live in poverty in the United States than in most other industrial and postindustrial nations.

Gender Tracking   A growing body of sociological research indicates that stereotypes and gender segregation are deeply ingrained in the American workplace, helping account for the wide disparity between the earnings of men and women (Fuller and

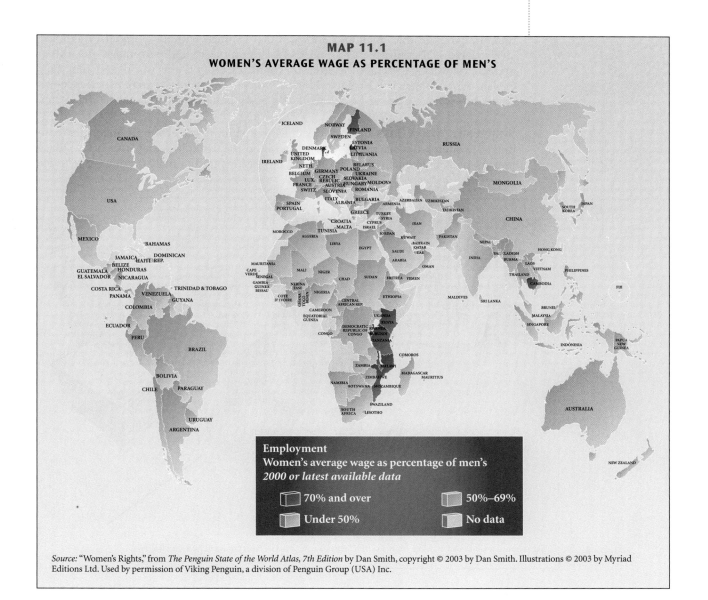

MAP 11.1
WOMEN'S AVERAGE WAGE AS PERCENTAGE OF MEN'S

Employment
Women's average wage as percentage of men's
2000 or latest available data

70% and over   50%–69%

Under 50%   No data

Source: "Women's Rights," from *The Penguin State of the World Atlas, 7th Edition* by Dan Smith, copyright © 2003 by Dan Smith. Illustrations © 2003 by Myriad Editions Ltd. Used by permission of Viking Penguin, a division of Penguin Group (USA) Inc.

Schoenberger, 1991; Bellas, 1994; Wellington, 1994; Ridgeway, 1997; Smith, 1997; McCall, 2000). In many cases this stereotyping has led to "gender tracking," or separate career ladders for men and women. In the corporate world, a "glass ceiling" blocks women from climbing the corporate ladder and entering upper-echelon positions beyond a particular point (Diprete and Soule, 1988; Garland, 1991). The Federal Glass Ceiling Commission reported that women account for a mere 5 percent of the senior managers of Fortune 1000 companies, and that despite Affirmative Action and other programs a barrier still exists at the highest levels of business for women and people of color (Kaufman-Rosen and Kalb, 1995). Moreover "glass walls" often prohibit women from moving laterally, depriving them of the supervisory experience necessary to advance vertically (Lopez, 1992).

Studies indicate that men and women may have different attitudes toward work and careers, but many of these differences may be attributed to the demands placed on married women in regard to domestic responsibilities (Bielby and Bielby, 1989; Desai and Waite, 1991; Glass and Estes, 1997). Women find themselves in the unenviable position of striving to maintain professional careers while not shirking the demands of their more traditional gender roles as wives and mothers (Keller, 1994; Warner, 2005; Quindlen, 2005). As one study noted, "More and more, women's professional potential is obstructed not by discrimination in the workplace but rather by obligations *outside* it" (Wilkins and Miller, 1985:46). This also affects women's decisions to enter into self-employment (Tanigachi, 2002). Numerous surveys of women with M.B.A.s have found that a large number of professional women opt out of the corporate fast-track because they cannot reconcile the strain it puts on their personal and family lives (Kaufman-Rosen and Kalb, 1995). When women with children remain in the labor force, they continue to earn less than men and even less than women without children (Waldfogel, 1997). Table 11.1 contrasts the amount of maternity leave and percentage of earnings granted to working women in selected countries around the world and may help explain why women in Germany, France, Norway, and Finland may experience less strain in reconciling domestic and work demands than do women in the United States.

Shattering the Glass Ceiling   While occupational and economic inequality continues, women today have more opportunities in the workplace than ever before. Each year more women enter occupations and professions traditionally dominated by men,

TABLE 11.1
CHILDBIRTH-RELATED LEAVE POLICIES IN THE UNITED STATES AND 10 PEER NATIONS

COUNTRY	TYPE OF LEAVE PROVIDED	TOTAL DURATION (IN MONTHS)	PAYMENT RATE
United States	12 weeks family leave	2.8	Unpaid
Canada	17 weeks maternity leave	6.2	15 weeks at 55% of prior earnings
	10 weeks parental leave		55% of prior earnings
Denmark	28 weeks maternity leave	18.5	60% of prior earnings
	1 year parental leave		90% of unemployment benefit rate
Finland	18 weeks maternity leave	36.0	70% of prior earnings
	26 weeks parental leave		70% of prior earnings
	Childrearing leave until child is 3		Flat rate
Norway	52 weeks parental leave	36.0	80% of prior earnings
	2 years childrearing leave		Flat rate
Sweden	18 months parental leave	18.0	12 months at 80% of prior earnings, 3 months flat rate, 3 months unpaid
Austria	16 weeks maternity leave	27.7	100% of prior earnings
	2 years parental leave		18 months of unemployment benefit rate, 6 months unpaid
France	16 weeks maternity leave	36.0	100% of prior earnings
	Parental leave until child is 3		Unpaid for one child; paid at flat rate (income-tested) for two or more
Germany	14 weeks maternity leave	39.2	100% of prior earnings
	3 years parental leave		Flat rate (income-tested) for 2 years, unpaid for third year
Italy	5 months maternity leave	11.0	80% of prior earnings
	6 months parental leave		30% of prior earnings
United Kingdom	18 weeks maternity leave	7.2	90% for 6 weeks and flat rate for 12 weeks, if sufficient work history; otherwise, flat rate
	13 weeks parental leave		Unpaid

Source: "Childbirth-Related Leave Policies in the United States and 10 Peer Nations" from *The Future of Children* by Jane Waldfogel, 2001. Reprinted by permission of *The Future of Children* as a publication of the David and Lucile Packard Foundation.

and an increasing percentage attain top-level management positions and own their own businesses. Today, women own approximately 40 percent of all small businesses and occupy almost one-fourth of corporate senior vice president positions. The glass ceiling is being cracked, if not shattered.

Yet it is still shocking how little things have changed for women since the mid-1970s. While more women are reaching upper-level jobs, fewer men are holding lower-level ones, which seem to be reserved for women (Steiger and Wardell, 1995). Moreover, some of the positive gains in nontraditional jobs for women have been somewhat offset by continued sexism, **sexual harassment** (*deliberate and unwelcome sexual comments, gestures, and actions that make a person feel uncomfortable*—see Focus box 11.2 on page 311), and other forms of prejudice and discrimination in the workplace.

SEXUAL HARASSMENT
Deliberate unwanted sexual gestures, comments, or actions that make an individual feel uncomfortable in her or his work environment.

TABLE 11.2
MEDIAN INCOMES OF MEN AND WOMEN IN SELECTED OCCUPATIONS: FULL-TIME WORKERS

FULL-TIME OCCUPATION	MEDIAN INCOME (DOLLARS)	
	WOMEN	MEN
All Occupations	28,704	36,140
Chief Executives	64,636	90,272
Computer Programmers	50,596	57,980
Architecture and Engineering Occupations	43,004	56,888
Lawyers	73,476	84,188
Elementary and Middle School Teachers	39,364	43,836
Waiters and Waitresses	16,536	20,020
Customer Service Representative	26,156	29,120
Postal Service Mail Carriers	39,780	40,664
Construction & Extraction Occupations	25,844	31,304
Bus Drivers	24,440	27,872
Physicians and Surgeons	51,428	87,204
Maids and Housekeeping Cleaners	16,484	19,292
Police and Sheriff's Patrol Officers	38,012	40,040

Source: Highlights of Women's Earnings in 2003, U. S. Department of Labor, Bureau of Labor Statistics, September 2004, Report 978.

Perhaps the most apparent and consistent inequality between men and women in the workplace is reflected in their salaries. Today, despite the fact that women earn more associate, bachelor's, and master's degrees than men, they continue to earn less on average than men who have comparable or less education (Castro, 1997; Bates et al., 2005).

The Wage and Earnings Gap

Despite greater opportunities for women in the workplace, income data indicate that even where there is equality of opportunity it has not translated into equality of earnings. After almost two decades in which the earnings gap between men and women was narrowing, U.S. Bureau of Labor Statistics indicate that the gap is widening once again. Women still lag far behind men in median income, earning approximately 70 cents for every dollar men earn, and are paid less even when performing the same work (U.S. Bureau of the Census, 1990a, 2000). Numerous explanations have been offered for this wage and earnings gap, but research indicates that gender segregation of occupations continues to emerge as one of the most important reasons (Cotter et al., 1997; Bielby, 2000; Bates et al., 2005). The four most lucrative occupations for women are lawyer, chief executive, physician or surgeon, and computer programmer, but they are still underrepresented in these male-dominated professions, and make less money than their male counterparts in them. Table 11.2 illustrates the discrepancies in median incomes for men and women in the same occupational categories. Interestingly, men in managerial positions where mostly women report to them earn less than their male counterparts who supervise mostly men (Ostroff and Atwater, 2003).

The wage and earnings gap between men and women in the same occupations and professions is not the only factor in income inequality. Bureau of Labor Statistics indicate that during the peak earning years (ages 25–54) the income gap widens between women and men (see Figure 11.1). These earning discrepancies not only have a dramatic impact on women's lives during that time period, but they also affect women's retirement years because they have paid in less to Social Security and can expect smaller incomes from private and corporate pension funds (Castro, 1997; Moos, 2006).

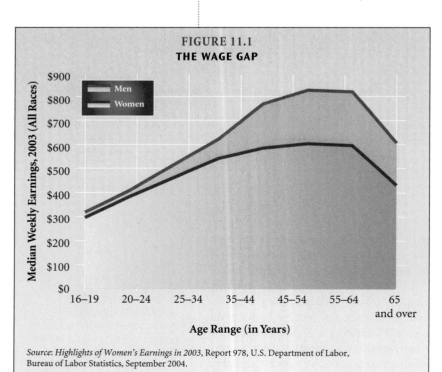

FIGURE 11.1
THE WAGE GAP

Source: *Highlights of Women's Earnings in 2003*, Report 978, U.S. Department of Labor, Bureau of Labor Statistics, September 2004.

Sexual harassment, or deliberate and unwelcome sexual comments, gestures, and actions that make a person feel uncomfortable, has probably been in the workplace as long as men and women have worked together. When "Rosie the Riveter" and thousands of other women left their homes to replace the young men who had marched off to World War II, many of them were greeted by sneers, jokes, lewd comments, references to sexy pinups, and even physical attacks by some of their male supervisors and fellow employees.

Sexual harassment comes in two forms. The first is the *quid pro quo* variety, which refers to the exchange of sexual favors for something else, for example, an employer offering an employee a raise or a promotion in exchange for sexual favors. Perhaps more commonly, an employer indicates that, unless sexual favors are granted, a deserved raise or promotion will be withheld or the employee may even be fired. This type of sexual harassment is clear-cut, and the courts have ruled that it is illegal and constitutes a violation of an individual's civil rights. Both males and females can be offenders in this type of sexual harassment, because the unlawful action is based not on a person's gender, but on her or his relative status in the workplace. Any individual who holds power over another and is in a position to use sex for leverage in the workplace can be guilty of this type of sexual harassment. Given the patriarchal structure of most work environments, where the people in positions of power tend to be men, it is more common for men to be in positions to sexually harass women at work than vice versa.

The second form of sexual harassment is much more ambiguous than the first and is called "creating a hostile environment." More subtle than an exchange for sexual favors, this type of sexual harassment involves unwanted gestures and comments, the telling of sexually laden jokes, sexual teasing, or the display of nude pinups, pornographic materials, or other offensive material that creates an uncomfortable work environment and hinders a person's performance on the job. This type of sexual harassment is linked to people's perceptions of sexual harassment, which may vary greatly as a result of gender-role socialization (Barr, 1993).

The issue of sexual harassment in the workplace captured widespread media attention and rose to national prominence during the U.S. Senate confirmation hearings for Supreme Court Justice nominee Clarence Thomas. A national debate was launched when a stunned television audience watched live coverage of University of Oklahoma law professor Anita Hill's testimony, which included a number of allegations of sexual harassment against Thomas, who had been her supervisor on two other jobs. Thomas vehemently denied the charges, and the all-male Senate Judiciary Committee eventually confirmed his nomination. Sexual harassment once again hit the media spotlight when Paula Jones sued former President Clinton for alleged sexual harassment while she was a State employee and he was the governor of Arkansas. In 1998 the U.S. Supreme Court heard a record number of sexual harassment cases (AP, Washington, 1998b; Carelli, 1998). And, although most attention on sexual harassment is focused on the United States, other countries are also grappling with this issue (Africa News Service, 2003).

The issue of sexual harassment is a complicated one, and it transcends the workplace. Sexual harassment can occur anywhere that males and females are in contact. It is a particular problem in educational and work environments, however, because of the ramifications that differences in power have in those arenas. While many victims suffer in silence, in other cases the careers of innocent people are ruined or ended by groundless accusations. Although the courts, federal agencies, and employers have worked to define guidelines more clearly and to end sexual discrimination and harassment in the workplace, most people agree that, with more women entering the workforce each year, and more women ascending to positions of power in the workplace, more allegations of sexual harassment against both men and women are likely to occur in the near future.

TAKE A CLOSER LOOK

Why is sexual harassment so difficult to define? Based on your reading of this chapter, are men and women likely to define it differently?

Source: Paula A. Barr. "Perceptions of Sexual Harassment." *Sociological Inquiry* 63 (Fall), 1993:400–470. Lincoln Kaplan. "Who Lied?" *Newsweek,* November 14, 1994:52–54. Lloyd R. Cohen. "Sexual Harassment and the Law." *Society* 28 (May/June), 1991:8–13. AP, Washington. "Sex-harassment Caseload Rises." *Dallas Morning News,* January 24, 1998:3A. Richard Carelli. "High Court Focused on Harassment." *Dallas Morning News,* June 28, 1998:9A. *Africa News Service,* "Sexual Harassment in Office and Schools," August 18, 2003.

If sexism persists in work, it is no less evident in play. Sports, too, reflect a long-standing tradition of patriarchy, gender stereotypes, and sexual inequality.

In Sports

The sexism and discrimination experienced by women in the world of work crosses over into the world of play, recreation, and professional sports. Sports represent a microcosm of society; sports, like the rest of society, have been and continue to be dominated by males. Although this attitude is less pronounced today, many families still socialize boys into participating in sports and girls away from them almost from birth. Boys are given footballs, helmets, baseball gloves, and bats as toys; girls are given pom-poms, batons, and cheerleader outfits. Boys are encouraged to fantasize about playing in the World Series or the Super Bowl; many girls are taught that their role in those games will be limited to the sidelines as spectators or cheerleaders.

Limited Opportunities In the past, opportunities in sports for females were severely limited. Until 1973, Little League baseball was an exclusively male domain, and it took a court battle to allow the first girl the opportunity to play (Eitzen and Sage, 2003). Even then, league officials attempted to maintain de facto segregation by passing safety rules that required all players to wear jockstraps. Gender barriers in sports have slowly tumbled, however, and girls now compete in soccer, volleyball, and gymnastics alongside boys. Still, despite more opportunities for girls, we are reminded of discriminatory rules and practices in sports. For example, in 1997, 12-year-old Melissa Raglin was temporarily suspended from playing on her coed Babe Ruth baseball team for violating the rule that catchers must wear a jockstrap and protective plastic cup; she was reinstated only after agreeing to wear a specially made protective device (AP, Boca Raton, 1997).

Title IX and Interscholastic Sports In schools, sex segregation and the most blatant violations of Title IX funding rules, which prohibit discrimination on the basis of sex, can be found in interscholastic athletics. Although schools have increased funding for girls' sports (volleyball, softball, and basketball) and some have created coeducational teams (usually in volleyball or swimming), few have opened the "rough" sports (football, hockey, and wrestling) to girls. The lion's share of athletic spending goes to these male-dominated or exclusively male sports. When female athletes participate in sports as aggressive and fierce competitors, they face social stigma for demonstrating the same attributes that bring male athletes praise. There is a widespread myth that competing in sports masculinizes females and may even cause them physical harm (Eitzen and Sage, 2003). Consequently, many female athletes attempt to emphasize their "femininity" while competing by wearing hair ribbons, jewelry, or makeup. Professional athletes such as tennis player Maria Sarapova and Anna Kornikova help dispel myths that female athletes are masculine, but critics contend that they are not famous for their athletic abilities, but for physical attractiveness.

Professional Sports Sexism in sports, as in the workplace, has had a pronounced economic impact on female participants. The first $100,000 athlete was Babe Ruth, who broke that barrier in the 1930s during the Great Depression; the first female athlete to earn $100,000 was tennis star Billie Jean King, who accomplished that feat some 40 years later, in 1971. In 1997, the Women's National Basketball Association (WNBA) was launched in the summer shortly after the men's NBA finals. Women's salaries were paltry when compared to the men's, and women found it difficult to lure television audiences, as their games competed with major league baseball. Similarly, a professional women's soccer league enjoyed a short-lived success after the Women's World Cup Championship, but it was disbanded in 2003. Even in women's sports, league commissioners, team owners, athletic directors, head coaches, referees, umpires, and others who wield power and make decisions are predominantly men. The patriarchal PGA was challenged in 2003 when Annika Sorenstam was allowed to compete in the U.S. Open, but she failed to qualify—reaffirming to critics of female sports that the best women athletes cannot compete with men. In 1973, when Billie Jean King defeated Bobby Riggs in tennis in the so-called battle of the sexes, many people thought that women's sports would benefit greatly. Three decades later, although advertising and prize monies for women's sports have increased, they still lag far behind those in men's sports (Jacob, 2003).

Michelle Wie became only the fourth woman and the youngest player ever to compete with men in a PGA tournament when she was invited to play in the Sony Open in Hawaii. She also became the first female to qualify for a men's USGA tournament.

Although some of the progress women have made in sports has been a result of changing public attitudes about gender, much of it has required lawsuits and reliance on politicians and the government to change discriminatory laws. Consequently, women find themselves in the precarious situation of turning from one patriarchal institution to another.

In Politics and Government

In every society, the institution most associated with power and authority is politics, and throughout history, in every culture, politics and government have been dominated by men (Harris, 2003). There are cultures with matrilineal descent patterns (tracing one's ancestry through the mother's side of the family), and European monarchies have had queens. In those cultures, women have tended to enjoy more opportunities and power than in patriarchal societies. However, anthropologists agree that there has never been a true **matriarchy,** *a system in which women dominate men politically, economically, and socially.*

The Barren Years (1925–1960) The founders of the United States excluded women from the political process, and it was not until 1920 that women won the right to vote. Voting rights did not significantly enhance women's political power, however; the period from 1925 to 1960 is referred to as "the barren years" by some feminists (Klein, 1984:17). Women made some political gains during those years: Miriam "Ma" Ferguson was elected governor of Texas in 1924 and 1932, and Nellie Tayloe Ross was elected governor of Wyoming in 1925. However, these elections were not the blows for political feminism they may appear: Ferguson was elected because of the popularity of her husband, a former governor of Texas, and Ross was elected to serve out the unexpired term of her late husband. Similarly, Lurleen Wallace was elected governor of Alabama in 1966, but mainly because the Alabama constitution prohibited her popular husband, George, from seeking another term (Doyle, 1985). In some of these cases it was popularly believed that the women's husbands "ran the show" from behind the scenes.

MATRIARCHY
A system in which women dominate men politically, economically, and socially.

Sandra Day O'Connor and Ruth Bader Ginsberg are the only women to have been appointed as members of this prestigious bench.

Political Gains in the 1970s, 1980s, and 1990s In 1974, Ella Grasso was elected governor of Connecticut without any political ties to her husband; later, Washington, Kentucky, and Vermont elected female governors on their own merits. Women have fared a bit better in national offices, but as of 1990 only 23 of the 435 members of the House of Representatives and 2 of the 100 senators were women. As a result of the 1992 elections, dubbed by the media as the "Year of the Woman," 24 women were added to the House and 4 women joined the 2 in the Senate. After the 1994 elections, women held 8 seats in the Senate and 48 seats in the House. And in 1996, the numbers increased slightly, to 9 women in the Senate and 51 in the House; however, none of the women chaired a single committee in either chamber (Camia, 1997).

The 1980s witnessed major political breakthroughs for women. Sandra Day O'Connor became the first U.S. Supreme Court justice in 1981, and Geraldine Ferraro won the vice presidential nomination from the Democratic party in 1984. Gender became a key issue in 1990 when Ann Richards was elected governor of Texas; some political observers called it the "biggest showdown of the sexes since the 1973 tennis match between Bobby Riggs and Billie Jean King in the Astrodome" (Attlesey, 1990:1A). Gender was less an issue in Richards's reelection bid in 1994, when she was defeated by George W. Bush, who is the son of former President Bush and was elected president in 2000 and 2004.

As you look at this photo of the justices who sit on the U.S. Supreme Court, what is the first thing that strikes you?

Former First Lady, Senator Hillary Rodham Clinton delivers a speech to the Council on Foreign Relations.

How has Senator Clinton helped redefine the role of women in politics in the United States?

In the 1990s, President Clinton appointed Janet Reno as the first woman to hold the office of U.S. Attorney General and Ruth Bader Ginsberg as the second woman to sit on the U.S. Supreme Court. During his second term, Clinton appointed Madeline Albright to become the first female U.S. Secretary of State. In Arizona in 1998, Jane Hull was elected Governor along with other women to the posts of Secretary of State, Attorney General, Treasurer, and Superintendent of Instruction— an all-female line of succession.

Women and Politics in the Twenty-First Century As a result of the 2000 elections, women made gains in the statehouses as well as in both houses of Congress (see Figure 11.2). The number of female governors increased from 3 to 5 and there was an increase from 9 to 13 in the number of women in the U.S. Senate. One of the most high-profile senatorial elections occurred in New York, where former First Lady Hillary Rodham Clinton was elected. Additionally, 7 new Congresswomen were elected, to bring the total of females in the House of Representatives to 59. Despite their political differences, President George W. Bush followed former President Clinton's lead and appointed 3 women to cabinet positions, naming Ann Veneman as Secretary of Agriculture, Gale Norton as Secretary of the Interior, and Elaine Chao as Secretary of Labor. Bush also appointed Condoleezza Rice as his National Security Advisor and Christine Todd Whitman as Director of the Environmental Protection Agency. Later, Rice became Secretary of State and one of the most highly visible women in politics in the United States and around the world. In 2002, the U.S. Senate gained 1 female member when Lisa Murkowski was appointed by her father to complete his term when he was elected Governor. The House gained 14 women members totalling 73 of the 535 members. As a result of the 2006 elections, there are 14 women serving in the Senate and 71 in the U.S. House of Representatives.

On a global basis, a major political event occurred in 2006 when Ellen Johnson Sirleaf became the first elected female head of state on the African continent (AP, Monrovia, 2006). And, that same year, Hillary Clinton emerged as the front-runner for the democratic party nomination for president, and Representative Nancy Pelosi became the first woman to rise to the rank of Speaker of the House of Representatives—third

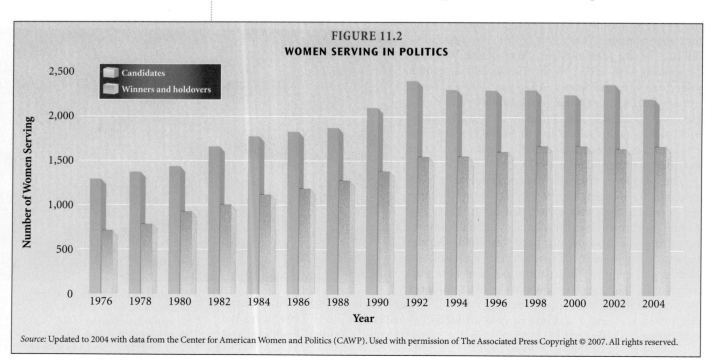

FIGURE 11.2
WOMEN SERVING IN POLITICS

Legend: Candidates; Winners and holdovers

Y-axis: Number of Women Serving (0, 500, 1,000, 1,500, 2,000, 2,500)

X-axis: Year (1976, 1978, 1980, 1982, 1984, 1986, 1988, 1990, 1992, 1994, 1996, 1998, 2000, 2002, 2004)

in line to the presidency. Still, worldwide, in the early twenty-first century, politics and government remains a patriarchal domain.

In the Military

Since 1973, when the Selective Service ended the draft and all branches of the military became dependent on volunteers, the number of women in the U.S. military has increased substantially. Today there are over a quarter of a million women on active duty in the military and approximately 15 percent of all commissioned officers are women. While opportunities for women in the military have increased over the past several years, the military is still a patriarchal environment where women sometimes find jobs and opportunities for advancement closed to them because of their sex.

Taking a Closer Look at the Numbers

Each year the U.S. Department of Defense releases data on personnel in all branches of military service. Despite the fact that the U.S. Coast Guard opens 100 percent of its job classifications to women, it does very little to recruit women; it has one of the lowest percentage (7 percent) of women of all the branches of service. The Air Force opens 97 percent of its jobs to women and fares much better in recruiting women, who constitute 19 percent of its ranks. The lowest in both percentage and number of women of all the branches of military service is the Marine Corps, which was the last branch to admit women, with approximately 10,000 women on active duty (approximately 6 percent of its members) and only 20 percent of jobs open to women. The Army and Navy stand at 15 percent and 14 percent, respectively, in terms of women in their ranks (Barta, 2003; U.S. Department of Defense, 2006).

Women who join the Marines find it is still saturated with the machismo image developed in World War II. Despite being open to women, the Marines tend to follow its longtime recruitment slogan: "The Marines are looking for a few good men." The slogan was changed to "The Few, The Proud, The Marines" in 1991, but sociology teaches us that it is much easier to change a slogan than an institution.

Taking a Closer Look at the Roles

Although no laws explicitly prohibit women from combat in the U.S. military, women's combat roles are limited. Public opinion polls show that approximately three-fourths of Americans believe women should be allowed to serve in combat. Nevertheless, all branches of the service have policies that limit women's access to combat roles. Public sentiment supported women participating in combat roles in the 2003 Iraqi war but questions were raised after two women were taken prisoners of war. In 2005, Congress voted to let the Pentagon decide what roles women could fill in combat zones as long as they notified Congress first (AP, Washington, 2004, 2005c, 2005d).

The Persian Gulf conflict in 1990 stimulated debate over the role of women in combat, and the military was required to review policies and procedures for recruitment, training, and deployment of women. All branches of the military stepped up their efforts to recruit women, and their numbers in the military increased. A series of scandals in the 1990s, however, rocked the military; accusations of sexual discrimination, sexual harassment, and even forcible rape became public. In the Army, where female recruits now comprise about 20 percent of all boot camps, high-ranking officials admit that new recruits must learn to say "Yes, sergeant" in

A U.S. soldier stands in front of the wreckage of a U.S. Army truck destroyed by Iraqi attackers in southern Baghdad. For the first time in American history, during the Iraqi war, women served in combat missions alongside men.

their sleep, and that sex among soldiers may be "as common as reveille at some bases" (Thomas and Vistica, 1997:41). With the pressure placed on recruits to obey their superiors, especially their drill sergeants, even consensual sex carries much ambiguity and because of imbalances in age and power may be defined as a form of rape (Thomas and Vistica, 1997). A Defense Department survey indicated that 70 percent of women in the military complained about crude behavior, raunchy jokes, and staring; 63 percent reported sexist or condescending attitudes; 41 percent reported unwanted touching; 13 percent had experienced sexual coercion; and 6 percent said they had been sexually assaulted (*USA Today*, 2003). In another survey, about half of all women in military academies reported being sexually harassed, while up to 6 percent reported being sexually assaulted (AP, Washington, 2005e). Women in the military complain that they are not afforded the same rights and protections against sexual harassment and assault as are their civilian counterparts.

The Double Standard: Are There Two Different Militaries?   Sexual integration of the military is sometimes compared to its racial desegregation in 1948—an analogy that some say is weak. Some observers contend that while the military may be sexually desegregated, disparities in the treatment of women and men have prevented true integration of the sexes. Instead, double standards in training, assignments, and promotion still exist.

Today the military remains one of the most patriarchal of all American social institutions. Americans indicate great confidence in the military and the vast majority support coeducational training, but over half say they believe that sexual harassment and sex discrimination are ingrained in military service. Part of this macho image may be attributed to how the military is portrayed in the media—another institution laced with sexism and gender inequality.

In the Media

The mass media play a powerful role in shaping attitudes, beliefs, values, and stereotypes about sex and gender. A major study conducted by the Gannett Foundation and the University of Southern California concluded that women are "symbolically annihilated by the media" (Beasley, 1994:216). This conclusion was based not only on stereotypical images of women on television and in magazines, but also on their glaring absence from some forms of media, especially from the front pages of major newspapers. Moreover, women's news, both in newspapers and on television, is often considered "soft news" (Beasley, 1994). Although this is changing, most forms of media remain dominated by men.

Masculinity and Femininity in the Media   In analyzing the media portrayals of gender over the last half century, we see that definitions of masculinity and femininity have changed to reflect such things as the shift from industrial to postindustrial society and women's growing political and economic influence. Yet beneath what appears to be a radical shift in the media's portrayal of gender is a common patriarchal theme that has changed very little over time: women are subordinate to men (Press, 1990, 1991; Carilli and Campbell, 2005). Whether women are presented as wives, attorneys, police officers, entrepreneurs, or sex objects, their statuses are validated by men. While all forms of the mass media play an influential role in portraying gender roles, after World War II motion pictures and television emerged as the major definers of masculinity and femininity. The media message was that real men were strong, silent, rough-and-tumble characters motivated by a strong sense of honor, loyalty, courage, and moral obligation to "right injustices." Femininity was portrayed as the art of being beautiful, alluring, and demure, yet cunning enough to attract reticent male heroes while staying out of their way. Focus box 11.3 discusses half a century of portrayals of women on television as an example.

Some contend that the sexual freedom won in the 1960s and 1970s may have resulted in a patriarchal backlash, creating a cultural climate that is more tolerant of aggression against women (Kaplan, 1990; Faludi, 1991; Baron and Richardson, 1994). In movies of this period, women's assertiveness had well-defined limits. Women who were too independent or aggressive—especially in sexual terms—were used and discarded or, worse, abused, raped, and murdered (Haskell, 1973). Nevertheless, significant changes occurred in the portrayal of women in movies: women were portrayed in nontraditional occupations and as being more aggressive, more prone to violence, and, in many ways, more stable and sensible than men (Rothman et al., 1993).

The 1980s and early 1990s saw masculine heroes in movies portrayed in both stereotypical and nonstereotypical ways. Mel Gibson, Kevin Costner, Michael Douglas, and other male stars were depicted as handsome, rugged, and sometimes ruthless—but they were also vulnerable and sometimes trapped by society's masculine stereotypes. For example, in *Fatal Attraction,* when the woman with whom Michael Douglas's character has had a "one-night stand" becomes obsessed with him, threatening his wife and child, many viewers forget that his infidelity created the problem in the first place. Instead, viewers see him as a *victim.*

Women were cast in more aggressive and important roles, and in movies such as *Thelma and Louise,* portrayed confident and independent nonstereotypical characters (Rothman et al., 1993). Still, for the most part, women in films were expected to be beautiful, alluring, and devoted to men. In *Fatal Attraction,* the wife, despite her husband's cheating on her at the first opportunity, fights to save both him and their marriage.

As we entered the twenty-first century, there was a resurgence of a familiar patriarchal theme in the movies: beautiful young women romantically involved with much older men. *A Perfect Murder* paired Michael Douglas (age 53) with Gwyneth Paltrow (age 25); Harrison Ford (57) was coupled with Anne Heche (29) in *6 Days/7 Nights; The Horse Whisperer* linked Robert Redford (60) with Kristin Scott-Thomas (37); in *Bulworth,* a 61-year-old Warren Beatty attracted the 29-year-old Halle Berry; and in *Entrapment,* 31-year-old Catherine Zeta-Jones (Michael Douglas's real-life wife) was paired with Sean Connery, who was in his early 70s. Meanwhile, in real life, forty-something Demi Moore married twenty-something Ashton Kutcher, raising eyebrows around the country in a way that never happened when older male stars married young starlets. The 2003 movie *Something's Gotta Give* toyed with conventional movie themes when Jack Nicholson's character dated the much younger Amanda Peet while the heart-throb doctor played by Keanu Reeves fell head over heels for her mother, played by Diane Keaton.

Sex, Gender, and Advertising   Advertisers in the mass media reinforce stereotypical gender roles (Lazier-Smith, 1989; Covell, 1992; Furnham and Bitar, 1993; Kolbe and Langefeld, 1993; Thomas and Treiber, 2000). In television, newspaper, and magazine advertisements, women advertise household products, secretarial equipment, and child-care products, while men advertise business equipment, computers, and medical, scientific, and technological products (Hawkins and Aber, 1993; Leppard et al., 1993). Men are depicted as serious, confident, competent, and self-assured, and even in commercials where women are more prominent than men they are likely to be pleasant, demure, and soft-spoken or provocative and sexy; most often the deep, resonant, authoritative voice-over that explains or sells the product, belongs to a man. The implications are clear: even in the domestic realm, "women are too dumb to know how to do things correctly" (Richmond-Abbott, 1986:124).

Erving Goffman (1979) pointed out that advertisers use photographs to underscore the message that men are more important, more aggressive, and, in most ways—physically, mentally, and socially—superior to women. Magazines also perpetuate these gender stereotypes. Content analyses of magazines aimed at teenage girls indicate that they promote the idea that "blonde is beautiful" and "blondes have more fun." These media images perpetuate what Naomi Wolf (1990) called the *beauty myth*—the cultural stereotype that women must attempt to fulfill almost unattainable standards of beauty and that a woman's physical appearance is the most important measure of her value. Moreover, these magazines' stories rarely portray men and women in anything other than traditional, stereotypical gender roles. Even popular greeting cards reflect the traditional gender stereotypes that Goffman linked to advertising (Mooney et al., 1993).

Sociological
FOCUS   11.3   Gender Socialization in the Media:
             Half a Century of Patriarchal Television

During the 1950s, television programs such as *The Donna Reed Show, I Love Lucy, Father Knows Best,* and *Leave It to Beaver* depicted "typical families": Men and women portrayed the idealized, stereotypical masculine and feminine roles. Men wore business suits, carried briefcases, and left their families each day for productive and challenging careers outside the home. Women were homemakers, wives, and mothers who were naive about finances, business, politics, and the world outside their homes. They cooked, sewed, cleaned, cared for children, and attempted to manage the households. The media made much of women being "feminine and domesticated" (Firth-Cozens and West, 1991:195). Programs focused on the inadequacies of women, even in handling routine family matters. When children had problems at school or things went awry at home, women made a few bungling attempts to fix the problem but the man of the household eventually returned home to resolve the crisis.

During the 1960s and early 1970s, gender roles in television families changed. Men still went off to work, made most of the major decisions, and untangled the messes their wives and children created during the day, but women were portrayed in less stereotypical roles. On programs such as *The Partridge Family* and *The Brady Bunch,* it was evident that women had jobs outside the home. But it was also clear that their most important roles were still those of wife and mother. The 1970s, however, ushered in the era of "career women" on television. Programs such as *The Mary Tyler Moore Show, Police Woman,* and even *Charlie's Angels*

showed women without husbands and families, working in businesses, solving crimes, taking risks, and participating in other nontraditional activities. Still, women worked for men who held power and authority over them and made all the important decisions (Tuchman et al., 1978). The new heroines of television were "typically women without men—single parents, separated or divorced . . . gathering around themselves the cobbled remnants of their own families' casualties" (Taylor, 1989:108)—a high price to pay for their independence.

Television in the 1980s portrayed women and men in family settings in both traditional and nontraditional gender roles. In Emmy Award–winning shows such as *Family Ties* and *The Cosby Show* and other situation comedies, females were depicted as "superwomen" who did it all: They maintained important professional careers; were perfect wives, mothers, and homemakers; and were incredibly bright, beautiful, and sexy. The men on these shows were depicted as having careers, but their most important roles were those of husband and father. In a role reversal from the 1950s and 1960s, these men often made bungling attempts to handle household problems and dilemmas before their wives could intervene and rectify the situation. In award-winning dramatic shows such as *Cagney and Lacey, Hill Street Blues,* and *L.A. Law,* women were depicted on equal career planes with men, performing effectively as police officers, attorneys, and judges.

As the 1990s began, five of the top ten television programs were about women: *Designing Women, Murder She Wrote, The Golden Girls, Roseanne,* and *Murphy Brown* (Funk, 1990). Most of these programs featured women who were strong, independent, intelligent, assertive, and in charge of their lives. Two of the shows were created by women. Diane English, creator of *Murphy Brown,* and Linda Bloodworth-Thomason, who created, directed, and wrote for *Designing Women,* portrayed women from a feminist perspective. Although *Designing Women* and *Murphy Brown* appear to portray the strong, independent women of the 1990s, from a sociological perspective an underlying patriarchal theme could still be detected. For example, on *Designing Women,* it was still a man—Anthony—who emerged as protector and level-headed decision

Television's portrayal of women and their roles in the family have changed dramatically from the times of *The Donna Reed Show* to those of *Desperate Housewives.*

Sex, Gender, and Music   An analysis of radio's most popular songs over the 1950s, 1960s, and 1970s indicated that they verbalized the same message (Stockard and Johnson, 1980). A content analysis of MTV, one of the most popular television channels among teenagers and young adults, found that men appeared twice as often as women; men were engaged in more aggressive and dominant behavior than women; women were engaged in more implicitly sexual and subservient behavior; and women

maker. And though *Murphy Brown* had a successful career, we were constantly reminded of its toll. Murphy was divorced and a recovering alcoholic, and she often sought validation from male characters on the show. In 1992 the theme of *Murphy Brown* focused on her pregnancy, and in one episode we were presented with several real-life television career women—Paula Zahn, Joan Lunden, Katie Couric, Mary Alice Williams, and Faith Daniels—attending a baby shower for Murphy, at which they cooed over baby gifts, played traditional baby shower games, and symbolically reasserted the importance of motherhood. In the final episode of that season, the centrality of motherhood was reinforced as Murphy gave birth to a son. The closing scene depicted Brown sitting in the hospital bed, infant cuddled to her breast, gazing into his eyes and softly singing the lyrics "You make me feel like a natural woman." This scene evoked a response from then–Vice President Dan Quayle, who accused *Murphy Brown* and the rest of Hollywood of representing all that was wrong in America by glorifying single mothers and denigrating the role of the father. This attack launched the "family values" motif for the Bush reelection campaign in 1992 and triggered a major controversy over women's roles and what constitutes a "family" in American society. In a 2001 *Newsweek* article, Dan Quayle contended that he still thought he was right in his contention that the media tend to denigrate the traditional family, and that today there is more pressure and turmoil on the family than ever before (Quayle, 2001).

Today, *ER, The King of Queens, CSI, Bones, Grey's Anatomy*, and a number of other popular television shows feature strong women as leading characters and portray them in less stereotypical and nontraditional roles. Nevertheless, even in the twenty-first century, these programs tend to continue the past half-century of patriarchal television. *ER* and *Grey's Anatomy* feature women as surgeons and hospital supervisors, but programming focuses on their love lives, pregnancies, romantic relationships, and marital problems more than their medical expertise. Despite the fact that the lead female character on *The King of Queens* is better educated and has a job with a law firm, it is clear that her retired father and delivery truck–driving husband make most of the important decisions that affect her life. All of the female forensic scientists on the various versions of *CSI* work for men, and the forensic anthropologist featured on

Bones is roundly criticized for being married to her work instead of the handsome FBI agent with whom she works. Reality television such as *Fear Factor, Survivor, Big Brother*, and other programs feature many women in important roles, often competing on equal grounds with men. Nevertheless, much of the programming capitalizes on showing the women participants in skimpy bikinis or their underwear and their physical attributes are highlighted far more often than their strategic or mental skills.

Emmy-winning *Desperate Housewives* emerged as one of the most popular television shows featuring several women in prominent roles. Some are professionals struggling to combine career aspirations with family obligations, while at least one is a stay-at-home mom, and another is a former fashion model and current spoiled diva. While the show has pushed the envelope on contemporary issues including suicide, alcoholism, homosexuality, and infidelity to name a few, all the women share a few common traits that reinforce decades old patriarchal themes: they are physically attractive; they view marriage and children as important to their self-actualization; and they are *desperate* for male attention and validation from males.

In summation, applying the critical thinking of sociological analysis, over a half-century of gender socialization in the media reveals that traditional female images and gender stereotypes have simultaneously been shattered and reinforced. In regard to television, while women may have come a long way, they still have a long way to go.

TAKING A CLOSER LOOK

Do you agree that over the past half-century, television has portrayed gender roles in a patriarchal fashion? If so, why? If not, what examples can you cite to support your claim?

Source: Gaye Tuchman, Arlene Kaplan Daniels, and James Benet. *Hearth and Home: Images of Women in the Mass Media.* New York: Oxford University Press, 1978. Ella Taylor. *Prime-Time Families: Television Culture in Postwar America.* Berkeley: University of California Press, 1989. Jenny Firth-Cozens and Michel A. West. "Women at Work: Reflections and Perspectives." In Firth-Cozens and West (eds.), *Women at Work: Psychological and Organizational Perspectives.* Philadelphia: Open University Press, 1991:192–200. Dan Quayle. "Why I Think I'm Still Right." *Newsweek*, May 28, 2001:52. Tim Funk. "Women in Change: Shows Catch Up to Society's Progress." *Dallas Morning News*, December 2, 1990:7c.

were more frequently the object of explicit, implicit, and aggressive sexual advances (Sommers-Flanagan et al., 1993). In the twenty-first century, the message seems clear: for women to succeed they need to be young, beautiful, sexy, and skimpily clad. Stars such as Beyonce Knowles, Jessica Simpson, and Christina Aguilera, set the standard. Popular rock star Pink bucked this trend in 2006 with her hit single and video *Stupid Girl*, which lampooned young women who give in to cultural sereotypes and are concerned with superficial aspects of physical beauty and obsessed with making or marrying money.

Television and Gender Socialization

Children's television programming is very influential in perpetuating stereotypical gender roles. Programs aimed at children are more likely to have male characters, usually portrayed as heroes; female characters are portrayed as submissive to and dependent on male characters (Stockard and Johnson, 1980; Basow, 1986). Do children pick up on these gender stereotypes? The evidence is that they do. One study indicated that children who watched television more than 25 hours per week were much more likely than their counterparts who watched less television to hold traditional stereotypical views of gender roles (Fruch and McGhee, 1975). A study of television advertising in Great Britain concluded that television can and does profoundly influence both children's and adult's perceptions of gender roles (Furnham and Bitar, 1993). Other research confirms that media stereotypes of women have lasting impact (Carilli and Campbell, 2005).

Pink's music video for her hit song "Stupid Girl" lampooned cultural and media stereotypes of girls and young women and their obsession with superficiality.

What messages about sex and gender roles does she send to young girls who would like to emulate her?

In summarizing media portrayals of women and men, Hilary Lips (1991:19) noted, "We are surrounded with the message that masculine males can be powerful, but feminine females cannot, or that women's only effective source of feminine influence is beauty and sex appeal." She asserted that these media images create a self-fulfilling prophecy and reinforce gender inequities—something that helped spawn a feminist movement for gender equality.

Sex, Gender, and the Technomedia

Many people believe that the so-called information superhighway has the potential to become the "great equalizer" in regard to sex, gender, and sexual orientation. Men, women, gays, straights, virgins, and prostitutes can go online and find other individuals, groups, or organizations with similar tastes and interests. Or they can go on-line and choose another identity if they wish. Remember the opening vignette in Chapter 5 in which Naughty Nina turned out to be a man?

The Internet has considerable potential for consciousness raising about gender. As Sherry Turkle (1995) noted, the Internet has given people the ability to suspend gender identities and to "gender swap"—becoming male, female, or "genderless" at their discretion. Consequently, on the Internet, people can gain insights into the power and meanings of gender in ways that would be impossible in real life. Gender is compelling, however, even on the Internet. As Turkle's study showed, in chat room discussions people need to get a "fix" on gender: to play a character that is neither male nor female is "disturbing and evocative" (Turkle, 1995:212). Research indicates there was a large "gender gap" in Internet usage during the 1990s with women lagging far behind men, but that gap narrowed significantly and disappeared by 2000 (Ono and Zavodny, 2003).

In much the same way, the Internet raises new questions and possibilities for sexual orientation. Virtual sex is very much a part of the Internet, and chat rooms devoted to sex proliferate. On the one hand, cybersex expands peoples' ideas about sex and sexual orientation, pushing them into uncharted territories restricted only by their imaginations and evolving Internet mores. But sex on the Internet raises disturbing questions as well, such as children's access to explicit sexual materials and their potential for encountering sexual predators online. Issues of sex and violence also have been raised. For example, can a person be sexually harassed over the Internet? What about "virtual rape"? These issues and others are likely to increase in the future.

Since the technomedia both shapes and is shaped by American and global society, many of the same issues that arise in society—problems in cross-gender communication, homophobia, sexual harassment, and sexual violence, for example—also exist in the technomedia. The majority of technomedia users, especially those who use the Internet, are white, middle-aged men. But increasing numbers of women are venturing into cyberspace. Their motives for Internet usage and types of use differ from those of men (Wasserman and Richmond-Abbott, 2005). In fact, the third wave of feminism in the United States and the future of global feminism and the struggle for gender equality may rely heavily on the technomedia. Our website provides links to a vast array of sites devoted to feminism, women's studies, and a wide variety of sex and gender issues.

FEMINISM: THE STRUGGLE FOR GENDER EQUALITY

The struggle for women's rights has been a long and hard-fought battle in the United States and around the globe. It has fostered a major social movement based on **feminism,** *an ideology aimed at eliminating patriarchy in support of equality between the sexes.* Let's look briefly at the feminist movements in the United States, and then turn to the global efforts of feminism as well as the resistance they have met.

Feminist Movements in the United States

The first major wave of feminism in the United States was linked to the pre–Civil War abolitionist movement. When it became clear that emancipation leaders were not seeking the same rights for women as for black men, however, Elizabeth Cady Stanton and Lucretia Mott organized a convention on women's rights at Seneca Falls, New York, in 1848. The main thrust of the early feminist movement was women's suffrage (the right to vote); with the passage of the Nineteenth Amendment in 1920 much of the movement's initial fervor dissipated.

The second major wave of feminism in the United States arose in the 1960s; again it was linked to the struggle for civil rights for African Americans and other minorities. Social activism of the times provided the milieu for contemporary feminism, and Betty Friedan's book *The Feminine Mystique* (1963) ignited public consciousness. Friedan described the relative isolation, discontent, and alienation of American women trapped in the stereotypical roles of housewife and mother. Many American women identified with the plight described by Friedan, and in 1966 the National Organization for Women (NOW) was formed. This organization and the women's movement attracted large numbers of women and men into their ranks.

Although the feminist agenda is diverse and feminists disagree about how best to accomplish its goals, there is consensus that laws, policies, regulations, and programs that discriminate against women should be abolished. A major goal of the contemporary feminist movement was the passage of an Equal Rights Amendment (ERA) to the U.S. Constitution. Initially proposed in 1923, during the Roaring Twenties—a period identified with sexual liberation and changing roles for women—the ERA simply states that equality under the law cannot be denied or abridged on the basis of sex. The amendment passed both houses of Congress in 1972, but despite widespread support by both men and women it fell 3 states short of the 38 needed for ratification, with feminists' only consolation being that women are protected by the Fourteenth Amendment.

Within the feminist movement, a more *radical* faction emerged that not only endorsed all reforms proposed by more moderate elements but also sought revolutionary social change. The ideological basis for radical feminism was spawned by Kate Millett's *Sexual Politics* (1970) and Germaine Greer's *The Female Eunuch* (1972), which concluded that the goals of feminism could not be accomplished without the abandonment of the institution of the family and elimination of the whole notion of gender. The more conservative *liberal feminists* and *socialist feminists* believe the institution of the family itself is not incompatible with gender equality as long as families change to accommodate the needs, goals, and ambitions of both females and males and the structured inequality in most families is eliminated.

Just over a decade ago, a feminist activist group calling itself *Guerrilla Girls* emerged. A network of women, mostly in the arts, who describe themselves as the female counterparts to Robin Hood, the Lone Ranger, and Batman, the *Guerrilla Girls* use humor and artistic talent to make posters that convey serious messages about problems related to sexism and gender inequality. The *Guerrilla Girls* started in the United States but through the World Wide Web have gained members and support throughout the world.

Feminism and feminist movements are most associated with the United States, but during the latter part of the twentieth century they gained impetus around the globe. As

FEMINISM
An ideology aimed at eliminating patriarchy in support of equality between the sexes.

with other aspects of globalization today, feminism has become even more diverse and multidimensional as it is defined and implemented in diverse social and cultural contexts (Bates et al., 2005).

Global Feminism

Although feminism in the United States and several European nations had much earlier roots, the first World Conference on Women was held in 1975 in Mexico City. It drew approximately 7,000 participants from around the globe, who gathered to discuss women's rights and the impact of gender discrimination on society. Resolutions adopted at that conference included the call for universal suffrage, equal access for women to education, and an increase in women's participation in both government and nongovernmental organizations. Subsequent World Conferences on Women were held in 1980 in Copenhagen and in 1985 in Nairobi, where additional global issues, such as increased representation of women in international organizations and conferences and the elimination of both *de jure* (legal) and *de facto* (in practice) discrimination against women in government and nongovernmental agencies.

The Fourth World Conference on Women was held in 1995 in Beijing, China. Some 8,000 American women joined Hillary Clinton and 28,000 other women from around the world to devise strategies for raising the status of women worldwide and ending gender discrimination on a global scale. This conference marked the largest and most diverse assemblage of feminists from around the world and resulted in a strong *Platform for Action* that reiterated unmet goals from the previous conferences and called for universal human rights for women. In addition, the platform condemned domestic violence, genital mutilation, and marital rape and indicated unwavering support for advances in health for women, economic equity, and the rights of girls. A fifth World Conference on Women has been called for but as of this writing has not been scheduled.

Since the 1995 conference, the United Nations has endorsed the conference platform, and a huge international network of government and nongovernmental organizations committed to global feminism has emerged. These organizations conduct research, dispense information, and provide social networks for feminists around the world.

Resistance to Feminism

The feminist movement has met with social resistance worldwide. For example, 41 nations and the Vatican have announced reservations regarding the World Conference on Women's platform stance on sexual and reproductive rights for women—especially those involving birth control and abortion. During the 1995 conference, dissension was so strong from the Vatican and the Islamic nations represented that all references to prohibition of discrimination on the basis of sexual orientation were dropped from the platform entirely.

In the United States, Phyllis Schlafly emerged in the 1970s as the leader of the antifeminist movement. She and her followers argued that passage of the Equal Rights Amendment and the rest of the feminist agenda would destroy the American family. Antifeminists not only oppose change but also believe that feminist ideas are "unnatural" because they violate traditional sex roles. In *Backlash,* Susan Faludi (1991:x) asserted that every positive stride women have made toward achieving equality has met with a social backlash by those who want to maintain the status quo; folk wisdom has it that "women are unhappy precisely because they are free." This, Faludi asserted, amounts to no less than an undeclared war against women.

A major form of resistance in the United States comes from men, some of whom want to maintain the benefits of gender inequality and others who argue that feminism is simply another form of sexism by a different name (Goldberg, 1976; Davidson, 1988). In *The Failure of Feminism* (1988), Nicholas Davidson proposed that radical feminism advocates man hating and the replacement of patriarchy with an equally intolerant matriarchy.

Despite resistance, feminism persists and is gaining international appeal and recognition. Moreover, as we note throughout this book, feminist scholarship is making important contributions to sociology. Feminists argue that gender, like social class, is one of the most important dimensions of social organization. Thus gender refers not only to the ways in which sex differences become socially significant but also to the social relationships between women and men, and the differing allocation of social power based on sex. Simply put, from the feminist perspective, power is a central aspect of gender relations; women have less access to most types of power than men, and most stereotypical gender differences are a result of this imbalance of power.

the FUTURE

LOOKING to

SEX AND GENDER IN THE TWENTY-FIRST CENTURY

The controversy over the extent to which biological and physiological differences in the sexes determine gender differences continues, and sociobiological research is likely to expand. A technological development that may offer unique research opportunities is the ability of parents not only to know the sex of an infant before its birth but also to choose the baby's sex. There is some research that suggests parents are more likely to want to pick the sex of a child if they already have two children of the same sex (Pollard and Morgan, 2002). This choice is medically possible today. What if it were to become a widely accepted cultural practice in the future? The world of genetic engineering, human cloning, and other technological developments offers fascinating and even frightening possibilities.

Many believe that the end of patriarchy and the establishment of a more egalitarian society in the twenty-first century are not only possible but inevitable. Popular psychologist Joyce Brothers dubbed the 1990s the "she-generation," claiming that women would set the agenda for the decade, in contrast to the nation's prior "he-generation," "me-generation," and "we-generation" periods (*Kansas City Times,* 1989). While the 1990s may have fallen short of her expectations, strides were made in that direction.

Marilyn French is less optimistic, but she concluded in *Beyond Power* (1985) that patriarchal structures will be altered as human needs and goals change. Most people agree that if equality between the sexes is achieved in this twenty-first century, economic factors and women's achievements in the workplace will be the driving force. Women have gained access to more powerful and prestigious positions in society largely because of their enhanced power in the labor market, and this may be accompanied in the future by major changes in the distribution of income between men and women. Research strongly suggests that education may have the most important impact on women's employment and earnings. Longitudinal studies show that women are now outpacing men at every level of educational credential (see Table 11.3) and that women

TABLE 11.3
ACADEMIC DEGREES CONFERRED BY SEX

YEAR	BACHELOR'S DEGREE					MASTER'S DEGREE				
	TOTAL	MEN	%	WOMEN	%	TOTAL	MEN	%	WOMEN	%
1968	632,289	357,682	57%	274,607	43%	176,749	113,552	64%	63,197	36%
1978	921,204	487,347	53%	433,857	47%	311,620	161,212	52%	150,408	48%
1988	994,829	477,203	48%	517,626	52%	299,317	145,163	48%	154,154	52%
1998	1,172,000	523,000	45%	649,000	55%	406,000	183,000	45%	223,000	55%
2003	1,312,503	537,079	41%	775,424	59%	512,645	211,381	41%	301,264	59%
2014*	1,582,000	633,000	40%	949,000	60%	693,000	275,000	40%	418,000	60%

*Projected

Source: Unpublished tabulations, Bureau of Labor Statistics, Current Population Survey. 2003 and 2014 (projected) data: Tables 27 & 28, "Projections of Education Statistics to 2014," National Center for Education Statistics, U.S. Department of Education.

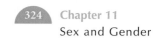

in their midtwenties to midthirties have nearly closed the wage gap with their male peers—a trend predicted to include most working-age groups in the future.

According to some analysts, feminism may contribute to enhanced economic equality. Whereas during the nineteenth century science emphasized the differences between the sexes, during the twentieth and twenty-first centuries it emphasizes sameness. Today's feminism reemphasizes differentness but focuses on different treatment based on gender rather than on any inherent differences between the sexes. Moreover, contemporary feminism encourages women not merely to attempt to get their "piece of the career success pie" but to transform the industries for which they work into more egalitarian structures.

Equality between the sexes will require more than economic equity; many people believe there must be significant changes in the political and legal structures as well. Gayle Binion (1991), for example, noted that feminist jurisprudence has passed through three distinct phases. During the first stage, which she called *conservative feminism,* the goal was to establish gender neutrality in public policy. In the second stage, *liberal feminism,* feminists demanded scrutiny of the impact of public policy on women. In the third stage, *progressive feminism,* which took us into the twenty-first century, women's values and experiences must be incorporated into jurisprudence. This final phase, Binion (1991:218) concluded, will be "uniquely sensitive to inequalities of power, and to the repression and lack of tolerance for diversity that that has entailed."

Will there be increased freedom, equality, and tolerance for those who violate traditional gender roles? Or will a conservative backlash and a renewed emphasis on genetics and biology attempt to reestablish traditional masculine and feminine roles? While these questions cannot be answered with any certainty, women's and men's roles have become much more flexible and are likely to continue to do so in the future. Women's use of technomedia will continue that increased flexibility with the ability to work from home, and take multi-tasking to a new unforeseen level. From a sociological perspective it is indisputable that changing attitudes toward sex and gender will continue to have an impact on people's daily lives—in America and throughout the world.

Summary

1. *Sex* refers to biological and physical differences between males and females, whereas *gender* refers to cultural and social definitions of masculinity and femininity. *Sexual orientation* refers to the choice of sexual partners and consists of heterosexuality (partners of the opposite sex), homosexuality (same-sex partners), and bisexuality (partners of both sexes). All societies differentiate people on the basis of sex and the accompanying gender roles learned through social interaction.

2. Sociologists explain gender differences in a variety of ways depending on their theoretical perspective. Those using the interactionist perspective focus on the socialization process and the development of gender identities. Functionalists emphasize gender differences and the need for clear-cut gender roles. The conflict perspective insists that gender is a form of stratification and promotes inequality.

3. Sexism is an ideology that maintains that one sex is inherently inferior to the other. It is exemplified by a patriarchal social structure in which men dominate women politically, economically, and socially. Sexism is pervasive in the family, religion, education, the workplace, sports, politics and government, the military, and the media.

4. Feminism grew out of the nineteenth-century women's movement, which initially fought for the abolition of slavery and women's suffrage. In the 1960s, a second wave of feminism developed, focusing on equality between the sexes, the passage of an Equal Rights Amendment, and the eradication of prejudice and discrimination against females. Femi-

nism crosses national and cultural boundaries and now is part of a global social movement to end gender inequality around the world.

5 Future directions in attitudes, values, and behavior toward sex and gender are difficult to predict, but notable changes are occurring. Many gender stereotypes have been challenged, and both men and women are actively pursuing endeavors not open to them only a few decades ago. Nevertheless, sex and gender remain major sources of inequality in the twenty-first century.

Key Terms

androgyny (p. 300)
bisexuality (p. 294)
femininity (p. 296)
feminism (p. 321)
gender (p. 293)
gender identity (p. 298)

gender roles (p. 296)
heterosexuality (p. 294)
homophobia (p. 295)
homosexuality (p. 294)
masculinity (p. 296)
matriarchy (p. 313)

patriarchy (p. 302)
sex (p. 293)
sexism (p. 302)
sexual harassment (p. 309)
sexual orientation (p. 294)

Summary

1 People in countries around the world, especially the United States, are enjoying longer life expectancies. The result is important demographic changes, including a dramatic increase in the number of people living past age 65. This increase in the elderly population has led to increased interest in gerontology, the scientific study of aging and the elderly. Gerontologists study the chronological, biological, psychological, and social dimensions of aging, focusing on the special problems that affect the elderly.

2 Attitudes toward aging and treatment of the elderly vary greatly from one type of society to another. Preindustrial societies tend to fall into two patterns: in nomadic food foraging societies, if the elderly become ill, decrepit, or infirm, they may be viewed as a burden to their families and may even threaten the survival of the group. In pastoral, horticultural, and agrarian societies, the elderly often are at the top of the social stratification scheme, owning most of the land and livestock and possessing most of the wealth, power, and prestige. Industrial societies tend to place tremendous emphasis on work and productivity—two things often associated with youth and vitality. Consequently, as people age they may be viewed as less productive and hence less valuable to society. As societies shift from industrial to postindustrial, with emphasis on knowledge, leisure, and service, however, the potential roles of the elderly are expanded.

3 The elderly face many of the problems experienced by others in society, but they also encounter unique age-related issues in the form of ageism, retirement (which may result in a fixed income and perhaps poverty), social isolation, elder abuse, declining health, and death.

4 The mass media, especially television, have traditionally either ignored the elderly or helped create and perpetuate negative stereotypes about them. Recently, television has begun to portray the elderly more positively, targeting the huge market that the elderly represent as consumers.

5 A number of sociological theories have been developed to explain the aging process. Social disengagement takes a functionalist perspective and posits that the elderly and the rest of society participate in a mutual withdrawal from interaction. Adopting a conflict approach, subculture theory views the elderly as a distinct subculture that experiences prejudice, discrimination, and inequality similar to those facing other minority groups. Activity theory borrows from the interactionist perspective and argues that the extent to which people remain socially active determines the quality of their lives in old age. Exchange theory combines elements of the three major sociological perspectives and explains that, at least in part, the disengagement and decreased power of older people is a result of their devaluation as partners in social exchange.

6 The twenty-first century will see changing demographics, and the over-65 population will increase dramatically throughout the world. In the United States, the huge baby boom generation will enter the ranks of the elderly, making the over-65 age group the largest single age cohort in this country. This "graying of America" promises to have a dramatic political, social, and economic impact that will affect virtually all aspects of American society and culture.

Key Terms

activity theory of aging (p. 349)

ageism (p. 340)

conflict approach to aging (p. 350)

elder abuse (p. 345)

euthanasia (p. 347)

exchange theory of aging (p. 350)

gerontocracy (p. 338)

gerontology (p. 328)

Gray Panthers (p. 341)

hospice (p. 347)

senescence (p. 332)

social disengagement theory (p. 349)

subculture theory of aging (p. 350)

thanatology (p. 346)

Chapter 13

Families

*"Family isn't about whose blood you have.
It's about who you care about."*
—*Trey Parker and Matt Stone (South Park)*

A 40-year-old single woman is "more likely to be killed by a terrorist than to ever marry!" proclaimed *Newsweek* magazine in its cover story entitled "The Marriage Crunch" in June 1986. Even in pre-9/11 America, that analogy seemed offensive to many, but it soon became embedded in the minds of single women everywhere, as well as part of the popular culture psyche as the subject of multiple news programs, television talk shows, and breakfast table discussions around the country. Based on studies conducted at Harvard and Yale by demographers who used past age cohorts' actions to predict future behaviors, the *Newsweek* article cited statistics on the rising trend of delayed marriage and non-marriage among professional women in the United States. According to the report, women who did not marry in their twenties faced "abysmal odds" of ever marrying at all. A woman who remained single at age 30 had only a 20 percent chance of ever marrying, and by the age of 35 that probability dropped to 5 percent. Women who were still single at age 40, it seemed, had almost no chance at all of ever marrying—hence, the infamous terrorist analogy. As sociologists warn, however, *things are not necessarily what they seem.*

In 2001, two Princeton sociologists conducted research on delayed marriage that concluded that 97.4 percent of women born between 1960 and 1964 who delayed marriage until after they completed college and began their careers would eventually marry. Subsequent sociological research confirms that although both women and men are delaying marriage, that does not spell impending doom for the institution, and although people are indeed delaying marriage for a variety of reasons, most plan to, and eventually do, get married, prompting *Newsweek* 20 years later to the week to run a cover article acknowledging: "The Marriage Crunch—we got it wrong" (McGinn, 2006).

It is not unusual today to see people delaying marriage into their thirties or forties, or remarrying during middle age to start new families.

Stephanie Coontz (2006:49), Director of Research at the Council on Contemporary Families, contends that "marriage has changed more in the last 30 years than in the previous 300." According to Coontz, the predictions made by the marriage researchers in the 1980s were valid, if people had continued to "play" by three "old rules" of marriage: (1) women who delayed marriage were condemning themselves to singlehood; (2) women who pursue advanced education and careers were less likely to marry; and (3) women who married later were less likely to have children and more likely to get divorced. Today, the average age for women to marry is 26 to 27 if they have a bachelor's degree, and 30 if they have a master's or professional degree. Also, today women with college degrees are more likely, not less likely, to marry than those who have high school educations or less. Finally, despite delaying marriage, most women plan to have, and eventually do have, children, and although divorce rates are slightly higher for women who marry much earlier or much later than the average age, women with higher education, careers, and higher earnings are more likely to choose husbands who support their careers and contribute to the marriage equally (Coontz, 2006).

In addition to the changes in marriage indicated in the opening vignette, the social institution of marriage and family life is changing globally as well as in America. In this chapter, we highlight several important themes. First, systems of marriage and the family are embedded within the larger society. Economic and political institutions and prevailing norms and values influence courtship behavior, family forms, sexual behavior and even the most intimate details of our lives. Second, rather than being fixed and immutable, the institutions of marriage and the family are adaptive and resilient (Eitzen and Baca-Zinn, 2005; Aulette, 2007; Skolnick and Skolnick, 2007).

In addition to choices, families face many constraints—including social inequality—as well as transitions in the larger society, such as corporate downsizing, job loss, and cutbacks in government assistance that have complicated and compounded many family problems. Technological and demographic changes—especially a progressive aging of populations in all industrial societies—have brought new challenges as well. So have new patterns of immigration and shifts in public attitudes about family and gender roles—many nurtured by the media—which have brought new opportunities and dilemmas. Given the powerful emotions and equally powerful rhetoric that have always been associated with the family, we begin by distinguishing real families from families of myth.

WHAT IS A FAMILY?

Because the family is the only institution with origins in biology, people tend to believe families are pretty much the same everywhere—or at least that families should suit their ideal images. But everywhere societies are highly selective in terms of which aspects of biology and "human nature" they emphasize, ignore, or downplay, hence the controversial nature of the family and the great diversity of families in the United States and around the world (Schultz and Lavenda, 2005).

At present, the U.S. Bureau of the Census defines the family as two or more persons related by blood, marriage, or adoption who share a common residence. But this definition ignores current living arrangements and the preferences of many people. While there may have been some consensus about the family several decades ago, what constitutes a family today is a matter of public debate. Is a couple who cohabit for many years but never marry a family? How about a mother and children? Are they a family, or an *incomplete* one, as some politicians would have us believe? Are gay and lesbian couples who are part of a domestic partnership a "family"? How about people who live alone: because they do not share a residence with kin, are they no longer "family members"? These and many other questions remain unresolved; the courts and all of us will have to decide the answers.

To account for the extraordinary diversity of families in contemporary society, we define **family** as *two or more people who are related by blood, marriage, or adoption or who are part of a relationship in which there is commitment, mutual aid and support, and, often, a shared residence.*

As in the past, most families today are formed through **marriage,** *a legally recognized economic and sexual relationship between two or more persons that includes mutual rights and obligations and is assumed to be permanent.* This definition highlights three important aspects of marriage. First, marriage includes not only the marrying parties but also the members of society who must approve of the union. Second, marriage provides for the regulation of sex and childbearing, and in most societies marriage and the family are the primary—and in many cases the only legitimate—contexts for both activities. Third, although Americans often emphasize romantic love and downplay the economic aspects of marriage, most societies acknowledge that economic exchanges are basic to the relationship (Schultz and Lavenda, 2005). As a popular German folk expression declares, "It is not man that marries maid, but field marries field, vineyard marries vineyard, cattle marry cattle" (Ember and Ember, 1996:190).

Sociologists distinguish two kinds of families, each with its own norms, roles, and relationships. During the life course, most Americans are members of both the **family of orientation,** which is *the family into which an individual is born,* and the **family of marriage,** *the family that a person forms at his or her marriage.*

FAMILY
Two or more people who are related by blood, marriage, or adoption or who are part of a relationship in which there is commitment, mutual aid and support, and often a shared residence.

MARRIAGE
A legally recognized economic and sexual relationship between two or more persons that includes mutual rights and obligations and is assumed to be permanent.

FAMILY OF ORIENTATION
The family into which an individual is born.

FAMILY OF MARRIAGE
The family that a person forms at his or her marriage.

FAMILY DIVERSITY: A GLOBAL PORTRAIT

At first glance, other people's cultural understandings about sex, marriage, and the family may appear strange. Only 100 years ago most Americans believed men had an uncontrollable sex drive, whereas women had none. Today, in the Middle East, most people hold the opposite view: women are the ones with a voracious sexual appetite and men must be protected from them. Moreover, in some societies men may marry men and women may marry women. And in some places, women may marry dead people ("ghost marriage") to perpetuate a family line (Evans-Pritchard, 1951; Schultz and Lavenda, 2005).

Families are equally diverse. In most industrial and postindustrial societies, family and kin groups tend to be small and loosely knit. By contrast, most industrializing societies define kin very broadly and dozens, even hundreds of people may be recognized as close kin. Moreover, families are usually much larger and younger and they fulfill many more functions than is common in industrial societies.

"If Heather has two mommies, and each of them has two brothers, and one of those brothers has another man for a 'roommate,' how many uncles does Heather have?"

Comparative studies over the last century have taught us several things. First, because people universally recognize marriage and family in moral as well as practical terms, it is necessary for all of us to guard against ethnocentric biases. Second, beliefs about marriage and the family are not random, but are related to particular historical and ecological contexts. Third, marriage and family patterns are not infinitely varied. If we look beyond the exotic and in many cases superficial differences, it becomes clear that all societies use a limited range of principles and norms: descent patterns; family patterns; courtship and marriage patterns; and residence and authority patterns.

Descent Patterns

Although we rarely think of it this way, most of us have more relatives than we could ever count. There are *consanguineal kin,* who are people related through biological or "blood" ties, and many people have *affinal kin* as well, who are people related by marriage, such as brothers- and sisters-in-law, parents-in-law, and step-relatives. There also are *adopted kin,* and many people have *fictive kin,* who are people that have gained kin status through special ties of friendship or through ritual (such as godparents). Combining all varieties of kin, your family tree and that of most others would include millions of people in the brief period that Europeans have inhabited America. It is impractical or impossible for Americans or members of any society to acknowledge kinship ties to so many people. Therefore, all societies narrow the pool of relatives into socially useful categories (Peoples and Bailey, 1997).

Bilineal Descent   In the United States, although most of us take our surname from the father's side, we trace descent through both father's and mother's families. This kinship system is called *bilineal descent.* In our system, few members of the middle class trace their ancestry back more than four or five generations. The upper class, members of Daughters of the American Revolution, and some others often trace kin back much further. But what they have constructed is not a comprehensive genealogy, but a *pedigree* that selectively acknowledges socially useful or prominent relatives, while omitting many others.

Patrilineal and Matrilineal Descent   Bilineal descent systems create a vast pool of potential kin, but they do not provide clear social boundaries for collective action or the transmission of property. Most preindustrial societies avoid this problem by tracing descent and transmitting property only through the father's or mother's lines. *Patrilineal descent* systems trace descent through male relatives only. Typically in such systems males are dominant and are favored in inheritance, politics, and other social arenas.

Matrilineal descent systems trace descent through women only. Matrilineal descent is associated with small-scale horticultural societies where women are primary producers and men are often absent for long periods, such as among the Navajo Indians of Arizona. At marriage, Navajo men move to the homes of their wives, and all future children become part of the wife's, not the husband's, kin groups. Fathers may be affectionate with their children and provide them with some goods, but their primary loyalties and lifelong commitments are not to them, but to their nephews and nieces—who are members of their matrilineal groups (Dutton, 1975).

Family Patterns

The key feature that distinguishes family patterns around the world, including advanced industrial societies, is the relative emphasis on marital and kin relationships. In the **nuclear family,** which consists of *parents and their children who live apart from other kin,* the couple's primary loyalties and strongest emotional attachments are to each other and their children. Despite the fact that they are residentially separate, however, the marital pair also visits and cooperates with a

NUCLEAR FAMILY
Parents and their children who live apart from other kin.

The Navajo trace descent through the female line. They also live together, share work, and at death pass their homes and other property to female relatives.

Can you think of any other groups that trace descent through women?

small core of close kin who "provide a variety of services and satisfactions that conjugal relationships by themselves do not provide" (Hill, 1988:740).

The **extended family** consists of *two or more closely related families who share a household and are economically and emotionally bound to others in the group*. For example, among the Navajo, relationships among sisters and other female kin often take precedence over the husband-wife relationship, not only because these relationships are defined as more satisfying but because women—not husbands and wives—live and work together and own property in common. Extended families take two major forms: *vertical extended families,* which include three or more generations—parents, their married children, grandchildren, and so on—and *joint families,* consisting of siblings and their spouses and their children.

While one or two family patterns often are the normative ideal in many societies, because the family is flexible and can be modified to suit a wide variety of conditions it is common for a multitude of patterns to coexist in most societies.

A **kinship group** is *a network of people whose social relationships are based on common ancestry (blood), marriage, adoption, and/or affiliation (e.g., godparents)*. In preindustrial societies a kin group may live and work together, share economic resources, and conduct religious and social activities in common. However, declines in household size are becoming more common in both developed and developing countries, because of lower fertility, increased migration, and much greater numbers of persons living alone than at any time in the past.

Today, with the exception of parents, siblings, and a handful of other "close kin," many white, middle-class Americans see relatives rarely—typically at family reunions or holiday celebrations. Moreover, they do not expect much of their more distant relatives, nor do they feel particularly obligated to them. By contrast, many ethnic groups, such as Mexican Americans, participate in large kinship networks whose members regularly visit and conduct exchanges—not only because they aid each other, but because relations with kin are deemed proper and enjoyable (Vega, 1990). For those at the top of the stratification hierarchy also, such as the DuPont and Kennedy families, kinship networks are important and often provide their members with homes, jobs, and other support. The chronically poor also maintain close ties with relatives, but as a means of coping with scarcity (Howard, 1989).

Courtship, Marriage, and Divorce Patterns

All societies have norms that regulate courtship and marriage. The most powerful is the **incest taboo**, *a norm that forbids people from mating with and marrying "close kin."* Social definitions of who is and who is not a "close relative" vary widely. The incest taboo applies almost universally to sexual intercourse and marriage between father and daughter, mother and son, and brother and sister. Exceptions include ancient Egyptians, the Inca of South America, and Hawaiians; all three societies permitted father-daughter and brother-sister marriages among royal families, because royalty were believed to be semi-divine and thus exempt from the norms of ordinary mortals (Middleton, 1962).

Other societies, however, expand the taboo to include more distant relatives. In the United States, for example, it is illegal to marry one's grandparents, uncles and aunts, nephews and nieces, and, in more than half the states, first cousins. Still other societies include categories of "relatives" that Americans do not consider close kin such as second cousins, and in some societies even people with the same surnames are included.

Exogamy and Endogamy   Societies that need to gain access to scarce goods or social and political networks beyond their immediate borders often practice **exogamy,** which is *a norm that requires people to find marriage partners outside their own group or social category*. Societies that wish to retain power, prestige, or property within groups usually take the opposite approach, establishing *norms that require people to find mates within a specific group or social category,* a pattern called **endogamy.** Because of social stratification, most societies exert strong pressures to marry within one's class as well as

EXTENDED FAMILY
Two or more closely related families who share a household and are economically and emotionally bound to others in the group.

KINSHIP GROUP
A network of people whose social relationships are based on common ancestry (blood), marriage, adoption, and/or affiliation (e.g., godparents).

INCEST TABOO
A norm that forbids people from mating with and marrying "close kin."

EXOGAMY
A norm that requires people to find marriage partners outside their own group or social category.

ENDOGAMY
Norms that require people to find mates within a specific group or social category.

racial, ethnic, and religious group. In the United States, exogamy continues to be rare for African Americans because of "socially constructed boundaries between black and white Americans" (Bankston and Henry, 1999:1). Low socioeconomic status and geographic concentration help perpetuate endogamy among Cajuns in Louisiana as well (Bankston and Henry, 1999).

In modern industrial societies most people have considerable freedom in choosing mates and strong physical and emotional attachments are considered essential ingredients for a successful marriage. In preindustrial societies (and among upper classes in industrial societies) where marital choices affect not only the couple but also the economic well-being, prestige, or power of entire kin groups, endogamy is often preferred, and the decision is made by family elders. Moreover, romantic love is deemed unimportant or, worse, a potential threat to both the marital relationship and the kin group. In China, for example, marriages are arranged, and despite scientific evidence to the contrary, there is widespread belief that "love matches start out hot and grow cold, while arranged marriages start out cold and grow hot" (Xiaohe Xu and Whyte, 1990).

Monogamy and Polygamy   In most industrial societies the only socially acceptable and legal form of marriage is **monogamy**—*the marriage of one woman and one man.* In America and many other industrialized countries, with high divorce rates, however, a large part of the population practices **serial monogamy**—*a marriage pattern in which a person has several spouses over a lifetime, but only one at a time.*

George Murdock's (1950) *World Ethnographic Sample* demonstrated that while most people were monogamous in virtually all societies, almost 70 percent of societies permitted or preferred **polygamy**—*a form of marriage in which a person has multiple spouses.* Polygamy has two variants: *Polyandry,* where one woman marries two or more men, is practiced by only a few societies; *Polygyny,* where a man marries two or more women, is the most common marital pattern throughout the preindustrial world.

There are numerous other forms of marriage that are historically rare, including *group marriage,* where two or more husbands have two or more wives, and same-sex marriages.

Some Plains Indian societies permitted men to marry *berdaches*—men who dressed and acted like women and assumed the social identity of women (Hoebel, 1960; Haviland, 2005). Among the Nuer of the Sudan it also was permissible for a woman to marry a "ghost"—a man who died without producing male heirs. Typically, a close male relative of the dead man helped perpetuate the "ghost's" line (Evans-Pritchard, 1951).

Dissolving Marriages   Just as norms regulate marriage and family relationships, they also specify conditions under which marriages may be dissolved. In many preindustrial societies in which children are of particular importance, sterility or impotence are grounds for divorce. In some traditional patriarchal Islamic societies, husbands needed only proclaim "I divorce thee" three times in front of two witnesses for marriages to end. By contrast, among Zuni Indians of Arizona, who are matrilineal, a woman only had to place her husband's belongings outside the door to proclaim that the marriage was over (Murdock, 1950).

Throughout most of American history, cruelty, desertion, or adultery were the most common legal grounds for divorce. Today in states with unilateral or *no fault divorce* neither party is required to admit wrongdoing—all that is needed is mutual consent. In the United States and Western societies in general, divorce is easy to obtain, spousal support is less common, there are increased efforts to improve payment compliance, and there is greater acceptance and encouragement for "shared parental decision-making authority" (Fine and Fine, 1994:249).

Residence and Authority Patterns

Societies also have norms that specify where newly married people should live and who should make important family decisions; in most cases residence and authority patterns are related. In industrial societies the most common pattern is *neolocal* residence, where married couples establish independent households. As women have entered the workplace in large numbers and gained greater economic independence, neolocal residence has become associated with *egalitarian* authority patterns, where husbands and wives

MONOGAMY
The marriage of one woman and one man.

SERIAL MONOGAMY
A marriage pattern in which a person has several spouses over a lifetime, but only one at a time.

POLYGAMY
A form of marriage in which a person has multiple spouses.

have equal say in most domestic decisions. Where a husband moves to the home of his wife and her kin group, it is called *matrilocal* residence, and when combined with matrilineal descent women often have considerable influence and power in domestic matters.

Of the 565 societies in Murdock's *World Ethnographic Sample,* 67 percent of married couples lived with or near the husband's family, in a *patrilocal* residence pattern (Ember and Ember, 1996). Patrilocal residence is associated with **patriarchal authority,** *where male elders dominate decision making and women have little control over their lives.* The historic and cross-cultural dominance of patriarchal authority, patrilineal descent, and patrilocal residence—and the many problems associated with this family form—has led many sociologists to question the functionalist emphasis on the social benefits that marriage and family bring to society as a whole. Sociologists have found that other approaches are needed, as we discuss in the next section.

SOCIOLOGICAL APPROACHES TO THE FAMILY

To understand contemporary families, sociologists take several different approaches. Some focus on family dynamics, while others emphasize social forces outside the family that also affect family relationships and family life and well-being.

Functionalism and the Family

From the functionalist perspective, the family is the foundation of the social order because it fulfills vital functions, including (1) defining and limiting who has sexual access to whom; (2) reproducing new members, integrating them into the social system, and replacing dying members; (3) providing for the care and support of the young, infirm, and elderly; (4) socializing new members; (5) providing people with ascribed statuses—social class, race, and ethnicity—that determine their place in society; and (6) providing people with emotional support, a sense of belonging, and fulfillment.

The functionalist perspective considers diverse marriage customs (such as polygamy and child betrothal in preindustrial societies) to be ecological "adaptations" believed to enhance individual and social survival. In much the same way, functionalists often describe the independent nuclear family as "well suited" to industrial society, where there are high levels of geographic and social mobility (Haviland, 2005). Functionalists do not believe every marriage custom and family form produces social benefits, and they describe those that deviate from normative expectations or produce instability as *dysfunctional.*

The Family from the Conflict Perspective

Conflict theorists agree that marriage and family institutions are shaped by environmental and other forces but emphasize that they also are rooted in structures of social inequality (Eitzen and Baca-Zinn, 2005). From the conflict perspective, marriage and the family are not static worlds of cooperation and harmony designed to serve the common good but arenas of conflict where families and family members struggle for wealth, power, and prestige. Friedrich Engels ([1884] 1902) had harsh words for the family, calling it an instrument of power and oppression by which men advance their interests and privileges at the expense of women and children (Collins, 1975).

With the emergence of stratified agrarian states, women came to be defined as "property" to be disposed of as men saw fit. As Randall Collins (1988:78) wrote, the modern term *family* is derived from the Latin *famulus,* which means "servant"; in Rome "the plebian form of marriage consisted of a man buying his wife, and she became recognized by law as part of his property—*his familia.*"

Even in contemporary industrial societies where women made great strides in the twentieth century, gender inequality and vestiges of patriarchy and male privilege persist in marriage and family relationships. In America, it is still customary for the bride's family to pay for the wedding, fathers often "give away" the bride, many wives continue to take their husbands' name, and there is still a strong preference (among many men and women) that the first child be a son. Likewise, many people believe that even when the husband's and wife's jobs are equal in terms of income and career advancement, the husband's job should take precedence (Machung, 1989).

PATRIARCHAL AUTHORITY
Where male elders dominate decision making and women have little control over their lives.

Marxist feminists contend that in contemporary society the oppression of women is vital to patriarchy and capitalism. From this perspective the special scorn and stigma associated with single-mother families reflects the intersection of sexism and racism—both of which benefit a "color conscious and color-privileged patriarchy" (Dowd, 1997:170). Feminist scholars contend that stigmatized single moms provide many benefits to capitalists, including cheap labor, social services not amenable to profit making, and new laborers for temporary and dead-end jobs. Patriarchal family structure and gender inequality in the labor force serve capitalists' interests in a more fundamental way, according to Janet Chafetz: the situation keeps the sexes and races "divided and competing with one another, rather than combining in a unified struggle against capitalism" (Chafetz, 1988:116).

Social Exchange

Social exchange, a microlevel approach, uses the marketplace metaphor, which sees people bargaining and negotiating to make the best deals they can in marriage and family relationships. This approach is well suited to the study of traditional societies, where marriage bargaining often is blatantly economic. Exchange theorists note, however, that even in societies where romantic love prevails and people are believed to be "swept off their feet" by intense emotions, the courtship process involves many rational calculations and much bargaining.

In many cultures, the economic aspects of marriage rather than "romantic love" are emphasized in the marriage ritual. In this photo, taken in Baghdad, Iraq, the bride's brother presents the dowry for the groom's inspection and approval.

According to the social exchange perspective, all of us bring personal and social resources to courtship, marriage, and family relationships, and we use them in our "negotiations" with others to maximize our benefits and minimize our costs (Lamanna and Riedmann, 1988). In contemporary industrial societies, the social resources that people bring to the marriage market include such traits as level of education, physical attractiveness, intelligence, and family status. In general, the *norms of reciprocity* guide marital exchanges. In *symmetrical exchanges* the prospective bride and groom exchange roughly similar traits, whereas in *complementary exchanges* people exchange different traits they believe are of equivalent value—for example, youth and beauty for wealth and status.

Symbolic Interactionism

The symbolic interactionist perspective also includes elements of bargaining and negotiation, but its primary focus is on "negotiated meanings" in marriage and family relationships. From this perspective, marriage and family have no fixed meanings, nor does every family member share the same meanings. Jesse Bernard (1982), for example, argued that men and women have such different ideas about marriage that there are in fact two marriages—his (how the husband understands the relationship) and hers (how the wife understands the relationship). Moreover, people's views of marriage and family may change over the life course as they shift from dating to being newlyweds, to raising a family, to adjusting to middle and old age. Likewise, as Eitzen and Baca-Zinn (2005) note, most couples now enter marriage without a blueprint for household responsibilities, and family members must make greater efforts to establish patterns of interaction and modify them to suit their changing interests and needs.

U.S. FAMILIES: IN THE LIFE COURSE

People expect a great deal of the family today, and social and economic changes—especially women's positions in the workplace and aging populations—have altered many family relationships. The ideal in traditional nuclear families was for husband-wife roles and responsibilities to be complementary. Husbands were expected to provide for their families' economic needs and wives were responsible for the household, the children, and the families' emotional well-being. Moreover, while roles and responsibilities changed over the life course, they did so in predictable stages: the preparental "newly-wed" stage, the parental stage, the postparental or "empty nest" stage, and the retirement stage (Menaghan and Parcel, 1990).

For much of the population the family life course has become more dynamic and complex. In the past several decades, co-provider families have increased—in response to both economic opportunities and declines in family incomes—and many couples choose to have fewer children or none at all. At the same time, high divorce and remarriage rates have added new stages and complex permutations to family relationships. Ironically, at a time when occupational and other responsibilities consume much of a couple's time, the quality and stability of marriages are becoming more rather than less dependent on the efforts of both husbands and wives to make them work. At the same time, social constraints against divorce have steadily diminished. And people are living much longer than in the past, presenting married couples with many new possibilities and problems that families in the past could not have imagined.

Dating and Mate Selection

Most Americans remain devoted to marriage and family institutions, and in an age of uncertainty and transient relationships the search for "romantic love" may be even more important than ever (see Map 13.1). In fact, nearly 80 percent of single men and women

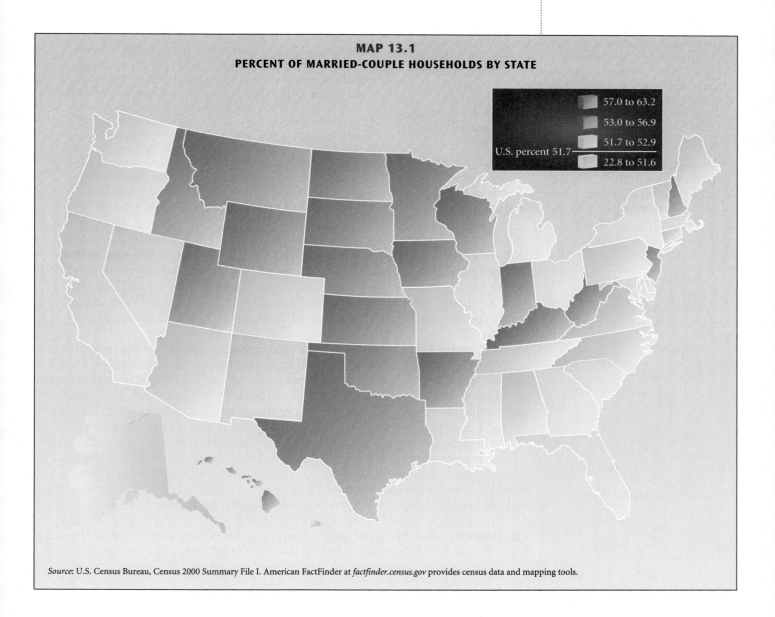

MAP 13.1
PERCENT OF MARRIED-COUPLE HOUSEHOLDS BY STATE

57.0 to 63.2
53.0 to 56.9
51.7 to 52.9
U.S. percent 51.7
22.8 to 51.6

Source: U.S. Census Bureau, Census 2000 Summary File I. American FactFinder at *factfinder.census.gov* provides census data and mapping tools.

A growing trend among college students, professionals, and other members of the middle class is to search for dates and prospective partners in novel, high-tech ways that include videodating and the Internet. These two electronic forms of courtship have something in common: They offer people the chance to meet hundreds or even thousands of other people and, for some, an opportunity to find prospective partners without the apprehensions and concerns that are a normal part of courtship and face-to-face social interaction (Woll and Young, 1989; Rheingold, 1993).

The Internet and videodating grant people special powers of impression management that would be impossible in everyday life (Woll and Young, 1989). Both computer keyboards and carefully crafted videotapes permit individuals to reveal the most favorable images of themselves and, at the same time, to conceal their undesirable qualities.

Today, many people begin computer dating as teenagers. Lynn Clark called these casual romantic interactions "chat room dating." In the thinking of some teens, "Internet dates" occur when a couple breaks away from others in an open chat room and visits "a separate chat room of only two persons." Clark conducted interviews with teens, observed them on-line, and even lurked in teen chat rooms and read e-mail exchanges to discover the nature of on-line dating as well as the meanings that teens associate with it.

She found that in many ways Internet dating mirrors real-life dating: Most teens adhered to what Clark (1998:180) called "heterosexism and sexism." Many teenage girls, however, felt empowered by the Net, telling Clark that it made them feel more assertive and in control and less constrained by peer groups, social status, and especially the currencies of "beauty and popularity."

Neither teenage boys nor girls recognized dating relationships on-line as either intimate or enduring. Instead, all of those surveyed said that Internet dating was meant to be "fun," and some would date only those whom they were certain they would never encounter off-line. Moreover, teens felt no sense of obligation to their "dates," and other than experimenting with roles and relationships, they believed that on-line dating had little consequence for their "real lives" (Clark, 1998:180).

Today, the Internet offers countless ways to find partners—including novel mobile "texting" phones that flash when a potential mate is in your vicinity (Rheingold, 2002). Busy professionals and even students wishing to find a partner now have access to cyberdating websites that list national and international dating services, personal websites, chat rooms, and singles travel sites. For example, the Internet Dating Guide for 2003 listed hundreds of sites including numerous ones that the website claims offer "religious" matches like <Christian Soul Mates>, <Christian Singles for U>, and <Singlesaints.com> (for LDS singles). Another site, <Cyberdating Home Page>, cautions about using any of these sites, noting that trust and credibility may be lacking in for-profit and personal websites alike. Paraphrasing their message, while cyberdating is cheap, minimizes peer pressure, and increases honest communication, when people choose cyberdating, "they need a lot more research" to compensate for a lack of social cues and information from

---

told pollsters that they would eventually find the "perfect mate" (Edwards, 2000:48). Whom we date and marry, however, is not entirely subject to chance. From our very first date to the day we marry (or remarry), demographic, social, and cultural factors influence our choices. One of them includes the media that are being used by an increasing number of students and professionals to find compatible mates (see Focus box 13.1).

Demography and Courtship
Structural factors, such as the size and composition of the population, are particularly important, as is the balance between numbers of men and women of marriageable age. For example, an oversupply of women, which has been called the *marriage squeeze* (Glick, 1988), is associated with higher rates of singlehood and divorce; conversely, an oversupply of men is associated with relatively high marriage rates and lower ages for first marriages (Guttentag and Secord, cited in Surra, 1990).

The billion-dollar cosmetics industry attests to the fact that physical attraction also is a factor in mate selection—especially during the early stages of courtship. Spatial nearness, or *propinquity*, is just as important because it increases chances of interaction. Shared or overlapping social networks also constrain our choices and attempt to ensure that when each of us finally discovers "true love" it is with the "right person" (Surra, 1990).

Homogamy and Heterogamy
Marriage patterns reflect the interplay of three major forces: (1) preferences of individuals; (2) the influence of social groups; and (3) the constraints of the marriage market in which people seek a spouse (Kalmijn, 1998). **Homogamy** refers to the *selection of a mate with personal and social characteris-*

HOMOGAMY
The selection of a mate with personal and social characteristics similar to one's own.

HETEROGAMY
The selection of a mate with social characteristics different than one's own.

family, friends, and social networks that is readily available in the off-line world.

Videodating, in which dating services help people construct video portraits of themselves to show prospective mates, also offers individuals greater powers of impression management. On a video, an individual can lock in a single image, perhaps that he or she is "athletic," "sexy," or "vulnerable," that cannot be challenged or contradicted by others—at least in the initial screening process. This, of course, would be impossible in live courtship arenas—even in virtual dating, where interaction and "teamwork" are involved.

Videodating is distinct in other important ways. While many college students may browse the Internet and flirt and chat with others when they are bored or have time to kill, it is unlikely that the majority are actively seeking marriage partners, especially with so many eligible partners nearby on college campuses. People who use videodating services have neither the time nor the opportunity to meet others. Most are busy upper-middle-class professionals—older, divorced, and single parents—who may work 60 or 70 hours a week and have family responsibilities as well.

Woll and Young's (1989) study of 80 clients of a Los Angeles–based service found that, rather than seeking to meet many people and expand their pool of potential marriage partners, most people used the service to screen out people and narrow their search for that one "Mr. or Ms. Right." They attributed this approach in part to the American cultural belief that there is a "perfect match" out there for everyone. That is why, in making videotapes, most people

spent little time rehearsing and few felt it necessary to alter or retape their original presentation. Most wanted the video portrait to be totally honest so that they would connect with that one ideal person who had matching or complementary traits (Woll and Young, 1989).

Ironically, Woll and Young's study found that, while there is little evidence that videodating services produce successful matches, they may actually reduce people's chances of finding partners: Clients are led to rule out—and are themselves screened out by—individuals whom, under most circumstances, they might wish to pursue" (Woll and Young, 1989:488).

TAKING A CLOSER LOOK

What is the likelihood that these forms of "dating" will catch on with members of all social classes? Also, can you think of any social trends that may result in videodating and love on the Internet gaining widespread popularity, and even replacing traditional person-to-person dating—perhaps even on college campuses?

Source: Stanley B. Woll and Peter Young. "Looking for Mr. and Ms. Right: Self-Presentation in Videotaping." *Journal of Marriage and the Family* 51(2) 1989: 483–488. Howard Rheingold. *The Virtual Community: Homesteading on the Electronic Frontier.* Reading, MA: Addison-Wesley, 1993. Copyright © 1993 by Howard Rheingold. Reprinted by permission of Addison-Wesley Publishing Company, Inc. Lynn S. Clark. "Dating on the Net: Teens and the Rise of 'Pure' Relationships," in Steven G. Jones (ed.), *Cybersociety 2.0: Revisiting Computer-Mediated Communication and Community.* New York: Sage, 1998: 159–183. Howard Rheingold. *Smart Mobs: The Next Social Revolution: Transforming Cultures and Communities in the Age of Instant Access.* New York: Perseus, 2002.

tics similar to one's own. Homogamous marriages, in which couples have similar religious backgrounds, educational level, ages, race, and social class, are the norm. As one study found, "mating requires meeting: the pool of available interaction partners is shaped by institutionally organized arrangements [school, work, neighborhood, social family networks, and voluntary associations] and these constrain the type of people with whom we form personal relationships"—and eventually marry (Kalmijn and Flap, 2001:1289). **Heterogamy,** which refers to *selection of a mate with social characteristics different than one's own,* however, has become somewhat more common over the last few decades.

For example, while the proportion of interracial marriages to all marriages remained small (less than 3 percent), interracial marriages in the mid-1990s were four times greater than in 1970. Most interracial marriages were between Asian American women and white men, with black-white interracial marriages much rarer. While black-white marriages are increasing—especially in the West and among black men and white women—they still account for only about 0.5 percent of all U.S. marriages. Native American intermarriage rates, however, have dramatically increased over the past four decades. In 1960, over three-fourths of Native American women were married to Native

Despite high-profile marriages such as that of Tiger Woods and his wife, Elin, and growing acceptance of interracial marriages, they still account for less than 3 percent of all marriages in the United States.

TABLE 13.1
ASIAN AMERICAN WOMEN: MARRIAGE AND COHABITATION

RACE/ETHNIC BACKGROUND OF PARTNER	MARRIED ASIAN WOMEN	COHABITATING ASIAN WOMEN
Asian	68.5%	42.4%
White	25.1%	44.6%
Hispanic	4.1%	5.9%
Black	1.8%	4.9%

Notice the different marriage and cohabitation rates.
Source: "Percentage of Asian Women with Partners from Selected Racial Groups." Reprinted with permission from the June 2000 issue of *American Demographics.* Copyright, Crain Communications Inc. 2000.

COHABITATION
Where two people live together without legal marriage.

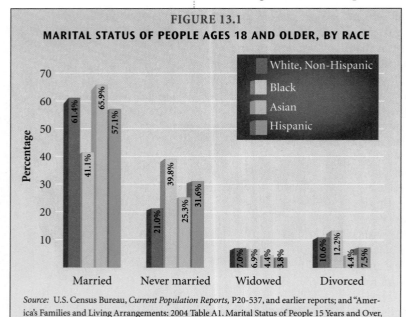

FIGURE 13.1
MARITAL STATUS OF PEOPLE AGES 18 AND OLDER, BY RACE

Source: U.S. Census Bureau, *Current Population Reports,* P20-537, and earlier reports; and "America's Families and Living Arrangements: 2004 Table A1. Marital Status of People 15 Years and Over, by Age, Sex, Personal Earnings, Race, and Hispanic Origin, 2004": published 29 June 2005; <http://www.census.gov> Reproduced by permission of the Population Reference Bureau.

American men; by the early 1990s these trends were reversed and more than 60 percent of Native American women were married to non-Indians (U.S. Bureau of the Census, 1995; *The Economist,* 1998e). Asian American cohabitation and intermarriage rates are also moderately high (see Table 13.1).

The intermarriage rate among people of different faiths rose as well, even among groups that were once strongly endogamous, such as Jews. Prior to 1960, Jews had only a 6 percent intermarriage rate. By the 1990s, slightly more than 50 percent of all Jews had married non-Jews, and in many cities intermarriage rates were much higher than that (Waxman, 1990; Legge, 1997; Shavit, 1997).

Social class is one of the most powerful factors in mate selection in most societies, and the United States is no exception. While the United States does not have a rigid caste system and people are free to date anybody they choose regardless of social class or status, people who live in working class neighborhoods, attend working class schools and social events, and fill working class jobs are not likely to meet, date, and marry members of the upper class. When people do meet and marry people from a higher social class or status, or marry up, as most people would call it, sociologists refer to this as *hyperogamy.* Conversely, the phenomenon of marrying down, or selecting a mate from a lower social class or status, is called *hypogamy.* Traditionally, because of the patriarchal nature of stratification in the United States, men often accumulate more wealth and power than women and therefore are more likely to marry down in social class, whereas women are more likely to marry up—although numerous exceptions to this trend can be found.

Some researchers see courtship as a filtering process in which individuals—seeking an equitable exchange—gradually narrow the field of eligible mates before making their final selection (Kerckhoff and Davis, 1962). For example, Bernard Murstein's (1976; 1987) *stimulus-value-role* theory maintains that courtship passes through three distinct stages: a *stimulus stage,* in which each member of a couple evaluates the other's observable qualities (appearance, reputation); a *value stage,* in which the pair determine whether they have compatible values; and a *role stage,* in which they see how well they function in various roles, such as lovers and companions (Murstein, cited in Surra, 1990). Others argue that courtship is not that neat; many of them prefer the *symbolic exchange perspective,* which "allows for alterations in shared perceptions, proposes no fixed sequence, [and] views similarity as negotiated rather than discovered by partners" (Surra, 1990:860).

Cohabitation: A New Courtship Stage?

For many, another stage in courtship is **cohabitation,** *where two people live together without legal marriage.* Since the 1960s, people have become more tolerant of alternative lifestyles, and the fear of sexually transmitted diseases has encouraged others to opt for longer-term relationships that may include cohabitation. Greater employment and educational opportunities for young people, economic hardships, and the decision by large numbers of women to delay marriage to pursue their careers have also boosted cohabitation rates. Higher divorce rates also have contributed to an increase in the number of unmarried couples living together. Figure 13.1 shows the marital status of persons ages 18 and older, by race, in 2004.

Cohabitation rates have increased dramatically over the past few decades. Today, the "majority of marriages and remarriages begin as cohabiting relationships" (Smock, 2000:1). The number of unmarried people living together increased 72 percent in the 1990s, according to the 2000 Census (Peterson, 2001). Further, "almost 40 percent of all births labeled 'nonmarital' occur in cohabiting families" (Smock, 2000:3). In fact, as the Census Bureau noted, U.S. women under 30 who become pregnant for the first time are now more likely to be "unmarried than married" (*The Futurist,* 2000c:9). Despite popular stereotypes that restrict cohabitation to college campuses, it is more common among working couples. Moreover, while most cohabitors are young adults (25–44), about 7 percent are age 65 and older. Although more than half have never married, about one-third are divorced and 40 percent of all cohabiting couples have one or more children present in the household (U.S. Bureau of the Census, 2000).

About one-third of all men and women in their thirties have lived with someone before marriage, a statistic that supports the view that cohabitation has become a new stage in the courtship process, one that for about 55 percent of all cohabitors is the final step before marriage (Gwartney-Gibbs, 1986; Smock, 2000). About 40 percent of cohabiting relationships end within five years. Many whose relationships dissolve, however, either enter or reenter the rapidly growing singles population.

Singlehood

Over the past few decades the number of single adults, including the never-married, divorced, and widowed, has dramatically increased. In a survey of Chicago singles that may reflect a growing urban trend, sociologist Edward Laumann found that "Chicagoans are destined to spend half their lives as single people, and half their single years will be spent alone" (Gorner, 2004:1). This is not only an American trend but one that is occurring throughout the industrial world. For example, in Japan, singles constitute about one-fifth of all households, and nearly one-fourth of Australians in their early forties remain single (*The Futurist,* 2000c:9).

Singles: Postponing Marriage Some of the rise in singles can be attributed to a growing tendency for young adults to postpone marriage. People are choosing to postpone marriage in industrial societies. Some prefer to focus on education and their careers, while others—in an unstable job market that has been characteristic of the early twenty-first century—are choosing to live with parents "as an advantageous alternative to early marriage" (Raymo, 2003: 302; Grossman, 2005). Today, in Japan, for example, the mean age of first marriage for men is about 29 years, whereas women on average marry at 27. Especially dramatic changes have occurred among women aged 25–29; in 1970 only about 20 percent of women in this age group were unmarried; three decades later, in 2000, half of women in this age group had yet to marry (Raymo, 2003). As noted in the opening vignette, U.S. men and women are delaying marriage for longer periods as well (McGinn, 2006). In 1960, for example, only about 28 percent of women and 53 percent of men aged 20–24 were unmarried; by 1990 more than 60 percent of women and 80 percent of men in that age group were still single (U.S. Bureau of the Census, 1996). And by the late 1990s, 40 percent of all adults were unmarried. As shown in Table 13.2, the median age of first marriage for women in 2000 was about 25 years, and for men 27 years—the highest figure in over a century (Waite, 2000; U.S. Bureau of the Census, 2001).

Furthermore, a small but growing segment of the population choose not to marry at all. For example, because of both

TABLE 13.2
MEDIAN AGE AT FIRST MARRIAGE, BY SEX, SELECTED YEARS BETWEEN 1890 AND 2003

YEAR	MEN	WOMEN
2003	27.1	25.3
2000	26.8	25.1
1990	26.3	24.1
1980	24.7	22.0
1970	23.2	20.8
1960	22.8	20.3
1950	22.8	20.3
1940	24.3	21.5
1930	24.3	21.3
1920	24.6	21.2
1910	25.1	21.6
1900	25.9	21.9
1890	26.1	22.0

Source: U.S. Census Bureau. "Marital Status and Living Arrangements, March 1993," *Current Population Reports*: *Population Characteristics*, Series P-20 , No. 472. Washington, DC: U.S. Government Printing Office, 1993, p.vii and the *Census and You 32* (5) May 1997:8. Updated: U.S. Bureau of the Census 2000.

a shortage and the economic marginality of African American men due to discrimination, only about 44 percent of African American adults were married in the early 1990s compared with about 64 percent in 1970. Moreover, "approximately 80% of adult whites are ever married, in comparison to 61% blacks, 70% of Latinos, and 72% of Asians" (Oropesa and Gorman, 2000:188).

Widowhood, Divorce, and Singles Widowhood has contributed to the growth in the singles population, since the elderly have become better able to care for themselves and maintain independent households. Divorce, however, has been a much more significant contributing factor. By 1995, single-person households accounted for about 25 percent of all American households (U.S. Bureau of the Census, 1997a). In 2000, the number of families headed by single mothers increased 25 percent over the 1990 figure to more than 7.5 million households (U.S. Bureau of the Census, 2000).

Some believe the rise in never-married singles reflects a growing disenchantment with the institution of marriage. Others contend that marriage remains desirable but has been assigned a lower priority due to greater educational and career opportunities for women and a growing need for both men and women to acquire the skills necessary to participate in the modern workplace. Still others argue that in postindustrial society a "surge of individualism" has reversed public attitudes about singlehood and marriage. Today, the deviant label is not attached to career-oriented singles but to those who rush into marriage and have children "too soon" (Horowitz, 1991; Warner, 2006).

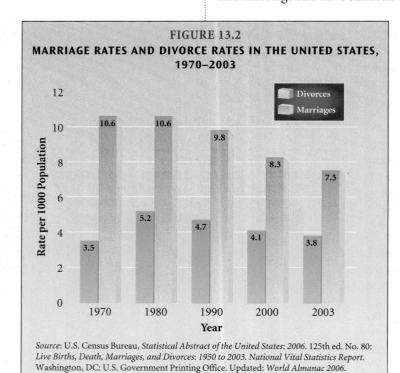

FIGURE 13.2
MARRIAGE RATES AND DIVORCE RATES IN THE UNITED STATES, 1970–2003

Source: U.S. Census Bureau, *Statistical Abstract of the United States: 2006*. 125th ed. No. 80: *Live Births, Death, Marriages, and Divorces: 1950 to 2003. National Vital Statistics Report.* Washington, DC: U.S. Government Printing Office. Updated: *World Almanac 2006.*

What factors in recent years may affect declining marriage and divorce rates?

Marriage and Divorce Rates

Most Americans still plan to marry, and more than 90 percent will do so at least once. Nevertheless, as Stephanie Coontz (1997:31) remarked, "marriage is certainly a *transformed* institution," in that it plays a much smaller role in organizing social and personal life than at any time in the past.

Marriage Rates *Marriage rates,* based on the number of marriages per 1,000 people, have steadily declined since the mid-1980s. While the 1990 rate of 9.8 marriages per 1,000 appears to be higher than the 8.5 recorded in 1960, this statistic includes remarriages, which have substantially increased over the last few decades and now account for more than 40 percent of the total (Bumpass et al., 1990). For a comparison of marriage and divorce rates from 1960 to 2003, see Figure 13.2.

Divorce Rates The *divorce rate* is the number of divorces per 1,000 people. In 1960, of a total population of 42.6 million married women, 393,000 women were granted divorces, for a divorce rate of 2.2 percent. In 1990 the number of divorces had increased to slightly over 1 million out of approximately 50 million marriages, for a divorce rate of 4.7 percent (U.S. Bureau of the Census, 1992c) (see Figure 13.2).

Moreover, redivorce rates are expected to be as high. Of the 70 percent of women who remarry, about 60 percent will get a second divorce. Divorce rates in the United States have increased dramatically over the past half-century and today are among the highest in the industrial world.

Families in the Middle and Later Stages of Life

Although people are delaying marriage and children to pursue educational goals and establish careers, the desire to have children has not diminished over the decades. Today, almost 90 percent of all married women will eventually have a child. What has changed in the past few decades is the close association between marriage and child-bearing: in the United States and many other postindustrial societies, one-third or more of the total births each year are to unmarried women (most in their twenties), who assume a major share of childrearing responsibilities (Aulette, 2007).

Parenting Richard Gelles (1995:269) remarked that "there are few, if any, other social roles that involve such a total and abrupt change of responsibilities and demands" than parenthood. Moreover, while having about two children is a cultural ideal, there are few clear guidelines on raising children successfully. This problem has been compounded in recent years, especially for women who must balance work, childrearing, and many other responsibilities. One family that may play a key role in alleviating some of these problems is the multigenerational family.

Families in Later Life Stages Underlying many changes in families and family relationships are shifts in population age structures in postindustrial nations. The numbers of both elderly and elderly families are increasing, resulting in a greater number of single persons living alone and many more child-free families. Traditionally, this stage of life has been called the postparental stage, referring to children leaving home, retirement, and widowhood.

But middle and later life stages of family life are changing. In many cases children delay leaving home, and in others elders merely shift from parental to grandparental or great-grandparental responsibilities. One writer called these emerging families "beanpole" or *multigenerational families,* because they include four or five living generations but have relatively few members in each generation. Demographers predict that sometime in the second decade of the twenty-first century America will experience a "great-grandparent boom," which may add a new stage in the family life course for many people. Will a growing number of elderly strain budgets and family relationships, as some family scholars have predicted? Or will healthier and more active elderly—even those in their eighties and nineties, assume major child-care, kin, and community responsibilities? It is too early to know the answer, but most sociologists believe the latter scenario is more likely (Gelles, 1995; Kinsella, 1995; Skolnick and Skolnick, 2007).

This photo of a three-generation family provides one model of family life in the United States, where families are highly diverse.

U.S. FAMILIES: A PORTRAIT OF SOCIAL DIVERSITY

"Raising a family is hard enough without having to live up to myths," wrote historian Stephanie Coontz (1996:37). The latest myth idealizes "intact families" of the past that politicians claim were once abundant, prosperous, and happy. Yet few families of any period in American history would have conformed to these families of popular nostalgia and political rhetoric.

Families of Myth and History

The much-maligned contemporary single-parent families and stepfamilies were very much in evidence during every phase of American history. Researchers estimate that a century ago one in three children spent part of their childhood in a single-parent home—although the primary cause was death rather than divorce. The colonial family was just as unstable. High mortality rates resulted in the majority of children spending some time in stepfamilies; many other children were apprenticed to other families as farm workers or domestic help.

Poverty encouraged many families to join in extended families and remain together during the Great Depression of the 1930s. During this period divorce rates fell, but desertion and domestic violence rose sharply, and economic hardship contributed to violence and murder rates comparable to those of the 1980s. Depression poverty also contributed to plummeting marriage and birth rates, as well as high rates of child abuse and neglect (Coontz, 1997).

The traditional nuclear family—a breadwinner father, homemaker mother, and children—popularized in television shows of the 1950s, such as *Leave It to Beaver* and *Father Knows Best,* had a brief reign during the postwar period: about 60 percent of families conformed to this pattern. But this family type was atypical of American family life. Few families enjoyed the carefree prosperity of the Cleavers and other TV families. Serious problems such as alcoholism, battering, and incest were in most cases swept under the rug, and discrimination against women, elders, gays, singles, and others was very common (Coontz, 1996, 1997; Skolnick and Skolnick, 2007).

During the 1950s divorce rates were low and unwed mothers were much less common than today. Yet 30 percent of American children and the elderly lived in poverty, nearly double the current rate. When the favorable socioeconomic and political climate of the 1950s and 1960s gave way to the hard times of the 1970s, diverse families reemerged—but not without a great deal of controversy (Coontz, 1996).

How do media families such as the one portrayed on the popular sitcom *Two and a Half Men* differ from the portrayal of families on television in previous decades?

Media Families: Compounding the Myths?

What is a family and how should family members behave? Our own families, kin, and neighbors provide some of the answers to these questions. But so do the media—especially television and, increasingly, computers and the World Wide Web.

Television and the Family More than any other medium, television has become almost synonymous with the family. It has been described as "a member of the family," "the focal point of American family life," and an "electronic babysitter." Perhaps because of its intimate association with our everyday lives, we have developed ambivalent feelings toward television that are usually reserved for our closest kin. Television has been praised for entertaining, informing, and educating us. But it has also been accused of "wrecking the family," "causing divorces," "destroying children's minds," "promoting family violence," and both overstimulating and dulling sexual desire (Abelman, 1990; Bryant, 1990; Kunkel, 1990).

Television both shapes and reflects social norms and values, and because it markets products to family audiences it is sensitive to demographic trends and changing public tastes. In 2006, for example, only two of the season's top-ten programs featured families at all—*Desperate Housewives* and *New Adventures of Old Christine*—hardly the television families of generations past.

In some ways, daytime soap operas are social pioneers, providing cutting-edge models of family diversity and family problems such as infidelity, homosexuality, and others. Watch a soap opera some afternoon and critically assess family images and gender roles, however. You will discover that few soaps have relinquished fundamental patriarchal themes. Men still control more of the action than women and women continue to be portrayed as more emotional than men. Soaps persist in the belief that women's value is directly related to their sexual allure and physical attractiveness.

The mainstream media play an important role in enlightening the public about family trends and problems. Polls show a strong correlation between media publicity and public concerns about domestic violence, date rape, child neglect, and a host of other important social problems. However, as noted in Chapter 1, for the most part mainstream media emphasize drama and novelty for entertainment purposes—not to critically assess or remedy family problems. And mainstream media frame issues in ways that emphasize the personal, rather than the social contexts in which family problems occur.

Families and the Technomedia Today, technomedia—including the World Wide Web, e-mail, cellular phones, and video cameras—have added new understandings and possibilities for family and kin relationships. With the help of cellular phones it is possible for parents to have almost constant contact with their children and to maintain close ties with kin all over the world as well. Video cameras enable parents to monitor their children at home or in day-care centers. E-mail has made computer marriages, on-line courtship, and even on-line divorce popular—if there are no disputes over property or children. According to one journalist, new on-line services promise not only divorce paperwork and general divorce information but also assistance in filling out "state-specific divorce forms they guarantee will be accepted by your local courts . . . you can't get divorced with the click of a button—you still have to go through the court system . . . but in counties where you can file by mail or fax, as in all counties in California, it is possible to be divorced without ever setting foot in court or a lawyer's office" (Mulrean, 2003:1–2). Early in the twenty-first century in the Middle East and Malaysia, considerable controversy ensued when some Muslim clerics ruled that men could divorce their wives by writing the text message ("I divorce thee" three times) on their mobile phones. Other Muslim religious and government officials disagreed, arguing the new short-messaging technology (SMS) that was sweeping Asia was not a valid form of divorce (Podger, 2001). E-mail correspondence has even become a grounds for divorce. For example, in 1996, a New Jersey man filed for divorce on grounds that his wife had had a "virtual affair" via e-mail (Black et al., 1997). "Cybercheating" has become a new form of marital infidelity.

The World Wide Web is a good resource, too. It gives instant access to different perspectives on marriage and the family—from Census Bureau data to a host of grassroots perspectives, and even ordinary people's opinions and interpretations of soap families and their problems. Nancy Baym (1998:46–47) maintains that chat room "discussion often evolves beyond the soap opera [into] . . . issues that are often highly personal and emotionally charged." Additionally, there are many websites that deal with children's issues, including the Children's Defense Fund, Children with AIDS Project, and Big Brothers–Big Sisters, to name just a few. Also, there are sites for singles, single parents, gay and lesbian families, and scores of other family interest groups and social movements. Go to the Web to take a closer look at some of these groups.

Families in the United States: The Reality

In analyzing living arrangements, the U.S. Bureau of the Census distinguishes between family and nonfamily households.

Nonfamily and Family Households According to the Census Bureau, *households* are places of residence (a home, apartment, or room). When individuals live alone or two or more unrelated people share a residence, they inhabit a *nonfamily household*. By contrast, *family households* consist of coresident persons who are related by blood, marriage, or adoption. Nonfamily households have more than doubled in the past four decades, but family households account for more than two-thirds of all U.S. households (see Figure 13.3).

American families have always been diverse and resilient, and they are even more so today. Many people shift from one family type to another over the life course to suit their changing interests and needs. A person may begin in a child-free, dual-earner family, then decide to have children, later divorce, and head a single-parent family, and still later to remarry and establish a blended family.

Nuclear Families   In 2000, married couple families accounted for about 52 percent of all households, down from 70 percent in the 1970 census. The nuclear family (married couple families with children) comprised about 25 percent of all American households, and **traditional nuclear families** *(breadwinner father, homemaker mother, and children)* had declined to fewer than 20 percent.

Child-Free Families   Today, the dominant family form in the United States is the **child-free family,** where *a couple resides together and there are no children present in the household.* With the aging of the baby boomer cohort, this family type is expected to increase over time. If current trends continue, nearly three of four U.S. households will be childless in another decade or so (U.S. Bureau of the Census, 2001).

In almost two-thirds of all households today, there are no children present. About 29 percent of all family households consist of a married couple with no children, and the proportion of childless families is increasing in the United States and among all other postindustrial nations. People now marry later and postpone having children, and due to increased life expectancy many more middle-aged and elderly couples in the postparental and retirement years live alone. In addition, increasing proportions of young adults choose to have fewer children or none at all.

Estimates of the proportion of married and unmarried women born in the 1960s who will remain childless range as high as 30 percent. This figure is only a few points higher than those of surveys that show about 10 percent of women plan to remain childless, and another 15 percent or so are undecided. Whether members of the latter group will eventually have children is uncertain, because many women—especially middle-class professionals—are torn between traditional family values and pragmatic, instrumental concerns.

Co-provider (Dual-Earner) Families   For much of the twentieth century the breadwinner-homemaker ideal was out of reach for some working-class couples, and since 1940 there have been steady increases in the number of coprovider families. In 1940, **co-provider families,** in which *both husband and wife had full-time jobs,* consti-

TRADITIONAL NUCLEAR FAMILY
A breadwinner father, homemaker mother, and children.

CHILD-FREE FAMILY
A couple resides together and there are no children present in the household.

CO-PROVIDER FAMILIES
Families in which both husband and wife have full-time jobs.

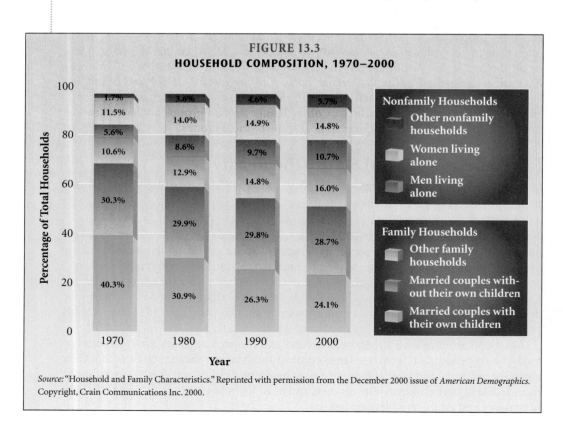

FIGURE 13.3
HOUSEHOLD COMPOSITION, 1970–2000

Source: "Household and Family Characteristics." Reprinted with permission from the December 2000 issue of *American Demographics.* Copyright, Crain Communications Inc. 2000.

tuted only 10 percent of all families. Today, dual-earner families are the fastest growing family type among white families, accounting for more than 50 percent. In more than 75 percent of married couple families with children both the husband and wife work (McLanahan and Casper, 1998). In many of these families, husbands earn less than $15,000 per year, consequently the wife's earnings do not supplement the family income but are essential to maintaining an adequate standard of living (Lechner and Creedon, 1994; Waite, 2000).

Another significant trend that began in earnest in the 1970s was for married women to embark on career tracks. Among the middle class, **dual-career families,** in which *husbands and wives have both family and career,* are no longer the exception but the rule. For some women, this means total devotion to career advancement and a relative deemphasis on the family. Others, who maintain separate households in what the media calls *commuter marriages,* tend to compartmentalize

© Gary Markstein, Milwaukee Journal-Sentinel.

their lives into two distinct categories: work and family. Still others want it all—a job they can opt in and out of during childrearing as well as a satisfying career (Eitzen and Baca-Zinn, 2005; Hochschild, 1997; Warner, 2006).

Blended Families Slightly more than one family in six (16 percent) is a **blended family,** in which *at least one member of the adult couple is a stepparent.* It is estimated that between one-third and one-half of today's young people will become stepchildren (Skolnick and Skolnick, 2007).

If current trends continue, about one out of every three adults in the United States will spend part of their lives in a blended family. People who are part of blended families must be both creative and flexible to make them work. Parents and stepparents in remarriages face a family situation in which roles and responsibilities are often uncertain and old stereotypes of wicked stepmothers or stepfathers abound. Blended families often begin with high expectations that this time they will "get it right," and it is not unusual for stepparents to try to be "supermoms" or "superdads" to the new stepkids (Kantrowitz and Wingert, 1990:30).

Likewise, often there is the expectation among stepparents that the various family members will blend and function much as they did in their previous families. But blended families have different family histories and expectations, and unlike the *Brady Bunch* on television most family members do not blend in the sense that they lose the character, identity, and emotional ties to their original families (Cherlin, 1998). For most blended families, "both patience and a strong support network are essential until sufficient time passes for collective experience to result in a shared (and, preferably positive) history" (Ihinger-Tallman and Pasley, 1994:242).

Single-Parent Families Of all family types, single-parent families have made the most gains during the past few decades. Between 1970 and 1995, the number of **single-parent families,** in which *one parent resides with and cares for one or more children,* almost tripled, from 3.8 million to almost 11 million. Today, approximately one-fourth of all families with children are single-parent families, and the number is rising.

At the beginning of the twentieth century most single-parent families were the result of the death of a spouse, compared with only about 10 percent today. Since World War II, more than 70 percent of single-parent families have been created by divorce and separation and the rest by unmarried mothers or fathers who have chosen to raise children by themselves. Although it is becoming more common among all classes, the single-parent family is the dominant family pattern of the economically disadvantaged. A small but growing number of single-parent families, however, are created by the deliberate choice of professional women who decide to have children through donor insemination.

DUAL-CAREER FAMILIES
Families in which husbands and wives have both family and career.

BLENDED FAMILY
A family in which at least one member of the adult couple is a stepparent.

SINGLE-PARENT FAMILIES
Families in which one parent resides with and cares for one or more children.

Most single-parent families are headed either by ex-spouses who have custody of the children and depend on inadequate child-care payments or by unmarried women. Despite media images that emphasize teenage single moms, only about one-third of unmarried single mothers are in fact teenagers. Thirty-five percent are ages 20–24 and the rest are 25 and older.

Despite political rhetoric about the benefits of marriage and family life, the number of poor, single mothers will likely increase. As Kathryn Edin (2000:130) observed:

> If men's employment opportunities and wages do not increase dramatically . . . [single] mothers might continue to opt for boyfriends, who can be replaced if they do not contribute, rather than husbands who cannot be so easily traded for a more economically productive man.

Minority Families Minority families—some by choice and others in response to discrimination and out of economic necessity—contribute to family diversity as well. While myths abound that all minority families are extended families with strong social support networks, ethnicity, race, class, and gender contribute to considerable diversity among minority families (Roschelle, 1997).

Severe poverty influences many minority families. For example, nearly one-third of all African Americans and Latinos live in poverty, and female-headed families represent almost three-quarters of all poor African American families. And more than 60 percent of African American children, in female-headed families, are currently classified by the government as poor (U.S. Bureau of Census, 2000).

Sharp declines in inner-city employment and cuts in government assistance to struggling families have taken a heavy toll on African American and Latino families and have contributed to declining marriage rates, rising divorce rates, and a much greater number of female-headed households. Some of these trends have reinforced long-term pragmatic attitudes about the family among some minority groups. For example, instead of the traditional middle-class emphasis on the nuclear family and husband-wife relationships, many African American families cope with scarcity and discrimination by seeking the assistance of extended families and fictive kin (close friends), as well as through flexible social networks (McAdoo, 1998).

Increasingly, African American and some Latino families place more emphasis on childrearing than on marriage. As a consequence, more than 50 percent of all African American women who head families have never married, and African American mothers tend to be younger than their white counterparts (Taylor, 1990; Dickerson, 1995).

At first glance, two-parent African American families, whose median adjusted incomes have grown relative to those of white families, may appear to be like white middle-class families. But these families, accounting for almost half of all African American families, provide much more progressive and flexible models of family life than the white majority. Of all families, they are among the most egalitarian, with complementary and flexible family roles that allow for much greater participation of husbands in domestic and child-care responsibilities than is characteristic of most white families (Taylor, 1994).

Many African American families also have stronger kin support systems—with many three-generation extended family households. Likewise, grandparents also may play greater roles in child care than they do in most white middle-class families. Because of economic marginalization and discrimination as well as cultural traditions, many Latino and Asian American groups also emphasize extended families. During the past few decades, many groups from around the world have used extended family networks and "circular migrations" to relocate from developing to developed countries, as well as to shift from rural to urban areas. But many remain anchored to kin in their home countries (Habenstein, 1998).

The strong emphasis on family is called *familism,* or a strong attachment and commitment to family and kin, which characterizes the attitudes of

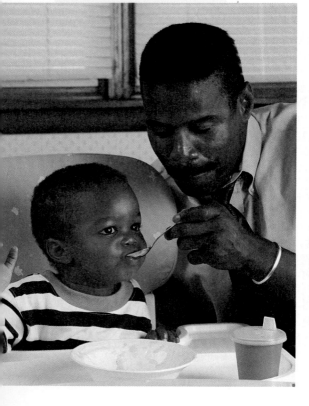

As this photo suggests, in addition to putting in long hours in the workplace, many fathers also take very active roles in child care, housekeeping, and other domestic chores.

many Latino groups toward family life. This is especially true of immigrants from Central and South America who make great efforts to keep in touch with kin, including sending much of their pay to support relatives in their home communities (Ortiz, 1995; Vega, 1995; Becerra, 1998; McAdoo, 1998).

Despite powerful stereotypes of close-knit, "multigenerational" Asian American families, there is considerable variation among Asian American groups. Many immigrants from war-torn southeast Asia do indeed stress extended family networks, and some groups are strongly patriarchal. Many other Asian American families who have been in the United States for generations, however, live in nuclear families and maintain kin ties that differ little from those of white middle-class Americans. On the surface, this is also true of many wealthy transplants and professionals from Hong Kong, Singapore, and other parts of Asia. Most of these families, however, maintain strong ties to widely dispersed kin throughout the Pacific, which may include regular family visitations and gifts, loans, and joint business ventures with relatives that most middle-class Americans would consider to be "distant kin" (Gelles; 1995; Wong, 1998).

Gay and Lesbian Families   One family type that has received little recognition until recently is the gay and lesbian family. More than 1.5 million homosexual and lesbian couples live together in the United States in stable and committed relationships, comprising almost 2 percent of all households, which a growing number of people recognize as families (McGinn, 2006). Philip Blumstein and Pepper Schwartz's (1983) research on American couples found that same-sex couples faced domestic concerns quite similar to those of their heterosexual counterparts—and they solved them in much the same ways. However, Judith Stacey (1999) contends that gay and lesbian relationships may offer new models for families in general, because—free of conventional norms and understandings—they have had to reflect on and resolve the meaning and purpose of intimate relationships. Compatibility is fundamental, and when there are conflicts over work and family, intimate relationships usually win—especially among lesbian couples. Stacey maintains that same-sex couples tend to share more interests and time together than do traditional married couples. And they are more likely to share household chores with less conflict—with gay males assuming tasks according to "abilities, schedules, and preference" (Stacey, 1999:397). But discrimination continues to create special problems for most gay and lesbian families.

Oliphant © 2003 Universal Press Syndicate. Reprinted with permission. All rights reserved.

More than two decades ago, in 1986, the U.S. Supreme Court ruled that states could retain sodomy laws and the criminalization of a variety of nonmarital sexual behaviors. In 1996, Congress passed what was billed as the Defense of Marriage Act, which withheld federal recognition of and many economic benefits in same-sex marriages.

Despite these setbacks, in 1997 legislators in Hawaii approved a reciprocal beneficiaries law, which made it possible for same-sex couples to qualify for health and other benefits. In the same year, a lawsuit brought by three gay couples who were denied marriage licenses went before Hawaii's state Supreme Court. Two years later, the Vermont Supreme Court ordered the legislature to grant gay and lesbian couples the same rights as heterosexuals, and state politicians enacted into law what they called "civil unions," which granted gay and lesbian couples "all the state-given rights of marriage like inheritance and next of kin status" (Rosenberg, 2000:56).

Hawaii and Vermont are not alone in granting benefits to same-sex couples. Domestic partnership legislation has won approval in many cities, and gay parents have won many custody suits across the country, as well as greater acceptance in many social arenas. Moreover, even within present government definitions many gay couples live in families, for many reside with their children. It is estimated that about 20 percent of the gay male population has been married and between 1 and 3 million lesbians and gay men are natural mothers and fathers (Bozett, 1987; Zimmerman, 1997; Strong et al., 1998).

In 2003, a U.S. Supreme Court ruling in *Lawrence v. Texas* struck down Texas's and the nation's anti-sodomy laws, which meant the states could no longer dictate an individual's private sexual conduct. The decision did not directly address gay marriage, but one of the high court's justices argued that the decision ended "the constitutional grounds for maintaining those prohibitions" (Von Drehle, 2003:2). Many argue that the court was catching up to public opinion, which had become more tolerant over the past few decades, but in 2004, Texas enacted a law prohibiting same-sex marriages. Some of America's largest corporations, including Wal-Mart, now offer benefits to gay partners.

By 2003, several states were more open to recognizing gay marriage. Vermont had what it called "civil unions" that bestowed many rights and obligations that are characteristic of legal marriage, and New Jersey and California were not far behind. And in 2003 the Massachusetts Supreme Court ruled the state's ban on gay marriage was unconstitutional. Of course, forces of resistance were marshalling as well. Conservative religious groups condemned the 2003 U.S. Supreme Court decision as immoral, and by early in the twenty-first century, 37 states and the federal government had passed a "Defense of Marriage Act," which defined marriage as between "a man and a woman," and barred recognition of same-sex marriage from other states (Thomas, 2003:43). Many of these laws and the fate of gay marriage itself will likely be contested. So will other issues, such as gay divorce: a couple who formed a "civil union" in Vermont has already filed for divorce in Texas. The Texas court ruled that it "cannot grant a divorce where no marriage existed" (Rosenberg, 2003:44). In the next few years, the high court will resolve similar issues including gay adoption and custody and gay rights in schools, the workplace, and the military, where part of the legal basis for its "don't ask, don't tell policies" had been federal anti-sodomy laws (Thomas, 2003:45). In 2006, Congress debated a constitutional amendment to ban same-sex marriages, but the bill failed in both houses.

FAMILY TRANSITIONS AND FAMILY PROBLEMS

Contemporary families are beset with many challenges and adjustments. In this section we focus on three that are of great concern to most Americans: domestic violence, divorce, and balancing work and family responsibilities.

Domestic Violence

There is no greater affront to cherished myths about the family than scenes of domestic violence depicted in newspapers and television. Globally, social activists have found violence against women and girls to be one of the most persistent human rights problems. Less than half of all nations have enacted laws and penalties for violence against women and girls including child abuse, sexual harassment, marital rape, and many other crimes that continue to be defined as private, domestic, and family matters.

In the United States family violence is an everyday occurrence committed by people often defined as "perfectly normal"—before their violent acts are publicly acknowledged. Research indicates that family violence may or may not involve alcohol and drugs. Moreover, while domestic violence cuts across all social classes, it does so unevenly; the poorest and most disadvantaged communities, with chronic unemployment, minimal institutional support structures, and high police surveillance, report a disproportionate share of the most horrific and dangerous acts of family violence (Gelles, 1996; Wallace, 1996; Straus et al., 2006). Many sociologists divide family violence into three major categories: spousal, child, and elder abuse.

Spousal abuse is one of the most common forms of violence in the United States. Since national studies began in the 1970s, "police reports of domestic violence by a husband or lover have ranged from 2 to 8 million per year, although the actual rate of spouse assault has been estimated as high as 18 million incidents per year" (Wallace, 1996:193). One study found that domestic violence has "a more serious impact on women's sense of well-being and control than it does on men in similar violent domestic relationships" (Umberson et al., 1998:449).

Child abuse rates are also very high. In most surveys 3 out of 4 parents reported they had struck their children at least once during the year, and 4 in 100 said that they had used severe violence on their children—punching, kicking, or biting them. From the early 1970s until the mid-1990s, reports of child abuse and neglect more than quadrupled to nearly 3 million (Besharov and Laumann, 1998). Focus box 13.2 takes a closer look at child abuse in the United States and the practice of "spanking," which is in the media spotlight today.

Gelles and Straus (1988) believe that family violence may be on the decline, or at least numerous factors reduced the severity of the problem during the 1980s. Many women have entered the workforce and have gained the means to leave abusive spouses. The rapid growth and expansion of treatment and prevention programs, such as shelters for battered women, in conjunction with higher arrest rates and stiffer penalties for abusers also may hold some promise for the future (Gelles and Conte, 1990). The media also have raised people's consciousness—especially through prime-time television shows, network news, and home videos that record shocking scenes of domestic violence; these, too, have helped change public policy.

Divorce

Around the world, divorce rates vary widely. In both Russia and Sweden the divorce rate is as high as 64 percent, whereas in Italy it is only 12 percent, and it is zero in Ireland where divorce is illegal. Today in the United States, about 50 percent of all marriages end in divorce (Kirn, 2000:76).

Throughout most of American history, cruelty, desertion, or adultery were the most common legal grounds for divorce. Today in states with *no-fault divorce* an admission of wrongdoing is not needed; all that is required is mutual consent. In the United States and Western societies in general, "marriage has become a choice instead of a necessity," and divorce has become more socially acceptable and easier to obtain (Schwartz and Kaslow, 1997:7).

People expect more of marriages today, and social and economic changes—especially women's gains in the workplace—have altered the nature of the marital relationship. Ironically, at a time when occupational and other responsibilities consume much of a couple's time, both the quality and stability of marriages are becoming more rather than less dependent on the sustained efforts of husbands and wives to make them work. And abundant opportunities outside the family have led many—especially upper-middle-class professionals—to reduce their investments and commitments to the family and to seek personal fulfillment elsewhere. At the same time, moral and social constraints against divorce have diminished, not only in the United States but in postindustrial nations around the globe (Goode, 1993; Fine and Fine, 1994).

Is spanking children a necessary part of parental discipline and a beneficial custom that teaches children obedience to authority? The Biblical adage "Spare the rod and spoil the child" seems to lend both the test of time and moral authority to the practice. Or is it, as Murray Straus contended in *Beating the Devil Out of Them,* yet another form of family violence and part of a major national and international social problem?

After years of study, Straus found what he considered to be a glaring omission in the data and literature on family violence—the widespread practice of corporal punishment against children. Surveys show that around 90 percent of American parents today spank toddlers, and most parents continue to spank their children well into adolescence. In fact, surveys showed that the majority of respondents believe that spanking was an appropriate "regular form of discipline," and a third of the parents even believed that spanking "helps children develop a better sense of self-control" (Springer, 2000:64; Brandon, 2002). Because the majority of spanking occurs in the privacy of the home, this form of corporal punishment is largely invisible to the public. When it becomes public and visible, however, at supermarkets and shopping malls, for example, many people are shocked and outraged at the level of the violence.

In most cases, Americans believe that spanking is necessary, either to stop children from misbehaving or to make them more obedient. Repeating what they were told as children, most parents tell their children that they spank them "for their own good." And many of those who were spanked offer themselves as living proof that the custom is beneficial: "My parents spanked me, and I turned out all right!" A study released by the American Medical Association, however, indicates that the more a parent spanks a child, the more likely they are to have additional discipline problems over time (Schulte, 1997). Another study, conducted by Columbia University, indicated that spanking leads to temporary compliance, but long-term defiance and aggression (*Washington Post,* 2002).

Child corporal punishment has the support of the law in every state in America, and it is legal in most nations as well. In Texas, for example, the penal code declares "The use of force, but not deadly force, against a child younger than 18 years is justified . . . to discipline the child or to safeguard or promote welfare" (cited in Straus, 1994:6).

Although corporal punishment is defined pretty much the same in most states, the exact meaning of the term *corporal punishment,* or "pain without injury," is variously interpreted. For example, "in a 1996 Iowa Supreme Court Decision, it was ruled that when a man, wishing to discipline his daughter for not bathing and washing her hair, paddled her with a wooden spoon so hard that it left marks . . . that is not child abuse" (*USA Today,* 1996:3A).

Straus's opposition to spanking and other forms of corporal punishment has been met with skepticism from many members of the public and some in academia as well. One of his conclusions, "that slapping a child and hitting wives were equivalent," was challenged by some of his feminist colleagues, who accused him of using corporal punishment "as a diversionary tactic" that takes away from the "real source" of the social problem of spouse abuse: male dominance and gender inequality (Straus, 1994:ix). Popular attacks on his thesis focus more on the nature of the punishment, with most critics contending that only corporal punishment that causes serious injury, which they claim is extremely rare, should be banned. Others contend that the true problem is not spanking but "incompetent parents." From this perspective, if "incompetent parents" learned good parenting skills, including how properly to discipline *and* spank their children, the problem would disappear. When "bad parents" spank, they typically use too much violence, which exacerbates rather than remedies domestic problems, according to those who want to retain the practice.

Straus (1994:xi) contends that even those who use "controlled violence" harm children in various ways. Straus wrote that often the harmful effects of spanking do not show up until later in life. Although there is no clear proof that corporal punishment produces violent individuals and future child and spouse abusers, the practice does predispose both individuals and entire societies to use violence and aggression in dealing with a wide range of social problems. Moreover, violence is often used not only as a last resort but as a routine response to problems of everyday life—especially in our dealing with youth—at home, in school, and in many other social arenas.

TAKING A CLOSER LOOK

Is corporal punishment a beneficial or harmful social practice? Take a position and focus on both the personal and social aspects of spanking to support your case.

Source: Murray A. Straus. *Beating the Devil Out of Them: Corporal Punishment in American Families.* New York: Lexington Books, 1994. "Spanking Ruling," *USA Today,* Thursday, June 20, 1996:3A). B. Schulte. "AMA: Spanking Kids May Make Them Worse." *Dallas Morning News,* August 15, 1997:1A, 18A. Karen Springen. "On Spanking." *Newsweek,* October 16, 2000:64. K. Brandon, "When Does Spanking a Child Become Abuse?" *Dallas Morning News,* Sept. 29, 2002:10A. Washington Post. "Spanking Causes More Problems than it Cures." *Dallas Morning News,* June 26, 2002:4A.

Divorce rates in the United States increased dramatically during the past half-century and are among the highest in the world. If these trends continue, it is estimated that between 50 and 60 percent of all recently contracted first marriages will end in divorce. Redivorce rates are expected to be about as high.

As noted earlier, because the American population has expanded by many millions, caution is required when interpreting contemporary divorce rates. In addition, divorce rates are expected to be much higher than in the past because they are based on marriages ending in divorce over a 40-year period and because increased life spans also contribute to rising divorce rates (Coontz, 1997).

Comparing divorce rates worldwide is problematic as well. For example, Japan's divorce rate is less than half that of the United States. Does this reflect the fact that the Japanese support traditional "family values" and make a determined effort to support two-parent families? To some extent they do. But most Americans would be unwilling to pay the high price for such stability. For example, many traditional marriages in Japan are arranged and few marriages are based on love and mutual passion. Husband-wife compatibility and shared interests are rare, which is not a big issue in Japan because husbands and wives spend very little time together. How do the Japanese describe the secret to their "successful" and stable families? Most mention three things, all of which would be perceived as "problems" in American families: "low expectations, patience, and shame" (Kristof, 1996:1, 12).

Cold statistics mask the emotional turmoil and devastating effects of divorce. While many people experience an increase in personal freedom and greater opportunities after divorce, others experience higher mortality rates, more accidents, more psychological problems, and higher disease rates than do the married, the single, and even the widowed. For many *displaced homemakers,* divorce also results in downward mobility and dramatic decreases in living standards—both in income and in overall economic and social well-being. Only about 60 percent of noncustodial parents pay child support, and considerably fewer receive alimony payments. Less than half of former husbands meet their obligations in full, whereas a quarter fail to pay anything—which means over half of the 16 million children living in single-parent families receive no financial support from the noncustodial parent (Ferree and Hess, 1994; Danzinger and Gottschalk, 1995:174; Coleman and Ganong, 2000).

Much more than money is involved, however. For children, who are present in almost 80 percent of families that divorce, confusion, self-doubt, and even self-blame can produce a legacy of bitterness that lasts for years and may even influence their own chances of marital happiness and success. Who gets divorced, and what factors are related to marital satisfaction? Although many factors are involved, researchers have focused on several independent variables that are especially important. Children of divorce are disproportionately likely to get a divorce. Moreover, marriages between two children of divorce are especially likely to fail. In both cases, research suggests that people from divorced families often marry under conditions that bode poorly for stability and a long-term relationship (Wolfinger, 2003:80). Age at marriage, family stage, low socioeconomic status, and loss of employment and economic hardships—which are related to low levels of marital satisfaction—also increase the likelihood of divorce.

In a survey of 130 newlywed couples John Gottman and colleagues (1998:20) found that marital happiness and stability were severely reduced by belligerence and defensiveness—especially on the part of husbands. Gottman recommended that any formula for success should include "changing the balance of power in favor of the husband's increased acceptance of influence from his wife."

During the late 1990s, a conservative religious movement encouraged a number of states, including Louisiana and Arizona, to enact "covenant marriage" bills to stem the rising tide of divorces that some claimed were "caused" by three decades of permissive, "no-fault divorce." Covenant marriage was part of the larger "Defense of Marriage Movement" that sought to resist gay marriage and reduce divorce rates by returning to "traditional marriages" of the past, where lifelong commitments were supposedly basic to the relationship. Today, in Arizona and Louisiana, couples may chose either conventional marriage (with unrestricted access to no-fault divorce) or the new "covenant marriage" contract (Nock et al., 1999).

Covenant marriages are designed to make it harder for people to both enter and exit marriages. They require premarital counseling and marital

This Phoenix, Arizona, mother waits to enroll her daughter in a school for homeless children. Nearly four out of five single-parent families are headed by women, and although some of them do quite well economically, many of them live below the poverty level.

counseling if problems arise during the marriage. The law requires that couples live separate and apart for two years (versus 6 months under most current marriage laws) or be legally separated for 18 months. Moreover, one person must prove fault: adultery, felony conviction, abuse, and abandonment are acceptable grounds for divorce. "Irreconcilable differences," or "we just don't get along" are not deemed acceptable grounds for divorce in covenant marriages (Nock et al., 1999). What do you think of covenant marriage? Do you agree that no-fault divorce—which gave women greater freedom and more options in marriage—"caused" rising divorce rates? While many sociologists agree that no-fault divorce in the 1970s may have produced a short-term rise in divorce rates, most believe that over the long term other factors were involved. Using your "sociological imagination," can you name some of these factors?

Balancing Family and Work

Today, almost 75 percent of married women with school-age children and more than 50 percent of women with preschool-age children are in the labor force (see Figure 13.4). The transition to coprovider families has not been without its problems, and in many ways it remains an unfinished experiment (Hochschild, 1997; Polatnick, 2000; Skolnick and Skolnick, 2007).

In the past few decades women have entered the paid labor force in unprecedented numbers and have entered virtually every profession. Despite these efforts, women's domestic responsibilities have changed little. Working wives continue to carry a disproportionate share of family responsibilities, such as child care, shopping, and housework.

There has been some improvement in men's participation in child care and other domestic responsibilities. In 1980 less than 15 percent of preschoolers were cared for by their fathers while mothers worked. That figure has risen to about 18 percent, or, as Linda Waite (2000:467) noted, the "housework gap" between married men and women has declined from 29 to 9 hours per week. When both parents are at home after work, however, women devote much more attention to child care than do men—about twice as much time—a situation that many women with economic resources and alternatives to marriage view as unjust and unacceptable (Lennon and Rosenfield, 1994).

It is estimated that women spend 32.7 hours per week on housework compared to 17 hours per week for men (see Figure 13.5). Although somewhat less unequal than in the past, this is not approaching equality (Shelton, 2000).

Gender inequality persists in other areas as well. Even when wives earn as much as or more than their husbands, many men still consider domestic matters to be the wife's responsibility. In addition, many husbands continue to see their wives' jobs as competing with their needs and those of the children. And families have yet to receive much help from either the government or corporate America in the form of flexible work schedules, funding for quality day care, and maternity and family leave benefits.

Almost half of preschool-age children are cared for by relatives—some of it "tag-team care" by parents. Seventeen percent are looked after by nonkin and 24.3 percent spend their formative years in day-care centers, which are highly uneven in quality. Babysitters, nannies, and the much rarer on-site day-care facilities are provided by 5,000 (out of 6 million) companies. Moreover, many facilities are unlicensed, overcrowded, and even dangerous. American businesses provide higher quality care, but they too are largely unregulated and of uneven quality (Collins and Coltrane, 1995; Garfinkel et al., 1996). And one in five children ages 6–12 are regularly left home after school—without adult supervision (*Dallas Morning News*, 2000:3A).

The government has not provided much help for working families with children. As Collins and Coltrane (1995) noted, although the Family Leave Act of 1993 took almost a

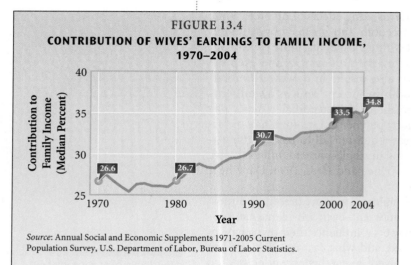

FIGURE 13.4
CONTRIBUTION OF WIVES' EARNINGS TO FAMILY INCOME, 1970–2004

Source: Annual Social and Economic Supplements 1971-2005 Current Population Survey, U.S. Department of Labor, Bureau of Labor Statistics.

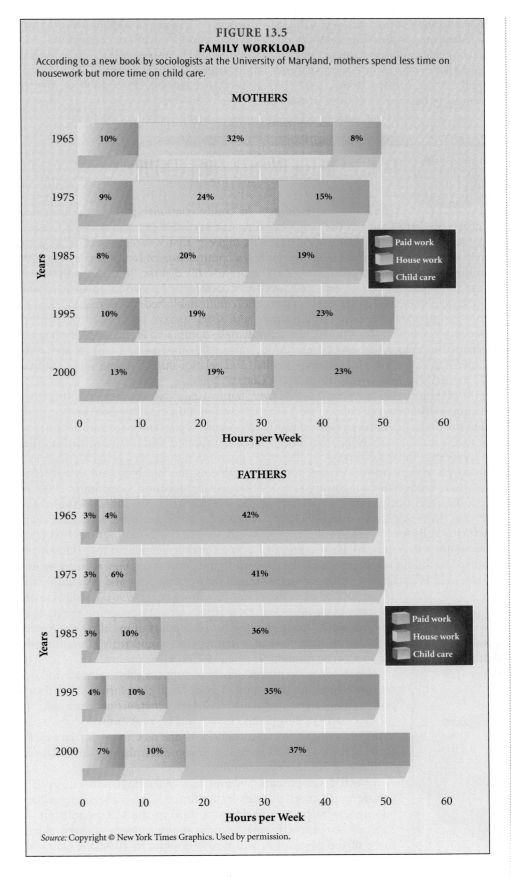

FIGURE 13.5
FAMILY WORKLOAD
According to a new book by sociologists at the University of Maryland, mothers spend less time on housework but more time on child care.

MOTHERS

Year	Paid work	House work	Child care
1965	10%	32%	8%
1975	9%	24%	15%
1985	8%	20%	19%
1995	10%	19%	23%
2000	13%	19%	23%

Years

Hours per Week

FATHERS

Year	Paid work	House work	Child care
1965	3%	4%	42%
1975	3%	6%	41%
1985	3%	10%	36%
1995	4%	10%	35%
2000	7%	10%	37%

Years

Hours per Week

Source: Copyright © New York Times Graphics. Used by permission.

decade to pass, it provided few substantive benefits: 12 weeks of *unpaid* parental leave for infant care or seriously ill family members and a few other minor concessions. Such benefits pale in comparison to family support policies in Sweden, which some sociologists believe is the most progressive and "family-friendly" environment in the industrial world (Acker, 1994; Coontz, 1997). Focus box 13.3 takes a closer look at Swedish attempts to balance family and work.

FAMILIES IN THE TWENTY-FIRST CENTURY

Given the many changes in family relationships over the past half-century, predictions about the family's future—or even that the family has a future—may seem unwise. But sociological research suggests that several scenarios are more likely than others. The most likely scenario is a continuation of long-term trends. First, families will continue to grow smaller and more socially diverse. Second, it will be even more acceptable for people, especially women, to delay marriage and child-rearing until they have completed higher levels of education and established their careers. Likewise, more people may choose to remain single, and single-parent families and cohabiting couples will increase. Traditional, hierarchical male-dominated families will decline and perhaps be replaced by egalitarian families and peer marriages, in which men's and women's roles become increasingly similar and relationships become more intimate and mutually supportive (McGinn, 2006; Countz, 2006).

Despite the highly politicized debate over "family values," young men and women are seeking realistic ways to balance work and family and individual freedom and commitment to others. As Kathleen Gerson (2000:187) wrote: "New family realities are producing a new set of family values that stress emotional support and justice within families, and tolerance for the diverse ways that individuals build their private lives." While specific kinds of families will experience many problems, the family system as a whole is likely to remain resilient (Schwartz, 1994; Goode, 1995; Murdock, 1995; Sollie, 2000).

In the short run, government social policies will play a key role in the fortunes of all families. However, as Goode (1993:336) remarked, "while we have witnessed many rhetorical calls for increased adherence to family values, concrete programs that really give support to family life have been rare." Some sociologists believe that limited and perhaps declining resources should be devoted to the poorest families, who are in desperate need of assistance. Others contend that aid for working poor and near-poor families would be more beneficial (Garfinkel et al., 1996). Theda Skocpol, for example, contends that "a family security program aimed at all families would likely gain the broad support of middle-class Americans and this, more than anything else, would truly strengthen the families of the future" (Skocpol, 1995:275).

At present, government efforts to support the family are focused on supplementing the wages of poor families, reforms in child support systems, and reducing child-care costs—but more will be needed. Barbara Bergmann (1996) calls for near-universal child care to replace current piecemeal subsidies. She recommends free care for those in the bottom 20 percent of income distribution and subsidies for those in the next two quintiles.

Several developments, however, may make improvements in child welfare much more difficult in the future. One is the aging of baby boomers, who constitute almost a third of the U.S. population. By 2030 all of them will have become senior citizens and the elderly share of the population will nearly double. In 2050, the estimated 400 million Americans will be even older, with one in five persons elderly, more ethnically diverse, and perhaps much poorer than today. Figure 13.6 shows how free or subsidized child care will have to address demographic changes.

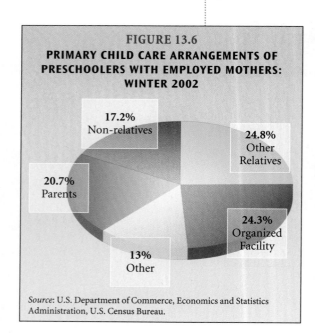

FIGURE 13.6
PRIMARY CHILD CARE ARRANGEMENTS OF PRESCHOOLERS WITH EMPLOYED MOTHERS: WINTER 2002

17.2% Non-relatives
24.8% Other Relatives
20.7% Parents
24.3% Organized Facility
13% Other

Source: U.S. Department of Commerce, Economics and Statistics Administration, U.S. Census Bureau.

Some sociologists believe that if any nation deserves the "pro-family" label, it is Sweden. In the past century the Swedish state, in cooperation with labor, industry, and the feminist and other social movements, has provided money and services to support family life and the employment of women. And to a lesser degree, it has sought to eliminate gender inequality and laws and customs that reinforce women's secondary place in society. As a result, wrote Joan Acker (1994:33), "Swedish women enjoy public programs and economic guarantees that have made Sweden a model for women in other countries."

Acker's study of Swedish reforms over the past few decades shows that many changes in the family were the result of conscious policy decisions. One of the most important began with labor shortages in the 1960s, which led the government to push for increased labor market participation of women. This was accomplished through a new tax policy that reduced tax deductions for wives and "encouraged" most to enter the workforce. The transition to work was also supported by the feminist movement, which saw work and financial independence as women's only hope of gaining equality with men (Acker, 1994:34).

To smooth the transition of women into the workforce, the Swedish government expanded welfare state services and new jobs—especially in a new sector called "caring work." These paid public sector jobs included nursing, child care, preschool teachers, and home helpers who make it possible for almost 90 percent of Swedish women to be gainfully employed—including similar percentages of women with children under 6 years of age.

The Swedish solution to the problem of combining family and labor market work is the most advanced in the world. No longer is there a worker and a housewife with separate but interdependent roles. Instead there are two workers—the classical, male-defined worker and a new worker in whose life the tasks of reproduction and production are intertwined (Acker, 1994:38).

The typical Swedish family today consists of two working parents, with the majority of women working part-time (67 percent of those with children) and more than 90 percent of men working full-time. To support women's and men's dual roles in the family and work, the state has devised a benefit package that all families receive, regardless of class or income. Some of the benefits are public-supported child care, including day-care centers and licensed family care homes (organized by local communities), and parental leave insurance available to both men and women. Parents of a newborn are entitled to 360 days of leave at normal sick pay, new fathers are entitled to 10 days of parental leave, and parents have the legal right to "reduce their hours on the job to three-quarters of normal pay, until the child reaches 8 years of age." Additionally all families are entitled to a basic child allowance per year of around $900, as well as a housing allowance that is based on income and number of children in the family (Acker, 1994).

Although Swedish attempts to balance family and work are the most progressive in the world, they remain an unfinished project. As Acker wrote (1994:40), "The new family model seems almost as firmly grounded in gender divisions as the old family model . . . The world of paid work is still primarily organized around the assumption of the male worker." For one thing, "Woman-friendly family work life coexists with sex segregation, a gendered wage gap, the concentration of women in low wage, low status jobs, and the same exclusions and invisibilities that women suffer in work organizations in the United States" (Acker, 1994:39).

As Acker's study found, most women are in part-time jobs, and more than half of Swedish women were in just 12 occupations—most low-level service jobs. And as in other industrial nations, the top administrative posts are still dominated by men, with women occupying only 5 percent of upper management positions. Similarly, white-collar women earn only about 75 percent of the wage of their male counterparts, and Swedish women continue to bear a disproportionate share of child-care and other domestic duties. Full-time employed mothers had a 73-hour work week, 34 of these hours at home; the men's work week totaled 60 hours, about 41 hours in the workplace and 19 hours on domestic chores (Acker, 1994).

Despite these deficiencies, Acker insists that the way Swedish women combine family and employment is far superior to the situations in most other countries. Nevertheless, Swedish women are fully aware that pro-family legislation and benefits can be erased by global competition, economic recessions, downsizing, and high unemployment. As Acker (1994:48) noted:

In response, some Swedish women [are] organizing within political parties and unions, as well as outside traditional organizations, to save welfare state programs and to reverse the decline of political power . . . These women warn that they will form a new women's party if the old parties do not actively work for women's interests. While the outcome is still unclear, the centrality of gender conflicts in welfare state politics is escalating in Sweden [as it is in the rest of the world].

TAKING A CLOSER LOOK

Why do you think the United States is not as family-friendly as Sweden? Do you believe the United States is shifting toward the Swedish model as more American women enter the workforce? What factors might encourage corporations and the government to move in this direction? Conversely, what factors might work against the United States adopting the Swedish model?

Source: "Women, Families, and Public Policy in Sweden," by Joan Acker from *Women, the Family, and Policy: A Global Perspective* by Ester Ngan-ling Chow and Catherine White Berheide (eds.), Stony Brook State University of New York Press, 1994, pp. 33–49.

Already, the four-generation family is becoming increasingly important; over the next few decades, extended families of various kinds may increase at the expense of the contemporary nuclear family model. Aging parents and the competing demands of work and children have popularized the phrase *the sandwich generation,* which describes the predicament of middle-aged parents who must provide for both children and elderly parents. As life spans increase and there are more divorces, remarriages, and blended families, we should expect even more complex family responsibilities. "In short, the sandwich generation, already feeling so much pressure in the 1990s, could give way to a multilayered club sandwich" (Wallis, 1996:28).

Family diversity will increase dramatically as minority populations increase. States will continue to struggle with issues over gay marriages and civil unions between members of the same sex. Will current trends toward a polarization of rich and poor families continue in the future? Will competition for scarce resources divide families in early stages from baby boomers in the later stages of life? Will politicians successfully promote constitutional amendments defining or redefining marriage?

Developments in reproductive technology may provide new shocks and challenges to the family as well. Since 1960 hundreds of thousands of children have been conceived through either *artificial insemination* or *in vitro fertilization,* in which a fetus is conceived in a lab dish and then transferred to the uterus to develop. In Los Angeles in the early 1980s, the first *embryo transplant* was made, in which a man donated sperm, a surrogate woman donated an ovum, and then the fertilized ovum was transplanted to the infertile woman. Since then, this technology has been so effective that it has produced an oversupply of unclaimed embryos, which some journalists have sensationalized as "orphan embryos." In 1996, British clinics found themselves under attack by anti-abortion groups and even the Vatican when they sought to destroy thousands of embryos that were more than 5 years old (*USA Today,* 1996:1A).

Even more controversial is the role of *surrogate mothers,* who for a fee are artificially inseminated and carry a child for a woman who is unable to carry her own child. At present, there are eight established commercial surrogate programs in the United States as well as numerous individuals who arrange surrogate contracts. Their numbers probably will increase in the future, perhaps adding to current controversies. Should human reproduction become commercial, a product to be bought and sold like any other product? Class issues are involved as well; and some have argued that surrogate motherhood is merely one more means by which the rich exploit the poor. Important gender issues are involved too (Ragone, 1994). The Human Genome Project, in which numerous international organizations have joined forces to map the 100,000 genes that control human development and provide a "complete set of instructions for making a human being" also has raised numerous social, legal, and ethical concerns (Jaroff, 1989:62).

While not yet as common as blood tests, genetic screening and genetic counseling, which identify whether prospective mates carry harmful genes that can be passed on to their offspring, are fast becoming part of the process of family formation. The new technology raises questions not only about who should be parents, but also about the characteristics we may want and demand in our children. We are at the point where parents have the ability both to screen fetuses for harmful diseases and to decide which sex the child will be (including deciding on a number of social characteristics).

As technology improves, we may demand perfect children or "designer babies," and perhaps perfect parents—with only a select few licensed to have children. New, high-tech eugenics might also be used to modify inherited characteristics in ways that society currently deems undesirable, and this technology raises the possibility of the creation of "a special class of persons who, from birth, were assumed to be superior" (Anderson, 2000:20). And what about the host of new technologies, including uterine transplants, which would offer an alternative to surrogacy, the ability to fertilize and grow embryos outside the human body, and perhaps even human cloning. While experts believe that cloning is unlikely to offer an option for infertile couples anytime soon—and it poses numerous ethical dilemmas—"they aren't saying that it necessarily can't be done (Stenson, 2003:6). Scientists and the courts will guide this debate, but all of us will have to make difficult choices (Bodmer and McKie, 1994). Arlene Skolnick (1991:224) put it best when she wrote:

There are no quick, easy, or cheap fixes for the problems of family life today. And there is good reason to believe that we may never solve some of the dilemmas of the family . . . But there is much that can be done to alleviate some of the major, outer sources of stress and strains; sooner or later, policymakers will translate rhetoric and genuine public concern about children and families into ways of addressing the new realities of family life.

Summary

1. Marriage and family are characterized by flexibility and resilience and are deeply embedded in the larger society.

2. All societies use a limited range of principles and norms to shape family and kinship relations, including descent patterns, courtship procedures, ways to establish and dissolve marriages, and residence and authority patterns.

3. Functionalists view marriage and family customs as adaptations to a variety of ecological contexts, whereas conflict theorists argue that marriage and family are arenas of conflict. Social exchange theorists use a marketplace metaphor that sees people bargaining to make the best deals. Symbolic interactionists emphasize that marriage and family relationships are negotiated during interaction.

4. The family life course has become more dynamic and complex than at any time in the past.

5. Many family sociologists contend that a normative family no longer exists in America and that people now create families of diverse styles, such as child-free families, dual-earner and dual-career families, single-parent families, blended families, and gay and lesbian families.

6. Although television's content has changed over the past few decades, patriarchal themes and a continued bias toward intact nuclear families continue to dominate prime-time TV. The World Wide Web offers a more realistic portrait of families and alternative approaches to family, as well as ways to help real families cope with the many challenges of modern life.

7. In the future, families may become more diverse and shift from patriarchal to egalitarian models. Developments in reproductive technology and aging baby boomers also challenge traditional understandings about courtship, marriage, parenthood, and the family—and they will continue to do so in the future.

Key Terms

blended family (p. 375)
child-free family (p. 374)
cohabitation (p. 368)
coprovider families (p. 374)
dual-career families (p. 375)
endogamy (p. 361)
exogamy (p. 361)
extended family (p. 361)

family (p. 359)
family of marriage (p. 359)
family of orientation (p. 359)
heterogamy (p. 367)
homogamy (p. 366)
incest taboo (p. 361)
kinship group (p. 361)
marriage (p. 359)

monogamy (p. 362)
nuclear family (p. 360)
patriarchal authority (p. 363)
polygamy (p. 362)
serial monogamy (p. 362)
single-parent families (p. 375)
traditional nuclear family (p. 374)

Chapter 14

Education

> *"Education's purpose is to replace an empty mind with an open one."*
> —*Malcolm Forbes*

Margot reads her e-mail, responds to a few questions, and then downloads the *Congressional Record* to her computer. She then completes her homework and faxes it to her teacher by modem. Next, she peruses one of the state university library's card catalogs, chooses a classic book from its stacks, and downloads it to be condensed into a book report due in two weeks. Later she will assist in a local private kindergarten, where she teaches reading as well as helps the students learn to tie their shoes and button up their coats. Some of Margot's classmates meet as a group at libraries, bookstores, or public parks before pursuing their internships, which include working alongside a professional horse trainer, a licensed massage therapist, and a wildlife biologist. Margot is 12 years old and is one of ten "cyberschool" students enrolled in the Puget Sound Community School in suburban Seattle. Her teacher and the founder of the school, 31-year-old Andy Smallman, believes that computer technology allows students and their parents to escape the fear of public school violence and the bureaucracy and mediocrity associated with public education, while providing state-of-the-art learning experiences (Hancock and French, 1994).

Students need not opt out of a public education to receive that same state-of-the-art learning opportunity. Take, for example, a model for urban schools, in Omaha, Nebraska, where fifth-grade students take courses in robotics and physics, and high schoolers "surf the Net" in schools that feature high-technology and computer science. What began as a desegregation plan in the late 1970s has developed into a highly competitive system where junior high students can choose to attend any of the high schools in the Omaha district. While all the schools offer the same basic core curriculum, some feature high-tech computer science curricula, while others focus on the humanities and fine arts (Barrett, 1993).

In Camden, New Jersey, a computer teacher urges her students to learn the keyboard on the standard Olympia manual typewriters that are in front of them, so that, if they ever get the opportunity to work on a real computer, the transition will be relatively easy. Down the hall, a science teacher instructs a class, half of whom have no textbooks, on how they would conduct an experiment on the rippling effects of water if they had the laboratory equipment. When it rains, the students get an idea of the outcome of the experiment as water pours in through the missing ceiling tiles in their classroom (Kozol, 1992, 1996, 2001, 2006).

The first public school established in the United States, in 1634, was in Boston. That school still exists today in the form of Boston Latin School, at a different location; the oldest public high school continues as the English High School. All white and all male, when founded in 1821, the school now is predominantly black and Hispanic, and is coed; since 1998 it has had a female Head Master, its first. In addition to the standard curriculum, English High offers a social club for its Somalian students, a day-care center for its students with children, and a program to help find summer jobs for students (Kantrowitz, 2005b).

How does this photo reflect the diversity and multiculturalism associated with educating children to live in a global society?

Today, many speak of the educational system of the United States as if it were some large, homogenous structure in which students have similar academic experiences regardless of where they attend school or what type of school they attend. As the four cases illustrate, however, *things are not necessarily what they seem.* Students in the United States may undergo a wide range of educational experiences, including home schooling, a vast array of religious and secular private schools, and public schools that range from decrepit and dangerous to state-of-the art facilities—and everything in between.

In this chapter we begin by looking at education in a global society, focusing on three major educational systems commonly believed to be among the best in the world: Great Britain, Japan, and the United States. We then analyze education as a social institution from the three major sociological perspectives. We apply the functionalist perspective to analyze education's manifest and latent functions; the conflict perspective to focus on education's role in creating and maintaining social inequality; and the interactionist perspective to examine education and its impact on everyday life. We continue by exploring some of the more important contemporary trends in American education and, finally, look to the future.

EDUCATION IN A GLOBAL SOCIETY

Ask almost any adult in any country around the world why they send their children to school and they are likely to respond, "To learn." When sociologists speak of education, however, they are not referring to learning, which is an ongoing process that includes every facet of the human experience. Instead, **education** is *the institutionalized process of systematically teaching certain cognitive skills and knowledge and transmitting them from one generation to the next.* Institutionalized education exists in every culture, from the simplest to the most complex, because it is vital to the survival of any society. In pre-

EDUCATION
The institutionalized process of systematically teaching certain cognitive skills and knowledge and transmitting them from one generation to the next.

literate societies education may be as simple as the adults in a tribe teaching traditional roles and basic hunting and domestic skills to younger tribal members. In industrial and postindustrial societies education is linked to formal *schooling,* and it may include a complex myriad of preschools, kindergartens, elementary and secondary schools, post-secondary vocational schools and technical institutes, two-year and four-year colleges, universities, graduate schools, and postdoctoral institutions. From a sociological view-point, education, like other social institutions, reflects a society's historical development and cultural values. For example, Map 14.1 depicts how illiteracy rates around the world are not randomly distributed, but linked to nations' political, economic, and social development. A brief overview of education in three postindustrial countries—Great Britain, Japan, and the United States—illustrates this point.

A Proper British Education

Great Britain has been a highly stratified society since the Norman invasion of 1066. Education in the form of formal schooling has traditionally been viewed as a *privilege* and not a *right,* and until the British Industrial Revolution in the mid-nineteenth century a proper British education was reserved for members of the upper class and nobility. Today, education is highly valued in the United Kingdom, and compulsory attendance laws similar to those in the United States require that children attend school from age 6 to 16 (or until they have finished a series of exams and portfolios taken at about age 16). Then, based on examination scores, students may be eligible to attend college (usually vocational or technical) or a university to pursue a degree in a specified area (e.g., law), for approximately 3 years. Those who desire to attend universities must pass A-level exams, which reflect mastery of academic subjects including reading, language, mathematics, science, and history. These exams cover much of what Americans would receive during their first two years of general education courses in college.

While British education is no longer reserved for the rich, it remains stratified on the basis of social class. Most wealthy families send their children to expensive public preparatory schools that are the equivalent of some of America's exclusive private boarding schools. These schools combine superior academic education with training in social etiquette, leadership, cricket, polo, and other aspects of life befitting their social standing. The British are fond of saying, for example, that World Wars I and II were won not on the battlefields but on the playgrounds of Eton (Britain's most exclusive and famous boys' school—the alma mater of Prince Charles, the heir to the British throne, and his two sons Prince William and Prince Harry). Meanwhile, sons and daughters of the working class and poor attend more modest state-supported day schools that focus on academic education and vocational training. Middle-class children are caught some-where in the middle, but they can attend some of the more exclusive public schools if they score high on standardized competitive examinations. And while theoretically even children of the poorest British families have the same opportunity, entrance into superior public and private schools is dominated by the upper and middle classes, who enjoy clear advantages in admissions policies.

Until the mid-1960s, British higher education was almost exclusively the domain of the upper class and nobility. Today, because of competitive entrance examinations, even England's most exclusive universities (Oxford and Cambridge) are open to students from working-class and middle-class backgrounds, but their rosters are still dominated by the descendants of lords and ladies, prime ministers, and the upper class—the vast majority of whom also attended those two schools. Meanwhile, the middle class are more likely to attend less prestigious universities, while working-class children attend college (vocational technical schools) or go to work right out of high school (only approximately 15 percent of the British population attend university).

Higher education has undergone some dramatic changes in Great Britain. These alterations were linked to the *Dearing Report,* a 1,700-page comprehensive 20-year blue-print that included 93 specific recommendations for overhauling Britain's higher educa-tion system. Among the more significant and hotly debated recommendations were ending free tuition for full-time students, increasing government spending on higher education, removing government-imposed caps on student recruitment; more flexible degree programs (ending the domination of the three-year program in one course of

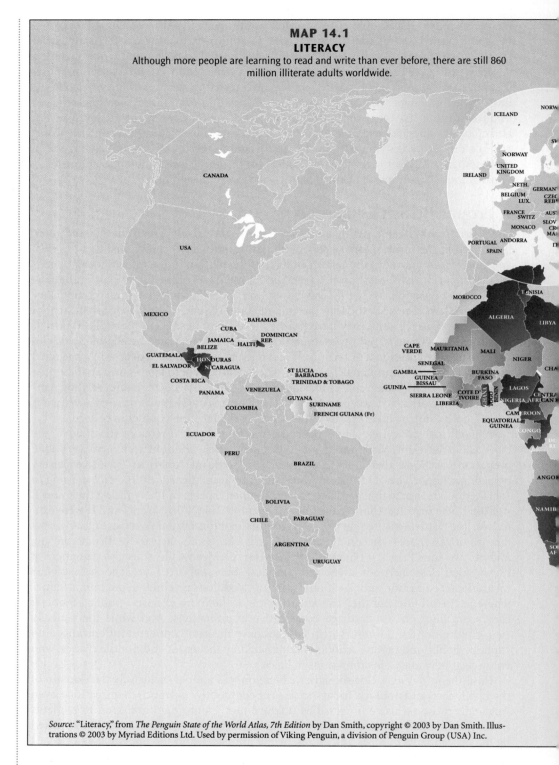

MAP 14.1

LITERACY

Although more people are learning to read and write than ever before, there are still 860 million illiterate adults worldwide.

Source: "Literacy," from *The Penguin State of the World Atlas, 7th Edition* by Dan Smith, copyright © 2003 by Dan Smith. Illustrations © 2003 by Myriad Editions Ltd. Used by permission of Viking Penguin, a division of Penguin Group (USA) Inc.

study), and increased emphasis on teaching skills through professional qualifications (O'Leary, 1997; Anderson, 2007).

While there is room for disagreement, the British seem satisfied with their education system from elementary through university levels. The most controversial of the British education overhauls is the charging of tuition for university education. Tuition for university education is not new to American students; most are shocked when they learn their British counterparts not only attend Cambridge and Oxford tuition-free or at a minimal cost, but also, if they qualify, receive living expenses from the government. On the other hand, Americans are surprised to learn how competitive entrance requirements are to universities in England. Consequently, although family status and income

Illiteracy
Rates of illiteracy among people aged 15 and over
2000

| | 70% and over | | 50%–69% | | 30%–49% |
| | 10%–29% | | under 10% | | no data |

still play important roles in the educational opportunities available to British students, the pursuit of higher education, especially admission to the most prestigious schools, is largely based on academic merit and standardized test scores. In that regard, higher education in Great Britain may share more in common with Japan than the United States.

Kanri Kyoiku in Japan

There was a time, especially during the 1950s, when the words *Made in Japan* stamped on a product elicited smirks, smiles, and ridicule. Although Japanese items caught on quickly in American and worldwide markets because they were inexpensive, their questionable quality caused people to consider them *cheap*. Today, Japanese products, especially automobiles, stereos, televisions, and other electronic devices have gained a worldwide reputation for their superior quality. Much of that turnaround is attributed to what is considered to be a first-rate educational system—especially mathematics and science, in which Japanese students rank among the highest in the world (Benjamin, 1997; Benton, 2001).

Ninety-nine percent of Japanese children attend public elementary schools, and polls indicate that Japanese people tend to be satisfied with the quality of education from elementary through university levels. As in any society, Japan's educational system reflects cultural values, and in their public schools one of the most important values taught can be summed up in two words: *kanri kyoiku,* or *rigid regimentation.* Primary grades focus on discipline, conformity, and respect for authority. These values encourage not only commitment to school but also devotion to family and government. Elementary school children are exposed to these values every day, six days a week, throughout the school year, which begins on April 1 and runs through the following March (Schoolland, 1990; Benjamin, 1997).

Compulsory school attendance ends after completion of the ninth grade, but about 95 percent of Japanese children attend high school, and nearly all of them graduate. Both public and private high schools charge tuition and fees, and entrance to both is determined through highly competitive entrance examinations. Public and private high schools are ranked throughout Japan based on the examination scores of their students as well as placement of their graduates in universities and employment. Discipline, conformity, and rigid regimentation are also stressed in Japanese high schools, and although corporal punishment is not officially sanctioned it is frequently used (Schoolland, 1990).

Admission to Japanese universities is based on extreme competition, and failure to gain admission to a desirable school can bring shame not only to students but to their families and ancestors as well. As a result, schooling in preparation for university education is all-consuming. Most students attend school all day, returning home to do homework through the evening or into the early morning hours. In addition they attend a *juku* (cram school) for 5–15 hours each week. A popular expression among Japanese junior high and high school students is "Pass with four, fail with five"—referring to the maximum number of hours of sleep allowed to pass examinations (Schoolland, 1990:20). Educational reforms launched in 2001, however, were designed to cut down on time and attention to core subjects such as math and science and use some of that time to help Japaneses students learn to think critically for themselves (Benton, 2001).

Gaining admission to a particular university is the most important goal of primary and secondary education. And since virtually everyone admitted goes on to graduate, once accepted into a university, students are relieved of the previous pressures of schooling and experience four of the most relaxed and enjoyable years of their lives. In fact, the more prestigious the university attended, the more relaxing and enjoyable the experience—an extended "decompression period," as Japanese educational experts put it, until the student graduates and enters a pressure-filled world of work, career, and familial responsibilities (James and Benjamin, 1988:33). As in the United States, academic credentials from Japan's more prestigious schools mean not only enhanced intellectual skills, but also important social networks that help ensure improved career opportunities (Ishida et al., 1997).

Education in the United States

There is no national education system in the United States. Many people are surprised to learn that the U.S. Constitution makes no mention of education whatsoever. Education was left up to individuals and families and today is considered the responsibility of the states—more accurately, in most cases, individual school districts.

Many Americans believe that Japan's emphasis on conformity, discipline, and rigid regimentation should serve as a model for education in the United States. Meanwhile, many Japanese educators believe that they should use American schools as their model as they strive to develop critical thinking and creativity in their students.

How do cultural values in the two countries make these goals difficult to accomplish?

To ensure that all American students receive an adequate and meaningful educational experience, many politicians and educational leaders believe the United States must establish a standardized academic curriculum and a set of national goals and standards to which all schools must adhere. Plans include enhanced training of teachers who must pass standardized tests for certification; preschool programs to ensure that students are adequately prepared to enter school when the time comes; and standardized curricula that include basic reading, writing, communication, and analytical skills as well as critical thinking skills and an understanding of the scientific method (Kennedy, 1997; Adler, 2007). Opponents of national educational goals, standards, and curricula argue, however, that those aims are at fundamental odds with American democracy, individualism, and the freedom of parents and local communities to determine what their children need to know and how they should be taught (Arons, 1997; Holt, 2007).

A host of American education's cheerleaders point with pride to model schools and successful students. Meanwhile, critics fear that much of what passes for education in the United States today is outdated, irrelevant, meaningless to students, and perhaps as much an impediment as a contributor to society's development and survival. When asked to assess American education, many Americans give it a failing grade (National Commission on Excellence in Education, 1983; Bloom, 1987; McLaren, 1989; Lounsbury and Clark, 1990; P. Smith, 1990; Bennett et al., 2006). But if American education or any other educational system deserves a passing or a failing grade, a fundamental question must be asked: Succeeding or failing to do what? To address that question, it is necessary to take a sociological look at what education is supposed to do in the United States and in all societies.

American teachers often feel overworked, underpaid, and unappreciated as government places more emphasis on standardized testing, and society puts more pressure on the schools to fulfill social functions once thought to be the domain of the family, church, and other social institutions.

THE ROLE OF EDUCATION: A FUNCTIONALIST PERSPECTIVE

Regardless of its structure or in what society it is located, as Neil Postman and Charles Weingartner (1969:207) noted, "the basic function of all education, even in the most traditional sense, is to increase the survival prospects of the group." Today, despite variation in social structures, politics, and economics, school curricula the world over are remarkably similar. From a functionalist perspective, education serves several important *manifest*, or intended, functions, including cultural transmission, anticipatory socialization, integration, and innovation, as well as numerous *latent*, or unintended, functions. Let's look first at the manifest functions and then at some unanticipated outcomes of education.

Cultural Transmission

Cultural transmission is *the process by which culture is passed from one generation to the next.* It is part of the socialization process discussed in Chapter 4. The family is the initial agent of socialization, but in most cultures relinquishes some responsibility to the schools early in a child's life. The educational institution assumes primary responsibility for transmitting cognitive culture (thoughts, ideas, and knowledge) and plays an important role in teaching normative culture (norms, values, attitudes, and beliefs).

Teaching Cognitive Skills: The "Three R's"
In small, homogeneous societies there is often general consensus about the skills and knowledge that should be taught to ensure survival. These societies place less emphasis on formal schooling, focusing instead on training youngsters to gather, hunt, and perform critical domestic skills to help ensure survival for themselves, their families, and their culture. Even in highly industrialized but relatively homogeneous societies, such as Japan, that place tremendous emphasis on formal schooling, there is still widespread consensus on curricular matters and what should or should not be taught in school.

CULTURAL TRANSMISSION
The process by which culture is passed from one generation to the next.

In large, heterogeneous nations such as the United States, however, there is much disagreement on what should be included in the educational curriculum. Yet even in the United States there is far more agreement about the teaching of cognitive culture than about the teaching of normative culture. Debates may develop over *how* to teach basic cognitive skills, such as the three R's (readin', 'ritin', and 'rithmetic), but almost everyone agrees that schools *should* be teaching them. In addition, most Americans agree that schools should teach history, geography, language, and literature. These are the basic courses of almost every American school curriculum. But should the schools be teaching more? More specifically, should they be teaching moral values?

Teaching Values and Norms: The "Other Two R's"   There is much less agreement in the United States and other heterogeneous countries about teaching the normative aspects of culture, especially the other two R's—right and 'rong. In the United States, children enter the public schools from a variety of cultural backgrounds. Public school teachers, however, represent a narrower segment of American society, predominantly coming from white, middle-class, Protestant backgrounds (Rothstein, 1996; Schuman, 2004). Consequently, when the issue of teaching values arises, at least two important questions emerge: First, which values do we teach? Second, how do we teach them? Some contend that American schools should concentrate on teaching cognitive skills and that the teaching of values should be the responsibility of other social institutions, namely the family and religion. Others, however, argue that there is a long tradition in American education of transmitting core values to students and that schools should teach honesty, loyalty, truthfulness, courtesy, obedience, ethical communication, and other time-honored moral virtues (Wynne, 1990; Purpel, 1991; Wong, 1991; Nazario, 1992; Townsend, 1992; Dabel, 1993; Lickona, 2006; Macedo, 2007).

An important function of education is the transmission of culture, which includes teaching norms and values so as to promote patriotism, nationalism, and cultural integration.

There is less controversy in private church-supported schools in the United States, which make a conscientious effort to teach specific theological beliefs and moral attitudes along with cognitive skills and knowledge. However, research on the use of the Bible as a textbook in Jewish schools both inside and outside of Israel suggests that despite strong consensus on the teaching of moral values a tension exists between the "ought" and "is," as teachers' and students' conceptions of values are often at odds (Shkedi, 1997). In the United States, cognitive skills and moral values have also become intertwined in the public schools, and the two are virtually inseparable in the curriculum. For example, when elementary students read about young George Washington confessing to his father that he chopped down a cherry tree, they are simultaneously learning to read, learning American history (although fictional in this case), and learning the virtue of honesty. Perhaps because the story is a national myth, teachers do not always recognize the irony of using a lie to teach the virtue of truth. An important aspect of American public education, sometimes referred to as the *hidden curriculum,* is discussed in the section on the conflict perspective on education.

Anticipatory Socialization

Another important function of education is anticipatory socialization: teaching the knowledge and skills necessary for the successful fulfillment of future roles and statuses. In Focus box 14.1, the overriding goal of kindergarten is seen as teaching the student role. If students learn and internalize this role, they are prepared not only for a successful school experience but also for adult work roles in factories, corporations, and other bureaucratic settings. Research suggests that parents contribute to this type of anticipatory socialization by structuring afterschool activities as well for their children (Adler and Adler, 1994).

Education has been defined by classical and contemporary sociologists as one of the major social institutions. Its most important function has been and remains today that of socializing people into becoming productive members of society through a formalized, standardized procedure.

Harry Gracey's research on kindergarten in a suburban school district in New York reveals that schools are large bureaucratic institutions. In the social organization of the schools, kindergarten is generally considered a year of preparation. A booklet prepared for parents by the staff of the school system that Gracey studied described the kindergarten experience as one that would "stimulate the child's desire to learn and cultivate the skills . . . for learning in the rest of [the] school career." But Gracey found that kindergarten's most critical function was to teach children the "student role":

> The unique job of the kindergarten in the educational division of labor seems . . . to be teaching children the student role . . . the repertoire of behavior and attitudes regarded by educators as appropriate to children in school. . . .
>
> By the end of the school year, the successful kindergarten teacher has a well-organized group of children. They follow classroom routines automatically, having learned all the command signals and the expected responses . . . in our terms, [they have] learned the student role.

Harry Gracey describes kindergarten as "academic boot camp."

Do you agree with this analogy?

The children have learned to go through routines and to follow orders with unquestioning obedience, even when these make no sense to them. They have been disciplined to do as they are told by an authoritative person without significant protest.

According to Gracey, children who submit to school-imposed discipline become defined as "good students," while those who refuse to submit become known as "bad students," "troublemakers," or "problem children." He also surmised that children's creativity, initiative, and spontaneity are systematically eliminated, while unquestioned obedience to authority and rote learning of meaningless material are encouraged and demanded. He concluded that learning the student role means "doing what you're told and never mind why."

Gracey contended that although kindergarten is designed to teach the student role, it may also be viewed as anticipatory socialization for adult life. Many children "will more than likely find themselves working in large-scale bureaucratic organizations, perhaps on the assembly line in the factory, perhaps in the paper routines of the white collar occupations, where they will be required to submit to rigid routines imposed by 'the company' which may make little sense to them." He concluded that those who learn to conform in school may also become successful bureaucratic functionaries as adults.

TAKING A CLOSER LOOK

Most schools (including those Gracey studied) contend that kindergarten is an enlightening experience for youngsters—a time when they learn to be away from parents; develop some prereading and premathematics skills; and learn to be independent, think for themselves, and develop the social and intellectual skills that will help them succeed in school and life. How does this view contrast with Gracey's findings? Do kindergarten and later school experiences produce bureaucratic human robots, as Gracey suggested? Is Gracey's research conducted in the 1970s still relevant in the twenty-first century?

Source: Harry L. Gracey. "Learning the Student Role: Kindergarten as Academic Boot Camp." In Harry L. Gracey, *Curriculum or Craftsmanship: Elementary School Teachers in a Bureaucratic System.* Chicago: University of Chicago Press, 1972:163–174.

Anticipatory socialization is not limited to teaching the student role. Less complex societies place very little importance on being a student, as the major function of education is to teach survival skills, sex roles, and the oral history and traditions of the tribe or village. Sometimes the family takes responsibility for these tasks, but even in small preindustrial societies responsibility for education often is removed from the family and relegated to people trained specifically for that purpose.

Education in industrial and postindustrial societies has a more difficult task in providing anticipatory socialization. Technological advancement is almost always accompanied by a sophisticated division of labor. Large numbers of skilled workers are needed to fill a variety of highly specialized occupational roles. Schools must attempt to match students' talents and abilities to an ever-changing job market in an effort to balance supply and demand in certain fields. Inevitably there is a lag between the needs of business and industry and the educational institution's ability to produce qualified people. Consequently, alternating "shortages" and "gluts" occur when schools produce either too few or too many specialists in certain fields. Still, employers contend that it is important that prospective employees possess the necessary cognitive and occupational skills that jobs in a high-tech and changing world demand.

Social and Cultural Integration

In relatively homogeneous societies, such as Japan, where people share common ethnic, religious, social, and cultural backgrounds, teachers worry little about education's integration function. In societies marked by social and cultural diversity, such as Great Britain and the United States, however, an important integrating force is a common educational experience. **Integration** means *bringing together people from diverse social backgrounds so that they share common social experiences and develop commonly held norms, attitudes, and beliefs.*

Education for Assimilation   It is no accident that most states in the United States implemented compulsory school attendance laws at a time when millions of immigrants were flocking to America's shores. Mandatory education in American public schools ensured that immigrants' children would learn to speak English, become acquainted with American history and government, and become at least partially acculturated, if not fully assimilated. Mandatory attendance laws did not guarantee, however, that children from different races, nationalities, and religions would be welcomed by other groups, nor did they ensure that all social classes would come into social contact, as neighborhood schools usually reflected community segregation patterns.

Education and Racial Desegregation   In the early 1950s, the racial integration function of American public education was underscored when a second grader named Linda Brown was not allowed to enroll in an elementary school only a few blocks from her home in Topeka, Kansas. Instead, she was forced to walk over half a mile to a bus stop and be transported to an all-black school over 2 miles away. Linda's parents filed suit, and in the 1954 case *Brown* v. *Board of Education of Topeka,* the U.S. Supreme Court rendered a unanimous decision that struck down the commonly held separate-but-equal doctrine, which had supported the racial segregation of public schools. The court ruled that separate schools were "inherently unequal" and that blacks were receiving inferior education compared to whites. While this ruling eliminated de jure (supported by law) segregation in American public schools, de facto (in fact) segregation continued well into the 1960s and 1970s—and in many areas, it persists today. Research indicates that in urban school districts large enrollments of whites in *nonpublic* schools lead to large minority enrollments in *public* schools (Bankston and Caldas, 2000; Hadnot and Parks, 2003). Despite polls showing that Americans overwhelmingly say they support integrated education, since the 1980s public schools have become increasingly *resegregated* (Hadnot and Parks, 2003). In fact in one school district in Omaha, Nebraska, a state legislator proposed to make resegregation official with three separate school boards: one white, one black, and one Hispanic (NBC, 2006).

Education and "Americanization"   The integration function of public schools in the United States extends well beyond racial desegregation. Mass public education involves assimilation and an *Americanization* process, teaching patriotism, nationalism, and basic American values and sharing a common academic curriculum. As we have noted, there is much debate over precisely what "basic" American values should be

INTEGRATION
Bringing together people from diverse social backgrounds so that they share common social experiences and develop commonly held norms, attitudes, and beliefs.

taught. Nevertheless, even extracurricular activities, especially high school athletics, help integrate students from diverse backgrounds: they wear common school colors, letter jackets, and other shared symbols that declare their sameness relative to some other group (Holland and Andre, 1991; McNeal, 1995).

Higher education continues the integration process. Different missions, academic specialties, and other unique characteristics distinguish colleges, universities, and other institutions of higher education, but most require a "core" of general education courses, many of which are transferable to other institutions and provide at least some common integrative elements for all who receive a college degree.

Innovation and Cultural Change

Besides being charged with transmitting what is already known, the schools are also supposed to develop students' intellectual skills and creativity and foster the production of new knowledge and technology. **Innovation** involves *creating new knowledge and finding new ways to use existing knowledge.* Even in the most traditional tribal societies, innovative ideas and inventions that provide a better way of performing a task or enhance the quality of life usually gain acceptance. In highly technological societies such as Great Britain, Japan, and the United States, schools—especially large research universities—play an important role in creating new knowledge and technology.

Educational institutions respond slowly to change, however, and schools often must perform the delicate balancing act of trying to preserve the status quo and teach tradition while promoting social innovation and cultural change. This is particularly true in countries like Great Britain and Japan where tremendous emphasis is placed on history, tradition, and social custom. One of the authors recalls touring the grounds of Cambridge with a British colleague who remarked that the "core" curriculum at Cambridge had remained relatively unchanged for the past 300 years; meanwhile the American university where the author taught had changed its general education requirements three times in the past decade.

Sometimes in the United States, innovative curricular changes and pedagogical techniques become so mired in the planning process that teachers get tired of them before they are ever implemented (Taylor, 1991). Also, as Focus box 14.2 depicts, in the United States, *educational reform* has become synonymous with more reliance on standardized testing (Parks, 2003). On the other hand, dramatic social and cultural changes have come from research. Innovative developments in medicine, robotics, engineering, genetics, chemistry, and biology have extended human life expectancy, and research in psychology, sociology, and the humanities has enhanced the quality of life.

INNOVATION
Creating new knowledge and finding new ways to use existing knowledge.

One of the latent functions of elementary schools in the United States is that they serve as one of the largest day-care systems in the world.

Latent Functions of Education

Social institutions not only fulfill the manifest functions for which they were intended but also perform latent functions with unintended and sometimes unrecognized consequences. In the United States, for example, public and private kindergartens and elementary schools constitute the largest day-care system in the world. Middle schools and high schools reinforce norms related to adolescence and help prolong the transition from childhood to adulthood (Rogers, 1985; Zastrow and Kirst-Ashman, 1990). Moreover, they help delay the entry of youths into the labor market, where they would compete with adults for jobs. Postsecondary education further delays

What are some of the other latent functions of American schools?

entry into the world of work, and institutions of higher education sometimes provide havens for the unemployed, divorced and widowed, and others who return to school, retrain for new occupations, or work on advanced degrees.

In 1983, the National Commission on Education Excellence published *A Nation at Risk,* concluding that the United States was suffering from a "rising tide of mediocrity." Reports from the American College Testing Program and other compilers of standardized test scores indicated that assessment might be overly generous.

Concerned about declining test scores and poor academic performance, task forces at the local, state, and national levels developed plans to strengthen curricula, extend school days, increase literacy, return to basics, and enhance students' abilities in mathematics and science. Despite these efforts, performance on standardized exams improved only slightly; in comparison to other industrial and postindustrial nations through the end of the twentieth century, American students rated among the lowest (Levine and Havighurst, 1992; Benton 2001; U.S. Department of Education, 2001).

In 2002, at the urging of President George W. Bush, Congress enacted the No Child Left Behind (NCLB) program, a series of federal laws mandating that all states implement standardized tests to assess student performance, evaluate schools, and improve education. NCLB promises that teachers must be "highly qualified" in the subjects they teach and that each year schools must demonstrate that increased numbers of students have achieved state standards. School districts are required to test students in math and English in grades 3 through 8 every year, and students in grades 10 through 12 must be tested in those subjects at least once.

Optimism about the reform benefits of No Child Left Behind waned when states and local school districts discovered the federal government failed to adeqately fund its ambitious mandates. Connecticut's Attorney General filed suit in federal court to block NCLB in his state arguing that the policy was "mistaken" and "misguided" (Reuters, 2006). He indicated that there was not adequate funding for the state to test in a way to maintain its already high standards, and that in fact, to adhere to NCLB, Connecticut would have to "dumb down" its tests to the point that they would be inadequate. In their book, *Many Children Left Behind,* editors Deborah Meir and George Wood (2004) offer a litany of America's most respected educators who view NCLB as a disaster for public education. For example, Linda Darling-Hammond points out that NCLB mistakes *measuring* schools for *fixing them,* and illustrates how many schools have been forced to lower their standards rather than increase them, while still others improve their performance by making sure that low performing students leave school. Ted Sizer argues that NCLB fails to address causes of school failure and ignores all meaningful reforms suggested by educators, focusing instead on standardized testing in only three subjects: English, mathematics, and beginning in 2007, science. Peter Schrag (2004) simply calls No Child Left Behind "Bush's educational fraud." Most educators agree that NCLB has transformed schools that used to emphasize critical thinking and writing skills, as well as developing well rounded graduates knowledgeable in history, literature, social sciences, fine arts and applied technology, into mere testing centers that focus on achieving passing scores on standardized examinations.

Sources: Paul E. Peterson, and Martin R. West (eds.). *No Child Left Behind?: The Politics and Practice of School Accountability.* Washington, DC: Brookings Institution, 2004; Peter Schrag. "Bush's Education Fraud." *The American Prospect* 15 (February), 2004. Deborah Meier, and George Wood (eds.). *No Child Left Behind: How the No Child Left Behind Act Is Damaging our Children and Our Schools.* Boston: Beacon Press, 2005; Reuters, New Haven. "State Seeks to Block 'No Child Left Behind'." Reuters, February 10, 2006.

College and university campuses also serve as large dating and marriage markets. People usually choose marriage partners of similar educational attainment and background, and many college graduates meet their spouses while attending school (Mare, 1991). A number of important social networks are created in college. Lifelong friendships are formed, and fraternity and sorority affiliations often pay off later in securing employment, promotions, raises, and other occupational opportunities. Again, as one of the authors walked the grounds at Cambridge, a British colleague remarked that students not only received an excellent education at Cambridge but could count on meeting classmates who would go on to powerful positions in the Anglican church, politics, and business—thus developing a network that may prove to be as important as their education. This is even more so the case in Britain than in Japan.

Finally, as we discuss next, the unequal allocation of educational resources and credentials and the channeling of high school students into either vocational education or college preparatory courses support and perpetuate basic patterns of social stratification (Parsons, 1959; Collins, 1971; Kozol, 1992, 2001, 2006). Sociologists generally agree that the present system bolsters existing social differences related to race, sex, ethnicity, and social class.

EDUCATION AND SOCIAL STRATIFICATION: A CONFLICT PERSPECTIVE

In Chapters 8 and 9 we analyzed social stratification, a form of inequality that results from the ranking of people and entire countries into a social hierarchy based on the distribution of scarce and valued resources. Education plays a crucial role in the stratification scheme of most societies, particularly those that place tremendous value on knowledge and technology. Consequently, from a conflict perspective, education is a valued resource, an end in itself, which is unequally distributed in a society; at the same time, it can be used as a means of achieving other socially desired attributes, such as wealth, power, prestige, and material possessions.

Conflict theorists point out that although mass education is emphasized and has the potential to promote equality, in both capitalist and socialist societies the educational institution promotes and perpetuates inequality. This analysis focuses on unequal access to schooling and inequality among schools, schools' hidden curriculum, how educational credentials enable schools to act as "screening devices" for society, and the link between educational attainment and unequal occupational opportunities (Collins, 1971; Illich, 1983; Sadovnik, 1991; Hanley and McKeever, 1997; Kozol, 2001, 2006).

Unequal Access to Schooling and Educational Inequality

Karl Marx and Friedrich Engels ([1848] 1964) argued for universal access to free education, believing that limited access to education served as a tool used by the bourgeoisie to dominate and exploit the proletariat. Indeed, historically, formal education was reserved for the wealthy, elite, and ruling classes and was associated more with leisure than with work. As our discussions of education in Great Britain and the United States indicated, it was not until after their industrial revolutions that mass education became a goal, and Japan did not embrace the concept until after World War II. Today, in the United States and many other countries, the belief in equal access to schooling is viewed as a measure of a nation's commitment not only to knowledge and technology but also to individual freedom and social mobility. But is that the case?

Unequal Access to Schools The United States was one of the first countries to embrace the goal of universal education, and a larger percentage of Americans graduate high school than in any other period of history. Yet the dream is far from realized. Unequal access to schooling still exists because of poverty, social isolation, and a number of other factors. Despite federal programs such as Head Start and others designed to enhance the educational opportunities of targeted minorities, members of those minorities continue to suffer unequal access to schooling, especially early childhood education for 3–5-year-olds (Bainbridge et al., 2005). Also, research indicates that "a Head Start does not last" and that "poor kids need intensive help long after they leave nursery school" in order to compete with the nonpoor (Kantrowitz and McCormick, 1992:44). Moreover, in 2003 the federal government developed a plan to give standardized tests to Head Start students to determine if funding should be continued—a controversial plan since most preschoolers cannot read (AP, Washington, 2003). A United States Department of Education study, *The Condition of Education, 2001,* indicates that there are disturbing gaps in educational participation and academic performance among different racial/ethnic and socioeconomic groups. These differences appear early and tend to persist (U.S. Department of Education, 2001a; Wertheimer, 2002).

Inequality between Private and Public Schools in the United States
Some of the most pronounced educational inequalities exist between private and public schools. James Coleman and Thomas Hoffer (1987) reported that in the United States, students who attend private schools score higher on standardized academic achievement tests and college entrance exams than students in public schools. This research also suggested that private schools, because they have more demanding college preparatory curricula, smaller class sizes, and stricter disciplinary policies, may be more effective than public schools. Because of high tuition, the cost of uniforms and books, and other

expenses, private schooling is beyond the reach of most lower-class and many middle-class families. Magnet schools with enhanced curricula have been developed in some public school districts to simulate the opportunities provided by private schools, but with a few notable exceptions they have done little to diminish the difference in opportunities available to children from lower- and upper-income families (Henig, 1990).

Not only do small private schools often provide better elementary and secondary education, they also enhance the likelihood of admission to some of the most prestigious universities. Sociologists point out that inequality in American education is not simply a result of the differences between private and public schools, however. Even among public schools designed to provide equal educational opportunities, there are great discrepancies in the quality of education.

Inequalities Among and Within America's Public Schools A team of researchers headed by sociologist James Coleman (1966) studied almost 650,000 students in over 4,000 schools. The *Coleman Report* stated that predominantly white schools were better funded and better equipped and had smaller classes, better laboratory facilities, better libraries, superior curricula, and more extracurricular activities. In *Savage Inequalities,* his exposé of inequality in the American educational system, Jonathan Kozol (1991) reported that very little had changed 25 years later. Moreover, while there is no organization called "Rich Parents against School Reform," there is mounting evidence that upper-middle-class parents have very little desire to rectify the educational inequalities that benefit their children at the expense of those who are less fortunate (Kohn, 1988; Kozol, 1991, 1996, 2001, 2006).

A surprising and controversial finding of the *Coleman Report* was that there appears to be very little relationship between the amount of money spent on a school and student achievement. Rather, a family's socioeconomic status, parental attitudes toward education, lack of availability of books in the home, and the overall social environment in poorer schools are linked to inequality in education. A later study appeared to confirm that inequality in the schools *reflects* rather than *causes* inequality in the larger society (Jencks et al., 1972). Other studies indicate that social variables related to the existing stratification largely determine educational aspirations and are the best predictors of educational success and attainment (Cerverno and Kirkpatrick, 1990; Alwin, 1991; Astone and McLanahan, 1991; Clausen, 1991; Crane, 1991; Karen, 1991; Hanson, 1994; Kalmijn, 1994; Pirog and Magee, 1997).

Kozol's book, *The Shame of the Nation* (2006), however, casts serious doubts on the idea that there is little relationship between school funding and educational inequality. He acknowledges that family socioeconomic status is linked to academic success, but even more important is the relative ability of local school districts to provide quality public education to children. In wealthy school districts, higher tax revenues provide better buildings, higher teacher salaries, and more and better instructional equipment and supplies. Kozol pointed out that while wealthy parents insist that spending more money on poor children's education would not increase its quality, they are convinced that spending any less on their children's education would seriously weaken its quality. Kozol is not alone in his dissent from the *Coleman Report*. A comprehensive study of data synthesized from the National Assessment of Educational Progress indicated that school spending is both directly and indirectly related to achievement: higher per-pupil expenditures provide more positive school environments and are linked to reduced class sizes, which in turn are linked to higher achievement (Wenglinsky, 1997).

School facilities vary greatly between school districts and among schools within a district. Many of America's public schools are in serious disrepair. In many districts, the so-called three R's are now regarded as readin', 'ritin', and renovation.

Unequal Access to Higher Education Beyond the elementary and secondary levels, unequal access to higher educational opportunities resurfaces as a major issue. In the United States, college attendance and graduation have steadily increased. Polls indicate that an overwhelming majority of parents in the United States aspire for their children to attend college, but college enrollments indicate that parents' aspirations exceed their children's opportunities. First-generation students who do not take a rigorous aca-

How do these two high school science labs reflect the inequality of education in the United States? What can be done to reduce the disparity in educational opportunities to students in different school districts?

demic high school curriculum are less likely to continue toward a bachelor's degree than their peers who have at least one parent with a college degree (U.S. Department of Education, 2001a). Despite scholarships, grants, and loans from federal, state, and private sources, parental education, family income, and the ability to acquire capital remain the most important variables in access to college (Mare, 1981; Steelman and Powell, 1989, 1991; Clausen, 1991; Karen, 1991; Duncan et al., 1998; Rouse, 2004).

Educational Credentials: Schools as a Screening Device

One of the recognized activities of schools is the awarding of educational credentials in the form of grades, certificates, diplomas, and degrees. In the United States, education promotes a fundamental American value that includes the belief in equal opportunities but not equal outcomes (Phelan et al., 1995). Thus, while the system is theoretically open to all, a decreasing proportion of Americans reach each level on the scale of educational credentials. For example, as Figure 14.1 illustrates, approximately 80 percent of Americans over the age of 25 hold a high school diploma, but only 24.4 percent have earned at least a bachelor's degree, 6.7 percent a master's degree, and less than 2 percent a doctorate (U.S. Bureau of the Census, 2006). Most of us would like to believe that this pyramidal distribution of educational credentials is directly linked to academic skills, intellectual abilities, and desire for education. Unfortunately, while those variables contribute to the awarding of academic credentials, other criteria are also quite important.

The "Hidden Curriculum" We have discussed the cognitive and normative aspects of education and some of the issues that surround the academic curriculum of both public and private schools. In most countries today, educational systems and individual schools publish their curricula and distribute them to prospective students and their parents, a variety of accrediting and governmental agencies, and other interested parties. As noted earlier, school curricula around the world, and across the United States, are remarkably similar in content. But, again, if we take a closer sociological look at education we discover that things are not necessarily what they seem.

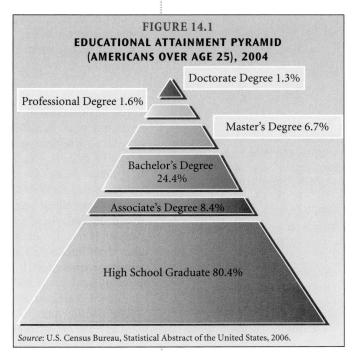

FIGURE 14.1
EDUCATIONAL ATTAINMENT PYRAMID
(AMERICANS OVER AGE 25), 2004

Doctorate Degree 1.3%

Professional Degree 1.6%

Master's Degree 6.7%

Bachelor's Degree 24.4%

Associate's Degree 8.4%

High School Graduate 80.4%

Source: U.S. Census Bureau, Statistical Abstract of the United States, 2006.

In addition to the stated curricula, sociologists using the conflict approach assert that all schools also contain a **hidden curriculum** *designed to teach the dominant values and norms of society and reinforce the status quo* (Apple, 1979, 1993; Illich, 1983). According to the conflict perspective, this hidden curriculum acts as a form of social control by promoting conformity, docility, obedience to authority, and legitimation of the existing social structure. For example, feminists argue that educational institutions bolster traditional gender roles and often promote and perpetuate gender stereotypes and inequities through a male-dominated curriculum and portrayal of gender roles in textbooks and teaching materials. Likewise, members of various racial and ethnic minority groups contend that **Eurocentrism,** *a focus on the contributions of Europeans to history, math, science, and literature,* is an essential part of the hidden curriculum in most American schools (Asante, 1997). Consequently, from the conflict perspective, inequalities in society are reinforced and perpetuated rather than eliminated by mass education. How? One way is the school's role as a screening device.

Screening in America's Public Schools Sociologist Howard Becker (1952) studied the Chicago public schools and found that curriculum, teachers, and administrators showed strong biases in favor of white middle-class children. Similarly, in *Death at an Early Age,* Jonathan Kozol (1967) exposed the cynicism, prejudice, and racism directed at lower-class black students in the Boston public schools by their middle-class white teachers. Research indicates that similar attitudes carry over into higher education, where members of minority groups and students from poor backgrounds experience both subtle and overt prejudice and discrimination (Nettles, 1990; Steele, 1992). Kozol (2006) contends that America's schools are restoring apartheid in the nation.

Edgar Friedenberg (1959) asserted that schools act as a screening device by filtering out students at different educational levels to fill positions of unequal status in society. While this process is viewed as legitimate because of its alleged link to academic and intellectual abilities, Friedenberg argued that it is more closely related to students' willingness to conform to middle-class white Anglo-Saxon Protestant (WASP) normative expectations. Thus Friedenberg determined that success or failure in school depends as much on racism, sexism, ethnocentrism, and conformity as on intellectual skills and academic abilities. An important study indicated that when employers seek white-collar professional workers, they view education as a screening device for desirable middle-class values, character, and demeanor (Collins, 1971). Thus from the conflict perspective a predominant goal of schools' hidden curricula is to teach the elite's culture, or at least a healthy respect for it, not to transmit knowledge and technical skills. The achievement of educational credentials, especially advanced university degrees, represents perseverance through the "educational pipeline," or what some might call "playing the academic game," which many minority segments of the population are not willing to do (McJamerson, 1991).

Tracking One of the ways elementary and secondary schools implement their screening process is through **tracking**—*placing students perceived to have similar intelligence and academic abilities in the same classroom.* On the basis of standardized test scores and previous academic performance, students viewed as having little or no chance of attending college are placed on vocational tracks designed to prepare them for trades, skilled labor, or admission to postsecondary vocational and technical schools. Students who seem more academically and intellectually suited for college are placed on a college preparatory track, and some schools provide advanced tracks, or Advanced Placement (AP) courses, for those viewed as "gifted and talented." While tracking is usually justified on academic grounds, numerous studies show that factors other than intellectual and academic abilities, such as race, socioeconomic status, and demeanor, often determine a child's placement and that tracking reinforces preexisting social inequalities (Oakes, 1985; Kohn, 1988; Gamoran and Mare, 1989; Kilgore, 1991; Hallinan, 1994; Scott, 2001).

The conflict perspective does not view schools as responsible for creating social inequality; it views the educational institution as reflecting and perpetuating the hierarchical social system outside schools. Moreover, much of the hidden curriculum is used

HIDDEN CURRICULUM
An aspect of education designed to teach dominant norms, values, and consensus ideology.

EUROCENTRISM
A focus on the contributions of Europeans to history, math, science, and literature.

TRACKING
Placing students perceived to have similar intelligence and academic abilities in the same classroom.

TABLE 14.1
MEDIAN INCOME IN 2003 BY EDUCATIONAL ATTAINMENT FOR PEOPLE 18 YEARS OLD AND OVER

EDUCATION LEVEL	AGE GROUP			
	25–34	35–44	45–54	55–64
High School Dropout	$15,253	$16,669	$16,077	$13,778
High School Diploma	$22,001	$25,929	$26,764	$22,056
Some College	$25,040	$30,705	$32,252	$29,010
Associate's Degree	$27,944	$32,272	$35,445	$30,798
Bachelor's Degree	$36,429	$45,419	$45,851	$42,268
Master's Degree	$42,800	$51,613	$56,881	$55,287
Doctorate	$51,790	$86,734	$92,372	$93,571
Professional Degree	$51,569	$71,514	$76,139	$75,791

Source: U.S. Census Bureau, www.census.gov/population/socdemo/education/cps2004/tab08-1.pdf, 10–21.

"to assign social rank" by teaching children to know their place and to stay in it (Illich, 1983:17). One of the most important ramifications of the schools is the relationship between educational attainment and occupational opportunities.

Education and Occupational Opportunities in the United States

What was your primary motivation for attending college? When first-year college students across the United States are asked that question, their most common responses are "To get a better job" and "To make more money." Was your answer similar? Data indicate that additional education indeed translates into additional income (see Table 14.1). Studies indicate that while formal schooling has always been linked to occupational access, it is more important today than ever before (Hunter, 1988; Schultz, 1994; Pirog and Magee, 1997; U.S. Bureau of Census, 2000).

Sociologist Randall Collins (1971) contends that Americans are obsessed with educational credentials, viewing them as the most tangible evidence of a person's ability to perform certain jobs and roles. He argues that diplomas, certificates, and degrees are important not because they reflect skills, abilities, and training but because they provide a mechanism for differentiating between job applicants. Because of this **credentialism**—an *overemphasis on educational credentials*—many individuals must settle for jobs for which they are overeducated. Some research, however, suggests that individuals' cognitive skills and abilities, and not solely their credentials, are directly related to better jobs and higher incomes (Farkas et al., 1997). Still other studies indicate that race, ethnicity, gender, and family's socioeconomic status account for much of the discrepancies in academic preparation, performance, grades, and attainment of credentials (Bankston et al., 1997; Bankston and Caldas, 1997; Pirog and Magee, 1997).

EDUCATION AND EVERYDAY LIFE: AN INTERACTIONIST VIEW

Sociologists who use the interactionist perspective are interested in the day-to-day activities that take place in schools and how they affect students, teachers, and administrators in those social worlds. In most countries by the time a child is age 5 or 6 the family relinquishes part of its socialization responsibilities to the school, and with the proliferation and popularity of preschools and kindergartens many children begin their educational careers even earlier. Consequently, a large portion of the most critical

CREDENTIALISM
Overemphasis on educational credentials.

period of personal and social development is spent in school. The average young person in the United States spends approximately 15,000 hours in school, so the social milieu of the schools is a very important contributor to a child's personal and social development.

Socialization: Personal and Social Development

In Chapter 4, we discussed the socialization process and how development of a self and a social identity occurs through interaction with others. Since children spend such a great deal of time in school, it follows that being a student is a critical part of a young person's identity.

Much of the educational experience is designed to produce conformity, transmit culture, reinforce social values and norms, and prepare students for roles they will assume as adults. Beyond these practical aspects, however, schools also provide young people with a society where they interact with peers, teachers, and administrators and learn to operate within the boundaries of both formal and informal normative systems. Through this process, students learn a great deal about themselves and others, and they develop attitudes, values, beliefs, and a sense of self that influence the rest of their lives. Research indicates that students who drop out of school often do so because they have been unable to become a meaningful part of the school social environment (Farrell, 1990). In fact, a longitudinal study of dropouts in Baltimore concluded that dropping out of school begins in the first grade and is "the culmination of a long-term process of academic disengagement" (Alexander et al., 1997:87).

Labeling Students: The Self-Fulfilling Prophecy

According to Greek mythology, the sculptor Pygmalion fell in love with a statue of a beautiful woman that he had created. In the George Bernard Shaw play *Pygmalion* (which was adapted into the musical *My Fair Lady*), a similar fate befell Professor Henry Higgins when he transformed the lower-class, uncultured Eliza Doolittle into the beautiful and charming lady of his dreams. In education, the **Pygmalion effect** *occurs when teachers who expect students to succeed and excel are motivated to work with them to ensure that they do;* teachers may ignore youngsters expected to fail until they, too, achieve the anticipated outcome. Thus labeling students often leads to a **self-fulfilling prophecy,** when *predictions about students' abilities shape the students' future actions and behaviors in such a way that the predictions come true.* Often these labels and prophecies may be inspired by nonacademic factors, such as race, gender, and social class.

How powerful are the labels that teachers attach to students? And what happens when students are mislabeled? Psychologists Robert Rosenthal and Lenore Jacobson (1968) devised an experiment to test the impact of labeling students. All students at an elementary school were administered a standardized IQ test. At the beginning of the next school term the teachers were given the names of the students who had been identified as extremely intelligent on the basis of their test scores. (The students' names were chosen randomly, without regard to the students' test scores or prior academic performance.) The teachers were told that these "special" students could be expected to learn at a far more rapid rate than their peers. At the end of the school year, the students labeled as more intelligent had achieved far greater academic gains than others in their classes, even though the only difference between them resided in the teachers' expectations. Other studies show that prior achievement, teacher expectations, and instructional support are linked to subsequent academic performance (Dusek, 1985; Whitener, 1989; Rossi, 1994; Oates, 2003).

Schools not only place academically oriented labels (e.g., smart, dumb, gifted, or slow learners) on students but also label students with regard to their personalities, appearance, demeanor, and level of conformity. Students perceived as smart alecks, troublemakers, or cheaters find it almost impossible to shake those negative labels, just as students considered sociable and intellectually gifted benefit from their accomplishments, both real and perceived. In addition to affecting grades and other academic credentials, the labeling process has a significant impact on social interaction among students, teachers, and administrators.

PYGMALION EFFECT
Occurs when teachers expect students to succeed and excel and are motivated to work with them to ensure that they do. Teachers may also ignore youngsters expected to fail until they, too, achieve the anticipated outcome (a form of self-fulfilling prophecy).

SELF-FULFILLING PROPHECY
When predictions about students' abilities shape the students' future actions and behaviors in such a way that the predictions come true.

An elementary teacher helps a student with her reading.

How would you apply the concept of labeling, "the Pygmalion effect," or self-fulfilling prophecy to this photo?

Student-Teacher Interaction

Many students simply tolerate going to classes, doing homework, and taking examinations. To them, the important business of school is maintaining their social lives. Studies show that students would rather be labeled star athletes, good-looking, and popular than smart or brilliant. Also, the boys and girls considered most popular in elementary school are those who most closely reflect the idealized images of masculinity and femininity. In an effort to structure their everyday world of social interaction in the schools, students often form social cliques based on common interests and activities and shared meaningful symbols. Being identified as a jock, Goth, skinhead, preppie, roper, doper, or nerd may have far more impact on an adolescent's self-concept and behavior in school than do other, more traditionally researched social variables, such as race, ethnicity, sex, or parents' social class. Cliques, usually formed during elementary school, become most pronounced during the middle school and high school years, and many of them even carry over into college (Coleman, 1961; Goodlad, 1984; Schwendinger and Schwendinger, 1985; Holland and Andre, 1991; Adler et al., 1992; Wooden, 1995; Desetta, 2006).

Many students who enter college directly after high school view this phase of their education also more in terms of its social significance than in terms of its academic importance. The growing ranks of nontraditional students (over age 25) in colleges and universities, however, are altering the social aspects of campus life across the United States and in many other countries. Trying to combine work, family, child rearing, and class attendance often leaves little time for social life, but even then being a student becomes an important part of a person's social identity.

While much student interaction is based on primary relationships with peers and teachers, it also occurs within a bureaucratic framework that shapes and affects everyday life.

Schools as Bureaucracy: Dehumanization of Education

When sociologist Max Weber coined the term, nothing could have been further from a *bureaucracy* than American schools. In most communities, the one-room schoolhouse, in which one teacher was charged with educating children in grades 1 through 8, was the norm. The teacher knew each child and his or her parents intimately, and because of the wide range of ages and abilities in the same classroom the teacher developed highly personalized curricula for individual students. Today, even in the most isolated rural areas, schools have been consolidated into large formal organizations that operate on the bureaucratic model. In metropolitan areas, large urban and suburban high schools issue photo identification cards to administrators, faculty, staff, and students, and they resemble major corporations more than their one-room forerunners.

The Advantages of Bureaucratic Structure

Organizing schools into bureaucratic structures has some advantages. Academic standardization meets the needs of a highly mobile society, allowing students to transfer from one school to another with only minor scholastic difficulties. Standardized policies and rules protect individual administrators, teachers, and students from the whims of school board members and others in positions of authority. Teachers must be certified to teach specific subjects and grade levels and are rarely asked to teach subjects beyond their academic training or expertise. In large school systems, students can choose from a variety of courses and can orient their education toward future academic, vocational, and professional goals.

Disadvantages of Bureaucratic Education

Bureaucratic education also has its drawbacks, however. When people are forced to operate within bureaucracies every day, they become engrossed in their bureaucratic roles, personally and socially alienated, and, to some extent, less human (Hummel, 1977). This alienation and dehumanization permeates much of contemporary education. Parents complain that they have lost control over the schools, whereas administrators often feel they are little more than bureaucratic functionaries (Wolcott, 1973). And teachers, faced with increased educational and certification requirements, mountains of paperwork, mounting discipline problems, and increasing threats of potential litigation by parents and students, feel they are only cogs in a heartless machine.

Perhaps the biggest losers in the educational bureaucracy are the students. In large schools, where students are treated more like numbers than individuals, many lose interest and give up. Others thread their way through the bureaucratic red tape that stands between them and their diplomas, and still others search for ways to humanize the educational process and manipulate the system to their own ends. And if teachers feel alienated, some of their frustrations may be taken out by becoming more authoritarian toward the one group less powerful than them—the students (Rothstein, 1996).

While it is naive and unfair to suggest that the widespread problems facing the schools today are caused entirely by their bureaucratic structure, researchers warn that bureaucratic structure leads to uniformity, emphasis on numbers, rigid expectations, and student passivity in the learning process (Sizer, 1984; Lounsbury and Clark, 1990). Educational reformers urge Americans to humanize their schools by reducing class size, making class schedules more flexible, increasing curricular offerings, and training teachers more broadly and encouraging them to become more socially involved with their students (Sizer, 1984; Wasley, 2003). Unfortunately, most of these reforms require additional money—something many school districts are either unable or unwilling to allocate.

CONTEMPORARY TRENDS IN AMERICAN EDUCATION

Trends in contemporary American education reflect both stability and change. Concern over declining test scores and poor academic performance has led to increased emphasis on standardized testing and rating public schools. Some public schools have rearranged their calendars to implement year-round schooling, while scores of parents have taken their children out of the public schools in favor of charter schools or home schooling. Diversity and multicultural education have become prominent issues in public education at all levels and the role of community colleges has expanded dramatically. Meanwhile, schools at all levels face numerous challenges including inadequate funding, lack of discipline, violence, drugs, and teacher shortages. Let's take a brief sociological look at each of these contemporary trends.

Standardized Testing

Declining test scores and poor academic performance by American students during the 1970s and 1980s prompted numerous studies and reports, almost all of which concluded that public schools in the United States were in need of serious revamping. Surveys showed that American children were less prepared to enter school than ever before (*Newsweek*, 1991a), while research indicated that Head Start and similar programs failed to adequately "catch up" unprepared children (Kantrowitz and McCormick, 1992), and the Third International Mathematics and Science Study concluded that American students were outperformed in those subjects by students in 14 industrialized and postindustrial nations (U.S. Department of Education, 2001a).

In 2002, fueled by reformers' demands that schools get "back to basics," Congress enacted the No Child Left Behind program which mandated that all states implement standardized testing to assess student performance (Stutz, 2002). For the first time, school funding, and in some cases, teachers' salaries, tenure, and professional futures, became directly related to students' performances on standardized tests. As Focus box 14.2 suggested, these developments shifted educational reform efforts away from a focus on cognitive and normative socialization in all academic areas including the applied arts, fine arts, and humanities, to a single-minded overemphasis on standardized testing in at first only two academic areas: English and mathematics, and later, a third: science (Meier and Wood, 2005; Stutz, 2006).

Conservatives, moderates, and liberals all seem to agree that there is a need for reform in American education. Many believe that meaningful reform requires a "back to basics movement," and call for a return to the curricula and teaching methods of the past—perhaps even returning to the one-room schoolhouse. Others argue that educational reform must look to the future and incorporate state-of-the-art technologies, mass media, and the technomedia to prepare students adequately for the world of tomorrow. While some education critics argued that the schools were failing to prepare students in the basic skills, and others argued that No Child Left Behind and standardized testing forced schools to emphasizing the wrong things, still others questioned why American students spend so little time in school as compared to their counterparts in other parts of the world.

Year-Round Education

Earlier in this chapter we looked briefly at schooling in Great Britain, Japan, and the United States—three countries whose schools are considered to be among the best in the world. Americans are concerned, however, that on standardized achievement tests and other academic performance indicators, American students often lag behind their British and Japanese counterparts. Some believe it is because American students spend less time in school. The average school year in Great Britain is 191 days. Japanese students, however, spend 240 days per year in school. The average school year in the United States is 178 days—two weeks shorter than in Britain and two months shorter than in Japan (*U.S. News & World Report,* 1996). Moreover, American students spend fewer hours per year in school than British students (1,460 compared to 1,800) and a little over one-third as many hours as Japanese students, who are in class approximately 3,200 hours per year (Hazleton, 1995).

Many Americans believe that schools in the United States may not be realizing their potential because they are held captive by an inefficient traditional nineteenth-century agrarian school calendar that has little relevance for twenty-first century urban America. In many small school districts across the United States, the largest and most expensive building in the community is the public school. Yet in many cases, that building is occupied for only 6 to 8 hours per day, 5 days per week, less than 180 days per year. The rest of the time it sits empty—unused by those whose taxes paid for it and those for whom it was built.

To address this issue, a growing number of school districts each year are adopting longer school days, extended calendars, or some other form of year-round education. **Year-round education** refers to *changing the traditional school calendar to extend instructional time or to rearrange the use of that time.* Initially met with resistance, various forms of year-round education are gaining popularity as school administrators and patrons realize they can more efficiently use school buildings, limited resources, and instructional time. Moreover, as one analyst noted, the trend toward year-round schooling reflects more than merely a desire to rearrange the educational calendar. It indicates a shift in educational philosophy "viewing time in school as a resource, not as a constraint, in providing continuous, flexible learning opportunities for all students" (Hazleton, 1995:21). For some, however, changes in the public schools represent too little, too late, as each year more parents opt to remove their children from the nation's public schools, and either have them attend private schools, start their own charter schools, or educate them at home.

Charter Schools and School Vouchers

When parents believe that the public schools are not meeting their children's needs or providing an adequate education, but they cannot afford to place their children in private schools, they must look for other alternatives. Two possible alternatives have emerged in the form of charter schools and school vouchers.

Charter schools are *schools created by a charter (a contract between those starting the school—either individuals, parent groups, or some other organization—with a governing body with the authority to grant the charter—often, state or local school boards) that receive state and federal tax monies and are open to all who wish to attend them.* Most charter schools share at least five common features: (1) they can be created by almost any individual or group of individuals; (2) they are exempt from most state and local regulations; (3) they can be attended by any students who want to enroll in them; (4) teachers and other employees are there by choice and not assigned by any school district; and (5) they must apply to get their charters renewed by the state and can be closed for not producing satisfactory results (Knoll 2003). Most states limit the number of charters they will issue, and although the charter schools operate independently of state and local school board control, they are accountable to them in order to have their charters renewed. Proponents of charter schools contend that they are "reinventing" public education by providing meaningful options to the standard public school system

YEAR-ROUND EDUCATION
Refers to changing the traditional school calendar to extend instructional time or to rearrange the use of that time significantly.

CHARTER SCHOOLS
Schools created by a charter (a contract between those starting the school—either individuals, parent groups, or some other organization—with a governing body with the authority to grant the charter—often, state or local school boards) that receive state and federal tax monies and are open to all who wish to attend them.

(Finn et al., 2007), while their critics argue that they potentially raise separation of church and state issues, may cause financial harm to small and poor public school districts, and may lead to resegregation of public education (Bernstein, 2007). At least one national study suggests that despite less funding and a heavy reliance on inexperienced teachers, charter schools may actually test higher academically than their counterparts in the regular public schools (Winter, 2003).

Another alternative to standard public school education involves school vouchers. Voucher programs can take several forms, but essentially **vouchers** *provide tax dollars to parents to offset some of the costs of transporting their children to public schools outside their district or to help defray the tuition costs of private schools.* Proponents of vouchers believe that they give parents alternatives to their closest public school and serve to help equalize access to private education for those who otherwise could not afford the tuition and other costs (Rosen, 2000). Opponents of vouchers argue that they do not provide enough money for poor parents to send their children to private schools, but provide tax-dollar subsidies to wealthier parents who already can afford to send their children to private schools. Moreover, critics contend that vouchers siphon away much needed funding for public schools and gives it to private schools (NEA, 2002). For many who are disgusted with public education, neither charter schools nor vouchers offer suitable alternatives, so they keep their children at home and educate them themselves.

Homeschooling

Early in America's history, the family assumed responsibility for educating its younger members. In settlements of any size, however, citizens pooled their resources, built schools, and relinquished most of their educational responsibilities to qualified teachers. By the 1830s, the renowned educator Horace Mann and his colleagues had outlined a plan for public school systems that would help the United States more closely realize its goal of mass education. From the beginning, however, some people have disagreed with the philosophies and methods of the public schools, and home schooling has persisted.

It is difficult to estimate the number of youngsters involved in **homeschooling,** *where children are not sent to school but receive their formal education from one or both parents,* but estimates put the number at approximately 1.7 million or approximately 3 percent of American school-aged children (Crawford, 2000; Pink, 2006). Once almost exclusively the domain of white families, today, thousands of African American families are deciding to educate their children at home (Jonsson, 2003). Legislation and court decisions have made it legally possible in most states for parents to educate their children at home, and each year more people take advantage of that opportunity. Some states require parents or a home tutor to meet teacher certification standards, and many require parents to complete legal forms and affidavits to verify that their children are receiving instruction in state-approved curricula (Hendrickson, 1989; Shepherd, 1990; Knowles et al., 1992; Hancock and French, 1994).

Supporters of home education claim it is less expensive and more efficient than mass public education. Moreover, they cite several advantages: alleviation of school overcrowding, curricular and pedagogical alternatives not available in the public schools, strengthened family relationships, lower dropout rates, the fact that students are allowed to learn at their own rate, increased motivation, higher standardized test scores, and reduced discipline problems (Dardick, 1990). Inexpensive computer technology that is readily available today is causing some to challenge the notion that homeschooling is in any way inferior to more highly structured classroom education, prompting *Newsweek* to proclaim, "The controversial concept of homeschooling has been taken into cyberspace, tethering children with technology rather than truant officers" (Hancock and French, 1994:67). Proponents of homeschooling also believe it provides parents with the opportunity to reinforce their moral values through education—something they are not satisfied the public schools will do (Ray, 2007).

Critics of homeschooling contend that it creates as many problems as it solves. They acknowledge that, in some cases, homeschooling may offer educational opportunities superior to those found in most public schools, but they argue that few parents can provide such educational advantages. Other critics argue that much of the homeschooling

VOUCHERS

Provide tax dollars to parents to offset some of the costs of transporting their children to public schools outside their district or to help defray the tuition costs of private schools.

HOMESCHOOLING

Where children are not sent to school but receive their formal education from one or both parents.

Homeschooling is an increasingly popular trend in contemporary American education.

What are some of the potential benefits of homeschooling? What are some of the potential disadvantages?

movement is driven more by the desire to instill conservative values than to provide a well-rounded education (Apple, 2007). Some parents who withdraw their children from the schools in favor of homeschooling have an inadequate educational background and insufficient formal training to provide a satisfactory education for their children. And, despite the availability of computers and other technologies, typically parents have fewer, not more, technological resources at their disposal than do schools. Finally, some critics believe the state relinquishes too much control to parents who, serving as both surrogate teachers and school administrators, can decide when their children graduate. For example, some Arkansas legislators were outraged when they learned that a 14-year-old billiard champion from their state had graduated early from homeschooling to pursue her career as a professional pool player, prompting them to reconsider whether such cases were in compliance with the state's compulsory attendance laws (Associated Press, Little Rock, 1997).

Sociologically, homeschooling is part of a larger social movement that emphasizes individualism, reliance on computer technology, and dissatisfaction not only with mass education but also with mass everything. This movement raises some important sociological questions. For example, what about the restricted social interaction experienced by children who are educated at home? Patricia Lines, a U.S. Department of Education policy analyst, believes that the possibilities provided by technology and the promise of homeschooling are exaggerated and insists that "technology will never replace the pupil-teacher relationship" (Hancock and French, 1994:67). Also, while relationships with parents and siblings may be enhanced, is it possible that children taught at home may develop a narrow view of society? What about children who live in homogeneous neighborhoods comprised of people of the same race, socioeconomic status, and religious background? Do they experience the diversity that can be provided in the social arena of the schools? Is that important? Will home-schooled students be equipped to function in the larger diverse multicultural world? For that matter, what about students who attend public and private schools? Are they being adequately prepared to live in the diverse global society of the twenty-first century?

Diversity and Multicultural Education

Multicultural education *recognizes cultural diversity and promotes an appreciation of all cultures.* It is projected that "minority" students will soon become the majority of the population in public schools in most large and middle-sized districts throughout the United States. Recognizing this, many people believe that to create a different and better future which reflects the contributions of many cultures, the educational curriculum will have to reflect more diversity (Gollnick and Chinn, 1990; Giroux and McLaren, 1994; Banks, 1997; Nieto, 2003). Many sociologists and leading educators urge colleges and universities to increase their emphasis on cross-cultural courses, and many states now require courses or demonstrated competence in multicultural education for teacher certification (Bennett and LeCompte, 1990).

Multicultural education requires curricular and pedagogical changes that reflect a diverse society made up of a mosaic of racial and ethnic groups. Since course content and pedagogical practices may reinforce existing social stratification and inequality, multicultural education is becoming increasingly important, and there is a special emphasis on broadening the study of world history and civilization to include non-Eurocentric and non-Western cultural contributions (Sadovnik, 1991; Hancock and Biddle, 1994).

One critic noted that multicultural education must be more than a rehash of the "intercultural education" of the 1940s, which focused on individual differences between cultures instead of exploring the collective ethnic identity that represents the diversity of the United States (Olneck, 1990). Multiculturalism has become a catchphrase in contemporary academic circles, and as Solomon and Solomon (1993:184) noted, it has become probably "the most important, the most stimulating, and at the same time, the silliest movement to hit the university since the beginning of democratic education." Instead of being based on solid anthropological and sociological theories and research, it has in some cases deteriorated into mere political correctness, and its implementation may have created more of an aversion to than a respect for cultural differences (Solomon and Solomon, 1993; McLaren, 1994; Famularo, 2003). This particularly seems to be the case with the highly politicized controversy over bilingual education (Leal and

MULTICULTURAL EDUCATION
Recognizes cultural diversity and promotes an appreciation of all cultures.

Hess, 2000). Nevertheless, with increased reports of overt racism on campuses across the country and the de facto segregation found among faculty, students, and administration in most elementary, secondary, and higher education systems, the heightened awareness of multiculturalism is a contemporary educational issue in our diverse and increasingly global society.

Expanding Role of Community Colleges

Diversity and multiculturalism are not new to America's community colleges. Immigrants, minorities, and women are more highly represented on community college campuses than at four-year colleges and universities (Bailey, 2002). Community colleges play an important and expanding role in postsecondary education today, and probably will become even more important in the future. At the turn of the twenty-first century, approximately one-half of all undergraduate students enrolled for credit in postsecondary institutions were enrolled in community colleges (Bailey, 2002). Matriculation agreements in most states allow students to take general education courses at community colleges and transfer them to four-year institutions to be applied toward degrees. Moreover, many community colleges offer valuable two-year programs and a variety of noncredit classes and programs that are not available at most four-year colleges and universities. In many cases, community colleges offer smaller classes, full-time teachers whose major interest is teaching instead of research, and they feature state-of-the-art technology and classroom facilities. Nevertheless, despite their growth and expanding role in American education, community colleges are experiencing many of the same challenges as the public schools and other components of higher education.

Challenges for Education

Public opinion polls indicate that inadequate financial support, lack of discipline, violence, drug use, declining test scores and poor academic achievement are viewed as major dilemmas facing American schools. Let's briefly take a closer look at each of these sociological issues. Figure 14.2 illustrates how three of these items have consistently ranked among the major problems facing public schools, with over 10 percent of the population citing them. We also will look at a rather new challenge facing schools: a shortage of qualified teachers.

Inadequate Funding Talk to school superintendents, building principals, and teachers across the country, and one of the few things they will agree on is that they need more money. While the federal government channels millions of dollars each year into the nation's public schools, the bulk of school funding has always been generated at the state and local levels. Consequently, school spending is inequitable from state to state and from district to district within states. One of the most popular ways to finance public schools is through *ad valorem* property taxes. This mechanism appraises the value of real estate and assesses a tax on property owners, a portion of which is allocated to the local school district. Under this funding scheme schools in wealthy districts (where there is expensive housing or large businesses and industries) receive larger revenues and can allocate more money per student than those in poorer districts. Thus, because of high property values one school district in a state may assess a low property tax rate and still be able to spend $10,000 or more per student per year, while another district in the same state may tax its residents at the highest rate allowable, but because of their low-valued property may be able to allocate only $2,500 per student. Such discrepancies have prompted lawsuits in several state legislatures under mandates from state and federal courts to find more equitable ways to finance their public schools. These suits have prompted a number of revenue sharing and "Robin Hood" plans that take monies from wealthier districts and distribute them to poorer ones, which have prompted yet other lawsuits from disgruntled parents and property owners who claim it is unfair that property taxes from their homes and property are used to finance the education of children in other school districts.

Proposals have been made for the federal government to provide school vouchers that would allow parents of children who attend public schools to attend private schools at public expense. While the voucher system is gaining support (approximately one-

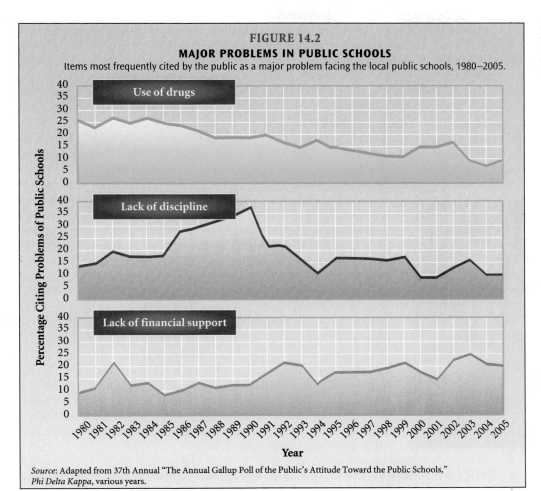

FIGURE 14.2

MAJOR PROBLEMS IN PUBLIC SCHOOLS

Items most frequently cited by the public as a major problem facing the local public schools, 1980–2005.

Source: Adapted from 37th Annual "The Annual Gallup Poll of the Public's Attitude Toward the Public Schools," *Phi Delta Kappa*, various years.

third of those surveyed say they support it), almost two-thirds of the public indicate that they believe most public schools are underfunded and that federal aid to public schools would be a much better way to improve education (Elam et al., 1996). What do you think? How should public schools be financed? What should be the role of state governments? What about the federal government?

Lack of Discipline   Many Americans believe that lack of adequate discipline is one of the most serious problems facing American public schools (Elam et al., 1996; Associated Press, 2003). Parents often blame the negative influences of mass media and celebrity role models who rebel against authority, publicly breaking rules and laws with few if any consequences. Some also blame teachers whom they believe to be reluctant to discipline students, choosing instead to ignore disruptive behavior, or send students to the office, for administrators to discipline. Teachers, on the other hand, often blame parents, who they see as failing to socialize their children with basic social skills and manners and relying on the schools to discipline their unruly children. Both teachers and administrators cite the United States' increasingly litigious culture and the number of lawsuits filed against teachers and school administrators as inhibiting discipline in both public and private schools.

What can be done? Educational reformers disagree, but there is general consensus that the risks and potential legal consequences of corporal punishment make it an unattractive alternative, and yet it is essential to return discipline and civility to the classroom. Proposals include requiring students to wear school uniforms; establishing clear-cut rules, regulations, and routines; removing seriously and habitually disruptive students from regular classrooms; involving parents in disciplinary policies and procedures; and hiring professional security (Wallis, 1995; Elam et al., 1996; Zirkel and Gluckman, 1997). Despite the implementation of some or all of these measures, school discipline remains a major concern, and violence is of major concern across the United States.

Violence in schools is a social reality. In some districts, students, faculty, and staff must show identification and either pass through a metal detector or be subjected to random checks for weapons before they may enter school buildings.

School Violence In many schools, vandalism of school property and physical assaults on students, teachers, and administrators are serious problems (Bayh, 1975; Foley, 1990; Elam et al., 1996). School violence steadily increased during the 1970s; tapered off during the 1980s, but dramatically increased again in the early 1990s, peaking in the 1992–1993 academic year. Shootings in schools across the country prompted many districts to install metal detectors at the doors through which all students, faculty, and administrators must pass before entering the building (Morganthau et al., 1992). Observers wrote, at many schools, "guns are as familiar as book bags" (Nordland, 1992:22), and gun violence in schools has increased to the point where "even fourth and fifth graders are arming themselves" (Morganthau et al., 1992:25). Violence in the Dallas schools reached epidemic proportions in 1991; a local television station aired a five-part series called *Education: The Four R's–Readin', 'Ritin', 'Rithmetic, and Revolvers.* By March 1992, the New York public schools had reported 56 shooting incidents (6 resulting in fatalities), making it the bloodiest school year in the district's history (Morganthau et al., 1992). In 1997 and 1998 multiple shooting murders in Paducah, Kentucky; Pearl, Mississippi; Jonesboro, Arkansas; Springfield, Oregon; and Littleton, Colorado, prompted school officials across the United States to make the reduction of school violence their number one priority (Stewart, 1998). During this same period, other countries, especially Japan, experienced similar increases in youth homicides and other forms of violence in the schools (Zielenziger, 1998). Violence in schools has been linked to violence in the larger society and to poverty, gang rivalries, drug sales, and drug abuse (Levine and Havighurst, 1992). In an effort to combat school violence, schools across the United States participate in a federally funded "zero-tolerance" campaign in an effort to establish schools as gun-free and drug-free zones (see Focus box 14.3).

Drugs in Schools Between the 1970s and the early 1990s, the overall use of illegal drugs declined in the United States. However, there were some disturbing trends that concerned parents and educators: age of first usage grew steadily younger; the use of illegal inhalants among adolescents increased; and although the use of alcohol and tobacco by students also declined slightly, age of first use and complications associated with usage increased. By the mid-1990s the nation witnessed a resurgence in the use of illegal drugs, and marijuana and hallucinogenic drug usage became increasingly popular among middle school and high school students. These trends prompted many school districts across the United States to implement zero-tolerance policies designed to make public and private schools drug-free zones. In these efforts, many schools hired professional security and routinely use trained dogs to "sniff out" drugs. Some school districts implemented random drug testing programs for athletes, students involved in extracurricular activities, and, in some cases, all students. At least one study suggests, however, that drug testing may not deter students from using drugs (*New York Times,* 2003a).

These programs, for the most part, have been met with public support, but they have not been without their problems and critics. In some high-profile cases, the zero-tolerance policies of individual schools have garnered widespread media attention for their bureaucratic absurdity. For example, in one case, a middle school student in Houston, Texas, was suspended after a drug-sniffing dog found a bottle of Advil in her backpack, and the same week a middle school student in Ohio received a 4-month suspension for sharing a Midol tablet with one of her friends who was experiencing menstrual cramps (*Washington Post,* 1996). Other highly publicized cases, such as the suspensions of a 13-year-old Oregon boy who took a sip of Scope mouthwash at lunch and a 5-year-old Virginia boy who took his mother's beeper on a school field trip, raise serious concern over the zero-tolerance policies (Katz, 1998).

The growing problems associated with drugs in schools have placed many school administrators in a damned-if-you-do, damned-if-you-don't situation. Parents and the public insist that schools be safer and drug-free, yet when students are suspended,

If ever there was a place where parents should believe that their children are safe, it should be the school. Yet schools are not immune to the violence that permeates American society. School violence peaked in the United States during the 1992–1993 academic year and has actually been on the decline since then, but a series of tragic shootings in American schools during the late 1990s and into 2001 focused worldwide attention on the issues of school violence and school safety. A 16-year-old boy who was rumored to be part of a Satanic cult shot nine of his high school classmates, fatally wounding two, in Pearl, Mississippi, in October 1997. Only 2 months later, three students were killed and five others were wounded in a shooting at Heath High School in West Paducah, Kentucky. Americans were still reeling from the shock of these two school shootings when, in March 1998, two boys, aged 11 and 13, killed four girls and a teacher and wounded ten other students during a false fire alarm at a middle school in Jonesboro, Arkansas. A month later, a science teacher was shot to death and two students were wounded at an eighth-grade dance in Edinboro, Pennsylvania. May of 1998 saw two fatal shootings within two days as an 18-year-old honors student killed a classmate in a high school parking lot in Fayetteville, Tennessee, and a 17-year-old boy in Springfield, Oregon, opened fire at a high school, killing two and wounding twenty others, after having murdered his parents in their home. On April 20, 1999, two students entered Columbine High School in Littleton, Colorado, clad in black trenchcoats and armed with several high-powered weapons and bombs. Before the rampage ended, 12 students and a teacher had been shot to death, 23 students had been wounded, and the two boys had turned the guns on themselves and committed suicide. Police estimated that if the killers had successfully discharged the bombs as planned, hundreds of students and teachers would have been killed or seriously wounded.

These events, like others that preceded them and still others that followed—including a shocking incident in which a first-grade girl was shot and murdered in a Michigan elementary school by a 6-year-old classmate—reminded Americans that children are not safe from violence even when at school. They also signaled a change in the nature of school violence. Before these mass shootings, violence in schools tended to be one-on-one and was usually motivated by some particular incident between the two students involved. By contrast, these later violent incidents involved large numbers of victims and were much more random in nature. Thus, although the number of specific violent incidents in schools actually decreased during the years 1993–2006, the numbers of students killed or injured in such incidents, the sensational nature of the violence in many of these episodes, and media coverage of those events increased dramatically (Lawrence and Birkland, 2004). Moreover, the seemingly random nature of these events and the fact that they occurred in small rural communities and upper-middle-class suburbs accentuated the fact that it is very difficult to predict where school violence is likely to occur and what type of student might bring weapons to school.

School officials are very aware of the necessity to provide a safe, secure environment for students, faculty, and all those who enter the school domain. In some schools this has prompted the stationing of full-time uniformed police officers or security guards within the schools. Other schools require all students, school personnel, and visitors to pass through metal detectors upon entrance to school buildings. Still others conduct random checks for weapons, drugs, or other forms of contraband and potentially dangerous items. Additionally, a number of schools prohibit the use of backpacks or book bags that might be used to conceal a weapon or some other dangerous or controlled substance. In an effort to reduce crimes and violence in schools, many school districts participate in a federally funded "zero-tolerance" program whose aim is to establish schools as "gun-free" and "drug-free" zones. Although it may be defined somewhat differently by various school districts, *zero tolerance* generally refers to school policies that prohibit the possession, use, sale, or supply of any type of weapon, alcohol, or illegal drug on school premises or at any school-related functions.

For the most part, the zero-tolerance movement has enjoyed fairly widespread public support, but it has not been without its problems and critics. Some argue that the presence of uniformed and armed guards in school buildings conveys precisely the wrong image for students, and may inadvertently create a more hostile and potentially violent atmosphere. Others argue that students' constitutional rights are violated when they are required to pass through metal detectors or are subjected to random stops and searches for weapons or drugs without probable cause. And the zero-tolerance policies of some schools have received widespread media attention for their bureaucratic absurdity as children have been suspended for possession of nail clippers, mouthwash, or over-the-counter pain relievers. Nevertheless, school administrators often find themselves in a very difficult situation when faced with the need to provide an open, inviting, and pleasant learning environment while at the same time trying to ensure that schools are safe and secure.

TAKING A CLOSER LOOK

Why does the public have the perception that school violence is on the increase when, in fact, it peaked during the 1992–1993 academic year? Do you agree with zero-tolerance programs? What can school administrators do to help ensure that schools are safe?

Source: Jack E. Bynum and William E. Thompson. *Juvenile Delinquency: A Sociological Approach* (7th ed.). Boston: Allyn & Bacon, 2008. Regina G. Lawrence and Thomas A. Birkland. "Guns, Hollywood, and School Safety: Defining the School Shooting Problem Across Public Arenas." *Social Science Quarterly* 85 (December), 2004:1193–1207. Pamela Wilcox Rountree. "Weapons at School: Are the Predictors Generalizable across Context?" *Sociological Spectrum* 20 (July–September), 2000:291–324.

especially for using or distributing legal over-the-counter medications, it prompts lawsuits and widespread public criticism.

Teacher Shortages   One of the most difficult challenges faced by many school districts today is finding adequate numbers of qualified teachers to fill their classrooms. Teacher shortages are a problem across the United States, and are expected to become worse as the Department of Education predicts that nearly half of the nation's 2.6 million elementary and secondary school teachers will retire and have to be replaced by the year 2010 (Kantrowitz and Wingert, 2000). Many of the large mass of baby boomers who flooded the teaching ranks in the late 1960s and early 1970s have left the profession for more lucrative careers, and those who remain are rapidly approaching retirement age. Shortages are most pronounced in lower-paying rural school districts, but even urban and rapidly growing suburban districts are struggling to find enough qualified teachers and administrators to meet their needs. Shortages are so severe in some areas that a spokesperson for the California state department of education declared, "This is not a shortage; this is a crisis" (Kantrowitz and Wingert, 2000:41). Particularly difficult to find and keep are teachers in the areas of mathematics, science, foreign languages, special education, and technology. And, for the first time in many decades some school districts are experiencing difficulty attracting and retaining principals, assistant principals, and other administrators (Steinberg, 2000).

As shrinking supplies of teachers and administrators couple with increasing demands for them, school districts are resorting to creative ways to develop a competitive edge in the market. Many school districts offer signing bonuses and additional stipends to new teachers, especially in the high-demand areas, and some even offer low-interest home mortgages and discounts from local merchants in an attempt to attract and keep teachers and administrators (Clemetson, 2000b; Kantrowitz and Wingert, 2000). Adding to the dilemma is the fact that today's teachers need not only a wealth of knowledge in content and pedagogy, but they must also be proficient in the use of mass media, computers, and other technomedia that permeate today's classrooms.

MASS MEDIA, COMPUTERS, AND THE TECHNOMEDIA

As we have indicated throughout this book, all forms of media now permeate all aspects of American as well as our global society. Some view technology as the answer to many of America's academic dilemmas, while others see it as simply another educational problem.

During the 1990s, schools turned to technology in hopes of redefining education, inspiring students, rejuvenating teachers, and transforming stale and stifling curricula into exciting hands-on experience. But today, many educators and others concerned about American education are asking whether technology is part of the solution or part of the problem.

The answer to that question varies depending on who you ask. However, almost everyone agrees that technology not only has failed as a panacea for all of the problems in American education, but it also has not been used to its full potential. Warren Hope (1997), a professor of education, concluded that technology has failed to live up to the hype and expectations ushered into the school because of a number of organizational and individual factors. The organizational factors include lack of leadership and vision of what

© Bruce Beattie, Copley News Service. Used with permission.

technology can and cannot accomplish, school cultures that mount obstacles to technology, limited resources, confusion in selecting and configuring the technology, confusion in selecting appropriate software, failure to provide training, development, and technical support, and failure to provide incentives to teachers for using the technology. Individual factors include teachers' lack of confidence in learning and using new technologies, faculty time constraints, and other demands. Hope points out that new technology disrupts existing organizational structures and instructional processes and notes that many academic environments are not compatible with new technology. He uses the analogy of a patient receiving an organ transplant. For the new organ to be accepted and function properly, it must match the chemistry of the host environment (the body) into which it is introduced. Otherwise, it is rejected. Similarly, simply interjecting new equipment into an existing school is not likely to work. When lack of planning, training, encouragement, and support combine with resistance to change and lack of time and ability to learn and use the new equipment, technology is likely to become part of the problem as much as part of the solution. Nevertheless, education is heavily dependent on mass media, computers, and technomedia.

Technomedia are a basic part of a child's education today.

What are some of the potential benefits of technology and the technomedia on education in the future? What are some of the potential drawbacks?

Mass Media and Education Reports by the American Pediatric Association indicate that children spend more time watching television than participating in any other single activity except sleeping (*CBS Morning News,* 1990; Churnin, 2006), and a 1990 Nielsen report showed that the average child had logged over 6,000 hours of television viewing by first grade (Jones, 1991). Parents and teachers worry that heavy television viewing is detrimental and threatens reading and writing skills. For example, A. Graham Down, president of the Council on Basic Education, claims that television is largely responsible for students' inability to concentrate on anything for any length of time (Jones, 1991). And some research suggests that television viewing may be linked to a decline in reading and verbal abilities (Glenn, 1994).

On the other hand, Patricia Greenfield (1984) contended that television can be an effective teaching aid and can be used to increase students' interest in reading. She asserted that television can motivate students to read short stories, novels, and literary classics that they would otherwise try to avoid. Similarly Susan Neuman (1991) suggested that fears that television viewing reduces literacy are based on the notion that there is only one avenue to achieving literacy. She summarized numerous studies indicating that, although it has its faults, television cannot be blamed for decreased literacy.

A survey of 247 junior high and high school teachers conducted by the Arts & Entertainment cable television network indicated that 96 percent of them saw television as complementary to their teaching (Jones, 1991). Other surveys also find that many teachers believe that because of students' fascination with television it makes an excellent educational vehicle (Jones, 1991).

Robert Hodge and David Tripp (1986) urged schools to integrate television into the educational curriculum in order to teach media literacy and to prepare students for the world of mass media that they will face as adults. The idea is not new: The use of educational films and videos that incorporate popular cultural forms has a long history and enjoys wide acceptance as a legitimate teaching strategy.

Some critics argue that the educational use of television and other forms of mass media provides even more pronounced opportunities for the development of a hidden curriculum based on a particular ideology or value system (Apple, 1993). Of particular concern is the introduction of commercial television into the schools and the debate over whether its primary focus is to provide academic instruction or socialize students to become consumers. The mass media are not merely ways of conveying knowledge but are methods for constructing and creating particular forms of knowledge.

Computers in the Classroom Thirty years ago, only large corporations and branches of the government could afford to own and operate computers. They were large, expensive, and difficult to operate and maintain. Today, miniature computers can be carried like briefcases to be used at home, in the office, on airplanes, and most certainly in classrooms. Some are as small as credit cards. In 1983, computers were available in most schools, but on average there was only one computer for every 125 students; by 1990, that ratio had dropped to one per 22 students, essentially one computer for every classroom (M. Rogers, 1990). Today, computers are commonplace equipment in most schools from kindergarten through college.

Children rarely suffer from the "computer phobia" exhibited by many adults, especially if they are exposed to computers at an early age, and they readily transfer skills learned in playing computerized video games to using educational computer software. Moreover, research indicates that computer-assisted teaching increases students' enthusiasm for learning; students learn at a faster pace and retain the acquired information longer than when they receive traditional instruction. The educational potential of computers for teaching math, science, reading, writing, art, and music is enormous. There is a fine line, however, between using computers for educational purposes to supplement curricula and teaching and merely using them as entertainment to replace teaching altogether. Most serious research shows that the computer is most effective as a supplemental tool, not as a replacement for human contact in the classroom (Trotter, 1991; Schofield et al., 1994; Comber et al., 1997; Means, 2006; Monke, 2007).

Technomedia and "Multimedia" Education   Hollywood filmmaker Robert Abel turned his creative talents from making feature-length films, television commercials, and rock music videos to a new venture: melding computers and television into an educational format called interactive multimedia. It mixes audio, video, and text, allowing students, using either a desktop mouse or a touch screen, to explore a multitude of topics as their curiosity dictates (M. Rogers, 1990). Students can explore classic poetry, art, and literature as well as history, science, and mathematics, and more educational software is being developed almost daily. Students interact with the computer, asking questions, learning at their own pace, and combining classic literature and poetry with contemporary rock music and videos. The combination of these computer developments with other forms of technology and mass media, especially television, offers mind-boggling possibilities for education. Today, schools from elementary to university level are incorporating multimedia classrooms into their educational repertoire.

Some worry that as teachers become more dependent on computers and multimedia programming, the "technocrats" who understand the technology may gain considerable influence over educational content, as well as enhanced control powers that neither teachers nor parents would willingly surrender under other circumstances (Kuhn, 1985; Ellsworth, 1989; Wartella, 1995; Monke, 2007). Educational psychologist Jane Healy (2003) worries that in the schools' "mad dash to compute," there may be some long-term ramifications that have not been considered.

The media and technomedia have become an integral part of most students' daily routine. If the past three decades are any indication, the mass media, computers, and other forms of technomedia promise to play an even more prominent role in the future of American education.

the FUTURE

LOOKING to

EDUCATION IN THE TWENTY-FIRST CENTURY

An important educational issue in every society is the preparation of younger generations for the changing social world in which they will live. While survival in a stable environment depends on remembering successful strategies of the past, survival in a rapidly changing environment requires a future orientation (Postman and Weingartner, 1969). In *Future Shock* (1970) and *The Third Wave* (1981), Alvin Toffler underscored the need for American education to become more future-oriented. He lamented that our schools look "backward toward a dying system rather than forward toward a new emerging society" (Toffler, 1970:399). Further, he argued that much of what passes for education today is hopeless in preparing people to cope with the future. To remedy this problem, Toffler (1970:405) insisted that we must "transform the organizational structure of our educational system, . . . revolutionize its curriculum, and . . . encourage a more future-focused orientation." The question is: have we?

Enrollments are growing at all levels of education. The National Center for Education indicates that over 54 million students are enrolled in U.S. private and public elementary and secondary schools. Another 15 million are enrolled in institutions of higher education, and that number probably will increase each year hereafter. This baby boom "echo" (the children of the baby boomers) has created a shortage of approximately 2 million public school teachers (Gerald and Hussar, 1990; Hirschfeld, 1997a; U.S. Department of Education, 2000, 2001a).

In addition, demographic trends indicate that the proportion of students who are members of racial and ethnic minority groups, especially Hispanics, will increase, placing even greater demands on schools for bilingual and multicultural education. It is expected that in the near future, when minority students will make up approximately one-third of the student population, only about 5 percent of the teaching force will be members of minority groups (Shane, 1990; Trent, 1990; Riley, 1998).

The number of nontraditional students in U.S. colleges and universities is expected to increase, and more adults are expected to return to the public secondary schools for adult basic education. These developments will require that schools become more accessible to adults and increase educational options with balanced and diversified programs (Best and Eberhard, 1990; Solomon and Solomon, 1993). Community college enrollments are predicted to grow as they play an ever-increasing role in postsecondary education (Bailey, 2002).

Increased technology, especially computers, mass media, and the new technomedia, is having a dramatic impact on curricula, pedagogy, and learning in both public and private schools, from kindergarten all the way through graduate schools. Even the poorest and most isolated rural school districts are now expanding their course offerings and learning opportunities to students through distance learning programs in which colleges and universities beam courses across the country by satellite. Television formats, although controversial because of their commercial aspects, are broadcast by cable and satellite to schools throughout the nation. Reliance on this type of technology and mass media is likely to increase substantially. Yet studies show that students want their future "high-tech" learning to be accompanied by "high-touch" personal contact with teachers and advisors (Suhler, 1997).

A growing trend across the country in higher education is to wire campuses so that library materials can be accessed from every room and office and teachers can post course syllabi and make assignments as well as conduct class "discussions" via computer networks. Likewise, students can converse with each other or with faculty through e-mail and other computerized means. On many campuses, without ever leaving the confines of their residence halls, students can access library catalogs; enroll in or drop courses; pay tuition, fees, and fines; and submit their homework and class projects. Additionally, on-line courses and degree programs are growing and will continue to do so in the forseeable future (see Focus box 14.3 on page 414).

How far technological advances will go in education remains to be seen. At the same time technology is propelling education into the future, some critics are urging that the only way to improve education is to get "back to basics."

Will American educational institutions be able to respond to rapid social change? Technological, curricular, and pedagogical developments are making dramatic changes in our educational experiences, but some people fear that nothing short of a total overhaul can salvage education as we know it today. One of the major concerns expressed by Americans regarding the education system is how to fund the nation's schools adequately. Thus educational reform promises to remain on the public agenda. Many state and federal plans for education in the future include private voucher systems that some fear would create an even more pronounced two-tiered educational system. One system would be the public schools, financed entirely by taxes, which would be open to all children, and would not require additional monies from parents;

Technology's impact on education from preschool through the levels of graduate and professional degrees has been profound, to say the least. An institution that less than two decades ago was dominated by chalkboards, overhead projectors, and 16 mm films, now uses desktop and laptop computers, programmable hand-held palm pilots and calculators, laser pointers, PowerPoint presentations, and the World Wide Web as standard pedagogical tools. Public elementary and secondary schools are taking advantage of the technological advances in computers and the Internet by posting homework assignments, class schedules, and even offering exams on-line, prompting one *Newsweek* article to proclaim that instead of "'the dog ate my homework,' teachers of today and the future are more likely to hear 'the Web ate my homework'" (Skipp and Campo-Flores, 2003:10).

Community colleges, four-year colleges, and universities are also on the technology bandwagon offering courses and entire degree programs on-line around the globe. People from around the world can go on-line and take courses ranging from introductory sociology to organic chemistry, and from culinary arts to quilting without ever setting foot on a college campus. Not only are high school, postsecondary, and graduate-level courses for credit offered on-line, but students sitting at home on their computers can now earn bachelor's degrees, master's degrees, M.B.A.s, and in some cases, even doctoral degrees, entirely on-line. Schools such as the University of Phoenix, Jones International University, and a host of others have revolutionized postsecondary education with their on-line offerings. In fact, Jones International University was founded in 1995 as the first entirely on-line university in the world, existing solely in cyberspace.

As with most technologies, these innovations in education have been met with mixed reviews. While some see increased technology as the salvation of tomorrow's schools (e.g., Means, 2001), others argue that the "mad dash to compute" raises serious questions about its future ramifications for the educational enterprise (Healy, 2006).

What does the future hold for technology, on-line teaching, and other innovations in education? Nobody knows for sure, but the use of computers and on-line instruction is probably analogous to toothpaste having been squeezed out of the tube. It is highly unlikely that education will ever go back to the way it used to be.

TAKING A CLOSER LOOK
What impact has technology had on education? Do you think this impact has been largely positive, or negative? What other technological developments do you see on the horizon for education in the near future?

Sources: Jane M. Healy. "The Mad Dash to Compute." In James W. Knoll (ed.), *Taking Sides: Clashing Views on Controversial Educational Issues*, 13th ed. Guildford, CT: McGraw-Hill/Dushkin, 2006:353–358. Barbara Means. "Technology Use in Tomorrow's Schools" in *Educational Leadership*, January 2001:1–7. Catharine Skipp and Arian Campo-Flores. "School: The Web Ate My Homework." *Newsweek*, August 4, 2003:10.

the other would be a private system financed through a combination of public and private funds—many of which would be created and run by private, profit-making corporations. As one critic noted, "This scenario of a two-tier education system in the year 2010—one tier for the haves and another for the have-nots—is ugly" (Cameron, 1992:32). Still, many education prognosticators believe that the privatization of what were formerly public schools by private, profit-seeking corporations will increase in this century.

As Focus box 14.2 described, President George W. Bush issued an educational plan titled No Child Left Behind that included the specific goals and objectives of: setting high standards and establishing accountability, putting reading first, improving teacher training and quality, improving math and science education, encouraging safe schools, enhancing education through technology, providing impact aid for underfunded schools, and providing for more parental options and innovative educational programs (U.S. Department of Education, 2001b). Only time will tell if these educational goals will be realized, but so far, most educational experts believe the No Child Left Behind program has failed to improve education (Dodge, 2003; Meier and Wood, 2005; Schrag, 2007).

In closing, as food for sociological thought we turn to anthropologist Gail Benjamin (1997:226–227), who poses an interesting and perplexing question regarding some of the major issues facing schools today and in the future:

People learn more in their first five years of life than at any later time. They do this, the world around, in the absence of an educational system, without formal schools, without grades or other special systems of rewards and punishments, without much rebellion, and without much thought on the part of either children or adults. . . . The question of learning in school might better be phrased, why don't children want to learn at school, when they so manifestly want to do so outside of school?

Summary

1   Education is an important global social institution that performs several important functions for all societies: cultural transmission, anticipatory socialization, social and cultural integration, and innovation and cultural change. In addition, in highly complex societies education serves latent functions that include providing day care for children, delaying the entry of young adults into the labor market, and offering an arena for dating, courtship, and mate selection.

2   The conflict perspective points out that education is directly linked to social stratification. Societies such as the United States do not provide equal access to schooling: youths from different social, cultural, racial, and ethnic backgrounds are not afforded the same educational experiences. The schools also act as screening devices that limit occupational opportunities and reinforce social inequality.

3   The schools play an important role in socialization and the personal development of students. The labels attached to students often result in self-fulfilling prophecies that greatly affect school performance and influence peoples' lives after they leave school. Interaction among students and between students and their teachers is one of the most important features of the educational experience. As the schools become more bureaucratized the educational experience is somewhat dehumanized, and many students, teachers, and administrators feel alienated from the educational process.

4   Several disturbing trends—including increased violence, drug problems, declining test scores, and lower academic achievement—have plagued schools in recent years. Mass education has experienced several other problems, and parents disenchanted with the public schools have sought alternatives for their children. One alternative, the homeschooling movement, reflects a return to traditional family-based education, which historically preceded the development of mass public education. Because of our nation's cultural diversity, multicultural education has become a prominent feature in most public school systems. Community colleges are playing an expanding role in postsecondary education. Perhaps the most significant trend in American education is the increased use of new technologies, which have brought about dramatic changes in instructional techniques.

5   The mass media and technomedia play an ever-increasing role in education. Television may represent a relatively untapped resource for educational innovation. Another viewpoint is that television, while attractive to children and an effective method of dispensing information, is more detrimental than beneficial.

6   The educational institution, which has traditionally looked to the past, must shift its focus to the future in order to be viable. Recent trends suggest that technological developments, especially in computers, mass media, and technomedia, will have a dramatic impact on the future of American education. Changing demographics and increasing global awareness will lead to changes in curricula and the structure of schools so that they will reflect multicultural diversity, an appreciation of critical thinking, and interdisciplinary instruction.

Key Terms

charter schools (p. 409)
credentialism (p. 405)
cultural transmission (p. 395)
education (p. 390)
Eurocentrism (p. 404)

hidden curriculum (p. 404)
homeschooling (p. 410)
innovation (p. 399)
integration (p. 398)
multicultural education (p. 411)

Pygmalion effect (p. 406)
self-fulfilling prophecy (p. 406)
tracking (p. 404)
vouchers (p. 410)
year-round education (p. 409)

PREPARE
TO
MEET
GOD

REV. GARY GREENE

Chapter 15

Religion

"Science without religion is lame, religion without science is blind."

—*Albert Einstein*

Sometime around the turn of the nineteenth century, a country preacher named George Hensley discovered a passage in the Bible that read "They shall take up serpents; and if they drink any deadly thing, it shall not harm them." Accepting everything in the Bible as the literal truth, Hensley decided that church services required rattlesnakes and other deadly vipers. Serpent handling soon spread throughout the southeastern United States, and the practice of drinking strychnine poison was added to religious services as well. Since then many worshipers have become violently ill and dozens have died from snakebites and drinking poison. Others have been arrested by authorities, which have banned serpent handling in many states. Despite these challenges, snake handler churches continue to attract new members and spread across the United States (LaBarre, 1962; Burton, 1993; Handwerk 2003).

In the mid-1990s, a devout Catholic from Australia purchased a fiberglass statue of the Virgin Mary while touring Thailand. In 2002, he noticed that a "rose-scented oil-like substance" began dripping from the statue's eyes. Shortly thereafter, the "weeping Madonna" was moved to a church in Perth, Western Australia, and since then, thousands of people from all over the world have made pilgrimages to the statue. The statue has been especially comforting to the sick and a parish priest reported that two hours after a dying priest was anointed with the oily tears: "he was sitting up in bed as cheerful as anything." Although scientists have tested the liquid, they still are not certain of its source (*BBC News Online,* September 13, 2002:1).

In 1997, 39 members of a new religious movement were found dead in a mansion in Rancho Santa Fe, California. Police found them wearing black running sneakers and their bodies were covered by purple shrouds. Nearby were overnight bags, seemingly

According to the snake handlers of West Virginia, the Bible requires that poisonous snakes be part of worship services.

packed for a trip, each containing clothes, $5 bills, rolls of quarters, and lip balm. As their Heaven's Gate website confirmed, they had decided to join a giant UFO that their leader had seen trailing the Hale-Bopp comet. Most media termed it a mass suicide but some surviving members contended that only their earthly vehicles were left behind. By dying, all had evolved to "The Next Level" (*Newsweek,* April 7, 1997).

Meanwhile, apparitions of the Virgin Mary have purportedly been discovered on tortillas, subway tunnel walls, and a grilled cheese sandwich that sold for over $15,000 on E-bay.

What is your reaction to these spiritual experiences? Do they agree with your views of the supernatural, or do you find them improbable, ridiculous, weird, or even dangerous? Some of you may wonder: what kind of religious group would drink poison or toss deadly rattlesnakes around during church services? And who could possibly believe in a weeping Madonna, or that a visiting UFO might transport a person to a "higher state"?

Religion is perhaps the most difficult subject to study from an objective point of view. In Chapter 2, we pointed out that a powerful source of knowledge is based on faith. Some of you may be deeply committed to your own religious beliefs and uninterested in examining alternative views. Perhaps you do not believe in supernatural beings or forces and are skeptical of sociology's concern with matters that seem to be beyond the realm of science. But once again, we caution that *things may not be what they seem.*

What is important to sociologists is not whether the supernatural exists, but that when people define supernatural beings and forces as real, *they become real in their consequences.* Moreover, sociology goes beyond the novel and exotic to explore religion in all of its richness and diversity—from mainstream churches that many of you know quite well, to folk traditions and new religious movements. In this chapter we examine the diversity of religious meanings and organizations in the United States and worldwide. We also describe how sociologists think about and study "one of the most powerful, deeply felt, and influential forces in human society"—religion (McGuire, 1992:3).

DEFINING RELIGION

On the surface, worldwide religious ideas and institutions seem to have little in common. In many preliterate societies people consider almost everything sacred. The ancient Greeks and Romans believed in a pantheon of gods, whereas Jews, Muslims, and Christians recognize only one supreme deity. The word *Christian* also has many meanings, and there are hundreds of Christian organizations. For some, Christianity consists of worship services, bible classes, and intellectual discussions; for others, it is more emotional, personal, and even ecstatic (Chalfant et al., 1994).

Early in his career, sociologist Émile Durkheim sorted through this maze of religious beliefs and practices—exploring both historical and diverse cultural examples—searching for something that was common to them all. His findings provide the basis for defining **religion** as *a system of socially shared symbols, beliefs, and rituals that address the sacred and the ultimate meaning of human existence.*

The Sacred and Profane

One of Durkheim's ([1912] 1965) initial findings, which remains basic to the sociological understanding of religion today, is that people everywhere make a distinction between the *sacred* and *profane.* According to Durkheim, religion pertains to the

RELIGION
A system of socially shared symbols, beliefs, and rituals that address the sacred and the ultimate meaning of human existence.

sacred, which are *uncommon and extraordinary aspects of social life that inspire in believers feelings of awe, reverence, and respect.* He contrasted this with the **profane,** which represents *ordinary, commonly understood, and routine activities that people take for granted as they go about their daily lives.*

Durkheim emphasized that an object, person, place, or event is not inherently sacred. Rather, "sacredness" is bestowed by a community of believers. Consequently, what is sacred to one group may be profane to another. For example, in the United States most people think of dairy cows in practical terms and most farmers do not hesitate to send them to a slaughterhouse when their milk production declines. In India, cows are sacred in Hindu theology. Not only may they not be eaten but their sacred status demands that government agencies maintain bovine rest homes for elderly, decrepit, and infirm cows (Harris, 1974).

Religious Symbols, Beliefs, and Rituals

Since the supernatural is beyond this sensory world, all religions include *religious symbols* that represent the sacred. They include such things as icons—holy pictures, statues, masks, and relics—as well as sacred words, places, food, clothing, people, and other tangible things that facilitate contact with the sacred. For Christians, two of the most potent religious symbols are bread and wine, which in church settings are symbolically transformed from ordinary food and drink into the body and blood of Christ.

Religious beliefs are symbolically demonstrated in a variety of ways.

All religions also include beliefs that guide people's perceptions and thinking about the natural and supernatural domains and serve as plans for action (McGuire, 1992; Johnstone, 2006). For example, most of us usually ignore strange sounds, interpreting them as being caused by wind or other natural forces. By contrast, many Native Americans pay particular attention to them, because they believe it is through such sounds that spirits communicate important messages to the living.

In Western societies much emphasis is placed on intellectual and formal beliefs that are fashioned into elaborate doctrines and creeds, and most historical religions also provide a general theory of the universe—or *cosmology*—which explains creation, how the world works relative to humans, and a vision of the future. Religion also includes many informal beliefs, including religious myths, legends, proverbs, and folktales (McGuire, 1992).

As belief and myth express the sacred order in words and images, ritual dramatizes them in performance. *Rituals* are formal, stylized enactments of beliefs that, in the case of religious rituals, detach people from the "ordinary" and focus their attention on the sacred. Prayers, chants, dances, fasting, and sacrifice are but a few of the many ritual expressions that enable people to make contact with the sacred and experience a deeper, more profound reality. Religious rituals may be brief and private or involve great collective celebrations, such as seasonal festivals or *rites of passage* of birth, puberty, marriage, and death that effect a permanent change in a person's position in society (Paden, 1988).

The Difference between Religion and Magic

Although religious rituals are future-oriented group activities, magical rituals are individual acts with short-term objectives. Moreover, rather than asking the supernatural to act on one's behalf—as in prayer and sacrifice—**magic** is *a ritual attempt to compel supernatural beings or forces to influence events in the natural world.* In preliterate societies, where much of life is uncertain, magical rituals and charms are used to minimize the risk of crop failure, sterility, sickness, and death. In contemporary industrial societies magic operates mostly at the margins of science and religion—or as a supplement to both.

SACRED
Uncommon and extraordinary aspects of social life that inspire in believers feelings of awe, reverence, and respect.

PROFANE
Ordinary, commonly understood, and routine activities that people take for granted as they go about their daily lives.

MAGIC
A ritual attempt to compel supernatural beings or forces to influence events in the natural world.

Do you use magic in your everyday life? Think about uncertain and high-risk activities where hard work and careful preparation may not be enough—perhaps that includes taking exams. You can be sure that in many professions where risk is great—such as Las Vegas gamblers, Wall Street speculators, or professional sports stars—magic is common. Professional athletes, for example, use scientific techniques to help them hit home runs or score goals in football and soccer. But many also wear lucky charms and repeat magical rituals that have brought success in previous attempts. So do many firefighters, police officers, and others in high-risk professions (Johnstone, 2006).

There is another important difference that distinguishes the two. Whereas magic rituals are employed to deal with current and specific problems—such as producing rain during a drought or getting an A on an exam—religion deals with the ultimate meaning of life (Chalfant et al., 1994).

Religion and Ultimate Meaning

Why do I exist, and why is there suffering and injustice in the world? Is death final or merely a transition to another kind of existence? Every religion deals with questions of ultimate meaning and provides answers for vital human concerns that have no answers in the natural world.

Rodney Stark and William Bainbridge (1985) contend that religious groups and organizations owe their existence to the fact that in all societies much of the population has far less of some rewards than they would like. And some intensely desired rewards, such as immortality, do not appear to be available at all.

In response to these universal conditions, people everywhere create religious organizations to provide themselves with *compensators,* which are "beliefs that a reward will be obtained in the distant future or in some other context that cannot be immediately verified" (Stark and Bainbridge, 1985:6). Most religions also provide *theodicies,* which are emotionally satisfying explanations for meaning-threatening experiences. For example, throughout history it has been common for leaders to promise soldiers that if they were "martyred" in combat they would go directly to heaven (McGuire, 1992). Can you think of any theodicies that might be part of your religious beliefs?

GLOBAL RELIGIOUS DIVERSITY

The earliest evidences of religion and magic appear in European caves dating back 35,000 years. Some contain burials with ritual objects that suggest a belief in an afterlife, including grave goods that many societies still employ in the *rite of passage of death.* To highlight differences and similarities in the tens of thousands of religions that have appeared over the millennia, sociologists have developed a classification system based on core religious beliefs that can be divided into four *ideal types:* animatism, animism, theism, and ethical religions based on abstract ideals.

Animatism

Animatism is *a system of beliefs in which supernatural "forces" rather than "beings" (gods or spirits) are the dominant power in the universe.* Beliefs in impersonal supernatural forces are mostly found in small-scale, preliterate societies, such as traditional societies in the Pacific Islands. Many believe in a diffuse and impersonal force called *mana* that lends supernatural power to events, objects, places, and people. To South Sea Islanders, mana, like electricity, is neither good nor evil. Instead, it is raw, concentrated supernatural energy that can be harnessed by individuals who have the knowledge and special gifts to make it work for good or evil purposes (Marett, 1909).

Although few people think of it this way, animatism is very much in evidence in contemporary industrial societies. Rabbits' feet and pyramid and crystal power are but a few of its modern expressions, and similar beliefs in mana-like powers can be found in many social arenas. Can the presense of four live rabbits end a baseball team's losing

ANIMATISM
A system of beliefs in which supernatural "forces" rather than "beings" (gods or spirits) are the dominant power in the universe.

streak? In 1991, the Milwaukee Brewers thought so—and with them, they began an extended winning streak.

Animism

Animism is *the belief in spirit beings that inhabit the same world as humans—but on another plane of existence.* Animistic religions are common in preindustrial societies that see humans as being very much a part of the natural world, rather than superior to it. Spirits include ghosts, souls of the dead, animal spirits, guardian angels, ancestral spirits, fairies, and demons. Because people believe that spirits have the ability to cross over into the world of the living to do good or evil, many feel the need to placate them or conduct rituals in their honor.

Of course, animistic beliefs are popular in modern industrial societies as well. Many Roman Catholics and other religious groups appeal to guardian angels. Polls taken in the 1990s showed that nearly 70 percent of Americans believed in angels, and nearly half of all respondents reported that they had personal guardian angels. Most Americans also believe in devils, and some groups conduct rituals to exorcise demons. In many other parts of the world, people also employ either oracles or spirit mediums to help them contact the dead and other spiritual beings (Bloom, 1996).

"You picked the wrong religion, period. I'm not going to argue about it."

Theism

Many religions recognize the existence of supernaturals that are even more powerful than ghosts and spirit entities. **Theism** is a *belief in one or more supreme beings or gods who, because of their power and influence in human affairs, deserve to be worshiped.*

Polytheism Around the world the most common form of theism is **polytheism,** *the worship of numerous gods who are believed to have varying degrees of power.* Quite a few, however—especially in complex, stratified societies—recognize a "high god" or "ultimate principle" that has greater power than the others. For example, *Hinduism,* the third largest religion in the world with almost 820 million adherents, is a good example of the latter. See Table 15.1 for estimated major religious populations and Map 15.1 for their global distribution.

Monotheism Three of most influential religions in the world today are **monotheistic religions**—*religions that acknowledge the existence of a single, supreme God.* These are Judaism, Christianity, and Islam. For Jews and Christians, this fundamental belief is contained in the first of the Ten Commandments, which proscribes, "I am the Lord thy God . . . Thou shall have no other gods before me." For Muslims, the same belief is expressed in the first of the Five Pillars—"There is no god but Allah, and Mohammed is his prophet." Despite official monotheism, in the unofficial or folk religious traditions of each there are clear leanings to polytheism, and many people believe in angels, or *jinns.*

Judaism, Christianity, and Islam share many religious beliefs and rituals, and over the years each has had great influence on the others. All three arose in the Middle East, with Judaism appearing first about 1500 B.C. Christianity emerged next as a sect of Judaism,

ANIMISM
The belief in spirit beings that inhabit the same world as humans—but on another plane of existence.

THEISM
Belief in one or more supreme beings or gods who, because of their power and influence in human affairs, deserve to be worshiped.

POLYTHEISM
The worship of numerous gods who are believed to have varying degrees of power.

MONOTHEISTIC RELIGIONS
Religions that acknowledge the existence of a single, supreme God.

TABLE 15.1
ADHERENTS OF ALL RELIGIONS BY SIX CONTINENTAL AREAS*, MID-2004

RELIGION	AFRICA	ASIA	EUROPE	LATIN AMERICA	NORTHERN AMERICA	OCEANIA	WORLD
Baha'is	1,929,000	3,639,000	146,000	813,000	847,000	122,000	7,496,000
Buddhists	148,000	369,394,000	1,634,000	699,000	3,063,000	493,000	375,440,000
Chinese Universists	35,400	400,718,000	266,000	200,000	713,000	133,000	402,065,000
Christians	401,717,000	341,337,000	553,689,000	510,131,000	273,941,000	26,147,000	2,106,962,000
Roman Catholics	143,065,000	121,618,000	276,739,000	476,699,000	79,217,000	8,470,000	1,105,808,000
Protestants	115,276,000	56,512,000	70,908,000	53,572,000	65,881,000	7,699,000	369,848,000
Orthodox	37,989,000	13,240,000	158,974,000	848,000	6,620,000	756,000	218,427,000
Anglicans	43,404,000	733,000	25,727,000	909,000	2,986,000	4,986,000	78,745,000
Independents	87,913,000	716,516,000	24,445,000	44,810,000	81,138,000	1,719,000	416,541,000
Confucianists	300	6,379,000	16,600	800	0	50,600	6,447,000
Ethnic religionists	105,251,000	141,589,000	1,236,000	3,109,000	1,263,000	319,000	252,769,000
Hindus	2,604,000	844,593,000	1,467,000	766,000	1,444,000	417,000	851,291,000
Jains	74,900	4,436,000	0	0	7,500	700	4,519,000
Jews	224,000	5,317,000	1,985,000	1,206,000	6,154,000	104,000	14,990,000
Muslims	350,453,000	892,440,000	33,290,000	1,724,000	5,109,000	408,000	1,283,424,000
New-Religionists	112,000	104,352,000	381,000	764,000	1,561,000	84,800	107,255,000
Shintoists	0	2,717,000	0	7,200	60,000	0	2,784,000
Sikhs	58,400	24,085,000	238,000	0	583,000	24,800	24,989,000
Spiritists	3,100	2,000	135,000	12,575,000	160,000	7,300	12,882,000
Taoists	0	2,702,000	0	0	11,900	0	2,714,000
Zoroastrians	900	2,429,000	89,900	0	81,600	3,200	2,605,000
Other religionists	75,000	68,000	257,500	105,000	650,000	10,000	1,166,000
Nonreligious	5,912,000	601,478,000	108,674,000	15,939,000	31,286,000	3,894,600	767,184,000
Atheists	585,000	122,870,000	22,048,000	2,756,000	1,997,000	400,000	156,656,000

*Continental Areas. Following current UN demographic terminology, which divides the world into the 6 major areas shown above. Note that "Asia" includes the former Soviet Central Asian states and "Europe" includes all of Russia, extending eastward to Vladivostok, the East Sea/Sea of Japan, and the Bering Strait.

Adherents. As defined in the 1948 Universal Declaration of Human Rights, a person's religion is what he or she says it is. Totals are enumerated following the methodology of the World Christian Encylopedias. 2nd ed. (2001) and World Christian Trends (2001), using recent censuses, polls, literature, and other data. Totals may conflict with some estimates for total populations.

Buddhists. 56% Mahayana, 38% Theravada (Hinayana), 6% Tantrayana (Lamaism). Chinese Universists (folk religionists). Followers of traditional Chinese religion (local deities, ancestor veneration, Confucian ethics, universism, divination, some Buddhist elements). Christians. Total Christians include those affiliated with churches not shown, plus other persons professing in censuses or polls to be Christians but not affiliated with any church. Figures for the subgroups of Christians do not add up to the totals because all subgroups are not shown and some Christians adhere to more than one denomination. Confucianists. Non-Chinese followers of Confucius and Confucianism, mostly Koreans in Korea. Ethnic religionists. Followers of local, tribal, animistic, or shamanistic religions, with members restricted to one ethnic group. Hindus. 70% Vaishnavites, 25% Shaivites, 2% neo-Hindus and reform Hindus. Independents. Members of churches and networks that regard themselves as postdenominationalist and neo-apostolic and thus independent of historic, organized, institutionalized denominationalist Christianity. Jews. Adherents of Judaism. Muslims. 83% Sunni Muslims, 16% Shia Muslims (Shi'ites), 1% other schools. New-Religionists. Followers of Asian 20th-cent. New Religions, New Religious movements, radical new crisis religions and non-Christian syncretistic mass religions, all founded since 1800 and most since 1945. Other religionists. Including a handful of religions, quasi-religions, pseudoreligions, parareligions, religious or mystic systems, and religious and semireligious brotherhoods of numerous varieties. Nonreligious. Persons professing no religion, nonbelievers, agnostics, freethinkers, uninterested, dereligionized secularists indifferent to all religion. Atheists. Persons professing atheism, skepticism, disbelief, or irreligion, including antireligious (opposed to all religion).

Source: The World Almanac and Book of Facts © 2006 by World Almanac Edition Group, Inc.

sometime around 33 A.D., and Islam was founded by the prophet Mohammed, who lived in the Arabian peninsula in the late sixth and early seventh centuries. Due to the active recruitment, or *proselytizing*, of new members by Christianity and Islam, monotheism has spread to the remote corners of the globe, and today more than three billion people are either Christians or Moslems (see Table 15.1).

Ethical Religions

Ethical religions originated in the Far East but, like other great religious traditions, have spread throughout the world—including the United States. Their largest followings are Buddhism, Taoism, and Confucianism. **Ethical religions** are *philosophical ideals that show how people may achieve enlightenment, peace, and harmony in this world.*

Buddhism, the fourth largest religion in the world, is based on the teachings of Siddhartha Gautama—the future Buddha—who was born a Hindu prince in 560 B.C. in what is now Nepal. He lived in a time of social turmoil. Like many others of his period he became disenchanted with traditional gods and rituals and set out on a quest for spiritual discovery. He found that the "self" and all earthly existence are illusions and that self-discipline, meditation, and a moral and virtuous life are the true paths to understanding and happiness. Today, Buddhist centers exist across the United States, and many people—including famous Hollywood actors such as Richard Gere—practice Zen or other forms of Buddhist meditation and ritual (Cavendish, 1980; Eckel, 1994).

Both Lao Tzu, the founder of *Taoism,* and K'ung Fu-tzu or Confucius, were contemporaries of the Buddha and both taught that meditation and selflessness were paths to spiritual enlightenment. In Taoism, spiritual wisdom is attained by relinquishing through discipline all desire and withdrawing from the world.

By contrast, *Confucianism* is guided by down-to-earth moral issues and the ideals of cooperation and social order. Confucius recommended active involvement and participation and, above all else, placed a special emphasis on *piety*—especially loyalty and devotion to one's parents, elders, ancestors, and other authority figures. Early on, Chinese officials incorporated Confucianism into the official state religion; since then many Confucian religious ideals have spread to virtually all East Asian religions—and, today, to the United States as well (Cavendish, 1980; Eastman, 1993; Ellwood, 1994).

THE SOCIAL ORGANIZATION OF RELIGION

The ideas of religious visionaries can capture the public imagination and inspire change, sometimes even social revolutions. But in the long run the relative influence of any religion also requires religious communities that are organized to promote religious ideals and objectives. Sociologists classify religious organizations into four ideal types: the *ecclesia, denomination (church), sect,* and *new religious movement.* Each can be distinguished by size and other organizational features; whether the group's norms and values resemble or are different from those of the majority; and whether a group claims to be uniquely legitimate or accepts other faiths (Stark and Bainbridge, 1985; Johnstone, 2006).

The Ecclesia

The **ecclesia** is *a large, formally organized religious body that includes most members of society and is supported by and closely allied with secular and state powers.* In some societies the ecclesia may become so powerful and well integrated into society that it is designated the official state religion. With the aid of the state, it attempts to maintain its religious monopoly by ignoring, suppressing, or coopting competing groups (Johnstone, 2006).

Ecclesiae were fairly common in the past. For example, prior to the Protestant Reformation the Catholic Church was an ecclesia. Likewise, religious officials maintain that the sacred and secular and church and state are virtually one and the same in the Islamic Republic of Iran.

The Denomination or Church

The **denomination (church)** is *an established, socially accepted religious organization that maintains tolerant relations with other denominations.* Because denominations tend to be large bureaucratic structures with considerable wealth and power and their members often play prominent roles in secular society, church and state interests are often intertwined. This is especially true of large, "mainstream" churches, which are considered by most Americans to be "legitimate faiths." Early in U.S. history, Episcopalian,

ETHICAL RELIGIONS
Philosophical ideals that show how people may achieve enlightenment, peace, and harmony in this world.

ECCLESIA
A large, formally organized religious body that includes most members of society and is supported by and closely allied with secular and state powers.

DENOMINATION
An established, socially accepted religious organization that maintains tolerant relations with other denominations.

Bishop Gene Robinson, shown here, was the first openly gay, elected bishop in Episcopal Church history.

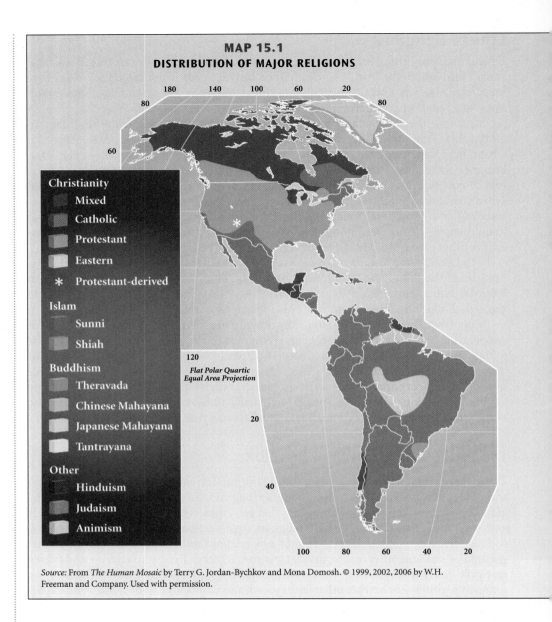

MAP 15.1
DISTRIBUTION OF MAJOR RELIGIONS

Christianity
- Mixed
- Catholic
- Protestant
- Eastern
- * Protestant-derived

Islam
- Sunni
- Shiah

Buddhism
- Theravada
- Chinese Mahayana
- Japanese Mahayana
- Tantrayana

Other
- Hinduism
- Judaism
- Animism

Flat Polar Quartic Equal Area Projection

Source: From *The Human Mosaic* by Terry G. Jordan-Bychkov and Mona Domosh. © 1999, 2002, 2006 by W.H. Freeman and Company. Used with permission.

Presbyterian, and Congregational denominations were considered by most people to be mainstream churches. Today, that label has been expanded to include many other religious organizations that began their lives as sects, such as Baptists, Methodists, and many other well-known American churches (Roof and McKinney, 1987).

The Sect

A **sect** is *a small, less formally organized religious group that usually has separated from a denomination and is in a negative tension with the larger society.* Sects often emerge as protests and challenges to churches (and sects) that some members claim have strayed too far from the original vision of the faith. Others splinter from mainstream churches because they believe the church has become too accommodating to secular society and, consequently, has grown decadent and corrupt. Sects do not see themselves as "new" but as "true" faiths (Stark and Bainbridge, 1985).

Unlike ecclesiae and denominations, whose members are born into the faith, sects usually have members who joined the religious organization because of their commitment to *charismatic* leaders. Also, they may join a sect because they prefer the spontaneity of worship, passion, and intimacy of smaller sect organizations (Stark and Bainbridge, 1985).

SECT
A small, less formally organized religious group that usually has separated from a denomination and is in a negative tension with the larger society.

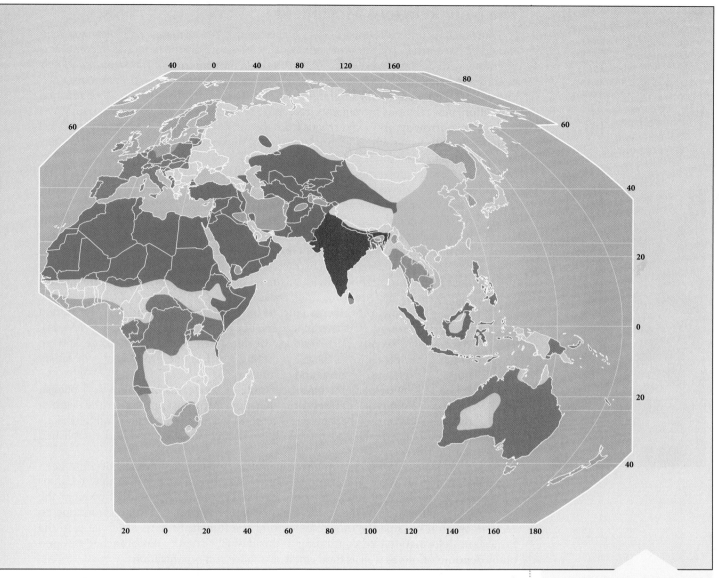

Does this map exaggerate the dominance of particular religions around the world? Or are almost all modern nations so religiously complex that it would be difficult to clearly mark off geographic divisions in any meaningful way?

Because they tend to be intolerant and claim to have a monopoly on the religious "truth," sects often encounter hostility and persecution from secular and religious authorities. Sect fervor burns hot, but it usually cannot be sustained beyond one generation or two, when the original leadership and highly committed followers begin to be replaced by those born into the faith. Those born into the faith are usually more willing to compromise with other religious groups and "the world." Moreover, to realize the visions of their leaders, most sects find that they must create formal organizations. This may lead to what Max Weber [(1922) 1963] termed the *routinization of charisma*, whereby the passion and dynamism of leadership is transformed into formal rules and procedures.

Some sects, such as the Amish, who have been around for centuries, survive by withdrawing from society and living in rural enclaves at the periphery of the secular world. Although they live in urban areas, the ultra-orthodox Jewish Hassidim maintain their distinctiveness by regulating contact with nonmembers and the rest of society. Many sects, after a period of religious challenge and isolation, surrender their claims to exclusive legitimacy and become socially acceptable. In doing so, they become denominations. If they accept the legitimacy of other groups but maintain a negative relationship with society, however, some become new religious movements (O'Dea and O'Dea Aviada, 1983; McGuire, 1992).

The New Religious Movement

H. Paul Chalfant and colleagues (1994) suggested that the term *new religious movement* should be used instead of the word *cult*, because in the media the latter has become synonymous with deviance and evil. A **new religious movement** is *a transient and loosely organized religious organization that includes religious beliefs and practices that are novel and at odds with mainstream religious traditions.* If sects look back to a time of spiritual perfection, new religious movements gaze into the future. They do so in two main ways. Either they borrow symbols and rituals from distant cultures, or they so transform local religious traditions—such as adding poisonous snakes to church services—that they appear alien and sometimes threatening to the majority.

New religious movements are often critical of society and consequently are negatively viewed by the mainstream. But unlike sects that protest and challenge other religious groups and society, new religious movements are usually on the receiving end of public hostility. Historically, new religious movements have been most attractive to the poor and underprivileged. However, in the twentieth century many members of the middle and upper-middle classes who became disenchanted with abstract religious doctrines and sterile rituals found the eclectic and highly individualistic religious movements much more appealing (Robbins and Anthony, 1988; Dawson, 2005).

New religious movements tend to be small, informal, and unstable. Often they form around charismatic leaders, but followers usually have low levels of commitment to any particular group. Most religious seekers come and go "where the spirit moves them," searching for that one group that will satisfy both their spiritual longings and earthly needs.

Some new movements have been able to create stable groups and persist. More commonly, though, new religious movements disappear after the death of their leaders, or they become sects or churches, as their exotic religious beliefs become mainstream and they develop formal organizations and established authorities.

It is noteworthy that many contemporary religions have at one time been organized in all four ways. For example, Christianity began as a sect or new religious movement, an offshoot of Judaism, with novel beliefs and practices that brought the wrath of the authorities. In the fourth century A.D., however, Christianity became an ecclesia, when it became the official religion of the Roman Empire. Much later, in the Protestant Reformation and continuing to this day, Christianity has branched out into many denominations as well as thousands of smaller sect organizations.

RELIGION AND SOCIETY: THREE PERSPECTIVES

Sociology was born in the nineteenth century in the midst of great changes brought by the Industrial Revolution, when religious and other institutions appeared to be either deteriorating or on the verge of collapse. Many nineteenth-century sociologists saw this as an inevitable historic trend. For example, Auguste Comte believed that society had advanced to the point that people were about to exit the *theological stage,* where the world was full of mysteries, ghosts, and spirits, and enter the *positive stage,* where people understood the world in terms of scientific laws. Three other pioneer sociologists—Émile Durkheim, Karl Marx, and Max Weber—built on these early studies. Today, their perspectives continue to have a strong influence on contemporary sociology as well as on the scientific study of religion.

Religion and Functionalism

Although many early scientists saw religion as "superstitions" that impeded progress and had other harmful effects, Durkheim ([1912] 1965) disagreed. Durkheim was aware the modern world was becoming more secular and individualistic, but he believed the functions religion performed were so important that all societies needed either religion or some means of re-creating the basic elements of religion in secular form.

Durkheim and Religion Like many social scientists at the turn of the twentieth century, Durkheim thought he could discover the essence of religion by examining "primitive" religions. After reviewing many, he decided *totemism,* which was practiced by Australian Aborigines and other preindustrial peoples, represented religion in its most basic and elementary form. According to Durkheim, when clan members gathered to worship their totem, which is an emblem or object that represents a clan's animal or plant ancestor from the dim mythical past, they were in effect worshiping their own society. Further, Durkheim reasoned that the very idea of the sacred was derived from the intense feelings of reverence and awe that people felt during collective rituals, when they witnessed and felt the extraordinary power of the group.

Although most sociologists question Durkheim's ideas about the origins of religion, those who adopt the functionalist perspective agree that religion serves a number of important functions for societies and individuals. For one thing, religion can promote social solidarity through common symbols, beliefs, norms, and collective rituals. It also may provide individuals and groups with emotional comfort and support, morale and motivation, and a sense of individual and group identity.

A civil religious shrine, the Vietnam War Memorial evokes feelings of reverence, awe, and respect among many visitors.

Modern Civil Religion Durkheim believed that with the appearance of large and complex nation-states, religious influences decline. However, he believed that all societies required collectively held sentiments and rituals for their cohesion and survival. One way that many modern, secular states accomplish this may be by creating what Robert Bellah (1967) termed *civil religions,* which associate a nation's institutions, history, and values with divine favor or some ultimate plan.

Civil religions often coexist with traditional religions, and some borrow religious symbols and rituals. All are distinct in that they include their own sets of sacred and national symbols, beliefs, and rituals. Civil religion in the United States, for example, includes its own "sacred" holidays—the Fourth of July, Memorial Day, Thanksgiving—myths, prophets, events, places, and even "martyrs" such as Lincoln and Kennedy (Bellah, 1967). Some would extend the civil religious domain further to include the modern corporation and secular organizations such as universities that are infused with religious rhetoric, including "mission statements" (Demerath et al., 1998:vii). Focus box 15.1 examines some contemporary versions of civil religion in the United States.

Whether American civil religion today promotes social cohesion in a Durkheimian sense is doubtful. Robert Wuthnow (1988), for example, contends that there may be at least two major competing versions of civil religion in America—a liberal and a conservative one. Each uses its own version of civil religion to boost its interests and challenge opposition groups. This approach is commonly employed by those who study religion from the conflict point of view (Demerath and Williams, 1985; Chalfant et al., 1994).

Religion from the Conflict Perspective

Karl Marx and other nineteenth-century German social theorists believed the world would be a better place without religion because, to their thinking, religion was a weapon by which wealthy and powerful groups maintained their privileged positions and oppressed those beneath them in the social hierarchy.

Karl Marx and Religion Marx was interested in how religion's comforting messages and promises of future rewards diverted people's attention from present social inequalities and injustices. In Marx's ([1848] 1964:42) words: "Religion is the sigh of the

Several researchers contend that in recent years civil religion in the United States has adapted to a variety of social and economic changes that have either altered traditional "sacred meanings" or added new ones that many Americans now hold dear. For example, John Hall and Charles Lindholm (1999:93) contend that Americans have a *deep sense of righteousness,* and believe that they live in a nation that is not only strong "but also a good place where 'being all you can be' is morally right" (Hall and Lindholm, 1999:93). Two other long-standing civil religious values are *social trust* (a general belief in the decency and goodwill of others) and *nonjudgmental tolerance.* The authors contend that these values are a legacy of Protestantism but have been secularized so that their goals are "no longer sanctity and salvation," but "being well-liked and getting along well with others" (Hall and Lindholm, 1999:97). Today both values translate into the characteristically American "smiley-faced niceness," according to Hall and Lindholm (1999:98), which allows perfect strangers from across the globe to "negotiate a social minefield where there are no clear status markers and where authority is decentralized and relatively weak." These authors also maintain that *emotional egalitarianism* is even more pronounced than in the past. This "sacred value" holds that individuals should follow the rules—especially in families and communities—not out of coercion and charisma, but because of caring, consensus, and affection (Hall and Lindholm, 1999:101). Today, these civil religious values even pervade politics. Many Americans believe that politics is not merely about power and deal making; rather, it is "the ethical center of a society where individuals, despite their differences, are joined together in a common humanity" (Hall and Lindholm, 1999:107).

Kathleen Lowney's book *Baring Our Souls* (1999) argues that television talk shows reveal a new twist on the American civil religious value of *individualism.* According to Lowney (1999:17), talk shows such as Oprah Winfrey's, Geraldo Rivera's, and Sally Jesse Raphael's are a novel sort of American revivalism. In the new "electronic tent," people assemble, watch sinners confess to deeds outside the realm of acceptable behavior, chastise the sinners, and sometimes grant them absolution and reinstatement into society. Lowney (1999:19) remarks that we should understand that this version of American civil religion is based on the Recovery Movement, which focuses almost exclusively on "healing one's inner child," usually with the help of counselors, therapy sessions, and support groups.

Lowney contends that although the television talk show version of civil religion is highly entertaining and popular, it is unlikely to address the important social problems that might truly improve people's lives. According to Lowney (1999:21):

> What kind of society can be constructed based on these 12-step prescriptions? Will it be one that can better tolerate others different than ourselves? Will it be a society that will create new solutions to long-term social problems like racism, sexism, and poverty? Or will it be a society so self-focused that the only time we talk to our neighbors in need will be to invite them to the next 12-step meeting?

TAKING A CLOSER LOOK

Do you agree or disagree that social trust, nonjudgmental tolerance, emotional egalitarianism, and talk show "self-help healing" are civil religious values?

Source: John A. Hall and Charles Lindholm. *Is America Breaking Apart?* Princeton, NJ: Princeton University Press, 1999. Kathleen S. Lowney. *Baring Our Souls: TV Talk Shows and the Religion of Recovery.* New York: Aldine de Gruyter, 1999.

oppressed creature, the sentiment of a heartless world, and the soul of soul-less conditions. It is the opiate of the people. . . ."

Marx argued that the economic base influenced all other social institutions. Most important, because the dominant class controlled politics and the economy, they also controlled religious ideologies, which promoted conformity and acceptance of poverty and injustice, until some future life. Sociologists who take a conflict perspective generally agree that in relatively small, homogeneous societies religion tends to promote cohesion and benefit society as a whole. In more complex, stratified societies, however, conflict theorists argue that rather than serving the common good, ruling elites often use religion as a means of promoting *their* interests and needs at the expense of the majority.

Conflict theorists have expanded Marx's analysis to account for the fact that while dominant groups have much influence in shaping religious ideologies they do not have total control, and subordinate groups also may use them to challenge existing social arrangements and enhance their power. For example, while the British used Protestant religion to denounce violence and disorder in the colonies, by appealing to these same traditions, "patriots mobilized the American people for revolution" (Divine et al.,

2005:145). In much the same way, while slave owners were citing their favorite biblical passages in support of slavery, abolitionists were reciting verses of their own to condemn it.

Religion's Two Faces   Dwight Billings (1990) found much the same thing when he compared religion's role in union struggles among textile workers and coal miners in the rural South after World War I. According to the Marxian model, religious leaders in both cases should have sided with the owners and opposed union activities as "ungodly and wicked." He found instead that while the evangelical Protestant clergy contributed to quiescence in mill towns, they helped promote activism in the coal fields. According to Billings (1990:27), religion is a "mediating variable" that may be used to support or challenge the status quo.

In the Appalachian coal fields, for example, workers abandoned the company church and formed their own church, with miners serving as lay ministers. In the North Carolina milltowns, churches and ministers were integrated into the community, which gave mill owners more influence in church affairs in general—and in setting ministers' salaries and other resources in particular (Flora et al., 1992).

Religion, Interactionism, and Social Change

Max Weber's comprehensive study of religions worldwide revealed that while some religious groups were highly conservative, others—in particular, Protestant Puritanism—inspired radical social and economic transformations in Western Europe and America. Using an interactionist approach, Weber concluded that not only do economic forces shape religion, but under certain circumstances the reverse can also occur, and religious values and beliefs may promote economic and social change—even revolutions.

In Weber's most famous work, *The Protestant Ethic and the Spirit of Capitalism* ([1904–1905] 1958a), he noted that capitalism arose in the Protestant nations of England, Holland, and Germany much faster than it did in European countries where Catholicism was dominant. Moreover, of all Protestant groups, Calvinists were at the forefront of the capitalist movement and were among the earliest and most successful business leaders. Weber asked how it was possible that Calvinism, with its ascetic moral code of self-denial and avoidance of material comforts, could inspire its members to pursue worldly activities, such as making a lot of money.

He found the key to this paradox in the Calvinist doctrine of *predestination.* This doctrine held that even before a person was born God had decided whether he or she was among the "elect" or the damned. In the original ideology, there was nothing a person could do to change the outcome. This belief was a radical departure from earlier Christian understandings that included numerous ways for individuals to gain divine favor—including gaining grace by paying church authorities. Without any of these advantages, there was great anxiety among many Calvinists.

According to Weber, people began to search for signs that they were among the chosen. Eventually, they decided worldly achievement gained by hard work, frugality, discipline, organization, and deferred gratification was evidence of both personal virtue and God's favor.

This combination of traits, which Weber labeled the *Protestant ethic,* made early Calvinists determined and successful capitalists: while their labors and discipline earned them great profits, they were unable to spend them on themselves or family members, but had to pour profits back into their business enterprises.

The publication of *The Protestant Ethic* in 1904 aroused considerable controversy, and some accused Weber of a one-sided religious interpretation. Weber denied this, arguing that he did not say religious beliefs *caused* capitalism but rather that they were part of a complex system of institutions that had a strong influence on its development. To lend additional support to his case, Weber undertook a massive study of Eastern religions. He discovered that one notable difference between Eastern and Western religions was their understandings of *salvation.* In Protestantism, at a personal level, salvation includes remaking one's spirituality and being "born again." Historically, it also has involved aggressive attempts at conquest and conversion, as well as periodic religious movements to reform a "sinful world" (Weber, [1904–1905] 1958a).

Most Eastern religions demanded just the opposite. Hinduism, Buddhism, and Confucianism emphasized harmony, conformity, and accommodation to authorities which, combined with structural factors, often discouraged change, including the development of industrial capitalism, at least in its early stages (Weber, [1922] 1968, 1951, 1958b).

RELIGIOUS MOVEMENTS IN FOCUS

The economic successes of Calvinists and other Protestant groups promoted the spread of the "Protestant ethic," and today the work ethic, acquisitiveness, and a rational approach to money and business have been adopted by many religious groups throughout the world. Early in his studies, Weber recognized the extraordinary material benefits that might be produced by the Protestant ethic. He could also see the dark side of the ethic, especially the possibility that the pursuit of wealth and material goods might one day be stripped of ethical and religious meanings and become ends in themselves. Some sociologists believe this has indeed occurred in much of the world, as societies have become more modern and secular.

The **secularization thesis** *maintains that the global spread of modernization and secularization inevitably leads to the decline of religious institutions.* The secularization thesis maintains that as modernization proceeds religion becomes *marginalized*—or disengaged from the dominant economic and political institutions. It also becomes *privatized,* in that people curtail their search for spiritual fulfillment in religious organizations and make religion a personal quest in such things as popular psychology, the paranormal, and other "new age" practices, which we discuss later in the chapter. Further, it becomes *desacralized,* and natural—not supernatural—forces are seen as causing almost everything in our everyday world (Wuthnow, 1989; Wald, 1997).

Not all sociologists agree that modernization has produced religious decline. For example, in religious surveys in the United States between 1988 and 2000, "over two-thirds (68 percent) of the adults with no religious preference expressed some belief in God or a higher power" (Marwell and Demerath, 2003:314). A *Newsweek* poll indicated that 70 percent of Americans described themselves as "spiritual," 67 percent believed that when people die they go to heaven or hell; and 80 percent believe God created the universe (Adler, 2005a). Stark and Bainbridge (1985) contend that while many mainstream religious denominations have indeed lost members, the level of religiosity has remained relatively constant in the United States. And according to Stark and Finke (2000), it is false reasoning to equate religious change with religious decline. Or, as Hadden and Shupe (1986:xv) put it, "Rather than some linear trend of secularization, . . . progressive forces of secularization generate the alienation and discontent that facilitate intermittent religious revival and revitalization."

Early Revivals and Religious Movements

Religion has undergone alternating cycles of secularization and fervor at every stage of American history. America's first mass religious revival—The Great Awakening—began in the 1730s in part as a response to the Enlightenment, with its emphasis on reason and a pragmatic approach to the world. The Great Awakening was first sparked by itinerant preachers who complained that mainstream church officials had become too preoccupied with dull, intellectual matters and worldly concerns. What people really needed were services that "touched the heart," which they brought to the masses in revivals that stimulated vast audiences publicly to experience a "spiritual rebirth" (Divine et al., 2005).

The Second Awakening began around 1800 and became more vigorous over the next half-century as economic and political changes brought many important religious movements that continue to this day. In many cities, rational and pragmatic approaches to the world gained new converts among those who benefited from the Industrial Revolution. However, those who derived few benefits from industrialization remained unfulfilled by nineteenth-century "progress." Moreover, many people in the new urban areas were confused about which path to the future was best; to some, religious messages that promised a return to a perfect past seemed the safest approach.

SECULARIZATION THESIS
Maintains that the global spread of modernization and secularization inevitably leads to the decline of religious institutions.

Perhaps the most extraordinary spiritual events occurred in western New York, a short distance from America's urban and industrial hub. In that region, cherished religious traditions confronted the forces of modernization and change to produce an extraordinary array of important religious movements (Ammerman, 1987; Johnson, 1989).

In 1830, in Palmyra, New York, Joseph Smith announced that he had experienced several holy visions. In one the whereabouts of the sacred texts that would become the *Book of Mormon* was revealed. The texts offered a radically new vision of history and morality that included the endorsement of plural marriage. Then in the 1840s in Oneida, New York, John Humphrey Noyes founded a utopian community whose members practiced free love instead of traditional marriage—because Noyes believed the Second Coming of Christ had already occurred and people were no longer bound to traditional morality (Divine et al., 2005).

About the same time, millenarian fever flared up among the Millerites, who predicted that the end of the world was at hand. A short time later, the Fox Sisters encountered Mr. Splitfoot, which led to the Spiritualist Movement. Even the normally staid Shakers, whose headquarters were in upstate New York, were affected by the unorthodox spiritual climate; instead of communicating with spirits during their dances, they became possessed by them and fell into trances and spoke in tongues (Divine et al., 2005).

The Holiness and Pentecostal Movements

Another major religious movement occurred at the beginning of the twentieth century, when many poor whites saw themselves being cut off from political power and the benefits of industrial growth. The Holiness Movement rejected religious hierarchies and formal church services, stressing instead "personal holiness" that was contained within the "foursquare" gospel of Christ as savior, baptizer, healer, and coming King (Marsden, 1988:154). Holiness revivals of the early twentieth century also helped inspire the Pentecostal Movement, in which persons who were "touched by the Holy Spirit" practiced faith healing, experienced trances and visions, and spoke in strange, unknown tongues (Marsden, 1988).

Evangelical and Fundamentalist Movements

Evangelical movements flourished throughout the twentieth century. They emphasize a personal relationship between church members and Jesus Christ. This relationship is expressed in such acts as being "born again" and public "testimonies" about one's commitment to Jesus and the church. A strong focus on the individual and personal prayer and testimony, however, has neither diminished evangelicals' concern for others nor deterred them from seeking converts to the faith. The "lost" are invited by a host of individuals, churches, and, most important, the evangelical media, to join the saved, follow Jesus, and win eternal salvation.

The Fundamentalist Movement emerged in response to the attempts of some progressive Protestant leaders who wanted to blend traditional beliefs with those of science and rational approaches of modern scholarship. These initiatives were met by a vigorous counterattack by fundamentalists who argued that accounts of creation, miracles, and everything else in the Bible was the "literal truth" (Ammerman, 1995).

During the 1980s and early 1990s many people experienced another resurgence of religious fervor—this one largely conservative. During such periods of major social change, fundamentalists sought to allay public fears of change by firming up boundaries having to do with women, children, and the family. Many religious leaders claimed that Christianity and the "American way of life" were under attack from "below"—in the form of feminist, gay and lesbian, and other "secular-humanist" movements. At the same time, Christianity was said to be under attack from "above"—especially "big government" and the mass media (K. M. Brown, 1994).

To resist these threats and other secular challenges, contemporary fundamentalists emphasize Scripture as the literal truth. Further, many fundamentalists believe it is their Christian duty to fight for the fundamentals of the faith, as well as resist new ideologies—both secular and religious. Historically, fundamentalists have disdained politics, but in recent years many groups have become involved at every political level. Some scholars claim that fundamentalism has been a third party in American politics for much of the nation's history. Fundamentalists have been very active on issues of abortion, school prayer, and sex education and other "family values" (Wuthnow, 1988; Wald, 1997). The New Life Church in Colorado openly promotes a conservative political agenda, endorsing conservative candidates and lambasting liberal ones, while practicing its fundamentalist faith. It became so popular that minister Ted Haggard became a media celebrity and the church offers two services each Sunday morning with approximately 6,000 people in attendance at each. In late 2006, Haggard was embroiled in a sex and drug scandal that caused him to resign and enter a rehabilitation program. Nevertheless, New Life Church and other fundamentalist churches remain an influential force in American politics, and many candidates court their favor, while others must develop political strategies to compensate for the evangelical vote that will go to their opponents.

A Contemporary Fundamentalist Movement

Of the many contemporary Christian fundamentalist movements, "Promise Keepers," a Christian men's movement aimed at reviving families and the male leadership role in the family, may be the best known. The movement was born in 1990, when officials of the Valley Vineyard Christian churches in Boulder, Colorado, decided to bring men back to Jesus and the Bible, as well as begin the process of merging thousands of Christian denominations in the United States into a single denomination (Spaulding, 1996; Swomley, 1997).

While the message is not entirely new, many of the group's tactics—especially their male-only events at football stadiums and mass rallies, such as the Stand in the Gap march on Washington in 1997—have attracted a great deal of public attention and interest. Sports figures, including Promise Keepers' founder and former University of Colorado football coach Bill McCartney, uses sports marketing tactics and military rhetoric to win millions of male converts, as well as picketing by the National Organization for Women (NOW). Promise Keepers' officials maintain that one of the movement's primary goals is to reimpose traditional male roles and authority (Abraham, 1997).

Contemporary Millenarian Movements

Another large segment of the fundamentalist movement looks to the end of the world and the Second Coming of Christ—or what some fundamentalists call the *Rapture*. This branch of fundamentalism studies the Bible for clues and prophecies about the future—especially the cataclysmic events that will mark the end of the world (Marsden, 1988; Wuthnow, 1993; Ammerman, 1995). Some believe that unrest in the Middle East and the Iraqi war signal the beginning of the end as prophesied. Focus box 15.2 takes a closer look at a few end of the world movements in the nineteenth and twentieth centuries.

Religious Movements in a Global Context

From the beginning of the discipline, sociologists have recognized a close relationship among religion, economics, and politics, as well as "the 'double function' of religion in the legitimation of power and privilege and in protest and opposition" (Billings and Scott, 1994:173).

Today, many parts of the world are experiencing a revitalization of religion that includes such diverse expressions as Islamic fundamentalism in the Middle East, liberation theology in Latin America, and environmental and peace movements in Europe; radical-traditionalist Catholic activism in the United States; and the renaissance of religious orthodoxy in the Russian Republic and elsewhere in Eastern Europe (Riesebrodt, 1993). Some sociologists see these and other contemporary religious movements as responses to various cycles of capitalist development, at the global as well as the national levels (Robertson, 1989a; Shupe and Hadden, 1989; Thomas, 1989).

For example, Irving Horowitz (1990) argues that fundamentalism is not a uniquely American phenomenon but part of a global pattern of popular religious movements against modernization, secularization, and elite visions of the future that provide ordinary people with few rewards and a disproportionate share of the costs of development. George Thomas (1989), though, contended that religious movements are not so much a rejection of modernization as they are attempts to construct a new sociocultural order in the face of large-scale change.

Throughout history there have been many outbreaks of "End of the World" fever in North America and other parts of the world. Some of the groups involved in these believe in progressive evolutionary change, but most adhere to catastrophic millenarian movements that stress that the earth must be destroyed and then re-created for human salvation (Wessinger, 1997). Many Americans may see the frenzied activities of groups planning for the world's end as something unexpected and new, but these activities have a long history, especially in America, where secular traditions that emphasize progress and perfectability intersect with biblical revelations that tell of Armageddon and the second coming of Christ to fan the flames of hope for a better future, perhaps even spark the dream of a "perfect world."

Although millenarian outbreaks have been common throughout American history, they have occurred with marked intensity during major social and economic transformations. Before the Civil War and the transition from agrarian to urban industrial society, for example, both millenarian and utopian fever burned especially hot. None caused a greater stir than the prophecies of William Miller, who not only announced the impending end of the world but gave the exact day it would occur.

In 1818, after reading his Bible and making a few simple calculations, Miller decided that the world would end on March 21, 1843. Over the next few decades, Miller recruited perhaps as many as 100,000 followers, some so certain of his prophecies that they left their families and gave away their possessions, seeing no need for either with the end so near. Miller and his disciples allegedly donned white "ascension robes" on the fateful day and waited on hilltops expecting to be transported directly to heaven. When nothing happened, Miller concluded that he had made a minor miscalculation and that the "true" end was March 21, 1844. When this prediction also failed, many left in disgust, but others became more committed to Miller and more certain of his prophecies (Barkun, 1986; Young, 1989; Haught, 1995).

Many contemporary expressions of millenarian fever have occurred worldwide. For example, in March 2000, in southwestern Uganda, the Movement for the Restoration of the Ten Commandments of God, which was founded by a former prostitute and several former priests and nuns, decided that the end was near and that the Virgin Mary was about to rescue them. Group members slaughtered cattle and purchased a large quantity of Coca-Cola, which they consumed at a final, farewell party. Shortly thereafter, an explosion and fire occurred, and because the doors to the building had been barricaded, more than 200 group members lost their lives in what has been described as either a "mass suicide or a mass homicide" (Melton, 2000:17).

J. Gordon Melton (2000) noted that a number of global apocalyptic movements and religion-related violence in the past few decades seem to be related to the withdrawal of colonial governments and the emergence of "new, often unstable, independent governments." In advanced industrial societies like Japan, the decline of established religious organizations and dramatic social change appears to have created a climate well suited to novel religious expression—including more than 200,000 new religious movements. Most include some blend of Buddhism, Christianity, folk religion, and science fiction. *Aum Shinrikyo* is the most well-known movement because it attempted to speed up the doomsday process by releasing sarin gas in the Tokyo subway system, killing 9 people and injuring 5,000. In 2003, another movement called *Pana Wave* caught the media's attention, when it too decided that the end was near: on May 15, 2003, a closer encounter with the "tenth planet" would set off earthquakes and tidal waves that would destroy most of humankind (Pigott, 2003:1–3).

Michael Barkun (1986) contends that apocalyptic visions, which insist that one world must die before a better world can begin, create special hazards in the nuclear age. Environmental problems and widespread public perceptions that science cannot solve all human ills, combined with religious dreams of a radically new and better spiritual era, may

induce self-fulfilling prophecies, for the millennial vision entails a struggle between normal desires for safety and routine and an anticipation of the climactic disasters to come. In a nuclear world, where human beings themselves possess the means for the world's destruction, fascination with the end of time may introduce a potentially fatal passivity into precisely those areas of political life most in need of decisive control (Barkun, 1986:160).

TAKING A CLOSER LOOK

Does a fascination with the end of time produce fatalism and political quiescence? Or does it produce political activism among believers? And is this activism a threat or a benefit to global society? Take a position and support it with empirical evidence.

Source: Michael Barkun. *Crucible of the Millennium: The Burned-Over District of New York in the 1840s.* Syracuse, NY: Syracuse University Press, 1986. Stanley Young. "The End." In Ted Schultz (ed.), *The Fringes of Reason: A Whole Earth Catalogue.* New York: Harmony Books, 1989:8–21. James A. Haught. *Holy Hatred: Religious Conflicts of the '90s.* New York: Prometheus, 1995. Philip Lamy. *Millennium Rage: Survivalists, White Supremacists, and the Doomsday Prophecy.* New York: Plenum, 1996. Gordon J. Melton. "Cult Mass Suicide/Homicide: Jonestown/Heaven's Gate Replay?" cited in the *Skeptic* 8(1), 2000:17–18. Catherine Wessinger, "Millennialism, without the Mayhem." In Thomas Robbins and Susan J. Palmer (eds.), *Millennium, Messiahs and Mayhem.* New York: Routledge, 1997:47–59.

Islamic Fundamentalism In much of the world, the line between religion and politics has become blurred, as have private and public domains. Politics has become infused with religious (and family) symbols, and religious groups have become active in politics—both at the national level and globally. In areas of the developing world where there are large Muslim populations—in the Middle East, North Africa, India, Pakistan, the former Soviet Union, and several Asian countries—the call for religious reform and the rejection of Western, secular values have been especially strong. Like Christianity, Islam has a long-standing activist tradition that encourages dissent, challenge, and, at times, *jihads,* or holy wars (Billings and Scott, 1994).

Prior to colonialism and the discovery of oil in the Middle East in the late nineteenth century, relations between priests (*ulema*) and secular rulers were for the most part harmonious and cooperative. In most Middle Eastern nations the ruling elite certified the country's Islamic character, and priests left matters of state to secular officials. After World War II, however, many secular rulers, including the Shah of Iran, decided that priests had to go and their societies had to be modernized "immediately." It is not surprising that Ayatollah Ruhollah Khomeni's call for revolution and a return to the days of Islamic justice, honor, and morality was heeded by so many—not only the dispossessed clergy, but also small merchants, students, Marxists, rural peasants, and many others. Highly visible but accessible to so few, Western goods and ideas became an easy target of fundamentalists, who mobilized people's anger and frustrations by attributing most of the world's problems to the corrupting influence of the West in general and the "Great Satan," America, in particular.

In many Muslim countries, religious movements involve more than the equitable redistribution of material benefits, however. They also involve struggles for power and influence among men and women in many social arenas (Riesebrodt, 1993). Some fundamentalist movements focus on the concerns and needs of particular societies. In contrast, the one in Iran and the larger movement led by the Muslim Brotherhood sought to export revolution to all Islamic countries and to alter the global human condition (Robertson, 1989a,b). Early in this century, the al-Qaeda terrorist network, run by Osama bin Laden, carried these goals to an extreme by pledging to overthrow all non-Islamic governments worldwide. And for a while, Afghanistan's fundamentalist Taliban party implemented severe anti-Western policies, such as forbidding the education of women and outlawing televisions and cell phones, until it was toppled by a U.S.-led coalition in 2001.

Liberation Theology In much the same way, the militant reformist movement within Catholicism known as liberation theology addresses the inequities in the global economy by teaching the poor that poverty and suffering are neither God's will nor the individual's fate, but the result of specific social, political, and economic forces (McGuire, 1992). The movement, which combines elements of theology and Marxist sociology, takes its name from the title of a 1971 book by Father Gustavo Gutierrez of Peru, *The Theology of Liberation.*

Although directed to inequities in the world system of stratification, liberation theology has received its strongest support in Latin America, where liberal elements of the Catholic church have become the primary institutional focus of dissent against a class system that has exploited peasants for centuries. Even more far-reaching are popular grassroots religious movements that have appeared all over Latin America. Most are small, autonomous, lay-directed groups and organizations called *Comunidades Eclesiales de Base* (CEBs), or Christian base communities. They meet regularly to discuss the social and political causes of their problems—especially authoritarian regimes and capitalist exploitation—"and consider solutions in the light of their readings of Scripture" (McGuire, 1992:243). With diverse goals and interests, CEBs have encountered suspicion and hostility not only from ruling elites but also at times from Catholic authorities.

Religious Movements in a "New Age"

At the beginning of the 1990s, a relatively small number of people had become part of the Witchcraft (Wicca) and Neopaganism religious movements. While an estimated 30,000 witches and neopagans in North America practice magic, psychic healing, astrology, and self-improvement, most modern witches have nothing to do with black magic or voodoo (Melton et al., 1990; Robbins and Anthony, 1990; Melton, 1996). Many, in fact, strive for gender equity. For example, Elizabeth Puttick (1997:245) wrote: "Paganism is the only religion that not only perceives the Goddess as equal or superior to the God, but follows through by giving women equal or superior spiritual status."

Satanism J. Gordon Melton (1986) described Satanism as an unusual cult with virtually no literature, little organization, and few members. Most satanic cults include three to five members, and their life spans are typically a few months or at most a few years. Even Anton LaVey's Church of Satan, founded in San Francisco in 1966, has less than 5,000 active members. As Melton (1996) observed, other than exotic rituals that center on Satan motifs, individual pragmaticism and hedonism are more important than devil worship.

Despite the fact that the number of Satanists is few and their influence is slight, many ordinary citizens remain convinced that satanic churches are growing and Satanism is a major threat to American society. James Richardson and colleagues (1991) examined the Satanism scare by asking, "Who is making claims about Satanists, and why are they making them?" They found that the combined interests and goals of many groups, including police officials, fundamentalist preachers, the mass media, anticult religious groups, "childsaver" groups, and some therapists and mental health workers, contributed to the "social construction" of Satanism as a severe "social problem."

New Age Many new religious movements offer two contrasting solutions to life in a highly individualistic society that is also characterized by bureaucratized work and rapid change. One solution offers what Dick Anthony and Thomas Robbins (1990:484) termed a "totalistic restored community," in which members are encouraged to live together, surrender all of their worldly possessions to the group, and create model communities. The Unification Church of Korean evangelist Sun Myung Moon (the "Moonies") is an example of this kind of religious movement.

The other branch is more eclectic and unstable. It may involve yoga, meditation, and religiotherapy groups, such as Scientology, EST (the Forum), and Lifespring. All three offer believers a sense of connectedness and belonging that transcends the fragmented conditions of modern life—but without the extreme costs and commitment demanded by communal groups.

The New Age Religious Movement has swept across America; today it includes hundreds of thousands of followers. **New Age** offers *a novel blend of magic and religion, ancient and futuristic beliefs, and utilitarian and mystical ethics and philosophies.* It confronts the apparent chaos, destructiveness, fragmentation, and dehumanization of contemporary society with a utopian vision of a New Age that will arrive "after enough individuals have evolved to a higher spiritual consciousness" (Robbins and Anthony, 1990:491).

New Age is a decentralized religious movement that includes an eclectic collection of orientations. Often, New Age disdains institutional religion, preferring religious experimentation and "new spiritual syncretisms" (Sutcliffe, 2003:29). Most are highly individualistic, and there is a strong emphasis on personal improvement and intuitive feelings over beliefs and doctrines. *Holism,* the belief that there is a latent unity of mind and body and all individuals are ultimately related to each other and nature, is particularly important. So is the notion that there is a "divine spark" in all individuals, and a "universal self" that is gradually understood according to the efforts and dedication each person brings to his or her spiritual quest. Just to name a few of the tools for personal and global transformation there is: meditation, wearing a crystal, charms, astrology, massage, herbs, a macrobiotic diet, and conversations with disembodied spirits or extraterrestrials through channels (Jorstad, 1990; Robbins and Anthony, 1990; Mayberry, 1991; Bloom, 1996).

Unlike the majority of new religious movements that have appealed to the poor and those outside the mainstream, New Age is a decidedly middle-class phenomenon whose largest constituency includes single, young, upwardly mobile urban adults—especially the "unchurched" who live on the West Coast and in major university cities (Jorstad, 1990). As J. Gordon Melton et al. (1990) observed, they are most accepting of the process of "transformation," having experienced it many times in career advancement

NEW AGE
A novel blend of magic and religion, ancient and futuristic beliefs, and utilitarian and mystical ethics and philosophies.

Tom Cruise and Katie Holmes helped make Scientology a household word during their highly publicized romance and wedding.

To what extent do the media shape people's view of religion? To what extent does religion shape people's view of the media?

and through geographic and social mobility. And, being affluent and entrepreneurial, they are most capable of disseminating the New Age message through networks, merchandising fairs, and at New Age retreats and spas. The movement has spread throughout the United States. Today, there are New Age restaurants, food stores, dating bureaus, and businesses of every description. Moreover, New Age training seminars for stress reduction are popular among Fortune 500 companies, and across the country New Age parents are choosing to teach their children at home rather than sending them to public or private schools.

Celebrities, too, have given the New Age movement a powerful boost. Actress Shirley MacLaine's books and television appearances introduced the public to the occult, channeling, and reincarnation. Another well-known New Age advocate is Oprah Winfrey; some might even include former First Lady Nancy Reagan, who "regularly consulted and followed the teachings of at least one astrologer" (Jorstad, 1990:174). Scientology boasts strong celebrity endorsements from the likes of John Travolta, Kirstie Alley, and Tom Cruise. Focus box 15.3 explores some critical approaches to "extraordinary phenomena."

But New Age celebrities do not have a monopoly on the mass media. Historically, Christian groups have been far more active at using the latest high-tech devices to bring conservative religious messages to mass audiences.

RELIGION AND THE MEDIA

Despite popular beliefs that the relationship between religion and the mass media is something unique and new, it is as old as the mass media itself; it began five centuries ago, when Johannes Gutenberg began mass printings of the Gutenberg Bible. Likewise, the "electronic church did not begin with Jim and Tammy Bakker's PTL (Praise the Lord) ministry, but with the first radio broadcast of a human voice in 1906, a Christmas service that included the singing of 'O Holy Night'" (Martin, 1988:1711). Today, religious organizations reach across the globe to influence hundreds of millions of viewers.

Evangelical Media

Although religious publication houses and broadcasters cannot control how viewers interpret their messages, it is clear the mass media shape people's understandings of religion in numerous ways. For one thing, Christian evangelists now control a disproportionate share of media offerings, and since the 1960s the more aggressive and entrepreneurial "Evangelicals have gained a virtual monopoly" purchasing over 90 percent of all broadcast time devoted to religion (Martin, 1988:1717). Evangelicals dominate the radio airwaves and produce the greatest number of religious magazines, books, record albums, music videos and, most of all, television programs with

> veritable smorgasbords of expression, everything from wrestlers for Jesus, doing physical deeds of prowess as testimony to their faith, and style shows with high-fashioned clothes emblazoned with religious mottoes to the other extreme of the subdued, understated preaching of Lloyd Ogilivie and Jack Hayford. (Wuthnow, 1993:112)

Mass Media, Religion, and Religious Messages
According to Wuthnow (1988:115), when religion is beamed into living rooms around the world from "sleek, high-technology studios via satellite hookups," it becomes the source of multiple paradoxes. For one thing, while many televangelists condemn modernization, they are the most high-tech and "modern" of all Christian groups. Likewise, the "hot rhetoric" of the tent preacher has given way to the cool demeanor of a talk show host in order to appeal to a mass audience (Wuthnow, 1988). As David Diekema (1991:143) observed, the absence of personal presence and other effects of a televised ministry transform what appears to be a charismatic relationship between minister and congregation into a pseudocharismatic one.

Almost daily the mass media report some "extraordinary phenomena" that concerns UFOs, crop circles, reincarnations, out-of-body experiences, and other paranormal happenings. One scientist argues that the odds are stacked when "science tries to debate pseudoscience"—especially in popular media debates. The reasons are many. In America many people have little knowledge of science and in a recent poll by the National Science Foundation, "half of Americans did not know that Earth orbits the Sun" (Krauss, 2002:1). Likewise, most Americans have the belief that "anything is possible," and many expect that scientific debate on any subject should be fair and that majority opinion should rule. As Lawrence Krauss (2002:1) observed, science is neither democratic nor fair, and it is unwilling to accept notions that have already been disproven by experiment or cannot be examined using the scientific method. Of course, "merely having a debate inevitably suggests that each side has some credibility"—and that too can be advantageous to pseudoscience—however fanciful or illogical the claims (Krauss, 2002:2).

Scientific reasoning cannot offer definitive proof that supports or rejects the merits of many claims. However, it can help you examine the evidence and judge whether these claims are logically compelling, and decide which hypothesis best suits the facts (Schick and Vaughn, 1995).

Theodore Schick and Lewis Vaughn (1995) propose that all popular claims about the "extraordinary" should be subject to the following four-step analysis:

1. *Is the claim clearly stated and can it be given an operational definition?* For example, when you examine extraordinary phenomena avoid vague and nonspecific statements, such as "ghosts are real." A more appropriate claim that can be specifically assessed might be, "disembodied spirits of dead persons exist and are visible to the human eye" (Schick and Vaughn, 1995:238).

2. *Is there empirical evidence or logical argument to support or refute claims of extraordinary phenomena?* When examining the merits of claims like "alien abductions and satanic ritual abuse are rampant in contemporary society," take a complete inventory of both the quantity and quality of the evidence. As the authors noted, "true believers" rarely take account of the limitations of empirical evidence—such as distortions of human perception and memory, biases in scientific research, and problems with ambiguous data. And, of course, in assessing the empirical evidence for such things as satanism, channeling abilities, and special psychic powers, be certain that the hypothesis is relevant to the evidence it is intended to explain (Schick and Vaughn, 1995).

3. *Always consider alternative hypotheses.* For example, if the evidence for UFOs is accepted without considering alternative hypotheses, it is possible that a fairly convincing case can be made for alien visitors. As Schick and Vaughn (1995:239) observed, often when people are confronted with some extraordinary phenomenon, they immediately conjecture that the paranormal or supernatural is involved. This giant step usually precludes any alternative hypothesis that may better explain the facts, as well as any further search for natural causes.

4. *According to the criteria of adequacy, rate each hypothesis.* The criteria of adequacy include: testability, accuracy, simplicity, and consistency with current evidence and scientific opinion. The hypothesis that is strongest by all of these measures usually has the greatest probability of being correct. Of course, the evidence may sometimes transform the improbable into the probable. Such was the case with black holes and antimatter, which most scientists believed were popular fantasies only a few decades ago.

TAKING A CLOSER LOOK

Apply the four-step plan to evaluate some "extraordinary religious phenomena" that interests you. Has this approach increased your skepticism, or conversely strengthened the certainty of your belief that the religious phenomenon in question is indeed probable?

Source: Theodore Schick, Jr. and Lewis Vaughn. *How to Think about Weird Things: Critical Thinking for a New Age.* Mountain View, CA: Mayfield, 1995.

The paradoxes do not end there. By exposing the public to an enormous variety of religious truths, media religion reinforces religious *privatization* and general consumerist trends in religion, where many see religion as one of many "private, leisure-time activities" (Wuthnow, 1988:116). At the same time, however, religious television has proved that it has the power to transform private morality into public issues and exert considerable influence on the political system.

To survive in a highly competitive marketplace, religious television must accommodate its message to the middle class and general TV viewers. At the same time, however, televangelists must not alienate their core constituency, which consists of approximately 13 million people (6 percent of the national television audience) who are for the most part poor, elderly, and disadvantaged.

This social composite bears a striking resemblance to the demographic portrait of the more than 80 million evangelicals in this country (Martin, 1988; Diekema, 1991), many of whom also exist at the margins of the mainstream but, thanks to television, are fully aware of both the material benefits and spiritual perils of the modern age. The Jim Bakker and Jimmy Swaggart sex scandals in the late 1980s resulted in declines in both viewers and contributions to religious television ministries. But by the turn of the century, one religious scholar argued that America was experiencing a fourth Great Awakening—and evangelical media was once again at the heart of the new religious revival. For example, in 2003, among the best-selling books in America was Tim LaHaye's Christian "left-behind" series about the apocalypse that sold about 50 million copies; and evangelist Benny Hind's television program was watched in 190 countries—making him "one of America's most prominent television personalities" (Kristof, 2003:1). Recent scandals also have had little effect on worldwide media ministries.

TECHNOMEDIA AND RELIGION

At the other end of the social spectrum are young, highly educated members of the upper middle class who may use the Internet and other information technologies to take religion in new, uncharted directions. If current trends toward isolation and social fragmentation continue among this group, they may shift increasingly to electronic congregations, which are proliferating in cyberspace.

In *The Soul of Cyberspace*, Jeff Zaleski (1997) contends that new information technologies are altering almost every aspect of religion. He notes that interactive television, CD-ROMs, the World Wide Web, and even pagers and cellular phones have altered religious organizations, how people pray and worship, and even people's ideas of the sacred.

Today, religious news and chat groups abound on the Net, daily exploring doctrines and beliefs of all major religions, as well as emerging religious movements that prior to the Net may have been known to only a few. Some groups use electronic pagers to signal the faithful that it is time to pray, while others use CD-ROMs and advanced computer graphics to fashion new, high-tech images of the supernatural (Zaleski, 1997).

Currently, Christian denominations—especially Roman Catholics—dominate cyberspace, accounting for almost 80 percent of the 10 million or so websites devoted to religion. But other religions from across the globe are catching up. According to Zaleski (1997:4), "it takes only the click of a mouse to jump from one temple, one mosque, or one church to the next." For example, one website, <beliefnet.com>, contains a portal "that allows visitors to choose from an A to Z of religions—that's A Course in Miracles to Zoroastrianism—and join in e-mail chats" (Sink, 2003:1).

"User name and password?"

RELIGIOUS DIVERSITY IN THE UNITED STATES

It is paradoxical that the most materialistic and highly industrial nation in the world also is one of the most religious. National surveys in the early 2000s revealed that over 80 percent of the U.S. population believe in God and nearly 70 percent are members of a church or synagogue. Although only about 35 percent of Americans attend a church or synagogue weekly, this is a much greater percentage than in most European countries. Moreover, over 60 percent of American respondents indicated that religion is "very important" in their lives. Further, 90 percent regularly pray, and 82 percent of those surveyed told pollsters they believed in life after death (Greeley and Hout, 1999; Moore, 2000; Adler, 2005a).

There are more than 1,000 denominations, sects, and new religious movements in the United States, although most of the religious population belong to only about two dozen major denominations (see Table 15.2). Eighty-seven percent of the population identify themselves as Christian, and the largest Christian denomination is the Roman Catholic Church, with about 67 million members. Judaism and Islam are the largest non-Christian denominations. (See Map 15.2.)

Some argue that the constitutional guarantee of religious freedom not only encourages religious tolerance but also promotes religious diversity in the larger society. In a free religious marketplace, membership in religious organizations has shifted over the

TABLE 15.2
MAJOR RELIGIOUS DENOMINATIONS IN THE UNITED STATES

DENOMINATION	NUMBER OF CHURCHES REPORTING	TOTAL MEMBERSHIP
African Methodist Episcopal Church	6,200	2,500,000
African Methodist Episcopal Zion Church	3,226	1,432,795
American Baptist Churches in the U.S.A.	5,836	1,433,075
Assemblies of God	12,133	2,729,562
Baptist Bible Fellowship International	4,500	1,200,000
Catholic Church	19,484	67,259,768
Christian Church (Disciples of Christ)	3,691	770,793
Church of God in Christ	15,300	5,499,875
Church of Jesus Christ of Latter-Day Saints (Mormons)	11,879	4,935,548
Churches of Christ	15,000	1,500,000
Episcopal Church	7,344	2,320,221
Evangelical Lutheran Church in America	10,721	4,984,925
Greek Orthodox	510	1,500,000
Jehovah's Witnesses	11,876	1,041,030
Jewish Reconstructionist Federation	103	180,000
The Lutheran Church–Missouri Synod	6,142	2,488,936
Muslims	N/A	4,657,000
National Baptist Convention U.S.A. Inc.	9,000	5,000,000
Presbyterian Church (U.S.A.)	11,097	3,241,309
Seventh-Day Adventist Church	4,619	935,428
Southern Baptist Convention	42,775	16,439,603
Union for Reform Judaism	900+	1,500,000
Union of Orthodox Jewish Congregations of America	1,000	1,075,000
United Church of Christ	5,850	1,296,652
United Methodist Church	35,102	8,251,175
United Synagogue of Conservative Judaism	760	1,500,000+

Source: From the *Yearbook of American & Canadian Churches,* 2000 edition. Edited by Eileen W. Lindner, (888) 870-3325.
© 2000 National Council of Churches. Used by permission.

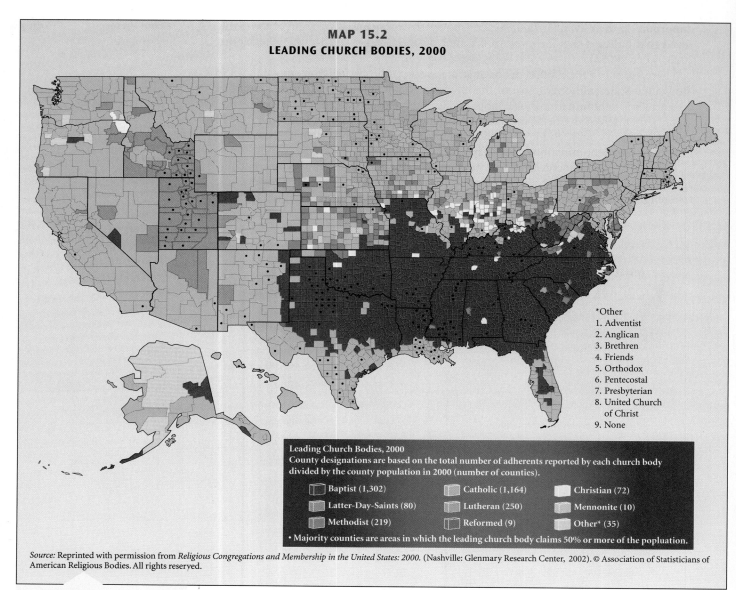

MAP 15.2
LEADING CHURCH BODIES, 2000

*Other
1. Adventist
2. Anglican
3. Brethren
4. Friends
5. Orthodox
6. Pentecostal
7. Presbyterian
8. United Church of Christ
9. None

Leading Church Bodies, 2000
County designations are based on the total number of adherents reported by each church body divided by the county population in 2000 (number of counties).

Baptist (1,302)	Catholic (1,164)	Christian (72)
Latter-Day-Saints (80)	Lutheran (250)	Mennonite (10)
Methodist (219)	Reformed (9)	Other* (35)

• Majority counties are areas in which the leading church body claims 50% or more of the population.

How might these denominational pockets affect social life in areas where one group is highly concentrated?

years, with denominations, sects, and new religious movements at times experiencing membership gains and at other times losses. Robert Wuthnow (1988) argued that there has been a steady decline since the denominational heyday of the 1950s, when most people identified with either the Protestant, Catholic, or Jewish faith. According to Wuthnow, over the last half-century, boundaries among these groups have blurred as baby boomers have adopted a more consumerist approach to religion and more people have married members of other faiths. There is some evidence that old boundaries have been replaced by a liberal-conservative polarization, in which denominational membership is less important than whether a person is a member of a mainline or evangelical church. As we show in Table 15.3, the once-dominant mainstream denominations have experienced membership declines of over 20 percent while some conservative, evangelical Christian churches have had gains of over 400 percent during the past quarter-century.

Social Correlates of Religion

Membership in religious organizations is not random but correlated with a number of social characteristics. For one thing, members of liberal mainline Protestant Episcopal, Presbyterian, Congregational, and Unitarian churches are disproportionately repre-

TABLE 15.3

**MEMBERSHIP CHANGES IN SELECTED EVANGELICAL AND
MAINSTREAM CHURCHES, UNITED STATES
AND CANADA, 1970 AND 2004**

SELECTED CHURCHES	1970	2004	CHANGE
Evangelical Churches			
Assemblies of God	625,027	2,779,095	+445%
Church of Jesus Christ of Latter-Day Saints (Mormons)	2,073,146	5,599,177	+270%
Seventh-Day Adventist Church*	420,419	935,428	+222%
Church of the Nazarene	383,284	631,253	+165%
Southern Baptist Convention	11,628,032	16,267,494	+140%
Mainstream Churches			
Lutheran Church, Missouri Synod	2,788,536	2,463,747	−12%
Presbyterian Church (U.S.A.)	4,045,408	3,139,573	−21%
United Methodist Church*	10,509,198	8,186,254	−22%

* 2003 Data

Source: "Membership Changes in Evangelical and Mainstream Churches, 1970 and 1995," adapted from the *Yearbook of American and Canadian Churches.* Updated with information from *Yearbook of American and Canadian Churches,* 2006.

sented at the top of the stratification system. In terms of annual income, however, Jews rank highest among all religious denominations, followed by several Catholic ethnic groups. Only Latinos, who comprise a minority of all Catholics and are in many cases recent immigrants to America, have relatively low incomes. They approach the income of conservative and evangelical Protestant groups, many of whom have incomes of $20,000 or less and little education (Johnstone, 2006).

Religion also correlates with age and political preference. In social surveys, married or widowed people age 50 and older attend church and define religion as important in their lives at much higher levels than do single people in the 18–24 age cohort. Moreover, the position of the three major religious groups on the political spectrum has not changed much over the last few decades: Protestants are still more likely to be Republican; Jews and Catholics more likely to be Democratic; Jews are more likely to be liberal on political issues, Protestants to be conservative, and Catholics to be in the middle (Johnstone, 2006).

Looking at all religious groups, political change has been greatest among evangelical denominations, which have moved dramatically toward the Republican Party over the last few decades (Kellstedt and Noll, 1990). As Jeffrey Hadden (1990a:467) observed, in the 1988 election evangelical Christians played a major role in former President George Bush's victory over Michael Dukakis, with Bush receiving more than 80 percent of the evangelical vote, and "their allegiance to the Republican Party is now approaching the strength of blacks' allegiance to the Democratic Party." Although former President Bill Clinton gained a share of the evangelical vote in the 1990s, George W. Bush's victory in the 2000 election owed much to white evangelicals, who voted overwhelmingly for the Republican ticket, as they did again in 2004.

Religion and Race: African American Religious Organizations

From the time of their arrival in the colonies in the seventeenth century until today, religion has been of central importance to African Americans. Historian Albert Raboteau (1978) called black religion an "invisible institution" during the slave era; under the cover of darkness, black preachers—men and women—combined African religious ritual with those of white evangelists, and emphasized biblical themes of deliverance and justice to produce a distinctly emotional, spontaneous, and joyous expression of the Christian faith. These beliefs, and the fact that racial inequality is inconsistent with most religious values, are ingrained in the cultural fabric of the church "and are given repeated expression through religious sermons, writings, music, testimonials, prayers, rituals, and emotional interactions" (Morris, 2000:447).

In 1816 in Philadelphia, the African Methodist-Episcopal (A.M.E.) Church was organized as the first black national church; a decade and a half later the first black national political organization also was organized in Philadelphia, at Bethel Church (Raboteau, 1988).

Following the Civil War, the church was fundamental to the advance of blacks from slavery to freedom, both leading and supporting African American community life. As centers of social, economic, and political life before and after the Civil War, the black church played a key role in the great migration of blacks from the rural South to Northern industrial centers. It also helped with the transition from rural to urban society, by securing jobs and housing for many people. There was an extraordinary proliferation of black Protestant denominations and sects soon after the turn of the twentieth century as blacks attempted to cope with segregation and ghetto life (Roof and McKinney, 1987; Montgomery, 1993). In subsequent years the black church was more complex with new institutions and leaders, but its influence in the black community was undiminished. In fact, the black church provided the great push toward real liberation, with the Reverend Martin Luther King Jr. and the Southern Christian Leadership Conference front-line leaders in the Civil Rights movement (Montgomery, 1993). Today, the black church remains a vital force in African American life and culture.

Women and Religion

Historically, women have remained in the background in mainstream churches, although in the last two centuries they have led many evangelical revivals and new religious movements and have assumed similar roles in most mainline religious organizations. Women challenged patriarchal religious institutions soon after the establishment of the first colonies. For example, in 1638 Anne Hutchinson argued for spiritual freedom and equality with men, which resulted in her banishment from the New England colony. Other seventeenth-century dissenters were kept in their place by periodic witchhunts and accusations of heresy.

Evangelical revivals of the eighteenth century, though, which emphasized women's spiritual and moral superiority over men, encouraged many women to play more active religious roles. From the mid-eighteenth to the mid-nineteenth centuries church attendance nearly doubled, from 17 to 33 percent, and women—mainly women under age 30—comprised about two-thirds of active church members (Blauvelt, 1981; Hackett, 1990). Moreover, the *feminization of piety* in the nineteenth century put women at the forefront of many new sect and religious movements, including Christian Science, Theosophy, Spiritualism, and Shakerism (Robbins and Anthony, 1990). Rosemary Keller (1988:1555) argued that women evangelists were well received "as long as they did not seek licenses to preach or be ordained," but this barrier began to dissolve as early as 1853, when Antoinette Brown was ordained by the Congregational Church.

After a century of being channeled into various lay minister, deaconess, and other subordinate positions, women have achieved fully ordained status in about half of all mainstream denominations, as well as among both Reform and Conservative Jewish denominations; by 1990 some 21,000 women served as ministers (Jorstad, 1990; Chaves, 1997). Today, only the Roman Catholic Church, Islamic, and Orthodox Jewish hierarchies, and some fundamentalist Christian sects and denominations continue to resist women's full participation in churches, mosques, and synagogues.

The reemergence of the feminist movement in the 1960s helped inspire a new era in the churches and people's ideas about religion in general. So did the supply-demand crisis, which, beginning in the 1980s, forced many church hierarchies that preferred middle-aged, white male clergy to consider women for clerical positions. By the 1980s, women comprised more than 50 percent of students at both liberal and conservative Protestant seminaries, and women clergy, such as Barbara Harris, the first woman bishop of the Anglican Church, are helping dismantle patriarchal religious institutions and beginning the process of reuniting masculine and feminine religious elements (Woodward, 1989). At the same time, women are participating in innovative religions in increasing numbers.

But gender discrimination continues in new guises. First, even in the most liberal denominations—such as the Episcopal Church, which has women bishops—many congregations still refuse to receive women ministers. As one woman minister described it, there is a "stained-glass ceiling" that continues to limit women clergy to either churches with small congregations or niche areas like hospitals or rural churches. Further, as is true of most other American occupations, women are "paid thousands less per year than men" (Sharn, 1997:1A). A notable exception is Unitarian Universalists, who routinely train and ordain women clergy and pay them the same as men.

Women, however, have made major advances in many new religious movements. In spiritualism, occultism, and paganism, they are in the majority as both followers and leaders. Women also predominate in channeling, healing, divination, and many other New Age groups that may have a major impact on our understanding of religion in the new century (Puttick, 1997).

Only relatively recently have women assumed top-level positions within mainstream churches. In 1989, Barbara Harris became the first female bishop in the Anglican Church. Her mother and Anglican officials appear at her side.

How have women altered the traditional clergy role?

the FUTURE
LOOKING to

RELIGION IN THE TWENTY-FIRST CENTURY

While participation in religious organizations varies considerably around the world, belief in the supernatural realm (and God) remains high. In only seven countries do more than 15 percent of the population "describe themselves as atheists" (Greeley, 2002:8). Even in Communist China, religious groups—both Muslim and

Christian—are on the ascendency, and "huge modern church centres are now prominent features of many cities" (Lambert, 2001:128). While the central government is concerned about "religion being used to subvert the party," and periodic repression of religious groups is likely to continue, "the overall trend of Chinese society, and of religious affairs, is toward plurality and greater openness (Lambert, 2001:128).

In the United States, some sociologists maintain that the trend toward religious pluralism, which began in the 1960s, has shifted toward "religious polarization." They attribute this development in part to declines in membership and influence of mainline denominations, which once provided a broad national consensus on moral issues but no longer do (Anthony and Robbins, 1990; Bellah, 1990). "Between 1990 and 2000, the proportion of adult Americans who report that they have 'no religious preference' (NRP) has approximately doubled" (Marwell and Demerath, 2003:314). Today, there are deep divisions on issues such as homosexuality, abortion, euthanasia, and research involving human stem cells.

Paradoxically, as Anthony and Robbins (1990) observed, the decline in moral consensus has increased demands for government regulation of morality, which in turn has discredited the secular ideal of segregating morality and government. For example, today, battles are being waged between evolution and "creationism." In many states there is support for organized school prayer and for years the chief justice of the Alabama Supreme Court battled with federal court justices over a granite monument with the Ten Commandments that he installed in his courthouse. The federal courts ruled that the monument was a religious monument, while the Alabama judge and his fundamentalist supporters argued that the Ten Commandments were the "moral foundation of America" (Gettleman, 2002).

Across the nation, old distinctions between sacred and secular organizations are no longer clear. Many organizations, such as Scientology and other "human potential groups," have straddled the fence between the sacred and secular and have defined themselves as "sort of religious," though they employ the term *spiritual* to describe group experiences (Greil and Rudy, 1990:223). No less problematic is the economic expansion and diversification of religious organizations—especially the giant media ministries—into health care, education, and other business enterprises, which also has blurred traditional church-state boundaries. Focus box 15.4 examines how the Human Genome Project has obscured traditional science and religion boundaries.

The Bush Administration's "faith-based initiative" presents similar dilemmas. It encourages religious organizations, such as the Salvation Army, Catholic Charities, and Lutheran Social Services, to provide assistance to the poor and needy with government funding and with few strings attached. Proponents of the plan argue that faith-based organizations alleviate serious social problems at home, like feeding the homeless, and overseas missions, many in remote areas, make a special contribution to solving a host of difficult problems, including HIV/AIDS (Green, 2003). But supporters of church–state separation contend that the government's no strings policy may lead to taxpayer-funded proselytizing by religious charities and job discrimination, in the form of such actions as hiring and firing employees based on their religious beliefs. Others take the more extreme view, believing that if left unchecked this policy may lead to governmental control of religious organizations or even to a new version of "state-sponsored religion" (Zimbrick, 2003:1). Further, some religious fundamentalists are opposed because they fear that federal money might help cults spread what they believe are dangerous messages (Adams, 2001; Curl, 2004). Despite these and other concerns, in 2004 President Bush ordered the Justice Department to release $3.7 billion to religious charities and faith-based programs (Curl, 2004).

One scholar contends that demographic trends, including adolescents at numbers higher than at any other time since the 1970s, may fuel new religious movements, much as they did decades earlier. And many aging baby boomers—in search of miracle cures and an extension of their lifespans—may provide an even richer market for new religious movements that purport to have answers to these human needs (Jenkins, 2000:20).

Perhaps with increasing state encroachment into moral and religious spheres, we will witness the growth of many more religious-political televangelical and Internet-based religious organizations. Ecumenism and greater interdenominational cooperation also

Since the beginning of the Enlightenment, science and religion have had an uneasy and sometimes contentious relationship. With the patenting of new life forms, human genes, and genetically engineered animals, this relationship has grown even more complex and strained. Today, the Human Genome Project, which assembled a world-renowned cast of scientists to map and sequence the approximately 30,000 human genes and identify their function, is at the center of this controversy. Sociologist Dorothy Nelkin (1996) contends that these scientists are trying to walk a fine line between scientific and religious groups, and until now their tactics have won few converts from either side.

Sociologist Barbara Katz Rothman (1995, 1998) has called the project a new, highly sophisticated version of biological determinism. Today, she says that whatever the question is, genetics seems to be the answer. Virtually every possible issue of our time—race and racism, addictions, war, disease, sexuality—all have been explained to some extent by genetics. It is not the claims that eventually science might discover a "gene for everything" that Rothman (1995:6) challenges, but the belief of many scientists that "the human condition, our body, and souls, our health and hopes, are genetically determined, that has consequences." Moreover, computer metaphors that describe DNA as a "program" that can be altered, fixed, and perhaps even reprogrammed to produce "perfect" people ignore our fundamental social nature and the importance of social interaction in the making of all human beings.

Perhaps because of attacks from those who say the Human Genome Project dehumanizes people and treats the body as a mechanical entity, other geneticists have chosen to emphasize traditional religious imagery to win over the public. As Dorothy Nelkin (1996:24) wrote, much of the language of geneticists emphasizes the "sanctity of the genes," and DNA "is treated in many ways as a secular equivalent to the Christian soul." For example, some scientists have described the human genome as "the Bible." Others have called it a "sacred text," and still others have said that to understand the genome is the ultimate answer to the Biblical mandate "Know thyself." In addition to finding "ultimate meaning" in the genes, others claim that they also hold the key to "eternal life." One biotech firm now offers to preserve a person's gene set for a future when science is capable of resurrecting the dead and perhaps even granting individuals "immortality." Other firms are already promoting the magical powers of genes by producing cards and jewelry that contain DNA cloned from famous rock stars and athletes (Nelkin, 1996).

Nelkin says that such practices will probably not "spread the faith of science." Instead, they will likely have the opposite effect. As Nelkin (1996:25) observed, such language and imagery are "encouraging the very image of DNA—its image as a sacred entity—that has attracted so much religious opposition. It is, ironically, scientists themselves who are providing weapons in the war between science and religion."

TAKING A CLOSER LOOK

Can you think of any language and imagery that scientists might use to promote the Human Genome Project and reconcile at least some of the differences between religious and scientific groups? What is wrong with using the language and imagery of traditional religions and melding them with scientific approaches to create a new reality and vision of the future? After all, that is what different religious traditions have done from the beginning of civilization. Take a position and build a logical argument for or against this possibility.

Source: Dorothy Nelkin and Susan Lindee. *The DNA Mystique: The Gene as a Cultural Icon.* New York: Freeman, 1995. Barbara Katz Rothman. "Of Maps and Imaginations: Sociology Confronts the Human Genome Project." *Social Problems* 42(1), 1995:1–10. Dorothy Nelkin. "Genetics, God, and Sacred DNA." *Society* 33(4), 1996:22–25. Barbara Katz Rothman. *Genetic Maps and Human Imaginations: The Limits of Science in Understanding Who We Are.* New York: W. W. Norton, 1998.

may be enhanced by government actions. William Petersen (2003) noted that in the 2000 election, when future president George W. Bush was asked what political authority had the greatest influence on him, he responded that "Jesus Christ" did. During that campaign, all of the candidates referred to God a total of 21 times. In 2004, when President Bush was asked if he had consulted his father, the first President Bush, before he ordered troops to invade Iraq, he replied that he had consulted a "higher father." Petersen (2003:57) contends that the politicians' embrace of "quasi-official Christianity" may, in fact, be a "facade." First, American Christianity and people's religious identities in the twenty-first century are complex: in a recent survey concerning personal faith, one person described himself as a "Christian Buddhist," while another said he was an Episcopalian, and "I think of myself as a practicing non-Jew." And, more important according to Petersen (2003:57), there is a widespread belief in religious tolerance and a growing certainty among many Americans that "all peoples, all cultures, all religions, all ethical systems are equivalent."

New telecommunication technologies and general trends toward the privatization of religion should boost "cyberchurches" as well—especially among professionals, baby boomers, and perhaps large segments of the elderly—in the United States and globally. But we should be cautious about predictions of an imminent decline or end of mainstream religious organizations. During the last few decades, an estimated two-thirds of the 8 million or so baby boomers dropped out of organized religion (Woodward, 1990). In the twenty-first century, however, more than one-third of the dropouts have returned. More educated and affluent, with strong consumerist values and more eclectic understandings of religion, many Americans are open to many spiritual possibilities, though most now see religion as a "personal quest" (Wuthnow, 1998; Adler, 2005a).

Today, the "spiritual" pervades popular culture and every group—Catholics, mainline Protestants, Jews, Latinos, 12 steppers, environmentalists, feminists—just about everybody—invokes the word *spiritual* (Roof, 1998:2). Baby boomers have linked their religious beliefs to political issues and concern for the environment (Scheitle, 2005; Bieland Nilsson, 2005).

New immigrants will fuel religious revivals as well. Already, immigrants from the Caribbean, Africa, and Latin America have brought new religious traditions from their home countries to urban America. And, in what sociologists call *religious syncretism*, they have blended elements of various religious traditions to suit life in the *diaspora*, where immigrants maintain dual or multiple residences—in their home countries and their adopted American homes. For example, Elizabeth McAlister (1999) describes how Haitian immigrants in New York City have blended Vodou, Catholicism, and new religious elements to suit their changing circumstances. As transnational migration proceeds in the twenty-first century, we can expect many new religious movements and practices that mirror the shifting needs and realities of transnational migrants (McAlister, 1999).

Will Americans become more tolerant and open to new religious ideas and organizations? Or, will the opposite occur and theological boundaries grow more rigid as some see Christianity beseiged by a diverse community of believers? Sociologists have no crystal ball to answer these important questions, but most would agree that, as in the past, religion will continue to play a vital role in American society.

Summary

1 Religion is a system of socially shared symbols, beliefs, and rituals directed toward a sacred, supernatural realm that addresses the ultimate meaning of life.

2 Religious belief systems can be categorized into four ideal types: animatism, animism, theism, and ethical religions.

3 Sociologists classify religious organizations into four ideal types: ecclesia and denominations, which tend to be large, formally organized religious bodies, and sects and new religious movements, which are usually smaller and exist in negative tension with society.

4 Functionalists argue that religion provides meaning and social solidarity, whereas conflict theorists contend that religion is an instrument of elite economic and political exploitation and oppression. Max Weber agreed that the economy influenced ideology but argued that religious beliefs also may promote economic and social change.

5 While the secularization thesis maintains that modernization inevitably leads to religious decline, religion in America and in a global context suggests that secularization also generates sects and new religious movements.

6 In the last few decades mainline congregations have lost members in the United States, while sects and new religious movements have flourished. Membership in religious organizations is correlated with social class, race, gender, and other social characteristics.

7 Today, by employing virtually all forms of mass communication, including the Internet, Christian religious groups and other religious entrepreneurs reach across the globe to influence billions of believers.

8 Sociologists see a continued growth of conservative denominations and sects, and new religious movements including "megachurches" as well as "cyberchurches" on the Net.

Key Terms

animatism (p. 426)
animism (p. 427)
denomination (p. 429)
ecclesia (p. 429)
ethical religions (p. 429)
magic (p. 425)

monotheistic religions (p. 427)
New Age (p. 441)
new religious movement (p. 432)
polytheism (p. 427)
profane (p. 425)

religion (p. 424)
sacred (p. 425)
sect (p. 430)
secularization thesis (p. 436)
theism (p. 427)

Chapter 16

Politics and War

"Politics is war without bloodshed, while war is politics with bloodshed."

—Mao Zedong

Military service—especially in times of war, has been a political issue and has figured into almost every presidential campaign. General George Washington's heroic deeds on the battlefields during the Revolutionary War earned him a seat in the first Continental Congress and led to his election as the first president of the United States. General Ulysses S. Grant's leadership of the Union troops during the Civil War helped propel him into the presidency, and General Dwight Eisenhower was sought out as a presidential candidate by both political parties after serving as Commander of the Allied Forces during World War II. Although a somewhat reluctant candidate, insisting that he was a military man, not a politician, he was nominated by the Republican party and elected thirty-fourth president of the United States. Political strategists and popular opinion after World War II and the election of "Ike" forever cemented the relationship between politics and war, and seemed to assure that no candidate without military service stood a chance of being elected to the House or Senate, much less the presidency. But as sociology teaches us, *things are not necessarily what they seem.*

In 1992, William Jefferson Clinton, governor of Arkansas sought and received the nomination of the Democratic party. Clinton differed from other post–World War II presidential candidates in two very important ways: he was the first baby boomer to seek the office, and he was the first major candidate who had no prior military service. In fact, while studying as a Rhodes Scholar at Oxford, he even participated in a demonstration protesting the Vietnam War. In a hotly contested campaign where Clinton's non–military record became an issue, Clinton defeated incumbent President George H. W. Bush, a former World War II fighter pilot. After Clinton's re-election, political pundits suggested that perhaps the link between military service and perceived fitness for the office of

Commander-in-Chief had been severed. Then, in 2004, we were reminded once again that things may not be what they seem. George W. Bush, son of the former president, ran for re-election against Senator John Kerry, a decorated soldier from the Vietnam War. During the younger Bush's first campaign, the status of his military service (he had been in the Texas National Guard) received little or no attention. But because the United States was engaged in a war in Iraq, the fact that President Bush had never served in combat—and neither his vice president, Dick Cheney, nor Secretary of Defense Donald Rumsfeld had served in the military at all—became a major campaign issue in 2004. As a counterattack, a group of Vietnam veterans and Bush supporters identifying themselves as the "Swiftboat Veterans" emerged charging that Kerry's military service was not as glorious as portrayed and suggesting that he did not deserve the Silver Star or three Purple Hearts that he had been awarded while serving as a Swift boat captain in Vietnam. As a result of the heated campaign rhetoric laced with charges and countercharges from both candidates and parties, a new political term, "swiftboating" was coined to describe the phenomenon of attacking political candidates' fitness to be president based on their military service record.

Arnold Schwarzenegger transformed his box office appeal and action star status into political power when he was elected governor of California. His wife, Maria Shriver, also a media personality, was no stranger to politics, having grown up as part of the Kennedy family.

In his farewell speech to the nation three days before leaving the Oval Office, career military man and decorated war hero, President Bwight D. Eisenhower warned:

> In the councils of government, we must guard against the acquisition of unwarranted influence, whether sought or unsought, by the military-industrial complex. The potential for the disastrous rise of misplaced power exists and will persist.

POWER AND POLITICS

Power and authority are fundamental to politics, and politicians and ordinary people use both to affect the actions of others. Those with power can compel obedience and force people to do what they may not wish to do. When people have authority others follow their commands not because they have to, but because they want to or believe it is their duty.

According to Max Weber (1968), **power** is *the ability to realize one's will even against the resistance and opposition of others.* If the focus shifts to power within groups and organizations, power also may be defined as the social capacity to make binding decisions that have far-reaching consequences for a society (Orum, 2001). **Politics,** of course, is about power; it is *a social process through which people and groups acquire, exercise, maintain, or lose power over others.* While power is channeled largely through **political institutions,** which are *relatively enduring social arrangements that distribute and exercise power,* it is also expressed in friendship, courtship, relations between parents and children, and in virtually all social interactions.

There are many sources of power. Income and wealth are vital sources. Because they control billions in corporate assets, in addition to their own personal fortunes, CEOs and other top executives have considerable political influence and power at every level of politics. In contemporary industrial societies, renown in science, sports, and entertainment can be converted to power as well. For example, can you think of a few Holly-

POWER
The ability to realize one's will even against the resistance and opposition of others.

POLITICS
A social process through which people and groups acquire, exercise, maintain, or lose power over others.

POLITICAL INSTITUTIONS
Relatively enduring social arrangements that distribute and exercise power.

wood celebrities and sports stars who became important political figures in recent years? Power can also come from the ballot box and collective organizations. With minimal resources and organizational structure, even the poorest of the poor—the homeless—"who have only their bodies and time as resources" can influence public policy (Wagner and Cohen, 1991:545).

While all of these resources may provide power, historically **governments,** which consist of *people and organizations that formulate and implement public policy,* often have placed special emphasis on coercion. Coercion and power are two sides of the same coin. Power is the *ability* or potential to use force to get one's way; whereas **coercion** is *the actualization of a threat.* Max Weber made the important point that coercion is a costly and inefficient means of controlling others, because the moment leaders fail to exercise it, followers invariably stop following their commands. In the long run, power is exercised more effectively through other means, and one of the most important is authority.

TYPES OF AUTHORITY

Authority is *a form of legitimate power that has widespread social approval and is obeyed because people believe that those who exercise it have a right to do so.* For example, although sociology instructors often explore controversial subjects that students may not wish to discuss, most do, because they believe their instructors have the "authority" to explore these issues. People in roles with more authority than teachers can usually get people to submit to even greater demands. For example, each day at airports around the world many people submit to intimate body searches and sometimes even strip-searches by perfect strangers—in part, because of their "authority."

Max Weber (1947:328–329) identified three major types of legitimate power, which he termed *traditional, legal-rational,* and *charismatic* authority. Because it has become increasingly important since Weber's death in 1920, we add *expertise* as the fourth major source of authority.

Traditional Authority

Traditional authority is *a form of authority based on custom and habit, which has its roots in the distant past and often is religiously sanctioned.* Christian fundamentalists, for example, use the Bible to support claims that men should have authority over women—arguing that not only is it divinely ordained, but also that it has been that way "since the time of Adam and Eve." Traditional authority is usually hereditary and based on ascriptive statuses (age, race, sex, religion), and people typically obey those who have it because they always have done so—not because their leadership is especially good, just, or wise.

Legal-Rational Authority

Legal-rational or bureaucratic **authority** is *authority based on explicit rules, regulations, and procedures that define who holds power and how power is to be exercised and distributed.* Legal-rational authority is legitimated by law rather than custom and stresses qualifications, credentials, and other achievements that entitle a person to occupy a position of authority. In legal-rational authority, people are elected or appointed to achieve specific objectives, and the relative powers of each office are stated in faculty handbooks, corporate charters, and constitutions.

Charismatic Authority

Charismatic authority is *authority based on unique personal qualities, which include the ability to excite and inspire followers.* When a person has it, he or she invariably becomes the center of attention wherever people are gathered. In the 1960s, while walking down a city street, one of the authors encountered Robert Kennedy. To this day, he remembers the charged atmosphere surrounding Kennedy and his entourage. The excitement was not caused by the fact that at the time

GOVERNMENTS
People and organizations that formulate and implement public policy.

COERCION
The actualization of a threat.

AUTHORITY
A form of legitimate power that has widespread social approval and is obeyed because people believe that those who exercise it have a right to do so.

TRADITIONAL AUTHORITY
A form of authority based on custom and habit, which has its roots in the distant past and often is religiously sanctioned.

LEGAL-RATIONAL AUTHORITY
Authority based on explicit rules, regulations, and procedures that define who holds power and how power is to be exercised and distributed.

CHARISMATIC AUTHORITY
Authority based on unique personal qualities, which include the ability to excite and inspire followers.

Max Weber believed that the best way to capture the essence of charisma was to define it in religious terms as a "gift of grace." One twentieth-century figure who had an abundance of charisma was the Rev. Dr. Martin Luther King Jr., who inspired people to work for social justice and equality.

Can you think of any other charismatic leaders?

Kennedy was Attorney General—a powerful but not especially glamorous role—but by his *charisma,* which in Greek means "gift of grace" (Thompson, 1990).

Because charismatic authority rests on the appeal and abilities of an individual, however, it is the most tenuous and unstable form of authority. Often short-lived, it may end suddenly with a leader's death or with a single incident that causes believers to lose faith in their leader's special "gifts," as did the sex scandals of Jim Bakker and Jimmy Swaggart in the late 1980s and early 1990s, and the sex and drug scandal involving Ted Haggard in 2006.

Expertise

Expertise is *a form of authority derived from the possession of specialized knowledge.* Today, almost all of us defer to the authority of experts, not only because they produce vaccines and send rockets into outer space, but also because they define problems and offer solutions to important concerns of modern life. The relative influence and power of experts is further enhanced by collective organizations such as the American Bar Association and the American Medical Association that not only restrict membership to those with proper credentials and monitor members' activities, but also attempt to codetermine major developments in government and industry (Haskell 1984; Rueschemeyer, 1986; Stryker, 1990).

Even a cursory examination of the fortunes and careers of political leaders demonstrates that the various ideal types of authority are by no means mutually exclusive. In real life, skilled politicians often employ them in various combinations to enhance their power. For example, Presidents Kennedy, Reagan, and Clinton combined charismatic and legal-rational authority to achieve many of their political objectives, and members of the Bush and Kennedy families can even draw on traditional authority by emphasizing their family's long history of service to the nation.

POLITICS AND INFLUENCE

Although it is more subtle and indirect than power, influence is a vital resource in contemporary politics. When it is properly employed, people may have no idea they are conforming to the wishes of others. **Influence** is *the ability to affect the behavior of others through persuasion, rewards, inducements, and appeals to reason.* Sometimes influence is employed in the absence of power or formal authority, for example by salespeople, who cannot force people to buy their products but must rely instead on persuasive skills. Even presidents, who have considerable power, use persuasion to convince members of Congress to support bills they favor and hold such events as fireside chats to sway public opinion.

Propaganda, Censorship, and Ideology

One well-known form of influence is **propaganda,** which is *"the communication of facts, ideas, and opinions not for the audience's sake but to benefit the communicator"* (Dye and Zeigler, 1983:17). Propaganda often appeals to peoples' emotions. Another well-known form of influence is *censorship,* in which information is withheld or altered. In what is called "psychological warfare," modern governments also conduct "misinformation" or "disinformation" campaigns, which include the selective leaking of false or misleading information to the mass media for specific political or military objectives.

A far more subtle and effective use of influence, however, is when governing elites use the mass media, churches, schools, museums, and other institutions to create political and other *ideologies.* These include beliefs, values, attitudes, and norms that rationalize and support elite power and privilege.

Politics, Influence, and the Mass Media

The mass media are most people's primary source of information about politics, politicians, and government activities around the world, and being the hub of the global communication industry, the United States is the primary source of that information. In

EXPERTISE
A form of authority derived from the possession of specialized knowledge.

INFLUENCE
The ability to affect the behavior of others through persuasion, rewards, inducements, and appeals to reason.

PROPAGANDA
The communication of facts, ideas, and opinions not for the audience's sake but to benefit the communicator.

the United States alone about 65 million people tune in the news on the three major broadcast networks and *CNN* each evening. For politicians in contemporary society, the media involves more than being seen and heard or even making news; they are now fundamental to governing.

Despite the many conflicts and strains, the interests, needs, and activities of media organizations and governments are, in fact, "reciprocal"; the media need politics and politicians for their news reports, and politicians, in turn, require the media to get elected, set the agenda, and shape public policy. Since the 1950s, when television aired the first 30-second campaign ads, and especially after the famous Kennedy-Nixon debate in 1960, television has dominated the electoral process, with media professionals—pollsters, consultants, advertisers, and image-makers—essential ingredients in any candidate's success. So are appearances on *Good Morning America,* the *Oprah Winfrey Show, Larry King Live,* MTV, and other popular television shows. And today a growing number of people—especially those between 18 and 29 years of age—get their information about presidential candidates from late-night comedy/talk shows.

Mass-media portrayals of politics are not so much about issues or party platforms but are "entertainment masquerading as news," wrote Dye and Zeigler (1983:26). On television, abstract political issues and dull "talking heads" are out; by contrast, campaign hoopla, American flags, emotionally charged rhetoric, entertaining personalities, and personal attacks against the opposition—including candidates' husbands, wives, children, and even family pets—are in. Even political messages of presidential candidates are becoming little more than "sound bites." As one study found, candidates' sound bites on network newscasts "dropped from 40 seconds in 1968 to 10 seconds in 1988 (*The Futurist*, 2000b:18).

Moreover, the media tend to reinforce stereotypes—especially gender stereotypes—that highlight the active role of men in the public arena. When women politicians are spotlighted, sex-role stereotypes often overwhelm the issues in question. If you look carefully at most media frames you will see that they usually highlight the "fact" that men and women have different areas of competence in public life; in the mainstream media, women politicians often address social issues of family and child care, education, and poverty, whereas male politicians tackle what are framed as vital national concerns such as defense and foreign policy matters (Bowen, 1996; Dietrich, 1997; Norris, 1997).

How has all of this affected American politics? Political scientist Larry Sabato (1991:23) contended that it has produced a "feeding frenzy" that not only reveals character flaws, but also damages the political fabric by "cheapening the public discourse, trivializing the campaign agenda, breeding cynicism, and discouraging able people from seeking public office." Michael Morgan (1989:251–252) contended that the audience also is affected: "Heavy viewers think like conservatives, want like liberals, and yet call themselves moderates."

Geena Davis won a Golden Globe for her portrayal of President of the United States, Mackenzie Allen, in the television drama *Commander in Chief,* but despite initially high ratings, the show failed to capture a large audience and soon was replaced. Some say the show's failure was due to poor writing and uninteresting plots as compared to the popular television show, *West Wing,* which preceded it. Others contend the American viewing public simply was not ready for a female president.

What do you think?

TECHNOMEDIA, INFLUENCE, AND CONTEMPORARY POLITICS

In the past decade, politics has gone on-line, creating a forum for political debate and an exchange of information that may alter politics everywhere on earth. According to one researcher:

A new postindustrial politics is emerging, one that resists big government and stresses social issues—gender equality, environmental concerns, and human rights, among other issues—that may or may not be linked in voters' thinking. Postindustrial politics will "use the media and Internet more actively." Moreover, social movements and policy experts will rise in salience, whereas traditional parties and interest groups will likely experience further declines. (Clark, 2000:48)

One political scientist contends that new technology has "broken government's monopoly on the collection and management of large amounts of information" (Haass, 1997:36). According to this view, new media, including the Internet, fax machines, and cellular phones, have made it impossible for political officials to restrict and control information. Moreover, it is much more difficult for them to monitor and control opposition groups. At the same time, two-way communication on the Web may offer people an unaccustomed voice in policy decisions. It gives politicians instant access to shifting public values, moods, and opinions (Castells, 1996; Haass, 1997).

Because contemporary information technologies are proliferating at such a rapid rate—including new personalized media that give millions of ordinary people worldwide access to information—even Mao Zedong's famous words, "Power comes from the barrel of a gun," no longer ring as true as they did a half-century ago. As one social activist told a *Newsweek* reporter, "What governments should really fear, is a communications expert" (Watson et al., 1995:36). Today that "expert" might be an MIT graduate who works for a government think-tank or an 11-year-old computer hacker who lives in Estonia, New Zealand, or the Bronx, New York.

Perhaps new media have the greatest potential for expanding public participation in the democratic process. One survey estimated that nearly three-fourths of potential voters were on-line during the 2000 election (White and Shea, 2000). Other analysts predict that sometime during the twenty-first century, voter registration, political conventions, fundraising, and elections at every level of government will be on-line (Bowen, 1996; Corrado and Firestone, 1996).

Do you think "on-line democracy" will empower ordinary people and enhance participatory democracy? Or, given current media trends, will new interactive technologies merely enhance the power of politicians, celebrity opinion makers, and corporations, whose proliferating websites receive far more attention and public visits than do third parties, let alone those devoted to more radical approaches to politics? Today, all serious politicians and their supporters, political interest groups, and grassroots activists have websites. Focus box 16.1 takes a closer look at the new information media and some of their negative affects on the political process. Today, although some political activists and interest groups may have very modest budgets, the Web enables them to launch large-scale advocacy campaigns, raise money, and bombard government agencies and congressional offices with e-mail messages in support of their causes (Johnson, 2000).

If you were a politician, what would you think would be the best way to appeal to this 24-year-old registered voter?

Political talk-show hosts are on-line as well; the Rush Limbaugh website provides the latest conservative views on political and other issues. Of course, there are numerous anti-Rush websites as well, which monitor and challenge his opinions and "facts" and provide alternative views of social and political issues.

Politics on-line raises many important concerns. For one thing, will computer access indeed be unrestricted and open to "all citizens"? Or, as one political scientist wrote, despite all of the hype and promises of the digital age, access to the media will remain stratified—by wealth and educational level. And information—including political information—"will be sold at a price" (Chan, 1997:337). What do you think?

Even if access to the Internet were free, would the majority of citizens have the time and skills to sort through the volumes of political information, opinion, and "facts"? The latter is particularly problematic, because the Internet presents extraordinary opportunities for politicians and others to spread rumors and misleading information that will test most people's critical thinking skills. And sheer information overload may overwhelm many voters. Others may be highly selective, visiting political websites that support their political preferences while ignoring all others—hardly the active and informed voters envisioned by the nation's founders.

The expansion of the Net presents other political challenges as well. As people gain greater access to global political channels and become politically involved around the

Some scholars believe that in the past decade new information technologies have radically changed political campaigns and perhaps politics itself. Today, modern telecommunications give politicians new ways to interact with voters, read the public mood, and react to public concerns. They also grant politicians and ordinary people extraordinary new ways to deceive, distort, and manipulate voters as well as their opponents.

With the insertion of a fictional character into important real-life political events, *Forrest Gump* became one of the most popular and successful films of the 1990s. In the same period, political ad campaigns did much the same—using similar technologies to doctor films and videos, not for entertainment value but to create a political advantage by manipulating voters' perceptions.

For example, in the 2000 New York Senate race between Democrat Hillary Clinton and Republican Rick Lazio, the Republican Leadership Council ran an ad that made it appear that Lazio was walking with Senator Daniel Patrick Moynihan, the retiring Democrat whose seat was being contested. Moynihan protested that he had never been photographed with Lazio. "The average voter can't tell the forgeries from the real images," says Darrell West, a political advertising expert at Brown University (Moore, 2000). Throughout the 2000 presidential election, both parties relied on computer-generated images for televised campaign advertisements.

During the same period, the political battleground shifted to the World Wide Web, where opportunities for political deception and abuse are even greater. Currently, websites, chat rooms, computer bulletin boards, electronic newsletters, e-mail, blogs, and other on-line services are fundamental in contemporary politics. Incumbents and challengers use these electronic resources to raise funds and discuss important policy issues. They are also important in winning votes—especially from narrowly cast target audiences or the growing number of uncertain and perhaps confused undecided voters.

Today, both major parties and most third parties have websites, as do the president of the United States, members of Congress, cabinet officers, state governors, and politicians at almost every level of government. Many also use chat rooms to meet with constituents and discuss important policy issues.

Although politics on-line may be promising, its openness and accessibility also make it politically vulnerable. Many politicians and candidates find that they are the targets of "rogue websites," nearly identical to their own sites but designed to mock or otherwise embarrass them. In April 1999, Zack Exley set up <GWBush.com>, a website that at first glance seemed to be candidate Bush's official site (which was actually at <GeorgeWBush.com>). Bush complained to the Federal Election Commission, and his lawyers threatened Exley with legal action. Exley responded by redesigning the site with more anti-Bush content, which stung Bush into proclaiming, "There ought to be limits to freedom."

Now that digital politics is widespread, many difficult questions need to be resolved—especially issues of information security and reliability. How can we guarantee that politics on-line will be safe without granting authorities so much power (e.g., cryptography "master keys" to all programs) that they might use to infringe on individual civil liberties? From the opposite angle, if we retain the current system, can we be certain that the newsletter or e-mail message that we received today from the Republican Party, National Organization for Women, or president of the United States is authentic? The same can be said for political messages on-line, chat room discussions, and even what you read on Democratic and Republican party websites. Likewise, the potential for voter fraud, electronic ballot box stuffing, and even electronic sabotage of elections is possible. How might such a catastrophe affect the political system and people's trust in on-line politics? And how might such events—or even the possibility that they might occur— affect democracy itself?

TAKING A CLOSER LOOK

In addition to some of the possibilities noted in this box, create your own scenarios, stressing either the positive or negative potentials of politics in the Information Age. Offer a plan that might help remedy some of your concerns about politics on-line. Or take the opposite tack, and argue why we should limit new technologies in politics.

Source: Michael Pfau and Allan Lauder. "Effectiveness of Adwatch Formats in Deflecting Political Attack Ads." *Communication Research* 21(3), 1994:325–341. Richard N. Haass. *The Reluctant Sheriff: The United States after the Cold War.* Washington, DC: Council on Foreign Relations, 1997. Wayne Rash, Jr. *Politics on the Net: Wiring the Political Process.* New York: W.H. Freeman, 1997. <www.rtmark.com.> Martha T. Moore. "Political Ads Practice Art of Half-Truth," *USA Today,* October 26, 2000.

world, will they cease to be active locally, or even recognize local political issues as being of much significance? And, in politics as in other social arenas, will new media technologies truly boost democracy? Or will they exaggerate social and political divisions— especially those between information haves and have-nots that are much in evidence today?

GLOBALIZATION AND POLITICAL SYSTEMS

Nation-states, which are *governments that have administrative reach across large territories over which sovereignty is claimed,* have been in existence for several centuries. Today, nation-states dominate the political landscape. When the United Nations was founded in 1945 there were 51 nation-states. Since then, the number has grown to over 200, with most new nations former European colonies and former members of the Soviet Union.

All contemporary nation-states share a number of features that distinguish them from *traditional states,* which were characterized by smaller territories, shifting boundaries, and less efficient systems of government—such as ancient city-states. First, each consists of an organized set of institutions that claim a monopoly on the legitimate use of force over relatively large geographic areas. Second, all depend on the capacity of their leaders to use symbols, ideologies, and mass communications to fashion a sense of nationhood and maintain the commitment and loyalty of their citizens. Third, contemporary nation-states have abundant resources and wealth, large and complex bureaucracies, and a pervasive influence on all social institutions (Kertzer, 1988; Orum, 2001).

Although nation-states share many common features, there are major differences in how states exercise and distribute power, as well as in relationships between rulers and ordinary citizens. Sociologists have found it useful to arrange **political systems,** which are *rules and policies that determine the organization, exercise, and transfer of government decision-making power,* along a continuum, with democratic systems that permit widespread public participation at one end and authoritarian systems, which operate without popular consent and suppress all opposition, at the other (Higley and Burton, 1989).

Authoritarian Systems

Many people today are ruled by **authoritarian regimes,** where *power is concentrated in the hands of a single leader, or is monopolized by a small elite (an oligarchy) who govern without constitutional limits and who recognize a responsibility only to themselves, rather than to the general public.* In such systems, people play no meaningful role in choosing leaders, nor do they have any legal means of removing them from office.

Today, most authoritarian systems are dictatorships or oligarchies. A **dictatorship** is *a political system of arbitrary rule by a single individual.* Most dictatorships, however, are short-lived and commonly give way to **oligarchies,** *a small group of elites who wield power and are accountable only to themselves.* According to the so-called *iron law of oligarchy,* elites always emerge in large organizations, because they possess assets of organizational skill, cohesion, and information that is unavailable to either individuals or the masses (Michels, cited in Levine, 1990). Today in South America, Asia, and Africa the most common form of oligarchy is the *military junta,* in which a small group of military leaders seize power from existing governments in coups d'états.

Totalitarian regimes are not content to rule, *they seek to regulate all aspects of people's lives and transform individuals and societies in the name of some utopian vision;* consequently they are the most extreme and repressive form of authoritarianism. To realize their visions, a dictator and a small party of ideological purists usually seize control of the economy, schools, mass media, and other institutions and use propaganda and terror to achieve their objectives. Some prominent examples in the twentieth century were Stalin's communist regime, Hitler's Nazi government, and the Khmer Rouge, which in the 1970s transformed Cambodia into a "Killing Field" in which millions of people lost their lives (Levine, 1990).

Authoritarian regimes often find it necessary to "prove" that they have the consent of the governed. Many contemporary authoritarian regimes now hold popular elections—although only a single party, and often only one candidate, is on the ballot for any given office. Likewise, regimes and groups of every political persuasion now proudly wave the democratic banner. To sort through this ideological maze, it is necessary to define *democracy* and establish some of the general features associated with this system of government.

NATION–STATES
Governments that have a unified administrative reach across large territories over which sovereignty is claimed.

POLITICAL SYSTEMS
Rules and policies that determine the organization, exercise, and transfer of government decision-making power.

AUTHORITARIAN REGIMES
Power is concentrated in the hands of a single leader, or, more commonly, is monopolized by a small elite (an oligarchy) who govern without constitutional limits and who recognize a responsibility only to themselves, rather than to the general public.

DICTATORSHIP
A political system of arbitrary rule by a single individual.

OLIGARCHIES
A small group of elites who wield power and are accountable only to themselves.

TOTALITARIAN REGIMES
They seek to regulate all aspects of people's lives and transform individuals and societies in the name of some utopian vision.

Democratic Systems

A **democracy** is *a political system based on popular participation in decision making, where ultimate authority is vested in the people.* Although democracies enjoy great popular appeal, only a few dozen nations have adopted this political system. They include a stable core of long-established democracies in Western Europe and a few former European colonies, such as Canada, Australia, New Zealand, and the United States, as well as Japan, India, Israel, and a few other nations that became representative democracies after World War II.

Conditions for Democracy

Since the 1950s, sociologists and political scientists have debated the conditions necessary for democracies to take root and flourish, and today there is general consensus that four factors are particularly important:

1. *Advanced Economic Development.* Seymour Martin Lipset's (1963, 1994) comparative study of 48 societies provided strong evidence that advanced economic development and widespread prosperity are important foundations of stable democracies. Lipset emphasized, however, that these conditions do not *guarantee* democratic forms of government. As a survey by Edward Muller (1988) found, where there are great disparities in income between the rich and the poor, democratic institutions tend to be replaced by authoritarian rule.

2. *A Diffusion of Power among a Diversity of Groups and Institutions.* Democracies work best when government powers are divided among many groups, and when people belong to diverse groups and organizations that have cross-cutting interests and loyalties (Blau and Schwartz, 1983).

3. *A Cultural Heritage that Emphasizes the Individual and Promotes Tolerance and Accommodation.* Democracies prosper in political climates that stress individual dignity, guard civil liberties, and emphasize "the desirability of citizen involvement in politics" (Orum, 2001). They also require a consensus among national elites concerning the "rules of the political game and the worth of political institutions" (Higley and Burton, 1990:423).

4. *Access to Information and Informed Citizens.* Democracy is best served when people have unrestricted access to diverse points of view. Since most people rely on the mass media for much of their information, the media can enhance the democratic process or, conversely, become instruments of oppression.

Contemporary Democracies

The word *democracy* is derived from the Greek and means "rule by the people," or majority rule. In the Greek system of *participatory* or *direct democracy,* all citizens regularly assembled and voted on all-important issues. This was possible in populous city-states because citizenship was restricted to a tiny minority of adult male property owners, with the majority—women, youths, slaves, and foreigners—excluded from the political process. Today, because direct democracy would be enormously time-consuming and costly, most democracies have attempted to involve citizens in the political process through *representative* or *indirect democracy,* in which voters delegate authority to elected officials who decide public policy on their behalf.

Democracy and Women's Political Rights

Like the ancient Greeks, most modern democracies initially granted *political rights* only to male property owners. Gradually, property restrictions were removed, but it was not until the feminist movement in the nineteenth and early twentieth centuries that women began to gain some—but not all—of their political rights. For example, during the 1992 election, which the media billed The Year of the Woman, four women were elected to the Senate—giving women a total of eight seats. By the 2000 election, that number had increased to 13 seats. Yet even with these gains, the Senate remained 87 percent male.

DEMOCRACY
A political system based on popular participation in decision making, where ultimate authority is vested in the people.

The National Organization for Women is a powerful interest group with millions of dedicated members. NOW's website details political and social issues that concern women and America.

How has the Internet increased the influence of political interest groups?

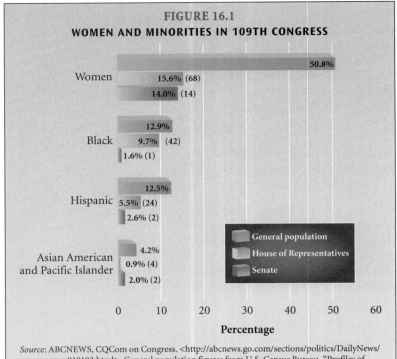

FIGURE 16.1
WOMEN AND MINORITIES IN 109TH CONGRESS

Women
50.8%
15.6% (68)
14.0% (14)

Black
12.9%
9.7% (42)
1.6% (1)

Hispanic
12.5%
5.5% (24)
2.6% (2)

Asian American and Pacific Islander
4.2%
0.9% (4)
2.0% (2)

☐ General population
☐ House of Representatives
☐ Senate

Percentage

Source: ABCNEWS, CQCom on Congress. <http://abcnews.go.com/sections/politics/DailyNews/newcongress010103.html>. General population figures from U.S. Census Bureau, "Profiles of General Demographic Characteristics, 2000 Census of Population and Housing, United States." Washington, DC: U.S. Department of Commerce, May 2001. Updated information from www.house.gov and www.senate.gov.

In the twenty-first century, women are making steady political gains. After the 2006 election, for example, a record 73 women (of 435 members) served in the House of Representatives and 14 women served in the Senate. In several states, including California, both senators were women. Figure 16.1 takes a closer look at the percentage of women and minorities in both Houses of the 109th Congress, as compared to their percentage in the general population.

Democracy, Social Rights, and the Welfare State In addition to granting citizens political rights, most Western-style democracies offer legal and constitutional protection for people's *civil rights,* including freedom of speech and the press, freedom of assembly and petition, the right to organize into groups, and equal justice under the law. In addition, *social rights,* including various benefits and services, have been extended to citizens in all democracies.

During the twentieth century, most industrialized and democratic nations expanded their social welfare responsibilities to the point that these nations are now termed *welfare states.* Since World War II, many European nations, such as Sweden, Denmark, and Great Britain, have institutionalized social rights by adopting comprehensive systems of universal benefits that guarantee workers a basic standard of living, adequate health care, educational benefits, housing, child-care provisions, and many other benefits.

Many Americans believe the U.S. social welfare system is out of control and that people who neither need nor deserve government "handouts" are living it up at taxpayer expense. What they do not understand or recognize is that in addition to poverty programs, there are programs for the elderly, farmers, veterans, and many others whom people do not ordinarily think of as "welfare recipients." Moreover, few realize that over the past several decades, federal and state aid to the poor steadily declined, whereas funding for programs that concerned the elderly and middle- and upper-class constituencies increased.

Conflict theorists argue that because of powerful corporate elites and interest groups, the American welfare state, which consists of a dual system of social insurance for the majority and social assistance for the "stigmatized poor," is far less generous than the aid provided by most European nations. Jill Quadagno (1994:8) contends that the U.S. welfare state is not a corrective to social inequality, but "a system of stratification" in its own right. By promoting competitive individualism and free markets with "winners" and a means-tested "class of failures," the U.S. welfare state reinforces social cleavages between the deserving and "undeserving poor," with the latter category linked to race.

At the beginning of this century, Myles and Quadagno (2000) contended that we were in the midst of the contraction of the welfare state. The clearest signal of this trend was the 1996 Personal Responsibility Act that shifted the focus from federal to state agencies, and ended most means-tested cash assistance programs and substituted workfare for the poor. In this program, most welfare recipients must move into the workforce within 2 years, and all benefits end after 5 years, "regardless of employment status." Should we expect further erosion in welfare and the welfare state? They contend that it is unlikely, because the remaining large programs (Social Security and Medicare) affect politically powerful baby boomers who are approaching old age, and relatively few other programs remain that can be cut (Myles and Quadagno, 2000).

DEMOCRACY: AMERICAN STYLE

Why do some individuals, groups, and organizations receive many benefits from government programs and policies, whereas others receive few? The popular view is that it is the will of the people, because ordinary people elect officials who, for the most part, carry out their wishes. But this idea further illustrates that *things may not be what they seem*. First, in most elections 40–50 percent of the voting age population doesn't vote—thus it is meaningless to talk of "popular sentiment." Further, public opinion polls consistently show that while some majority sentiments become public policy, many others, such as those favoring strict gun control and a balanced federal budget, may not.

To understand American politics, it is necessary to examine not only the formal system of government but also unofficial processes that affect political outcomes. Borrowing Edward Lehman's (1988) complex organizational model of politics, the American political system can be described as having four levels of power (see Figure 16.2). At the top is the state, which includes the three branches of government, various government agencies, and "congeries of associations, bureaus, and corporations that pursue policy outcomes favorable to their interests" (Knoke, 1990:150). Next in power and organizational assets are political parties, and just beneath them are interest groups. At the bottom is the *public* that includes millions of ordinary citizens—each armed with little more than a vote. The public also includes categories of people with similar interests and concerns, such as teachers, firefighters, and the homeless, who have the potential of being mobilized into political parties, interest groups, and social movements.

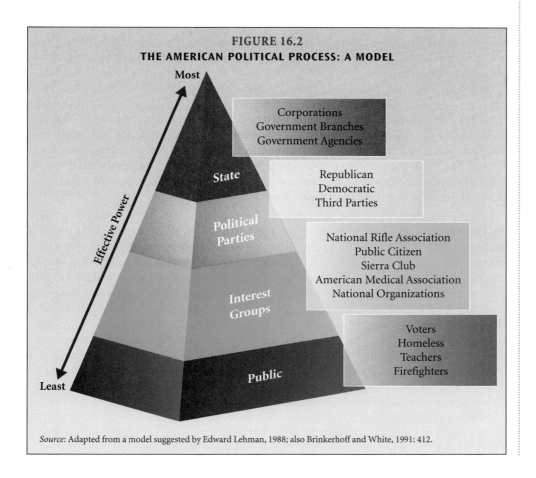

FIGURE 16.2
THE AMERICAN POLITICAL PROCESS: A MODEL

Most

Effective Power

State

Corporations
Government Branches
Government Agencies

Republican
Democratic
Third Parties

Political Parties

National Rifle Association
Public Citizen
Sierra Club
American Medical Association
National Organizations

Interest Groups

Voters
Homeless
Teachers
Firefighters

Public

Least

Source: Adapted from a model suggested by Edward Lehman, 1988; also Brinkerhoff and White, 1991: 412.

Political Participation and the American Voter

When he visited the United States in 1831, Alexis de Tocqueville was struck by Americans' passion for politics (Conway, 1991). If he could return, de Tocqueville would be shocked at how much things have changed. Today, the United States "stands 139th out of 163 democracies in the rate of voter participation" (Gans, 2000:44). Other studies show that as much as 22 percent of the population engage in no political activities at all (Orum, 2001). Voter turnout in nonpresidential elections averages between 40 to 50 percent of eligible voters, and turnout for general elections has been only slightly higher, with presidential elections attracting 50–65 percent of eligible voters. Voter turnout in the United States is, in many cases, more related to convenience than any other factor (Dyck and Gimpel, 2005).

The California Recall election in 2003 proved that voter apathy could be overcome to some extent—especially with an angry electorate and the added bonus of a celebrity candidate. In a rare recall election, about 60 percent of California's registered voters turned out to remove Governor Gray Davis from office and replace him with Hollywood action hero Arnold Schwarzenegger (Kiely, 2003:1).

Even long-standing popular beliefs in the power of "one person, one vote" have been challenged—especially in the 2000 presidential election, when a host of voting machine and other problems in Florida put the presidential election on hold until the U.S. Supreme Court resolved the dilemma. While the media made much of ballot problems in Florida and some other states, two political scientists found that there were other serious problems as well. In their research of the Georgia election, they discovered that "counties with large numbers of new registrants, lower education levels, and a higher proportion of African American voters . . . had higher error rates" (Bullock and Hood, 2002:981).

Voter Behavior: Class, Age, Race, and Ethnicity

Socioeconomic status (income, education, and occupation) is strongly associated with both the type and frequency of political participation as well as party affiliation. With more income, knowledge about issues, time, and other resources, those at the top of the social hierarchy vote at higher rates and participate in a much broader range of political activities than do those at the bottom.

Voter participation also is influenced by age, ethnicity, and race. Although related to other social characteristics, including income and educational attainment, young adults age 18–24 vote at somewhat lower rates than middle-age people or those 65 or older.

Until the Civil Rights movement in the 1960s, voter registration and other laws aimed at hindering minority participation effectively barred many African Americans from the political process. Since their repeal, black voter turnout has increased dramatically. With the exception of affluent and better-educated Cuban Americans, Latino political participation has been much lower.

A Gender Gap?

Since gaining the right to vote in 1920, women have steadily increased their voting rate, for the first time in 1980, exceeding that of men. In 2000, the turnout for women was 61 percent—compared to 58 percent for men—and demographic trends suggest that these voting patterns will continue well into the future. In what some have called a *gender gap,* women's voting patterns also have begun to diverge from those of men. According to an analysis by the Center for Policy Alternatives, a nonpartisan policy center that tracks the gender gap, if only women's votes were counted in the 2000 presidential election, Al Gore would have won the popular and electoral vote in 32 states and would have tied in Colorado. This would have given Gore a landslide victory, with 402 electoral votes to George Bush's 128. The analysis also showed that women cast 52 percent of all votes in the November 2000 election and 54 percent of all votes in the 2004 presidential election.

Women's political influence did not stop at the ballot box; it was greatly expanded by the activities of interest groups such as the National Organization for Women (NOW). Three decades ago, health care, peace, child care, reproductive freedom, and the environment were "women's issues"—"now they top the national agenda" (Hall, 1991:8A).

Interest Groups

The Constitution makes no mention of **interest groups,** which are *groups or organizations that seek to influence government policy and public opinion.* Today, there are over 15,000 registered lobbyists and an estimated 25,000 part-time lobbyists in Washington; they represent interest groups by dealing with public officials, sometimes as the name implies, by directly engaging politicians in "lobbies" outside of legislative chambers, or by wining and dining them in Washington and far more exotic locations, despite laws limiting such activities.

Single-Interest and Public Interest Groups

Interest group activities reflect the diversity of interests and opinions in American society. *Single-interest groups* have narrowly defined causes; an example is the National Rifle Association (NRA), which focuses on gun legislation. Others represent large segments of the population, such as the National Association for the Advancement of Colored People (NAACP). Still others are *public interest groups,* or citizens' lobbies, such as Ralph Nader's group Public Citizen. Globalization has produced many others, and today virtually all nation-states pay lobbyists to represent their interests in Washington (Flammang et al., 1990).

Political Action Committees

Congressional efforts to check "influence peddling" inadvertently encouraged the formation of thousands of additional interest groups called Political Action Committees (PACs). The Campaign Reform Act of 1974, which limited individual contributions to $1,000 and group contributions to $5,000, encouraged wealthy interests—in particular "corporation-established committees"—to collect small contributions from many sources to be donated to candidates who support their causes (Sherman and Kolker, 1987:229). In addition, the Supreme Court ruled that PACs could spend unlimited funds on media campaigns for their favorite candidates—as long as they did not directly collaborate with the candidates' campaign organizations (Edwards, 1988).

INTEREST GROUPS
Groups or organizations that seek to influence government policy and public opinion.

In 1976, PAC contributions to congressional candidates amounted to $23 million. Today through PACs, corporations, labor unions, and citizen's groups annually funnel over $1 billion to candidates of their choice, supplying about a third of the funding for House campaigns and over 20 percent for Senate races. With Senate races costing in excess of $10 million dollars, PAC support has become essential for serious candidates. While PACs favor candidates who support their interests, they also tend to back incumbents who *might* support them in the future. In short, PACs stack the deck against challengers, who usually are fortunate if their campaign contributions amount to half those of incumbents.

To counter the growing clout of powerful interests and what they called "soft money" contributions to political campaigns from corporations, unions, and wealthy individuals, Congress passed the McCain-Feingold Campaign Finance Law of 2002. Although some of the bill's provisions have been challenged in court, it did limit the use of "soft money" (funds raised outside the limits set by federal law) from corporations and wealthy individuals—especially those used to fund issue-ads and "attack-ads" within 60 days of a general election. These ads have become

"*Listen, pal! I didn't spend seven million bucks to get here so I could yield the floor to you.*"

important in swaying "undecided" voters and perhaps even deciding close elections (Willis, 2003; *Congressional Record,* 2003). While some believe that this will be beneficial, others contend that limiting campaign funding did little to affect the larger sums spent by lobbying, and, "If anything, well-funded campaigns provide a counterbalance to special-interest lobbying" (Bailey, 2003:1).

Those who take a pluralist perspective argue that PACs and other interest groups are what democracy is all about because they give everyone input into the political process. Conflict theorists, however, challenge these claims on two grounds. First, they note that PACs do not represent a broad spectrum of interests but favor upper-middle- and upper-class constituencies. Second, they are not all equal: small, poorly funded groups win occasional battles, but when major policy issues are involved, well-organized and well-funded corporate PACs usually prevail.

Some argue that PACs and other interest groups now rival political parties in terms of power and influence. Others contend that while parties have lost power over the last few decades, they have "retained their role as conduits of political power and as links between masses and elites" (Sherman and Kolker, 1987:233).

Political Parties

Political parties, which are *enduring coalitions of individuals who organize to win elections and shape public policy,* are almost as old as the nation itself. The United States was the first representative democracy to adopt mass political parties, and "With few exceptions, two major parties have accounted for about 90 percent of the vote since the 1800s" (Schmidt, 1985:220).

Third party and Independent candidates have a difficult time capturing media attention and getting enough signatures on petitions to even get on the ballot, much less get elected. Name recognition and media attention were not problems for Kinky Friedman, however, when he ran for governor of Texas in 2006. Nevertheless, the popular singer, songwriter, and author received less than 13 percent of the vote. This does not mean that Kinky's candidacy was irrelevant, however, as the incumbent candidate won by a margin of less than 11 percent.

Third Parties
This is not to say that *third parties* have not been plentiful, for in the same period more than 1,000 have made brief appearances. Whether it was a movement or a third party, the 19 million votes that Ross Perot garnered (19 percent of the total) in the 1992 election represented the strongest showing by a non-Democrat or non-Republican since 1912, when Theodore Roosevelt's Progressive (Bull Moose) Party captured about 24 percent of the popular vote.

Over the years, however, most third parties have not even come close to these numbers. In 1988, for example, voters gave 16 third parties less than 1 million votes (of 91 million votes cast), and 7 parties received fewer votes than "none of the above" (*Congressional Quarterly,* 1988). Despite these statistics, third parties can have a powerful effect on close elections; they can siphon off votes from one party or another and play a decisive role in which party prevails in the election. Some contend that is what occurred in the 2000 presidential election, when votes for third-party candidates Ralph Nader and Patrick Buchanan "may have changed the election outcome in Florida and the nation" (Bailey, 2003:1). Research suggests that support for third parties might increase if the electoral college was eliminated and electoral rules changed (Donovan et al., 2005).

Parties and Proportional Representation
In most other democracies—even those dominated by two parties—minor parties, such as the environmentally minded Green Party in Germany, have been able to attract sizeable minority votes and play significant political roles. This is partially true because in Germany, Great Britain, and many other parliamentary democracies, elections are based on *proportional representation,* in which each party gains seats in parliament in proportion to its share of the popular vote. The power of minority parties is further enhanced by an additional rule that if no party is able to win a majority (more than 50 percent of the seats in parliament), several parties must combine to form a coalition government. To accomplish this, large parties often must make important political concessions to smaller parties, or face new elections (Lipsitz and Speak, 1989).

POLITICAL PARTIES
Enduring coalitions of individuals who organize to win elections and shape public policy.

Winner Take All At almost all levels of government in the United States, the outcome of elections is based on a *plurality,* or winner-take-all principle, even if the margin of victory is a single vote. (The exact nature of this system of choosing America's president and other candidates could not have been clearer than during the 2000 election.) Electoral laws and the mass media also place third parties at a disadvantage. In most states, third parties face a rather complex petition process to get on the ballot, and during primaries they must win more than 5 percent of the vote to qualify for federal campaign funds. In addition, even when they raise important issues the mass media virtually ignore them—preferring to cover only "serious candidates" put forth by the two major parties.

With the exception of Roosevelt's New Deal Coalition during the Great Depression, parties have been unable to generate much popular interest. Still, many people continue to identify with parties, and there is a fairly strong association between the Democratic Party and "ordinary working people." It also continues to receive strong support among African Americans, Hispanics, Jews, and women voters. Republicans, while still largely perceived as "the party of business interests and the rich," have steadily eroded Democratic support (Francia et al., 2005).

A comprehensive nonpartisan study by the Pew Research Center reveals that simplistic models that divide the United States into Blue (Democratic) and Red (Republican) states, are at best short-sighted and misleading, and at worst, imply deep political divisions that may not actually exist. Their data indicate that the American political divide is more accurately portrayed when viewed on a spectrum (see Figure 16.3). Figure 16.4 shows voting trends by sex, race, age, and income in the 2004 presidential election.

Analyzing postelection survey results, journalist Richard Ostling (2001) found that "overall, three-fourths of the Bush vote came from all types of white churchgoers who attended church regularly, plus a slim majority of less observant white Protestants." But Bush's strongest supporters were white Evangelicals, 85 percent of whom voted for the Republican candidate. By contrast, nearly two-thirds of religious minority groups—especially black Protestants and Hispanic Catholics—as well as those who define themselves as "secular," and white Catholics who do not attend church regularly, voted for Gore and the Democratic ticket.

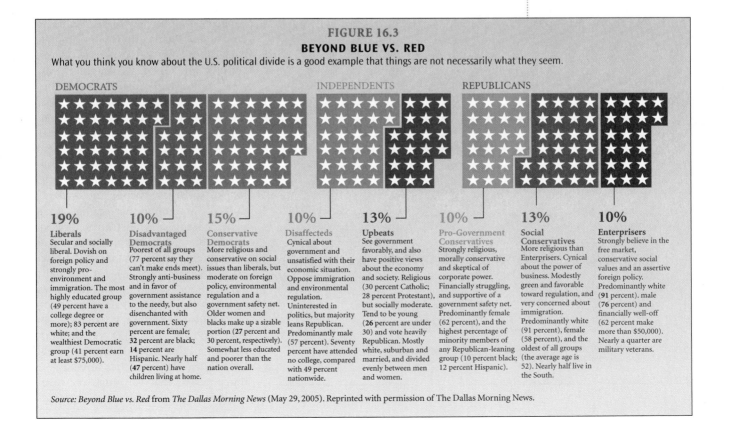

FIGURE 16.3

BEYOND BLUE VS. RED

What you think you know about the U.S. political divide is a good example that things are not necessarily what they seem.

DEMOCRATS   INDEPENDENTS   REPUBLICANS

19%

Liberals
Secular and socially liberal. Dovish on foreign policy and strongly pro-environment and immigration. The most highly educated group (49 percent have a college degree or more); 83 percent are white; and the wealthiest Democratic group (41 percent earn at least $75,000).

10%

Disadvantaged Democrats
Poorest of all groups (77 percent say they can't make ends meet). Strongly anti-business and in favor of government assistance to the needy, but also disenchanted with government. Sixty percent are female; **32 percent are black;** **14 percent are** Hispanic. Nearly half (**47 percent**) have children living at home.

15%

Conservative Democrats
More religious and conservative on social issues than liberals, but moderate on foreign policy, environmental regulation and a government safety net. Older women and blacks make up a sizable portion (**27 percent and** 30 percent, respectively). Somewhat less educated and poorer than the nation overall.

10%

Disaffecteds
Cynical about government and unsatisfied with their economic situation. Oppose immigration and environmental regulation. Uninterested in politics, but majority leans Republican. Predominantly male (**57 percent**). Seventy percent have attended no college, compared with 49 percent nationwide.

13%

Upbeats
See government favorably, and also have positive views about the economy and society. Religious (30 percent Catholic; 28 percent Protestant), but socially moderate. Tend to be young (**26 percent are under** 30) and vote heavily Republican. Mostly white, suburban and married, and divided evenly between men and women.

10%

Pro-Government Conservatives
Strongly religious, morally conservative and skeptical of corporate power. Financially struggling, and supportive of a government safety net. Predominantly female (62 percent), and the highest percentage of minority members of any Republican-leaning group (10 percent black; 12 percent Hispanic).

13%

Social Conservatives
More religious than Enterprisers. Cynical about the power of business. Modestly green and favorable toward regulation, and very concerned about immigration. Predominantly white (91 percent), female (58 percent), and the oldest of all groups (the average age is 52). Nearly half live in the South.

10%

Enterprisers
Strongly believe in the free market, conservative social values and an assertive foreign policy. Predominantly white (**91 percent**). male (**76 percent**) and financially well-off (62 percent make more than $50,000). Nearly a quarter are military veterans.

Source: Beyond Blue vs. Red from *The Dallas Morning News* (May 29, 2005). Reprinted with permission of The Dallas Morning News.

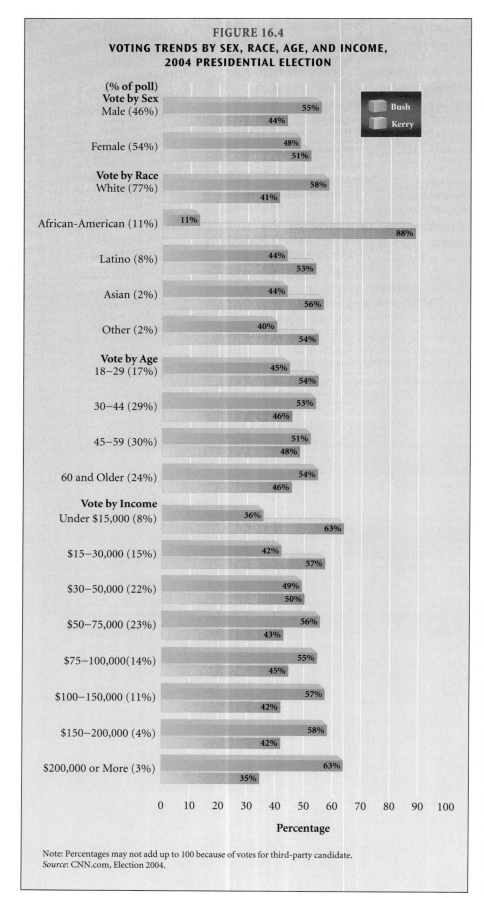

FIGURE 16.4

VOTING TRENDS BY SEX, RACE, AGE, AND INCOME, 2004 PRESIDENTIAL ELECTION

(% of poll)

Vote by Sex
- Male (46%): Bush 55%, Kerry 44%
- Female (54%): Bush 48%, Kerry 51%

Vote by Race
- White (77%): Bush 58%, Kerry 41%
- African-American (11%): Bush 11%, Kerry 88%
- Latino (8%): Bush 44%, Kerry 53%
- Asian (2%): Bush 44%, Kerry 56%
- Other (2%): Bush 40%, Kerry 54%

Vote by Age
- 18–29 (17%): Bush 45%, Kerry 54%
- 30–44 (29%): Bush 53%, Kerry 46%
- 45–59 (30%): Bush 51%, Kerry 48%
- 60 and Older (24%): Bush 54%, Kerry 46%

Vote by Income
- Under $15,000 (8%): Bush 36%, Kerry 63%
- $15–30,000 (15%): Bush 42%, Kerry 57%
- $30–50,000 (22%): Bush 49%, Kerry 50%
- $50–75,000 (23%): Bush 56%, Kerry 43%
- $75–100,000 (14%): Bush 55%, Kerry 45%
- $100–150,000 (11%): Bush 57%, Kerry 42%
- $150–200,000 (4%): Bush 58%, Kerry 42%
- $200,000 or More (3%): Bush 63%, Kerry 35%

Percentage

Note: Percentages may not add up to 100 because of votes for third-party candidate.
Source: CNN.com, Election 2004.

Who Governs? Models of State Power

In Lehman's model, the state and a relatively small number of powerful people were described as sitting atop the political pyramid. Lehman (1988) called the state a "supraorganization," in that most organizations fall under its jurisdiction. At another level of analysis, the state can be described as a decision-making arena where individuals and groups compete for influence and power. Finally, the state can be analyzed at the societal level "beyond the visible appearances of legal structures, governmental decision-making, and political behavior" (Alford and Friedland, 1985:6). These levels of power are represented in the *organizational, pluralist,* and *elite* approaches to contemporary American politics (see Table 16.1).

The Organizational Approach

The organizational approach sees the state as being composed of organizations that differ in their legal and political capacities to control funds and personnel, as well as their abilities to mobilize popular support. From the organizational point of view, power is structural and is observed in the capacity of politically biased state and corporate organizations to dominate each other. Although powerful organizations and interests fragment the state, the overall historical development of the state in industrial societies has been toward bureaucratic centralization (Alford and Friedland, 1985:9).

Although few would accord them unlimited policymaking powers, scholars who subscribe to the *state-centered model,* such as Skocpol and Amenta (1986), maintain that rather than being passive administrative tools of groups that gain government power or instruments of dominant classes, government bureaucracies are "partially autonomous actors" with their own structures and capacities to affect society (Gilbert and Howe, 1991:205). Gregory Hooks (1990: 373), for example, contended that since the end of World War II, the Pentagon has amassed so much power that its budgetary insu-

TABLE 16.1
THREE APPROACHES TO AMERICAN POLICYMAKING: A COMPARISON

	ORGANIZATIONAL APPROACH	PLURALIST APPROACH	ELITE APPROACH
Basic political units	Government agencies and other bureaucratic organizations	Interest groups	Institutional elites
Sources of power	Bureaucracies, laws, and rules	Multiple sources, depending on policy areas and issues	Wealth, power, and control of cultural industries
Decision-making positions	Relatively open	Open	Relatively closed
Basis of power	Position in bureaucratic structure	Motivation, talents, and skill grant access to power	Class position
Limits on power	Checked by elites and occasionally by the public	"Veto groups" check each other's power	Class conflict and social and political protest movements
Ways power is demonstrated	Actual decisions, rules, and regulations	Actual policy outcomes	Decisions and "nondecisions" that never enter the formal political arena

lation enables "high-ranking military officers to operate as relatively autonomous bureaucrats . . . [pursuing] . . . a distinct agenda in key industrial sectors."

Functionalism and the Pluralist Approach   Functionalists argue that power is distributed among many groups and organizations—businesses, labor unions, government agencies, religious groups, and so on. Each has political clout only in certain policy areas and not others. Consequently, no group or organization is able to dominate the system.

Functionalists stress that the vast proliferation of interest groups and the emergence of policy experts and mass media as political forces have made the democratic process even more complex. The world of politics, according to functionalist theory, is an arena of fierce competition and struggle. However, in contrast to the natural world, where the largest and most powerful emerge victorious, functionalists postulate that compromise and stability is the norm. This is because interest groups protect narrow territories or sometimes act in concert with others to act as *veto groups,* which prevent larger, more powerful groups from getting their way (Dahl, 1981, 1982, 1989).

Dahl's study, and pluralist theory in general, has been much criticized by elite theorists, who argue that the pluralist issue-oriented approach and emphasis on formal government reveals only the middle levels and "visible" aspects of power (Bachrach and Baratz, 1962).

Conflict Approaches   According to the conflict approach, there are far more politically powerful actors who operate behind the scenes and exert great influence when it comes to key policy decisions. They control the agenda so the potential issues that do not serve their interests are kept out of the political process. Conflict theorists maintain that real power is concentrated in the hands of a small segment of the population who "are more unified, more conscious, and more manipulative than the pluralists would have us believe" (Domhoff 1970:299).

The Power Elite   C. Wright Mills (1956) argued that a **power elite,** *a small triumvirate of top corporate, political, and military leaders,* dominates American politics. According to Mills, members of the power elite—almost exclusively middle-aged or older white Anglo-Saxon Protestant men—circulate back and forth among government, major corporations, and the military. These men know one another, meet regularly, and informally decide such things as whether America should promote war or peace, whether taxes should be raised or lowered, and all other significant policy matters.

POWER ELITE
A small triumvirate of top corporate, political, and military leaders.

What role do you think lobbyists play in today's political climate?

Not all conflict theorists are willing to limit the size of the elite to such a small number of politically powerful actors, nor do they agree that all members of the elite must regularly interact to decide major policy issues. Dye (1990:10), for example, contended that there are a little more than 7,000 individuals "who occupy the top positions in the institutional structure of American society," who set the agenda and decide the issues that count. According to Dye, three major sectors contribute to the "institutional elite": the *corporate sector* (major banks, industries, and investment firms), which supplies more than 4,000 leaders; the *public interest sector* (mass media, education, foundations, law, and civic and cultural organizations), which provides an additional 3,000; and the *government sector,* which donates several hundred top military and political leaders. Further, studies have shown that there are substantial linkages, or "interlocks, among elites in the corporate, government and civil (nonprofit) sectors" (Moore et al., 2002:726). As Gwen Moore and her colleagues (2002:726) wrote, of these three, major corporations and their directors are the best integrated, and despite considerable growth in the nonprofit sector and foundations in recent years, "nonprofit organization linkages fail to offer compelling evidence of elite pluralism in the United States." Focus box 16.2 examines "diversity and the power elite."

The Governing Class G. William Domhoff (1970, 1990) and Michael Useem (1979, 1983) contend that the ruling elite is a great deal larger than several thousand. They believe the ruling group in the United States includes all members of the upper class. Domhoff calls this group "the governing class," noting that while upper-class families comprise about 1 percent of the population, their representatives use their assets as a base for wielding power in government, industry, the mass media, foundations, and think tanks directly and indirectly to create and implement public policy. To Domhoff, whether one asks *who governs, who benefits* and receives goods and services of highest value in American society, or *who wins* when significant policies are at stake, the answer is always the same—the upper class (Domhoff, 1990).

Some contend that with the dismantling of communism, the end of the Cold War, and the vast expansion of transnational corporations to the remote corners of the globe, the capitalist upper class has the potential to experience not only unprecedented economic growth but also perhaps a further consolidation and intensification of its power as well. Others are not so sure. They contend that the contradictory "logics" of capitalism, bureaucracy, and democracy have begun to produce serious strains among bureaucratic rules, the law, market rights, and democratic freedoms. Some predict that such tensions and strains will grow worse and present insurmountable problems in the future, perhaps even leading to war, even nuclear war (Alford and Friedland, 1985).

WAR, NUCLEAR WAR, AND SOCIETY

In popular usage, *war* has many meanings: sportscasters often call hard-fought football games "wars," the government has declared a "war" on drugs, and television newscasters report on such things as the "war" between the sexes, "gang wars," and even "pizza wars." But none of these are wars in a sociological sense. To sociologists, **war** means *sustained armed conflicts among politically organized groups that involve large-scale violence and many fatalities.* Wars may involve nations, coalitions of nations, or groups and factions within a society, such as combatants in civil wars.

Perspectives on War

Because war has the power to cause large-scale suffering and death and alter peoples' everyday lives, people have always sought to explain it. Theories attribute war to external factors such as overpopulation and scarcity, or, conversely, to something inside people—emotions, drives, sex hormones, or instincts. Unlike theorists who focus on a single cause, sociologists emphasize that specific political and social contexts define, condition, and legitimate either nonviolence or aggression and warfare (Robarchek, 1989), and that "norms and values about violence and the availability of

WAR
Sustained armed conflicts among politically organized groups that involve large-scale violence and many fatalities.

It has been over a half century since C. Wright Mills (1956) formulated his "power elite" hypothesis: that a small group of males who were white and almost entirely Christian dominated American political life. Mills could hardly have imagined the powerful changes that the civil rights movement, the women's movement, and other social movements would soon have on American life. And in the 1950s it is doubtful that he could have foreseen events such as the collapse of the Soviet Union or the powerful impact of technological change. But have these changes affected the domain of power and the power elite? In the 1990s, and again in the twenty-first century, Richard Zweigenhaft and G. William Domhoff (1998, 2006) sought to answer this question by reexamining the power elite.

To determine whether the power elite had become more culturally diverse, the authors examined the top positions at the nations' Fortune 500 and 1000 corporations, as well as the board of directors of these companies. Additionally, they surveyed the top levels of political and military power. They found that the contemporary power elite exhibited considerable diversity, "at least as compared to its state in the 1950s." However, they cautioned that "its core group continues to be wealthy, white, Christian males, most of whom are still from the upper third of the social ladder" (Zweigenhaft and Domhoff, 1998:6, 2006:7).

Early in the twenty-first century, only a handful of women had gained CEO positions in the nation's top Fortune 500 or 1000 companies; in both cases they still accounted for around 1 percent of the total. Similar statistics hold for the nation's highest ranking military officers. Women have done better in the court system, winning slightly more than 20 percent of U.S. Supreme Court positions, and a similar number of federal judgeships. And in the same period, there were 14 women senators and 59 women members of the House of Representatives, and several women on President Bush's cabinet—all substantial gains from the 1950s, when only a handful of women held such positions (Stanley, 2002).

No African American served on the board of directors of a major corporation until 1964. By the early twenty-first century, African Americans held little more than 3 percent of the total seats on Fortune 1000 companies. Likewise, before the 1990s, only five African Americans had served on presidential cabinets. Presidents Clinton and Bush more than doubled that number during their presidencies. Similar gains were achieved in top military positions and Colin Powell has served as both chairman of the Joint Chiefs of Staff and Secretary of State; followed by Condoleezza Rice. However, there were only two African American senators in the twentieth century, the same number of Supreme Court Justices, and early in the twenty-first century, only 35 (of 435) House members were African American, or about 8 percent of the total.

Only recently have openly gay men and women entered the corporate and political elites, although they continue to be excluded from the military elite. Likewise, with the exception of Jews, all other minority groups have assumed few positions in the power elite over the past 50 years. Based on the percentage of Jews in the population (2.3 percent), people with Jewish backgrounds hold many top corporate positions, comprising around 8 percent of the total early in the twenty-first century. Since the 1950s, Jews have also held more than 15 cabinet posts and they have made it to the top of the military elite and the CIA. Likewise, there were 11 men and women senators and more than 25 members of the House, a sizeable gain even from 1975, when there were only 10 House members with Jewish backgrounds (Zweigenhaft and Domhoff, 1998:38).

Although Latinos constitute more than 10 percent of the population, by the early twenty-first century, they held 181 seats on Fortune 1000 companies, or about 2 percent of the total. There were no Latino cabinet officers until 1988, although two served in the administrations of George Bush and Bill Clinton. There were ten Latino generals in the U.S. military, although none of them were women. In the twentieth century there were only two Latino senators (none from 1978 to 2004 when two were elected), and by 2000 there were 21 House members with Latino backgrounds.

Asian Americans have fared somewhat better than Latinos. Asian Americans make up about 3 percent of the population, but early in the twenty-first century they held over 200 seats on Fortune 1000 companies. However, only a few Asian Americans have ever been appointed to a presidential cabinet, and there are few in the military elite. A total of five senators and eight House members served in the twentieth century. Despite these statistics, Zweigenhaft and Domhoff (1998:2006) predict that in the future many more Asian Americans, Chinese Americans in particular, will become increasingly important members of the power elite. When an Asian Indian was elected to the House of Representatives from Louisiana, one commentator stated, "Asian Americans [may] now fall on the white side of the racial divide" (Zweigenhaft and Domhoff, 2006:196).

Zweigenhaft and Domhoff (2006:248) concluded, "the increased diversity in the power elite hs not generated any changes in [the] underlying class system . . . [and] intertwined dilemmas of class and race lead to a nation that celebrates individualism, equal opportunity, and diversity but is, in reality, a bastion of class privilege . . ."

TAKING A CLOSER LOOK

What social factors do you think are most important for minority group entry into the contemporary power elite? Do you believe that they affect all groups equally?

Source: C. Wright Mills. *The Power Elite.* New York: Oxford University Press, 1956. Richard L. Zweigenhaft and G. William Domhoff. *Diversity and the Power Elite: Have Women and Minorities Reached the Top?* New Haven, CT: Yale University Press, 1998. Alessandra Stanley. "For Women, To Soar Is Rare To Fall Is Human." *The New York Times on the Web,* Sunday, January 13, 2002:1–5. Richard L. Zweigenhaft and G. William Domhoff. *Diversity and the Power Elite: How It Happened, Why It Matters.* Lanham, MD: Rowman and Littlefield, 2006. From Nelson and Chowdhury (eds.) *Women and Politics Worldwide.* Copyright © 1994. Reprinted by permission of Yale University Press.

institutionalized means for resolving conflicts shape the strategies adversaries choose to pursue their goals" (*Footnotes*, 1992:9).

Conflict theorists who adopt a decision-making approach emphasize that nations resort to armed conflict when political elites decide that war is an attractive means of achieving goals in conflicts with others. In the oft-repeated words of the nineteenth-century Prussian general and military theorist Carl von Clausewitz (1975), "War is a continuation of political activity by other means." While sociologists agree that political elites calculate the costs and benefits of war, they stress that they do so within a larger political and socioeconomic framework that influences their choices.

Marxist theorists, by contrast, stress the relationship between war and inequality, noting that domestic and international inequalities provide fertile ground for violence and war and that war both produces and sustains social inequalities. Some go even further, arguing that capitalist countries *need* war to stimulate their economies when they are heading into depressions, or that global competition for markets inevitably leads to imperialist wars (Brown, 1987).

Others argue that the causes of war must be sought in the nature of the modern state and the structure of international relations. In Charles Tilly's model, for example, states are not only instruments of class rule, they are "autonomous and omnivorous institutions" whose agents constantly seek to expand their wealth, power, and influence—both at home and abroad (Kimmel, 1990). As Tilly (1985:169) wrote, state makers are "coercive and self-seeking entrepreneurs" whose personal mobility depends on state expansion; since war making is one of the chief functions of the capitalist state, eras of capitalist expansion have often been eras of war (Kimmel, 1990).

Functionalism emphasizes order and equilibrium and treats war as dysfunction, or a temporary aberration in global political relations. Functionalists maintain that since no global authority has the power to adjudicate conflicts and enforce agreements, prudent national elites arm their states to deter the actions of others and provide themselves with the option of physical coercion (Gochman, 1990). When necessary, they also form alliances to enhance their power in competition with others (Mesquita and Lalman, 1990). Sociologists who take a functionalist approach argue that when there is a balance of power among states, peace normally prevails. Conversely, when a state develops sufficient military strength to threaten all other powers combined, wars commonly occur (Morgan and Levy, 1990:45).

The Development of War

Before the sixteenth century, armed conflicts rarely involved more than 50,000 men, and battles were for the most part brief and sporadic.

Limited and Total Wars   The *industrialization of war* in the nineteenth century, however, which included mass-produced weaponry and improvements in transportation and communications systems, meant that wars could be sustained for years. Nevertheless, until World War I, most wars were *limited wars*, which affected only combatants and civilians living in areas where battles were fought. Since then, the full-fledged alliance of science, the military, and industry has made *total wars* possible, where many nations engage in sustained armed combat and entire societies mobilize for war.

Guerrilla, Proxy, and Unilateral Wars   Although there have been no total wars among superpowers since 1945, scores of local and regional conflicts have produced an estimated 20 to 50 million fatalities. State-sponsored killings, however, have produced far more casualties. **Guerrilla wars** are *small-scale, irregular armed struggles against larger, better-armed government military forces.* Many people assume that guerrilla wars in developing nations are strictly local or regional conflicts, but from World War II until the early 1990s most were part of the global rivalry between the United States and the Soviet Union. During this period and continuing in some parts of the world today, state sponsorship of guerrilla wars has assumed two basic forms. Some are **proxy wars,** where *major powers do not participate directly in Third World conflicts; rather, one side assists government forces while the other supports guerrillas.* Many others are **unilateral wars,**

GUERRILLA WARS
Small-scale, irregular armed struggles against larger, better-armed government military forces.

PROXY WARS
Major powers do not participate directly in developing nations' conflicts; rather, one side assists government forces while the other supports guerrillas.

UNILATERAL WARS
One superpower becomes directly involved in a conflict with guerrillas, whereas the other stays out—but clandestinely supplies the opposition with arms, money, training, and, in recent years, satellite intelligence.

where *one superpower becomes directly involved in a conflict with guerrillas, whereas the other stays out—but clandestinely supplies the opposition with arms, money, training, and, in recent years, satellite intelligence* (Babiuch, 1993; Haass, 1997).

Terrorism and the "New Wars" of the Twenty-First Century As has been the case with many guerrilla conflicts, modern-day and future wars may not involve nation-states against nation-states, but smaller cells of groups and individuals who are fighting for social, political, economic, or religious ideologies. Labeled as *terrorists,* these groups and individuals tend to view themselves as "freedom fighters," "liberationists," or in some other positive light. Their acts and deeds, however, involve force and violence against both military and civilian targets, and, indeed, strike terror in the hearts and minds of those whom they oppose.

Terrorism is difficult to define, with some experts offering as many as 109 different meanings for the term (Schmid and Jongman, 1988; Hoffman, 1998). There are, however, some common terms and phrases associated with the concept, with almost all definitions including some reference to violence, force, political motives, fear, terror, and differentiated targets. Sociologically, **terrorism** can be defined as *deliberate threats or acts of violence intended to create fear and terror in order to bring about political and social change.* There are well over a thousand known terrorist groups around the globe today. The mass media tend to focus on religious terrorism and there has been a rise in religious violence that employs "religious images of divine struggle and places them in the service of worldly political battles" (Juergensmeyer, 2000:1). But state-sponsored terrorism—which uses threats, death squads, and mass murder to intimidate and subjugate a nation's own citizens as well as people in other countries—is on the rise as well. Early in the twenty-first century, the U.S. State Department designated several countries including Iraq, North Korea, Iran, Libya, Syria, Cuba, and the Sudan as sponsors of global terrorism. The 2003 invasion of Iraq and removal of the Saddam Hussein regime was defined by the second Bush administration as part of the United States' struggle against global terrorism (U.S. State Department, 2003). In the same year, Libya's decision to renounce efforts to acquire nuclear weapons and permit United Nations inspectors to verify compliance, seemed to offer hope for a reduction in global terror (Slevin and Frankel, 2003). At the time of this writing, the war in Iraq continues and Iran and North Korea pose nuclear threats to world peace.

Today, experts argue that the most potent threat to superpowers such as the United States comes from *postmodern terrorism,* which is less ideological, more apocalyptic, and potentially more lethal, armed with new weapons of mass destruction that include the possibilities of chemical and biological warfare (Laqueur, 1997). The 1993 bombing of New York City's World Trade Center, the 1995 nerve gas attack on the Tokyo subway system, the 1997 bombing of the Murrah Federal Building in Oklahoma City, and the 2001 attacks on the Pentagon outside Washington, D.C., and the World Trade Center buildings in New York City, and, later, bombings in Madrid and London ushered in a new era of terrorism. The tragic events of September 2001 and subsequent attacks by small groups against states worldwide, prompted U.S. officials and political leaders around the world to call terrorism a new form of warfare.

The Military-Industrial Complex

In 1945, war expenditures accounted for one out of every three dollars of the U.S. gross national product, and much of the civilian population and virtually all major industries were involved in military production. As World War II came to an end, many recommended that, as was the case following all previous wars, there be vast cutbacks in the

Early on, the Iraqi war was purportedly linked to the 9/11 attacks on the World Trade Center, and was portrayed as the major front of a global "war against terrorism." Popular support for the war waned, however, as it became seen more as a "political war" than a military one.

How would you compare the Iraqi war to the Vietnam War some four decades earlier?

TERRORISM
Deliberate threats or acts of violence intended to create fear and terror in order to bring about political and social change.

military and a return to a civilian economy. Some corporate leaders, however, offered convincing arguments that a rapid demobilization and return to a civilian economy would lead to an economic depression—perhaps one as destructive as the Great Depression (Neubeck, 1991). Military officials were more fearful of the former Soviet Union, which they claimed was intent on "world domination."

For four decades, the war with Russia remained a **cold war,** where *hostile nations sought to destabilize and destroy the other—but without engaging in direct armed combat.* However, the U.S. military (and that of the Soviet Union as well) expanded so dramatically that President Eisenhower, a former general, became alarmed at the "unwarranted influence . . . economic, political, and even spiritual," of what he called the "military-industrial complex" (Davis, 1971:80–81).

The **military-industrial complex** includes *mutually beneficial relationships among the uniformed military, defense industries, corporations, universities, national security and defense agencies, and Congress and the executive branches of government.* While each of these organizations has considerable influence and power, their shared and overlapping interests and in many cases circulating personnel have resulted in their becoming a combined pressure group—and a potent political force (Adams, 1982).

Following the media's line, it is easy to focus on the Pentagon's failures—the faulty gas masks and $500 million planes that cannot fly. But we should not neglect the other side of the picture: the military-industrial complex produces extraordinary weapons of mass destruction. Despite the end of the Cold War, the Pentagon's budget remains in the hundreds of billions of dollars, and hundreds of thousands of workers and many of the nation's most distinguished scientists continue to seek improvements in high-tech weaponry. Although the mass media exaggerated the technological aspects of the first Persian Gulf War, high-tech weaponry, which combines rocket and gas turbine technology, computers, and electronic sensors and guidance systems, are indeed highly efficient and lethal (O'Connell, 1989). One writer in *The Futurist* magazine envisions twenty-first century weapons such as the "gray cloud," which uses nanotechnology to create solid barriers that potentially could block sun from the earth. And new nanotechnologies and artificial intelligence may eventually reach the point "where a single human will have the power to kill all other humans (Magalhaes, 2002:42). Today, the military-industrial complex is shifting from a domestic to a global enterprise, led by both mergers among giant defense industries and collaborative arms ventures among many industrial nations (Bitzinger, 1999). Figure 16.5 examines U.S. military spending compared to that of other nations in 2005.

COLD WAR
Hostile nations seeking to destabilize and destroy the other—but without engaging in direct armed combat.

MILITARY-INDUSTRIAL COMPLEX
Mutually beneficial relationships among the uniformed military, defense industries, corporations, universities, national security and defense agencies, and Congress and the executive branches of government.

Technomedia and "Infowar" The 9/11 terrorist attacks on the World Trade Center and the subsequent wars in Afghanistan and Iraq demonstrated that new mobile-phone and Internet technologies can be employed to "help or harm," provide vital information or gossip, or even disinformation and hoaxes. Mobile phones were used to alert passengers on highjacked flights of the impending suicide mission and helped them thwart yet another potential attack; they were also used by emergency workers, victims, and families to coordinate and update their responses to the attack—which saved many lives. Websites and e-mail gave millions of other people across the globe minute-by-minute developments and allowed them to offer assistance, concern, and condolences. But mobile phones and the Internet were also used to make false emergency claims and bomb threats, as well as to circulate stories about government conspiracies. Later, these same technologies became essential to the military in both the war against the Taliban in Afghanistan and the war in Iraq—providing vital communication among troops in the field as well as generals as far away as Quatar and the Pentagon in Washington, D.C. (Katz and Rice, 2002:120–122).

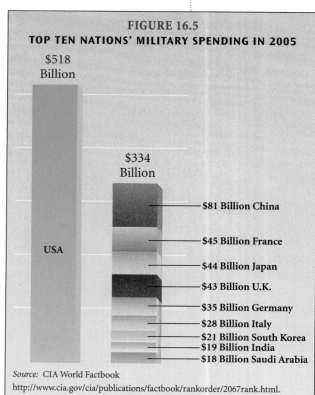

FIGURE 16.5

TOP TEN NATIONS' MILITARY SPENDING IN 2005

$518 Billion

USA

$334 Billion

$81 Billion China
$45 Billion France
$44 Billion Japan
$43 Billion U.K.
$35 Billion Germany
$28 Billion Italy
$21 Billion South Korea
$19 Billion India
$18 Billion Saudi Arabia

Source: CIA World Factbook
http://www.cia.gov/cia/publications/factbook/rankorder/2067rank.html.

David Altheide (1994) claims that the combination of telecommunications, computers, and high-tech weaponry has altered many of the strategies, perspectives, and activities of war—perhaps even the fundamental nature of war itself. For one thing, the success or failure of military campaigns now relies heavily on telecommunications. For example, the Gulf War was the first satellite war in which both military and network television signals traveled through the airwaves and mediated the conflict. Media impact was obvious even to television viewers, who watched generals and key political figures use CNN and network TV broadcasts to help guide military strategies. In some cases, these news broadcasts were the *only* reliable guide to what was happening on the battlefield (Couch, 1996). Writer Frank Rich (2000:60) contends the new prominence of the media in warfare became obvious in the first Gulf War, which was "the first war to have its own logos, theme music, and telegenic overnight stars." He called this media version of war a "mediathon," where a real war was played out and interpreted in real-time by the media in the simple, classic American archetypes of American pulp entertainment for a national audience (Rich, 2000:60). During the second invasion of Iraq and the subsequent occupation, media people were "embedded" in U.S. troops, sending instant coverage of skirmishes and battles around the globe.

Global telecommunications permit political and military officials to assess the consequences of their actions many thousands of miles away—in an instant. Telecommunication formats and their "logics" are now basic to military planning and strategies, sometimes with tragic consequences. Altheide (1994:671) gives the example of the U.S. Navy's mistaken downing of an Iranian civilian airliner in 1988:

> Notwithstanding disclaimers by the Navy and government officials that the error was "human" and due to "stress," the outcomes can also be interpreted as a feature of training with tapes that simulate battle situations, none of which included overflights by civilian airliners—a common occurrence in the Gulf.

A looming possibility is what one military analyst called "infowar," where military outcomes have much more to do with the destruction of telecommunications systems than they do with armies and weaponry. Again, this possibility was hinted at in the first Gulf War, where many early battle tactics were not aimed at soldiers but at command centers and either destroying or preserving telecommunications systems. In the near future, if it has not already come to pass, military campaigns may be directed at these systems, and winners or losers will be determined by who controls information processing when the battle ends (Couch, 1996). And now that equipment for ordinary soldiers includes cellular phones, laptops, and maps on CD-Roms, this is even more true today than a decade ago. Even video games are part of the Pentagon's expanding arsenal. In 2001, the military helped create "Real War" to help train troops for conflicts with terrorist cells—before September 11. In the future, the military plans to use "strategic games" for a host of purposes, including scenarios that are too dangerous for real-life training. Former Navy Seals and other military consultants are now helping create games for the general public that simulate real combat down to the smallest detail (Sieberg, 2001; Marriott, 2002). Focus box 16.3 takes a closer look at the thesis that wars of the twenty-first century will be "netwars."

The United States once enjoyed the status of being the only nuclear power on earth. When the Soviet Union developed nuclear weapons of mass destruction, the result was a nuclear "stand-off" between the U.S. and the U.S.S.R. known as the "Cold War." In 2006, North Korea tested nuclear missiles, reminding Americans and the world that nuclear weapons are not exclusive to major world powers. Events such as these and the potential of nuclear weapons in the Middle East prompted the Bulletin of Atomic Scientists to move the "doomsday clock" to 5 minutes.

Nuclear War and Society

After a half-century of living in the shadow of "the bomb," most people are aware of the awesome destructive power of nuclear weapons and see them as radically different than conventional weapons. Unfortunately, this kind of thinking has not been characteristic of some political leaders and military tacticians. Over the last half-century, such leaders have made every effort to define nuclear weapons as "large-scale" conventional weapons,

In the 1991 war against Iraq, the U.S. media showcased "smart weapons," including cruise missiles, stealth bombers, satellite-guided bombs and other high-tech weaponry that at least on television "never missed their targets." Similar images dominated "Operation Iraqi Freedom" in 2003, with *CNN* and other mainstream media highlighting technological warfare, with "Shock and Awe" bombing campaigns and tales of personal heroism—like the dramatic nighttime helicopter rescue of Private Jessica Lynch. To many Americans, these images proved why the United States and its allies won the war. They also hinted at the future of war, where superpowers do battle with the most sophisticated weaponry, and military outcomes are largely determined by whose weapons are the most advanced. But compelling media images may be misleading, according to military analysts.

Many analysts believe that military conflicts in the future will not be dominated by superpowers attacking each other with laser-guided missiles or protecting themselves with satellite shields in space. They believe it is far more likely that future wars and terrorist attacks will involve both nations and small groups, ranging from criminal gangs to rebels and dissenters, who will not only recruit terrorist bombers through the Internet, but also will exploit information technologies to confound, confuse, and perhaps even defeat established powers.

Military analysts have called these conflicts "cyberterrorism" and "netwars." Some contend that in addition to radically altering the economy, politics, and social relations, advances in telecommunications have fundamentally transformed the nature of war itself—blending elements of both terrorism and war into something entirely new. Instead of preserving oneself and wiping out the enemy, as in traditional war, in the information age the goal of war will be to preserve oneself and *control* various enemies. In the near future, some military analysts claim, total wars and "final victories" will be rare or nonexistent. Instead, national leaders will routinely conduct battles on many telecommunications fronts with the primary weapons of war: tactical deception, strategic deterrence, propaganda, psychological warfare (misinformation and disinformation), and sabotage. One U.S. general claims that information wars have already begun, with routine Russian attacks on computers at Kelly Air Force Base in Texas, which houses the military's top information warfare center (Arquilla and Ronfeldt, 1997; Zuckerman, 1997).

Computers will be the preferred weapons of war for criminals, revolutionaries, and terrorists as well. While these groups have always organized in loosely knit networks, new technologies now enable them to expand their networks worldwide to challenge national leaders on many fronts. Arquilla, Ronfeldt, and Zanini (2000:179) contend that new media have given birth to a new generation of transnational terrorists, who are developing global leagues of computer-hacking "cyboteurs." Some of these cyberterrorist networks employ a steady stream of propaganda that challenges and threatens established authorities on the Internet. Others seek to use the Web to disrupt social and democratic institutions across the globe or to promote "violent netwar," which uses information and communication technologies to destroy civilian, military, and police targets. Netwars of sabotage, perhaps the collapsing power grids or a software bomb that knocks out Wall Street for days or weeks, may damage cities or perhaps entire nations. Likewise, a daily barrage of disturbing videoclips of public disturbances, severe military defeats, or soldiers being abused or killed by hostile forces—which may or may not have occurred—may erode legitimate authority and public morale (Craddock, 1997).

Of course, there is little likelihood that state leaders will ignore these powerful new means of "war." The Pentagon and other powerful militaries have already established Internet commands and more integrated information technologies into their defense plans (CBS News, 2007). And the National Security Agency has developed "Echelon," a global eavesdropping operation, which can intercept all e-mail, telephone, and fax communications (Richelson, 2000:48). Another possibility is that smaller states, realizing the extraordinary potential of information technologies to level the military playing field, may adopt them and align themselves with others to augment their power. Or they may join forces with global terrorists and criminal organizations, "who serve as their proxies in a grim new era of chronic, low-cost, and low-intensity" campaigns of cyberterrorism and netwars (Craddock, 1997:3).

TAKING A CLOSER LOOK

Critically assess the "netwar-cyberterrorism" thesis. Has information technology given terrorists and "drug lords" new ways to harass, destabilize, and perhaps even defeat powerful nations and militaries? Or is this thesis yet another way for political leaders to generate more funds to expand their high-tech surveillance and military capabilities? Examine various perspectives on wars of the future. Then browse the Internet—including government and military websites—and see if you can build a case either for or against the netwar thesis.

Source: John Arquilla and David Ronfeldt. "A New Epoch—and Spectrum—of Conflicts." In John Arquilla and David Ronfeldt (eds.), *In Athena's Camp: Preparing for Conflict in the Information Age.* Santa Monica, CA: Rand, 1997: 1–20. Ashley Craddock. "Netwar and Peace in the Global Village," *Wired,* May 1997:1–5. M. J. Zuckerman. "Targeting Cyberterrorism," *USA Today,* October 20, 1997:17A-18A. John Arquilla, David Ronfeldt, and Michele Zanini. "Information Age Terrorism," *Current History* 99 (636), April 2000:179–185. Jeffrey Richelson. "Desperately Seeking Signals," *The Bulletin of the Atomic Scientists* 56(2), 2000:47–51. CBS News. *60 Minutes,* March 4, 2006.

integrate them with conventional weapons, and use them in support of traditional military and political objectives.

Mutually Assured Destruction

In the 1950s, when the United States had a clear monopoly in deliverable nuclear weapons, they were seen as a substitute for conventional forces in deterring a broad range of Soviet threats. A few years after the Cuban missile crisis, however, when the Soviet Union had achieved nuclear parity, America's nuclear posture changed. First, President Kennedy's Secretary of Defense Robert McNamara promoted a costly policy that dominated strategic planning for over 30 years. Following McNamara's logic of **mutually assured destruction (MAD),** the United States (and the Soviet Union) developed *a strategic triad of ballistic missiles buried in hardened silos and carried on submarines and in human-piloted bombers that would provide a "survivable" second strike that would obliterate the attacking nation.*

As both sides discovered, MAD offered little security, as new technologies threatened the reliability of the triad and required new defenses and many more missiles to ensure a second strike capability. Even worse in the minds of many military planners, for all their efforts, and at a cost of billions of dollars, they achieved little more than a stalemate. So Pentagon planners found a new and even more costly solution to the nuclear dilemma, called the *Strategic Defense Initiative (SDI),* nicknamed "Star Wars." President Reagan's plan called for building trillion-dollar battle stations in space that, using advanced laser and particle beam technologies, would destroy *all* incoming missiles and thus create an impenetrable defensive shield around the United States. In the midst of the debate over whether Star Wars would make the world safer or increase the chances of a Soviet "first strike," the Soviet Union collapsed and the Cold War ended, with the result that both sides cut or scaled back many weapons systems—including the Star Wars program (Mendelsohn, 1991).

Despite a more peaceful climate, arms reduction treaties have not rescinded what amounts to a suicide-pact among superpowers. Even with large-scale reductions in nuclear arsenals over the last few years, Russia and the United States alone still possess thousands of nuclear warheads. Today, the United States continues to develop a "missile-proof umbrella," this time to protect the nation against so-called "rogue states" or "unauthorized or accidently fired missiles (Shen, 2000:21). Moreover, North Korea, possibly Iran, and other nations are capable of producing nuclear weapons, and because nuclear weapons have expanded both technologically and bureaucratically and no individual or organization has the capacity to control them completely, a nuclear accident caused by "Murphy's law," a computer glitch, or human error remains a possibility.

Society in the Nuclear Age

In the 1950s, the government and mass media encouraged ordinary people to dig bomb shelters in their basements or backyards, and elementary schools conducted "duck and cover" drills, where children were instructed to hide under their desks and in hallways or auditoriums during nuclear attacks. As absurd as these activities may seem today, during the late 1980s a Reagan administration official insisted that people could construct makeshift shelters in their backyards "by digging a hole and covering it with a wooden door and dirt" (Beckman et al., 1989:182). Yet, most nuclear experts agree that even the heavily fortified North American Defense Command (NORAD) that sits under the Rocky Mountains probably would not survive the destructive power of contemporary, third-generation nuclear weapons. Moreover, the Pentagon added the B-61-11 "nuclear earth penetrator" to its arsenal that burrows into the earth before exploding. It destroys targets several hundred feet beneath the earth's surface (Hall, 1998).

Although it is a remote possibility, there is still a chance that some nation with nuclear bombs will use its weapons. Using the functionalist perspective, Sheets and Bynum (1989) conclude that following a nuclear attack there would be social collapse, and in such an environment individual survival would be the dominant concern. They note, in a society of specialists, those with the skills to acquire food and potable water or

MUTUALLY ASSURED DESTRUCTION (MAD)
A strategic triad of ballistic missiles buried in hardened silos and carried on submarines and in human-piloted bombers that would provide a "survivable" second strike that would totally obliterate the attacking nation.

even build a fire without matches would be in short supply. Sheets and Bynum suggested that perhaps after a period of shock and lawlessness, small, purposive groups might reemerge to gain and maintain possession of scarce foodstuffs in a highly competitive and violent atmosphere—"with the size of the groups being regulated by the land's carrying capacity" (Sheets and Bynum, 1989:18).

The Doomsday Clock With the collapse of the Soviet Union and the end of the Cold War in 1992, *The Bulletin of the Atomic Scientists* reset its *doomsday clock* to 17 minutes to midnight. In the twenty-first century, with terrorism on the rise and nuclear weapons proliferating in both developed and emerging nations, the organization reset the doomsday clock to around 7 minutes. Today, it is set at 5 minutes. Many sociologists believe that global political organizations and peace movements in particular may become more important in ensuring humanity's future in the new century.

PEACE ORGANIZATIONS AND PEACE MOVEMENTS

Peace is neither the absence of war nor something fixed and permanent. Rather, **peace** is *a process by which politically organized groups develop and maintain positive, constructive, and mutually beneficial relationships that enable them to transcend collective violence.*

As Figure 16.6 shows, peace involves nonviolent and constructive means of conflict management, as opposed to those methods at the opposite end of the continuum that rely on coercion and violence. Peace is sustained by numerous factors, including cultural compatibility, beliefs by each side that the relationship is fair and just, and structural mechanisms that promote cooperation, positive reform, and the peaceful resolution of conflicts.

There is much evidence that many of these elements are in place among democracies in what Kenneth Boulding (1987:58) described as "a great triangle of stable peace, stretching roughly from Australia to Japan, across North America, to Finland, with about eighteen countries which have no plans whatever to go to war with each other." Unfortunately, they comprise but a small segment of contemporary nation-states and their relationships are uncharacteristic of those of the rest of the world. Globally, peace is fragile and often dependent on emerging political structures whose promise for maintaining peace and stability largely remains unfulfilled.

The United Nations and the Search for Peace

Two of the most important global political organizations are the United Nations and the International Court of Justice, or World Court, established in 1945 during the latter stages of World War II. At that time, virtually all national leaders recognized a need for global organizations that could mediate disputes among nation-states and serve as effective international peacemaking and peacekeeping bodies. The United Nations includes representatives from over 200 nation-states that are members of the General Assembly. In addition to the Assembly, the United Nations includes a Security Council

PEACE
A process by which politically organized groups develop and maintain positive, constructive, and mutually beneficial relationships that enable them to transcend collective violence.

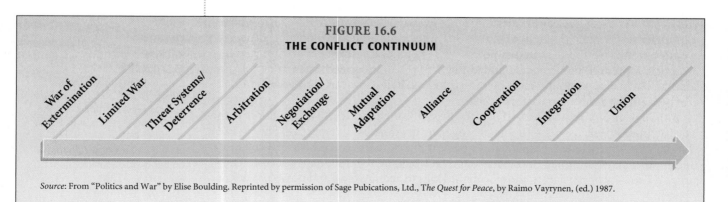

FIGURE 16.6
THE CONFLICT CONTINUUM

War of Extermination · Limited War · Threat Systems/Deterrence · Arbitration · Negotiation/Exchange · Mutual Adaptation · Alliance · Cooperation · Integration · Union

Source: From "Politics and War" by Elise Boulding. Reprinted by permission of Sage Pubications, Ltd., *The Quest for Peace*, by Raimo Vayrynen, (ed.) 1987.

that until recently had as permanent members the United States, Russia, China, Britain, and France. Each had the power to veto any decision it did not like, but when all five were in agreement their decisions were binding on all other members. In 1997, Japan and Germany were added to the council; in addition, the United States proposed that three representatives from developing countries be made permanent members of the Security Council in the near future. However, there is little consensus about whether veto power should be given to the three representatives of poor nations and whether this vote would strengthen or weaken the United Nation's traditional role as a mediator of global political disputes.

Such concerns have led many to see greater possibilities outside formal political channels, in social movements that have as their goal peace and justice for *all* people.

Peace Movements

Peace movements are *loose and shifting combinations of individuals and groups who come together to promote peace or prevent war.* Some peace movements include no more than a few dozen dedicated pacifists. Others have widespread popular appeal and at various times have mobilized thousands or even millions of ordinary citizens as well as a broad coalition of peace organizations.

In 1828, Quakers, evangelical preachers, and enlightenment intellectuals joined forces to form the American Peace Society, a national organization that promoted not only world peace but also abolitionism and women's rights. Later in the century they were joined by feminists, suffragettes, and social reformers such as Jane Addams, who in addition to founding Hull House in Chicago for the urban poor also helped found and became the first president of the Women's International League for Peace and Freedom (DeBenedetti, 1986). In 1923, feminist and socialist Jessie Wallace Hughan founded the War Resisters League to oppose war and social injustice, and two twentieth-century "peace heroes"—Mohandas Gandhi and Martin Luther King Jr.—promoted *nonviolent resistance* and stressed the inherent linkages among peace, social justice, civil rights, and a respect for human dignity (DeBenedetti, 1986; Young, 1987). Nigel Young (1987) remarked that while peace movements have been unable to get any state to demilitarize, they have pressured national elites on such issues as the Vietnam War, conscription, nuclear weapons testing and other nuclear issues.

Some believe that peace activism is at an all-time low. For example, one researcher claims that from the 1980s to 2000, membership in various peace organizations declined from "170,000 paid-up members" to about 50,000 members (Lortie, 2000:52). As one peace activist remarked, "There's been a proliferation of groups and causes: People pick their one or two issues, and that's it" (Lortie, 2000:52). The end of the Cold War influenced the level of activism, but so did media framing. According to Adam Eidinger, a media consultant with Project Abolition, when mainstream media covered the group's *Wall of Denial* protest event, they ignored the connection between nuclear weapons and the end of the Cold War. Instead, they focused their coverage on "democracy and human rights (the 'Western triumphs' of the Cold War) rather than the difficulties ahead" (Lortie, 2000:54).

Antinuclear protestors around the world, like Taiwan protestors in this photo who seek to block a controversial nuclear power plant, have not been able to get any government to demilitarize. However, they have pressured many national leaders to reduce nuclear weapons and limit or abolish the testing of nuclear weapons.

PEACE MOVEMENTS
Loose and shifting combination of individuals and groups who come together to promote peace or prevent war.

the FUTURE
LOOKING to

GLOBAL POLITICS IN THE TWENTY-FIRST CENTURY

Although the modern nation-state remains the focus in the study of politics, a comprehensive understanding of the political process requires that we expand our analysis to include relations among nation-states, their economic, political, and organizational assets, and their relative ranking vis-à-vis other nation-states. We have witnessed extraordinary political events in the last 2 decades that suggest we are entering a new era of international relations. Some argue that the use of force will diminish in the future—especially among superpowers (Schell, 2003). Others believe that stable political structures and "politics as usual" in the United States and across the globe may be a thing of the past. Manuel Castells (2002) contends that with the help of the Internet and electronic media nation-states too are transforming themselves by creating coalitions and merging these coalitions into "supra-national" institutions that allow them to manage the global processes that will be important in the twenty-first century.

Nuclear proliferation, however, may provide serious threats to all people. Critics argue that even with recent cuts in nuclear weapons, thousands still remain, and scientists and engineers around the world remain hard at work improving nuclear, biological, and chemical weapons. Moreover, given the power and prestige attached to a nation's having nuclear weapons, it is unlikely that many emerging nations will halt their efforts to become members of the "nuclear club." In 1998, India and Pakistan detonated nuclear devices and became members. North Korea too is a member. How many other nations will follow in the twenty-first century?

Even poor nations have no intention of being left out of the arms race. The poorest nations—and even small terrorist groups—have stockpiled antipersonnel mines, while many others have attempted to purchase or produce state-of-the-art chemical and biological weapons—like anthrax or sarin (Lavoy et al., 2000). Many nations, including the United States, have stockpiled vaccines against these and other biological agents, in anticipation of future biological attacks.

During the Iraqi war, journalists embedded with the troops transmitted war updates to media outlets around the clock. Moreover, soldiers and civilians on the scene also contributed to media reports of the war via e-mails, cell phones, and small hand-held videos transmitted in the heat of battle and shortly thereafter.

Will the technomedia along with high-tech weaponry continue to revolutionize the nature of war? How do the technomedia contribute to the further politicization of war?

At the close of the twentieth century, political scientists projected that wars of the future would more likely be terroristic in nature, as opposed to one nation-state battling another. On September 11, 2001, the future became the present when the United States experienced the worst terrorist attack in history. Terrorists hijacked four commercial airliners and crashed two of them into the twin towers of the World Trade Center in New York City. The towers collapsed soon afterward, and almost 3,000 people were killed and many thousands injured. A third jet was nose-dived into the Pentagon, destroying part of the building and killing close to 200. The fourth plane, whose target was evidently another important federal building in Washington, D.C., perhaps the White House, crashed in rural Pennsylvania after passengers on the plane struggled to overtake the terrorists aboard. President Bush, and political leaders around the world, declared these acts the start of the twenty-first century's first war.

Theodore Caplow (1989:5) argued that instead of concentrating most of our efforts on "war games" and preparation for future biological, chemical, and nuclear catastrophes, we should invent "peace games," the object of which "is to go from the existing war system of independent nations, to a new system that excludes industrial war without passing through a nuclear exchange on the way." As opposed to most war games, Caplow's "game" demands two conditions that make it relevant to the real world: "existing nations may not be removed from the board except by voluntary merger; [and] existing conflicts may not be ignored."

Some social theorists, however, contend that state power has been eclipsed by global capitalism. For example, Ross and Trachte (1990:2–3), maintain that in the past the state was jealous of centers of competing authority. In the future, however, variations in social conditions may be welcome—perhaps even encouraged—because powerful corporations can use uneven regional development as a bargaining lever. There is a growing privatization of the military, with companies like DynCorp, AirScan, and other large defense contractors able to "put troops in the field, build and run military bases, train guerrilla forces, [and] conduct air surveillance" operations anywhere in the world (Murphy, 2003:137). Historically, state "terror" has been the domain of the police and military or paramilitary. In global capitalism it is downsizing, unemployment, wage cuts, and factory transfers. Likewise, states historically have been permeated with irrational commitments to hierarchy, status, and the privilege of birth. As we discuss in Chapter 17, in global capitalism the new focus is on rational calculation, property, and profit.

Summary

1. Power is fundamental to politics. Power is the ability to get one's way wherein coercion is the actualization of a threat.

2. One form of power is authority, which can be divided into four ideal types: traditional, legal-rational, charismatic, and expertise.

3. Influence is also a vital resource in contemporary politics and elites rely on the mass media and personalized media to influence audiences.

4. Contemporary nation-states emerged in the sixteenth century and continue to dominate the political landscape. Globally many nations are ruled by authoritarian regimes whose power is concentrated in the hands of a single leader or elite group, whereas democratic systems are based on popular participation in decision making.

5. The American political system can be described as a kind of pyramid with four levels of power. The state is at the top, political parties are on the next level, and beneath them are interest groups and unorganized citizens, who are armed with little more than their votes.

6. Sociologists take three major approaches to contemporary American politics: the organizational, pluralist, and elite approaches.

7. War consists of sustained armed conflicts among politically organized groups that involve large-scale violence and many fatalities. Some believe the best chances for peace exist outside of the nation-state in emerging global political organizations and peace movements that seek to demilitarize society and remove the conditions that contribute to conflict and violence.

8. In some scenarios, stable political structures are becoming a thing of the past. Others argue that state power has been eclipsed by global capitalism, and in the future, warfare, terrorism, and peace will assume new meanings and forms.

Key Terms

authoritarian regimes (p. 462)
authority (p. 457)
charismatic authority (p. 457)
coercion (p. 457)
cold war (p. 476)
democracy (p. 463)
dictatorship (p. 462)
expertise (p. 458)
governments (p. 457)
guerrilla wars (p. 474)
influence (p. 458)

interest groups (p. 467)
legal-rational authority (p. 457)
military-industrial complex (p. 476)
mutually assured destruction (MAD) (p. 479)
nation-states (p. 462)
oligarchies (p. 462)
peace (p. 480)
peace movements (p. 481)
political institutions (p. 456)
political parties (p. 468)

political systems (p. 462)
politics (p. 456)
power (p. 456)
power elite (p. 471)
propaganda (p. 458)
proxy wars (p. 474)
terrorism (p. 475)
totalitarian regimes (p. 462)
traditional authority (p. 457)
unilateral wars (p. 474)
war (p. 472)

Chapter 17

The Economy and Work

"Economics is extremely useful as a form of employment for economists."

—John Kenneth Galbraith

*R*ick was not ecstatic about selling shoes, but after 14 months of drawing unemployment checks, he was glad to be working again. Plus he was working on a commission versus salary basis, so if he sold enough shoes, he could increase his paycheck substantially. So far, however, after 2 months on the job, he not only had never made a commission check, but because his deficit in sales commission rolled over from month to month, it was unlikely that he ever would receive more than minimum wage for the hours he worked. Nevertheless, it felt good to be working. The economy was supposedly in good shape, retail sales were up across the board, and the unemployment rate was only 5 percent, but Rick had just spent over one full year applying for and being turned down for job after job. Every morning the newspapers reported massive layoffs in the aerospace, automobile, airline, and telecommunications industries, and the evening news reverberated with stories of middle-aged engineers, autoworkers, advertising executives, and others who had lost their jobs and joined the ranks of the unemployed. Rick owed the government some back taxes and penalties, and still owed his student loans, but he was lucky to be working—or was he? Again, *things are not necessarily what they seem.*

While Rick was not unemployed, he certainly was underemployed. With a bachelor's degree in advertising and marketing Rick had joined a small advertising firm right out of college, drawing an annual salary of just under $40,000—a sum that seemed attractive then, since he had just finished 5 years of college and had been living off part-time jobs, student loans, and a small monthly allowance from his parents. Two years out of college, however, Rick hit the jackpot. A small, but rapidly growing telecommunications firm based in Miami offered Rick a $10,000 bonus to sign a

one-year contract with their firm for an annual salary of $85,000 per year. Tossing in a monthly car allowance, a cell phone, and a laptop computer for good measure, it did not matter to Rick, who was only 25 years old, that technically he was an independent contractor, and received no health insurance, retirement plan, or any other fringe benefits. Even income taxes were not withheld from his check, but at that amount of money, Rick would not have any difficulty saving back what he needed—although that proved more difficult than he had imagined. After the end of his first year, Rick signed a new contract for $95,000, bought a new $50,000 car, took out a 30-year mortgage on a new condominium, promised himself that he would save some money, and could see nothing ahead but smooth sailing and a fast track to a successful career and early retirement.

Then the bottom fell out. The 42 people in Rick's Miami office were flown first class to the corporate headquarters in Atlanta. They were wined and dined and sat in luxury boxes as the Atlanta Braves beat the Pittsburgh Pirates in extra innings. The next morning they were called into the CEO's office one by one, where they received their severance package and a form letter of recommendation along with a handshake and "best wishes" from their former boss. The company, along with dozens of other telecommunications companies across the country, was going out of business. All contracts of employment were null and void. Rick was told by the boss that he had been an "asset to the company," that he should "keep his head up," and that he wished him "good luck." Good luck had indeed come a little over a year later. Rick was selling shoes.

Unemployment rates do not always accurately reflect the state of the economy and the world of work. Many Americans are underemployed, such as Rick in the opening vignette.

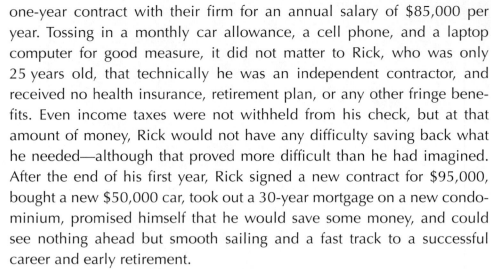

The economy is one of the basic social institutions that exist in every society. Consequently, sociologists are interested in the economy and how it affects society and social life. Because the economy and work shape the content and rhythm of people's lives as well as their very identities, we hope you agree that "the relations of 'economic' life are too important to be left to economists" (Ross and Trachte, 1990:4).

In this chapter, we first look at how sociologists define the economy, then compare and contrast the traditional economic systems of capitalism and socialism to see how they are combined to form the mixed economies that comprise our contemporary global economy. Next, we turn our attention to the American economy and work, including the concepts of unemployment and underemployment introduced in the opening vignette. We then explore work as a social phenomenon and look at how the functionalist, conflict, and interactionist perspectives view the economy and work. Finally, we explore the economy and work in the twenty-first century.

SOCIOLOGY AND THE STUDY OF THE ECONOMY

From its beginning, sociology has borrowed many important concepts from economics. For example, Karl Marx and the conflict perspective were influenced by economic studies, and much of their analyses of human social behavior is based on economic

Sociology
and the Study
of the Economy

487

determinism—that is, social class is of paramount importance in shaping people's values, behavior, and life chances. The structural functionalist perspective also was influenced by economics; Talcott Parsons, its American founder and spokesperson, studied at the London School of Economics. Exchange theory, developed by George Homans and Peter Blau, uses rational choice theory and incorporates many of the tenets of utilitarian economics in an effort to explain human behavior. In fact, it would be almost impossible for any sociologist, regardless of his or her specific interests or theoretical orientation, to ignore the economy and its powerful impact on human social life.

The **economy** consists of *the systematic production, distribution, and consumption of goods and services in a society.* Goods include the basic necessities of life, such as food, clothing, and shelter, as well as a wide array of manufactured commodities ranging from simple tools to home computers. Services, which are provided by some people for the benefit of others, include activities ranging from child care and house cleaning to brain surgery and psychotherapy. Together, goods and services are the things people want and need to enhance their lives. Let's look briefly at three important aspects of the economy: production, distribution, and consumption.

Production

Production is *the process by which goods and services are brought into existence.* Production is usually divided into three types: primary, secondary, and tertiary. Primary production involves the extraction of natural resources and the means of survival directly from the physical environment by hunting, gathering, fishing, farming, and mining. Secondary production means transforming raw materials into manufactured goods, for example turning clay into pottery, transforming iron ore into steel and subsequently into automobiles and other products, and converting crude oil into usable fuel and a host of petroleum-based products. Tertiary production involves the creation and distribution of services, such as education, sports, and entertainment. Of course, producing goods and services is of little value without a way of distributing them.

Distribution of Goods and Services

Distribution is *the allocation of goods and services to societal members.* Perhaps one of the most important aspects of the economy is the determination of who gets what. In Chapters 8 and 9 we discussed social stratification as the inevitable outcome of the unequal distribution of goods and services within a society and across the globe. While some societies strive to distribute goods and services equitably, in virtually every society some people receive and accumulate a disproportionate share and hence enjoy higher social status and an enhanced quality of life.

Consumption

Consumption is *the process of accumulating and using goods and services.* Every society's economy depends on consumers who want, need, and use goods and services. The basic staples of an economy—food, clothing, and shelter—have inherent value, since people cannot survive without them. In contrast, most objects produced in industrial and postindustrial societies are valued not because they are needed but because they are wanted. Over a century ago, sociologist Thorstein Veblen (1899) coined the term **conspicuous consumption** to describe *consumers' desire to express their social standing by acquiring goods and services simply for the purposes of having, displaying, and consuming them.* Focus box 17.1 analyzes how conspicuous consumption has led to what contemporary sociologist George Ritzer (1995) referred to as the worldwide "credit-carditization" of society.

The Economic System

Because production, distribution, and consumption are vital to all societies, they are institutionalized into an **economic system** that includes *the ideology, values, norms, and activities that regulate an economy.* The economic system holds the same interest for

ECONOMY
The systematic production, distribution, and consumption of goods and services in a society.

PRODUCTION
The process by which goods and services are brought into existence.

DISTRIBUTION
The allocation of goods and services to societal members.

CONSUMPTION
The process of accumulating and using goods and services.

CONSPICUOUS CONSUMPTION
Consumers' desire to express their social standing by acquiring goods and services simply for the purposes of having, displaying, and consuming them.

ECONOMIC SYSTEM
The ideology, values, norms, and activities that regulate an economy.

Several years ago, a popular internationally recognized credit card developed the slogan "Don't leave home without it" as its trademark, and millions of people around the globe have apparently taken that message to heart. Sociologist George Ritzer (1995:xii) used the analysis of credit cards as a "window on society" and pointed out that a sociological analysis of the widespread use of credit cards sheds light on some of "the most essential problems in modern society—crime, debt, threats to privacy, rationalization, and homogenization."

Drawing on the rich sociological theories of C. Wright Mills, Karl Marx, Georg Simmel, and Max Weber, Ritzer (1995:1, i) described how the credit card has become not just "an American icon," but "the premier symbol of American lifestyle that much of the rest of the world is rushing to emulate."

In *The Sociological Imagination* (1959), Mills differentiated between personal troubles and social issues and demonstrated how individuals with the same or similar problems can affect the social structure to the point of creating a major social issue. Such is the case, Ritzer argued, with the widespread use of credit cards and the personal and social consequences associated with their use and abuse. Ritzer (1995:18) agreed with a suggestion that perhaps, like cigarette packs, credit cards should bear the warning: "Caution. Financial experts have determined that continued bank card use can lead to debt, loss of property, bankruptcy, plus unhealthful effects on long-lived standards and virtues."

The German social theorist Karl Marx warned that exploitation was an inherent characteristic of capitalistic systems, and Ritzer used this premise to demonstrate how the prolif-

eration of credit cards and sophisticated advertising techniques have encouraged consumers to spend more money, far beyond their means of available cash, for goods and services they may not need or, in some cases, even want. Simmel's theory on the money economy also provides a critical framework for the analysis of credit cards. Simmel believed that the use of money, as opposed to bartering and other systems, encouraged what he called "mean machinations": social problems linked to imprudence, bribery, fraud, and increased secrecy in commercial transactions. Ritzer demonstrated that these consequences are even more likely to arise through the widespread use of credit cards.

Credit cards have become the mainstay of a global economic system.

sociologists as other major institutions—the family, education, religion, and politics—because it is part of the social fabric that shapes and defines human social interaction. Economic systems can be placed on a continuum ranging from the ideal type of capitalism at one end to that of socialism at the other (see Figure 17.1). Those that fall somewhere in the middle are referred to as *mixed economies*.

THE GLOBAL ECONOMY

If you travel to Russia you may sip a Coca-Cola while washing your clothes in one of the many laundromats that sell locally manufactured Tide detergent. Or you may walk a few blocks down the street to the Pizza Hut and contemplate the rapid growth of the

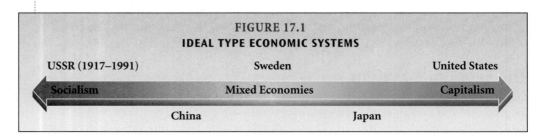

FIGURE 17.1
IDEAL TYPE ECONOMIC SYSTEMS

USSR (1917–1991)	Sweden	United States
Socialism	Mixed Economies	Capitalism
	China Japan	

Finally, Ritzer turned to the theories of Max Weber and his emphasis on the rationalization process and its implications for analyzing and critiquing a global economy that is so highly dependent on the use of credit cards. Describing the development of bureaucracies and the increased rationalization of society as being linked to dehumanization as people become "faceless cogs" in the "iron cage of rationalization," Ritzer (1995:21) contended that credit cards' impact on banking, the way consumer loans are acquired, and the purchase of goods through catalogs and on television has helped to create a massive worldwide consumer culture that has transformed many otherwise sensible people into "stupefied" consumers "immersed in the mindless pursuit of goods and services." Ritzer argued that the rampant expansion of the consumer culture through the globalization of the credit card industry is contributing to burgeoning private and public debt, increased fraud and other credit card–related crimes, widespread invasion of privacy, and increased rationalization and dehumanization—very high prices to pay for the convenience credit cards afford. Moreover, Ritzer (1995:177) warned that the increased global use of credit cards leads to homogenization—a process of Americanizing the globe. He concluded:

> The credit card is, like many other goods and services, a quintessentially American product that is sweeping across the world. In the process, although it can help to sustain cultural differences, the credit card is helping to Americanize the world and erode national differences. This erosion of national differences, this homogenization of the world's cultures to at least some degree, is a great threat to us all. A world of increasing sameness is a world of decreasing interest.

In a later work, *The Globalization of Nothing* (2004), Ritzer contended that major credit cards epitomize *nothingness*. For example, most people obtain credit cards through unsolicited preapproved offers that set a predetermined credit limit. Thousands, hundreds of thousands, and perhaps even millions of people receive identical credit offers. The results? Ritzer (2004:144) concludes:

> For some users, credit cards open up a magical world of a cornucopia full of life's delights, but for others it becomes a nightmarish void where it is impossible to extricate themselves from debt in a world characterized by a continuous round of often empty and unfulfilling consumption of unneeded and unnecessary goods and services.

TAKING A CLOSER LOOK

How have American credit cards contributed to creating a global economy? Is there such a thing as an "American" credit card? Do you agree with Ritzer's assessment that credit cards have helped to "homogenize" the world? What would happen if retail merchants and banks around the globe suddenly refused to accept major credit cards? Credit card debt is a rapidly growing problem among American college students. To what extent does the "global credit card society" contribute to this problem?

Source: C. Wright Mills. *The Sociological Imagination.* New York: Oxford University Press, 1959. George Ritzer. *Expressing America: A Critique of the Global Credit Card Society.* Thousand Oaks, CA: Pine Forge, 1995. George Ritzer. *The Globalization of Nothing.* Thousand Oaks, CA: Pine Forge, 2004.

global economy. Many of the major corporations with which you are familiar, that once manufactured and sold products exclusively in the United States, are now enjoying the benefits of worldwide production, marketing, and sales. Consider the following facts: two-thirds of all sales of the Colgate Palmolive Company and Coca-Cola are outside the United States; Procter & Gamble leads the market among all shampoos, soaps, and detergents sold in China; MTV has regional production centers in Brazil, Europe, Japan, and India; the National Football League, the National Basketball Association, and the National Hockey League are all pursuing franchise teams outside of North America; Pringles potato chips are shipped to more than 40 countries around the globe; Kentucky Fried Chicken is sold in Paris, London, and Beijing; McDonald's can be found in almost every major city in the world; and hundreds of other companies that once operated solely in the United States have expanded their markets into a worldwide global economy that since 1990 has increased U.S. exports by almost 30 percent and promises to continue to grow (Ritzer, 2000).

Many economists believe that the influence of a global economy could not have come at a better time. Japan and many Western European nations have been battling an economic slump for almost a decade, a slump that has caused record-level unemployment rates and discouraged domestic economic growth. Japan's economy has also suffered from uncontrolled real estate and stock market speculation. Meanwhile,

Perhaps two of the most recognized trademarks around the globe are those of Pepsi and Coca-Cola.

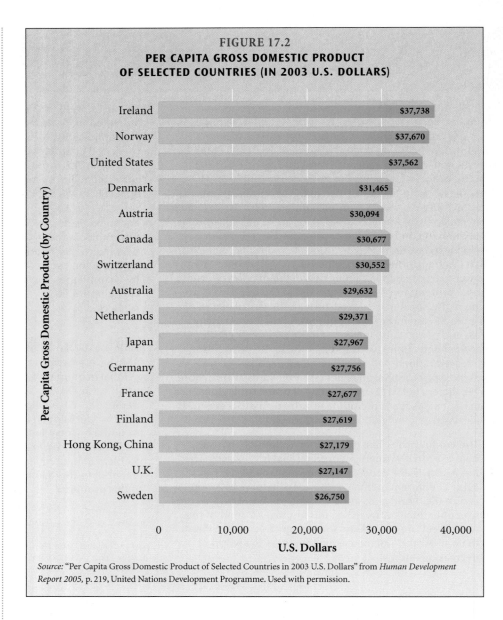

FIGURE 17.2

PER CAPITA GROSS DOMESTIC PRODUCT OF SELECTED COUNTRIES (IN 2003 U.S. DOLLARS)

Per Capita Gross Domestic Product (by Country)	U.S. Dollars
Ireland	$37,738
Norway	$37,670
United States	$37,562
Denmark	$31,465
Austria	$30,094
Canada	$30,677
Switzerland	$30,552
Australia	$29,632
Netherlands	$29,371
Japan	$27,967
Germany	$27,756
France	$27,677
Finland	$27,619
Hong Kong, China	$27,179
U.K.	$27,147
Sweden	$26,750

Source: "Per Capita Gross Domestic Product of Selected Countries in 2003 U.S. Dollars" from *Human Development Report 2005*, p. 219, United Nations Development Programme. Used with permission.

several Latin American countries as well as countries in the former Soviet Union have attempted to establish democratic governments based on capitalist economies. A strong and expanding global economy can restore faith in local and domestic economies while providing jobs, higher living standards, and capital for both international and national investment. Figure 17.2 shows the per capita gross domestic product of selected countries.

In October 1997, a sudden drop in the Asian stock market sent the Dow Jones Industrial Average into a tailspin; for the first time in its history the New York Stock Exchange was forced to cease all trading for one hour midday and then close down altogether a full hour earlier than usual. In early 2007, Asian markets experienced another major downturn and the Dow Jones Average recorded major losses. Still, many economists are confident that the global market economy will return to a growth mode. This optimism is based on the widespread acceptance on the part of national governments and private corporations, especially in the United States, Japan, China, and throughout Europe, that the global marketplace is and will continue to be the best source of domestic and local economic success. It is also based on the fact that many traditional economic barriers have been eradicated and others continue to dissolve every day. This is due to the blending of traditional economic systems of capitalism and socialism and the dissolution of national economic barriers in an effort to create a mixed, global economy. Let's take a moment to compare and contrast these economic systems.

Capitalism

Capitalism is *an economic system in which the means of production are privately owned and goods and services are distributed competitively for profit.* The United States is often cited as an example of the success that can be attained through "free enterprise." Every social institution must be supported by a compatible ideology; three key elements of capitalistic ideology are private ownership, competition, and profit.

In predominantly capitalist societies, private ownership is the hallmark of the economy and extends to the ownership of natural resources (e.g., forests, mines, and land), means of production (e.g., factories, industrial plants, and manufacturing sites), and businesses that provide important services. As an ideal type, capitalism promotes competition by allowing the relative value and cost of goods and services to be determined by their supply and demand in the marketplace. In its pure form, free economic competition requires a laissez-faire (hands-off) policy that allows the economy to be guided solely by the "laws" of the marketplace. In practice, most capitalist economies are subtly and sometimes forcefully guided by government leaders and agencies that regulate the distribution and consumption of goods and services. Despite government intervention, profit remains the driving force behind a capitalistic economy.

Most supporters of capitalism agree that the profit motive is essential to a dynamic and efficient society. Because private producers and owners of businesses are forced to compete for profits, they must search for ways to cut costs and increase their share of the consumer market. Hence capitalism is almost always accompanied by dynamic growth. Since Max Weber's classic work on *The Protestant Ethic and the Spirit of Capitalism* (1958a), sociologists have been intrigued with the relationship among capitalism and religion and other social institutions (Tester, 2000).

When American businesses like McDonald's entered the former Soviet Union, long lines formed as people got their "first taste" of capitalism.

Socialism

Socialism is *an economic system in which the means of production are owned and controlled by the state and goods and services are distributed as a cooperative enterprise without regard to personal profit.* No country practices pure socialism, but between 1917 and 1991 the Soviet Union was the premier example of a socialist economy. Today, China has assumed that role and promotes the ideology that state ownership, government regulation, and collective goals provide the greatest benefits for the masses although capitalism is making noticeable inroads there. Under socialism, the state restricts private ownership to only a few personal items and thus limits social stratification based on wealth. Through state ownership of factories and service agencies, revenue generated from production is put back into the economic system for the benefit of all citizens. This does not mean socialist countries are without stratification, however, as party membership, the region of the country, and urban versus rural residence create important economic differences (Kerblay, 1983; Mathews, 1986; Gerber, 2002).

According to socialist ideology, capitalism is fueled by short-run hedonism and is ultimately doomed to fail as individuals compete for personal profit. In contrast, socialism is supported by the social value that the common good is more important than individual desires. Hence socialists believe that the collective goals of society can be accomplished better through state planning and economic cooperation. When countries undergo a transition from socialism to capitalism, as in the republics of the former Soviet Union and to a lesser extent in China, power and privilege are no longer the sole domain of the state and the managers in charge of redistribution but are shared by the workers involved in production and the market economy (Nee, 1989, 1991).

Mixed Economies

A **mixed economy** *combines central elements of capitalism and socialism and allows private ownership and free enterprise to compete with businesses, industries, and services owned and operated by the state.* While all societies are mixed to some degree, Sweden is often considered as the model of a mixed economy.

CAPITALISM
An economic system in which the means of production are privately owned and goods and services are distributed competitively for profit.

SOCIALISM
An economic system in which the means of production are owned and controlled by the state and goods and services are distributed as a cooperative enterprise without regard to personal profit.

MIXED ECONOMY
Combines central elements of capitalism and socialism and allows private ownership and free enterprise to compete with businesses, industries, and services owned and operated by the state.

Through democratic socialism, Sweden combines large government-regulated businesses, industries, and social services with participatory democracy, strong labor organizations, private ownership, and personal profit. Because Sweden remained neutral during both world wars, Swedish officials were able to concentrate on economic development and stability. Remarkably, the country avoided much of the agony of the Great Depression, which dramatically affected the United States and most of Europe. Moreover, Sweden is viewed as one of the most humane and progressive nations in the world; it combines socialism and capitalism to provide cradle-to-grave social assistance for its citizens, including generous health-care benefits, low-cost housing, child-care provisions for working parents, and many other benefits.

Although we used the United States as our example for a capitalist economy, in reality it, too, has a mixed economy. Despite the fact that Americans embrace capitalism, free enterprise, and competition, the U.S. government has massive landholdings and operates a host of businesses and services, subsidizes numerous others, and regulates even more. For example, the U.S. Postal Service is owned and operated by the federal government and, with a few exceptions, enjoyed a monopoly during the nineteenth and twentieth centuries. Nevertheless, capitalism thrives even in the highly regulated delivery of mail and packages, as United Parcel Service, Federal Express, and other private companies both cooperate and compete with the U.S. Postal Service for overnight and express delivery services. In contrast, health care has been provided in the United States from its inception by private citizens in a competitive manner for personal profit. As health-care costs increased, privately owned for-profit insurance companies were created to provide medical insurance to help individual consumers faced with the high costs of health care and catastrophic illness. Nevertheless, over the years, medical practice has become increasingly subject to government regulations, and the government is one of the largest medical insurers. The government provides health coverage in the form of Medicare, Medicaid, and subsidized disability programs. Government-sponsored clinics, along with the massive welfare system, have led some economists to refer to America's economic system not as free enterprise but as *welfare capitalism.*

Some social scientists argue that economic and political circumstances have changed so much that the socialism-versus-capitalism debate may be obsolete (Davies, 1989). Yet the strong conflicting ideologies behind capitalism and socialism do not die easily, and many government leaders and citizens still argue that one system or the other is inherently superior.

Transnational Corporations and the Global Economy

In today's world, socialism and traditional capitalism, characterized by small businesses and factories owned by the state or privately owned by individual entrepreneurs, have given way to a global economy characterized by corporate capitalism. Manufacturing is now dominated by **corporations,** *large business concerns owned by thousands of stockholders and managed by boards of directors.* As we noted earlier, many giant corporations have merged with others to form **transnational corporations,** which are *corporations that operate worldwide,* and **corporate conglomerates,** which are *huge corporations that produce hundreds of different products under a variety of trade and brand names.* These megacorps, as they have been called, are extremely powerful; they dominate capitalist economies through investments, control of production, price setting, and employment (Deprez, 1991; Cuyvers and DeBeule, 2006). Their power is enhanced through **corporate interlocks,** *situations that occur when directors sit on more than one major corporate board, linking the corporations in ownership, management, and political and economic activities.*

Today, huge transnational corporations are part of a "global web" and conduct business in every major country in the world (Morgan et al., 2003). A transnational corporation might own forests in America's Pacific Northwest, steel mills in the northeastern United States, rubber plantations in South America, banking interests in Japan, and manufacturing plants in Korea and Mexico. It might market its goods in the United States, Europe, the Middle East, and several Asian and African

CORPORATIONS
Large business concerns owned by thousands of stockholders and managed by boards of directors.

TRANSNATIONAL CORPORATIONS
Corporations that operate worldwide.

CORPORATE CONGLOMERATES
Huge corporations that produce hundreds of different products under a variety of trade and brand names.

CORPORATE INTERLOCKS
Situations that occur when directors sit on more than one major corporate board, linking the corporations in ownership, management, and political and economic activities.

Think the Volkswagen Beetle is a German car? Think again. These new Beetles await inspection at Volkswagen's factory in Puebla, Mexico.

countries. A prime example of a transnational corporation can be found in Volkswagen, the German automobile manufacturer whose Beetle is manufactured in Puebla, Mexico, and is one of the hottest selling vehicles in the United States. General Motors, considered an American corporation, is also transnational. It manufactures and markets cars throughout Europe and in Mexico. Toyota and Honda have huge production plants in the United States.

Although everyone is affected by transnational corporations and the global economy, most people's economic concerns are more local and personal in nature. The reason is, at least in part, that people's most direct link to the economy is through their work and the struggle to maintain a satisfactory quality of life.

THE AMERICAN ECONOMY AND WORK

Since its beginnings, the United States has moved from a rural nation, with the majority of its citizens involved in agriculture, to an urban-oriented society, in which less than 3 percent of the workforce participates in farming (U.S. Bureau of Labor Statistics, 2000).

From an Agrarian to an Industrial Economy

In the early 1800s, over 80 percent of the U.S. labor force was engaged in agriculture (Divine et al., 2005). With the exception of the cotton gin, sophisticated technology and machinery were virtually nonexistent, and labor was primarily performed by animals and humans. People who lived in the cities and were not directly involved in trade often participated in small cottage industries, making handcrafted goods. Others cured meat, ran bakeries, or otherwise produced needed goods and commodities. Blacksmiths, silversmiths, buggy makers, candle makers, and other artisans worked in their homes or barns, relying on the help of family members, or apprentices who worked for room and board.

Perhaps no single phenomenon brought more widespread and lasting change to American society than the Industrial Revolution. American industrial growth hinged on several economic factors. First, industry requires an abundance of natural resources, especially coal, iron ore, water, petroleum, and timber—all readily available in North America. Second, factories demand a large labor supply. Between the 1870s and World War I, approximately 23 million immigrants streamed to the United States, settled in cities, and went to work in American factories and mines. They also helped build the vast network of canals and railroads that crisscrossed the American continent and linked the important trade centers essential to industrial growth (Divine et al, 2005).

Factories also offered a reprieve from the back-breaking work and financial unpredictability associated with farming. Many young adults, poor and disillusioned with farm life, were *pulled* to the cities by promises of steady employment, regular paychecks, increased access to goods and services, and expanded social opportunities for recreation, entertainment, courtship, and marriage. Others were *pushed* there when new technologies made their farm labor cheap or expendable; inventions such as steel plows and mechanized harvesters allowed one farmhand to perform work that had previously required several, thus making farming capital-intensive rather than labor-intensive.

Both European and American investors were eager to provide the capital necessary to extract and transport raw materials as well as to construct and operate new factories. So were government officials, who joined forces with the emerging class of factory owners, railroad magnates, and other entrepreneurs. J. P. Morgan, Jay Gould, Andrew Carnegie, and John D. Rockefeller were touted by some as captains of industry—and others called them robber barons.

Over a period of a few decades, the American economy underwent a massive transition, and the nature of work was permanently altered. Whereas cottage industries relied on a few highly skilled craftworkers who slowly and carefully converted raw materials into finished products from start to finish, factories relied on specialization. Factory workers performed one or two relatively simple tasks over and over again, making only a partial contribution to the finished product. While factory work was less creative and more monotonous, it was also more efficient and allowed the mass production of goods at less expense. By the end of the nineteenth century, the United States emerged as a major industrial nation, and by the end of the two world wars, it became the world's leading industrial and manufacturing country.

Technological innovations, mechanical inventions, and mass production of manufactured goods had another lasting effect on the American economy and the world of work. Not only was a vast labor market needed to mass-produce goods, but the Industrial Revolution also required a large consumer market to buy the increased output. This requirement gave rise to the new occupations of advertising and marketing.

Advertising and the Media

With the advent of mass production, capitalism needed a mass market and higher levels of consumption. Advertising arose to meet that need. Newspapers, circulars, and billboards touted the virtues of certain products, and companies strove to make their brand names into household words. In 1867, businesses and industry spent approximately $50 million for advertising; by 1900, that figure had increased tenfold, to over $500 million; today it exceeds $500 billion (Larson, 1992; Divine et al., 2005; U.S. Bureau of the Census, 2000).

Print Advertising   Newspapers, magazines, catalogs, and circulars were the first and most popular forums for mass advertising. The publisher of one magazine remarked at the turn of the twentieth century that if he could get 400,000 subscribers, he could sell enough advertising to give his magazine free to anyone willing to pay the postage (Goodrum and Dalrymple, 1990). By the 1900s, magazines had become the major outlet for advertising, but producers and advertisers longed for a medium that would "reach the home and the adult members of the family in their moments of relaxation." That medium was found in radio, which brought "to the audience its program of entertainment or its message of advertising" (Czitrom, 1982:77).

Radio and Television   By the 1920s, radio was the ultimate advertising medium, and it continued in that role until after World War II. Radio was a dream come true for mass advertisers, but television offered the ultimate advertising avenue by combining the tried-and-true methods of radio with visual images and celebrity endorsements to pique consumer interest. A popular trend is to use technomedia to resurrect dead celebrities (e.g., John Wayne, Elvis Presley) to endorse products that were produced and developed after their lives had ended. Not only do these ads appeal to the nostalgia of viewers, but companies find it is safer to have dead celebrities whose positive images are permanently etched in the minds of viewers than to use living ones who might get arrested or otherwise offend consumers (Gellene, 1997). From its inception, television advertising represented a boon to retailers—but after only two full decades, it had almost sounded the death knell of print advertising (Goodrum and Dalrymple, 1990). Television ads are fast-paced, lively, sensuous, and stimulating—powerful ingredients to whet consumer appetites. Although many viewers leave the room during commercials or Tivo their favorite programs so they can fast-forward through ads, marketers are convinced that television advertising is effective enough to warrant the billions of dollars that are spent on it annually.

Advertising and the Technomedia   Today, the technomedia are reshaping the world of business and advertising. Online advertising, marketing, and promotion have become a multibillion-dollar industry. Major transnational corporations place on-line advertisements on all of the most popular search vehicle websites, and as Internet users browse various popular websites they are inundated with full-color advertisements and marketing promotions that are updated daily, in some cases hourly, and tailored to the demographics of the Internet subscriber.

Small businesspersons and the self-employed are also cashing in on the on-line advertising bonanza. Websites provide free tips for registering websites and also offer free general marketing guides and on-line marketing handbooks. On-line advertising has increased significantly over the past few years making it difficult to search out a website without being bombarded by "pop-up" ads. Whereas traditional print media as well as radio and television can reach millions of potential consumers, on-line advertis-

Mastercard aired this ad during the 2006 Super Bowl as part of their "Priceless" campaign. Super Bowl ads are not priceless, however. They cost approximately $3 million for 30 seconds, and almost twice that for a full minute advertisement.

Why are corporations willing to spend so much money on advertising during the Super Bowl?

ing provides the added dimension of providing interactive advertising. Consumers not only are made aware of the product, but also can simultaneously make purchases, exchange goods, register complaints and suggestions, file warranties, process rebates, and provide information about themselves and others for consumer research and the development of future marketing campaigns.

Taking a Closer Look at Advertising Soon after its inception, advertising through the mass media came under heavy scrutiny. As early as the 1920s, consumer groups attacked deceptive advertising and attempted to force the Federal Communications Commission (FCC) and the Federal Trade Commission (FTC) to enact stricter regulations governing commercial advertisements (Pope, 1991). Consumer groups received little assistance from these agencies, however, and even through the 1960s and 1970s, when an organized consumer movement was under way, most of the rules that applied to media advertising relied on voluntary compliance and industry self-regulation. In 1978, the FTC attempted to ban television advertising geared to vulnerable, prepubescent children, but the issue became protection of the marketplace versus protection of children, and the marketplace won (Kunkel and Roberts, 1991).

We have a tendency to take advertising for granted, but sociologists are interested in its social impact and have studied it since the appearance of Vance Packard's book *The Hidden Persuaders* (1957). From a functionalist perspective, advertising has the manifest function of stimulating the sale of goods and services. It also performs several latent functions, including ideological support for capitalism, consumerism, affluence, and conspicuous consumption. These latent functions have both positive and negative consequences for society. The conflict perspective points out that advertising manipulates and exploits consumers to generate massive profits, and that media advertising helps create and maintain a false consciousness about the quality of life of the average person in the United States. Finally, the interactionist perspective focuses on how advertising creates a particular definition of the situation for consumers, persuading the public that everyone needs certain products to enhance his or her quality of life—thus creating "wants" and "needs" that did not previously exist. This is particularly true of advertisements that promote the multibillion-dollar over-the-counter health and beauty aids industry, as consumers strive to achieve the idealized looks and body shapes of the movie stars and fashion models who are used to advertise the products.

Advertising has played an increasingly important role over the past six decades. The somewhat predictable mass market of the 1950s "exploded into smaller micromarkets of unfathomable consumers—blacks, Asians, empty-nesters, yuppies, dinks, and so forth—who don't play by the old rules" (Larson, 1992:5). These diverse domestic and international markets, coupled with the technology of the technomedia, which makes it possible to reach hundreds of millions of consumers around the globe, have helped advertisers ease the transition of moving from an industrial to a postindustrial economy dominated by service industries.

Postindustrialism and Service Work

Sociologists contend that the United States has passed its industrial peak and represents a postindustrial economy, in which the service industries provide a large proportion of jobs and generate a vast amount of revenue for individuals, businesses, and the government (Eitzen and Baca-Zinn, 2006). There was little or no job growth in manufacturing during the 1970s and 1980s. Newly created jobs were almost exclusively in the high-technology and service industries.

Postindustrial societies depend on service industries and the manufacture of information and knowledge. As indicated at the beginning of this chapter, they are characterized by large transnational corporations, business conglomerates, and agribusiness, which compete in a global market economy and emphasize science, technology, and education. In 2000, less than 20 percent of the U.S. workforce was employed in manufacturing—the lowest proportion since 1900. The vast majority of Americans now earn their living as part of a service economy (see Figure 17.3).

In a postindustrial economy manufacturing involves the use of computers and robotics, and a much smaller human workforce is needed in factories. An example of the tremendous change in manufacturing can be seen in the Owens Corning Plant in

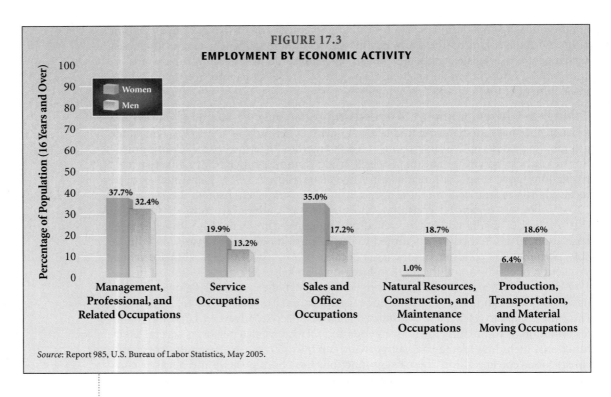

FIGURE 17.3
EMPLOYMENT BY ECONOMIC ACTIVITY

Percentage of Population (16 Years and Over)

Women
Men

Management, Professional, and Related Occupations	Service Occupations	Sales and Office Occupations	Natural Resources, Construction, and Maintenance Occupations	Production, Transportation, and Material Moving Occupations
37.7% / 32.4%	19.9% / 13.2%	35.0% / 17.2%	1.0% / 18.7%	6.4% / 18.6%

Source: Report 985, U.S. Bureau of Labor Statistics, May 2005.

Jackson, Tennessee. This thriving fiberglass plant once had over 500 employees, compared with 80 today. Three of the four levels of management that once ran the plant have been eliminated; in fact, every employee in the plant now reports to one person. The once strong labor union that negotiated wages, fringe benefits, and retirement plans for plant employees has been disbanded, and some have claimed that the plant signifies the "end of blue-collar labor." This dramatic change in manufacturing has prompted some economic analysts to proclaim that the United States is undergoing a second industrial revolution—one that will be no less significant in terms of its economic, political, social, and cultural impact than the one that occurred during the nineteenth century.

As the need for physical labor is reduced, more people are needed to work in computer programming, data processing, advertising, and sales to teach the information and knowledge necessary to build the sophisticated machines and technology on which manufacturing depends. Many high-income Americans are reluctant to spend their leisure time on routine household tasks such as housecleaning, child care, yard work, and home maintenance; they provide occupational opportunities to people who lack the educational background and technical skills to assume advanced technological jobs. However, the pay is low, there are no benefits and no security, and these occupations do not begin to provide jobs for the millions of undereducated members of the "underclass." This type of employment often becomes part of the "hidden economy" discussed later in this chapter.

Work in industrial and postindustrial economies is highly stratified. Workers in factories, businesses, and corporations are supervised by people who are accountable to others further up the chain of command. One scheme sociologists use to classify types of jobs is to divide them into the categories of blue-collar, white-collar, and pink-collar occupations and to differentiate between vocations and professions.

Blue-Collar, White-Collar, and Pink-Collar Occupations

Traditionally, a convenient way to distinguish between types of jobs was to divide them into two categories: blue collar and white collar. Generally speaking, a **blue-collar occupation** *involves manual labor or factory work,* whereas a **white-collar occupation** *involves office work or nonmanual labor.*

At the beginning of the twentieth century, blue-collar workers made up almost half of the workforce; only about 20 percent of workers held white-collar jobs. By 2000, those figures had changed dramatically, with blue-collar workers making up less than one-fourth of the labor market, while over 70 percent of all American workers were employed in

BLUE-COLLAR OCCUPATION
An occupation that involves manual labor or factory work.

WHITE-COLLAR OCCUPATION
An occupation that involves office work or nonmanual labor.

white-collar occupations. Sociologist Jessie Bernard (1981) contended that the blue-collar–white-collar dichotomy is misleading because it inaccurately implies that the majority of American workers are employed in high-paying, prestigious jobs. She added a new category to the occupational classification scheme, dubbing clerical work a **pink-collar** occupation because it is so *heavily dominated by women.* Many service jobs are also pink-collar occupations: nurses, waiters, flight attendants, child-care workers, and household servants are predominantly women, and consequently these jobs are devalued (Baron and Newman, 1990; Kemp, 1994). Research also shows that in the postindustrial service sector, while more women are reaching upper-level jobs, fewer men are working in the lower-level and lowest-paying jobs (Steiger and Wardell, 1995).

Primary and Secondary Labor Markets and the Rise of Professions

Whereas Bernard alerted us to the stratification of labor based on sex, sociologists also distinguish between the **primary labor market,** which comprises *occupations that provide high income, prestige, and extensive benefits,* and the **secondary labor market,** which includes *jobs that provide low wages and few benefits.* This scheme recognizes that although the proportion of blue-collar workers is shrinking, the number of workers employed in the secondary labor market is ballooning. This segment of the labor market includes traditional blue-collar jobs, pink-collar occupations, and a number of other low-paying, dead-end jobs. It is also heavily populated by members of ethnic enclaves in major cities. Their strong ethnic ties confer some safeguards against "difficult work conditions, health hazards, low pay, and gender and ethnic segregation" (Edwards 1979; Lamphere et al., 1994:18).

The primary labor market includes upper-level management positions in business and industry as well as the members of professions. Technically, anybody who is paid to do something is a professional (as opposed to being an amateur, who participates in an activity for no compensation). To sociologists, a **profession** is *a white-collar occupation that is prestigious, is relatively high-paying, and requires advanced formal education and specialized training.* For example, law and medicine have been considered professions for quite some time, as has college teaching. More recently, schoolteachers, social workers, law enforcement officers and morticians have sought to enhance their occupational status by proclaiming their jobs to be professions (see Focus box 17.2).

Some occupations suffer from "occupational status insecurity" (Ritzer, 1977:9). Pine (1975:28) noted, "because professionalization is highly respected in American society, the word 'profession' tends to be used as a symbol by occupations seeking to improve or enhance the lay public's conception of that occupation." Moreover, because of the prestige associated with professions, it is generally considered an insult to call someone "unprofessional" (Pavalko, 1988).

There is debate over whether certain occupations are vocations or professions. George Ritzer (1977) identified four qualities that characterize a profession: theoretical knowledge, self-regulation, authority, and community orientation. People in vocations that strive to be recognized as professions but do not fully meet all four criteria are sometimes referred to as paraprofessionals. Medical technicians, legal assistants, and teaching assistants, for example, often work alongside physicians, attorneys, and college professors but are not accorded the same professional status.

Partly because autonomy and self-regulation are associated with high status, many people prefer jobs in which they are not directly supervised by others. In addition, in economically turbulent times, job security is tenuous and unemployment rates rise. This is another reason some Americans prefer to work for themselves.

Self-Employment

During the eighteenth century, over three-fourths of Americans were self-employed, mostly in agriculture or small cottage industries, but with the Industrial Revolution that proportion declined dramatically (Mills, 1951). In 1990, less than 10 percent of the workforce was self-employed. Although small, that figure represented a slight increase over the previous two decades, especially in the number of people who owned and

Today, many men and women are employed in occupations that once were closed to them because of institutionalized discrimination in the workplace based on a person's sex.

How do you think this "blue-collar" job influences this woman's social identity? What about men who work in so-called "pink-collar" occupations?

PINK-COLLAR OCCUPATION
An occupation heavily dominated by women.

PRIMARY LABOR MARKET
Occupations that provide high income, prestige, and extensive benefits to workers.

SECONDARY LABOR MARKET
Jobs that provide low wages and few benefits.

PROFESSION
A white-collar occupation that is prestigious, is relatively high-paying, and requires advanced formal education and specialized training.

Until the 1900s in the United States, people usually died at home, and their bodies were prepared for burial by family members and close friends. As the medical profession grew, however, and the care of the sick and elderly became viewed as something that required skilled professionals with advanced education and specialized training, deaths increasingly occurred outside the home in hospitals and nursing homes. As society changed its attitudes about those who handled the sick and the dying, views toward people in related occupations—such as druggists or apothecaries, who worked with physicians to provide needed medicines, and undertakers, who cared for the dead—also changed. Druggists became professional pharmacists, and undertakers became licensed and certified embalmers and funeral directors.

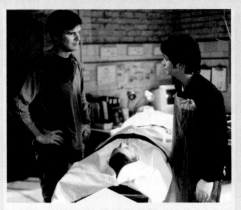

How has the popular HBO series *Six Feet Under* changed public perception of morticians and funeral directors?

There is a national association of funeral directors, as well as state and local professional organizations. They hold annual conventions, sponsor professional activities, produce professional journals, and provide candidates for election to state, regional, and national governing and regulating boards. Every member of the funeral industry is expected to adhere to its professional code of ethics, which has been approved by the national association.

Because of their specialized training, licensure, and certification requirements, funeral directors have been given almost sole authority over American funeral practices. Their clients come to them relatively ignorant of embalming and burial laws and generally rely on the funeral director for guidance of what "must" and "should" be done at the time of death. Agreements between local funeral directors and cemetery officials often call for burial vaults or specific types of containers for transportation and cremation of bodies; although not required by state law, these agreements may in fact dictate certain burial procedures.

The occupational status and prestige of doctors and pharmacists steadily increased during most of the twentieth century. Embalmers and funeral directors, however, have struggled with the stigma associated with handling the dead that plagues their jobs. William E. Thompson conducted ethnographic interviews with morticians and funeral directors in four states to discover how they handle the stigma associated with their work and to examine their methods of attempting to define their occupation from a vocation to a profession.

In an effort to manage stigma, members of the funeral industry work diligently to professionalize their occupation and enhance its prestige. Their efforts involve implementing all the criteria associated with professions: theoretical knowledge, self-regulation, authority, and community orientation.

Despite the relative simplicity of the embalming process, the funeral industry in most states lobbied successfully to require licensure and certification for its members. Most states require at least 60 college hours; some colleges and universities offer bachelor's degrees in mortuary arts or mortuary sciences. Additionally, most states now require a 1-year apprenticeship under a licensed embalmer and passage of a state board examination to become a certified embalmer. An applicant who also wishes to become a licensed funeral director must take additional courses and pass a different examination.

Finally, few occupations work harder at promoting an image of community orientation than do funeral directors. Downplaying the commercial interests of their business, funeral directors wrap themselves in what Thompson called a "shroud of service," relentlessly promoting their roles as "pre-need counselors," "grief therapists," and professional caretakers of the deceased and their loved ones in the time of most need.

TAKING A CLOSER LOOK

Why is there so much stigma associated with handling the dead in American society? Can you think of other occupations that have sought to enhance their occupational status by redefining a vocation as a profession? How has this process been similar to that experienced by morticians and funeral directors? In what ways has it been different? What other strategies might members of an occupation use to enhance its social status?

Source: William E. Thompson. "Handling the Stigma of Handling the Dead: Morticians and Funeral Directors." *Deviant Behavior* 12 (4), 1991:403–429.

operated small service businesses. Today, estimates put the number of self-employed Americans around 15 million (U.S. Bureau of Labor Statistics, 2003).

There could be several reasons for the slight increase in rates of self-employment. Sociologists recognize that several American values may be involved. For one thing, owning a small business and working for oneself reflects and reinforces Americans' emphasis on independence. Even though self-employment may mean working harder and putting in longer hours, many people feel this is a small price to pay to avoid time clocks, supervisors, and the risk of being fired or laid off at someone else's discretion. And although Americans spend millions of dollars on labor-saving devices, they still claim to value hard work. Americans also value innovation, a characteristic associated with the success of small-business and manufacturing ventures. In addition, corporate layoffs and the reduction in number of full-time job opportunities have discouraged some people from pursuing full-time employment, opting instead to start their own businesses. Finally, while most Americans are skeptical of "rags-to-riches" stories, H. Ross Perot, the late Mary Kay Ash, and Sam Walton, all of whom started out as small independent business owners and later became millionaires (or billionaires), inspire them to go it alone. Self-employment is not without risks, and the self-employed know that even minor fluctuations in a nation's economy have a direct impact on the lives of its citizens. In the United States, self-employment simultaneously ranks among the *best* and *worst* jobs in the labor market (McManus, 2000). Owners of small businesses and family farms often feel the first pains of inflation, recession, and other economic problems. Americans marvel at the success of small businesses that begin in garages or spare bedrooms and grow into successful ventures, but the reality is that the majority of small businesses are far less successful, and many fail each year.

Unemployment and Underemployment

According to Richard Barnet (1994:162), "Between 1979 and 1992, Fortune 500 Companies presented 4.4 million of their employees with pink slips, a rate of around 340,000 a year." In the same period, more than one-half of all men 16 and older who lived in high-poverty areas were not working, more than one in three reporting that they had not worked even a single day for an entire year (Reich, 1994). By 1998, U.S. unemployment rates had fallen to 4.3 percent and in 2000 they dropped to 4.0 percent—their lowest level since 1970 (Seaberry, 1998; McGinn and Naughton, 2001a). The economy took a sharp downturn, however, and by 2003, unemployment rates had reached 6.4 percent. In 2006, the unemployment rate hovered around 4.8 percent with 7.2 million unemployed Americans actively seeking jobs (U.S. Bureau of Labor Statistics, 2006). The U.S. government considers an unemployment rate of less than 5 percent as representing "full employment," but that assessment ignores the fact that even that small percentage, especially when combined with those who are working part-time jobs, includes millions of people seeking employment who are unable to find full-time jobs.

Unemployment   During difficult economic times, many workers, especially those employed in blue-collar occupations and the secondary labor market, lose their jobs. (Figure 17.4 shows U.S. unemployment rates and Map 17.1 shows global unemployment.)

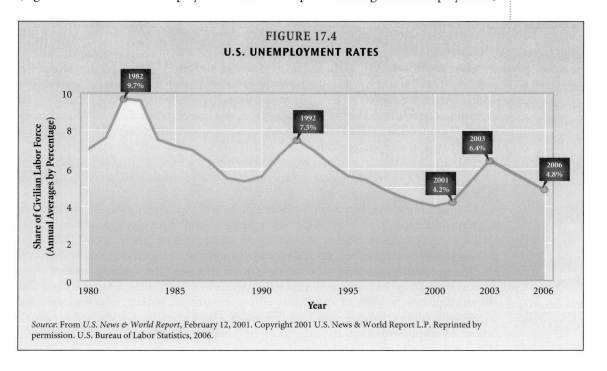

FIGURE 17.4
U.S. UNEMPLOYMENT RATES

Source: From *U.S. News & World Report*, February 12, 2001. Copyright 2001 U.S. News & World Report L.P. Reprinted by permission. U.S. Bureau of Labor Statistics, 2006.

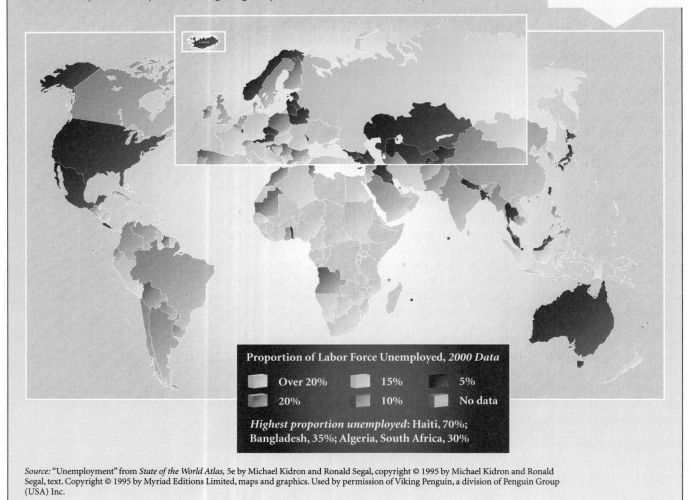

MAP 17.1

UNEMPLOYMENT RATES

As this map illustrates, poor nations tend to have much higher unemployment rates than wealthy nations. The United States government considers an unemployment rate of 5 percent or less as full employment; however, the United States and many other wealthy nations are beginning to experience an increase in underemployment.

How do unemployment and underemployment affect a nation's economy and work?

Proportion of Labor Force Unemployed, *2000 Data*

- Over 20%
- 15%
- 5%
- 20%
- 10%
- No data

Highest proportion unemployed: Haiti, 70%; Bangladesh, 35%; Algeria, South Africa, 30%

Source: "Unemployment" from *State of the World Atlas,* 5e by Michael Kidron and Ronald Segal, copyright © 1995 by Michael Kidron and Ronald Segal, text. Copyright © 1995 by Myriad Editions Limited, maps and graphics. Used by permission of Viking Penguin, a division of Penguin Group (USA) Inc.

An assembly line worker on the kill floor of a large beef-processing plant told one of the authors, "This job ain't much, but it beats the hell out of being unemployed!" Several economic factors are related to unemployment, including recession, market instability, and economic uncertainty. Also, as Flint, Michigan, discovered, when General Motors relocated a number of its plants to Mexico, where labor and production costs were cheaper, many American workers were displaced, and Flint's economy suffered dramatically. Further, in rapidly changing societies many workers become unemployed when their skills become obsolete or technological advancements replace human workers with machines or robots.

Although economic factors contribute significantly to unemployment, sociologists are more interested in its social dimensions. From a conflict perspective, wealthy industrialists, chief executive officers of large corporations, and members of other powerful groups always reap more benefits than members of the working class in a capitalist society. Thus, regardless of economic conditions, unemployment is far more common in the secondary than in the primary labor market. Moreover, conflict theorists point out that the unemployment rates of racial and ethnic minorities, women, and teenagers are consistently higher than the rates for white males. Although ethnicity, sex, and age are all linked in important ways to differences in unemployment rates, race consistently

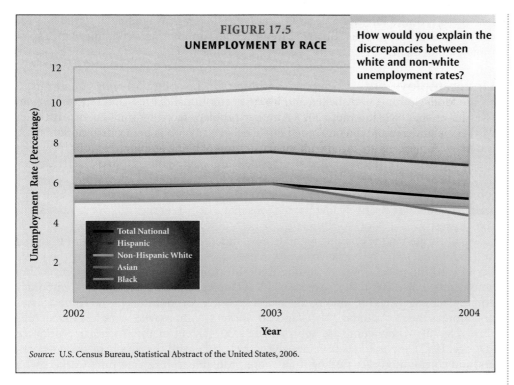

FIGURE 17.5
UNEMPLOYMENT BY RACE

How would you explain the discrepancies between white and non-white unemployment rates?

Unemployment Rate (Percentage)

12
10
8
6
4
2

Total National
Hispanic
Non-Hispanic White
Asian
Black

2002   2003   2004

Year

Source: U.S. Census Bureau, *Statistical Abstract of the United States, 2006.*

Because of plant closings in many northern industrial cities, large numbers of unemployed workers moved away from the "Rust Belt" for the warmer climates and anticipated better economic opportunities in the "Sun Belt."

appears to be most significant; since the mid-1960s the unemployment rates of African Americans have been almost double those of whites (see Figure 17.5).

Several factors may explain why racial and ethnic minorities have higher unemployment rates than whites. One explanation is racism and its correlates of the reduced educational, economic, social, and employment opportunities for minorities (Willie, 1990). Sociologist William J. Wilson (1978), however, argued that the occupational and economic discrepancies between blacks and whites in the United States are attributable more to social class than to race. He argued that a small, well-educated portion of the black population has capitalized on increased educational and occupational opportunities and that its members have joined the ranks of the middle class. He noted that a large urban underclass, composed primarily of uneducated and unskilled African American men, has become locked in the grip of low-paying, menial jobs or—worse—unemployment. Others point out that blacks are disproportionately represented in manufacturing jobs, the hardest hit by a sluggish economy, while Hispanics are more likely to hold service jobs (Solis, 2003).

John Kasarda (1980, 1983) observed that urban labor markets have been polarized by the shift to a postindustrial economy. American cities are no longer centers of the production and distribution of manufactured goods but are focal points for the creation and distribution of information, financial services, and government services. Poorly educated and unskilled blacks and other minorities are heavily concentrated in urban areas, but many unskilled and semi-skilled industrial jobs for which they would have been qualified have been replaced by professional, technical, and administrative jobs requiring higher education and certification credentials; the result is high unemployment rates for urban minorities.

The secondary labor market, racial and ethnic minorities, and blue-collar workers are not the only ones experiencing the pains of unemployment. During the economic slowdown of 2000–2003, many high-tech industries such as the computer industry, telecommunications, marketing, advertising, and others experienced financial difficulties and terminated large numbers of highly educated and highly skilled employees (McGinn and Naughton, 2001b; Sloan, 2001; Shah, 2003). While many of those who

What impact does this type of migration have on the economy of the states the workers leave? What impact does it have on the states to which they move?

lose these types of jobs are able to find new employment, it is often at a much lower salary than their previous job. This trend has led to another economic hardship—underemployment.

Underemployment Unemployment threatens the ability of many Americans to secure food, clothing, and shelter, and it causes emotional distress and low self-esteem (Kessler et al., 1989; Konrad, 2002). Another problem faced by millions of American workers is underemployment. Some people believe any job is better than no job at all, but many Americans are faced with the frustration of being employed in jobs for which they are overeducated, overskilled, overtrained, and overqualified (Sloan, 2001; Dooley and Prause, 2004). In the twenty-first century, college graduates are finding increased job opportunities as compared to a decade earlier, but many of the jobs for which they are being hired are relatively low-paying jobs that a decade earlier did not require a college degree.

We illustrated in the opening vignette how underemployment exacts both a financial and emotional toll. The social costs of underemployment include increasing the number of working poor as well as adding to health problems such as depression, alcohol abuse, low self-esteem, and even suicide (Dooley and Prause, 2004). Temporary employment agencies are among the fastest growing corporations in the United States and around the world today. "Nonstandard workers"—those who work less than a full-time schedule—now comprise approximately 30 percent of the American workforce (Dodge, 1997). Job markets have not always kept pace with the supply of skilled workers, and corporations are finding it far more profitable to hire part-time workers who can be paid lower wages and not be provided health insurance, retirement benefits, and other benefits that come with full-time employment. According to Janice Castro (1994:191), temporary staffers, whose numbers have grown dramatically with corporate downsizing in the last two decades, "have more in common with the unemployed than with people who have jobs."

When workers are unemployed or underemployed and must settle for temporary or part-time jobs, they often must find other ways to raise money for basic necessities, and they must supplement their low wages to enjoy a higher standard of living. This situation has contributed to a legion of working poor and the development of a large underground, or hidden, economy in the United States.

America's Hidden Economy

When government officials and the media mention the state of the economy or cite unemployment figures, they are referring to the massive data collected by governmental and private agencies. These data are the official records on the economy and work in the United States. The government keeps track of national production figures, international trade ratios, the gross national product, and wholesale and retail sales. In addition, the Internal Revenue Service requires Americans to report all income from salaries, wages, tips, interest, dividends, and other sources, and the U.S. Bureau of Labor Statistics annually releases statistics on employment figures and income.

What is missing from these official data is the vast **hidden** or **underground economy**—the *exchange of goods and services and the generation of income that goes unreported to the government.* The hidden economy may account for as much as 10 percent of the total American economy, or over $1 trillion, and may cost the U.S. government close to $200 billion in uncollected taxes.

Part of the hidden economy is a result of illegal activities. For example, it is estimated that the sale of illegal drugs such as cocaine, heroin, marijuana, and amphetamines amounts to several billion dollars per year (Abadinsky, 2003). When the income generated by other criminal activities is added, the total exceeds the gross national product of some nations. The bulk of the hidden economy, however, consists of work and other activities performed off the record. Many teenagers and illegal immigrant mow lawns, babysit, clean houses, and perform other jobs for income that goes unreported. And each year, thousands of families across the country hold yard and garage sales to gener-

HIDDEN ECONOMY (UNDERGROUND ECONOMY) Exchange of goods and services and generation of income that goes unreported to the government.

ate a few extra dollars to supplement the family budget. The combined revenue generated by these sales may amount to more than a billion dollars per year.

More significant, much of the income generated by self-employment is untraceable, and the government must rely on the honor system. The government can seize and scrutinize people's financial records, but unreported income can be "lost" to official records. Even more difficult to document is income from tips received by bartenders, waiters, topless dancers, housekeepers, cab drivers, and others who either inadvertently or intentionally underreport their earnings. You might ask yourself how much you and your family have contributed to the hidden economy through unreported earnings from babysitting, lawn mowing, garage sales, tips, and other sources of unreported income. Now multiply that by the number of families like yours in the United States, and you will begin to get a picture of the underground economy.

The government downplays the existence of the hidden economy and generally portrays it "as a temporary phenomenon that will disappear when circumstances return to 'normal'" (Wiegand, 1992:1). Yet sociological and economic scholars agree that the hidden economy is an enduring institution in American society.

Garage sales comprise a large part of America's "hidden economy" where millions of dollars a year exchange hands without the government collecting taxes from the sellers.

Have you ever been part of the hidden economy?

WORK AS A SOCIAL PHENOMENON

In the United States and most industrial and postindustrial nations, the largest single portion of most adults' waking hours is spent on their jobs. Consequently, while government officials and economists view work as an economic activity, sociologists focus on its social importance. There are at least four important dimensions of sociological interest: work as a social role, how work links an individual to the larger social structure, work as a source of identity, and the extent of the satisfaction or alienation people experience in their work. We look briefly at each of these aspects of work as a social phenomenon.

Work as a Social Role

Just as norms govern our actions when we perform the roles of women or men, mothers or fathers, and friends or neighbors, they also accompany our occupational roles as doctors, lawyers, teachers, accountants, police officers, social workers, assembly line workers, construction workers, flight attendants, or oil field roughnecks. Although we say our favorite professor was "born to teach" or that Sir Laurence Olivier had acting "in his blood," occupational roles, or the expectations that accompany a particular job, must be learned through socialization.

A Functionalist View Working from a functionalist perspective, Robert Merton and colleagues described socialization in medical schools as a process of steady and incremental change in attitudes and behaviors during which students progressively assume the role of physician as they move through their training (Merton et al., 1957). On entering medical school, Merton's subjects were students who wanted to be doctors. As they progressed through the curriculum, they gained knowledge, competence, and confidence, and they became doctors in training, acting and being treated as junior colleagues by the physicians with whom they worked. By the end of medical school, they had acquired the knowledge, skills, and experience required to become full-fledged physicians.

The Interactionist Perspective Howard Becker and associates used an interactionist perspective to study the same phenomenon. They focused on the symbolic transformation that occurred during medical school. Specifically, they described the social interactions between and among students, physicians, nurses, and patients, and they considered important rituals that allowed medical students to be symbolically transformed into medical doctors (Becker et al., 1961).

A Conflict/Feminist Approach   Jane Leserman (1981) also examined the socialization process in medical school, focusing on value changes and the differences between the experiences of male and female students. Her study revealed that medical school environments are very conservative and that faculty serve as traditional and powerful role models, especially for men, reflecting the conservative values of the profession. Other studies on socialization into medical careers have also generally found that an important part of the education and training of doctors and nurses involves traditional gender role behavior (e.g., Stein, 1967; Coombs, 1978; Astor, 1995).

Occupational Socialization   While these studies focused on the medical profession, every occupation, whether professional or blue collar, high-status or low-status, well-respected or even deviant or illegal, includes the socialization of new members. An important part of police officer training occurs in academies, where cadets learn the role expectations associated with law enforcement (Hopper, 1977), and military academies concentrate as much on shaping the personalities of cadets to conform to the idealized role of the officer as they do on education and skill training (Wamsley, 1972). Bartenders and waiters need little training in mixing and serving drinks, but they undergo extensive on-the-job socialization by club owners, bartenders, and other waiters on how to handle customers effectively (Spradley and Mann, 1975). Similarly, strippers and topless dancers must learn to simultaneously play the roles of entertainer, seductress, hustler, and even bouncer if they are going to maximize their tips while effectively handling the heckling and sexual advances of intoxicated customers (Skipper and McCaghy, 1970; Boles and Garbin, 1974; Thompson and Harred, 1992, 2003).

In addition to providing an important social role, work also links the individual to the larger social structure in terms of social stratification and social relationships.

Work and the Social Structure

Because few occupations are performed in social isolation, work links individuals to others with whom they interact both on and off the job. These social networks become important for mobility within the workplace (Podolny and Baron, 1997; Mouw, 2003). Work also links individuals to both the national and international economy; waiters in Dallas, plumbers in Nashville, and stockbrokers in New York City are affected by economic factors such as recession, inflation, and the prices of gold and oil on world markets. The work group is recognized as a powerful influence on individuals' attitudes and behavior. In Chapter 2, we discussed the famous studies at the Western Electric plant near Chicago, where researchers discovered the Hawthorne effect (workers' production increases simply because they are being studied) and learned that norms among workers govern individual output and productivity (Jones, 1990). Often people share a common social bond with those with whom they work. For example, Jeffrey Riemer (1979:41) studied construction workers and noted: "Learning the culture of one's trade and its location within the larger social structure of the building construction industry provides an occupational identity for the worker. Whereas the work structure makes distinctions between workers, the work culture socially bonds them together."

Occupational Subcultures   In some occupations, strong occupational subcultures develop. Co-workers share common values, norms, and attitudes not only toward their work but also toward life in general. As a result, the members of a particular occupational subculture often spend most of their off-the-job time with others in the same line of work. A work subculture can become the dominant force in a person's life, shaping his or her attitudes, beliefs, and actions on and off the job; sociologists refer to this as "occupational encapsulation" (Pavalko, 1988).

Simply sharing the workplace does not necessarily create a social bond, however. In an effort to maximize efficiency and profits in industry, the assembly line was developed. Workers along the line perform specialized tasks, each contributing in a small way to the finished product. As Focus box 17.3 illustrates, although assembly lines are effi-

One of the most demanding, demeaning, demoralizing, and dehumanizing jobs is working on an assembly line. William Thompson (1983) described and analyzed work on an assembly line in a major beef-packing plant and its impact on the workers. His research showed that day-dreaming, horseplay, and occasional sabotage were tactics used by workers to deal with the monotonous and demeaning nature of their work in an attempt to maintain a sense of dignity, individuality, and self-respect.

The monotony of the line was almost unbearable. With the exception of a scheduled 15-minute break and a 30-minute lunch period (and sporadic brief gaps in the line), the work was mundane, routine, and continuous. It was not unusual to look up or down the line and see workers at various stations singing to themselves, tapping their feet to imaginary music, or carrying on conversations with themselves. In visiting with other workers, I found that daydreaming was the norm. Some would think about their families, while others fanta-sized about sexual escapades, fishing, or anything unrelated to the job. Daydreaming was not inconsequential, however. During these periods, items were most likely to be dropped, jobs improperly performed, and accidents incurred.

Perhaps the most devastating aspect of working at the beef plant was the dehumanizing and demeaning elements of the job. In a sense, the assembly line worker became a part of the assembly line. The assembly line is not a tool used by the workers, but a machine that controls them. When workers are viewed as mere extensions of the machines with which they work, their human needs become secondary in impor-tance to the smooth mechanical functioning of the produc-tion process. Workers on the assembly line are seen to be as interchangeable as the parts of the product on the line itself.

It is fairly common knowledge that assembly-line work sit-uations often lead to employee sabotage. At the beef plant, I quickly learned that there was an art to effective sabo-tage. Subtlety appeared to be the key. Despite formal norms against sabotage, it was not uncommon for workers to deliberately cut chunks out of pieces of meat for no reason (or for throwing at other employees). The workers practically made a game out of doing forbidden things simply to see if they could get away with them. New workers were routinely socialized into the subtle art of

rule-breaking as approved by the line workers. At my par-ticular work station, it was a fairly common practice for other workers who were covered with beef blood to come over to the tub of swirling water designed to clean the [cows'] tongues, and as soon as the inspector looked away, wash their hands, arms, and knives in the tub. This proce-dure was strictly forbidden by the rules. If witnessed by a foreman or inspector, the tub had to be emptied, cleaned, and refilled, and all the tongues in the tub at the time had to be put in the "inedible" tub. All of that would be a time-consuming and costly procedure, yet the workers seemed to absolutely delight in successfully pulling off the act. This artful sabotage served as a symbolic way in which the workers could express a sense of individuality, and hence, self-worth.

TAKING A CLOSER LOOK

Why is assembly line work more demeaning and dehu-manizing than other forms of blue-collar labor? Why is sabotage fairly common among assembly-line workers? What are some of the possible consequences of this sab-otage? What steps might factory owners take to "human-ize" the production process?

Source: "Hanging Tongues: A Sociological Encounter with the Assembly Line," by William E. Thompson. *Qualitative Sociology* 6 (Fall) 1993:215–237. Reprinted by permission of Human Sciences Press, Inc.

cient they greatly reduce social interaction and have an alienating and dehumanizing impact on workers (Hummel, 1977; King, 1978; Thompson, 1983). Many factory work-ers view their jobs as something to endure and see their co-workers as scarcely different from the machines they operate.

Labor Unions Historically, worker identity was created and enhanced by the forma-tion of labor unions to represent the interests of workers against those of factory owners and managers. Labor unions got their start in the 1860s; by the 1890s, the American Fed-eration of Labor (AFL) had emerged as one of the most powerful labor groups in the country. Labor unions gained strength, and by the end of World War II approximately one-third of the labor force was unionized. The Civil Rights movement of the 1960s revitalized labor militancy (Isaac and Christiansen, 2002). Union membership reached almost 25 million during the early 1970s but declined during the 1970s and 1980s (Divine et al., 2005). Part of the decline in union membership can be explained by the failure of unions to negotiate successfully with management for higher wages, better benefits, shorter hours, and better working conditions. Massive layoffs in the steel and automobile industries during the 1970s led union leaders to agree to wage and benefit cuts—and even then, many union workers lost their jobs. During the same period, the rank and file began to distrust the motives of union leadership amid scandals involving alleged bribery, misuse of pension funds, and other criminal activities.

The recession of the 1980s created waves of factory closings, and in some cases union workers were coaxed into making further concessions (including disbanding union membership) to retain their jobs. Perhaps the crowning blow to the decline of labor unions was dealt in 1981, when President Reagan ordered the striking members of the Professional Air Traffic Controllers Organization (PATCO) to return to work or lose their jobs. The union stood its ground and the president stood his—and thousands of air traffic controllers were fired and replaced by nonunion substitutes. The PATCO strikers were further punished with a permanent ban on employment as air traffic controllers.

Although economic and political events of the 1980s and 1990s took their toll on labor union strength, in both membership and power, they did not spell their death. As the twenty-first century dawned, labor unions, like most other organizations in the United States and the rest of the world, discovered the power and importance of the World Wide Web. AFL-CIO was one of the first of the major unions to offer Internet access to its members, and it was quickly followed by a host of others. Sociologist and labor expert Arthur Shostak (1999) believes that in addition to empowering union members, networking through advanced technologies by members of these new "CyberUnions" will help revitalize the political power of labor unions by making them a powerful voice for labor once again (Wagner, 2000).

The "Team" Concept The decline of labor unions in the United States did not necessarily signal a weakening of the importance of the work group, however. In fact, American businesses and industries, frustrated by their inability to compete with foreign manufacturers, have attempted to revitalize the importance of work groups by means of the team concept of production. Impressed by the loyalty of Japanese workers, many American corporations have attempted to copy the Japanese style of management and production. In some cases, large-scale assembly lines have been replaced with smaller teams of workers who build a particular product from start to finish "together."

One of the most interesting experiments is the Saturn automobile plant established by General Motors in Spring Hill, Tennessee. At Saturn, the corporate president wears a polo shirt, the workers call him "Skip," and he refers to himself as a "member of the team." The rank-and-file workers do not punch a time clock, and during off-work hours they run an outdoor obstacle course on the plant's grounds and participate in group "hugging sessions." Workers who develop a bad attitude receive a paid day off to think about what is bothering them (Gwynne, 1990). Some American corporations have experienced great difficulty trying to implement the "team" concept, however, because American management styles tend to be hierarchial in nature (Vallas, 2003). And, the Saturn experiment has not revolutionized the auto industry as expected.

How does the team concept of car building compare to the traditional assembly line process? Which do you think is most rewarding to the workers? Which do you think is the most efficient? Why haven't all auto makers switched to the "team" concept?

Corporate image and product image are important in shaping the public's perception of manufactured goods and also have an impact on how people regard themselves and others. One of the powerful ways work links individuals to the larger social structure is by shaping their social identity.

Work and Identity

In modern complex societies, an important part of a person's identity is linked to work. In hunting-gathering and other preindustrial societies, when strangers met they identified themselves in terms of tribal membership, location of village, or kinship. In industrial and postindustrial nations, however, two people are most likely to "'break the ice' by indicating the kind of work they do, and [the question] 'Who am I?' is increasingly likely to be answered in occupational terms" (Pavalko, 1988:4).

Regardless of whether people perform menial tasks in a factory, are skilled craftpersons, make powerful decisions in a boardroom, or are chronically unemployed, their concept of themselves is affected by their occupational status and their work role. In *Working* (1972), Studs Terkel included interviews with over 130 people who talked about their jobs and how they felt about them. Although the feelings ranged from disgust and hostility through ambivalence to outright pride and pleasure, a common element in all the interviews was the impact of work on identity:

> The blue-collar blues is no more bitterly sung than the white-collar moan. "I'm a machine," says the spot-welder. "I'm caged," says the bank teller, and echoes the hotel clerk. "I'm a mule," says the steelworker. "A monkey can do what I do," says the receptionist. "I'm less than a farm implement," says the migrant worker. "I'm an object," says the high-fashion model. Blue-collar and white call upon the identical phrase: "I'm a robot." . . . [And yet a waitress beaming with pride proclaims,] "When I put the plate down, you don't hear a sound. When I pick up a glass, I want it to be just right. When someone says, "How come you're just a waitress?" I say, 'Don't you think you deserve being served by me?'" (Terkel, 1972:xi–xii)

"Work provides identities as much as it provides bread for the table" (R. Friedland and Robertson, 1990:25). As a result, people in high-status jobs are accorded prestige and respect in nonwork situations as well. For example, physicians are addressed as "doctor" not only in clinics and hospitals but also in society at large. Doctors are treated with respect by nurses, staff, and patients in their work environments, and if they make hotel or restaurant reservations using their title they most often receive the same treatment from bellhops, desk clerks, maître d's, and waiters. Similarly, when people occupy lower-status occupations and that fact is conveyed to others, they may be treated off the job the same way they are treated at work.

Because occupational title is linked to identity and makes such an important impression on others, members of lower-status occupations sometimes attempt to improve their prestige by creating lofty-sounding titles to refer to their work. For example, janitors and custodians may insist on being called "maintenance engineers," and garbage collectors may refer to themselves as "sanitation workers." Few people are deceived by these titles, but on the other hand certain occupations have removed some of the stigma associated with their work by changing their job titles and reshaping the public image of their work. For example, "funeral director" does not elicit the same negative connotations as "undertaker," and "animal patrol officer" does not sound as demeaning as "dogcatcher."

Of course, occupation is not the sole source of a person's identity. Nora Watson, a 28-year-old staff writer, summarized as follows: "I think most of us are looking for a calling not a job. Most of us . . . have jobs that are too small for our spirit. Jobs are not big enough for people" (Terkel, 1972:xxiv).

Worker Satisfaction

In addition to exploring the impact of work on a person's identity, a common theme of Terkel's book is the negative feelings and dissatisfaction many people experience on the job:

> This book, being about work, is by its very nature, about violence—to the spirit as well as to the body. It is, above all (or beneath all), about daily humiliations. To survive the day is triumph enough for the walking wounded among the great many of us. (Terkel, 1972:xi)

Hardly a rousing endorsement for worker satisfaction, this statement may summarize the attitudes of many working Americans. Numerous people live for the weekends, holidays, and annual vacations, and Monday is dreaded by many because it signifies the beginning of a new work week. If work indeed is an important social role linking us to

the larger social structure—and it is perhaps the single most important element in shaping our adult identity—why is it viewed so negatively?

From a conflict perspective, the answer points to worker alienation—a feeling of powerlessness and separation from what one produces. Assembly line work seems to be particularly dehumanizing and demeaning (see Focus box 17.3), and workers involved in it often express a high degree of alienation (Terkel, 1972; King, 1978; Thompson, 1983). Worker dissatisfaction is not limited to assembly line work, however; elements of alienation can be found among unskilled blue-collar workers, skilled pink-collar workers, and white-collar professionals. In most cases, people seem less satisfied with their jobs when they lack autonomy and control over what they do. Yet, while there is consensus that technology affects the nature of work, studies are mixed as to whether technology is directly related to worker satisfaction.

Despite the many studies that document worker alienation and the commonly accepted notion that people generally feel negatively about work, the majority of American workers express far more satisfaction about their work than is expected. This is especially true of white-collar professionals: almost 90 percent indicate that if they had it all to do over again they would choose the same line of work (Tausky, 1984). The high level of satisfaction among this group could be attributed to high salaries, but research indicates that salary is only one of many factors that relate to job satisfaction (Halaby, 2003; Jencks et al., 1988; Mortimer and Lorence, 1989; Loscocco and Spitze, 1991).

What factors lead to the highest worker satisfaction? Exchange theorists insist that satisfaction is highest when workers feel they are operating under norms of reciprocity, where they receive fair compensation for their work. Salary and other fringe benefits are important, but opportunities for advancement, job security, flexible hours, and autonomy—the ability to make important decisions affecting work and being relatively free of direct supervision—are also rated as very important (Mortimer and Lorence, 1989; Loscocco and Spitze, 1991; Smith, 1997; Ross, 2000; Halaby, 2003).

TAKING A CLOSER LOOK AT THE ECONOMY AND WORK

At various points in this chapter we have discussed how sociologists using each of the three major theoretical perspectives in sociology might view advertising, occupational socialization, and other particular aspects of the economy or work. At this point, it might be useful to provide a brief general analysis of the economy and work from each of these perspectives.

A Functionalist View

We began this chapter by defining the economy as one of the basic social institutions in every society, then analyzed it in the context of economic systems. Both of these approaches reflect the functionalist view, which focuses on the structure of the economic system and its manifest (production, distribution, and consumption of goods and services) and latent (maintenance of social classes) functions.

Work is functional in that it integrates individuals into the overall social structure of the economic system, providing us with meaningful social roles and an important part of our social identities. The development of a global economy and transnational corporations is also functional in that it serves similar functions for nations. From the functionalist perspective, a strong economy contributes to the overall functioning of society and its other interdependent institutions such as the family, education, religion, and government. Conversely, economic problems such as runaway inflation, recession or depression, and high rates of unemployment are dysfunctional and have negative consequences for virtually all other aspects of society.

The Conflict Perspective

By now, it should come as no surprise that sociologists who apply the conflict perspective to the economy and work focus on economic inequality, social stratification, and the exploitation and alienation of workers. Conflict theorists contend that most economic systems, especially capitalism, are driven by power, greed, unfair competition, and exploitation of the masses (workers who both produce and consume the goods and services) by the elites (who control the capital, own the means of production, and reap the profits from the labor and consumption of the masses).

Conflict theorists point out that although both the economic elite and the masses apparently benefit during economic booms, the disparities between corporate executives and workers at the bottom of the corporate ladder grow larger, not smaller. In fact, during the 1990s, despite the fact that the U.S. economy was quite strong, the Dow Jones expanded to record levels, and corporate profits exploded beyond almost everyone's expectations, America's largest companies laid off workers and converted full-time positions to part-time and temporary jobs. And, of course, during economic busts it is the lowest-paid workers and small-business people who suffer the most, while corporate owners and those at the top of the employment ladder remain somewhat insulated from economic hard times. Corporate scandals involving Enron, WorldCom, and even Martha Stewart reinforce the conflict perspective on the economy and the world of work.

In a global economic system, rich nations assume the role of the economic elite (bourgeoisie), while poor, developing nations become the masses (proletariat). Most core nations (the United States, Japan, and most of Western Europe) extract raw materials from poor developing nations, produce and manufacture parts, then export the parts to developing nations, where they are assembled by uneducated and untrained laborers at slave wages and the goods packaged and distributed worldwide and sold for huge profits.

An Interactionist Approach

Much of our earlier analysis of work as a social phenomenon reflects an interactionist approach to the economy and work. For example, viewing work as an important social role and part of our social identity illustrates how work symbolically reflects not only what we do, but also who we are. Symbolic interactionists contend that work is simply another form of social interaction—thus, like any other form of interaction it helps shape, define, and give meaning to our social worlds and our selves.

What differentiates a job from a profession? The characteristics of a profession (e.g., prestige, education, self-regulation, and community orientation) illustrate that these terms are subjectively determined as much as they are objectively defined. Moreover, workers in any particular occupation may symbolically define and redefine their jobs until they and the public come to view them as professions.

Worker satisfaction is perhaps the ripest area for symbolic interactionist analysis. While most of us assume that high pay is linked to high job satisfaction and worker morale, research indicates that a wide variety of other, less tangible variables are equally or more important. Of utmost importance, it seems, is a sense of personal autonomy (control over one's work) and a feeling of accomplishment (pride in what has been done). These, of course, are largely subjective conditions, defined primarily by the worker, not by the employer or type of work.

LOOKING to the FUTURE

THE ECONOMY AND WORK IN THE TWENTY-FIRST CENTURY

Economic sociology has a rich tradition and will continue to become even more important in the future (Carruthers and Uzzi, 2000). Predictions about the economy and work, however, are as unreliable as a weather forecast. For example, three decades ago, who would have predicted the collapse of the Soviet Union and the large-scale demise of socialism around the globe? Nevertheless, some current trends lead economists and sociologists to make tentative projections.

For one thing, people worldwide seem to be aware of and concerned about economic problems, on both an international and a national scale. Moreover, while Americans have traditionally viewed unemployment, recession, inflation, and other economic concerns in national terms, today there is more interest in the world economy, international

Do you recognize this familiar American icon in Moscow?

trade agreements, and other transnational economic issues. Today, people worldwide are increasingly becoming part of a worldwide labor market within a global economy.

Political and economic events in the early 1990s signaled major economic changes for countries in central and Eastern Europe and had economic ramifications around the world. These events marked an increased emphasis on the market decentralization of socialist economies that had begun several years earlier. As a result, the lines between capitalism and socialism became even further blurred. Moreover, these developments contributed to a growing belief that future East-West relations may hinge on economics more than any other single factor. During the early 1990s, the United States, Mexico, and Canada agreed to the North American Free Trade Agreement (NAFTA), the U.S. Congress renewed China's most favored nation status for trade purposes, and the European Union became a reality (Grinspun and Cameron, 1994). Today, China is a major economic "player," and no doubt will become an even more powerful global economic power in the future.

What impact will these and other economic pacts have on the global economy? Some predict that in the short run they will accelerate "deindustrialization," with additional plant closings and worker layoffs from many blue-collar and low-skill jobs. There may be a continued "deskilling" of jobs in the high-growth service sector, although technical, professional, and managerial job growth should benefit a small group of highly educated and highly skilled workers. Career opportunities for technicians and professional, managerial, and service workers are likely to increase, while jobs for machine operators and other blue-collar laborers continue to decline and are outsourced overseas. The workplace may see a gradual demise of hierarchies, careers, and corporate ladder climbing. Work structures will become more flexible, and the "ladder" will be replaced with a "web," or team of workers who temporarily join forces with teams of technicians and professionals to complete jobs—in many cases all over the globe (Reich, 1994; V. Smith, 1997). As Figure 17.6 illustrates, it is also predicted that home-based workers will become an even larger percentage of the workforce (Joyce, 2002).

The media—especially television and the Internet—have played an increasingly important economic role, not only in regard to advertising but also in helping define the state of the economy. Media reports and forecasts on international trade deficits, new housing starts, unemployment rates, the stability of world currencies, recession and inflation, and other economic indicators have an important influence on consumer confidence in the state of the economy and affect individuals' investment strategies, purchases, and consumption. It is likely that in a global society, where the instantaneous dispersal of information is possible, the media, especially television and the technomedia, will play an even greater economic role.

What will the world of work look like in the future? Nobody knows for sure, but some projections based on current trends are in order. Despite deindustrialization, some economists predict that the United States may face a labor shortage in the early part of this century. Because of demographic trends, the number of teenagers in the workforce has already been reduced, and the number of workers in their early twenties is declining noticeably. Meanwhile, although life expectancies are increasing each year, corporations are making it easier and more attractive for employees to take early retirement. Moreover, some research indicates that the discontinuance of many work-related perquisites, as well as the mental fatigue and stress that people associate with work today, is causing many people to jump off the "fast track" in an attempt to regain their humanity—a phenomenon likely to increase in the future. At the same time, *downsizing, rightsizing, restructuring, outsourcing,* and other buzzwords foretell of a growing *disposable work-*

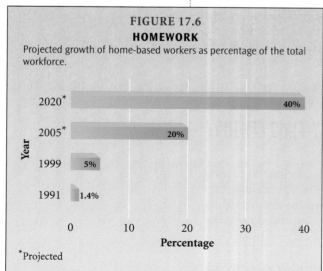

FIGURE 17.6
HOMEWORK
Projected growth of home-based workers as percentage of the total workforce.

Year	Percentage
2020*	40%
2005*	20%
1999	5%
1991	1.4%

*Projected

Source: "Home, Projected growth of home-based workers as a percentage of the total work force." Reprinted with permission from the June 2000 issue of *American Demographics.* Copyright, Crain Communications Inc. 2000.

Sociological
FOCUS   17.4   Telework: The Technomedia and the Changing Face
of Work in the Twenty-First Century

The Industrial Revolution brought about the largest transformation of the workplace in American history. Large numbers of semiautonomous rural farm workers, who had been living and working in relative isolation, moved to urban areas to work in factories with rigid hierarchical structures, work schedules, policies, and procedures. Today, with the massive influence of technomedia, the workplace is experiencing another revolution.

In October 2000 the U.S. Department of Labor held a national symposium in New Orleans on "Telework: The New Workplace of the Twenty-First Century." More than 150 leading experts—academics, social scientists, practitioners, public officials, corporate executives, and representatives from organized labor—met and discussed telework, in which workers stay at home and use computers, e-mail, fax machines, cellular phones, and other forms of technomedia to perform their jobs.

By some estimates, there are somewhere between 13 and 19 million teleworkers in the United States today. Some work out of their homes exclusively; a larger number telework one or two days per week and then go in to the office on the other days. According to available data, the typical teleworker tends to be a college-educated white male between the ages of 34 and 55 who owns a home computer and earns more than $40,000 per year. These workers are most often employed in information-based jobs at mid-level and senior-level positions. There is evidence that the trend is expanding, however, and teleworking may eventually spread to virtually all types and levels of employment.

From a sociological viewpoint, telework may have both positive and negative ramifications for workers and the larger society. Working from the home can provide more flexibility, helping to reduce some of the role overload experienced by so many working parents who are trying to balance job and family responsibilities. It can also reduce or eliminate many of the pressures associated with commuting, office politics, and other work-related hassles. It may contribute to diversity as some who have been shut out of the workplace because of their age, race, sex, or other variables find broader employment opportunities. On the other hand, telework may also blur the boundaries between home and work, essentially putting workers on 24-hour duty as e-mails, pagers, fax machines, and computers continue to pile up work responsibilities and provide work opportunities. Organized labor is particularly concerned that the concept of overtime will become obsolete as work time spills over into personal time for teleworkers on a regular basis.

TAKING A CLOSER LOOK

How are the new technomedia changing the face of work? As these new forms of technology continue to advance and spread, what impact are they having on the social dimensions of work? If people work at home alone and interact with fellow workers only through cyberspace, how might this affect social identities, social roles, social interaction, and the social networks that often develop in the workplace? Is telework truly the future of the workplace?

Source: U.S. Department of Labor, 2001. <www.dol.gov>.

force of temporary and part-time workers in the twenty-first century, where the expectations and obligations that link people to their jobs are forever changing (Moore, 1996; *Newsweek*, 2001, 2002).

Demographic trends indicate that an increasing number of minority workers will join the workforce in the remainder of the twenty-first century. Women, African Americans, Hispanics, and Asians will account for the largest percentage of new entrants into the world of work. Of these categories, women, many of whom will be members of racial and ethnic minorities, will represent the largest proportion of new workers.

It has been projected that companies of the future will use even more cable television, satellite linkups, computer technology, and other technomedia to decrease the need for face-to-face interaction. They will instead make increased use of teleconferencing, decentralization of the workplace, and autonomous working conditions (perhaps out of individuals' homes). Today, already over 13 million employees work out of their homes for major corporations that have decided it is more sensible and less expensive to transport data and information than people from home to workplace (see Focus box 17.4). These developments may change methods of supervision and the role of supervisors, increasing the pressure to support creativity, increase worker morale, and help develop a sense of humanity. In production jobs, the work group may become more significant. The team concept of manufacturing is spreading, and individual workers are more cognizant of the importance of cooperation and teamwork in producing goods of superior quality while at the same time increasing their sense of satisfaction with their work. In some cases, this may mean even larger numbers of people choosing to leave the corporate "rat race" for self-employment and for more self-fulfilling jobs and careers.

Changes in organizational structure may also bring about increasing interdependence among major businesses and corporations because of their need to share information and technology. The result could be the centralization of major planning and decision making, as well as a simultaneous decentralization into smaller organizational units that will operate more efficiently and be independent of direct supervisory control by top executives.

It will be interesting to watch future developments in the economy and in work. One contemporary trend suggests that sociologists, who increasingly focused their attention on organizational structure over the last three decades, will focus more of their attention on workers. Whatever the nature of the specific changes, it seems clear that the future of the economy and of work will depend less on local and national economic factors and increasingly be linked to international events and their impact on the world economy.

Summary

1. The economy has long been of sociological interest because of its impact on virtually all aspects of social life. The economy includes the production, distribution, and consumption of goods and services. An economic system comprises the ideology, values, norms, and activities that regulate the economy.

2. Two ideal types of economic systems are capitalism and socialism. Most societies mix elements of capitalism and socialism; in countries like Sweden, the economic system is best described as a mixed economy. Today, national and local economies are part of a massive global economy dominated by transnational corporations that manufacture, distribute, advertise, and sell goods and services around the world.

3. The American economy has moved from being predominantly agrarian to industrial. Advertising and the mass media played a very important role in this transition. Many economists and sociologists contend that despite its industrial output, the United States is in a transition to becoming a postindustrial economy dominated by service industries and the manufacture of information and knowledge. Work in the American economy is differentiated into a secondary labor market, characterized by blue-collar, pink-collar, and lower-level management white-collar jobs, and a primary labor market, comprising middle- and upper-level management positions and professions. The United States also has a large hidden economy, which involves a variety of work and other economic activities that take place "off the record."

4. While work is an economic activity, it is also an important social phenomenon that links individuals to the social structure, serves as an important source of social identity, and provides various levels of satisfaction to different people.

5. When we take a closer look at the economy and work from the functionalist perspective, we focus on the manifest and latent functions of the economic system. Conflict theorists point out that the economic system contributes to social inequality and work involves exploitation of workers by the economic elites, who control the means of production and reap the profits from workers' labor. Interactionists point out that work is an important part of our social identity and that people define and redefine the world of work through social interaction and the manipulation of meaningful symbols.

6. Current trends and patterns indicate that there will be dramatic shifts in the workforce in this century. More minorities, especially African Americans, Hispanics, and women, will enter the labor market. Changes are also likely to occur in communication in the workplace, supervision, the work group, organizational structure, and management. There is a consensus among sociologists and economists that in the future an interdependent global economy will have an increasingly dramatic impact on the lives of individuals, groups, and nation-states.

Key Terms

blue-collar occupation (p. 496)
capitalism (p. 490)
conspicuous consumption (p. 487)
consumption (p. 487)
corporate conglomerates (p. 492)
corporate interlocks (p. 492)
corporations (p. 492)

distribution (p. 487)
economic system (p. 487)
economy (p. 487)
hidden economy (p. 502)
mixed economy (p. 491)
pink-collar occupation (p. 497)
primary labor market (p. 497)

production (p. 487)
profession (p. 497)
secondary labor market (p. 497)
socialism (p. 491)
transnational corporations (p. 492)
underground economy (p. 502)
white-collar occupation (p. 496)

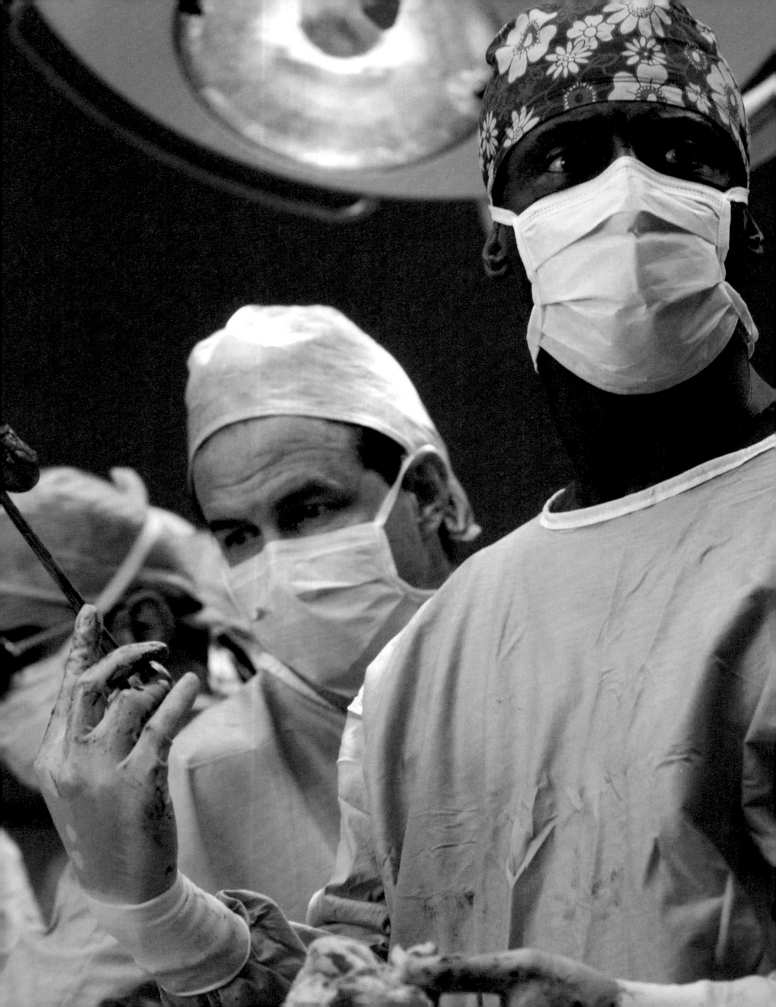

Chapter 18

Health and Medicine

"Health is not simply the absence of sickness"

—*Hannah Green*

You have been diagnosed with a chronic, degenerative, crippling form of arthritis. Three of the most respected specialists in the United States say there is nothing they can do except put you on a regimen of high-dosage anabolic steroids that will relieve some of the symptoms, but also produce some potentially dangerous side effects. Surgeons at the most highly rated and technologically sophisticated hospital in the world told you that there is no cure for your disease and that your condition will worsen.

But today, you have been given a slim ray of hope: it is called *spontaneous healing.* Not only will it relieve your symptoms, but it also may beat the disease entirely, returning you to a state of optimum health. To achieve it, you must change your lifestyle. You must dramatically alter your diet, and take a wide variety of natural herbs and tonics as well as an array of over-the-counter vitamin and mineral supplements. You must dispose of your microwave oven and remove the electronic clock radio from your bedroom. You are to drink only bottled water and substitute green tea for your coffee. Each week you must buy fresh flowers for your home, take a sauna or steambath, spend at least one entire day in which you do not read a newspaper or watch television, and be involved in volunteer work in the community. On a daily basis, you must take at least a 40-minute walk, stretch or do yoga, meditate, and think pleasant and healing thoughts (Weil, 1998, 2000, 2001, 2007).

Think you've just come out of the inner sanctum of a New Age guru who studies crystals, reads tea leaves, and consults Tarot cards? If so, think again, remembering sociology's admonition that *things are not necessarily what they seem.* You've just emerged from the office of Andrew Weil, M.D., a graduate of Harvard College and Harvard Medical School. He has worked for the National

515

Institute of Mental Health for 20 years, traveled throughout the world collecting information on medicine and healing, founded the Center for Integrative Medicine in Tucson, is director of the Integrative Medicine Program at the University of Arizona, is an author of several best-selling health books, and maintains his own website.

HEALTH AND SICKNESS: A GLOBAL VIEW

When you are having a bad day or feeling depressed, a friend may try to cheer you up by saying, "Be thankful, at least you have your health!" Good health is often viewed as the most valuable commodity a person can have. But what exactly is good health? What does it mean to be healthy? At first, the answer seems obvious: to be healthy simply means to be free from **disease,** or *a medically diagnosed illness.* But, again, *things are not necessarily what they seem.* Health is far more complex than being disease-free, because it has physical, psychological, and sociocultural dimensions. From a sociological viewpoint, **health** is *the absence of disease and infirmity and the ability to respond effectively to one's environment.* To be healthy, then, means to be physically, mentally, and socially capable of satisfactorily performing the routine activities of everyday life.

Definitions of health and illness vary cross-culturally.

How do you think this American medical team must adapt to successfully treat patients in this clinic in rural Honduras?

Health and Sickness in Poor Nations

Cultural definitions of health and sickness are linked to a country's level of wealth, technology, and ability to meet the needs of its population. In impoverished nations, where **infant mortality rates**—*the number of deaths in the first year of life for each 1,000 live births per year*—are high, life expectancies are low, and vaccines against controllable diseases are scarce, health and sickness take on different meanings than in nations where advanced medical technologies have made good health a normative expectation for most people. Also, as a consequence of differences in access to health care due to social stratification, the wealthy and the poor within a particular culture often hold different notions of health and sickness. Map 18.1 shows infant mortality rates around the globe.

In Mozambique, a developing country in southern Africa, for example, the gross domestic product (GDP) per capita is roughly equivalent to 870 International dollars per year and total health expenditures are approximately 5.0 percent of the country's total GDP. The infant mortality rate approaches 163 per 1,000 live births, approximately 4 percent of all mothers die during childbirth, and over one-third of deaths of children under age 5 are attributed to measles and other preventable diseases. Diarrhea, pneumonia, malaria, tetanus, and a number of parasite-related diseases also take a huge toll, and life expectancy is approximately 35–40 years. It is estimated that 30 percent of Mozambique's population is malnourished, and most of its citizens are infected with *Giardia,* hookworm, *Ascaris,* and other intestinal parasites (World Health Organization, 2006). These health problems are shared by a host of other countries, especially those with depressed economies (e.g., Pearce, 1994; World Health Organization, 2006). Map 18.2 (on page 518) provides a global view of outbreaks of infectious and parasitic diseases. By Western standards, every person living in Mozambique would be defined as "sick." Yet because these conditions are the norm in Mozambique, their definition of illness is quite different from that of the United States and most other contemporary industrial countries. In Mozambique and many other poor and developing countries, persons are not considered ill until their symptoms are so serious that they become bedridden or so weak that they can no longer function independently. In fact, there may be no social recognition of a person's illness at all: he or she is simply alive one day and dead the next.

DISEASE
A medically diagnosed illness.

HEALTH
The absence of disease and infirmity and the ability to respond effectively to one's environment.

INFANT MORTALITY RATE
The number of deaths in the first year of life for each 1,000 live births per year.

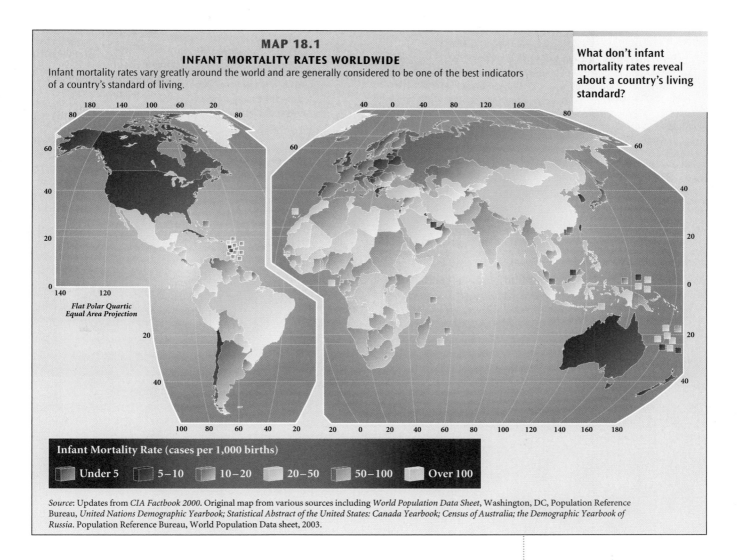

MAP 18.1

INFANT MORTALITY RATES WORLDWIDE

Infant mortality rates vary greatly around the world and are generally considered to be one of the best indicators of a country's standard of living.

Flat Polar Quartic Equal Area Projection

Infant Mortality Rate (cases per 1,000 births)

| Under 5 | 5–10 | 10–20 | 20–50 | 50–100 | Over 100 |

Source: Updates from *CIA Factbook 2000*. Original map from various sources including *World Population Data Sheet*, Washington, DC, Population Reference Bureau, *United Nations Demographic Yearbook; Statistical Abstract of the United States: Canada Yearbook; Census of Australia; the Demographic Yearbook of Russia*. Population Reference Bureau, World Population Data sheet, 2003.

What don't infant mortality rates reveal about a country's living standard?

Health and Sickness in Wealthy Nations

Contrast people's conceptions of health and sickness in Mozambique with those who live in wealthy nations such as the United States, the United Kingdom, Sweden, Norway, or Japan. When surveyed, over two-thirds of Americans indicate that they are in "excellent" or "good" health and almost half (48 percent) say they are healthier than their parents were (Research America, 2006). The GDP per capita measured in International dollars in these nations ranges from $27,959 per year (Great Britain) to $35,056 (United States). Although infant mortality is higher in the United States than in several other developed nations, at approximately 8 per 1,000 live births the rate is still relatively low. The United Kingdom's infant mortality rate is even lower, at 6.5; Norway's is 4.0; Japan's is 4.0; and Sweden's is among the lowest in the world, at 3.5. Less than 1 percent of mothers die in childbirth in each of these countries (approximately 8 per 100,000). Life expectancy for males in most developed nations is in the mid-seventies, and for women ranges from 79 to 82 years (World Health Organization, 2006). Measles, mumps, whooping cough, tuberculosis, and other diseases that ravage many developing nations are preventable, and anyone in these countries who suffers from them is considered sick and in need of medical treatment. And imagine the concern most American, British, Swedish, or Japanese parents would express if a physician informed them their children were infected with hookworms, roundworms, or other intestinal parasites. Finally, consider that whereas 30 percent of Mozambique's population suffers from malnutrition, approximately 70 percent of Americans are overweight (1 in 50 Americans is at least 100 pounds overweight), and problems related to obesity are among the major health concerns in the United States today (Associated Press, Chicago, 2003; Jacobson, 2003).

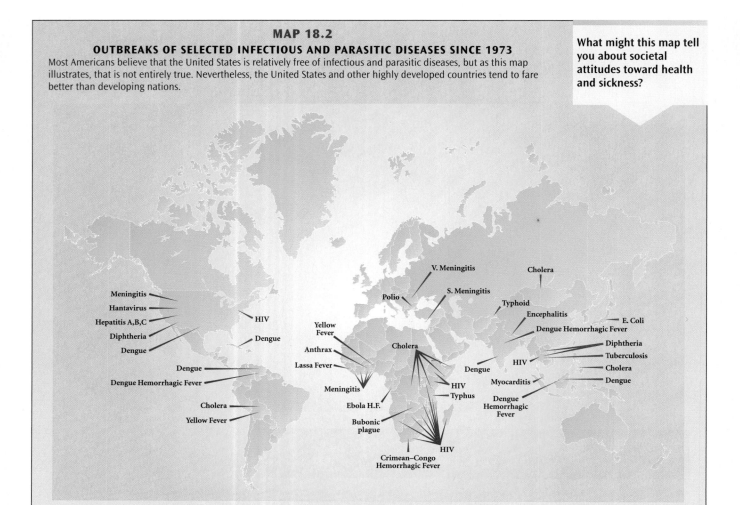

MAP 18.2
OUTBREAKS OF SELECTED INFECTIOUS AND PARASITIC DISEASES SINCE 1973

Most Americans believe that the United States is relatively free of infectious and parasitic diseases, but as this map illustrates, that is not entirely true. Nevertheless, the United States and other highly developed countries tend to fare better than developing nations.

What might this map tell you about societal attitudes toward health and sickness?

Source: From *Population Bulletin* 52(2) 1997:21. Reprinted by permission of the Population Reference Bureau; TB/HIV Research Project Thailand, October 6, 2000.

Map 18.3 shows the tremedous increase in obesity in the United States over the past several years.

HEALTH AND SICKNESS IN THE UNITED STATES

Expectations about what is "normal" and desirable as opposed to "abnormal" and undesirable play an important role in defining health, and just as these expectations vary greatly from one culture to another, they also change over time within a particular culture. Changing values and norms related to health and sickness in the United States are reflected in attitudes toward cigarette smoking. In the seventeenth century, European settlers in America were introduced to tobacco smoking by Native Americans, who used it primarily for ceremonial purposes. Over the next two centuries, recreational use of tobacco increased in both Europe and the United States, and it became popular among the upper classes: some people even believed it possessed medicinal value (Payne et al., 1991).

By the early 1900s, cigarette smoking had become widespread among males, and throughout much of the twentieth century smoking was viewed almost as a rite of passage for boys into manhood. Interestingly, one of the factors that contributed to an increase in the popularity of smoking over chewing tobacco was a health issue. People pursued other methods of ingesting tobacco because of rising rates of tuberculosis and the link between contamination from spitting and the disease (Payne et al., 1991). Although some evidence of health risks emerged in the 1930s, smoking was not associated with illness or disease by either the public or the medical community. By the mid-

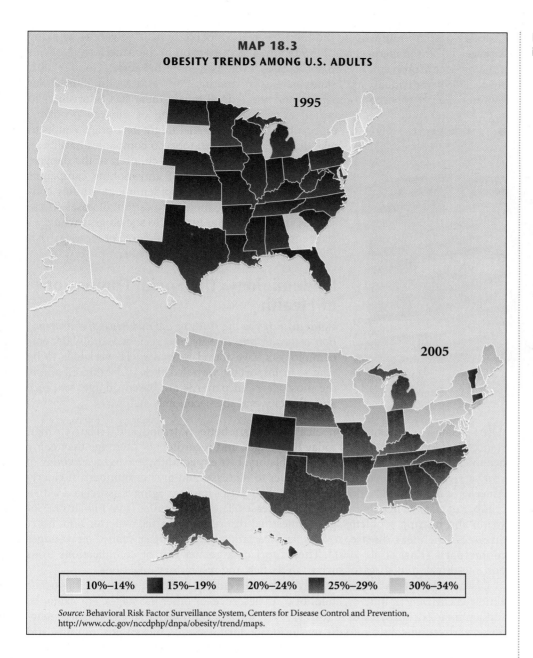

MAP 18.3
OBESITY TRENDS AMONG U.S. ADULTS

1995

2005

	10%–14%		15%–19%		20%–24%		25%–29%		30%–34%

Source: Behavioral Risk Factor Surveillance System, Centers for Disease Control and Prevention,
http://www.cdc.gov/nccdphp/dnpa/obesity/trend/maps.

1960s, however, research linked cigarette smoking to several major health problems, including bronchitis, emphysema, heart disease, and cancer of the mouth, throat, and lungs. The U.S. Surgeon General issued a report in 1964 that concluded that cigarette smoking was injurious to health and contributed to increased health problems and mortality rates among men. Moreover, the public became increasingly aware of the addictive nature of nicotine when U.S. Surgeon General C. Everett Koop declared that nicotine is as addictive as heroin. This drug acts as a stimulant in mild doses and a depressant in larger quantities, and it is toxic and even lethal in large doses (Payne et al., 1991; Avis, 1993).

In 1971, cigarette advertisements were banned from television and radio, and the public perception of cigarette smoking changed. As more studies linked smoking to a variety of preventable diseases, its popularity waned, and increased health concerns led the American public to view smoking in moral terms as well as in terms of health. When the surgeon general's 1986 report confirmed that nonsmokers also suffer increased health risks due to passive second-hand smoking, smoking became viewed as not only self-destructive but harmful to others. As a consequence, many states and municipalities passed laws against smoking in public places, and many corporations moved toward establishing smoke-free workplaces.

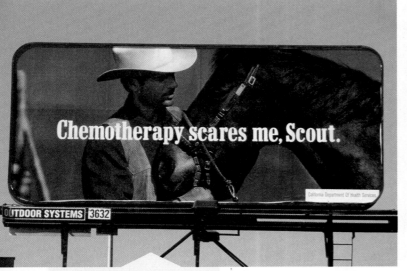

Chemotherapy scares me, Scout.

Today, despite arguments to the contrary by the tobacco industry, cigarette smoking is perceived by the medical community and a large portion of the American public as a major health problem, and in some cases, even as deviant behavior (Goode, 2001; Thio, 2006). Individuals and states have won multimillion- and multibillion-dollar lawsuits against tobacco companies, and the federal government has intervened to curtail even further advertising of tobacco products, especially ad campaigns that might encourage youths to take up smoking. In fact, tobacco companies have been required to warn teenagers and children of the dangers of smoking and a number of antismoking campaigns have been launched. Social epidemiology studies continue to link cigarette smoking to certain diseases. These studies are of particular interest to sociologists who specialize in **medical sociology**, *a subarea of sociology that links social structure and social life to health.*

Epidemiology: The Social Dimensions of Health

Epidemiology is *the study of the incidence and distribution of health and disease in a society.* Worldwide, epidemiologists have found several social variables to be related in important ways to levels of health. Of these, the most clear-cut patterns are based on age, sex, race and ethnicity, and socioeconomic status.

Age   Because of advances in medical technology, better nutrition, and a relatively high standard of living, Americans today live longer, and regardless of their age they enjoy healthier lives than at any other time in history. **Life expectancy,** *the average number of years a person is expected to live,* continues to increase, and greater numbers of elderly Americans enjoy good health throughout their lives. However, aging is associated with a number of chronic health problems and diseases. The elderly suffer from higher rates of vision and hearing problems, gastrointestinal disorders, arthritis, hypertension, heart disease, Alzheimer's disease, strokes, and certain types of cancer than their younger counterparts (Kart et al., 2001). They also face a greater risk of complications from non-life-threatening diseases such as colds, flus, and respiratory infections.

Diseases do not discriminate solely against the elderly, however; some illnesses occur almost exclusively in infancy, childhood, adolescence, or other life stages. For example, sudden infant death syndrome (SIDS) is a respiratory problem that causes some newborns and young children to die mysteriously during sleep. Chicken pox, mumps, and measles can be contracted at any age but are generally considered childhood diseases. Sexually transmitted diseases (STDs) can attack anyone who is sexually active, but they are most common among teenagers and young adults.

Sex and Gender   Many medical problems and diseases differ in their distribution among the population according to sex. Some of the more obvious are illnesses, diseases, and medical complications related to menstruation, pregnancy, and childbirth. Likewise, ovarian, fallopian, cervical, and uterine cancer claim only female victims, and although men can contract breast cancer, over 99 percent of its victims are women. Conversely, impotence and testicular and prostate cancer are exclusively male problems. Perhaps the most important health difference between males and females is the difference in their life expectancy, with women outliving men an average of 7 to 10 years in the United States. In general, women's illnesses are more likely to be linked to **morbidity** (*chronic debilitation*), while men's diseases are linked to **mortality** (*death*). And research indicates that women are more likely than men to go to the doctor with their ailments, thus potentially catching serious diseases before they become fatal (Clements and Hales, 1997).

Race and Ethnicity   While sex is the strongest predictor of life expectancy in the United States, race is also an important factor. On average, whites can expect to live

MEDICAL SOCIOLOGY
A subarea of sociology that links social structure and social life to health.

EPIDEMIOLOGY
The study of the incidence and distribution of health and disease in a society.

LIFE EXPECTANCY
The average number of years a person is expected to live.

MORBIDITY
Chronic debilitation.

MORTALITY
Death.

approximately 5 years longer than nonwhites. Infant mortality rates are higher for Native Americans, African Americans, and Mexican Americans than for whites and are higher for these groups in the United States than in some developing nations. And the rates of illness and death from preventable diseases in the United States are much greater for minorities than for whites.

Social epidemiologists have found that Native Americans suffer the poorest health in the United States, with higher rates of infant mortality, influenza, typhoid fever, diphtheria, pneumonia, alcoholism, malnutrition, and secondary infections than any other racial or ethnic category. African Americans experience higher infant mortality rates than whites and are more likely to contract pneumonia, influenza, diabetes, and tuberculosis and to suffer from sickle cell anemia. Mexican Americans report higher incidences of influenza, pneumonia, and tuberculosis than whites, and in some Hispanic neighborhoods as many as one in five suffer from diabetes (Nash, 1990). Mexican American infant mortality rates are higher than the national average, and Mexican American children are less likely to be vaccinated against preventable diseases such as mumps, measles, whooping cough, diphtheria, and typhoid fever, especially in towns in southern Texas, New Mexico, Arizona, and California along the U.S.–Mexican border.

Although a few health problems are attributed to genetic causes (e.g., higher rates of sickle cell anemia among blacks), most of the racial and ethnic differences in health and sickness depend on social variables, including poverty, social inequality, lifestyle, and the fact that racial and ethnic minorities often are not provided the same level of health care as whites (Stohlberg, 2002; Quaye, 2005).

Socioeconomic Status Several centuries of data document differential life expectancies and levels of health based on social class. As one might expect, those at the top of the social hierarchy fare better than those toward the middle, who enjoy longer lives and better health than those at the bottom. Just as the impact of poverty on health can be seen when we compare poor countries with wealthier nations, within the United States health and access to health care are unequally distributed on the basis of socioeconomic status.

Money, or the lack of it, explains much of the disparity in the physical health of the rich and the poor. The costs of medical care are soaring, and more than 43.5 million Americans (more than 15 percent of the population) have no medical or health insurance coverage; among those who are insured, almost half indicate that they self-medicate because it is too expensive to go to the doctor and they fear they would not have enough money or insurance to pay for a major surgery or catastrophic illness (Wekesser, 1994; Clements and Hales, 1997; Pugh, 1999; CNN, 2003). Although the poor are not the only ones who lack medical insurance, they are least likely to be able to afford adequate health care without it. Poor women have the highest rates of pregnancy and childbirth in the United States, but they are the least able to afford birth control, prenatal care, routine immunizations, regular medical checkups, prescription medicines, and even over-the-counter medications. Infant mortality rates are far higher among the poor than among the wealthy in the United States. The overall U.S. infant mortality rate is higher than that of Singapore or Costa Rica, where the medical expenditure per person per year is approximately one-tenth the amount spent in the United States (World Health Organization, 2006).

The middle class and the wealthy are not immune to illness. Some high-status professions, such as medicine and dentistry, are linked to high stress and increased rates of alcoholism, drug abuse, mental disorders, and suicide, and middle-level managers and corporate executives seem prone to hypertension, ulcers, and heart attacks. Regardless of one's place in the social hierarchy, socioeconomic status is linked to health. Perhaps part of the reason is the impact that social class exerts on people's attitudes toward health and illness.

Social Attitudes toward Health and Illness

Ask yourself, "What are my expectations regarding health?" Unless you suffer a chronic debilitating disease, you probably are like millions of other Americans who take good health for granted. We expect to go about our daily lives without suffering pangs of hunger and free of pain and other physical discomforts. This does not necessarily mean that most Americans view themselves as healthy or free of the need of medical care, however. Americans spend billions of dollars annually for professional health care, as well as billions more for vitamins, laxatives, and over-the-counter medications and pain remedies. The total national expenditure on health is 14.6 percent of the GDP (World Health Organization, 2006).

Health and Fitness Americans today seem obsessed with health and fitness. This has been accompanied by behavior that has had positive effects on the overall health of American citizens. For example, although two-thirds of Americans are overweight, health consciousness has had a noticeable impact on the American diet. Studies linking high levels of dietary fat and cholesterol to increased rates of hypertension, heart disease, and strokes have made most Americans painfully aware of the need to eat more nutritious foods.

In the United States, doctors and nutritionists have for years been urging Americans to change their eating habits. In fact, the healthful eating movement has gained so much momentum that today even most fast-food chains offer low-fat, low-cholesterol, and even low-carb entrees and desserts in addition to their traditional fare of hamburgers, french fries, and milk shakes.

Change in diet is not the only weapon in Americans' battle to maintain health and fitness. Interest in health and physical fitness has never been higher in the United States. Millions of Americans jog, take aerobics classes, lift weights, work out, and participate in wellness programs in an effort to enjoy better health and live longer while warding off disease. Physical exercise has long been linked to better health, but in the 1980s it enjoyed unprecedented popularity. Health clubs, spas, racquet clubs, and fitness centers sprang up almost overnight in communities across the country, and more people than ever before began participating in routine exercise, including walking, jogging, bicycling, swimming, weight training, and aerobics. Today, thousands of celebrity home workout videos are on the market, and exercise programs can be found on cable and network stations almost any time of day or night. Despite the emphasis on fitness and the plethora of health and medical information available today, millions of Americans continue to live very unhealthy lifestyles that include overeating, smoking, drinking, and other pleasurable but unhealthy practices. Some medical sociologists attribute part of this resistance to healthy living to America's emphasis on individual rights, freedom of choice, "information overload," which desensitizes people by confusing them, and daily bombardments by mass media and advertising that promote unhealthy habits.

The Wellness Movement Many people believe that one of the more positive outcomes of the health and fitness movement has been the **wellness movement,** which *emphasizes preventive health care by combining knowledge about health and nutrition with sensible eating and exercise programs.* Many employers realize that well employees are more productive and miss fewer days of work, so they have initiated wellness programs in the workplace to discourage smoking and encourage good health and physical exercise. Several insurance companies have joined the movement by offering reduced rates to companies or employees who participate in wellness programs.

From a sociological viewpoint, one of the most interesting developments has been how attitudes have shifted from viewing sickness, obesity, and other health problems as a result of bad genes or bad luck toward seeing them as consequences of poor health practices and unhealthy lifestyles. In other words, those stricken by disease or otherwise in poor health have gone from being viewed as victims to being seen as contributors to their own illness. This is especially the case for diseases related to smoking, drinking, sexual behavior, overeating, or other "controllable" behaviors.

Consequently, a certain amount of stigma may be attached to being sick. While some stigma may be associated with almost any illness, people with AIDS provide an example of the relationship between stigma and disease in American society.

Disease and Stigma: AIDS

Stigma is the phenomenon whereby people are discredited or denied full social participation and acceptance because of some socially devalued attribute (Goffman, 1963). Leprosy in ancient times and cancer in more recent years are diseases that have brought

WELLNESS MOVEMENT
Emphasizes preventive health care by combining knowledge about health and nutrition with sensible eating and exercise programs.

stigma to their victims, mainly because of misconceptions and fear about the diseases. In the early 1980s, a new terminal disease—AIDS—appeared on the American scene. It has been accompanied by as much fear, misunderstanding, anxiety, and stigma as any previous disease. Initially, AIDS was so highly stigmatizing that studies show that, in addition to the general public, even some physicians shunned people who are HIV-positive, and those who had the disease were required to work at managing the stigma on their social identities (Rubin, 1992; Tewksbury, 1994, 2004). One reporter noted: "AIDS brought out the worst in us at first, but ultimately it brought out the best, and transformed the nation" (Jefferson, 2006).

AIDS (acquired immune deficiency syndrome) is *a spectrum of disorders and symptoms that result from a progressive breakdown of the body's immune defense system.* The virus that causes AIDS, first identified in 1981, is the human immunodeficiency virus (HIV), and it can be carried in the body for years before a person becomes sick with AIDS. Although the virus and AIDS are not technically direct causes of death, they break down the body's immune system to the point that the infected person is unable to fight off other infections, which become fatal. Those who test positive for HIV, if their positive status becomes known, are often stigmatized even before becoming sick.

In 1981, only 199 AIDS cases were reported in the United States; by 1990, it was estimated that over 120,000 Americans were living with AIDS, and over 70,000 cases had resulted in death. In 1995, the Centers for Disease Control and Prevention (CDC) reported that approximately 500,000 Americans were afflicted with AIDS. By 1997 that number had risen to over 612,000, with almost 380,000 total deaths. After 1997, AIDS deaths per year began to decline in the United States, and each year more money has been poured into research for a cure for the deadly disease. Nevertheless, the AIDS epidemic is far from over. HIV infections and deaths from AIDS-related diseases continue to take their toll in the United States (see Figure 18.1). In 2001, 890,000 adults and another 10,000 children were living with AIDS and 15,000 deaths were attributed to AIDS-related causes (World Health Organization, 2003). In 2002, there was a 2.2 percent increase in AIDS cases in the United States (Stein, 2003). Advances in drugs and treatment programs have provided increased hope for those infected with HIV. At the same time, some medical experts worry that the advent of these drugs and their appealing television advertisements, implying that it is possible to live longer and healthier lives while infected, may have led to complacency on the part of racial and ethnic minorities and those who participate in behaviors that put them most at-risk for contracting AIDS and could lead to even higher infection rates in the future (Begley, 2001; Jacobson, 2001; Ornstein, 2001).

AIDS
Acquired immune deficiency syndrome, a spectrum of disorders and symptoms that result from a progressive breakdown of the body's immune defense system.

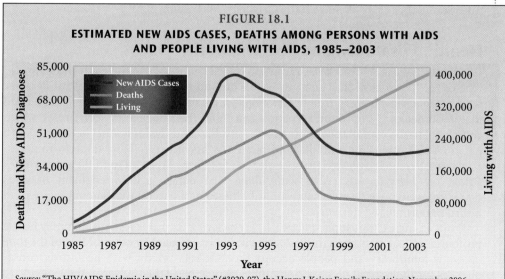

FIGURE 18.1

ESTIMATED NEW AIDS CASES, DEATHS AMONG PERSONS WITH AIDS AND PEOPLE LIVING WITH AIDS, 1985–2003

Source: "The HIV/AIDS Epidemic in the United States" (#3029-07), the Henry J. Kaiser Family Foundation, November 2006. This information was reprinted with permission from the Henry J. Kaiser Family Foundations. The Kaiser Family foundation, based in Menlo Park, California, is a nonprofit, private operating foundation focusing on the major health care issues facing the nation and is not associated with Kaiser Permanente or Kaiser Industries.

Map 18.4 shows the worldwide geographic distribution of reported AIDS cases. The World Health Organization (WHO) estimates that 47 million people worldwide have been infected with HIV/AIDS (900,000 in the United States) and that over 25 million deaths can be attributed to the disease. In 2005, there were 5 million new cases of AIDS and 3 million deaths worldwide (WHO, 2006). Approximately 95 percent of new HIV infections occur in developing nations. The African continent leads in the number of infections and AIDS-related deaths, but Asia is predicted to become the epicenter of the disease. Predictions vary, but even the most conservative estimates predict that AIDS will become the most serious health epidemic in modern times, perhaps rivaling the plagues that wiped out almost one-fourth of Europe's population in the fourteenth century (Cowley and Hager, 1994; CDC, 1997; Begley, 2001; World Health Organization, 2006).

AIDS is highly infectious, but it is transmitted only through the exchange of body fluids, especially blood and semen (Meyer-Bahlburg et al., 1991). Americans are understandably fearful of the AIDS epidemic, but their fears are exacerbated by misinformation related to its cause and transmission, as well as by popular misconceptions and negative stereotypes about those who have the disease. It is not surprising that many of those who are HIV-positive practice what sociologists call **passing,** *an attempt to hide their stigmatizing attribute* from others in an attempt to avoid the negative labels and reactions associated with the disease. This may become impossible, however, when the disease progresses to a stage that forces them to disclose their illness (Tewksbury, 1994).

One study on American attitudes toward persons with AIDS found that over half the population and most of the public health community and gay community favor distribution of sex education information, condoms, and sterile needles. Approximately 20 percent of Americans urge compassion but are opposed to these measures, and about 6 percent believe that punitive actions, including quarantine, should be implemented against those with AIDS (Herek and Glunt, 1991). As one group of social scientists noted, attitudes toward AIDS and those who suffer from it reflect "the interaction between culture and the total disease process—affecting body, spirit, self, and social relations" (Herdt et al., 1991:167). One of the biggest fears of medical experts is that a new attitude of complacency may lead to increases in HIV infection in the future (Begley, 2001; Ornstein, 2001; Stein, 2003).

AIDS-related deaths have increased so dramatically in Zambia that this coffin dealer sells his wares alongside the road.

How do you think Americans would react to such a roadside business?

Health, Disability, and Social Identity

What does it mean to be sick or disabled in a society obsessed with health and wellness? One of the first sociological analyses of this question was provided by Talcott Parsons, who approached the topic from a functionalist perspective. Parsons (1951) contended that good health is important so people can fulfill their obligatory social roles, which contribute to the overall functioning of society. Illness is dysfunctional because when a person is sick others must fill the void created by his or her inability to perform necessary roles. Parsons suggested that people who fall ill are expected to fulfill a **sick role,** *a pattern of behavior associated with illness* that entails acknowledgment of one's deviance, exemption from social responsibilities, a desire to get well, and taking steps to return to normality.

From an interactionist perspective, being sick or disabled is a status that may have a profound impact on how an individual is viewed and treated by others. Most of the time illness is temporary and people occupy the sick role briefly, with no lasting consequences for their social identity. Sometimes people place themselves in the sick role to take advantage of its accompanying normative expectations. For example, it is common for college students to fall ill before major examinations; this often means they will take the test at a later date. Such "illnesses" are usually tolerated once or twice and do not

PASSING
An attempt to hide a stigmatizing attribute.

SICK ROLE
A pattern of behavior associated with illness.

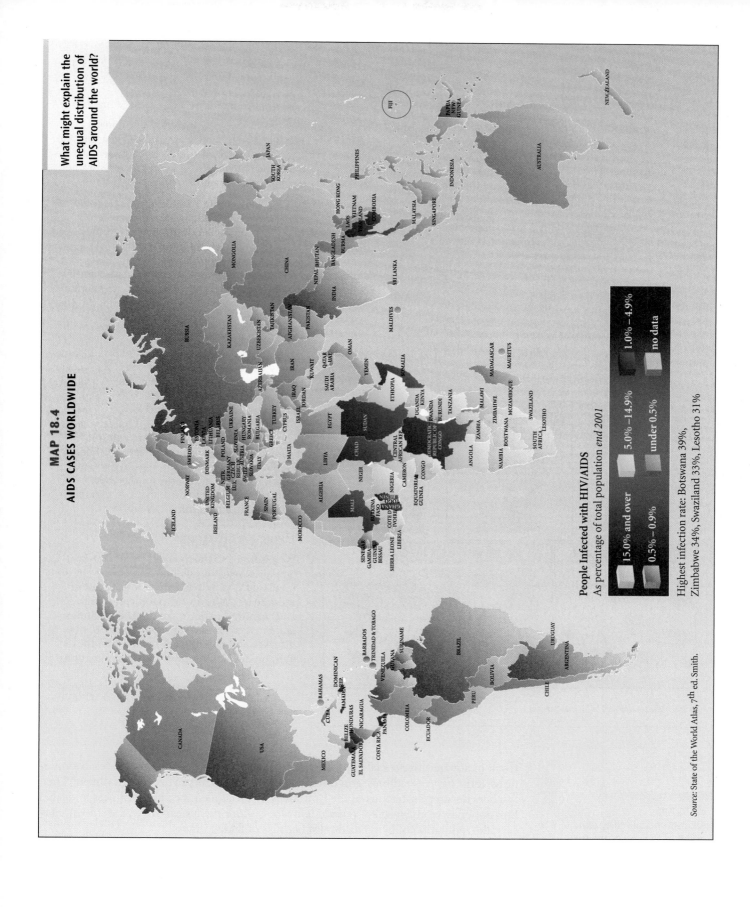

MAP 18.4

AIDS CASES WORLDWIDE

What might explain the unequal distribution of AIDS around the world?

People Infected with HIV/AIDS
As percentage of total population *end 2001*

15.0% and over	5.0% – 14.9%
0.5% – 0.9%	under 0.5%
1.0% – 4.9%	no data

Highest infection rate: Botswana 39%,
Zimbabwe 34%, Swaziland 33%, Lesotho 31%

Source: State of the World Atlas, 7th ed. Smith.

Every generation experiences the fear of an epidemic of some dreaded disease for which there is no known cure—and in some cases, no known cause. Over the centuries, the bubonic plague, smallpox, malaria, tuberculosis, polio, cancer, AIDS, and even measles, mumps, whooping cough, and other diseases have spread widely through countries, wiping out large numbers of people and, in some cases, almost entire populations. These epidemics are generally met, at least initially, with widespread fear and misunderstanding, and then, after years of research and increasing medical technology, are often brought under control and sometimes virtually eliminated.

On two different occasions, one of the authors, when preparing to go to England to teach in the university's British Studies Program, was warned that he should not go because in one case, England was besieged with a "flesh-eating virus" (there had been one or two confirmed cases),

and in the other, that he would most certainly contract "Mad Cow Disease." The second fear extends even into the medical community, as to this day, he is not allowed to donate blood because he has spent 5 weeks each summer over an 11-year period in Great Britain.

More recent scares in the United States have included Lyme disease, E-coli bacteria, hantavirus, anthrax, monkeypox, SARS, West Nile virus, and Avian (Bird) flu. Fear of these diseases has caused panic, altered people's travel plans, shut down businesses and airports, and in some cases almost paralyzed entire communities, cities, states, and countries (Beil, 2003). In order to squelch fears and rumors that you could get SARS from eating Chinese food, the Los Angeles mayor and several city council members dined in Chinatown with media coverage (Kalb, 2003).

While the media can help shatter myths and alleviate some of the fears of new diseases and epidemics, popular television shows like *ER,* and movies like *Outbreak,* not to mention nightly news coverage of potentially deadly biological terrorism after September 11, 2001, and the Iraqi war, have contributed to social panic and cultural change regarding health concerns. While the medical community scrambles to find antidotes, vaccines, and cures for diseases, new diseases continue to arise that can create social panic and cultural change.

© Stuart Carlson/Milwaukee Journal-Sentinel.

TAKING A CLOSER LOOK

Why is there so much widespread fear of new diseases and possible epidemics? Do the media tend to help alleviate or exaggerate these fears? Why do the people in wealthy and "healthy" nations like the United States and most of Europe react differently to new diseases and possible epidemics than those in poor, developing, and "unhealthy" nations?

Source: Laura Beil. "Welcome to a World of Emerging Diseases Like Monkeypox, SARS," *Dallas Morning News,* June 12, 2003:20A. Claudia Kalb. "The Mystery of SARS," *Newsweek,* May 5, 2003:26–32.

MEDICINE
An institutionalized system designed to prevent and treat disease and illness.

HEALTH–CARE SYSTEM
The social institution charged with the maintenance of a society's health and standard of well-being.

result in any negative social consequences. What if a student routinely misses examinations, term paper deadlines, and other academic requirements because of illness? Then teachers become suspicious of the legitimacy of the student's claims of illness and label him or her as an unconscientious student who is shirking duties. Worse, the student may earn the reputation of being dishonest because of faking illness.

Illness may develop into a master status that subsumes all other statuses and becomes the dominant feature of a person's social identity (Becker, 1963). From our earlier discussion of disease and stigma, we can see how a disease such as AIDS may dominate a person's life. Testing positive for HIV alters a person's self-concept, and almost everyone who is made aware of the disease treats the person differently. Disabilities can be permanent and people who are morbidly obese, wheelchair-bound or otherwise disabled often face social stigma and spoiled identities (Goffman, 1963; Goode, 2004; Barnartt et al., 2004).

From an interactionist perspective, health and sickness are subjective concepts reliant on interpretations and judgments made by members of the medical community as well as by patients themselves. Once a set of symptoms is labeled a disease, there is an immediate jump in the number of people who suffer from that illness. It is common for those who suffer from chronic and terminal diseases to experience a sudden downturn in health on being informed of the diagnosis. New diseases also can affect a society or the entire world, as Focus box 18.1 illustrates.

Early in this chapter we illustrated how perceptions of health are linked to cultural definitions. In addition, within any culture individuals interpret health and illness in relative terms. What some people identify as routine aches and pains may send others to their doctor for relief. Doctors long have recognized the psychosomatic nature of some health problems; this illustrates the importance of a definition of the situation, in which illnesses become real when people define them as real. Medical experts are often puzzled by some patients' ability to go on living when all medical data indicate that death is imminent and should already have taken place; other patients, convinced they are ill or about to die, either remain sick or perish, despite the lack of any apparent medical cause.

Although the nature of health and sickness is subjective, some important objective conditions affect both a person's likelihood of suffering certain diseases and the overall quality of health in a society. We have already discussed many of them; now we turn to one of the most important factors—the availability and quality of medicine and health care.

The SARS outbreak in 2003 caused widespread panic throughout much of Asia and around the world as people donned surgical masks in an effort to avoid the deadly virus.

MEDICINE AND HEALTH CARE: A CROSS-CULTURAL VIEW

It is very difficult to compare and contrast medicine and health care cross-culturally, as both are rooted in the history, economics, politics, and culture of the particular nation in which they occur. Yet, in a world of more than 200 countries, some points of convergence can be discerned as nations throughout the world are struggling to promote better health, reduce health-care inequalities, reduce medical costs, increase efficiency and effectiveness, promote health, and provide better health-care delivery. These efforts focus on improving medicine and health care. **Medicine** is *an institutionalized system designed to prevent and treat disease and illness.* In most countries, medicine is part of a larger **health-care system,** *the social institution charged with the maintenance of a society's health and standard of well-being.* Medicine and health-care systems vary around the world, from reliance on folk beliefs and practices (e.g., voodoo, witchcraft, and faith healing by local shamans) to complex, multibillion-dollar networks with millions of health-care professionals (paramedics, nurses, doctors, surgeons, dentists, psychiatrists, etc.) as well as insurance companies, clinics, and a host of hospitals and agencies linked to public and private health maintenance. A brief description of medicine and health care in Japan, Sweden, Norway, and Great Britain provides an informative cross-cultural comparison of health-care systems.

CHARLIE

PLACEBO CRANK

"Thank you, Nurse, right there feels much better."

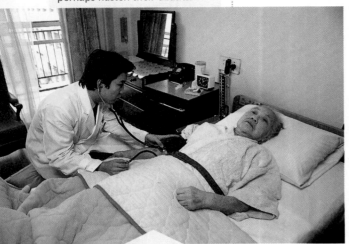

How would most American patients react if they discovered that their doctors had not informed them that they had a terminal disease?

Japan: Scientific Medicine and *Kanpo*

Since World War II, perhaps no country in the world has undergone more dramatic social change than Japan. At the turn of the twentieth century, the country's infant mortality rate hovered around 150–160 per 1,000 live births, and during the 1930s and early 1940s it varied between 90 and 100. In the 1980s, the infant mortality rate dropped to 6–7 per 1,000 live births—lower than in the United States and many Western European nations. As noted earlier, today it hovers around 4.0, among the lowest in the world. Life expectancy has also dramatically increased in Japan since World War II, with one out of every two babies born in 1990 expected to live beyond age 80. According to the World Health Organization, the people in Japan enjoy the longest healthy life expectancy of any country in the world. Life expectancy is 78 years for males and 85 years for females. In keeping with increased technological development, Japan's leading causes of death are now cardiovascular disease, cancer, and stroke (World Health Organization, 2006).

The Japanese government and general population place health care at or near the top of their list of priorities, and by all standard measures overall health and the quality of private and public health care in Japan are excellent. In Japan's health-care system, advanced medical, dental, surgical, and pharmaceutical care are available to most of the population. In addition, *kanpo*—a traditional form of Japanese medicine introduced in the sixth century, which relies on herbs, acupuncture, meditation, and other non-Western medical practices—is still widely respected and routinely used. Over 90 percent of the total expenditure for health care in Japan (which accounts for approximately 7.9 percent of the nation's GDP) comes from public funds, and every village, town, and city is required by law to provide health insurance for its citizens; this requirement reflects the tremendous commitment of the Japanese government to providing adequate medical and health care for its citizens (Steslicke, 1988; World Health Organization, 2006).

The doctor–patient relationship in Japan is very different from that in the United States. Japanese physicians believe mental attitude is important in the healing process, so they rarely share bad news with their patients. Rather, they often conspire with family members to keep the seriousness of illness secret from patients (Darnton and Hoshia, 1989).

Sweden and Norway: Prenatal to Postmortem Health Care

Sweden and Norway operate sophisticated health-care systems of socialized medicine that provide cradle-to-grave—or, more accurately, prenatal to postmortem—coverage for their citizens. **Socialized medicine** is *a system in which public funds are used to provide a state-owned and state-operated health-care system available to all citizens.*

Sweden Like other aspects of the Swedish economy, the health-care system combines both public and private elements. All Swedish citizens are covered by national health insurance, and they have the option of securing medical services from either public clinics and hospitals or private practitioners and health-care facilities. Children receive free dental care until age 16, and the national dental insurance program pays for half of all dental work thereafter. Prescription drugs and other medications are usually free. Approximately 9.2 percent of Sweden's GDP goes for health-care expenditures, and it is estimated that over 97 percent of all medical costs are paid for by the government. Consequently, the Swedes pay a substantial amount in taxes to support the health-care system (Zimbalist et al., 1989; World Health Organization, 2006).

Sweden's commitment to medicine and health care is reflected in many of its health-care statistics. The small nation has almost 2,000 physicians, and government-funded state-of-the-art medical care is readily available throughout the country. Sweden's infant mortality rate is relatively low, around 4 per 1,000 live births, and the average life expectancy is approximately 78 years for men and 83 years for women. Sweden's health-care system is viewed by some as the model toward which the rest of the world should strive. It is not without problems, however, and the Swedish government is experimenting with new health-care organizational structures and delivery systems to improve quality and efficiency (Saltman, 1988; Hoffman, 1991; World Health Organization, 2006).

Norway   Norway's state-funded health-care system is similar to Sweden's but more extensive in coverage. Approximately 9.6 percent of Norway's GDP is expended on health care. The infant mortality is 4.0 per 1,000 live births. Life expectancy is approximately 77 years for men and 82 years for women. Although Norwegians pay high taxes, most believe it is money well spent, especially in regard to health-care coverage, which begins when the state pays for the pregnancy test at conception and ends when the state has paid all the funeral expenses. After a child is born, both parents can take six months off work at full salary or an entire year off at 80 percent of their salaries—all paid for by the state. Not only are all routine medical expenses covered, but if a child is ill the state pays the full salary of one parent, or half the salary of both parents, to stay home and care for the child. If adults are ill, the government pays all their medical costs plus their salary while they recuperate. And if the doctor decides a change of climate would be beneficial the government will not only continue to pay salary and medical expenses but also underwrite a trip to a Norwegian-owned spa in Turkey on the Mediterranean. In short, Norway's health-care system may be the most comprehensive program of socialized medicine anywhere in the world (CBS News, 1997; World Health Organization, 2006).

Great Britain: Socialized Medicine in a Capitalist Society

Great Britain also has a system of socialized medicine. Unlike Norway, however, where all citizens are guaranteed access to the very best health care available, the British health-care system blends elements of private capitalism with their version of socialized medicine. Thus, in keeping with Britain's capitalistic approach to business and enterprise, while the government provides at least a minimum level of health care for all citizens, those who can afford it have access to private physicians and hospitals and may seek out elective surgeries and state-of-the-art medical treatments not provided for by the government.

Approximately 7.7 percent of Britain's GDP is spent on health care, about 85 percent of which is government expenditure. Infant mortality rates are around 6.0 per 1,000 live births. Life expectancy is approximately 76 years for men and 81 years for women. As in most industrial and postindustrial nations, children are routinely vaccinated against preventable diseases, and the most common causes of death are cardiovascular diseases and cancer (World Health Organization, 2006). In this regard, Great Britain is not unlike the United States.

MEDICINE AND HEALTH CARE IN THE UNITED STATES

Despite many flaws in the American medical and health-care system, people in the United States are among the healthiest in the world. Life expectancy is 75 years for men and 80 for women, and the infant mortality rate, although much higher than in some countries, is about 8 per 1,000 live births. Deaths from smallpox, whooping cough, and other communicable diseases for which vaccinations are available have been all but eliminated in the United States, although occasional outbreaks of measles occur in areas where children have not been vaccinated. Also, in the early 1990s, the United States experienced an alarming increase in the number of cases of tuberculosis (Hoffman, 1991; Cowley et al., 1992; World Health Organization, 2006).

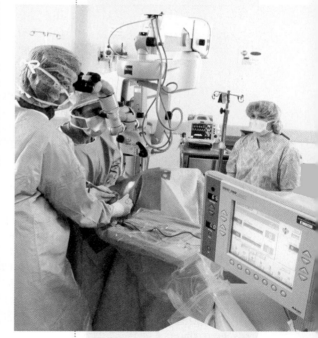

Today's hospitals are filled with sophisticated high-technology equipment and teams of highly trained and highly paid medical specialists.

What are some of the positive impacts of technology on medical care? Have there been any negative effects?

Health care accounts for 14.6 percent of the U.S. GDP, and this figure is projected to rise soon to close to 20 percent; however, the government's share of the expenditure is less than half (Thomas, 1993; Wekesser, 1994; World Health Organization, 2006). Although the government operates Medicare and Medicaid programs for the elderly and indigent, there is no system of national health insurance, and America's health-care costs of $5,274 per person per year, most of which are borne by the individuals who receive it, are the highest in the world (World Health Organization, 2006). One sociologist says that the government's regulating of health care while endorsing private enterprise is the "paradox of liberal intervention" (Ruggie, 1992). Health care is provided mostly by private individuals and corporations for profit; one of the major criticisms of medicine and health care in the United States is their unequal distribution.

To understand America's health-care system, we need to look at its origins, from early folk remedies to the development of modern medicine.

The Development of Modern Medicine

In Colonial America, as in the rest of Western society, the art of healing was practiced by a handful of European-trained doctors along with midwives, druggists, herbalists, ministers, faith healers, and sometimes barbers. Infection was common, and "the fever" was a frequent cause of death. Superstition, folk remedies, and the notion of being possessed by demons played a prominent role in early health care in the United States. Even trained doctors used unsterilized and unsanitary instruments, and bleeding patients or using leeches—to rid them of the "bad blood" thought to be the cause of many diseases—was a common treatment. Sometimes the treatment was worse than the disease, and numerous deaths were either caused or hastened by unsafe medical practices.

By the early 1800s, a better understanding of anatomy, physiology, biology, and chemistry revolutionized the field of medicine, and more of its practitioners embraced a scientific approach to illness and disease. Perhaps the most important contribution to the development of modern medicine was Louis Pasteur's germ theory, which postulated that most diseases are linked to the presence of bacteria. Germ theory shifted physicians' focus away from caring for the sick and toward the scientific study of disease. The new approach permanently altered the nature of professional health care in the United States, as elsewhere. In 1847, the American Medical Association (AMA) was founded, and by 1900 it took charge of licensing and certification procedures for medical doctors and curricula in medical schools. As the AMA grew in power and prestige, so did the scientific medical community. The roles of midwives, herbalists, and others fell into disfavor while physicians gained social status. Because certified medical schools were located in large cities and their tuition and fees were quite expensive, medicine drew most of its trainees from a narrower segment of the population; "certified doctors" were predominantly white men from urban upper- and middle-class backgrounds—a demographic characteristic still true of the medical profession today.

From the early 1900s to the 1950s, scientific medicine grew in power and influence. Medical technology made tremendous advances during both world wars—especially in emergency and reconstructive surgeries. As medical research moved forward and scientific knowledge grew, vaccines were developed to prevent many of the country's most dreaded and deadly diseases. Although the general practitioner, or "family doctor," was the mainstay of the American medical community, as medical knowledge increased and medical practice became increasingly sophisticated a wide variety of medical specialties arose. **Specialization** involves *advanced education and training allowing doctors to focus on one particular aspect of medicine (e.g., pediatrics, obstetrics, surgery, or psychiatry).*

The Age of Specialization

Beginning in the 1960s, the United States experienced three decades of increased specialization in the fields of medicine and health care. By 1990, more specialists than general practitioners were practicing medicine (Hoffman, 1991). Advanced knowledge and technology led some doctors to specialize in treating certain diseases and health problems. Advanced medical technology also poses many ethical issues (see Focus box 18.2). Another contributing factor was the enhanced prestige and increased income of spe-

SPECIALIZATION (MEDICAL)
Advanced education and training allowing doctors to focus on one particular aspect of medicine (e.g., pediatrics, obstetrics, surgery, or psychiatry).

TABLE 18.1
PHYSICIAN SPECIALTIES

PERCENT DISTRIBUTION OF PHYSICIANS BY SPECIALTY, 2003	PERCENT	MEDIAN TOTAL COMPENSATION OF PHYSICIANS BY SPECIALTY, 2004	LESS THAN 2 YEARS IN SPECIALTY	OVER 1 YEAR IN SPECIALTY
TOTAL	100.0	Anesthesiology	$259,948	$321,686
PRIMARY CARE	40.8	Surgery: General	228,839	282,504
Family medicine and general practice	12.8	Obstetrics/gynecology: General	203,270	247,348
Internal medicine	15.1			
Obstetrics & gynecology	5.3	Psychiatry: General	173,922	180,000
Pediatrics	7.6	Internal medicine: General	141,912	166,420
SPECIALTIES	59.2	Pediatrics: General	132,953	161,331
Anesthesiology	5.4	Family practice (without obstetrics)	137,119	156,010
Psychiatry	5.4			
Surgical specialties, selected	14.6			
All other specialties	33.9			

Source: U.S. Department of Labor, Bureau of Labor Statistics, Occupational Outlook Handbook, http:www.bls.gov/oco/ocos074.htm

cialists in certain fields. Table 18.1 indicates the proportion of doctors and their annual incomes for selected medical specialties.

The trend toward medical specialization has affected many American families. Middle-class children visit a pediatrician for their health care. Their mother sees a gynecologist for her annual physical. She visits an ear, nose, and throat specialist for her allergies; a dermatologist for a skin condition; an orthopedic surgeon for her broken wrist; and a psychiatrist for emotional distress. The children's father sees a specialist in family medicine when he has a common viral infection, but throughout the course of the year he also visits a proctologist, a urologist, an internist, and a psychiatrist. For dental care the family uses the services of a family dentist, an orthodontist for the children's braces, an endodontist for root canals, a periodontist for gum disease, and an oral surgeon should tooth extraction be necessary. Specialization has contributed to an overall increase in the costs of medical care. Consequently, certain types of medical care are inaccessible to a large segment of the population. Moreover, the rise of scientific medicine and specialization, along with mass media portrayals, has contributed to an interesting social phenomenon in the United States—the medicalization of American society.

Media and the Medicalization of American Society

Media portrayals of medicine, doctors and health care, heavy media advertising of over-the-counter remedies, and the dramatic rise in the power and influence of scientific medicine have had a far-reaching impact on American society. One consequence of interest to sociologists has been **medicalization,** *a process in which behavior, activities, and problems previously dissociated from health and medicine are now viewed from a medical perspective and seen within the domain of doctors, hospitals, and other elements of the health-care system.* Let's turn first to how the media portrays medicine and health care, then look at how these images and perceptions have promoted the medicalization of American society.

Early Media Portrayals of Medicine and Health Care: Creating a Positive Image
How much of our perception of medical care and image of doctors comes from the media? As one media expert noted, "While the relation between fiction and fact is invariably subtle, the medical genre on television expresses, reflects, and compensates for practices of formal medicine and health care in the 'real world'" (Real,

MEDICALIZATION
A process in which behavior, activities, and problems previously dissociated from health and medicine are now viewed from a medical perspective and seen as within the domain of doctors, hospitals, and other elements of the health-care system.

With sirens blaring and lights flashing, the ambulance skids to a halt in front of the hospital emergency room entrance. A swarm of medical personnel descends on the ambulance as its drivers and the paramedics who are aboard fling open its door and unload the cargo. The patient is wheeled through the automatic doors of the hospital and rushed down the corridor toward the emergency room triage. While nurses and emergency room physicians monitor vital signs and start an intravenous solution, one doctor races over to a desk and hands a clipboard to a staff person who is sitting in front of a computer and who carefully begins to enter data.

The computer program is referred to simply as RIP. In emergency rooms across the country and around the world, this computer program is helping doctors make informed decisions about whether to administer life-saving treatments or simply allow patients to die. Using statistical probability, the program analyzes all of the input on a particular patient and makes a prognosis on the likelihood of survival. If the probability is 95 percent or better that the patient is going to die regardless of treatment, it is recommended that treatment not be administered. On the other hand, if the odds are greater than 5 percent that the patient will survive, the computer not only indicates the probability of survival but also prints out recommended treatment procedures. All of this happens in milliseconds.

Critics of the new computerized system contend that it is a frightening example of overreliance on computer technology to make decisions that were once reserved for human judgment. Medical ethicist Arthur Caplan of Philadelphia argues that computers should not be used to make decisions about the allocation of medical resources to patients and points out that the computer will be wrong in about 5 percent of all cases. Supporters of the new technology insist that the computer does not make any decisions. Rather, it provides data and information that allow trained medical personnel to make more informed decisions about how to allocate very expensive treatment procedures and how to use most effectively limited medical resources, such as intensive care beds and organs for transplants. Armed with this information, doctors can better determine who should and should not be treated. David Bihari, a critical care specialist in England, points out that because of a lack of intensive care facilities, as many as one in four patients may have to be turned away from British hospitals. A computer program such as RIP provides physicians with vital information about who is most likely to benefit from treatment and who is not.

While medical doctors and ethicists debate the merits of using a computer program such as RIP, sociologists are more interested in the social ramifications of such procedures. Decisions about whom to treat and how to treat them have always been part of the dynamics of emergency rooms. How important have social variables such as race, gender, age, and social class been in the past? Might a computer be less likely to discriminate on the basis of these and other social characteristics? On the other hand, what is lost when the human dimension is subordinated to computer technology in medical decision making? These and other sociological issues are likely to become even more pronounced as more sophisticated medical technology, combined with an increasing demand on medical services, forces physicians and health-care workers around the world to make even more decisions about who should and should not receive their services.

Less controversially, emergency rooms across the United States routinely use a doctor-friendly computerized database that, within 60 seconds of inputting symptoms, pro-

1977:137). One of television's first portrayals of a medical doctor was the kind but cantankerous Doc Adams on the series *Gunsmoke*. This paternalistic image gave way to a younger, more urbane and sophisticated stereotype in television's *Ben Casey* and *Dr. Kildare*. Robert Young's portrayal of *Marcus Welby, M.D.*, was reminiscent of his earlier role on *Father Knows Best* and became the epitome of the television medical genre from 1969 to 1976. Unlike real-life doctors, Marcus Welby made house calls, was on a first-name basis with all of his patients, and often did not charge for his medical services. Marcus Welby was so beloved and trusted that Robert Young received an average of 5,000 letters per week from viewers seeking both medical and personal advice (Real, 1977). These early television characters and programs both reflected and promoted the *deification* of medical doctors in American society (Real, 1977; Howitt, 1982). Their positive images promoted the public notion that scientific medicine is not only necessary and important for those who are ill, but powerful and indispensable for virtually all aspects of society; doctors are not only helpful to the sick, but nearly omnipotent.

The Medicalization of Birth and Death
Media portrayals of doctors, along with billions of dollars spent on advertising by drug manufacturers, have contributed to the public's increasing reliance on scientific medicine and drugs to help everyone

vides a diagnosis and preferred method of treatment in pediatric emergency cases (*USA Today,* 1995; Noonan, 2002). And what contemporary doctor's office, medical clinic, or hospital would be complete today without computers, X-ray machines, and even sophisticated magnetic resonance imaging and laser technologies?

The question is not whether technology is going to alter the future course of health and medical care in the United States and around the world but, more important, where we draw the line. Medical ethicists today are debating issues ranging from the use of biogenetic engineering to create life, to the use of fetal organs for transplant and the treatment of Alzheimer's disease, to euthanasia and doctor-assisted suicides. The world was stunned when the parents of a teenage daughter who needed a kidney transplant but couldn't find a perfect match decided to have another child for the express purpose of providing an organ donor. Reports that starving people in developing nations may sell their organs on a black market, from which the organs eventually find their way to the United States and Europe for transplant, provide frightening science fiction–like scenarios for the future. The rapid development of medical knowledge and technology has created what some call an "ethical minefield" (Woodward et al., 1993:52). From a sociological viewpoint, these and other issues may be ruled on from medical, legal, and religious perspectives but will continue to be debated and ultimately decided in a larger social arena, where attitudes, values, beliefs, and important norms regarding technology, health, and medical care are created, transmitted, and transformed through the process of social interaction.

Sociologists have long understood that technology often develops at a much faster rate than the public's ability to grasp its consequences and to rethink the important values,

attitudes, norms, and beliefs that surround its uses (Ogburn, 1922, 1964). Nowhere is this cultural lag more evident than in the case of the revolutionary technological developments in medical and health care. As one sociologist noted, "medical ethics is an arena in which sociologists can revisit issues about the doctor-patient relationship . . . the meaning of death and dying, and the character of the medical profession" (Zussman, 1997:171).

TAKING A CLOSER LOOK

Some people contend that the major purpose of health care and medicine is to sustain and prolong life and that technological developments that allow us to do so should be used without hesitation. Others argue that medical technology has developed at such a rapid pace that the most important issue today is not whether we *can* sustain and prolong life almost indefinitely, but whether we *should.* On which side of this debate would you most closely align your position? Why? What do you think of computer programs such as RIP? How will they affect emergency room care? What ethical dilemmas are presented by this and other types of medical technology?

Source: William F. Ogburn. *Social Change.* New York: Viking Press, 1922. William F. Ogburn. "Culture Lag as Theory," in William F. Ogburn (ed.), *Culture and Social Change.* Chicago: University of Chicago Press, 1964, pp. 86–95. *USA Today,* "Emergency Medicine Goes High-Tech," 123 (February) 1995:5. Staci Elder and Martha Collar. "American Health Watch 2000." *USA Today,* 119 (September) 1990:50–52. Sharon Begley, Jennifer Foote, Daniel Glick, et al. "Cures from the Womb." *Newsweek,* February 22, 1993:48–51. Kenneth L. Woodward, Mary Hager, and Daniel Glick. "A Search for Limits." *Newsweek,* February 22, 1993:52–53. Robert Zussman. "Sociological Perspectives on Medical Ethics and Decision-Making." In John Hagan and Karen S. Cook (eds.), *Annual Review of Sociology* 23. Palo Alto, CA: Annual Reviews, Inc., 1997, pp. 171–189. David Noonan. "Wiring the New Docs," *Newsweek,* June 24, 2002:59–62.

through the daily activities of life. Changes in childbirth practices, for example, reflect the medicalization of what was once viewed as a natural life event not associated with doctors, nurses, or hospitals. Throughout most of the country's history, American women, like women throughout the world, gave birth at home, usually with the aid of a friend, family member, or midwife. Doctors rarely participated unless complications arose. In post–World War II America, however, obstetrics and gynecology emerged as medical specialties, and women routinely reported to hospitals for the births of their babies. Today, although natural childbirth and home birthing have regained popularity, 99 percent of births still occur in hospitals under the supervision of certified medical personnel (World Health Organization, 2006). Even childhood has become increasingly medicalized. Once pediatricians spent their time fighting infectious diseases; today they deal with problems such as temper tantrums, sibling rivalry, cursing, bedwetting, school difficulties, and running away (Pawluch, 2003).

Death also once took place in the home, surrounded by one's loved ones. This was especially the case when the elderly died from what was described as "old age" or "natural causes." Over time, however, with the expansion of hospitals, nursing homes, and other health-care facilities, death came to be viewed as an event that requires the attendance of medical personnel. In most states today, if death is unattended by a physician

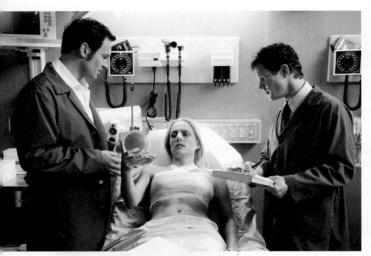

How does television's portrayal of doctors in popular programs such as *Nip/Tuck* affect viewers' ideas about health, medicine, and health care?

an autopsy must be performed to establish the legal cause of death. Consequently, when signs of death are imminent, the terminally ill are usually placed in a hospital, nursing home, or hospice so their death can be monitored and certified by a physician. Moreover, as technology has produced new life-saving equipment and techniques, death has come to be viewed as unnatural in our society, and medical personnel are called on to postpone death or to make it as painless as possible.

The Medicalization of Deviance In Chapter 7, we discussed another example of the medicalization of society: the *medical model* of deviance. This model defines problems such as stress, mental disorders, alcoholism, drug abuse, and even crime as individual pathologies and diverts attention away from the social and structural factors that help create and sustain them. The rise of psychiatry contributed to the medical model of deviance, as certain types of deviants and criminals who committed "sick" acts were viewed as mentally ill. Since a criminal cannot be convicted unless he or she has the ability to distinguish right from wrong, the insanity defense entered the legal arena. Testimony by medical experts is used to determine a criminal's state of mind at the time of the commission of a crime.

The medical model of deviance—especially as applied to alcoholism and drug abuse—had unprecedented influence in the United States during the 1980s. Research linking predisposition to alcoholism with certain genetic patterns supported the view that alcoholism is a disease, but social definitions and media portrayals of alcoholism and other types of drug abuse as pathological behaviors had an even greater influence. By the 1980s, thousands of medical personnel were trained as specialists in dealing with alcohol and drug abuse, and thousands of vacant hospital beds were occupied by "sick" alcoholics and drug abusers in need of medical attention. Some hospitals were converted to specialize in the treatment of specific "illnesses" of alcoholism and drug abuse. They advertised on television for new "patients," and insurance coverage of these "diseases" led to higher premiums. Today, alcoholism, drug abuse, obesity, and a wide array of what used to be considered behavioral disorders are now considered to be medical problems.

Elective Plastic Surgery Plastic surgery also reflects the medicalization of society. Although plastic surgery was developed to correct birth defects and treat accident victims and soldiers wounded in war, today it is most often associated with aesthetics. Botox injections are so common that suburban housewives now have "Botox parties" instead of Tupperware parties. Television talk shows offer panels of famous and ordinary people who have undergone plastic surgery. In 1992, talk show host Jenny Jones disclosed details of her breast augmentation, and Geraldo Rivera underwent minor cosmetic surgery on the air. These topics are presented for their titillating and entertainment value—because the hosts and participants discuss them in technical and sterile-sounding medical terms under the pretense of medical professionalism, their guests may be allowed to show bare breasts or buttocks, or before and after photos of nude body parts that normally would not make it past network censors. In 2003, FX network premiered *Nip/Tuck,* a program about two fictional plastic surgeons that immediately became a major television hit.

Over-the-Counter Remedies The medicalization of society supports the multibillion-dollar over-the-counter pharmaceutical industry, as Americans turn to medical solutions to handle routine problems of everyday living. With the help of the mass media, Americans have become obsessed with pills and other medications. The typical American medicine cabinet contains an arsenal of unused prescription medications and over-the-counter remedies—some with a dangerous and even lethal potential. And advertising in the mass media, especially on television, has bombarded us with the "take-a-pill" mentality. There are pills to help us get to sleep and pills to make us more alert; pills to help us lose weight and pills to increase our body size; laxatives to cure constipation and other medications that have the opposite effect; and pain relievers in every form, shape, and size.

Contemporary Media Portrayals of Medicine and Health Care

To what extent can the medicalization of American society be attributed to the mass media? Robert Nisbet (1976:76) asserted, "We live in a world of ideas, and ideas, stereotypes, and images have far greater directive forces in our lives, generally, than do the conditions they are supposed to reflect." In their quest for health, Americans have become dependent on medicine and the health-care system. In this vein, the media have helped "create, extend, and confirm . . . 'common sense' beliefs and practices" related to health care in American society (Real, 1977:138). Contemporary media portrayals of doctors, medicine, and health care have changed from the highly positive images of the past. Media coverage of gross overbilling, unnecessary surgery, medical malpractice, collusion between unscrupulous doctors and drug companies, and other medical scandals (largely as a result of television programs such as *60 Minutes, 20/20,* and *Dateline*) have altered public attitudes toward doctors and health care. In some cases public images are probably more realistic—and sometimes even cynical. Television programs began to portray doctors differently in the 1970s and 1980s; characters on *M*A*S*H, St. Elsewhere,* and *Northern Exposure* were likable but not beyond reproach. The 1990s spawned intense dramatical medical series such as *ER* and *Chicago Hope,* which focused on the stress, tension, and physical and emotional trauma associated with the medical profession. They also portrayed doctors as fallible and health care as less than perfect. Today, *Grey's Anatomy* is one of the most popular medical television programs; it has been joined by *Scrubs* which parodies the life of doctors, nurses, and patients, and *Nip/Tuck* which pushes the boundaries of believability and network censors. *House* portrays a doctor as socially inept but infallible in his ability to diagnose illness. Viewers also can watch real-life emergency room procedures as well as a host of other medical specials. Media coverage of rising costs, medical malpractice, and other problems associated with medicine and health care in the United States also have helped make the public more aware of what many describe as a health-care crisis in American society.

Popular television shows like *Scrubs* satirize contemporary medicine and hospital routines, but they also deal with timely medical issues.

The Health-Care Crisis: A Functionalist Viewpoint

The manifest functions of medicine and health care are the prevention and treatment of disease and the maintenance of health in society. The American health-care system has done a creditable job of fulfilling these functions, but it is not without its problems. Sociologists who analyze the health-care crisis from a functionalist perspective identify several factors at the heart of the problem: lack of education, unequal geographic distribution of doctors and health-care facilities, bureaucratization and inefficiency, the high costs of health care, and inadequate resources for research and development.

Lack of Education Many Americans, especially those in poverty, remain uneducated about health maintenance and disease prevention. They do not understand the importance of immunizing their children or know about public health clinics and other programs that provide free vaccinations and other medical care.

Geographic Distribution Each year, some Americans die because of lack of medical attention when they cannot reach a doctor or an adequate health-care facility. The AMA insists there is no shortage of doctors and hospitals, but there is a problem in their geographic distribution. Every major city has a large number of general practitioners and doctors representing virtually every medical specialty. There are plenty of clinics, hospitals, laboratories, and other facilities in most urban areas. However, in many isolated rural areas, where there are approximately 31 doctors for every 100,000 people, adequate health and medical care is unavailable (NBC News, 1997).

Small communities often share doctors, and their residents may have to drive hundreds of miles to the nearest clinic or hospital. Moreover, studies show that there is a serious shortage of nurses nationwide (Underwood, 2005), and that a large number of doctors practicing in the United States do not speak English as their first language, creating communication problems with patients (Underwood and Adler, 2005).

Bureaucratization and Inefficiency

Even where adequate health care is available, it is often accompanied by myriad forms, paperwork, red tape, and long lines of waiting people; the situation creates frustration, hostility, and inefficiency. Bureaucratization is functional to the extent that it aids in organizing and coordinating efficient medical care, but it becomes dysfunctional when it impedes the efficient delivery of health care. Many complain that huge health-care organizations and insurance companies are becoming increasingly bureaucratic, as more decisions about treatments, referrals to specialists, and length of hospital stays are being made by insurance company employees or hospital managers, as opposed to doctors. While providing the best possible health care is supposed to be the goal of all parties, some fear this may result in health-care decisions being motivated primarily by cost and efficiency, as opposed to medical reasons. A study conducted by the Rand Corporation and reported in the *New England Journal of Medicine* indicated that many U.S. doctors ignore treatment guidelines for common illnesses such as high blood pressure and diabetes (McConnaughery, 2003).

High Costs of Health Care

Doctors blame the high costs of medical equipment and overhead, especially malpractice insurance premiums, for driving up their fees. Likewise, hospital administrators say that increased operating costs are directly linked to what they charge patients. From a functionalist perspective, malpractice litigation, large settlements and court awards, the cost of high-tech equipment, problems in the insurance industry, and stiffer federal regulations concerning medical practice have all contributed to the skyrocketing costs of health care. But functionalists argue that high salaries are necessary to induce individuals to make the sacrifices necessary to become medical doctors and highly trained specialists.

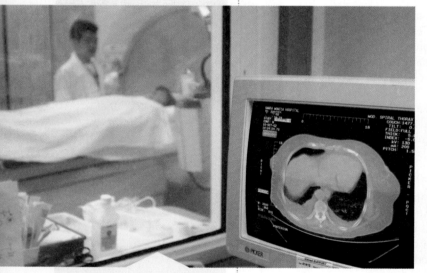

Highly sophisticated medical equipment such as this medical resonance imaging (MRI) unit are partially responsible for the rising costs of health care.

What other factors contribute to the high costs of medical care?

Inadequate Resources for Research and Development

The high costs of health care are partly due to the high costs of medical research and the development of new technologies. Just as research on diabetes, cancer, and other serious diseases appeared to be succeeding, AIDS appeared on the medical scene, requiring billions more dollars for research and the development of new drugs for prevention and treatment. Medical researchers lament that not enough money is devoted to research and the development of new technology.

The problems cited by functionalists are readily acknowledged by most of those familiar with the American health-care system, but the sources of these problems are viewed quite differently when analyzed from the conflict perspective.

The Health-Care Crisis from the Conflict Perspective

From the conflict perspective, the American health-care crisis is linked to structural inequality. From this viewpoint, the most serious flaws in American health care can be attributed to unequal access to medicine and health care, high costs linked to large profits, bureaucratization and its resulting alienation, and the use of scientific medicine as an ideology to reinforce social inequality.

Unequal Access   Conflict theorists point out that in a capitalist society where medicine and health care are commodities to be bought and sold, inequality in health care is inevitable. That is, the availability of health care in the United States depends on one's social class and ability to pay. Although there are subsidized public health clinics for the poor and programs such as Medicare to help the elderly, most people obtain medical services either through a direct fee payment system, where individuals pay for whatever treatment they can afford, or through third-party fee payment, which requires health insurance. Insurance is another commodity that must be purchased by the individual or provided by his or her employer. Because medical care and health insurance are expensive, millions of Americans who are least able to afford it must bear the entire cost of their illnesses—or, as often is the case, ignore or suffer them without care. Because poor people usually do not have a regular physician, they more often use hospital emergency rooms for nonemergency treatment, thus helping to clog an already overcrowded system and driving up the costs for those who have insurance or can afford to pay for hospital services. The Institute of Medicine released a report that indicated that even when they have insurance, racial and ethnic minorities in the United States get worse medical care, leading some minority groups to allege that some of the unequal access to health care amounts to "medical racism" (Stohlberg, 2002).

High Costs and Large Profits   While conflict theorists acknowledge that medical providers have a high operating overhead, they ascribe much of the cost of insurance and health care to the greed of private businesses and practitioners. X-rays and other medical tests have become routine in health care, but many people contend that part of the high cost of health care in the United States can be attributed to unnecessary tests ordered by doctors and hospital staff. Many critics of the American medical profession cite unnecessary surgery, overreliance on certain prescription medications, consultation and referral fees, and physicians' and surgeons' investments in pharmaceutical companies and medical laboratories as major contributors to soaring medical costs.

Bureaucratization and Alienation   U.S. health care has become increasingly bureaucratized. People without health insurance may be denied necessary medical services. Even people with insurance may be unable to document their coverage properly or may become so frustrated with the process of filing forms that they either do not seek needed health care or are not properly reimbursed for its expense. In addition, bureaucratization in health care and the difference in status in doctor-patient relations contribute to a feeling of dehumanization and alienation. Even during our sickest moments, most of us have seriously considered getting up and leaving a crowded waiting room one or two hours after the designated appointment time has passed. Two studies in different parts of the nation found that 8–15 percent of emergency room patients left before seeing a doctor because of long waits—in some cases up to 17 hours (*USA Today*, 1991d). Another study found that because of America's "fragmented and chaotic" healthcare system, patients receive proper medical care only about 55 percent of the time (Pugh, 2006).

Scientific Medicine as Ideology   From the conflict perspective, strict adherence to scientific medicine has created an ideology that serves as a form of social control and reinforces structural inequality. The belief that illness, disease, and shorter life expectancy are attributable to smoking, viruses, and bacteria precludes the serious consideration of the effects of poverty, malnutrition, racism, and sexism, which also help account for disparities in health and longevity. Further, the medical model of deviance illustrates how medicine can be used to control deviants and other nonconformists with the use of isolation, drugs, and even surgery. The conflict perspective sees the AMA as a powerful agency of social control with a vested interest in limiting who can practice medicine, what procedures can be used, and what constitutes acceptable health care, often dismissing less expensive alternatives to conventional health care.

Alternative medicine includes treatments aimed to restore and maintain health that lie outside conventional medicine and includes therapeutic practice such as biofeedback, vitamins and herbs, massage, magnets, and yoga. Alternative medicine also includes divergent systems that have their own underlying philosophies, training, and treatments—such as acupuncture, chiropractic, and homeopathy. Other elements that make alternative medicine "alternative" include:

1. *Vitalism*—a belief in a vital force that maintains health in the body. (Acupuncture calls this "ch'i;" chiropractic refers to this as "Innate Intelligence.")

2. *Holism*—practitioners that address the whole patient, including emotions, diet, and the environment, not just bodily symptoms.

3. A concern for the mind-body connection, or an understanding that a patient's psychological state and attitudes may affect health outcomes.

4. Disease being seen as a natural process, with recovery being an opportunity for personal growth and exploration.

5. A view that patients should take responsibility and become involved in their own health, rather than passively rely on physicians.

6. Treatments that are natural (drugless) and stimulate the body's ability to heal itself.

Each year there are more visits to unorthodox medical practitioners than to orthodox ones. Most patients of alternative medical practitioners are nonblack, have high levels of education, and are willing to pay for these services out-of-pocket (Eisenberg, 1993). Many patients view alternative medical practitioners as "doctors of last resort," seeking treatment for chronic ailments that conventional methods have not helped.

Increased use has accompanied more acceptance. Today, many alternative medical treatments are covered by insurance, practitioners often go through a credentialing or licensing process, and some treatments have been scientifically verified. This level of acceptance is quite a change, because only a few decades ago alternative medicine was considered quackery, cultism, or charlatanism. Hundreds of chiropractors were persecuted and imprisoned for practicing medicine without a license in the early 1900s and the American Medical Association (AMA) formed a Committee on Quackery in 1964 to "control and eliminate" questionable and unproven medical practices.

In the 1970s, the cries of quackery were tempered and replaced by the term "alternative" (meaning "in place of" orthodox medicine). This change was fueled by patient demands: the self-help movement, demands for more participation in the health care encounter, and a cultural backlash against medicine's excesses.

In the 1990s, the term *complementary medicine* (meaning "together with" orthodox medicine) emerged, signaling the interest and inquiry of orthodox medicine into alternative medicine. As increased scientific research was aimed at testing the efficacy of alternative medicine, the legitimacy of specific treatments improved, but the underlying philoso-

Is There a Health-Care Crisis? An Interactionist Approach

In contrast to the functionalist and conflict perspectives, sociologists using the interactionist approach are less concerned about identifying the causes of problems in the health-care system and more likely to ask: Is there a health-care crisis? If so, what does that mean? Perhaps more important, who decides? As we have discovered in this chapter, people around the globe define health and sickness differently, and even within any particular culture, individuals hold vastly disparate views of what it means to be sick or well. Similarly, we have seen that different countries have varying degrees of abilities and commitments, not to mention delivery systems, for providing health care to their citizens. Consequently, from an interactionist perspective, health, sickness, medicine, and health care, like everything else, are social constructions that are subjectively defined and redefined through social interaction.

From the interactionist perspective, the process of determining whether health care in the United States is in crisis is as subjective as defining health and illness. Interactionists agree with the functionalists that lack of availability, high costs, and inefficiency are serious health-care problems, but they maintain that the dehumanization and alienation experienced by both doctors and patients who must deal with huge bureaucratic insurance companies and health-care providers are far more serious. Likewise, interac-

phies of alternative medicine, like "Innate Intelligence" remained unsubstantiated (Villanueva-Russell, 2005).

The term *integrative medicine* (meaning "seamless binding of two parts") has emerged. In 1996, a program in Integrative Medicine within the Department of Medicine at the University of Arizona was created with similar programs soon to follow all over the country. Does this signal that patients will now have the best of both worlds—receiving alternate and orthodox treatments in equal measure? Are orthodox physicians more tolerant of alternative medicine and willing to incorporate holism, vitalism, and considerations of the mind-body connection into their biomedical model?

Probably not. Remember, *things are not necessarily what they seem.* As long as alternative medicine has divergent philosophies like ch'i and Innate Intelligence that do not fit into current medical practice and cannot be measured by science, the fluid meshing of alternative medicine into orthodox medicine seems unlikely. Wolpe's (1985) research on acupuncture shows that orthodox medicine may "permanently borrow" the treatments it believes are beneficial and scientific, (e.g., using acupuncture for anesthesia) while renouncing the bulk of other practices and philosophies that are deemed less useful or less scientific (e.g., ch'i). Integration in this case may actually mean a reinforcement of orthodox medicine's power to control a subordinate discipline rather than a cooperative union between them.

Schneirov and Geczik (2005) studied an alternative health program "integrated" into a hospital and found that increased status of these services were countered by second-class treatment. The services were offered in the basement—which implied inferiority—and many orthodox physicians were skeptical of the program.

Although it is clear that the acceptance of alternative medicine has grown, its future as "integrative" medicine is far from certain. As Schneirov and Geczik (2005: 368) ask, "Will orthodox medicine accommodate alternative medicine, or, will alternative medicine be more likely to accommodate orthodox medicine?"

TAKING A CLOSER LOOK

Can alternative medicine be integrated into orthodox medicine while still preserving the ideas and practices that made it "alternative" in the first place?" Why have the AMA and conventional medical practitioners scorned alternative medicine?

Source: David Eisenberg, Ronald C. Kessler, Cindy Foster, Frances E. Norlock, David R. Calkins, and Thomas L. Dlebanco. "Unconventional Medicine in the United States," *New England Journal of Medicine* 328 (4), 1993: 246–252. Matthew Schneirov and Jonathan David Geczik. "Alternative Health and the Challenges of Institutionalization." In Peter Conrad, (ed.), in *The Sociology of Health and Illness* (7th) ed.). New York: Worth Publishers, 2005, 366–377. Yvonne Villanueva-Russell. "Evidence-Based Medicine and Its Implications for the Profession of Chiropractic," *Social Science and Medicine* 60 (February), 2005: 545–561. James Whorton. "From Cultism to CAM: Alternative Medicine in the Twentieth Century," in Robert Johnston (ed.), *The Politics of Healing.* New York: Routledge, 2005, pp. 287–305. Paul Root Wolpe. "The Maintenance of Professional Authority: Acupuncture and the Medical Physicians," *Social Problems* 35(5), 1985: 409–424.

*This previously unpublished piece was written especially for Society in Focus, reprinted by permission of Yvonne Villanueva-Russell, Texas A&M University–Commerce.

tionists agree with the conflict perspective that much of the power of scientific medicine and the AMA is linked to political ideology and largely ignores the growing array of widely used and socially acclaimed alternative medical practices of millions of people across the country.

Integrative Medicine and Alternatives to Conventional Health Care

Although scientific medicine as approved and practiced by the AMA dominates health care in the United States, Americans also participate in a variety of alternatives to conventional health care. For example, osteopathic doctors, once snubbed by the medical profession because they combine spinal manipulation and acupressure with more conventional practices, now are a vital part of the health-care system. Chiropractic medicine, which uses massage, spinal manipulation, acupressure, and sometimes acupuncture, enjoys a wide following in the United States but is still denigrated by the AMA and many medical doctors.

Perhaps one of the fastest-growing alternatives to conventional medicine is **integrative** or **holistic medicine,** which *emphasizes the prevention of disease and focuses treatment on patients as whole persons in an effort to maintain good physical, emotional,*

INTEGRATIVE MEDICINE (HOLISTIC MEDICINE)
Emphasizes the prevention of disease and focuses treatment on patients as whole persons in an effort to maintain good physical, emotional, and spiritual health.

and spiritual health. Holistic medicine recognizes the need to seek professional medical help and go to the hospital for serious illnesses, but as our opening vignette illustrates, its practitioners (many of whom are medical doctors) emphasize that people need to take personal responsibility for their own health and well-being. Holistic medicine is part of the wellness movement, and its advocates use diet, nutrition, meditation, relaxation, and exercise to maintain good health. Whereas traditional scientific medicine tends to be *reactive,* responding to poor health and disease, holistic medicine and some other alternative approaches are *proactive* in their approach, with an emphasis on preventive medicine and the maintenance of good health. Johns Hopkins has even launched a study on the impact of prayer on healing, especially with patients suffering from cancer and other life-threatening diseases (Hales, 2003). Integrative medicine and other alternative forms of health care are likely to play a larger role in the future. In fact, the National Institutes of Health, the embodiment of scientific medicine, has established an Office of Alternative Medicine to investigate promising alternatives to conventional medical treatments, and future doctors are already taking courses in alternative medicine at over 55 U.S. medical schools (Rosenfeld, 1997).

the FUTURE
LOOKING to

HEALTH AND MEDICINE IN THE TWENTY-FIRST CENTURY

"Forecasting a future for public health is like betting on a horse race" (Pickett and Hanlon, 1990:553). Some scenarios are more likely than others, but there is still a high probability of being wrong no matter what your prediction. Nevertheless, most medical forecasters believe that current trends in medicine, health care, and public health will lead to more emphasis on prevention, with social epidemiology playing an important role. They predict that government at all levels—local, county, state, federal, and international—will become more involved in health care and that government agencies will play a more important role in linking various health-care agencies, community groups, and individuals through computer networks (Banister et al., 1988; Pickett and Hanlon, 1990).

In the United States, the Clinton administration pledged to cut health costs and make health care more accessible to all, and during the 2000 and 2004 presidential campaigns George W. Bush promised reforms in health care, especially regarding the high costs of prescription drugs. Despite these pledges, actual health-care reforms have been modest and quite slow in coming. Thus, despite increased biomedical research and new medical technology that has improved the techniques of diagnosing and treating disease, many Americans share a sense of fatalism about the nation's health problems.

Responding to changing health-care needs, many employers have turned to **health maintenance organizations (HMOs)** and **preferred-provider organizations (PPOs),** *insurance programs that emphasize preventive care and attempt to reduce medical costs by pooling funds and contracting with participating physicians who manage their patients' total health care.* While patients lose some flexibility in managing their health care and choosing medical practitioners, lower insurance premiums and reduced out-of-pocket expenses for routine medical care often offset the perceived inconvenience. In the early twenty-first century, many HMOs have come under fire as being too rigid and even interfering with doctors' decisions about patient health care. Some have been involved in major lawsuits and some have even gone bankrupt. Nevertheless, HMOs have become powerful players in the health-care field.

Numerous alternatives to traditional hospitalization have been developed to reduce medical expenses. Outpatient surgery has become the norm for minor operations, and Connecticut and Texas have experimented with subacute care facilities for those who are too well to remain hospitalized but too sick or incapacitated to return home. These "halfway hospitals" cost about half as much as a regular hospital and are predicted to become the fastest-growing segment in health care over the next decade. There has been an economic restructuring of elite dominance in health care, but it has occurred unevenly across states and regions.

HEALTH MAINTENANCE ORGANIZATION (HMO) and PREFERRED-PROVIDER ORGANIZATION (PPO)
Insurance programs that emphasize preventive care and attempt to reduce medical costs by pooling funds and contracting with participating physicians who manage their patients' total health care.

In the early 1990s, *U.S. News & World Report* (1991:94–99) listed seven predictions for medical trends: using genetics to cure disease, stopping cancer before it starts, turning back nature's clock, insurance for the uninsured, new ways to defeat heart disease, the growth of patient power, and death with dignity. None of the seven has been fully realized, hence they may still be seen as goals for the future. Clearly, biomedical developments and other techno-scientific developments will play an important role in medicine and health care in the future (Clarke et al., 2003; *Newsweek,* 2005).

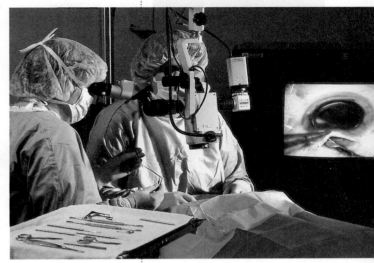

Television is everywhere. Here, through the use of miniature cameras, surgeons perform intricate procedures by viewing them on a television monitor.

Today, many communities provide computerized reference services for physicians, specialists, and dentists, and in some locations patients correspond with their doctors and medical teams via e-mail (Friend, 1995). Also, millions of Americans seek and obtain medical advice from a wide array of on-line services and Internet websites (see Figure 18.2). Today, medical technology is available to use fetal tissue to treat Alzheimer's patients, and doctors may predetermine the sex of a baby. Perhaps we are only a few years away from being able to genetically program a genius or gifted athlete, implant artificial organs, and prolong life indefinitely. Also, medical technology is on the verge of creating synthetic substitutes for blood, or "artificial blood" that can be used in transfusions without fear of transmitting HIV, hepatitis, or other blood-borne diseases (Underwood, 2002). But these developments will impose even more responsibility on doctors and present many more ethical questions (Wright, 1990; Begley et al., 1993; *Newsweek,* 2005).

The costs of health care are likely to increase, and the portion of the U.S. gross national product devoted to health care will increase as well. Many people predict that with current demographic trends toward longer life expectancies and with baby boomers entering the later stages of life, there will be a tremendous need for more doctors and other health-care practitioners in the future, and the United States may experience a severe shortage in some areas (Ginzberg, 1990; Underwood, 2005). Some of the slack will be taken up by the expanded role of physicians' assistants, dieticians, nutritionists, physical therapists, clinical pharmacists, and nurse practitioners. Others

FIGURE 18.2

THE HEALTH-CONSCIOUS

More than one third of all on-line users currently retrieve health information from the Web.

Legend:
- All on-line adults
- Retrieve health/medical content

All on-line adults (in millions):
1999: 74.5; 2000: 83; 2001: 90.5; 2002: 99.1; 2003: 109.4

Retrieve health/medical content (in millions):
1999: 24.8; 2000: 33.5; 2001: 39.7; 2002: 45.9; 2003: 52

X-axis (Year): 1994, 1995, 1996, 1997, 1998, 1999, 2000, 2001, 2002, 2003

Y-axis: Number of U.S. Adult Users (In Millions) — 0 to 120

Source: "The Health-Conscious" as appeared in *American Demographics*, July 2000. Reprinted by permission of Cyber Dialogue.

What are some of the risks associated with seeking health information on the Internet?

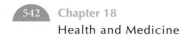

predict that there may be too many doctors (especially specialists) in the future; this prompted the federal government to initiate a plan in 1997 whereby medical hospitals were paid *not* to train doctors, receiving a fixed amount of money for each slot they did not fill (NBC News, 1997).

Regardless of whether all or only a few of these predictions prove true in the future, it is certain that social institutions related to health and medicine will continue to be important social concerns in the United States and worldwide.

Summary

1 Health and sickness are viewed differently in various cultures. People's definitions of healthy and sick are closely linked to a society's level of wealth and technology and its ability to meet the health needs of its population.

2 In the United States, as in other countries, what is considered healthy is closely tied to cultural values and definitions of what is normal. Conversely, sickness often is linked to attributes and conditions deemed undesirable. The historical development of attitudes toward cigarette smoking and its link to illnesses illustrates how changing values affect attitudes toward health issues. Epidemiologists study the distribution of health and disease and show that health varies by age, sex, race, ethnicity, and socioeconomic status. Social attitudes toward health have led to a wellness movement in the United States, and victims of certain diseases, especially AIDS, have been stigmatized because of fear, anxiety, and the phenomenon of blaming the victim for his or her condition. Health and illness are closely linked to a person's identity. Sometimes individuals assume a sick role, which affects their self-concept.

3 Medicine and health care represent institutionalized efforts to combat disease and maintain a society's health. They vary cross-culturally in philosophy, form, and content, from heavy dependence on mysticism and magic to reliance on highly sophisticated scientific procedures and technology. Japan, Sweden, Norway, Great Britain, and the United States offer contrasting examples of medicine and health care.

4 The United States is committed to scientific medicine, which is dominated by the AMA and characterized by specialization. These facts, coupled with mass media influence, have contributed to an increasing medicalization of life activities not previously associated with medicine and health care. Most Americans believe there is a crisis in American health care, but this crisis is viewed quite differently from the functionalist, conflict, and interactionist perspectives. There have always been forms of medicine and health care that are alternatives to the dominant scientific approach, and recent decades have seen increased acceptance of some of these unorthodox approaches. Especially popular is the holistic approach, which emphasizes the prevention of disease and illness and which incorporates the patient fully into his or her own health care.

5 Current trends and patterns in medicine and health care indicate that research and technology will play an even more important role in medicine and health care in the future. Sociologists whose teaching and study center on medicine and health care are encouraged to rethink their approach and to emphasize the human dimension of medicine and health care.

Key Terms

AIDS (p. 523)
disease (p. 516)
epidemiology (p. 520)
health (p. 516)
health-care system (p. 526)
health maintenance organization
    (HMO) (p. 540)
infant mortality rate (p. 516)

integrative medicine (holistic
    medicine) (p. 539)
life expectancy (p. 520)
medicalization (p. 531)
medical sociology (p. 520)
medicine (p. 526)
morbidity (p. 520)
mortality (p. 520)

passing (p. 524)
preferred-provider organization
    (PPO) (p. 540)
sick role (p. 524)
socialized medicine (p. 528)
specialization (medical) (p. 530)
wellness movement (p. 522)

Chapter 19

Population, Urbanization, and Ecology

"The chief obstacle to the progress of the human race is the human race."

—Don Marquis

*I*magine your whole world crashing down on you: your home demolished, pets lost, personal possessions damaged, ravaged, or destroyed; neighbors, friends, and perhaps family members killed—your life forever changed in a matter of moments. The people along the Gulf Coast of the United States do not have to imagine such a horrible nightmare. In August 2005, Hurricane Katrina barreled across the coastlines of Louisiana, Mississippi, and Alabama leaving in its wake over 1,800 people dead and over $75 billion in property damage. Entire cities disappeared; schools, hospitals, municipal buildings, supermarkets, and locally owned businesses and industries ceased operation— some never to be reopened. Thousands fortunate enough not to lose their lives, lost their livelihoods. Hurricane Katrina and its aftermath, like most natural disasters, seemed inexplicable and unavoidable, but as we know well by now, *things are not necessarily what they seem.*

In Chapter 7, we looked at how Hurricane Katrina exposed America's social stratification system and class differences, but those are not the only sociological lessons to be learned from such a disaster. The breached levees, flooding, looting, price gouging, and perhaps even the ferocity of the hurricane itself, were as much social disasters as a natural one, and they involve the three components of this chapter: population, urbanization, and environment. People band together in tribes, villages, towns, and cities to increase their personal safety, to have access to goods and services, and to enhance the quality of their lives. Ironically, the same forces that bring people together—population growth, urbanization, and technology that alters the environment—may also threaten the quality of life, and life itself. Take the city of New Orleans, for

DEMOGRAPHY
The scientific study of the size, composition, distribution, and changes in human population.

FERTILITY
The extent of reproduction in a society.

MORTALITY
Death

CRUDE BIRTHRATE
The number of live births per year for every 1,000 people in a specific population.

CRUDE DEATH RATE
The number of deaths per year for every 1,000 people in a specific population.

MIGRATION
Population movement across political boundaries.

MIGRATION RATE
The number of emigrants (people leaving a country) subtracted from the number of immigrants (those entering it) per 1,000 population.

Hurricane Katrina showed what can happen when increased population and urbanization disrupt natural ecosystems. New Orleans is often described as the "city built in a bowl," and Katrina reminded the world that human engineering and technology is sometimes no match for nature's more powerful forces.

example. Built in a "bowl," 80 percent of New Orleans population lies below sea level along Lake Pontchartrain. FEMA officials and the Army Corps of Engineers had warned for decades that a direct strike from a hurricane that was category 3 or higher (Katrina was a category 5) might breach the levies or produce a storm surge that would sweep over the tops of the levees and flood the entire city (Drye, 2005). Scientists also warned that fluorocarbon emissions and other technological developments were depleting the ozone layer, which cause ocean temperatures to rise, resulting in much stronger, longer lasting, and more intense tropical storms and hurricanes (Schwartz, 2006). Hurricane Katrina illustrates how altering the natural environment to accommodate growing populations and urban development can have devastating consequences.

Sociologically, important questions arise from such a disaster. Can humans propagate the species, live together in large urban areas, and learn to live in harmony with the environment? Or are we destined to destroy ourselves through overpopulation, massive urbanization, and the accompanying problems of poverty, disease, crime, stress, and destruction of the ecosystem? In this chapter we explore population growth and the growth of cities and how urban sociology and human ecology study problems related to urbanization and the environment. Finally, we look to the future and explore sociological aspects of population, urbanization, and ecology in the twenty-first century. Let's begin by looking at demography and how sociologists study population.

DEMOGRAPHY AND GLOBAL POPULATION

Sociologists are keenly interested in **demography,** *the scientific study of the size, composition, distribution, and changes in human population.* These factors have far-reaching consequences for the quality of human life:

> Lines at the supermarket, the price of gas at the pump, the chances that you will marry, have children, and divorce, the kind of housing you find, the choices that you might have for a mid-life career change, and the kind of social support you can expect in old age are only a few examples of the tremendously broad demographic foundation of our lives. (Weeks, 1999:4)

Demographers are interested in a number of population factors, but they concentrate on fertility, mortality, migration, and population composition and density.

Fertility, Mortality, and Migration

Fertility is *the extent of reproduction in a society.* It is usually expressed as **crude birthrate,** *the number of live births per 1,000 people in a population per year.* With this standardized formula, we can compare countries or compare birthrates in a single country over time.

Demographers are also interested in **mortality,** or death. They calculate **crude death rate** as *the annual number of deaths per year for every 1,000 people in a specific population.*

Birthrates and death rates ignore the numbers of people who move from one place to another. To obtain these figures, demographers must look at **migration,** or *population movement across political boundaries.* Demographers calculate a **migration rate,** as *the number of emigrants (people leaving a country) subtracted from the number of* *immigrants (those entering it) per 1,000 population.* From a sociological viewpoint, migration rates depend on two interacting factors. *Push factors* are undesirable events or situations, such as droughts, famines, plagues, and political, economic, and social upheaval. These encourage people to leave a country for a better life elsewhere. Conversely, *pull factors* attract people. These may include enhanced economic prospects, political and religious freedom, and aesthetic and creature comfort factors, such as climate, landscape, and amenities. Map 19.1 shows annual natural changes in the global population.

Population Composition and Density

Demographers do not simply count people; they are also concerned about how population factors affect people's lives. Two factors are of particular interest to sociologists. The **composition of a population** refers to *the numbers and types of people, classified by characteristics such as age, sex, race, and ethnicity.* **Population density** describes *how a population is dispersed geographically (e.g., the number of people per square mile).*

One of the simplest measures of population composition is the **sex ratio,** *the number of males per 100 females.* In most countries the sex ratio is below 100 because women have longer life expectancies than men. In the United States the sex ratio is approximately 95, indicating that there are about 95 males for every 100 females.

The age composition of the population is undergoing dramatic changes. The fact that the worldwide population is becoming increasingly aged is more than an interesting demographic fact. In the United States, for example, more people are entering the over-65 age bracket, and the elderly will soon become the single largest population category. As we noted in Chapter 12, this demographic shift has created increased demands and

COMPOSITION OF A POPULATION
The numbers and types of people, classified by characteristics such as age, sex, race, and ethnicity.

POPULATION DENSITY
How a population is dispersed geographically (e.g., the number of people per square mile).

SEX RATIO
The number of males per 100 females.

Why are demographers and sociologists interested in these statistics? What important information about population does this map reveal?

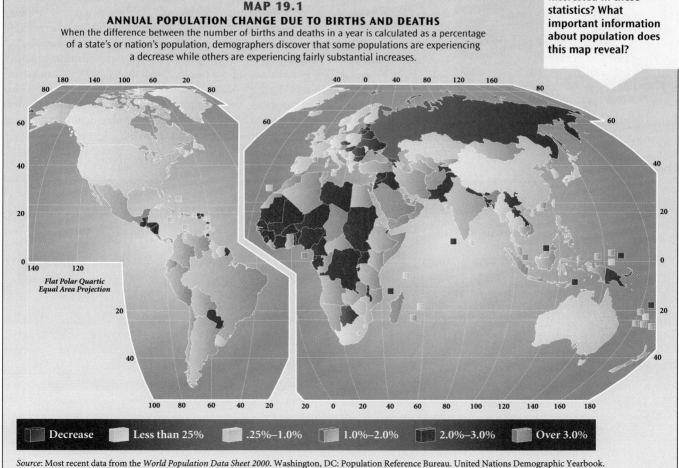

MAP 19.1
ANNUAL POPULATION CHANGE DUE TO BIRTHS AND DEATHS
When the difference between the number of births and deaths in a year is calculated as a percentage of a state's or nation's population, demographers discover that some populations are experiencing a decrease while others are experiencing fairly substantial increases.

Flat Polar Quartic Equal Area Projection

Decrease | Less than 25% | .25%–1.0% | 1.0%–2.0% | 2.0%–3.0% | Over 3.0%

Source: Most recent data from the *World Population Data Sheet 2000.* Washington, DC: Population Reference Bureau. United Nations Demographic Yearbook. Statistical Abstract of the United States. Canada Yearbook. Census of Australia. Demographic Yearbook of Russia. Update: U.S. Census Bureau, Statistical Abstract of the United States, 2006.

problems related to health care, Social Security, housing, and other social issues regarding the elderly.

When combined, data on age and sex characteristics provide a wealth of demographic and social information about a given population. This information is often expressed in an age-sex pyramid. Figure 19.1 depicts an age-sex pyramid for the United States and a typical developing country.

POPULATION GROWTH

The world's population stands at over 6.5 billion people, and it is increasing by nearly 90 million a year, with over 250,000 babies born every day (World Health Organization, 2006). Population growth is of major concern to sociologists because many believe that as the number of people on the planet increases the quality of life goes down. Figure 19.2 illustrates the dramatic nature of world population growth.

Growth Rates and Doubling Time

Population **growth rate** is *the difference between the numbers of people added to and subtracted from a particular population,* expressed in annual percentages. In most industrialized nations today the population growth rate is less than 1 percent; in many developing nations it is over 3 percent. Worldwide, birthrates are declining, but the population is growing at an annual rate of approximately 1.6 percent (Cone, 1999; World Health Organization, 2006).

Growth rate figures do not tell the whole story; another important measure of population growth is its **doubling time,** *the number of years it takes for a population to double in size.* The United States will double its current population in roughly 90 years, reaching 500 million around the end of the twenty-first century. A country with a 1 percent growth rate will double its population in approximately 70 years and a country with a 2 percent growth rate in about 35 years. Kenya, with a growth rate of 4.2 percent, will double its current population of 24 million in less than 17 years. If current trends continue, 82 countries will double their populations in 30 years or less. The world's population has doubled over the past 40 years, and at current rates could double again in the next half-century (Mitchell, 1998; World Health Organization, 2006).

What do age-sex population pyramids tell us about a country?

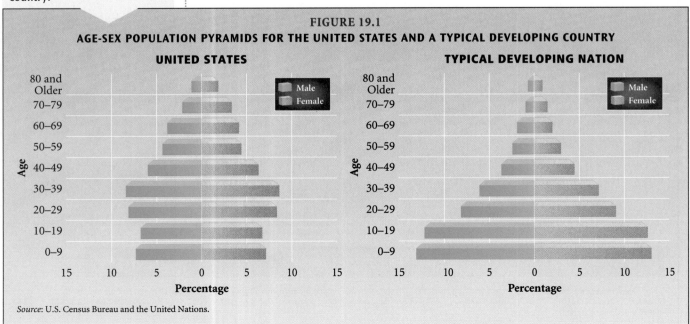

FIGURE 19.1

AGE-SEX POPULATION PYRAMIDS FOR THE UNITED STATES AND A TYPICAL DEVELOPING COUNTRY

Source: U.S. Census Bureau and the United Nations.

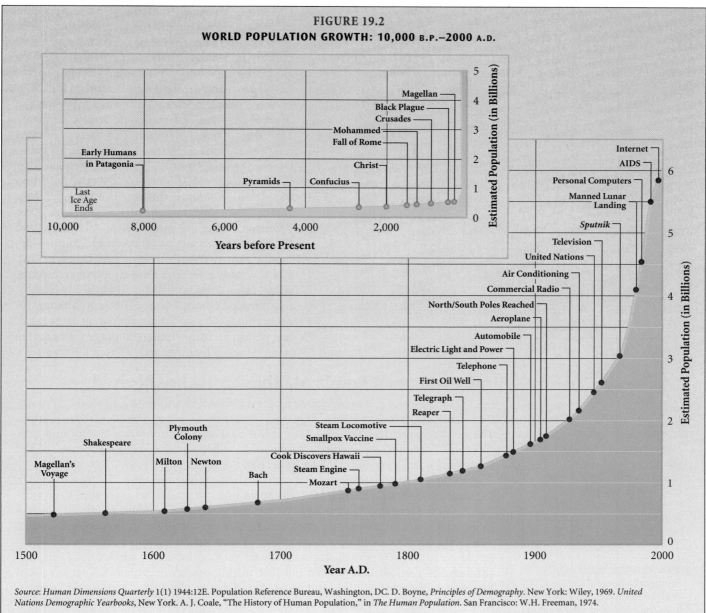

FIGURE 19.2
WORLD POPULATION GROWTH: 10,000 B.P.–2000 A.D.

Source: *Human Dimensions Quarterly* 1(1) 1944:12E. Population Reference Bureau, Washington, DC. D. Boyne, *Principles of Demography*. New York: Wiley, 1969. *United Nations Demographic Yearbooks*, New York. A. J. Coale, "The History of Human Population," in *The Human Population*. San Francisco: W.H. Freeman, 1974.

Many people are alarmed by current growth rates and doubling times. They fear that unless steps are taken to further curb birthrates around the world, the quality of life on the planet will decline. Such thinking is not new; it can be traced to one of the earliest theories of population growth.

Malthusian Theory

Perhaps the first important theory to explain population growth was proposed by Thomas Malthus in 1798. Malthus argued that the most critical factor in population growth is the available food supply; he warned that when population growth outstrips a nation's ability to feed its people, social chaos will reign. He predicted that the food supply would grow arithmetically, that is, in an additive fashion, in standard increments. Population, on the other hand, grows geometrically, in an exponential fashion. This means that in a given time frame the food supply increases or is added to, while the population has multiplied—doubled, tripled, or quadrupled (see Figure 19.3). In this way, the population outpaces the available food supply.

GROWTH RATE
The difference between the numbers of people added to and subtracted from a particular population.

DOUBLING TIME
The number of years it takes for a population to double in size.

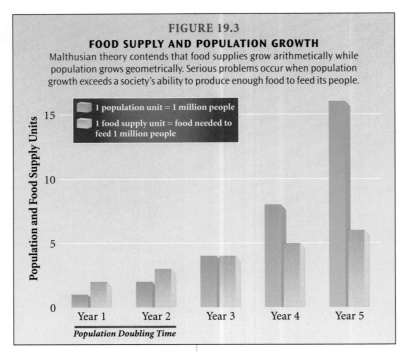

FIGURE 19.3

FOOD SUPPLY AND POPULATION GROWTH

Malthusian theory contends that food supplies grow arithmetically while population grows geometrically. Serious problems occur when population growth exceeds a society's ability to produce enough food to feed its people.

Population and Food Supply Units

- 1 population unit = 1 million people
- 1 food supply unit = food needed to feed 1 million people

15

10

5

0

Year 1   Year 2   Year 3   Year 4   Year 5

Population Doubling Time

Malthus reasoned that the population would outgrow the food supply unless *preventive checks,* such as delayed marriage or celibacy, intervened. Otherwise, Malthus predicted, *positive checks,* such as war, plagues, and famine, would bring population growth and the food supply more in line.

Some people rejected Malthusian theory as the "dismal theorem," but many demographers contend that it may be sound. The theory remains untested because unforeseen factors intervened to change the population-to-food supply equation in Western Europe. Malthus could not have predicted the massive migration during the early nineteenth century that sent millions of Europeans to other countries, including Australia, South Africa, and the United States, nor advances in agriculture during the early twentieth century that increased crop yields enormously. The food supply increased, in some cases, exponentially, not additively. Finally, modifications in cultural values and changes in economic factors no longer encourage large families, and an increased understanding of conception and contraception allows people to marry, be sexually active, and yet limit family size.

The Population Bomb: Malthusian Theory Revived

In 1968, Paul Ehrlich, a professor of biology at Stanford University, wrote *The Population Bomb,* a book that earned him the reputation of being a modern-day Malthus. The book's cover depicted an infant inside a glass "bomb" with a lit fuse and proclaimed, "While you are reading these words five people, mostly children, have died of starvation—and forty more babies have been born."

Although more scientifically and statistically sophisticated, Ehrlich's thesis is much the same as Malthus's. Ehrlich (1971:3) noted that "no matter how you slice it, population is a numbers game," and as far as he was concerned, the numbers predicted a dismal future unless drastic measures were taken. Ehrlich calculated that if trends continued, in over 900 years the earth's population would grow to 60 million billion people. This would be "about 100 persons for each square yard of the earth's surface, land and sea" (Ehrlich, 1971:4). Ehrlich pointed out that world population growth has far outpaced increases in food production, and he predicted that by the 1990s there would be thousands of deaths due to starvation and malnutrition. Ehrlich went beyond Malthusian theory by insisting the problem is more than a matter of food production and population growth; he noted that the quality of the environment, especially the availability of clean air and water, is also an important variable.

ZERO POPULATION GROWTH (ZPG)
An organization dedicated to reaching the population replacement level of approximately two children per family.

Overpopulation and the depletion of natural resources have contributed to starvation in many developing nations.

Zero Population Growth   Ehrlich offered his own version of preventive checks to control population growth. His primary recommendation was the implementation of government policies to limit population growth, and he encouraged people to join **Zero Population Growth (ZPG),** *an organization dedicated to reaching the population replacement level of approximately two children per family.*

Although the U.S. government has not been aggressive in curbing population growth, organizations such as ZPG and Planned Parenthood promote birth control, and large segments of the American public (especially the middle class) have internalized the goals of ZPG. In fact, the United States and parts of Western Europe have reached the overall goal of population replacement, averaging approximately 1.8–2.1 children per family.

The Population Explosion   Paul Ehrlich teamed with his wife, sociologist Anne Ehrlich, to write *The Population Explosion* (1990), which declares that the population bomb has been detonated. The Ehrlichs pointed out that although birthrates have declined in many industrialized nations, worldwide population growth is still out of control. Moreover, while each year brings almost 100 million more mouths to be fed, there are "hundreds of billions fewer tons of topsoil and hundreds of trillions fewer gallons of groundwater" than existed in 1968, when Ehrlich sounded his initial alarm (Ehrlich and Ehrlich, 1990:9).

In a later work, the Ehrlichs contend that today's world population figure of 6 billion is about three times the "optimal" number, and has taken and will continue to take a severe toll on the world's nonrenewable natural resources, the environment, and even the climate (Ehrlich and Ehrlich, 2006).

The president of the Population Institute echoed the Ehrlichs' concerns:

> The world has a built-in demographic time bomb. Three billion people, the equivalent of the entire population on this planet as recently as 1960, will enter their childbearing years within the next generation. (Fornos, 1997:1)

Others are not so bleak. The theory of demographic transition, for example, offers an alternative to the Malthusian model.

The Theory of Demographic Transition

The **demographic transition theory** contends that *population growth develops through three distinct stages: high birth and death rates; high birthrates and low death rates; low birth and death rates.* Figure 19.4 depicts the stages of demographic transition.

Stage 1   Stage 1 is characterized by high birthrates and high death rates. This stage is illustrated by Colonial America, when it was not unusual for women to bear 13 or 14 children. Because of high infant mortality rates and the toll of infectious diseases, however, half or fewer of these children reached adulthood. Life expectancies were short, so despite high birthrates, the high death rates kept population growth at a stable level.

DEMOGRAPHIC TRANSITION THEORY
Population growth develops through three distinct stages: (1) high birth and death rates, (2) high birthrates and low death rates, and (3) low birth and death rates.

Stage 2   Stage 2 is marked by high birthrates and low death rates. The United States during the onset of industrialization typified a country in stage 2. Cultural values still encouraged large families, and women continued to bear many children. Because of reduced infant mortality rates, however, more of those children survived to have children, and at the same time life expectancy steadily increased. Fortunately, the United States had vast land areas where its population could expand.

Stage 3   Eventually, the United States entered stage 3 of demographic transition, which is characterized by low birthrates and low death rates. In complex industrialized societies, large families impede geographic mobility, and children often become economic liabilities. Also there tends to be widespread information about and accessibility to birth control. Consequently, values change, encouraging parents to have only a few children. Nations in stage 3 experience moderate levels of population growth.

Demographic transition theory implies that eventually all countries will progress through all three stages. While it is far more optimistic about population growth than Malthusian theory, until the final

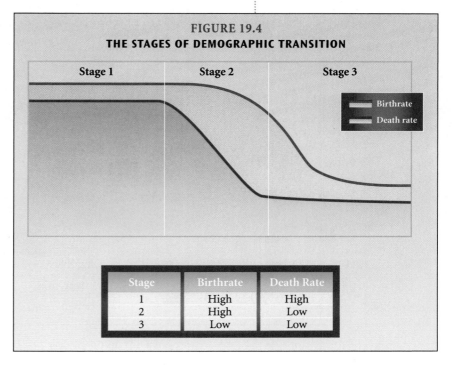

FIGURE 19.4
THE STAGES OF DEMOGRAPHIC TRANSITION

Stage	Birthrate	Death Rate
1	High	High
2	High	Low
3	Low	Low

transition is made population trends portend dire consequences. In the meantime, because so many countries are caught in the demographic trap of stage 2, millions of people die of starvation and disease as population outstrips the available land, pure water, and food supplies. Nevertheless, research indicates that as these less-developed countries experience modernization, there is a general decline in birth and death rates, thus lending support to demographic transition theory (Crenshaw et al., 2000).

Population Growth in the United States

Benjamin Franklin estimated in 1751 that America's population was doubling approximately every 25 years. He remarked that if population expansion continued at such a high rate, "The greatest number of Englishmen will be on this side [of] the water" (Divine et al., 2005:96).

From the Colonial Years to World War II Accurate population data for the American colonies are difficult to ascertain; it was not until 1790 that the first systematic census was taken. Thereafter it has been taken every 10 years. Since the first official Census, which counted 3.9 million Americans, the U.S. population has expanded continuously (see Figure 19.5). It grew quite rapidly at first, almost doubling by 1810 and almost tripling, to approximately 9.6 million, by 1820 (Nam and Gustavus, 1976). By 1900, the U.S. population had reached 76.2 million; then growth rates dropped, reaching an all-time low during the Great Depression of the 1930s.

The Post–World War II Baby Boom The years following World War II witnessed a demographic anomaly in the United States: the baby boom. Birthrates jumped dramatically during the late 1940s and 1950s. In 1950, the U.S. population numbered over 150 million for the first time. The **baby boomers,** *the age cohort in the United States comprising those born roughly between 1945 and 1964,* continue to leave an indelible mark on society as they progress through the life stages. During the late 1960s and early 1970s, demographers recorded another noticeable increase in birthrates (although smaller than the original baby boom) as the baby boomers began having children. The

BABY BOOMERS
The age cohort in the United States comprising those born roughly between 1945 and 1964.

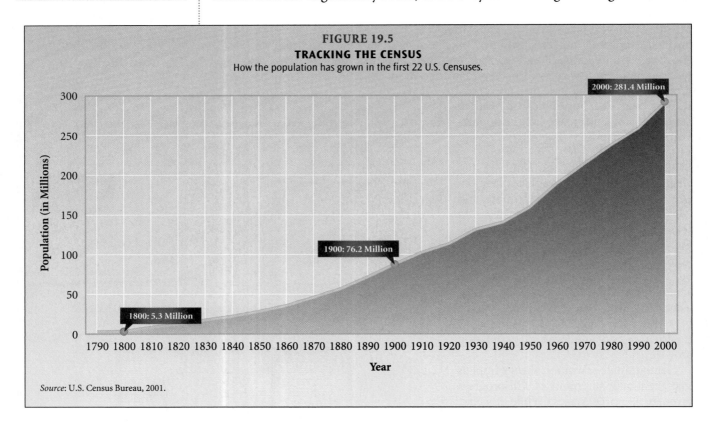

FIGURE 19.5
TRACKING THE CENSUS
How the population has grown in the first 22 U.S. Censuses.

2000: 281.4 Million

1900: 76.2 Million

1800: 5.3 Million

Source: U.S. Census Bureau, 2001.

media dubbed this demographic event the *baby boom echo,* but by the 1980s, birthrates had once again declined.

2000 and Beyond   The 2000 Census officially counted (281,463,269) Americans—a 13.2 percent increase over the 1990 Census figure (U.S. Bureau of the Census, 2000). Map 19.2 shows the percent change in population for the 50 states, the District of Columbia, and Puerto Rico from 1990 to 2000. In 2006, U.S. population reached over 298 million and is projected to surpass 300 million soon (WHO, 2006).

Social scientists also point out that even though America's population growth may be in check, our sheer numbers, especially in light of our lifestyle, pose an ecological problem. For example, despite accounting for slightly less than 6 percent of the world's population, the United States consumes more than one-third of the world's energy and produces one-half of all pollution. From an ecological viewpoint, this makes population control even more important in the United States than in developing countries. The average U.S. citizen consumes over 50 times as much as the average Kenyan, thus making the prevention of an unwanted birth in the United States 50 times more important in terms of global impact than the prevention of one birth in Kenya (Porritt, 1991).

Rapid population growth is accompanied by a variety of social developments. Among them are the increasing importance of cities and the process of urbanization.

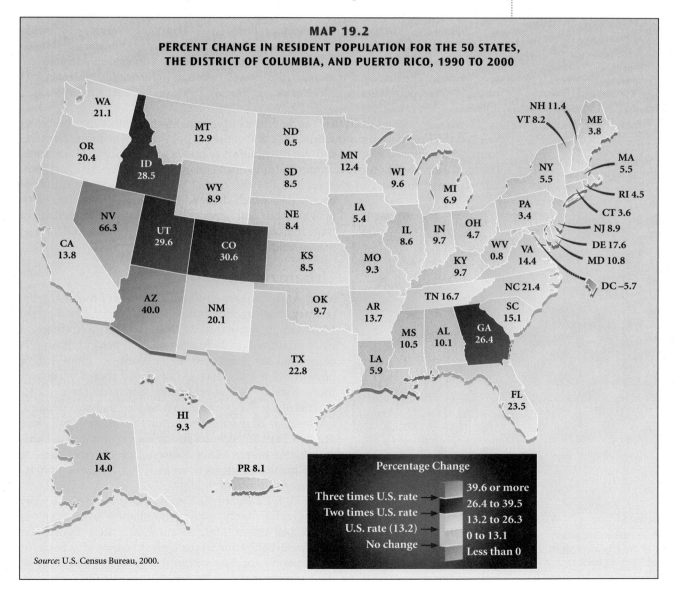

MAP 19.2

PERCENT CHANGE IN RESIDENT POPULATION FOR THE 50 STATES, THE DISTRICT OF COLUMBIA, AND PUERTO RICO, 1990 TO 2000

WA 21.1 · OR 20.4 · MT 12.9 · ND 0.5 · MN 12.4 · WI 9.6 · MI 6.9 · NH 11.4 · VT 8.2 · ME 3.8 · MA 5.5 · RI 4.5 · CT 3.6 · NY 5.5 · ID 28.5 · SD 8.5 · WY 8.9 · NE 8.4 · IA 5.4 · IL 8.6 · IN 9.7 · OH 4.7 · PA 3.4 · NJ 8.9 · DE 17.6 · MD 10.8 · NV 66.3 · UT 29.6 · CO 30.6 · KS 8.5 · MO 9.3 · KY 9.7 · WV 0.8 · VA 14.4 · DC −5.7 · CA 13.8 · AZ 40.0 · NM 20.1 · OK 9.7 · AR 13.7 · TN 16.7 · NC 21.4 · SC 15.1 · MS 10.5 · AL 10.1 · GA 26.4 · TX 22.8 · LA 5.9 · FL 23.5 · HI 9.3 · AK 14.0 · PR 8.1

Percentage Change

Three times U.S. rate → 39.6 or more
Two times U.S. rate → 26.4 to 39.5
U.S. rate (13.2) → 13.2 to 26.3
No change → 0 to 13.1
Less than 0

Source: U.S. Census Bureau, 2000.

THE GROWTH OF CITIES AND URBANIZATION

The dominance of cities is relatively recent. Yet, cities have been in existence for approximately 9,000–10,000 years, and human cultural development is directly linked to them. In fact, the word *civilization* comes from the Latin *civis,* which means "a person living in a city."

The Rise of Cities

Even though much of the world's population remains rural, when human accomplishments are chronicled it is the cities that capture the most attention. The first cities developed in the fertile valley of the Tigris and Euphrates Rivers, and cities formed along the Indus River and parts of ancient China as much as 4,000 years ago. These cities resembled overgrown villages of 5,000–10,000 people more than modern-day cities (Schwab, 1982). Nevertheless, these early population centers served many of the same functions that contemporary cities do, including providing a centralized government, property rights, an expanded division of labor, and a relatively stable market for the exchange of goods and services. Important empires throughout the world were marked by the growth of cities. In ancient times, while Greek citizens lived throughout the countryside, the cities of Athens and Sparta epitomized Greek life, and they are still remembered for their contributions to Western culture. As populations have grown throughout the world, cities have increased in importance. In 1950, less than 30 percent of the world's population lived in cities; in the twenty-first century, that percentage has already risen to just under one-half; and the United Nations and Population Institute predict that, by the year 2025, for the first time in human history well over half (approximately 60 percent) of the world's population will live in cities (Fornos, 1997; Hall, 2002; Knight Ridder, 2006).

The rise of cities is linked to (1) agricultural improvements that reduce the number of workers needed in food production; (2) stabilization of political and economic institutions, which enhances safety and the distribution of goods and services; (3) improvements in transportation and communication, which enhance trade and social interaction among large numbers of people; and (4) the rise of industrial and postindustrial economies, which demand concentrated populations to provide labor and services. As cities grow and increase in importance society undergoes the powerful social force of urbanization.

Urbanization

Many Americans have romantic notions of moving to the country to escape the hustle and bustle of city life (see Focus box 19.1), but the United States is becoming increasingly urbanized. In 1790, only about 5 percent of Americans lived in cities and fewer than 25 cities had a population of more than 25,000. Two hundred years later those figures had substantially changed. Over three-fourths of the U.S. population now lives in towns or cities, and another 20 percent live within the sphere of influence of a city. The United States clearly has experienced **urbanization,** *the movement of masses of people from rural to urban areas and an increase in urban influence over all spheres of culture and society.*

The U.S. Bureau of the Census continues to classify any demographic entity with a population over 2,500 as urban and under 2,500 as rural, but these figures are almost meaningless in understanding urbanization in the United States today. Sociologists recognize that the number of people residing within the political boundaries of cities is less important than the complex communication, transportation, economic, and social networks that link people in cities and towns to those in suburbs and sur-

---

URBANIZATION
The movement of masses of people from rural to urban areas and an increase in urban influence over all spheres of culture and society.

Author and naturalist Henry David Thoreau's cabin in the idyllic setting of Walden Pond in Concord, Massachusetts, represents the fantasy of many urbanites who long to escape crowds and polluted cities for the peacefulness and solitude of nature. Thoreau lived in his cabin for only 2 years and 2 months, however, before moving back to the city to write *Walden.*

Why do so many urbanites return to the city after short stints of "getting back to nature"?

In the preface of *The Pursuit of Loneliness,* Philip Slater tells of a man who so desperately wanted to escape the hassles of overpopulation and urban life that he went to live alone in the forest, where he built a small hut. The man loved the peace and solitude, but when summer came, he cursed the heat and the bitter harshness of the elements. He made a small garden and kept a few chickens, and all was well until the food in his garden attracted rabbits that stole his produce. So he trapped a fox and taught it to catch the rabbits. Unfortunately, the fox also developed a fondness for the man's chickens, so he eventually shot the fox and cursed all animals.

Because he threw garbage on the floor, his hut swarmed with vermin. To alleviate the problem, the man suspended his waste from the ceiling, but because of the weight and strain, the roof collapsed, forcing him to leave his home and build a new one. One day while visiting a village, the man boasted of the beauty and peacefulness of his forest home. Impressed by his description, several villagers visited there for picnics and hunting excursions. This angered the man, so he posted "No Trespassing" signs and shot at sightseers who invaded his privacy.

Out of revenge, boys from the village sneaked around the man's hut at night to vandalize his property and steal from him. The man decided to sleep with a loaded shotgun, but he then accidentally shot himself in the foot. This made the villagers very fearful, and they decided to leave him alone. Crippled and isolated, the man became extremely lonely and depressed and cursed the unfriendliness of the villagers as he yearned for human companionship.

In some ways, the experiences of the man in Slater's story reflect the history of humankind and the problems we face in trying to live together, yet have peace and solitude, and in trying to live in harmony with nature, yet at the same time conquer and manipulate it. Ironically, many Americans who yearn to "get away from it all" often end up taking much of "it" with them.

TAKING A CLOSER LOOK

How does the mythical character in Slater's book reflect contemporary American values, attitudes, and beliefs? Why do so many urban Americans dream of escaping it all? Why is it so difficult to fulfill that dream? What is the message behind Slater's story for us in the twenty-first century?

Source: Philip Slater. *The Pursuit of Loneliness.* Boston: Beacon Press, 1976.

---

rounding rural areas. Acknowledging this fact, the U.S. Bureau of the Census collects and analyzes data from **metropolitan statistical areas (MSAs),** *a city, or a city and its surrounding suburbs, with a population of 50,000 or more.* The Census Bureau refers to *the largest MSAs (those containing over a million people)* as **consolidated metropolitan statistical areas (CMSAs).**

The Metropolis, the Megalopolis, and the Suburbs

From the beginning of the twentieth century through the mid-1960s, urbanization patterns reflected a steady migration from rural to urban areas. Since the mid-1960s, however, while cities have continued to grow, most migration has been into the fringe areas around major cities. The traditional concept of the city grew inadequate to describe American urbanization, and the newer term *metropolis* was coined to describe the bulging urban areas that were once cities.

The Metropolis   A **metropolis** is *a major urban area that includes a large central city surrounded by several smaller incorporated cities and suburbs that join to form one large recognizable municipality.* The greater metropolitan area of New York City, for example, has a population of over 16 million and includes people who live in the city's five boroughs—Manhattan, the Bronx, Brooklyn, Queens, and Staten Island—as well as surrounding suburbs in Long Island and Westchester Counties and in the states of Connecticut and New Jersey. Similarly, Los Angeles has absorbed the communities of Anaheim, Beverly Hills, and several other satellite cities; today metropolitan Los Angeles includes over nine separate cities and 60 self-governing communities. Even the Dallas metroplex, which cherishes its Western tradition and rural roots, boasts a population of well over a million and includes the cities of Garland, Mesquite, Irving, Arlington, Plano, and Las Colinas, to mention only a few, as part of its greater metropolitan area.

METROPOLITAN STATISTICAL AREAS (MSAS)
A city, or a city and its surrounding suburbs, with a population of 50,000 or more.

CONSOLIDATED METROPOLITAN STATISTICAL AREAS (CMSAS)
The largest MSAs (those containing over a million people).

METROPOLIS
A major urban area that includes a large central city surrounded by several smaller incorporated cities and suburbs that join to form one large recognizable municipality.

The Megalopolis As major metropolitan areas have continued to absorb smaller surrounding cities, an even larger urban unit has developed. The **megalopolis** consists of *two or more major metropolitan areas linked politically, economically, socially, and geographically.* Along the Eastern Seaboard, a chain of hundreds of cities and suburbs now stretches from Boston through Washington, D.C., to Richmond, Virginia, in an almost continuous urban sprawl (see Map 19.3). Similarly, much of Florida is almost one continuous city, from Jacksonville through Tampa to Miami. Dallas and Fort Worth, once two distinct cities 30 miles apart, are now linked by an international airport and a nearly unbroken band of businesses, industries, and suburban communities. Urban sprawl joins Chicago to Pittsburgh. Along the West Coast, a huge megalopolis stretches from San Diego through Los Angeles and up to San Francisco and Oakland, with only a few breaks. Migration patterns reflect a move from older cities in the Northeast (sometimes dubbed the rust belt because of its decaying factories) to cities in the sun belt of the South and the Southwest. In fact, over half the U.S. population growth during the 1980s and 1990s occurred in three states: California, Texas, and Florida. It is predicted that if those trends continue even more megalopolises or "supercities" will emerge in the sun belt states.

The Suburbs Prior to World War II, less than one-fifth of the U.S. population lived in **suburbs,** *residential areas surrounding cities, which expand urban lifestyles into previously rural areas.* By 2000, however, half of all Americans could be classified as suburbanites. The rush to the suburbs by urban dwellers and rural residents alike can be explained by several factors. After World War II, Americans wanted to raise the families they had deferred during the Great Depression and the war—and they produced a huge baby boom and a demand for housing. The expansion of interstate highway systems, including loops around major cities, made it easier for disenchanted city dwellers to leave the congestion of the city and move into surrounding neighborhoods, from which they could easily commute to their jobs. The shortage of desirable housing in many cities, combined with rapid economic expansion and the availability of cheap land, government-subsidized loans, and moderately priced housing in outlying areas, made

MEGALOPOLIS
Two or more major metropolitan areas linked politically, economically, socially, and geographically.

SUBURBS
Residential areas surrounding cities, which expand urban lifestyles into previously rural areas.

Do you anticipate more or fewer megalopolises? What areas are most likely to experience this type of urban growth?

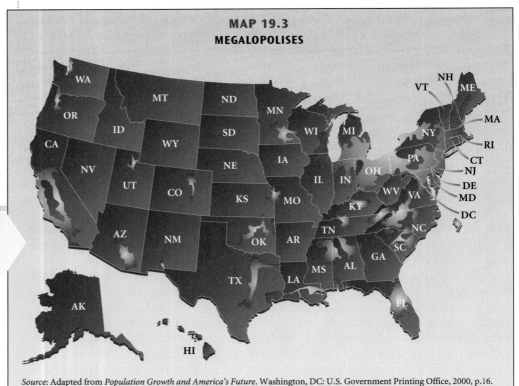

MAP 19.3
MEGALOPOLISES

Source: Adapted from *Population Growth and America's Future.* Washington, DC: U.S. Government Printing Office, 2000, p.16.

suburban living attractive and economically practical for working-class and middle-class families.

Another important variable was the idyllic stereotype of suburban living promoted by the mass media. According to television, motion pictures, and popular magazines, the suburbs provided all the amenities of urban life yet were far enough from the central city that people could avoid the hassles and problems of the city.

Problems in American Cities and Suburbs

Perhaps the greatest problem facing major cities is generating enough revenue to provide adequate services and protection for their residents. Suburban growth exacerbated the financial woes of many cities, because urban dwellers who leave the city limits reduce the city's property tax base and still demand services. Most cities raise taxes to compensate for shrinking revenues, but tax increases encourage more residents and businesses to flee the city and locate in the surrounding suburbs. For example, New York City residents have fled in large numbers to New Jersey, and the hardiest among them live as far away as eastern Pennsylvania, some 100 miles and two states away. This move out of the city has led New York City and other cities to institute "commuter taxes" to offset revenue losses.

"It's so lovely out here you wonder why they have it so far from the city."

Urban Decay and Poverty   Urban decay hits the central city as major businesses move from the downtown area to more profitable suburban locations. Old buildings often remain vacant and deteriorate or become multiple-unit slum housing, low-rent hotels, "adult" bookstores and theaters, centers for drug distribution and other criminal activities, and repositories for the urban homeless.

The 2000 Census revealed that over 32 million Americans, or over 12 percent, lived in poverty. While many of the poor reside in rural areas, the proportion of the urban poor increased between 1990 and 2000. Much urban poverty is a result of a growing urban underclass of poorly educated and unskilled minorities who lack the skills and education to make the transition from an industrial to a service economy.

Poverty is accompanied by other urban problems, especially chronic unemployment, homelessness, violent crimes, alcohol and drug abuse, suicide, terrorism, and other forms of deviance. While estimates vary from 500,000 to 1.5 million, a 1992 report indicated that "on any given night, up to 600,000 Americans are literally homeless" (Task Force, 1992). Today, most agree that may be a conservative estimate.

Revitalization Efforts   There have been numerous attempts to revitalize central cities. During the 1950s and 1960s, federal funding assisted many cities in urban renewal projects intended to clean up inner cities. Most of these projects involved razing dilapidated buildings and replacing them with modern high-rise office buildings and apartment complexes. Though these efforts seemed successful, they rarely solved the problems of inner-city decay. The street people, drug dealers, and prostitutes who had inhabited those areas did not disappear—either they were displaced to other parts of the cities or they vanished during the daytime and reappeared after dark.

In their effort to eliminate urban blight, city planners often ignored the fact that many inner-city areas provided an important ecological niche for minorities who had

Many cities have turned what were once rundown debilitated areas into attractive enclaves replete with upscale boutiques, restaurants, clubs, and apartment complexes.

What happens to the people and businesses that are displaced by urban renewal?

created their own cities in the form of ethnic enclaves. The razing of old tenement buildings and shops meant the destruction of meaningful social networks and communities that were "home" to thousands of urban residents.

During the 1970s and 1980s, several major cities embarked on rehabilitation programs, selling buildings in historical areas of the city (sometimes for as little as $1) with the requirement that the buyers renovate the buildings and either open shops or restaurants in them or convert them into single-family housing units and live in them. Conflict theorists point out that although such gentrification projects pump new life into a particular part of a city, they also contribute to overall woes by displacing many of the inner-city poor and adding to the number of homeless.

Urban distress is one of the most perplexing and challenging problems that city officials and residents face. A number of cities that attempted revitalization in the 1980s were heralded as "success stories" in the 1990s, but based on objective indicators of the economic and social well-being of their residents, with the possible exception of Atlanta, Baltimore, and Boston, there is no evidence that these cities have performed any better than other cities with similar problems that did not undergo revitalization. In fact, in some cases, the so-called revitalized cities have performed even worse (Wolman et al., 1994).

Urban sociologists as well as architectural historians and other experts on cities contend that revitalization of a city requires far more than simply the beautification and regentrification of its streets and buildings. Rather, for cities to be socially viable, they must not only have a solid infrastructure that meets all of the economic and political needs of their inhabitants, but they must also be able to take on an important sense of *place* in the hearts and souls of those who live there (Jacobs, 1992; Rykwert, 2000).

Problems in the 'Burbs The suburbs—once viewed as the great escape from the cities—are not immune to problems associated with urban living (see Focus box 19.2). As increasing numbers of people flee the cities, suburban areas are running out of affordable housing, and many building sites originally designated for single-family dwellings now contain apartment complexes and condominiums. Multiple-unit housing brings the traffic and noise associated with urban living. Moreover, as more members of racial and ethnic minorities move to the suburbs, once-homogeneous neighborhoods are encountering racial strife and religious controversies.

Real estate speculation, accompanied by the recession of the 1980s and the early 1990s, resulted in the bankruptcy of some large suburban shopping malls. Some suburban commercial districts mirror the urban decay of the central city. Suburban crime rates have also increased, especially the rates of property crimes such as burglary and vandalism. Many suburban neighborhoods grew up around small municipalities outside the main city, and their police forces and volunteer fire departments are ill equipped to handle the burgeoning growth of the suburbs. Likewise, many suburban schools are woefully overcrowded; their small tax base cannot support rapid enrollment growth.

These urban and suburban problems are the focus of two areas of specialization in sociology: urban sociology and human ecology.

URBAN SOCIOLOGY AND HUMAN ECOLOGY

Sociologists' interest in cities began with the inception of the discipline, but in 1929, Pitirim Sorokin and Carle Zimmerman (1929) identified the need for a specialty within general sociology to study cities. They created **urban sociology** *to identify, study, and explain the specific traits of urban social phenomena.* Even before the creation of urban sociology, however, sociologists compared and contrasted rural and urban societies.

Shortly after World War II, America's steady trend of urbanization was transformed into one of suburbanization as millions of families moved from the central cities to their edges and beyond, seeking what they hoped would be the best of both urban and rural living. Sociologists note that the new suburban lifestyle was accompanied by a barrage of new norms, values, attitudes, and beliefs to support it; and today, suburban sprawl continues to be one of the more powerful forces on the American social landscape.

Some view the massive suburbanization of America as the hallmark of social progress. People enjoy the freedom that suburban living provides. Mass migration to the suburbs may represent not only people's desire to leave the hustle and bustle of city life as well as the crime and pollution of cities, but also their attempts to express independence and mobility while exercising their basic property rights (Gordon and Richardson, 2000). In short, a move to the suburbs represents an attempt to realize what many view almost as a birthright: the "American Dream."

Critics of suburbanization view things differently. They contend that social civility has suffered as cities have declined and suburbs have prospered. Time that previously was spent interacting with other people is now spent in an automobile, driving to and from work, school, and social activities. And, as many can attest, people are not necessarily at their most civil when behind the wheel of an automobile. Moreover, some critics note, it doesn't take a sociology degree to predict the sort of culture that is created by suburban housing subdivisions where not only all the houses look alike, but because of pricing strategies, people are strictly segregated by income (Andres et al., 2000; Minerd, 2000).

TAKING A CLOSER LOOK

What has been the impact of suburbanization on American society? Does it represent social progress? Or are you more inclined to agree with its critics who view it as symptomatic of social decline? Can it be both?

Source: Duany Andres, Elizabeth Plater-Zyberk, and Jeff Speck. *Suburban Nation: The Rise of Sprawl and the Decline of the American Dream.* New York: North Point Press, 2000. Peter Gordon and Harry W. Richardson. *Critiquing Sprawl's Critics,* Washington, DC, Cato Institute, 2000. Jeff Minerd. "Impacts of Sprawl." *The Futurist* 34 (July–August), 2000:10–11.

Toennies's *Gemeinschaft* and *Gesellschaft*

Ferdinand Toennies developed a theoretical continuum to analyze the differences between rural and urban living. At one pole is *Gemeinschaft, a community characterized by a relatively small population, a simple division of labor, face-to-face interaction, and informal social control.* At the other end is *Gesellschaft, a society made up of a large population characterized by loose associations, a complex division of labor, secondary relationships, and formal social control.* According to Toennies ([1887] 1961), *Gemeinschaft* communities share a strong sense of community, common values, and a commitment to strive for the common good. Cities, on the other hand, tend to be *Gesellschaft* communities and more heterogeneous in values, with much less emphasis on common goals. Toennies's ideas influenced Durkheim and other European sociologists who sought to understand the social experiences of people undergoing the rapid industrialization that accompanied the Industrial Revolution.

Durkheim's Mechanical and Organic Solidarity

Borrowing from Toennies's theoretical continuum, Émile Durkheim ([1893] 1964) made a similar distinction between rural and urban societies, but he focused on social solidarity, or the extent to which members of a society are bound together. He believed that a society's social solidarity was based on its level of division of labor. In predominantly rural societies, where there is very little division of labor, people are bound together through **mechanical solidarity,** *characterized by tradition, unity, consensus of norms and values, and strong informal pressure to conform.* Durkheim contrasted this to highly diverse urban areas where people are bound by **organic solidarity,** *characterized by a highly sophisticated division of labor that makes individuals interdependent with one another.* Both Toennies's and Durkheim's ideas provided a theoretical foundation for urban and rural sociology in the United States; investigators focused on differences

GEMEINSCHAFT
A community characterized by a relatively small population, a simple division of labor, face-to-face interaction, and informal social control.

GESELLSCHAFT
A society made up of a large population characterized by loose associations, a complex division of labor, secondary relationships, and formal social control.

MECHANICAL SOLIDARITY
Characterized by tradition, unity, consensus of norms and values, and strong informal pressure to conform.

ORGANIC SOLIDARITY
Characterized by a highly sophisticated division of labor that makes individuals interdependent with one another.

between rural communities and urban areas and how these disparities affected basic social structure, institutions, and interaction.

Redfield's Folk and Urban Societies

Anthropologist Robert Redfield (1941) studied the peasants of Yucatan. Borrowing from Toennies and Durkheim, he developed a rural-urban continuum that distinguished between **folk societies,** which *emphasize tradition, consensus, and primary relationships,* and **urban societies,** *based on change, diversity, and secondary relationships.*

Urban studies in the United States gained momentum during the 1920s and 1930s and became closely identified with **human ecology,** *a subfield of sociology that focuses on recurring spatial, social, and cultural patterns within a particular social environment—* in this case, cities. Human ecologists view a city as an **ecosystem,** *a community of organisms sharing the same physical environment.* Spatial relations are the analytical basis for human ecology, which focuses on the physical shape of cities, the economic and social relations between cities, and social relations and interactions. The study of human ecology became synonymous with the Chicago School of sociology. Its founders and early proponents developed theories and applied them to urban studies, especially within their local sociological laboratory: the city of Chicago.

The Chicago School and Ecological Studies

The founder of the Chicago School of human ecology was Robert Ezra Park (1916), who joined the department of sociology and anthropology at the University of Chicago in 1914 and established a research agenda that dominated urban studies for decades. An influential work associated with the Chicago School was an essay by Louis Wirth entitled "Urbanism as a Way of Life." Influenced by Toennies's work, Wirth (1938) asserted that rather than being a simple reflection of a shift from rural to urban residency patterns, **urbanism** entailed *a way of life in which the city affects how people feel, think, and interact.* As noted earlier, urbanization refers to an increase in the proportion of people living in cities; *urbanism* reflects changes in attitudes, values, and lifestyles resulting from urbanization. According to Wirth, urbanism affects people negatively because the city's large size, high population density, and great heterogeneity lead to impersonality, anonymity, and such individual problems as loneliness, alcoholism, and suicide.

Some modern-day sociologists disagree with Wirth's assertions. They counter that large urban areas comprise a mosaic of smaller communities, fairly homogeneous neighborhoods characterized by shared values, strong interpersonal relationships, and common racial, ethnic, and socioeconomic identities. Such patterns of urban develop-

FOLK SOCIETIES
Emphasize tradition, consensus, and primary relationships.

URBAN SOCIETIES
Societies based on change, diversity, and secondary relationships.

HUMAN ECOLOGY
A subfield of sociology that focuses on recurring spatial, social, and cultural patterns within a particular social environment.

ECOSYSTEM
A community of organisms sharing the same physical environment.

URBANISM
A way of life in which the city affects how people feel, think, and interact.

An aerial view of Chicago shows the dynamic urban setting of the "Chicago School" of urban development and human ecology.

How did living and working in Chicago influence sociologists' view of how cities develop?

ment and their impact on the people who live in and around cities are of particular interest to sociologists.

The Concentric Zone Model

Ernest Burgess, a sociologist at the University of Chicago, was interested in how the ecological arrangement of cities affects the economic resources of groups and individuals and the degree to which people can profitably use urban space. He noticed that land use influences residential patterns and segregation based on race, social class, and other characteristics of people and places of business. According to Burgess's (1925) concentric zone model, cities develop in a series of zones represented by concentric circles radiating out from the central business district. Zone 1 is the central business district—the heart of the city and the center of distribution of goods and services; it is the location of important businesses, financial institutions, and retail outlets (see Figure 19.6).

Zone 2 is the zone of transition because it is subject to rapid social change. In many major cities, this area has been where immigrants first settled and established urban enclaves, such as a Chinatown or Little Sicily. Zone 2 often reflects the cultures of numerous foreign countries, and as a result of the marginality experienced by many of its inhabitants it is characterized by high rates of delinquency, crime, alcoholism, drug abuse, suicide, and other forms of deviant behavior. Factories also often locate in and around zone 2, adding increased rail and truck traffic, more transients, and pollution. The zone of transition is marked by urban decay, in part because speculators and absentee landlords who own the land and buildings there do not invest in their maintenance.

Factory workers and other blue-collar laborers live in zone 3, which contains residential hotels, apartments, trailer parks, and other working-class housing. As immigrants become assimilated, find jobs, and can afford permanent housing, they often move into zone 3.

Zone 4 is a middle-class and upper-class residential area. Since World War II, people living in zone 4 have found it

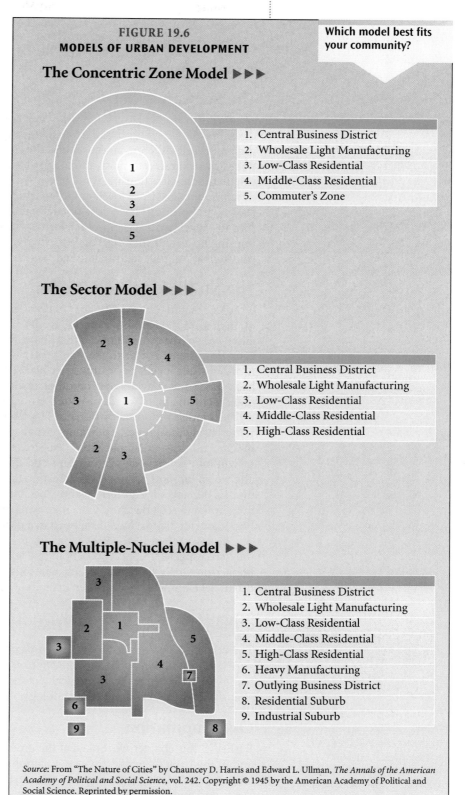

FIGURE 19.6
MODELS OF URBAN DEVELOPMENT

The Concentric Zone Model ▶▶▶

1. Central Business District
2. Wholesale Light Manufacturing
3. Low-Class Residential
4. Middle-Class Residential
5. Commuter's Zone

The Sector Model ▶▶▶

1. Central Business District
2. Wholesale Light Manufacturing
3. Low-Class Residential
4. Middle-Class Residential
5. High-Class Residential

The Multiple-Nuclei Model ▶▶▶

1. Central Business District
2. Wholesale Light Manufacturing
3. Low-Class Residential
4. Middle-Class Residential
5. High-Class Residential
6. Heavy Manufacturing
7. Outlying Business District
8. Residential Suburb
9. Industrial Suburb

Which model best fits your community?

Source: From "The Nature of Cities" by Chauncey D. Harris and Edward L. Ullman, *The Annals of the American Academy of Political and Social Science*, vol. 242. Copyright © 1945 by the American Academy of Political and Social Science. Reprinted by permission.

inconvenient and undesirable to drive downtown to shop, bank, and receive necessary services, so branch banks, shopping malls, medical clinics, hospitals, and other services have sprung up in and around zone 4.

Zone 5 is a commuter zone, where people live in suburban areas or smaller incorporated towns far enough away to avoid the undesirable elements of the city (e.g., crime and drugs), yet close enough to enjoy its amenities (e.g., theater, professional sports, and necessary goods and services) as well as to commute to their places of work.

Burgess's ecological model provided sociological insight into urban development. Since then, other urban sociologists have offered models they believe more accurately illustrate the process.

The Sector Model

According to Homer Hoyt (1939), the center of the city develops in much the way Burgess described. But Hoyt proposed that cities grow outward in several wedge-shaped sectors, each reflecting different land uses and the congregation of fairly homogeneous populations based on race, ethnicity, and social class (see Figure 19.6). Hoyt contended that suburban middle-class housing is not likely to develop next to inner-city ghettos but instead develops outward from lower-middle-class housing areas. Likewise, after these middle-class neighborhoods have developed, wealthier suburban housing often develops adjacent to them. Factories and other forms of industry are not allowed to locate in these housing areas and therefore develop in another sector, usually along major arteries of transportation (especially major highways and railroad lines).

The Multiple-Nuclei Model

C. D. Harris and Edward Ullman (1945) offered yet another explanation of urban development with their multiple-nuclei model (see Figure 19.6). According to their model, cities evolve from several nuclei that shape the character and structure of the areas surrounding them. For example, the central business district serves as one important nucleus, while a college or university across town serves as another. If the community has a prison, it may serve as another distinct nucleus for development, and a major manufacturing plant would provide the nucleus for yet another area.

The models proposed by Burgess, Hoyt, and Harris and Ullman are just that: models representing ideal types. They may or may not accurately describe the specific developmental patterns of actual cities. Nevertheless, they provide important sociological insight into how spatial relationships and different land uses affect population patterns and social life. You may find it interesting to make transparencies based on each of the models depicted in Figure 19.6 and place them one at a time over a map of your city or hometown to see how closely the map conforms to one of the models. Perhaps you will find that your city or town developed in a different fashion altogether.

These sociological theories focus on urban development and human ecology, and they are especially concerned about the spatial arrangements of cities and how they impact on social life. Human ecologists also apply the ecological perspective to how urban development affects the environment.

HUMAN ECOLOGY AND THE ENVIRONMENT

The **ecological perspective** provides *a theoretical model for analyzing the interdependence between human beings and the physical environment.* In the case of human society, two of the most important ecological factors are growth in population and our ability to alter the environment through technology.

Overpopulation

Earlier in this chapter we looked at the growth of human population around the globe and in the United States. Why is population growth a concern to human ecologists? As human populations grow, we alter our physical environment in order to obtain sufficient food and shelter. In the United States alone, billions of acres of land once covered with trees, grasses, flowers, marshes, and streams have been covered with asphalt, con-

ECOLOGICAL PERSPECTIVE
A theoretical model for analyzing the interdependence between human beings and the physical environment.

crete, steel, wood, and glass to build cities and residential areas and to create millions of miles of highways. Moreover, worldwide, there is mounting evidence that population growth is the most significant cause of environmental damage, ranging from topsoil loss and diminishing water supply to global climate change (Fornos, 1997; Nierenberg, 2003).

In many developing nations trapped in stage 2 of demographic transition, overpopulation threatens to bring about widespread starvation and millions of deaths. As populations increase and urban areas expand, farmers are forced onto marginal lands. They may burn forests to grow crops or raise cattle or may cut down the trees for fuel. Either way, deforestation often leads to overcultivation and soil erosion. Moreover, larger populations demand not only more food and wood, but also more petroleum and other fossil fuels, electricity, water, and other scarce commodities. While some argue that human ingenuity has enabled the earth to sustain more people at higher living standards than ever before (Lambert, 1995), others insist that we have missed numerous opportunities to confront the problems of overpopulation, food scarcity, and related issues that will continue to plague us during the twenty-first century (Brown et al., 2001; Brown, 2006).

Depletion of Natural Resources

One of the consequences of overpopulation is the depletion of natural resources. Worldwide, population growth and urbanization have led to problems of deforestation, desertification, and the extinction of many species of plants and wildlife.

Deforestation
Forest land around the globe is being destroyed at a rate of one acre per second, and tropical forests are shrinking by 14 million hectares per year (United Nations Fund for Population Activities, 1991; Gore, 1992; Brown, 2006). Particularly disturbing is the fact that tropical forests, which cover only 7 percent of the earth's surface, may house as much as 80 percent of the planet's species (Linden, 1989). Worldwide, this massive *deforestation* (destruction of forests) is linked to population growth and migration; it results in land degradation where the forests are stripped, and in greenhouse gases where they are burned for fuel (Fornos, 1997; Bonnicksen, 1998). In North America, deforestation results from massive logging operations to provide lumber for housing and pulp for paper; in tropical rainforest areas it often follows the burning of trees to clear land for crops and animals. Overgrazing, deforestation, and agricultural mismanagement account for almost three-fourths of the damage to the world's soil (Fornos, 1997). And, the burning of tropical rain forests may contribute as much as 10 percent of the global greenhouse buildup (Bonnicksen, 1998).

Desertification
One side effect of the depletion of tree cover is accelerated soil erosion, resulting in an estimated loss of 26 billion tons of topsoil per year. The U.S. Department of Agriculture discovered in the early 1980s that American farmers were losing 3.1 billion tons of topsoil annually to wind and water erosion and that for every ton of grain produced 6 tons of topsoil were lost (Brown et al., 1988). Soil mismanagement has also contributed to desertification in many parts of the globe—most noticeably in Sub-Saharan Africa.

Desertification, the creation of a desert in what was once arable land, can be partially attributed to the loss of fresh groundwater and the destruction of natural lakes. As overpopulation and expanded use of agricultural irrigation increase the demand for fresh water, water tables are falling at a rate of 20 meters per year. Some

Scientists contend that destruction of the world's rain forests has had devastating effects on the earth's ozone layer. Although some of the damage can be attributed to fires and the stripping of forests to provide farmland, much of it can be linked to commercial logging operations and the building of roads, housing developments, cities, and huge agribusinesses.

How long do you think it would take to replace a tree this size?

natural aquifers are being drained at a rate faster than the water can be replaced (UNFPA, 1991; Fornos, 1997; Brown, 2006).

Extinction of Species   As human population expands, more than half the world's other primate population is declining (Tuxill, 1997). Humans' greatest impact on other species, especially other primates, is the alteration of their natural environments for our use. As a consequence, species are becoming extinct at a rate 1,000 times greater than the pace that has prevailed since prehistory; it is predicted that over the next three decades *every* day humans will drive 100 species into extinction. Many distinguished ecologists, such as E. O. Wilson and Norman Myers, are concerned that entire ecosystems are being destroyed (Linden, 1989; Diamond, 1990; Brown et al., 1997, 2001).

Some skeptics insist that environmentalists exaggerate the depletion of natural resources, extinction of species, and environmental doomsday prophecies (Bailey, 1995; Simon, 1995). Julian Simon (1983, 1995), for example, asserts that life on earth is getting better, not worse, and argues that many so-called finite natural resources are replenishable. However, even he reluctantly agreed that lumber and oil are becoming scarce and that, while we should avoid alarmism, that does not mean we need not worry about endangered species (Simon, 1983).

Pollution: Water, Air, and Land

Pollution now affects almost every aspect of life. Its most serious manifestations affect the three major givers of life: water, air, and land.

Water Pollution   The three major sources of water pollution are domestic wastewater, industrial discharges, and agricultural runoff (World Resources Institute, 1990). Urbanization creates a heavy concentration of human waste, which is discharged into sewage systems that empty into nearby bodies of water. Unfortunately, other municipalities downstream rely on those same bodies of water for their major supply of drinking water. Even small amounts of pollutants from paper, chemical, petrochemical, refining, textile, and metalworking industries can be toxic when they are discharged into freshwater supplies. Despite strict regulations and heavy fines, illegal disposal of toxic waste is second in profits only to trafficking in illegal drugs in the United States (ABC News, 1995).

In the early 1960s, Rachel Carson's book *The Silent Spring* startled the American public into awareness of some of the problems that advanced technology posed for the environment. Carson (1962) traced a reduction in the number of birds and the extinction of some bird species to the use of chemical pesticides, especially the most popular and powerful among them: DDT. She warned that the short-term benefits of heavy pesticide use could not possibly offset their long-term harm to the environment. Eventually, other environmentalists joined the chorus and pressured government agencies to ban the use of DDT in the United States, and restrictions were placed on the production, storage, shipment, and use of many other chemical pesticides. Nevertheless, some American chemical companies with warehouses of deadly DDT averted financial losses by sell-

ing the chemical to other nations. Studies show that fertilizer use continues to increase worldwide, especially in China, the Indian subcontinent, and parts of the former Soviet Union. One of the major problems associated with the heavy use of these toxic chemicals, along with a host of commercial fertilizers and other chemicals used in agriculture, is the devastating effect as they run off into streams, rivers, and lakes and seep into underground water tables (Brown et al., 1997, 2001).

Each year, millions of gallons of petroleum, industrial chemicals, and other toxic substances are either intentionally dumped or accidentally spilled into the world's oceans. One of the most alarming and highly publicized disasters occurred in 1989, when the *Exxon Valdez* oil tanker ran aground, split its hull, and dumped millions of gallons of oil into the pristine waters of Prince William Sound in Alaska. Several years and billions of dollars later, cleanup efforts were still under way, and both plants and wildlife in the area still suffered repercussions of the spill. The *Exxon Valdez* and other tanker accidents pale in comparison to the intentional dumping of billions of gallons of oil each year during tank cleaning, ballasting, and other routine tanker operations (World Resources Institute, 1990). Clean, fresh water is becoming scarcer around the world—a problem that could cause global food prices to soar in the future (Johnson, 2000). The United Nations projects that up to 7 billion people in 60 countries will face water scarcity in the next half-century (Sawin, 2003).

Air Pollution Los Angeles smog has provided material for comedians for decades, but the worldwide problem of urban air pollution is generating very few laughs. Mexico City, one of the largest and most beautiful cities in the world, is almost permanently enveloped in a haze of smog. Other major cities around the world suffer from similar problems.

Emissions of lead, sulfur dioxide, and nitrogen oxides produce air pollution that is aesthetically displeasing as well as threatening to human health. These pollutants are most heavily concentrated in urban areas and have been directly linked to lung damage and respiratory diseases. Moreover, they pose a significant environmental threat because they contain acids that help form acid rain, which is altering the chemistry of streams, rivers, and lakes and has caused irreparable damage to crops and forests (World Resources Institute, 1990).

Damage to the earth's ozone layer has received increasing attention since the mid-1970s. This layer is a band of ozone molecules in the stratosphere 10–30 miles from the earth's surface; it filters out the sun's most dangerous rays. In 1985, researchers reported the existence of a large hole in the ozone layer over Antarctica, where as much as 50 percent of the ozone had been depleted. Scientists warn that the hole is spreading, and today ozone damage is detectable over populated and agricultural areas. The results could be devastating for human and plant and animal life. Damage to the ozone layer allows more ultraviolet radiation from the sun to reach the earth's surface. Ultraviolet light has been linked to sunburn, skin cancer, cataracts, and damage to the immune system as well as increased carbon dioxide production, which may contribute to **global warming,** *an increase in the earth's overall average temperature due to a greenhouse effect produced by increased exposure to ultraviolet light* (Lemonick, 1989; World Resources Institute, 1990; Brown et al., 1997, 2001). Although a few government officials contend that the threat of global warming has been exaggerated, most scientists do not (World Watch, 2003). The nonprofit World Resources Institute found in 2005 that most scientists believe that the world has gone past a dangerous tipping point in global warning (Zabarenko, 2006).

Land Pollution By the end of the 1980s, the United States was producing over 178 million metric tons of municipal waste per year and facing a major problem of waste disposal. The Environmental Protection Agency estimates that one-third of America's landfills are already full and that by 2010 four-fifths of them will be closed (D. Grossman and Shulman, 1990). Another problem is the type of waste materials produced, many of

Air pollution in Mexico City has become so severe that schoolchildren sometimes must don protective masks.

Can you think of other areas where air pollution disrupts people's daily lives?

GLOBAL WARMING
An increase in the earth's overall average temperature due to a greenhouse effect produced by increased exposure to ultraviolet light.

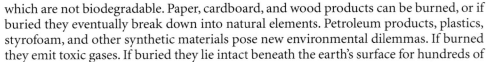

Former Vice President Al Gore's film An *Inconvenient Truth* won critical acclaim, and an Oscar, and drew worldwide attention to the problem of global warming.

which are not biodegradable. Paper, cardboard, and wood products can be burned, or if buried they eventually break down into natural elements. Petroleum products, plastics, styrofoam, and other synthetic materials pose new environmental dilemmas. If burned they emit toxic gases. If buried they lie intact beneath the earth's surface for hundreds of years, because they are not biodegradable. Environmentalists urge the recycling of these materials.

In an effort to meet energy needs and decrease dependence on fossil fuels, several nuclear reactors have been put on-line since the early 1970s, creating a new environmental and human problem. Fear associated with nuclear energy was underscored in the United States in 1979 when a problem at the Three Mile Island reactor in Pennsylvania forced its closure and the evacuation of nearby areas. Although officials reassured the public that the problem was minor and the plant had never approached a "meltdown," the incident highlighted the potential threat of a nuclear catastrophe. In 1986, the threat of a massive nuclear disaster was realized when the Chernobyl nuclear plant in Ukraine experienced a core meltdown. The North American continent had another scare in December 1994, when Canada's oldest nuclear reactor, the Pickering Nuclear Power Plant near Toronto, experienced an "incident" causing it to be shut down. In 1995, Japan's Monju plant experienced a major accident during start-up testing.

Today there are almost 450 nuclear reactors listed as grid-connected and on-line, and despite the scares of Three Mile Island, Chernobyl, and Monju, nuclear generated electricity increases every year. Nuclear reactors pose a hazardous waste problem even when plants operate safely and efficiently. Radioactive waste was once sealed in lead containers and dumped miles out into the ocean, but nature reminded us that the earth is a giant ecosystem: some of the sealed conisters drifted ashore.

Remote desert areas in Nevada—near nuclear bomb test sites—have become a popular dump site for nuclear waste, but Nevada residents and government officials are beginning to fight such practices. Some people have proposed that radioactive waste be launched into outer space, but scientists reminded public officials that the earth is part of a large ecosystem and when it comes to nuclear waste, "out of sight" should not mean "out of mind." Much of the material we launch into space finds its way back to earth as debris. Because of its potentially devastating effects, the mass media have focused a great deal of attention on environmental concerns—especially those related to nuclear power.

The Media and Environmental Concerns

What is the state of planet Earth? Are environmental conditions stable, improving, or approaching a crisis in which human numbers and activities threaten fundamental life-support systems and perhaps even life itself? The answer to all of these questions can be found in the mass media and technomedia, which have become a "reality test" through which many of us learn about and evaluate the relative seriousness of problems beyond our immediate environments (Ryan, 1991).

Why the Media Embrace Environmental Issues

Why do the media, especially television, love environmental issues? Most have compelling visuals, hot rhetoric, conflict, and human drama that evoke people's deepest hopes, dreams, and fears. Herbert Gans (1979a) found that of the four major segments of network "news" each evening, two concern environmental issues: either "disorder news" that involves "natural disasters," such as floods, earthquakes, and volcanic eruptions, or serious technological breakdowns like the nuclear disaster at Chernobyl and the Bhopal, India, chemical explosion. Today, environmental issues often take a backseat to the more sensational crime and violence stories, but they still attract media attention especially if protestors chain themselves to trees or create some other media attraction.

The Case of Nuclear Power   Perhaps no environmental concern has captured as much mass media attention as the potential problems associated with nuclear energy. After the massive destruction of Hiroshima and Nagasaki at the end of World War II, the vision of the towering mushroom cloud associated with a nuclear bomb was indelibly etched into the American consciousness. Consequently, in 1953, when President Eisenhower addressed the United Nations on the development and use of nuclear energy during peacetime, he was faced with the challenge of changing the public's destructive image of nuclear power. In what the media dubbed his "atoms for peace" speech, Eisenhower framed the development of nuclear energy within the context of progress, touting its potential for the betterment of humankind, not only in America but throughout the world (Gamson and Modigliani, 1989).

Throughout the 1950s and 1960s, as the Cold War with the former Soviet Union heightened, the media provided a dualistic discourse on the development of nuclear energy that vacillated between the potential horror of civilization vanishing in a "cataclysmic nuclear holocaust" and an atomic future that would be "unimaginably bright" and cost-efficient (Boyer, 1985:125). The dualistic dialogue has continued in the media, with antinuclear and environmental groups promoting the runaway technology image of a nuclear industry fraught with the possibilities of massive death and destruction, while the proponents of nuclear energy have framed the development of nuclear power within the context of progress (Gamson and Modigliani, 1989).

In 1969, *CBS News* aired a special program entitled *Can the World Be Saved?* By the mid-1970s every major television network and every major magazine, ranging from *Reader's Digest* to *Playboy,* had run regular segments or special features on the development of nuclear power and other important environmental issues (Rubin and Sachs, 1973). The motion picture industry also focused public interest on nuclear issues with movies such as *Silkwood,* which dealt with the mysterious death of Karen Silkwood, an employee at a nuclear fuel processing plant in Oklahoma that could not account for approximately 40 pounds of plutonium, and *The China Syndrome.* This 1979 movie portrayal of the potential horrors associated with a possible meltdown at a nuclear power plant gave moviegoers a fictional preview of the real-life scare that occurred at Three Mile Island just a few weeks after the movie's release, as well as of the 1986 Chernobyl disaster.

Taking a Closer Look at the Media, Technomedia, and the Environment

If we use the critical thinking approach of sociology, it becomes apparent that, as in other areas, media time constraints and the emphasis on entertainment dominate media coverage of environmental issues. Moreover, media portrayals may be used by others to shape and distort social reality as well as to influence public opinion and governmental policies by framing stories in different contexts. For example, opponents of the nuclear industry capitalized on those media accounts of the events at Three Mile Island and Chernobyl that underscored the risks associated with nuclear energy. Some replayed visual images of the mushroom cloud, while others included frequent pictures of food and people being checked for radioactive contamination. The proponents of the nuclear industry, on the other hand, used media coverage of the events to reassure the public that the safety systems at Three Mile Island averted disaster despite a string of highly improbable errors, and to underscore the wisdom of the American nuclear industry in constructing large, fortified containment structures far superior to the one at Chernobyl (Gamson and Modigliani, 1989).

While most of the debate and media discourse was dominated by major corporate and political entities, ecoactivists, who understand the power of the media in shaping public opinion and influencing governmental policies, use the media—especially the technomedia—more to their advantage in disseminating information and gaining

Actress Darryl Hannah chained herself to a walnut tree to protest the destruction of an urban farm in south-central Los Angeles.

What impact do celebrities have on attitudes of the American and world public when they lend their support to environmental and ecological issues?

popular support for environmental movements. By staging media events such as demonstrations or chaining themselves to the gates of a nuclear power plant, activists are assured of getting a photograph and an article in the newspaper and possibly even 30–60 seconds of coverage on the television evening news. While they risk being depicted in a negative way, they also know that such coverage is vital if they hope to garner support for their cause and to contribute to the development of a powerful social movement—a calculated risk that social activists are likely to be willing to take even more in the future.

With today's widespread access to the technomedia, environmental activists have established a multitude of websites where environmental causes and concerns are defined and discussed and information is given on how to become involved in environmentalist organizations and contemporary ecological social movements. These aspects of social movements are discussed further in Chapter 20.

Al Gore championed environmental causes during the 2000 presidential campaign, as did Green party candidate Ralph Nader in 2000 and 2004. When George W. Bush was elected President and Dick Cheney as Vice President, both with strong ties to the oil business, environmentalists feared this was a major step backward. Despite assurances from Bush's Director of the Environmental Protection Agency that the administration was very concerned about the environment, decisions to rescind some of the restrictions on drilling for oil on protected lands and easing some of the restrictions on various pollutants confirmed many of the environmentalists' fears. In 2006, Al Gore's documentary *An Inconvenient Truth* raised international awareness of the problems of global warning.

the FUTURE

LOOKING to

POPULATION, URBANIZATION, AND ECOLOGY IN THE TWENTY-FIRST CENTURY

The United Nations Population Division predicts that by 2025, world population will increase to about 9 billion people (United Nations, 2003). More disturbing, whereas the United Nations earlier predicted that the world population would stabilize at around 10 billion, it has revised its estimate to closer to 11 billion, or even as high as 14 billion. These projections have prompted concerns that overpopulation and food scarcity are the principle threats to the planet's future (Brown et al., 1997, 2001; Brown, 2006). The United Nations sponsored an International Conference on Population and Development held in Cairo in 1994. There, a World Programme of Action was developed to shift the focus of dismal demographic projections toward concern about a gender-sensitive, humanistic approach to population control (Chen et al., 1995; Sen, 1995). In 2000, the United Nations adopted eight Millenium Goals to be achieved by 2015, two of which addressed population and environmental concerns (United Nations, 2006).

The population problem is most pronounced on the African continent; if the present annual growth rate of 3.1 percent continues, the current population of 650 million will triple by the year 2028. Meanwhile, the continent's food supply is expanding by only 1.1 percent each year. China's largest cities continue to grow to almost unimaginable numbers. Approximately 20 million people live in Shanghai, and Beijing has a population in excess of 15 million. Meanwhile, India, already over the 1 billion mark, is expected to add another 300 million to its population by the year 2020, and Bangladesh will add another 100 million (Wehrfritz, 1994; Brown et al., 1997; Mitchell, 1998; United Nations, 2006). Whereas developed nations represented approximately one-third of the world's total population in 1950, by 2025 this figure will be reduced to about 16 percent of the total (Mitchell, 1998; United Nations, 2006).

Most urban sociologists predict that the United States will continue to see an increase in suburban development around large metropolitan areas. Thus, while the population of some major cities may decline, increased suburbanization around those cities may perpetuate their importance. And although some argue that urbanization and even suburbanization are slowing, most sociologists believe they will continue to dominate American life.

U.S. cities are likely to play five very important roles in the future: (1) headquarters for large multinational corporations; (2) innovation centers for important research and development; (3) module production places where unique natural, physical, or human resources allow the city to assemble, produce, or distribute specific goods; (4) Third World entrepôts where large immigrant populations provide a significant low-wage labor force for assembly-type jobs; and (5) retirement centers, as evidenced by the large wave of retirees who continue to migrate from northern snow belt cities to sun belt cities in the South and Southwest (Logan and Molotch, 1987; Gottdiener, 1994; Hall, 2002).

Worldwide urbanization is predicted to grow at unprecedented rates. In mid-2006 the United Nations issued a report announcing that for the first time in world history, by 2007, more people would live in cities than rural areas, and predicted that by 2030, over 62 percent of the world's population would be urban. The majority of urban growth and new "megacities" (populations of 10 million or more) will be in poverty-stricken developing nations least equipped to deal with them (Knight Ridder, 2006).

A major concern for the future is the impact of the increased population and concentration of people in cities and suburbs will have on the environment. For the first time in our existence, our lifestyle may threaten the existence of life on the planet.

Although not everyone is this pessimistic, Katsuhide Kitatani, deputy executive director of the United Nations Population Fund, noted that developing countries now produce one-third of the world's carbon dioxide and one-sixth of the world's chlorofluorocarbons (CFCs). By the year 2025, these countries could raise their share to two-thirds of a much higher level of carbon dioxides and more than one-third of a dangerously high level of CFCs. He continued, "Growing populations may be responsible for as much as 80 percent of the loss of forest cover in countries like Brazil and Indonesia; for rapidly diminishing water resources in countries like Egypt . . . for soil erosion and desertification in areas as far apart as the Sahel and the Himalayas" (WPNS, 1991d:1). Moreover, some wildlife conservationists believe that more than half of all existing species will be extinct or endangered by the middle of the twenty-first century (Diamond, 1990; Brown et al., 1997, 2001; Brown, 2006). A United Nations (1992:16A) report indicated that the environment is far worse than it was 20 years ago and that "the fouling of the Earth's air, water and farmland is accelerating."

These projections emphasize the need for environmental education and resocialization toward an ecological perspective on human life, and research indicates that these are indeed taking place (Kanagy et al., 1994). Environmental problems have renewed interest in the study of demography and ecology, which led one sociologist to contend that ecological demography, a combination of the two subfields, may become the most important paradigm in sociology (Namboodiri, 1988). Scientists around the world are experimenting with methods to reduce the depletion of natural resources, find alternatives to chemical fertilizers and pesticides, halt the process of global warming, recycle waste, protect the ozone layer, and slow the extinction of species. Additionally, the global institutionalization of the principle that nation-states are responsible for environmental protection is bringing about an increase in national activities and policies to protect the natural environment (Frank et al., 2000). There is some evidence that ozone erosion is slowing (NY Times, 2003b), but virtually all scientists agree that modernity is taking a tremendous toll on the environment (York et al., 2003; Zabarenko, 2006). As Al Gore's 2006 documentary, An Inconvenient Truth pointed out, global warming poses a serious threat to our future and must be addressed on a world-wide basis.

Can humans overcome the bleak prospects of overpopulation, urban decay, depletion of natural resources, pollution, and other environmental concerns? If left unchecked, do current trends doom our species to certain extinction? Focus box 19.3 explores these two disparate possibilities for the future. Meanwhile, concern over these and other questions has led to social movements designed to bring about social change, the topic of Chapter 20.

Welcome to the future. Uncontrolled population growth has led to massive starvation throughout not only sub-Saharan Africa, but also most of India and much of Asia. The desertification of Africa, Russia, India, and parts of South America is complete, and acid rain combined with other forms of pollution has led to the widespread depletion of natural resources and the extinction of many plant and animal species. Aquifers in the United States have been drained, so there is widespread drought throughout the once fertile Midwest, and massive dikes have been constructed around several important American cities to hold back the rising seawater that is a consequence of continued global warming. "Nightmare cities" in China, India, Russia, Mexico, Europe, and the United States are characterized by overcrowding, inadequate housing, widespread unemployment, homelessness, racial and ethnic tension, and skyrocketing crime rates that all but paralyze its inhabitants (Rifkin, 1989; Ehrlich and Ehrlich, 1990; Brown, 1995; Doerr, 1995).

Or—welcome to the future. As has always been the case, the continued increase in population has led to a marked increase in scientific discoveries, innovation, and technology, which have raised the average person's standard of living to the highest it has ever been. Natural resources have not been depleted but are, in fact, more abundant. Improved technology in agriculture has bolstered our ability to feed the world's population, and the scourge of famine that plagued the developing nations during the twentieth century has been all but eliminated. There are, of course, some local environmental concerns but no serious global threats. The earth's average temperature has increased less than 1 degree Fahrenheit over the last century, and there has been no significant global warming or melting of polar icecaps. Around the globe, cities and their burgeoning suburbs, far from becoming decayed enclaves of hate, pollution, and crime, have become the hub of social and cultural activities for their residents and for the ever-growing rural population, who, connected to their jobs and urban services through computer technology, have moved out of the cities for the serenity of country life (Fondersmith, 1988; Bailey, 1995; Simon, 1995).

Now that we are in the twenty-first century, neither of these conflicting scenarios, which were promoted by experts in a variety of the natural and social sciences as well as by leaders of various economic, political, and social organizations, has turned out to be accurate. Which of these predictions most accurately describes the world today? Some conclude that we may already be living in the cities of the future and that, well into the twenty-first century, cities will continue their tendencies toward large urban sprawl characterized by decentralization, unemployment, homelessness, crime, and a large urban underclass largely deprived of social and economic justice (Flanagan, 1995). Nobody can say for sure. Most sociologists are skeptical that either extreme prediction is ever likely to come true. Rather, from a sociological

viewpoint, it is highly probable that society will have to continue to wrestle with the social aspects of population, cities, and the environment, constantly defining and redefining the problems and solutions that make life possible on this planet.

Others believe that cities are changing and taking on a revitalized importance in a global society. Today, large metropolitan centers surrounded by clusters of growing suburban areas are developing unabated around the globe. Silicon Valley in California, the Oxbridge complex in England, and the Scuba complex outside Tokyo have become the "command and control centers of the world economy" (Gottdiener, 1994:334).

In 1990 a symposium on "Sustainable Cities: Preserving and Restoring Urban Biodiversity" was held in Chicago. It drew geographers, ecologists, architects, forestry and wildlife management experts, and social and behavioral scientists together in an effort to identify (1) the functions of biodiversity within urban areas, (2) the impacts of urbanization on biodiversity, and (3) ways to design cities compatibly within their ecological contexts. Organizers and participants offered models for ecological cities of the future designed to preserve and restore urban biodiversity (Platt, 1994).

Although urban sociologists disagree on what the future holds for cities and urban dwellers, most agree that issues of planning, policy development, and social equity must be addressed. One future prospect for American cities is the sociospatial approach, in which decisions are made by the majority rather than by the few select politicians and profiteers who currently dominate urban and suburban planning (Gottdiener, 1994).

TAKING A CLOSER LOOK

How can scientists and futurists come up with such diametrically opposed views of life in the twenty-first century? Which of these scenarios seems the more likely to you? Or do you foresee a different future entirely—perhaps somewhere between these two extremes?

Source: Ronald Bailey. "Seven Doomsday Myths About the Environment." *The Futurist* 29 (January/February) 1995:14–18. Lester R. Brown. "Earth Is Running Out of Room." *USA Today Magazine* 123 (January) 1995:30–32. Edd Doerr. "Curbing Population: An Opportunity Missed." *USA Today Magazine* 123 (January) 1995:36–37. Paul Ehrlich and Anne H. Ehrlich. *The Population Explosion.* New York: Simon & Schuster, 1990. William C. Flanagan. *Urban Sociology: Images and Structure.* Boston: Allyn & Bacon, 1995. John Fondersmith. "Downtown 2040: Let's Make Cities Fun." *The Futurist* 22 (March/April) 1988:7–18. Mark Gottdiener. *The New Urban Sociology.* New York: McGraw-Hill, 1994. Rutherford H. Platt. "The Ecological City: Introduction and Overview." In Rutherford H. Platt, Rowan A. Rowntree, and Pamela C. Muick (eds.), *The Ecological City: Preserving and Restoring Urban Biodiversity.* Amherst: University of Massachusetts Press: 1994:1–17. Jeremy Rifkin. *Entropy: Into the Greenhouse World* (rev. ed.). New York: Bantam, 1989. Julian L. Simon. "Why Do We Hear Prophecies of Doom from Every Side?" *The Futurist* 29 (January/February) 1995:19–23.

Summary

1 Demography, the scientific study of human population, is concerned with fertility, mortality, migration, and population composition and density, especially with regard to how these factors affect the quantity and quality of human life.

2 World population growth is of particular interest to demographers and sociologists. Two important variables are growth rate (the percentage increase in population) and doubling time (the number of years it takes for a population to increase twofold). Two major theories have dominated ideas on population growth. Malthusian theory contends that population grows geometrically while food production increases arithmetically. Demographic transition theory views population changes as progressing through three distinct stages.

3 Cities have played an important role in human civilization. Sociologists have developed three theoretical models to explain urban development in the United States. The concentric zone model views urban development as radiating from a central core in concentric circular patterns; the sector model views cities as developing in distinct sections; and the multiple-nuclei model contends that various parts of a city grow around several important centers.

4 The growth of cities and the contrast between rural and urban life have long been of interest to sociologists. Ferdinand Toennies developed a rural-urban continuum to compare gemeinschaft communities to those with gesellschaft characteristics; Durkheim viewed the continuum as ranging from mechanical to organic solidarity; and Robert Redfield saw the two ends of the spectrum as consisting of folk versus urban societies. Sociological studies of urban areas gained impetus at the University of Chicago when Robert Park applied an ecological perspective to urban development and fostered the development of what became known as the Chicago School. Later urban studies have focused on the development of huge metropolises and megalopolises, which link several major cities. The 1950s and 1960s witnessed a population migration from many major cities to surrounding suburbs; today, sociologists see many of the same problems that plague cities spreading into the suburbs.

5 Population growth, urban development, and suburban lifestyles have had a devastating impact on the natural environment. Some of the most serious environmental problems include overpopulation, depletion of natural resources, and pollution. The mass media embrace environmental concerns because they contain all of the high drama that television and motion pictures demand. For example, concern about the use of nuclear power arose shortly after World War II, and both proponents and opponents have used mass media discourse to shape public opinion and policy. As with other major social issues, media constraints on time and the focus on entertainment have helped shape how the media frame nuclear issues. Ecoactivists use the mass media to focus public attention on nuclear issues as well as to rally support for social movements related to nuclear and other environmental concerns.

6 Population growth, urbanization, and the environment promise a multitude of challenges that must be faced as we begin the twenty-first century. Of major concern are skyrocketing population increases in developing countries, uncontrolled and unplanned urban and suburban growth, and continued deterioration of the planet's environment. Concern over these issues has led to the development of several social movements aimed at reducing these problems through collective action and environmental education.

Key Terms

baby boomers (p. 552)
composition of a population (p. 547)
consolidated metropolitan statistical area (CMSA) (p. 555)
crude birthrate (p. 546)
crude death rate (p. 546)
demographic transition theory (p. 551)
demography (p. 546)
doubling time (p. 548)
ecological perspective (p. 562)
ecosystem (p. 560)

fertility (p. 546)
folk societies (p. 560)
Gemeinschaft (p. 559)
Gesellschaft (p. 559)
global warming (p. 565)
growth rate (p. 548)
human ecology (p. 560)
mechanical solidarity (p. 559)
megalopolis (p. 556)
metropolis (p. 555)
metropolitan statistical areas (MSAs) (p. 555)

migration (p. 546)
migration rate (p. 546)
organic solidarity (p. 559)
population density (p. 547)
sex ratio (p. 557)
suburbs (p. 556)
urbanism (p. 560)
urbanization (p. 554)
urban societies (p. 560)
urban sociology (p. 558)
Zero Population Growth (ZPG) (p. 550)

Chapter 20

Social Change, Collective Behavior, and the Future

"Nothing endures but change."
—Heraclitus

*T*he cameras are familiar to most people, perhaps even comforting to some. They are perched high atop almost every lamppost, rooftop, and street light. Elsewhere, they are undetectable, except to the authorities. Videocameras are never turned off. They pan up and down, left and right, surveying traffic, pedestrians, and everything else in public view, day and night.

You might be thinking this scene offers a glimpse of the future. Perhaps it is a dark, futuristic vision, much like George Orwell's nightmare of Big Brother monitoring and controlling people's lives down to the smallest details. But by now you are aware that *things are not necessarily what they seem.*

This is not some grim, dystopian vision of the future, but a growing trend almost everywhere in the world—including most shopping malls and stores, almost all government and corporate offices, and many other social arenas. In the name of public security, the British have been most active of all nations in installing surveillance monitoring systems. In the beginning, they were tried in a handful of "trouble spots." Now more than a million cameras have been installed throughout Britain, and the average Londoner can expect their picture to be taken hundreds of times each day (EPIC, 2003:1).

Since the 9/11 terrorist attacks, the United States has been trying to catch up. Times Square in New York and the nation's capitol have seen a proliferation of surveillance cameras installed in public places. Experiments in face-recognition technology have been expanded and "photo radar" that uses cameras and computers to photograph license plates, identify traffic violators, and issue citations is catching on as well. And in all cases, the technology has also grown more sophisticated. The "Patriot Act," passed after 9/11 and renewed in 2006, expanded the government's authority to "spy" on private citizens. In the private sector, where cameras and computers are most abundant and socially accepted, sociologist

William Staples calls them "Tiny Brothers" (Murphy, 2002:1). Today, there are millions of tiny private security cameras at hotels, malls, parking lots and everywhere businesses and shoppers can be found. And new digital surveillance systems are more sophisticated than they were just a few years ago. Today's technology not only can scan businesses and malls, but also analyze what it is watching and recording and, if something is unusual, alert security (Schiesel, 2003). Likewise, digital security systems can now record, store, and index images making it possible for security personnel to "instantly retrieve images of every person who passed through a door on any given day" (Flynn, 2003:2).

Today, surveillance cameras are so common in stores, apartments, and office buildings that most of us hardly notice their presence.

Many Americans are certain that technology holds the key to the future—either for better or for worse. The latest pronouncements from Silicon Valley or Bill Gates about the technological wonders of the future are often treated by the press and the public not as possibilities but as statements of fact. For example, sociologist Arthur Shostak (2000a:3) cites one futurist who predicted that technology will change an astounding "90 percent of our culture and society" in the next 10 years. Few sociologists would disagree that new technologies are bringing sweeping changes to societies everywhere on earth. However, despite mainstream media reports and images suggesting that technology is the major and perhaps even the *only* significant agent of social change, many other factors are involved.

In this chapter, we use a variety of sociological perspectives to examine the complex factors that contribute to social change. They include the powerful economic and political organizations that produce and control many of the technological wonders of the Information Age. We review the impact of several other key agents of change, such as the globalization of the economy, demography, wars, and natural disasters. Our special emphasis in this chapter concerns collective behavior and social movements, or "politics from below." In both forms of collective action large numbers of ordinary people join forces to challenge the mainstream, as well as promote or resist change. Throughout history these social forces have had a profound impact on society, and most sociologists believe they will have an even greater impact in the future.

WHAT IS SOCIAL CHANGE?

Social change is *a process through which patterns of social behavior, social relationships, social institutions, and systems of stratification are altered over time.* Everything changes, and, like nature, all societies are in a constant state of flux. The *rate of change,* however, varies from one society to another. For much of human history change was slow, and while hunting-gathering societies adopted new ways and relinquished customs and traditions, they did so very gradually over the course of centuries or even millennia.

With the origin of agriculture and the emergence of cities the pace of change quickened, and with industrialization social changes that once took generations or more occurred in the space of decades or even a few years. C. Wright Mills's (1959:4) comment that no society on earth had experienced such "earthquakes of change" at such a rapid pace as contemporary American society is even more poignant today than when he wrote it five decades ago.

Macro-change

Macro-changes are gradual, large-scale, and, because they take place over long periods of time, imperceptible to people as they go about their daily lives. *Modernization,* a process through which societies become more internally differentiated and complex as they

SOCIAL CHANGE
A process through which patterns of social behavior, social relationships, social institutions, and systems of stratification are altered over time.

move from simple to complex social institutions, is a good example of this kind of macro-change. Other kinds of macro-change may take less time, spanning only a few generations, such as the current shift from industrial societies based on manufacturing to postindustrial societies based on information and service economies.

Micro-change

Micro-changes involve small, rapid changes produced by the countless decisions people make as they interact with others in the course of their daily lives. Micro-change occurs in the everyday lives of millions of ordinary people, as people make business, family, and countless other decisions. With the exception of movers and shakers whose decisions may have an immediate effect on our lives, the small acts of ordinary people may slowly and imperceptibly alter social institutions and, eventually, entire societies.

Like other aspects of culture, people's understandings of the future are paradoxical. While the future is the repository of people's collective hopes and dreams, it also represents people's collective fears. Consequently, while some individuals and groups view change as positive and beneficial, others perceive it as harmful and a potential threat to their interests, needs, and "futures." Even when there is widespread agreement and change is carefully planned, it often has social consequences that were never intended or imagined.

Change may be desired and pursued or reviled and resisted—but it can never be halted. The speed and direction of change, however, are never random. As Clark Kerr observed, every society "moves towards its future in terms of its past, its own institutions, and traditions" (cited in McCord, 1991:58). Put another way, when societies confront a new situation, they do so in a context of existing sociocultural constraints, which influence their members' perceptions and choices (Barrett, 1991).

SOCIOLOGICAL APPROACHES TO SOCIAL CHANGE

Novel ideas and radically new visions of the world sometimes emerge during periods of intense conflict and social turmoil. The Industrial Revolution in the nineteenth century, for example, provided fertile ground for a "new science" that could explain the remarkable social changes that were taking place in Europe and America. The growth and respectability of science also generated a great deal of optimism that sociology—like the natural sciences—would discover "laws" that would not only explain social change but lead to the creation of "better societies" (Turner et al., 1989).

Cyclical Approaches

For most of human history, cyclical understandings of social change dominated people's thinking. Before the invention of clocks and the Industrial Revolution, the basic rhythms of people's lives were attuned to the repetitive cycles of nature. The sun rose and set, the seasons changed, and these and other natural cycles guided people's everyday lives and influenced their understandings of social change. Even today, many Native Americans make no clear distinctions between the past and future. To them, they are one and the same, because—like nature—history is forever repeated in endless cycles.

Classical Cyclical Theories   Early scientists and historians rejected these ideas, although some borrowed biological metaphors that held that societies have their own "inherent life spans" and that each is born, matures, and then experiences decay and death (Toynbee and Caplan, 1972). They, in turn, are replaced by societies in their youth and prime—a cycle that Oswald Spengler's *The Decline of the West* ([1922] 1962) predicted would lead to the decline of Western European culture. Another cyclical theorist, historian Arnold Toynbee, held similar views but renounced the "inevitability" of decline and proposed that "creative efforts" by people might enable civilizations to survive.

Sociologist Pitirim Sorokin (1941) took the cyclical theory of change a step further, arguing that civilizations oscillated among three types of "mentalities," or worldviews: *ideational,* which emphasizes faith and spirituality; *sensate,* which stresses practical and

utilitarian approaches to reality; and *idealistic,* which balances the practical and transcendental. According to Sorokin, in all cultural systems change occurs when a particular mode of thinking reaches its logical limits. For example, when a sensate society becomes too hedonistic and sensual people "turn to ideational systems as a refuge" (Ritzer, 1992a:202).

Contemporary Cyclical Approaches

Theodore Caplow (1991:3) found similar oscillations in contemporary industrial societies, noting their occurrence in such diverse phenomena as "the rise and decline of scholarly theories, clothing fashions, fads and crazes, the fluctuation of party strength in two-party systems, changes in nutritional patterns, and shifts in public opinion."

Cyclical understandings of change have experienced something of a revival among New Age groups, as well as in popular expressions such as "everything that goes around comes around." Most contemporary sociologists, however, believe that in addition to describing change we must take the next step and explore the complex processes that have taken us from the Stone Age to the space age.

Functionalism and Evolutionary Perspectives

With the widespread distribution of clocks and watches during the Industrial Revolution, linear views, which hold that time proceeds in a straightforward, nonrepetitive fashion, became popular. Businesspeople, of course, favored linear models because they facilitated industrial production and the pursuit of profit. In linear models, time can be divided into discrete units and "made better use of," or it can be "lost," "wasted," or "squandered." Linear views also make planning important, and the "future"—not the past—is the dominant orientation.

Classical Evolutionary Models

Borrowing models from the biological sciences, which had gained great prestige in the nineteenth century, many sociologists subscribed to the popular theory called *unilineal evolution,* which held that all forms of life—and, by analogy, all societies—"progressed" from simple to complex forms, with each form an *advance* over its predecessors. Just as biologists classified life forms according to complexity, social scientists developed ranking systems of their own, each showing humankind's "steady ascent up a ladder of predictable stages" (Caplow, 1991:11).

One popular nineteenth-century scheme emphasized that all societies passed through three main stages: *savagery, barbarism,* and *civilization.* Auguste Comte, often referred to as the founder of sociology, developed a similar scheme. He argued that all societies passed through *theological, metaphysical,* and *positivistic* stages, and that European societies were in the latter stage—which was the highest and final stage of human development.

Herbert Spencer, a contemporary of Comte, also was influenced by biological theories of evolution. Coining the term "survival of the fittest" before it became associated with Charles Darwin and biological evolution, Spencer saw the survival of organisms and societies as linked to their ability to *adapt* to a changing environment. To Spencer, Western societies had advanced to the highest social level because they were "better suited" to nineteenth-century conditions than non-Western ones. Not surprisingly, these ideas gained widespread popularity during European colonization and industrial expansion, and they added ideological support when European colonial powers redefined their activities from conquest and exploitation to the moral duty of a "superior race" to assist natives in making the difficult journey from "savagery" to "civilization."

Not everyone was convinced that industrialization and the new emphasis on competition, profit, and self-interest would lead to social advancement. In fact, German sociologist Ferdinand Toennies ([1887] 1961) maintained that modernization led to a progressive loss of community, or *Gemeinschaft,* where social life was characterized by primary ties and a strong sense of solidarity. These bonds were replaced by fleeting and impersonal ties based on self-interest, or the modern *Gesellschaft* social type (Toennies, [1887] 1961). Toennies argued that modern societies might give people greater opportunities and material benefits, but the costs would include a growing sense of isolation, uncertainty, and powerlessness, which had the potential of producing unmanageable social problems, social decay, and collapse.

Another classical theorist, Émile Durkheim, disagreed that economic competition would lead to chaos. He argued that new varieties of *social solidarity,* or feelings of collective conscience, would emerge to maintain social order. According to Durkheim's two-part model, in simple societies every member performed the same tasks, was interchangeable, and shared similar beliefs and values. Homogeneity, or what he called *mechanical solidarity,* served to integrate society. During the nineteenth century, it was clear that industrialization, increased population growth, and competition were destroying traditional forms of social solidarity. Durkheim argued that those who survived the bitter economic competition were progressively assuming specialized roles and exchange relations with one another, and thus were in the process of developing what he called *organic solidarity* (Turner et al., 1989). This same theme was echoed in the works of Robert Redfield (1953), who viewed society as evolving from "folk" to "urban," and Carl Becker (1933), who linked social change to the transition from "sacred" to "secular." Likewise, industrialization and modernization also have transformed small-scale, *traditional societies* into modern *mass societies* everywhere on earth. Table 20.1 compares the two types of societies along a number of social dimensions.

Neoevolutionary Perspectives During the twentieth century, unilineal models that described social change as continuous and inevitable were replaced by more sophisticated and less ethnocentric ones. Current *neoevolutionary theories,* for example, acknowledge that societies differ according to levels of social complexity and that over time there has been a general trend toward *social differentiation,* where various social institutions (economic, religious, political, and others) have become separate and distinct from one another.

Unlike nineteenth-century evolutionary theorists, however, neoevolutionists neither describe one form of society as superior to another nor maintain that societies inevitably progress to some higher state. Likewise, few associate modernization with an inevitable

TABLE 20.1
FROM TRADITIONAL SOCIETIES TO MODERN MASS SOCIETIES: A COMPARISON

CHARACTERISTICS FOR COMPARISON	CHARACTERISTICS OF TRADITIONAL SOCIETIES	CHARACTERISTICS OF MODERN MASS SOCIETIES
Size	Small-scale	Large-scale
	Sparsely populated	Densely populated
	Predominantly rural	Predominantly urban
Technology	Human and animal power	Machine, microchip, nuclear power
Economy	Agrarian	Industrial
	Small-scale cottage industries	Mass production
		Postindustrial information and service economies
Roles and Statuses	Roles are simple; few are specialized.	Roles are highly specialized.
	Most statuses are ascribed.	There are many achieved as well as ascribed statuses.
Groups	Family and kin groups predominate.	Formal organizations predominate.
Relationships	Primary	Secondary and primary
Communication and Interaction	Direct, face-to-face communication. Interaction is local, personal, familial, and mainly egalitarian.	Impersonal, bureaucratic, and mass-mediated communication and interaction.
Values and Norms	Religion and customs guide a fairly consistent worldview; people are "tradition-oriented," and most of their understanding of the world is recognized as "truth."	Rational-scientific worldview with many subcultures and countercultures; there are many questions, few answers, and even fewer "certainties."

shift in the opposite direction: from a nostalgic past of warm personal relations to the cold indifference of the city. Instead, they stress that there are many paths to development and change. Perhaps the major proponents of contemporary evolutionary thinking are Gerhard and Jean Lenski (1987), who contend that at various stages of history, technological and economic changes have set in motion a series of other changes, including population growth, increased population density, more complex organizations, and new ideologies.

The Conflict Perspective

Like most nineteenth-century social theorists, Karl Marx was influenced by evolutionary theory. He agreed that societies had to adapt to survive and stressed that the economy served as the foundation for the social order. Further, he believed that social arrangements and people's ideas reflected their material conditions. Conforming to the linear models of evolution popular in his time, he also believed that societies inevitably advanced toward a higher and final state—in his model, from class to classless society.

Class Warfare and Change
Marx, however, interpreted the consequences of the Industrial Revolution and social change in a dramatically different fashion than most of his peers. To Marx, the most significant processes of change centered on the tensions, strains, and conflicts among individuals, groups, nations, and, especially, social classes.

In Marx's model of revolutionary change, as capitalists bought off competitors they would grow stronger and more ruthless in their search for profits, and workers would suffer progressively lower wages, higher rates of unemployment, and poverty and destitution. This, in turn, would produce rising levels of alienation, discontent, and severe economic crises—each more serious than the last—until in the end workers everywhere would recognize their common enemy and join in a revolutionary movement to overthrow capitalists and the system of private property, ultimately taking charge of the economy and running it for the good of all.

Where did Marx go wrong? Despite monopoly capitalism, cyclical economic crises, and disgruntled workers in many industrial societies, there have been no revolutions in industrial capitalist nations and capitalism seems to be expanding rather than contracting—even into territories where socialism once reigned supreme. To Marxists, one key reason the revolution has been stalled is dramatic advances in transportation and communication, which have brought the whole world into the capitalist orbit and enabled Transnational corporations to exploit global resources, labor, and profits undreamed of a century ago.

Revolutionary Change
Marx also seems to have overemphasized economic factors in his model of revolutionary change. In her study of revolutions in France, Russia, and China, Theda Skocpol (1979:19) found that where revolutionary change occurred not only were there serious economic crises and class conflicts, but in all cases national political and economic elites were unable to meet the challenges of transnational or international relations, which "helped shape revolutionary struggles and outcomes."

The collapse of the Soviet Union seems to support Skocpol's thesis. Not only did national economic crises and internal conflicts fuel revolutionary change in the Soviet Union and Eastern Europe, but also so did military competition with the United States. This led to massive spending by both nations, which helped bankrupt the former Soviet Union as well as put severe economic pressures on Western economies. Despite short-term gains, however, most conflict theorists agree that while capitalism seems to be prospering at present, "crises can only be put off, not evaded entirely" (Collins and Makowsky, 1993:44).

While contemporary conflict theorists continue to explore the social consequences of class conflict, they have expanded their analysis to include all forms of social conflict—

Despite considerable anti-American sentiment toward most things American—and American megacorporations—Starbucks opened its first coffee shops in Paris in 2003. Today Starbucks and other major American chains can be found in almost every country around the globe.

racial, ethnic, religious, gender, age, and others examined throughout this book. Again, the collapse of the Soviet Union is instructive, as current ethnic and religious struggles in many parts of Eastern Europe—and efforts by some groups at "ethnic cleansing"—bear out the compelling nature of ethnic conflict as a force for social change.

Contemporary Perspectives on Change

Today few sociologists subscribe to a single "grand theory" of social change. Some borrow elements of neoevolutionary theory and stress adaptation and economic factors in the process of change. Most also emphasize class-based and other forms of conflict both within and among nations. Likewise, instead of attempting to explain change in terms of a single factor, most agree that the complex interaction among many factors—both internal and external to a nation—produce change, although in varied specific historical and social contexts specific factors may sometimes exert more influence than others.

Sources of Change   In addition to war, which we discussed in Chapter 16, some of the most important sources of change are the physical environment, technology, population, cultural innovation, and social conflict.

The *physical environment* includes cataclysmic events such as floods, droughts, volcanic eruptions, and earthquakes. Human activities, especially industrial activities in the last two centuries, which have produced acid rain, global warming, massive deforestation, desertification, and holes in the ozone layer, also produce social change and have the potential of causing profound changes in the next century.

Technology, which is the application of knowledge for practical ends, has been a powerful force for social change since the invention of the first tool. Lasers, fiber optics, biotechnology, genetic engineering, computer-assisted technologies, and other technological advances have the potential of vastly improving the quality of people's lives. As we discuss in Focus box 20.1, while technology can enhance our lives, it also has the potential to give giant organizations powers of surveillance and social control that were impossible and even unimaginable just a few years ago.

Population and *changes in the size and composition of populations, migration,* and other *demographic forces* are also important sources of change. As noted in Chapter 19, one of the most important trends related to modernization has been the steady expansion of the global population over the past two centuries, which now approaches 6 billion people.

Cultural innovation, including discovery, and invention, and diffusion—*or cultural borrowing*—is an important source of social change as well. Today, tourism, international commerce, and the global telecommunications industry have introduced the world to a steady stream of Western products, goods, ideas, and values—especially consumerism, individualism, and popular culture. Of course, diffusion is rarely a one-way process, and goods and ideas from all of the world's cultures affect the foods we eat, the clothes we wear, the music we listen to, and most other aspects of American culture and society.

Social conflict in a global society includes racial, ethnic, religious, and gender conflicts, as well as nationalist struggles. Because they have strong vested interests in the status quo, elites often resist change and suppress subordinates who desire it. When elites become divided or lose legitimacy, however, significant social change becomes possible. War and terrorist activities also can bring sudden change, and so can ordinary people—when they join forces to alter the conditions of their lives.

As we discuss in the next section, when ordinary people join forces to protest and challenge the status quo, they too can become powerful agents of social change. What do the following activities have in common: rioting, rumors of UFO medical experiments on humans, satanism, a lynch mob, and the feminist and civil rights movements? The answer is that they are all forms of *collective action* involving two related but distinctive forms of social behavior. One, **collective behavior,** consists of *relatively spontaneous and noninstitutionalized responses by a large number of people to uncertain and problematic situations.* The other form, **social movements,** involve *organized, goal-directed efforts by a large number of people to promote or resist change outside of established institutions.* We examine them one at a time, beginning with the more volatile and spontaneous collective behavior.

COLLECTIVE BEHAVIOR
Relatively spontaneous and noninstitutionalized responses by a large number of people to uncertain and problematic situations.

SOCIAL MOVEMENTS
Organized, goal-directed efforts by a large number of people to promote or resist change outside of established institutions.

We began this chapter with a vignette that described a few of the high-tech surveillance devices that are becoming more common across the urban landscape. While many people may be wary of these devices, few are aware that they are but a small part of surveillance technologies that now routinely monitor all of our personal histories, daily routines, and tastes. And 9/11 and global terrorist threats have increased public willingness for added security and new surveillance technologies.

Police and military surveillance is impressive—with videoscanners, electronic ankle monitors, night-vision goggles, and pilotless airborne spy vehicles, to name just a few of the new technologies. But high-tech surveillance has expanded well beyond the police and military to thousands of corporations, government agencies, and even individuals who routinely monitor the workplace, marketplace, and almost all other social arenas (Staples, 1996). As one sociologist noted, "Being able to hide and remain anonymous has become more difficult . . . we are moving toward a glass village in which everyone is available for view online" (Hurst, 2005:51).

Today, corporations and government agencies routinely share databases. In "computer matching," organizations swap back and forth personal information on different kinds of populations and combine them to suit their own needs. The Pentagon's "Total Information Awareness Program" is one the most ambitious plans to combine computer databases. The Pentagon maintains that it relies mainly on information from government, law enforcement, and intelligence databases to "forestall terrorism," but as of 2003, its use of other kinds of data—like personal financial and health records—remained unresolved (Clymer, 2003:1).

Critics argue that because such a system could also tap into Internet mail, culling records, and credit card and banking transactions as well as travel documents, it poses a direct threat to civil liberties.

Similar arguments were made after the Passage of the Patriot Act in 2001, which gave the government the right to "search suspected terrorists' library records—and add them to government databases—without the patron ever knowing" (Sebastian, 2003:3). By early 2002, one study found that over 85 libraries had already been asked for information on patrons in connection with the 9/11 investigation (Sebastian, 2003).

Post-9/11 surveillance surfaced as a controversial political issue in 2006 when it was discovered that after the 9/11 attacks, the government gave approval to the highly secretive National Security Agency (NSA) to solicit phone records of private citizens from the nation's largest phone companies (Hosenball and Thomas, 2006). Only weeks later it was revealed that the government also had begun monitoring the banking habits of private citizens in an effort to thwart terrorist activities. Open debates developed over how much personal privacy Americans were willing to relinquish for the promise of safety from terrorism.

The government is not the only one in the spying business. Some of the most sophisticated surveillance devices are available to the public and can be ordered from retail catalogues. For example, night-vision goggles can be had for the price of a good videocamera. High-tech scanners are available that can trace ink patterns and read the content of letters "without ever breaking the seal" (Brin, 1996:308). And Brin (1996:309) believes there is a good possibility that as

COLLECTIVE BEHAVIOR

Most of our lives are spent in small social groups or large formal organizations where we interact with others in patterned and predictable ways. During the course of our everyday lives, we also become part of **collectivities**—*large numbers of people who interact briefly and superficially in the absence of clearly defined norms*—such as shoppers at a supermarket or mall.

What transforms an ordinary gathering of people into a panic-stricken crowd? How is it possible for conservative and frugal people to become so caught up in a fad they are willing to pay almost any price to acquire a Beanie Baby, a Teenage Mutant Ninja Turtle, or a Razor scooter? What led more than 900 members of the People's Temple to drink cyanide-laced Kool-Aid and commit mass suicide? What could possibly induce a group of people to commit inhuman acts such as the angry Brazilian mob in 1991 that not only viciously beat three kidnappers, but also covered them with gasoline and burned them alive? How do we explain the riots and mayhem that often break out during European or South American soccer matches?

COLLECTIVITIES
Large numbers of people who interact briefly and superficially in the absence of clearly defined norms.

Interpreting Collective Behavior

Social scientists take several approaches to these and other forms of collective behavior. They include contagion theory, convergence theory, emergent norm theory, and value-added theory.

cameras get smaller and more mobile, we should expect "mosquito-scale drones" that fly in and out of office and home windows, making privacy difficult or impossible. Of course, mobile phones with digital cameras have proliferated, as have pinhole cameras, microvideo systems, and wireless video that potentially could make everyone part of the security apparatus (Miller, 2003).

While journalists have largely focused their attention on how surveillance relates to political citizenship and "privacy" issues, much more is involved. According to sociologist David Lyon (1994:15), new surveillance systems have expanded to the point at which they have become a major social institution that affects all social relationships, as well as people's very identities, personal space, freedom, and dignity. Increasingly, data images—computer-integrated profiles of each individual's finances, health, consumer preferences, ethnicity, neighborhood, education, criminal record, and other "significant" characteristics—are the "looking-glass" that provide social judgments about "who we are" and our life changes. Using the old South Africa as his guide, Lyon (1994:211) asks, will the new "non-persons," segregated by surveillance systems, be bankrupt individuals or perhaps nonconsumers?

Many people see the benefits of new surveillance as far outweighing the risks and argue that only criminals and terrorists should be concerned about the intensification of surveillance. They assert, "Why should I worry about privacy? I have nothing to hide" (Garfinkel, 2000:3). Lyon (1994) himself makes the point that dark visions about corporate and government Big Brothers may be counterproductive in that they may produce nothing more than paranoia, fatalism, and inaction. New surveillance, in fact,

both constrains and enables. Although it is unequally distributed, with large organizations controlling most information technologies, these same technologies have given ordinary people access to many new channels of participation and protest, not only nationally but globally. Today's increases in identity theft, spying, selling personal information, and other technological invasions of privacy prompted one sociologist to conclude that "public access to private information has taken on even more ominous tones" (Hurst, 2005:53).

TAKING A CLOSER LOOK

Can new information-gathering technologies be used to protect the public and provide for national security without infringing on people's privacy and personal freedoms? Take a position and support it using one of the sociological perspectives mentioned earlier in the chapter.

Source: David Lyon. *The Electronic Eye: The Rise of Surveillance Society.* Minneapolis: University of Minnesota Press, 1994. David Brin. "Society." *Wired,* December, 1996:303–309. William A. Staples. *The Culture of Surveillance.* New York: Basic Books, 1996. Stephen G. Jones. "Information, Internet, and Community: Notes toward Understanding of Community in the Information Age." In *Cybersociety 2.0: Revisiting Computer-Mediated Communication and Community,* pp. 1–34. Thousand Oaks, CA: Sage, 1998. "Private Eye, Public View." *The Bulletin of the Atomic Scientists* 56(2), March–April 2000:6–7. Simson Garfinkel. *Database Nation: The Death of Privacy in the 21st Century.* Sebastopol, CA: O'Reilly and Associates, 2000. Adam Clymer. "Pentagon Surveillance Plan Is Described as Less Invasive." *The New York Times on the Web,* Wednesday, May 7, 2003:1–2. Matt Sebastian. "Living in a Surveillance Society." *Emporia Gazette,* Section 3, June 7–8, 2003:3. Stephen C. Miller. "Hold It Right There, My Camera's Ringing." *The New York Times on the Web,* Thursday, March 20, 2003:1. Charles E. Hurst. *Living Theory: The Application of Classical Social Theory to Contemporary Life.* Boston: Allyn & Bacon, 2005. Mark Hosenball and Evan Thomas. "Hold the Phone." *Newsweek,* May 22, 2006: 22–32.

Contagion Theory Most early scientific approaches to collective behavior focused on "crowd psychology." For example, Gustav LeBon's ([1895] 1960) *contagion theory* stressed powerful and "contagious" emotions, which when combined with the anonymity of the crowd enabled people to act irresponsibly or even brutally. According to contagion theory, this transformation occurs through the power of suggestion, which makes people susceptible to crowd emotions.

Although the theory is more than a century old, it was used during the past decade in the Reginald Denny trial. Defense lawyers contended that when the people of South Central Los Angeles heard that police officers had been found not guilty in the beating of Rodney King, many took to the streets to express their anger and rage. Under the powerful influence of the crowd, some became prone to violence—including those who dragged Denny out of his truck and threw a brick at his skull.

Although most social theorists agree that emotions are important in such crowds, few believe there is *total uniformity* in people's moods and behaviors in crowds, or even that there is a common emotional response in crowds (Miller, 1985; McPhail, 1994b). Ralph Turner and Lewis Killian (1987:27), however, agree with contagion theory in one regard: the more uncertain the situation, the more individuals become susceptible to "the suggestions of others."

Convergence Theory *Convergence theory* maintains that mobs are comprised not of ordinary citizens caught in the grip of powerful emotions, but of segments of the

How would the various theories on collective behavior explain the riots and police confrontations that occur during rival soccer matches?

population who already share certain attitudes and interests that predispose them to converge and act in violent and destructive ways. This theory might be used to explain the violence that followed Danish newspapers' printing of cartoons that depicted the Islamic prophet Mohammed. Sociologists, however, have found little difference between the attitudes and beliefs of participants and nonparticipants in most forms of collective behavior.

Emergent Norm Theory According to *emergent norm theory,* in situations where collectivities become crowds people neither are overwhelmed by emotions nor are simply imitating each other. Instead, they look to each other during interaction for clues as to how they should behave and establish new or emergent "group norms of judgement" (Turner and Killian, 1987:27). For many years, Chinese officials were strong proponents of emergent norm theory. For example, when crowds gathered, Chinese authorities arrested and detained suspected militants, believing their tactics and the potentially violent norms they might seek to establish were far more dangerous than the crowd itself.

Value-Added Theory Neil J. Smelser's (1962) *value-added theory* requires not only an understanding of crowd dynamics but also an examination of the larger social context in which collective behavior occurs. According to Smelser's model, several conditions increase the likelihood of collective behavior:

1. *Structural Conduciveness*—where institutions are organized in such a way that they encourage collective behavior. For example, democratic states that permit legal rallies and assemblies are structurally more conducive to rioting and mob behavior than authoritarian regimes that outlaw and brutally repress all public gatherings. In much the same way, the mass media can dramatize events, heighten emotions, and encourage crowd behavior, rumors, fads, and fashions.

2. *Social Control Factors*—either government inactivity, confusion, and vacillation or active encouragement by elites may boost collective behavior. In considering the case of the Brazilian mob violence mentioned earlier, it is helpful to know that the police turned the kidnappers over to the mob and that violence against the poor and even urban children is widespread and often condoned by Brazilian authorities.

3. *Structural Strains*—which include any social condition that strains social relations, such as poverty, injustice, discrimination, and economic uncertainty.

4. *Generalized Beliefs*—about their situation that define the nature of the problem, identify who is responsible for it, and offer some plan of action.

5. *Mobilization for Action*—which usually occurs when leaders emerge and mobilize curious or sympathetic observers into active participants. Often a *precipitating event* triggers collective behavior—such as Martin Luther King Jr.'s assassination in 1968, which touched off urban riots in 125 cities across the United States.

Marx and McAdam caution against viewing crowds and masses as the very opposite of formal organizations, noting that the two are often linked in important ways. First, formal organizations create communication channels and social networks that encourage—or retard—collective action should some unusual event occur. Second, "organizations are a major source of strains, grievances, dissatisfaction, and frustrations that lie behind social unrest" (Marx and McAdam, 1994:14). Third, organizations such as the media, government agencies, corporations, and social movement organizations may intentionally generate collective behavior to promote their interests and agendas (Marx and McAdam, 1994).

Crowds, Masses, and Collective Behavior

Following John Lofland's (1985) model, sociologists have combined two major characteristics in classifying various forms of collective behavior: (1) the *dominant emotion expressed*—joy, anger, fear, and other emotions; and (2) the *type of collectivity* involved. In a **crowd,** *people are in close proximity;* in a **mass,** *large numbers of people are widely dispersed* (Turner and Killian, 1987). Table 20.2 lists various kinds of collective behavior and their characteristic emotions. We caution you that these are *ideal types,* which may mask the volatile emotional states characteristic of many forms of collective behavior.

Crowds and Collective Behavior Some kinds of crowds produce collective behavior, while others do not. *Casual crowds,* such as a gathering of people who witness an accident, may share a common focus but too briefly to qualify as collective behavior. *Conventional crowds,* in which people are gathered to watch a sports event, concert, or theater performance, also do not qualify but for the opposite reason: these events occur so often that they are routine and governed by established norms. But under the conditions mentioned by Smelser, even conventional and casual crowds can quickly change to emotionally charged, nonconforming crowds—either expressive or acting (Blumer, 1969a).

An *expressive crowd* gathers for the purpose of expressing emotions. As Turner and Killian (1987:98) noted, "The crowd creates a permissive setting in which the individual can express feelings more freely and with less regard for conventional formality." Rock concerts and sports events, for example, are common settings where members of expressive crowds chant, hug perfect strangers, and even take off their clothes in response to the joyous mood.

Unlike expressive crowds, where emotional release is the only goal, *acting crowds* are emotionally aroused gatherings that direct their attention and activity toward some event or goal. For example, if expressive members of a crowd at a rock concert notice that police officers are attempting to remove an overly exuberant fan, anger may replace joy, and in minutes they may become an acting crowd.

In *mob behavior* an acting crowd threatens violence or engages in violent and destructive acts; it is referred to as a *mob.* If the violence becomes widespread, sustained, and includes large numbers of people, it is called a *riot.* McPhail (1994b:25) contends that during riots "violent actors are neither hapless victims of structural strains nor [victims] of psychological deindividuation. [Instead] purposive actors adjust their behaviors to make their perceptions match their objectives."

Revolutions are "attempts by subordinate groups to transform the social foundations of political power" (Kimmel, 1990:6). Successful revolutions include the American and

At rock concerts and some sports events, a highly emotional and joyous mood often transforms crowds like this one into an "expressive crowd."

Can you think of any other events that might have the same effect on crowds?

CROWD
A large number of people in close enough proximity to interact and influence one another's behavior.

MASS
Large numbers of people widely dispersed.

Can you name current urban legends and identify their "hidden messages"?

TABLE 20.2
FORMS OF COLLECTIVE BEHAVIOR

ORGANIZATIONAL FORM	FEAR	HOSTILITY	JOY	OTHER (GRIEF, ANXIETY, DESPAIR, ETC.)
Crowd	Localized panics (escaping fires, concert exclusion)	Mob attacks, public protests, ghetto riots	Toga parties, rock concerts, New Year's celebrations, carnival celebrations	Rumors concerning death of leaders, loss of jobs, or company relocations
Mass	Mass hysteria, "Red Scares," ecohysteria, space invasions, crime waves	Large-scale multi-city riots, mass vilification or condemation of a person, group, or nation	Postelection celebrations, holiday celebrations, fads, fashions	Urban legends such as "window-pitting" or woman broiled in tanning salon, mass rumors (conspiracy theories), cancer and food scares

Source: Reprinted by permission of Transaction Publishers. Adapted from *Protest: Studies of Collective Behavior and Social Movements* by John Lofland. Copyright © 1985 by Transaction Publishers; all rights reserved.

French Revolutions and the more recent street protests and uprisings in Iran that toppled the Shah's regime and ushered in the current Islamic Republic.

In a *panic*, which is a "collective flight based on a hysterical belief," fear, rather than anger, is the predominant emotion (Smelser, 1962:131). Panics occur whenever crowds believe they must immediately escape a perceived danger or avoid being excluded from a highly desired event. The panics most of us are familiar with involve fires in theaters, nightclubs, or businesses, where exits are limited and people develop the belief that the only course of action is immediate escape by any available means. Increasingly in contemporary society, crowd members panic when they fear they are being excluded from some desirable event or perhaps denied a consumer product.

For example, in 1997, when a crowd that had gathered outside a McDonald's restaurant in Belarus, Russia, heard the news that only a few Big Macs remained, they panicked and rushed into the restaurant injuring several people. Similar panics occur during blockbuster sales—especially at Christmas, when many shoppers may fear the last Nano Ipod or Play Station 3 is about to be sold.

Members of the "Heaven's Gate" religious movement took their lives in the belief that their souls would be transported to a better place by a UFO.

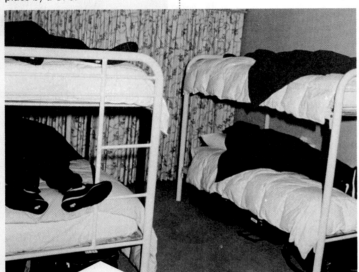

How might theories of collective behavior explain this mass suicide?

Panics have become quite common at rock concerts and sports events as well. For example, in 1989, when hundreds of soccer fans waiting to enter a stadium in Sheffield, England, heard rumors that they were about to be excluded from the event, they frantically pushed into the stadium and crushed those at the front of the stadium against heavy wire fences, causing the deaths of almost 100 people. And we continue to hear of such tragic events at soccer matches worldwide.

The rarest and most dramatic form of crowd behavior is *mass suicide.* Historically, such events have been associated with members of apocalyptic religious communities who are convinced the end of the world is imminent and an armed assault by a hostile government force is about to take place. This was the context of the 1978 mass suicide of more than 900 members of the People's Temple sect in Jonestown, Guyana, who committed suicide by drinking cyanide-laced Kool-Aid (Robbins, 1986). Although the exact cause of the conflagration that took the lives of David Koresh and almost 90 members of the Branch Davidians is still uncertain, the Waco tragedy involved an armed millenarian group that found itself threatened and under siege by government forces (Haught, 1995).

Collective Behavior and Masses Unlike crowds, where people affect one another directly, in **mass behavior** *people are not in the same locality, yet through a common source of information or communication medium they can indirectly influence one another.* Although personal networks remain important, television, cellular phones, and other forms of communication have become key agents in many forms of mass collective behavior. We want to make it clear again that while the mass media may promote collective action it can discourage it as well. For example, Gary Fine and Ryan White (2002) examined how the mainstream media use "human interest stories" to create collective attention, provoke public discussion, and foster communal identification. Media favorites for over a century include stories about people and animals that have become trapped, a child lost in the woods, a missing climber, or a baby who needs unusual medical attention. But human interest stories—just like media stories that detail the trials and tribulations of celebrities—rarely produce collective action. In fact, because human interest stories are highly personal and seem to have little social importance, "the call for collective action and political action is muffled and muted." This may be of increasing significance with the growing "tabloidization of the media." Today, important forms of collective action include: fads, fashions, rumors, urban legends, and mass hysteria (Goode, 1992).

MASS BEHAVIOR
People are not in the same locality, yet through a common source of information or communication medium they can indirectly influence one another.

Fads are *short-term, frivolous, and unconventional collective behaviors that usually provide pleasure and involve only a small segment of the population.* Many challenge tradition and authority—such as young people dressing like popular rock stars. College students "streaking" (running naked through public places) and youths dyeing their hair green are other examples of fads. Some fads are more respectable and more profitable to businesses and other interests. These may involve objects such as crystals, ferret pets, in-line skates, or Razor scooters, or activities such as bungee jumping or dances like the Macarena or Lambada. The future will be marked by global fads and trends, according to *The Futurist* magazine.

Fashions are *relatively enduring styles and behaviors that enjoy widespread popularity, often in cycles,* such as dress and hair styles and automobile and home designs. Fashions are acutely sensitive to shifting economic and demographic trends. In the United States, shifts in the values, tastes, and concerns of baby boomers are of special importance. In the 1960s, for example, many youthful and rebellious baby boomers found miniskirts and bikinis fashionable. Early in the twenty-first century, more affluent baby boomers switched to jacuzzis, BMWs, and designer sunglasses. Today, fashions reflect middle-age concerns, such as the powerful emphasis on saving, dieting, travel, and other leisure activities.

Rumors tend to be the opposite of fashion in many ways. While fashions are often associated with the "high-brow" domain, popular rumors are "low-brow" and commonplace—the stuff of ordinary people, popular culture, tabloids, and "trash TV." **Rumors** are *unconfirmed items or media reports that spread by word of mouth and cannot be verified* (Goode, 1992). They can arise on a large scale in periods of change or when people lack reliable or trustworthy information. Rumors reflect people's deep-seated concerns, prejudices, hopes, and fears. They also can be spread by activists and others to alert the public to social problems or to promote or resist change. For example, following the 9/11 World Trade Center attacks, rumors and "conspiracy theories" spread across the Middle East that the event either never occurred or the U.S. government was responsible. A short time later, a French author, described by the French press as a "left-wing activist," published a book that rose to the top of that country's best-seller list, that claimed that "no terrorists were involved in the 9/11 attacks, no airplanes crashed into the Pentagon on 9/11, and the whole affair was a hoax orchestrated by a cabal of right-wing CIA rogues" (Hagen, 2002:1). On a global scale, the poor and disadvantaged "have not remained silent in the face of threats to their bodily integrity, security, and dignity," wrote anthropologist Nancy Scheper-Hughes (2000:201). "Organ-stealing" rumors have been one collective response to these threats. This urban legend was perpetuated by a story line on the popular television show *Nip/Tuck*.

Many rumors are introduced on radio and television but the Internet is now the favored source. Websites spread both facts and rumors about corporations, the government, celebrities, and a host of other public concerns each day. Because of their growing influence in contemporary life, website rumors about corporate activities are especially popular. In 1997, for example, someone began spreading the rumor that "Mrs. Field's Cookies had donated cookies to O. J. Simpson's victory party." As *Newsweek* reported, "The Utah-based cookiemaker hired *eWatch* to find where the rumor was spreading on the Internet to help them issue electronic denials. The rumors stopped in a few days, averting a threatened boycott" (Tanaka, 1997:80).

Urban legends are *complex popular tales that often contain implicit warnings and messages.* Today, they are favorites of tabloids and talk-show hosts. For example, during the 1980s reports circulated about the hapless woman who discovered to her horror that the chicken she thought she was eating at a fast-food restaurant was actually "batter-fried rat"; or the tale of the man who called a computer company to report that his computer "cup-holder" (the CD-ROM drive) was broken (Brunvand, 1999:287). Such stories express collective anxieties and concerns about mass society and things beyond people's control—such as the hidden dangers of modern technology and the subtle costs of the hurried pace of modern life.

Many rumors also are fabricated or sustained by businesses, the government, and other organizations and movements. During the 1980s, for example, some fundamentalist

Fads and fashions come and go. While baby boomers have embraced the "low carb" and fitness craze, their children's and grandchildren's generations seem to be more fascinated with tattoos, piercings, and unusual hairdos.

FADS
Short-term, frivolous, and unconventional collective behaviors that usually provide pleasure and involve only a small segment of the population.

FASHIONS
Relatively enduring styles and behaviors that enjoy widespread popularity, often in cycles.

RUMORS
Unconfirmed items or media reports that spread by word of mouth and cannot be verified.

URBAN LEGENDS
Complex popular tales that often contain implicit warnings and messages.

Some call it "bad information"—bogus flyers, faxes, and e-mails that detail some imminent threat that is supposedly based on scientific fact and irrefutable evidence that is often attributed to scientists, high government officials, a television news show, or some recent research report. Jan Brunvand adds to this list what he calls "xeroxlore," anonymously produced flyers that are posted on bulletin boards or handed around neighborhoods, faxed, or e-mailed to friends—often within minority communities—that warn about some terrible community threat. As Brunvand noted, these forms of "xeroxlore" are a kind of hybrid between "too good to be true" urban legends, and unverified rumors, that have no well developed narrative content but resonate with meanings within minority communities.

In addition to the message itself, "xeroxlore" often comes with handwritten additions such as "Warning!!!" Or "Please Read and Circulate!!!" Or "This Is Not a Joke!!!" (Brunvand, 1999:386). Patricia Turner (1993) describes one that circulated in New York City about a dangerous soft drink called either "Top Pop" or "Tropical Fantasy" that was supposedly manufactured by the Ku Klux Klan and distributed "only in Harlem and other black neighborhoods" to "sterilize black males." It ended with "You Have Been Warned, Please Save the Children" (Brunvand, 1999:387). Brunvand notes that

similar rumors about sterilizing agents were associated with a national fast-food chain and an athletic-wear manufacturer. In the same period, another bogus warning concerned dire threats to a much wider audience: America's children. During the height of the body piercing and tattooing craze, one circular warned parents about a tattoo called "Blue Star" that was being sold to school children. According to the circular, "They are the size of a pencil eraser and each star is soaked with L.S.D." (Brundvand, 1999:390). Today, e-mail messages have become the most popular ways to mass-circulate similar hoaxes.

TAKING A CLOSER LOOK

Are such flyers, posters, and e-mails about bogus threats and conspiracies "bad information"? Or, in the context of this chapter, can they be understood as either an important form of collective behavior or perhaps even grass-roots social activism?

Source: From Jan H. Brunvand. *Too Good To Be True: The Colossal Book of Urban Legends.* New York: W.W. Norton, 1999. Patricia A. Turner, *I Heard it Through the Grapevine: Rumor in African-American Culture.* Davis, CA: University of California Press, 1993.

religious groups gained new members and increased contributions by promoting false rumors that Procter & Gamble's logo was a satanic symbol. Focus box 20.2 examines bogus e-mails and flyers—circulated by ordinary people—that describe threats to the community.

At first glance, **mass hysteria,** which involves *widespread anxiety and the frantic reactions of large numbers of people to some perceived threat,* seems to be completely irrational and to have no logic. Typically, the dangers involved—witches, UFOs, and Satanists—are either greatly exaggerated or nonexistent. James Richardson and colleagues (1991) argue that to understand these forms of hysteria fully, it is useful to take into account some of the more organized and goal-oriented forms of collective action that sociologists call *social movements.*

For example, the *anticult movement*—a religious movement aimed at containing the spread of New Age and other novel approaches to religion—promoted the idea that Satanists had infiltrated almost every American community. About the same time, the *childsaver movement* focused public attention on missing and abducted children, introducing the public to a whole range of issues—perhaps including some, such as UFO abductions and UFO medical experiments, that never happened. The fact that some parents, school officials, police officers, and segments of the public became convinced that Satanists and sinister aliens from outer space had become a threat to society attests to the power and influence of these and other social movements. Let's take a closer look at social movements and their special contributions to social change.

MASS HYSTERIA
Widespread anxiety and the frantic reactions of large numbers of people to some perceived threat.

SOCIAL MOVEMENTS

Social movements, as we noted earlier, are organized goal-directed efforts by a large number of people to promote or resist change outside of established institutions. Unlike fads, riots, panics, and other forms of spontaneous social action, social movements are relatively enduring and have an organizational base, leadership, and an ideological blueprint for collective action. Because they are well organized and enduring, social movements have been major agents of social change (Goldberg, 1991; Della Porta and Diani, 2006).

Social movements are "noninstitutional challenges to the mainstream." Unlike the activities of lobbyists, political parties, and interest groups, which are integral parts of the political order, social movement organizations are not part of the formal political process. Instead, they are political outsiders, and their ideas and alternative visions of the future are either at the margins of mainstream society or excluded and deemed socially unacceptable (Lofland, 1996; Meyer, 2006).

Establishment officials typically ignore emerging social movements—at least initially. If their ideas become widespread and somewhat socially acceptable, officials may ridicule movement leaders and their ideas. Today, they often do so with the help of the media—which may frame movement leaders and their ideas as silly, outrageous, unpatriotic, or even treasonous. Those that strike a chord with the public, however, may receive much closer scrutiny from authorities: perhaps close monitoring of movement leaders and their activities, and sometimes even official and unofficial violence. Successful movements must find ways to overcome these and other obstacles, as well as challenges from competing social movements (Lofland, 1996; Meyer, 2006).

Perspectives on Social Movements

According to *relative deprivation theory,* social movements appear when people feel deprived relative to others or the way life was in the past. In fact, social movements are more common in relatively affluent societies than in those experiencing severe poverty. Often they occur when conditions are improving but expected benefits are not materializing as rapidly or to the degree that people wish.

Sociologists who adopt the *resource mobilization* perspective disagree that grievances and alienation are at the heart of social movements. For example, McCarthy and Zald (1977) contended that whereas discontent is widespread in all societies, collective action is relatively uncommon. They maintained that when deprived groups mobilize it is not because of rising levels of discontent but because they have found effective ways to mobilize people and resources—leadership, money, organizing skills, and media coverage— to their causes. The resource mobilization perspective places special emphasis on the strategies and tactics used by leaders to mobilize resources from within and outside their ranks, rally supporters, neutralize external challenges, and gain the support of elite groups.

David Snow and Robert Benford (1988) pointed out that a movement's success is also dependent on ideology and what they termed *frame alignment.* This is a process in which the values, beliefs, and goals of potential recruits are made congruent and complementary to a movement's value orientation and put in the service of the movement (Snow et al., 1980, Snow et al., 1986). According to Snow and Benford (1988), commitment to a social movement is an ongoing, interactive process in which leaders must provide potential recruits with reasons they should join or remain members. To be successful, a movement must develop what the authors call "core framing" that negotiates the nature of a problem, who is responsible for it, and an alternative set of arrangements and plans for action (Benford and Snow, 2000:615). In effect, movements are engaged in the production of meaning for participants, and their relative success depends on how well their messages compete with those of other movements and, most importantly, with those of the established political forces they attack.

In short, social movements should be considered part of the political process because they, like political parties and interest groups, seek to affect public policy. But unlike parties and interest groups, which are part of the formal political process, social movements include "irregular players" who have fewer resources than their competitors and minimal access to traditional avenues

Protesters outside the World Trade Organization meeting held in the United States.

of influence and power. As Robert Goldberg (1991:3) observed: "Aware of power realities, movement leaders mobilize recruits to pursue goals in unorthodox and innovative ways."

Social Movement Organizations

Depending on their tactics and relationships with authorities, whether they look to the future or past, and how much change they advocate, social movements can be classified into four ideal types: *Reform movements* are the most common and socially acceptable type of social movement. They aim at limited reforms in existing institutions, such as the Children's Rights Movement, which has worked for several centuries to improve the health and welfare of American children (Hawes, 1991). Reform movements attempt to work within established political channels, although they often have militant branches.

Utopian movements seek to create "perfect societies," often by establishing communities apart from the larger society that promise to fulfill *all* of their members' needs and desires, as well as serve as models for future social behavior.

Revolutionary movements have both utopian visions and specific plans for governing a society once they have assumed power. Revolutionary movements have as their goal the elimination of old institutions and their replacement with new ones that conform to a radically different vision of society. Few revolutionary movements succeed in achieving their visions, but those that have (e.g., the American and French Revolutions) have brought extraordinary changes that have reshaped societies virtually everywhere on the globe.

Resistance movements, or *countermovements,* seek to reverse or resist change and restore "traditional values" that presumably prevailed at some time in the past. Resistance movements often emerge to resist reform movements. For example, Phyllis Schlafly's conservative Eagle Forum opposes the goals of the National Organization for Women (NOW), and there are other well-organized movements both for and against abortion rights, gun control, capital punishment, civil rights, and gay rights. These movements and others have websites where they dispense information, sign up recruits, and link to other social movements' sites.

Grassroot and Professional SMOs

When grievances are widely shared and there are abundant resources to attract many followers, social movements and countermovements proliferate (McAdam et al., 1988). Moreover, successful movements typically produce many separate *social movement organizations (SMOs)* with the same general goals but diverse tactics. For example, in the United States alone, there are 7,000 groups concerned with animal rights and some 3,000 organizations devoted to gay and lesbian issues (Goode, 1992; Meyer, 2006).

There are two major kinds of SMOs: volunteer and professional. The former are supported and run by ordinary women and men who volunteer their time, money, and services and who are committed to a cause that directly affects their lives. For example, homeowners can join forces to stop a company from dumping toxic chemicals in their neighborhood. In contrast, professional SMOs are formal organizations such as the NAACP or the National Audubon Society that include full-time professional activists who derive much of their income from foundations, grants, and agencies, in addition to contributions from the people they represent.

McCarthy and Zald (1973) believe the success of many professional SMOs hinges less on how deeply their members feel about issues than on their gaining the support of elite groups. In fact, many contemporary professional SMOs have relatively few active members. They rely on expertise donated by think tanks, on media support, and on funds supplied by foundations and middle- and upper-class "conscience constituents," who contribute to but do not directly benefit from a movement's success

Environmental activists represent both grassroot movements and SMOs.

such groups presents new dilemmas for the movement that leaders must resolve if the movement is to persevere and achieve its goals.

The Life Course of Social Movements

In some ways, it is remarkable that social movements ever get launched, because during their early stages all movements find themselves in a classic Catch-22 situation: protest leaders must convince members to join, "but the incentive for individuals to cooperate in an organized movement depends first on a demonstration that collective action is a worthwhile investment" (Chong, 1991:234). How is this dilemma resolved? Chong argued that a history of successful collective action and past political mobilization, which provides hope and inspiration, is one way. The other centers on leaders, who Chong calls "unconditional cooperators," who are so committed to the cause that they are willing to pay the heavy start-up costs, which may include getting fired by employers and being persecuted by authorities or opposition forces.

In his study of the Civil Rights movement, Aldon Morris (1984) found that many were also attracted to Dr. Martin Luther King Jr. because he possessed *charisma,* as well as the talent to articulate his visions of a new society devoid of racism. At the same time, King was able to mobilize the support of churches, labor unions, the media, and others essential for the movement's development and growth.

Early on, leaders must overcome what is known as the *free-rider problem:* many people who stand to benefit from a movement let others do the hard work while they sit on the sidelines. Leaders try to gain the support of free-riders by winning "quick victories" and concessions from authorities (Chong, 1991). Leaders can also gain new recruits and resources by aligning their causes with churches, colleges, and other powerful organizations.

In his book *Soul of a Citizen,* Paul Loeb (1999:34–35) contends that the media and popular culture portray famous civil rights activists such as Rosa Parks as larger-than-life figures who come out of nowhere to take dramatic stands. Such portrayals imply that unique individuals, acting alone, have the greatest social impact. Yet Rosa Parks—whose refusal to give up her bus seat to a white man helped set in motion the Montgomery, Alabama, bus boycott—had a long history of social activism. As Loeb (1999) and many social researchers have found, prior to this historically important incident, Parks had spent many years helping lead the local chapter of the NAACP, and she had close links to union, church, and many other groups and social movements. Loeb (1999:37) argues that we should honor heroes such as Rosa Parks, but we should recognize that "social change is the product of deliberate, incremental action whereby we join together to try to shape a better world." For example, Focus box 20.3 takes a closer look at the anti–death penalty movement, which has had its ups and downs in American history but appears to have lost ground during the past few decades.

Social networks that facilitate participation in social movements are fundamental to recruitment as well (Knoke and Wisely, 1990; Cable, 1992). There are three kinds of networks: networks of individuals, networks of organizations, and networks of collectivities and events, according to Diani and McAdams (2003:4). Though people may recognize the benefits of joining social movements, most tend to participate out of a sense of obligation to family members, friends, and associates who already belong. Member commitment, in turn, is bolstered by a variety of group processes such as group decision making, group discussions, and confrontations with authorities, which often enhance protester "commitment to the cause and their belief in the noninstitutional tactics that further the cause" (Hirsh, 1990:243).

To augment their resources and gain new sources of funding and recruits, successful movement leaders—especially in professional SMOs—commonly employ a strategy called *bloc mobilization,* whereby resources are shared with other organizations with similar beliefs and goals. By sharing computer mailing lists, underdogs now have instant access to thousands or even millions of potential supporters and contributors, as well as access to political friends in high places, celebrities, and experts.

Almost everywhere in the world, capital punishment is on the decline. Today, only China, Iran, Cuba, some nations in the Middle East, and the United States execute people for a host of crimes, from various forms of personal violence, including murder, to crimes against the state, such as treason and political assassination. In his study of capital punishment, sociologist Herbert Haines found that public support for capital punishment in the United States has waxed and waned over the centuries, including most of the twentieth century. However, since the 1960s, when capital punishment advocates were decidedly in the minority, popular enthusiasm for the death penalty, including what Haines (1996:3) called "ordinary crimes of violence," steadily increased. In a 2003 poll, for example, 74 percent of Americans supported the death penalty, whereas only 24 percent opposed it "for a person convicted of murder" (Jones, 2000; Jones, 2003).

What caused this shift in public attitudes? In *Against Capital Punishment,* Haines argues that numerous factors were involved, including economic restructuring and rising crime rates—including about 20,000 homicides per year throughout the 1990s. But early in the twenty-first century, DNA tests, which exonerated some wrongly convicted death-row inmates and led hundreds of others to seek tests to prove their innocence, may have shifted public opinion somewhat in the other direction (Chebium, 2000). Record low crime rates—especially violent crimes—which fell to about 23 victims per 1,000 U.S. residents, less than half of victims reported in 1993 (Anderson, 2003:1), may have also contributed to the shift.

Most of Haines's book focuses on the tactics and problems within the Anti–Death Penalty Movement (ADPM). His investigations provide an excellent case study of the inner workings of a social movement and how movement activists and their tactics influence both public attitudes

and public policy. Haines discovered that the ADPM comprises several important groups and organizations that sometimes cooperate and occasionally work at cross-purposes. One large group includes criminal attorneys who specialize in capital defense cases. Policy advocates who lobby against the death penalty are another important component of the movement. Equally important are the more than 20 religious denominations that actively seek to abolish capital punishment, as well as several key human rights groups, including the National Coalition to Abolish the Death Penalty, Amnesty International, and the American Civil Liberties Union.

Haines contends that one serious problem the movement faces is that it is not a mass movement on the order of the civil rights movement or the feminist movements. As Haines (1996:15) remarked, "Its major advocates are neither death-sentenced inmates nor former convicts." Instead, it is largely a professional social movement organization. There are a handful of "moral entrepreneurs," such as Sister Helen Prejean, whose work was portrayed in the Hollywood movie *Dead Man Walking.* Most members, however, are "paper contributors," and the vast majority of them are "multi-issue contributors." Consequently, the movement's resource base is highly erratic, and funds are often scarce, as they have been during much of the past three decades.

Because it is not a traditional mass movement, the ADPM has other drawbacks. One potential difficulty is that the movement has no "radical flank" that employs disruptive and strategically violent tactics, which generate widespread publicity and media attention. Of course, the movement's nonviolent philosophy largely precludes these tactics. Instead, activists must rely on lobbying, letter writing, and public education programs on behalf of death-sentenced inmates to reach the public, often in the face of sensational media images of crime scenes and their victims. Haines also

Factors Related to Movement Success

In 1975, William Gamson completed an in-depth study of 53 social movements active between 1800 and 1945. He found that several factors were related to a movement's success. First, large, bureaucratically organized movements were somewhat more successful than small, loosely organized ones. Historical conditions, such as wars and depressions, boosted social movements as well. Movements that effectively used "strategic violence" tended to fare somewhat better than their more peaceful counterparts. Of course, violence is a double-edged sword that may backfire and generate public outrage rather than support. For example, do you remember what ordinary people and the media called those responsible for bombing the federal building in Oklahoma City in 1996 that caused the deaths of hundreds of men, women, and children? Finally, single-issue challengers advocating minor reforms generally do much better than movements that demand significant social change (Goldberg, 1991; Della Porta and Diani, 2006).

Robert Goldberg's (1991:230) study of the Ku Klux Klan, NOW, the Berkeley free-speech movement, and five other twentieth-century movements generally supported Gamson's findings. However, Goldberg found that three interrelated variables were crit-

found that whereas anti–capital punishment organizations were relatively strong at the national and international levels, they were weak at the state and local levels.

Haines contends that frame alignment difficulties and activist decisions to focus on issues that had little public appeal also eroded public support. Many activists in the 1980s also misunderstood the media, naively assuming that the media would objectively present both sides of the capital punishment debate. They found that the media much preferred violent images that were geared to entertainment and ratings points. An emphasis on morality and human rights also produced mixed results, especially in a climate of fear and anger over violent crime and hot political rhetoric about getting tough on crime and criminals. Now, however, with falling crime rates, enthusiasm for capital punishment may have begun to wane.

Radelet and Borg (2000:57) contend that there is an accelerating worldwide decline in the acceptance of the death penalty. They believe that the number of executions in the United States may increase in the short term but that trends point toward abolition of the death penalty. Further, they maintain that popular support for the death penalty could erode quickly "if there emerged absolute, incontrovertible proof that an innocent prisoner had been executed" (Radelet and Borg, 2000:57). The final thrust might come from conservative politicians who turn against the death penalty out of budgetary concerns or perhaps in the name of religious principles (e.g., a more consistent pro-life position) (Radelet and Borg, 2000:57).

Haines (1996:165) and other activists maintain that the following frames may help to shift public sentiment against the death penalty in the United States:

1. The *fairness frame* claims that the death penalty is applied in a discriminatory way. For example, in one U.S. poll, 51 percent of respondents said the death penalty was applied fairly; however, 41 percent said that it was applied unfairly (Jones, 2000:64).

2. The *anti-violence frame* argues that the death penalty is so brutal that it enhances rather than reduces violence in America.

3. The *high-cost frame* maintains that the criminal justice system that includes the death penalty is extremely expensive and a heavy burden for taxpayers.

4. The *public safety frame* insists that the death penalty has not made the public safer, particularly in states with the highest execution rates.

TAKING A CLOSER LOOK

Do you believe the four frames would convince people who are largely neutral on the subject to support the anti–death penalty cause? What about "pro–capital punishment" advocates? Do you think these four or any frames might weaken their position and shift them even slightly toward the anti–death penalty cause?

Source: Adapted from Herbert H. Haines, *Against Captial Punishment: The Anti-Death Penalty Movement in America, 1972–1994.* Copyright © 1996. Reprinted by permission of Oxford University Press. Jeffrey M. Jones. "Slim Majority of Americans Think Death Penalty Applied Fairly in This Country." *The Gallup Poll Monthly,* No. 417, June 2000:64–68. Michael L. Radelet and Marian J. Borg. "The Changing Nature of Death Penalty Debates." *The Annual Review of Sociology* 26 2000:43–61. Raju Chebium. "DNA Provides New Hope for Wrongly Convicted Death Row Inmates." *CNN.com Law Center,* June 16, 200:1–6. Curt Anderson. "2002 Crime Rates Lowest Since Records Kept." *Yahoo.com News,* Sunday, August 24, 2003:1–4. Jeffrey M. Jones. "Support for the Death Penalty Remains High at 74%; Slight Majority Prefers Death Penalty to Life Imprisonment as Punishment for Murder." *Gallup Poll Analysis.* The Gallup Organization, May 19, 2003:1–7.

ical to a movement's fate: the support of powerful sponsoring groups and organizations, linking a movement's ideology to a society's core values and traditions, and a multitude of resources to overcome government attempts to silence or co-opt the movement's leadership and either make them part of the political establishment or get them to return to "normal life."

Social Movements and Change

Although the forces opposed to grassroots protest and challenge are formidable, it should be obvious that some social movements, such as the civil rights and feminist movements, have brought significant changes to American society. Even obscure grassroots movements may generate important changes in people's lives. For example, Sherry Cable (1992:39), who studied a women's environmental protest movement in rural Kentucky, found that by assuming leadership roles rural activists not only forced a local tannery to stop polluting local streams, but they also "experienced changes in their perceptions and grievances, of themselves, and of their own SMO roles." Many of the women also experienced a sense of empowerment that led to additional changes in their domestic lives.

Moreover, even movements that appear to have been crushed, such as Poland's Solidarity movement during the early 1980s, may set in motion a series of events that pave the way for significant political change. According to Piotr Sztompka (1991:156), even at its low point, when its leaders were in prison, Solidarity had already "succeeded in infusing the system with the 'logic of reform,' enlarged the scope of participation in political life, and transformed the balance of forces in political elites."

Perhaps, as Goldberg (1991) noted, the United States and other major industrial nations have become more tolerant of protest movements because they see themselves as beneficiaries of social movements and collective activities in Eastern Europe and elsewhere. Whether these movements will persist, die out, or spread to other parts of the world is uncertain, though there is plenty of evidence that democratic ideals that legitimate protest are spreading across the globe. Moreover, waves of protests, strikes, and "food riots" are becoming more common throughout the developing world as international economic competition intensifies.

Boswell and Dixon (1990) contended that in the absence of intense state repression, protests and rebellions will increase as nations modernize, income inequality and class polarization become more pronounced, and greater resources become available to the lower classes for organizing protests. Verta Taylor (2000:227) contends that the United States is becoming a "social movement society," in which grassroots protests are "routine" and serve as vital sources of community, meaning, and multicultural citizenship. There is also some evidence that protests are spreading worldwide because intervention by national elites is becoming less cost-effective and more politically hazardous, due to the unprecedented rise of mass anti-interventionist and human rights movements (Kowalewski, 1991).

LOOKING to the FUTURE

THE MEDIA, SOCIAL CHANGE, AND LIFE IN THE TWENTY-FIRST CENTURY

What will life be like in the future? Our opinions and views depend on many social factors, but in contemporary society many people rely on the media for answers.

Mass Media Visions of the Future

Science fiction and popular movies offer some hints and possibilities. One of the most popular movies of all time, *Star Wars*, and its sequels used myth and the timeless struggle between good and evil—and good's victory—to offer moviegoers a vision of hope. So did blockbuster films such as *E.T. the "Extraterrestrial," Close Encounters of the Third Kind, Independence Day*, and the 2005 version of *War of the Worlds*.

Dark visions of the future, though, were much more in evidence. A persistent theme of twentieth-century novels and science fiction movies was the threat of technology, "big government," the military, and foreign enemies to the lives of ordinary people. Movies such as *Frankenstein* and *2001: A Space Odyssey* expressed public anxieties about out-of-control technology long before the era of computers and sophisticated surveillance devices.

Hollywood movies and television shows often reflect the media's fascination with technology and dark visions of the future.

Similarly, George Orwell's 1949 novel *1984* captured public anxieties about the expansion of government and fears of Big Brother. Fears of government conspiracies were no less evident in 1998, with Hollywood's release of the *X-Files*. Sometimes public anxieties reflect very real conditions; for example, in the context of Nazi military threats on the eve of World War II, Orson Welles and the Mercury Theater's broadcast of the radio drama *War of the Worlds* offered convincing proof that under the right conditions media could create panic among millions of people—even with fanciful tales of Martian landings.

Since the late 1940s, the potential horror of nuclear war has been a favorite media theme both in films and on television. Most shows, including the television movie *The Day After*, portrayed the extraordinary destructive potential of nuclear weapons but allayed public fears with the comforting but false message that after a brief period of instability and suffering, people's lives would return to normal. Similar messages were attached to futuristic movies such as *Terminator, Robocop,* and *Bladerunner,* which showed urban wastelands dominated by lawless gangs and minorities. Some analysts argue that the success of all of these films was due to very real twentieth-century social and political concerns, as well as racial and ethnic prejudices, which were projected onto outlaw gangs, monsters, robots, and aliens (Skal, 1993).

New surveillance technologies and their potential impact on people's lives and identities did not escape Hollywood's notice. In 1998, *The Truman Show* and Jim Carrey portrayed real life as a soap opera. Ironically, ordinary people also record their everyday lives with Web cameras, and several of these sites are now on the Web.

Although futuristic novels and films captured deep-seated public fears and even collective nightmares, it is unlikely that the majority of Americans saw them as anything other than entertainment fantasies. For "realistic" views of the future, most of us seek the opinions of experts who appear regularly on network news or who write about future trends in newspapers and magazines such as *The Futurist*. For complex issues, like biotechnology debates and their role in the future, mainstream media "experts" currently employ a number of *frames* to help organize and guide public interpretations of "scientific truth." For most medical issues, in both Europe and the United States, the mainstream media typically employ *progress frames*. In other cases, *economic* or *globalization frames* are common, and *ethical* and *public accountability frames* are used for more controversial issues. When major institutions are threatened by some biotechnology advance—like stem cell research or cloning—the media often use two other frames to question or challenge their use: either a *runaway technology frame* that spells out known dangers that a new technology may set in motion; or, in the case of more radical technological change, the media often employ a *pandora's box frame,* that hints at the many unknown and dire consequences that a new technology may unleash on humanity (Priest and Eych, 2003:30–32). In *Futurehype,* Max Dublin (1991) asserted that a small group of media prophets, including "pop futurologists" and consultants for establishment think tanks such as the Rand Corporation, have assumed great influence in defining and shaping how Americans perceive the future. By now you are well aware that social activists rarely qualify as "experts" and this usually disqualifies them as media consultants on network news. There are exceptions, however, such as environmental activists who address the "toxic pollution" issues that are discussed in Focus box 20.4.

Some "experts" offer visions of a future that are pretty much a continuation of what is happening today, although they predict that people's fortunes will gradually improve over time. This is especially true for advancements in medical technology that futurists claim will go beyond cloning and include such bioengineering wonders as organ regeneration and even the manufacture of body parts, which would have a profound impact on "human life, evolution, and civilization" (Mironov, 2003:37). Others present utopian visions of a high-tech postindustrial future where robots, cyborgs, and the new information superhighway will forever banish adversity and want, and where the lives of ordinary people will be much happier and more fulfilling (Penley and Ross, 1991; Gandy, 1994). Will the Information Age bring beneficial social changes that until now people have only dreamed about?

Some scholars maintain that the media, with their emphasis on dramatic action and compelling visuals, have tilted the balance among social movements toward those with the most militant and violent approaches to social change. According to their view, all contemporary movements must compete to get the media's attention, and in the media spotlight, conflict and violence can often be the difference between movement success and failure.

One of the most effective movements in the 1970s and 1980s was the anti–toxic waste movement. According to Andrew Szasz (1994), the media were attracted to Love Canal, the Chernobyl nuclear disaster, and the *Exxon Valdez* oil spill because such issues were "made for television." Most had compelling visuals, hot rhetoric, and even elements of myth. Often, there were "good guys" (homeowners and community members—the victims) and "bad guys" (big corporations and big government—the victimizers). Most of all, there were conflict and angry confrontations between the two, who along with social movement activists, helped make "toxic waste a household word and hazardous industrial waste a mass issue" (Szasz, 1994:5).

Social activist concerns about new technologies, such as new surveillance technologies and their threat to personal privacy, attracted far less media attention. For example, during the early 1990s many social movement activists sought a dialogue with government and business, using traditional approaches such as letter-writing campaigns and enlisting academic experts to alert politicians and the public to potential problems. But these tactics failed to attract the mainstream media's attention. This was not the case with Theodore Kaczynski, the "Unabomber," who sought to resist technological change by sending mail bombs to scientists and others, causing three deaths and 23 injuries. His one-man crusade against a growing "technological society"

Violence and militant branches of social movements usually get a great deal of media attention. During the 1990s, while some social activists sought a dialogue on technological change, the mainstream media focused most of their attention on Theodore Kaczynski, known as the Unabomber, who sought to resist technological change by sending mail bombs to scientists and others he believed were proponents of a "technological society."

TECHNOMEDIA AND THE FUTURE

In *The Road Ahead*, Microsoft billionaire Bill Gates painted an optimistic vision of the future, where computers and interactive networks transform work, the family, and all other aspects of life in the twenty-first century—almost all of it for the better. Because these extraordinary benefits would require little effort and have no costs for ordinary people, we should treat them much as we do futuristic Hollywood films—as popular fantasies.

Today, much of the debate about the future centers on new information technologies and the spectacular benefits or dangers they may bring. Advocates associate a high-tech future with prosperity, equality, and justice (Gilder, 2000). By contrast, detractors often envision poverty, Big Brother, and oppression. Certainly, new information technologies will accelerate such trends as economic globalization, a restructuring of work, and many other social transformations. Some predict that we will continue to witness the most striking technological advances in history. And "e-fads" and "e-crazes," and what the media termed "flash mobs," will continue.

Few would disagree that the World Wide Web has great potential for erasing political and geographical boundaries as well as facilitating global interaction and understanding. For the first time in history, the Internet provides ordinary people oppor-

received intense media coverage, and even today, his comments from prison appear in newspapers and magazines and on the evening news.

Global activists annually protest the World Trade Organization meetings, advocating global equality, social justice, and ways to achieve these goals. But most of these messages go unheeded in the mainstream media. For example, the WTO protest in Seattle in 1999 drew over 40,000 men and women who peacefully expressed opposition to various world trade policies. However, the mainstream media—from network news to late-night comic routines—focused on violent confrontations and the activities of a few dozen masked protestors who spray-painted buildings, challenged police, and otherwise disrupted the ordinary routines of Seattle shoppers and businesses (Nacos, 2000:194).

Since this event, which the media dubbed "The Battle in Seattle," there have been scores of other globalization protests noted in websites like ZNET and Protest.Net. But like the Seattle protest most received similar media coverage with a focus on violence and the destruction of property. Ironically, even antiwar protests sometimes receive similar attention but more often the focus is on the "odd," "the unusual," and the "unpopular." For example, during the spring of 2003 antiwar protests against the Iraq war, the *Philadelphia Inquirer* noted that there were many "fringe groups" including: "Apologists for North Korea . . . Anarchists, [and people carrying] giant cardboard skeleton heads, [and] mock oil derricks spouting blood and scores of placards scrawled with capital-*P* cries for peace,"—and wondered, was "such inclusiveness a strength or a distraction?" (Gammage, 2003:1).

Of course, such attention can be a double-edged sword. Mainstream TV and newspaper coverage may confer a kind of legitimacy on a movement and enhance its credibility, and media attention can raise rank-and-file morale and facilitate recruitment efforts and resource building by reaching many millions of people. But if the rewards are great, so too are the risks—especially for activists who prefer militant tactics. While some movements may be labeled silly or utopian, militant tactics often result in others being framed by mainstream media as "extremist," threatening American jobs, families, or even the "American way of life" (Goldberg, 1991). Such framing rarely promotes movement goals, although even these challenges are now being planned for by savvy activists who recognize both the media's propensity for dramatic action and their typical responses to militant social action.

TAKING A CLOSER LOOK

Examine a militant social protest and how it was portrayed in either mainstream or alternative media. After describing media framing, discuss whether you believe the movement's tactics were effective or ineffective in gaining public attention and support of its cause.

Source: Robert A. Goldberg. *Grassroots Resistance: Social Movements in Twentieth Century America.* Belmont, CA: Wadsworth, 1991. Andrew Szasz. *EcoPopulism: Toxic Waste and the Movement for Environmental Justice.* Minneapolis, MN: University of Minnesota Press, 1994. Brigette L. Nacos. "Accomplice or Witness? The Media's Role in Terrorism." *Current History* 99(636), 2000:174–178. Jeff Gammage. "The Fringe Factor." *The Philadelphia Inquirer, Philly.com,* Saturday, March 29, 2003:1–7.

tunities to communicate with people across the globe and organize large-scale social movements in a matter of hours or days. For example, it took just a few days for "over thirty thousand organizations and one hundred thousand individuals from all around the United States to form an on-line coalition in response to the Congressional effort to censor speech on the Internet" (Berman and Weitzen, 1997:1315). And as Howard Rheingold (2002:xviii) wrote: "Location-sensing wireless organizers, wireless networks, and community supercomputing all have one thing in common; they enable people to act together in new ways and in new situations where collective action was not possible before." This only hints at the potential of on-line and other forms of "techno-mediated" activism in the future. But the dark side of the Information Age is just as evident.

For millions of Americans, advanced telecommunications have not produced greater prosperity and more satisfying lives—but declining fortunes. If current trends are any guide, corporate downsizing, high unemployment, and reductions in government assistance may continue to affect the lives of millions of people well into the twenty-first century. Likewise, income disparities between high-tech and manual workers may widen. Today, Silicon Valley and other highly skilled workers earn three times the overall average wage in the United States. Will this wage gap widen in the next stage of the Information Age?

As noted in Focus box 20.1, new technologies pose many threats to ordinary people, including round-the-clock electronic monitoring, even in the privacy of people's homes.

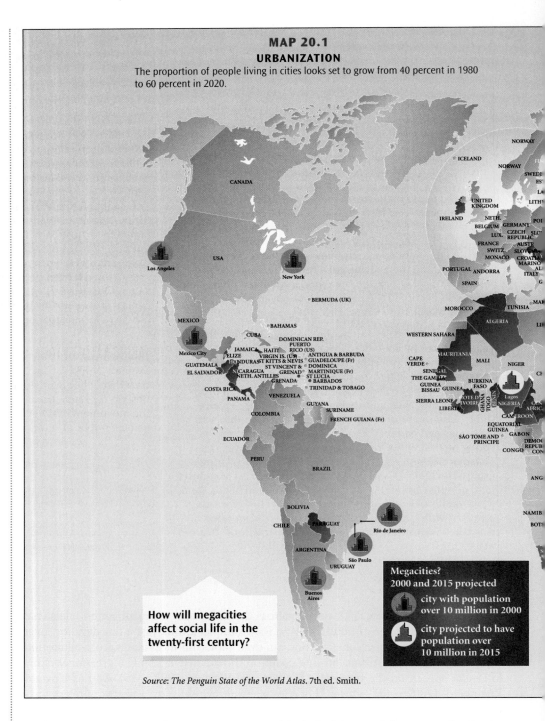

MAP 20.1

URBANIZATION

The proportion of people living in cities looks set to grow from 40 percent in 1980 to 60 percent in 2020.

How will megacities affect social life in the twenty-first century?

Megacities?
2000 and 2015 projected

city with population over 10 million in 2000

city projected to have population over 10 million in 2015

Source: *The Penguin State of the World Atlas.* 7th ed. Smith.

Perhaps an even greater threat is a growing public belief that proliferating technologies are a kind of contemporary "juggernaut" that are beyond people's control. As Leo Marx (1997:984) observed, technology "really serves as a surrogate agent, as well as a mask, for the human actor actually responsible for the developments in question. As in the past, both individuals and powerful organizations—not technology—are making the decisive choices that will determine the speed and direction of social change in the future."

Social Trends:
The Next Twenty-Five Years

No one can chart future trends with precision, but Theodore Caplow (1991:216) asserted that several key assumptions will improve the accuracy of our forecasts in the future: the persistence of social institutions such as religion, the family, and state should

People living in cities
As a percentage of total population 2000

Over 80%   61%–80%

41%–60%   21%–40%

20% and under   no data

be taken for granted; change is always channeled and circumscribed by the limited availability of material resources; the future is not determined by the past but is rather an amalgam of probabilities based on past experience and of contingencies arising from accident and free will; and events in history do not depend on "great causes" linked by some mysterious "chain of fatality" but are produced by "human actions."

Caplow (1991:215) also argued that "the longer a trend has been running, the further out it can be projected, and the greater the probability the projection will be accurate." Given the fact that the globalization of the economy is now several centuries old, it is fairly safe to predict that trends toward global economic and political interdependence will continue (Rosenau, 1990; Brown, 2006). So will urbanization, with the further growth of "megacities" not just in the United States but globally, as we show in Map 20.1. This is also reflected in the recent emergence of several global social movements, including the environmental, antinuclear, and world citizen movements as well as in the internationalization of human rights. Doubtless, as these trends proceed, there will be revivals of nationalism—and calls by national elites to return to a glorious national past. Regional power blocs such as the European Union are also likely to expand. Whether they are precursors of a more unified global political economy—perhaps even a world government—remains to be seen.

In this century, wars, economic depressions, and social movements opposed to current understandings of "progress" may retard technological innovations and national or even global development. At the core of many of these movements is a critique of materialism and instrumentalism that weaves together what Smelser calls "the threads of secular religiosity, bourgeois compassion, rage, and anti-modernism" (Jasper and Nelkin, 1992). These movements—from Christian Fundamentalism to radical feminism—"insist that policies and decisions must be guided by moral values and social needs, not by profits, technological feasibility, or bureaucratic inertia" (Jasper and Nelkin, 1992:5). Because of media attention, the most militant branches of the environmental movement are perhaps the best known of all such movements. According to media reports, early in the twenty-first century, "ecoterrorists" were conducting sensational arson attacks across the country: on housing construction projects, ski resorts, and even sports utility vehicle dealerships—to protest what some environmental activists believed were assaults on the environment and America's "natural heritage" (Reuters New Service, Yahoo.com, *Yahoo News,* 2003).

Firth-Cozens and West (1991) believe the Green movement and related social movements have established more nurturant and holistic visions of people's relationships to the environment and each other that will guide us in the future. Basic to this new paradigm is a shift away from linear, evolutionary views and beliefs that technology and "science" will lead us into the future or even that "science" can be spoken in a "singular universal voice." Instead it argues for "multiple methodologies as well as multiple class, race, and gender perspectives on problems" (Agger, 1991:121). However, according to Michael Buroway (2000:349), these diverse voices can only be effective if they are "woven together around universalistic interests such as human rights or environmental justice."

In 2006, *Newsweek* asked 15 leaders in the fields of science, technology, education, and business to assess the challenges the United States faces in the future and how best to address those challenges. While each of the experts' offerings differed in regards to specifics, some common elements could be found among them, including:

1. We must fix our educational system so that our children are competitive in reading, mathematics, science, and technology with the best and brightest in the world.

2. We must encourage, promote, and reward creativity, not only in science and technology, but in all fields of endeavor.

3. We must face fiscal realities, thinking long-term instead of short-term.

4. We must recognize and accept our place in the global political and economic arenas and realize that some competitors can become our partners.

5. We must spend more money on research and development in all areas of science and technology.

"Daddy and I wish you'd spend less time with your computer and more time watching T.V."

Futuristic visions, such as this one or others, are not inevitabilities but are social constructions guided by the choices and decisions of human actors.

In the twenty-first century, will all nations and all people be included in this optimistic vision of the future?

6. We must come to respect and even revere scientists, engineers, and innovators in the way that we now reserve for famous athletes, television celebrities, and movie stars.

7. We must think in a future-oriented mode.

Sociologists have no crystal ball and no way of predicting with any certainty what life will be like in this century. What the sociological perspective offers is the knowledge that the process of change is not beyond the understanding of ordinary people, nor is it "out of control" or charted in some "inevitable" direction. Instead, it is a social construction guided by the choices and decisions of human actors. We agree with C. Wright Mills's (1959:193) assertion that sociology may not be able to "save the world," but it can help provide the level of human understanding that is necessary to help avoid wars, address major social problems, and "rearrange human affairs in accordance with the ideals of human freedom and reason." Sociological analysis, which includes critical thinking, a greater understanding and appreciation of history and cultural diversity, and the knowledge that basic social values and norms determine the course of social action, provides the necessary intellectual tools for understanding social change. While this knowledge may not allow us to shape the future exactly as we desire, it will help us make informed decisions and choices that offer the possibility of a better future—not just for individuals or particular nations, but for the global community as a whole.

Summary

1 Everything changes and societies are in a constant state of flux. However, the rate of change differs from one society to another, depending on the complex interaction among various sources of change. Some changes, macro-changes, are large-scale, while others that sociologists call micro-changes, are small, rapid changes produced in social interaction.

2 Understanding global dynamics is fundamental to the study of social change. Functionalism sees change as a gradual process as industrial societies and science and technology guide social development. By contrast, conflict theories stress the role of social conflict—class, ethnic, gender, and national struggles—as important sources of change.

3 Collective behavior involves socially shared—but nonroutine—responses by a large number of people to uncertain and problematic situations, such as fashions, fads, panics, and rumors.

4 Social movements involve large numbers of people who use noninstitutional means to promote or resist social change. Social movements are often well-organized and goal-directed and may involve a broad range of organizations from local grassroots organizations, to large, well-financed professional SMOs.

5 In contemporary society the media play a key role in defining and shaping public visions of the future. While sociologists have no crystal ball, the sociological perspective can help people make informed choices. This offers the possibility of a better future—not just for developed nations but the global community as a whole.

Key Terms

collective behavior (p. 579)
collectivities (p. 580)
crowd (p. 583)
fads (p. 585)

fashions (p. 585)
mass (p. 583)
mass behavior (p. 584)
mass hysteria (p. 586)

rumors (p. 585)
social change (p. 574)
social movements (p. 579)
urban legends (p. 585)

Glossary

ABSOLUTE POVERTY When people fall below a minimum subsistence level and are unable to function as members of society.

ACHIEVED STATUSES Statuses secured through effort and ability.

ACTIVITY THEORY OF AGING Contends that it is the extent to which an individual remains engaged in meaningful social activity that determines the quality of life in old age.

AFROCENTRISM The perspective that emphasizes the preeminence of African and African American culture in human development.

AGEISM The belief that people in a particular age category are inferior to people in other age categories.

AGENTS OF SOCIALIZATION Those groups and institutions that both informally and formally take on the task of socialization.

AGGREGATE A collection of people who happen to be in the same place at the same time.

AGRARIAN SOCIETY A society that depends on crops raised with plows, draft animals, and intensive agricultural methods.

AIDS Acquired immune deficiency syndrome, a spectrum of disorders and symptoms that result from a progressive breakdown of the body's immune defense system.

ANDROGYNY A blending of masculine and feminine attributes.

ANIMATISM A system of beliefs in which supernatural "forces" rather than "beings" (gods or spirits) are the dominant power in the universe.

ANIMISM The belief in spirit beings that inhabit the same world as humans—but on another plane of existence.

ANOMIE A state of social strain, normative confusion, or rapid change in norms, when people's behavior is no longer restrained by conventional norms.

ANTICIPATORY SOCIALIZATION Learning designed to prepare an individual for the fulfillment of future statuses and roles.

APPLIED SOCIOLOGY Using sociological principles, social ideals, and ethical considerations to improve society.

ASCRIBED STATUSES Statuses assigned to individuals without reference to their abilities or efforts.

ASSIMILATION A process in which minority groups lose their distinctive identities and conform to cultural patterns of the dominant group.

AUTHORITARIAN REGIMES Power is concentrated in the hands of a single leader or, more commonly, is monopolized by a small elite (an oligarchy) who govern without constitutional limits and who recognize a responsibility only to themselves, rather than to the general public.

AUTHORITY A form of legitimate power that has widespread social approval and is obeyed because people believe that those who exercise it have a right to do so.

BABY BOOMERS The age cohort in the United States comprising those born roughly between 1945 and 1964.

BELIEFS Assertions about the nature of reality.

BIOLOGICAL RACE A population that differs from others in the frequency of certain hereditary traits.

BISEXUALITY Attraction to partners of both sexes.

BLENDED FAMILY A family in which at least one member of the adult couple is a stepparent.

BLUE-COLLAR OCCUPATION An occupation that involves manual labor or factory work.

BUREAUCRACY A large-scale organization that uses rules, hierarchical ranking, and a rational worldview to achieve maximum efficiency.

BUREAUCRATIC RITUALISM Workers conform to rules and procedures to such a degree that they become more important than goals.

CAPITALISM An economic system in which the means of production are privately owned and goods and services are distributed competitively for profit.

CASE STUDIES Qualitative techniques that involve intensive observation of a particular person, group, or event.

CASTE SYSTEM Ranking is hereditary and permanent, and marriage between members of different categories is prohibited.

CATEGORY People with similar social characteristics or a common status.

CHARISMATIC AUTHORITY Authority based on unique personal qualities, which include the ability to excite and inspire followers.

CHARTER SCHOOLS Schools created by a charter (a contract between those starting the school—either individuals, parent groups, or some other organization—with a governing body with the authority to grant the charter—often, state or local school boards) that receive state and federal tax monies and are open to all who wish to attend them.

CHILD-FREE FAMILY A couple resides together and there are no children present in the household.

CLASS SYSTEM The economic factor and achieved statuses (gained by ability and merit) are the principal means of ranking.

COERCION The actualization of a threat.

COHABITATION Where two people live together without legal marriage.

COLD WAR Hostile nations seeking to destabilize and destroy the other—but without engaging in direct armed combat.

COLLECTIVE BEHAVIOR Relatively spontaneous and noninstitutionalized responses by a large number of people to uncertain and problematic situations.

COLLECTIVITIES Large numbers of people who interact briefly and superficially in the absence of clearly defined norms.

COLONIALISM An economic and political system in which powerful nations dominate and exploit weaker ones in trade and other relations.

COMPOSITION OF A POPULATION The numbers and types of people, classified by characteristics such as age, sex, race, and ethnicity.

CONFLICT PERSPECTIVE Views society as composed of diverse groups with conflicting values and interests.

CONFLICT THEORIES OF DEVIANCE View deviance as arising when groups with power attempt to impose their norms and values on less powerful groups.

CONFORMITY Adherence to social norms.

CONSOLIDATED METROPOLITAN STATISTICAL AREAS (CMSA) The largest msas (those containing over a million people).

CONSPICUOUS CONSUMPTION Consumers' desire to express their social standing by acquiring goods and services simply for the purposes of having, displaying, and consuming them.

CONSUMPTION The process of accumulating and using goods and services.

CONTENT ANALYSIS Research that examines and analyzes communications.

CONTROL GROUP Subjects not exposed to the experimental variable in an experiment.

COPROVIDER FAMILIES Families in which both husband and wife have full-time jobs.

CORPORATE CONGLOMERATES Huge corporations that produce hundreds of different products under a variety of trade and brand names.

CORPORATE INTERLOCKS Situations that occur when directors sit on more than one major corporate board, linking the corporations in ownership, management, and political and economic activities.

CORPORATIONS Large business concerns owned by thousands of stockholders and managed by boards of directors.

COUNTERCULTURES Groups that reject the conventional wisdom and standards of behavior of the majority and provide alternatives to mainstream culture.

CREDENTIALISM Overemphasis on educational credentials.

CRIME Any act that violates a criminal law.

CRITICAL THINKING Objectively assessing ideas, statements, and information.

CROWD A large number of people in close enough proximity to interact and influence one another's behavior.

CRUDE BIRTHRATE The number of live births per year for every 1,000 people in a specific population.

CRUDE DEATH RATE The number of deaths per year for every 1,000 people in a specific population.

CULTURAL ECOLOGICAL APPROACH An approach that examines the relationship between a culture and its total environment.

CULTURAL HEGEMONY The domination of cultural industries by elite groups.

CULTURAL LAG Inconsistencies in a cultural system, especially in the relationship between technology and nonmaterial culture.

CULTURAL PLURALISM When racial and ethnic groups cooperate while still retaining their distinctive identities and lifestyles.

CULTURAL RELATIVISM A perspective which asks that we evaluate other cultures according to their standards, not ours.

CULTURAL TRANSMISSION The process by which culture is passed from one generation to the next.

CULTURE The learned set of beliefs, values, norms, and material goods shared by group members.

CULTURE OF POVERTY A set of norms, beliefs, values, and attitudes that trap a small number of the urban poor in a permanent cycle of poverty.

CULTURE SHOCK Feelings of confusion and disorientation that occur when a person encounters a very different culture.

DEFINITION OF THE SITUATION The idea that when people define situations as *real* they become real in their consequences.

DEGRADATION CEREMONY A process in which an individual is stripped of his or her former self, publicly stigmatized, and assigned a new identity.

DEMOCRACY A political system based on popular participation in decision making, where ultimate authority is vested in the people.

DEMOGRAPHIC TRANSITION THEORY Population growth develops through three distinct stages: (1) high birth and death rates, (2) high birthrates and low death rates, and (3) low birth and death rates.

DEMOGRAPHY The scientific study of the size, composition, distribution, and changes in human population.

DENOMINATION An established, socially accepted religious organization that maintains tolerant relations with other denominations.

DEPENDENCY THEORY Maintains that rich industrialized nations keep poor countries from advancing through various dependency relationships.

DEPENDENT VARIABLE A variable that is changed by the independent variable (i.e., the effect).

DESOCIALIZATION The "unlearning" of previous normative expectations and roles.

DETERRENCE THEORY States that deviance will be effectively deterred if negative social sanctions (especially punishment) are perceived to be certain, swift, and severe.

DEVELOPMENTAL SOCIALIZATION Learning better to fulfill the roles we already occupy.

DEVIANCE Violation of a social norm.

DICTATORSHIP A political system of arbitrary rule by a single individual.

DISCRIMINATION Unequal treatment of people because of their group membership.

DISEASE A medically diagnosed illness.

DISTRIBUTION The allocation of goods and services to societal members.

DOUBLING TIME The number of years it takes for a population to double in size.

DRAMATURGICAL ANALYSIS Uses the analogy of the theater to analyze social behavior.

DRAMATURGY Analyzes social interaction as though participants were actors in an ongoing drama.

DUAL-CAREER FAMILIES Families in which husbands and wives have both family and career.

DYAD A two-person group.

ECCLESIA A large, formally organized religious body that includes most members of society and is supported by and closely allied with secular and state powers.

ECOLOGICAL PERSPECTIVE A theoretical model for analyzing the interdependence between human beings and the physical environment.

ECONOMIC SYSTEM The ideology, values, norms, and activities that regulate an economy.

ECONOMY The systematic production, distribution, and consumption of goods and services in a society.

ECOSYSTEM A community of organisms sharing the same physical environment.

EDUCATION The institutionalized process of systematically teaching certain cognitive skills and knowledge and transmitting them from one generation to the next.

ELDER ABUSE Mistreatment of older persons; it may be physical, psychological, or financial, or it may take the form of neglect or financial exploitation.

ELITE DEVIANCE Includes all aspects of white-collar crime as well as other deviant acts perpetrated by those in power.

ENDOGAMY Norms that require people to find mates within a specific group or social category.

EPIDEMIOLOGY The study of the incidence and distribution of health and disease in a society.

ESTATE SYSTEM A social hierarchy centered on the monopoly of power and ownership of land by a group of religious and political elites.

ETHICAL RELIGIONS Philosophical ideals that show how people may achieve enlightenment, peace, and harmony in this world.

ETHNIC GROUP A category of people set apart from others because of distinctive customs and lifestyles.

ETHNICITY Statuses based on cultural heritage and shared "feelings of peoplehood."

ETHNOCENTRISM The tendency to evaluate the customs of other groups according to one's own cultural standards.

ETHNOGRAPHIC INTERVIEW A qualitative technique where the researcher talks with people in an effort to learn as much as possible about them and their behavior.

ETHNOMETHODOLOGY A way of analyzing the "taken-for-granted" aspects that give meaning to social interaction.

EUROCENTRISM The belief that European cultures have contributed the most to human knowledge and are superior to all others.

EUROCENTRISM A focus on the contributions of Europeans to history, math, science, and literature.

EUTHANASIA "Gentle death" or "merciful death"; helping the terminally ill to die free of pain and with as much dignity as possible.

EVALUATION RESEARCH Research that measures the effectiveness of a program.

EXOGAMY A norm that requires people to find marriage partners outside their own group or social category.

EXPERIMENTAL DESIGN A research design that attempts to discover a cause-and-effect relationship between two variables.

EXPERIMENTAL GROUP Subjects exposed to the independent variable in an experiment.

EXPERTISE A form of authority derived from the possession of specialized knowledge.

EXTENDED FAMILY Two or more closely related families who share a household and are economically and emotionally bound to others in the group.

FADS Short-term, frivolous, and unconventional collective behaviors that usually provide pleasure and involve only a small segment of the population.

FAMILY Two or more people who are related by blood, marriage, or adoption or who are part of a relationship in which there is commitment, mutual aid and support, and often a shared residence.

FAMILY OF MARRIAGE The family that a person forms at his or her marriage.

FAMILY OF ORIENTATION The family into which an individual is born.

FASHIONS Relatively enduring styles and behaviors that enjoy widespread popularity, often in cycles.

FEMININITY Attributes traditionally associated with appropriate behavior for females.

FEMINISM An ideology aimed at eliminating patriarchy in support of equality between the sexes.

FEMINIST THEORY Studies, analyzes, and explains social phenomena from a gender-focused perspective.

FEMINIZATION OF POVERTY Women and girls constitute a disproportionate share of the poor.

FERTILITY The extent of reproduction in a society.

FOLK SOCIETIES Emphasize tradition, consensus, and primary relationships.

FOLKWAYS Informal rules and expectations that guide peoples' everyday behavior.

FORMAL ORGANIZATIONS Secondary groups that are formally organized to achieve specific goals.

GEMEINSCHAFT A community characterized by a relatively small population, a simple division of labor, face-to-face interaction, and informal social control.

GENDER Cultural understanding of what constitutes masculinity and femininity in a society.

GENDER IDENTITY Acknowledging one's sex and internalizing the norms, values, and behaviors of the accompanying gender expectations.

GENDER ROLES The social and cultural expectations associated with a person's sex.

GENERALIZED OTHERS The dominant attitudes and expectations of most members of society.

GENOCIDE Deliberate and systematic elimination of minority group members.

GERONTOCRACY A society in which the elderly control most of society's wealth, power, and prestige.

GERONTOLOGY The scientific study of aging and the elderly.

GESELLSCHAFT A society made up of a large population characterized by loose associations, a complex division of labor, secondary relationships, and formal social control.

GLOBAL STRATIFICATION SYSTEM Nations are ranked in a hierarchy on the basis of their access to the world's wealth, power, and prestige.

GLOBAL WARMING An increase in the earth's overall average temperature due to a greenhouse effect produced by increased exposure to ultraviolet light.

GOVERNMENTS People and organizations that formulate and implement public policy.

GRAY PANTHERS An organization with the goal of eliminating ageism in all its forms.

GROUPTHINK Decision making that ignores alternative solutions in order to maintain group harmony.

GROWTH RATE The difference between the numbers of people added to and subtracted from a particular population.

GUERRILLA WARS Small-scale, irregular armed struggles against larger, better-armed government military forces.

HATE CRIMES Criminal acts against people and their property that are motivated by racial and ethnic prejudices and other social biases.

HAWTHORNE EFFECT The phenomenon where subjects' behavior is influenced by the fact that they are being studied.

HEALTH The absence of disease and infirmity and the ability to respond effectively to one's environment.

HEALTH MAINTENANCE ORGANIZATION (HMO) AND PREFERRED-PROVIDER ORGANIZATION (PPO) Insurance programs that emphasize preventive care and attempt to reduce medical costs by pooling funds and contracting with participating physicians who manage their patients' total health care.

HEALTH-CARE SYSTEM The social institution charged with the maintenance of a society's health and standard of well-being.

HETEROGAMY The selection of a mate with social characteristics different than one's own.

HETEROSEXUALITY Attraction to partners of the opposite sex.

HIDDEN CURRICULUM An aspect of education designed to teach dominant norms, values, and consensus ideology.

HIDDEN ECONOMY (UNDERGROUND ECONOMY) Exchange of goods and services and generation of income that goes unreported to the government.

HIGH-INCOME NATIONS Nations with advanced industrial economies and high living standards.

HOME SCHOOLING Where children are not sent to school but receive their formal education from one or both parents.

HOMOGAMY The selection of a mate with personal and social characteristics similar to one's own.

HOMOPHOBIA Hatred and discrimination directed against homosexuals, based on exaggerated fears of homosexuality.

HOMOSEXUALITY Sexual attraction to partners of the same sex.

HORTICULTURAL SOCIETY A society in which hand tools are used to grow domesticated crops.

HOSPICE An environment designed for the care of the terminally ill, where individuals are allowed to die a relatively pain-free, comfortable, and dignified death.

HUMAN ECOLOGY A subfield of sociology that focuses on recurring spatial, social, and cultural patterns within a particular social environment.

HUNTING-GATHERING SOCIETY A society in which people make their living by hunting, collecting wild foods, and fishing with simple technologies.

IDEAL CULTURE What people should do, according to group norms and values.

IDEAL TYPE A conceptual model or typology constructed from the direct observation of a number of specific cases and representing the essential qualities found in those cases.

IMPRESSION MANAGEMENT Ways that people use revelation and concealment to make a favorable impression on others.

INCEST TABOO A norm that forbids people from mating with and marrying "close kin."

INDEPENDENT VARIABLE A variable that brings about change in another variable (i.e., the cause).

INDUSTRIAL SOCIETY A society that relies on machines and advanced technology to produce and distribute food, information, goods, and services.

INFANT MORTALITY RATE The number of deaths in the first year of life for each 1,000 live births per year.

INFLUENCE The ability to affect the behavior of others through persuasion, rewards, inducements, and appeals to reason.

INFOTAINMENT A combination of information and entertainment.

IN-GROUP A group with which people identify and have a sense of belonging.

INNOVATION Creating new knowledge and finding new ways to use existing knowledge.

INSTITUTIONAL DISCRIMINATION Unequal treatment of a group that is deeply embedded in social institutions.

INTEGRATION Bringing together people from diverse social backgrounds so that they share common social experiences and develop commonly held norms, attitudes, and beliefs.

INTEGRATIVE MEDICINE (HOLISTIC MEDICINE) Emphasizes the prevention of disease and focuses treatment on patients as whole persons in an effort to maintain good physical, emotional, and spiritual health.

INTEREST GROUPS Groups or organizations that seek to influence government policy and public opinion.

INTERVENING VARIABLES Variables that may come between the independent and dependent variables in an experiment.

KINSHIP GROUP A network of people whose social relationships are based on common ancestry (blood), marriage, adoption, and/or affiliation (e.g., godparents).

LABELING APPROACH Contends that people attach various labels to certain behaviors, individuals, and groups that become part of their social identity and shape others' attitudes about and responses to them.

LABELING THEORIES View deviance and conformity primarily as labels assigned to certain people and certain acts.

LANGUAGE A complex system of symbols with conventional meanings that people use for communication.

LATENT FUNCTIONS Unintended or unrecognized consequences of social institutions.

LAWS Formal rules enacted and enforced by the power of the state, which apply to members of society.

LEGAL DISCRIMINATION Minority group members are denied lawful access to public institutions, jobs, housing, and social rewards.

LEGAL-RATIONAL AUTHORITY Authority based on explicit rules, regulations, and procedures that define who holds power and how power is to be exercised and distributed.

LIFE CHANCES Opportunities for securing such things as health, education, autonomy, leisure, and a long life.

LIFE COURSE A process in which individuals move from one biological and social stage to another as they grow and develop.

LIFE EXPECTANCY The average number of years a person is expected to live.

LIFESTYLES The distinctive ways in which group members consume goods and services and display rank.

LOOKING-GLASS SELF Cooley's concept that individuals use others like mirrors and base their conceptions of themselves on what is reflected back to them during social interaction.

LOW-INCOME NATIONS Nations that are poor, agrarian, and benefit least from their participation in the global economy.

MACROLEVEL ANALYSIS Examines broader social structures and society as a whole.

MAGIC A ritual attempt to compel supernatural beings or forces to influence events in the natural world.

MANIFEST FUNCTIONS Anticipated or intended consequences of social institutions.

MARRIAGE A legally recognized economic and sexual relationship between two or more persons that includes mutual rights and obligations and is assumed to be permanent.

MASCULINITY Attributes considered appropriate for males.

MASS Large numbers of people widely dispersed.

MASS BEHAVIOR People are not in the same locality, yet through a common source of information or communication medium they can indirectly influence one another.

MASS HYSTERIA Widespread anxiety and the frantic reactions of large numbers of people to some perceived threat.

MASS MEDIA Forms of communication that transmit standardized messages to widespread audiences (e.g., newspapers, magazines, books, radio, television, and movies).

MASTER STATUS A status that dominates all other statuses.

MATERIAL CULTURE Artifacts, art, architecture, and other tangible goods that people create and assign meanings.

MATRIARCHY A system in which women dominate men politically, economically, and socially.

MECHANICAL SOLIDARITY Characterized by tradition, unity, consensus of norms and values, and strong informal pressure to conform.

MEDICAL MODEL Views deviance as analogous to illness.

MEDICAL SOCIOLOGY A subarea of sociology that links social structure and social life to health.

MEDICALIZATION A process in which behavior, activities, and problems previously dissociated from health and medicine are now viewed from a medical perspective and seen as within the domain of doctors, hospitals, and other elements of the health-care system.

MEDICINE An institutionalized system designed to prevent and treat disease and illness.

MEGALOPOLIS Two or more major metropolitan areas linked politically, economically, socially, and geographically.

METROPOLIS A major urban area that includes a large central city surrounded by several smaller incorporated cities and suburbs that join to form one large recognizable municipality.

METROPOLITAN STATISTICAL AREAS (MSA) A city, or a city and its surrounding suburbs, with a population of 50,000 or more.

MICROLEVEL ANALYSIS Focuses on the day-to-day interactions of individuals and groups in specific social situations.

MIDDLE-INCOME NATIONS Nations that are newly industrialized and have moderate wealth and living standards.

MIGRATION Population movement across political boundaries.

MIGRATION RATE The number of emigrants (people leaving a country) subtracted from the number of immigrants (those entering it) per 1,000 population.

MILITARY-INDUSTRIAL COMPLEX Mutually beneficial relationships among the uniformed military, defense industries, corporations, universities, national security and defense agencies, and congress and the executive branches of government.

MINORITY GROUP A category of people who are set apart for unequal treatment because of physical or cultural characteristics.

MIXED ECONOMY Combines central elements of capitalism and socialism and allows private ownership and free enterprise to compete with businesses, industries, and services owned and operated by the state.

MODERNIZATION THEORY Recognizes global development as a process in which advanced industrial nations and technology help poor nations advance.

MONOGAMY The marriage of one woman and one man.

MONOTHEISTIC RELIGIONS Religions that acknowledge the existence of a single, supreme god.

MORBIDITY Chronic debilitation.

MORES Salient norms that people consider essential to the proper working of society.

MORTALITY Death.

MULTICULTURAL EDUCATION Recognizes cultural diversity and promotes an appreciation of all cultures.

MULTICULTURALISM A movement that encourages respect and appreciation for cultural differences.

MUTUALLY ASSURED DESTRUCTION (MAD) A strategic triad of ballistic missiles buried in hardened silos and carried on submarines and in human-piloted bombers that would provide a "survivable" second strike that would totally obliterate the attacking nation.

NATION-STATES Governments that have a unified administrative reach across large territories over which sovereignty is claimed.

NATURE Heredity. Nurture environment.

NEW AGE A novel blend of magic and religion, ancient and futuristic beliefs, and utilitarian and mystical ethics and philosophies.

NEW RELIGIOUS MOVEMENT A transient and loosely organized religious organization that includes religious beliefs and practices that are novel and at odds with mainstream religious traditions.

NONMATERIAL CULTURE Mental blueprints that serve as guidelines for group behavior.

NONVERBAL COMMUNICATION The body movements, gestures, and facial expressions that we use to communicate with others.

NORMS Expectations and rules for proper conduct that guide behavior of group members.

NUCLEAR FAMILY Parents and their children who live apart from other kin.

OLIGARCHIES A small group of elites who wield power and are accountable only to themselves.

ORGANIC SOLIDARITY Characterized by a highly sophisticated division of labor that makes individuals interdependent with one another.

OUT-GROUP A group that people do not identify with and consider less worthy and less desirable than their own.

PARADIGM A set of assumptions and ideas that guide research questions, methods of analysis and interpretation, and the development of theory.

PARTICIPANT OBSERVATION A qualitative method in which the researcher systematically observes the people being studied while participating with them in their activities.

PASSING An attempt to hide a stigmatizing attribute.

PASTORAL SOCIETY A society that depends for its livelihood on domestic animals.

PATRIARCHAL AUTHORITY Where male elders dominate decision making and women have little control over their lives.

PATRIARCHY A system in which males dominate females in most spheres of life (politics, economics, family, and so on).

PEACE A process by which politically organized groups develop and maintain positive, constructive, and mutually beneficial relationships that enable them to transcend collective violence.

PEACE MOVEMENTS Loose and shifting combinations of individuals and groups who come together to promote peace or prevent war.

PERSONAL DISCRIMINATION Attacks on minority group members, from social slights and insults to murder.

PERSONAL SPACE An area around our body that we reserve for ourselves, intimate acquaintances, and close friends.

PERSONALITY A dominant pattern of attitudes, feelings, and behaviors. **Self** a person's conscious recognition that he or she is a distinct individual who is part of a larger society. **I** in Mead's schema, the unsocialized self as subject. **Me** in Mead's schema, the socialized self as object.

PINK-COLLAR OCCUPATION An occupation heavily dominated by women.

POLITICAL INSTITUTIONS Relatively enduring social arrangements that distribute and exercise power.

POLITICAL PARTIES Enduring coalitions of individuals who organize to win elections and shape public policy.

POLITICAL SYSTEMS Rules and policies that determine the organization, exercise, and transfer of government decision-making power.

POLITICS A social process through which people and groups acquire, exercise, maintain, or lose power over others.

POLYGAMY A form of marriage in which a person has multiple spouses.

POLYTHEISM The worship of numerous gods who are believed to have varying degrees of power.

POPULATION An entire body of people to which the sociologist would like to generalize research findings.

POPULATION DENSITY How a population is dispersed geographically (e.g., the number of people per square mile).

PORNOGRAPHY Sexually explicit materials intended solely for sexual arousal.

POSITIVISM The use of observation, comparison, experimentation, and the historical method to analyze society.

POSTINDUSTRIAL SOCIETY A society where service industries and the manufacture of information and knowledge dominate the economy.

POWER The ability to realize one's will even against the resistance and opposition of others.

POWER ELITE A small triumvirate of top corporate, political, and military leaders.

PREJUDICE Preconceived judgments about a category of people.

PRESTIGE The respect and admiration people attach to various social positions.

PRIMARY DEVIANCE When an individual violates a norm and is viewed as deviant but rejects the deviant label and maintains a conformist conception of himself or herself.

PRIMARY GROUP People who regularly interact and have close and enduring relationships.

PRIMARY LABOR MARKET Occupations that provide high income, prestige, and extensive benefits to workers.

PRIMARY SOCIALIZATION The learning of human characteristics and behaviors and the development of a concept of self.

PRODUCTION The process by which goods and services are brought into existence.

PROFANE Ordinary, commonly understood, and routine activities that people take for granted as they go about their daily lives.

PROFESSION A white-collar occupation that is prestigious, is relatively high-paying, and requires advanced formal education and specialized training.

PROPAGANDA   The communication of facts, ideas, and opinions not for the audience's sake but to benefit the communicator.

PROXY WARS   Major powers do not participate directly in developing nations' conflicts; rather, one side assists government forces while the other supports guerrillas.

PURE SOCIOLOGY   The study of society in an effort to understand and explain the natural laws that govern its evolution.

PYGMALION EFFECT   Occurs when teachers expect students to succeed and excel and are motivated to work with them to ensure that they do. Teachers may also ignore youngsters expected to fail until they, too, achieve the anticipated outcome (a form of self-fulfilling prophecy).

QUALITATIVE RESEARCH DESIGN   A research design that uses systematic observation and focuses on the meanings people give to their social actions.

QUANTITATIVE RESEARCH DESIGN   A research design that emphasizes the use of numbers and statistics to analyze and explain social events and human behavior.

RACES   Categories of people set apart from others because of socially defined physical characteristics.

RACISM   Beliefs and attitudes that one racial category is inherently superior or inferior to another.

RANGE OF TOLERANCE   A scope of behaviors considered acceptable and defined as conformity.

REAL CULTURE   What people do in everyday social interaction.

REFERENCE GROUPS   Groups that people refer to when evaluating their personal qualities, circumstances, attitudes, values, and behaviors.

RELATIVE POVERTY   A lack of resources relative to others and the overall standards of a society.

RELIGION   A system of socially shared symbols, beliefs, and rituals that address the sacred and the ultimate meaning of human existence.

RESOCIALIZATION   Learning a radically different set of norms, attitudes, values, beliefs, and behaviors.

RITES OF PASSAGE   Ceremonies that symbolically acknowledge transitions from one life stage to another.

ROLE   A set of expectations, rights, and duties that are attached to a particular status.

ROLE CONFLICT   When a person cannot fulfill the roles of one status without violating those of another.

ROLE DISTANCE   When people play a role but remain detached from it to avoid any negative aspects of the role.

ROLE EMBRACEMENT   When a person's sense of identity is partially influenced by a role.

ROLE MERGER   When a role becomes central to a person's identity and the person literally becomes the role he or she is playing.

ROLE SET   Multiple roles that are attached to almost every status.

ROLE STRAIN   Contradictory expectations and demands attached to a single role.

ROLE TAKING   The ability to anticipate what others expect of us, and to act accordingly.

RUMORS   Unconfirmed items or media reports that spread by word of mouth and cannot be verified.

SACRED   Uncommon and extraordinary aspects of social life that inspire in believers feelings of awe, reverence, and respect.

SAMPLE   A segment of the population.

SANCTIONS   Penalties or rewards society uses to encourage conformity and punish deviance.

SCAPEGOAT   A weak, convenient, and socially approved target.

SECONDARY ANALYSIS   The analysis of existing data.

SECONDARY DEVIANCE   The internalization of a deviant label and the assumption of a deviant role. Social learning theories contend that all behavior (including deviance) is learned through social interaction.

SECONDARY GROUP   Two or more people who interact on a formal and impersonal basis to accomplish a specific objective.

SECONDARY LABOR MARKET   Jobs that provide low wages and few benefits.

SECT   A small, less formally organized religious group that usually has separated from a denomination and is in a negative tension with the larger society.

SECULARIZATION THESIS   Maintains that the global spread of modernization and secularization inevitably leads to the decline of religious institutions.

SEGREGATION   Physical or social exclusion of minority groups from dominant group activities.

SELF-FULFILLING PROPHECY   When predictions about students' abilities shape the students' future actions and behaviors in such a way that the predictions come true.

SENESCENCE   Natural deterioration of cells and organs as a result of aging.

SERIAL MONOGAMY   A marriage pattern in which a person has several spouses over a lifetime, but only one at a time.

SEX   Biological and physical differences between females and males.

SEX RATIO   The number of males per 100 females.

SEXISM   The ideology that one sex is inherently superior or inferior to the other.

SEXUAL HARASSMENT   Deliberate unwanted sexual gestures, comments, or actions that make an individual feel uncomfortable in her or his work environment.

SEXUAL ORIENTATION   Preference of sex partners.

SICK ROLE   A pattern of behavior associated with illness.

SIGNIFICANT OTHERS   Specific people with whom we interact and whose response has meaning for us.

SINGLE-PARENT FAMILIES   Families in which one parent resides with and cares for one or more children.

SITUATED SELF   The self that emerges in a particular situation.

SLAVE SYSTEM   A society with two distinct strata—a category of people who are free and a category of people who are legally the property of others.

SOCIAL ACTS   Behaviors influenced or shaped by the presence of others.

SOCIAL BOUNDARIES   Material or symbolic devices that identify who is inside or outside a group.

SOCIAL CHANGE   A process through which patterns of social behavior, social relationships, social institutions, and systems of stratification are altered over time.

SOCIAL CONTROL   Mechanisms people use to enforce prevailing social norms.

SOCIAL CONTROL THEORIES   Contend that deviance is normal and conformity must be explained.

SOCIAL DIFFERENTIATION   A process in which people are set apart for differential treatment by virtue of their statuses, roles, and other social characteristics.

SOCIAL DISENGAGEMENT THEORY   Contends that, as people age, they gradually withdraw from social participation and simultaneously are relieved of social responsibilities.

SOCIAL GROUP   Two or more people who interact in patterned ways, have a feeling of unity, and share interests and expectations.

SOCIAL INEQUALITY   A condition in which people have unequal access to wealth, power, and prestige.

SOCIAL INSTITUTIONS   Relatively enduring clusters of values, norms, social statuses, roles, and groups that address fundamental social needs.

SOCIAL INTERACTION The mutual influence of two or more people on each other's behavior.

SOCIAL LEARNING THEORY The idea that much human behavior is learned from modeling others.

SOCIAL MOBILITY The movement of people from one social position to another in the stratification system.

SOCIAL MOVEMENTS Organized, goal-directed efforts by a large number of people to promote or resist change outside of established institutions.

SOCIAL NETWORK The total web of an individual's relationships and group memberships.

SOCIAL PATHOLOGY A problem that potentially threatens the survival of society.

SOCIAL PERCEPTION The process by which we form impressions of others and of ourselves.

SOCIAL STRATIFICATION A form of inequality in which categories of people are systematically ranked in a hierarchy on the basis of their access to scarce but valued resources.

SOCIAL STRUCTURE The ordered relationships and patterned expectations that guide social interaction.

SOCIALISM An economic system in which the means of production are owned and controlled by the state and goods and services are distributed as a cooperative enterprise without regard to personal profit.

SOCIALIZATION A process in which we learn and internalize the attitudes, values, beliefs, and norms of our culture and develop a sense of self.

SOCIALIZED MEDICINE A system in which public funds are used to provide a state-owned and state-operated health-care system available to all citizens.

SOCIETY People who live in a specific geographic territory, interact with one another, and share many elements of a common culture.

SOCIOBIOLOGY A field that integrates theories and research from biology and sociology in an effort to better understand human behavior.

SOCIOCULTURAL EVOLUTION A process in which societies grow more complex in terms of technology, social structure, and cultural knowledge over time.

SOCIOECONOMIC STATUS A ranking that combines income, occupational prestige, level of education, and neighborhood to assess people's positions in the stratification system.

SOCIOLOGICAL IMAGINATION Quality of mind that provides an understanding of ourselves within the context of the larger society.

SOCIOLOGICAL THINKING Asking questions and questioning answers.

SOCIOLOGY The systematic and scientific study of human behavior, social groups, and society.

SPECIALIZATION (MEDICAL) Advanced education and training allowing doctors to focus on one particular aspect of medicine (e.g., pediatrics, obstetrics, surgery, or psychiatry).

SPLIT-LABOR MARKET An economic situation in which two groups of workers are willing to do the same work for different wages.

STATUS A socially defined position in a social structure.

STATUS INCONSISTENCY Two or more statuses that a society deems contradictory.

STATUS SET All of the statuses a person has at a given time.

STEREOTYPES Static and oversimplified ideas about a group or a social category.

STIGMA Any characteristic that sets people apart and discredits or disqualifies them from full social acceptance and participation.

STRAIN THEORIES The view that deviance is a result of the tensions or strain experienced by people because of their position in the social structure.

STRUCTURAL FUNCTIONALIST PERSPECTIVE Views society as a system of interdependent and interrelated parts (often referred to simply as the functionalist perspective or functionalism).

STRUCTURAL MOBILITY Large-scale changes in occupational, educational, and corporate social structures that enable people to move up or down in the stratification system.

SUBCULTURES Groups that share many elements of mainstream culture but maintain their own distinctive customs, values, norms, and lifestyles.

SUBURBS Residential areas surrounding cities, which expand urban lifestyles into previously rural areas.

SURVEY RESEARCH Research using a questionnaire or interview to obtain data.

SYMBOL Anything to which group members assign meaning.

SYMBOLIC INTERACTIONIST PERSPECTIVE Views social meaning as arising through the process of social interaction (often referred to as *interactionism*).

TABOOS Prohibitions against behaviors that most members of a group consider to be so repugnant they are unthinkable.

TECHNOMEDIA Newer and more personalized information technologies (e.g., personal computers, CD-ROMs, fax machines, video games, handheld databanks, cellular phones, the Internet, fiber optic communications, and interactive television).

TERRORISM Deliberate threats or acts of violence intended to create fear and terror in order to bring about political and social change.

THANATOLOGY The scientific study of death and dying.

THEISM Belief in one or more supreme beings or gods who, because of their power and influence in human affairs, deserve to be worshiped.

THEORETICAL PERSPECTIVE A viewpoint or particular way of looking at things.

TOTAL INSTITUTIONS Places where people carry out virtually all of their activities.

TOTALITARIAN REGIMES They seek to regulate all aspects of people's lives and transform individuals and societies in the name of some utopian vision.

TRACKING Placing students perceived to have similar intelligence and academic abilities in the same classroom.

TRADITIONAL AUTHORITY A form of authority based on custom and habit, which has its roots in the distant past and often is religiously sanctioned.

TRADITIONAL NUCLEAR FAMILY A breadwinner father, homemaker mother, and children.

TRANSNATIONAL CORPORATIONS Corporations that own companies and search for profits all over the globe.

TRIAD A three-member group.

TRIANGULATION The use of multiple (usually three) techniques to gather or analyze research data.

UNILATERAL WARS One superpower becomes directly involved in a conflict with guerrillas, whereas the other stays out—but clandestinely supplies the opposition with arms, money, training, and, in recent years, satellite intelligence.

URBAN LEGENDS Complex popular tales that often contain implicit warnings and messages.

URBAN SOCIETIES Societies based on change, diversity, and secondary relationships.

URBAN SOCIOLOGY A subdivision of sociology that identifies, studies, and explains the specific traits of urban social phenomena.

URBANISM A way of life in which the city affects how people feel, think, and interact.

URBANIZATION The movement of masses of people from rural to urban areas and an increase in urban influence over all spheres of culture and society.

VALUES Shared ideas about what is socially desirable.

VOUCHERS Provide tax dollars to parents to offset some of the costs of transporting their children to public schools outside their district or to help defray the tuition costs of private schools.

WAR Sustained armed conflicts among politically organized groups that involve large-scale violence and many fatalities.

WEALTH A person's or family's total economic assets.

WELLNESS MOVEMENT Emphasizes preventive health care by combining knowledge about health and nutrition with sensible eating and exercise programs.

WHITE-COLLAR OCCUPATION An occupation that involves office work or nonmanual labor.

WORLD SYSTEM THEORY Maintains that all nations are part of a worldwide division of labor.

YEAR-ROUND EDUCATION Refers to changing the traditional school calendar to extend instructional time or to rearrange the use of that time significantly.

ZERO POPULATION GROWTH (ZPG) An organization dedicated to reaching the population replacement level of approximately two children per family.

Bibliography

Abadinsky, Howard. *Drugs: An Introduction*, 5th ed. Belmont, CA: Wadsworth/Thomson, 2003.

———. *Drugs: An Introduction*. 4th ed. Chicago: Nelson-Hall, 1989.

Abbott, Andrew. "Reflections on the Future of Sociology." *Contemporary Sociology* 29 (March) 2000:296–300.

ABC News. *Prime-Time Live*. February 8, 1995.

———. "Junk Science: What You Know May Not Be So." January 9, 1997a.

———. *Turning Point*. May 22, 1997b.

ABCNews/Beliefnet Poll. "Public Backs Stem Cell Research." (Gary Langer, Analysis). June 26, 2001:1.

Abelman, Robert. "Determinants of Parental Mediation of Children's Television Viewing," in Jennings Bryant (ed.), *Television and the American Family*. Hillsdale, NJ: Erlbaum, 1990, pp. 311–326.

Abt, Vicki, and Mel Seesholtz. "Talking the Talk: Sociological Messages on T.V. Talk Shows." *Footnotes* 25 (February) 1997:4.

Abzug, Bella (with Mim Kelber). *Gender Gap: Bella Abzug's Guide to Political Power for American Women*. Boston: Houghton Mifflin, 1984.

Acker, Joan. "Women, Families, and Social Policy in Sweden," in Ester Ngan-ling Chow and Catherine White Berheide (eds.), *Women, the Family, and Policy: A Global Perspective*. Stony Brook: State University of New York Press, 1994, pp. 33–50.

Acs, Gregory, Katherin Ross Phillips, and Sandi Nelson. "The Road Not Taken? Changes in Welfare Entry During the 1990s." *Social Science Quarterly* 86 (Special Issue), 2005:1060–1079.

Adams, Gordon. *The Iron Triangle: The Politics of Defense Contracting*. New Brunswick, NJ: Transaction, 1982.

Adams, Michael. "Salvation Army Controversy Is Just the Tip of 'Faith-Based Initiative' Iceberg." *Lambda Legal.org, Lambda Legal Defense and Education Fund*, July 11, 2001:1–3.

Adams, Mike S., James D. Johnson, and T. David Evans. "Racial Differences in Informal Labeling Effects." *Deviant Behavior* 19 (April–June) 1998:157–171.

Adelman, Robert M. "The Roles of Race, Class, and Residential Preferences in the Neighborhood Racial Composition of Middle-Class Blacks and Whites." *Social Science Quarterly* 86 (March) 2005:209-228.

Adler, Jerry. "In Search of the Spiritual." *Newsweek*, September 5, 2005a:46-64.

Adler, Jerry. "Hitting 60." *Newsweek*, November 14, 2005b :50-58.

Adler, Mortimer J. "The Paideia Proposal: Rediscovering the Essence of Education," in James W. Noll (ed.), *Taking Sides: Clashing Views on Controversial Educational Issues*, 14th ed. Guilford, CT: McGraw-Hill Dushkin, 2006. pp. 18–24.

Adler, Patricia A., and Peter Adler. "Social Reproduction and the Corporate Other: The Institutionalization of Afterschool Activities." *Sociological Quarterly* 35 (2) 1994:309–328.

Adler, Patricia A., Steven J. Kless, and Peter Adler. "Socialization to Gender Roles: Popularity among Elementary School Boys and Girls." *Sociology of Education* 65 (July) 1992:169–187.

Africa News Service. "Sexual Harassment in Office and Schools." August 18, 2003.

African Development Foundation. "Grassroots Development: The Way Up from Poverty," Washington, DC: African Development Foundation, 1993.

Agger, Ben. "Critical Theory, Poststructuralism, Postmodernism: Their Sociological Relevance." *Annual Review of Sociology* 17, 1991:105–131.

Akers, Ronald L. *Deviant Behavior: A Social Learning Approach*, 3rd ed. Belmont, CA: Wadsworth, 1985.

Alba, Richard D. *Ethnic Identity: The Transformation of White America*. New Haven, CT: Yale University Press, 1990.

Albas, Daniel, and Cheryl Albas. "Aces and Bombers: The Post-Exam Impression Management Strategies of Students." *Symbolic Interaction* 11, 1988:289–302.

Aldrich, Howard E., and Peter V. Marsden. "Environments and Organizations," in Neil J. Smelser (ed.), *Handbook of Sociology*. Newbury Park, CA: Sage, 1988, pp. 361–392.

Alesci, Nina L. "'Socumentaries' Prove Pictures Worth a Thousand Words." *ASA Footnotes* 22 (Summer) 1994:7.

Alexander, Karl L., Doris R. Entwisle, and Carrie S. Horsey. "From First Grade Forward: Early Foundations of High School Dropout." *Sociology of Education* 70 (April) 1997:87–107.

Alford, Robert A., and Roger Friedland. *Powers of Theory: Capitalism, the State, and Democracy*. New York: Cambridge University Press, 1985.

Alonzo, Angelo A. "Why Do Americans Resist a Healthy Lifestyle?" *USA Today: Your Health* (special newsletter) 123 (October) 1994:1–2.

Altheide, David L. "An Ecology of Communication: Toward a Mapping of the Effective Environment." *Sociological Quarterly* 35 (4) 1994:665–683.

Alwin, Duane F. "Family of Origin and Cohort Differences in Verbal Ability." *American Sociological Review* 56 (October) 1991:625–638.

Amato, Paul R., and Alan Booth. "Changes in Gender Role Attitudes and Perceived Marital Quality." *American Sociological Review* 60 (February) 1995:58–66.

Ambrose, Sue Goetinck. "Anti-Aging Hormone in Mice Might Benefit Us in Old Age." *Dallas Morning News*, August 25, 2005:1A.

American Academy of Pediatrics. "Media Violence." *Pediatrics* 108 (November) 2001: 1222–1226.

Amir, Yehuda. "Contact Hypothesis in Ethnic Relations." *Psychological Bulletin* 71 (May) 1969:319–342.

Ammerman, Nancy T. *Bible Believers: Fundamentalists in the Modern World*. New Brunswick, NJ: Rutgers University Press, 1987.

———. "North American Protestant Fundamentalism," in Andrew M. Greeley (ed.), *Sociology and Religion: A Collection of Readings*. New York: HarperCollins, 1995, pp. 416–425.

Andersen, Margaret L. *Thinking about Women: Sociological Perspectives on Sex and Gender*, 3rd ed. New York: Macmillan, 1993.

Andersen, Margaret L., and Patricia Hill Collins. "Social Change and the Politics of Empowerment," in Margaret L. Andersen and Patricia H. Collins (eds.), *Race, Class, and Gender: An Anthology*. Belmont, CA: Wadsworth, 1992, pp. 450–455.

Anderson, Clifton E. "Dangers and Opportunities." *The Futurist* (March/April) 2000:20–25.

Anderson, Craig A., Nicholas L. Carnagey, and Janie Eubanks. "Exposure to Violent Media: The Effects of Songs with Violent Lyrics on Aggressive Thoughts and Feelings." *Journal of Personality and Social Psychology* 84 (5) 2003:960–971.

Anderson, Curt. "2002 Crime Rate Lowest Since Records Kept." *Yahoo.com News*, Sunday, August 24, 2003:1–4.

Anderson, Robert. *British Universities Past and Present*. London: Hambledon & London, 2007.

Angel, Ronald, and William Gronfein. "The Use of Subjective Information in Statistical Models." *American Sociological Review* 53 (June) 1988:464–473.

Anthony, Dick, and Thomas Robbins. "Civil Religion and Recent American Religious Ferment," in Thomas Robbins and Dick Anthony (eds.), *In Gods We Trust: New Patterns of Religious Pluralism in America*, 2nd ed. New Brunswick, NJ: Transaction, 1990, pp. 475–502.

Apgar, Mallon IV. "The Alternative Workplace: Changing Where and How People Work." Harvard Business Review 76 (3) 1998:39–50.

Apple, Michael W. *Ideology and Curriculum*. Boston: Routledge & Kegan Paul, 1979.

———. *Official Knowledge: Democratic Education in a Conservative Age*. New York: Routledge, 1993.

———. "The Cultural Politics of Home Schooling." Pp. 219-231 in in Knoll, James Wm. (ed.), *Taking Sides: Clashing Views on Educational Issues* (14th ed.), Guilford, CT: McGraw-Hill/Dushkin, 2007.

Araghhi, Farshad A. "Global Depeasantization, 1945–1990." *Sociological Quarterly* 36 (2) 1995:337–368.

Aronowitz, Stanley. *The Knowledge Factory: Dismantling the Corporate University and Creating True Higher Learning*. Boston, MA: Beacon Press, 2000.

Arons, Stephen. "Constitutional Implications of National Curriculum Standards," in James W. Noll (ed.), *Taking Sides: Clashing Views on Controversial Educational Issues*, 9th ed. Guilford, CT: Dushkin, 1997, pp. 125–132.

Arquilla, John, and David Ronfeldt. "A New Epoch—and Spectrum—of Conflict," in John Arquilla and David Ronfeldt (eds.), *In Athena's Camp: Preparing for Conflict in the Information Age*. Santa Monica, CA: Rand, 1997, pp. 1–20.

ASA. Code of Ethics. Washington, DC: American Sociological Association, 2001.

Asante, Molefi Kete. "The Afrocentric Idea in Education," in James W. Noll (ed.), *Taking*

Sides: Clashing Views on Controversial Educational Issues, 9th ed. Guilford, CT: Dushkin, 1997, pp. 206–218.

Asch, Solomon E. *Social Psychology.* Englewood Cliffs, NJ: Prentice-Hall, 1952.

Associated Press, Atlanta. "Life Expectancy is Up, but There's Bad News." *Dallas Morning News,* December 9, 2005:2A.

Associated Press, Boca Raton, FL. "Change in Equipment Could Put Girl Ballplayer Back Behind Plate." *Dallas Morning News,* May 23, 1997:11A.

Associated Press, Boston. "Feminist Professor Ordered to Let Men Join Her Classes." *Dallas Morning News,* February 26, 1999:14A.

Associated Press, Charleston, SC. "2 Female Cadets at Citadel Say Their Clothes Were Sprayed with Flammable Liquid, Set on Fire." *Dallas Morning News,* December 14, 1996:3A.

————. "Citadel Female Hazing Case Won't Be Prosecuted." *Dallas Morning News,* January 24, 1998:3A.

————. "Making History." *Dallas Morning News,* May 9, 1999:4A.

Associated Press, Chicago. "Extreme Obesity on Rise." *Dallas Morning News,* October 14, 2003:8A.

Associated Press, Fort Lauderdale, FL. "Boy Who Used Pro Wrestling Defense Guilty of Murder." *Dallas Morning News,* January 26, 2001:4A.

Associated Press, Lexington, VA. "First Woman Drops Out of VMI." *Dallas Morning News,* August 22, 1997:8A.

————. "Female Cadet Chosen to be VMI Leader." *Dallas Morning News,* March 24, 2000:4A.

Associated Press, Little Rock. "Lawmaker Rebukes Home Schooling after Pool Champion Graduates at 14." *Dallas Morning News,* September 7, 1997:55A.

Associated Press, Monrovia. "Liberia's New Leader Vows Break with Past." *Dallas Morning News,* January 17, 2006:9A.

Associated Press, New York. "Poll Backs Women in Military." *Dallas Morning News,* March 1, 1997a:10A.

————. "Telecommuters Revolutionize Workplace with Offices at Home." *Dallas Morning News,* September 21, 1997b:8H.

Associated Press, Seattle. "Lawyers Urge Death Penalty Changes." *Dallas Morning News,* February 9, 2003:4A.

Associated Press, Washington. "Same-Sex Classes Not Necessarily Better for Girls." *Dallas Morning News,* March 13, 1998a:8A.

————. "Sex-Harassment Caseload Rises." *Dallas Morning News,* January 24, 1998b:3A.

————. "Life Expectancy on Rise for Most." *Dallas Morning News,* September 10, 2002a:3A.

————. "Students' Poor Showing on History Test Generates Concerns." *Dallas Morning News,* May 10, 2002b:4A.

————. "Incarcerations Exceed 2 Million for the First Time." *Dallas Morning News,* April 7, 2003a:1A.

————. "Head Start Students to Face Testing." *Dallas Morning News,* January 18, 2003b:9A.

————. "Teacher Morale, Unruly Students Are Concerns, Study Shows. *Dallas Morning News,* April 24, 2003c:9A.

————. "Study: Media Glut Starts Early." *Dallas Morning News,* October 29, 2003d:11A.

————. "Female Combat Roles Expanding." *Dallas Morning News,* January 3, 2004:17A.

————. "U.S. Murder Rate Lowest in 40 Years." *Dallas Morning News,* October 18, 2005a: 6A.

————. "Inmate Population Grows 2.3% in U.S." *Dallas Morning News,* April 25, 2005b:6A.

————. "Women in Combat? Bill Calls for Congress to Decide." *Dallas Morning News,* May 20, 2005c:14A.

————. "Policy on Women's Combat Role Stands." *Dallas Morning News,* May 26, 2005d: 23A.

————. "Poll: Female Military Students Abused." *Dallas Morning News,* December 24, 2005e: 10A.

————. "Poll: Progress Mad on King's Dream." *Dallas Morning News,* January 15, 2006:13A.

Astin, Helen S. "Educating Women: A Promise and a Vision for the Future." *American Journal of Education* 98 (August) 1990:479–493.

Astone, Nan Marie, and Sara S. McLanahan. "Family Structure, Parental Practices and High School Completion." *American Sociological Review* 56 (June) 1991:309–320.

Astor, Kathy K. "No Cure for Sexism in the Medical Profession," in Paula S. Rothenberg (ed.), *Race, Class, and Gender in the United States: An Integrated Study,* 3rd ed. New York: St. Martin's Press, 1995, pp. 112–116.

Attlesey, Sam. "A His and Hers Battle: Gender a Key Issue in Governor's Race." *Dallas Morning News,* April 29, 1990:1A, 20A.

Attorney General's Commission on Pornography. *Final Report.* Washington, DC: Government Printing Office, 1986.

Aulette, Judy R. *Changing American Families* (2nd ed.). Boston: Allyn and Bacon, 2007.

Austin, Elizabeth. "Why Homer's My Hero." *Washington Monthly* 32 (10) October 2000: 30–35.

Avis, Harry. *Drugs and Life,* 2nd ed. Madison, WI: Wm. C. Brown, 1993.

Axtell, James. *The European and the Indian: Essays in the Ethnohistory of Colonial North America.* New York: Oxford University Press, 1981.

Babiuch, William. "The American Power Elite and the Iraq-Coalition War," in Mathew Kanjirathinkal (ed.), *Politics at the End of History.* New York: Peter Lang, 1993, pp. 247–271.

Baca-Zinn, Maxine, and D. Stanley Eitzen. *Diversity in American Families.* New York: HarperCollins, 1987.

————. *Diversity in Families,* 5th ed. New York: HarperCollins, 1993.

Bachrach, Peter, and Morton S. Baratz. "Two Faces of Power." *American Political Science Review* 51 (December) 1962:947–952.

Bailey, Kathleen C. *Doomsday Weapons: In the Hands of Many.* Urbana: University of Illinois Press, 1991.

Bailey, Michael. "Campaign Finance Reform: What Next?" Hoover Institution: Public Policy Inquiry—Campaign Finance, August 26, 2003:1–2.

Bailey, Ronald. "Seven Doomsday Myths about the Environment." *The Futurist* 29 (January/ February) 1995:14–18.

Bailey, Thomas. "Community Colleges in the 21st Century: Challenges and Opportunities," in *The Knowledge Economy and Postsecondary Education: Report of a Workshop.* Center for Education, 2002, pp. 59–76.

Bainbridge, Jay, Marcia K. Meyers, Sakiko Tanaka, Jane Waldfogel. "Who Gets an Early Education? Family Income and the Enrollment of Three- to Five-Year-Olds from 1968-2000." *Social Science Quarterly* 86 (September): 724–745.

Bales, Kevin. "Because She Looks Like a Child," in Barbara Ehrenreich and Arlie Hochschild (eds.), *Global Woman: Nannies, Maids, and Sex Workers in the New Economy.* New York: Metropolitan Books, 2002, pp. 207–229.

Bales, Robert F. "Channels of Communication in Small Groups." *American Sociological Review* 1951:461–468.

Baltzell, E. Digby. *Philadelphia Gentlemen: The Making of a National Upper Class.* New York: Free Press, 1958.

————. "Upperclass and Elites." *Society* 27 (January/February) 1990:72–75.

Bandura, Albert J. "Influence of Models' Reinforcement Contingencies on the Acquisition of Imitative Responses." *Journal of Personality and Social Psychology* 1, 1965:589–595.

————. *Aggression: A Social Learning Analysis.* Englewood Cliffs, NJ: Prentice-Hall, 1973.

————. *Social Learning Theory.* Englewood Cliffs, NJ: Prentice-Hall, 1977.

Bandura, Albert J., and R. H. Walters. *Social Learning and Personality Development.* New York: Holt, Rinehart & Winston, 1963.

Banister, Eric W., Murray Allen, and Samia Fadl, et al. *Contemporary Health Issues.* Boston: Jones & Bartlett, 1988.

Banks, James A. "Multicultural Education: Development, Dimensions, and Challenges," in James W. Noll (ed.), *Taking Sides: Clashing Views on Controversial Educational Issues,* 9th ed. Guilford, CT: Dushkin, 1997, pp. 88–97.

Bankston, Carl L. III, Stephen J. Caldas, and Min Zhou. "The Academic Achievement of Vietnamese American Students: Ethnicity as Social Capital." *Sociological Focus* 30 (February) 1997:1–16.

Bankston, Carl L., III, and Jacques Henry. "Endogamy among Louisiana Cajuns: A Social Class Explanation." *Social Forces* 77 (4) June 1999:1317–1338.

Barcus, F. Earle. *Images of Life on Children's Television: Sex Roles, Minorities, and Families.* New York: Praeger, 1983.

Barker, Chris. *Television, Globalization and Cultural Identities.* Philadelphia, PA: Open University Press, 1999.

Barnartt, Sharon, Kay Schriner, and Richard Scotch. "Social Movements of People with Disabilities," in Alex Thio and Thomas C. Calhoun (eds.), *Readings in Deviant Behavior,* 3rd ed. Boston: Allyn and Bacon, 2004, pp. 343–345.

Barnet, Richard J. "The End of Jobs: Employment Is One Thing the Global Economy Is Not Creating." *Annual Editions, Sociology 94/95,* 23rd ed. Guilford, CT: Dushkin, 1994, pp. 161–166.

Barnet, Richard J., and John Cavanagh. *Global Dreams: Imperial Institutions and the New World Order.* New York: Simon & Schuster, 1994.

Baron, James N., and Andrew E. Newman. "For What It's Worth: Organizations, Occupations, and the Value of Work Done by Women and Non Whites." *American Sociological Review* 55 (April) 1990:155–175.

Baron, Robert A., and Deborah R. Richardson. *Culture and Conduct: An Excursion in Anthropology,* 3rd ed. Belmont, CA: Wadsworth, 1994.

Barr, Paula A. "Perceptions of Sexual Harassment." *Sociological Inquiry* 63 (Fall) 1993: 400–470.

Barrett, Richard A. *Culture and Conduct: An Excursion in Anthropology,* 2nd ed. Belmont, CA: Wadsworth, 1991.

Barrett, Todd. "Be Careful What You Ask For." *Newsweek,* February 15, 1993:43–45.

Barta, Carolyn. "Public's Refusal Rate May Skew Results of Phone Surveys." *Dallas Morning News,* March 15, 1998:1J, 10J.

———. "Changes for Women at Home and Abroad." *Dallas Morning News,* October 19, 2001:1A, 7A.

Bartos, Omar J. "Postmodernism, Postindustrialism, and the Future." *Sociological Quarterly* 37 (2) 1996:307–325.

Basow, Susan A. *Gender Stereotypes: Traditions and Alternatives,* 2nd ed. Pacific Grove, CA: Brooks/Cole, 1986.

Bates, Oklu U. Florence L. Denmark, Virginia Held, Dorothy O. Helly, Shirley Hune, Susan H. Lees, Frances E. Mascia-Lees, Sarah, B. Pomeroy, and Carolyn M. Somerville. *Women's Realities, Women's Choices: An Introduction to Women's Studies* (3rd ed.). New York: Oxford University Press, 2005.

Baubock, Rainer. *Transnational Citizenship: Membership and Rights in International Migration.* Brookfield, VT: Edward Elgar, 1994.

Baxter, Janeen. "Is Husband's Class Location and Class Identity Enough?: Class Location and Class Identity in the United States, Sweden, Norway, and Australia." *American Sociological Review* 59 (2) 1994:220–235.

Bayh, Birch. "Our Nation's Schools: A Report Card: 'A' in School Violence and Vandalism." *Preliminary Report of the Subcommittee to Investigate Juvenile Delinquency.* Washington, DC: Government Printing Office, 1975.

Baym, Nancy K. "The Emergence of On-Line Community," in *Cybersociety 2.0: Revisiting Computer-Mediated Communication and Community.* Thousand Oaks, CA: Sage, 1998, pp. 35–68.

BBC News Online (Asia-Pacific). "Mystery of Australia's Weeping Madonna," Friday, September 13, 2002:1–2.

Beasley, Chris. *What Is Feminism?: An Introduction to Feminist Theory.* Thousand Oaks, CA: Sage, 1999.

Beasley, Maurine H. "Women Audiences," in Erwin K. Thomas and Brown H. Carpenter (eds.), *Handbook on Mass Media in the United States: The Industry and Its Audiences.* Westport, CT: Greenwood Press, 1994, pp. 207–230.

Beaubier, Jeff. "Biological Factors in Aging," in Cary S. Kart and Barbara B. Manard (eds.), *Aging in America: Readings in Social Gerontology,* 2nd ed. Sherman Oaks, CA: Alfred, 1981, pp. 155–175.

Becerra, Rosina M. "The Mexican American Family," in Charles H. Mindel, Robert W. Habenstein, and Roosevelt Wright Jr. (eds.), *Ethnic Families in America: Patterns and Variations,* 4th ed. Upper Saddle River, NJ: Prentice-Hall, 1998, pp. 153–171.

Beck, Melinda. "The New Middle Age." *Newsweek,* December 7, 1992:50–56.

Beck, Melinda, Mary Hager, and Patrick Rogers, et al. "Doctors under the Knife." *Newsweek,* April 5, 1993:28–33.

Beck, Melinda, Karen Springen, and Lucille Beachy, et al. "The Losing Formula." *Newsweek,* April 30, 1990:52–58.

Becker, Carl. "Progress." *Encyclopedia of the Social Sciences,* vols. 11, 12. New York: Macmillan, 1933.

Becker, Ernest. *The Denial of Death.* New York: Free Press, 1973.

Becker, Howard S. "The Career of the Chicago Public School Teacher." *American Journal of Sociology* 57 (March) 1952:470–477.

Becker, Howard S., Blanche Geer, and Everett C. Hughes, et al. *Boys in White: Student Culture in Medical School.* Chicago: University of Chicago Press, 1961.

———. *Outsiders: Studies in the Sociology of Deviance.* New York: Free Press, 1963.

———. "What Should Sociology Look Like in the (Near) Future?" *Contemporary Sociology* 29 (March) 2000:333–336.

Beckfield, Jason. "Inequality in the World Polity: The Structure of International Organization." *American Sociological Review* 68 (3) June 2003:401–424.

Beckman, Peter R., Larry Campbell, and Paul W. Crumlish, et al. *The Nuclear Predicament: An Introduction.* Englewood Cliffs, NJ: Prentice-Hall, 1989.

Bedell, Doug. "Surrendering to Mob Mentality." *Dallas Morning News,* July 22, 2003:1A.

Beeghley, Leonard. *The Structure of Social Stratification in the United States* (4th ed) Boston: Allyn & Bacon, 2005.

Begley, Sharon. "Gray Matters." *Newsweek,* March 27, 1995:48–54.

———. "How to Build a Baby's Brain." *Newsweek* special issue (Spring/Summer) 1997:28–32.

———. "AIDS at 20." *Newsweek,* June 11, 2001: 35–37.

Begley, Sharon, Mary Hager, and Daniel Glick, et al. "Cures from the Womb." *Newsweek,* February 22, 1993:49–51.

Beil, Laura. "The Youth Age: Promise or Field of Dreams?" *Dallas Morning News,* September 16, 2002:1F, 6F.

Bell, Daniel. *The Coming of Postindustrial Society.* New York: Basic Books, 1973.

Bellah, Robert N. "Civil Religion in America." *Daedalus* 96 (1) 1967:1–21.

———. "Religion and the Legitimation of the American Republic," in Thomas Robbins and Dick Anthony (eds.), *In Gods We Trust: New Patterns of Religious Pluralism in America,* 2nd ed. New Brunswick, NJ: Transaction, 1990, pp. 411–426.

Bellas, Marcia L. "Comparable Worth in Academia: The Effects on Faculty Salaries of the Sex Composition and Labor-Market Conditions of Academic Disciplines." *American Sociological Review* 59 (December) 1994:807–821.

Belson, W. A. *Television Violence and the Adolescent Boy.* Westmead, England: Saxon House, 1978.

Benford, Robert D., and David A. Snow. "Framing Processes and Social Movements: An Overview and Assessment." *Annual Review of Sociology* 26 2000:611–639.

Benjamin, Gail R. *Japanese Lessons: A Year in a Japanese School through the Eyes of an American Anthropologist and Her Children.* New York: New York University Press, 1997.

Bennett, Kathleen P., and Margaret D. LeCompte. *How Schools Work: A Sociological Analysis of Education.* New York: Longman, 1990.

Bennett, William J., Willard Fair, and Chester E. Finn, et al. "A Nation Still at Risk," in James W. Noll (ed.), *Taking Sides: Clashing Views on Controversial Educational Issues,* 13th ed. Guilford, CT: McGraw-Hill Dushkin, 2006, pp. 177–183.

Bennis, Warren G., and Philip E. Slater. *The Temporary Society.* New York: HarperCollins, 1968.

Bensman, Joseph, and Bernard Rosenberg. *Mass, Class, and Bureaucracy: An Introduction to Sociology.* New York: Praeger, 1976.

Benton, Joshua. "Despite Educational Success, Japan Plans to Change System." *Dallas Morning News,* December 3, 2001:1A, 14A.

Berberoglu, Berch. *Political Economy of Development: Development Theory and the Prospect for Change in the Third World.* Albany, NY: State University of New York Press, 1992.

———. *Class Structure and Social Transformation.* Westport, CT: Greenwood Press, 1994.

Berger, Bennet M. *The Survival of a Counterculture.* Berkeley: University of California Press, 1981.

Berger, Peter L. *Invitation to Sociology: A Humanistic Perspective.* New York: Doubleday, 1963.

Bergmann, Barbara R. *In Defense of Affirmative Action.* New York: Basic Books, 1996.

Berman, Jerry, and Daniel Weitzen. "Technology and Democracy." *Social Research* 64 (3) 1997:1313–1319.

Bernard, Jessie. *The Female World.* New York: Free Press, 1981.

———. *The Future of Marriage,* 2nd ed. New Haven, CT: Yale University Press, 1982.

Bernard, L. L. *Instinct.* New York: Holt, Rinehart & Winston, 1924.

Bernstein, Marc F. "Why I'm Wary of Charter Schools," in James W. Noll (ed.), *Taking Sides: Clashing Views on Controversial Educational Issues,* 14th ed. Guilford, CT: McGraw-Hill Dushkin, 2007, pp. 209–215.

Berryman-Fink, Cynthia, Deborah Ballard-Reisch, and Lisa H. Newman (eds.). *Communication and Sex-Role Socialization.* Hamden, CT: Garland, 1993.

Bertman, Stephen. *Hyperculture: The Human Cost of Speed.* Westport, CT: Praeger, 1998.

Besharov, Douglas J., and Lisa A. Laumann. "Don't Call It Child Abuse If It's Really Poverty," in Andrew J. Cherlin (ed.), *Public and Private Families: A Reader.* Boston: McGraw-Hill, 1998, pp. 257–271.

Best, Fred, and Ray Eberhard. "Education for the Era of the Adult." *The Futurist* (May/June) 1990:23–28.

Best, Joel. *Damned Lies and Statistics: Untangling Numbers from the Media, Politicians, and Activists.* Berkley: University of California Press, 2001.

Best, Joel, and David F. Luckenbill. *Organizing Deviance,* 2nd ed. Englewood Cliffs, NJ: Prentice-Hall, 1994.

———. "The Rhetorical Appeal of Random Violence," in Joel Best and Donileen R. Loseke (eds.), *Social Problems: Constructionist Readings.* New York: Aldine de Gruyter, 2003, pp. 113–119.

Biel, Anders and Andreas Nilsson. Religious Values and environmental Concern: Harmony and Detachment. *Social Science Quarterly* 86 (March), 2005:178-191.

Bielby, William T. "Minimizing Workplace Gender and Racial Bias." *Contemporary Sociology* 29 (January) 2000:120–129.

Bielby, William T., and Denise D. Bielby. "Family Ties: Balancing Commitments to Work and Family in Dual Earner Households." *American Sociological Review* 54 (October) 1989: 776–789.

Biggart, Nicole W. *Charismatic Capitalism: Direct Selling Organizations in America.* Chicago: University of Chicago Press, 1989.

Billings, Dwight B. "Religion as Opposition: A Gramscian Analysis." *American Journal of Sociology* 96 (July) 1990:1–31.

Billings, Dwight B., and Shauna L. Scott. "Religion and Political Legitimation." *Annual Review of Sociology* 20, 1994:173–234.

Billingsley, Andrew. *Climbing Jacob's Ladder: The Enduring Legacy of African-American Families.* New York: Simon & Schuster, 1992.

Binder, Amy. "Media Depictions of Harm in Heavy Metal and Rap Music." *American Sociological Review* 58 (December) 1993: 753–767.

Binion, Gayle. "Toward a Feminist Regrounding of Constitutional Law." *Social Science Quarterly* 72 (June) 1991:207–220.

Bitzinger, Richard A. "Globalization in the Post-Cold War Defense Industry: Challenges and Opportunities," in *Arming the Future: A Defense Industry for the 21st Century.* New York: Council on Foreign Relations Press, 1999, pp. 305–333.

Black, Jay, Jennings Bryant, and Susan Thompson. *Reinventing Media,* 4th ed. Madison, WI: Brown & Benchmark, 1997.

Black, Thomas R. *Doing Quantitative Research.* Thousand Oaks, CA: Sage, 1999.

Blakely, Edward J., and Mary Gail Snyder. *Fortress America: Gated Communities in the United States.* Washington, DC: Brookings Institute Press, 1997.

Blalock, Hubert M., Jr. "The Real and Unrealized Contributions of Quantitative Sociology." *American Sociological Review* 54 (June) 1989:447–460.

Blank, Renee, and Sandra Slipp. *Voices of Diversity.* New York: Amacom, 1994.

Blau, Joel. *The Visible Poor: Homelessness in the United States.* New York: Oxford University Press, 1992.

Blau, Peter M. *The Dynamics of Bureaucracy: A Study of Interpersonal Relations in Two Government Agencies,* 2nd ed. Chicago: University of Chicago Press, 1963.

———. *Exchange and Power in Social Life.* New York: Wiley, 1964.

Blau, Peter M., and Otis Dudley Duncan. *The American Occupational Structure.* New York: Wiley, 1967.

Blau, Peter M., and Joseph E. Schwartz. *Cross-Cutting Social Circles: Testing a Macrostructural Theory of Intergroup Relations.* New York: Academic Press, 1983.

Blauvelt, Martha T. "Women and Revivalism," in Rosemary R. Ruether and Rosemary S. Keller (eds.), *Women and Religion in America: Vol. 1, the Nineteenth Century.* New York: Harper-Collins, 1981, pp. vii–xiv.

Bloch, Marc. *Feudal Society.* London: Routledge & Kegan Paul, 1961.

Bloom, Allan. *The Closing of the American Mind.* New York: Simon & Schuster, 1987.

Bloom, Harold. *Omens of the Millennium: The Gnosis of Angels, Dreams, and Resurrection.* New York: Riverhead Books, 1996.

Blumer, Herbert G. "Collective Behavior," in Alfred McClung Lee (ed.), *Principles of Sociology,* 3rd ed. New York: Barnes & Noble, 1969a, pp. 65–121.

———. *Symbolic Interactionism: Perspective and Method.* Englewood Cliffs, NJ: Prentice-Hall, 1969b.

Blumstein, Philip, and Pepper W. Schwartz. *American Couples: Money, Work, Sex.* New York: Simon & Schuster, 1983.

Bodmer, Walter, and Robin McKie. *The Book of Man: The Human Genome Project and the Quest to Discover Our Genetic Heritage.* New York: Scribner, 1994.

Bogart, Leo. "American Media and Commercial Culture." *Society* 28 (September/October) 1991:62–73.

———. *Commercial Culture: The Media System and Public Interest.* New York: Oxford University Press, 1995.

Boles, Jacqueline, and A. P. Garbin. "Stripping for a Living: An Occupational Study of the Night Club Stripper," in Clifton Bryant (ed.), *Deviant Behavior: Occupational and Organizational Bases.* Chicago: Rand McNally, 1974, pp. 312–335.

Boli, John, and George M. Thomas. "World Culture in the World Polity: A Century of International Non-Government Organizations." *American Sociological Review* 62 (2) 1997: 171–190.

Bonacich, Edna. "A Theory of Ethnic Antagonism: The Split-Labor Market." *American Sociological Review* 37, 1972:547–559.

Bonacich, Edna, and Richard P. Appelbaum. *Behind the Label: Inequality in the Los Angeles Apparel Industry.* Berkeley, CA: University of California Press, 2000.

Bonanno, Alessandro, Lawrence Busch, and William H. Friedland, et al. "Introduction," in Alessandro Bonanno, et al. (eds.), *From Columbus to ConAgra.* Lawrence: University Press of Kansas, 1994, pp. 1–26.

Bonnicksen, Thomas. "A Closer Look at Problems of Rain Forests." *Dallas Morning News,* July 10, 1998:31A.

Bork, Robert H. "Multiculturalism Is Bringing Us to a Barbarous Epoch." *The Chronicle of Higher Education,* (October 11) 1996:11.

Bose, Christine E. *Jobs and Gender: A Study of Occupational Prestige.* New York: Praeger, 1985.

Boston College Chronicle. "Mary Daly Ends Suit, Agrees to Retire." February 15, 2001:4.

Boswell, Terry, and William J. Dixon. "Dependency and Rebellion: A Cross-National Analysis." *American Sociological Review* 55 (August) 1990:540–559.

Bosworth, Barry, and Gary Burtless. "Population Aging and Economic Performance," in Barry Bosworth and Gary Burtless (eds.), *Aging Societies: The Global Dimension.* Washington, DC: Brookings Institution, 1998, pp. 1–32.

Boulding, Elise. "Learning Peace," in Raimo Vayrynen (ed.), *The Quest for Peace.* Newbury Park, CA: Sage, 1987, pp. 317–329.

Boulding, Kenneth E. "Peace and the Evolutionary Process," in Raimo Vayrynen (ed.), *The Quest for Peace.* Newbury Park, CA: Sage, 1987, pp. 48–62.

Bowen, Charles. *Modem Nation: The Handbook of Grassroots American Activism Online.* New York: Random House, 1996.

Boyer, Ernest L. *High School: A Report on Secondary Education in America.* New York: HarperCollins, 1983.

Boyer, Paul. *By the Bomb's Early Light.* New York: Pantheon, 1985.

Boyle, Elizabeth H. *Female Genital Cutting: Cultural Conflict in the Global Community.* Baltimore, MD: Johns Hopkins University Press, 2002.

Boyle, Karen. *Media and Violence: Gendering the Debates.* Thousand Oaks, CA: Sage, 2005.

Bozett, Frederick W. "Gay Fathers," in Frederick W. Bozett (ed.), *Gay and Lesbian Parents.* New York: Praeger, 1987, pp. 3–22.

Brandon, Karen. "U.S. Fringe Groups Praising Terrorist Actions." *The Chicago Tribune Online Edition,* October 27, 2001:1–2.

Braun, Denny. *The Rich Get Richer: The Rise of Income Inequality in the United States and the World.* Chicago: Nelson-Hall, 1991.

Brecher, Jeremy. "Foreword," in *Panic Rules: Everything You Need to Know About the Global Economy.* Cambridge, MA: South End Press, 1999, pp. vii–x.

Brimelow, Peter. "Cutting the Pie." *Forbes,* September 4, 2000:86.

Brines, Julie. "Economic Dependency, Gender, and the Division of Labor at Home." *American Journal of Sociology* 100 (November) 1994:652–688.

Brinkerhoff, David B., and Lynn H. White. *Sociology,* 3rd ed. New York: West, 1991.

Brown, Gordon. "How to Embrace Change." *Newsweek,* June 12, 2006:69.

Brown, Heidi Nolte. "Can Violent Films Help Troubled Teens?" *Dallas Morning News,* March 11, 1990:4C.

Brown, J. David. "The Professional Ex-: An Alternative for Exiting the Deviant Career." *Sociological Quarterly* 32 (2) 1991:219–230.

Brown, Karen M. "Fundamentalism and the Control of Women," in John S. Hawley (ed.), *Fundamentalism and Gender.* New York: Oxford University Press, 1994.

Brown, Lester R. *Vital Signs 1994: The Trends That Are Shaping Our Future.* New York: Norton, 1994.

———. *Plan B2.0: Rescuing a Planet Under Stress and a Civilization in Trouble.* New York: W.W. Norton, 2006.

Brown, Lester R., Christopher Flavin, and Edward C. Wolf. "Earth's Vital Signs." *The Futurist* (July/August) 1988:13–20.

Brown, Lester R., Christopher Flavin, and Hilary French (eds.). *State of the World 2001.* New York: W. W. Norton, 2001.

Brown, Lester R., Michael Renner, and Christopher Flavin. *Vital Signs 1997: The Environmental Trends That Are Shaping Our Future.* New York: Norton, 1997.

Brown, Seyom. *The Causes and Prevention of War.* New York: St. Martin's Press, 1987.

Brown, Susan L., and Alan Booth. "Stress at Home, Peace at Work: A Test of the Time Bind Hypothesis." *Social Science Quarterly* 83 (December) 2002:905–920.

Brunvand, Jan H. *Curses! Broiled Again! The Hottest Urban Legends Going.* New York: Norton, 1989.

———. *Too Good to Be True: The Colossal Book of Urban Legends.* New York: W. W. Norton, 1999.

Bryman, Alan. *The Disneyization of Society.* Thousand Oaks, CA: Pine Forge Press, 2004.

Bryant, Adam, and Erika Check. "How Parents Raise Boys and Girls." *Newsweek* special issue (Fall/Winter) 2000:64–65.

Bryant, Jennings (ed.). "Preface," in *Television and the American Family.* Hillsdale, NJ: Erlbaum, 1990, pp. xiii–xvii.

Bryman, Alan. *The Disneyization of Society.* Thousand Oaks, CA: Pine Forge Press, 2004.

Bryson, Bethany. "Anything But Heavy Metal: Symbolic Exclusion and Musical Dislikes." *American Sociological Review* 61 (5) 1996: 884–899.

Budiansky, Stephen, Art Levine, and Ted Gest, et al. "The Numbers Racket: How Polls and Statistics Lie." *U.S. News and World Report* July 11, 1988:44–47.

Bullock, Charles S. III, and M. V. Hood III. "One Person—No Vote; One Vote; Two Votes: Voting Methods, Ballot Types, and Undervote Frequency in the 2000 Presidential Election." *Social Science Quarterly* 83 (4) December 2002: 981–993.

Bumpass, Larry, James A. Sweet, and Teresa C. Martin. "Recent Trends in Divorce and Remarriage." *Journal of Marriage and the Family* 52 (August) 1990:747–756.

Burdett, Hal, Werner Fornos, and Sheila Kinkade, et al. "A Continent in Crisis: Building a Future for Africa in the 21st Century." *Toward the 21st Century: A Special Report by the Population Institute to the 101st Congress.* Washington, DC: Population Institute, 1988, pp. 1–2.

Burgess, Ernest W. "The Growth of the City: An Introduction to a Research Project," in Robert Park, R. D. McKenzie, and Ernest Burgess (eds.), *The City*. Chicago: University of Chicago Press, 1925, pp. 47–62.

Buroway, Michael. "Grounding Globalization," in Michael Buroway, Joseph A. Blum, and Sheba George, et al. (eds.), *Global Ethnography: Forces, Connections, and Imaginations in a Postmodern World*. Berkeley, CA: University of California Press, 2000, pp. 337–350.

Burton, Thomas. *Serpent-Handling Believers*. Knoxville: University of Tennessee Press, 1993.

Butler, Judith. *Gender Trouble: Feminism and the Subversion of Identity*. New York: Routledge, 1990.

Button, James W., and Barbara A. Rienzo. "The Impact of Affirmative Action: Black Employment in Six Southern Cities." *Social Science Quarterly* 84 (1) March 2003:1–31.

Bynum, Jack E., and William E. Thompson. *Juvenile Delinquency: A Sociological Approach*, 7th ed. Boston: Allyn & Bacon, 2007.

———. *Juvenile Delinquency: A Sociological Approach*, 6th ed. Boston: Allyn and Bacon 2008.

Cable, Sherry. "Women's Social Movement Involvement: The Role of Structural Availability in Recruitment and Participation Processes." *Sociological Quarterly* 33 (1) 1992:35–50.

Cameron, Don. "Preserving the American Dream." *Educational Horizons* 71 (Fall) 1992:31–36.

Camia, Catalina. "A Tough Hill to Climb." *Dallas Morning News*, August 24, 1997:1J, 10J.

Campbell, Anne. "Cultural Identity as a Social Construct." *Intercultural Education* 11 (1) 2000:31–39.

Caplow, Theodore. *Peace Games*. Middletown, CT: Wesleyan University Press, 1989.

———. *American Social Trends*. New York: Harcourt Brace Jovanovich, 1991.

Cappell, Charles L., and Thomas M. Guterbock. "Visible Colleges: The Social and Conceptual Structure of Sociology Specialties." *American Sociological Review* 57 (April) 1992:266–273.

Carelli, Richard. "High Court Focused on Harassment." *Dallas Morning News*, June 28, 1998:9A.

Carilli, Theresa and Jane Campbell, *Women and the Media: Diverse Perspectives*. Lanham, MD: University Press of America, 2005.

Carmichael, Stokely, and Charles V. Hamilton. *Black Power: The Politics of Liberation in America*. New York: Vintage Books, 1967.

Carnegie Foundation for the Advancement of Teaching. *Report on Higher Education*. Princeton, NJ: Carnegie Foundation for the Advancement of Teaching, 1977.

Carruthers, Bruce G., and Brian Uzzi. "Economic Sociology in the New Millennium." *Contemporary Sociology* 29 (May) 2000:486–494.

Casper, Lynne M., Sara S. McLanahan, and Irwin Garfinkel. "The Gender-Poverty Gap: What We Can Learn from Other Countries." *American Sociological Review* 59 (August) 1994:594–605.

Cassata, Mary. *Television Looks at Aging*. New York: Television Information Office, 1985.

Castells, Manuel. *The Rise of the Network Society*. Malden, MA: Blackwell, 1996.

———. "Materials for an Exploratory Theory of the Network Society." *British Journal of Sociology* 51 (1) January/March 2000:5–24.

———. "The Internet and the Network Society," in Barry Wellman and Caroline Haythornwaite (eds.), *The Internet in Everyday Life*. Malden, MA: Blackwell, 2002, pp. xx–xxxi.

Castro, Ida. "Worth More than We Earn." *National Forum* 77 (Spring) 1997:17–21.

Castro, Janice. "Disposable Workers." *Annual Editions, Sociology 94/95*, 23rd ed. Guilford, CT: Dushkin, 1994:191–194.

Cavan, Ruth Shonle. "The Concepts of Tolerance and Contraculture as Applied to Delinquency." *Sociological Quarterly* 2 (Spring) 1961: 243–258.

Cavanagh, John, and Jerry Mander (co-chairs). *Alternatives to Economic Globalization: (A Better World Is Possible)*. San Francisco: Berritt-Koehler, 2002.

Cavender, Gray. "Reality Television Constructs Crime," in Joel Best and Donileen R. Loseke (eds.), *Social Problems: Constructionist Readings*. New York: Aldine de Gruyter, 2003, pp. 29–36.

Cavendish, Richard. *The Great Religions*. New York: Arco, 1980.

CBS Morning News, April 15, 1988. CBS News. Report by American Pediatric Association on television watching by children.

———. April 17, 1990.

CBS News. "Welfare à la Carte." *60 Minutes*, September 21, 1997.

———. November 30, 1999.

Census and You. "More Empty Nests," 31 (6) June 1996:1.

Census Bureau News. *United States Department of Commerce News*, 2003.

Centers for Disease Control and Prevention online, <http://www.cdc.gov>, 1997.

Cerverno, Ronald M., and Thomas E. Kirkpatrick. "The Enduring Effects of Family Role and Schooling on Participation in Adult Education." *American Journal of Education* 99 (November) 1990:77–94.

Chafetz, Janet Saltzman. *Feminist Sociology: An Overview of Contemporary Theories*. Itasca, IL: Peacock, 1988.

———. "Feminist Theory and Sociology: Underutilized Contributions for Mainstream Theory," in John Hagan and Karen S. Cook (eds.), *Annual Review of Sociology* 23. Palo Alto, CA: Annual Reviews, 1997, pp. 97–120.

Chalfant, H. Paul, Robert E. Beckley, and C. Eddie Palmer. *Religion in Contemporary Society*, 3rd ed. Itasca, IL: Peacock, 1994.

Chambers, James A. *Blacks and Crime: A Function of Class*. Westport, CT: Praeger, 1995.

Chambliss, William, and Milton Mankoff (eds.). *Whose Law, What Order? A Conflict Approach to Criminology*. New York: Wiley, 1976.

Chan, Ying. "NII," in O'Reilly et al. (eds.), *The Internet and Society*. Cambridge: Harvard University Press, 1997, p. 337.

Charles, Camille Z. "Neighborhood Racial-Composition Preferences: Evidence from a Multiethnic Metropolis." *Social Problems* 47 (3) August 2000:379–407.

Charles, Maria, and Karen Bradley. "Equal but Separate? A Cross-National Study of Sex Segregation in Higher Education." *American Sociological Review* 67 (August) 2002:573–599.

Chaves, Mark. *Ordaining Women: Culture and Conflict in Religious Organizations*. Cambridge, MA: Harvard University Press, 1997.

Chebium, Raju. "DNA Provides New Hope for Wrongly Convicted Death Row Inmates." *CNN.com, Law Center*, June 16, 2000:1–6.

Chemers, Martin M., Robert W. Rice, and Eric Sundstrom, et al. "Leader Esteem for the Least Preferred Co-Worker Score, Training, and Effectiveness: An Experimental Examination." *Journal of Personality and Social Psychology* 31 (3) 1975:401–410.

Chen, Lincoln G., Winifred M. Fitzgerald, and Lisa Bates. "Global Management: The Cairo Conference." *Environment* 37 (January/February) 1995:4–9; 31–33.

Chen, Wenhong, Jeffrey Boase, and Barry Wellman. "Remarriage," in Andrew Cherlin (ed.), *Public and Private Families: A Reader*. Boston: McGraw-Hill, 1998, pp. 295–296.

———. "The Global Villagers: Comparing Internet Users and Uses around the World," in Barry Wellman and Caroline Haythornthwaite (eds.), *The Internet in Everyday Life*. Malden, MA: Blackwell, 2002, pp. 74–113.

Chernow, Ronald. *Titan: The Life of John D. Rockefeller, Sr*. New York: Random House, 1998.

Cherry, Andrew L. *The Socializing Instincts: Individual, Family, and Social Bonds*. Westport, CT: Praeger, 1994.

Chia, Rosing C., Jamie L. Moore, and Ka Nei Lam, et al. "Cultural Differences in Gender Role Attitudes between Chinese and American Students." *Sex Roles* 31 (July) 1994:23–30.

Chomsky, Noam. *Year 501: The Conquest Continues*. Boston: South End Press, 1993.

Chong, Dennis. *Collective Action and the Civil Rights Movement*. Chicago: University of Chicago Press, 1991.

Chowdhury, Najma, Barbara J. Nelson, and Kathryn A. Carver, et al. "Redefining Politics: Patterns of Women's Political Engagement from a Global Perspective," in Barbara J. Nelson and Najma Chowdhury (eds.), *Women and Politics Worldwide*. New Haven, CT: Yale University Press, 1994:3–24.

Chua, Amy. *World on Fire: How Exporting Free Market Democracy Breeds Ethnic Hatred and Global Instability*. New York: Doubleday, 2003.

Church, Diana K., Mark A. Siegel, and Carol D. Foster (eds.). *Growing Old in America*. Wylie, TX: Information Aids, 1988.

Churchill, Ward. *Indians 'R' Us? Culture and Genocide in Native North America*. Monroe, ME: Common Courage Press, 1994.

Churnin, Nancy. "Tot TV Comes with Parental Guidance." *Dallas Morning News*, May 25, 2006:1A;6A.

Civin, Michael A. *Male, Female, Email: The Struggle for Relatedness in a Paranoid Society*. New York: Other Press, 2000.

Clark, Terry N. "Is Materialism Rising in America?" *Society* 37 (6) September/October 2000: 47–48.

Clarke, Adele E., Laura Mamo, Jennifer R. Fishman, Janet K. Shim, and Jennifer Ruth Fosket. "Biomedicalization: Technoscientific Transformations of Health, Illness, and U.S. Biomedicine." *American Sociological Review* 68 (April) 2003:161–194.

Clausen, John S. "Adolescent Competence and the Shaping of the Life Course." *American Journal of Sociology* 96 (January) 1991:805–842.

Clausewitz, Carl von. *On War*. Paret and Howard (trans.). Princeton: Princeton University Press, 1975.

Clayman, Steven E., and Ann Reisner. "Gatekeeping in Action: Editorial Conferences and Assessments of Newsworthiness." *American Sociological Review* 63 (April) 1998:178–199.

Clements, Mark, and Dianne Hales. "How Healthy Are We?" *Parade*, September 7, 1997:4–7.

Clemetson, Lynette. "Mixing It Up in the Burbs." *Newsweek*, January 17, 2000a:61–62.

———. "Wooing Them with Elvis: How the Nation's Fastest-Growing Districts Tempt Teachers." *Newsweek*, October 2, 2000b:39.

Clinard, Marshall B., and Robert F. Meier. *Sociology of Deviant Behavior*, 12th ed. Belmont, CA: Wadsworth, 2003.

Clore, George C., Robert M. Bray, and Stuart M. Itkin, et al. "Interracial Attitudes and Behavior at a Summer Camp." *Journal of Personality and Social Psychology* 36, 1978:107–116.

Cloward, Richard A., and Lloyd E. Ohlin. *Delinquency and Opportunity*. New York: Free Press, 1960.

Clymer, Adam. "Pentagon Surveillance Plan Is Described as Less Invasive." *The New York Times* on the Web, Wednesday, May 7, 2003:1–2.

CNN. "Aging Prisoners a Growing Problem." *CNN News*, September 21, 1995.

———. *Headline News*, September 30, 2003.

Cochran, John K., Peter B. Wood, Christine S. Sellers, Wendy Wilkerson, and Mitchell B. Chamlin. "Academic Dishonesty and Low Self-Control: An Empirical Test of a General Theory of Crime." *Deviant Behavior* 19 (July–September), 1998:227–255.

Cohen, Albert K. *Delinquent Boys: The Culture of the Gang*. New York: Free Press, 1955.

Cohen, Lloyd R. "Sexual Harassment and the Law." *Society* 28 (May/June), 1991:8–13.

Coleman, James S. *The Adolescent Society*. Glencoe, IL: Free Press, 1961.

———. *Intimate Relationships, Marriage, and Family*, 2nd ed. New York: Macmillan, 1988.

Coleman, James S., et al. *Equality of Educational Opportunity (The Coleman Report)*. U.S. Department of Health, Education and Welfare. Washington, DC: Government Printing Office, 1966.

Coleman, James, and Thomas Hoffer. *Public and Private High Schools: The Impact of Communities*. New York: Basic Books, 1987.

Coleman, Marilyn, and Lawrence H. Ganong. "Changing Families, Changing Responsibilities?" *National Forum* 80 (3) (Summer) 2000: 34–37.

Coles, Clifton. "Government: Testing the Limits of Tolerance." *The Futurist* (March–April) 2003: 14–15.

Collins, Randall. "Functional and Conflict Theories of Educational Stratification." *American Sociological Review* 36 (December) 1971: 1002–1019.

———. *Conflict Sociology: Toward an Explanatory Science*. New York: Academic Press, 1975.

———. *Sociology of Marriage and the Family: Gender, Love, and Property*, 2nd ed. Chicago: Nelson-Hall, 1988.

Collins, Randall, and Scott Coltrane. *Sociology of Marriage and the Family: Gender, Love, and Property*. Chicago: Nelson-Hall, 1995.

Collins, Randall, and Michael Makowsky. *The Discovery of Society*, 5th ed. New York: Random House, 1993.

Coltrane, Scott. "Families and Gender Equity." *National Forum* 77 (Spring) 1997:31–34.

Comber, Chris, Ann Colley, and David J. Hargreaves, et al. "The Effects of Age, Gender and Computer Experience upon Computer Attitudes." *Educational Research* 39 (Summer) 1997:123–133.

Congressional Quarterly. Congressional Research Service, April 1988:863.

Congressional Record (Senate). *McCain Feingold Campaign Finance Law*. S5738–S5740. May 5, 2003:1–6.

Conly, Catherine, and J. Thomas McEwen. "Computer Crime." *National Institute of Justice Reports* 218 (January/February) 1990:2–7.

Connell, R. W. "Charting Futures for Sociology." *Contemporary Sociology* 29 (March) 2000: 291–296.

Conrad, Karen Smith, and Andrew J. Houtenville. "Out with the Old, in with the Old: A Closer Look at Younger Versus Older Elderly Migration." *Social Science Quarterly* 84 (June) 2003: 309–328.

Considine, Mark, and Iva Ellen Deutchman. "The Gendering of Political Institutions: A Comparison of American and Australian State Legislators." *Social Science Quarterly* 75 (December) 1994:854–866.

Conway, M. Margaret. *Political Participation in the United States*, 2nd ed. Washington, DC: Congressional Press, 1991.

Cook, Timothy E. *Governing with the News: The News Media as a Political Institution*. Chicago, IL: University of Chicago Press, 1998.

Cooley, Charles H. *Social Organization*. New York: Scribner, 1909.

———. *Human Nature and the Social Order*. New York: Scribner, [1902] 1922.

Coombs, Robert H. *Mastering Medicine: Professional Socialization in Medical School*. New York: Free Press, 1978.

Coontz, Stephanie. "Where Are the Good Old Days?" *Modern Maturity* 39 (3) 1996:36–43.

———. *The Way We Really Are: Coming to Terms with America's Changing Families*. New York: Basic Books, 1997.

———. "Three 'Rules' that Don't Apply." *Newsweek*, June 5, 2006:49.

Corcoran, Mary, Sandra K. Danziger, Ariel Kalil, and Kristin S. Seefeldt. "How Welfare Reform is Affecting Women's Work." *Annual Review of Sociology* 26 2000:241–269.

Corn, Joseph J. *Imagining Tomorrow: History, Technology, and the American Future*. Cambridge: Massachusetts Institute of Technology Press, 1986.

Corn, Joseph J., and Brian Horrigan. *Yesterday's Tomorrows: Past Visions of the American Future*. New York: Summit Books, 1984.

Corrado, Anthony. *Elections in Cyberspace: Toward a New Era in American Politics*. Aspen: Aspen Institute, 1998.

Cose, Ellis. "The Prison Paradox." *Newsweek*, November 13, 2000:40–49.

———. "The Black Gender Gap." *Newsweek*, March 3, 2003:47–51.

Coser, Lewis A. *The Functions of Social Conflict*. New York: Free Press, 1956.

Costanzo, Mark. *Just Revenge: Costs and Consequences of the Death Penalty*. New York: St. Martin's Press, 1997.

Cotter, David A., JoAnn DeFiore, and Joan M. Hermsen, et al. *Information Technologies and Social Orders*. New York: Aldine de Gruyter, 1996.

———. "All Women Benefit: The Macro-Level Effect of Occupational Integration on Gender Earnings Equality." *American Sociological Review* 62 (October) 1997:714–734.

Coughlin, Ellen K. "Making Business a Belief: A Sociologist Examines the Direct-Selling Industry in America." *Chronicle of Higher Education* 35 (July) 1989:A4–A6.

Covell, Katherine. "The Appeal of Image Advertisements: Age, Gender, and Product Differences." *Journal of Early Adolescence* 12 (February) 1992:46–60.

Cowley, Geoffrey. "Made to Order Babies." *Newsweek* special issue (Winter/Spring) 1990: 94–100.

———. "It's Time to Rethink Nature and Nurture." *Newsweek*, March 27, 1995:52–53.

———. "How to Live to 100." *Newsweek*, June 30, 1997:56–62.

———. "For the Love of Language." *Newsweek* special issue (Fall/Winter) 2000:12–15.

Cowley, Geoffrey, and Mary Hager. "The Ever-Expanding Plague." *Newsweek*, August 22, 1994:37.

———. "The Biology of Beauty," *Newsweek*, June 3, 1996:61–66.

Cowley, Geoffrey, Elizabeth Ann Leonard, and Mary Hager. "Tuberculosis: A Deadly Return." *Newsweek*, March 16, 1992:53–57.

Cox, Harold G. "Roles for Aged Individuals in Post-Industrial Societies." *Journal of Aging and Human Development* 30 (1) 1990:55–62.

——— (ed.). *Aging: Annual Editions*, 11th ed. Guilford, CT: Dushkin, 1997.

Crampton, Thomas. "China's 'Great Firewall' Limits Internet." *International Herald Tribune*, Tuesday, October 1, 2002:1–3.

Crandall, Richard C. *Gerontology: A Behavioral Science Approach*, 2nd ed. New York: McGraw-Hill, 1991.

Crane, Jonathan. "The Epidemic Theory of Ghettos and Neighborhood Effects on Dropping Out and Teenage Childbearing." *American Journal of Sociology* 96 (March) 1991:1226–1259.

Cravey, Altha J. *Women and Work in Mexico's Maquiladoras*. Lanham, MD: Rowman and Littlefield, 1998.

Crawford, Selwyn. "Home Is Where the Classroom Is." *Dallas Morning News*, December 24, 2000:1J, 6J.

Crenshaw, Edward M., Matthew Christenson, and Doyle Ray Oakey. "Demographic Transition in Ecological Focus." *American Sociological Review* 65 (June) 2000:371–391.

Crossen, Cynthia. *Tainted Truth: The Manipulation of Fact in America*. New York: Simon & Schuster, 1996.

Crystal, Stephen, and Dennis Shea. "Cumulative Advantage, Cumulative Disadvantage, and Inequality among Elderly People." *Gerontologist* 30 (August) 1990:437–443.

Cumming, Elaine, and William Henry. *Growing Old: The Process of Disengagement*. New York: Basic Books, 1961.

Cundy, Donald T. "Televised Political Editorials and the Low-Involvement Viewer." *Social Science Quarterly* 70 (December) 1989:911–922.

Curl, Joseph. "Bush Orders Cash Flow to Faith-Based Programs," *The Washington Times.com*, January 16, 2004:1–2.

Curra, John and Paul Paolucci. *Engaging the Sociological Imagination: An Invitation for the Twenty-First Century*. Dubuque, IA: Kendall/Hunt, 2006.

Current Population Reports. Series P-70, no. 42. Washington, DC: Government Printing Office, 1995.

Cuyvers, Ludo and Pilip De Beule (Eds.). *Transnational Corporations and Economic Development: From Internationalisation to Globalisation*. Hampshire, England: Palgrave Macmillan, 2006.

Cylwik, Helen. "Notes from the Field: Emotions of Place in the Production and Interpretation of Text." *International Journal of Social Research Methodology* 4 (3) 2001:243–250.

Czitrom, Daniel J. *Media and the American Mind*. Chapel Hill: University of North Carolina Press, 1982.

Dabel, Michelle. "Ethical Communication in the Classroom." *Kapp. Delta Pi Record* (Spring) 1993:80–84.

Dahl, Robert A. *Who Governs?* New Haven, CT: Yale University Press, 1961.

———. *Democracy in the United States,* 4th ed. Boston: Houghton Mifflin, 1981.

———. *Dilemmas of Pluralist Democracy: Autonomy vs. Control.* New Haven, CT: Yale University Press, 1982.

———. *Democracy and Its Critics.* New Haven, CT: Yale University Press, 1989.

Dahrendorf, Ralf. *Class and Class Conflict in Industrial Society.* Palo Alto, CA: Stanford University Press, 1959.

———. *Life Chances.* Chicago: University of Chicago Press, 1979.

Dallas Morning News. "1 in 5 Kids Home Alone After School, Survey Finds." Monday, September 11, 2000:3A.

Danigelis, Nicholas L., and Alfred P. Fengler. "Homesharing: How Social Exchange Helps Elders Live at Home." *Gerontologist* 30 (April) 1990:162–170.

Danziger, Shelton, and Peter Gottschalk. "Introduction," in Shelton Danziger and Peter Gotts-chalk (eds.), *Uneven Tides: Rising Inequality in America.* New York: Sage, 1993, pp. 3–17.

———. *America Unequal.* Cambridge: Harvard University Press, 1995.

Dardick, Geeta. "Home Study and the Public Schools," in Anne Pedersen and Peggy O'Mara (eds.), *Schooling at Home: Parents, Kids, and Learning.* Santa Fe: John Muir, 1990, pp. 86–91.

Darnton, Nina, and Yuriko Hoshia. "Whose Life Is It, Anyway?" *Newsweek,* January 13, 1989:61.

Darwin, Charles. *On the Origin of Species.* New York: Mentor, [1859] 1964.

Davidson, Nicholas. *The Failure of Feminism.* Buffalo, NY: Prometheus, 1988.

Davis, Kenneth S. "The Military-Industrial Complex: Critical Descriptions," in Kenneth S. Davis (ed.), *Arms, Industry and America.* New York: H. W. Wilson, 1971, pp. 81–83.

Davis, Kingsley. "Extreme Social Isolation of a Child." *American Journal of Sociology* 45, 1940:554–564.

Davis, Kingsley, and Wilbert E. Moore. "Some Principles of Stratification." *American Sociological Review* 10, 1945:242–249.

———. "Final Note on a Case of Extreme Isolation." *American Journal of Sociology* 50, 1947:432–437.

Davis, Nanette J., and Clarice Stasz. *Social Control of Deviance: A Critical Perspective.* New York: McGraw-Hill, 1990.

Davis, Richard H., and James A. Davis. *TV's Image of the Elderly: A Practical Guide for Change.* Lexington, MA: Lexington Books, 1985.

Davies, S. N. G. "The Capitalism/Socialism Debate in East Asia." *Society* 26 (March/April) 1989:29–37.

Dawson, Lorne L. *Comprehending Cults: The Sociology of New Religious Movements* (2nd ed.). New York: Oxford University Press, 2005.

Day, Sherri. "Pepsi Looks to Pop Stars to Reach Minorities and Mainstream." *The New York Times* on the Web, Tuesday, August 27, 2002:1–2.

DeWitt, Karen. "Government Tea Taster Targeted by Deficit Busters." *Wichita Eagle,* October 1, 1995:13A.

DeBenedetti, Charles. "Introduction," in Charles DeBenedetti (ed.), *Peace Heroes in Twentieth Century America.* Bloomington: Indiana University Press, 1986, pp. 1–27.

DeFina, Robert H., and Thomas M. Arvanites. "The Weak Effect of Imprisonment on Crime: 1971–1998." *Social Science Quarterly* 83 (September) 2002:635–653.

DeFleur, Melvin L. *Social Problems.* Boston: Houghton Mifflin, 1983.

Delamont, Sara. *Feminist Sociology.* Thousand Oaks, CA: Pine Forge Press, 2003.

Delamont, Sara. *Feminist Sociology.* Thousand Oaks, CA: Pine Forge Press, 2003.

Della Porta, Donatella and Mario Diani. *Social Movements: An Introduction* (2nd ed.). Malden, MA: Blackwell, 2006.

Demerath, N. J. III, and Rhys H. Williams. "Civil Religion in an Uncivil Society," in Erica Ginsburg (ed.), *Annals of the American Academy of Political and Social Science* 480 (July) 1985:154–166.

Demerath, N. J., Peter D. Hall, Terry Schmitt, and Rhys H. Williams (eds.). "Preface," in *Sacred Companies: Organizational Aspects of Religion and Religious Aspects of Organizations.* New York: Oxford University Press, 1998:v–xiii.

Dentler, Ronald, and Kai Erikson. "The Functions of Deviance in Groups." *Social Problems 7* (Fall) 1959:98–107.

Denzin, Norman K. *The Research Act in Sociology: A Theoretical Introduction to Research Methods.* London: Butterworth, 1970.

Denzin, Norman K., and Yuonna S. Lincoln. *Handbook of Qualitative Research,* 2nd ed. Thousand Oaks, CA: Sage, 2000.

Deprez, Johan. "The Macrodynamics of Advanced Market Economies: The Post-Keynesian Perspective of Alfred Eichner." *Social Science Quarterly* 72 (September) 1991:415–430.

Desai, Sonalde, and Linda J. Waite. "Women's Employment during Pregnancy and after the First Birth: Occupational Characteristics and Work Commitment." *American Sociological Review* 56 (August) 1991:551–566.

Desetta, Al. *The Courage to Be Yourself: True Stories By Teens About Cliques, Conflicts, and Overcoming Peer Pressure.* Minneapolis: Free Spirit Publishing, 2006.

DeVault, Marjorie L. "Talking Back to Sociology: Distinctive Contributions of Feminist Methodology," in John Hagan and Karen S. Cook (eds.), *Annual Review of Sociology,* 22. Palo Alto, CA: Annual Reviews, 1996, pp. 29–50.

Diamond, Jared. "Playing Dice with Megadeath." *Discover* 11 (April) 1990:55–59.

Diani, Mario, and Douglas McAdams. Introduction in Mario Diani and Douglas McAdams (eds.), *Social Movements and Networks: Relational Approaches to Collective Action.* New York: Oxford University Press, 2003, pp. 1–12.

Dickerson, Bette J., *African American Single Mothers: Understanding Their Lives and Families.* Thousand Oaks, CA: Sage, 1995.

Diekema, David A. "Televangelism and the Mediated Charismatic Relationship." *Social Science Journal* 28 (2) 1991:143–162.

Dietrich, Dawn. "(Re)-Fashioning the Techno-Erotic Woman: Gender and Textuality in the Cybercultural Matrix," in Steven G. Jones (ed.), *Virtual Culture: Identity and Communication in Cybersociety.* Thousand Oaks, CA: Sage, 1997, pp. 169–184.

DiNitto, Diane M. *Social Welfare: Politics and Public Policy,* 4th ed. Boston: Allyn & Bacon, 1995.

Dinnerstein, Leonard, and David M. Reimers. *Ethnic Americans: A History of Immigration,* 3rd ed. New York: HarperCollins, 1988.

DiPrete, Thomas A., and Whitman T. Soule. "Gender and Promotion in Segmented Job Ladder Systems." *American Sociological Review* 53 (February) 1988:26–40.

Divine, Robert A., T. H. Breen, and George M. Fredrickson, et al. *America: Past and Present,* 7th ed. New York: Longman, 2005.

Dizard, Wilson, Jr. *Old Media, New Media: Mass Communications in the Information Age,* 2nd ed. New York: Longman, 1997.

DMN. "Doctors Now Allowed to Kill Terminally Ill." *Dallas Morning News,* September 24, 2002:7A.

Dodge, Robert. "Labor Complications." *Dallas Morning News,* Oct. 4, 1997:1–2D.

———. "Retirees' Costs to Drain Surplus, Report Warns." *Dallas Morning News,* February 7, 2001:1A, 13A.

———. "No Child Left Behind Leaves Schools in Lurch." *Dallas Morning News,* October 5, 2003:1A, 22A.

Domhoff, G. William. *The Higher Circles: The Governing Class in America.* New York: Random House, 1970.

———. *The Bohemian Grove and Other Retreats: A Study in Ruling-Class Cohesiveness.* New York: Harper & Row, 1974.

———. *The Power Elite and the State: How Policy Is Made in America.* New York: Aldine de Gruyter, 1990.

Dominick, Joseph R. *The Dynamics of Mass Communication,* 2nd ed. New York: Random House, 1987.

Donahue, Phil. *The Human Animal.* New York: Simon & Schuster, 1985.

Donovan, Todd, Janine A. Parry, and Shaun Bowler. "O Other, Where Art Thou? Support for Multiparty Politics in the United States." *Social Science Quarterly* 86 (March), 2005:147-159.

Dooley, David, and JoAnn Prause. *The Social Cost of Underemployment.* Cambridge: Cambridge University Press, 2004.

Dotter, Daniel. "Creating Deviance: Scenarios of Stigmatization in Postmodern Media Culture." *Deviant Behavior* 23 (September–October) 2002:419–448.

Douglas, Jack D. *Investigative Social Research.* Beverly Hills, CA: Sage, 1976.

Dowd, James J. "Aging as Exchange: A Preface to Theory." *Journal of Gerontology* 30, 1975: 584–594.

———. "Exchange Rates and Old People." *Journal of Gerontology* 35, 1980:596–602.

Dowd, James, and Laura Dowd. "From Subcultures to Social Worlds." *Teaching Sociology* 31 (1), January 2003:20–37.

Doyle, "Our Marriage Barely Survived." *Newsweek,* May 12, 2003:53.

Doyle, Sir Arthur Conan. *The Adventures of Sherlock Holmes.* Stanford, CT: Longmeadow Press, [1892] 1987.

Doyle, James A. *Sex and Gender: The Human Experience.* Dubuque, IA: Brown, 1985.

Dreben, E. K., S. T. Fiske, and R. Hastie. "The Independence of Evaluative and Item Information: Impression and Recall Order Effects in Behavior-Based Impression Formation." *Journal of Personality and Social Psychology* 37, 1979:1758–1768.

Dreier, Peter, and Richard Appelbaum. "American Nightmare: Homelessness." *Social Problems: Annual Editions.* Guilford, CT: Dushkin, 1994, pp. 35–42.

Drye, Willie. "Hurricane Katrina Pulls Its Punches in New Orleans."<http://news.nationalgeographic.com/news/2005/08/0829_050829_hurricane.html> *National Geographic,* August 29, 2005.

DuBois, W. E. B. *The Souls of Black Folk.* New York: Vintage Books, [1903] 1990.

Dublin, Max. *Futurehype: The Tyranny of Prophecy.* New York: Dutton, 1991.

Duncan, Greg J., Jeanne Brooks-Gunn, W. Jean Yeung, and Judith R. Smith. "How Much Does Childhood Poverty Affect the Life Chances of Children?" *American Sociological Review* 63 (June) 1998:406–423.

Dunn, Samuel L. "The Virtualizing of Education." in *The Futurist,* March/April 2000:34–38.

Durand, Jorge, Douglas S. Massey, and Fernando Charvet. "The Changing Geography of Mexican Immigration to the United States: 1910–1996." *Social Science Quarterly* 81 (1) March 2000:1–15.

Durkheim, Emile. *Suicide: A Study in Sociology.* John A. Spaulding and George Simpson (trans.), George Simpson (ed.). New York: Free Press, [1897] 1951.

———. *The Division of Labor in Society.* Glencoe, IL: Free Press, [1893] 1964.

———. *The Elementary Forms of Religious Life.* New York: Free Press, [1912] 1965.

Durkin, Keith F., and Clifton D. Bryant. "'Log on Sex': Some Notes on the Carnal Computer and Erotic Cyberspace as an Emerging Research Frontier." *Deviant Behavior* 16 (July–September) 1995:179–200.

Dusek, Jerome B. (ed.). *Teacher Expectancies.* Hillsdale, NJ: Erlbaum, 1985.

Dutton, Bertha P. *Navahos and Apaches: The Athabascan Peoples.* Englewood Cliffs, NJ: Prentice-Hall, 1975.

Dvorchak, Robert. "Workers Say, 'Enough.'" *The Wichita Eagle Beacon,* February 19, 1995: 1E–2E.

Dyck, Joshua, J. and James G. Gimpel. "Distance, Turnout, and the Convenience of Voting." *Social Science Quarterly* 86 (September), 2005:531–548.

Dye, Thomas R. *Who's Running America: The Bush Era,* 5th ed. Englewood Cliffs, NJ: Prentice-Hall, 1990.

Dye, Thomas R., and L. Harmon Zeigler. *American Politics in the Media Age.* Monterey, CA: Brooks/Cole, 1983.

Eagleton, Terry. *The Making of Culture.* Malden, MA: Blackwell, 2000.

Easterlin, Richard A. "Retirement Prospects of the Baby Boom Generation: A Different Perspective." *Gerontologist* 30 (December) 1990: 776–783.

Eastman, Roger. "Confucianism: An Ideal of Moral Order," in Roger Eastman (ed.), *The Ways of Religion: An Introduction to the Major Traditions,* 2nd ed. New York: Oxford University Press, 1993, pp. 145–147.

Eckel, Malcolm D. "Buddhism in the World and in America," in Jacob Neusner (ed.), *World Religions in America: An Introduction.* Louisville, KY: Knox Press, 1994, pp. 203–218.

Edin, Kathryn. "What Low-Income Single Mothers Say About Marriage." *Social Problems* 40 (1) February 2000:112–133.

Edin, Kathryn, and Laura Lein. "Work, Welfare, and Single Mothers' Economic Survival Strategies." *American Sociological Review* (February) 1997:253–266.

Edwards, David V. *The American Political Experience: An Introduction to Government,* 4th ed. Englewood Cliffs, NJ: Prentice-Hall, 1988.

Edwards, Mike. "As Good As It Gets." *AARP, The Magazine,* Vol 47 (November/December), 2004:43-49.

Edwards, Richard. *Contested Terrain: The Transformation of the Workplace in the Twentieth Century.* New York: Basic Books, 1979.

Edwards, Tamala M. "Flying Solo." *Time* 156 (9) August 28, 2000:47–53.

Ehrenreich, Barbara, and Annette Fuentes. "Life on the Global Assembly-Line," in James Henslin (ed.), *Down to Earth Sociology,* 9th ed. New York: Free Press, 1997, pp. 367–375.

Ehrenreich, Barbara, and Arlie R. Hochschild. "Introduction," in Barbara Ehrenreich and Arlie R. Hochschild (eds.), *Global Woman: Nannies, Maids, and Sex Workers in the New Economy.* New York: Metropolitan Books, 2002, pp. 1–13.

Ehrlich, Paul R. *The Population Bomb,* rev. ed. New York: Ballantine, 1971.

Ehrlich, Paul R., and Anne H. Ehrlich. *The Population Explosion.* New York: Simon & Schuster, 1990.

———. *One With Nineveh: Politics, Consumption, and the Human Future.* Washington, DC: Island Press, 2006.

Eisenstein, Zillah R. (ed.). *Capitalist Patriarchy and the Case for Socialist Feminism.* New York: Monthly Review Press, 1979.

Eitzen, D. Stanley, and Maxine Baca-Zinn. (eds.). *The Reshaping of America: Social Consequences of the Changing Economy.* Englewood Cliffs, NJ: Prentice-Hall, 1989.

———. *Diversity in American Families,* 7th ed. Boston: Allyn & Bacon, 2005.

———. *Social Problems,* 10th ed. Boston: Allyn & Bacon, 2006.

Eitzen, D. Stanley, and George H. Sage. *Sociology of North American Sport,* 7th ed. Woodland Hills, CA: McGraw-Hill, 2003.

Elam, Stanley M., Lowell C. Rose, and Alec M. Gallup. "The 28th Annual Phi Delta Kapp. Gallup Poll of the Public's Attitudes toward the Public Schools." *Phi Delta Kappan* September 1996:41–59.

Elder, Staci, and Martha Collar. "American Health Watch 2000." *USA Today Magazine* 119 (September) 1990:50–52.

Electronic Privacy Information Center (EPIC.Org), "Video Surveillance," EPIC Video Information Page, August 8, 2003:1–6.

Ellis, Desmond. *The Wrong Stuff.* New York: Macmillan, 1987.

Ellsworth, Elizabeth. "Educational Media, Ideology, and the Presentation of Knowledge through Popular Cultural Forms," in Henry A. Giroux and Roger I. Simon (eds.), *Popular Culture, Schooling, and Everyday Life.* Granby, MA: Bergin & Garvey, 1989, pp. 47–66.

Ellwood, Robert S. "East Asian Religions in Today's America," in Jacob Neusner (ed.), *World Religions in America: An Introduction.* Louisville, KY: Knox Press, 1994, pp. 219–241.

Ember, Carol R., and Melvin Ember. *Cultural Anthropology,* 8th ed. Upper Saddle River, NJ: Prentice-Hall, 1996.

Emporia Gazette. "Women at Record High in House and Senate." May 4, 1998:18.

Engels, Friedrich. *The Origin of the Family.* Chicago: Charles H. Kerr, [1884] 1902.

Englehardt, Tom. "The Shortcake Strategy," in Todd Gitlin (ed.), *Watching Television.* New York: Pantheon, 1986, pp. 68–110.

Entwisle, Doris R., Karl L. Alexander, and Linda Steffel Olson. "The Gender Gap in Math: Its Possible Origins in Neighborhood Effects." *American Sociological Review* 59 (December) 1994:822–838.

Epstein, Cynthia Fuchs. "Inevitabilities of Prejudice." *Society* 23 (6) 1986.

Epstein, Jonathan S. (ed.). *Adolescents and Their Music: If It's Too Loud, You're Too Old.* Hamden, CT: Garland, 1994.

Erikson, Erik H. *Childhood and Society.* New York: Norton, 1963.

Erikson, Kai J. *Everything in Its Path: Destruction of Community in the Buffalo Creek Flood.* New York: Simon & Schuster, 1976.

———. *A New Species of Trouble: Explorations in Disaster, Trauma, and Community.* New York: Norton, 1994.

Ermann, M. David, and Richard J. Lundman (eds.). *Corporate and Governmental Deviance.* New York: Oxford University Press, 1996.

Eron, L. D., and L. R. Huesmann. "Adolescent Aggression and Television." *Annals of the New York Academy of Sciences* 347, 1980:319–331.

———. "The Role of Television in the Development of Prosocial and Antisocial Behavior," in D. Olweus, M. Radke-Yarrow, and J. Block (eds.), *Development of Antisocial and Prosocial Behavior.* Orlando, FL: Academic Press, 1985.

Erwin, Kirstin J. "Children's Attitudes toward Violence on Television." *Journal of Psychology* 131 (4) 1997:411.

Etzioni, Amitai. *A Comparative Analysis of Complex Organizations.* Glencoe, IL: Free Press, 1975.

Evans, Ellis D., Judith Rutberg, and Carmela Sather, et al. "Content Analysis of Contemporary Teen Magazines for Adolescent Females." *Youth and Society* 23 (September) 1991: 99–120.

Evans, Peter, and James E. Rauch. "Bureaucracy and Growth: A Cross-National Analysis of the Effects of 'Weberian' State Structures on Economic Growth." *American Sociological Review* 64 (5) October 1999:748–765.

Evans-Pritchard, E. E. *Kinship and Marriage Among the Nuer.* Oxford: Oxford University Press, 1951.

Evelyn, Jamilah. "Last All-Male Military College in the U.S. Will Accept Women in 2006." *Chronicle of Higher Education,* http://chronicle.com/daily/2005/10/2005102405n.htm.

Evra, Judith Van. *Television and Child Development.* Hillsdale, NJ: Erlbaum, 1990.

Ezekiel, Raphael S. *The Racist Mind: Portraits of American Neo-Nazis and Klansmen.* New York: Viking, 1995.

Fairbank, Katie. "Dancing for Dollars." *Dallas Morning News,* February 22, 2003:2F, 3F.

Faludi, Susan. *Backlash: The Undeclared War against American Women.* New York: Crown, 1991.

———. "Looking Beyond the Slogans." *Newsweek,* December 28, 1992.

———. "The Naked Citadel." *The New Yorker,* September 5, 1994:62–81.

Famularo, Thomas J. "The Intellectual Bankruptcy of Multiculturalism," in James W. Noll (ed.), *Taking Sides: Clashing Views on Controversial Educational Issues,* 12th ed. Guilford, CT: McGraw-Hill Dushkin, 2003, pp. 126–130.

Farber, Susan L. *Identical Twins Reared Apart: A Reanalysis.* New York: Basic Books, 1981.

Farkas, George, Paula England, and Keven Vicknair, et al. "Cognitive Skill, Skill Demands of Jobs, and Earnings among Young European American, African American, and Mexican American Workers." *Social Forces* 75 (March) 1997:913–940.

Farley, John E. *Majority-Minority Relations,* 3rd ed. Englewood Cliffs, NJ: Prentice-Hall, 1995.

Farrell, Edwin. *Hanging In and Dropping Out: Voices of At Risk High School Students.* New York: Teachers College, Columbia University, 1990.

Feagin, Joe R. "Foreword," in Otto Santa Ana, *Brown Tide Rising: Metaphors of Latinos in*

Contemporary American Discourse. Austin, TX: University of Texas Press, 2002:xi–xiv.

Feagin, Joe R., and Hernán Vera. *White Racism: The Basics.* New York: Routledge, 1995.

Fears, Darryl. "Hue and Cry on Whiteness Studies' Classes. "*Washington Post.com,* Friday, June 20, 2003:A01.

Featherman, David L., and Robert M. Hauser. *Opportunity and Change.* New York: Academic Press, 1978.

Feemster, Ron. "The Problem with Public Housing: Is Chicago Solving It?" *Ford Foundation Online Report,* (Spring) 2003:1–5.

Feinberg, Walter. *On Higher Ground: Education and the Case for Affirmative Action.* New York: Teachers College, Columbia University, 1998.

Feld, Scott L. "Why Your Friends Have More Friends Than You Do." *American Journal of Sociology* 96 (May) 1991:1464–1472.

Feldman, Leonard C. *Citizens Without Shelter: Homelessness, Democracy, and Political Exclusion.* NY: Cornell University Press, 2006.

Felson, Richard B. "Mass Media Effects on Violent Behavior," in John Hagan and Karen S. Cook (eds.), *Annual Review of Sociology* 22. Palo Alto, CA: Annual Reviews, 1996, pp. 103–128.

Felson, Richard B., and Mark D. Reed. "Reference Groups and Self-Appraisals of Academic Ability and Performance." *Social Psychology Quarterly* 49 (2) 1986:103–109.

Felson, Richard B., and Lisa Trudeau. "Gender Differences in Mathematics Performance." *Social Psychology Quarterly* 54 (June) 1991: 113–126.

Fenigstein, A. "Does Aggression Cause a Preference for Viewing Media Violence?" *Journal of Personality and Social Psychology* 37, 1979: 2307–2317.

Ferdman, Bernardo M., and Angelica C. Cortes. "Culture and Identity Among Hispanic Managers in an Anglo Business," in Paul Rosenfeld, Amy Culbertson, and Stephen S. Knouse (eds.), *Hispanics in the Workplace.* Newbury Park, CA: Sage, 1992:246–277.

Fernandez, Roberto M., Emilio J. Castilla, and Paul Moore. "Social Capital at Work: Networks and Employment at a Phone Center." *American Journal of Sociology* 105 (5) March 2000:1288–1356.

Ferraro, Gary. *Cultural Anthropology,* 4th ed. Belmont, CA: Wadsworth, 2001.

Ferree, Myra Marx, and Beth B. Hess. *Controversy and Coalition,* rev. ed. New York: Twayne, 1994.

Fields, Gary, and Charisse Jones. "Studies Find Death Penalty Links to Race." *USA Today,* June 4, 1998:3A.

Fine, Gary A. "Negotiated Orders and Organizational Cultures," in Ralph H. Turner (ed.), *Annual Review of Sociology* 10, 1984, pp. 239–262.

Fine, Gary Alan, and Ryan D. White. "Creating Collective Attention in the Public Domain: Human Interest Narratives and the Rescue of Floyd Collins." *Social Forces* 81 (1) September 2002:57–85.

Fine, Marka, and David R. Fine. "An Examination and Evaluation of Recent Changes in Divorce Laws in Five Western Countries: The Critical Role of Values." *Journal of Marriage and the Family* 56 (May) 1994:249–264.

Finke, Roger, and Rodney Stark. "Religious Economies and Sacred Canopies: Religious Mobilization in American Cities, 1906." *American Sociological Review* 53 (1) 1988: 41–49.

Finn, Chester E., Jr., Bruno V. Manno, and Gregg Vanourek. "The Radicalization of School Reform." Pp. 200–208 in Knoll, James Wm. *Taking Sides: Clashing Views on Educational Issues* (14th ed.). Guilford, CT: McGraw-Hill Dushkin, 2007.

Firth-Cozens, Jenny, and Michael A. West. "Women at Work: Reflections and Perspectives," in Jenny Firth-Cozens and Michael A. West (eds.), *Women at Work: Psychological and Organizational Perspectives.* Philadelphia: Open University Press, 1991, pp. 192–200.

Fischer, Claude S. *To Dwell among Friends: Personal Networks in Town and City.* Chicago: University of Chicago Press, 1982.

Fisher, Arthur. "Sociobiology—A Special Report: A New Synthesis Comes of Age." *Mosaic* 22 (Spring) 1991:3–9.

Fisher, Robert Leslie. *The Research Productivity of Scientists: How Gender, Organization Culture, and the Problem Choice Process Influence the Productivity of Scientists.* Lanham, MD: University Press of America, 2005.

Fitzpatrick, Jackie. "Caring for Aging Loved Ones," in Harold Cox (ed.), *Aging: Annual Editions,* 11th ed. Guilford, CT: Dushkin, 1997, pp. 211–215.

Fix, Michael, George C. Galster, and Raymond J. Struyk. "An Overview of Auditing for Discrimination," in Michael Fix and Raymond Struyk (eds.), *Clear and Convincing Evidence: Measurement of Discrimination in America.* Washington, DC: Urban Institute, 1993, pp. 1–49.

Flaherty, Michael G. "Two Conceptions of the Social Situation: Some Implications of Humor." *Sociological Quarterly* 31 (1) 1990: 93–106.

Flammang, Janet, Dennis R. Gordon, and Timothy J. Lukes, et al. *American Politics in a Changing World.* Pacific Grove, CA: Brooks/Cole, 1990.

Flora, Cornelia B., Jan L. Flora, and Jacqueline D. Spears, et al. *Rural Communities: Legacy and Change.* Boulder, CO: Westview, 1992.

Flowers, Ronald B. *Minorities and Criminality.* Westport, CT: Praeger, 1990.

Fluehr-Lobban, Carolyn. "Cultural Relativism and Human Rights." *The Chronicle of Higher Education,* June 9, 1995, B1–2.

———. "Cultural Relativism and Human Rights." *Annual Editions: Anthropology/20th ed.* Guilford, CT: Dushkin Publishing, 1997:33–35.

Flynn, Laurie J. "Now Digital, Spy Camera Technology Widens Gaze." *The New York Times* on the Web, Monday, April 21, 2003:1–3.

Foley, D. "Danger: School Zone." *Teacher* 1 (8), 1990:57–63.

Fondersmith, John. "Downtown 2040: Making Cities Fun." *The Futurist* 22 (March/April) 1988:9–17.

Foot, David K. *Boom, Bust & Echo 2000.* Toronto, Canada: Macfarlane, Walter & Ross, 2000.

Footnotes. "American Sociological Association." 20 (3) 1992:9.

Forbes, H. D. *Ethnic Conflict: Commerce, Culture, and the Contact Hypothesis.* New Haven, CT: Yale University Press, 1997.

Forbes. "The Forbes 400." October 23, 1989: 145–358.

———. "Forbes 400." October 13, 1997.

———. "Forbes 400." October, 1994.

Form, William. "Institutional Analysis: An Organizational Approach," in Maureen T. Hallinan, David M. Klein, and Jennifer Glass (eds.), *Change in Societal Institutions.* New York: Plenum, 1990, pp. 257–271.

Fornos, Werner. "1996 World Population Overview." www.populationinstitute.org, 1997.

Fox, Maggie. "Don't Base Drug Policy on Race, Geneticists Say." *Yahoo News,* Reuters News Service, Thursday, July 24, 2003:1.

Francia, Peter L., John C. Green, Paul S. Herrnson, Lynda W. Powell, and Clyde Wilcox. "Limousine Liberals and Corporate Conservatives: The Financial Constituencies of the Democratic and Republican Parties." *Social Science Quarterly* 86 (December), 2005:761–778.

Frank, David John, Ann Hironaka, and Evan Schofer. "The Nation-State and the Natural Environment over the Twentieth Century." *American Sociological Review* 65 (February) 2000:96–116.

Frank, Thomas. *The Conquest of Cool, Business Culture, Counterculture, and the Rise of Hip Consumerism.* Chicago, IL: University of Chicago Press, 1998.

Franklin, Clyde W. II. *Men and Society.* Chicago: Nelson-Hall, 1988.

Free, Marvin D., Jr. "Religiosity, Religious Conservatism, Bonds to School, and Juvenile Delinquency among Three Categories of Drug Users." *Deviant Behavior* 15 (April/June) 1994:151–170.

Freeman, Lance. "Black Homeownership: The Role of Temporal Changes and Residential Segregation at the End of the 20th Century." *Social Science Quarterly* 86 (June), 2005: 403–426.

Freud, Sigmund. *The Ego and the Id.* London: Hogarth, [1923] 1947.

Friedan, Betty. *The Feminine Mystique.* New York: Norton, 1963.

———. *The Fountain of Age.* New York: Simon & Schuster, 1993.

Friedenberg, Edgar Z. *The Vanishing Adolescent.* New York: Dell, 1959.

Friedkin, Noah E. "Choice Shift and Group Polarization." *American Sociological Review* 64 (5) December 1999:856–875.

Friedland, Roger, and A. F. Robertson. "Beyond the Marketplace," in Roger Friedland and A. F. Robertson (eds.), *Beyond the Marketplace: Rethinking Economy and Society.* New York: Aldine de Gruyter, 1990, pp. 3–49.

Friend, Tom. "Patients Find 'Direct Line' to Doctors." *USA Today,* February 8, 1995:1A–2A.

Fruch, Terry, and Paul E. McGhee. "Traditional Sex Role Development and Amount of Time Spent Watching Television." *Developmental Psychology* 11 (1) 1975:109.

Fry, Douglas P. "Intercommunity Differences in Aggression among Zapotec Children." *Child Development* 59, 1988:1008–1019.

Fucini, Joseph J., and Suzy Fucini. *Working for the Japanese: Inside Mazda's American Auto Plant.* New York: Free Press, 1990.

Fuller, Rex, and Richard Schoenberger. "The Gender Salary Gap: Do Academic Achievement, Internship Experience, and College Major Make a Difference?" *Social Science Quarterly* 72 (December) 1991:715–737.

Funk, Tim. "Women in Change: Shows Catch Up to Society's Progress." *Dallas Morning News,* December 2, 1990:7C.

Furnham, Adrian, and Nadine Bitar. "The Stereotypical Portrayal of Men and Women in British Television Advertisements." *Sex Roles* 29 (August) 1993:297–310.

Furstenberg, Frank F., Jr. "Good Dads, Bad Dads: Two Faces of Fatherhood," in Andrew J. Cherlin (ed.), *The Changing American Family and Public Policy.* Washington, DC: Urban Institute Press, 1988.

Gable, Donna. "Prime-Time Hispanic Portrayals Found Lacking." *USA Today,* September 7, 1994:3D.

Gabler, Neal. "The World Still Watches America." *The New York Times* on the Web, Thursday, January 9, 2003:1.

Gallagher, Winifred. "How We Become What We Are." *The Atlantic Monthly* 274 (September) 1994:38–55.

Gallup, George, Jr., and Jim Castelli. *The Gallup Poll: Public Opinion, 1997.* Wilmington, DE: Scholarly Resources, 1998.

Gammage, Jeff. "The Fringe Factor." *The Philadelphia Inquirer, Philly.com,* Saturday, March 29, 2003:1–7.

Gamoran, Adam, and Robert D. Mare. "Secondary School Tracking and Educational Inequality: Compensation, Reinforcement, or Neutrality." *American Journal of Sociology* 94 (March) 1989:1146–1183.

Gamson, William A., and Andre Modigliani. "Media Discourse and Public Opinion on Nuclear Power: A Constructionist Approach." *American Journal of Sociology* 95 (July) 1989:1–37.

Gandy, Oscar H. "The Information Superhighway as the Yellow Brick Road." *National Forum* 74 (2) 1994:24–27.

Gans, Curtis. "Table for One, Please." *Washington Monthly,* July/August 2000:44–45.

Gans, Herbert J. *Essays on Urban Problems and Solutions.* New York: Basic Books, 1971.

———. *Popular Culture and High Culture: An Analysis and Evaluation of Taste.* New York: Basic Books, 1975.

———. *Deciding What's News: A Study of CBS Evening News, NBC Nightly News, Newsweek and Time.* New York: Pantheon, 1979a.

———. "Symbolic Ethnicity: The Future of Ethnic Groups and Cultures in America." *Ethnic and Racial Studies* 2 (January) 1979b: 1–20.

———. "Sociology in America: The Discipline and the Public." *American Sociological Review* 54 (February) 1989:1–16.

———. "No, Poverty Has Not Disappeared." In Leonard Cargin and Jeanne H. Ballantine (eds.), *Sociological Footprints: Introductory Readings in Sociology,* 6th ed. Belmont, CA: Wadsworth, 1994, pp. 173–177.

Garbarino, Merwyn S. *Native American Heritage.* Boston: Little, Brown, 1976.

Garfinkel, Harold. "Conditions of Successful Degradation Ceremonies." *American Journal of Sociology* 61 (March) 1956:420–424.

———. *Studies in Ethnomethodology.* Englewood Cliffs, NJ: Prentice-Hall, 1967.

Garfinkel, Irwin, Jennifer L. Hochschild, and Sara S. McLanahan. "Introduction," in Irwin Garfinkel, Jennifer L. Hochschild, and Sara S. McLanahan (eds.), *Social Policies for Children.* Washington, DC: Brookings Institution, 1996, pp. 1–32.

Garland, Susan B. "Throwing Stones at the 'Glass Ceiling.'" *Business Week,* August 19, 1991:29.

Geen, R. G. "Aggression and Television Violence," in R. G. Geen and E. I. Donnerstein (eds.), *Aggression: Theoretical and Empirical Reviews,* vol. 2. New York: Academic Press, 1983, pp. 103–125.

Geertz, Clifford. "The Impact of the Concept of Culture on the Concept of Man," in Yehudi A. Cohen (ed.), *Man in Adaptation: The Cultural Present.* Chicago: Aldine de Gruyter, 1968b, pp. 16–29.

Gegax, T. Trent, Debra Rosenberg, and Pat Wingert, et al., "The War Over Gay Marriage." *Newsweek,* July 7, 2003:39–45.

Gellene, Denise. "Firms Tap into Film Nostalgia to Market Products." *Dallas Morning News,* September 20, 1997:1F, 11F.

Gelles, Richard J. *Contemporary Families: A Sociological View.* Thousand Oaks, CA: Sage, 1995.

———. *The Book of David: How Preserving Families Can Cost Children's Lives.* New York: Basic Books, 1996.

Gelles, Richard J., and Jon R. Conte. "Domestic Violence and Sexual Abuse of Children: A Review of Research in the Eighties." *Journal of Marriage and the Family* 52 (November) 1990:1045–1058.

Gelles, Richard J., and Claire P. Cornell. *Intimate Violence in Families,* 2nd ed. Newbury Park, CA: Sage, 1990.

Gelles, Richard J., and Murray A. Straus. *Intimate Violence.* New York: Simon & Schuster, 1988.

Gelman, David. "Why We All Love to Hate." *Newsweek,* August 28, 1989.

Gerald, Debra E., and William J. Hussar. *Projections of Education Statistics to 2001: An Update.* National Center for Education Statistics, Washington, DC: Government Printing Office, 1990.

Gerber, Jerry, Janet Wolff, and Walter Klores, et al. *Lifetrends: The Future of Baby Boomers and Other Aging Americans.* New York: Macmillan, 1989.

Gerber, Theodore P. "Structural Change and Post-Socialist Stratification: Labor Market Transitions in Contemporary Russia." *American Sociological Review* 67 (October) 2002: 629–659.

Gerbner, George, and L. Gross. "Living with Television: A Violence Profile." *Journal of Communications* 26 (2), 1976:173–200.

Gerson, Kathleen. "Resolving Family Dilemmas and Conflicts: Beyond Utopia." in *Contemporary Sociology* 29 (1) January 2000:180–187.

Gettleman, Jeffrey. "Judge's Biblical Monument Is Ruled Unconstitutional." *The New York Times* on the Web, Tuesday, November 19, 2002:1–3.

Gibbs, Jack P. *Crime, Punishment, and Deterrence.* New York: Elsevier, 1975.

———. "Testing the Theory of Status Integration and Suicide Rates." *American Sociological Review* 47 (April) 1982:227–237.

Giddens, Anthony. *The Nation-State and Violence,* vol. 2. Berkeley: University of California Press, 1985.

Gilbert, Dennis, and Joseph A. Kahl. *The American Class Structure: A New Synthesis,* 3rd ed. Chicago: Dorsey, 1987.

Gilbert, Jess, and Carolyn Howe. "Beyond 'State vs. Society': Theories of the State and New Deal Agricultural Policies." *American Sociological Review* 56 (April) 1991:204–220.

Gilder, George. *Telecosm: How Infinite Bandwidth Will Revolutionize Our World.* New York: Free Press, 2000.

Gilliard, Darrell K., and Allen J. Beck. "Prison and Jail Inmates at Midyear 1997." *Bureau of Justice Statistics Bulletin* (January) 1998:1–11.

Gilligan, Carol. *In a Different Voice: Psychological Theory and Women's Development.* Cambridge, MA: Harvard University Press, 1982.

———. "Mommy, I know You." *Newsweek,* January 30, 2006:53.

Gilligan, Carol, Janice Victoria Ward, and Jill McLean Taylor. *Mapping the Moral Domain: A Contribution to Women's Thinking to Psychological Theory and Education.* Cambridge, MA: Harvard University Press, 1989.

Giordano, Peggy, Monica A. Longmore, and Wendy D. Manning. "Gender and the Meanings of Adolescent Romantic Relationships: A

Focus on Boys." *American Sociological Review* 71 (April), 2006:260-287.

Ginzberg, Eli. *The Medical Triangle: Physicians, Politicians, and the Public.* Cambridge, MA: Harvard University Press, 1990.

Giroux, Henry A., and Peter McLaren (eds.). *Between Borders: Pedagogy and the Politics of Cultural Studies.* New York: Routledge, 1994.

Gitlin, Saul. "Ground Shifts in California." *Advertising Age* 71 (40) September 25, 2000:78.

Gitlin, Todd. *The Twilight of Common Dreams: Why America Is Wracked by Cultural Wars.* New York: Metropolitan Books, 1995.

Glass, Jennifer. "Envisioning the Integration of Family and Work: Toward a Kinder, Gentler Workplace." *Contemporary Sociology* 29 (January) 2000:129–142.

Glass, Jennifer L., and Sarah Beth Estes. "The Family Responsive Workplace," in John Hagan and Karen S. Cook (eds.), *Annual Review of Sociology* 23. Palo Alto, CA: Annual Reviews, 1997, pp. 289–313.

Gleick, James. "Society: Living Faster and Faster." *The Futurist* (March–April) 2000:18–19.

Glenn, Norval D. "Television Watching, Newspaper Reading and Cohort Differences in Verbal Ability." *Sociology of Education* 67 (3): 216–229.

Glenn, Norval D., and Kathryn B. Kramer. "The Marriages and Divorces of the Children of Divorce." *Journal of Marriage and the Family* 49 (November) 1987:811–825.

Glick, Paul C. "Fifty Years of Family Demography: A Record of Social Change." *Journal of Marriage and the Family* 50 (November) 1988: 861–873.

———. "Remarried Families, Stepfamilies, and Stepchildren: A Brief Demographic Analysis." *Family Relations* 38, 1989:7–26.

Gochman, Charles S. "Prometheus Bound: The State and War," in Charles S. Gochman and Alan N. Sabrosky (eds.), *Prisoners of War? Nation-States in the Modern Era.* Lexington, MA: Lexington Books, 1990, pp. 287–308.

Godinez, Victor. "Hate Groups Wooing Teens by Making a Game out of Racism." *The Dallas Morning News,* Thursday, March 14, 2002:1A, 13A.

Goffman, Erving. *The Presentation of Self in Everyday Life.* New York: Doubleday, 1959.

———. *Asylums: Essays on the Social Situation of Mental Patients and Other Inmates.* Garden City, NY: Doubleday, 1961a.

———. *Encounters.* Indianapolis: Bobbs-Merrill, 1961b.

———. *Stigma: Notes on the Management of Spoiled Identity.* Englewood Cliffs, NJ: Prentice-Hall, 1963.

———. *Gender Advertisements.* New York: HarperCollins, 1979.

Goldberg, Herb. *The Hazards of Being Male: Surviving the Myth of Masculine Privilege.* New York: Signet, 1976.

Goldberg, Robert A. *Grassroots Resistance: Social Movements in Twentieth Century America.* Belmont, CA: Wadsworth, 1991.

Goldberg, Steven. "Reaffirming the Obvious." *Society* 23 (6) 1986:4–7.

Goldsmith, Marshall. "Global Communications and Communities of Choice," in Frances Hesselbein, Marshall Goldsmith, and Richard Beckhard, et al. (eds.), *The Community of the Future.* San Francisco: Jossey-Bass, 1998, pp. 101–114.

Goldstein, Alan. "African-Americans Double their Use of Internet." *Dallas Morning News,* October 23, 2000:D1.

Gollnick, Donna M., and Philip C. Chinn. *Multicultural Education in a Pluralistic Society,* 3rd ed. New York: Merrill, 1990.

Goode, Erich. "Cigarette Smoking as Deviant Behavior," in Alex Thio and Thomas C. Calhoun (eds.), *Readings in Deviant Behavior,* 2nd ed. Boston: Allyn and Bacon, 2001, pp. 128–136.

———. "The Stigma of Obesity," in Alex Thio and Thomas C. Calhoun (eds.), *Readings in Deviant Behavior,* 3rd ed. Boston: Allyn and Bacon, 2004, pp. 176–182.

———. *Collective Behavior.* Fort Worth: Harcourt Brace Jovanovich, 1992.

Goode, William J. *World Changes in Divorce Patterns.* New Haven, CT: Yale University Press, 1993.

———. *Deviant Behavior,* 5th ed. Saddle River, NJ: Prentice-Hall, 1997.

Goodlad, John I. *A Place Called School: Prospects for the Future.* New York: McGraw-Hill, 1984.

Goodman, Paul. *Growing Up Absurd.* New York: Random House, 1956.

Goodrum, Charles, and Helen Dalrymple. *Advertising in America: The First 200 Years.* New York: Abrams, 1990.

Gootman, Elissa. "Twins Reunite after 20 Years." *The New York Times* on the Web, March 3, 2003.

Gordon, Milton M. *Assimilation in American Life.* New York: Oxford University Press, 1964.

———. *Human Nature, Class and Ethnicity.* New York: Oxford University Press, 1978.

Gore, Albert. "The Ecology of Survival," in Hugh F. Lena, William B. Helmreich, and William McCord (eds.), *Contemporary Issues in Society.* New York: McGraw-Hill, 1992, pp. 492–496.

Gorner, Peter. "U. of C. sex study sees love, loneliness." *Chicago Tribune Online Edition,* Friday, January 9, 2004:1.

Gottman, John M., James Coan, and Sybil Carrere, et al. "Predicting Marital Happiness and Stability from Newlywed Interactions." *Journal of Marriage and the Family* 60 (1) 1998:5–22.

Gouldner, Alvin W. "The Norm of Reciprocity: A Preliminary Statement." *American Sociological Review* 39, 1960:86–101.

Graber, Doris A. "Media Impact on the Political Status Quo: What Is the Evidence?" in Robert Y. Spitzer (ed.), *Media and Public Policy.* Westport, CT: Praeger, 1993, pp. 19–29.

Gracey, Harry L. "Learning the Student Role: Kindergarten as Academic Boot Camp," in Dennis H. Wrong and Harry L. Gracey, *Readings in Introductory Sociology,* 3rd ed. New York: Macmillan, 1977, pp. 215–226.

Granovetter, Mark. *Getting a Job: A Study of Contacts and Careers,* 2nd ed. Chicago: University of Chicago Press, 1975.

Graves, Joseph L. Jr. *The Race Myth: Why we Pretend Race Exists in America.* New York: Penquin, 2004.

Greeley, Andrew M. "The Great Story and Its Discontents." *Society* 40 (November/December) 2002:45–48.

Greeley, Andrew M., and Michael Hout. "Americans' Increasing Belief in Life After Death: Religious Competition and Acculturation." *American Sociological Review* 64 (5) December 1999:813–835.

Green, Bryan S. *Gerontology and the Construction of Old Age.* Hawthorne, NY: Aldine de Gruyter, 1993.

Green, Edward C. "Faith-Based Organizations: Contributions to HIV Prevention, *Harvard Center for Population and Development Studies. USAID,* September, 2003:1–18.

Greenberg, Bradley S. "Children's Reactions to T.V. Blacks." *Journalism Quarterly* 49, 1972:5–14.

Greer, Colin. "We Can Save Jobs," *Parade Magazine,* May 21, 1995:4–5.

Greer, Germaine. *The Female Eunuch.* New York: Bantam, 1972.

Greider, William. *One World, Ready or Not! The Manic Logic of Global Capitalism.* New York: Simon & Schuster, 1997.

Greider, William, Jeffrey H. Garten, and Ted C. Fishman. "Global Roulette (A Colloquy)." *Harper's Magazine* 296 (1777) 1998:39–50.

Grinspun, Ricardo, and Maxwell A. Cameron. "The Political Economy of North American Integration: Diverse Perspectives, Converging Criticisms," in Ricardo Grinspun and Maxwell A. Cameron (eds.), *The Political Economy of North American Free Trade.* New York: St. Martin's Press, 1994, pp. 3–26.

Grossman, Dan, and Seth Shulman. "Down in the Dumps." *Discover* 11 (April) 1990:36–41.

Grossman, Lawrence K. *The Electronic Republic.* New York: Penguin, 1995.

Grossman, Lev. "Grow Up? Not so Fast." *Time,* Vol. 165, No. 4 (January 24), 2005:42-54.

Gurevitch, Michael, and Jay G. Blumbler. "Political Communication Systems and Democratic Values," in Doris Graber (ed.), *Media Power in Politics,* 3rd ed. Washington, DC: Congressional Quarterly, 1994, pp. 25–36.

Guttentag, Marcia, and Paul F. Secord. *Too Many Women? The Sex Ratio Question.* Beverly Hills, CA: Sage, 1983.

Gwartney-Gibbs, Patricia A. "The Institutionalization of Premarital Cohabitation: Estimates from Marriage License Applications, 1970 and 1980." *Journal of Marriage and the Family* 48 (May) 1986:423–434.

Gwynne, S. C. "The Right Stuff." *Time,* October 29, 1990:74–84.

Haass, Richard N. *The Reluctant Sheriff: The United States After the Cold War.* New York: Washington, DC: Council on Foreign Relations, 1997.

Habenstein, Robert W. "A Then and Now Overview of the Immigrant Family in America," in Charles H. Mindel, Robert W. Habenstein, and Roosevelt Wright, Jr. *Ethnic Families in America: Patterns and Variations.* Upper Saddle River, NJ: Prentice-Hall, 1998, pp. 13–38.

Haber, Carole, and Bran Gratton. *Old Age and the Search for Security: An American Social History.* Bloomington: University of Indiana Press, 1994.

Hackett, David G. "Rodney Stark and the Sociology of American Religious History." *Journal for the Scientific Study of Religion* 29 (September) 1990:372–376.

The Hactivist.com. "What is Hacktivism?" The Hactivist.com, 2006.

Hadden, Jeffrey K. "Televangelism and Political Mobilization," in Quentin J. Schultze (ed.), *American Evangelicals and the Mass Media.* Grand Rapids, MI: Academie Books, 1990a, pp. 215–229.

Hadden, Jeffrey K., and Anson Shupe. "Introduction," in Jeffrey K. Hadden and Anson Shupe (eds.), *Prophetic Religions and Politics.* New York: Paragon, 1986, pp. i–xv.

Hadnot, Ira J. "Turning the Clock on Culture: Hip Consumerism Transforms Rebels into Emblems of Cool." *Dallas Morning News,* Sunday Reader, Sunday, January 5, 2003:1J, 6J.

Hadnot, Ira J., and Scott Parks. "Public Schools Resegregating, Research Finds." *Dallas Morning News,* January 19, 2003:23A.

Hafner, Katie. "Wiring the Ivory Tower." *Newsweek,* January 30, 1995:62–66.

———. "Look Who's Talking." *Newsweek,* February 17, 1997:70–72.

Hagen, L. Kirk. "French Follies." *Skeptic* 9 (4) April 2002:1–6.

Hahnel, Robin. *Panic Rules: Everything You Need to Know about the Global Economy.* Cambridge, MA: South End Press, 1999.

Halaby, Charles N. "Where Job Values Come From: Family and Schooling Background, Cognitive Ability, and Gender." *American Sociological Review* 68 (April) 2003:252–278.

Hales, Dianne. "Why Prayer Could Be Good Medicine." *Parade,* March 23, 2003:4–5.

Hall, Brian. "Overkill Is Not Dead." *The New York Times Magazine,* Section 6, March 15, 1998:42–85.

Hall, Edward T. *The Silent Language.* New York: Doubleday, 1959.

Hall, John R., and Mary Jo Neitz. *Culture: Sociological Perspectives.* Englewood Cliffs, NJ: Prentice-Hall, 1993.

Hall, Peter. *Cities of Tomorrow,* 3rd ed. New York: Blackwell, 2002.

Hall, Richard A. *Organizations: Structures, Processes, and Outcomes, 8th ed.* Upper Saddle River, NJ: Prentice-Hall, 2002.

Hallinan, Maureen T. "Tracking: From Theory to Practice." *Sociology of Education* 67 (April) 1994:79–84.

Halter, Marilyn. *Shopping for Identify: The Marketing of Ethnicity.* New York: Schocken Books, 2000.

Hamer, Dean, and Peter Copeland. *The Science of Desire: The Search for the Gay Gene and the Biology of Behavior.* New York: Simon & Schuster, 1994.

Hampton, Keith N., and Barry Wellman. "The Not So Global Village of Netville," in Barry Wellman and Caroline Haythornthwaite (eds.), *The Internet in Everyday Life.* Malden, MA: Blackwell, 2002, pp. 345–371.

Hancock, Lee. "Death Sentence Debate Centers on Gender." *Dallas Morning News,* January 25, 1998:1A, 9A.

Hancock, LynNell, and Archer Biddle. "It's a Small World, After All." *Newsweek,* November 14, 1994:59.

Hancock, LynNell, and Rob French. "The Dawn of Online Home Schooling." *Newsweek,* October 10, 1994:67.

Hancock, LynNell, and Betsy McKay. "The Caviar Curriculum." *Newsweek,* December 5, 1994:66–68.

Hancock, LynNell, and Melissa Roberts. "Fishing for Freshmen." *Newsweek,* November 21, 1994:104–105.

Handwerk, Brian. "Snake Handlers Hang on in Appalachian Churches." *National Geographic News,* April 7, 2003.

Hanley, Eric, and Matthew McKeever. "The Persistence of Educational Inequalities in State-Socialist Hungary: Trajectory-Maintenance versus Counterselection." *Sociology of Education* 70 (January) 1997:1–18.

Hannon, Lance E. "Extremely Poor Neighborhoods and Homicide." *Social Science Quarterly* 86 (Special Issue), 2005:1418-1434.

Hansen, Marcus L. "The Third Generation in America." *Commentary* 14 (November) 1952:492–500.

Hanson, Sandra. "Lost Talent: Unrealized Educational Aspirations and Expectations among

U.S. Youths." *Sociology of Education* 67 (July) 1994:159–183.

Harmon, Amy. "Racial Divide Found on Information Highway." *New York Times*, April 17, 1998:A1, A22.

Harris, C. D., and Edward L. Ullman. "The Nature of Cities." *Annals of the American Academy of Political and Social Science* 242, 1945:7–17.

Harris, David R., and Jeremiah J. Sim. "Who Is Multiracial? Assessing the Complexity of Lived Race." *American Sociological Review* 67 (August) 2002:614–627.

Harris, Diana K. *Sociology of Aging*, 2nd ed. New York: HarperCollins, 1990.

Harris, Louis, et al. *The Myth and Reality of Aging in America.* Washington, DC: National Council on Aging, 1976.

Harris, Marvin. *Cows, Pigs, Wars and Witches: The Riddles of Culture.* New York: Vintage, 1974.

Harris, Marvin, and Orna Johnson. *Cultural Anthropology*, 6th ed. Boston: Allyn & Bacon, 2003.

Hart, C. W. "Fieldwork among the Tiwi, 1928–29," in G. Spindler (ed.), *Being an Anthropologist: Fieldwork in Eleven Cultures.* New York: Holt, Rinehart & Winston, 1970.

Harvey, Neil. *The Chiapas Rebellion: The Struggle for Land and Democracy.* Durham, NC: Duke University Press, 1998.

Haskell, Molly. *From Revenge to Rape: The Treatment of Women in Movies.* New York: Holt, Rinehart & Winston, 1973.

Haskell, Thomas L. *The Authority of Experts.* Bloomington: Indiana University Press, 1984.

Hathaway, Andrew D., and Michael F. Atkinson. "Tolerable Differences Revisited: Crossroads in Theory on the Social Construction of Deviance." *Deviant Behavior* 22 (July–August) 2001:353–377.

Hattemer, Barbara, and Robert Showers. *Don't Touch That Dial.* Lafayette, LA: Huntington House, 1993.

Haught, James A. *Holy Hatred: Religious Conflicts of the '90s.* New York: Prometheus, 1995.

Hauser, Robert M., Shu-Ling Tsai, and William H. Sewell. "A Model of Stratification with Response Error in Social and Psychological Variables." *Sociology of Education* 56, 1989:20–46.

Havighurst, Robert. "Personality and Patterns of Aging." *Gerontologist* 8, 1968:20–23.

Haviland, William A. *Cultural Anthropology*, 7th ed. Fort Worth: Harcourt Brace Jovanovich, 1993.

———. *Cultural Anthropology*, 8th ed. Forth Worth, TX: Harcourt Brace, 1998.

———. *Cultural Anthropology*, 9th ed. Fort Worth, TX: Harcourt, 2000.

———. *Anthropology*, 11th ed. Belmont, CA: Wadsworth, 2005.

Hawes, Joseph M. *The Children's Rights Movement: A History of Advocacy and Protection.* Boston: Twayne, 1991.

Hawkins, Joellen W., and Cynthia S. Aber. "Women in Advertisements in Medical Journals." *Sex Roles* 28 (February) 1993:233–242.

Hayden, Thomas. "Sense of Self." *Newsweek* special issue (Fall/Winter) 2000:57–62.

Haythornthwaite, Caroline, and Barry Wellman. "The Internet in Everyday Life: An Introduction," in Barry Wellman and Caroline Haythornthwaite (eds.), *The Internet in Everyday Life.* Malden, MA, 2002, pp. 3–41.

Hazleton, Jared E. "Year-Round Schools: A Matter of Time?" *School Business Affairs* (November) 1995:15–16, 18–21.

Healy, Jane M. "The Mad Dash to Compute," in James W. Noll (ed.), *Taking Sides: Clashing*

Views on Controversial Educational Issues, 12th ed. Guilford, CT: McGraw-Hill Dushkin, 2003, pp. 353–358.

Heath, Christian, Hubert Knoblauch, and Paul Luff. "Technology and Social Interaction: The Emergence of Workplace Studies." *The British Journal of Sociology* 51 (2) June 2000:299–320.

Heckert, Teresa M., Heather E. Droste, Patrick J. Adams, Christopher M. Griffin, Lisa L. Roberts, Michael A. Mueller, and Hope A. Wallis. "Gender Differences in Anticipated Salary: Role of Salary Estimates for Others, Job Characteristics, Career Paths, and Job Inputs." *Sex Roles* 47 (August) 2002:139–151.

Heller, Celia S. *Structured Social Inequality: A Reader in Comparative Social Stratification*, 2nd ed. New York: Macmillan, 1987.

Hellman, Chan M., and Wayne L. McMillin. "Newcomer Socialization and Affective Commitment." *Journal of Social Psychology* 134 (April) 1994:261–262.

Hendrickson, Borg. *Home School: Taking the First Step.* Kooskia, ID: Mountain Meadow Press, 1989.

Henig, Jeffrey R. "Choice in Public Schools: An Analysis of Transfer Requests among Magnet Schools." *Social Science Quarterly* 71 (March) 1990:69–82.

Henshaw, Stanley K. "Unintended Pregnancy in the United States." *Family Planning Perspectives* 30 (January/February) 1998:24–39.

Henslin, James. "Trust and Cabbies," in James M. Henslin (ed.), *Down to Earth Sociology: Introductory Readings*, 7th ed. New York: The Free Press, 1993, pp. 183–196.

Herdt, Gilbert (ed.). *Ritual Homosexuality in Melanesia.* Berkeley: University of California Press, 1984.

Herdt, Gilbert, William L. Leap, and Melanie Sovine. "Introduction: Anthropology, Sexuality, and AIDS." *Journal of Sex Research* 28 (May) 1991:167–169.

Herek, Gregory M., and Eric K. Glunt. "AIDS-Related Attitudes in the United States: A Preliminary Conceptualization." *Journal of Sex Research* 28 (February) 1991:99–123.

Herman, Edward S., and Noam Chomsky. *Manufacturing Consent: The Political Economy of the Mass Media.* New York: Pantheon, 1988.

Herrnstein, Richard J., and Charles Murray. *The Bell Curve: Intelligence and Class Structure in American Life.* New York: Free Press, 1994.

Hess, John. "Geezer-Bashing: Media Attacks on the Elderly." *Extra* (August/September) 1991. <http://www.fair.org/extra/best-of-geezer-bashing.html>

Hesse-Biber, Sharlene Nagy, and Michelle L. Yaiser (eds.). *Feminist Perspectives on Social Research.* New York: Oxford University Press, 2004.

Heyck, Denis Lynn. *Barrios and Borderlands: Cultures of Latinos and Latinas in the United States.* New York: Routledge, 1994.

Hickey, Joseph V., and William E. Thompson. "Personal Space: The Hidden Dimension of Cowboy Demeanor." *Midwest Quarterly* 24 (Winter) 1988:264–272.

Hickson, David J. "Decision Making at the Top of Organizations," in W. Richard Scott (ed.), *Annual Review of Sociology* 13, 1987, pp. 165–192.

Higley, John, and Michael G. Burton. "The Elite Variable in Democratic Transitions and Breakdowns." *American Sociological Review* 54 (February) 1989:1732.

———. "In Defense of Elite Theory: A Reply to Cammack." *American Sociological Review* 55 (June) 1990:421–426.

Hill, Malcolm D. "Class, Kinship Density, and Conjugal Role Separation." *Journal of Marriage and the Family* 50 (August) 1988:731–741.

Hillenbrand, Barry. "War Is Hell." *Time*, September 25, 1989:87.

Hinton, Mick. "Moore Legislator Seeking Warning on Records Deemed Objectionable." *Oklahoman*, February 24, 1990:1A, 9A.

Hirschfeld, Julie. "Enrollment in U.S. Schools Expected to Hit Record Level." *Dallas Morning News*, August 22, 1997a:5A.

———. "Report Says U.S. Students Slipping in Reading, Writing." *Dallas Morning News*, August 31, 1997b:8A, 9A.

Hirschi, Travis. *Causes of Delinquency.* Berkeley: University of California Press, 1969.

Hirsh, Eric L. "Sacrifice for the Cause: Group Processes, Recruitment, and Commitment in a Student Social Movement." *American Sociological Review* 55 (April) 1990:243–254.

HND. "Media Violence Predicts Aggressive Behavior." *Health News Digest*, 2003. <http://www.healthnewsdigest.com/>

Hochschild, Arlie. *The Time Bind: When Work Becomes Home and Home Becomes Work.* New York: Metropolitan Books/Holt, 1997.

Hochschild, Arlie, and Anne Machung. *The Second Shift: Inside the Two-Job Marriage.* New York: Avon, 1990.

Hodge, Robert, and David Tripp. *Children and Television: A Semiotic Approach.* Cambridge, UK: Polity Press, 1986.

Hoebel, E. Adamson. *The Cheyennes: Indians of the Great Plains.* New York: Holt, Rinehart & Winston, 1960.

Hoffman, Bruce. *Inside Terrorism.* New York: Columbia University Press, 1998.

Hoffman, Mark S. (ed.). *The World Book Almanac and Book of Facts 1992.* New York: Pharos Books, 1991.

Hoffman, Saul D., and Greg J. Duncan. "What Are the Economic Consequences of Divorce?" *Demography* 25, 1988:641–645.

Holland, Alyce, and Thomas Andre. "Is the Extracurriculum an Extra Curriculum?" *American Secondary Education* 19 (2) 1```991:6–12.

Holliday, Ruth. "We've Been Framed: Visualizing Methodology." *The Sociological Review* 48 (November) 2000:503–521.

Holstein, William J. "How Consumer Culture Sets Up Its Young Ducks." *The New York Times* on the Web, Sunday, January 26, 2003:1.

Holt, John. "Escape from Childhood," in James W. Noll (ed.), *Taking Sides: Clashing Views on Controversial Educational Issues*, 14th ed. Guilford, CT: McGraw-Hill Dushkin, 2007, pp. 25–30.

Homans, George C. *The Human Group.* New York: Harcourt Brace Jovanovich, 1950.

———. *Social Behavior: Its Elementary Forms.* New York: Harcourt Brace Jovanovich, 1961.

hooks, bell. *Black Looks: Race and Representation.* Boston: South End, 1992.

Hooks, Gregory M. "The Rise of the Pentagon and U.S. State Building: The Defense Program and Industrial Policy." *American Journal of Sociology* 96 (September) 1990:358–404.

Hooyman, Nancy R., and H. Asuman Kiyak. *Social Gerontology: A Multidisciplinary Perspective*, 7th ed. Boston: Allyn & Bacon, 2005.

Hope, Warren C. "Why Technology Has Not Realized Its Potential in Schools: A Perspective." *American Secondary Education* 25 (June) 1997:1–9.

Hopper, Marianne. "Becoming a Policeman: Socialization of Cadets in a Police Academy." *Urban Life* 6 (July) 1977:149–170.

Horowitz, Irving L. "The Limits of Modernity," in Thomas Robbins and Dick Anthony (eds.), *In Gods We Trust: New Patterns of Religious Pluralism in America,* 2nd ed. New Brunswick, NJ: Transaction, 1990:63–76.

———. "Chance, Choice, Civility and Coleman." *Society* 28 (January/February) 1991:80–84.

Horton, Hayward D., Beverly L. Allen, Cedric Herring, and Melvin E. Thomas. "Lost in the Storm: The Sociology of the Black Working Class: 1850 to 1990." *American Sociological Review* 65 (1) February 2000:128–137.

Hostetler, John. *Amish Society,* 3rd ed. Baltimore: Johns Hopkins University Press, 1980.

Hostetler, John, and Gertrude E. Huntington. *Children in Amish Society: Socialization and Community Education.* New York: Holt, Rinehart & Winston, 1971.

Hout, Michael, and William R. Morgan. "Race and Sex Variations in the Causes of the Expected Attainments of High School Seniors." *American Journal of Sociology* 81 (September) 1975:364–394.

Howard, Michael C. *Contemporary Cultural Anthropology,* 3rd ed. New York: Harper-Collins, 1989.

Howard, Michael C., and Janet Dunaif-Hattis. *Anthropology: Understanding Human Adaptation.* New York: HarperCollins, 1992.

Howard, Philip N., and Steve Jones. *Society Online: The Internet in Context.* Thousand Oaks, CA: Pine Forge Press, 2004.

Howe, Harold II. "Sins of Omission in 'America 2000.'" *Phi Delta Kappan* 73 (November) 1991:192–203.

Howitt, Dennis. *The Mass Media and Social Problems.* New York: Pergamon Press, 1982.

Hoyt, Homer. *The Structure and Growth of Residential Neighborhoods in American Cities.* Washington, DC: Federal Housing Authority, 1939.

Huber, Evelyne, and John D. Stephens. "Partisan Governance, Women's Employment, and the Social Democratic State." *American Sociological Review* 65 (June) 2000:323–342.

Huber, Joan. "Macro-Micro Links in Gender Stratification." *American Sociological Review* 55 (February) 1990:1–10.

Hughes, Donna Rice, and John D. McMickle. "Pornography Incites Violent Sexual Crime," in Carol Wekesser (ed.), *Pornography: Opposing Viewpoints.* San Diego: Greenhaven Press, 1997, pp. 36–39.

Hughes, Everett C. *Men and Their Work.* Glencoe, IL: Free Press, 1958.

Hulbert, Ann. *Raising America: Experts, Parents, and a Century of Advice About Children.* New York: Knopf, 2003.

Hummel, Ralph. *The Bureaucratic Experience.* New York: St. Martin's Press, 1977.

Humphreys, Laud. *Tearoom Trade: Impersonal Acts in Public Places.* New York: Aldine de Gruyter, 1970.

Humphry, Derek. *Final Exit,* 3rd ed. New York: Random House, 2002.

Hunt, Darnell M. *Channeling Blackness: Studies on Television and Race in America.* New York: Oxford University Press, 2004.

Hunt, Larry L., and Janet G. Hunt. "African Americans," in Andrew M. Greeley (ed.), *Sociology and Religion: A Collection of Readings.* New York: HarperCollins, 1995, pp. 467–479.

Hunter, Alfred A. "Formal Education and Initial Employment: Unravelling the Relationships between Schooling and Skills over Time." *American Sociological Review* 53, 1988: 753–765.

Hurst, Charles E. *Social Inequality: Forms, Causes, and Consequences,* 3rd ed. Boston: Allyn & Bacon, 1998.

———. *Living Theory: The Application of Classical Social Theory to Contemporary Life.* Boston: Allyn and Bacon, 2005.

Idler, Ellen L., and Stanislav V. Kasl. "Religion, Disability, Depression, and the Timing of Death." *American Journal of Sociology* 97 (January) 1992:1052–1079.

Ihinger-Tallman, Marilyn, and Kay Pasley. "Building Bridges, Reflections on Theory, Research, and Practice," in Kay Pasley and Marilyn Ihinger-Tallman (eds.), *Stepparenting: Issues in Theory, Research, and Practice.* Westport, CT: Greenwood, 1994, pp. 239–250.

Illich, Ivan D. *Deschooling Society.* New York: HarperCollins, 1983.

IMDiversity Website, Hispanic American Village. "Few Seats for Latinos at Fortune 500 Board Tables," November 2, 2002:1–3.

Inglehart, Ronald. *Modernization and Postmodernization: Cultural, Economic, and Political Change in 43 Societies.* Princeton, NJ: Princeton University Press, 1997.

Inglehart, Ronald, and Wayne E. Baker. "Modernization, Culture Change, and the Persistence of Traditional Values." *American Sociological Review* 65 (1) February 2000:19–51.

Inter-Parliamentary Union. Women in National Parliaments, World and Regional Averages, Interparliamentary.org website, May 31, 2003.

Irwin, John. *The Felon.* Englewood Cliffs, NJ: Prentice-Hall, 1970.

Isaac, Larry, and Lars Christiansen. "How the Civil Rights Movement Revitalized Labor Militancy." *American Sociological Review* 67 (October) 2002:722–746.

Ishida, Hiroshi, Seymour Spilerman, and Juo-Hsien Su. "Educational Credentials and Promotion Chances in Japanese and American Organizations." *American Sociological Review* 62 (December) 1997:866–882.

Jackson, Jeffrey M., and Stephen G. Harkins. "Equity in Effort: An Explanation of the Social Loafing Effect." *Journal of Personality and Social Psychology* 49, 1985:1199–1206.

Jacob, Matt. "To Some, the Fight Is Still Far from Over." *Dallas Morning News,* September 20, 2003:1C, 10C.

Jacobs, David, and Jason T. Carmichael. "The Political Sociology of the Death Penalty: A Pooled Time-Series Analysis." *American Sociological Review* 67 (February) 2002:109–131.

Jacobs, Jane. *Death and Life of Great American Cities.* New York: Vintage, 1992.

Jacobs, Jerry. *Fun City: An Ethnographic Study of a Retirement Community.* Prospect Heights, IL: Waveland, 1983.

Jacobs, Jerry, Marie Lukens, and Michael Useem. "Organizational, Job, and Individual Determinants of Workplace Training: Evidence from the National Organizations Survey." *Social Science Quarterly* 77 (March) 1996: 159–176.

Jacobsen, Joyce P. "Trends in Work Force Sex Segregation, 1960–1990." *Social Science Quarterly* 75 (March) 1994:204–211.

Jacobson, Sherry. "AIDS Rates Escalating among Minority Groups." *Dallas Morning News,* June 4, 2001:1A, 6A.

———. "Surgeon General Says Obesity Top Health Threat." *Dallas Morning News,* January 24, 2003:4A.

James, Estelle, and Gail Benjamin. *Public Policy and Private Education in Japan.* New York: St. Martin's Press, 1988.

Janis, Irving L. *Victims of Groupthink.* Boston: Houghton Mifflin, 1972.

Jankowski, Martin Sanchez. *Islands in the Street: Gangs and American Urban Society.* Berkeley: University of California Press, 1991.

Janofsky, Michael. "Women in the Marines Join the Firing Line." *New York Times,* April 1, 1997:A10.

Jaroff, Leon. "The Gene Hunt." *Time,* March 20, 1989:62–67.

Jaschik, Scott. "U. Of California to Limit Racial Preferences in Admissions, Hiring." *Chronicle of Higher Education* XLI (45) 1995:A25.

Jasper, James M., and Dorothy Nelkin. *The Animal Rights Crusade: The Growth of a Moral Protest.* New York: Free Press, 1992.

Jefferson, David. "How AIDS changed America." *Newsweek,* May 15, 2006:36-41.

Jehl, Douglas. "It's Heavy Going for Sex, Satan and Heavy Metal." *New York Times,* February 11, 1997:A–4.

Jencks, Christopher. *Rethinking Social Policy: Race, Poverty, and the Underclass.* New York: Harper Perennial, 1993.

———. *The Homeless.* Cambridge: Harvard University Press, 1994.

Jencks, Christopher, Lauri Perman, and Lee Rainwater. "What Is a Good Job? A New Measure of Labor-Market Success." *American Journal of Sociology* 93, 1988:1322–1357.

Jencks, Christopher, Marshall Smith, and Henry Acland, et al. *Inequality: A Reassessment of the Effect of Family and Schooling in America.* New York: Basic Books, 1972.

Jenkins, Philip. *Mystics and Messiahs: Cults and New Religions in American History.* New York: Oxford University Press, 2000.

Jennings, James. "Conclusion: Racial Hierarchy and Ethnic Conflict in the United States," in James Jennings (ed.), *Blacks, Latinos, and Asians in Urban America: Status and Prospects for Politics and Activism.* Westport, CT: Praeger, 1994, pp. 143–157.

Jennings, Lane. "Finding Better Ways to Die." *The Futurist,* March/April, 2005:43-47.

Jensen, Mike. "Making the Connection: Africa and the Internet." *Current History* 99 (637) May 2000:215–220.

Jensen, Robert. "Pornography and Sexual Violence." National Electronic Network on Violence Against Women, *Applied Research Forum,* July, 2004:1-8.

Jewell, K. Sue. *From Mammy to Miss America and Beyond.* New York: Routledge, 1993.

Johnson, Cathryn. "Gender, Legitimate Authority, and Leader-Subordinate Conversations." *American Sociological Review* 59 (February) 1994:122–135.

Johnson, Curtis D. *Islands of Holiness: Rural Religion in Upstate New York, 1790–1860.* Ithaca: Cornell University Press, 1989.

Johnson, Dan. "Clash of Trends: Disappearing Water vs. Super Farms." *The Futurist* 34 (September–October) 2000:16–17.

Johnston, David C. "Very Richest Share of Income Grew Even Bigger, Data Show," *New York Times,* Business, June 26, 2003:1–3.

Johnston, Jerome, and James S. Ettema. "Using Television to Best Advantage: Research for Prosocial Television," in Jennings Bryant and Dolf Zillmann (eds.), *Perspectives on Media Effects.* Hillsdale, NJ: Erlbaum, 1986, pp. 143–164.

Johnston, Paul. "Citizenship Movement Unionism: For the Defense of Local Communities in a Global Age," in Bruce Nissen (ed.), *Unions in a Globalized Environment: Changing Borders,*

Organizational Boundaries, and Social Roles. New York: M. E. Sharpe, 2002, pp. 236–263.

Johnstone, Ronald L. *Religion in Society: A Sociology of Religion,* 8th ed. Upper Saddle River, NJ: Prentice-Hall, 2006.

Jones, Dylan. "Schools Tune In to TV." *USA Today,* March 20, 1991:7A.

Jones, James E., Jr. "The Rise and Fall of Affirmative Action," in Herbert Hill and James E. Jones, Jr. (eds.), *Race in America: The Struggle for Equality.* Madison: University of Wisconsin Press, 1993, pp. 345–369.

Jones, Jeffrey M. "Support for the Death Penalty Remains High at 74%; Slight Majority prefers death penalty to life imprisonment as punishment for murder." *Gallup Poll Analysis.* The Gallup Organization. May 19, 2003:1–7.

Jones, Mildred. "Trained and Untrained Secondary School Teachers in Barbados: Is There a Difference in Classroom Performance?" *Educational Research* 39 (Summer) 1997: 175–184.

Jones, Stephen R. G. "Worker Interdependence and Output: The Hawthorne Studies Revisited." *American Sociological Review* 55 (April) 1990:176–190.

Jones, Steven G. "Introduction," in *Cybersociety 2.0: Revisiting Computer-Mediated Communication and Community.* Thousand Oaks, CA: Sage, 1998a, pp. xi–xvii.

———. "Information, Internet, and Community: Notes Toward Understanding of Community in the Information Age." in *Cybersociety 2.0: Revisiting Computer-Mediated Communication and Community.* Thousand Oaks, CA: Sage, 1998b, pp. 1–34.

Jonsson, Patrik. "The New Face of Home Schooling." *Christian Science Monitor,* April 29, 2003. http://www.csmonitor.com/2003/0429/p01s01-ussc.html

Jorstad, Erling. *Holding Fast/Pressing On: Religion in America in the 1980s.* New York: Praeger, 1990.

Joyce, Amy. "Interest in Telecommuting Rises." *Dallas Morning News,* January 8, 2002:2C.

Juergensmeyer, Mark. *Terror in the Mind of God: The Global Rise of Religious Violence.* Berkeley, CA: University of California Press, 2000.

Kalmijn, Matthijs. "Mother's Occupational Status and Children's Schooling." *American Sociological Review* 59 (April) 1994:257–275.

Kalmijn, Matthijs, and Henk Flap. "Assortative Meeting and Mating: Unintended Consequences of Organized Settings for Partner Choices." *Social Forces* 79 (4) June 2001: 1289–1312.

Kanagy, Conrad L., Craig R. Humphrey, and Glenn Firebaugh. "Surging Environmentalism: Changing Public Opinion or Changing Publics?" *Social Science Quarterly* 75 (December) 1994:804–819.

Kane, Emily W. "Education and Beliefs about Gender Inequality." *Social Problems* 42 (February) 1995:74–90.

Kantrowitz, Barbara. "Sociology's Lonely Crowd." *Newsweek,* February 3, 1992:55.

———. "Off to a Good Start." *Newsweek* special issue (Spring/Summer) 1997:7–9.

———. "The New Middle Age." *Newsweek,* April 3, 2000:57–59.

———. "Living Longer: Health for Life." *Newsweek* special issue (Fall/Winter) 2001:5–9.

———. "Sex and Science." *Newsweek,* January 31, 2005a:36-38.

———. "The 100 Best High Schools in America." *Newsweek,* May 16, 2005b:50-59.

Kantrowitz, Barbara, and Claudia Kalb. "Boys Will Be Boys." *Newsweek,* May 11, 1998:55–60.

Kantrowitz, Barbara, and John McCormick. "A Head Start Does Not Last." *Newsweek,* January 27, 1992:44–45.

Kantrowitz, Barbara, and Pat Wingert. "Step by Step." *Newsweek* special issue (Winter/Spring) 1990:24–34.

———. "Teachers Wanted." *Newsweek,* October 2, 2000:37–42.

———. "Unmarried with Children." *Newsweek,* May 28, 2001:46-54.

Kantrowitz, Barbara, Pat Wingert, and Patrick Houston. "Sexism in the Schoolhouse." *Newsweek,* February 24, 1992:62.

Kapinus, Carolyn A., and Michael P. Johnson. "Personal, Moral, and Structural Commitment to Marriage: Gender and the Effects of Family Life Cycle Stage." *Sociological Focus* 35 (May) 2002:189–205.

Kaplan, Abraham. *The Conduct of Inquiry.* Scranton, PA: Chandler, 1964.

Kaplan, E. Ann. "Sex, Work and Motherhood: The Impossible Triangle." *Journal of Sex Research* 27 (August) 1990:409–425.

Kaplan, Lincoln. "Who Lied?" *Newsweek,* November 14, 1994:52–54.

Karen, David. "The Politics of Class, Race, and Gender: Access to Higher Education in the United States, 1960–1986." *American Journal of Education* 99 (February) 1991:208–237.

Karrfait, Wayne. "A Multicultural Mecca." *American Demographics* 25:4 (May) 2003:54–55.

Kart, Cary S., Eileen K. Metress, and Seamus P. Metress. *Aging, Health and Society.* Boston: Jones & Bartlett, 2001.

Kasarda, John D. "The Implications of Contemporary Redistribution Trends for National Urban Policy." *Social Science Quarterly* 61 1980:373–400.

———. "Caught in the Web of Change." *Society* 21, 1983:41–47.

Kastenbaum, Robert J. *Death, Society, and the Human Experience* (9th ed.). Boston: Allyn and Bacon, 2007.

Katz, James E., and Ronald E. Rice. "Syntopia: Access, Civic Involvement, and Social Interaction on the Net," in Barry Wellman and Caroline Haythornthwaite (eds.), *The Internet in Everyday Life.* Malden, MA, 2002, pp. 114–138.

Katz, Jesse. "Schools' Zero-Tolerance Stance Lacks Common Sense, Critics Say." *Dallas Morning News,* March 1, 1998:9A.

Katz, Michael B. *Improving Poor People: The Welfare State, the "Underclass," and Urban Schools as History.* Princeton: Princeton University Press, 1995.

Katz-Gerro, Tally. "Highbrow Cultural Consumption and Class Distinctions in Italy, Israel, West Germany, Sweden, and the United States." *Social Forces* 81 (1) September 2002: 207–229.

Kaufman-Rosen, Leslie, and Claudia Kalb. "Holes in the Glass Ceiling Theory." *Newsweek,* March 27, 1995:24–25.

Kaye, Lenard W., and Jeffrey S. Applegate. *Men as Caregivers to the Elderly.* Lexington, MA: Lexington Books, 1990.

Keister, Lisa A., and Stephanie Moller. "Wealth Inequality in the United States." *Annual Review of Sociology* 26 2000:63–81.

Kelle, Helga. "Gender and Territoriality in Games Played by Nine- to Twelve-Year-Old School Children." *Journal of Contemporary Ethnography* 29 (April) 2000:164–197.

Keller, Kathryn. *Mothers and Work in Popular American Magazines.* Westport, CT: Greenwood Press, 1994.

Keller, Rosemary S. "Women and Religion," in Charles H. Lipp. and Peter W. Williams (eds.), *Encyclopedia of the American Religious Experience: Studies of Traditions and Movements,* vol. 3. New York: Scribner, 1988, pp. 1547–1562.

Kellstedt, Lyman A., and Mark A. Noll. "Religion, Voting for President, and Party Identification, 1948–1984," in Mark A. Noll (ed.), *Religion and American Politics: From the Colonial Period to the 1980s.* Oxford: Oxford University Press, 1990, pp. 355–379.

Kemp, Alice Abel. *Women's Work: Degraded and Devalued.* Englewood Cliffs, NJ: Prentice-Hall, 1994.

Kennedy, Edward M. "On the Common Core of Learning," in James W. Noll (ed.), *Taking Sides: Clashing Views on Controversial Educational Issues,* 9th ed. Guilford, CT: Dushkin, 1997, pp. 120–124.

Kerblay, Basile. *Modern Soviet Society.* New York: Pantheon, 1983.

Kerbo, Harold R. *Social Stratification and Inequality: Class Conflict in Historical and Comparative Perspective,* 2nd ed. New York: McGraw-Hill, 1991.

Kerckhoff, Alan C., and Keith E. Davis. "Value Consensus and Need Complementarity in Mate Selection." *American Sociological Review* 27 (June) 1962:295–303.

Kern-Foxworth, Marilyn. "Magazines," in Erwin K. Thomas and Brown H. Carpenter (eds.), *Handbook on Mass Media in the United States: The Industry and Its Audiences.* Westport, CT: Greenwood Press, 1994, pp. 73–91.

Kertzer, David I. *Ritual, Politics, and Power.* New Haven, CT: Yale University Press, 1988.

Kessler, Ronald C., J. Blake Turner, and James S. House. "Unemployment, Reemployment, and Emotional Functions in a Community Sample." *American Sociological Review* 54 (August) 1989:648–657.

Kiang, Peter Nien-Chu. "When Know-Nothings Speak English Only: Analyzing Irish and Cambodian Struggles for Community Development and Educational Equity," in Karin Aguilar San Juan (ed.), *The State of Asian-Americans: Activism and Resistance in the 1990s.* Boston: South End, 1994, pp. 125–145.

Kiely, Kathy. "Triumphant Schwarzenegger Vows: 'I Will Not Fail You.'" *USAToday.com* Politics, October 8, 2003:1–4.

Kilgannon, Corey. "Authors Never Left Queens on Three-Year Trip Around the World. *New York Times.com/books.* December 29, 2003:1–2.

Kilgore, Sally B. "The Organizational Context of Tracking in Schools." *American Sociological Review* 56 (April) 1991:189–203.

Killias, Martin, Marcelo F. Abei, and Denis Ribeand. "Learning Through Controlled Experiments: Community Service and Heroin Prescription in Switzerland." *Crime and Delinquency* 46 (April) 2000:233–251.

Kim, Tia E., and Sharon G. Goto. "Peer Delinquency and Parental Social Support as Predictors of Asian American Adolescent Delinquency." *Deviant Behavior* 21 (July–August) 2000:331–348.

Kimmel, Michael S. *Revolution: A Sociological Interpretation.* Philadelphia: Temple University Press, 1990.

Kincheloe, Joe L. *The Sign of the Burger: McDonald's and the Culture of Power.* Philadelphia: Temple University Press, 2002.

King, Rick. "In the Sanding Booth at Ford," in John Perry and Erna Perry (eds.), *Social Problems in Today's World*. Boston: Little, Brown, 1978, pp. 199–205.

Kinsella, Kevin G. *Older Workers, Retirement, and Pensions*. Washington, DC: U.S. Bureau of the Census, 1995.

Kinsey, Alfred C., Wardell B. Pomeroy, and Clyde E. Martin. *Sexual Behavior in the Human Male*. Philadelphia: W.B. Saunders, 1948.

Kinsey, Alfred C. and staff of Kinsey Institute. *Sexual Behavior in the Human Female*. Philadelphia: W. B. Saunders, 1953.

Kirkpatrick, Curry. "It's No Way to Live." *Newsweek*, March 6, 1995:52.

Kirn, Walter. "Should You Stay Together for the Kids?" *Time* 156 (3) September 25, 2000:75–82.

Kiser, Edgar, and Michael Hechter. "The Role of General Theory in Comparative-Historical Sociology." *American Journal of Sociology* 97 (July) 1991:1–30.

Klatz, Abram. "Negative Attitudes on TV Toward Aging Affect Elderly." *The Bristol Press*, Global Action on Aging, 2005.

Klein, Ethel. *Gender Politics: From Consciousness to Mass Politics*. Cambridge, MA: Harvard University Press, 1984.

Klein, Fritz. *The Bisexual Option: A Concept of One Hundred Percent Intimacy*. New York: Arbor House, 1979; 2nd edition, Haworth Press, 1994.

Knight Ridder. "World to Soon Have Urban Majority." *Dallas Morning News*, June 17, 2006: 2A.

Knoke, David. *Political Networks: The Structural Perspective*. New York: Cambridge University Press, 1990.

Knoke, David, and Nancy Wisely. "Social Movements," in David Knoke and Mark Granovetter (eds.), *Political Networks: A Structural Perspective, Social Science Series, No. 4*. New York: Cambridge University Press, 1990: 57–84.

Knoll, James W. "Can Charter Schools Revitalize Public Education?" in James W. Noll (ed.), *Taking Sides: Clashing Views on Controversial Educational Issues*, 12th ed. Guilford, CT: McGraw-Hill Dushkin, 2003, pp. 216–217.

Knowles, J. Gary, Stacey E. Marlow, and James A. Muchmore. "From Pedagogy to Ideology: Origins and Phases of Home Education in the United States, 1970–1990." *American Journal of Education* 100 (February) 1992:195–235.

Koblinsky, Sally A., and Alan I. Sugawara. "Non-sexist Curricula, Sex of Teacher, and Children's Sex-Role Learning." *Sex Roles* 10, 1984:357–367.

Kohlberg, Lawrence. *The Psychology of Moral Development: The Nature and Validity of Moral Stages*. New York: Harper & Row, 1981.

Kohn, Alfie. "Only for My Kid: How Privileged Parents Undermine School Reform." *Phi Delta Kappan*, April 1988:569–577.

Kolbe, Richard H., and Carl D. Langefeld. "Appraising Gender Role Portrayals in TV Commercials." *Sex Roles* 28 (April) 1993: 393–417.

Konrad, Rachel. "From High-Tech to Blue Collar." *CNet News*, February 8, 2002.

Korgen, Kathleen Odell. *From Black to Biracial: Transforming Racial Identity Among Americans*. Westport, CT: Praeger, 1998.

Kortenhaus, Carole M., and Jack Demarest. "Gender Role Stereotyping in Children's Literature: An Update." *Sex Roles* 28 (February) 1993:219–232.

Kottak, Conrad P. *Anthropology: The Exploration of Human Diversity*, 4th ed. New York: Random House, 1987.

———. *Mirror for Humanity: A Concise Introduction to Cultural Anthropology*, 2nd ed. New York: McGraw-Hill, 1998.

Kowalewski, David. "Core Intervention and Periphery Revolution, 1821–1985." *American Journal of Sociology* 97 (July) 1991:70–95.

Kozol, Jonathan. *Death at an Early Age*. New York: Bantam Books, 1967.

———. *Savage Inequalities: Children in America's Schools*. New York: Perennial, 1992.

———. *Amazing Grace: Lives of Children and the Conscience of a Nation*. New York: Perennial, 1996.

———. *Ordinary Resurrections: Children in the Years of Hope*. New York: Perennial, 2001.

———. *The Shame of the Nation: The Restoration of Apartheid Schooling in America*. New York: Crown, 2006.

Krauss, Lawrence M. "Odds Are Stacked When Science Tries to Debate Pseudoscience." *The New York Times* on the Web, Tuesday, April 30, 2002:1–3.

Krebs, Nina Boyd. *Edgewalkers: Defusing Cultural Boundaries on the New Global Frontier*. Far Hills, NJ: New Horizon Press, 1999.

Kristof, Nicholas D. "Who Needs Love! In Japan Many Couples Don't." *New York Times*, February 11, 1996:1, 12.

———. "God, Satan, and the Media." *The New York Times* on the Web, March 4, 2003:1–2.

Kubey, Robert, and Mihaly Csikszentmihalyi. *Television and the Quality of Life: How Viewing Shapes Everyday Experience*. Hillsdale, NJ: Erlbaum, 1990.

Kübler-Ross, Elizabeth. *Living with Death and Dying*. New York: Macmillan, 1981.

Kuhn, Annette. *The Power of the Image: Essays on Representation and Sexuality*. London: Routledge & Kegan Paul, 1985.

Kumar, Krishan. *From Post-Industrial to Post-Modern Society: New Theories of the Contemporary World*. Oxford, UK: Blackwell, 1995.

Kunkel, Dale. "Child and Family Regulator Policy," in Jennings Bryant (ed.), *Television and the American Family*. Hillsdale, NJ: Erlbaum, 1990, pp. 349–368.

Kunkel, Dale, and Donald Roberts. "Young Minds and Marketplace Values: Issues in Children's Television Advertising." *Journal of Social Issues* 47 (1) 1991:57–72.

Kurth, Joel, and Jodi Upton. "Does Diet Obsession Make Americans Fat?" *The Detroit News.com*, Health and Fitness, Sunday, January 11, 2004:1–4.

Kurz, Karin, and Walter Muller. "Class Mobility in the Industrial World." *Annual Review of Sociology* 13, 1987:417–442.

Kushner, Tony. "Fireworks and Freedom." *Newsweek*, June 27, 1994.

LaBarre, Weston. *They Shall Take Up Serpents*. Minneapolis: University of Minnesota Press, 1962.

Lamanna, Mary A., and Agnes Riedmann. *Marriage and Families: Making Choices and Facing Changes*, 3rd ed. Belmont, CA: Wadsworth, 1988.

Lambert, Thomas. "What They Missed in Cairo: Defusing the Population Bomb." *USA Today Magazine* 123 (January) 1995:333–335.

Lambert, Tony. "The Present Religious Policy of the Chinese Communist Party." *Religion, State and Society* 29 (2) 2001:121–129.

Lamont, Michele, and Marcel Fournier. *Cultivating Differences: Symbolic Boundaries and the Making of Inequality*. Chicago: University of Chicago Press, 1992.

Lamphere, Louise, Alex Stepick, and Guillermo Grenier. "Introduction," in Louise Lamphere, Alex Stepick, and Guillermo Grenier (eds.), *Newcomers in the Workplace: Immigrants and the Restructuring of the U.S. Economy*. Philadelphia: Temple University Press, 1994, pp. 1–24.

Laqueur, Walter. *The Age of Terrorism*. Piscataway, NJ: Transaction Books, 1997.

Larson, Erik. *The Naked Consumer: How Our Private Lives Become Public Commodities*. New York: Henry Holt, 1992.

Latané, Bibb, and Steve Nida. "Ten Years of Research on Group Size and Helping." *Psychological Bulletin* 89, 1981:308–324.

Laub, John H., and Robert J. Sampson. "The Sutherland-Glueck Debate: On the Sociology of Criminological Knowledge." *American Journal of Sociology* 96 (May) 1991: 1402–1440.

Lavoy, Peter R., Scott D. Sagan, and James J. Wirtz. *Planning the Unthinkable: How New Powers Will Use Nuclear, Biological, and Chemical Weapons*. Ithaca, NY: Cornell University Press, 2000.

Lazier-Smith, Linda. "Advertising: Women's Place and Image," in Pamela J. Creedon (ed.), *Women in Mass Communication: Challenging Gender Values*. Newbury Park, CA: Sage, 1989, pp. 247–262.

Leal, David L., and Frederick M. Hess. "The Politics of Bilingual Education Expenditures in Urban School Districts." *Social Science Quarterly* 81 (December) 2000:1064–1072.

Leavitt, Robin Lynn, and Martha Bauman Power. "Emotional Socialization in the Postmodern Era: Children in Day Care." *Social Psychology Quarterly* 52 (Spring) 1989:35–43.

LeBon, Gustave. *The Crowd: A Study of the Popular Mind*. New York: Viking Press, [1895] 1960.

Lebra, Takie Sugiyama. "Mother and Child in Japanese Socialization: A Japan–U.S. Comparison," in Patricia M. Greenfield and Rodney R. Cocking (eds.), *Cross-Cultural Roots of Minority Child Development*. Hillsdale, NJ: Erlbaum, 1994, pp. 259–274.

Lechner, Viola M., and Michael A. Creedon. *Managing Work and Family Life*. New York: Springer, 1994.

Ledeen, Barbara J. "Hens, Eggs, Roosters, Astrological Bodies, and Other Problems of Cause and Effect." *National Forum* 77 (Spring) 1997:9–11.

Lee, Christopher, and Bruce Nichols. "Taking One Sex Out of the Classroom." *Dallas Morning News*, September 17, 2002:1A, 10A.

Lee, Jennifer B. "Guerrilla Warfare, Waged with Code." *The New York Times* on the Web, Thursday, October 10, 2002:1–4.

Legge, Jerome S. "The Religious Erosion—Assimilation Hypothesis: The Case of U.S. Jewish Immigrants." *Social Science Quarterly* 78 (2) 1997:472–486.

Lehman, Edward W. "The Theory of the State versus the State of Theory." *American Sociological Review* 53 (December) 1988:807–823.

Lehman, Edward W., and Amitai Etzioni (eds.). *Sociology of Complex Organizations*, 3rd ed. New York: Holt, Rinehart & Winston, 1980.

Lehrer, Warren, and Judith Sloan. *Crossing the Blvd: Strangers, Neighbors, Aliens in a New America*. New York: W. W. Norton, 2003.

Leland, John. "Blessed Be the Bull." *Newsweek*, April 27, 1998:51–53.

Lemert, Charles. *Social Things: An Introduction to the Sociological Life* (3rd ed.). New York: Rowman & Littlefield, 2005.

Lemert, Edwin. *Social Pathology*. New York: McGraw-Hill, 1951.

———. *Human Deviance, Social Problems and Social Control*, 2nd ed. Englewood Cliffs, NJ: Prentice-Hall, 1972.

Lemonick, Michael D. "Deadly Danger in a Spray Can." *Time,* January 2, 1989:42.

Lengermann, Patricia Madoo, and Ruth A. Wallace. *Gender in America: Social Control and Social Change.* Englewood Cliffs, NJ: Prentice-Hall, 1985.

Lennon, Mary Clare, and Sarah Rosenfield. "Relative Fairness and the Division of Housework: The Importance of Options." *American Journal of Sociology* 100 (September) 1994: 506–531.

Lenski, Gerhard. "Rethinking Macrosociological Theory." *American Sociological Review* 53 (April) 1988:163–171.

Lenski, Gerhard, and Jean Lenski. *Human Societies: An Introduction to Macrosociology,* 4th ed. New York: McGraw-Hill, 1982.

———. *Human Societies: An Introduction to Macrosociology,* 5th ed. New York: McGraw-Hill, 1987.

Leonard, Fran, and Laura Loeb. "Heading for Hardship: The Future of Older Women in America," in Harold Cox (ed.), *Aging: Annual Editions.* Guilford, CT: 1997, pp. 224–226.

Leonhardt, David. "Globalization Hits a Speed Bump." *The New York Times* on the Web, Sunday, June 1, 2003:1.

Leppard, Wanda, Shirley Matile Ogletree, and Emily Wallen. "Gender Stereotyping in Medical Advertising: Much Ado about Something?" *Sex Roles* 29 (December) 1993:829–838.

Leserman, Jane. *Men and Women in Medical School: How They Change and How They Compare.* New York: Praeger, 1981.

Leslie, Connie. "From the Lab to the Library." *Newsweek,* December 7, 1992:58.

LeVay, Simon. "A Grieving Scientist's Labor of Love Convinces Him That Biology Is Destiny." *Newsweek,* February 24, 1992:49.

Levin, Jack, and William C. Levin. *Ageism: Prejudice and Discrimination against the Elderly.* Belmont, CA: Wadsworth, 1980.

Levine, Daniel U., and Robert J. Havighurst. *Society and Education,* 8th ed. Boston: Allyn & Bacon, 1992.

Levine, Herbert M. *Political Issues Debated: An Introduction to Politics,* 3rd ed. Englewood Cliffs, NJ: Prentice-Hall, 1990.

Levine, John M., and Richard L. Moreland. "Small Groups," in Daniel T. Gilbert, Susan T. Fiske, and Gardner Lindsey (eds.), *The Handbook of Social Psychology, Volume II,* 1998, pp. 415–469.

Levinson, Daniel J. *The Seasons of a Man's Life.* New York: Knopf, 1978.

Levinthal, Dave. "More Adults Under Supervision." *Dallas Morning News,* July 24, 2000a:5A.

———. "Some Colleges Shifting Focus Away From Standardized Tests." *Dallas Morning News,* August 19, 2000b:1A.

Levy, Becca R., Martin D. Slade, Suzanne R. Kunkel, and Stanislav V. Kasl. "Longevity Increased by Positive Self-Perceptions of Aging." *Journal of Personality and Social Psychology* 83, 2002:261-270.

Lewin, Ellen. *Lesbian Mothers: Accounts of Gender in American Culture.* Ithaca: Cornell University Press, 1993.

Lewis, Diane. "Minority Professionals Plan Effort Aimed at Diversifying Corporate Boards." *HireDiversity.com,* July 11, 2003:1–2.

Lewis, Oscar. *Five Families: Mexican Case Studies in the Culture of Poverty.* New York: Basic Books, 1959.

———. *La Vida: A Puerto Rican Family in the Culture of Poverty: San Juan and New York.* New York: Random House, 1966.

Lewis, James R. *Satanism Today: An Encyclopedia of Religion, Folklore, and Popular Culture.* Santa Clara, CA: ABC-Clio, 2001.

Leyens, J. P., L. Camino, and R. D. Parke, et al. "Effects of Movie Violence on Aggression in a Field Setting as a Function of Group Dominance and Cohesion." *Journal of Personality and Social Psychology* 32, 1975:346–360.

Liazos, Alexander. "The Poverty of the Sociology of Deviance: Nuts, Sluts, and Perverts." *Social Problems* 20, 1972:102–120.

Lichter, Daniel T. "Poverty and Inequality among Children." *Annual Review of Sociology* 23, 1997:121–170.

Lichter, Daniel T., Zhenchao, Qian, and Martha L. Crowley. "Child Poverty Among Racial Minorities and Immigrants: Explaining Trends and Differentials." *Social Science Quarterly* 86 (Special Issue), 2005:1037–1059.

Lichter, Robert S., Linda S. Lichter, and Stanley Rothman. *Prime Time: How TV Portrays American Culture.* Washington, DC: Regnery Press, 1994.

Lickona, Thomas. "The Return of Character Education," in James Wm Noll (ed.), *Taking Sides: Clashing Views on Controversial Educational Issues,* 14th ed. Guilford, CT: McGraw-Hill Dushkin, 2006, pp. 94–101.

Lie, John. "Globalization and Its Discontents." *Contemporary Sociology* 25 (5) 1996:585–587.

Lieberson, Stanley. "Einstein, Renoir, and Greeley: Some Thoughts about Evidence in Sociology." *American Sociological Review* 57 (February) 1992:1–15.

Lieberson, Stanley, and Mary C. Waters. *From Many Strands: Ethnic and Racial Groups in Contemporary America.* New York: Sage, 1988.

Lieberson, Stanley, Susan Dumais, and Shyon Baumann. "The Instability of Androgynous Names: The Symbolic Maintenance of Gender Boundaries." *American Journal of Sociology* 105 (March) 2000:1249–1287.

Liebert, Robert M., and Joyce Sprafkin. *The Early Window: Effects of Television on Children and Youth,* 3rd ed. New York: Pergamon, 1988.

Lilley, Rozanna. "Teaching Elsewhere: Anthropological Pedagogy, Racism, and Indifference in a Hong Kong Classroom." *The Australian Journal of Anthropology* 12 (2) 2001:127–154.

Limerick, Patricia N. *The Legacy of Conquest: The Unbroken Past to the American West.* New York: Norton, 1987.

Linden, Eugene. "The Death of Birth." *Time,* January 2, 1989:32–35.

Linton, Ralph. *The Study of Man.* New York: Appleton-Century-Crofts, 1936.

Lippitt, Ronald, and Ralph K. White. "An Experimental Study of Leadership and Group Life," in Eleanor E. Maccoby, Theodore M. Newcomb, and Eugene L. Hartley (eds.), *Social Psychology.* New York: Holt, Rinehart & Winston, 1958.

Lips, Hilary M. *Women, Men, and Power.* Mountain View, CA: Mayfield, 1991.

Lipset, Seymour Martin. *Political Man.* New York: Doubleday, 1963.

———. "Social Mobility in Industrial Societies." *Public Opinion* 5 (June/July) 1982:41–44.

Lipsitz, Lewis, and David M. Speak. *American Democracy,* 2nd ed. New York: St. Martin's Press, 1989.

Liska, Allen E., and Barbara D. Warner. "Functions of Crime: A Paradoxical Process." *American Journal of Sociology* 96 (May) 1991:1441–1463.

Livingston, Gretchen, and Joan R. Kahn. "An American Dream Unfulfilled: The Limited Mobility of Mexican Americans." *Social Science Quarterly* 83 (4) December 2002: 1003–1012.

Loeb, Paul R. *Soul of a Citizen: Living With Conviction in a Cynical Time.* New York: St. Martin's Press, 1999.

Loewen, James W. *The Mississippi Chinese: Between Black and White,* 2nd ed. Prospect Heights, IL: Waveland, 1988.

Lofland, John. *Protest: Studies of Collective Behavior and Social Movements.* New Brunswick, NJ: Transaction, 1985.

———. *Social Movement Organizations: Guide to Research on Insurgent Realities.* New York: Aldine de Gruyter, 1996.

Logan, John R., and Harvey L. Molotch. *Urban Fortunes: The Political Economy of Place.* Berkeley: University of California Press, 1987.

Long, J. Scott. "The Origins of Sex Differences in Science." *Social Forces* 68 (June) 1990:1297–1315.

Longino, C. F., K. A. McClelland, and W. A. Peterson. "The Aged Subculture Hypothesis: Social Integration, Gerontophilia and Self-Conception." *Journal of Gerontology* 35 (5) 1980:758–767.

Loomis, Burdett A., and Allan J. Cigler. "Introduction: The Changing Nature of Interest Group Politics," in Burdett A. Loomis and Allan J. Cigler (eds.), *Interest Group Politics,* 4th ed. Washington, DC: Congressional Quarterly, 1995, pp. 1–31.

Lopez, Julie Amparano. "Study Says Women Face Glass Walls as Well as Glass Ceilings." *Wall Street Journal,* March 3, 1992:B1.

Lortie, Bret. "Where's It Gone? The Peace Movement at the Turn of the Century." *Bulletin of the Atomic Scientists* 56 (2) March/April 2000:47–51.

Loscocco, Karyn A., and Glenna Spitze. "The Organizational Context of Women's and Men's Pay Satisfaction." *Social Science Quarterly* 72 (March) 1991:3–19.

Lounsbury, John H., and Donald C. Clark. *Inside Grade Eight: From Apathy to Excitement.* Reston, VA: National Association of Secondary School Principals, 1990.

Lovell, Jeremy. "One Million Children Trafficked Each Year." *Yahoo News,* Wednesday, July 30, 2003:1–2.

Low, Setha. *Behind the Gates: Life, Security, and the Pursuit of Happiness in Fortress America.* New York: Routledge, 2003.

Lowenthal, Marjorie, Majda Thurnher, and David Chiriboga. *Four Stages of Life.* San Francisco: Jossey-Bass, 1975.

Lowie, Robert H. *Indians of the Plains.* New York: Natural History Press, [1954] 1963.

Lowney, Kathleen. "Satanism as Oppositional Youth Subculture." *Journal of Contemporary Ethnography* 23 (January) 1995:453–484.

Lowney, Kathleen S. "Television Talk Shows Construct Morality," in Joel Best and Donileen R. Loseke (eds.), *Social Problems: Constructionist Readings.* New York: Aldine de Gruyter, 2003, pp. 66–73.

Ludtke, Melissa. *On Our Own: Unmarried Motherhood in America.* New York: Random House, 1997.

Ludwig, Jack. "Perceptions of Black and White Americans Continue to Diverge Widely On Issue of Race Relations in the U.S." *The Gallup Poll Monthly* 413, February 2000:53–63.

Lull, James. *China Turned On: Television, Reform, and Resistance.* New York: Routledge, 1991.

Lynxwiler, John, and David Gay. "Moral Boundaries and Deviant Music: Public Attitudes Toward Heavy Metal and Rap." *Deviant Behavior* 21 (January–February) 2000:63–86.

Maccoby, Eleanor E. *Social Development, Psychological Development: Psychological Growth and the Parent-Child Relationship.* New York: Harcourt Brace Jovanovich, 1980.

Macedo, Donaldo P., and Lilia I. Bartolomé. *Dancing With Bigotry: Beyond the Politics of Tolerance.* New York: St. Martin's Press, 1999.

Macedo, Stephen. "Crafting Good Citizens." Pp. 68-75 in Knoll, James Wm. (ed.), *Taking Sides: Clashing Views on Controversial Educational Issues* (14th ed.). Guilford, CT: McGraw-Hill/Dushkin, 2007.

Machlup, Fritz. "Are the Social Sciences Inferior?" *Society* 25 (May/June) 1988:57–65.

Machung, Anne. "Talking Career, Thinking Job: Gender Differences in Career and Family Expectations of Berkeley Seniors." *Feminist Studies* 15 (1) 1989:35–58.

Mackie, Gerry. "Ending Footbinding and Infibulation: A Convention Account." *American Sociological Review* 61 (6) December 1996: 999–1017.

MacKinnon, Neil J., and Tom Langford. "The Meaning of Occupational Scores: A Social Psychological Analysis and Interpretation." *Sociological Quarterly* 35 (2) 1994:215–245.

Magalhaes, Joao P. "The One-Man Rule." *The Futurist* 36 (6) November/December 2002: 41–45.

Maguire, Brendan, Sandage, Diane, and Georgie Ann Weatherby. "Violence, Morality, and Television Commercials." *Sociological Spectrum* 20 (January–March) 2000:121–143.

Mahler, Sarah J. *American Dreaming: Immigrant Life on the Margins.* Princeton: Princeton University Press, 1995.

Maines, David R. "Social Organization and Social Structure in Symbolic Interactionist Thought," in Alex Inkeles (ed.), *Annual Review of Sociology* 3. Palo Alto, CA: Annual Reviews, 1977: 235–259.

Mangum, Garth L., Stephen L. Magnum, and Andrew Sum. *The Persistence of Poverty in the United States.* Baltimore: Johns Hopkins University Press, 2003.

Marcano, Tony. "Judge Drops Charges against Danish Mother." *The New York Times*, May 14, 1997:B3.

Marden, Charles F., Gladys Meyer, and Madeline H. Engle. *Minorities in American Society*, 6th ed. New York: HarperCollins, 1992.

Mare, Robert D. "Change and Stability in Educational Stratification." *American Sociological Review* 46 (February) 1981:72–87.

———. "Five Decades of Educational Assortative Mating." *American Sociological Review* 56 (February) 1991:15–32.

Mare, Robert D., and Meei-Shenn Tzeng. "Fathers' Ages and the Social Stratification of Sons." *American Journal of Sociology* 95 (1) 1989:108–131.

Marett, R. R. *The Threshold of Religion.* London: Methuen, 1909.

Marriott, Michel. "Beyond War's Hell, the Bedevilling Details." *The New York Times* on the Web, Thursday, October 3, 2002:1–3.

Marsden, George M. "Fundamentalism," in Charles H. Lipp. and Peter W. Williams (eds.), *Encyclopedia of the American Religious Experience: Studies of Traditions and Movements,* vol. 1. New York: Scribner, 1988, pp. 947–962.

Marshall, Ann. "Organizing across the Divide: Local Feminist Activism, Everyday Life, and the Election of Women to Public Office." *Social Science Quarterly* 83 (September) 2002:707–725.

Marshall, Nancy L. (ed.). "The Social Construction of Gender in Childhood and Adolescence." *American Behavioral Scientist* 46 (June) 2003.

Martin, William. "Mass Communications," in Charles H. Lipp. and Peter W. Williams (eds.), *Encyclopedia of the American Religious Experience: Studies of Traditions and Movements,* vol. 3. New York: Scribner, 1988, pp. 1711–1726.

Marwell, Gerald, and N. J. Demerath III. "Secularization by Any Other Name." *American Sociological Review* 68 (2) April 2003: 314–316.

Marx, Gary T., and Douglas McAdam. *Collective Behavior and Social Movements: Process and Structure.* Englewood Cliffs, NJ: Prentice-Hall, 1994.

Marx, Karl, and Friedrich Engels. *The German Ideology.* New York: International Publishers, [1846] 1947.

Marx, Leo. "Technology: The Emergence of a Hazardous Concept." *Social Research* 64 (3) 1997:965–988.

Massey, Douglas, and Nancy Denton. *American Apartheid.* Cambridge, MA: Harvard University Press, 1993.

Mastro, Dana E. and Susannah Stern. "Representations of Race in Television Commercials." *Journal of Broadcasting and Electronic Media* 47, 2003:129-151.

Matei, Sorin, and Sandra J. Ball-Rokeach. "Belonging in Geographic, Ethnic, and Internet Spaces," in Barry Wellman and Caroline Haythornthwaite (eds.), *The Internet in Everyday Life.* Malden, MA, Blackwell, 2002: pp. 404–427.

Mathews, Mervyn. *Poverty in the Soviet Union.* Cambridge, UK: Cambridge University Press, 1986.

May, Christopher. *The Information Society: A Skeptical View.* Cambridge, UK: Polity, 2002.

May, Hazel. "Murderers' Relatives: Managing Stigma, Negotiating Identity." *Journal of Contemporary Ethnography* 29 (April) 2000:198–221.

Mayberry, Maralee. *New Age Thought and Cultural Production.* Paper presented at the 33rd Annual Conference of the Western Social Science Association. Reno, NV, April 24–27, 1991:1–9.

McAdam, Doug, John D. McCarthy, and Mayer N. Zald. "Social Movements," in Neil J. Smelser (ed.), *Handbook of Sociology.* Newbury Park, CA: Sage, 1988, pp. 695–737.

McAdams, Robert. "Introduction: Moral and Political Issues." *Social Research* 64 (3) 1997a:1310–1315.

———. "Social Contexts of Technology." *Social Research* 64 (3) 1997b:947–964.

McAdoo, Harriet Pipes. "African-American Families," in Charles H. Mindel, Robert W. Habenstein, and Roosevelt Wright Jr., *Ethnic Families in America: Patterns and Variations.* Upper Saddle River, NJ: Prentice-Hall, 1998, pp. 361–383.

McAlister, Elizabeth. "The Madonna of 115th Street Revisited: Vodou and Haitian Catholicism in the Age of Transnationalism," in R. Stephen Warner and Judith G. Wittner (eds.), *Gatherings in Diaspora: Religious Communities and the New Immigration.* Philadelphia: Temple University Press, 1999:123–160.

McAneny, Leslie. "Ethnic Minorities View the Media's View of Them." *Gallup Poll Monthly*, 347 (August) 1994:31–41.

McCaffrey, Shannon. "Ruling: Filter Internet Porn in Libraries or Forfeit Funding." *Dallas Morning News*, July 24, 2003:16A.

McCaghy, Charles H., and Timothy A. Capron. *Deviant Behavior: Crime, Conflict, and Interest Groups*, 3rd ed. New York: Macmillan, 1994.

McCall, George, and Jerry Simmons. "Social Perception and Appraisal," in Howard Robboy, Sidney L. Greenblatt, and Candace Clark (eds.), *Social Interaction: Introductory Readings in Sociology.* New York: St. Martin's Press, 1979, pp. 66–78.

McCall, Leslie. "Gender and the New Inequity: Explaining the College/Non-College Wage Gap." *American Sociological Review* 65 (April) 2000:234–255.

McCarthy, John D., and Mayer N. Zald. *The Trend of Social Movements in America: Professionalization and Resource Mobilization.* Morristown, NJ: General Learning Press, 1973.

———. "Resource Mobilization and Social Movements: A Partial Theory." *American Journal of Sociology* 82 (May) 1977:1212–1241.

McConnaughey, Janet. "Study: U.S. Doctors Often Ignore Treatment Guidelines." *Dallas Morning News*, June 26, 2003:8A.

McCord, William. "The Asian Renaissance." *Society* 28 (September/October) 1991:50–61.

McCrea, Frances B., and Gerald E. Markle. *Minutes to Midnight: Nuclear Weapons Protest in America.* Newbury Park, CA: Sage, 1989.

McElroy, Wendy. "Pornography Does Not Incite Violent Sexual Crime," in Carol Wekesser (ed.), *Pornography: Opposing Viewpoints.* San Diego: Greenhaven Press, 1997, pp. 40–44.

McGinn, Daniel. "Guilt Free TV." *Newsweek,* November 11, 2002:53–59.

———. "Marriage by the Numbers." *Newsweek,* June 5, 2006:40-48.

McGinn, Daniel, and Keith Naughton. "How Safe Is Your Job?" *Newsweek*, February 5, 2001a: 37–43.

McGuire, Meredith B. *Religion: The Social Context*, 2nd ed. Belmont, CA: Wadsworth, 1987.

———. *Religion: The Social Context*, 3rd ed. Belmont, CA: Wadsworth, 1992.

McJamerson, Evangeline McConnell. "The Declining Participation of African-American Men in Higher Education: Causes and Consequences." *Sociological Spectrum* 11 (January/March) 1991:45–65.

McLanahan, Sara S., and Lynne Casper. "Growing Diversity and Inequality in the American Family," in Andrew J. Cherlin (ed.), *Public and Private Families: A Reader.* Boston: McGraw-Hill, 1998, pp. 5–17.

McLanahan, Sara S., and Gary Sandefur. *Growing Up with a Single Parent: What Hurts, What Helps.* Cambridge: Harvard University Press, 1994.

McLaren, Peter. *Life in Schools: An Introduction to Critical Pedagogy in the Foundations of Education.* New York: Longman, 1989.

———. "Multiculturalism and the Post-Modern Critique: Toward a Pedagogy of Resistance and Transformation," in Henry A. Giroux and Peter McLaren (eds.), *Between Borders: Pedagogy and the Politics of Cultural Studies.* New York: Routledge, 1994, pp. 192–222.

McLean, Scott L. "Afterword," in Scott L. McLean, David A. Schultz, and Manfred B. Steger (eds.), *Social Capital: Critical Perspectives on Community and Bowling Alone.* New York: New York University Press, 2002, pp. 281–287.

McLemore, S. Dale. *Racial and Ethnic Relations in America.* Boston: Allyn & Bacon, 1980.

McManus, Patricia A. "Market, State, and the Quality of New Self-Employment Jobs Among Men in the U.S. and Germany." *Social Forces* 78 (March) 2000:865–906.

McNeal, Ralph B., Jr. "Extracurricular Activities and High School Dropouts." *Sociology of Education* 68 (January) 1995:62–81.

McNeil, Elton B. *Human Socialization.* Belmont, CA: Brooks/Cole, 1969.

McPhail, Clark. "The Dark Side of Purpose: Individual and Collective Violence in Riots." *Sociological Quarterly* 35 (1) 1994:1–32.

McQuail, Denis. *Mass Communication Theory: An Introduction.* London: Sage, 1983.

Meachum, Jon. "The New Face of Race." *Newsweek,* September 18, 2000:38–41.

Mead, George H. *Mind, Self, and Society.* Chicago: University of Chicago Press, 1934.

Mead, Margaret. *Sex and Temperament in Three Primitive Societies.* New York: Morrow, [1935] 1963.

Means, Barbara. "Technology Use in Tomorrow's Schools." Pp. 346–352 in James Noll (ed.), *Taking Sides: Clashing Views on Controversial Educational Issues* (13 ed.). Dubuque, IA: McGraw-Hill, 2006.

Medved, Michael. *Hollywood vs. America: Popular Culture and the War on Traditional Values.* New York: HarperCollins/Zondervan, 1992.

Melson, Gail F., and Alan Fogel. "Learning to Care." *Psychology Today* 22 (January) 1988:39–45.

Melton, J. Gordon. *Encyclopedic Handbook of Cults in America.* New York: Garland, 1986.

———. *Encyclopedic Handbook of Cults in America,* rev. ed. New York: Garland, 1992.

———. *Encyclopedia of American Religions.* Detroit, MI: Gale Research, 1996.

Melton, J. Gordon, Jerome Clark, and Aidan A. Kelly. *New Age Encyclopedia.* New York: Gale Research, 1990.

Menaghan, Elizabeth G., and Toby L. Parcel. "Parental Employment and Family Life: Research in the 1980s." *Journal of Marriage and the Family* 52 (November) 1990:1079–1098.

Mendelsohn, Jack. "Senate Will Grouse, Then Ratify." *Bulletin of the Atomic Scientists* 47 (January/February) 1991:8–10.

Merrill, John C., and Everette E. Dennis. *Social Theory and Social Structure,* 2nd ed. New York: Free Press, 1968. pp. 346–352 in James Wm. Knoll (ed.), *Taking Sides: Clashing Views on Controversial Educational Issues* (13th ed.). Dubuque, IA: McGraw-Hill, 2006.

———. "Globalism Harms National and Local Media and Can Impair Freedom of Expression and Individual Liberty," in Everette E. Dennis and John C. Merrill (eds.), *Media Debates: Issues in Mass Communication,* 2nd ed. New York: Longman, 1996, pp. 223–228.

Merrow, John, and Jonathan Kozol. *Choosing Excellence: "Good Enough" Schools are Not Good Enough.* New York: Scarecrow Press, 2001.

Merton, Robert K. "Social Structure and Anomie." *American Sociological Review* 3, 1968:672–682.

———. "Discrimination and the American Creed," in *Sociological Ambivalence and Other Essays.* New York: Free Press, 1976, pp. 189–216.

Merton, Robert, George G. Reader, and Patricia L. Kendall. *The Student-Physician.* Cambridge: Harvard University Press, 1957.

Mesquita, Bruce B., and David Lalman. "Dyadic Power, Expectations, and War," in Charles S. Gochman and Alan N. Sabrosky (eds.), *Prisoners of War? Nation-States in the Modern Era.* Lexington, MA: Lexington Books, 1990, pp. 161–176.

Meyer, David. *The Politics of Protest: Social Movements in America.* New York: Oxford University Press, 2006.

Meyer, Madonna Harrington. "Family Status and Poverty among Older Women: The Gendered Distribution of Retirement Income in the United States." *Social Problems* 37 (November) 1990:551–563.

Meyer-Bahlburg, Heino F. L., and Theresa M. Exner, et al. "Sexual Risk Behavior, Sexual Functioning, and HIV-Disease Progression in Gay Men." *Journal of Sex Research* 28 (February) 1991:3–27.

Michener, H. Andrew, John D. DeLamater, and Shalom H. Schwartz. *Social Psychology.* New York: Harcourt Brace Jovanovich, 1986.

Middleton, Russell. "Brother-Sister and Father-Daughter Marriage in Ancient Egypt." *American Sociological Review* 27, 1962:103–111.

Miller, Alan S., and Rodney Stark. "Gender and Religiousness: Can Socialization Explanations Be Saved?" *American Journal of Sociology* 107 (May) 2002:1399–1423.

Miller, Barbara D. *Cultural Anthropology* (3rd ed.). Boston: Allyn and Bacon, 2005.

Miller, David L. *Introduction to Collective Behavior.* Belmont, CA: Wadsworth, 1985.

Miller, Joanne. "Jobs and Work," in Neil J. Smelser (ed.), *Handbook of Sociology.* Newbury Park, CA: Sage, 1988, pp. 327–359.

Miller, Matthew. "Explaining California's Mississippification." *U.S. News and World Report,* 124 (May 18) 1998:32.

Miller, Stephen C. "Hold It Right There, My Camera's Ringing." *The New York Times* on the Web, Thursday, March 20, 2003:1.

Miller, Warren E., and J. Merrill Shanks. *The New American Voter.* Cambridge, MA: Harvard University Press, 1996.

Millett, Kate. *Sexual Politics.* Garden City, NY: Doubleday, 1970.

Mills, C. Wright. *White Collar: The American Middle Classes.* New York: Oxford University Press, 1951.

———. *The Power Elite.* New York: Oxford University Press, 1956.

———. *The Sociological Imagination.* New York: Oxford University Press, 1959.

Minerd, Jeff. "The Rise of Cyber Civility." *The Futurist* 34 (January–February) 2000:6.

Mingione, Enzo, and Enrico Pugliese. "Rural Subsistence, Migration, Urbanization, and the New Global Food Regime," in Alessandro Bonanno, Lawrence Busch, and William H. Friedland, et al. (eds.), *From Columbus to ConAgra: The Globalization of Agriculture and Food.* Lawrence: University Press of Kansas, 1994, pp. 52–68.

Mironov, Vladimir. "Beyond Cloning: Toward Human Printing." *The Futurist* (May/June) 2003:34–37.

Mishel, Lawrence, Jared Bernstein, and John Schmitt. *The State of Working America, 2000/2001.* Ithaca, NY: Cornell University Press, 2001.

Mitchell, Jennifer D. "Before the Next Doubling." *World Watch* 11 (January/February) 1998:21–27.

Mittelstadt, Michelle, and Catherine K. Enders. "Postal Workers Get Bad Rap, According to Violence Study." *Dallas Morning News,* September 1, 2000:4A.

Monke, Lowell. "The Human Touch." Pp. 345-351 in in Knoll, James Wm. (ed.), *Taking Sides: Clashing Views on Educational Issues* (14th ed.), Guilford, CT: McGraw-Hill/Dushkin, 2007.

Monte, Philip. "Attitudes toward the Voluntary Taking of Life: An Updated Analysis of Euthanasia Correlates." *Sociological Spectrum* 11 (July/September) 1991:265–277.

Montgomery, William E. *Under Their Own Vine and Fig Tree: The African-American Church in the South 1865–1900.* Baton Rouge: Louisiana State University Press, 1993.

Mooney, Linda A., Sarah Brabant, and Susan Moran. "Gender and Age Displays in Ceremonial Tokens." *Sex Roles* 29 (November) 1993: 617–627.

Moore, David W. *The Superpollsters: How They Measure Public Opinion in America.* New York: Four Walls Eight Windows, 1992.

———. "Two of Three Americans Feel Religion Can Answer Most of Today's Problems." *The Gallup Poll Monthly* 414 March 2000:53–61.

Moore, Gwen, Sarah Sobieraj, J. Allen Whitt, Olga Mayorova, and Daniel Beaulieu. "Elite Interlocks in Three U.S. Sectors: Nonprofit, Corporate, and Government." *Social Science Quarterly* 83:3 (September) 2002:726–744.

Moore, Marvin E. "The Family as Portrayed on Prime-Time Television, 1947–1990: Structure and Characteristics." *Sex Roles* 26 (1–2) 1992:41–61.

Moore, Ryan. "Alternative to What?: Subcultural Capital and the Commercialization of a Music Scene." *Deviant Behavior* 26 (May-June), 2005:229-252.

Moore, Thomas S. *The Disposable Work Force: Worker Displacement and Employment Instability in America.* New York: Aldine de Gruyter, 1996.

Moos, Bob. "The Gender Gap Endures, Even in Retirement." *Dallas Morning News,* June 18, 2006:1A; 10A.

Morgan, Glenn, Peer Hull Kristensen, and Richard Whitley (eds.). *The Multinational Firm.* New York: Oxford University Press, 2003.

Morgan, Michael. "Television and Democracy," in Ian Angus and Sut Jhally (eds.), *Cultural Politics in Contemporary America.* New York: Routledge, 1989, pp. 240–253.

Morgan, T. Clifton, and Jack S. Levy. "Base Stealers versus Power Hitters: A Nation-State-Level Analysis of the Frequency and Seriousness of War," in Charles S. Gochman and Alan N. Sabrosky (eds.), *Prisoners of War? Nation-States in the Modern Era.* Lexington, MA: Lexington Books, 1990, pp. 43–56.

Morganthau, Tom, Peter Annin, and John McCormick, et al. "It's Not Just New York . . . Big Cities, Small Towns: More and More Guns in Younger and Younger Hands." *Newsweek,* March 9, 1992:25–29.

Morris, Aldon D. *The Origins of the Civil Rights Movement: Black Communities Organizing for Change.* New York: Free Press, 1984.

———. "Charting Futures for Sociology: Social Organizations, Reflections on Social Movement Theory: Criticisms and Proposals." *Contemporary Sociology* 29 (3) May 2000:447.

Mortimer, Jeylan T. *Changing Attitudes toward Work.* Scarsdale, NY: Work in America Institute, 1979.

Mortimer, Jeylan T., and Jon Lorence. "Satisfaction and Involvement: Disentangling a Deceptively Simple Relationship." *Social Psychology Quarterly* 52, 1989:249–265.

Mouw, Ted. "Social Capital and Finding A Job: Do Contacts Matter?" *American Sociological Review* 68 (December), 2003:868-898.

Moses, Stephen A. "The Fallacy of Impoverishment." *Gerontologist* 30 (February) 1990:21–25.

Muller, Edward. "Democracy, Economic Development, and Income Inequality." *American Sociological Review* 53, 1988:50–68.

Mulrean, Jennifer. "Get an Online Divorce." *MSN.Com Money Central,* July 23, 2003:1–5.

Murdock, George P. "Comparative Data on the Division of Labor by Sex." *Social Forces* 15 (May), 1937:551–553.

———. "Family Stability in Non-European Cultures." *Annals of the American Academy* 272, 1950:195–201.

Murdock, Steve H. *An America Challenged: Population Change and the Future of the United States.* Boulder, CO: Westview, 1995.

Murphy, Cullen. "Feudal Gestures." *The Atlantic Monthly* 292 (3) October 2003:135–137.

Murphy, Dean E. "As Security Cameras Sprout, Someone's Always Watching." *The New York Times* on the Web, Sunday, September 29, 2002:1–3.

Murstein, Bernard I. *Who Will Marry Whom: Theories and Research in Marital Choice.* New York: Springer, 1976.

Myers, David G. *Social Psychology,* 4th ed. New York: McGraw-Hill, 1993.

Myers, David G., and H. Lamm. "The Group Polarization Phenomenon." *Psychological Bulletin* 83, 1978:602–627.

Myles, John, and Jill Quadagno. "Envisioning a Third Way: The Welfare State in the Twenty-First Century." *Contemporary Sociology* 29 (1) January 2000:256–167.

Nack, Adina. "Damaged Goods: Women Managing the Stigma of STDs" *Deviant Behavior* 21 (March–April) 2000:95–122.

Nam, Charles B., and Susan O. Gustavus. *Population: The Dynamics of Demographic Change.* Boston: Houghton Mifflin, 1976.

Namboodiri, Krishnan. "Ecological Demography: Its Place in Sociology." *American Sociological Review* 53 (August) 1988:619–633.

Nash, Madeleine. "Special Report: Diabetes, A Slow, Savage Killer." *Time,* November 26, 1990:52–54.

National Council of Churches of Christ in the USA. *Yearbook of American and Canadian Churches: Religious Pluralism in the New Millennium,* 68th ed. Eileen W. Linder (ed.). Nashville, TN: Abbington Press, 2000.

National Center for Education Statistics. *Digest of Education Statistics, 2003.* Washington, DC: Government Printing Office, 2005.

National Center on Elder Abuse. "Elder Justice and Protection." *Newsletter* 5 (September) 2006.

National Commission on Excellence in Education. *A Nation at Risk: The Imperative for Educational Reform.* Washington, DC: Government Printing Office, 1983.

National Education Association. "School Vouchers: The Emerging Track Record." *A Report of the National Education Association,* 2002.

National Institute of Justice. *Research in Action.* Washington, DC: National Institute of Justice, 1995.

National Institute of Mental Health. *Television and Behavior: Ten Years of Scientific Progress and Implications for the Eighties,* vols. 1, 2. Washington, DC: Government Printing Office, 1982.

Nazario, Sonia L. "Right and Wrong." *Wall Street Journal,* September 11, 1992:B4–B5.

NBC News. "Readin', 'Ritin' and Renovation." *NBC Nightly News,* February 2, 1995.

———. "In-Depth: Schools and Technology." *NBC Nightly News,* August 26, 1997.

———. *The Today Show.* September 5, 2003.

———. "In God They Trust." *NBC News Special with Tom Brokaw,* October 28, 2005.

———. "Resegregating Schools in Omaha." *NBC Nightly News,* April 19, 2006.

Nee, Victor. "A Theory of Market Transition: From Redistribution to Markets in State Socialism." *American Sociological Review* 54 (October) 1989:663–681.

———. "Social Inequalities in Reforming State Socialism: Between Redistribution and Markets in China." *American Sociological Review* 56 (June) 1991:267–282.

Neihardt, John G. *The Sixth Grandfather.* Raymond J. DeMallie (ed.). Lincoln: University of Nebraska Press, 1984.

Nelkin, Dorthy, and Susan Lindee. *The DNA Systique: The Gene as a Cultural Icon.* New York: Freman, 1995.

Nelson, E. Anne, and Dale Dannefer. "Aged Heterogeneity: Fact or Fiction? The Fate of Diversity in Gerontological Research." *Gerontologist* 32 (February) 1992:17–23.

Nettles, Michael T. "Success in Doctoral Programs: Experiences of Minority and White Students." *American Journal of Education* 98 (August) 1990:494–522.

Neubeck, Kenneth J. *Social Problems: A Critical Approach,* 3rd ed. New York: McGraw-Hill, 1991.

Neuman, Susan B. *Literacy in the Television Age: The Myth of the TV Effect.* Norwood, NJ: Ablex, 1991. New York: Oxford University Press, 1992.

Neuman, W. Lawrence. *Basics of Social Research: Qualitative and Quantitative Approaches* (2nd ed.). Boston: Allyn and Bacon, 2007.

Newman, Katherine S. *Declining Fortunes: The Withering of the American Dream.* New York: Basic Books, 1993.

Newman, Katherine. *No Shame in My Game: The Working Poor in the Inner City.* New York: Knopf, 2002a.

———. "No Shame: The View From the Left Bank." *American Journal of Sociology* 107 (6) May 2002b:1577–1599.

Newsweek. "An 'F' for the Nation's Kindergartners." December 16, 1991a:59.

———. "Education: A U.S. Gold Medal in Math." August 1, 1994:63.

———. "Perspectives." January 30, 1995.

———. "After the Millennium . . ." January 27, 1997a:73.

———. "Living in the Twenty-First Century." January 27, 1997b:57.

———. "The Next Level." April 7, 1997c:28.

———. "Jobs of the Future." *Newsweek* special edition, April 30, 2001.

———. "Companies of the Future." *Newsweek* special edition, April 29, 2002.

———. "Beyond the Horizon." *Newsweek,* December 12, 2005:82-84.

———. "15 Ideas to Recharge America." *Newsweek,* June 12, 2006:53-60.

Newton, Chris. "Bush Likely to Sign Violent-lyrics Proposal." *Dallas Morning News,* June 7, 1997:33A, 38A.

New York Times News Service. "Recession, Dim Prospects Worry Many in U.S., Poll Shows." *Dallas Morning News,* April 7, 1991:3A.

———. "Women's Pay Falls Further Behind Men's." *Dallas Morning News,* September 15, 1997:1A.

———. "Decline in Executions in U.S. May Reflect Change in Attitudes." *Dallas Morning News,* December 11, 2000:3A.

———. "Blondes Get Last Laugh After Media Gaffe." *Dallas Morning News,* October 2, 2002:18A.

New York Times. "Services Becoming the Goods in Industry." January 7, 1997:D1–5.

———. "Drug Testing May Not Deter Students." *Dallas Morning News,* May 17, 2003a:16A.

———. "Scientists Say Ozone Erosion Is Slowing." *Dallas Morning News,* July 30, 2003b:8A.

Nichols, Mark. "Studies Show that Pornography Causes Violence," in Carol Wekesser (ed.), *Pornography: Opposing Viewpoints.* San Diego: Greenhaven Press, 1997, pp. 45–47.

Niebuhr, Gustav. "A Shift in Hierarchy." *Dallas Morning News,* April 25, 1999:8A–9A.

Nierenberg, Danielle. "Factory Farming in the Developing World." *World Watch* 16 (May–June) 2003:10–19.

Nieto, Sonia. "What Does It Mean to Affirm Diversity?" in James W. Noll (ed.), *Taking Sides: Clashing Views on Controversial Educational Issues,* 12th ed. Guilford, CT: McGraw-Hill Dushkin, 2003, pp. 122–125.

Nimmo, Dan. *Political Communication and Public Opinion in America.* Santa Monica, CA: Goodyear, 1978.

Nisbet, Robert. *The Social Bond.* New York: Knopf, 1970.

———. *Sociology as an Art Form.* London: Oxford University Press, 1976.

Nisbett, Richard E. "Race, Genetics, and IQ," in Christopher Jencks and Meredith Phillips (eds.), *The Black–White Test Score Gap.* Washington, DC: Brookings Institute, 1998:86–102.

Niven, David. "Bolstering an Illusory Majority: The Effects of the Media's Portrayal of Death Penalty Support." *Social Science Quarterly* 83 (September) 2002:671–689.

Njaim, Julie. "Surveys Show Widespread Cheating among High Schoolers." *Dallas Morning News,* December 1, 1996:7F.

Nock, Steven L., James D. Wright, and Laura Sanchez. "America's Divorce Problem." *Society* 36 (4) May/June 1999:43–53.

Noggle, Gary, and Linda Lee Kaid. "The Effects of Visual Images in Political Ads: Experimental Testing of Distortions and Visual Literacy." *Social Sciences Quarterly* 81 (December) 2000: 913–927.

Noonan, David. "Wiring the New Docs." *Newsweek,* June 24, 2002:59–62.

Nordheimer, Jon. "Downsized, But Not Out: A Mill Town's Tale." *New York Times,* March 9, 1997:sec. 3, 1, 12.

Nordland, Rod. "Deadly Lessons." *Newsweek,* March 9, 1992:22–24.

Noriega, Chon. "Citizen Chicano: The Trials and Titillations of Ethnicity in the American Cinema, 1935–1962." *Social Research* 58 (Summer) 1991:413–438.

Norris, Pippa. "Introduction: Women, Media, and Politics," in Pipp. Norris (ed.), *Women, Media, and Politics.* New York: Oxford University Press, 1997, pp. 1–18.

Novak, Mark. Issues in Aging. Boston: Allyn and Bacon, 2006.

O'Connell, Robert L. *Of Arms and Men: A History of War, Weapons, and Aggression.* Oxford: Oxford University Press, 1989.

O'Leary, John. "End Signalled to 50 Years of Free Tuition in College." *London Times,* July 24, 1997:11.

Oakes, Jeannie. *Keeping Track: How Schools Structure Inequality.* New Haven, CT: Yale University Press, 1985.

Oates, Gary L. "Teacher-Student Racial Congruence, Teacher Perceptions, and Test Performance." *Social Science Quarterly* 84 (September) 2003:508–525.

Ogburn, William F. *Social Change.* New York: Viking Press, 1922.

———. "Culture Lag as Theory," in William F. Ogburn (ed.), *On Culture and Social Change.* Chicago: University of Chicago Press, 1964, pp. 86–95.

Ogletree, Charles J., Mary Prosser, Abbe Smith, William Talley, and NAACP. *Beyond the Rodney King Story: An Investigation of Police Misconduct in Minority Communities.* Boston: Northeastern University Press, 1995.

Ojita, Mirta. "They're Not in Denmark Anymore." *New York Times,* May 18, 1997:D2.

Okun, Morris A., Joseph F. Melichar, and Martin D. Hill. "Negative Daily Events, Positive and Negative Social Ties, and Psychological Distress among Older Adults." *Gerontologist* 30 (April) 1990:193–199.

Oliver, Melvin L., Thomas M. Shapiro, and Julie E. Press. "Them That's Got Shall Get: Inheritance and Achievement in Wealth Accumulation." *Research in Politics and Society* 5, 1995:69–95.

Omoto, Allen Martin and Howard S. Kurtzman (Eds.) *Sexual Orientation and Mental Health: Examining Identity and Development in Lesbian, Gay, and Bisexual People.* Washington, DC: APA, 2006.

Olneck, Michael R. "The Recurring Dream: Symbolism and Ideology in Intercultural and Multicultural Education." *American Journal of Education* 98 (February) 1990:147–174.

Ong, Aihwa. *Spirits of Resistance and Capitalist Discipline: Factory Women in Malaysia.* Albany: State University of New York Press, 1987.

———. "Cultural Citizenship as Subject-Making." *Current Anthropology* 17 (5) 1996: 737–762.

Ong, Aihwa, and Donald M. Nonini. "Toward a Cultural Politics of Diaspora and Transnationalism," in Aihwa Ong and Donald M. Nonini (eds.), *Ungrounded Empires: The Cultural Politics of Modern Chinese Nationalism.* New York: Routledge, 1997, pp. 323–332.

Ong, Paul, Edna Bonacich, and Lucie Cheng (eds.). "Preface," in *The New Asian Immigration in Los Angeles and Global Restructuring.* Philadelphia: Temple University Press, 1994, pp vii–xi.

Ono, Hiroshi, and Madeline Zavodny. "Gender and the Internet." *Social Science Quarterly* 84 (March) 2003:111–121.

Oppenheimer, Valerie Kincade. "Women's Employment and the Gain to Marriage," in John Hagan and Karen S. Cook (eds.), *Annual Review of Sociology 23.* Palo Alto, CA: Annual Reviews, 1997, pp. 431–453.

Orcutt, James D. "Differential Association and Marijuana Use: A Closer Look at Sutherland (with a Little Help from Becker)." *Criminology* 25 (2) 1987:341–358.

Ornstein, Charles. "AIDS: A Growing Complacency." *Dallas Morning News,* June 3, 2001:1A, 22A.

Oropesa, R. S., and Bridget K. Gorman. "Ethnicity, Immigration, and Beliefs about Marriage as a 'Tie That Binds,'" in Christine Bachrach, Michelle Hindin, Elizabeth Thomson, and Arland Thornton (eds.), *Ties That Bind: Perspectives on Marriage and Cohabitation.* New York: Aldine De Gruyter, 2000, pp. 188–211.

Ortiz, Vilma. "The Diversity of Latino Families," in Ruth E. Zambrana (ed.), *Understanding Latino Families: Scholarship, Policy, and Practice.* Thousand Oaks, CA: Sage, 1995, pp. 18–39.

Orum, Anthony M. *Introduction to Political Sociology: The Social Anatomy of the Body Politic,* 4th ed. Englewood Cliffs, NJ: Prentice-Hall, 2001.

Osgood, D. Wayne, Janet K. Wilson, and Patrick M. O'Malley, et al. "Routine Activities and Individual Deviant Behavior." *American Sociological Review* 61 (August) 1996:635–655.

Ostling, Richard N. "U.S. Voters Religiously Polarized." *Yahoo! News, Politics/News,* Thursday January 25, 2001.

Ostroff, Cheri, and Leanne E. Atwater. "Does Whom You Work with Matter? Effects of Referent Group Gender and Age Composition on Managers' Compensation." *Journal of Applied Psychology* 88 (4) 2003:725–740.

Otten, Michael C. *Power, Values, and Society: An Introduction to Sociology.* Glencoe, IL: HarperCollins, 1981.

Overby, L. Marvin, Robert D. Brown, John M. Bruce, Charles E. Smith, Jr., and John W. Winkle, III., "Race, Political Empowerment, and Minority Perceptions of Judicial Fairness." *Social Science Quarterly* 86 (June), 2005: 444–462.

Packard, Vance. *The Hidden Persuaders.* New York: McKay, 1957.

Padavic, Irene. "Attractions of Male Blue-Collar Jobs for Black and White Women: Economic Need, Exposure, and Attitudes." *Social Science Quarterly* 72 (March) 1991:33–49.

Paden, William E. *Religious Worlds: The Comparative Study of Religion.* Boston: Beacon Press, 1988.

Palac, Lisa. "Feminists Should Embrace Pornography's Liberating Effects," in Carol Wekesser (ed.), *Pornography: Opposing Viewpoints.* San Diego: Greenhaven Press, 1997, pp. 164–169.

Palazzolo, Charles S. *Small Groups: An Introduction.* New York: Van Nostrand, 1981.

Palmore, Erdman. "Predictors of Successful Aging." *Gerontologist* 19 (October) 1979: 427–431.

Pampel, Fred C. "Population Aging, Class Context, and Age Inequality in Public Spending." *American Journal of Sociology* 100 (July) 1994: 153–195.

Pan, Philip P. "Poisoned Back into Poverty: As China Embraces Capitalism, Hazards to Workers Rise." *Washington Post,* August 4, 2002.

Paradiso, Louis V., and Shauvan M. Wall. "Children's Perceptions of Male and Female Principals and Teachers." *Sex Roles* 14, 1986:1–7.

Parenti, Michael. *Power and the Powerless.* New York: St. Martin's Press, 1978.

———. *Make-Believe Media: The Politics of Entertainment.* New York: St. Martin's Press, 1992.

Park, Robert E. "The City: Suggestions for the Investigation of Human Behavior in the Urban Environment." *American Journal of Sociology* 20, 1916:577–612.

———. "Human Migration and the Marginal Man." *American Journal of Sociology* 33 (May) 1928:893.

Parkinson, C. Northcote. *Parkinson's Law and Other Studies in Administration.* New York: Ballantine, 1957.

Parks, Scott. "Out-of-the-Box Ideas on Education." *Dallas Morning News,* August 18, 2003:1B, 2B.

Parrillo, Vincent N. *Strangers to These Shores: Race and Ethnic Relations in the United States,* 8th ed. Boston, MA: Allyn & Bacon, 2006.

Parsons, Talcott. *The Social System.* New York: Free Press, 1951.

———. "The School Class as a Social System: Some of Its Functions in American Society." *Harvard Educational Review* 29 (4) 1959: 297–318.

Paterniti, Debora A. "The Micropolitics of Identity in Adverse Circumstance." *Journal of Contemporary Ethnography* 29 (February) 2000: 93–119.

Patterson, James T. *America's Struggle against Poverty, 1990–1994.* Cambridge: Harvard University Press, 1994.

Patterson, Karen. "Facing Up to Fate." *Dallas Morning News,* September 16, 2002.

———. "Piling on the Violence: Link Between Media and Aggression Clear, Experts Say." *Dallas Morning News,* April 12, 2004:1E.

Patterson, Orlando. *Slavery and Social Death: A Comparative Study.* Cambridge: Harvard University Press, 1982.

Pattison, E. Mansell. *The Experience of Dying.* Englewood Cliffs, NJ: Prentice-Hall, 1977.

Pavalko, Ronald M. *Sociology of Occupations and Professions,* 2nd ed. Itasca, IL: Peacock, 1988.

Pawluch, Dorothy. "Medicalizing Childhood," in Joel Best and Donileen R. Loseke (eds.), *Social Problems: Constructionist Readings.* New York: Aldine de Gruyter, 2003, pp. 219–225.

Payne, Wayne A., Dale B. Hahn, and Robert R. Pinger. *Drugs: Issues for Today.* St. Louis: Mosby Year Book, 1991.

PBS Frontline/World. "India, Hole-in-the-Wall: Story." July 23, 2003:1–3.

Pearlin, Leonard I. "Structure and Meaning in Medical Sociology." *Journal of Health and Social Behavior* 33 (March) 1992:1–9.

Pedrick-Cornell, Claire, and Richard J. Gelles. "Elder Abuse: The Status of Current Knowledge," in Beth B. Hess and Elizabeth W. Markson (eds.), *Growing Old in America: New Perspectives on Old Age,* 3rd ed. New Brunswick, NJ: Transaction, 1985, pp. 401–414.

Peek, Charles W., George D. Lowe, and L. Susan Williams. "Gender and God's Word: Another Look at Religious Fundamentalism and Sexism." *Social Forces* 69 (June) 1991: 1205–1221.

Peet, Richard. *Global Capitalism: Theories of Societal Development.* New York: Routledge, 1991.

Penley, Constance, and Andrew Ross (eds.). *Technoculture.* Minneapolis: University of Minnesota Press, 1991.

Peoples, James, and Garrick Bailey. *Humanity: An Introduction to Cultural Anthropology,* 4th ed. Belmont, CA: West/Wadsworth, 1997.

Peraino, Kevin. "Berkeley's New Colors." *Newsweek,* September 18, 2000:61.

Perkins, Ken P. "Establishing a Presence in Films and TV Is an Ongoing Struggle with No Big Breaks in Sight." *Dallas Morning News,* July 1, 1990.

Perrow, Charles. *Complex Organizations: A Critical Essay,* 3rd ed. New York: Random House, 1986.

———. "An Organizational Analysis of Organizational Theory." *Contemporary Sociology* 29 (3) May 2000:469–476.

Perrucci, Robert, and Earl Wysong. *The New Class Society.* Oxford, UK: Rowman and Littlefield, 1999.

Pescosolido, Bernice A., and Beth A. Rubin. "The Web of Group Affiliation Revisited: Social Life, Postmodernism, and Sociology." *American Sociological Review* 65 (1) February 2000:52–76.

Peter, Laurence J., and Raymond Hull. *The Peter Principle: Why Things Always Go Wrong.* New York: Morrow, 1969.

Petersen, William. "Social Consequences of Religion." *Society* 40 (2) January/February: 2003:53–58.

Peterson, Karen S. "Cohabitation Is Increasing, Census Data Confirm." *USA Today Census 2000,* May 24, 2001:15.

Peterson, Peter G. *Gray Dawn.* New York: Times Books, 2000a.

———. "Does an Aging Society Mean an Aging Culture?" *The Futurist* 34 (1) January/February 2000b:20–22.

Peterson, Richard A., and Roger Kern. "Changing Highbrow Taste: From Snob to Cultural Omnivore." *American Sociological Review* 61 (5) 1996:900–907.

Peterson, Thane. "A Lesson in Computer Literacy from India's Poorest Kids." *BusinessWeek Online,* Paul Judge (ed.), March 2, 2000:1–7.

Pettit, Arthur G. *Images of the Mexican American in Fiction and Film.* College Station: Texas A&M University Press, 1980.

Phelan, Jo, Bruce G. Link, and Ann Stueve, et al. "Education, Social Liberalism, and Economic Conservatism: Attitudes toward Homeless People." *American Sociological Review* 60 (February) 1995:126–140.

Phillips, David P. "The Influence of Suggestion on Suicide: Substantive and Theoretical Implications of the Werther Effect." *American Sociological Review* 39 (June) 1974:350–354.

———. "The Impact of Mass Media Violence on U.S. Homicides." *American Sociological Review* 48 (August) 1983:560–568.

Phillips, Kathryn. "Why Can't a Man Be More Like a Woman . . . and Vice Versa?" *Omni* 13 (November) 1990:42–68.

Phillips, Susan A. *Wallbangin': Graffiti and Gangs in L.A.* Chicago, IL: The University of Chicago Press, 1999.

Piaget, Jean. *The Construction of Reality in the Child.* New York: Basic Books, 1954.

Pickett, George, and John J. Hanlon. *Public Health: Administration and Policy.* St. Louis: Times Mirror/Mosby, 1990.

Pigott, Robert. "Rise of Japanese Cults." *BBC Online, World Edition,* Wednesday, May 14, 2003:1–3.

Pine, Vanderlyn R. *Caretaker of the Dead: The American Funeral Director.* New York: Irvington, 1975.

Pink, Daniel H. "School's Out" Pp. 78-87 in James Wm. Noll (Ed.), *Taking Sides: Clashing Views on Controversial Educational Issues* (13th Ed.). Dubuque, IA: McGraw-Hill/Dushkin, 2006.

Pinkney, Alphonso. *Black Americans,* 3rd ed. Englewood Cliffs, NJ: Prentice-Hall, 1987.

Pirog, Maureen A., and Chris Magee. "High School Completion: The Influence of Schools, Families, and Adolescent Parenting. *Social Science Quarterly* 78 (September) 1997:710–724.

Pirsig, Robert M. *Zen and the Art of Motorcycle Maintenance.* New York: Bantam Books, 1974.

Piven, Frances Fox, and Richard A. Cloward. *Regulating the Poor: The Functions of Public Welfare.* New York: Random House, 1971.

———. *Why Americans Don't Vote.* New York: Pantheon Books, 1988.

———. *The Breaking of the American Social Contract.* New York: Free Press, 1997.

Podger, Corinne. "Anger over Mobile Divorce Ruling." *BBC/World Online,* Wednesday, July 11, 2001:1.

Podolny, Joel M., and James N. Baron. "Resources and Relationships: Social Networks and Mobility in the Workplace." *American Sociological Review* 62 (October) 1997:673–693.

Polatnik, M. Rivka. "Working Parents: Issues for the Next Decade." *National Forum* 80 (3) Summer 2000:38–41.

Pollack, William S., and Todd Shuster. *Real Boys' Voices.* New York: Random House, 2000.

Pollard, Michael S., and S. Philip Morgan. "Emerging Parental Gender Indifference? Sex Composition of Children and the Third Birth." *American Sociological Review* 67 (August) 2002:600–613.

Pope, Daniel. "Advertising as a Consumer Issue: An Historical View." *Journal of Social Issues* 47 (1) 1991:41–56.

Porritt, Jonathon. "Save the Earth: Population Growth Is too Serious to Ignore." *Dallas Morning News,* September 8, 1991:4J.

Portes, Alejandro, and Alex Stepick. *City on the Edge: The Transformation of Miami.* Berkeley: University of California Press, 1993.

Portes, Alejandro. "The Hidden Abode: Sociology as Analysis of the Unexpected." *American Sociological Review* 65 (February) 2000:1–18.

Postman, Neil, and Charles Weingartner. *Teaching as a Subversive Activity.* New York: Dell, 1969.

Poveda, Tony G. *Rethinking White-Collar Crime.* Westport, CT: Praeger, 1994.

Powell, A. D. *"Passing" For Who You Really Are.* Palm Coast FL: Backintyme, 2005.

Prasas, Pushkala, and Albert J. Mills. "From Showcase to Shadow: Understanding Dilemmas of Managing Workplace Diversity," in Pushkala Prasad, Albert J. Mills, and Michael Elmes, et al. (eds.), *Managing the Organizational Melting Pot: Dilemmas of Workplace Diversity.* Thousand Oaks, CA: Sage, 1997, pp. 3–27.

Press, Andrea L. "Class, Gender and the Female Viewer: Women's Response to *Dynasty,*" in Mary Ellen Brown (ed.), *Television and Women's Culture.* Newbury Park, CA: Sage, 1990, pp. 158–182.

Priest, Susanna Hornig, and Toby Ten Eych. "News Coverage of Biotechnology Debates." *Society* 40 (6) September/October 2003:29–34.

Prokos, Anastasia H. and Jennifer Reid Keene. "The Long-Term Effects of Spousal Care Giving on Survivors' Well-Being in Widowhood." *Social Science Quarterly* 86 (September), 2005:664-682.

Pugh, Tony. "Ranks of Uninsured Grew in '98 U.S. Says." *Dallas Morning News,* October 4, 1999.

———. "Study Finds U.S. Health Care Lacking for All Major Groups." *Dallas Morning News,* March 16, 2006:1A;5A.

Purpel, David E. "Moral Education: An Idea Whose Time Has Gone." *Clearing House* 64 (May/June) 1991:309–312.

Putnam, Robert D. *Bowling Alone: The Collapse and Revival of American Community.* New York: Simon and Schuster, 2000.

Putnam, Robert D., and Lewis M. Feldstein, with Don Cohen. *Bowling Alone: The Collapse and Revival of American Community.* New York: Simon and Schuster, 2001.

Puttick, Elizabeth. *Women in New Religions: In Search of Community, Sexuality, and Spiritual Power.* New York: St. Martin's Press, 1997.

Quadagno, Jill. "Race, Class, and Gender in the U.S. Welfare State: Nixon's Failed Family Assistance Plan." *American Sociological Review* 55 (February) 1990:11–28.

———. *The Color of Welfare: How Racism Undermined the War on Poverty.* New York: Oxford University Press, 1994.

Quaye, Randolph K. *African Americans' Health Care Practices, Perspectives, and Needs.* Lanham, MD: University Press of America, 2005.

Quindlen, Anna. "The Essentials of Sane Parenthood." *Newsweek,* February 21, 2005:50.

Quinn, James F. and Craig J. Forsyth. "Describing Sexual Behavior in the Era of the Internet: A Typology for Empirical Research." *Deviant Behavior* 26 (May-June), 2005:191-207.

Quinn, Lois M., and John Pawasarat. "Racial Integration in Urban America: A Block Level Analysis of African American and White Housing Patterns." Employment and Training Institute, School of Continuing Education, University of Wisconsin, Milwaukee, December 2002, revised 2003:1–32.

Quinney, Richard. *Criminology: Analysis and Critique of Crime in America.* Boston: Little, Brown, 1975.

———. *Class, State, and Crime,* 2nd ed. New York: Longman, 1980.

Raboteau, Albert J. *Slave Religion: The Invisible Institution in the Antebellum South.* New York: Oxford University Press, 1978.

———. "Black Christianity in North America," in Charles H. Lipp. and Peter W. Williams (eds.), *Encyclopedia of the American Religious Experience: Studies of Traditions and Movements,* vol. 1. New York: Scribner, 1988, pp. 635–638.

Ragone, Helena. *Surrogate Motherhood: Conception in the Heart.* Boulder, CO: Westview, 1994.

Rainwater, Lee. *What Money Buys: Inequality and the Social Meanings of Income.* New York: Basic Books, 1974.

Rakow, Lana F. "A Bridge to the Future: Re-Visioning Gender in Communication," in Pamela J. Creedon (ed.), *Women in Mass Communication: Challenging Gender Values.* Newbury Park, CA: Sage, 1989, pp. 299–312.

Ramage, James. "Berkeley and UCLA See Sharp Drops in Admission of Black and Hispanic Applicants." *Chronicle of Higher Education* 64 (31) April 10, 1998:A43.

Rash, Wayne, Jr. *Politics on the Net: Wiring the Political Process.* New York: W. H. Freeman, 1997.

Ray, Brian D. "Home Schooling for Individuals' Gain and Society's Common Good." Pp. 232-250 in Knoll, James Wm. (ed.), *Taking Sides: Clashing Views on Educational Issues* (14th ed.), Guilford, CT: McGraw-Hill/Dushkin, 2007.

Raymo, James M. "Premarital Living: Living Arrangements and the Transition to First Marriage in Japan." *Journal of Marriage and Family* 65 (2) May 2003:302–315.

Raz, Aviad E. *Riding the Black Ship: Japan and Tokyo Disneyland.* Cambridge, MA: Harvard University Press, 1999.

Real, Michael R. *Mass-Mediated Culture.* Englewood Cliffs, NJ: Prentice-Hall, 1977.

———. *Super Media: A Cultural Studies Approach.* Newbury Park, CA: Sage, 1989.

Reckless, Walter. "A New Theory of Delinquency and Crime." *Federal Probation* 25 (December) 1961:42–46.

Redfield, Robert. *The Folk Culture of Yucatan.* Chicago: University of Chicago Press, 1941.

———. *The Primitive World and Its Transformations.* Ithaca, NY: Cornell University Press, 1953.

Reibstein, Larry, Gregory Beals, and Marc N. Peyser, et al. "Public Glory, Secret Agony." *Newsweek,* March 6, 1995:48–51.

Reich, Robert B. "Hire Education: The Secretary of Labor Tells You Where the Jobs Will Be in the New Economy." *Rolling Stone,* October 20, 1994:119–125.

Reiman, Jeffrey H. *The Rich Get Richer and the Poor Get Prison,* 7th ed. Boston: Allyn & Bacon, 2004.

Renzetti, Claire M., and Daniel J. Curran. *Women, Men, and Society.* Boston: Allyn & Bacon, 1995.

Research America. *American Health Poll,* 2006 <www.ResearchAmerica.org>.

Reskin, Barbara F., and Patricia A. Roos. *Job Queues, Gender Queues: Explaining Women's Inroads into Male Occupations.* Philadelphia: Temple University Press, 1990.

Retsinas, Joan. "A Theoretical Reassessment of the Applicability of Kübler-Ross's Stages of Dying." *Death Studies* 12, 1988:207–216.

Reuters News Service. "Number of Web Users Doubled from a Year Ago." On the Internet, April 25, 1997.

———. "E-Mail Brings Together Flash Mob at N.Y. Toy Store," *Yahoo.com, Yahoo News,* Saturday, August 9, 2003:1–3.

———. "SUVs Destroyed by Environmental Radicals in Calif." *New York Times.com News* August 22, 2003:1.

Rheingold, Harriet L. "The Social and Socializing Infant," in D. H. Goslin (ed.), *Handbook of Socialization Theory and Research.* Chicago: Rand McNally, 1969, pp. 779–790.

Rheingold, Howard. *The Virtual Community: Homesteading on the Electronic Frontier.* Reading, MA: Addison-Wesley, 1993.

———. *Smart Mobs: The Next Social Revolution.* Cambridge, MA: Perseus, 2002b.

———. "The Virtual Community in the Real World," in Barry Wellman and Caroline Haythornthwaite (eds.), *The Internet in Everyday Life.* Malden, MA: Blackwell, 2002, pp. xxvii–xxviii.

Rich, Frank. "The Age of the Mediathon." *New York Times Magazine,* October 29, 2000:58–65, 84–94.

Richards, Lynne. "The Appearance of Youth Subculture: A Theoretical Perspective on Deviance." *Clothing and Textiles Research Journal* 6 (Spring) 1988:56–64.

Richardson, James T., Joel Best, and David G. Bromley. "Satanism as a Social Problem," in James T. Richardson, Joel Best, and David G. Bromley (eds.), *The Satanism Scare.* New York: Aldine de Gruyter, 1991, pp. 3–17.

Richmond-Abbott, Marie. *Masculine and Feminine: Sex Roles over the Life Cycle.* New York: Random House, 1986.

Ridgeway, Cecelia L. "Interaction and the Conservation of Gender Inequality: Considering Employment." *American Sociological Review* 62 (April) 1997:218–235.

Ridgeway, Cecilia L., and Shelley J. Correll. "Limiting Inequality through Interaction: The End(s) of Gender." *Contemporary Sociology* 29 (January) 2000:110–119.

Riding, Alan. "Why *Titanic* Conquered the World," *New York Times,* 1998:sec. 2, 1; 28–29.

Ridley, Matt. *Nature Via Nurture: Genes, Experience, and What Makes Us Human.* New York: HarperCollins, 2003.

———. "Filmmakers Seek Protection from U.S. Dominance." *The New York Times* on the Web, Wednesday, February 5, 2003:1.

———. *Nature Via Nurture: Genes, Experience, and What Makes Us Human.* New York: Harper Collins, 2003.

Riemer, Jeffrey W. *Hard Hats: The Work World of Construction Workers.* Beverly Hills, CA: Sage, 1979.

Riesebrodt, Martin. *Pious Passion: The Emergence of Modern Fundamentalism in the United States and Iran.* Berkeley: University of California Press, 1993.

Rifkin, Jeremy. *Entropy: Into the Greenhouse World,* rev. ed. New York: Bantam Books, 1989.

Riggins, Stephen H. "Introduction," in Stephen H. Riggins (ed.), *Ethnic Minority Media: An International Perspective, Communication and Human Values Series,* vol. 13. Thousand Oaks, CA: Sage, 1992:1–12.

Riley, Richard W. *A Back to School Report: The Baby Boom Echo.* On-line, U.S. Department of Education, http://nces.ed.gove/bbecho/index.html/, June 22, 1998.

Ritzer, George. *Working: Conflict and Change,* 2nd ed. Englewood Cliffs, NJ: Prentice-Hall, 1977.

———. *Classical Sociological Theory.* New York: McGraw-Hill, 1992a.

———. *Sociological Theory,* 3rd ed. New York: McGraw-Hill, 1992b.

———. *Expressing America: A Critique of the Global Credit Card Society.* Thousand Oaks, CA: Pine Forge, 1995.

———. *The McDonaldization of Society* (New Century Edition). Thousand Oaks, CA: Pine Forge Press, 2000.

———. *The Globalization of Nothing.* Thousand Oaks, CA: Pine Forge Press, 2004.

Robarchek, Clayton A. "Primitive Warfare and the Ratiomorphic Image of Mankind." *American Anthropologist* 91 (December) 1989:903–920.

Robbins, Thomas. "Religious Mass Suicide before Jonestown: The Russian Old Believers." *Sociological Analysis* 47, 1986:1–20.

Robbins, Thomas, and Dick Anthony. "Cults in the Late Twentieth Century," in Charles H. Lipp and Peter W. Williams (eds.), *Encyclopedia of the American Religious Experience: Studies of Traditions and Movements,* vol. 2. New York: Scribner, 1988, pp. 741–754.

———. "Introduction: Conflict and Change in American Religions," in Thomas Robbins and Dick Anthony (eds.), *In Gods We Trust: New Patterns of Religious Pluralism in America,* 2nd ed. New Brunswick, NJ: Transaction, 1990, pp. 1–41.

Roberts, Dexter, and Aaron Bernstein. "A Life of Fines and Beating." *Business Week* October 2, 2000:122–128.

Robertson, Roland. "Global Aspects of the Contemporary Politicization of Religion," in James A. Beckford and Thomas Luckmann (eds.), *The Changing Face of Religion.* Newbury Park, CA: Sage, 1989a.

———. "A New Perspective on Religion and Secularization in the Global Context," in Jeffrey K. Hadden and Anson Shupe (eds.), *Secularization and Fundamentalism Reconsidered: Religion and the Political Order,* vol. 3. New York: Paragon, 1989b, pp. 63–77

Robinson, Bill. "Beleaguered Citadel Freshmen Finish Tense 1st Year." *Dallas Morning News,* May 18, 1997:12A.

Robinson, William I., and Jerry Harris. "Towards a Global Ruling Class? Globalization and the Transnational Capitalist Class." *Science and Society* 64 (1) Spring 2000:11–54.

Rodriguez, Gregory. "Where the Minorities Rule." *The New York Times* on the Web, Sunday, February 10, 2002:1.

Roethlisberger, Fritz J., and William J. Dickson. *Management and the Worker.* Cambridge, MA: Harvard University Press, 1939.

Rogers, Dorothy. *Adolescents and Youths,* 5th ed. Englewood Cliffs, NJ: Prentice-Hall, 1985.

Rogers, Michael. "MTV, IBM, Tennyson and You." *Newsweek* special edition (Fall/Winter) 1990:50–52.

Roof, Wade C., and William McKinney. *American Mainline Religion: Its Changing Shape and Future.* New Brunswick, NJ: Rutgers University Press, 1987.

Roof, Wade Clark. *A Generation of Seekers: The Spiritual Journeys of the Baby Boom Generation.* New York: HarperSanFrancisco, 1993.

———. "Looking Forward: Trends in American Religion: A Summary of the SSA Plenary Presentation." *Southwestern Sociological Association Presentation Newsletter* 24 (2) 1998:2.

Ropers, Richard H. *Persistent Poverty: The American Dream Turned Nightmare.* New York: Plenum, 1991.

Roschelle, Anne R. *No More Kin: Exploring Race, Class, and Gender in Family Networks.* Thousand Oaks, CA: Sage, 1997.

Rose, Arnold M. "The Subculture of Aging," in Arnold M. Rose and Warren A. Peterson (eds.), *Older People and Their Social World.* Philadelphia: F. A. Davis, 1965.

Rose, Peter I. *They and We: Racial and Ethnic Relations in the United States,* 4th ed. New York: McGraw-Hill, 1990.

Rose, Peter I., Myron Glazer, and Penina Migdal Glazer. *Tempest-Tost: Race, Immigration, and the Dilemmas of Diversity.* New York: Oxford University Press, 1997.

———. "In Controlled Environments: Four Cases of Intensive Resocialization," in Peter I. Rose (ed.), *Socialization and the Life Cycle.* New York: St. Martin's Press, 1979, pp. 323–325.

Rose, Tricia. "Rap Music Is Unfairly Blamed for Society's Violence," in Carol Wekesser (ed.), *Violence in the Media.* San Diego: Greenhaven Press, 1995, pp. 169–174.

Rosen, Gary. "Are School Vouchers Un-American?" *Commentary* (February) 2000.

Rosenau, James N. *Turbulence in World Politics: A Theory of Change and Continuity.* Princeton: Princeton University Press, 1990.

Rosenbaum, James E., and Amy Binder. "Do Employers Really Need More Educated Youth?" *Sociology of Education* 70 (January) 1997:68–85.

Rosenberg, Debra. "State of the 'Union.'" *Newsweek,* October 23, 2000:56–57.

———. "Breaking Up Is Hard to Do." *Newsweek,* July 7, 2003:44.

Rosenfeld, Isadore. "Alternative Medicine: Some Worth Trying." *USA Today,* March 20, 1997:13A.

Rosenthal, Robert, and Lenore Jacobson. *Pygmalion in the Classroom.* New York: Holt, Rinehart & Winston, 1968.

Rosman, Abraham, and Paula G. Rubel. *The Tapestry of Culture: An Introduction to Cultural Anthropology*, 7th ed. Boston, MA: McGraw Hill, 2001.

Ross, Catherine E. "Occupations, Jobs, and the Sense of Control." *Sociological Focus* 33 (October) 2000:409–419.

Ross, Robert J. S., and Kent C. Trachte. *Global Capitalism: The New Leviathan*. Albany: State University of New York Press, 1990.

Rossi, Robert J. *Schools and Students at Risk: Context and Framework for Positive Change*. New York: Teachers College, Columbia University, 1994.

Rossides, Daniel W. *Social Stratification: The Interplay of Class, Race, and Gender*, 2nd ed. Upper Saddle River, NJ: Prentice-Hall, 1998.

Rothman, Stanley, Stephen Powers, and David Rothman. "Feminism in Films." *Society* 30 (March/April) 1993:66–72.

Rothstein, Edward. "Damning (Yet Desiring) Mickey and the Big Mac." *The New York Times* on the Web, Saturday, March 2, 2002:1.

Rothstein, Stanley William. *Schools and Society: New Perspectives in American Education*. Englewood Cliffs, NJ: Merrill, 1996.

Rouse, Cecilia Elena. "Low-Income Students and College Attendance: An Exploration of Income Expectations. *Social Science Quarterly* 85 (December):1299-1317.

Rubin, David M., and David P. Sachs. *Mass Media and the Environment*. New York: Praeger, 1973.

Rubin, Rita. "Doctors Live with Risk, Fear of Treating AIDS Patients." *Dallas Morning News*, March 22, 1992:1A, 15A.

Rubinowitz, Leonard, and James E. Rosenbaum. *Crossing the Class and Color Lines: From Public Housing to White Suburbia*. Chicago: University of Chicago Press, 2000.

Rueschemeyer, Dietrich. *Power and the Division of Labour*. Palo Alto, CA: Stanford University Press, 1986.

Ruggie, Mary. "The Paradox of Liberal Intervention: Health Policy and the American Welfare State." *American Journal of Sociology* 97 (January) 1992:919–944.

Ruggiero, Vincent Ryan. *The Art of Thinking: A Guide to Critical and Creative Thought*, 6th ed. New York: Longman, 2000.

Rumbault, Rubin G. "The New Immigration." *Contemporary Sociology* 24 (4) 1995:307–311.

Russell, Charles H. *Good News about Aging in America*. New York: Wiley, 1999.

Rutter, Michael, Barbara Maughan, and Peter Mortimore, et al. *Fifteen Thousand Hours: Secondary Schools and Their Effects on Children*. Cambridge: Harvard University Press, 1980.

Ryan, Charlotte. *Prime-Time Activism Media Strategies for Grassroots Organizing*. Boston: South End, 1991.

Rykwert, Joseph. *Seduction of Place: The City in the Twenty-first Century and Beyond*. New York: Pantheon, 2000.

Rytina, Steven. "Is Occupational Mobility Declining in the U.S.?" *Social Forces* 78 (4) June 2000:1227–1276.

Sabato, Larry J. *PAC Power*. New York: Norton, 1985.

———. *Feeding Frenzy: How Attack Journalism Has Transformed American Politics*. New York: Free Press, 1991.

Sachs, Susan. "Arab Media Portray War as a Killing Field." *The New York Times* on the Web, Friday, April 4, 2003:1–4.

Sadovnik, Alan R. "Basil Bernstein's Theory of Pedagogic Practice: A Structuralist Approach." *Sociology of Education* 64 (January) 1991: 48–63.

Safire, William. "On Media Giantism." *The New York Times* on the Web, Monday, January 20, 2003:1–2.

Salholz, Eloise, Daniel Glick, and Lucille Beachy, et al. "The Power and the Pride." *Newsweek*, June 21, 1993:54–60.

Saltman, Richard B. "Sweden," in Richard B. Saltman (ed.), *The International Handbook of Health-Care Systems*. New York: Greenwood Press, 1988, pp. 285–294.

Sampson, Robert J., and John H. Laub. "Crime and Deviance over the Life Course: The Salience of Adult Social Bonds." *American Sociological Review* 55 (October) 1990:609–627.

Samuelson, Robert J. "The Mysterious Merger Frenzy." *Newsweek*, October 16, 2000:55.

Sandberg, Jared. "What Do They Do On-Line?" *Wall Street Journal*, December 9, 1996:R6.

Sapir, Edward. "The Status of Linguistics as a Science." *Language* 5, 1929:207–214.

———. *Selected Writings of Edward Sapir in Language, Culture and Personality*. David G. Mandelbaum (ed.). Berkeley: University of California Press, 1949.

Sassen, Saskia. *Cities in a World Economy*. Thousand Oaks, CA: Pine Forge, 1994.

———. *Globalization and Its Discontents*. New York: New Press, 1998.

Sasson, Theodore. "Crime Frames and Their Sponsors," in Joel Best and Donileen R. Loseke (eds.), *Social Problems: Constructionist Readings*. New York: Aldine de Gruyter, 2003, pp. 88–92.

Savage, Mike, Gaynor Bagnall, and Brian J. Longhurst. *Globalization and Belonging*. Thousand Oaks, CA: Pine Forge Press, 2005.

Sawin, Janet L. "Water Scarcity Could Overwhelm the Next Generation." *World Watch* 16 (July–August) 2003:8.

Sayers, Janet. "Science, Sexual Difference, and Feminism," in Beth B. Hess and Myra Marx Ferree (eds.), *Analyzing Gender: A Handbook of Social Science Research*. Newbury Park, CA: Sage, 1987, pp. 68–91.

Scanlan, James P. "Race and Mortality." *Society* 37 (2) January/February 2000:29–35.

Schaefer, Richard T. *Racial and Ethnic Groups*, 5th ed. New York: HarperCollins, 1993.

Scheff, Thomas J. "Shame and Conformity: The Deference-Emotion System." *American Sociological Review* 53 (June) 1988:395–406.

Scheider, Matthew C. "Moving Past Biological Determinism in Discussions of Women and Crime During the 1870s–1920s: A Note Regarding the Literature." *Deviant Behavior* 21 (September–October) 2000:407–427.

Scheitle, Christopher P. "In God We Trust: Religion and Optimism Toward Biotechnology." *Social Science Quarterly* 86 (December), 2005:846-856.

Schell, Jonathan. "No More unto the Breach—Part I." *Harper's Magazine* 306 (1834) March 2003:33–46.

Schell, Orville. "Sending 'Liberal Media' Truism to the Fact-Checker." *The New York Times* on the Web, March 20, 2003:1–3.

Scheper-Hughes, Nancy. "The Global Traffic in Human Organs." *Current Anthropology* 41 (2) April 2000:191–224.

Schick, Theodore, Jr., and Lewis Vaughn. *How to Think About Weird Things: Critical Thinking for a New Age*. Mountain View, CA: Mayfield, 1995.

Schiesel, Seth. "Security Cameras Now Learn to React." *The New York Times* on the Web, Thursday, March 6, 2003:1–2.

Schlesinger, Arthur M., Jr. *The Disunity of America: Reflections on a Multicultural Society*. New York: Norton, 1992.

Schmid, Alex P., and Albert J. Jongman. *Political Terrorism: a New Guide to Actors, Authors, Concepts, Data Bases, Theories, and Literature*. New Brunswick, NJ: Transaction Books, 1988.

Schmidt, Steffen W., Mack C. Shelley II, and Barbara A. Bardes. *American Government and Politics Today*. New York: West, 1985.

Schofield, Janet Ward, Rebecca Eurich-Fulcer, and Cheri L. Britt. "Teachers, Computer Tutors, and Teaching: The Artificially Intelligent Tutor as an Agent for Classroom Change." *American Educational Research Journal* 31 (Fall) 1994:579–607.

Schoolland, Ken. *Shogun's Ghost: The Dark Side of Japanese Education*. New York: Bergin & Garvey, 1990.

Schrag, Peter. "Bush's Education Fraud." Pp. 120-126 in in Knoll, James Wm. (ed.), *Taking Sides: Clashing Views on Educational Issues* (14th ed.), Guilford, CT: McGraw-Hill/Dushkin, 2007.

Schultz, Emily A., and Robert H. Lavenda. *Cultural Anthropology: A Perspective on the Human Condition*, 6th ed. New York: Oxford University Press, 2005.

Schultz, Fred. "A Look to the Future," in Fred Schultz (ed.), *Annual Editions, Education 94/95*, 21st ed. Guilford, CT: Dushkin, 1994, pp. 222–223.

Schuman, David. *American Schools, American Teachers: Issues and Perspectives*. Boston: Allyn & Bacon, 2004.

Schur, Edwin M. *Labeling Deviant Behavior*. New York: HarperCollins, 1971.

Schwab, William A. *Urban Sociology: A Human Ecological Perspective*. Reading, MA: Addison-Wesley, 1982.

Schwartz, Barry. "Capitalism, the Market, the 'Underclass,' and the Future." *Society* 37 (November/December) 1999:33-42.

Schwartz, John. "Two New Studies Link Hurricane Intensity and Global Warming." http://www.iht.com/articles/2006/05/31/news /storms.php *New York Times*, May 31, 2006.

Schwartz, John, and Matthew L. Wald. "'Groupthink' Is 30 Years Old, and Still Going Strong." *The New York Times* on the Web, Sunday, March 9, 2003:1–2.

Schwartz, Pepper. *Peer Marriage: How Love between Equals Really Works*. New York: Free Press, 1994.

Schwartz, Pepper, and Virginia Rutter. *The Gender of Sexuality*. Thousand Oaks, CA: Pine Forge Press, 1998.

Schwendinger, Herman, and Julia Schwendinger. *Adolescent Subcultures and Delinquency*. New York: Praeger, 1985.

Scott, John. "Networks of Corporate Power: A Comparative Assessment." *Annual Review of Sociology* 17, 1991:181–203.

Scott, Ralph. "Tracking in Schools: Can American Social Scientists Objectify Such a Sensitive Topic?" *Mankind Quarterly* 42 (December), 2001:47-52.

Seaberry, Jane. "U.S. Unemployment Rate Falls to 4.3%, Lowest Level since '70." *Dallas Morning News*, May 9, 1998:1A, 20A.

Seabrook, Jeremy. *Victims of Development: Resistance and Alternatives*. London: Verso, 1996.

Sebald, Hans. *Adolescence: A Sociological Analysis*. New York: Appleton-Century-Crofts, 1968.

———. "Adolescents' Shifting Orientation toward Parents and Peers: A Curvilinear Trend over Recent Decades." *Journal of Marriage and the Family* 48, 1986:5–13.

Sebastian, Matt. "Living in a Surveillance Society." *Emporia Gazette*, Section 3, June 7–8, 2003:3.

Seccombe, Karen. *"So You Think I Drive a Cadillac?": Welfare Recipients' Perspectives on the System of Welfare Reform.* Boston, MA: Allyn & Bacon, 1999.

Seeman, Melvin, Teresa Seeman, and Marnie Sayles. "Social Networks and Health Status: A Longitudinal Analysis." *Social Psychology Quarterly* 48 (3) 1985:237–248.

Seligmann, Jean. "Variations on a Theme." *Newsweek* special issue (Winter/Spring) 1990:38–46.

Sella, Marshall. "The Stiff Guy vs. the Dumb Guy." *New York Times Magazine*, September 24, 2000:72–80, 102.

Sen, Gita. "The World Programme of Action: A New Paradigm for Population Policy." *Environment* 37 (January/February) 1995:10–15, 34–37.

Seper, Jerry. "Racist Ways Die Hard at Lawmen's Retreat: Annual 'Good O' Boys Roundup' cited as evidence of 'Klan Attitude' at ATF." *Washington Times*, July 11, 1995:1.

Settersten, Richard A., Jr., and Karl Ulrich Mayer. "The Measurement of Age, Age Structuring, and the Life Course," in John Hagan and Karen S. Cook (eds.), *Annual Review of Sociology* 23. Palo Alto, CA: Annual Reviews, 1997, pp. 233–261.

Shah, Angela. "Tech Job Squeeze Goes White-Collar." *Dallas Morning News*, August 1, 2003:1A, 24A.

Shane, Harold G. "Improving Education for the Twenty-First Century." *Educational Horizons* 69 (Fall) 1990:11–15.

Shaoguang, Wang, and Hu Angang. *The Political Economy of Uneven Development: The Case of China*. Armonk, New York: M. E. Sharpe, 1999.

Shapiro, Laura. "Guns and Dolls." *Newsweek*, May 28, 1990:56–65.

Sharn, Lori. "Clergy Still Tough Career for Women." *USA Today*, July 9, 1997:1A.

Sharp, Susan F. "Relationships with Children and AIDS-Risk Behavior Among Female IDUs." *Deviant Behavior* 19 (January–March), 1998: 3–28.

Shattuck, Roger. *The Forbidden Experiment*. New York: Farrar, Straus & Giroux, 1980.

Shavit, Ari. "Vanishing." *New York Times Magazine*, June 8, 1997:52.

Sheehy, Gail. *Passages: Predictable Crises of Adult Life*. New York: Bantam Books, 1976.

———. *The Silent Passage: Menopause*. New York: Pocket Books, 1993.

———. "Life Begins at 60." *Parade Magazine*, December 11, 2005:4-6.

Sheets, Gregory L., and Jack Bynum. "The Social Consequences of Nuclear War: Toward a Theoretical Understanding." *Quarterly Journal of Ideology* 13 (November) 1989:13–21.

Shelton, Beth Anne. "Understanding the Distribution of Housework Between Husbands and Wives," in Christine Bachrack, Michelle Hindin, Elizabeth Thomsom, and Arland Thornton (eds.), *Ties That Bind: Perspectives on Marriage and Cohabitation*. New York: Aldine De Gruyter, 2000:343–355.

Shen, Dingli. "What Missile Defense Says to China." *Bulletin of the Atomic Scientists* 56 (4) July/August 2000:20-21.

Shepherd, Michael S. "Home Schooling: A Legal View," in Anne Pedersen and Peggy O'Mara (eds.), *Schooling at Home: Parents, Kids, and Learning*. Santa Fe: John Muir, 1990, pp. 57–66.

Sherif, Muzafer. *The Psychology of Social Norms*. New York: HarperCollins, 1936.

Sherman, Arnold K., and Aliza Kolker. *The Social Bases of Politics*. Belmont, CA: Wadsworth, 1987.

Shirk, Martha, Neil G. Bennett, and J. Lawrence Aber. *Lives on the Line: American Families and the Struggle to Make Ends Meet*. Boulder, CO: Westview, 1999.

Shkedi, Asher. "The Tension between 'Ought' and 'Is': Teachers' Conceptions of the Encounter between Students and Culturally Valued Texts." *Educational Research* 39 (Spring) 1997: 65–76.

Shostak, Arthur B. *CyberUnion: Empowering Labor Through Computer Technology*. New York: M. E. Sharpe, 1999.

———. *Cyberunion: Empowering Labor Through Computer Technology*. Armonk, NY: M. E. Sharpe, 2000a.

———. "Teaching Utopia." *The Futurist* 34 (September–October) 2000b:68.

"Show-Guide: Married by America," *AllYourTV.com*, June 24, 2003.

Shrum, Wesley. "Critics and Publics: Cultural Mediation in Highbrow and Popular Performing Arts." *American Journal of Sociology* 97 (September) 1991:347–375.

Shupe, Anson, and Jeffrey K. Hadden. "Is There Such a Thing as Global Fundamentalism?" in Jeffrey K. Hadden and Anson Shupe (eds.), *Secularization and Fundamentalism Reconsidered: Religion and the Political Order*, vol. 3. New York: Paragon, 1989, pp. 109–122.

Sieberg, Daniel. "War Games: Military Training Goes High-Tech." *CNN.com*, Sci-Tech, November 23, 2001:1–2.

Siegfried, Tom. "Of Mice, Men and Behavior: Scripting Reveals Flaws of Nature vs. Nurture Debate." *Dallas Morning News*, May 12, 2003:1E.

Simmel, Georg. *Conflict and the Web of Group Affiliations*. New York: Free Press, [1908] 1955.

Simmons, Rachel. *Odd Girl Out: The Hidden Culture of Aggression in Girls*. New York: Harvest Books, 2003.

Simmons, William Paul. "Beliefs in Conspiracy Theories Among African Americans: A Comparison of Elites and Masses." *Social Science Quarterly* 86 (September), 2005:582-598.

Simon, David R. *Elite Deviance*, 8th ed. Boston: Allyn & Bacon, 2006.

Simon, Julian L. "Life on Earth Is Getting Better, Not Worse." *The Futurist* 17 (August) 1983:7–14.

———. "Why Do We Hear Prophecies of Doom from Every Side?" *The Futurist* 29 (January/February) 1995:19–23.

Simon, Richard K. *Trash Culture: Popular Culture and the Great Tradition*. Berkeley, CA: University of California Press, 1999.

Simpson, George E., and J. Milton Yinger. *Racial and Cultural Minorities*, 4th ed. New York: HarperCollins, 1972.

Singer, Eleanor. "Reference Groups and Social Evaluation," in Morris Rosenberg and Ralph Turner (eds.), *Social Psychology*. New York: Basic Books, 1981.

Singer, Eleanor, and Phyllis Endreny. "The Reporting of Social Science Research in the Mass Media," in Sandra J. Ball-Rokeach and Muriel G. Cantor (eds.), *Media, Audience, and Social Structure*. Newbury Park, CA: Sage, 1986, pp. 293–312.

Singley, Susan, Glenn Firebaugh, and Anna Chase. "American Sociological Review Authorship Patterns: Are There Gender Differences?" *ASR Footnotes* 26 (April) 1998:1, 6.

Sinick, David. "Attitudes and Values in Aging." *Counseling and Values* 24 (3) 1980:148–154.

Sink, Mindy. "Spiritual Issues Lead Many to the Net." *The New York Times* on the Web, September 6, 2003:1.

Sizer, Theodore R. *Horace's Compromise: The Dilemma of the American High School*. Boston: Houghton Mifflin, 1984.

Skal, David J. *The Monster Show: A Cultural History of Horror*. New York: Norton, 1993.

Skerry, Peter. *Counting the Census? Race, Group Identity, and the Evasion of Politics*. Washington, DC: Brookings Institution Press, 2000.

Skill, Thomas, Samuel Wallace, and Mary Cassata. "Families on Prime-Time Television: Patterns of Conflict Escalation and Resolution across Intact, Nonintact, and Mixed Family Settings," in Jennings Bryant (ed.), *Television and the American Family*. Hillsdale, NJ: Erlbaum, 1990, pp. 129–164.

Skipp. Catharine, and Arian Campo-Flores. "The Web Ate My Homework," *Newsweek*, August 4, 2003:10.

Skipper, James K., Jr., and Charles H. McCaghy. "Stripteasers: The Anatomy and Career Contingencies of a Deviant Occupation." *Social Problems* 17 (3) 1970:391–404.

Skocpol, Theda. *States and Social Revolutions: A Comparative Analysis of France, Russia, and China*. New York: Cambridge University Press, 1979.

———. *Social Policy in the United States: Future Possibilities in Historical Perspective*. Princeton: Princeton University Press, 1995.

———. *The Missing Middle: Working Families and the Future of American Social Policy*. New York: W. W. Norton, 2000.

Skocpol, Theda, and Edwin Amenta. "States and Social Policies." *Annual Review of Sociology* 12, 1986:131–157.

Skogan, Wesley G. *Community Policing: Chicago Style*. New York: Oxford University Press, 1997.

Skolnick, Arlene S. *Embattled Paradise: The American Family in an Age of Uncertainty*. New York: Basic Books, 1991.

Skolnick, Arlene S. and Jerome H. Skolnick. *Family in Transition* (14th ed.). Boston: Allyn and Bacon, 2007.

Slater, Philip. *The Pursuit of Loneliness*. Boston: Beacon, 1976.

Slevin, Peter, and Glenn Frankel. "Libya Vows to Give Up Banned Weapons." *Washingtonpost.com*. Saturday, December 20, 2003: *A01–A06.

Sloan, Allan. "A Blissful Dream, a Rude Awakening." *Newsweek*, February 5, 2001:45.

Smeeding, Timothy M. "Public Policy, Economic Inequality, and Poverty: The United States in Comparative Perspective." *Social Science Quarterly* 86 (Special Issue), 2005:955-983.

Smelser, Neil J. *Theory of Collective Behavior*. New York: Free Press, 1962.

———. "Culture Coherent or Incoherent," in Richard Munch and Neil J. Smelser (eds.), *Theory of Culture*. Berkeley: University of California Press, 1992, pp. 3–28.

Smith, Allen C., III, and Sherryl Kleinman. "Managing Emotions in Medical School: Students'

Contacts with the Living and the Dead." *Social Psychology Quarterly* 52 (March) 1989: 56–69.

Smith, Craig. "Beware of Cross-Cultural Faux Pas in China." *The New York Times* on the Web, Tuesday, April 30, 2002:1–3.

Smith, Joel. "A Methodology for Twenty-First Century Sociology." *Social Forces* 70 (September) 1991:1–17.

Smith, Page. *Killing the Spirit: Higher Education in America*. New York: Viking Penguin, 1990.

Smith, Vicki. "New Forms of Work Organization." *Annual Review of Sociology* 23. Palo Alto, CA: Annual Reviews, 1997.

Smock, Pamela J. "Cohabitation in the United States: An Appraisal of Research Themes, Findings, and Implications." *Annual Review of Sociology* 26 2000:1–20.

Snow, David A., and Robert D. Benford. "Ideology, Frame Resonance, and Participant Mobilization." *International Social Movement Research* 1, 1988:197–217.

Snow, David A., E. Burke Rochford Jr., and Steven K. Worden, et al. "Frame Alignment Processes, Micromobilization, and Movement Participation." *American Sociological Review* 51 (August) 1986:464–481.

Snow, David A., Louis A. Zurcher Jr., and Sheldon Ekland-Olson. "Social Networks and Social Movements: Differential Recruitment." *American Sociological Review* 45 (October) 1980: 787–801.

So, Alvin Y. *Social Change and Development: Modernization, Dependency, and World System Theories*. Newbury Park, CA: Sage, 1990.

So, Alvin Y., and Stephen W. K. Chiu. "Modern East Asia in World-Systems Analysis." *Sociological Inquiry* 66 (4) 1996:471–485.

"Social Science and the Citizen." *Society* 40 (5) July/August 2003:1–8.

Solis, Dianne. "African-Americans Being Hurt Most by Joblessness." *Dallas Morning News*, July 21, 2003:1D, 2D.

Solis, Dianne and Isabel C. Morales. "Hispanic-White Job Divide Grows." *Dallas Morning News*, December 15, 2005:1A; 4A.

Sollie, Donna L. "Beyond Mars and Venus: Men and Women in the Real World." *National Forum* 80 (3) Summer 2000:42.

Solomon, Robert, and Jon Solomon. *Up the University: Re-creating Higher Education in America*. Reading, MA: Addison-Wesley, 1993.

Sommers-Flanagan, Rita, John Sommers-Flanagan, and Britta Davis. "What's Happening on Music Television? A Gender Role Content Analysis." *Sex Roles* 28 (June) 1993:745–754.

Sorokin, Pitirim. *The Crisis of Our Age*. New York: Dutton, 1941.

Sorokin, Pitirim, and Carle Zimmerman. *Principles of Rural-Urban Sociology*. New York: Holt, Rinehart & Winston, 1929.

South, Scott J., and Glenna Spitze. "Housework in Marital and Nonmarital Households." *American Sociological Review* 59 (June) 1994: 327–347.

Spanier, Bonnie B. "Sexism and Scientific Research." *National Forum* 77 (Spring) 1997:26–30.

Spaulding, John D. "Bonding in the Bleachers: A Visit to the Promise Keepers." *Christian Century* 113 (8) 1996:260–265.

Spengler, Oswald. *The Decline of the West*. New York: Knopf, [1922] 1962.

Spicker, Paul. *Poverty and Social Security: Concepts and Principles*. New York: Routledge, 1993.

Spitzer, Steven. "Toward a Marxian Theory of Deviance," in Delow H. Kelly (ed.), *Criminal Behavior: Readings in Criminology*. New York: St. Martin's Press, 1980, pp. 175–191.

Spradley, James P. *The Ethnographic Interview*. New York: Holt, Rinehart & Winston, 1979.

———. *Participant Observation*. New York: Holt, Rinehart & Winston, 1980.

Spradley, James P., and Brenda J. Mann. *The Cocktail Waitress: Woman's Work in a Man's World*. New York: Knopf, 1975.

Springen, Karen. "On Spanking." *Newsweek*, October 16, 2000:64.

———. "Why We Tuned Out." *Newsweek*, November 11, 2002:60.

Squitieri, Tom. "Africa's Quandary: More People, Less Food." *USA Today*, August 31, 1994:2A.

Srivastava, Sanjay, Oliver P. John, Samuel D. Gosling, and Jeff Potter. "Development of Personality in Early and Middle Adulthood: Set Like Plaster or Persistent Change?" *Journal of Personality and Social Psychology* 84 (5) 2003:1027–1040.

St. Jean, Yanick, and Joe R. Feagin. *Double-Burden: Black Women and Everyday Racism*. New York: M. E. Sharpe, 1998.

Stacey, Judith. "Gay and Lesbian Families Are Here: All Our Families Are Queer; Let's Get Used to It!" in Stephanie Coontz, Maya Parson, and Gabrielle Raley (eds.), *American Families: A Multicultural Reader*, New York: Routledge, 1999, pp. 372–405.

Stack, Steven. "Celebrities and Suicide: A Taxonomy and Analysis, 1948–1983." *American Sociological Review* 52 (June) 1987a:401–412.

———. "Publicized Executions and Homicide, 1950–1980." *American Sociological Review* 52 (August) 1987b:532–540.

———. "Execution Publicity and Homicide in South Carolina: A Research Note." *Sociological Quarterly* 31 (4) 1990a:599–611.

———. "New Micro-Level Data on the Impact of Divorce on Suicide, 1959–1980: A Test of Two Theories." *Journal of Marriage and the Family* 52 (February) 1990b:119–127.

———. "The Effects of Gender on Publishing: The Case of Sociology." *Sociological Focus* 27 (February) 1994:81–83.

———. "Gender and Scholarly Productivity: 1970–2000." *Sociological Focus* 35 (August) 2000:285–296.

———. "Media Impacts on Suicide: A Quantitative Review of 293 Findings." *Social Science Quarterly* 81 (December) 2000:957–971.

Stanley, Alessandra. "For Women, To Soar Is Rare, To Fall Is Human." *The New York Times* on the Web, January 13, 2002:1–5.

Staples, William G. *The Culture of Surveillance: Discipline and Control in the United States*. New York: St. Martin's Press, 1997.

Stark, Rodney, and William S. Bainbridge. *The Future of Religion: Secularization, Revival and Cult Formation*. Berkeley: University of California Press, 1985.

Stark, Rodney, and Roger Finke. *Acts of Faith: Explaining the Human Side of Religion*. Berkeley, CA: University of California Press, 2000.

Starr, Mark, and Martha Brant. "It Went Down to the Wire and Thrilled Us All." *Newsweek*, July 19, 1999:46–54.

Steele, Claude M. "Race and the Schooling of Black Americans." *The Atlantic Monthly* 269 (April) 1992:68–78.

Steelman, Lala Carr, and Brian Powell. "Acquiring Capital for College: The Constraints of Family Configuration." *American Sociological Review* 54 (October) 1989:844–855.

———. "Sponsoring the Next Generation: Parental Willingness to Pay for Higher Education." *American Journal of Sociology* 96 (May) 1991:1505–1529.

Steiger, Thomas L., and Mark Wardell. "Gender and Employment in the Service Sector." *Social Problems* 42 (February) 1995:91–123.

Stein, Leonard I. "The Doctor-Nurse Game." *Archives of General Psychiatry* 16, 1967:699–703.

Stein, Rob. "AIDS Increase is First in a Decade." *Dallas Morning News*, July 29, 2003:4A.

Steinberg, Jacques. "Schools Nationwide Struggle with Principal Shortage." *Dallas Morning News*, September 3, 2000:11A.

———. "After 25 Years, a Road Map for Diversity on Campus." *The New York Times* on the Web, Politics, June 24, 2003:1–4.

Steinberg, Stephen. *Turning Back: The Retreat from Racial Justice in American Thought and Policy*. Boston: Beacon, 1995.

Steitz, Jean A., and Tulita P. Owen. "School Activities and Work: Effects on Adolescent Self-Esteem." *Adolescence* 27 (Spring) 1992:37–50.

Stengel, Richard. "Resentment Tinged with Envy." *Time*, July 8, 1985:56.

Stenson, Jacqueline. "The Future of Babymaking," *MSN, MSNBC News, Health/Fertility*, July 23, 2003:1–7.

Stephens, Lowndes F. "Children and Youth Audiences," in Erwin K. Thomas and Brown H. Carpenter (eds.), *Handbook on Mass Media in the United States: The Industry and Its Audiences*. Westport, CT: Greenwood Press, 1994, pp. 231–250.

Steslicke, William E. "Japan," in Richard B. Saltman (ed.), *The International Handbook of Health-Care Systems*. New York: Greenwood Press, 1988, pp. 173–197.

Stevenson, Richard, W. "Bush Urges Congress to Extend Welfare Law, with Changes." *The New York Times* on the Web, Wednesday, January 15, 2003:1–2.

Stewart, Jocelyn Y. "School Officials Taking Verbal Threats More Seriously." *Dallas Morning News*, May 3, 1998:4A.

Stiglitz, Joseph E. *Globalization and Its Discontents*. New York: W. W. Norton, 2002.

Stiles, Beverly L., and Howard B. Kaplan. "Stigma, Deviance, and Negative Social Sanctions." *Social Science Quarterly* 77 (September) 1996:685–696.

Stockard, Jean, and Miriam M. Johnson. *Sex Roles: Sex Inequality and Sex Role Development*. Englewood Cliffs, NJ: Prentice-Hall, 1980.

Stockard, Jean, and Robert M. O'Brien. "Cohort Effects on Suicide Rates: International Variations." *American Sociological Review* 67 (December) 2002:854–872.

Stohlberg, Sheryl Gay. "Medical Racism Alleged." *Dallas Morning News*, March 21, 2002:1A, 17A.

Stone, Brad. "The Keyboard Kids." *Newsweek*, June 8, 1998:72–74.

Stonequist, Everett H. *The Marginal Man*. New York: Scribner, 1937.

Stoner, James A. F. *A Comparison of Individual and Group Decisions Involving Risk*. Unpublished master's thesis, Massachusetts Institute of Technology, 1961.

Straus, Murray A., *Beating the Devil Out of Them: Corporal Punishment in American Families*. New York: Lexington Books, 1994.

Straus, Murray A., and Richard J. Gelles. "Societal Change and Change in Family Violence from

1975 to 1985 as Revealed by Two National Surveys." *Journal of Marriage and the Family* 48 (August) 2006:465–479.

Straus, Murray A., Richard J. Gelles, and Suzanne K. Steinmetz. *Behind Closed Doors: Violence in the American Family.* Somerset, NJ: Transaction Publishers, 2006.

Strong, Bryan, Christine DeVault, and Barbara W. Sayad. *Marriage and Family Experience: Intimate Relationships in a Changing Society,* 7th ed. Belmont, CA: Wadsworth, 1998.

Strossen, Nancy. *Defending Pornography: Free Speech, Sex, and the Fight for Women's Rights.* New York: Scribner, 1995.

Stryker, Robin. "Science, Class, and the Welfare State: A Class-Centered Functional Account." *American Journal of Sociology* 96 (November) 1990:684–726.

———. "Rules, Resources, and Legitimacy Processes: Some Implications for Social Conflict, Order, and Change." *American Journal of Sociology* 99 (January) 1994:847–910.

Stryker, Sheldon. "The Vitalization of Symbolic Interactionism." *Social Psychology Quarterly* 50 (March) 1987:83–94.

Stutz, Terrence. "TAAS Rated Second-Best in Nation." *Dallas Morning News,* June 10, 2002:19A.

———. "Most Say School Testing Overemphasized." *Dallas Morning News,* February 22, 2006:3A.

Sudnow, David. *Passing On: The Social Organization of Dying.* Englewood Cliffs, NJ: Prentice-Hall, 1967.

Suhler, Jayne Noble. "Survey Finds Collegians Want High-Tech Learning." *Dallas Morning News,* September 4, 1997:25A.

Sullivan, John. "Charges against Danish Mother Dropped." *New York Times,* May 17, 1997:A23.

Sumner, William Graham. *Folkways.* Boston: Ginn, 1906.

Surette, Ray. *Media, Crime and Criminal Justice: Images and Realities.* Belmont, CA: Brooks/Cole, 1992.

Surra, Catherine A. "Research and Theory on Mate Selection and Premarital Relationships in the 1980s." *Journal of Marriage and the Family* 52 (November) 1990:844–865.

Sutcliffe, Steven J. *Children of the New Age: A History of Spiritual Practices.* New York: Routledge, 2003.

Sutherland, Edwin, and Donald Cressey. *Principles of Criminology.* Philadelphia: Lippincott, 1978.

Svensson, Peter. "Men Take on Responsibility for Aging Parents." *Dallas Morning News,* July 29, 2003:2E.

Swann, William B., Jr. "The Self is Not a Bowling Ball," in John M. Darley and Joel Cooper (eds.), *Attribution and Social Interaction: The Legacy of Edward E. Jones.* Washington, DC: American Psychological Association, 1998, pp. 399–407.

Swartz, Marc J., and David K. Jordan. *Anthropology: Perspective on Humanity.* New York: Wiley, 1976.

Sweeney, Richard. *Out of Place: Homelessness in America.* New York, HarperCollins, 1993.

Swomley, John M. "Storm Troopers in the Cultural War." *The Humanist* (September/October) 1997:8–13.

Sykes, Gresham M., and David Matza. "Techniques of Neutralization: A Theory of Delinquency." *American Sociological Review* 22 (December) 1957:664–670.

Sztompka, Piotr. *Society in Action: The Theory of Social Becoming.* Chicago: University of Chicago Press, 1991.

Talwar, Jennifer P. *Fast Food, Fast Track: Immigrants, Big Business, and the American Dream.* Boulder, CO: Westview, 2002.

Tan, Alexis S. "Social Learning of Aggression from Television," in Jennings Bryant and Dolf Zillmann (eds.), *Perspectives on Media Effects.* Hillsdale, NJ: Erlbaum, 1986, pp. 41–55.

Tanaka, Jennifer. "Foiling the Rogues." *Newsweek,* October 27, 1997:80.

Taniguchi, Hiromi. "Determinants of Women's Entry into Self-Employment." *Social Science Quarterly* 83 (September) 2002:875–893.

Tannen, Deborah. *You Just Don't Understand: Women and Men in Conversation.* New York: Harper Paperbacks, 2001.

———. "Interview." *Dallas Morning News,* April 12, 1998:1J, 10J.

———. *You're Wearing That?: Understanding Mothers and Daughters in Conversation.* New York: Random House, 2006.

Tarrant, David. "Mixed Messages: Should Race Still Matter to Generation Y?" *Dallas Morning News,* January 12, 2006:4A.

Task Force. *Outcasts on Main Street: Report of the Federal Task Force on Homelessness and Severe Mental Illness.* Washington, DC: U.S. Department of Health and Human Services, 1992.

Tausky, Curt. *Work and Society: An Introduction to Industrial Sociology.* Itasca, IL: Peacock, 1984.

Taverner, William J. (Ed.). *Taking Sides: Clashing Views on Controversial Issues in Human Sexuality* (9th ed.). Guilford, CT: McGraw-Hill/Dushkin, 2006.

Taxpayers for Common Sense Website. "The Golden Fleece Award," July 12, 2003.

Taylor, Ella. *Prime-Time Families: Television Culture in Postwar America.* Berkeley: University of California Press, 1989.

Taylor, Robert J., Linda M. Chatters, and M. Belinda Tucker, et al. "Developments in Research on Black Families: A Decade Review." *Journal of Marriage and the Family* 52 (November) 1990:993–1014.

Taylor, Ronald L. "Black American Families," in Ronald L. Taylor (ed.), *Minority Families in the United States: A Multicultural Perspective.* Englewood Cliffs, NJ: Prentice-Hall, 1994, pp. 19–45.

Taylor, Rosemarye. "Instructional Innovation: Components for Accelerated Implementation." *American Secondary Education* 19 (2) 1991:13–15.

Taylor, Verta. "Mobilizing for Change in a Social Movement Society. "*Contemporary Sociology* 29 (1) January 2000:219–230.

———. *Working: People Talk About What They Do All Day and How They Feel about What They Do.* New York: Pantheon, 1972.

Terkel, Studs. *Race: How Blacks and Whites Think and Feel About the American Obsession.* New York: New Press, 1992.

Tester, Keith. "Between Sociology and Theology: The Spirit of Capitalism Debate." *The Sociological Review* 48 (February) 2000:43–57.

Tetrault, Mary Kay Thompson. "Levels of Feminist Phase Theory," in Jodi Wetzel, Margo Linn Espenlaub, and Monys A. Hagen, et al. (eds.), *Women's Studies: Thinking Women,* rev. ed. Dubuque, IA: Kendall Hunt, 1993, pp. 21–24.

Tetzlaff, David. "Popular Culture and Social Control in Late Capitalism," in Paddy Scannell, Philip Schlesinger, and Colin Sparks (eds.), *Culture and Power: A Media, Culture and Society Reader.* Newbury Park, CA: Sage, 1992, pp. 48–72.

Tewksbury, Richard. "'Speaking of Someone With AIDS . . .': Identity Constructions of Persons with HIV Disease." *Deviant Behavior* 15 (October/December) 1994:337–355.

Tewksbury, Richard. "Bareback Sex and the Quest for HIV: Assessing the Relationship in Internet Personal Advertisements of Men Who Have Sex with Men." *Deviant Behavior* 24 (September/October) 2003:467–482.

The Dallas Morning News. Thursday, January 16, 2003:4A.

The Economist. "Chinese Tunnel Through the Net." February 7, 1998a:43.

———. "Cultural Food Preferences." February 7, 1998b:31.

———. "The Keenest Recruits to the Dream." April 25/May 1998c:25–27.

———. "I, Thee, We, Them." June 20–26, 1998e:31.

———. "The World as a Single Machine," June 20–26, 1998f:3–4.

———. "The Poor Who Are Always With Us." 356 (8177) July 1, 2000:46.

———. "Take It Block by Block," January 25, 2003a:35.

———. "Bush, Hero or Hypocrite?" May 31, 2003b:67–68.

The Futurist. "Fads and Trends." March/April 2000a:67.

———. "Society: Living Faster and Faster." March/April 2000b:18–19.

———. "Trends in Premarital Childbearing." March/April 2000c:9.

Theo, Alex. *Sociology,* 5th ed. New York: Longman, 1998.

The Irish Times. "The Hidden Downside of Santa's Little Helpers." December 21, 2002.

The World Bank. "World Development Report 2000/2001." New York: World Bank Reports, 2000.

Thio, Alex. *Deviant Behavior* (8th ed.). Boston: Allyn & Bacon, 2006.

Thomas, Evan. "The War Over Gay Marriage," *Newsweek,* July 7, 2003:39–45.

Thomas, Evan, and Gregory L. Vistica. "A Question of Consent." *Newsweek,* April 28, 1997.

Thomas, George M. *Revivalism and Cultural Change: Christianity, Nation Building, and the Market in the Nineteenth-Century United States.* Chicago: University of Chicago Press, 1989.

Thomas, Melvin E., and Linda A. Treiber. "Race, Gender, and Status: A Content Analysis of Print Advertisements in Four Popular Magazines." *Sociological Spectrum* 20 (July–September) 2000:357–371.

Thomas, Rich. "A Walk in Space." *Newsweek,* October 4, 1993:46–49.

Thomas, Susan L. *Gender and Poverty.* New York: Garland, 1994.

Thomas, William I. *The Unadjusted Girl.* Boston: Little, Brown, 1931.

Thomas, William I., and Dorothy Thomas. *The Child in America.* New York: Knopf, 1928.

Thompson, Kenneth W. "Ubiquity of Power." *Society* 28 (November/December) 1990:56–65.

Thompson, William E. "The Oklahoma Amish: Survival of an Ethnic Subculture." *Ethnicity* 8 (December) 1981:476–487.

———. "Hanging Tongues: A Sociological Encounter with the Assembly Line." *Qualitative Sociology* 6 (Fall) 1983:215–237.

———. "Old Order Amish in Oklahoma and Kansas: Rural Tradition in Urban Society."

Free Inquiry in Creative Sociology 12 (May) 1984:39–43.

———. "Deviant Ideology: The Case of the Old Order Amish." *Quarterly Journal of Ideology* 10 (1), 1986:29–33.

———. "Handling the Stigma of Handling the Dead: Morticians and Funeral Directors." *Deviant Behavior* 12 (Spring) 1991:403–429.

———. *The Glass House.* Campbell, TX: Seasons of Harvest, 2006.

Thompson, William E., and Jackie L. Harred. "Topless Dancers: Managing Stigma in a Deviant Occupation." *Deviant Behavior* 13 (Summer) 1992:291–311.

Thompson, William E., Jack L. Harred, and Barbara E. Burks. "Managing the Stigma of Topless Dancing: A Decade Later." *Deviant Behavior* 24 (6) 2003:1–20.

Thorne, Barrie. *Gender Play: Girls and Boys in School.* New Brunswick, NJ: Rutgers University Press, 1993.

Thornton, Arland. "Influences of the Marital History of Parents on the Marital and Cohabitational Experiences of Children." *American Journal of Sociology* 96 (January) 1991:868–894.

Thurow, Lester C. "Appearing Soon on a Computer Near You." *USA Today,* February 26, 1997:13A.

Thye, Shane R. "Reliability in Experimental Sociology." *Social Forces* 78 (June) 2000:1277–1309.

Tichi, Cecelia. *Electronic Hearth: Creating an American Television Culture.* New York: Oxford University Press, 1991.

Time. "Not Coed—or Dead." May 28, 1990:27.

Tocqueville, Alexis de. *Democracy in America.* J. P. Mayer and Max Lerner (eds.). New York: HarperCollins, [1835] 1966.

Toennies, Ferdinand. "Gemeinschaft and Gesellschaft," in Talcott Parsons, et al. (eds.), *Theories of Society,* 3rd ed., vol. 1. Glencoe, IL: Free Press, [1887] 1961, pp. 190–201.

Toffler, Alvin. *Future Shock.* New York: Bantam Books, 1970.

———. *The Third Wave.* New York: Bantam Books, 1981.

Tomasson, Richard F. "Reaching the Top." *Society* 37 (5) July/August 2000:9–18.

Torres-Gil, Fernando. "Aging in an Ethnic Society: Policy Issues for Aging Among Minority Groups," in Donald E. Gelfand and Charles M. Barresi (eds.), *Ethnic Dimensions of Aging.* New York: Springer, 1987, pp. 121–132.

Toufexis, Anastasia, J. Madeleine Nash, and Dick Thompson. "Older—But Coming on Strong." *Time,* February 22, 1988:76–79.

Townsend, Kathleen Kennedy. "Why Johnny Can't Tell Right from Wrong." *Washington Monthly,* December, 1992:29–32.

Toynbee, Arnold J., and Jane Caplan. *A Study of History.* New York: Oxford University Press, 1972.

Travis, Jeremy. *But They All Come Back.* Washington, DC: Urban Institute, 2005.

Treas, Judith, and Eric D. Widmer. "Married Women's Employment Over the Life Course: Attitudes in Cross-National Perspective." *Social Forces* 78 (June) 2000:1409–1436.

Treiman, Donald J. *Occupational Prestige in Comparative Perspective.* New York: Academic, 1977.

Trent, William. "Race and Ethnicity in the Teacher Education Curriculum." *Teachers College Record* 91 (Spring) 1990:361–369.

Trotte, William Monroe, National Association for the Advancement of Color, Criminal Justice Institute of Harvard Law School, and the University of Massachusetts. *Beyond the Rodney King Story: An Investigation of Police Conduct in Minority Communities.* Boston: Northeastern University Press, 1995.

Trotter, Andrew. "Technology in Classrooms: 'That's Edutainment'!" *Executive Educator* 13 (June) 1991:20–24.

Truelsen, Stewart. "Food under Attack." *The Tennessee Farm Bureau News,* July, 2003:5.

Tuchman, Gaye, Arlene Kaplan Daniels, and James Benet. *Hearth and Home: Images of Women in the Mass Media.* New York: Oxford University Press, 1978.

Turk, Austin. *Criminality and Legal Order.* Chicago: Rand McNally, 1969.

Turkle, Sherry. *The Second Self: Computer and the Human Spirit.* New York: Simon & Schuster, 1984.

———. *Life on the Screen: Identity in the Age of the Internet.* New York: Simon & Schuster, 1995.

Turnbull, Colin M. *Man in Africa.* Garden City, NY: Doubleday (Anchor Books), 1977.

———. *Mbuti Pygmies: Change and Adaptation.* Fort Worth: Holt, Rinehart & Winston, 1983.

Turner, Jeffrey S., and Donald B. Helms. *Contemporary Adulthood,* 4th ed. Fort Worth, TX: Holt, Rinehart & Winston, 1989.

Turner, Jonathan H., "Inequality and Stratification," in Dana Dunn and David V. Waller (eds.), *Analyzing Social Problems: Essays and Exercise.* Englewood Cliffs, NJ: Prentice Hall, 1997, pp. 80–87.

Turner, Ralph H., and Lewis M. Killian. *Collective Behavior,* 3rd ed. Englewood Cliffs, NJ: Prentice-Hall, 1987.

Turque, Bill, Carolyn Friday, and Jeanne Gordon, et al. "Gays under Fire." *Newsweek,* September 14, 1992:35–40.

Tuxill, John. "Death in the Family Tree." *World Watch* 10 (September/October) 1997:12–21.

Tyre, Peg. "Bringing Up Adultolescents." *Newsweek,* March 25, 2002:39–40.

———. "The Trouble With Boys." *Newsweek,* January 30, 2006:44-52.

Tyre, Peg, and Daniel McGinn. "She Works, He Doesn't." *Newsweek,* May 12, 2003:45–52.

U.S. Bureau of the Census. "Persons of Spanish Origin in the United States." *Current Population Reports, Population Characteristics,* Series P–20 no. Washington, DC: Government Printing Office, 1985:396.

———. *Statistical Abstract of the United States.* Washington, DC: Government Printing Office, 1988.

———. *Population Studies.* Washington, DC: Government Printing Office, 1990a.

———. *Census and You* 26 (February) 1991a.

———. *Census and You* 26 (October) 1991b.

———. *Current Population Reports,* P-60, no. 188. Washington, DC: Government Printing Office, 1993a.

———. "Marital Status and Living Arrangements: March 1993." *Current Population Reports, Population Characteristics,* Series P-20, no. 472. Washington, DC: Government Printing Office, 1993b:vii.

———. *Statistical Abstract of the United States, 1996,* 116th ed. Washington, DC: Government Printing Office, 1996.

———. *Current Population Reports,* Series P-70, no. 54. Washington, DC: Government Printing Office, 1997a.

———. *Statistical Abstract of the United States, 1997,* 117th ed. Washington, DC: Government Printing Office, 1997b.

———. "Voting and Registration." *Current Population Reports,* Series P-20, no. 504. Washington, DC: Government Printing Office, 1997c.

———. *Statistical Abstract of the United States, 1998.* Washington, DC: Government Printing Office, 1998.

———. *Statistical Abstract of the United States, 2000.* Washington, DC: Government Printing Office, 2000.

———. "Overview of Race and Hispanic Origin." Census 2000 Brief (Elizabeth M. Grieco and Rachel C. Cassidy). United States Department of Commerce. Washington, DC: March, 2001a.

———. "The Two or More Races Population: 2000." Census 2000 Brief (Nicholas A. Jones and Amy Symens Smith). United States Department of Commerce. Washington DC: November, 2001b.

———. "Money Income in the United States: 2001." *Current Population Reports,* P60–218. Washington, DC: Government Printing Office, 2002a.

———. "Poverty in the United States: 2001." *Current Population Reports,* P60–219. Washington, DC: Government Printing Office, 2002b.

U.S. Bureau of Labor Statistics. "Employment Hours and Earnings, United States," *Employment and Earnings* (September) 2003:975.

U.S. Bureau of Labor Statistics. *Unemployment News.* www.bls.gov/news.release, 2006.

U.S. Department of Defense. 2006. www.Defense.gov.

U.S. Department of Education. *America 2000: An Education Strategy.* Washington, DC: U.S. Department of Education, 1991a.

———. *The Condition of Education, 2001.* Washington, DC: Government Printing Office, 2001a.

———. http://www.ed.gov, 2001b.

U.S. News and World Report. "Top Ten." *U.S. News and World Report,* May 20, 1991:94–99.

———. "The Case for Tough Standards." *U.S. News and World Report,* April 1, 1996:52–56.

U.S. State Department. "Patterns of Global Terrorism, 2002." Washington, DC, April 3, 2003.

Uchitelle, Louis. "Keeping Up with the Gates?" *New York Times,* May 3, 1998:12B.

Umberson, Debra, Kristin Anderson, and Jennifer Glick, et al. "Domestic Violence, Personal Control, and Gender." *Journal of Marriage and the Family* 60 (2) 1998:442–452.

Underwood, Anne. "The Quest for Artificial Blood." *Newsweek,* June 24, 2002:68–70.

———. "Diagnosis: Not Enough Nurses." *Newsweek,* December 12, 2005:80.

Underwood, Anne and Jerry Adler. "When Cultures Clash." *Newsweek,* April 25, 2005:68-72.

Uniform Crime Reports. *Crime in the United States: Uniform Crime Reports, 2005.* Washington, DC: FBI, Government Printing Office, 2006.

United Nations Development Report. *Human Development Report 1995.* New York: United Nations, 1995.

United Nations Development Report. *Human Development Report 2003.* "Millennium Development Goals: A Compact Among Nations to End Poverty," July, 2003.

United Nations. *United Nations Millennium Goals Report,* 2006.

United Nations Fund for Population Activities. *Population and the Environment: The Challenges Ahead.* New York: Author, 1991.

United Nations. *World Population Prospects, 1988.* Population Studies, no. 106. New York: United Nations Department of International Economic and Social Affairs, 1989.

———. "Environment in Worse Shape Than 20 Years Ago, U.N. Reports." *Dallas Morning News,* May 8, 1992:16A.

———. *Report on the World Social Situation: 1993.* New York: United Nations Department of International Economic and Social Affairs, 1993.

———. "The Progress of Nations," 1997.

Urry, John. "Mobile Sociology." *British Journal of Sociology* 51 (1) January/March 2000:185–203.

USA Today. "Number of New Magazines Down Last Year." January 29, 1991a:B2.

———. August 26, 1991b:B1.

———. August 28, 1991c.

———. December 5, 1991d:B2.

———. "Good Ol' Boys Round Up." July 18, 1995.

———. "British to Destroy Frozen Embryos," July 29, 1996:1.

———. "Outdated Sex-Crime Laws Leave Military Women at Risk." *USA Today,* April 17, 2003:12A.

Useem, Michael. "The Social Organization of the American Business Elite and Participation of Corporate Directors in the Governance of American Institutions." *American Sociological Review* 44 (August) 1979:553–572.

———. *The Inner Circle: Large Corporations and the Rise of Business Political Activity in the U.S. and U.K.* New York: Oxford University Press, 1983.

Vallas, Steven P. "Why Teamwork Fails: Obstacles to Workplace Change in Four Manufacturing Plants." *American Sociological Review* 68 (April) 2003:223–250.

Van Biema, David. "The Citadel Still Holds." *Time,* 144, 1994:61.

Van Gennep, Arnold. *The Rites of Passage.* M. B. Vizedom and G. L. Caffee (trans.). Chicago: University of Chicago Press, [1908] 1960.

Van Poppel, Frans, and Lincoln H. Day. "A Test of Durkheim's Theory of Suicide—Without Committing the 'Ecological Fallacy.'" *American Sociological Review* 61 (June) 1996:500–507.

Vander Zanden, James W. *American Minority Relations,* 4th ed. New York: Knopf, 1983.

Vaquera, Elizabeth and Grace Kao. "Private and Public Displays of Affection Among Interracial and Intra-Racial Adolescent Couples." *Social Science Quarterly* 86 (June), 2005: 484–505.

Veblen, Thorstein. *The Theory of the Leisure Class.* New York: Macmillan, 1899.

Vega, William A. "Hispanic Families in the 1980s: A Decade of Research." *Journal of Marriage and the Family* 52 (November) 1990:1015–1024.

———. "The Study of Latino Families: A Point of Departure," in Ruth E. Zambrana (ed.), *Understanding Latino Families: Scholarship, Policy, and Practice.* Thousand Oaks, CA: Sage, 1995, pp. 3–17.

Vetter, Betty M. "Women in Science—Ferment: Yes; Progress: Maybe; Change: Slow." *Mosaic* 23 (Fall) 1992:34–41.

Viano, Emilio C. "Violence Among Intimates: Major Issues and Approaches," in Emilio C. Viano (ed.), *Intimate Violence: Interdisciplinary Perspectives.* Washington, DC: Hemisphere Publishing, 1992.

Vidmar, Neil, and Milton Rokeach. "Archie Bunker's Bigotry: A Study in Selective Perception and Exposure." *Journal of Communication* 24 (1) 1974:36–47.

Vogel, Lise. *Marxism and the Oppression of Women: Toward a Unitary Theory.* New Brunswick, NJ: Rutgers University Press, 1983.

Vold, George B., and Thomas J. Bernard. *Theoretical Criminology,* 3rd ed. New York: Oxford University Press, 1986.

Von Drehle, David. "Debate on Marriage and More Looms." *WashingtonPost.com,* June 27, 2003:1–5.

Wacquant, Loic. "Scrutinizing the Street: Poverty, Morality, and the Pitfalls of Urban Ethnography." *American Journal of Sociology* 107 (6) May 2000:1468–1532.

Wade, Carole, and Carol Tavris. *Psychology,* 5th ed. New York: Addison-Wesley, 1998.

Wagner, Cynthia G. "Cyberunions: Organized Labor Goes Online." *The Futurist* 34 (January/February) 2000:7.

Wagner, David, and Marcia B. Cohen. "The Power of the People: Homeless Protesters in the Aftermath of Social Movement Participation." *Social Problems* 38 (November) 1991:543–561.

Wahl, Jenny B. "From Riches to Riches: Intergenerational Transfers and the Evidence from Estate Tax Returns." *Social Science Quarterly* 84 (2) June 2003:278–296.

Wald, Kenneth D. *Religion and Politics in the United States,* 3rd ed. Washington, DC: Congressional Quarterly Press, 1997.

Waldfogel, Jane. "The Effect of Children on Women's Wages." *American Sociological Review* 62 (April) 1997:209–217.

Wallace, Harvey. *Family Violence: Legal, Medical, and Social Perspectives.* Boston: Allyn & Bacon, 1996.

Waller, James. *Face to Face: The Changing State of Racism Across America.* New York: Plenum Press, 1998.

Wallerstein, Immanuel. *The Modern World System: Capitalist Agriculture and the Origins of the European World Economy in the Sixteenth Century.* New York: Academic, 1974.

———. "The Present State of the Debate on World Inequality," in Michael A. Seligson (ed.), *The Gap between the Rich and Poor.* Boulder, CO: Westview, 1984.

———."Where Should Sociologists Be Heading?" *Contemporary Sociology* 29 (March) 2000:306–308.

Wallis, Claudia. "The Traditional Family Will Be Less Prevalent," in David Bender and Bruno Leone (eds.), *America beyond 2001: Opposing Viewpoints.* San Diego: Greenhaven Press, 1996, pp. 25–35.

Wallis, Stephen. "Discipline and Civility Must be Restored to America's Public Schools." *USA Today Magazine,* (November) 1995:32–34.

Wallraff, Barbara. "What Global Language?" *The Atlantic Monthly* 286 (5) November 2000:52–66.

Walsh, Robert H., Mary Z. Ferrel, and William L. Tolone. "Selection of Reference Group, Perceived Reference Group and Personal Permissiveness, Attitudes and Behavior: A Study of Two Consecutive Panels (1967–1971; 1970–1974)." *Journal of Marriage and the Family* 38, 1976:495–507.

Wamsley, Gary L. "Contrasting Institutions of Air Force Socialization: Happenstance or Bellwether?" *American Journal of Sociology* 78 (September) 1972:399–417.

Warner, Judith. "The Myth of the Perfect Mother." *Newsweek,* February 21, 2005:42-49.

Warner, Judith. *Perfect Madness: Motherhood in the Age of Anxiety.* New York: Riverhead Books, 2006.

Warschauer, Mark. *Technology and Social Inclusion: Rethinking the Digital Divide.* Cambridge, MA: MIT Press, 2003.

Wartella, Ellen. "The Commercialization of Youth: Channel One in Context." *Phi Delta Kappan* 76 (February) 1995:448–451.

Washington Post. "Schools' Anti-Drug Policies Extend to Legal Medications." *Dallas Morning News,* October 13, 1996:8A.

———. "Day Care Doesn't Hurt Kids' Learning, Study Says." *Dallas Morning News,* April 4, 1997:1A, 19A.

———. "Study: Violent Media Targeting Young Buyers." *Dallas Morning News,* August 27, 2000:7A.

———. "Black Men Show Deep Divide on Selves, Society." *Dallas Morning News,* June 4, 2006:12A.

Wasley, Patricia A. "Small Classes, Small Schools: The Time Is Now," in James W. Noll (ed.), *Taking Sides: Clashing Views on Controversial Educational Issues,* 12th ed. Guilford, CT: McGraw-Hill Dushkin, 2003, pp. 268–272.

Wasserman, Ira M. and Marie Richmond-Abbott. "Gender and the Internet: Causes of Variation in Access, Level, and Scope of Use." *Social Science Quarterly* 86 (March), 2005:252-270.

Waters, Harry F. "Family Feuds." *Newsweek,* April 23, 1990:58–62.

Watson, James L. "Introduction: Transnationalism, Localization, and Fast Foods in East Asia," in *Golden Arches East: McDonald's in East Asia,* James L. Watson (ed.). Stanford, CA: Stanford University Press, 1997, pp. 1–38.

Watson, John B. *Behavior.* New York: Norton, 1924.

Watson, Russell, John Barry, and Christopher Dickey, et al. "When Words Are the Best Weapon." *Newsweek,* February 27, 1995: 36–40.

Waxman, Chaim I. "Whither American Jewry?" *Society* 28 (November/December) 1990:34–41.

Webb, R. K. *Harriet Martineau, A Radical Victorian.* New York: Columbia University Press, 1960.

———. *Economy and Society,* vol. 3. New York: Bedminster, [1922] 1968.

Weber, Max. *Max Weber: Essays in Sociology.* H. H. Gerth and C. Wright Mills (eds. and trans.). New York: Oxford University Press, 1946.

———. *The Theory of Social and Economic Organization.* New York: Free Press, 1947.

———. *The Religion of China.* New York: Free Press, 1951.

———. *The Protestant Ethic and the Spirit of Capitalism.* New York: Scribner, [1904–1905] 1958a.

———. *The Religion of India.* New York: Free Press, [1904] 1958b.

———. *Economy and Society: An Outline of Interpretive Sociology,* vol. 1. Guenther Roth and Claus Wittich (eds.). New York: Bedminster Press, 1968.

———. *Economy and Society,* vol. 2. Guenther Roth and Claus Wittich (eds.). Berkeley: University of California Press, 1978.

Weeks, John R. *Population: An Introduction to Concepts and Issues,* 7th ed. Belmont, CA: Wadsworth, 1999.

Wehrfritz, George. "China: Nightmare Cities." *Newsweek,* December 26, 1994:107–108.

Weil, Andrew. *Eight Weeks to Optimum Health: A Proven Program for Taking Full Advantage of Your Body's Natural Healing Power.* New York: Ballantine, 1998.

Weil, Andrew. *Spontaneous Healing: How to Discover and Embrace Your Body's Natural Ability to Heal Itself.* New York: Ballantine, 2000.

———. *Eating Well for Optimum Health.* New York: Quill, 2001.

———. *Healthy Aging: A Lifelong Guide to Your Physical and Spiritual Well-Being.* NY: Anchor, 2007.

Weiss, Carol H., and Eleanor Singer. *Reporting of Social Science in the National Media.* New York: Sage, 1988.

Wekesser, Carol (ed.). *Health Care in America: Opposing Viewpoints.* San Diego: Greenhaven Press, 1994.

———, ed. *Violence in the Media.* San Diego: Greenhaven Press, 1995.

———. *Pornography: Opposing Viewpoints.* San Diego: Greenhaven Press, 1997.

Welch, Susan, and Lee Sigelman. "Getting to Know You: Latino-Anglo Social Contact." *Social Science Quarterly* 81 (1) March 2000:67–81.

Wellington, Alison J. "Accounting for the Male/Female Wage Gap Among Whites: 1976–1985." *American Sociological Review* 59 (December) 1994:839–848.

Wellman, Barry, and Caroline Haythornthwaite (eds.). *The Internet in Everyday Life.* Malden, MA: Blackwell, 2002.

Wellman, Barry, Janet Salaff, and Dimitrina Dimitrova, et al. "Computer Networks as Social Networks: Collaborative Work, Telework, and Virtual Community." *Annual Review of Sociology* 22. Palo Alto, CA: 1996:213–238.

Wenglinsky, Harold. "How Money Matters: The Effect of School District Spending on Academic Achievement." *Sociology of Education* 70 (July) 1997:221–237.

Wertheimer, Linda K. "Grad Schools Struggle to Narrow Minority Gap." *Dallas Morning News,* June 24, 2002:1A, 18A.

Wertheimer, Linda K., and Christy Hoppe. "College Race Policy Withheld." *Dallas Morning News,* Tuesday, June 24, 2003:1A, 16A.

Wheelan, Charles, J. *Naked Economics: Undressing the Dismal Science.* New York: W. W. Norton, 2002.

White, John K., and Daniel M. Shea. *New Party Politics: From Jefferson and Hamilton to the Information Age.* Boston, MA: Bedford/St. Martin's Press, 2000.

Whitener, Ellen M. "A Meta-Analytic Review of the Effect on Learning of the Interaction between Prior Achievement and Instructional Support." *Review of Educational Research* 59 (Spring) 1989:65–86.

Whiting, Robert. "You've Gotta Have 'Wa.'" *Sports Illustrated,* September 24, 1979:58–71.

———. *You Gotta Have Wa.* New York: Macmillan, 1989.

Whorf, Benjamin L. "Selected Writings of Benjamin Lee Whorf," in John B. Carroll (ed.), *Language, Thought, and Reality.* Cambridge MA: MIT Press, 1956.

Whyte, William Foote. *Street Corner Society.* Chicago: University of Chicago Press, 1943.

Wichita Eagle. "In Italy, Gestures Speak Louder than Words Do." December 18, 1994b:5D.

Wickipedia. "Underground Economy." *Wickipedia, 2006.*

Wiegand, Bruce. *Off the Books: A Theory and Critique of the Underground Economy.* Dix Hills, NY: General Hall, 1992.

Wilkins, Shirley, and Thomas A. W. Miller. "Working Women: How It's Working Out." *Public Opinion* (October–November) 1985: 44–48.

Williams, Frederick, Robert LaRose, and Frederica Frost. *Children, Television, and Sex-Role Stereotyping.* New York: Praeger, 1981.

Williams, Gregory H. *Life on the Color Line: The True Story of a White Boy Who Discovered He Was Black.* New York: Dutton, 1995.

Williams, Patricia. *The Rooster's Egg: On the Persistence of Prejudice.* Boston: Harvard University Press, 1996.

Williams, Robin M., Jr. *American Society: A Sociological Interpretation,* 3rd ed. New York: Knopf, 1970.

———. "The Sociology of Ethnic Conflicts: Comparative International Perspectives." *Annual Review of Sociology* 20, 1994:49–79.

Williams, Walter. *The Spirit and the Flesh: Sexual Diversity in American Indian Culture.* Boston: Beacon Press, 1986.

Williams-Myers, A. J. *Destructive Impulses: An Examination of an American Secret in Race Relations: White Violence.* New York: University Press of America, 1995.

Willie, Charles V. "The Inclining Significance of Race," in Kurt Finsterbusch and George McKenna (eds.), *Taking Sides: Clashing Views on Controversial Social Issues.* New York: Dushkin, 1990, pp. 141–145.

Willis, Derek. "Devil's in the Details." *Hoover Institution,* campaignfinancesite.com. Excerpted from Campaign Finance Information Center. August 26, 2003:1–3.

Wilson, Brian. "The Canadian Rave Scene and Five Theses on Youth Resistance." *Canadian Journal of Sociology* 27 (3) 2003:373–391.

Wilson, Clint C. II, Felix Gutierrez, and Lena Chao. *Racism, Sexism, and the Media: The Rise of Class Communication in Multicultural America.* Thousand Oaks, CA: Pine Forge, 2004.

Wilson, Edward O. *On Human Nature.* Cambridge: Harvard University Press, 1978.

Wilson, John. "The Problem of Minority Groups." In Ralph Linton (ed.), *The Science of Man in the World Crisis.* New York: Columbia University Press, 1945, pp. 347–372.

———. "The Sociological Study of American Religion," in Charles H. Lippy and Peter W. Williams (eds.), *Encyclopedia of the American Religious Experience: Studies of Traditions and Movements,* vol. 1. New York: Scribner, 1988, pp. 17–30.

———. *When Work Disappears.* New York: Knopf, 1996.

———. *The Bridge over the Racial Divide: Rising Inequality and Coalition Politics.* Berkeley, CA: University of California Press, 1999.

———. "Volunteering." *Annual Review of Sociology* 26 2000:215–240.

Wilson, William Julius. *The Declining Significance of Race: Blacks and Changing American Institutions.* Chicago: University of Chicago Press, 1978.

Wilton, Tamsin. *Sexual (Dis)Orientation: Gender, Sex, Desire and Self-Fashioning.* Palgrave Macmillan, 2005.

Wingert, Pat. "Oh to be a Knob!" *Newsweek,* August 22, 1994:22.

Winn, Marie. *The Plug-In Drug.* New York: Bantam, 1977.

Winick, Charles (ed.). *Deviance and the Mass Media.* Beverly Hills, CA: Sage, 1978.

Winslade, William J. "Best Support for Assisted Suicide Is Rooted in Cherished Heritage of Individual Liberty." *Dallas Morning News,* June 17, 1990:1J.

Winter, Greg. "Charter School Students Academically Ahead, Study Finds." *Dallas Morning News,* 2003:6A.

———. "Ruling Provides Relief, but Less Than Hoped." *The New York Times* on the Web, Education, June 24, 2003:1–3.

Wire Reports, Washington. "VMI Chief Calls Women Disruptive." *Dallas Morning News,* June 14, 1998:4A.

Wire Service. "AIDS Researchers Say Vaccine Likely in '90s." *Dallas Morning News,* June 22, 1991:19A.

Wirth, Louis. "Urbanism as a Way of Life." *American Journal of Sociology* 44 (July) 1938:1–24.

———. "The Problem of Minority Groups," in Ralph Linton (ed.), *The Science of Man in the World Crisis.* New York: Columbia University Press, 1945, pp. 347–372.

Wolcott, Harry F. *The Man in the Principal's Office: An Ethnography.* New York: Holt, Rinehart & Winston, 1973.

Wolf, Naomi. *The Beauty Myth: How Images of Beauty Are Used Against Women.* New York: Morrow, 1990.

Wolfinger, Nicholas H. "Family Structure Homogamy: The Effects of Parental Divorce on Partner Selection and Marital Stability." *Social Science Research* 32 (1) March 2003: 80–98.

Woll, Allen L. "Bandits and Lovers: Hispanic Images in American Film," in Randall M. Miller (ed.), *The Kaleidoscopic Lens: How Hollywood Views Ethnic Groups.* New York: Jerome Ozer, 1980, pp. 54–72.

Woll, Stanley B., and Peter Young. "Looking for Mr. and Ms. Right: Self-Presentation in Videotaping." *Journal of Marriage and the Family* 51 (May) 1989:483–488.

Wolman, Harold L., Coit Cook Ford III, and Edward Hill. "Evaluating the Success of Urban Success Stories." *Urban Studies* 31 (June) 1994:835–850.

Wong, Morrison G. "The Chinese American Family," in Charles H. Mindel, Robert W. Habenstein, and Roosevelt Wright Jr. (eds.), *Ethnic Families in America,* 4th ed. Upper Saddle River, NJ: Prentice-Hall, 1998, pp. 284–310.

Wong, Sandra C. "Evaluating the Content of Textbooks: Public Interests and Professional Authority." *Sociology of Education* 64 (January) 1991:11–18.

Wood, Erica F. "The Availability and Utility of Interdisciplinary Data on Elder Abuse: A White Paper for the National Center on Elder Abuse." National Center on Elder Abuse, May, 2006.

Wood, Julia T. *Gendered Lives: Communication, Gender, and Culture.* Belmont, CA: Wadsworth, 1994.

———. *Gendered Lives: Communication, Gender, and Culture,* 3rd ed. Belmont, CA: Wadsworth, 1998.

Wood, Robert E. "Tourist Ethnicity: A Brief Itinerary." *Ethnic and Racial Studies* 21 (2) 1998: 218–242.

Wooden, Wayne S. *Renegade Kids, Suburban Outlaws: From Youth Culture to Delinquency.* Belmont, CA: Wadsworth, 1995.

Woodward, Kenneth L. "Feminism and the Churches." *Newsweek,* February 13, 1989: 58–61.

———. "Is God Listening?" *Newsweek,* March 31, 1997:57–64.

Worchel, Stephen, Joel Cooper, and George R. Goethals. *Understanding Social Psychology,* 5th ed. Pacific Grove, CA: Brooks/Cole, 1991.

World Almanac and Book of Facts 2000. Ken Park (ed.). New York: World Almanac Books, 1999.

World Almanac and Book of Facts 2003. Ken Park (ed.). New York: World Almanac Books, 2002.

World Bank. *World Bank Atlas,* 2006. Washington, DC: The World Bank, 2006.

World Health Organization on-line, http://www .who.int/whosis/statistics/menu.cfm, 2006.

World Population News Service. "Dr. Sadik Attributes Wave of Disasters to Overpopulation." *Popline* 13 (July/August) 1991a:4.

———. "Megacities Multiply in Developing World." *Popline* 13 (July/August) 1991b:3.

———. "1.3 Billion Births Expected in 1990s." *Popline* 13 (July/August) 1991c:3.

———. "Population Crisis Seen Spreading." *Popline* 13 (September/ October) 1991d:1.

World Resources Institute. *World Resources, 1990–91.* New York: Oxford University Press, 1990.

World Watch. "Interviews with Rajendra Pachauri and Robert Watson." *World Watch* 16 (March–April) 2003:10–15.

Wright, Richard A. "The Doctor's Dilemma in the 21st Century." *USA Today Magazine,* 119 (September) 1990:53–54.

Wright, Wynne and Elizabeth Ransom. "Stratification on the Menu: Using Restaurant Menus to Examine Social Class." *Teaching Sociology* 33 (July), 2005:310–316).

Wrong, Dennis. "The Functional Theory of Stratification: Some Neglected Considerations." *American Sociological Review* 24, 1959: 772–782.

———. "The Oversocialized Conception of Man in Modern Sociology." *American Sociological Review* 26, 1961:183–193.

———. "Adversarial Identities and Multiculturalism." *Society* 37 (2) January/February 2000:10–14.

Wuthnow, Robert. *The Restructuring of American Religion: Society and Faith since World War II.* Princeton: Princeton University Press, 1988.

———. *The Struggle for America's Soul: Evangelicals, Liberals, and Secularism.* Grand Rapids, MI: Eerdmans, 1989.

———. *Christianity in the Twenty-First Century: Reflections on the Challenges Ahead.* New York: Oxford University Press, 1993.

———. *God and Mammon in America.* New York: Free Press, 1994a.

———. *Sharing the Journey: Support Groups and America's New Quest for Community.* New York: Free Press, 1994b.

———. *After Heaven: Spirituality in America Since the 1950s.* Berkeley, CA: University of California Press, 1998.

Wynne, Edward A. "The Great Tradition in Education: Transmitting Moral Values," in Kurt Finsterbusch and George McKenna (eds.), *Taking Sides: Clashing Views on Controversial Social Issues,* 6th ed. Guilford, CT: Dushkin, 1990, pp. 13–20.

Wynter, Leon E. *American Skin: Pop Culture, Big Business, and the End of White America.* New York: Crown, 2002.

Xiaohe, Xu, and Martin K. Whyte. "Love Matches and Arranged Marriages: A Chinese Replication." *Journal of Marriage and the Family* 52 (August) 1990:709–722.

Yamaguchi, Kazuo, and Yantao Wang. "Class Identification of Married Employed Women and Men in America." *American Journal of Sociology* 108 (2) September 2002:440–475.

Yetman, Norman R. (ed.). *Majority and Minority: The Dynamics of Race and Ethnicity in American Life,* 4th ed. Boston: Allyn & Bacon, 1985.

Yinger, J. Milton. *Countercultures.* New York: Free Press, 1982.

Yinger, John. "Housing Discrimination Is Still Worth Worrying About." *Housing Policy Debate* (Fannie Mae Foundation) 9 (4) 1998:893–923.

York, Richard, Eugene A. Rosa, and Thomas Dietz. "Footprints on the Earth: The Environmental Consequences of Modernity." *American Sociological Review* 68 (April) 2003:279–300.

Young, Nigel. "Peace Movements in Industrial Societies: Genesis, Evolution, Impact," in Raimo Vayrynen (ed.), *The Quest for Peace.* Newbury Park, CA: Sage, 1987, pp. 303–316.

Young, Stanley. "The End," in Ted Schultz (ed.), *The Fringes of Reason: A Whole Earth Catalog.* New York: Harmony Books, 1989, pp. 8–21.

Zabarenko, Deborah. "Global Warming Reaches a 'Tipping Point': A Report." *Reuters on-line news service,* March 15, 2006.

Zaleski, Jeff. *The Soul of Cyberspace.* New York: HarperCollins, 1997.

Zastrow, Charles, and Karen K. Kirst-Ashman. *Understanding Human Behavior and the Social Environment,* 2nd ed. Chicago: Nelson-Hall, 1990.

Zellner, William W. *Countercultures: A Sociological Analysis.* New York: St. Martin's Press, 1995.

Zhang, Sheldon, and Chin Ko-Lin. "Enter the Dragon: Inside Chinese Human Smuggling Organizations." *Criminology* 40 (4) 2002:737–769.

Zhao, Shanyang. "Metatheory, Metamethod, Meta-Data-Analysis: What, Why, and How?" *Sociological Perspectives* 34 (Fall) 1991:377–390.

Zia, Helen. *Asian Americans: The Emergence of an American People.* New York: Farrar, Straus, and Giroux, 2000.

Zielenziger, Michael. "Schools in Japan Grapple with Increasing Violence." *Dallas Morning News,* April 19, 1998:43A.

Zimbalist, Andrew, Howard J. Sherman, and Stuart Brown. *Comparing Economic Systems: A Political-Economic Approach,* 2nd ed. San Diego: Harcourt Brace Jovanovich, 1989.

Zimbardo, Philip. "Pathology of Imprisonment." *Society* 9 (April) 1972:4–8.

Zimbrick, Emily Louise. "Faith-Based Roadblocks," *The Washington Times.com,* October 7, 2003: 1–4.

Zimmerman, Janet. "Hawaii OKs Benefits to Same-Sex Couples." *USA Today,* July 8, 1997:2A.

Zirkel, Perry A. and Ivan B. Gluckman. "Is Corporal Punishment Child Abuse?" in Fred Schultz (ed.), *Annual Editions: Education 97/98,* 24th ed. Guilford, CT: Dushkin, 1997, pp. 147–148.

Zuckoff, Mitchell. "Toxic Traders Turn Developing Nations into Dump Sites." *Wichita Eagle,* September 11, 1994a:1–2F.

Zuo, Jiping, and Shengming Tang. "Breadwinner Status and Gender Ideologies of Men and Women Regarding Family Roles." *Sociological Perspectives* 43 (Spring) 2000:29–43.

Subject Index

Name Index

Credits

Text credits

p. 269: From "Human Family," copyright © 1990 by Maya Angelou, from *I Shall Not Be Moved* by Maya Angelou. Used by permission of Random House, Inc.

Photo credits

Chapter 1

p. xx: Ryan McVay/Getty Images; p. 2: Monty Brinton/CBS/Landov LLC; p. 3: Bettmann/Corbis; p. 5: Ace Stock Limited/Alamy Images; p. 10: Benno Grieshaber/VISUM/The Image Works; p. 13, top: Bettman/Corbis; p. 13, bottom: Hulton-Deutsch Collection/Corbis; p. 14, top: Wlliam E. Thompson; p. 14, bottom: Bettmann/Corbis; p. 15: Culver Pictures; p. 16: Bettman/Corbis; p. 17: David Young Wolff/PhotoEdit Inc.; p. 20: Yaroslava Mills

Chapter 2

p. 26: David Young-Wolff/PhotoEdit Inc.; p. 28: Ethel Wolvovitz/The Image Works; p. 29: AP Images; p. 31: AP Images/Mel Evans; p. 34: Spencer Grant/PhotoEdit Inc.; p. 40: Michael Newman/PhotoEdit Inc.; p. 41: Richard Lord/The Image Works; p. 44: Ted Soqui/Corbis; p. 46: Corbis Royalty Free; p. 47: Michael Kleinfeld/UPI Photo/Landov LLC

Chapter 3

p. 54: Sonda Dawes/The Image Works; p. 54: Rudi Von Briel/PhotoEdit Inc.; p. 57: Estelle Klawitter/Corbis Zefa Collection; p. 59: Stephen Cardinale/Corbis; p. 60: Deanne FitzmauriceCorbis; p. 63: Ali Imam/Reuters/Landov LLC; p. 65: Photo Courtesy of Marilyn Rae Thompson; p. 71: Andrew Rakoczy/Bruce Coleman, Inc.; p. 77: Radu Sigheti/Reuters/Landov LLC

Chapter 4

p. 82: Karen Preuss/The Image Works; p. 84: AFP Photo/Matt Campbell/ Getty Images; p. 88: David Young Wolff/PhotoEdit Inc.; p. 89: IndexOpen Royalty Free; p. 90: Stewart Cohen/Stone/Getty Images; p. 91: Network Productions/The Image Works; p. 94: AP Images/Charles Rex Arbogast; p. 97: Michael Newman/PhotoEdit Inc.; p. 98: Peter Hvizdak/The Image Works; p. 100: David Young-Wolff/Photo Edit Inc.; p. 103: HENGHAMEH FAHIMI/Agence France Presse/Getty Images, Inc.; p. 104: Joel Stettenheim/Corbis; p. 107: David Livingston/Getty Images

Chapter 5

p. 112: David Young-Wolff/Getty Images; p. 114: Michael Newman/PhotoEdit Inc.; p. 117: Murray Andrew/Corbis/Sygma; p. 120: Corbis Royalty Free; p. 123: Colin Young-Wolff/PhotoEdit Inc.; p. 124: Melissa Moore/The Image Works; p. 126: Chromosohm Media/Stock Boston, LLC; p. 128, left: Ed Kashi/Corbis; p. 128, right: Fujifotos/The Image Works; p. 129, top: Rommel Pecson/The Image Works; p. 129, bottom: Bonnie Kamin/PhotoEdit Inc.; p. 131: Chris Pizzello/Corbis; p. 134: AP Images

Chapter 6

p. 138: SuperStock/Alamy Images; p. 140: Michael Wolf/Aurora Photos; p. 142: Jim Bryant/epa/Corbis; p. 146: Lynne Fernandes/The Image Works; p. 148: Fujifotos/The Image Works; p. 151: Reuters/Colin Braley; p. 153: Joel Stettenheim/Corbis; p. 156: Michelle Pedone/Corbis; p. 157: Spencer Grant/PhotoEdit Inc.

Chapter 7

p. 162: Design Pics Inc/Alamy Images; p. 164: AP Images; p. 166: Scott McKiernan/Black Star; p. 169, top left: Art Wolfe/Stone/Getty Images; p. 169, top right: Fujifotos/The Image Works; p. 169, bottom: Sean Cayton/The Image Works; p. 171: Paramount/The Kobal Collection/The Picture Desk; p. 173: Paramount/Everett Collection; p. 174: Brad Rickerby/Sipa Press; p. 176: Courtesy Dr. Albert Bandura, Stanford University; p. 182: Ron Sachs/Corbis; p. 191: Doug Menuez/Getty Images; p. 194: AP Images/Frank Franklin II

Chapter 8

p. 198: Andrew Lichtenstein/Corbis; p. 200: AP Images/Rick Bowmer; p. 202, left: © The Star-Ledger; p. 202, right: Ira Wyman/Corbis; p. 209: AP Images; p. 210: © Brent Jones; p. 212: Paul Colangelo/Corbis; p. 215: Steven Rubin/The Image Works; p. 218: Brooks Kraft/Corbis; p. 224, left: Mark Peterson/Corbis; p. 224, right: Nina Berman/Sipa Press

Chapter 9

p. 228: Peter Treanor/Alamy Images; p. 230: Nina Berman/Sipa Press; p. 233: Cameramann International, Ltd.; p. 234: Carter Kevin/Sygma/Corbis; p. 237: AP Images; p. 239: Gary Way/Sygma/Corbis; p. 240: AP Images; p. 245: AP Images/Ahn Young-joon; p. 249: AP Images; p. 252: Andres Hernandez/Liaison/Getty Images

Chapter 10

p. 256: De Yonker/The CW/Landov LLC; p. 258: Dave G. Houser/Corbis; p. 260: Dr. Gregory Howard Williams, President, The City College of New York, and author of *Life on the Color Line;* p. 261: Monika Graff/UPI Photo/Landov LLC; p. 265, left: Doug Benc/Getty Images; p. 265, right: AP Images; p. 267, both: AP Images; p. 276: Lions Gate/Everett Collection; p. 277: AP Images/Kirsty Wigglesworth; p. 282: Jason Reed/Corbis

Chapter 11

p. 290: Sean Cayton/The Image Works; p. 292: Roberto Schmidt/AFP/ Getty Images; p. 293: Bill Strode/Woodfin Camp & Associates; p. 299, top: Robert Brenner/PhotoEdit Inc.; p. 299, bottom: Myrleen Ferguson Cate/PhotoEdit Inc.; p. 303: Myrleen Ferguson Cate/PhotoEdit Inc.; p. 305, top: Jim West/The Image Works; p. 305, bottom: AP Images; p. 312: Christian Liewig/Liewig Media Sports/Corbis; p. 313: Brooks Kraft/Corbis; p. 314: AP Images/Kathy Willens; p. 315: AP Images; p. 318, left: Picture Desk, Inc./Kobal Collection; p. 318, right: Brakha Moshe/ABC/Picture Desk, Inc./Kobal Collection; p. 320: Georgios Kefalas/Keystone/AP Wide World Photos

Chapter 12

p. 326: Ariel Skelley/Corbis; p. 333, bottom: Novosti/Sovefoto/ Eastfoto; p. 333, bottom :Roberto Schmidt/Agence France Presse/ Getty Images, Inc.; p. 335: Myrleen Ferguson Cate/PhotoEdit Inc.; p. 336: AP Images/Tom Bauer/Missoulian; p. 337: Amy Wilton/ Aurora Photos; p. 341: Paul Conklin/PhotoEdit Inc.; p. 343: Barry Bland/Alamy Images; p. 348: Blake Discher/Sygma/Corbis; p. 349: Bill Aron/PhotoEdit Inc.

Chapter 13

p. 356: Bill Aron /PhotoEdit Inc.; p. 358: Francis Dean/Dean Pictures/ The Image Works; p. 360: David Young-Wolff/PhotoEdit Inc.; p. 364: Francoise de Mulder/Corbis; p. 367: Justin Lane/Corbis; p. 371: David Young-Wolff/PhotoEdit Inc.; p. 372: Tony Esparza/CBS/ Picture Desk, Inc./Kobal Collection; p. 376: Ed Bock Photography; p. 381: Jack Kurtz/The Image Works

Chapter 14

p. 388: photos_alyson/Taxi/Getty Images; p. 390: Bill Aron/PhotoEdit; p. 393: Robert Wallis/Corbis Saba; p. 394: Charles Gupton/ ImageState; p. 395: Bob Dammerich Photography; p. 396: Sean Cayton/The Image Works; p. 398: Aristide Economopoulos/Star Ledger/Corbis; p. 402, left: Frank Siteman; p. 402, right: David Young-Wolff/PhotoEdit Inc.; p. 405: Jeff Greenberg/PhotoEdit Inc.; p. 409: Ellen B. Senisi /The Image Works; p. 413: Bob Dammerich/ The Image Works; p. 417: Tony Freeman/PhotoEdit Inc.

Chapter 15

p. 422: Robin Nelson/PhotoEdit Inc.; p. 424: Renato Rotolo/Getty Images; p. 425: Romeo Ranoco/Reuters/Corbis; p. 429: Jim Bourg/ Corbis; p. 432: AP Images/Max Nash; p. 433: Lawrence Migdale Photography; p. 435: Jeff Greenberg/PhotoEdit Inc.; p. 442: Allstar Picture Library/Alamy Images; p. 448: © Brent Jones; p. 449: Reuters/Corbis

Chapter 16

p. 454: Hank Parker/Polaris Images; p. 456: Kenneth James/Corbis; p. 457: Cham/Sipa Press; p. 459: ABC/Picture Desk, Inc./Kobal Collection; p. 460: Peter Hvizdak/The Image Works; p. 463: National Organization for Women; p. 468: AP Images/Donna McWilliam; p. 472: AP Images/Gerald Herbert; p. 475: Salient Images/Alamy Images; p. 477: Kim Kyung-Hoon/Reuters/Landov LLC; p. 481: Copyright 2004 Corbis; p. 482: Jose Henao/Getty Images

Chapter 17

p. 484: Monika Graff/The Image Works; p. 486: Jose Galvez/ PhotoEdit Inc.; p. 488: Martha Bates/Stock Boston, LLC; p. 489: Baldev/Sygma/Corbis; p. 491: Mark I. Stephenson/Corbis; p. 492: AP Images; p. 494: Courtesy of Mastercard/McCann Erickson; p. 497: Bob Dammerich Photography; p. 498: Everett Collection; p. 501: Mark Richards/PhotoEdit Inc.; p. 503: Willie Hill, Jr./The Image Works; p. 505: Jim Pickerell/Stock Boston, LLC; p. 506: Danny Lehman/Corbis; p. 510: Klaus Reisinger/Black Star

Chapter 18

p. 514: ABC/Picture Desk, Inc./Kobal Collection; p. 516: Bob Dammerich Photography; p. 520: A. Ramey/PhotoEdit Inc.; p. 524: Joao Silva/Sygma/Corbis; p. 527: AP Images; p. 528: Milt & Joan Mann/Cameramann International, Ltd.; p. 529: Tom Stewart/Corbis; p. 534: © FX/Everett Collection; p. 535: © NBC-TV/Scott Humbert/The Kobal Collection/ The Picture Desk; p. 536: David Young-Wolff/PhotoEdit Inc.; p. 541: Matthew Borkoski/Stock Boston, LLC

Chapter 19

p. 544: Alexander Farnsworth/The Image Works; p. 546: Wesley Bocxe/The Image Works; p. 548: Robert Frerck/Odyssey/Chicago; p. 550: Gianni Giansanti/Sygma/Corbis; p. 554: Corbis Bettmann; p. 558: Jeff Greenberg/The Image Works; p. 560: Mark Segal/ Panoramic Images, Chicago; p. 563: David Austen/Woodfin Camp & Associates; p. 565: Fred Carol/Getty Images; p. 566: AP Images/Vincent Yu; p. 567: Robyn Beck/ Agence France Presse/Getty Images, Inc.

Chapter 20

p. 572: Ron Lowery/Corbis; p. 574: GmbH & Co.KG/Alamy Images; p. 578: AP Images; p. 582: Yury Kochetkov/epa/Corbis; p. 584: AP Images; p. 585: Topham/The Image Works; p. 587: AP Images/Kin Cheung; p. 588: Janine Wiedel Photolibrary/ Alamy Images; p. 592: Dreamworks/Paramount/Picture Desk, Inc./ Kobal Collection; p. 594: Corbis. All Rights Reserved; p. 596: Marilyn Humphries/The Image Works